Of the writing systems of the ancient world which still await deciphering, the Indus script is the most important. It developed in the Indus or Harappan Civilization, which flourished *c.*2500–1900 BC in and around modern Pakistan, collapsing before the earliest historical records of South Asia were composed. Nearly 4,000 samples of the writing survive, mainly on stamp seals and amulets, but no translations.

Professor Parpola is the chief editor of the *Corpus of Indus Seals and Inscriptions*. His ideas about the script, the linguistic affinity of the Harappan language, and the nature of the Indus religion are informed by a remarkable command of Aryan, Dravidian and Mesopotamian sources, archaeological materials, and linguistic methodology. He outlines what is known about the Harappan culture and its script, presents a decipherment of a small number of interlocking Indus signs, and proposes a method which will permit further progress in decipherment.

His fascinating study confirms that the Indus script was logo-syllabic and that the Indus language belonged to the Dravidian family. He also argues that Indian astronomy was started by the Harappans, and that the Indus religion was genetically related to those of the ancient Near East and Hindu India.

Deciphering the Indus script

Deciphering the Indus script

Asko Parpola

CAMBRIDGE
UNIVERSITY PRESS

Published by the Press Syndicate of the University of Cambridge
The Pitt Building, Trumpington Street, Cambridge CB2 1RP
40 West 20th Street, New York, NY 10011-4211, USA
10 Stamford Road, Oakleigh, Melbourne 3166, Australia

First published 1994
Reprinted 1997

Printed in Great Britain at the University Press, Cambridge

A catalogue record for this book is available from the British Library

Library of Congress cataloguing in publication data

Parpola, Asko.
Deciphering the Indus script / Asko Parpola.
p. cm.
Includes bibliographical references and index.
ISBN 0 521 43079 8
1. Indus script. 2. Indus Civilization. 3. Harappan site (Pakistan). 4. Pakistan – Antiquities. I. Title.
PK119.5.P37 1994
491'.1 – dc20 92-37773 CIP

ISBN 0 521 43079 8 hardback

VN

Contents

List of figures — *page* ix
List of tables — xiv
Preface — xv
Credits for illustrations and quotations — xviii
List of abbreviations — xx

PART I INTRODUCTION — 1

1 The Indus Civilization and its historical context — 3
1.1 Problems, objectives and strategies of research — 3
1.2 Rediscovery of a forgotten civilization — 4
1.3 Life in the Indus cities and villages — 6
1.4 Contacts with the Near East — 9
1.5 The land of Meluḫḫa — 12
1.6 Rise and fall of the Harappan culture — 15

PART II THE INDUS SCRIPT — 27

2 Early writing systems — 29
2.1 Evolution of communication — 29
2.2 The Sumerian writing system — 31
2.3 Creation of syllabic and alphabetic scripts — 34

3 Deciphering an unknown script — 40
3.1 Early breakthroughs — 40
3.2 Linear B — 43
3.3 Etruscan and the theory of decipherment — 45
3.4 Maya hieroglyphs — 49

4 Approaches to the Indus script — 52
4.1 Evolution of the Indus script and later Indian scripts — 52
4.2 Trial and error: attempts at decipherment — 57
4.3 Preparation of basic research tools — 61
4.4 The direction of writing — 64

5 Internal evidence for the type of script used in the Indus Valley 68
5.1 Graphemic analysis 68
5.2 Composite signs 79
5.3 Segmentation of texts 82
5.4 The type of writing system 84

6 Internal evidence for the structure of the Indus language **86**
6.1 Typological linguistics as a tool in decipherment 86
6.2 A positional classification of phrases 88
6.3 The problem of inflection 92
6.4 A computerized syntactic analysis 97

7 External clues to the Indus script 102
7.1 Basic methodology for deciphering the Indus script 102
7.2 The iconic meaning of the signs 103
7.3 Inscribed objects other than seals 106
7.4 Seals 113
7.5 Seal inscriptions 116

PART III THE LINGUISTIC CONTEXT 123

8 In search of the Indus language 125
8.1 Restriction of the search 125
8.2 Languages of the ancient Near East and the Iranian plateau 126
8.3 Languages of South Asia 133
8.4 The coming of the Aryans 142
8.5 The horse argument 155

9 Dravidian languages and the Harappan culture **160**
9.1 The Brahui problem and North Dravidian 160
9.2 Linguistic convergence in South Asia 167
9.3 Dravidian substratum influence on Old Indo-Aryan 167
9.4 Archaeological identification of Proto-Dravidian speakers 169
9.5 South Dravidian and the archaeology of peninsular India 171
9.6 Dravidian and decipherment of the Indus script 174

PART IV INTERPRETATIONS OF INDUS PICTOGRAMS 177

10 The 'fish' signs of the Indus script 179
10.1 Fish = star: astral divinities 179
10.2 Fish as an emblem of 'Proto-Śiva', Enki, Varuṇa and Kāma 184
10.3 Fish offerings 190
10.4 The sign sequences of 'number' + 'fish' 194
10.5 The planets Mercury and Saturn 195

11 The astronomical and astrological background 198
11.1 Planetary worship in India 198
11.2 The Vedic star calendar 201
11.3 Vernal equinox, due east and the asterism of the new year 205
11.4 Astral proper names in India 207

12 The trefoil motif: further evidence for astral religion 211
12.1 Indus bull figurines and dresses 211
12.2 'Liṅga-stands': the Seven Sages and the Great Bear 218

13 Evidence for Harappan worship of the god Muruku 225
13.1 Murukaṉ and the bangle cult 225
13.2 Murukaṉ's name and the planet Venus: a case for cross-checking 230
13.3 The 'seizer' 232
13.4 The name of Rudra 233
13.5 The goat-faced god 237

14 Evidence for Harappan worship of the Goddess 240
14.1 The North Star 240
14.2 The 'contest' motif and Durgā's fight with the Buffalo demon 246
14.3 Iconography of the 'fig deity' seal 256
14.4 The inscription on the 'fig deity' seal: the star of the Goddess, the carp and the red dot on the forehead 261

15 Epilogue 273

Appendix: Compounds ending in the word mīṉ *in* Tamil Lexicon 279
Bibliographical notes 284
References 303
Index of Indus signs and sign sequences 349
Index 353

Figures

1.1 The Persian empire under the Achaemenids. *page* 5
1.2 (a–b) The first known Indus seal. 6
1.3 Sites of the Indus Civilization (Mature Harappan and late Kot Dijian cultures). 7
1.4 Layout of the Indus cities of Mohenjo-daro and Harappa. 8
1.5 Sites where Indus seals and inscriptions have been discovered. 10
1.6 An Indus-style cylinder seal from Tell Asmar (Mesopotamia) with Indian animals. 11
1.7 (a–c) A typical Gulf seal discovered at Lothal. 11
1.8 Layout of the Indus town of Lothal. 12
1.9 Traditional houseboats used today on the Indus. 13
1.10 An amulet from Mohenjo-daro showing a ship. 14
1.11 Traffic routes and archaeological sites in the Indo-Iranian borderlands. 16
1.12 Archaeological sites of Elam, *c*.3000–2000 BC. 17
1.13 Early Harappan sites and cultural complexes in the Greater Indus Valley. 20
1.14 Three zebu bulls tethered to different trees on a painted jar from Nausharo ID. 21
1.15 Fig tree and a humped bull tied to a stand on Kulli-style ware from Mehi. 21
1.16 (a–b) Distribution of 'intercultural-style' carved steatite vessels, *c*.2500 BC. 23
1.17 Late and Post-Harappan cultures in the Indo-Iranian borderlands and the northwestern parts of the Indian subcontinent *c*.1900–1400 BC. 25
2.1 Comparison of discoid clay tokens and archaic Sumerian pictograms. 30
2.2 Numerical markings in successive layers at Susa, *c*.3300–2900 BC. 31
2.3 An archaic Sumerian economic tablet from Uruk III 2, with translation. 32
2.4 An archaic Sumerian economic tablet from Uruk with a summary on the reverse. 32
2.5 The Linear Elamite portion of a bilingual inscription of King Puzur-Inšušinak. 35
2.6 (a–b) A computer-drawn Proto-Elamite tablet from Tepe Yahya and its transliteration. 36

2.7 Correspondences between Egyptian, West Semitic, Greek and Indian (Brāhmī) alphabets. 37
3.1 Cartouches of Ptolemy and Cleopatra: the Egyptian hieroglyphs and their transliterations. 41
3.2 Noun paradigms in Linear B texts as analysed by Alice Kober. 44
3.3 Alice Kober's syllabic grid based on variation in inflection. 45
3.4 Tablet PY TA 641 from Pylos in Linear B script and in transliteration. 46
3.5 Bishop Landa's 'Maya alphabet' (AD 1566). 49
3.6 'Turkey' = Maya *ku-tzu* in the Dresden Codex (*c.* AD 1250). 50
3.7 'Dog' = Maya *tzu-lu* in the Madrid Codex. 50
4.1 Early Harappan painted and incised potter's marks from Bala-kot. 53
4.2 A 'fish' sign incised on a copper 'anthropomorph' from Sheorajpur. 55
4.3 A Late Harappan seal from Daimabad, Maharashtra, with one Indus sign. 55
4.4 (a–b) Outlined St Andrew's cross with crossbars from Mohenjo-daro and Navdatoli. 55
4.5 A woman of the South Indian Kuṟavar caste drawing an auspicious diagram (*kōlam*). 56
4.6 (a–h) The 'endless knot' motif in India and in the ancient Near East. 57
4.7 Similar-looking signs in different pictographic scripts, with their phonetic and semantic values. 58
4.8 Part of a concordance to the occurrences of the Indus sign . 63
4.9 (a–b) Overlaps in lines of Indus signs incised on pottery. 65
4.10 An Indus seal from Harappa inscribed along three sides. 65
4.11 An Indus seal with cramping of the last inscribed sign. 65
4.12 An Indus seal with cramping of the last two signs and one written beneath them. 66
4.13 An Indus seal with a boustrophedon two-line inscription. 66
4.14 (a–b) Indus seals paralleling the sequence of the two-lined seal in fig. 4.13. 66
5.1 A sign list of the Indus script, with principal graphic variants. 70
5.2 Absence and presence of the sign | at the beginning of 18 sign sequences. 80
5.3 (a–b) Functional correspondence between ligatures and their component signs. 81
5.4 An Indus seal with a single 'man' ligature. 82
5.5 The longest continuous Indus inscription: a seal from Mohenjo-daro. 83
6.1 A 'grid' analysis of some Indus inscriptions illustrating the positional slots I–III. 89
6.2 (a–b) Two unusually long texts with more than one 'cycle' of positions I–III. 90
6.3 (a–c) An amulet with three sides, each showing a deity and the same single Indus sign. 91
6.4 (a–f) Three seals with the initial portion of their obverse inscription repeated on the reverse. 92
6.5 The signs that occur immediately before the sign and the sequence 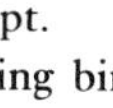. 93
6.6 An analysis of the 'final phrases' that occur after the different 'fish' signs. 94
6.7 Paradigmatic alternation at the end of some recurring sequences of Indus signs. 94
6.8 Indus language inflection pattern proposed by the Finnish team in 1969. 94
6.9 Indus language inflection pattern proposed by the Soviet team in 1968–81. 96
6.10 An Indus text analysed syntagmatically according to the pairwise frequencies of its signs. 98
6.11 Branching of alternative continuations after each phoneme in English phrases beginning in the same way. 98
6.12 Syntactic morph boundaries and the number of possible continuations after each phoneme in the English sentence 'Dogs were indisputably quicker.' 99
6.13 An Indus text analysed according to the 'Harris method'. 99
6.14 Labelling nodes of a syntactic tree according to the obligatory constituent. 99
6.15 Rule-forming in the paradigmatic approach. 100
6.16 Parsing a string of signs according to an intermediate grammar. 100
6.17 The first 50 pairs of signs most similar to each other in the Indus corpus, obtained by means of paradigmatic analysis on the first iteration. 101
6.18 List of the first ten groups of similar signs in the Indus corpus obtained after several iterations. 101
7.1 (a–c) An Indus sign and the palm squirrel. 103
7.2 (a–b) The graphic variants of an Indus sign and hoeing in Egypt. 105
7.3 (a–d) The 'flying bird' motif on painted pottery from Iran and Baluchistan. 105
7.4 (a–i) Frontal images of animal heads with horns and ears on a seal from Iran and painted potsherds from Rahman Dheri. 106
7.5 The solar 'wheel' as a symbol of royalty: a relief from Jaggayyapeṭa. 106
7.6 An inscribed shaft-hole axe from Tchoga-Zanbil near Susa. 107
7.7 An inscribed axe-adze from Ras Shamra (ancient Ugarit), Syria. 107
7.8 (a–f) A distinctive sign sequence on copper axes and seals from Mohenjo-daro. 108
7.9 (a–b) A typical 'miniature tablet' from the lower levels of Harappa. 109
7.10 The reverse of a moulded tablet from Harappa. 109
7.11 'Number two' and a kneeling man with the 'vessel' sign on an Indus tablet. 109
7.12 'Sacrificial vessel' in the iconography and text of an Indus tablet. 109
7.13 (a–b) The 'sacrificial vessel' and 'yoke carrier' signs

on an Indus tablet whose iconography on the reverse shows the worship of the 'fig deity'. 110
7.14 A typological analysis of the copper tablets from Mohenjo-daro. 111
7.15 (a–b) The monumental inscription from the city gate complex of Dholavira, with a close-up of the first three signs on the left. 113
7.16 (a–b) A clay tag from Umma, Iraq, with the impression of a square Indus seal on the obverse and of cloth on the reverse. 113
7.17 An analysis of the seal impressions on clay tags from the burnt-down warehouse at Lothal, showing interconnected inscriptions. 114
7.18 Method of securing the integrity of a commodity container in third millennium Mesopotamia. 114
7.19 An ancient customs house in Bahrain, with find spots of seals and weights. 115
7.20 (a–d) Analysis of house I, HR-A area, Mohenjo-daro, with find spots of seals. 118
7.21 Seal inscriptions that appear more than once. 120
8.1 Languages spoken in the ancient Near East. 127
8.2 Approximate distribution of the Iranian languages. 129
8.3 (a–b) A squarish Indus-style stamp seal from Ur, with a cuneiform inscription. 131
8.4 The Akkadian-style cylinder seal of 'Šu-ilišu, Meluḫḫa interpreter'. 132
8.5 (a–b) Square stamp seals with an identical sequence of Indus signs, from Kish and Mohenjo-daro. 132
8.6 A round stamp seal from Ur with common Indus signs in a unique sequence. 132
8.7 Modern Indo-Aryan and Nuristani languages. 135
8.8 Present-day distribution of the Dravidian languages. 136
8.9 Microlithic sites in South Asia and the areas in which the relict languages Nahāli, Iruḷa, Vedda and Rodiya are or were spoken. 138
8.10 Distribution of the Austro-Asiatic languages. 139
8.11 Distribution of Eastern Neolithic cultures of South Asia and their external relationships. 140
8.12 Area in which the Burushaski language is spoken today; the Northern Neolithic of South Asia; the Yang Shao Neolithic of China; and ancient trade routes in Inner Asia. 141
8.13 Distribution of the Sino-Tibetan languages. 143
8.14 The spread of the Proto-Indo-European language *c.*3000–2800 BC, according to Marija Gimbutas. 144
8.15 Distribution of the Timber Grave and Andronovo cultures. 146
8.16 The Mitanni kingdom and its neighbours. 147
8.17 A horse-drawn two-wheeled chariot on a cylinder seal from Tepe Hissar IIIb. 148
8.18 Ground-plan of the 'temple-fort' at Dashly-3 in Bactria, *c.*1900–1700 BC. 150
8.19 Ground-plan of the Achaemenid fortress at Kutlug-Tepe in Bactria. 150
8.20 An Early Andronovo chariot burial at the Sintashta cemetery in the southern Urals. 152
8.21 Distribution of Painted Grey Ware (*c.*1100–350 BC) and Northern Black Polished Ware (*c.*700–100 BC) in northern South Asia. 153
8.22 Places and peoples mentioned in the Vedic texts, *c.*1500–500 BC. 154
8.23 (a–b) Antennae-hilted copper swords from Bactria (Afghanistan) and Fatehgarh (India). 155
8.24 (a–c) Formation of the Aryan branch of Indo-European in three hypothetical stages. 155
8.25 A horse-headed macehead from plunder excavations in northern Afghanistan. 158
8.26 Shaft-hole axe with horse head from Afghanistan, early second millennium BC. 158
8.27 (a–b) Horse on painted pottery from Bīr-kōṭ-ghwaṇḍai, Swat, *c.*1700–1400 BC. 158
9.1 Two views of the formation of North Dravidian. 161
9.2 Migration pattern of nomadic people in Baluchistan at the end of the nineteenth century. 164
9.3 Major linguistic areas in South Asia as defined by the retroflex systems; also, the distribution of the inclusive / exclusive distinction in the pronoun of the first person plural. 166
9.4 (a–b) The Dravidian kinship system based on cross-cousin marriage. 171
9.5 Principal Megalithic sites in peninsular India. 173
9.6 Family tree of the principal Dravidian languages, with the number of their speakers in 1971. 175
10.1 (a–e) The fish-eating alligator (gavial) in Harappan art. 180
10.2 An Indus seal with a naturalistically depicted fish above joined animals. 181
10.3 A bird over a 'unicorn' bull and a fish over a bison on an Indus-style cylinder seal from Tell as-Sulema. 181
10.4 A fish in front of a 'unicorn' bull on an Indus-style cylinder seal from Ur. 181
10.5 (a–b) 'Fish' and 'star' motifs combined on Indus pottery from Amri III. 183
10.6 An Early Harappan goblet with three 'star' symbols from Mehrgarh VII. 183
10.7 An Indus-inspired round Dilmun seal from Ur, showing a water carrier with a star on either side. 183
10.8 A naked anthropomorphic figure, with streams flowing from his shoulders and a star on either side of his head, on a Syrian-style cylinder seal of *c.* eighteenth century BC. 184
10.9 An Indus seal with a deity sitting in a 'yogic' posture and a star in both loops of his buffalo-horned head-dress, which also bears a fig branch. 185
10.10 An Indus-style cylinder seal from the Near East with two anthropomorphic figures: one wears a crown of water buffalo horns with the leafed branch of a fig and sits on a throne with hoofed legs, surrounded by a pair of horned snakes, a pair of fishes and a pair of water buffaloes; the other figure stands, fighting two tigers, and surrounded by trees, a markhor goat and a vulture above a rhinoceros. 186

10.11 An Indus amulet showing a horned deity who sits in 'yogic' posture on a throne with hoofed legs, surrounded by fishes, gavials and snakes. 186
10.12 The symbol of 'two fish' among Buddhist auspicious signs in necklaces depicted at the stupa of Sāñcī, Central India, first century BC. 186
10.13 A man carrying two fishes in either hand in the mosaic 'Peace' panel from Ur. 187
10.14 Fish and the water-god in an early Iranian seal from Susa B. 187
10.15 Fish swimming in a river on a Proto-Elamite seal. 187
10.16 The Mesopotamian water-god Enki (Ea) on an Akkadian cylinder seal, depicted with fish swimming in the streams of water that issue from his shoulders. 187
10.17 Five fishes surround Enki on an Akkadian cylinder seal from Tell Asmar. 187
10.18 The 'Proto-Śiva' seal from Mohenjo-daro. 188
10.19 A priest masked as Enki, half-fish and half-man, in a relief of Assurnasirpal II (883–859 BC) from Calah. 190
10.20 (a–u) Painted and incised fish motifs on pottery from the Greater Indus Valley in Early and Mature Harappan periods. 192
10.21 (a–b) Possible recording of fish offerings in 'miniature tablets' from Harappa. 194
10.22 A fish-shaped tablet from Harappa, incised with an Indus inscription. 194
10.23 (a–c) Archaic Sumerian tablets from Uruk with numbers and fish signs. 195
10.24 Inscription consisting of just the signs '7' + 'fish' on a seal from Harappa. 195
11.1 Worship of the planet Saturn in a Śiva temple at Tiṭṭaguḍi, South India. 199
11.2 The traditional images and symbols of the nine planets, arranged in a gridiron of nine directions, on a contemporary South Indian metal plate. 200
11.3 Map of the calendrical stars of the Veda in 2250 BC. 202
12.1 The 'priest-king' statue from Mohenjo-daro. 212
12.2 A bull statuette with trefoil inlays from Uruk, *c.*3000 BC. 213
12.3 A bull decorated with trefoils on a steatite bowl from Ur, *c.* twenty-first century BC. 213
12.4 Fragment of a trefoil-decorated bull statuette from Mohenjo-daro. 213
12.5 Fragments of alabaster mosaic in the form of a bull ornamented with trefoils, from the 'palace' of Dashly-3 in north Afghanistan, *c.*1900–1800 BC. 213
12.6 A gold rosette with four holes for fixing it on clothing, from an Uruk period tomb at Tepe Gawra. 214
12.7 Inscription on a moulded terracotta amulet from Mohenjo-daro (the two other sides of this triangular prism show a fish-eating alligator and a ship). 215
12.8 A 'liṅga stand' from Mohenjo-daro decorated with 'trefoil' inlays. 218
12.9 A standing human couple in sexual intercourse on a tablet from Mohenjo-daro. 219
12.10 A standing human couple in sexual intercourse on an Early Dynastic seal from Ur. 219
12.11 A standing human couple in sexual intercourse on a Dilmun seal from Failaka. 219
12.12 A round seal with Indus script and the motif of a bull mating with a cow. 219
12.13 Worship of Śiva's liṅga with trefoil bilva leaves. Roof painting from Tiṭṭaguḍi, South India. 220
12.14 Seven fire-altars on a ceremonial platform in Kalibangan. 222
12.15 The fireplaces of the 'seven sacrificial priests' in the Vedic Soma sacrifice. 223
13.1 (a–b) An incised 'miniature tablet' with the Indus sign of 'intersecting circles'. 226
13.2 (a–b) An Indus tablet with the sign sequence ;on the reverse, a deity sitting on a throne, flanked by cobras and worshippers. 226
13.3 (a–b) An Indus tablet with the sign sequence  on both sides: on the obverse with 'a man in front of a tiger', on the reverse with a row of swastikas. 227
13.4 (a–b) 'Intersecting circles' in traditional Lamaistic art: auspicious symbols representing the ear-rings of the king and the queen. 227
13.5 The Indus sign of 'intersecting circles' on a stoneware bangle. 227
13.6 The signs of 'fireplace' and 'intersecting circles' on a seal from Harappa. 228
13.7 A domestic sanctuary of the Tharu in Nepal, with a pair of glass bangles representing Curinyā, a female spirit that menaces children and pregnant women. 228
13.8 A sacred tree with a railing, in a moulded tablet from Harappa. 229
13.9 Worship of a sacred Bodhi tree in a medallion from the stupa of Bhārhut, second century BC. 229
13.10 The sign sequence 'fig tree' + 'fish' on a seal from Mohenjo-daro. 231
13.11 The sequence 'fig tree' + 'two long vertical strokes' on a seal from Harappa. 231
13.12 (a–b) Two variants of the ligature composed of the 'fig tree' and 'crab' signs on Indus seals from Harappa and Lothal. 232
13.13 The ligature of 'fig tree' + 'crab' signs corresponding to the motif of 'horned archer' in two sets of copper tablets from Mohenjo-daro. 234
13.14 (a–c) A terracotta mask from Mohenjo-daro, representing a male deity with a human face, elongated eyes, the horns of a bull and a goat's beard. 235
13.15 Allographs of the 'fig tree' sign and of its ligature with the 'crab' sign. 235
13.16 (a–i) 'Three-branched fig tree' as a motif on Early, Mature and Late Harappan pottery. 236
13.17 The goat-headed fertility-god Naigameṣa in early Jaina art from Mathurā. 238
13.18 A ram-faced deity with long arms, standing inside a fig tree, on a tablet from Harappa. 239

14.1 Vaṭa-Sāvitrī in a picture drawn after traditional models about 1905. 241
14.2 The banyan tree (*Ficus indica* = *F. bengalensis*) with its aerial roots. 242
14.3 The sequence 'fig tree' + 'fish' in the inscription of a seal from Mohenjo-daro. 243
14.4 Circumpolar stars and the celestial pole between 5000 BC and AD 2000. 243
14.5 An anthropomorphic deity within a fig tree, with stars placed in horn-like loops on either side of the fig on a tablet from Harappa. 244
14.6 (a–b) A tablet from Harappa with the sequence of '4' + 'fig tree' on the obverse and the sign or motif of 'fig leaf' on the reverse. 246
14.7 The 'contest' of a nude hero (with six locks of hair) and tigers on a seal from Mohenjo-daro. 247
14.8 The 'contest' motif on the ivory handle of a flint-bladed knife, found at Gebel el-ʿAraq in Upper Egypt. Carved in Egypt in the Sumerian style of the Jemdet Nasr period. 247
14.9 An Early Dynastic III seal from Susa with the 'contest' motif. 247
14.10 The 'contest' motif on an Early Dynastic II votive plaque from the temple of the goddess Inanna at Nippur. 248
14.11 An Early Dynastic II / III seal from Fara, showing a hero with six locks of hair checking two bulls, while a bull-man checks two lions. 248
14.12 (a–b) The 'contest' of lion and bull on Proto-Elamite seals from Susa. 249
14.13 An 'intercultural-style' bowl from Khafajeh, Mesopotamia, with three scenes: (a) Fight between a lion and a bull. (b) A deity sits, with his legs bent underneath, upon two humped bulls. He holds in his hands streams of water and there is the sickle moon and a rosette-formed star in front of his head. In the background, there are ears of corn (or trees). (c) A deity stands upon two lionesses or other felines and holds attacking serpents in his hands. In front of his head is a rosette-shaped star. 249
14.14 (a–b) Proto-Elamite seals from Susa, with bulls and other animals represented in sitting posture, in profile and as seen from the front with their legs turned to either side. 250
14.15 (a–c) Proto-Elamite seals from Susa, with bulls sitting with legs bent double and fully turned to either side, seen from the front. 250
14.16 An Indus seal with a multifaced anthropomorphic god whose sitting posture resembles that of the Proto-Elamite bulls. The deity's arms are full of bangles, the crown on his head has buffalo horns and a fig branch, and the throne has hoofed legs. 250
14.17 Seal impression on a potsherd from Tepe Yahya IVA, with a male deity whose hoofed legs are bent double beneath and turned out to either side; dots surround the head. 250
14.18 An Early Harappan pot from Lewan Dheri in north Pakistan, showing two goats and the heads of a buffalo and a zebu with fig leaves rising from between the horns. 251
14.19 (a–d) Water buffalo on Early Harappan pottery from Kot Diji, Gumla and Burzahom. 251
14.20 (a–b) Water buffalo on two late Akkadian cylinder seals with the 'contest' motif. 252
14.21 Late Akkadian seal of the royal scribe Ibnišarrum, showing the hero with six locks of hair as slaking the thirst of the buffalo with water flowing from the pot of Enki. 252
14.22 The water-god Enki sits between two water buffaloes subdued by two six-locked heroes, who each place a foot on the head of the subdued beast: a late Akkadian cylinder seal. 252
14.23 (a–c) The spearing of water buffalo in Harappan glyptic art. 252
14.24 The goddess Durgā, riding on a lion, defeats the Buffalo demon. Rock-cut relief in Mamallapuram, South India, *c.* AD 650. 253
14.25 A cylinder seal from Kalibangan, with two warriors in the act of spearing each other; both are held by the hand by a goddess, also shown with the body of the tiger. 253
14.26 A square stamp seal with the tiger-bodied goddess from Kalibangan. 254
14.27 Sumerian electrum helmet from the Royal Cemetery at Ur. 254
14.28 A late Akkadian cylinder seal showing the war-goddess Ishtar with one foot on a lion. 254
14.29 (a–b) A golden seal with a winged goddess and lions from Bactria. 255
14.30 Ground-plan of the 'palace' in Dashly-3, Bactria. 255
14.31 The Tantric maṇḍala of Mahākālī. 255
14.32 A bison bull about to have intercourse with a prostrate priestess on an Indus seal from Chanhujo-daro. 256
14.33 A Lamaist *thang-ka* with the ithyphallic god Yama upon a buffalo which mates with an old woman. 257
14.34 A cylinder seal from Bactria with mating couples, human and animal. 256
14.35 The 'fig deity' seal from Mohenjo-daro. 260
14.36 Statue of Narunde, the Elamite goddess of victory, from Susa, *c.*2220 BC. 262
14.37 The 'snakehead' fish, *Ophiocephalus striatus* (Sanskrit *śakula*, *śāla*). 264
14.38 The carp, *Cyprinus rohita(ka)*, alias *Labeo rohita* (Sanskrit *rohita*). 264
14.39 Hindu forehead marks with lunar crescents. 265
14.40 (a–b) Women wearing a forehead mark in the early historical art of India. 266
14.41 (a–b) A 'third eye' on bull figurines from the Quetta Valley, Baluchistan, *c.*2600 BC. 269
14.42 A traditional brass mask representing the goddess Durgā. 271
15.1 (a–e) A cuneiform tablet with the impression of a Dilmun seal, mentioning Amorite proper names, and with an early second millennium date in its inscription. 274
15.2 Interpretations of (partially interconnected) Indus signs and sign sequences. 275

Tables

		Page
1.1	Chronologies and cultural periods of the ancient Near East (Mesopotamia) and the Indus Valley (the Kachi plain) and the times of appearance of the different scripts. *page*	18
2.1	Percentages of logograms, syllabic signs and determinatives in Sumerian and Akkadian texts.	35
3.1	Conventional typology of decipherments.	48
5.1	Frequency distribution of the 417 graphemes distinguished by I. Mahadevan.	78
5.2	Basic types of writing system and the Indus script.	84
6.1	Implicational universals of language.	88
6.2	The first ten pairs of words most similar to each other in an English text, obtained by means of the paradigmatic analysis on the first iteration.	100
8.1	Ungulates represented by faunal remains at sites in the Greater Indus Valley.	157
10.1	Representation of the etyma **mīn* 'fish' and **mīn* / **vīṉ* / **vīṉṭ-V-kk-* 'star', **min* / **vin* / **miṉ* / **viṉ* 'to glitter, shine, flash' in Dravidian languages.	182

Preface

In March 1964, my friend Seppo Koskenniemi, of IBM, offered to do the programming for a study of the enigmatic Indus script, which had interested me ever since I read John Chadwick's fascinating book *The decipherment of Linear B*. My brother Simo Parpola (now Professor of Assyriology at the University of Helsinki) immediately joined the team which took up the Indus script as a hobby. (Five years later we learnt that a Soviet team had, independently of us, also embarked upon a computer-assisted study of the Indus script in 1964.)

In 1968, after finishing my doctoral thesis on ancient Indian ritual texts, I moved from Helsinki to Copenhagen to take up an appointment at the Scandinavian Institute of Asian Studies (SIAS). I was now in a position to review some aspects of our Indus studies. The draft was read by Simo as well as by my teacher, Professor Pentti Aalto. Their comments prompted me to try to read some Indus signs, and, as the approach seemed to lead to sensible results, I wanted to publish a preliminary report on the findings. The acting director of the SIAS, Professor Kristof Glamann, encouraged the idea and kindly provided me with all necessary facilities. Three successive progress reports were sent out in 1969.

Written in the first flush of enthusiasm, those reports were premature and incautious. They prompted justified criticism, but also support and important advice:

> What we shall need is not more possible or even plausible interpretations of signs based upon this theory, but the clearest possible demonstration that these meanings, and only these meanings, are correct. Once this foundation is unshakeable, it will be safe to build on it, but we must not be led into admiring a house of cards, which, elegant as it seems, will collapse if one prop is withdrawn. The authors of this booklet have a lot to learn about the presentation of their case; but the case itself looks extremely promising and we shall await developments with keen interest. (Chadwick in Clauson and Chadwick 1969: 207)

Heeding this advice, I have examined various aspects of the problem in depth and published both detailed studies and short summaries over the past twenty years. This book is the first integrated synthesis of the results. It proposes specific solutions to various problems related to the Indus script and its historical context. At the same time, it is intended to serve as a general introduction to the study of the Indus script, as it presents a fairly comprehensive selection of data that will also be relevant to any other approach. In the interests of readability, I have left out altogether a number of side issues and less compelling sign interpretations. Moreover, with the focus on the decipherment of the Indus script, the treatment of other relevant but complex issues is briefer than in an earlier draft of this book. Among these other topics is the correlation of the archaeological and linguistic models of Indian pre- and protohistory (part III). In a lengthy paper in 1988, I discussed the central but very vexed problem of the coming of the Aryans, synthesizing what was known already and proposing a number of new solutions; the summary given in sections 8.4–5 makes some adjustments in the light of the most recent research and continued deliberation. Reconstruction of the pre-Vedic religion of India is another major task, which will be touched on here and there, but a systematic and more extensive treatment must be left for another book.

The book chiefly reflects my own work, but its basic ideas stem from our early collective work. My brother Simo has continually helped me in questions regarding the ancient Near East. The original three-man team also collaborated in producing the first computerized concordance to the Indus script (1973). It was revised and complemented in three publications by Seppo's brother Kimmo Koskenniemi (now Professor of Computer Linguistics at the University of Helsinki) and me in 1979–82. My observations on the Indus script in part II are mostly based on these working tools. Kimmo has also developed further Seppo's ideas for a computerized analysis of the Indus inscriptions; these plans are now being realized by my daughter Päivikki Parpola, M.Sc. Section 6.4 is entirely based on their work and writings.

Many other friends too have made important contributions. First I want to acknowledge an old debt that goes back to the 'prehistory' of this book. In 1969, while working at the SIAS in Copenhagen, I felt the need of an index to those elements of compounds that do not occur initially but are recorded in the *Tamil Lexicon*, a work comprising seven volumes. My colleague Dr Eric Grinstead volunteered to compile such a research tool with the help of the computer. Dr R. Panneerselvam and Dr P.R. Subramaniam, both visiting scholars at the SIAS, took part in the project along with Mrs Setsuko Bergholdt, and in 1973 Dr Grinstead handed me a printout of the completed index. (This useful working tool remains unpublished, but I shall try to remedy that.)

Dr Juha Janhunen gave valuable comments in the early phase of writing this book. To Dr Bertil Tikkanen I owe useful criticism, especially regarding Indian linguistics. He also readily agreed to my request for a survey of the major areal isoglosses in South Asian languages, based on his own current research. I had originally planned to include this summary in section 9.2, but with much regret I finally excluded it as too specialized. This comprehensive and up-to-date catalogue will nevertheless be accessible to the interested reader as Dr Tikkanen will publish it shortly elsewhere. I am very grateful for being able to include at least a map that details the evidence most relevant for the present book (fig. 9.3). With similar generosity, Dr Paul Kent Andersen made many substantial amendments to sections 6.1–3. Dr Dominique Collon provided a commentary on the iconography of a particularly significant Akkadian seal (fig. 8.4).

Special thanks are due to Dr Jane R. McIntosh, Dr Andrew Robinson and Dr Margaret Deith, who have put their editorial skills at my disposal. Andrew in particular doggedly commented on draft after draft, and very substantially helped to improve the quality. Dr Robert Whiting and Mrs Margaret Whiting, M.Phil., also kindly checked the manuscript and suggested amendments, particularly in regard to the Near Eastern seals. Dr Peter Richards and Dr Jessica Kuper of the Cambridge University Press have helped with advice.

I am very much obliged to Mrs Virpi Hämeen-Anttila, B.A., who has skilfully drawn and redrawn many maps and figures to meet my wishes. Professor K. A. Hämeen-Anttila of the Department of Astronomy, University of Oulu, computed the positions of the stars for the stellar map in fig. 11.3. Pictures taken for the *Corpus of Indus Seals and Inscriptions* (§ 4.3), especially by Ms Erja Lahdenperä, Mr Jyrki Lyytikkä and Mr Arto Vuohelainen, have also been used in the illustration of the present book. I am most grateful to all the copyright holders for allowing the illustrations to be reproduced here. Credits are given on pp. xviii–xix.

Over the years and in various ways, many other friends and colleagues have helped me in my studies of the Indus script and its historical context. I cordially thank them all but can mention by name here only a few whose encouraging interest and help have benefited the book: Mr Harry Halén, Lic. Ph., Professor Jorma Koivulehto, Mr Petteri Koskikallio, M.A., Dr Klaus Karttunen and Mr R. Sivalingam in Helsinki; Mr Oppi Untracht in Porvoo; Mr Karl-Reinhold Haellquist in Copenhagen / Lund; Dr F.R. Allchin, Dr B. Allchin, Professor K.R. Norman and Professor Sir H.W. Bailey in Cambridge; Dr J. R. Knox and Dr J. E. Reade in London; Dr A. Ardeleanu-Jansen and Dr M. Jansen in Aachen; Professor H. J. Nissen and Dr U. Franke-Vogt in Berlin; Dr H. Falk in Freiburg; Professor W. Rau in Marburg; Professor J. Elfenbein in Mainz; Dr Paul Yule in Bochum; Professor K. V. Zvelebil, Professor H. W. Bodewitz and Dr Teun Goudriaan in Utrecht; Professor M. Tosi in Rome; Professor Pierre Amiet and Mme Francine Tissot in Paris; Dr V. I. Sarianidi in Moscow; Professor C. C. Lamberg-Karlovsky, Dr R. Meadow and Professor M. Witzel in Cambridge, Mass.; Professor G. L. Possehl in Philadelphia; Professor M. B. Emeneau and Professor G. F. Dales in Berkeley; Professor J. M. Kenoyer in Wisconsin; Professor W. A. Fairservis in Poughkeepsie; Professor D. Potts in Sydney; Dr. M. Rafique Mughal in Lahore; Professor A. H. Dani in Islamabad; Professor Sayid Ghulam Mustafa Shah, Dr M. Ishtiaq Khan and Dr Ahmad Nabi Khan in Karachi; Dr Shashi Asthana, Dr R. S. Bisht, Dr J. P. Joshi, Dr M. C. Joshi, Dr B. M. Pande and Professor Romila Thapar in Delhi; and Mr I. Mahadevan in Madras.

It remains for me to express my gratitude to the institutions that have sponsored my work on the Indus script over the years. Here I mention those directly connected with the present book. I started writing it in 1982, when I had a six months' senior research fellowship at the Academy of Finland. In 1983, the Wihuri Foundation awarded a grant for drawing maps and other illustrations; these were revised in 1991 with a grant from the Finnish Ministry of Education. The writing was interrupted by urgent field research on Vedic rituals in South India in 1983–7. A three months' British Academy exchange fellowship granted by the Academy of Finland enabled me to complete most of the remaining chapters at Churchill College and the Faculty of Oriental Studies, University of Cambridge, at the end of 1987. With another senior research fellowship at the Academy of Finland, I was able to concentrate on revising the book in 1989–90. The Academy of Finland has further contributed a subvention towards the printing of the illustrations and, together with the Finnish Ministry of Education, funds for language revision and editing the text. My sincere thanks also go to the Syndicate of the Cambridge University Press for publishing this book.

My family has paid a price for this work, so if there is any *puṇya* in it, that is hereby transferred to my wife Marjatta and our daughters Päivikki and Mette.

Credits for illustrations and quotations

I would like to thank the authors (mentioned in the captions) as well as the following copyright holders for their courtesy in permitting figures (quoted here with plain numbers) and other illustrative material to be reproduced:

P. K. Agrawala (Varanasi): 7.5; 10.12; Roshen Alkazi (New Delhi): 14.40b; F. R. and B. Allchin (Cambridge): 10.20.1; 14.18; American Institute of Indian Studies (Varanasi): (courtesy of the Archaeological Survey of India) 13.17; *American Journal of Archaeology* (Concord, N.H.): 3.2–3 and quotation from Kober 1948 in § 3.2; American Museum of Natural History (New York): 10.20m–n; 14.41; American Oriental Society (New Haven): 14.32; Pierre Amiet (Paris): 14.34; Archaeological Survey of India (New Delhi): 1.2a; 1.4; 1.8; 4.6c–e; 4.11; 4.14b; 7.15; 10.21b; 12.1; 12.14; 13.8–10; 14.23a–b; table 5.1; (photographs by Erja Lahdenperä for the University of Helsinki): 1.7; 4.9b; 4.12; 6.4a–b; 7.9a–b; 7.13; 8.5b; 10.1a; 10.9; 13.1–2; 13.6; 13.12b; 14.6; 14.25–6; (photographs by Jyrki Lyytikkä for the University of Helsinki): 4.10; 5.4–5; 10.1d; 10.21a; 10.24; 13.18; 14.3; Ashmolean Museum (Oxford): (Department of the Ancient Near East) 7.16; (Department of Eastern Art) 10.11; 14.33; Geoffrey Bibby (Århus): 7.19 (drawing by Bente Højholt Fischer); Warwick Bray (London): quotation from Bray 1968 in § 4.1; Bristol Classical Press (Bristol): 3.4; Trustees of the British Museum (London): 1.2b; 8.3; 8.6; 10.13; 10.16; 12.12; 14.13; Cambridge University Press (Cambridge): 9.4; George F. Dales (Berkeley): 4.1; Deccan College Postgraduate and Research Institute (Pune): 4.4b; (photograph by Erja Lahdenperä for the University of Helsinki): 4.3; Délégation Archéologique Française en Afghanistan (Paris): 13.16a–c; Department of Archaeology and Museums, Government of Pakistan (Karachi): 4.13; 4.14a; 13.12a; (photographs by Jyrki Lyytikkä for University of Helsinki): cover ill.; 7.1a; 13.5; 14.35; (photograph by J. C. M. H. Moloney): 7.1b; (photographs by Arto Vuohelainen for the University of Helsinki): 7.10; 14.16; Deutsches Archäologisches Institut, Abteilung

Baghdad (Berlin): 12.2; Editions du Centre National de la Recherche Scientifique (Paris): 4.6g–h; 10.14–15; 12.10; 13.7; 14.12; 14.14; 14.15b–c; Josef Elfenbein (Mainz): 9.1 and quotations in § 9.1; Faber and Faber Ltd (London): quotation from Burrow 1973 in § 9.3; Forschungsprojekt Mohenjo-daro, Lehrstuhl für Baugeschichte und Denkmalpflege, Rheinisch-Westphälische Technische Hochschule (Aachen): 1.10; 7.20; 12.3–5 (drawings by R. Bunse); 13.14; Richard N. Frye (Cambridge, Mass.): 1.1; Lamia al Gailani-Werr (London): 10.3; Marija Gimbutas (Los Angeles): 8.14; the President and Fellows of Harvard College: 2.6; Heras Institute of Indian History and Culture, St Xavier's College (Bombay): quotations from Heras 1953 in § 4.2; Indian Museum (Calcutta): (photographs by Erja Lahdenperä for the University of Helsinki): 4.4a; 7.12; (photographs by Jyrki Lyytikkä for the University of Helsinki): 7.9; Iraq Museum (Baghdad): 1.6; 8.5a; 10.4; 14.22; Istituto Italiano per il Medio ed Estremo Oriente (Rome): 8.27; 10.20d; 13.16h; Othmar Keel (Fribourg): 14.20a; Poul Kjærum (Højbjerg): 12.11; Philip L. Kohl (Wellesley): 1.16; Kimmo Koskenniemi (Helsinki): 6.10; 6.13–14; 6.16; Kimmo Koskenniemi and Asko Parpola (Helsinki): 4.8; Librairie C. Klincksieck (Paris): 10.1e; 10.5; 13.16f; Librairie Orientaliste Paul Geuthner (Paris): 14.15a; Gösta Liebert (Sävsjö): 14.4; Ligabue Collection, Centro Studi Ricerche Ligabue (Venice): 14.29; Jyrki Lyytikkä (Helsinki): 1.9; Macmillan Press Ltd (Basingstoke, Hampshire): 7.18; Richard Meadow (Cambridge, Mass.): table 8.1; Metropolitan Museum of Art (New York): (Rogers Fund, 1915) 7.2b; (Norbert Schimmel Trust, 1989) 8.26; Mission Archéologique de l'Indus (Paris): title page; 1.11 (drawn by Gonzague Quivron); 1.14; 10.6; 10.20a–c; 13.16e; Musée Guimet (Paris): 14.40a (photograph by J. Auboyer); Musée du Louvre, Département des Antiquités Orientales (Paris): 7.6–7; 8.4; 10.10; 14.21; 14.36; National Museum of India (New Delhi): (photograph by the Archaeological Survey of India): 10.2; (photographs by Erja Lahdenperä for the University of Helsinki): 4.9a; 6.3; 6.4c–d; 10.1b; 13.11; (photographs by Jyrki Lyytikkä for the University of Helsinki): 7.11; 10.18; 12.9; 13.3; 14.5; 14.23c; Hans J. Nissen (Berlin): 2.3; Oriental Institute, University of Chicago (Chicago): 10.17; 14.20b; 14.28; Asko Parpola (Helsinki): 8.23; 11.1; 12.8; 12.13; 14.2; table 3.1; table 5.2; table 6.1; (photograph by Jyrki Lyytikkä): 11.2; Asko Parpola (planning) and Virpi Hämeen-Anttila (drawing) (Helsinki): 1.3; 1.5; 1.12–13; 1.17; 2.7; 3.1; 3.5–7; 4.6a; 4.7; 5.1–3; 6.1–2; 6.5–9; 7.2a; 7.3–4; 7.8; 7.14; 7.17; 7.21; 8.1–2; 8.7–13; 8.15–16; 8.21–2; 8.24; 9.5–6; 10.20e–k, o–p, t; 10.22; 11.3; 13.13; 13.15; 13.16g, i; 14.7–8; 14.10–11; 15.2; table 1.1; Päivikki Parpola (Helsinki): 6.11; 6.15; 6.17–18; table 6.2; Peabody Museum of Archaeology and Ethnology, Harvard University (Cambridge, Mass.): 14.17; Stuart Piggott (Wantage, Oxfordshire): 8.20; Edith Porada (New York): 10.8; Gregory L. Possehl (Philadelphia): 1.15; 4.6b; 10.20q–s; T. J. Roberts: 7.1c; Viktor Sarianidi (Moscow): 8.18–19; 8.25; 14.30; Denise Schmandt-Besserat (Austin): 2.1; Fred Scholz (Berlin): 9.2; Society for South Asian Studies (London): 10.23; State Museum (Lucknow): (photograph by Jyrki Lyytikkä for the University of Helsinki): 4.2; Thames and Hudson Ltd (London): 10.20u; Bertil Tikkanen, Asko Parpola and Virpi Hämeen-Anttila (Helsinki): 9.3; University of California Press (Berkeley): quotation from Hart 1975 in § 10.5; University Museum, University of Pennsylvania (Philadelphia): 8.17; 10.1c; 10.7; 12.6–7; 14.27; Oppi Untracht (Porvoo) (photograph by Timo Ripatti): 14.42; François Vallat (Paris): 2.2; 2.5; John Wiley and Sons, Inc.: 6.12; Rita P. Wright (New York): 13.16d (drawn by Lise Poirier); Yale Babylonian Collection (New Haven): 15.1. The Indus signs in the text have been drawn by Virpi Hämeen-Anttila.

Abbreviations

Ancient Indian texts

AĀ = *Aitareya-Āraṇyaka*
AB = *Aitareya-Brāhmaṇa*
ĀgniveśyaGS = *Āgniveśya-Gṛhyasūtra*
Akam = *Akanāṉūṟu*
ĀpGS = *Āpastamba-Gṛhyasūtra*
ĀpŚS = *Āpastamba-Śrautasūtra*
AS = *Atharvaveda(-Saṁhitā)*
ĀśvGS = *Āśvalāyana-Gṛhyasūtra*
BĀU = *Bṛhad-Āraṇyaka-Upaniṣad*
BaudhDhS = *Baudhāyana-Dharmasūtra*
BaudhGS = *Baudhāyana-Gṛhyasūtra*
BaudhŚS = *Baudhāyana-Śrautasūtra*
GB = *Gopatha-Brāhmaṇa*
GGS = *Gobhila-Gṛhyasūtra*
HGS = *Hiraṇyakeśi-Gṛhyasūtra*
HŚS = *Hiraṇyakeśi-Śrautasūtra*
JB = *Jaiminīya-Brāhmaṇa*
JGS = *Jaiminīya-Gṛhyasūtra*
JŚS = *Jaiminīya-Śrautasūtra*
JUB = *Jaiminīya-Upaniṣad-Brāhmaṇa*
KapS = *Kapiṣṭhala-Kaṭha-Saṁhitā*
KāṭhGS = *Kāṭhaka-Gṛhyasūtra*
KB = *Kauṣītaki-Brāhmaṇa*
KP = *Kālikā-Purāṇa*
KS = *Kaṭha-Saṁhitā*
KSS = *Kathāsaritsāgara* by Somadeva
KŚS = *Kātyāyana-Śrautasūtra*
LŚS = *Lāṭyāyana-Śrautasūtra*
MBh = *Mahābhārata*
MGS = *Mānava-Gṛhyasūtra*
MS = *Maitrāyaṇī Saṁhitā*
MŚS = *Mānava-Śrautasūtra*
PB = *Pañcaviṁśa-Brāhmaṇa*
Perumpāṇ. = *Perumpāṇāṟṟuppaṭai*
PGS = *Pāraskara-Gṛhyasūtra*

Puram = *Puranāṉūṟu*
R̥S (= RV) = *R̥gveda(-Saṁhitā)*
RV (= R̥S) = *R̥gveda(-Saṁhitā)*
ŚĀ = *Śāṅkhāyana-Āraṇyaka*
ṢB = *Ṣaḍviṁśa-Brāhmaṇa*
ŚB = *Śatapatha-Brāhmaṇa*
ŚGS = *Śāṅkhāyana-Gr̥hyasūtra*
ŚŚS = *Śāṅkhāyana-Śrautasūtra*
SVB = *Sāmavidhāna-Brāhmaṇa*
TĀ = *Taittirīya-Āraṇyaka*
TB = *Taittirīya-Brāhmaṇa*
TS = *Taittirīya-Saṁhitā*
UMS = *Uttaramīmāṁsāsūtra*
(= Brahmasūtra = Vedāntasūtra)
VaikhGS = *Vaikhānasa-Gr̥hyasūtra*
VārGS = *Vārāha-Gr̥hyasūtra*
VS(M) = *Vājasaneyi-Saṁhitā* (Mādhyandina-śākhā)
Yāḻ. aka. = *Yāḻppāṇattu māṉippāy akarāti* = Pulavar 1842

Journals and publication series

AA = *American Anthropologist*. Menasha.
AASF = Annales Academiae Scientiarum Fennicae. Helsinki.
AASOR = *Annual of the American Schools of Oriental Research*. New Haven.
ABIA = *Annual Bibliography of Indian Archaeology*. Leiden.
AI = *Ancient India. Bulletin of the Archaeological Survey of India*. New Delhi.
AIUON = *Annali [dell'] Istituto Universitario Orientale di Napoli*. Naples.
AJA = *American Journal of Archaeology*. Concord.
ALB = *The Adyar Library Bulletin*. Madras.
AMAW = Akademie der Wissenschaften und der Literatur, Abhandlungen der Geistes- und sozialwissenschaftlichen Klasse. Mainz.
AO = *Acta Orientalia*. Leiden and Copenhagen.
APAMNH = Anthropological Papers of the American Museum of Natural History. New York.
ARASI = *Annual Report of the Archaeological Survey of India*. Calcutta and Delhi.
BASOR = *Bulletin of the American Schools of Oriental Research*. Baltimore.
BAVA = *Beiträge zur allgemeinen und vergleichenden Archäologie*. Bonn.
BDCPGRI = *Bulletin of the Deccan College Post-Graduate and Research Institute*. Pune.
BDCRI = *Bulletin of the Deccan College Research Institute*. Pune.
BEFEO = *Bulletin de l'Ecole Française d'Etrême-Orient*. Hanoi and Paris.
BIA = *Bulletin of the Institute of Archaeology, University of London*. London.
BSL = *Bulletin de la Société de Linguistique de Paris*. Paris.
BSO(A)S = *Bulletin of the School of Oriental (and African) Studies, University of London*. London.
CA = *Current Anthropology*. Chicago.
CISI = *Corpus of Indus Seals and Inscriptions*. 1 = Joshi and Parpola 1987; 2 = Shah and Parpola 1991.
DED = *Dravidian Etymological Dictionary* = Burrow and Emeneau 1961.
DEDR = *Dravidian Etymological Dictionary*, revised edn = Burrow and Emeneau 1984.
ERE = *Encyclopaedia of Religion and Ethics* = Hastings 1908–26.
EW = *East and West*. Rome.
GJ = *The Geographical Journal*. London.
Grundriss = Grundriss der Indo-Arischen Philologie und Altertumskunde. Strasburg.
IA = *The Indian Antiquary*. Bombay.
IAR = *Indian Archaeology – A Review*. New Delhi.
IASCCAIB = *International Association for the Study of the Cultures of Central Asia, Information Bulletin*. Moscow.
IHQ = *The Indian Historical Quarterly*. Calcutta.
IIJ = *Indo-Iranian Journal*. The Hague.
IJDL = *International Journal of Dravidian Linguistics*. Trivandrum.
IL = *Indian Linguistics*. Pune.
ILN = *The Illustrated London News*. London.
IS = *Indische Studien*. Berlin.
IT = *Indologica Taurinensia*. Torino.
JA = *Journal Asiatique*. Paris.
JAOS = *Journal of the American Oriental Society*. New Haven.
JAS = *Journal of Asian Studies*. New York.
JASB = *Journal of the Asiatic Society (of Bengal)*. Calcutta. See also *JRASB*.
JESHO = *Journal of the Economic and Social History of the Orient*. Leiden.
JIES = *Journal of Indo-European Studies*. Austin.
JNES = *Journal of Near Eastern Studies*. Chicago.
JRAS = *Journal of the Royal Asiatic Society*. London.
JRASB = *Journal of the Royal Asiatic Society of Bengal, Letters*. Calcutta.
JSFOu = *Journal de la Société Finno-Ougrienne*. Helsinki.
JTS = *Journal of Tamil Studies*. Madras.
LMB = *Lahore Museum Bulletin*. Lahore.
MAGW = *Mitt(h)eilungen der Anthropologischen Gesellschaft in Wien*. Vienna.

MASI = Memoirs of the Archaeological Survey of India. Calcutta and Delhi.
ME = *Man and Environment*. Pune.
MSFOu = Mémoires de la Société Finno-Ougrienne. Helsinki.
NBS = *Newsletter of Baluchistan Studies*. Naples and Rome.
OLZ = *Orientalistische Literatur-Zeitung*. Berlin.
PA = *Pakistan Archaeology*. Karachi.
PAPS = *Proceedings of the American Philosophical Society*. Philadelphia.
PEFEO = Publications de l'Ecole Française d'Etrême-Orient. Hanoi and Paris.
PIFI = Publications de l'Institut Français d'Indologie. Pondicherry.
QJMS = *The Quarterly Journal of the Mythic Society*. Bangalore.
RA = *Revue d'Assyriologie et d'Archéologie Orientale*. Paris.
RLA = *Reallexikon der Assyriologie und vorderasiatischen Archäologie*. Berlin.
SA = *Sovetskaya Arkheologiya*. Moscow.
SAA 1971 = *South Asian Archaeology [1971]* = Hammond 1973.
SAA 1973 = *South Asian Archaeology 1973* = van Lohuizen-de Leeuw and Ubaghs 1974.
SAA 1975 = *South Asian Archaeology 1975* = van Lohuizen-de Leeuw 1979.
SAA 1977 = *South Asian Archaeology 1977* = Taddei 1979.
SAA 1979 = *South Asian Archaeology 1979* = Härtel 1981.
SAA 1981 = *South Asian Archaeology 1981* = B. Allchin 1984.
SAA 1983 = *South Asian Archaeology 1983* = Schotsmans and Taddei 1985.
SAA 1985 = *South Asian Archaeology 1985* = Frifelt and Sørensen 1989.
SAA 1987 = *South Asian Archaeology 1987* = Taddei with Callieri 1990.
SAA 1989 = *South Asian Archaeology 1989* = C. Jarrige 1992.
SAA 1991 = *South Asian Archaeology 1991* = Gail, in press.
SBE = Sacred Books of the East. Oxford.
SÈ = *Sovetskaya Ètnografiya*. Moscow.
SLS = *Studies in the Linguistic Sciences*. Bloomington.
SO = *Studia Orientalia*. Helsinki.
SÖAW = Österreichische Akademie der Wissenschaften, Philos.-hist. Klasse, Sitzungsberichte. Vienna.
TC = *Tamil Culture*. Madras.
TL = *Tamil Lexicon*, I–VI and Supplement. Published under the authority of the University of Madras. Madras 1924–39.
TPS = *Transactions of the Philological Society*. London.
TSBA = *Transactions of the Society of Biblical Archaeology*. London.
VKAW = Verhandelingen der Koninklijke (Nederlandse) Akademie van Wetenschappen (te Amsterdam), Afdeling Letterkunde. Amsterdam.
WA = *World Archaeology*. London.
WZKM = *Wiener Zeitschrift für die Kunde des Morgenlandes*. Vienna.
WZKS(O) = *Wiener Zeitschrift für die Kunde Süd(- und Ost)asiens*. Vienna.
ZA = *Zeitschrift für Assyriologie und Vorderasiatische Archäologie*. Berlin.
ZDMG = *Zeitschrift der Deutschen Morgenländischen Gesellschaft*. Halle and Wiesbaden.

Other abbreviations and symbols

ASI = Archaeological Survey of India
BM = The British Museum
BMAC = Bactria and Margiana Archaeological Complex
C = (unspecified) consonant
CDr = Central Dravidian
Drav. or Dr = Dravidian
IE = Indo-European
IsMEO = Istituto Italiano per il Medio ed Estremo Oriente
OCP = Ochre Coloured Pottery
PCDr = Proto-Central Dravidian
PDr = Proto-Dravidian
PGW = Painted Grey Ware
PIE = Proto-Indo-European
PSDr = Proto-South Dravidian
SDr = South Dravidian
Skt = Sanskrit
V = (unspecified) vowel
: = represents / stands for / is related to / is associated with
* = the word or form following the asterisk is not actually attested anywhere, being a purely hypothetical reconstruction
< = comes from, is derived from
> = develops into, is changed into
≈ = is approximately the same as, nearly equal to, is roughly similar to

Part I

Introduction

1 The Indus Civilization and its historical context

1.1 Problems, objectives and strategies of research

In 1921, excavations at Harappa in the Punjab brought to light the ruins of a large brick-built city, and soon an unknown civilization was uncovered in and around the Indus Valley. The Indus (or Harappan) Civilization, now dated to *c*.2550–1900 BC, collapsed before the composition of the hymns collected in the Ṛgveda-Saṁhitā, the oldest historical document of India. No unambiguous information has been preserved to tell us the names of the Indus kings or their subjects, the names of the gods they worshipped, or even what language they spoke. The Harappan language and religion continue to be among the most vexing problems of South Asian protohistory.

The Indus people used a writing system of their own. Nearly 4,000 specimens of this script survive on stamp seals carved in stone, on moulded terracotta and faience amulets, on fragments of pottery and on a few other types of inscribed object. In addition to writing, the seals and amulets often contain iconographic motifs, mostly realistic pictures of animals apparently worshipped as sacred, and a few cultic scenes, including anthropomorphic deities and worshippers. The preserved texts are all very short (§ 5.3). There is no bilingual translating an Indus text into a known script and language. In the added absence of historical information on the Indus Civilization, it is no wonder the prospects of a successful decipherment have been considered meagre at best.

Yet it is necessary to keep on trying to find a solution. To be convincing, it must agree with generally accepted knowledge, and the methods by which such a solution has been reached must be scientific and open to scrutiny. Reduced to its barest essence, the scientific method of solving a problem consists of two operations: (1) devising theoretically justifiable hypotheses and (2) testing them. Contrary to common belief, it is not good research strategy to make carefully non-committal hypotheses, for these are difficult to test. Guesses that are as bold and detailed as possible are not only the easiest kind to test but also wield the maximum explanatory power if they turn out to be right. Excesses are kept under control by the simultaneous requirements of theoretical justification and testability: 'the question is not to minimize hypotheses but to maximize their control' (Bunge 1967: 287). This need for various kinds of tests is one reason why the Indus script should be studied from many different angles.

I turn in the Introduction to a survey of the present state of knowledge of the Harappan culture. This will define a number of premisses, some of which have changed substantially since the initial discoveries in the 1920s. I shall stress the Harappan contacts with ancient Western Asia, which provide relevant parallels and potential sources of information on the Harappan culture.

There follows in part II a brief history of writing and decipherment, as applied to other ancient scripts, for the benefit of those readers not acquainted with them. After that comes an analysis of the Indus script, discussing theoretical issues and summarizing some results to date. The main objectives are to chart ways of defining the type of writing and language represented by the Indus script and discovering the meaning of individual signs.

I come in part III to the problem of the Harappan language and consider its potential relationship to languages spoken in the Near East and South Asia. Most of this section is an attempt to correlate the linguistic protohistory with the typological and archaeological evidence. The aim is to see whether any of the languages known from this area is likely to have been spoken by the Harappans.

The coming of the Aryans to India is here considered at some length, so as to throw light on the gap between the Indus Civilization and the historical period that begins with the compilation of the Ṛgveda around 1200 BC. As we shall see, the textual, archaeological and linguistic evidence converges to suggest that the Ṛgvedic Aryans were preceded in India by another wave of Indo-European-speaking invaders, and that these earlier 'Aryans' (who called themselves Dāsa) penetrated further to the east than did the Ṛgvedic Aryans.

This inference provides a new basis on which to reconstruct the pre-Vedic religion of India. Such a reconstruction is vital, because we have good reason to expect the names of Harappan deities to be mentioned on Indus inscriptions. Personal names, both in the ancient Near East and in historical India, often contain gods' names as their building blocks, and the signs on Indus seals probably show the names and titles of their owners. One source for reconstructing the Harappan religion is the archaeological remains of the Indus Civilization, especially the motifs of the glyptic and plastic arts whose meaning may be elucidated by comparison with Near Eastern material. Another major source is the Vedic and later Indian texts and living cultic practices.

The pre-Vedic religion that emerges anticipates much of the later worship and mythology of Rudra-Śiva and the Goddess, especially as deities of war and fertility, with parallels in Western Asia. Religious issues particularly relevant to the decipherment of the Indus script will be dealt with in this book as the occasion arises, but a more comprehensive reconstruction of the pre-Vedic religion has to be left for a separate publication; an outline of the basic theses is available elsewhere (Parpola 1988a).

The book concludes (part IV) with some suggested readings of a few Indus signs, and a detailed presentation of the inscriptional, linguistic and religious evidence for them.

1.2 Rediscovery of a forgotten civilization

The Indus Valley has occupied a pivotal position in the early cultural history of the Indian subcontinent. Until colonial times, the mountain passes of the northwest were the gateway through which wave after wave of foreign invaders came. The plains of the Indus were the first area to be annexed to dominions in the Iranian plateau or Central Asia. This political unification of the two sides of the Hindu Kush mountains opened the way for widespread cultural exchange in both directions. When the invaders extended their rule into India, they usually lost contact with their origins and the exchange ceased. This historical pattern has repeated itself many times, and can be expected to have some validity even in prehistory.

When Darius the Great conquered the southern Indus Valley around 520 BC, he annexed it to the Persian empire as a satrapy called in Old Persian *Hinduš* (fig. 1.1). In Sanskrit or Old Indo-Aryan, the language spoken in North India at that time, the word *sindhu-* means primarily 'river'; as a proper name it refers both to the river Indus and to the southern Indus Valley, the modern province of Sind(h) in Pakistan. Through Old Persian, this name immediately passed into the language of the Ionian Greeks, who were also subjects of the Persian empire. Persian *Hinduš* became *Indós* 'Indus river' and *Indíē* 'country of the Indus river and beyond'.

Both India and its earliest civilization are therefore called after the Indus. With its yearly floods this mighty snow-fed river, like the Nile and the Euphrates and Tigris, made possible large-scale cultivation and thereby urbanization. But unlike its counterparts in Egypt and Mesopotamia, the Indus Civilization did not survive until historical times. Flourishing from about 2550 BC, it collapsed around 1900 BC and was soon totally forgotten. All that remained were the mounds of deserted towns and cities, which even today are up to 30 metres high.

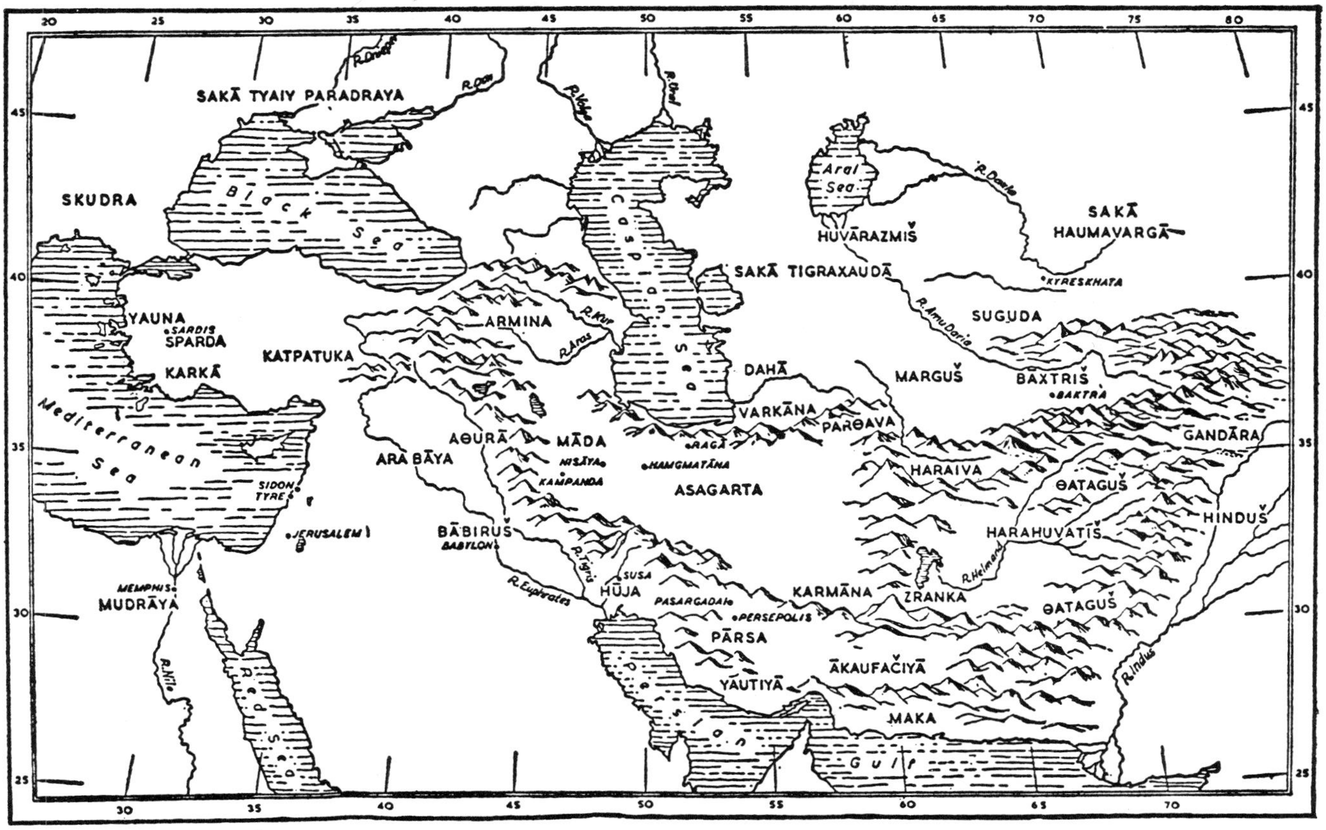

Fig. 1.1. The Persian empire under the Achaemenids. After Frye 1966: 286. ('Dahā' is placed too far to the west, in its later (Parthian period) location; for earlier times, see § 8.4.)

The earliest documents of India, Vedic texts dating from *c.*1200–500 BC, speak of ancient ruin mounds (*arma*) in various ways: as widely scattered habitations of foreign people who have gone away to some other country (TB 2,4,6,7–8); as haunts of sorceresses (ṚS 1,133,3); and as find-places of potsherds in the wilderness (KS 19,5; TS 5,1,6,2), located along the banks of the rivers Indus (JB 3,238), Sarasvatī (PB 25,10,16–18) and Dṛṣadvatī (LŚS 10,19,4–9). The settlements of the Indus Civilization cluster along the old beds of these very rivers. Sent on an excursion by Alexander the Great in 326 BC, Aristoboulos, too, 'found an abandoned country, with more than a thousand towns and villages deserted after the Indus had changed its course' (Strabo xv,1,19).

Not until 2,000 years later are the ruin mounds of the Indus Valley mentioned again in historical sources. In the early nineteenth century several Britons travelled in the Indus Valley, publishing detailed accounts of their journeys. The most noteworthy was that of the young Scottish officer Alexander Burnes, who in 1831 drew the first scientific maps of the Indus and its tributaries. During his travels, Burnes made an excursion to the huge ruin mounds of Harappa about 100 miles to the southwest of Lahore on the dry bed of the river Ravi.

The ancient ruins of Harappa had by then already supplied the bricks used in building the nearby modern village of 5,000 inhabitants. The site was, however, extensive enough to furnish ballast for more than 100 miles of the Punjab railway, the stretch between Multan and Lahore, laid between 1856 and 1863 by the British engineer William Brunton.

Few British officials were as insensitive to the cultural history of India as Brunton. Serious study had been strongly urged as early as 1774 by Dr Samuel Johnson in a letter to Warren Hastings. The most significant initiatives were taken by Sir William Jones (1746–94) of the Supreme Court of Bengal. Jones founded the Asiatic Society in 1784 and initiated the translation of Indian classical literature, the study of the Sanskrit language, and comparative Indo-European linguistics. Another remarkable pioneer was James Prinsep (1799–1840), an official of the Calcutta Mint, who studied the coins of the Indo-Greek kings and the inscriptions of the emperor Asoka. Asoka's edicts, carved on rocks and

Fig. 1.2. The first known Indus seal (BM 1892-12-10,1): (a) in a drawing of its impression as published by Cunningham (1875: pl. 33, 1), and (b) in a newly made impression.

stone pillars all over his vast empire, are the earliest directly preserved historical documents of India, dating from *c.*250 BC. Prinsep deciphered the two forms of writing used in these and other early monuments, the Brāhmī and the Kharoṣṭhī scripts (§§ 2.3 and 4.1).

General Alexander Cunningham (1814–93) was in his youth an eager assistant of Prinsep, but his special hobby was studying ruin mounds. Cunningham was able to devote himself fully to this task after his retirement in 1862, first as an official and later as the Director of the newly founded Archaeological Survey of India. After three visits to Harappa from 1853 onwards, in 1875 he published a description of the site, with a map and illustrations of the few antiquities discovered. These included a curious seal, with characters in an unfamiliar script (fig. 1.2).

Two further seals of this type were found at Harappa and published in 1886 and 1912. The origin of the seals intrigued Sir John Marshall (1876–1958), Director General of the Archaeological Survey of India from 1902. Marshall directed D. R. Sahni to begin excavations at Harappa in January 1921. More seals were immediately discovered, from beneath the levels representing the oldest archaeological assemblage known in India at that time. R. D. Banerjee discovered similar seals in 1922–3 at Mohenjo-daro in Sind, some 650 kilometres to the southwest of Harappa, while examining the ruin mounds surrounding a Buddhist stupa built in the first or second century AD.

As soon as Marshall had been able to study the material unearthed at Harappa and Mohenjo-daro, he wrote an article on it, published in 1924 in *The Illustrated London News*. The brick-built cities shattered the belief that India had been inhabited only by primitive savages before the nomadic Aryans brought their culture to the subcontinent some time in the second millennium BC. But how ancient were these cities? What was their relation to the early civilizations in other countries? What language did their people speak and what did they call themselves? Answers could perhaps be found in the inscriptions carved on the seals. But nobody could read them.

These tantalizing discoveries led to large-scale mass excavations at the two sites. The digs at Harappa in 1921–5 were led by Sahni, in 1926–34 by M. S. Vats, those at Mohenjo-daro in 1924–31 were directed first by Marshall himself, and from 1927 onwards by Ernest Mackay. In spite of their defective methods, these excavations still constitute the basis of our knowledge of the Indus Civilization. But later discoveries during the past several decades have constantly changed our perceptions of it.

1.3 Life in the Indus cities and villages

More than a thousand settlements of the Indus Civilization have been discovered over an area of some 1.25 million square kilometres, larger than today's Pakistan or the Egyptian and Mesopotamian empires of the third millennium BC (fig. 1.3). We do not know whether this whole domain was politically unified or consisted of several states, but culturally it was surprisingly uniform, though recent research has brought to light many examples of regional variety too. Cities like Mohenjo-daro and Harappa covered more or less a square kilometre, housed some 40,000 inhabitants and were among the greatest metropolises of their time. Still untouched sites of almost the same size are Judeirjo-daro in Sind, Lurewala Ther and Ganweriwala Ther on the dried-up course of the ancient river Hakra in the desert of Cholistan and Rakhigarhi in Haryana; indeed, the pattern suggests a regular network of settlements, with major cities at an average distance of *c.*250 kilometres from each other.

Many Harappan towns and cities shared a common layout (fig. 1.4). An acropolis, the administrative and ritualistic centre, was built upon a high platform of mud and mud-brick. Like the lower town with living quarters, workshops and bazaars, it was surrounded by walls, needed for protection against both human and animal aggression and the periodic floods of the Indus. In smaller towns like Lothal (with about 2,500 inhabitants), the acropolis and the lower town were separated only by a wall (fig. 1.8). The buildings and streets were carefully orientated according to the cardinal directions (§ 11.2).

The famous Great Bath in the acropolis of Mohenjo-daro was undoubtedly used for religious rites. Built of burnt brick, it was made watertight with bitumen. At each of the short ends, a flight of steps led into the water, which was drained off through an underground outlet under a high corbelled archway. The basin was surrounded by brick columns supporting the roof of a covered corridor. On three sides there were smaller rooms, one containing a well.

Grain was presumably the basis of economic transactions, as in contemporary Mesopotamia. Taxes levied in the form of corn had to be stored. A building next to the Great Bath on the west, adjoining the wall, may be such a treasury. The floor has

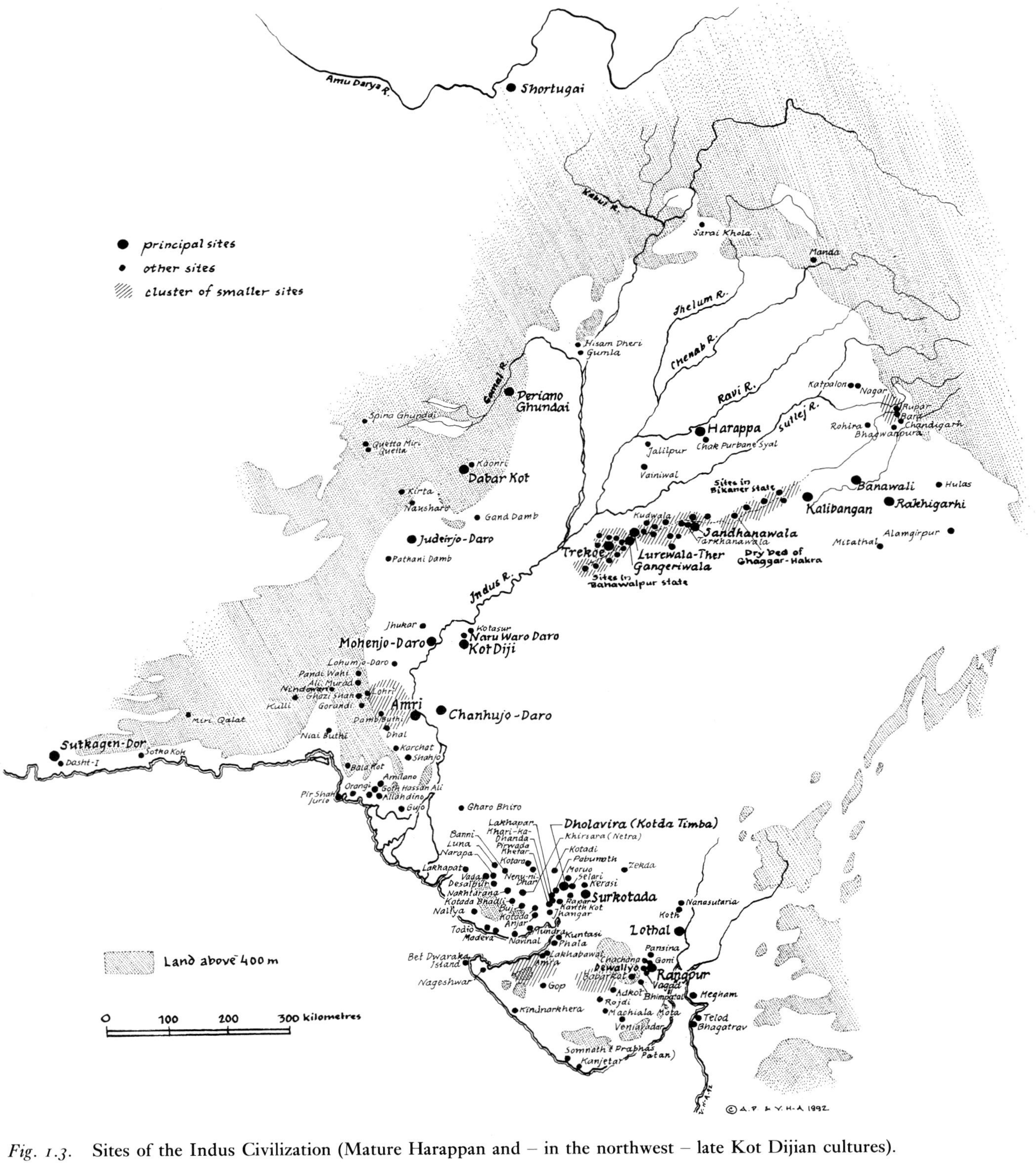

Fig. 1.3. Sites of the Indus Civilization (Mature Harappan and – in the northwest – late Kot Dijian cultures).

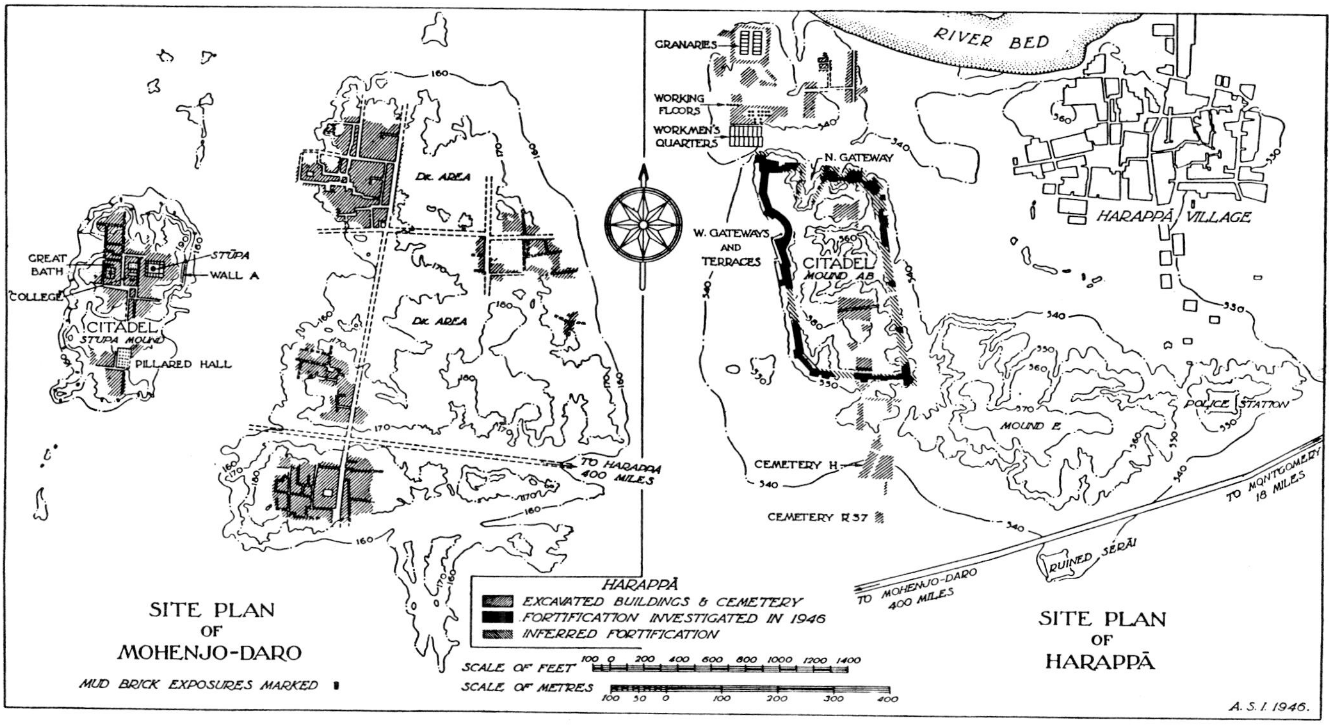

Fig. 1.4. Layout of the Indus cities of Mohenjo-daro (in Sind) and Harappa (in the Punjab). After Wheeler 1947a: 63, fig. 2.

numerous rectangular masonry platforms which probably supported a timber floor, with open passages beneath, which would have kept the bottom free from ground moisture.

The analogous 'Great Granary' at Harappa is somewhat surprisingly situated outside the citadel walls, near the main gate on the bank of the old bed of the river Ravi. This position may have been chosen to facilitate transport by boat. Close by, there were at least five rows of circular platforms, paved with burnt brick, for pounding grain on a large scale. In one of the central holes of the 18 surviving platforms, once furnished with wooden basins, remains of burnt wheat and husked barley have been identified.

The private houses, too, were mostly built of expensive baked brick. Considerable attention was paid to privacy and comfort. No doors or windows opened on to the broad main streets, noisy and dusty with traffic; the entrances were from small side lanes. Then, as today in Sind, the focus of domestic activities was the inner courtyard, surrounded by several smaller rooms and stairs leading to the upper storey.

The residences of well-to-do people had good wells of their own and bathrooms with paved floors. Pottery pipes carried waste water to the covered baked-brick drains running along the streets. Their soak-pits were undoubtedly emptied municipally, like the pottery receptacles outside the house walls, into which the dirt from rubbish-chutes running through the walls emptied. Harappan water engineering was far more advanced than that in many oriental towns today.

Different occupational groups probably had their own areas within the city, as in India and Pakistan today. In Harappa, remains of 14 barrack-like houses in two rows, and of 16 furnaces used for metal-working have been found near the Great Granary. Some craftsmen's workshops have been identified, for example those of a coppersmith and a bead-maker in Lothal, a Harappan coastal town in Gujarat. Harappan craftsmen were competent, specialized and conservative. Their occupations are likely to have been hereditary. The mass-produced and standardized objects were sometimes quite inefficient, but little effort was made to improve them. For instance, the Harappans continued to use an axe with a flat bronze blade that was tied to the shaft, even though they knew from imported examples a much more efficient type of axe with a hole in the blade for inserting the shaft.

The millions of bricks used to construct the cities were made in standardized and convenient sizes. They could each be lifted in one hand, and their proportions (1:2:4) are ideal for a firm bond. The weights, polished cubes of stone, were highly standardized, too. The same can be said of the metal, stone and pottery artefacts. Neolithic flint tools were not abandoned; on the contrary, cheap chert blades outnumber metal implements. Copper, often alloyed with tin or arsenic as bronze, was worked into different kinds of vessels, tools and weapons. In addition to metal arms, soldiers and city guards probably used slings with clay pellets, as do the hunters of present-day Sind.

Copper was also cast by the lost-wax method into statuettes, a sensuously modelled nude dancing girl and lifelike buffaloes and bulls being the finest examples. Numerous terracotta and faience models of animals (fig. 7.1b) and humans undoubtedly had a religious significance, like the few stone sculptures (fig. 12.1). With the exception of a magnificent stone urial ram about 1 metre long that has recently come to light, all surviving art objects are on a very small scale. Miniature clay carts with solid wheels, and pottery whistles and rattles, may have been children's toys. Game-pieces and a fragment of a board with squares drawn on it attest adult pastimes. The most common personal ornaments were bangles, rings and beads of various types, made of faience, shell, terracotta, steatite, gold, etc.

The majority of pots found in Harappan cities are small, plain water pitchers produced in great quantities, but not all ceramics were so severe. Many vessels were made of carefully prepared clay, often covered with red slip, and painted in black. Among the favourite motifs are geometrical figures, like intersecting circles or fish scales, naturalistic paintings of peacocks, snakes and fig trees, and some more stylized objects that are difficult to recognize.

The people in the cities, specializing in arts and crafts, trade, religion and administration, were fed from the surplus produced by farmers. The main plants under cultivation were barley and wheat, or (in Gujarat only) rice; different types of pea were also grown, and possibly sesamum for oil. A small piece of woven cotton cloth dyed red with madder attests the antiquity of India's famous cotton and dyeing industry. The plough was used, and the flooding of the Indus may have been exploited in the same way as today: barley and wheat are grown immediately after the floods in the autumn and reaped in March to April, while cotton and sesamum are sown at the beginning of the floods and harvested at their end.

The most important domestic animals were cattle, sheep and goats; but fowls, dogs and probably water buffaloes were also kept. Deer, gazelle and wild boar were the main hunted game. The tiger and rhinoceros depicted on the Indus seals and tablets have been used as an argument for a slightly more humid climate in Harappan times than today's semi-arid one, which receives less than 200 mm of annual rainfall. But the tiger is still occasionally found in Sind, and Babur, the first of the Great Mogul emperors, speaks of rhinoceros-hunting in the Punjab. The need for fuel to bake the huge quantity of bricks used in building the Harappan cities has been cited as another indication of more luxuriant vegetation. However, the fuel output of the present-day riverine forest has been shown to be sufficient to satisfy that need.

The rivers have certainly changed their courses many times since the third millennium. The system of the ancient Sarasvatī river (modern Ghaggar) was in Harappan times perennial and probably emptied itself into the Indian Ocean east of the Indus, which by Vedic times it no longer did. Large numbers of fish bones found at Mohenjo-daro and Harappa prove that fishing, with nets and copper fish-hooks, provided an important source of food. The rivers also provided irrigation and transport, carrying cedar pine used as timber at Harappa down from the Himalayan foothills and heavy loads of chert from the working sites in the Rohri hills. The rivers were indeed vital to the Harappan cities, which were almost invariably situated on ancient river-beds, despite the risk of floods.

Thus the Harappans could effectively harness the Indus with all its economic potential. This secured for most inhabitants of the Indus cities a fairly high standard of living. One feature that is quite unusual for ancient times is the relatively even distribution of this wealth. There is little evidence of extreme poverty or of extreme luxury.

1.4 Contacts with the Near East

When he announced the discovery of the Indus Civilization, Sir John Marshall expressed the hope that archaeologists working in other countries might suggest clues to its date and external contacts. He was not disappointed. Just one year earlier, in 1923, Ernest Mackay (who was soon to excavate Mohenjo-daro) had unearthed a Harappan-type seal with an Indus inscription at Tell Uhaimir, ancient Kish, under a pavement built by Hammurapi's son, King Samsu-iluna (1749–1712 BC) (fig. 8.5a). Two other 'Indus seals', discovered at Tello and Susa, were published in 1925. By 1932 the number of seals found in the Near East and supposed to be related to the Indus Civilization was 30, and the next half-century has added a dozen more. Of the 11 seals from Mesopotamia that can be dated with any degree of certainty, nine have been attributed to the Akkadian period (2334–2154 BC) and two to the time of the Isin and Larsa dynasties (nineteenth to eighteeenth century BC).

Several different types can be distinguished among the 'Indus seals' found outside the Indus Valley (fig. 1.5). One could be called 'native Harappan' type, because it is like the great majority of the Indus seals found in India and Pakistan, consisting of *square* stamp seals with a bipartite high boss on the reverse, an inscription in Indus characters, and a characteristically Harappan iconographic motif, such as the 'unicorn' bull (fig. 8.5). Such native Harappan-type seals have been discovered at several sites in the Near East and were

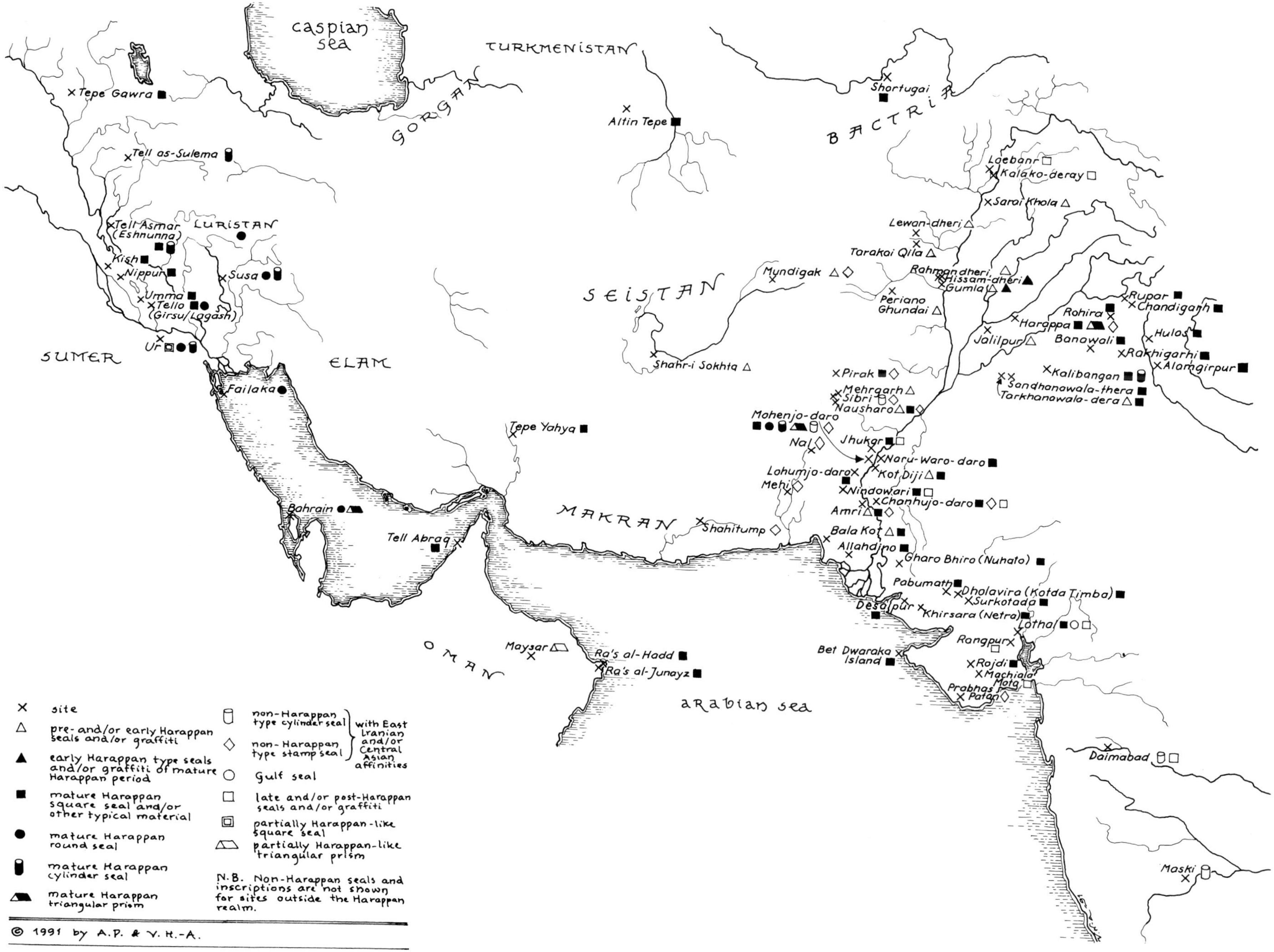
caspian sea
TURKMENISTAN
GORGAN
BACTRIA
SEISTAN
LURISTAN
SUMER
ELAM
MAKRAN
OMAN
arabian sea
Tepe Gawra
Tell as-Sulema
Tell Asmar (Eshnunna)
Kish
Nippur
Umma
Tello (Girsu/Lagash)
Susa
Ur
Failaka
Bahrain
Tell Abraq
Maysar
Ra's al-Hadd
Ra's al-Junayz
Altin Tepe
Tepe Yahya
Shahr-i Sokhta
Mundigak
Shortugai
Laebanr
Kalako-deray
Sarai Khola
Lewan-dheri
Tarakai Qila
Rahman dheri
Hissam-dheri
Gumla
Periano Ghundai
Harappa
Jalilpur
Rohira
Banawali
Rupar
Chandigarh
Hulas
Rakhigarhi
Alamgirpur
Kalibangan
Sandhanawala-thera
Tarkhanawala-dera
Pirak
Mehrgarh
Sibri
Nausharo
Mohenjo-daro
Nal
Jhukar
Naru-Waro-daro
Kot Diji
Lohumjo-daro
Mehi
Nindowari
Chanhujo-daro
Amri
Shahitump
Bala Kot
Allahdino
Gharo Bhiro (Nuhato)
Pabumath
Dholavira (Kotda Timba)
Surkotada
Desalpur
Khirsara (Netra)
Lothal
Rangpur
Bet Dwaraka Island
Rojdi
Machiala
Prabhas Patan
Mota
Daimabad
Maski
site
pre- and/or early Harappan seals and/or graffiti
early Harappan type seals and/or graffiti of mature Harappan period
mature Harappan square seal and/or other typical material
mature Harappan round seal
mature Harappan cylinder seal
mature Harappan triangular prism
non-Harappan type cylinder seal
non-Harappan type stamp seal
with East Iranian and/or Central Asian affinities
Gulf seal
late and/or post-Harappan seals and/or graffiti
partially Harappan-like square seal
partially Harappan-like triangular prism
N.B. Non-Harappan seals and inscriptions are not shown for sites outside the Harappan realm.
© 1991 by A.P. & V.H.-A.

Fig. 1.5. Sites where Indus seals and inscriptions have been discovered.

Fig. 1.6. Impression of a cylinder seal (IM 14674) from Tell Asmar (in Mesopotamia), with Indian animals carved in Harappan style: rhinoceros, elephant and gavial (fish-eating alligator). 'Glazed steatite', height 3.4 cm. Cf. Frankfort 1955: no. 642; Collon 1987: no. 610.

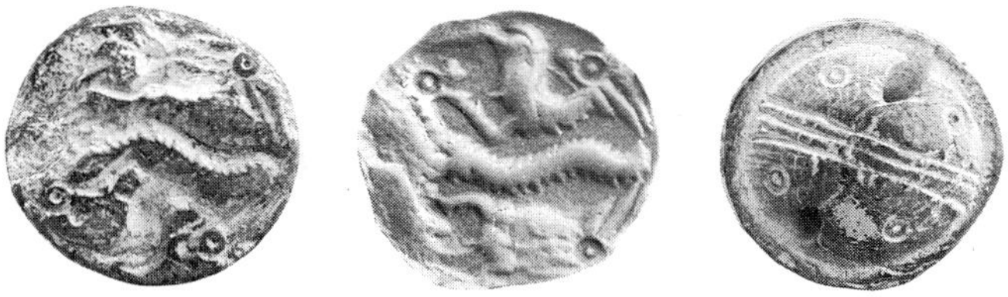

Fig. 1.7. A typical Gulf seal (L-123) discovered at Lothal (in Gujarat): (a) obverse, (b) impression, (c) reverse.

probably transported there from the Indus Valley. Some other Indus seals, found in Ur, Susa, Tell Asmar and Tell as-Sulema, were undoubtedly locally made, for although they bear Indus script and / or iconographic motifs that are clearly of Harappan inspiration, their form agrees with the main type of Mesopotamian seals: they are *cylinders*, rolled over wet clay rather than pressed upon it (fig. 1.6). However, most of the foreign-style Indus seals found in the Near East are *round* stamp seals, a type that is rare both in the Indus Valley and in Mesopotamia. They come mainly from the coastal city of Ur and from the Gulf. The iconographic motif on these round seals is the 'bison feeding from a manger' (fig. 8.6), a typically Harappan motif, but not nearly as common in the Indus Valley as the 'unicorn' bull.

Some of the round seals excavated at Ur were of a type not known at all from the Indus Valley; they had on the reverse a low, pierced boss, engraved with one to three parallel lines flanked by two dots-in-circles on either side. (An untypical Gulf seal from Ur is shown in fig. 10.7.) The mystery of their provenance was solved in the 1950s during Danish excavations on the islands of the Gulf. Over 500 round stamp seals have by now been discovered on Failaka and Bahrain, which have turned out to be centres of a previously unknown 'Dilmun Civilization'. One of the Indus seals found at Bahrain was associated with a small cuneiform tablet containing three Amorite proper names (§ 8.2), datable on the grounds of the forms and combinations of its signs to *c.*2050–1900 BC.

In the early 1960s one 'Gulf seal' (fig. 1.7) was discovered at Lothal in Gujarat. Among other finds from this Harappan coastal site is a water-basin measuring 219 × 37 metres and 4.5 metres deep, built of baked brick and situated immediately beside the acropolis (fig. 1.8). One interpretation sees it as a dockyard, where ships could find harbour sheltered from the strong tide; another as a fresh-water reservoir.

Immediately adjoining the water-basin in the acropolis of Lothal is a 'warehouse' with a floor area of 1,930 square metres (fig. 1.8). Its ground-plan resembles that of the 'granaries' of Harappa and Mohenjo-daro and originally comprised 64 cubes of mud-brick, separated from each other by metre-wide brick-paved passages. The superstructure, built partly of timber, partly of mud, has burnt down. Among the ashes on the floor were found nearly a hundred clay tags, bearing impressions of native Indus seals on one side and of packing materials (bamboo, reeds, mattings, woven cloth and twisted cords) on the other (figs. 7.16–17).

Lothal, situated some 700 kilometres southeast of Mohenjo-daro, has been termed a 'gateway settlement'. It functioned not only as an outpost for sea trade but also as an exchange point between the Harappans and the hunter-gatherers of Gujarat, who collected raw materials for them. Whole and partly sawn elephant tusks were discovered at a workshop in Lothal. The trading network of the Harappans must have extended as far as South India, for northern Karnataka is the most likely source of their fuchsite: a vase made of this rare mineral was found at Mohenjo-daro.

But chief among the raw materials procured from Saurashtra and Gujarat are various kinds of semi-precious stones, especially agate and carnelian. Beads were manufactured on an extensive scale at Lothal. A bead factory identified in the lower town yielded many unfinished specimens as well as drills and other tools, including a stone anvil and a furnace. The Harappans had learnt to stain white designs on the red carnelian: the pattern was first drawn on the stone with soda, and the stone was then heated until the alkali entered it, making the pattern permanent. This industry of 'etched' carnelian has survived at Sehwan in Sind until this century. Such 'etched' carnelian beads have been found in the Royal Cemetery of Ur, dating from *c.*2500–2334 BC; they constitute the earliest evidence of trade contacts between Mesopotamia and the Indus Civilization.

Lothal is not the only Harappan town on the coast of the Indian Ocean. Trading outposts identified in Pakistani Makran (up to Sutkagen-dor near the border of Iran) bridge

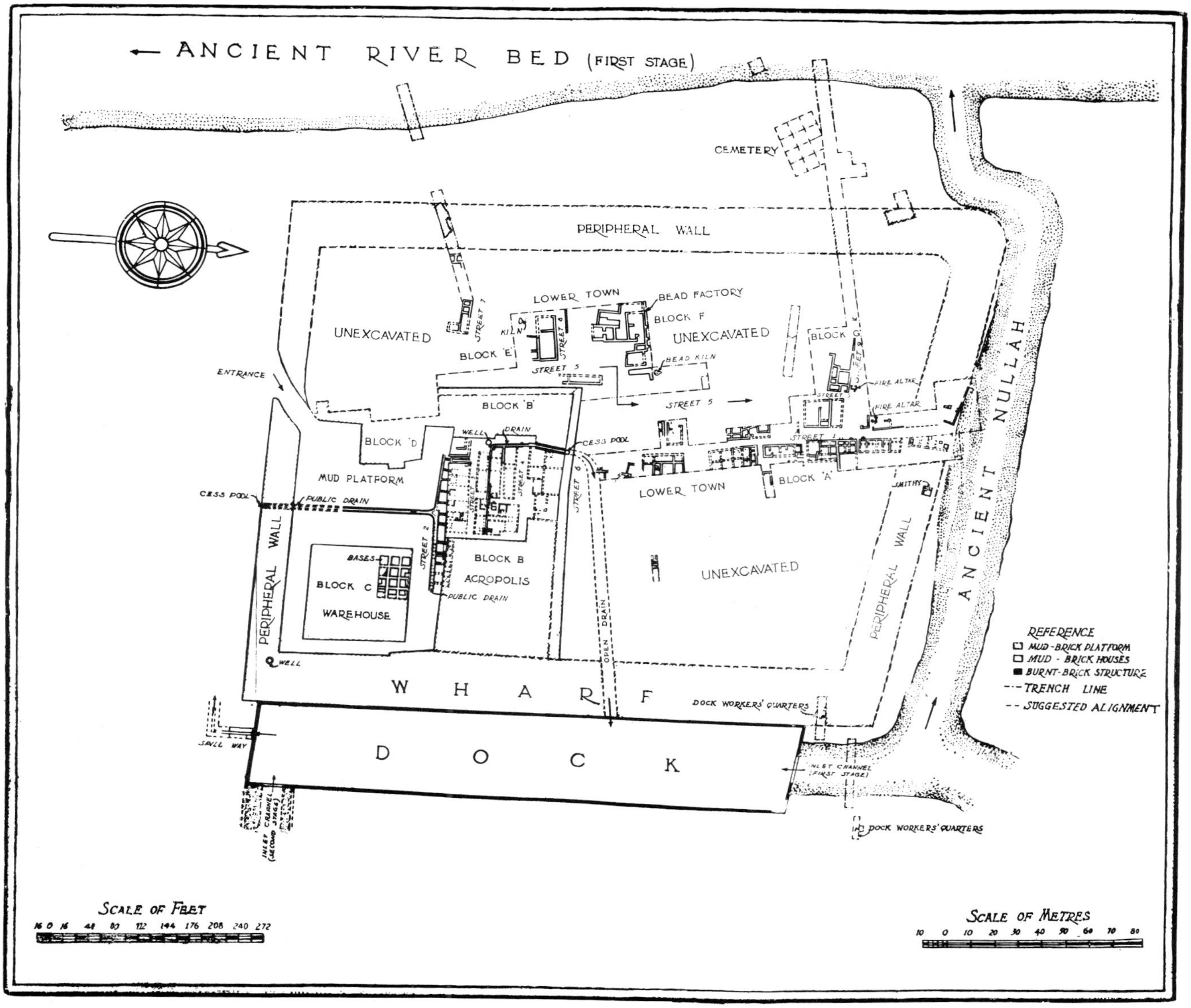

Fig. 1.8. Layout of the Indus town of Lothal (in Gujarat). After Rao 1979: I, pl. 38.

the distance to the Gulf and Mesopotamia (fig. 1.3). In 1981 an Indus inscription on a large potsherd was discovered at Ra's al-Junayz in Oman (fig. 1.5). That the Harappans were a seafaring people is suggested also by representations of ships, both in terracotta models found at Lothal, and on Indus seals and sealings from Mohenjo-daro (figs. 1.9–10).

1.5 The land of Meluḫḫa

The discoveries of the Gulf culture and Lothal directed attention to the cuneiform references to sea trade. Three foreign countries were the main participants in this trade from the twenty-fourth to the nineteenth century BC: Dilmun, Magan and Meluḫḫa. The fixed order of reference to these countries is usually understood to reflect their respective locations. The following identifications are now widely agreed:

Dilmun = the Gulf culture, especially the islands of Tarut, Bahrain and Failaka;

Magan = the Oman peninsula and the Iranian Makran across the Gulf;

Meluḫḫa = the Indo-Iranian borderlands and the Indus Civilization.

Dilmun (see also § 8.2) must have been nearest to Mesopotamia, for it is usually mentioned first, most frequently and

Fig. 1.9. The Harappan ships (fig. 1.10) were very similar to the traditional houseboats (Sindhi *ḍū̃nḍī* or *beṟī*) with a rectangular cabin (Sindhi *thaṟo*) used today on the Indus by the aboriginal Sindhi tribe of fishermen and sailors called Mohāna. It is the name of this tribe that figures in the name of *Mohenjo-daro* (spelt also *Mohan-jo-daro* in the 1920s) 'the mound [situated in the area] of the Mohānas'. The widely current interpretation of the name as 'the mound of the dead', Sindhi *Moen-jo-daro*, appears to be a misunderstanding.

as a trading emporium which supplied goods from more distant lands. Recently Dilmun has been found mentioned in the archaic texts of Uruk III, dated to *c*.3200 BC. The name occurs in several contexts tentatively interpreted as follows: 'tax collector of Dilmun', 'Dilmun axe', 'one bale of Dilmun garments' and 'prince of the good Dilmun-house (or temple)'. Archaeological and textual evidence has suggested that until *c*.2400 BC Dilmun was the island of Tarut and the nearby coast of the eastern Arabian mainland. Between *c*.2400 and 1500 BC, the expanded 'Dilmun Civilization' would have stretched from Failaka island in the north to Bahrain island in the south, with Bahrain as its centre (fig. 1.5). During the latter half of the second millennium BC, Dilmun seems to have become displaced northwards, its centre shifting to Failaka island.

Magan is quoted especially as the source of copper, and recent excavations and surveys have shown Oman to be the largest known site of copper production in the third millennium BC. Magan is supposed to designate Oman in the third and early second millennium BC, and southeastern Iran as well around the middle of the second millennium. The name *Magan* / *Makan* / *Makkan* may be etymologically related to the place-name *Makrān*: this early Islamic spelling goes back to Old Persian *Maka*, one of the satrapies of the Achaemenid empire (fig. 1.1). Greek authors place the people called *Mákai* in Oman and on the opposite coast of Karmania in Iran. An item of trade supporting this identification is 'the *mêsu* wood of Magan', which, according to the trilingual inscriptions of Darius the Great, was imported from northwest India (Gandāra) and eastern Iran (Karmāna) and called *yakā-* in Old Persian: in modern Iranian the cognate word *jag* denotes sissoo (*Dalbergia sissoo* Roxburgh), a large tree growing in the mountains of Oman, southern Iran and Pakistan.

Meluḫḫa is mentioned in cuneiform sources for the first time when one of the most famous rulers of Mesopotamian history, Sargon of Akkad (2334–2279 BC), the founder of the

Akkadian dynasty, boasts in one of his inscriptions: 'Ships from Meluḫḫa, ships from Magan (and) ships from Dilmun he [i.e. Sargon] made lay anchor at the harbour of Akkad.' The order of enumerating the countries is exceptional. Apparently the most distant country was mentioned first to impress the reader.

A historical text relates how almost the whole world rebelled against Sargon's grandson, Narām-Sīn (2254–2218 BC), towards the end of his rule. A newly identified fragment of this text, published in 1976, enumerates the names of mutinous kings, among them '[. . .]ibra, man of Meluḫḫa', in a passage where all geographical names refer to places east of Mesopotamia.

Gudea, the Sumerian king of Lagash in 2144–2124 BC, states in his inscriptions that 'the Meluḫḫans came from their country' and supplied *ušū* wood, gold dust, carnelian and other luxury items for the construction of the main temple in Gudea's capital. The Meluḫḫans seem to have stayed in Lagash and established a colony there, for a village called Meluḫḫa existed near the city for at least 35 years (2105–2071 BC) in the time of the Third Dynasty of Ur.

Literary texts dating from *c.*2000 BC contain interesting information on Meluḫḫa. A composition called 'Enki and the world order' describes how the wise water-god Enki moves around organizing the world, decreeing the fate of different countries. The participants in the sea trade figure prominently; their ships are mentioned in verses 124–30. But the most noteworthy passage is in verses 219–35:

He crossed to the land (*kur*) of Meluḫḫa.
Enki, the king of the Sweet-Water Ocean, decrees its fate:
'Black land (*kur*), your trees will be large trees,
they will be *mêsu*-groves of the highland (*kur*),
their thrones will be set in royal palaces.
Your reeds will be large reeds,
they will be reeds of the highland (*kur*),
heroes work them as weapons in the battlefields.
Your bulls will be large bulls,
they will be the bulls of the highland (*kur*),
their roar will be the roar of the bulls of the highland (*kur*).
The great laws (*me*) of the gods will be perfected for you.
All *dar*-birds (i.e. fowls) of the highland (*kur*) [wear] carnelian beards;
your birds will be *ḫaia*-birds,
their cries will fill the royal palaces.
Your silver will be gold, your copper will be bronze-tin.
Land (*kur*), everything you have will [increase],
your people will [multiply],
your male will go after his fellow male like a bull.'
(trans. based on Kramer 1963: 178, and Kramer and Maier 1989: 46f.)

Fig. 1.10. A Harappan ship with a rectangular cabin (cf. fig. 1.9), with birds aboard. A later Buddhist story (Jātaka no. 339) relates how 'some [Indian] merchants came to the kingdom of *Bāveru* [= *Bābilu* in Babylonian], bringing on board ship with them a direction-crow'. Such a crow was released if the sailors wandered too far towards the open sea from the coast; by flying towards the land, the bird would show the right direction. One side of a moulded terracotta amulet in the form of a triangular prism from Mohenjo-daro (M-1429). Length 4.6 cm. (For the two other sides, see figs. 10.1c and 12.7.)

The word 'highland' (*kur*), occurring many times in this passage, usually refers to the Iranian plateau and to the foreign countries east of Mesopotamia. The expression 'black country' (*kur-gi*$_6$) may mean 'country of dark soil' or 'country of dark-skinned people'. It recurs as an attribute of Meluḫḫa in the text called 'Curse over Akkad' (lines 48–9): 'In the days of Narām-Sīn . . . ships kept bringing goods to Sumer . . . The Meluḫḫans, the men of the black country, brought to him all kinds of exotic wares.'

The divine *ḫaia*-bird (^{d}*ḫa-ia*^{mušen}) whose sound is to be heard in the royal palaces could be the peacock. The Buddhist Bāveru-Jātaka speaks of Indian merchants who 'came to the kingdom of *Bāveru* [fig. 1.10] [and] brought a royal peacock which they had trained to scream at the snapping of the fingers and to dance at the clapping of the hands'; the Babylonians bought it for a thousand gold coins, and paid the royal peacock high honour. This Indian parallel may date from the Achaemenid times, because the name *Bāveru* for Babylonian *Bābilu* may owe its *r* to Old Persian *Bābiru*.

The cuneiform text called 'Enki and Ninḫursag' (lines 3–5) says: 'May the land of Meluḫḫa bring to you tempting precious carnelian, sissoo wood of Magan, fine sea-wood (and) large boats.' The meaning 'carnelian' for ^{na_4}*gug* (= Akkadian *sāmtu*, lit. 'red stone') is considered as certain; we have seen that 'etched' carnelian beads of Harappan origin had found their way to Ur already in Early Dynastic times. The 'sea-wood' imported from Meluḫḫa for making chairs and dagger sheaths in the times of the Third Dynasty of Ur was in all likelihood the very hard wood of the mangrove tree growing on the coast of east Baluchistan and Sind.

Ivory was also among the products of Meluḫḫa. After the end of the Isin-Larsa dynasty around 1760 BC, ivory was no longer imported via the Gulf. Nor is the name of Meluḫḫa mentioned again before the fifteenth century BC, when it started to denote the new source of ivory, Nubia or Ethiopia, unknown to Mesopotamians in the third millennium BC. The texts now speak of 'black men of Meluḫḫa'.

1.6 Rise and fall of the Harappan culture

When the discovery of the Indus Civilization was first announced, Assyriologists drew attention to a number of traits that it seemed to share with early Mesopotamia. It was quickly recognized, however, that the resemblances are mainly general features of urbanization, while numerous differences establish the independent character of the Indus Civilization.

At Mohenjo-daro many attempts to reach the lowest levels in order to establish the origins of the city have been frustrated by the high water-table, which has risen several metres during the past millennia. But at Amri an older culture stratified under the Harappan layers was recognized by N. G. Majumdar as early as 1929. Similar sites have since been located in increasing numbers (fig. 1.13).

Recent work has clearly shown that the Indus Civilization grew out of earlier local cultures, and that these represent an essentially indigenous development. Most important have been the French excavations carried out under the direction of Jean-François Jarrige since 1974 at Mehrgarh and Nausharo on the Kachi plain, along the route to the Bolan Pass that leads from western Sind to the highlands of Baluchistan and beyond (fig. 1.11). These excavations have for the first time created an unbroken cultural sequence from the end of the eighth to the beginning of the second millennium BC (table 1.1).

While summarizing the cultural evolution in the Greater Indus Valley on this basis, we shall naturally pay attention to contacts with the external world. These, too, have been adequately charted only from the past few decades' explorations and excavations in the Iranian plateau and in Central Asia. Acquaintance with the archaeological background of the Indus Civilization is indispensable not only for attempts at defining the linguistic prehistory of the Greater Indus Valley (chapter 8). We have to be aware that certain of the cultural traits of the Harappans have a long prehistory. The dates given here (i.e. in this chapter and in table 1.1) have been calibrated to the traditional Near Eastern chronology. References to the Mesopotamian periods help to correlate the events in Indus Valley with those of Western Asia (table 1.1).

Neolithic period

The earliest level of Mehrgarh (IA, *c.*7000–6000 BC) was aceramic. Small houses with a quadrangular plan and several rooms were built of air-dried mud-brick. Naked six-row barley and other indigenous grains including bread wheat were harvested on a large scale with sickles whose flint blades were fixed in place with bitumen. Both wild and partially domesticated varieties of cereals have been identified. The animal bones discovered belong mainly to hunted wild species, but herding of sheep, goats and above all cattle (zebu) had started by the end of the aceramic period. Small human figurines were made of unbaked clay. The burials were made in simple pits dug in cemetery areas. The grave goods comprise young goats, ground stone axes and ornaments. Necklaces made of marine shells, lapis lazuli and turquoise attest contacts with the Arabian Sea and Afghanistan. Similarities of a general nature connect these earliest farming communities of Baluchistan with those of the Zagros region and northern Iran.

The earliest layers of Kili Ghul Muhammad (KGM, 1,500 metres above sea-level) appear to represent this same phase. This would mean that sedentary life was started simultaneously in the highlands and the plains (Mehrgarh is 150 metres above sea-level).

The second major phase of Mehrgarh (IB–IIA, *c.*6000–5000 BC) is also Neolithic. It is characterized by a limited amount of pottery, handmade from rough clay with plenty of straw, very similar to the earliest pottery of the Near East and the Iranian plateau. Baskets coated with (local) bitumen were also used. The site now covered several hectares and included large granaries (compartmented storage buildings with remnants of charred grain), which remained a characteristic cultural trait until the end of period III. Jujube and date were also cultivated now. Remains of domesticated animals, especially bovids, greatly outnumber the bones of wild animals. Besides the human figurines already present in the earlier phase, there are also clay statuettes of the zebu from 6000 BC onwards. Conceptions of the afterlife must have changed, for the dead were now buried without any grave goods.

Chalcolithic period

The next major phase at Mehrgarh (IIB–III, *c.*5000–3600 BC) is Chalcolithic. There is now evidence for copper-smelting. Awls, knife blades and hooks were made of metal. A bow drill was used in specialized lapidary workshops. Mehrgarh covered dozens of hectares in period III. Some sort of irrigation undoubtedly existed, required by the cotton cultivation evidenced by large amounts of cotton seeds. The pottery, now wheel-thrown, was plain at first. From about 4000 BC, ceramics were painted with geometric and soon also with animal motifs, evolving into complex friezes. The rather homogeneous KGM II–III / Togau A Ware is known not only from the Kachi plain but also from many sites in Baluchistan (the highland plateaux as well as the valleys of Kalat, Quetta, Zhob and Loralai) and from the lowest levels of

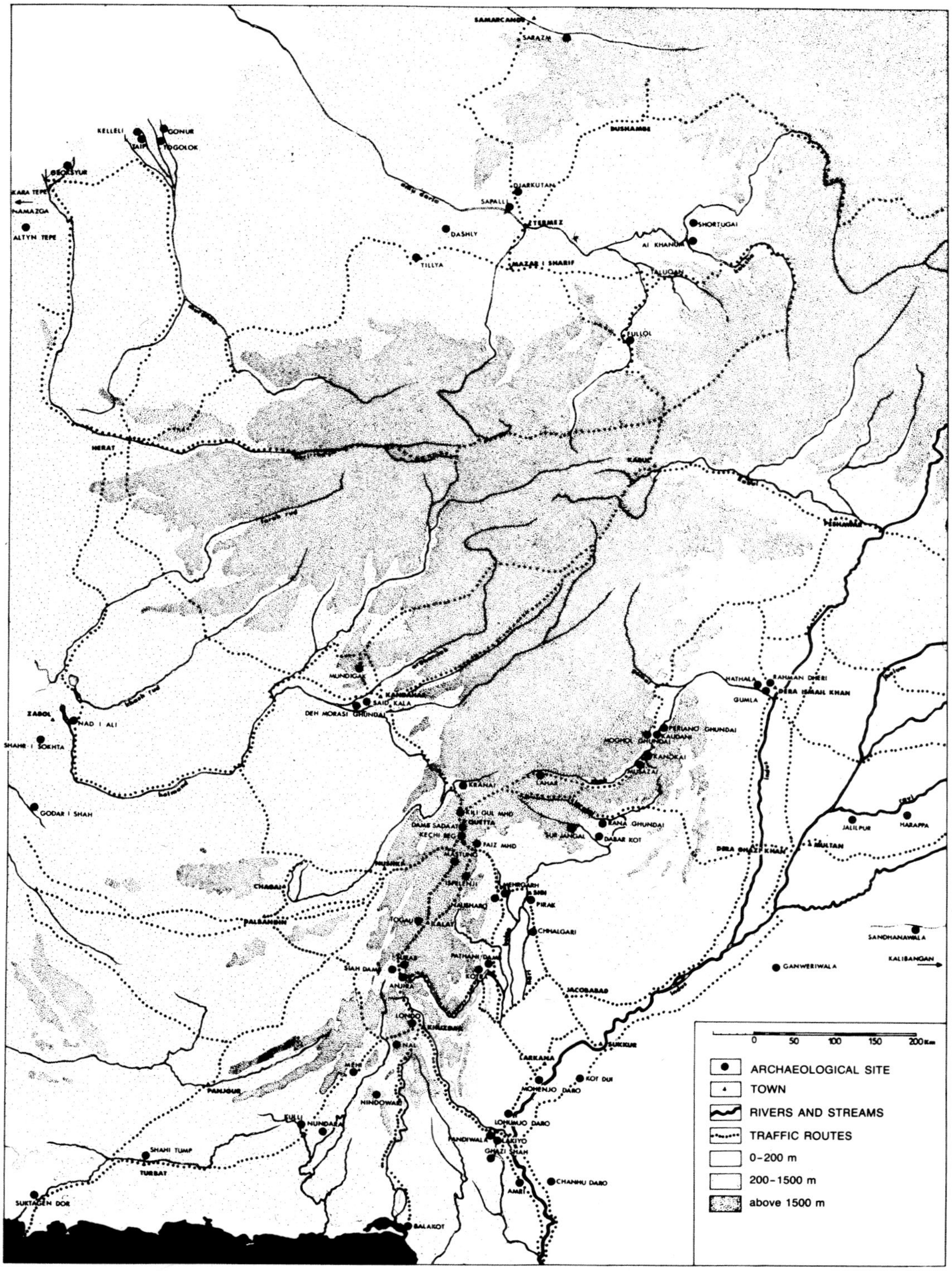

Fig. 1.11. Traffic routes and archaeological sites in the Indo-Iranian borderlands. Mehrgarh on the Kachi plain occupies a position that is strategic from the point of view of intercourse between the Iranian plateau / Central Asia and the Indus Valley. After Jansen et al. 1991: 99, pl. 84.

Mundigak in southern Afghanistan. This suggests the seasonal migration that has remained the basis of the economy in this area, with summers spent in the mountains and winters on the alluvial plains (fig. 9.2).

Mobility is seen also in the affinities of painted pottery motifs between Baluchistan, southern Turkmenistan (Namazga II–III) and northern Iran (Sialk style). The technical excellence of the Baluchistan pottery and its local antecedents precludes the earlier assumed hypothesis of a colonization from the northwest, but these areas evidently maintained commercial relations and perhaps shared a common ideology.

Early Harappan period

During the next phase (Mehrgarh IV–V, *c.*3600–3200 BC) there is evidence for the construction of irrigation canals. This enabled the extension of agricultural activities beyond the floodplain, and many new sites came into existence throughout the Greater Indus Valley. This proliferation of settlements was accompanied by social changes as well. Communal granaries disappear, while large storage jars appear in more compact house units that seem to have belonged to families. Potter's marks appear at many sites (fig. 4.1), also suggesting private ownership (§ 2.1). Round and rectangular stamp seals, made of stone, terracotta and bone and bearing geometrical motifs, point to development in administration. Advances were made in all the crafts, including metallurgy and pottery. The fine polychrome Kechi Beg style is diagnostic of Baluchistan ceramics in this period.

Around 3600 BC, population pressure drove farmers from Baluchistan to the Indus Valley, the marshes and jungles of which had been less attractive before the fourth millennium. Vessels of a developed variety of the KGM / Togau Ware, undoubtedly coming from the southern parts of the Kachi plain, occur beside local handmade bichrome pottery at Amri, one of the first villages on the Indus plain.

In the following phase (Mehrgarh VI–VII, Nausharo I, Amri II, lower layers of Kot Diji, *c.*3200–2600 BC) the development continued and trade increased. There are more stamp seals, not only round and rectangular but of many different forms; their motifs are mainly geometric, but one depicts five seated human figures, two others (one compartmented copper seal) zebus. The potters of Mehrgarh mastered the technique of air reduction and produced high-quality luxury ceramics, such as the Quetta Ware, the polychrome Nal Ware (fig. 10.20 o–p), and the Faiz Mohammad Ware (fig. 10.20a–b); Quetta Ware has geometrical, the other two also plant and animal motifs.

All these ceramics are important in documenting the connections between the Greater Indus Valley and the Iranian plateau and Central Asia at this time. Technological analyses have proved that Faiz Mohammad ceramics produced in centralized workshops on the Kachi plain were exported to sites in the Quetta Valley (Damb Sadaat, Faiz Mohammad), to Mundigak (II–III) in southern Afghanistan, and in small numbers even to Shahr-i Sokhta (I) in Iranian Seistan, where local imitations were made (fig. 10.20d). On the other hand, Emir Ware, which predominates on the western margins of the Indo-Iranian borderlands from Oman and Makran via Kerman to Seistan, was produced at Shar-i Sokhta and Bampur and exported to Mundigak and possibly even Kalat in Pakistani Baluchistan. The geometric decorations of Quetta Ware have close parallels both in Seistan (Shahr-i Sokhta I) and in southern Turkmenistan (Geoksyur and Namazga III), where, however, the pottery is handmade.

Such interregional similarities, which comprise also human and animal figurines, stamp seals, beads, and other things, are now thought to result from an intensive caravan trade that was at its peak *c.*3000 BC. This trade benefited the intermediaries. Shahr-i Sokhta in Seistan became a great city of 100 hectares. Clay tablets with Proto-Elamite script have been found at this site (fig. 2.6). This shows that Shahr-i Sokhta was associated with the Proto-Elamite Civilization that had its centre at Susa in western Iran, but extended its influence widely over the Iranian plateau (fig. 1.12). Lapis lazuli mined in Afghanistan

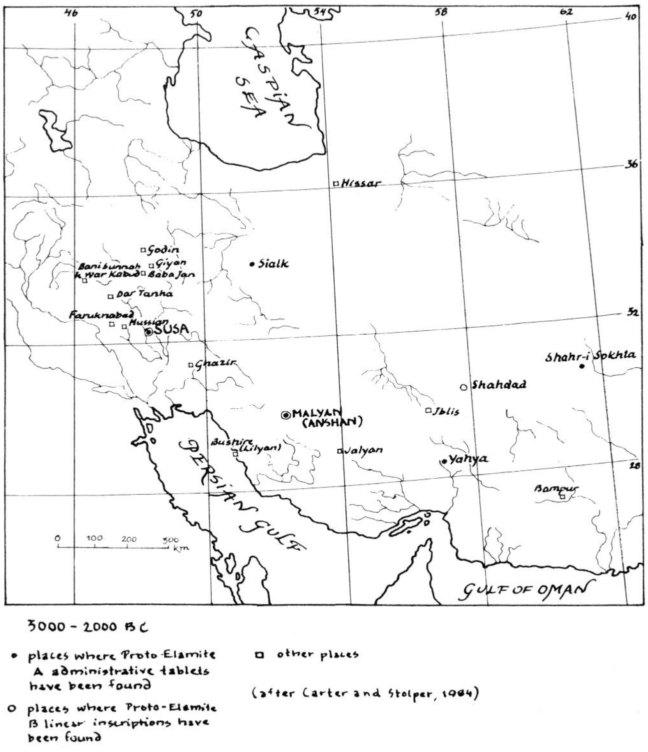

Fig. 1.12. Archaeological sites of Elam, *c.*3000–2000 BC. Redrawn after Carter and Stolper 1984.

Table 1.1. *Chronologies and cultural periods of the ancient Near East (Mesopotamia) and the Indus Valley (the Kachi plain) and the times of appearance of the different scripts used in and around these regions*

History of writing (l-s = logo-syllabic; s = syllabic; a = alphabetic)	Years BC	Cultural periods in (southern) Mesopotamia	
	100		
Brahmi (a)	200		
	300		HELLENISTIC *c*.330–
	400		
	500		ACHAEMENID *c*.539–330
	600		NEO-BABYLONIAN *c*.626–539
	700		
	800		
Greek alphabet (a)	900		NEO-ASSYRIAN *c*.1000–612
	1000		
	1100	Isin II	
	1200	*c*.1155–1026	
Ugaritic cuneiform (a)	1300		MIDDLE BABYLONIAN
Hittite hieroglyphic (s)	1400		
Linear B (s)	1500	Kassites	*c*.1600–1000
Semitic alphabet (a)	1600	*c*.1730–1155	
	1700	Hammurapi dynasty	
Linear A (s)	1800	*c*.1894–1595	
Minoan hieroglyphic	1900	Isin and Larsa	OLD BABYLONIAN
	2000	*c*.2017–1763	*c*.2000–1600
	2100	Ur III *c*.2112–2004	NEO-SUMERIAN
Linear Elamite (s)	2200	Gudea *c*.2144–2124	*c*.2154–2000
Eblaite cuneiform (s)	2300	Sargon *c*.2334–2279	(OLD) AKKADIAN *c*.2334–2154
	2400	ED III B: Royal Tombs of Ur I	
Indus script	2500	*c*.2500–2334	
	2600	ED III A *c*.2600–2500	EARLY DYNASTIC
	2700	ED II *c*.2750–2600	*c*.2900–2334
	2800	ED I *c*.2900–2750	
	2900		
Egyptian hieroglyphs (l-s)	**3000**	Uruk III	JEMDET NASR
Proto-Elamite (l-s)	3100	*c*.3100–2900	*c*.3100–2900
	3200		
Archaic Sumerian (l-s)	3300		
(bullae with tokens and seal impressions)	3400	Uruk IV	
(cylinder seals in the Near East)	3500	*c*.3500–3100	
(stamp seals and potter's marks in Baluchistan)	3600		URUK *c*.3700–3100
	3700		
	3800		
	3900		
	4000		
	4100		ʻUBAID *c*.4400–3700
	4200		
	4300		
	4400		
	4500		HALAF *c*.5000–4400
	4600		(northern Mesopotamia)
	4700		
	4800		
	4900		
	5000		HASSUNA-SAMARRA
	5100		*c*.5700–5000
	5200		(northern Mesopotamia)
	5300		
(stamp seals in the Near East)	5400		
(tokens in the Near East from *c*.8000)	5500		
	5600		
	5700		

Table 1.1. (*cont.*)

Archaeological sequence in the Kachi plain (MR = Mehrgarh; NS = Nausharo)		Years BC	Cultural periods	
		100		
		200		
		300	MAURYAN *c.*322–183	
		400		
Dur Khan II *c.*600–300		500		
		600		
Dur Khan I *c.*800–600		700	IRON AGE *c.*1100–	
		800		
		900		
		1000		
Pirak III *c.*1400–800		1100		
		1200		
		1300		
		1400		
Pirak II *c.*1600–1400		1500	POST HARAPPAN *c.*1800/1400–1100	
		1600		
Pirak I *c.*1800–1600		1700	LATE HARAPPAN *c.*1900–1800/1400	
		1800		
MR VIII	NS III *c.*1900–1800	1900		
		2000		
		2100	Intermediate	
	NS II B *c.*2300–1900	2200	*c.*2300–1900	MATURE HARAPPAN *c.*2550–1900
		2300	Early	
	NS II A *c.*2550–2300	2400	*c.*2550–2300	
		2500		
	NS ID	2600	transition *c.*2600–2550	
MR VII C =	NS IC	2700		
MR VII B =	NS IB	2800	Kot Dijian	
MR VII A =	NS IA	2900	*c.*3200–2550	EARLY HARAPPAN *c.*3600–2550
		3000		
MR VI *c.*3200–3000		3100		
		3200		
MR V *c.*3300–3200		3300		
		3400		
MR IV *c.*3600–3300		3500		
		3600		
		3700		
		3800		
		3900		
MR III *c.*4500–3600		**4000**		
		4100		
		4200		
		4300	CHALCOLITHIC *c.*5000–3600	
		4400		
		4500		
		4600		
MR IIB *c.*5000–4500		4700		
		4800		
		4900		
		5000		
		5100		
MR IIA *c.*5500–5000		5200		
		5300	POTTERY NEOLITHIC *c.*6000–5000	
		5400		
		5500		
MR IB *c.*6000–5500		5600		
		5700		

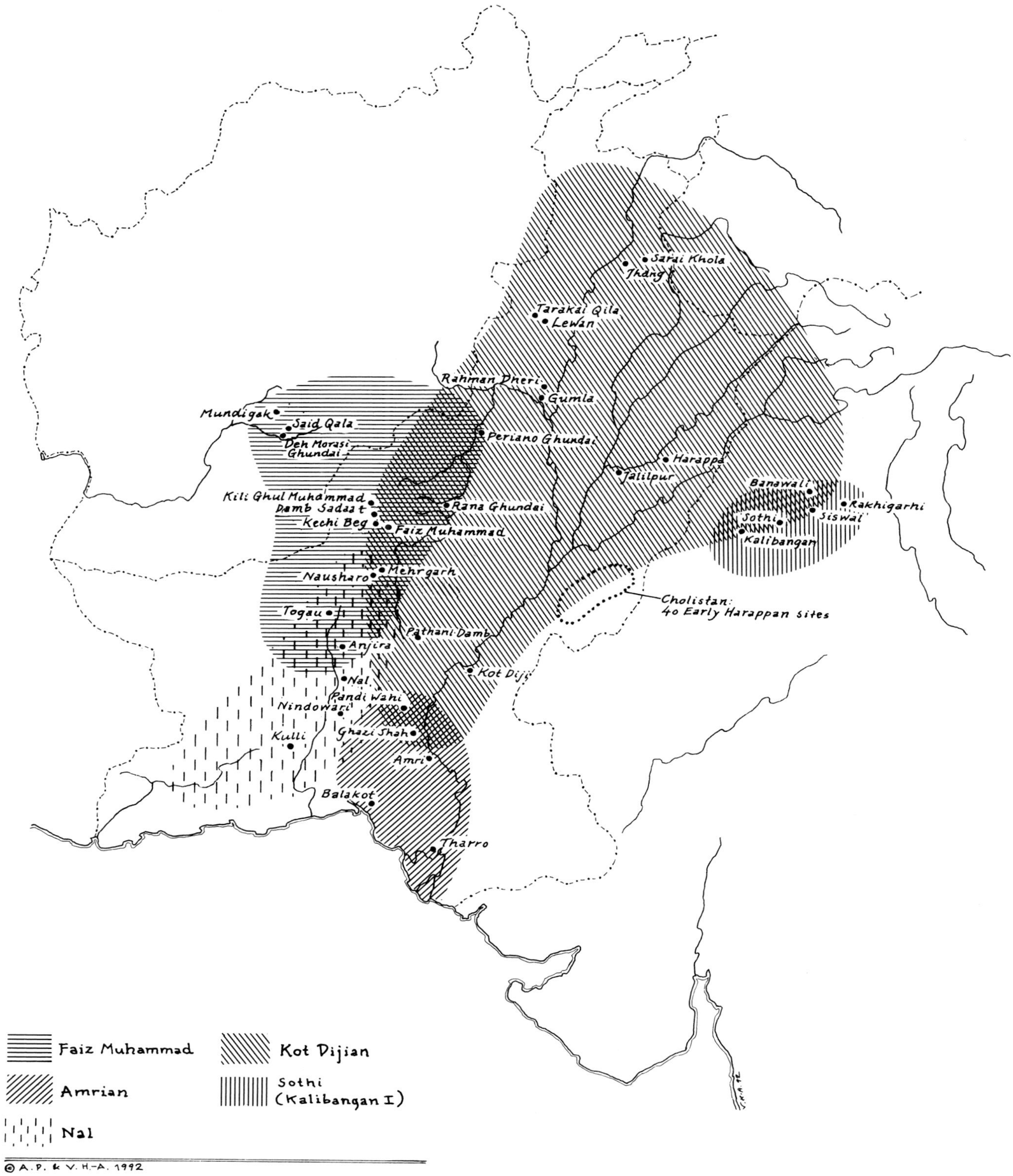

Fig. 1.13. Sites and cultural complexes of the Early Harappan phase in the Greater Indus Valley. Mainly based on Mughal 1990b and Wright 1984: fig. 3.1.

was one of the main attractions of these distant places for the Proto-Elamites. Mundigak, which was closer to Baluchistan, also prospered and became a walled town with monumental architecture. In the Indus Valley, one of the earliest towns was Rahman Dheri in the Gomal Valley, on the route to Seistan and Central Asia. Built *c.*3300 BC, it anticipates the Indus cities with its walls and streets laid out on a grid pattern.

In the Indus Valley, population increased greatly and many new sites were founded (fig. 1.13). Communications and trade developed, resulting in a surprising degree of cultural uniformity over a very wide area. The ceramic style most widespread in the Indus Valley is Kot Dijian Ware, characterized by globular vessels with a wide black band painted around the neck. Such pottery was found in the 1950s in the early levels of Kot Diji near Mohenjo-daro (fig. 14.19a). Related to Kot Dijian is Sothi Ware, found along the Ghaggar-Hakra river and known especially from Kalibangan I. In southern Sind, Amrian Ware predominates.

This last phase has appropriately been called Early Harappan, because in many respects it prefigures the following Indus Civilization or Mature Harappan phase. Common features include towns along rivers, built with mud-brick walls on stone foundations, citadels and monumental architecture; standardization of brick sizes (usually 30 × 20 × 10 centimetres, not yet in the ratio 1:2:4); bullock carts (in terracotta models); stamp seals; animal and (female and male) human figurines; triangular terracotta 'cakes' (heated in fire and put into pots to cook liquids); and mass-production of plain pottery.

M. Rafique Mughal, who coined the term 'Early Harappan' in 1970, has recently suggested extending it to include the preceding phase, so that it would cover approximately the time 3600–2550 BC. (The earlier term 'pre-Harappan', still used by some scholars, is misleading as it suggests discontinuity, like pre-Aryan vs. Aryan.)

Transition

The Early Harappan period closes with a transitional phase (Nausharo ID, Amri IIIA, *c.*2600–2550 BC). Radiocarbon dates from many sites suggest that the transitional phase leading to Mature Harappan was very short. At Nausharo, the ongoing excavations of the ID phase have revealed impressive architecture on massive foundations and rooms full of ceramics *in situ*. There is a great deal of (locally produced) Kot Dijian pottery, some decorated with the 'fish scale' and 'concentric circle' motifs, which remain among the hallmarks of the succeeding Mature Harappan period. Diagnostic of this phase are big dishes with 'radiating elongated leaves'. The vessels painted with animals tethered to trees (fig. 1.14) are interesting not only as prototypes of the later Kulli Ware of southern Baluchistan (fig. 1.15), but also because they prefigure the principal iconographic motifs in the Indus seals. It is noteworthy that the tree to which the animal is tied is in the Kulli vessels replaced by a stand rather similar to the mysterious 'cult object' in front of the 'unicorn' in the Indus seals (fig. 8.5). Perhaps it is a sacrificial post, like that to which the victims are tied in the Vedic and Hindu rituals (§ 12.2).

Considering the dramatic changes with which the following Mature Harappan period opens, something crucial must have taken place around this time that triggered the process of full urbanization and led to the creation of the Indus Civilization. What was it? Most probably the adoption of water transport

Fig. 1.14. Three zebu bulls tethered to different trees. Motif painted in black directly on the reddish-buff ware characteristic of the transitional ID period from Nausharo (structure II locus 4), *c.*2600–2550 BC. After Jarrige 1988b: 188, fig. 4.4.

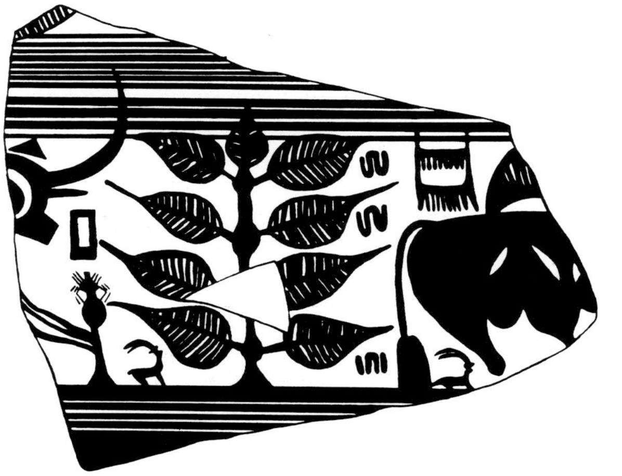

Fig. 1.15. Fig tree and, in front of it, a humped bull tied to a stand (sacrificial stake?), which resembles the 'cult object' associated with the 'unicorn' bull in the Indus seals. The triangle between the bull's horns has a parallel in the triangular inlay on the forehead of some bull statuettes from the ancient Near East (the significance of this mark is discussed in § 14.4). Fragment of a black-painted coarse red ware of the Kulli style from Mehi, second half of the third millennium BC. After Possehl 1986: 46, fig. 18 (Mehi II.4.5), based on Stein 1931: pl. 30.

and a concomitant shift in the orientation and volume of trade. Two major changes in the external contacts of the Harappans happened simultaneously during the transitional phase. On the one hand, previously flourishing overland connections with Seistan and Central Asia withered, with a consequent collapse of sites (such as Rahman Dheri, Mundigak and Shahr-i Sokhta) along these trade routes. On the other hand, maritime contacts were established with the Gulf region for the first time. Goods almost certainly of Harappan manufacture ('etched' carnelian beads, including the long, barrel-shaped beads which are technically difficult to produce) reached Mesopotamia towards the end of the Early Dynastic III period.

A parallel reorientation of foreign trade took place also in Mesopotamia about the same time. From that time on, the Sumerians imported raw material by sea from the Gulf, rather than by land from the Iranian plateau. The overland routes on the western side of the Iranian plateau were apparently controlled by the successors of the Proto-Elamites. Their sphere of influence seems to be reflected by the distribution of the luxury steatite (or chlorite) vessels carved in the so-called 'intercultural style': they have been found all over the ancient Near East, including one in the lower levels of Mohenjo-daro (fig. 1.16) and also Nausharo ID. The only workshop for their manufacture identified with certainty so far is at Tepe Yahya in southeastern Iran.

Mature Harappan period

The term 'Indus Civilization' is nowadays understood to cover three major subphases. In the narrow sense it is synonymous with Mature Harappan, subdivided into Early Mature Harappan and Intermediate Harappan phases, while in a broader sense it encompasses also a third, Late Harappan or Post-Urban phase.

The Early Mature Harappan phase (Nausharo IIA = Amri IIIA, *c*.2550–2300 BC) represents the climax of the Harappan culture. As we have already described this zenith in some detail (§ 1.3), only a few aspects, important from the diachronic and interregional point of view, will be highlighted here. At Nausharo, a substantial new settlement was built on a new site, with mighty walls and an impressive gate. Drains made of baked brick, typical Indus seals (with the Indus script and the 'unicorn' motif) and standardized weights make their first appearance. Everything, however, speaks for an unbroken cultural continuity from the preceding phase.

The founding of Mohenjo-daro at this time gives us an idea of the scale of the communal projects. Its 'citadel' stands on a huge mud-brick platform which measures 400 × 200 × 7 metres. Michael Jansen (in press) estimates that this artificial foundation must have taken several years to construct even assuming that some 15,000–20,000 people were working on it. He thinks that it was possible to build big cities in the floodplain only because the adoption of naval transport enabled sufficient amounts of grain and other necessary materials from long distances to be imported, and because the organization of the society could cope at state level. Jansen considers the superb water engineering one of the most important innovations of this phase. It is exemplified by the ring-wells, ingeniously constructed with tapering bricks that made them stronger than the Roman wells (square in section). With 60 wells encountered in excavations that may cover only 10 per cent of the total area, Mohenjo-daro had perhaps a greater density of wells than any other city has ever had.

The Indus Civilization resulted in a surprisingly uniform culture almost everywhere in the Greater Indus Valley, including much of Baluchistan. A significant change in comparison to the extent of the Kot Dijian culture in the Early Harappan period, in other respects largely identical with that of the Indus Civilization, is the expansion towards the coastal areas to include both Makran and Gujarat. This is clearly a consequence of the new orientation towards sea trade, and contrasts with the situation in the northernmost Indus Valley, which remained Kot Dijian even during the Mature Harappan period. However, northern Afghanistan with its lapis lazuli mines interested the Indus people sufficiently for them to found a small outpost (Shortughai) there. Otherwise their activity in this direction seems to have been rather limited, even if some Mature Harappan material (ivory game-pieces and dice and two Indus-type stamp seals at Altin Tepe) has been found in Central Asia from late Namazga V contexts (*c*.2100–1900 BC).

On the other hand, clear evidence of a Harappan presence in Oman comes from Ra's al Junayz in the form of Harappan-type black-and-red pottery with such motifs as the pipal leaf and the peacock (6 per cent of the total assemblage, which is mostly of Omani origin) and two Indus graffiti, a square copper stamp with 'unicorn' and Indus script, ivory combs with concentric circles, and 'etched' carnelian beads. In 1987, remains of typically Harappan large storage jars were discovered at Wadi Asimah in the Oman mountains, a considerable distance from the seashore.

At several sites, e.g. Nausharo and Kot Diji, the town of the transitional phase was burnt down and destroyed with all its artefacts when the Mature Harappan settlement was founded. While the once popular idea of a conquest by foreign invaders bringing the idea of urbanization from the Near East into the Indus Valley has been conclusively rejected, one may still ask to what extent the entirely internal transition from Early to Mature Harappan culture was a peaceful one. The change was very abrupt over a wide area and it is difficult to see what could have persuaded people to burn down their own towns in many places if it did not happen by force. In any case it is clear that

(a)

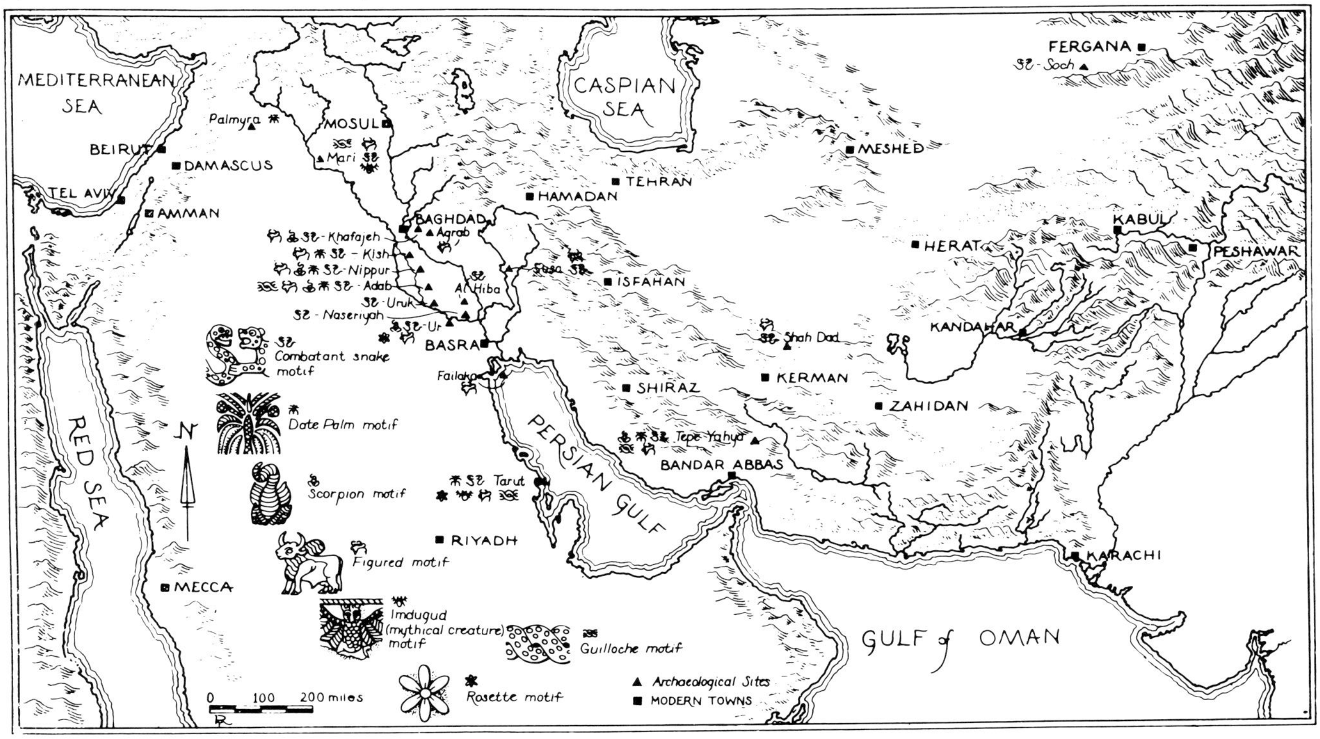

(b)

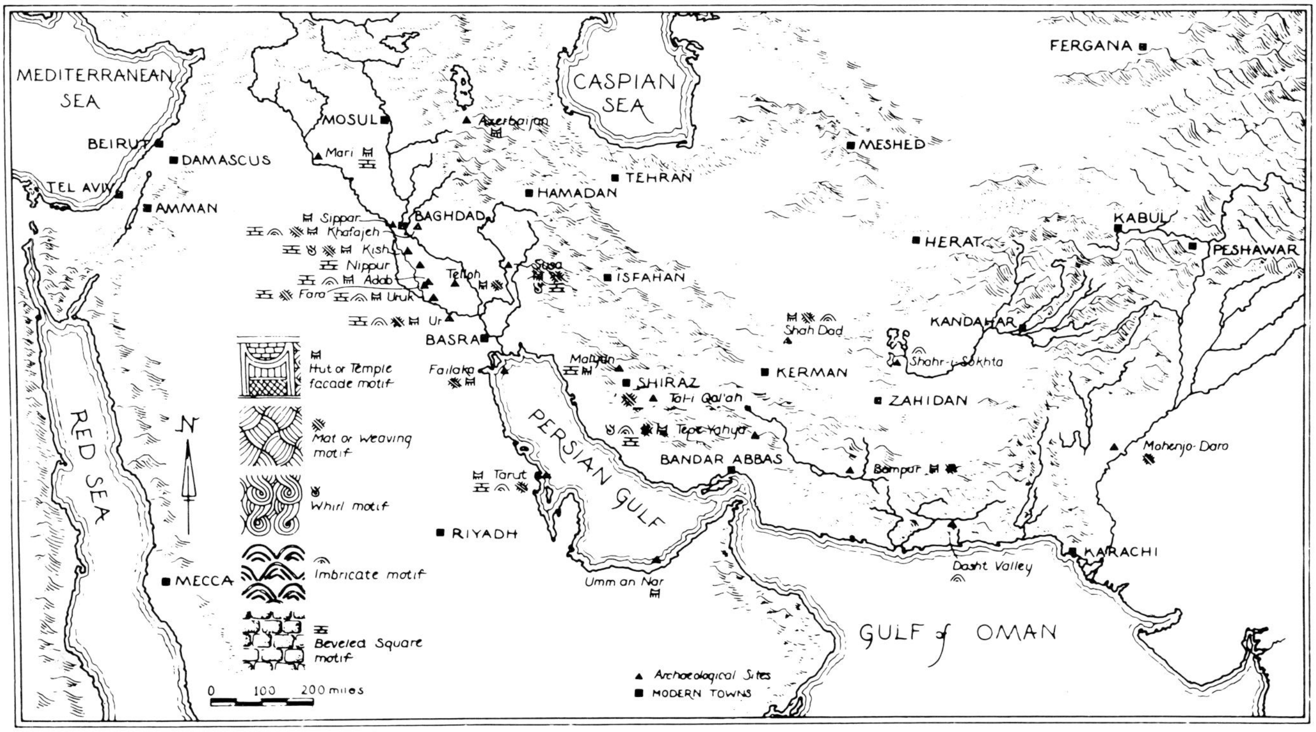

Fig. 1.16. Distribution of 'intercultural-style' carved steatite vessels, *c.*2500 BC: (a) vessels with representational designs; (b) vessels with non-representational designs. After Kohl 1979: 1, 60–1, figs. 1–2.

the Indus Civilization was based on systematic planning and that it was strongly centralized. Relatively few weapons have been found, but some support for militaristic ideology is provided by the cylinder seal from Kalibangan (see fig. 14.25) and the finely made bronze statuette of a man with a spear and a 'double bun' hairstyle that has recently been located among the unpublished finds from Chanhujo-daro by Mark Kenoyer.

Some degree of militarism and the concomitant worship of war deities may be postulated even on the basis of other, better known city civilizations. In a comparative analysis of the ancient cultures of Peru, Mesoamerica, Mesopotamia, Egypt and China, Julian H. Steward developed the theory of the multilinear evolution of human culture. Steward's premiss was that, under a given set of environmental and technological conditions, the structure and function of most other aspects of culture are likely to vary within a fairly limited range. With the emergence of new levels of organization as his criterion, Steward distinguished between several successive eras in the evolution of the early irrigation civilizations: 'era of incipient agriculture', 'formative era', 'era of regional florescence' and 'era of conquest'. His aim was 'to suggest cause-and-effect relationships between the cultural phenomena of the successive eras and to formulate as basic regularities those relationships which are common to all areas' (Steward 1955: 187). Steward's pioneering classic is naturally outdated in many respects now. In the study of the Harappan culture, the functional analyses by the archaeological specialists of the area are certainly much more reliable. But because the preserved archaeological evidence is lacunary and textual evidence is virtually lacking, the comparative perspective can provide useful insights, and here we may still have something to learn from Steward.

The following Intermediate Harappan phase (Nausharo IIB–III, Amri IIIB, *c.*2300–1900 BC) appears to have been far less innovative and dynamic than the Early Mature phase. The impression agrees with Steward's characterization of his 'era of conquest':

> In this era, all aspects of culture were increasingly regimented at the expense of creative effort . . . Laws were codified, learning was systematized (astronomy, theology, mathematics, medicine, writing), art became standardized, and goods were mass-produced by specialists. (Steward 1955: 204f.)

In the absence of tangible evidence for them (see, however, § 11.2), it is not surprising that astronomy, mathematics, medicine and law find little mention in studies of the Indus Civilization. Yet they have played an important role in all early civilizations (see also § 4.1).

Unfortunately the large-scale excavations of Mohenjo-daro and Harappa ignored the true stratification of the sites. Knowledge of the internal development of the Indus Civilization has therefore long remained somewhat imprecise. The excavations of George F. Dales at Mohenjo-daro in 1964–5 and the excavations he has been directing at Harappa since 1986 together with J. M. Kenoyer are, however, improving our understanding of these important sites. Another major undertaking that is contributing significantly to this aim is the Research Project Mohenjo-Daro directed by Michael Jansen of the Technical University of Aachen from 1979 onwards. This project has completed an extensive photographic documentation of the finds and the site (including surveys from hot-air balloons), carried out more than 600 deep drillings and a surface survey of more than a hundred hectares in collaboration with the Istituto Italiano per il Medio ed Estremo Oriente (Rome); the unpublished excavation diaries have been computerized, and the building plans are being fed into the computer.

Late Harappan period

The uppermost level of Mohenjo-daro (*c.*1900–1800 BC, corresponding to Amri IIIC and the last phase of Chanhujo-daro) consists of poorly constructed huts made of used and often broken bricks. Kilns were built in the middle of streets. Although the artefacts are typically Harappan, the standard of workmanship is lower than before. Painted pottery, for example, was largely replaced by plain wares. Finely carved steatite seals with Indus script and animal motifs to a great extent gave way to seals bearing nothing but geometrical motifs such as the swastika. Just beneath the surface, many groups of unburied skeletons have been found. By *c.*1800 BC Mohenjo-daro was abandoned.

What happened? Many explanations have been offered. The Harappans may have been over-exploiting their environment and causing gradual deterioration. Irrigation, for example, may have caused the fields to become saline. Drastic changes in the course of the river may have left some areas under water. Several layers of silt at Mohenjo-daro do testify to a series of floods. If vast areas became uncultivable, food shortages would eventually have made city life impossible and led to a social and political crisis. The squatter-like huts on top of quite habitable houses filled with rubble and dirt have been interpreted as a desperate attempt to raise the occupational level above the height of floodwater. Waterlogging in its turn would have brought various diseases. A recent study of the unburied skeletons in Mohenjo-daro suggests death from malaria.

Finally, the weakened cities would have been easy victims for raiders. We shall return to the much-debated question of a foreign invasion later (§§ 8.4–5). At this point it is sufficient to note that the recent excavations in the Kachi plain (Mehrgarh period VIII, Sibri, Nausharo III) and Quetta have provided

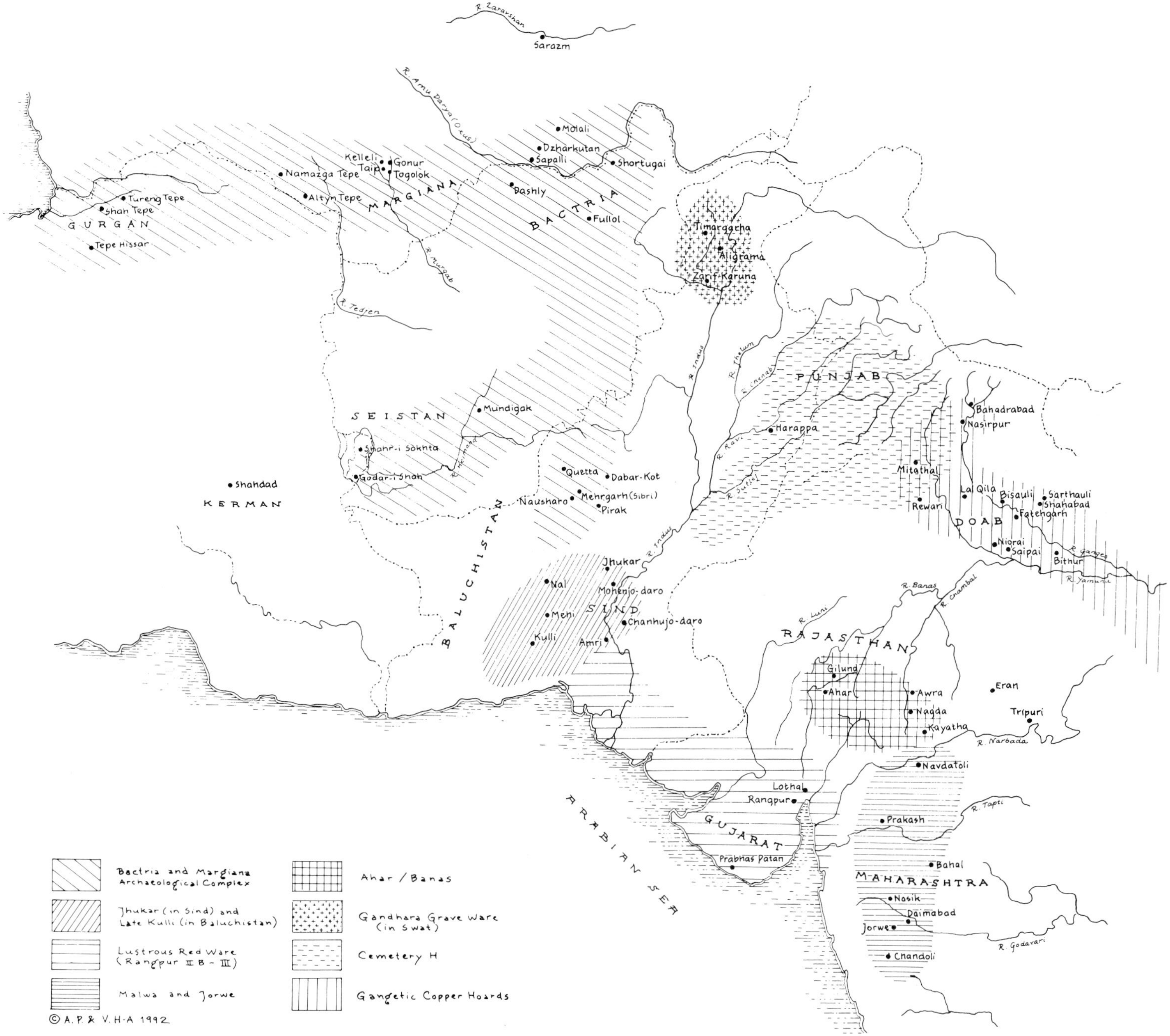

Fig. 1.17. Late and Post-Harappan cultures in the Indo-Iranian borderlands and the northwestern parts of the Indian subcontinent *c.* 1900–1400 BC. Based on various sources including Mughal 1990b and Yule 1985b.

evidence for the arrival of immigrants from Central Asia. An entire cultural complex, intrusive in Baluchistan and the Indus Valley, is now in evidence, with close parallels in Bactria and Margiana, and further off in Seistan and Kerman and in southern Turkmenistan and northern Iran.

While some of these immigrants obviously settled in the Kachi plain, some of them proceeded further to Sind and elsewhere in the Indian subcontinent. They could not have been very numerous, but sufficiently so for their arrival and integration into the Harappan population to make a difference.

The Late Harappan period marks a cultural fragmentation in the Greater Indus Valley. The interconnections between the different Harappan areas break down. This is exemplified by the fact that not a single example of the mass-produced 'goblets' with pointed ends typical of late Mohenjo-daro has been found at Nausharo III in the Kachi plain. The relative cultural uniformity of the Mature Harappan phase is gradually replaced by a variety of distinct regional cultures (see fig. 1.17). The traditions of the Indus Civilization continue without a break, but are transformed by some intrusive traits. The processes of city life, such as centralized government, with the collection of taxes and organization of trade, gradually ceased to function. The thousands of countryside villages, however, persisted, although there was an increase in nomadism: the number of habitation sites decreased and that of camp sites increased. In peripheral regions, especially in Gujarat and Maharashtra, Mature Harappan traits lingered much longer than in the Indus Valley (§§ 4.1 and 9.4), until the unevenly distributed Late Harappan cultures (*c.*1900–1500 BC) gave way to more or less clearly Post-Harappan traditions (§ 8.4).

Part II

The Indus script

2 Early writing systems

2.1 Evolution of communication

The invention of a visual communication system based on the representation of spoken language by conventional marks of some durability has enabled accurate storage of information and this in its turn eventually advanced technology. Inventions usually represent responses to particular needs and tend to result from gradual improvements upon previous achievements. This is certainly true of writing. The following brief outline sets the early scripts in a proper time perspective and explains the specific background of the oldest writing system, which will be discussed in detail. The sketch is restricted to the concrete archaeological evidence.

Though writing is one of our most powerful tools, it remains secondary to, and dependent on, that superb communication system which is common to the whole of the human race, language. In the absence of modern technology, spoken language is transitory and restricted to short distances. Human memory, too, sets limits to the conveyance of information in verbal form. These difficulties may be overcome by putting the message into a more durable form. This can be done by assigning a symbolic meaning to concrete objects or by means of drawing, engraving or painting pictures or marks. The earliest evidence for such activities is preserved in sculptures and wall paintings more than 20,000 years old. Similarly, incisions on Palaeolithic bone artefacts are assumed to have served for reckoning time. These markings are grouped in recurring sequences that coincide with the number of days in successive phases of the moon.

Neolithic potter's marks (see § 4.1) suggest that the communal ownership that is assumed to have prevailed in earlier times started giving way to private property (§ 1.6). In Western Asia, between the eighth and the late fourth millennium BC, debts were recorded with an increasingly complex accounting system that utilized small, standardized clay tokens. Large numbers of such tokens have been found at some Neolithic sites (1,153 at Jarmo). At Tell Abada of the

'Ubaid period levels (fifth millennium BC), clay tokens have been recovered from the temple. Here altogether 90 tokens of various shapes and sizes were placed in 11 pottery vessels. It appears that the temple administration had at their disposal a large supply of tokens, whose different sizes and shapes (including spheres, discs, cones, biconoids, ovoids, cylinders and pyramids) represented the various commodities of daily life in different quantities ('one bushel of grain', 'one jar of oil', etc.). When a person brought goods to the temple, a number of tokens corresponding to their value were placed in a vessel representing his account as a reminder of what he had paid.

The distribution of about 800 tokens discovered at Uruk, dating between *c*.4000 and 3200 BC, testifies to the development of such accounting: until 3500 BC the tokens are relatively few and comprise only simple types, while by 3200 BC there are about 250 different kinds of token, divisible into 16 basic types. Quite a few tokens bear incised or punched markings, some of which survive in the archaic Sumerian script. If these markings may be equated with the script, then a small clay disc with a cross on it stands for sheep, and one with parallel lines across it for wool (fig. 2.1).

The evolution of hierarchical society and irrigation agriculture produced surplus wealth and encouraged arts and crafts as well as local and long-distance trade. Transactions were increasingly performed through intermediaries, and the parties involved had to be accurately identified even when they were not present. Precautions against fraud also became necessary. The earliest stamp seals invented to satisfy this need date from *c*.5500 BC (Hassuna II in northern Mesopotamia); they were used for impressing identification marks upon wet clay and for sealing bales of goods by this means. Around 3500 BC stamp seals were replaced by cylinder seals, used to seal large surfaces. Occasional impressions of more than one seal suggest the use of witnesses.

Starting with Uruk IVa and Susa 18 (*c*.3300 BC), about 300 hollow clay balls have been discovered at nine sites distributed in Iran, Iraq, Syria, Israel and Saudi Arabia. Some of these fist-sized bullae have been sawn open or X-rayed to reveal assortments of clay tokens inside. With four exceptions, all the clay envelopes have carried impressions of cylinder seals on their outsides. Since so many bullae have been found intact, they were clearly kept in archives as records of transactions: tokens could not be added or taken away by stealth. But once the bullae had been closed and sealed, the number and type of the clay tokens inside could not be checked without breaking the envelope. Therefore, markings corresponding in shape and number to the tokens inside were made on the outer surface, in addition to the seal impressions.

The bullae were soon replaced by small clay tablets bearing impressions of seals and nothing other than repeated symbols arranged in rows. These numerical marks (deep and shallow circles, long and short wedges, ovals and triangles) thus replaced the tokens as signs of the commodities and amounts. Around 200 such 'numerical tablets' have been discovered from temples and private houses at ten sites scattered along the main trade routes in Iran, Iraq and Syria. They were quickly followed by more developed tablets, in which archaic pictograms accompany numerical signs.

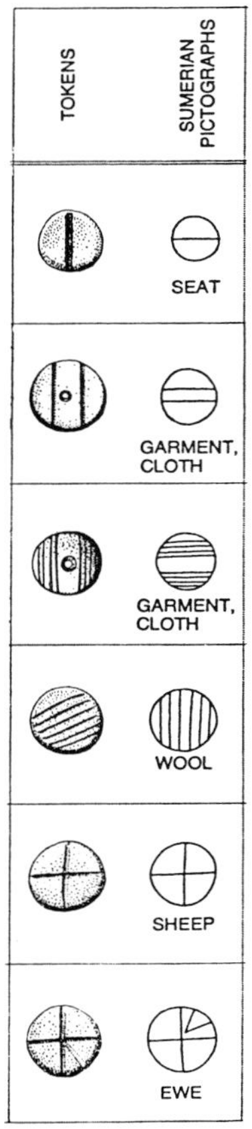

Fig. 2.1. A comparison of discoid clay tokens and archaic Sumerian pictograms from Uruk. After Schmandt-Besserat 1978: 56.

At Uruk in southern Mesopotamia complex tokens and bullae are found in stratum IV (*c*.3300–3100 BC), but not in stratum III (*c*.3100–2900 BC). The bullae are accompanied by tablets bearing numbers only, as well as by tablets with pictograms. This method of communication was quickly adopted at Susa in Elam, where a parallel development can be observed. Here two 'numerical tablets' were found together with a bulla filled with tokens in a bowl in level 18 (*c*.3300 BC). In level 17 (*c*.3200 BC) the bullae disappear, but the tablets continue. In level 16 (*c*.3100 BC) they are replaced by tablets bearing Proto-Elamite pictograms (fig. 2.2).

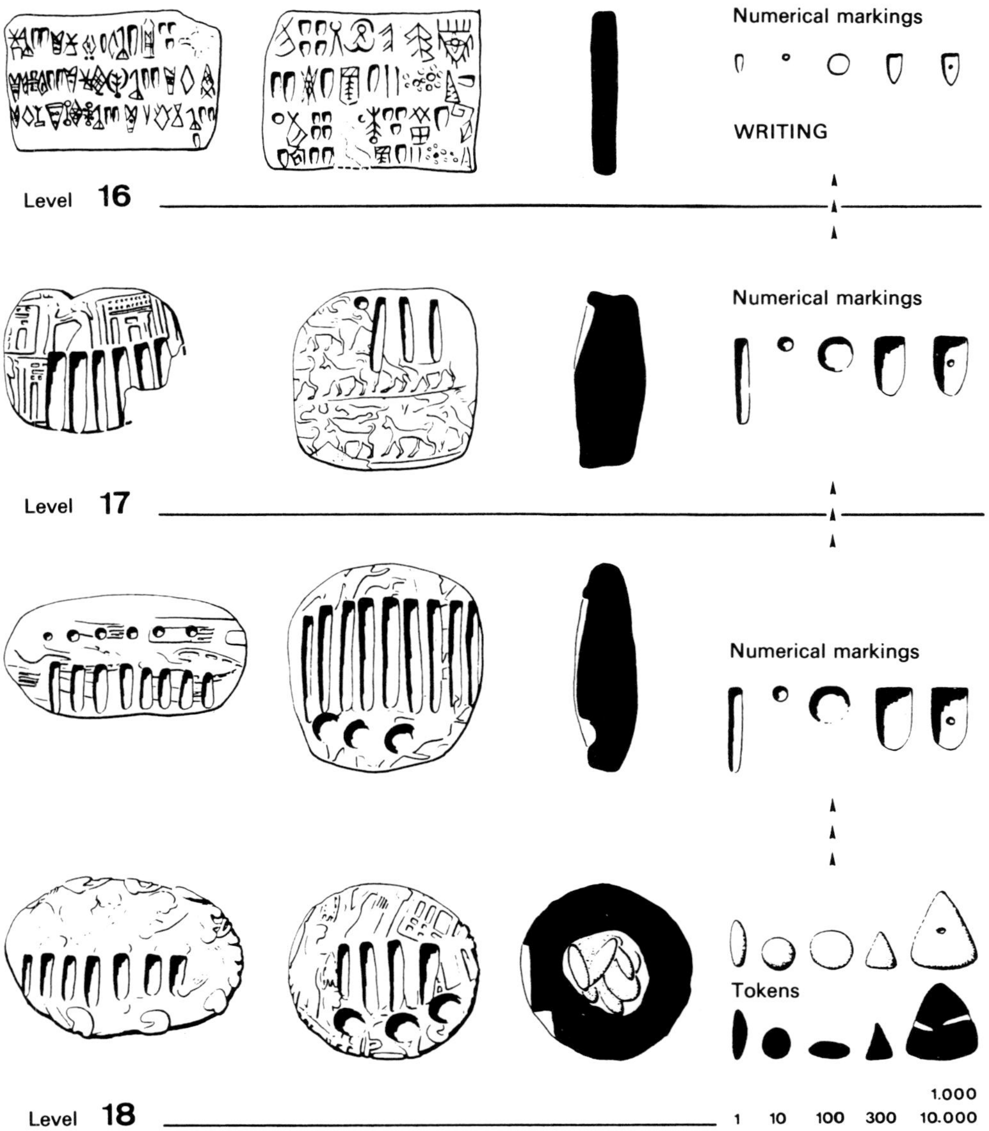

Fig. 2.2. Numerical markings in successive layers at Susa, *c.*3300–2900 BC. Level 18: (a) bullae with tokens and numerical markings, and (b) tablets with numerical markings. Level 17: tablets with numerical markings. Level 16: tablets with numerical markings and Proto-Elamite script. After Vallat 1986: 337, fig. 1.

2.2 The Sumerian writing system

The archaic Sumerian script is the oldest writing system in the world. Sumerian is the name of the language spoken by the people who lived in the alluvial plains of the lower Euphrates and Tigris at least from the Uruk III period onwards, but very probably also in the Uruk IV period and even earlier (§ 8.1). No other language is known to be cognate to Sumerian, yet we know what Sumerian may have sounded like. This is possible because the Semitic-speaking scribes of later times found difficulty in understanding Sumerian, 'the monastic Latin of the ancient Near East', and compiled extensive sign lists, lexicons and grammars as well as translations. The existence of these bilingual documents alone has given modern scholars access to the Sumerian language.

Most experts now believe that the Sumerian script has grown out of the system of clay envelopes containing tokens of debt, and out of the 'numerical tablets' replacing that system (§ 2.1). Some of the numerical tablets are perforated, suggesting that they were strung on to goods for transport. Only possessors of seals were able to send goods in this way,

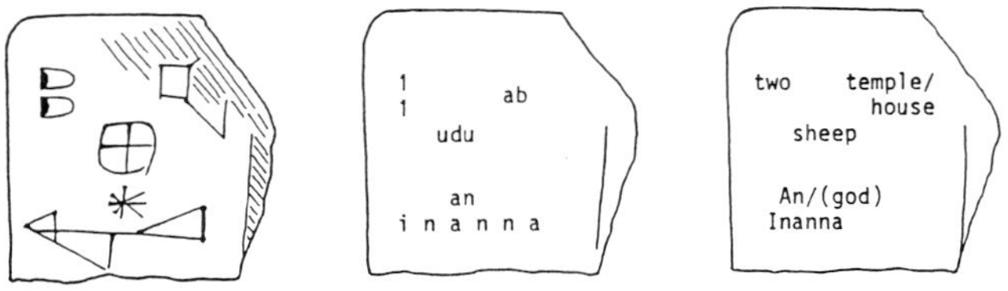

Fig. 2.3. An archaic Sumerian economic tablet from Uruk III 2. The fragmentary text probably reads: 'Two sheep (delivered to, or received from) the house (i.e. temple) of the goddess Inanna (or, [the gods] An and Inanna)'. After Nissen 1986a: 330, fig. 6.

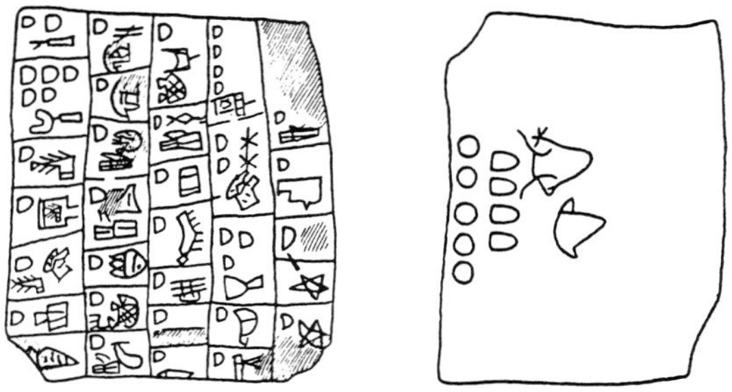

Fig. 2.4. An archaic Sumerian tablet from Uruk detailing on one side economic transactions summarized on the other side: '54 oxen and cows'. After Falkenstein 1936: pl. 31, no. 339; cf. Gelb 1963: 64.

and the recipient had to recognize the seal and know its owner. The recipient was aware of the nature of the goods delivered, and was chiefly concerned about getting the correct amount. The primitive tablets satisfied that need. The small and often perforated tags could also be stored.

But once the transaction was completed, the significance of the numbers was difficult to remember. This earliest type of tablet was therefore soon replaced by a more sophisticated one. Added to the numbers is a pictogram or two, occasionally a few more. One such sign corresponds to the earlier token or its impression and expressed the commodity, while another sign replaces the earlier seal impression, indicating who or which institution was responsible (fig. 2.3).

The scribes had discovered that they could greatly expand the range of written symbols and make them more explicit by drawing pictures with a pointed stylus. Iconic signs (from Greek *eikōn* 'picture'), which represent things or actions pictorially, may be termed 'pictograms'. Pictograms have the potential to express an 'idea' visually, through their 'iconicity' or similarity with the objects depicted. Signs that represent a meaning in this way may be termed 'ideograms'; in principle, they can be vaguely understood independently of any particular language, in contrast to 'phonograms' or phonetic signs, which express a meaning through the sound of the respective words in a specific language.

Some of the archaic Sumerian signs are unmistakable pictures of natural objects. For example, the sign  represents 'fish'. But even when it is used ideographically, a sign does not necessarily denote the primary meaning of its picture ('fish' might also mean 'water', or the 'god of water', as in Sumerian art; see §10.2). A characteristic part may represent the whole:  (female organ) means 'woman', and  (frontal view of a bull's head with horns but no other details) means 'bull'. Others, like  'sheep', whose shape is completely unrecognizable, seem to derive directly from the early tokens (fig. 2.1). So in practice even the 'reading' of ideograms requires acquaintance with culture-specific conventions.

The need to summarize individual transactions or accounts in collective records that register subtotals and grand totals (fig. 2.4) caused the tablets to become bigger as early as the Uruk IV period. To avoid confusion in interpretation, the signs were divided into groups separated by straight lines. Horizontal rows were subdivided by vertical lines into compartments, each containing one entry; the rows were read from right to left, so that most pictograms face to the right, pointing towards the beginning of the text.

The great majority (*c*.85 per cent) of the more than 4,200 archaic texts now known are such economic accounts. They come from Uruk IV–III and from Jemdet Nasr, contemporaneous with Uruk III (*c*.3100–2900 BC). Later texts still counted as archaic Sumerian come from Early Dynastic I levels (*c*.2900–2600 BC) at Ur and from Early Dynastic II–III levels (*c*.2600–2400 BC) at Fara and other sites.

The urge for greater ease, rapidity and efficiency in writing brought about a transformation of the archaic Sumerian script around the beginning of the Jemdet Nasr (= Uruk III) period (*c*.3100–2900 BC). Curved lines are difficult to draw neatly and quickly on wet clay, so the signs became angular: they were made by a few strokes of a stylus with a triangular tip, the shape of which gave the signs a wedge-like or 'cuneiform' appearance. The cuneiform sign for 'bull' is 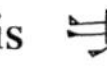, corresponding to the archaic sign 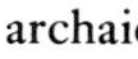. The pictorial meaning of the cuneiform signs would be difficult to discern, were it not clear from the shape of the early pictograms.

Many archaic pictograms could be equated with their later cuneiform counterparts by means of lexicographic texts existing in earlier and later versions. Lexical lists, used in scribal schools and for reference, enumerate, for example, all known plants or animals. In their contents as well as in their arrangement, the lexical texts of the Uruk IV–III period (comprising about 15 per cent of the entire material) are virtually identical with the lexical lists of the Early Dynastic II–III period (*c*.2600–2400 BC) which can be read and understood. Another factor that made an essential contribution to the understanding of the archaic texts is that certain kinds of text, e.g. the yearly inventories of cattle herds, were made according to the same formula, which was later followed in cuneiform.

The 'bull' sign illustrates another reason why the signs become unrecognizable, namely that they were turned 90° anticlockwise. This seems to have happened in the following way. As the size of the tablet continued to grow, it eventually became too large for the scribe to hold in the left hand (at an angle of 45° to the body). The tablet had to be laid on the table. It was rotated 45° so that the direction of the rows became vertical, read from top to bottom, and the orientation of the signs changed.

In its formative stage, the Sumerian script is thought to have had some 1,200 distinct signs (=graphemes). In the latest sign list by M. W. Green and Hans J. Nissen (1987), the number is 771+58 (numerals), with a further 28 in the supplementary list by Robert K. Englund (1987). Graphic variants (=allographs) are common, since different scribes had different ways of drawing the same sign, but an effort to restrain variation was clearly made.

As with the Chinese script and the later varieties of cuneiform, a wide discrepancy between theory and practice exists: the number of signs in use depends on both the kind of text and the scribe. Many of the archaic signs are attested only in lexical lists. Elimination of rare signs was one of the ways in which the extensive repertory of signs was gradually reduced, so that it became easier to learn and use. Another was to conflate two or more signs that were graphically and semantically close to each other, e.g. 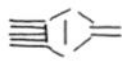 'fire' and  'torch'.

Reduction in the number of signs had to be compensated for by devising ways to meet the need to express new concepts. A sign could be modified by the addition of a diacritic: for example, hatchings inside the pictogram  'jar' may indicate the contents,  'beer'.

The primary meaning of a sign could be extended to include connotations of the object represented. Thus the sign  *kur* depicting 'mountains', and meaning primarily 'mountains, mountain region', also denotes 'foreign country' (because the mountains around the plains of Mesopotamia were inhabited by foreign people) and '(captured) inhabitant of a foreign country, slave'. The pictogram of a leg, , stands for the verbs *du* / *gin* 'to go', *gub* 'to stand' and *túm* 'to carry off'. One sign can thus have several phonetic values: this is polyphony. (On the other hand, several signs can have the same phonetic value but different meanings: this is polysemy. In transcription, different signs sharing one and the same pronunciation are distinguished by subscript numbers. The list begins with the most common signs, and the first three, e.g. tu_1, tu_2, tu_3, may also be written *tu*, *tú*, *tù*.)

Two signs could be combined to form a ligature (from Latin *ligare* 'to tie together') with a new meaning: 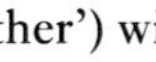 *geme* 'slave girl'. This method was especially used to express verbal and abstract notions (e.g. 'head'+'bread'='to eat'). Originally, there were several ways to indicate a ligature, such as connecting lines between the joined signs; later, one sign was usually written inside the other.

Abstract concepts, foreign proper names and grammatical elements are difficult to express pictographically. Recourse was made to a homophone with a second meaning that was easy to draw. An early example of this 'phonographic' use in the texts of the Uruk III period is the pictogram  *gi* 'reed', apparently meaning the verb *gi* 'to return, reimburse', since it is used in parallel with the sign  *ba* 'to divide, give' in documents mentioning numerical amounts. This way of expressing the phonetic shape of a word or syllable is known as *rebus* (Latin 'by means of things').

Rebus writing thus makes use of homophones, that is, words pronounced alike but having a different meaning. (Retained historical spellings keep apart the written forms of many homophones in modern English and show that in earlier phases of the language these words were not pronounced alike, e.g. *rite*, *write*, *right*, *wright*. Those homophones which have a different meaning but are both pronounced and written alike, such as *can* 'be able to' and *can* 'metal container', are called homonyms.) There are Sumerian myths based on homophones (§ 7.1), and it is virtually certain that punning was cultivated by ancient Mesopotamians in their oral literature long before they used it in writing. Along with other stylistic devices such as rhyme and alliteration, punning is found in oral literature all over the world, including the traditions of primitive hunter-gatherers.

A rebus pun is not always exact. To take an English example, the sound of the word *belief* could be approximated by depicting a *bee* and a *leaf*, but the vowel in the first syllable would not be rendered exactly. In Sumerian, the script keeps the different phonemes strictly apart, but some signs had morphophonemic and allophonic latitude (*mu* / *ŋu*, *mi* / *ŋi*, etc.).

The rebus principle was a crucial step in the phonetization of the Sumerian script. The phonetization was a lengthy process in which the graphic signs became systematically correlated to the acoustic signs of the language. The prehistoric tokens and the earliest pictograms that replaced them referred to physical objects and numbers. They had counterparts in the spoken language, namely the sounds of words naming those objects and numbers. But in the beginning, the order of the written signs was fortuitous and did not follow a linguistic pattern; it took centuries before they were arranged in orderly lines and in an appropriate syntactic sequence.

For a long time, written documents remained simple shorthand-like memorandums, in which only indispensable 'catchwords' (i.e., word stems, usually monosyllabic roots, which carry the main weight of information) were written down. Such signs, which express a complete word, are called logograms, 'word signs'. Grammatical morphemes seem to be entirely absent from the earliest documents. Some uncertain examples of the genitive and dative suffixes can be quoted from the early archaic texts, but even these were usually omitted, though later they were always written.

The functionally manifold use of signs (phonetic as well as ideographic in both a primary and a semantically extended meaning) had a major disadvantage – ambiguity – when grammatical affixes were not marked and the order of the signs was haphazard. To overcome this, the Sumerians started attaching semantic determinatives to some signs with multiple meanings. These classifiers were simply aids to reading, with no phonetic counterpart in speech. Among the earliest determinatives used in this way is the picture for star, ✳, prefixed to names of divinities perhaps as early as the Uruk IV period, but certainly by the Uruk III period. In such a context its sound *dingir* (meaning 'god') would not have been pronounced. At this time started being used as the determinative of place-names.

Later, every word belonging to any of the following classes – men, women, gods, mammals, birds, fishes, trees, plants, wood, leather, stones, rivers, towns, countries, amongst others – had, as a rule, its determinative. Its position was initially free, but in the Early Dynastic II–III period (*c.*2600–2400 BC) it became fixed: the determinative of city names, *uru*, is placed before the name, for instance, but the determinative of places (other than city, country or river), *ki*, is placed after. The scribe could refer to comprehensive lexical lists that catalogue every known word written with a given determinative.

Phonetic indicators, too, were added, on the same principle as semantic determinatives: not to alter the pronunciation of a sign but to distinguish the various meanings of a sign with a single sound. For example, in *ú-uga*, the sign *ú* merely indicates that from the various possible ways of reading the following sign the reader should choose that which begins with the sound *u*, i.e. *uga*. Similarly, in *alim-ma*, the sign *ma* approximates the final sound (*m*) of the preceding sign. One possible example of this device from the Uruk IV period is the sign *men* 'crown', where the ligatured picture of a throne, , stands for the word *en* 'lord', and might have functioned as a phonetic determinative. But this ligature can also be interpreted as a compound of

ŋá + *en* = *ŋaen* > *ŋen*.

In the twenty-sixth century, Sumerian writing still expressed only those elements of a phrase that were indispensable for its comprehension. This can be illustrated by comparing the form of a recurrent phrase in the Early Dynastic texts from Fara with its expression in later 'classical' Sumerian

^{d}en-ki isimud gù dé
^{d}en-ki-<u>ke$_4$</u> ^{d}isimud-<u>ra</u> gù <u>mu-un-na</u>-dé-<u>e</u>
'god Enki (lit. Lord [*en*] Ground [*ki*]) calls (lit. emits [*dé*] call [*gù*]) to Isimu'

In the early version, the text consists almost entirely of logograms or word signs; the only other sign type is the determinative of divine names, *dingir* (abbreviated in transliteration with superscribed ^{d}). Only the roots are written; the subject and dative suffixes as well as the verbal affixes are all omitted. The Sumerian reader, acquainted with the content either from its context (in an economic text) or from oral tradition (in a literary text), could presumably supply the missing elements without difficulty. In the later version, syllabic signs (underlined) are mixed with logograms to record all the elements of the spoken language.

The distinction between logograms and syllabic signs is theoretically useful, but difficult to maintain in practice. It must be stressed that many signs were both logographic and syllabic. They were also pictographic, early on. But as the signs lost their pictorial form, their ideographic use became less important than their phonetic use. This development of syllabic signs constituted another vital step in the process of the phonetization of the script. It increased the phonetic correspondence between the written symbols and their meaning and compensated for the decrease in the visual correspondence caused by the development of pictograms into abstract cuneiform signs.

Thus written signs were transformed from pictograms to groups of individually meaningless phonetic symbols. Logograms started being replaced by syllabic spellings (e.g. *ga - ar$_3$* for earlier *ga'ar* 'cheese'). Syllabic spelling reduced the range of graphemes in the writing system, but increased the number of signs required to write a given message. The logograms, on the other hand, are a convenient shorthand. Cuneiform is thought to have remained a logo-syllabic script as a compromise between these two conflicting ways of writing that affect its expressiveness and efficiency.

2.3 Creation of syllabic and alphabetic scripts

Akkadian cuneiform

The Akkadians, a Semitic-speaking people (§ 8.2), had for a long time been close neighbours of the Sumerians. They eventually infiltrated and took over Sumer, and after a long

Table 2.1. *Percentages of logograms, syllabic signs and determinatives in Sumerian and Akkadian texts*

Sign types	Sumerian texts	Akkadian texts
Logograms	60.3–42.8	6.5–3.5
Syllabic signs	36.4–54.3	85.6–95.7
Determinatives	3.1–2.9	7.6–0.7

After Civil 1973: 26.

period of bilingualism, Sumerian as a spoken language died out by around 1900 BC. The cuneiform script, which the Akkadians had adopted around 2500 BC or earlier, continued in use. The adoption of a script created for one spoken language by a completely dissimilar language brought about some mismatch between spoken and written Akkadian. For example, cuneiform does not systematically distinguish between the voiced, voiceless and emphatic quality of the Akkadian consonants, because these phonetic oppositions did not exist in Sumerian. Thus the Sumerian sign  *ig* has the values *ig*, *ik* and *iq* in Akkadian. At the same time, the cuneiform signs acquired new values, and the proportion of phonetically used signs increased considerably (table 2.1). The writing system thus changed from chiefly logographic to chiefly syllabic, with a trend towards consistent spelling. In the early first millennium BC, an Assyrian scribe could manage fairly well with just 120 graphemes.

Linear Elamite

In an ideal syllabic writing system each sign has, in principle, just one phonetic value. Among the earliest known 'syllabic' scripts is Linear Elamite, known from only 19 inscriptions belonging to the twenty-third century BC (fig. 2.5). Its decipherment is incomplete, but it seems likely that the script was created by Puzur (alias Kutik)-Inšušinak (*c*.2260–2225 BC), the last king of Awan, who is mentioned in most of the texts: a reaction against the centuries-old cultural (and occasionally political) domination of Elam by Mesopotamia. The outward appearance of Linear Elamite is similar to that of the old Proto-Elamite script (fig. 2.6), used in 3100–2900 BC, and in its structure close to archaic Sumerian. But instead of the hundreds of signs found in the Proto-Elamite system, the total number of recorded signs in Linear Elamite is 103, out of which about one-half can be read with the help of bilinguals. Linear Elamite is essentially syllabic, with open and closed syllables, interspersed by a few logograms. In principle, it is based upon a simplification of Akkadian cuneiform, which replaced it after the conquest of Elam *c*.2200 BC.

Fig. 2.5. The Linear Elamite portion of a bilingual inscription of Puzur-Inšušinak, the last Elamite king of the dynasty of Awan (*c*.2260–2225 BC). The Akkadian portion of the inscription reads 'To the god Inšušinak, his lord, Puzur-Inšušinak, Governor of Susa, Regent of the land of Elam, son of Šimbišhuk, dedicated a bolt of bronze (and) cedar-wood.' The two identical sequences of four signs in the first two columns (I 7–10 and II 5–8) were read *šu-ši-na-ak* by F. Bork in 1905, immediately after the text had been published by V. Scheil in 1905. After Vallat 1986: 341, fig. 3.

Egyptian hieroglyphs

By contrast to the relatively simple pictograms of archaic Sumerian, the Egyptian hieroglyphs (literally, 'sacred carvings') are elaborate, following the conventions of Egyptian art. Their monumental forms were conserved for almost three and a half millennia, from *c*.3000 BC to AD 400. However, a cursive form called 'hieratic' developed as early as the First Dynasty for writing texts with a reed pen on papyrus scrolls. Around 700 BC, hieratic was replaced by a more rapidly written variant called 'demotic', in which pictorial forms are unrecognizable. These three scripts were used to write the now extinct Egyptian language, which belonged to the Afroasiatic family and was distantly related to the Semitic languages (§ 8.2). The latest form of Egyptian, called Coptic, died out as a living language in the sixteenth century AD, but survives in the Coptic Church. Written in the Greek alphabet, Coptic has served as the key to Pharaonic Egyptian (§ 3.1).

In an astonishingly short time, the early hieroglyphs developed into a fully-fledged writing system. There are

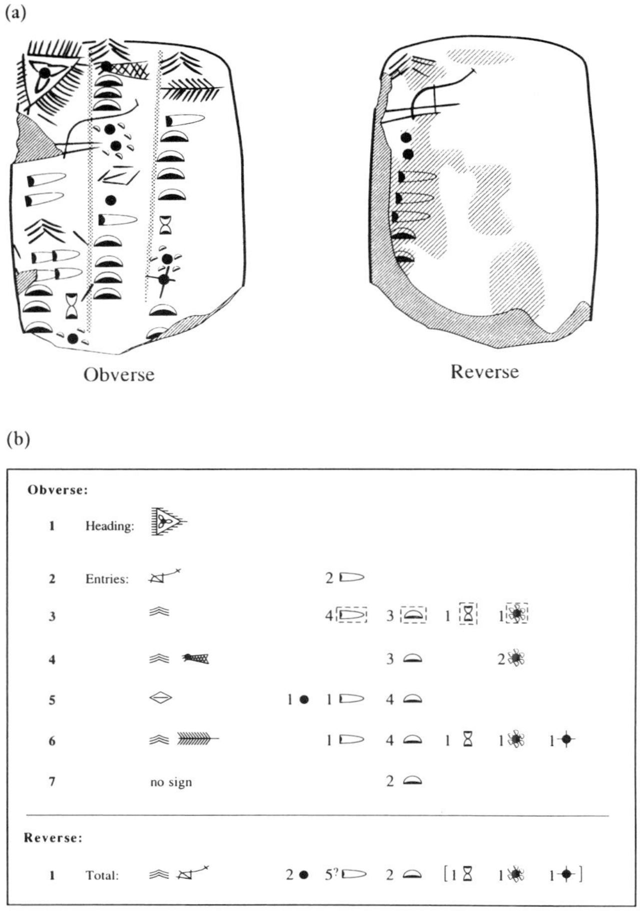

Fig. 2.6. (a) A computer drawing of a Proto-Elamite tablet from Tepe Yahya (TY 1) and (b) its transliteration. After Damerow and Englund 1989: 33, fig. 8.

reasons to suspect Sumerian influence on the birth of writing in Egypt. A superbly carved flint knife from Gebel el-ʿAraq in Upper Egypt depicts on its handle a man in Sumerian dress conquering two lions (fig. 14.8), a common Mesopotamian motif (figs. 14.9–10), and (on the reverse) a naval battle in which Sumerian-type ships defeat Egyptian ships. Some pottery and seals found in Upper Egypt are clearly imports from Sumer. These finds immediately predate the First Dynasty of Egypt, which started *c.*3000 BC.

The earliest examples of Egyptian writing are on votive stone palettes, used for grinding pigments for eye-paint. Historical scenes, which can be understood by those acquainted with Egyptian culture and its artistic conventions, have been carved on the palettes. Hieroglyphs have been added here and there in these pictures, enabling particular persons and places to be identified.

In the fully developed Egyptian script, semantic determinatives were quite regularly added after phonetically written sign sequences. For instance, in writing 'the sun-god Rᶜ' (ᶜ stands for the pharyngeal fricative, a 'weak' consonant produced in the throat, called *ᶜain* in Arabic), two determinatives are used: 'god' (the picture is of a person in a seated posture, which expresses honorific status) and ⊙ 'sun' (which by extension also means 'day'). The first two signs write the Egyptian word *rᶜ* 'sun' phonetically: the sign depicts 'mouth' = *r* in Egyptian, and the sign 'forearm' = ᶜ. In this example, 'god' indicates the class of concepts to which the word belongs. About a hundred such classifying determinatives were used, and in Middle Egyptian only the commonest words lack one. 'Sun' in the above example determines the specific meaning of the word. The ideographic use of a pictogram was often indicated by an optional short stroke, in which case phonetic signs could be omitted: means 'sun' or 'day'.

The ancient Egyptian language had vowels, as every language does, but in the original hieroglyphic writing system the vowels were ignored. Only the consonantal root (which stays constant in the inflection of Afroasiatic languages) was written. But in Late Egyptian, known as Coptic, which was written with the alphabetic Greek script, all vowels are written. Thus the hieroglyph , transcribed *mn*, may stand for any of the following Coptic sound sequences: *man*, *mīn*, *men*, *mūn*, *mon*, *mēne*, *mīne* and *mno*. Here the root consists of two consonants, *m* and *n*. Most hieroglyphs represent roots with two or three consonants, but a small number, 24 signs in all, stand for roots with just one consonant. These uniconsonantal signs form the so-called 'hieroglyphic alphabet'.

West Semitic alphabet

The complexities of the Egyptian writing system could be ignored by Egyptian-trained West Semitic scribes when they devised a writing system for their own language. Taking over the idea of one-consonant signs, they created a consonantal alphabet. This took place probably towards the end of the Hyksos rule (*c.*1730–1580 BC), when Sinai and Syria were inhabited by West Semitic-speaking peoples and were part of Lower Egypt. In this process, the number of graphemes needed in writing was radically reduced to only 22. Many (but not all) signs of the West Semitic alphabet resemble Egyptian hieroglyphs (these similarities are not restricted to the one-consonant signs); their phonetic values, however, are different (fig. 2.7). It seems that the Egyptian model and the principle of acrophony ('A as in apple') underlie the creation of the Semitic alphabet. Thus the hieroglyphic sign *n* is a picture of water (*nt* in Egyptian), but in the Semitic script , stands for *m*, because the Semitic word for 'water', *mw*, begins with *m*.

The West Semitic alphabet, documented in longer

Development of the Alphabet

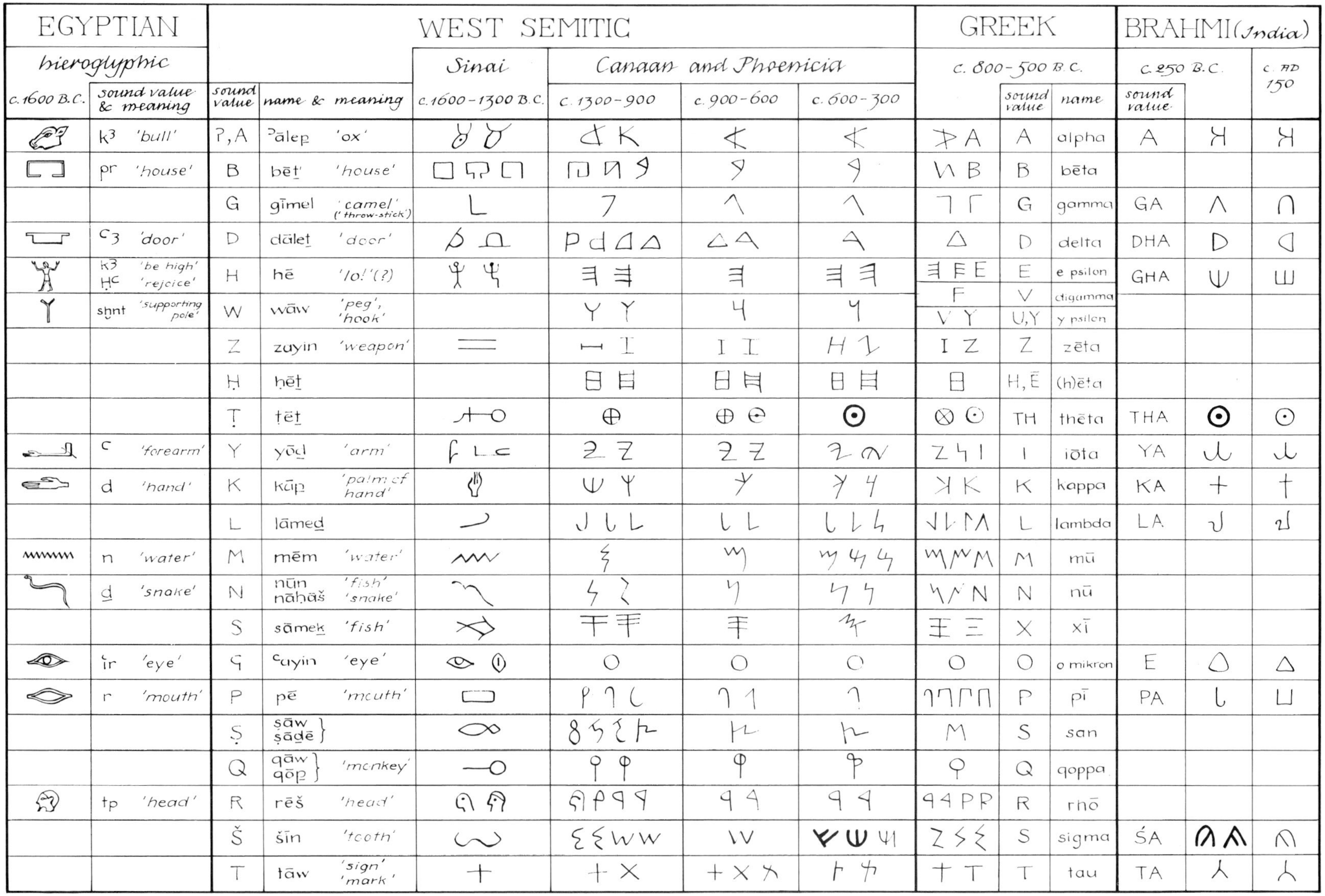

Fig. 2.7. Correspondences between Egyptian, West Semitic, Greek and Indian (Brāhmī) alphabets.

inscriptions from *c.*1000 BC, is supposed to have been invented in the second quarter of the second millennium BC, perhaps in Canaan. The earliest extant examples are about three dozen short texts in the Proto-Sinaitic alphabet (*c.* fifteenth century BC) and a few short texts in the Canaanite Linear alphabet (*c.* thirteenth century BC). The alphabetic script discovered at Ugarit in northern Syria consists of 30 cuneiform signs and probably dates from the fourteenth century BC. It is thought that the Ugaritic scribes, who were accustomed to writing the cuneiform script, devised this script in imitation of the slightly earlier Proto-Canaanite alphabet.

The consonantal alphabet suited the writing of Semitic languages tolerably well, so it is still used for this purpose. The vowels are usually ignored, as in Egyptian, but in ambiguous cases long vowels are occasionally indicated by means of the 'weak' consonants like semivowels or laryngeals, for instance by writing *'bj* instead of *'b* to express / *'bī* / 'my father'. This device was invented when Northwest Semitic languages lost short vowels in the final position: the form / *'abija* / 'of my father', written *'bj*, was reduced to / *'abij* /, which in pronunciation converged with / *'bī* / 'my father'.

Greek alphabet

Fully alphabetic writing came into being when the Greeks adopted the Phoenician alphabet around 1100–800 BC and while doing so regularized the marking of the vowels, because the consonantal alphabet was too ambiguous for the Greek language. The writing of long vowels became the rule, and short vowels also started to be written. Since there was no consonant like the Semitic laryngeal *'āleph* in the Greek language, the sign for *'āleph* (renamed *alpha* by the Greeks), along with other superfluous consonant signs, came to be used exclusively for writing a vowel (fig. 2.7).

Indian alphabets

The Semitic consonantal alphabet is the model for the Indian alphabets too. Two different adaptations of the Semitic consonantal alphabet are used in the earliest directly preserved historical documents of India, Asoka's inscriptions dated *c.*250 BC (§§ 1.2, 8.3). One, known (in Sanskrit) as Kharoṣṭhī, is restricted to northwest India; it is based on the Aramaic script used by clerks all over the Achaemenid empire, which extended from the Nile to the Indus *c.*520–330 BC. The other, called Brahmi (Brāhmī), is ultimately based on the West Semitic alphabet, and seems to have been adopted sometime after *c.*600 BC, probably via sea trade. All the modern Indian scripts go back to Brahmi. The greater number of phonemes in Indian languages demanded the creation of many new consonant signs, and led to considerable modifications. The correspondences suffice, however, to establish the Semitic origin, and the shapes of Brāhmī *tha* and *śa* even narrow the date of adoption to between 600 and 250 BC (fig. 2.7). The vowels are systematically marked in the Indian scripts, too, but by a rather complicated method (§ 4.1).

Writing developed in stages over a long period in the ancient Near East. In the system of debt tokens (*c.*8000–3100 BC), the individual tokens had a conventional meaning, but no systematic relationship prevailed between them and the signs of spoken language. Writing came into being with the phonetization of some pictograms in archaic Sumerian (*c.*3300–3100 BC) through the rebus principle. Some signs of this earliest phase can still be understood ideographically, independently of the spoken language. The system may be characterized as 'logographic', since it mainly expresses lexical units of the language, i.e. 'words'. But as some grammatical morphemes are occasionally expressed too, especially in the later stage of the development of Sumerian writing (*c.*3100–2500 BC), it may be better to call the system 'morphemic', the lexical roots being also morphemes. The use of phonetic signs in various contexts (particularly affixes, abstract words and foreign names), mixed with logograms, also legitimizes the widely used term 'logo-syllabic'. The script still requires a relatively large number of signs and an apparatus of semantic and phonetic determinatives.

With the increased marking of grammatical affixes in classical cuneiform (from *c.*2500 BC onwards), many script signs regularly begin to denote syllables. Cuneiform, however, remains a mixed 'logo-syllabic' writing system. With their much smaller number of logograms, the recently discovered Eblaite cuneiform of Syria (twenty-fourth century BC), Linear Elamite (*c.*2350 BC) and the Aegean scripts (from *c.*2000 BC) are more distinctly 'syllabic'. When West Semitic scribes, devising a new script for their own language, drastically simplified the model provided by the Egyptian logo-syllabic script, 'phonemic' writing came into being; with the full marking of vowels, the Greeks completed this invention.

The evolution of writing from logographic to morphemic / logo-syllabic to syllabic to alphabetic writing systems displays increasing phonetization in representing linguistic units (table 5.2). The alphabetic stage has never been reached immediately unless cultural contact (through colonization, for instance) has offered a short cut. In this evolution, the number of graphemes has become smaller and the capacity to represent speech has increased. The greater the reduction of the number of graphemes, the easier writing became to learn and use. At the same time, the shape of the graphemes tended to change from elaborate pictograms to more abstract symbols to radically simplified signs.

This progressive development has its inner logic, based as it is on successive improvements upon earlier systems. But the systematizations have been the result of improvisation rather than consciously planned. None of the ancient scripts is purely 'logographic', 'morphemic', 'syllabic' or 'phonemic', and scripts of any one type differ from the others not only in outer form but also in structure. By definition, a system of visual communication can only be called 'writing' when it represents speech. In other words, all scripts are partially phonetic, and there is no such thing as an 'ideographic' script independent of speech: certainly not Chinese, as some imagine. The origins of writing appear to be similar everywhere. The Central American scripts, which have evolved independently of those of the Old World, are of particular interest in this regard. Their decipherment has properly begun only in the past few decades, but enough is known to be sure that the Mayans and Aztecs, too, used such devices as pictography, the rebus principle, syllabic signs and determinatives (§ 3.4).

Chinese script

Specific scripts have been created to write specific languages and to reflect their structure. The Chinese script came into being, probably in the second millennium BC, as a largely pictographic and logo-syllabic writing system comparable to archaic Sumerian and Egyptian. It developed into a morphemic script so well fitted to write the largely monosyllabic Chinese language that it has remained in use until the present day. Over 80 per cent of the 9,353 signs listed in the first comprehensive Chinese dictionary compiled around AD 100 are combinations of semantic and phonetic components, and so are over 90 per cent of the more than 50,000 signs now in existence. The semantic determinative 木 (originally 木 'tree with roots and branches'), for example, indicates a kind of tree, a part of tree, an object made of wood, or an action associated with trees. When the phonetic complement 安 *àn* (originally meaning 'peace': the sign depicts 'a woman under a roof') is added, the resulting combined sign 案 represents *àn* 'table'.

The way in which these semantic / phonetic combinations work is extremely varied and complex, often not following either semantic or phonetic rules, but the method has secured an effective graphic distinction between the many homophonous words of the Chinese language. This is the principal reason why the Chinese have been unwilling to adopt a syllabic or alphabetic script. The frequently emphasized effectiveness of the alphabetic script needs some qualification: ideographic logograms are making their comeback in the communication of the twentieth century, for instance in traffic signs.

3 Deciphering an unknown script

3.1 Early breakthroughs

To attack the problem of the Indus script one needs to be familiar with other decipherments. A study of them makes it clear that methodologies vary with the circumstances and available materials. At the same time, both successful and unsuccessful attempts at deciphering ancient scripts have demonstrated that there are some rules and principles that cannot be ignored.

Proper names occurring in bilingual inscriptions have most often provided the crucial key to a decipherment. In 1714, an appropriate methodology was for the first time outlined by G. W. von Leibnitz:

In Palmyra and elsewhere in Syria and its neighbouring countries there exist many ancient double inscriptions, written partly in Greek and partly in the language and characters of the local people. These ought to be copied with the greatest care from the original stones. It might then prove possible to assemble the alphabet, and eventually to discover the nature of the language. For we have the Greek version, and there occur proper names, whose pronunciation must have been approximately the same in the native language as in the Greek. (Leibnitz in a letter of 1714, cited in Pope 1975: 95)

Egyptian hieroglyphs

The seventeenth- and eighteenth-century rescue and study of Coptic manuscripts prepared the way for the decipherment of Egyptian hieroglyphs, making the language of ancient Egypt accessible through its latest, but already extinct, form. In 1799, the year after Napoleon's invasion of Egypt, his soldiers discovered at Rosetta a stone bearing an inscription from the year 196 BC, written in three different scripts, Greek, demotic and hieroglyphic, and in two languages, Greek and Egyptian. Partially successful attempts to decipher the two unknown Egyptian scripts were made by A.I. Silvestre de Sacy, J. D. Åkerblad and Thomas Young.

In 1802, de Sacy tried to identify the proper names with the help of their approximate locations and repetitions in the

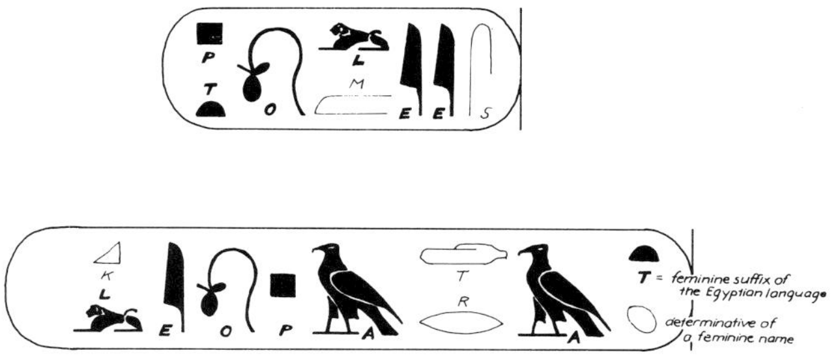

Fig. 3.1. Cartouches of Ptolemy and Cleopatra: the Egyptian hieroglyphs and their transliterations (with repetitions shown in bold).

Greek version. He further reasoned that if any letter occurred twice or more in the Greek spelling of a name, it might do so in the Egyptian spelling too. Nine years later de Sacy observed that the Chinese had to write foreign proper names with phonetic signs, and that they used to mark such instances specifically. Therefore, the circular line around a group of hieroglyphs in the Rosetta Stone might have a similar function. Such 'cartouches' were known from obelisks, too, and they had been thought to contain proper names of kings or gods (fig. 3.1).

Decipherment was achieved by Jean-François Champollion (1790–1832), who had prepared himself for this task from the age of 11. For a long time, he supposed (like everybody else) that the hieroglyphs represented ideas, not sounds. This preconception was mainly due to statements made by Graeco-Roman authors. In 1821, Champollion finally realized that there had to be phonetic elements: the hieroglyphic part of the Rosetta Stone contains about three times as many signs as there are words in the corresponding Greek version, so a hieroglyphic sign could not stand for a single word. He was then in a position to transcribe the Greek names into hieroglyphic and ascribe phonetic values to the signs.

Ptolemy's cartouche was the only one extant on the Rosetta Stone, so it did not suffice to cross-check the decipherment. But in 1822 Champollion was able to see copies of an obelisk with two cartouches, the names of Ptolemy and Cleopatra (fig. 3.1). The sound values which Champollion obtained from these cartouches enabled him to read both foreign and Egyptian kings' names in the cartouches of other texts. In 1824, Champollion published his *Précis du système hiéroglyphique*, but this was not generally accepted until much later.

Cuneiform

The cuneiform script had been completely forgotten even earlier than the hieroglyphs and was rediscovered only at the beginning of the seventeenth century. The Spanish ambassador to the Abbasid court, Don Garcia Silva Figueroa (1620) was the first to identify the ruined site of Takht-i Jamshīd in Persia with the palace of the Achaemenid king Darius in Persepolis; he referred to the ancient description given by Diodorus Siculus (17, 70–2). Don Garcia also speaks of the many local inscriptions written in strange triangular but long characters that only differed from one another in their placing and grouping.

The decipherment of cuneiform was made possible by the careful copies of trilingual inscriptions at Persepolis published by Carsten Niebuhr in 1778. Niebuhr recognized three different writing systems in these inscriptions, all to be read from left to right: he suspected that they represented three different languages. The first script comprised, according to Niebuhr's count, only 42 graphemes; the second was somewhat more complex; while the third had a great number of different signs. In 1798, Frederik Münter (1801) suggested that the three scripts were alphabetic, syllabic and ideographic respectively, that each text said the same thing in three different developmental stages of the Persian language: Zend, Pehlevi and Parsi. Eventually they were discovered to have been written in the Old Persian, Neo-Elamite and Neo-Babylonian languages.

As Münter's suggestion implies, the ancient language of the Persians (§ 8.2) was partially understood by the end of the nineteenth century. This was due to A.H. Anquetil Duperron's publications, above all his partial translation of *Zend-Avesta, ouvrage de Zoroastre* (1771), based on original manuscripts and other information that he had collected during seven years among the Parsees of India. Another crucial step towards deciphering the cuneiform script was taken by Silvestre de Sacy (1793), who read and translated Middle Persian (Pehlevi) inscriptions of the Sassanid kings (third century AD) with the help of Greek versions of them. As at Persepolis, these texts accompanied sculptured representations of kings, and contained royal names and titles, including that of 'king of kings'.

In 1802, Georg Friedrich Grotefend (1775–1853) succeeded in deciphering the simplest of the three cuneiform scripts. Like Münter, he recognized the often-repeated oblique stroke as a word divider. The length of the words, up to ten signs, and the limited number of different signs, made it likely that the script was alphabetic. Münter had sought the typically Persian title 'king of kings' in a recurring group of seven signs. Grotefend recognized that two words were required for this title: Münter's word, and a longer form of the same word that followed it. Having thus identified the word for 'king', he concluded that the words preceding it were proper names of kings. Grotefend followed Münter in believing that the Persepolis inscriptions had been left by the Achaemenid kings, and that the three most frequently occurring signs represented vowels. One of these, identified by Münter as *a* / *e* on the basis of its frequency in Zend Avesta, occurred as the second character of a royal name, and Grotefend assumed this to be Darius.

At the beginning of an inscription the royal name and the title following it were likely to be in the nominative, while the altered forms of these words, occurring in the middle of the inscription, represented case endings, probably that of the genitive singular. In the Sassanid inscriptions read by de Sacy, the king states whose son he is. Grotefend could now recognize the inscriptional formula to be 'X, great king, king of kings, son of Y (the king)'. Comparing the descent of the Achaemenid kings known from the Greek historians to the names and genealogies of the different inscriptions (where one king's father lacked the royal title), he could identify 'Xerxes, son of Darius the king', and 'Darius, son of Hystaspes (who was not a king)'. To establish the sound values of the respective signs, Grotefend referred to Anquetil Duperron's Zend vocabulary, which gave *Gustasp* or *Goshtasp* for Hystaspes and *khscheïô* for 'king'. The words Grotefend had suggested for 'king' and 'Xerxes' began with the same sign, now read as *khsch*, and closely corresponding to the pronunciation of Greek ξ. Although only 12 of the 29 sound values suggested by Grotefend in 1802–3 were correct, and many of his readings and interpretations raised severe and justified criticism, he is considered to be the decipherer of cuneiform, because his solution contained internal means of validation: some sound values (such as *r*) allotted to individual signs interlocked to form proper names (e.g. those of Darius and Xerxes) and words whose forms were plausible for Old Persian, as far as it could be reconstructed from external sources. Moreover, he clearly understood the most important parts of the Old Persian inscriptions: their names and titles.

Rasmus Rask (1787–1832), one of the founders of comparative linguistics, made an important contribution in 1823. Correcting the sound values of some signs, he read the genitive plural in the phrase 'king of kings' as *-ānām*. Its identity with the genitive plural in Sanskrit led Rask to infer that the two languages were related. This discovery led to great advances, because it allowed a more accurate reconstruction of Avestan as well as Old Persian. Henry C. Rawlinson (1810–95), the 'father of Assyriology', discovered the great trilingual rock inscription of Darius the Great at Bīsutūn. A young officer of the East India Company's army, who served as military adviser to the Shah of Persia's brother in 1833–9, Rawlinson's knowledge of Persian and his organizational skills were outstanding. He copied the long edict at risk of his life, suspended by ropes 100 metres above the ground. He had heard of Grotefend's decipherment of Achaemenid names in cuneiform inscriptions, but had no further details. Rawlinson's analysis of his newly found texts repeated Grotefend's decipherment and greatly improved upon it, translating for the first time 414 lines of Old Persian and publishing them in 1846–7.

In 1837 Grotefend identified the ideogram for 'king' and recognized the single vertical wedge as the determinative of proper names in the second, Neo-Elamite script of the Persepolis inscriptions. The values of its apparently syllabic signs could now be partly determined on the basis of the Old Persian sound values. The publication of the Bīsutūn inscription raised the number of identified proper names from about 40 to 90, which sufficed to determine the phonetic value of most signs. The absence of cognate languages known from other sources, however, has been a great hindrance in Elamite studies.

The third version of cuneiform script in the trilingual inscriptions, in the Neo-Babylonian language, with over 300 signs, was of cardinal importance, for its decipherment opened up the understanding of thousands of cuneiform tablets found in excavations all over Western Asia from the 1840s onwards. Once again, the key lay in the proper names of the Old Persian inscriptions. The Semitic character of the language was suspected by Isidore Löwenstern in 1845 and proved beyond doubt by Rawlinson in 1850–1. The multiple meanings of the cuneiform signs caused immense difficulties, but these obstacles were overcome by the efforts of Rawlinson, Edward Hincks and others. Four consistent independent interpretations of a newly discovered cuneiform inscription in 1855–7 confirmed the power of the decipherment. In the consolidation and expansion of the results, study of the grammatical, lexical and graphical lists prepared by the ancient scribes (§ 2.2) played a decisive role. In these earliest dictionaries, word signs were ordered according to their pronunciation, outer form, and meaning.

Hittite hieroglyphs

The Hittite hieroglyphic script, used *c.*1400–700 BC in Syria and Anatolia, was most probably invented by the Luvians in western Anatolia (§ 8.2). After the publication of the first hieroglyphic inscriptions in 1872, A. H. Sayce determined that the script was syllabic, although it also contained some logograms. He argued that the length of the words and the number of graphemes tallied with those of the classical Cypriot script, which had recently been deciphered (§ 3.2). He was able to reach this conclusion, which was never seriously doubted, because the Egyptian, cuneiform and Cypriot scripts were already known. Sayce also argued that the inventors of the hieroglyphs were Hittites, known from the Bible and other sources to have ruled in Syria, whence the inscriptions came. New finds in Anatolia enabled Sayce to extend the known boundaries of the Hittite empire and to collect over 100 Hittite proper names, chiefly from cuneiform sources.

A short bilingual seal and rock carvings of deities at Boğazköy in western Anatolia, with hieroglyphic and cuneiform labels, enabled Sayce to identify the determinatives for king, country and god. Such determinatives have played a role similar to that of bilinguals in the decipherment of Hittite hieroglyphs. Many Hittite names of individual gods, kings, towns and countries were known from external sources, and sign groups standing for such names could be identified in the texts with the help of the determinatives. As in the Egyptian and Old Persian decipherments, the control was eventually provided by the interlocking of syllables that happened to occur in several different names.

In 1890, J. Ménant remarked that the sign  depicting a human figure who points to himself with his arm is similar to the Egyptian sign  signifying 'I', the pronoun of the first person singular. Since it occurs at the beginning of inscriptions, these texts could now be assumed to follow the well-known pattern of many Western Asiatic royal edicts starting 'I (am) N.N., the king of the COUNTRY (or CITY) N.N.'. The recognition in 1892 of the word divider |(, which unfortunately is often omitted, and of the mark of ideograms, | | (two vertical strokes on either side of the sign), assisted the analysis of the texts. After Piero Meriggi (1930: 199) identified the sign for the word 'son', royal genealogies could be read.

The language of the Hittites was as unknown as their hieroglyphic script until the discovery of cuneiform tablets in 1887/8 at Tell el-Amarna in Upper Egypt. Among these texts were two letters sent by Ḫatti kings from Arzawa in Asia Minor to the Pharaoh. They were written in Akkadian cuneiform and could therefore be read phonetically even though their language was unknown. J. A. Knudtzon, who published the letters in 1902, read into them the stereotyped introductory formula known from other letters found at Tell el-Amarna: 'I (the sender) am well, my house, my wives (etc.) are well. May you (the addressee) be well, may your house, your wives (etc.) be well.' Knudtzon suggested that the Hittite language was Indo-European, because the suffixes *-mi* and *-ti* evidently meant 'my' and 'your', and *e-es-tu* 'may (he / she / it) be' seemed to correspond to Sanskrit *astu*, Greek *éstō* and Latin *estō*. Discouraged by severe criticism, however, Knudtzon withdrew the suggestion.

The language was identified with certainty after Hugo Winckler's excavations at Boğazköy in 1906–7 and 1911–12 had revealed the Hittite state archives, comprising some 20,000 cuneiform tablets. Bedřich Hrozný, sent to copy these tablets in 1914, expected their language to belong to the Caucasian family. The reading of the texts did not cause serious difficulties, since the values of many signs were known: they were Sumerian logograms, with or without Hittite suffixes written with syllabic signs, Akkadian words and phonetically written Hittite words, with both open and closed syllables. The logograms, Akkadian words and determinatives provided a meaningful context for guessing the unknown Hittite elements.

The language turned out to be Indo-European, and Hrozný could utilize the 'etymological method' (i.e. comparison with related languages) in interpreting it. He was not, however, quite familiar with Indo-European linguistics, and was often misled by wrong etymologies. But criticism soon established Hittite studies on a secure basis.

The knowledge of the Hittite language thus gained from cuneiform sources was introduced into the decipherment of the Hittite hieroglyphs. After this had been worked out, the decipherment was subsequently confirmed by a long bilingual inscription in Phoenician and hieroglyphic Hittite, discovered in 1946–7 at Karatepe.

3.2 Linear B

The earliest Aegean script was probably inspired by Egyptian hieroglyphic writing. The Minoan 'hieroglyphic' came into being around 2000 BC with the first palaces of Middle Minoan I in Crete. It is mainly known from seals, but a few clay accounting documents also exist. Linear A, a descendant of this script, was used in Crete and the surrounding islands *c.*1850–1450 BC. Though both scripts are undeciphered, they appear to transcribe the non-Greek language of the Minoan Civilization. Apart from the numerals and metrical signs, a few logograms depicting agricultural commodities, and some ligatures, a little under 100 syllabic signs exist in Linear A, all apparently representing open syllables like the signs of its descendants, Linear B, Cypro-Minoan and classical Cypriot.

The classical Cypriot script, used in Cyprus between the seventh and second centuries BC, was quickly deciphered with the aid of a bilingual published in 1871. George Smith demonstrated that the script is not alphabetic but syllabic. Starting with proper names, he worked out phonetic values for 18 signs and, applying these to short inscriptions on medallions, was able to read in them Greek proper names. Moriz Schmidt (1874) revised and systematized Smith's work. He established that the classical Cypriot syllabic signs stand for open syllables only and have five different vowels. (The Cypro-Minoan script, known from Cyprus and Ugarit and dated *c.*1500–1200 BC, has remained little understood until recently and does not concern us here.)

The decipherment of the Linear B script in 1952 without the help of any bilingual and without any conception of the underlying language ranks as a great achievement and the model of a methodological approach deserving careful study.

Sir Arthur Evans (1851–1941), excavating at Knossos in Crete in 1900 and 1904, had discovered over 3,000 clay tablets in the Linear B script. Some of these were published but the majority were not made available for study until 1952. The tablets are all inventories recording numbers of persons, animals and commodities. The numerals consist of strokes and circles and follow a decimal system. The direction of writing runs from left to right. The lines on the tablets usually consist of words written with phonetic signs, followed by one or more logograms and numbers. The logograms can be distinguished from the phonetic signs by their position (they generally stand alone) and by the fact that they are usually associated with numbers; moreover, they often depict recognizable things. The logograms usually allow the general sense of the tablet to be understood immediately. Some variants in the logograms for livestock seem to correspond with gender differentiation. The phonetically written words preceding the ideograms may be related to them, perhaps standing for the names of the objects. The words are clearly divided by means of word dividers consisting of vertical strokes. Word length varies from two to seven signs. There are about 90 phonetic signs, of which about 70 are in common use. About ten signs are practically identical with signs in classical Cypriot. For these reasons, the phonetic signs in all likelihood stand for open syllables.

Some of these fundamental observations and conclusions were put forward at the outset by Evans, some by other scholars. In 1927 A. E. Cowley tried to find out whether the comparable signs in the classical Cypriot script had the same phonetic value in Linear B. Enlarging on Cowley's work in 1935, Evans discovered 'good evidence for declension' in the frequent alternation of the signs 𐀍 and 𐀊 at the end of otherwise identical sign groups. Evans even noted that two signs, followed by the logogram of 'maneless horse' and the number 2, could, with the syllabic values of the Cypriot script, be read *po-lo*, giving the Greek word for 'foal' (*pōlō* in the dual, which is now known to be the correct reading). But he dismissed this as coincidence, because he was convinced that Linear B rendered the non-Greek Minoan language.

Between 1943 and 1950, Alice J. Kober was able to take some quite decisive steps. The words in which she defined her goal are worth quoting:

> Let us face the facts. An unknown language written in an unknown script cannot be deciphered, bilingual or no bilingual. It is our task to find out what the language was, or what the phonetic values of the signs were, and so remove one of the unknowns . . . If, as seems probable, it [i.e. the language of Linear B] was highly inflected language, it should be possible to work out some of the inflection pattern. Once this is done, two possibilities exist. The inflection pattern may prove a clue to the language used, or, at any rate, to the language group. In that case we have a more or less known language written in an unknown script. On the other hand, the inflection pattern will also furnish some information about the phonetic relationship of the signs . . . In that case, we would have an unknown language in a more or less known script. (Kober 1948: 102)

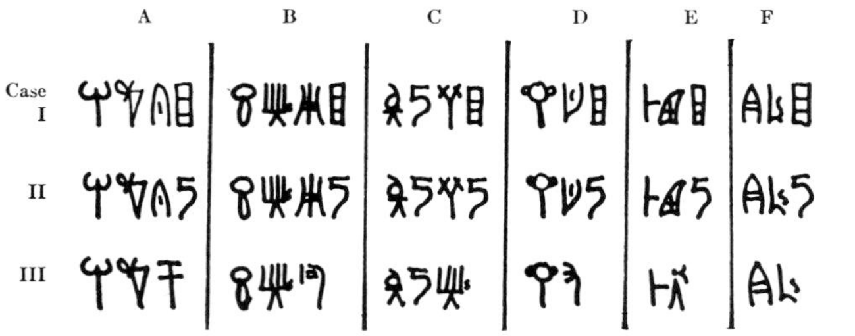

Fig. 3.2. Noun paradigms in Linear B texts as analysed by Alice Kober. After Kober 1948: 97, fig. 8.

Kober found evidence for gender distinction in the fact that the totals of women and female animals had a form different from that of the totals of men and male animals. This discovery also confirmed that the gender was marked in the logograms by adding marks for the female to the respective male ideogram. Kober also discovered systematic paradigmatic alternation that suggested inflection (fig. 3.2): in each word, cases I and II ended in two signs, the first suffix sign being the same in both cases, while case III ended with only one sign, which was different from the first suffix sign of cases I and II. Kober compared this pattern with partial paradigms drawn, just for the sake of illustration, from Latin and Middle Akkadian:

Latin		Middle Akkadian	
sg. nom.	*ser*-**vu**-*s*	pl. nom.	*ša*-**dā**-*nu*
sg. acc.	*ser*-**vu**-*m*	pl. obl.	*ša*-**dā**-*ni*
sg. dat.-abl.	*ser*-**vo**	sg. nom.	*ša*-**dū**

Written in a syllabic script of the Cypriot type, the first suffix sign of cases I and II on the one hand and the only suffix sign of case III on the other were therefore likely to share a common consonant but have a different vowel in each word. This hypothesis enabled Kober to arrange ten signs into a grid according to the internal relationships of their consonantal and vocalic components, although she did not know their phonetic values; this grid (fig. 3.3) proved to be 100 per cent correct.

Alice Kober died in 1950, but her line of argument led ultimately to the decipherment. It was taken up and developed by Michael Ventris (1922–56), whose ambition it

Fig. 3.3. Alice Kober's syllabic grid based on variation in inflection. After Kober 1948: 98, fig. 10.

had been to decipher the Knossos tablets ever since, at the age of 14, he had heard Sir Arthur Evans talk about the Minoan Civilization. From January 1951 to June 1952 Ventris prepared his famous 20 'work notes', privately distributed to a group of experts.

Ventris's methodology consisted above all in completing, as fully as possible, the syllabic grid started by Alice Kober. In addition, he prepared statistical analyses of the frequency of each sign in different positions within the words. Thus he could spot the characters that were almost exclusively limited to the initial position and therefore probably stood for pure vowels. Every word beginning with a vowel had to begin with a vowel sign, but in the middle of a word most vowels are preceded by a consonant and will therefore be written with a consonant + vowel sign, as in the classical Cypriot script. Also on the basis of statistical and distributional analysis, Ventris correctly identified the postfixed connective particle and some prefixes.

Ventris finally used the analogy of the clay tablets of the same type and age from Ugarit on the coast of Syria to guess that certain words, regularly repeated after hypothetical personal names, were the towns and occupations of those persons. The identification of words probably standing for as yet unknown place-names suggested that they might be matched with Cretan place-names known from classical sources.

In one four-sign place-name, Ventris had a pure vowel, probably *a*, at the beginning, while the third sign could, on the basis of classical Cypriot, have been *ni*. These clues suggested the reading *a-mi-ni-so* for *Amnisos*, a harbour town near Knossos. Reference to the grid then suggested that if these values were correct, another word likely to be a place-name would read *?o-no-so*, which Ventris guessed to be *ko-no-so* = *Knossos*, and *??-?i-so* similarly *tu-li-so* = *Tulissos*. Transferred to the grid, these readings determined the phonetic values of many other signs through shared consonantal and vocalic components. When all these phonetic values were applied to the texts, Ventris found he could read Greek personal names, names of Greek deities, Greek words and Greek inflectional suffixes.

To the very end, Ventris had not anticipated finding Greek in the texts. (He had thought that the language might be related to Etruscan, assumed to have come to Italy from Asia Minor.) In fact about one-quarter of the signs were wrongly placed in the grid as it stood at the time of the breakthrough. The essential correctness of the decipherment was nevertheless proved by the power of the phonetic values in the grid to generate consistent and sensible readings of the texts. External corroboration soon came in the form of new texts that had not been available to Ventris and his collaborator John Chadwick, whose expert knowledge of Greek Ventris had wisely drawn upon in the final stage (fig. 3.4).

3.3 Etruscan and the theory of decipherment

Etruscan provides a classic example of the difficulties raised by texts whose language is not related to any reasonably well-known language. The Etruscan language is unknown in this sense, although the Etruscan script is well understood. The decipherment of the Etruscan script was not difficult, because it is the model for Latin and other Italic alphabets. Annio of Viterbo (1437–1502) could already *read* Etruscan inscriptions tolerably well, and the last problems of the script were sorted out by 1936.

The longest Etruscan text is about 1,300 words. The only known example of a book written on linen cloth (later wrapped around a mummy in Egypt), it deals with Etruscan rituals. All other texts are epigraphic. Apart from a sacrificial calendar with more than 300 words legible, there are half a dozen texts of between 20 and 130 words, and about 10,000 shorter inscriptions. The majority are from graves, and show the name of the dead person, possibly with an account of his title, age and family relationships. About 30 Etrusco-Latin bilinguals are similar short funerary inscriptions. In addition, Greek and Latin authors have preserved about 60 glosses of Etruscan words. Greek names and words taken over into Etruscan and Latin borrowings from Etruscan have yielded valuable information about Etruscan phonology. The discovery in 1964 of three similar, though not exactly matching, texts in Punic and Etruscan on gold plates, reporting a temple dedication at Pyrgi, north of Rome, provides a semi-bilingual.

But the bulk of the Etruscan language remains unknown. Etruscan bilinguals may translate the words that appear on them, but they fail to translate unknown words appearing elsewhere. On the Rosetta Stone, by contrast, the understood text (in Greek) translates words of an unknown language (Old

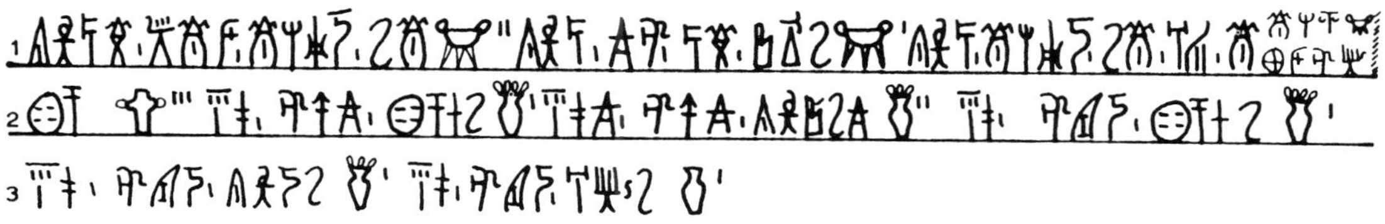

ti-ri-po-de ai-ke-u ke-re-si-jo we-ke TRIPOD 2 ti-ri-po e-me po-de o-wo-we TRIPOD 1 ti-ri-po ke-re-si-jo we-ke a-pu ke ke-re-a₂ TRIPOD ka-u-me-no

qe-to PITHOS 3 di-pa me-zo-e qe-to-ro-we JAR 1 di-pa-e me-zo-e ti-ri-o-we-e JAR 2 di-pa me-wi-jo qe-to-ro-we JAR 1

di-pa me-wi-jo ti-ri-jo-we JAR 1 di-pa me-wi -jo a-no-we JAR 1

Fig. 3.4. Tablet PY Ta 641 in the original Linear B script and in transliteration. This three-lined clay tablet was discovered at Pylos in 1952 and made available for study in 1953. It provided a kind of 'pictorial bilingual' that proved the correctness of Ventris's decipherment, already accomplished without its help. The Greek words *ti-ri-po-de* = *trípode* 'two three-legged (cauldrons)', *ti-ri-po* = *trípōs* 'one three-legged (cauldron)', *ti-ri-o-we-e* = *trió̄wee* 'two (vessels) with three handles', *ti-ri-jo-we* = *trió̄wes* 'one (vessel) with three handles', *qe-to-ro-we* = *q*[u]*etrō̃wes* 'one (vessel) with four handles', and *a-no-we* = *anō̃wes* 'one (vessel) without handles' are each accompanied by the corresponding ideograms and numbers. After Hooker 1980: 129–32.

Egyptian) that is related to another language (Coptic, descended from Old Egyptian) whose vocabulary and grammar are known. The systematic relationship between the 'unknown' language and its known relative implies that a translation of one word helps to predict the translation of other words in the unknown language.

Genetic relationship of languages

A short discussion of the concept of genetic relationship may be of help to appreciate this important point. The languages of the world, past and present, are classified genetically into various language families. Genetically related languages are descended from a common protolanguage. Their ultimate origin lies in dialects of an ancient language that have lost contact with each other and therefore diverged to such an extent that their speakers can no longer (or only defectively) understand each other.

In the course of time, all languages change in their lexicon, phonology, morphology and syntax. Phonological changes usually start with an assimilation, dissimilation, metathesis or some other alteration in a word which occurs with a high frequency and in which the changing sound does not have a grammatical function. The sound change then becomes systematic and spreads to other words, allowing, however, exceptions due to morphological or semantic analogy.

The determination of whether a genetic relationship exists between any given languages or not depends on whether systematic correspondences can be established between their sound systems. If the relationship between the languages concerned is sufficiently close, the comparative method allows reconstruction of the earlier protolanguage. In the decipherment of the Linear B script, for example, knowledge of the reconstructed prehistory of the Greek language proved to be of vital significance.

But why can Etruscan not be distantly related to some known language? It is true that in some cases it may be possible to reconstruct even several successive protolanguages. Thus Italian, Spanish, Portuguese, French and Romanian form the Romance group of languages, whose protolanguage is Latin; Latin in its turn is descended from the same Italic protolanguage as the little-known ancient languages Venetic, Oscan and Umbrian; Italic, finally, is just one of the daughter languages of Proto-Indo-European.

Some scholars have argued (but not been able to prove) that Proto-Indo-European has similarly branched off from a still more ancient protolanguage called 'Nostratic'. The Nostratic 'phylum' would consist of the following language families, all assumed to be genetically related to each other: Indo-European (§ 8.4), Afroasiatic (§ 8.2), Uralic, Altaic (assumed to comprise the Turkic, Mongolian and Tungusic languages, sometimes also Korean and even Japanese), Kartvelian (South Caucasian) and Dravidian (§§ 8.3 and 9.1–6). The idea of a Nostratic phylum is not improbable in itself; the geneticist L. L. Cavalli-Sforza (1991) in fact argues quite forcefully that 'the family tree relating human populations corresponds to another relating the languages of the world. Both trees imply a series of migrations; the biological evidence indicates a homeland in Africa.' It is the proving of such a distant relationship by linguistic means that seems impossible at present. The application of the comparative method becomes critical as the distance of the relationship increases: the longer the related languages develop apart from each other, the smaller becomes the number of shared words and morphemes that have been inherited from the common protolanguage.

Proto-Uralic, spoken perhaps about 8,000–6,000 years ago around the Ural mountains, may be the oldest language reconstructable with certainty. The reconstruction of Proto-Uralic is based on about 140 fairly secure etymologies shared by Proto-Finno-Ugric (*c*.4000–3000 BC) (§ 8.4) and the much more recently differentiated Proto-Samoyedic spoken in Siberia. Only a fraction of these 140 words can be expected to be derived from a still earlier protolanguage and to be shared by related language families (as assumed by the Nostratic hypothesis), and such a number is too small for a reliable reconstruction of systematic sound correspondences.

It is not enough to have well over a hundred similar words in two languages or language families to establish their genetic relationship. Amateurs often draw far-reaching conclusions on the basis of superficial phonetic resemblances, but, contrary to their expectations, cognate words have often diverged so much in distantly related languages that they hardly resemble each other: compare, for example, English *wheel*, Greek *kúklos* and Sanskrit *cakraḥ*, all derived from Proto-Indo-European **k^{w}ek^{w}los* (the asterisk indicates that the following word is not actually attested but only a hypothetical reconstruction). The words on which the comparison is based have to fulfil certain requirements. In distant relationships, the words on either side must be reconstructable in the respective protolanguage (which implies, among other things, that they are found in several languages, preferably as distant from each other as possible, and / or in ancient documents) and the reconstructed forms should bear a reasonable resemblance to each other in both sound and meaning. Only if these basic requirements are fulfilled can one proceed to the all-important test and see whether the phonemic correspondences are regular.

The requirements demanded of words taken as the basis of comparisons aiming at the establishment of distant relationships have now been further refined. They may be illustrated by the case of the 'Altaic' languages. Eminent linguists have long argued for a genetic relationship between the Turkic, Mongolian and Manchu-Tungusic families, but nowadays experts think that the extensive similarities are more likely to result from long and intensive contacts which have led to massive borrowings and structural convergences. Distant comparisons, therefore, have to be limited to core vocabulary that is not easily borrowed (grammatical morphemes, kinship terms, names for the principal parts of the body, important natural phenomena, directions of space, etc.); cultural loanwords as well as onomatopoeic expressions with iconic similarity (e.g. *cuckoo*) must be excluded.

Etruscan (continued)

The absence of obviously related languages well known from other sources is coupled with another major limitation in Etruscan studies: the scantiness and repetitive nature of the written material. Much of the vocabulary and morphology of the Etruscan language is not used in inscriptions (and thus not available for linguistic study), while numerous words and forms appear only once, defying interpretation.

Yet it would be a mistake to say that Etruscan is a totally unknown language. The number of plausible hypotheses concerning all aspects of the Etruscan language is currently considerable. This became so after the 'etymological method' was abandoned as the primary means of studying the Etruscan language. Yet it still continues to be the favourite method of many dilettantes, who, year after year claim to have 'solved the Etruscan problem' by 'proving' that Etruscan is related to this or that language. (Etymology remains necessary, of course, to sort out loan contacts between Etruscan, Italic languages and Greek in particular.)

It is the 'combinatory method' that has yielded substantial results. This requires that the Etruscan language be interpreted chiefly in terms of itself, through a multi-sided internal analysis of the inscriptions, taking into account all possible contextual clues. The Etruscologist must be acquainted with linguistics, philology, history, archaeology, art history and religion. Within this general methodological framework an important sideline is the use of Latin, Oscan, Umbrian and Greek parallels to interpret specific categories of Etruscan texts. We have already seen how fruitful the exploitation of stereotype 'routines' has proved in deciphering ancient scripts: it is quite warranted to expect similar texts within a single cultural milieu to share similar formulae and phraseology, even if their languages differ. This 'quasi-bilingual' method has been successfully employed in the study of the linen book.

Etruscan studies also provide a good example of the importance of carefully laid epigraphic foundations in decipherment. The revision of the first volume of the *Corpus Inscriptionum Etruscarum* showed that about 20 per cent of the material in the old edition had been misread; a number of linguistic and philological hypotheses had been based on 'ghost words' which did not exist at all in reality.

Types of decipherment

Expositions of decipherment of ancient scripts usually distinguish three types of decipherment, according to whether the script, the language or both script and language are unknown. In order of increasing difficulty, the scheme looks as follows (table 3.1):

Table 3.1. *Conventional typology of decipherments*

type	script	language	example(s)
1	unknown	known	Egyptian hieroglyphic
2	known	unknown	Etruscan
3	unknown	unknown	Linear B; Indus script

Such a typology of decipherments is, however, grossly over-simplified. In the first place, the terms 'known' and 'unknown' are inexact. Many 'unknown' languages have later proved to be members of well-known language families, enabling them to be worked out by linguistic methods.

In the case of type 2, unknown language and known script, there are therefore two possibilities: the language can be recognized as belonging to a known family and can therefore be worked out; or it can be found, like Etruscan, to belong to an unknown or little known language family. In the latter case, its whole grammar and lexicon have to be worked out from scratch. Experience has shown that this is possible only if extremely extensive bilinguals are available, as in the case of Sumerian. A modest number of bilinguals, as in the case of Etruscan, will not take one further than their own coverage. If no bilinguals at all are available and the underlying language is an isolated one, a decipherment is absolutely impossible.

Type 3 cannot be deciphered unless painstaking work and a few clues make possible the identification either of the language or of the script, thus converting it into either type 1 (as was the case with Linear B) or type 2. In practice the methodology to be followed in types 1 and 3 will be much the same, with this important difference: in type 1 efforts can be concentrated on matching the script with the known language or language group, whereas in type 3, efforts must be dissipated in probing various possibilities, and the use of linguistic clues is always accompanied by a very much greater range of uncertainty.

Prospects of decipherment vary also according to the type of unknown script. An alphabetic script, with very few graphemes and a nearly one-to-one fit with the phonemes of the underlying language, offers the smallest number of possibilities for tentative reading and is therefore the easiest type of script to decipher. Statistical and distributional features of the phonemic and graphemic systems can be directly compared.

Ugaritic cuneiform alphabet

Tablets written in a previously unknown cuneiform alphabet were discovered at Ugarit in Syria in 1929. Within a week one of its decipherers, Hans Bauer (1878–1937), a cryptographer in the First World War, could determine correctly the phonetic values of half of the signs. The script had to be a consonantal alphabet, because there were only 27 (eventually 30) graphemes, and because the words, separated by single vertical strokes, were short (often one or two signs only). Bauer first isolated all signs that appeared to represent prefixes, suffixes and monosyllabic words. He compared these signs with the consonants that served in these functions in West Semitic, which he assumed to have been spoken in Ugarit. Discriminating the alternatives on the basis of frequency and distribution, he got partly right, partly wrong sound values, which he applied to the texts. Bauer identified the introductory preposition as *l* 'to', and looked for words likely to occur, especially *mlk* 'king' (containing *l*) and *bn* 'son'. Their location led to the words $b^{c}l$ 'god' and $b^{c}lt$ 'goddess', providing a good beginning to the decipherment.

Types of decipherment (continued)

In a syllabic script, too, the signs usually have just one phonetic value, but the relation to the phonemic system is not as direct as in the alphabetic script. There are more variables, so more material is needed for the determination of their values. Nevertheless, the number of syllables in a given language is much smaller than the number of words. If its syllable structure happens to be of a simple type (as in Japanese), the language can be represented quite well with relatively few signs (the Japanese syllabary today consists of 46 basic signs and a few diacritic marks). Compromises have been made when languages with a complex syllable structure have been written with a syllabic script, so that the number of syllabograms used at one time rarely exceeds 120. Thus the signs of a syllabic script are integrated into a closed system, where phonetic interrelationships between the signs can be worked out and tabulated, as Kober and Ventris did in their grids. When a breakthrough has been achieved in the decipherment of alphabetic and syllabic scripts, it has soon been possible to work out the phonetic values of other signs on the basis of a few initial clues. One important reason for this is that the clues are scattered all over phonetically written texts, which do not leave too much of the language unrepresented.

A logo-syllabic script is much more difficult to decipher. There is a large number of signs, which do not form such a tightly coherent system and which, moreover, generally have more than one phonetic and / or semantic value. In the absence of effective aids, such as extensive bilinguals, native lexica or descendants of the signs with known values, complete decipherments of logo-syllabic writing systems are usually impossible. The degree of difficulty depends further on the number, length and diversity of the texts and the extent to which there are semantic and phonetic determinatives, grammatical elements that have been marked, words written phonetically, and the like. The degree to which the pictograms are stylized is also crucial: recognizable pictures give clues to sound values if the underlying language is known, and to primary meanings even if it is not.

3.4 Maya hieroglyphs

The decipherment of the hieroglyphic script of the Maya has been controversial for a long time, but considerable agreement and progress have been achieved during the past few decades. The Maya script is a complex logo-syllabic writing system with no real bilinguals which would provide translations. The methods used in its decipherment and in controlling the decipherment are therefore particularly interesting and relevant for the study of the Indus script.

Proto-Mayan speakers had settled in the lowlands of Central America by about 1500 BC. The social changes that took place around 250 BC transformed forest villages into powerful cities possessed of writing. The script of the Maya, used from the second century BC, was based on the hieroglyphic writing that had been developed by their western neighbours by *c*.700 BC. Although the classical Maya Civilization collapsed around AD 900, writing continued to be used, probably until the seventeenth century. After the Spanish conquest, however, a great number of Mayan books written on bark-paper were ruthlessly destroyed. Only four such manuscripts or codices have survived, but fortunately there are more than a thousand inscriptions on beautifully carved stone monuments. In 1566 Bishop Diego de Landa compiled a work that was to become the 'Rosetta Stone' of Maya writing. In his *Relación de las cosas de Yucatán*, Landa explained the rudiments of the Maya calendar and 'the Maya alphabet', equating certain glyphs with A, B, C, etc. (fig. 3.5).

The clearly recognizable numbers provided the starting-point for the first major breakthroughs. Landa explains the sophisticated counting system of the Maya, based on the idea of place-value that increases in multiples of 20, i.e. 1, 20, 400, 8000, etc. The numeral signs consist of a picture of a shell for zero, a dot for one, and a bar for five. Landa drew the symbols which the Maya used for their 20 days and their 18 + 1 months, and also gave the corresponding names in Yucatec Maya. But Landa's book became available only after a copy of it had been discovered in Madrid and published together with a French translation in 1864 by Charles Etienne Brasseur de Bourbourg (1814–74). Brasseur did also other great services to Maya studies. While serving as an Abbé in Guatemala he had learned the Maya language, and had already published most important pre-conquest Maya texts, the great creation epic Popol Vuh (from a manuscript) and the drama Rabinal Achi (from an oral source) in 1861–2. In 1869 he was to publish the famous Maya Codex he had also discovered in

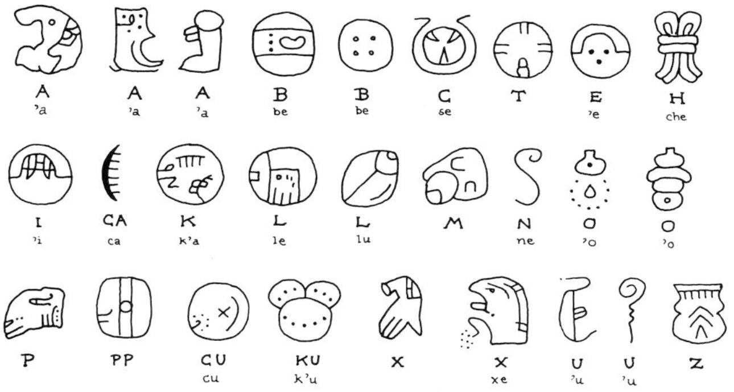

Fig. 3.5. Bishop Landa's 'Maya alphabet' (AD 1566). Drawn after a facsimile in Houston 1989: 16, fig. 7.

Madrid and to make an unsuccessful attempt to read the Maya script as an alphabetic system of writing. On the basis of Landa and the Dresden Codex, Ernst Förstemann (1823–1906) and others could work out the exact structure of the Maya calendar. The calendar is based on paired cycles of $(20 \times 13 =)$ 260 days and of $((18 \times 20) + (1 \times 5) =)$ 365 days. A date is usually expressed by noting its position in both cycles. But because each combination repeats itself every 52 years, the Maya chroniclers also recorded the position of a date in a 'long count', i.e. a great cycle starting in 3114 BC and ending in AD 2012.

The Dresden Codex, Förstemann's main source, has turned out to be an almanac for divination. Each day is linked to other days by astronomical calculations, involving the eclipses and cycles of Venus. Their astrological significance is expressed through connected deities and animals, of which there is a great variety.

The parallelism between partly ideographic glyphs and the pictorial illustrations which accompany them in the codices and monuments has provided 'pictorial bilinguals' for the decipherment of the Maya script. Particularly important are parallel passages, where one variable element in the text corresponds to one variable element in the iconography. In this way, it has been possible to determine the approximate meaning of quite a number of glyphs. Besides numbers and calendrical and astronomical signs, they include compass points, colours, deities, animals, plants, artefacts, parts of the body, and so on.

Some 25 Maya languages are still spoken by about 5 million people in the area of the classical Maya Civilization, enabling reconstruction of the Proto-Mayan language. This unbroken linguistic continuity and the linguistic research carried out since colonial times have made a phonetic decipherment possible.

The breakthrough here was achieved in the 1950s by the Soviet scholar Yurij V. Knorozov, who had studied Egyptian hieroglyphs and who was later to work on the Indus script too

Fig. 3.6. 'Turkey' = *ku-tzu* in the third section of the uppermost row on leaf 7a of the Dresden Codex (*c.* AD 1250). The image of the turkey and the double glyph corresponding to it are emphasized.

Fig. 3.7. 'Dog' = *tzu-lu* in the middle section in the uppermost row on leaf 90a of the Madrid Codex. The image of the dog and the double glyph corresponding to it are emphasized.

(§4.2). Knorozov assumed that Bishop Landa's 'alphabet' was in fact a list of syllabic signs, whose phonetic values correspond to the Spanish names of the letters involved. For example, when Landa had asked 'What is B (*beh*) in your writing?' his native informant would have drawn the Maya sign with the phonetic value *beh*.

Comparative work had equated the picture of 'turkey' with a two-glyph word written over it (fig. 3.6). The first glyph is Landa's K. In modern Yucatec Maya, 'turkey' is *kutz*, so Knorozov supposed that the K glyph stands for the syllable *ku*. The second glyph he read as *tzu*. This was the first of two glyphs assumed to mean 'dog', while the second was Landa's glyph for L (fig. 3.7). This agreed with the old Yucatec word for 'dog', *tzul*. Most Maya words end in consonants, so Knorozov assumed, on the basis of these and some other interlocking examples, that the word-final consonants were written syllabically by means of signs containing the same vowel as the word-initial syllable.

Knorozov's interpretations were published in 1952, but at that time in Russian only, and not all of them were by any means as convincing as those quoted above. For other reasons, too, it took more than 25 years before his assumptions about the syllabic nature of the phonetic glyphs and their 'synharmony' became widely accepted. Meanwhile, other approaches were developed.

In spite of progress made in understanding the Maya calendar and astronomy, the general purpose of the monuments remained problematic for a long time. Then, in 1958, Heinrich Berlin identified 'emblem glyphs' standing for specific places or their ruling families. Two years later, Tatiana Proskouriakoff analysed 35 inscriptions which all came from a single place and fell architecturally into seven groups. She noticed that the time span of the dates within each group never exceeded the average lifetime of a human being, which suggested that the monuments in question had been raised within a single reign. One stela in each group shows a person seated on a platform, and the inscription records two dates, both accompanied by a specific glyph; these have been deciphered as denoting 'birth' and 'accession to power'. With the identification of a prefix for female names and titles (the face of a woman), it became possible to pick out names of queens and queen mothers (distinguishable from the accompanying dates). King lists could then be compiled, and family relationships charted. Subsequent research has shown that warfare and rituals are among the other main topics recorded in the inscriptions.

One of the grave difficulties that has been obstructing the decipherment of the Maya script is the complex composition of its signs, or 'glyphs', usually square in form, numbering 750–850 in all. At least 400 of them are 'main signs', which may appear in three variant forms, with no apparent semantic difference: besides depicting in considerable detail the 'head' or the 'full figure' of a human being, animal or deity, a glyph may have a more abstract 'symbolic' form. In addition there are at least 250 smaller 'affix signs', which may be added to the main signs, the whole forming a square 'glyph block'. Affix signs added on the left side or above the main sign are called 'prefixes', those on the right side or below 'postfixes', and signs placed inside the main glyph 'infixes'. There is a lot of variation, and constituent signs are extremely difficult to recognize with certainty.

In addition, the same thing may be written in many different ways. This variation is partly due to the fact that words could be written ideographically as well as syllabically. Syllabic signs (e.g. *ba*) could also be added as phonetic determinatives to logograms (e.g. the head of a jaguar = *balam* 'jaguar'). Finally, logograms can also be used as rebuses. Thus there are three (nearly) homophonous words in Maya with the phonetic shape *kan* / *kān*, meaning 'snake', 'sky' and '4', and the respective glyphs may be substituted for each other. Thus, for example, the 'sky' glyph is used in a context requiring the meaning '4'.

Many of the Maya glyphs remain undeciphered. The known glyphs, though few in number, are used as a clue to the subject-matter dealt with in a given text. Clarification of sequences dealing with deities and rituals, for example, has been sought from Spanish sources, the Maya creation epic Popol Vuh that survived the conquest, and the religions of the present-day Maya. Longer texts have been analysed syntactically. Even totally unknown signs can with some confidence be interpreted as belonging to specific grammatical categories (nouns, verbs, adjectives, numerical classifiers, etc.) on the basis of 'positional schematism' (§ 6.2). Grammatical affixes, too, have been identified, those of the possessive and locative markers most securely. It is apparent, however, that not nearly all the affixes of the spoken language have been represented in writing.

The nature of the Maya script has not permitted a complete and simultaneous decipherment of the entire writing. One has to proceed gradually, deciphering the glyphs one by one. Nevertheless, 'any addition to our knowledge of the glyphs tends to have a feedback effect, helping us to achieve additional results . . . All glyphs have some sort of relevance to the decipherment of other glyphs' (Kelley 1976: 248).

A full decipherment of a Maya glyph involves four aspects:

1 recognition of the object depicted by the glyph,
2 knowledge of its phonetic value,
3 knowledge of its meaning(s), and
4 understanding how the three are interrelated.

It is possible to decipher a glyph only partially, i.e. achieve one or two of the first three requirements without the others.

The routine decipherment procedure, again, has been described as follows:

1 The pictorial meaning of the glyph is determined, mainly from Maya art.
2 A phonetic reading is looked for by reconstructing the Proto-Maya word for the object represented.
3 The homophones of the phonetic reading are determined.
4 The meanings of the words in points 2 and 3 are compared in the different contexts in which the glyph occurs.
5 Conversely, when two or more different meanings of a glyph can be concluded from the contexts, an explanation is sought from a possible Proto-Maya homophony.

At the end of the book we shall briefly compare the methods and premisses in deciphering the Maya script to those that are here applied to the Indus script. We are now ready to turn our attention to this subject.

4 Approaches to the Indus script

4.1 Evolution of the Indus script and later Indian scripts

The potter's marks on the ceramics of Neolithic societies may be considered as forerunners of writing, but only in the sense that they trained people to use incised or painted symbols, and that some of these traditional local symbols may have been models for the signs of a real writing system when such a system was devised. From the period dated *c.*3600–2600 BC, thousands of Early Harappan potsherds with potter's marks have been discovered, usually on utilitarian unpainted ware. The marks were incised on the wet clay before firing, with a sharp instrument, a fingernail, or both; marks painted before firing are much rarer. Graffiti scratched on pottery after firing also occur: they may have been made by the potter or the owner.

Incised and painted marks are found on vessels from many early sites in the Indus region and the Indo-Iranian borderlands, including Amri IA–IIB, Kot Diji, Bala-kot I (fig. 4.1), Mehrgarh IV–VII, Damb Sadaat I–III, Kili Ghul Muhammad IV and other Quetta Valley sites, Mundigak I–IV, Rahman Dheri, Sarai Khola II and Jalilpur. About 50 to 150 different signs are known in some sites or areas. Comparable and roughly contemporaneous pot-marks are known from Shahr-i Sokhta in Seistan and from elsewhere in Iran.

Many of the Early Harappan potter's marks seem to be numerals, especially the groups of vertical strokes, whose numerical value varies from one onwards. The lower numbers are marked in this way in the Indus script, too (§ 5.2), and a large part of the Mature Harappan graffiti on potsherds consists solely of such numerals (§ 7.3). It seems that the larger numbers (tens?) were expressed in the Indus script by means of semicircles standing on their open ends, often repeated one above another (fig. 7.8b and d). Did they develop from the (often repeated) fingernail impressions among the Early Harappan potter's marks?

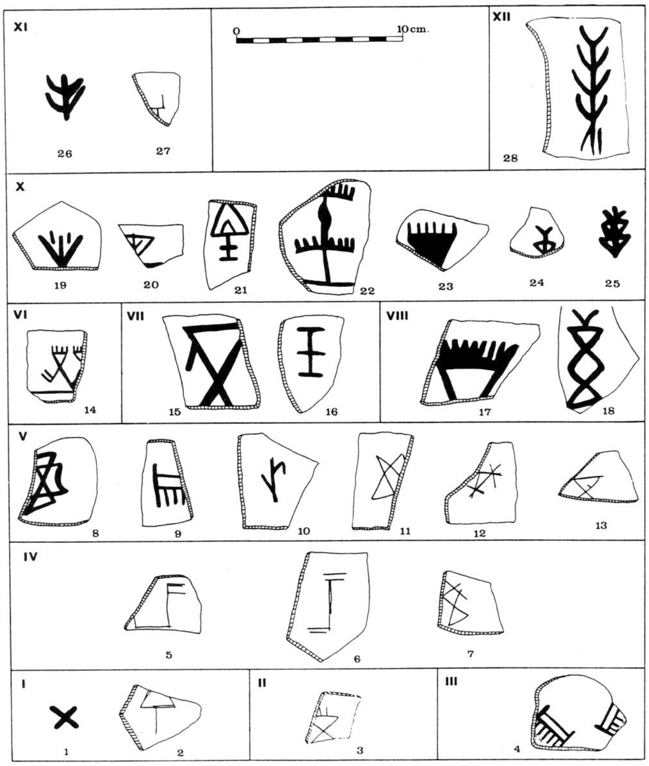

Fig. 4.1. Early Harappan painted and incised potter's marks from Bala-kot (in Sind), layers I–XII, period I, *c.*3500–2600 BC. After Dales 1979: 256, fig. 6.

Resemblances between relatively simple linear signs in different marking systems cannot be given much weight in an assessment of genealogical relationship. For example, signs of the Vinča culture in southeast Europe (Winn 1981) resemble the Indus script in ways at least as close as the Early Harappan pot-marks. On the whole, the signs that characterize the Indus script are not present in the Early Harappan graffiti. A few interesting exceptions do deserve special attention, however.

One (unfortunately broken) Early Harappan graffito from Bala-kot (fig. 4.1 no. 5) resembles the most common and most characteristic Indus sign Ʊ, except that the Bala-kot sign is angular. But other Early Harappan potter's marks from Rahman Dheri (*CISI* 2: Rhd-139 to 141) suggests that the sign surviving on the Bala-kot sherd may be complete, in which case there is no match with the Indus sign. Another Indus sign usually occupying the final position in the inscriptions, the 'spearhead', ↑, is also found on a slightly broken potsherd from Bala-kot (fig. 4.1 no. 2), and on a number of sherds from Rahman Dheri (Rhd-88 to 93). In Rahman Dheri, again, there are several examples of 'triangles', which are like the 'spearhead' sign but without the 'shaft' (Rhd-81 to 85).

Potter's marks were in existence over a vast area in the Greater Indus Valley for many centuries, if not a millennium, before the creation of the Indus script, and there is an unbroken continuity in the stratigraphic sequence from the Early Harappan period to the Mature Harappan period at many sites. Even so, nowhere do we find clear evidence of a gradual progress towards real writing in the Early Harappan layers. Unpublished miniature seals from Rahman Dheri, dated to the early third millennium BC, are said to bear symbols that herald the Indus script, but this remains to be verified, and in fact other evidence does not support the hypothesis that the Indus script developed here in the north. No Indus inscriptions of two or more signs have been discovered in the Mature Harappan layers of the Late Kot Dijian sites of the upper Indus Valley. Only the Harappan symbol of 'two intersecting circles' (discussed in § 13.1) is represented among the painted symbols on the pottery of Gumla in the Gomal Valley (*CISI* 2: G-8), and of Sarai Khola II near Taxila (Halim 1972: pl. 20 B 1).

A dozen potsherds from the large Kulli site of Nindowari in southern Baluchistan each have between one and five marks painted on them. The excavator, Jean-Marie Casal, thought that these graffiti might represent a local script, because they contain some recurring sign sequences. The specimens, however, are too few and the signs too linear and cursive to inspire confidence in this hypothesis. Moreover, the Nindowari graffiti belong to the Mature Harappan period. Nevertheless, they are interesting in the light of the close connection between the Kulli culture and the transitional phase between the Early and Mature Harappan periods (figs. 1.14–15).

On present evidence, the Indus script cannot be directly derived from any other known script. The geographically closest and vaguely similar Proto-Elamite script (figs. 2.2 and 2.6), which has often been mentioned in this connection, is many centuries older. The historical situation in the twenty-sixth century BC, when the Indus script came into being, and particularly the establishment of sea contact with the Gulf region (§ 1.6), makes it likely that the Indus script was inspired by a Near Eastern script. The source of inspiration could have been the cuneiform script, but it could equally well have been an as yet unknown later variety of the Proto-Elamite script that may have been used somewhere within the Elamite realm *c.*2600 BC. The survival of the Proto-Elamite script in some form after 2900 BC is suggested by its being the source for the signs of the Linear Elamite syllabic script created in the middle of the twenty-fourth century BC (§ 2.3). The 'Late Proto-Elamite' alternative is supported by the evident influence that Proto-Elamite glyptic art exerted upon the iconography of the Harappan seals (figs. 14.15–16).

When the Harappan traders were establishing trade

relations with the Near Eastern merchants in the Gulf area, they undoubtedly saw how their western colleagues used writing to draw up contracts and to register the goods. This would have been sufficient stimulus for them to create their own communication system quickly. Whatever the particular source of inspiration for the Indus script, its influence was probably limited to the basic idea of how scripts work, while the external forms of the Indus signs are likely to be predominantly native Harappan invention. (At least some of the earlier local symbols of the Greater Indus Valley, including decorative motifs painted on pottery, seem to have been adopted as pictograms in the Indus script; see figs. 13.15–16.) We have a parallel in early Egyptian writing, which developed in a very short time from native elements *c*.3000 BC once some Sumerian adventurers had imported the idea of writing, together with a few Sumerian iconographic motifs (§ 2.3).

In the available evidence, the Indus script emerges almost fully standardized. Only a few signs on the 'miniature tablets' in the lower levels of Harappa differ slightly from their later forms, e.g.  for later ; this change may be due to an effort to save space (§ 7.2). The 'miniature tablets' have been considered the earliest Indus texts, but the 1991 excavations at Harappa showed that they were stratigraphically preceded by a square stamp seal with Indus script and a boldly carved bison.

Except for stylistic variation determined by the different materials of artefacts bearing inscriptions, the Indus script did not change much during the Mature Harappan period. Specimens of the script have survived only on seals and a few other objects that will be discussed in detail later on (§§ 7.3–5). Some scholars have maintained that there never were any other kinds of documents. On the analogy of 'empires' comparable to the Indus Civilization (§ 1.6), this seems unlikely. The Aztecs of the classical period, for instance, used writing for many purposes. Ixtlilxochitl, a hispanized brother of the last native Aztec ruler of Texcoco, who wrote in the sixteenth century, has left us the following graphic description:

> They had scribes for each branch of knowledge. Some dealt with the annals, putting down in order the things which happened each year, giving the day, month, and hour. Others had charge of the genealogies, recording the lineage of rulers, lords and noblemen, registering the newborn and deleting those who had died. Some painted the frontiers, limits, and boundary markers of the cities, provinces and villages, and also the distribution of fields, whose they were and to whom they belonged. Other scribes kept the law books and those dealing with the rites and ceremonies which they practised when they were infidels. The priests recorded all matters to do with the temples and images, with their idolatrous doctrines, the festivals of their false gods, and their calendars. And finally, the philosophers and learned men which there were among them were charged with painting all the sciences which they had discovered, and with teaching by memory all the songs in which were embodied their scientific knowledge and historical traditions. (quoted by Bray 1968: 91)

We do not possess any such historical record of the activities of the Harappan scribes and scholars, so we can only speculate on what has been lost from the Indus Valley of the third millennium. The normal writing material is likely to have been the perishable palm leaf, as it was in India until this century, or cotton cloth (Sanskrit *paṭ(ṭ)a*). But the Mesopotamians wrote on clay, and their surviving documents and literature testify that writing was used in the Akkadian empire in much the same way as it was in the Aztec empire.

In the Late Harappan period, the centralized Harappan administration in the Greater Indus Valley seems to have been disrupted (§ 1.6). Around 1900 BC, the political power appears to have largely passed over to a new group of people representing the expanding Bactria and Margiana Archaeological Complex (=BMAC) who came via Baluchistan (§ 8.4). In spite of the magnificent prestige objects it produced, the BMAC had no writing. To judge from their characteristic cylinder and stamp seals (of both the BMAC and Jhukar type), which continued to be without inscriptions, the newcomers were at least partially still illiterate. On the other hand, at Nausharo a BMAC cylinder seal was found on the floor of the same room as a small stamp seal that contained two signs of the Indus script, but no iconographical motif; the sequence of the two signs occurs in many Harappan texts and undoubtedly represents the official Indus language, but the 'spearhead' sign has an unusual form. In the urban centres that survived after the mature phase of the Indus Civilization had ended, the Harappan traditions continued but the standard of workmanship became lower. Thus at Lothal (periods IV and V), the Indus signs are carelessly incised, on crude terracotta seals instead of neatly carved stone seals.

The incisions on pottery from Rangpur II–III and other Post-Urban sites of Gujarat that have been quoted as examples of a 'Late Harappan linear script' cannot be considered as real writing. Some of these symbols are similar to, or even identical with, some rarely occurring Indus pictograms, but characteristic signs and above all sign sequences are lacking. These Late Harappan symbols, like the graffiti incised on the Chalcolithic pottery of the Deccan, and the 'fish' sign engraved on a copper 'anthropomorph' from Sheorajpur in the upper Ganges Valley (fig. 4.2), are likely to be just echoes of the Indus script used as potter's or owner's marks, comparable to those on the Early Harappan ceramics. It seems that the script was forgotten when urban centres and with them the administrative bureaucracy ceased to exist.

However, a Late Harappan seal from Daimabad with its

Fig. 4.2. A 'fish' sign incised on an 'anthropomorph' from Sheorajpur (Kanpur District, U.P., India), typical of the Gangetic Copper Hoards. 47.7 × 39 × 2.1 cm, *c.* 4 kg. Early second millennium BC. State Museum, Lucknow (O.37).

Fig. 4.3. A single sign of the Indus script on a Late Harappan seal (DMD-1) from Daimabad (in Maharashtra), period II, *c.*1700 BC. ASI.

(a)

(b)

Fig. 4.4. The survival of a complex Harappan motif in the Malwa culture of the Deccan. (a) An outlined St Andrew's cross with crossbars in an inscribed tablet from Mohenjo-daro (M-457). The Indian Museum, Calcutta. (b) The same on a painted sherd of Malwa Ware from Navdatoli in Maharashtra: period III, *c.*1700–1400 BC. After Sankalia et al. 1971: 216 f., fig. 87: D 585 (sherd 8355 I A 13/5).

single typically Harappan pictogram (fig. 4.3) constitutes an interesting exception. This seal shows that isolated signs of the Indus script, at least, survived longer far to the south in Maharashtra. One motif on Chalcolithic pottery also testifies to a Harappan tradition (fig. 4.4). Unambiguous longer texts are needed to verify whether Daimabad remotely parallels Cyprus, where the Linear B script survived until historical times, having disappeared elsewhere soon after the collapse of the Mycenaean Civilization. It has been claimed that the Indus script survives even in the signs scratched on Iron Age Megalithic pottery in western and southern India. Again, similarities concern only rather general shapes, and there cannot be any question of real writing. In those relatively few cases where as many as three signs have been incised, the signs are always the same, but their order varies.

The earliest North Indian coins, which go back to the late sixth century BC, have between one and five symbols punched separately upon them. Some 300 different punch-marks, pictographic and geometrical, have been distinguished. In spite of claimed similarities, these signs do not constitute a communication system that could be considered some sort of 'degenerate variant' of the Indus script. This is not to deny the possibility that isolated Indus signs could have survived into historical times in the form of religious and other symbols, including the punch-marks on the coins. Unfortunately, however, the punch-marks are in any case of little help in the decipherment of the Indus script, since their own significance is relatively obscure.

One medium through which traditional motifs have passed from generation to generation all over India is the folk custom of drawing auspicious designs in courtyards and on house walls with dry or wet flour, possibly mixed with colour (fig. 4.5). In North India this is done on festive occasions only, but in South India every day. Unfortunately, the ephemeral nature of this sacred art usually makes it impossible to check

Fig. 4.5. A woman of the Kuṟavar caste drawing an auspicious diagram (*kōlam*) with rice powder on the street in front of the house in the morning of a marriage festival. After Hatch 1928: facing p. 88.

the age of the tradition. In a few rare cases, some concrete evidence has survived from earlier times to demonstrate the unbroken continuity from Harappan times up to the present day. One such example involves a complex, maze-like closed pattern, called 'Brahma's knot', which can ultimately be traced back to third-millennium Mesopotamia (fig. 4.6).

Comparable ancient religious symbols, which have survived through the ages in an ephemeral form, sometimes apparently going back to the Indus Civilization (§ 14.4), are the Hindu 'sectarian marks' painted on the forehead:

> Then there is the custom of painting the forehead and other parts of the body with different figures and emblems in various colours ... which vary according to the different castes, sects, and provinces. It would be difficult to explain the origin and meaning of the greater number of these symbols; those who wear them are often themselves ignorant of their meaning... Anyway, the Hindu code of good breeding requires that the forehead shall be ornamented with a mark of some sort. To keep it quite bare is a sign of mourning. It is also a sign that the daily ablutions have not been performed, that a person is still in a state of impurity, or that he is still fasting. If one meets an acquaintance after noon with his forehead still bare, one always asks if it is because he has not yet broken his fast. It would be rude to appear before decent people with no mark whatever on the forehead. (Dubois [1815] 1906: 333–5)

The earliest preserved inscriptions from India after those in the Indus script are the edicts of Emperor Asoka, dating from *c.*250 BC. Two different scripts, both of Semitic origin, are used in these edicts. The use of the Kharoṣṭhī script was always restricted to the northwest of India, where it died out *c.* AD 200 (and in Central Asia *c.* AD 600). The northwest had been part of the Achaemenid empire, where Aramaic was the language of administration. The Asokan term for 'inscription', *dipi* (whence later *lipi* 'writing'), is an Iranian loanword going back to Achaemenid inscriptions. Such considerations, together with the similarity of sign forms and the direction of writing from right to left, have left little doubt that the Kharoṣṭhī script is based on the Aramaic script. The word *kharoṣṭhī* may be a folk-etymological distortion (Sanskrit *kharoṣṭha* means 'donkey's lip') of a Semitic term (cf. Hebrew *ḥrṣ* 'to engrave').

According to the Indian tradition, writing was invented by Brahma; the Brahmi script, named after this Hindu god of creation, is the basis of all subsequent 'native' scripts of India, including the Devanāgarī script used for writing Hindi. The ultimately Semitic origin of the Brahmi has often been called into question, but seems to be established by the close similarity in form and sound value of several signs (fig. 2.7). On the other hand, the small number of Semitic-looking signs, along with several other arguments which cannot be detailed here, make it likely that the Brahmi script as it is known to us represents the conscious creation of a writing system fitted to Indian languages and monumental inscriptions. Probably commissioned by emperor Asoka, this writing system was devised by Brahmins trained in phonetics; its basis may have been an earlier, less satisfactory script used by merchants.

The Semitic consonantal alphabet did not mark vowels at all (excepting long vowels in ambiguous cases). The Brahmi and the later Indian scripts based on it may be called syllabic alphabets, for they do not mark the most frequently occurring vowel, the short *a*; it is included in the basic consonant sign, while all the other vowels are indicated by means of different diacritics added to the basic sign. Thus, for example, we have in the Brahmi script 𑀓 *ka*, 𑀓𑀸 *kā*, 𑀓𑀺 *ki*, 𑀓𑀻 *kī*, 𑀓𑀼 *ku*, 𑀓𑀽 *kū*, 𑀓𑁂 *ke*, 𑀓𑁄 *ko*. Consonant clusters with no intervening vowels are indicated by ligaturing the respective consonant signs, as in the Brahmi character 𑀓𑁆𑀬𑀸 *kyā* < 𑀓 *ka* + 𑀬𑀸 *yā*.

Shortly after the discovery of the Indus Civilization, leading experts on Brāhmī epigraphy denied any possibility of the Brāhmī script's being a descendant of the Indus script. Many authors have nevertheless insisted on such a connection, and attempted to read the Indus script as a syllabic alphabet. One of their arguments has been the alleged similarity or identity of several signs in these two scripts. A closer examination shows that most of these comparisons are based on mistaken readings. The similarity is restricted to a few very simple linear signs, which naturally converge independently of any historical connection. Another argument has been the apparent structural similarity in the diacritical modification of basic signs (cf. the Indus signs 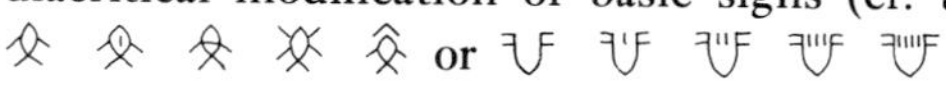) and in their ligatures (e.g. Indus ). But diacritics and ligatures also characterize archaic Sumerian and other early

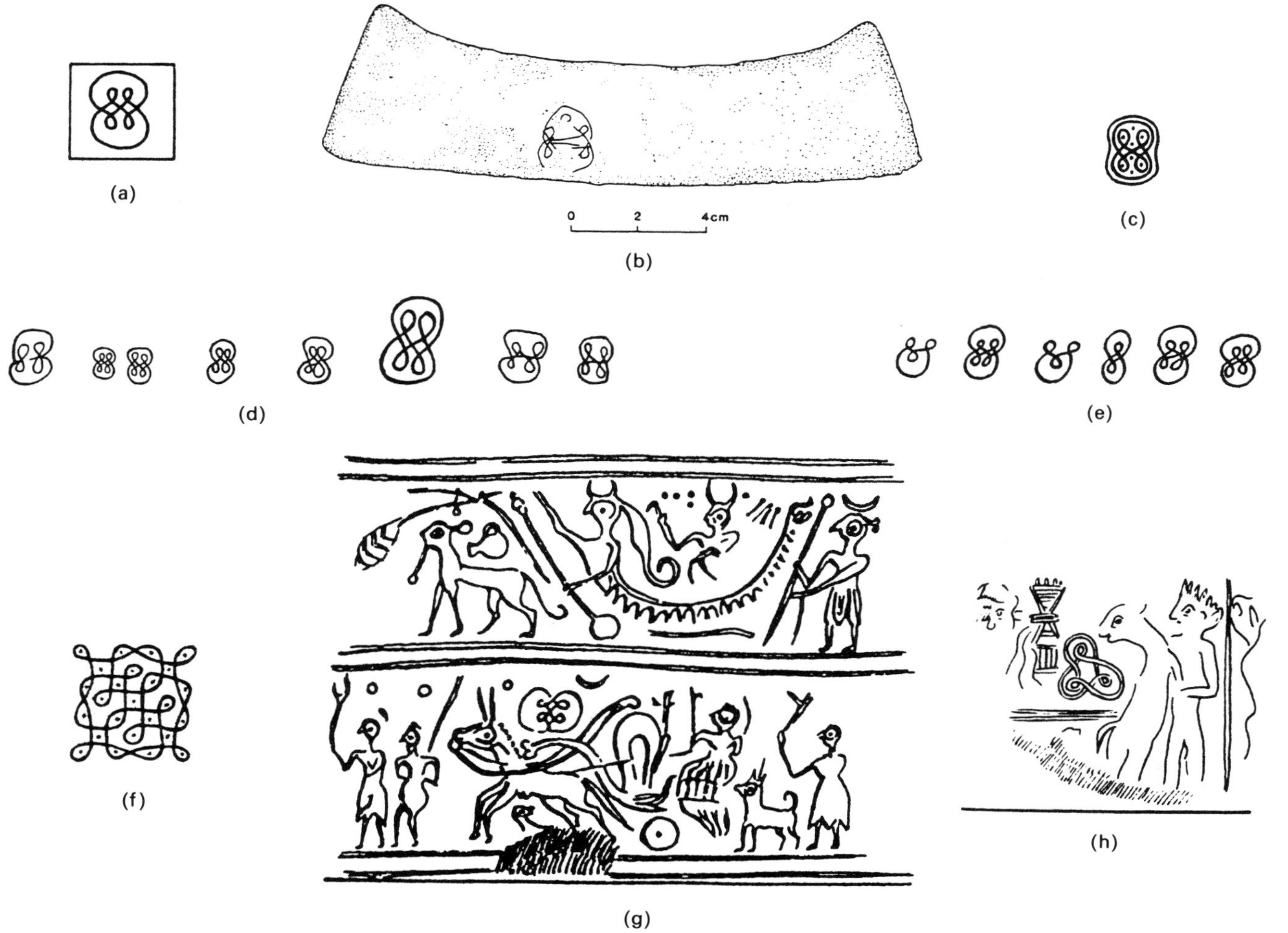

Fig. 4.6. The 'endless knot' motif in India and in the ancient Near East. (a) Reverse of a Harappan copper tablet from Mohenjo-daro (M-507), late third millennium BC. 2.8 × 2.8 × 0.3 cm. (b) A Harappan axe-head or knife of copper from Rojdi in Gujarat, early second millennium BC. Length 17.4 cm. After Possehl and Raval 1989: 162, fig. 77. (c) A terracotta stamp seal from Taxila in the upper Indus Valley, from the beginning of the Christian era. (d) Rāṣṭrakūṭa inscriptions from Gujarat, ninth century AD. (e) Mason's marks in Mughal buildings, seventeenth century AD. After Sarkar and Pande 1969–70; cf. Gorham s.a.; Heras 1953: li. (f) A complex variant of the 'endless knot' motif among the daily drawn auspicious figures (*kōlam*) of South India. After *Piranṭs navīna kōlaṅkaḷ* (Madras, n.d.): 29. (g) Impression of a Sumerian cylinder seal (*c.*2500 BC), with the 'endless knot' motif. After Amiet 1980a: pl. 108, no. 1435. (h) Variant of the 'endless knot' motif on an Early Dynastic seal from Lagash. After Amiet 1980a: pl. 83, no. 1099.

logo-syllabic scripts. In contrast to the Semitic derivation, there is thus no positive evidence whatsoever for a Harappan origin of the Brāhmī script.

4.2 Trial and error: attempts at decipherment

All kinds of answers have been offered to the questions posed by unsolved scripts ever since Graeco-Roman times. Thus in 1580, Goropius Becanus of Amsterdam tried to prove that the language of the ancient Egyptians was Dutch. In the case of the Indus script, connections have been sought with the manuscripts of the Lolos living in southern China and in Southeast Asia, dating back to the sixteenth century AD; with Proto-Elamite accounting tablets; with ideograms carved some two centuries ago on Easter Island in the southeastern Pacific Ocean; with Etruscan pot-marks; with the numeral system of Primitive Indonesian; with Egyptian, Minoan and Hittite hieroglyphs; with the auspicious symbols carved on a 'footprint of the Buddha' in the Maldivian archipelago; and with the glyphs of ancient Central America.

Certain attempted solutions are evidently less likely than others, but even obvious failures may contain some pertinent and stimulating observations amidst absurd or uninformed statements. Reading what has been published with a critical but open mind yields a crop of useful ideas. Detailed sifting cannot be undertaken here, but another kind of survey may be worth while. Incorrect hypotheses have seduced even well-informed scholars, and some of them have been put forward repeatedly. To point out clearly how those schemes are mistaken may help to eliminate them from future work on the subject.

Many hypotheses are simply outdated. Sir Alexander Cunningham (1875), for instance, considered the first published Indus seal (fig. 1.2) to be a foreign import because the bull carved on it lacked a hump, and later (1877) supposed that it might bear 'archaic Indian letters of as early an age as Buddha himself'. Another example is the 'Indo-Sumerian' hypothesis prevalent shortly after the discovery of the Indus Civilization (§ 1.6), out of date in spite of recent attempts by the Assyriologist James Kinnier Wilson to revive it (§ 10.4). In 1925 it provided a natural starting-point for L. A. Waddell, a Tibetologist, who 'read' all the published inscriptions in his book *The Indo-Sumerian seals deciphered.* Waddell (1) identified the Indus signs with similar-looking Sumerian signs; (2) read the inscriptions with the phonetic values of the Sumerian signs substituted; and (3) interpreted the resulting sequences as 'revised forms' of the names of Sumerian kings, and of Aryan kings mentioned in the Vedas and in Sanskrit epics. The last step gave him occasion to revise rather radically the entire early history of mankind, as indicated by the subtitle of his book: *Discovering Sumerians of the Indus Valley as Phoenicians, Barats, Goths and famous Vedic Aryans 3100–2300 BC.*

Waddell's method is among those most often used in attempts at decipherment. Transferring the phonetic values of signs in a known script to similar-looking signs in an unknown one is likely to work only if the two scripts are genetically closely related, and even then similar signs may have quite different phonetic values, as do *P* and *H* in the Greek alphabet, compared to their values in the Latin alphabet. A comparison between signs that look alike in non-alphabetic scripts demonstrates that their phonetic values are usually quite different, because different scripts for the most part reflect different languages (fig. 4.7).

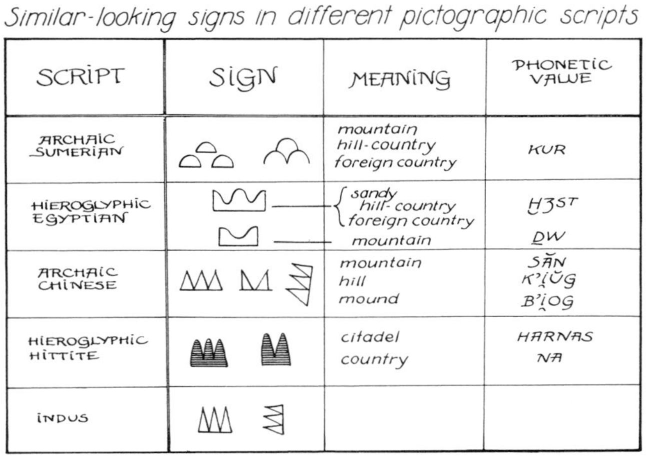
Similar-looking signs in different pictographic scripts
SCRIPT
SIGN
MEANING
PHONETIC VALUE
ARCHAIC SUMERIAN
mountain
hill-country
foreign country
KUR
HIEROGLYPHIC EGYPTIAN
sandy
hill-country
foreign country
mountain
ARCHAIC CHINESE
mountain
hill
mound
HIEROGLYPHIC HITTITE
citadel
country
HARNAS
NA
INDUS

Fig. 4.7. Similar-looking signs in different pictographic scripts, with their phonetic and semantic values. After Parpola 1988a: 128, fig. 1b.

Another frequently used approach is to interpret an Indus sign pictorially and then assign it a syllabic value taken from the corresponding word of a chosen language by the principle of acrophony. This has been the favourite approach of many Indian scholars. Nationalistic bias makes it difficult for some North Indians to admit even the possibility of the Indus Civilization being pre-Aryan; they deny the very concept of Aryan immigration (§ 8.4–5) and insist that the Harappan and Vedic cultures are one and the same. So the language chosen has usually been Sanskrit. This approach has been encouraged by the parallel (alleged as a survival of the Indus script) provided by pictorial figures used in Tantric texts more than two millennia later. The symbols of this 'Tantric code' thus stand for syllables in Sanskrit mantras; many of them are derived from the initial or final syllables of the Sanskrit word for the object depicted, e.g. frog = *ma* < *maṇḍūka* 'frog', or moon = *dra* < *candra* 'moon'. The ambiguities in matching Tantric symbols and Harappan signs, not to speak of their frequently allowed polyvalence, provide ample scope for the wildest imagination.

Towards the end of his life the Czech orientalist Hrozný, who in 1915 had brilliantly established cuneiform Hittite as an Indo-European language and had later played a less responsible part in the reading of hieroglyphic Hittite, began to lose his critical faculties and embarked on a wholesale attack on the remaining undeciphered scripts of the world. His readings of the then-published Linear B tablets (1940–9) are a painful hotch-potch of Hittite and Babylonian words, which it has proved only too easy to discredit. From this occupational disease of decoders we may all wish to be preserved. (Ventris in Ventris and Chadwick 1956: 12f.)

Bedřich Hrozný derived the Indus script from the Hittite hieroglyphs (which actually are a thousand years younger) on the basis of superficial similarities. Hrozný's example cautions us against adopting polysemy (§ 2.2) as the working principle: he assumed that individual signs usually have many different phonetic and semantic meanings, and that many different signs exist with exactly the same meaning. Hrozný then quite arbitrarily assigned the phonetic value *s*(*i*) to more than 25 completely different-looking signs; and in 309 inscriptions he 'read' the fictitious 'Indo-European' name of the sun-god, alleged to mean 'goer', explaining away the obvious discrepancies in the respective sequences as being due to the name having more than 50 variant forms.

Such liberties naturally grant the decipherers a convenient licence to read whatever they choose into the inscriptions, and then to use these fancies as a basis for revising history. This willingness to vary sounds and meanings takes away one of the few real tests to which hypothetical readings of Indus signs can be subjected. The question 'Do the interpretations, when they are put together, yield meaningful sequences or not?' loses its point. The absence of internal or external control is the tell-tale sign of uncritical attempts.

Sir John Marshall (1924) was the first to suggest that the Indus Civilization was non-Aryan and that its language most probably belonged to the Dravidian family. (Dravidian languages are nowadays spoken mainly in South India, where Tamil has a literary history of two millennia: §§ 8.3, 9.1ff.) In 1934, Piero Meriggi considered the Dravidian language of Brahui spoken in Baluchistan (§ 9.1) as the only reasonable contender, but renounced hopes of a phonetic decipherment, on the grounds that Brahui has changed so much during the past 4,000 years. Meriggi was involved in the decipherment of the Hittite hieroglyphs and tried to apply the same methods to an ideographic interpretation of the Indus script. While his approach is in general one of the soundest ever made, the particular solutions he proposed (e.g. seal 1111: 'Grain for officer corps' table') are not convincing. For example, the graphic variants of the sign (fig. 5.1 no. 87) hardly support Meriggi's contention that it depicts a horse. Some variants of the basic sign (fig. 5.1 no. 86) rather suggest an enraged cobra with expanded hood; moreover, the number of the added strokes (Meriggi's 'feet') is not always four, and they are sometimes placed as if they represented hair. This might also be a parallel to archaic Sumerian, Linear B and Maya scripts, where diacritic additions to a basic animal pictogram denote female gender; such as assumption would not be far-fetched even if a snake is in fact meant, for Vedic texts speak of a 'Serpent Queen' and equate her with the goddess Earth (PB 4, 9; KB 27, 4; AB 5, 23). The sign , again, is a composite sign (§ 5.2) rather than a picture of 'table'. Meriggi's principal clues were Hittite hieroglyphs that looked similar to some of the Indus signs, and he held the correspondences to be too systematic to result from mere chance. Another leading idea was the identification of word dividers (criticized in § 5.3).

The Spanish Jesuit Henry Heras spent most of his life in India. His numerous publications on the Indus script culminated in 1953 in a book called *Studies in Proto-Indo-Mediterranean culture.* Taking up Marshall's suggestion, Father Heras correctly thought that it would be possible to reconstruct Proto-Dravidian by comparing its surviving daughter languages (§ 9.6), though his own efforts to do so are amateurish. Heras characterizes the Indus script as a 'picto-phonographic' writing system, whose signs 'do not stand for syllables and much less for consonant sounds only, but express full words' (p. 66). In practice, however, he entertains quasi-phonological assumptions about the nature of the Indus script, which are in conflict with the established history of writing. His analysis of the signs and his method of determining their phonetic value (from their pictorial shape, as in the following extract, or from similar-looking signs in other scripts) has its own logic, but cannot be accepted, because it is not supported by the principles on which known scripts are based:

> The sign reads *naṇḍ* and means 'crab' ... Let us turn the sign to the left, thus . Now ... we must read *naṇḍ* in the opposite direction, thus *danan*, which means 'a generous or liberal man'. Let us now shorten a little the two ends of the front of the crab, like this . This will be equivalent to suppressing a sound in the reading. By cutting the sound *d* we have *nan*, which means 'good'. (Heras 1953: 100f.)

By such methods, Father Heras turned more than 1,800 Indus texts into 'Proto-Dravidian' sentences. It is easy to understand why his decipherment has not been accepted, especially when one reads some of his translations: 'The mother of the middle of the year walking ant-like' (p. 97); 'There is no feast in the place outside the country of the Mīnas of the three fishes of the despised country of the woodpeckers' (p. 98). Common sense says that phrases like this are not elaborately carved on seals.

Some of Father Heras's readings anticipate other, later ones (§ 10.1):

> There are some signs in our script whose values can only be explained in Dravidian languages. To give an instance, let us take the three following signs which are evident pictographs of a fish:
>
> *mīn*, 'fish', 'the Fish'.
> *min*, 'shining', 'glittering', 'glorious'.
> *mīn*, 'star' and proper name or title of a king.
>
> Only in Dravidian languages these three signs have the same phonetic values corresponding to the different meanings, according to the three differences shown in the signs themselves. If we suppose for a moment that the language of Mohenjo-Daro was Sanskrit, we should read the three above signs *mātsya* [*sic*] or even *mīna* – a word borrowed from Dravidian languages; but these two words in Sanskrit have no other meaning than fish, and therefore we shall not be able to assign a proper meaning to the other two signs. (*Mīna* means also 'constellation' in Sanskrit, but even then one of the signs would remain without proper explanation.) (Heras 1953: 99f.)

The problem with these interpretations by Heras is that he has no independent means of checking the meanings he has assigned to the signs. In other words, why should the sign  mean 'shining'? One inscription starting with the sign  is translated, 'This (is) the weak toddy of the Mīnas' (p. 97). Thus useful observations are inextricably mixed with clearly impossible 'solutions'.

One of the most methodical attempts at decipherment was launched in 1964 by a group of Soviet scholars headed by Yurij V. Knorozov, famed for his work on the Mayan script (§ 3.4). Based on the number of different signs they distinguished (315), the Russians supposed the Indus script to be of the logo-syllabic type rather than syllabic or alphabetic. Carrying out a statistical computer analysis of sign distribution in a sample of Indus texts, they interpreted the results by analogy with ancient Egyptian material that had been processed in a similar way. The signs occurring with a high frequency were supposed to represent grammatical markers and signs with a low frequency root morphemes, as in Egyptian.

With the help of interval statistics, the texts were divided into 'blocks' of one to five signs, assumed to correspond to words in the Indus language. An internal comparison of the blocks led to a distinction between 'constant' and 'variable' signs, supposed to stand for root morphemes and inflectional suffixes respectively. In addition, the Soviet scholars identified 'semivariable' signs, supposed to stand for adjectives when occurring before 'constant' signs, and for word-forming derivative suffixes when occurring between the 'constant' and 'variable' signs. (A critical examination of these hypotheses will follow in § 6.3.)

The Soviet scholars identified the Indus language as belonging to the Dravidian family on the basis of this structural analysis. Dravidian, alone among the languages of the ancient Near East and India, also displays those typological characteristics thought to be found in the Indus texts. (For a modified typological approach of this kind, see §§ 6.1 and 8.1.) The most frequent sign of the Indus script, , a 'variable' after which other 'variables' may or may not be added, is equated with the Proto-Dravidian oblique case suffix (corresponding to Tamil *-attu* and Telugu *-ti*). On the basis of the iconography in the 'fig deity' seal (fig. 14.35), the sign  is considered to be a stylized rendering of a fig tree (for criticism, see § 7.2), and one kind of fig tree is called *ati* or *atti* in Dravidian languages. The suggested phonetic reading of the suffix, *-at(tu)*, is based on a rebus.

This approach has been criticized for its insufficient differentiation between script and language (the 'variable' signs, for example, might well have been used to express something other than suffixes), for its application of statistics relevant only to the Egyptian script and language to the elucidation of an entirely different script and language, for the lack of explicit documentation, and for various defects in details. Nevertheless, the proposed analyses, assumptions and conclusions of this first stage of the Soviet attempt at decipherment have been found 'thought-provoking' and 'possible', but 'entirely hypothetical' and 'absolutely unverifiable' by Kamil Zvelebil, who concluded his detailed review with the following observation:

> Proof that the readings and translations are correct may be offered only in the following way: (a) either a *bilingual* inscription or inscriptions will confirm the correctness of the 'Dravidian hypothesis'; (b) or, in the absence of a bilingual text, a much greater amount of material must be read, translated and interpreted, and this large sum of *translated data* must form a *meaningful, logical and internally consistent corpus of data.* Until then, the Dravidian affinity of the Proto-Indian language remains only a very attractive and quite plausible *hypothesis.* (Zvelebil in Zide and Zvelebil 1976: 138)

The latest Soviet report from 1981 has tried to meet this demand by proposing concrete Dravidian readings for most of the Indus signs, with counter-productive results. Unlike the first few readings, which were put forward rather cautiously, the new readings are presented with few reservations, although they are mostly based on insufficiently checked guesses, and there are gaps or weak links in the chain of argument. For instance, the sign  (*sic*) is interpreted as depicting 'star' and read as *sukka* 'star'. However, the sign  is likely to be a combination of the signs || and × (§ 5.2); it is at least doubtful whether 'star' is depicted by any Indus sign (§ 10.1). There are, moreover, other Dravidian words to choose for the meaning 'star' and the word *sukka* is not a genuine Dravidian word but a loanword from Middle Indo-Aryan (< Sanskrit *śukra*). And is it likely that a seal text reads, for example, 'The red (or great) glittering monsoon's power'? A longer 'sacrificial inscription' is supposed to read: 'Our sun (asterism), the first (60-day) season, for the shining seven, increasing rage of thunderstorms, storm, the second sacrifice.'

Several other people have published Dravidian-based decipherments in recent years. Among them, from 1970, has been Iravatham Mahadevan, a pioneer in Old Tamil epigraphy, who has contributed remarkably to the documentation of the Indus script (§ 4.3) and the analysis of its technical aspects. His Dravidian readings are based on parallels offered by Old Tamil inscriptions and literature, especially personal names, titles and administrative terminology, which he considers as very likely to occur in the Indus seals. Mahadevan argues that the Indo-Aryan tradition is Post-Harappan, but may preserve reminiscences of Harappan expressions in loanwords or early translations from Dravidian. He lays special stress on the pictorial meaning of the Indus signs and seeks clues to their interpretation from the symbolic uses of the depicted objects in later Indian tradition, especially in so far as they relate to the official titles of various ruling dynasties.

There is nothing inherently improbable in these basic assumptions of Mahadevan, but the concrete interpretations he has proposed have failed to produce convincing internal proofs. He starts from the hypothesis that the most frequent final signs of the seal inscriptions stand for seal owners and in particular for their official titles. He interprets the sign  as depicting a 'jar' (this is criticized in § 7.2). Considering it as a symbol of sacrifices he takes it to mean 'priest', while the 'spear' sign  he takes to represent 'soldier'. The 'yoke carrier' sign 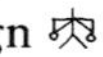 is compared to later Indian expressions referring to the official's bearing the 'load of responsibility'. There are, Mahadevan points out, many royal names and titles, such as Bharata (from the Sanskrit root *bhar-* 'to carry'), which he considers as derived from a Harappan notion concerning the burdens of high office. The ligature of 'jar' + 'yoke carrier', , supposedly meant 'official with priestly duties', that of 'spear' + 'yoke carrier', , 'official with military duties'.

Mahadevan sees a confirmation of his hypotheses in the dynastic titles *Sāta-vāhana* and *Sāli-vāhana*. The former he derives from **sata-vahana* 'jar bearer' and the latter from **śalya-vahana* 'spear bearer'. However, neither of these assumed primary compounds is attested in any texts, and these etymologies are in any case most questionable. Previous researchers have usually considered the titles *Sāta-vāhana* and *Sāli-vāhana* as synonymous variants and connected their components with words meaning 'horse' and 'son' respectively, the horse being the emblem of this relatively late dynasty, which ruled around the beginning of the Christian era in Central India. Nor is there any linguistic foundation for Mahadevan's fictitious Proto-Dravidian word **cāta<u>n</u>*, based merely on his interpretation of the ligature  as **sata-vahana*, and presented as the etymology of the word *āta<u>n</u>*, an important element in Old Tamil proper names. Thus the ligatures have been used as clues rather than as tests.

It is usual for Tamil names to start with the name of one's home town or village. On the basis of this, and the meaning 'city' for the similar-looking Egyptian hieroglyph , Mahadevan has interpreted the initially occurring sign  as 'lower town', and inferred that the common initial sign  means 'citadel'. Critics have already pointed out that the find spots of the texts containing these signs do not at all correspond with these assumed meanings. One may also ask for Old Tamil parallels for place-names of this kind as parts of personal proper names and question their utility as addresses.

Since 1976, Walter A. Fairservis, one of the leading archaeologists specializing in the Harappan culture, has both elaborated general assumptions and principles relevant to the decipherment of the Indus script and attempted concrete Dravidian readings. Many of the former appear sound, but the actual readings and the resulting 'sentences', stretched to yield some sense, fail to convince (e.g. 'the first harvest guardian, lineage of the sun'). The approach has been justly criticized for its inadequacies in handling Dravidian.

The attempts of Fairservis (and of some others as well) are characterized by a far-fetched analysis of pictograms. For example, he considers the Indus sign  as a combination of (1) the 'arrow' in the sign  and (2) one-half of the sign  depicting a fig leaf. 'Arrow' is *ampu* in Dravidian, and *ara(cu)* means 'pipal fig'. Their combination produces *amp-ara*, a Dravidian word meaning 'public space', and this is considered as the meaning of the 'composite' sign and as a proof for the correctness of the analysis. But there is no other reason why the sign should mean 'public space'. Such questionable interpretations form the basis of an elaborate sociopolitical reconstruction.

In summary, none of the attempts at deciphering the Indus script made so far (including that of our Finnish team) has gained wide acceptance. Not all work on the Indus script can be disqualified, however. There are solid contributions on various aspects of the script by a number of scholars, and these will be examined next.

4.3 Preparation of basic research tools

Successful decipherments have always been preceded by patient and often extensive preparatory work. In every case, it is eventually necessary to start guessing, but the method consists initially of proceeding as far as possible without making guesses. When the time for guessing comes, the range of the guesses will have been limited by the preparatory analysis. It must be admitted, though, that a completely objective preparatory analysis is impossible; the preparation always involves a number of subjective estimations and decisions. Some fundamental tasks that can and must be undertaken, and the achievements made so far, will be reviewed in this section and the ones that follow.

First is the collection of material into a corpus. Comprehensiveness must be the aim, because the extent and diversity of the available material directly affect the chances of a solution. What looks possible from an inspection of a small amount of data may be disqualified by the discovery of new material (§ 6.3). A single text may contain a crucial clue.

Accuracy is vital in such a corpus. This may seem obvious, but publications dealing with the Indus script frequently contain quite incorrect copies of inscriptions; and conclusions based on such distorted versions are, of course, invalid. A critical edition of the texts must therefore be based on primary sources, i.e. the original objects and their impressions and the photographs taken of them. Many an Indus text is broken, but this does not always show in a photograph; if the text is then taken to be complete, it will lead to wrong conclusions. Its other, uninscribed sides have to be examined to ascertain the integrity of the text and to estimate the extent of the missing portion.

But even a most careful inspection of the original cannot solve all the problems of text editing. Some signs on a given document may be too indistinct to be read with certainty. However, there may be other, identical inscriptions that can establish the reading; such parallels have to be traced. A given sign may look quite similar but not wholly identical with one or more other signs: are they variants of a single grapheme, or distinct graphemes? In which order are the signs to be read in a given text?

It is necessary, for the sake of serious analysis, to make definite decisions on these and other questions. They can be reached only by means of a careful comparative study of the entire material. For this, one needs a classified index or concordance giving all occurrences of every sign, with their contexts; and this tool must be constantly updated, as the text edition upon which it is based is revised. The preparation of a text edition is thus in practice inseparable from the task of processing other research tools needed for the analysis of the inscriptions and the objects upon which they are found. The work is most economically done with the aid of a computer, which can be programmed also to draw or print the Indus signs.

In 1934 G. R. Hunter included in his analysis of the Indus script a good text edition and concordance to the approximately 800 texts then available; and the reports of excavations at Mohenjo-daro and Harappa included much less thorough, but still helpful, sign lists. These are all now outdated, and their graphemic analysis in particular is no more acceptable. In recent years new concordances have been compiled with the help of a computer by I. Mahadevan (1977) and by our Finnish teams (S. Koskenniemi et al. 1973; K. Koskenniemi and A. Parpola 1979–82) (fig. 4.8).

Certain decisions in establishing the readings of the texts are bound to be subjective, open to criticism and improvement, so checking of the originals remains vital. This is now becoming easier with the new photographic *Corpus of Indus Seals and Inscriptions* (*CISI*), published by the Finnish Academy of Sciences and Letters in collaboration with the Archaeological Survey of India and the Department of Archaeology and Museums, Government of Pakistan (Joshi and Parpola 1987; Shah and Parpola 1991; a third volume is yet to appear). Here Indus inscriptions are quoted either from the *CISI* (these references have a letter + number code) or from the edition / concordance of K. Koskenniemi and A. Parpola (1979–82) (a four-digit numeral code); in some exceptional cases, excavation or museum numbers are used.

The checking of the readings against the original objects in the museums of India and Pakistan, undertaken separately in 1971 by me and by I. Mahadevan, proved to be more important than could have been anticipated. We discovered many hundreds of Indus seals and inscriptions recovered in excavations at Mohenjo-daro (DK-I and DK-B areas) between 1931 and 1938 and at Harappa between 1934 and 1941, of which only brief notices were published in the Annual Reports of the Archaeological Survey of India. These finds, left forgotten in the museums for almost 40 years, have now been included in the computer concordances and the photographic *Corpus*.

On the other hand, a considerable number of the objects reported from various sites, especially from Mohenjo-daro, Harappa and Chanhujo-daro, have still not been traced. In 1975 it was realized that the photographic archive of the Archaeological Survey of India contains extensive and largely unpublished documentation of Indus seals and inscriptions. Sometimes these photographs, mostly taken immediately after the discovery, show objects in a better state of preservation than they are now. Wherever relevant, this important source material has been included in the *CISI*.

The great majority of the Indus texts are seals and tablets, which, in addition to an inscription, often display an iconographic motif. These glyptics constitute one of the most important primary sources for the study of Harappan art and religion. Since the seals form an important category of artefacts in their own right, relevant to the study of both the external relations of a culture and its internal processes, including administration and trade, the *CISI* contains all the Harappan seals, including those without any inscriptions: a good number have just a geometrical motif, such as the swastika. The category of 'Indus seals' in the *CISI* has been extended to include a handful of imported seals of foreign types coming from Harappan sites. A selection of Early and Late Harappan potter's marks is also included.

In a new book on 'the glyptics of Mohenjo-daro' (1991 [1992]), Ute Franke-Vogt has documented the seals, amulets and other inscribed material (altogether 2,371 objects) from this major site in great detail. Together with her multifaceted quantitative and qualitative analyses of all non-textual aspects of this material, it constitutes an important and useful working tool.

The available inscriptional material comes from over 40 Harappan sites and almost 20 foreign ones (fig. 1.5). The vast majority, more than 3,500 objects, come from Mohenjo-daro and Harappa, while Lothal and Kalibangan have both produced about 300 objects, Chanhujo-daro 83 and Banawali 37. Excluding the Early and Late Harappan potter's marks, the uninscribed and the completely broken or otherwise quite illegible objects, there are approximately 3,700 more or less

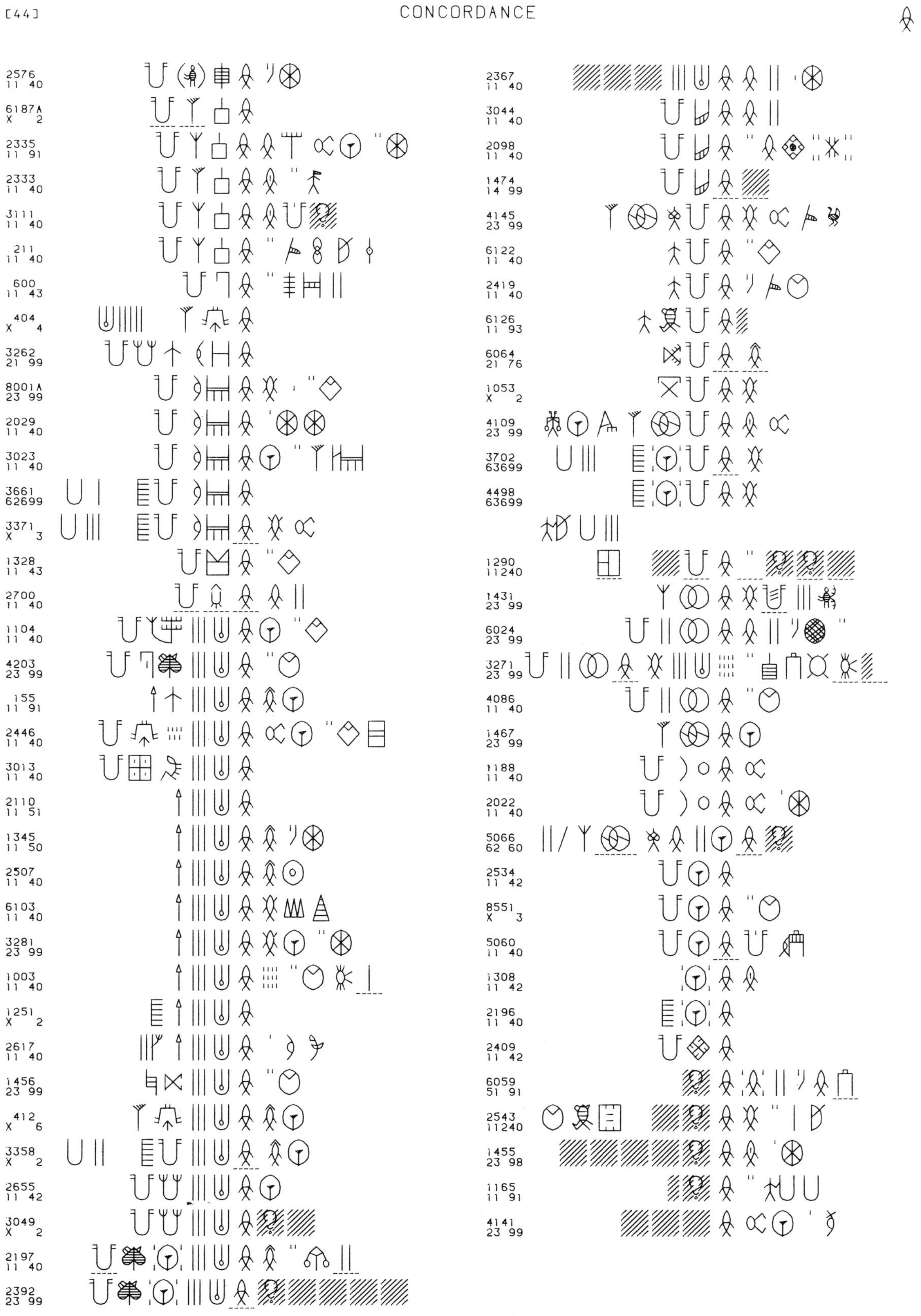

Fig. 4.8. Part of a concordance to the occurrences of the Indus sign ⟨sign⟩. After Koskenniemi and Parpola 1982: 44.

legible inscriptions, but in linguistic analysis several hundred of these must be left out of account as too uncertain. More than 500 different texts, moreover, are variously repeated, so that they occur altogether nearly 1,900 times, which means that there are some 1,400 duplicate inscriptions.

Besides a concordance to all occurrences of each sign, it is useful to generate various kinds of statistics – frequencies of the individual signs (see also table 5.1) and sign combinations (grand totals and totals in different positions within the inscriptions), of texts with different lengths, of object types, of iconographic motifs, etc. – and to tabulate the distributions of signs and other variables in relation to different criteria, as has been done by I. Mahadevan (1977: 717–82). Another major purpose of preparing a computerized text edition is to make a linguistic analysis of the inscriptions; duplicate inscriptions must be excluded from such an analysis, since the results may be severely distorted if repetitions are retained.

Such repetitions, with the possible variation in accompanying iconography etc., do, however, provide valuable clues to the probable function of the objects and the probable meaning of the texts, and they merit study in their own right. The reason for the existence of many identical inscriptions is cultural (e.g. identical amulets are distributed to visitors at a temple) and does not add to the linguistic information. In this respect the repetitions fall into the same class as the type, shape, material, colour and size of an inscribed object, its archaeological context, the accompanying iconography, the iconic shape of the pictograms, and the comparative material from other cultures and languages adduced as relevant to the study of the Indus inscriptions. These data are all 'external evidence', as opposed to the purely linguistic 'internal evidence' of sign order, number of signs in an inscription, sign repetition within an inscription, etc. This distinction will be maintained in our structural analysis, where the 'internal evidence' will be dealt with first (§§ 5.1–6.4), before the 'external evidence' (§§ 7.1–5). Both kinds of evidence are drawn upon to determine the direction of writing, an important preliminary task and one of the few points about which there is unanimity among almost all researchers.

4.4 The direction of writing

Before the texts can be subjected to linguistic analysis one has to know in which direction the signs were intended to be read, for texts read in the wrong direction will distort the evidence and the conclusions.

The seal texts (and the accompanying iconographic motifs, if any) are sunk (intaglio) in the originals, i.e. engraved in the negative (reversed). Their positive impressions on clay, a number of which survive in ancient examples, stand out in relief. It is the latter that represent the text as it was intended to be read. We know this because the sign sequences and sign orientations of seal impressions generally match those of inscriptions meant to be read directly, such as pottery graffiti and engravings on metal implements. A reference to a 'seal' (inscription) in this book always means the impression made with the respective seal stamp, unless otherwise specified.

The order of signs long remained unpredictable in the earliest known writing system, that of the Sumerians. In the Indus inscriptions, by contrast, even the earliest examples available in larger numbers – the miniature tablets from the low levels at Harappa – are written in lines with regular, repeated sequences of signs. On the other hand, vacillation between opposite directions of writing is found in the earliest accessible Mature Harappan documents. The most frequently occurring sequence on these miniature tablets is ; but on some tablets this sequence is written in reverse order, with signs reversed at the same time , in a mirror image. This mirror correspondence clearly shows that the same sequence is involved in both cases. If the signs in the sequence happen to be symmetrical, e.g.  and , another very frequent sequence (fig. 7.9), which of these two directions is the regular one? And how can the direction be ascertained in each case?

Both external and internal criteria exist to determine the direction of Indus writing. When signs were incised on pots, the lines drawn first could become partially obliterated by those drawn later. These overlaps can demonstrate that the signs were drawn from right to left, as on a potsherd from Kalibangan (fig. 4.9a). It has rightly been pointed out, however, that this much-quoted external proof for the direction of writing is valid only for this particular inscription. In fact, another potsherd from Kalibangan (fig. 4.9b) provides evidence for the opposite direction: the 'body' of the fish was clearly drawn from left to right, before the 'fins' were added. (Internal evidence of the sign sequences confirms that this inscription really is to be read from left to right.)

Another external criterion proposed for the determination of writing direction is even less conclusive than the overlapping of signs. This is the idea (suggested by the Egyptian tradition) that the animals depicted on the Indus seals and the pictograms in the accompanying inscriptions should face in the direction in which the writing was to be read. Examining this hypothesis in the light of other evidence, we find it to be generally though not invariably true of the animals, but not true of the pictograms, which include both left-facing and right-facing signs such as  and . Neither animals nor pictograms are a reliable indication of the direction of writing.

More dependable external evidence is supplied by the spacing, both in individual signs (e.g.  versus ) and in

(a)

(b)

Fig. 4.9. Overlaps in lines of Indus signs incised on pottery. (a) A potsherd from Kalibangan with a post-firing graffito (K-100); (b) another potsherd from Kalibangan incised in wet clay before firing (K-96).

Fig. 4.10. Impression of a square Indus seal from Harappa (H-103) inscribed along three sides.

Fig. 4.11. Impression of a seal (M-735) from Mohenjo-daro, with cramping of the last inscribed sign.

inscriptions. Sometimes the inscription is shorter than the allotted space. Texts starting from the right edge and leaving an unused space to the left may reasonably be expected to run from right to left. The direction right to left is beyond any doubt in the case of the square seal H-103 (fig. 4.10), in which a long inscription runs anticlockwise along two whole sides and part of a third, while the rest of the third and part of the fourth side are left blank. At each corner the signs are turned through 90° so that their tops are always towards the edge. Only the first side is filled by the inscription from edge to edge, and must therefore be the one with which the engraver started his work.

Sometimes, however, the text may be longer than the engraver of a seal had estimated and, running short of space at the end of the line, he has been forced to cramp the last sign, as in seal M-735 (fig. 4.11), or even place some of the last signs beneath the line, as in seal M-66 (fig. 4.12). In both cases the external evidence suggests that the script runs from right to left, and that the sign U ends the inscription. This conclusion is corroborated by the internal evidence of the sign sequences, which we shall now examine.

First of all, it is important to establish the fact that the sign U is the most frequent of all in the Indus script, chiefly found in the furthest left position, never furthest right in the inscriptions (except in a minority of inscriptions with reversed sequence and sign orientation, where it would be expected to occur in the furthest right position). If the location of the sign U can be proved to be the end and not the beginning of an

Fig. 4.12. Impression of a seal from Mohenjo-daro (M-66), with cramping of the last two signs of the line and one sign written beneath them.

Fig. 4.13. Impression of an Indus seal from Mohenjo-daro (M-892) with a two-line inscription, where the direction of writing goes boustrophedon: the upper line from right to left, the lower from left to right.

(a)

(b)

Fig. 4.14. Impression of (a) a seal from Harappa (H-515) and of (b) a seal from Mohenjo-daro (M-665) with lines ending in the same sequence of four signs as the two-lined seal in fig. 4.12.

inscription, we can go on to establish the direction of the large majority of the inscriptions. It also provides a good number of further clues. For instance, some of the most common sign sequences in the Indus script, like [sign] or [sign], often occur at the far right in inscriptions with [sign] as the sign furthest left, and these can then be regarded as beginning markers and will in their turn give further clues.

If we read inscription M-66 (fig. 4.12) from left to right, placing the sign [sign] of the second line after [sign], which is at the far right of the first line, the resulting sequence [sign] [sign] is almost unique. (It is found only once elsewhere, in the middle of an inscription.) The sequence [sign], on the other hand, is nowhere else found in the furthest left position, whereas [sign] – a sequence of three signs, much less likely to occur by chance – is found 76 times.

An even more forceful example is seal M-892 (fig. 4.13), which provides clear proof of boustrophedon writing ('the way the ox turns [in ploughing]'). Read in the normal way from right to left, the sequence [sign] [sign] is unique, but its converse [sign] [sign] (the boustrophedon reading after being normalized right to left) occurs elsewhere over 40 times: 13 times in the same long series of four signs as here, for instance in seals H-515 (fig. 4.14a) and M-665 (fig. 4.14b).

Boustrophedon is, however, rather rare; only about ten cases exist in all. In most instances, as in the last quoted (seal M-665 in fig. 4.14b), the second line is to be read from right to left like the first. If the inscription is read boustrophedon, the text ends in the sequence [sign] [sign] (here normalized to read from right to left). This sequence is otherwise unknown, while [sign] [sign] occurs over 30 times, and [sign] is often found at the end of an inscription, and another twice in addition to this at the end of a second line. Plain [sign] is also found, even more frequently, at the end of a second line (on the left), and another ligature of it [sign] also occurs in the same position.

Thus numerous tests agree in establishing right to left as the preponderant direction of writing in the Indus inscriptions. This was already clear in the early 1930s to Gadd and Smith, Marshall and Hunter, and can now be considered as sufficiently established.

It goes without saying that all reversed sequences must be normalized accordingly; this has been done in both of the two recent concordances, though a few uncertain cases still remain. Mahadevan, who has carefully recorded the direction of the original in each of his 3,573 lines, distinguishes 2,974 lines running right to left (83.23 per cent) and 235 going left to right (6.57 per cent), in addition to such ambiguous sequences as 190 single-sign lines, 12 symmetrical sequences and 155 cases that are doubtful on account of damaged or illegible lines. A top-to-bottom sequence is recorded for seven lines.

Usually the order of lines on a given side of an object is from top to bottom (more examples in § 5.3). But in a few cases the order is inverted. Thus the single line of seal 2348  is in seal 2564 divided into two lines so that the sequence  forms the upper line and the sequence  the lower line.

5 Internal evidence for the type of script used in the Indus Valley

5.1 Graphemic analysis

After completing the preliminary tasks of collecting and critically editing the material and establishing the direction of writing, we may attempt a structural analysis of the Indus texts. But I should first clarify exactly what I am trying to achieve.

The history of writing (chapter 2) and successful decipherments (chapter 3) make it clear that one of the principal objects must be finding out what kind of writing system the Indus script represents. Here the principal parameters that need to be established by means of a structural analysis of the inscriptions are (a) the number of graphemes and (b) the 'word' length. I shall address the first of these problems in sections 5.1 and 5.2, dealing with graphemic analysis and composite signs respectively, and the second in section 5.3 on the segmentation of texts, and draw my conclusions regarding these fundamental questions in section 5.4.

After this, I shall deal with the other main tasks in a structural analysis of the Indus inscriptions, namely the attempt to discover linguistic patterns that can help in the identification of the language(s) in which the texts have been written (chapter 6) and then to establish the meaning which individual signs and sign sequences were intended to convey (chapter 7).

The first task, then, relates to the number of graphemes. There are many signs in the Indus script that more or less resemble other signs. How can one distinguish between different signs (graphemes) and variants of a single sign (allographs)? In a distributional analysis, false conflation of two graphemes into one is as detrimental as false distinction of two allographs. The analyst must take both possibilities into account with equal care and search for optimal solutions. So as to allow readers to make their own decisions, while avoiding the drawback of treating allographs as different signs, the

Finnish concordances have retained the principal allographs in the lists, but treated them as the same sign for purposes of analysis.

Graphic variation has many causes. To begin with, a single object can be represented in different ways pictorially, depending on the viewpoint, and on the selection and emphasis of characteristic features. Then there are variations resulting from gradual historical development, typically involving the simplification of pictures; from regional styles; from the effect of the material and of the technique of inscribing (wood and clay, for instance, favour angular forms, while palm leaves – the traditional South Asian writing material that may well have been used by Indus people – favour rounded forms); from the type and use of the object and the status of its owner (elaborate and monumental versus simple and crude forms); from scarcity of writing space on small objects like seals (compact and turned variants); and from personal styles of handwriting.

The following criteria seem appropriate for identifying two or more graphs as variants of a single grapheme. (1) The potential variants (e.g. and) bear a reasonable resemblance to each other, so that they can be assumed to represent one and the same object. The likelihood of their being identical is increased if intermediate forms establish a continuum between the variants (e.g. , , and). (2) Two signs meeting the above condition occur only in almost identical contexts. (In our example, the signs and are each found paired with much the same two dozen signs. The signs also occur interchangeably in other contexts, such as the very common sequence : , or preceded by numerals, or as the last sign in an inscription.) Allographs may have a complementary distribution among different types of object, i.e. one may not appear in the same situations as the other (for instance, the copper tablets have only the variant). (3) If there are any ligatures (composite signs) composed of the same signs, they may behave in the same way as the simple signs. (Thus, when the signs and are ligatured with a circle, their distribution shows that the resulting signs and behave as allographs.)

Application of the context criterion can be very convincing if the signs have a high frequency, but when they occur a few times only, the conclusion is bound to remain open to doubt unless the contexts are long and unique (cf. the inscriptions 2436 and 2654 cited in § 7.2). Signs found once only constitute a difficult problem, and require rigorous inspection. The sign , for instance, looks like 'a man with phallus', and there is evidence for the practice of phallic cults by the Harappans (§§ 12.2, 14.2). However, as this sign is unique, and the seal (1321) carelessly carved, the extra stroke is more likely to ligate the 'man' sign with the preceding sign , though the connecting line is usually added to the hand of the 'man' sign: .

Allocation of sign boundaries does not usually present difficulties even when a sign consists of a group of strokes or lines: whenever the sign occurs, the grouping repeats itself, making a characteristic integrity that is easy to recognize. In a few cases unclear spacing between signs, especially linear signs, may cause doubt, but such texts can generally be sorted out by an examination of similar inscriptions and sequences. Text 1218, , for example, could *a priori* be read as three, four or five signs – all of which occur elsewhere in the script – as follows: , , , , . But because the sequence is the only inscription on other objects, because the single long stroke is often found at the beginning of texts before integral sequences (fig. 5.2), and because none of the other potential sign sequences , , , is separately documented, this seal can only be read as having the following three signs: , , .

Distinguishing as a single sign instead of three requires some further explanation. First, it is clear that the 'man' sign often forms ligatures with other signs. Secondly, the vertical strokes on either side of it can be compared to other 'circumgraphs' that are always found in pairs, on both sides of an enclosed sign or signs. Thus, for instance, the graph sequences and [or and] never occur outside the sequence [or its variant], except where the simple sign is once (in seal 5025) juxtaposed with . It is obvious that [=] is a ligature of the signs and or . The sequence may therefore be assumed to be a similar ligature of the signs and . These are examples of a class of signs formed by inserting one sign between two elements of another; a parallel example is , which is a ligature of the sign inserted within the sign .

Circumgraphs may enclose more than one sign: for example, , and . Are the last two ligatures allographs in spite of the different order of the enclosed signs? A single idea is apparently expressed by such contiguously joined ligatures as , which is put together from the separately occurring signs , and (or ?).

On the other hand, the identity of context in seals 1348 and 1373 suggests that writing conventions could vary. For the sake of consistency, the sign has been treated as one grapheme, although it appears to be an exceptional spelling for . This particular spelling is valuable, however, in confirming that the four circumscribed strokes belong to the sequence (occurring without the four circumscribed strokes in 6059), and not just to the 'fish' sign, and that this should be so also in the case of other integral sequences occurring with and without the four strokes around the 'fish' sign (compare the pairs : ; : ; and :). Indeed, other evidence suggests that the four strokes around the 'fish' sign may in fact be understood to be read after it, and that

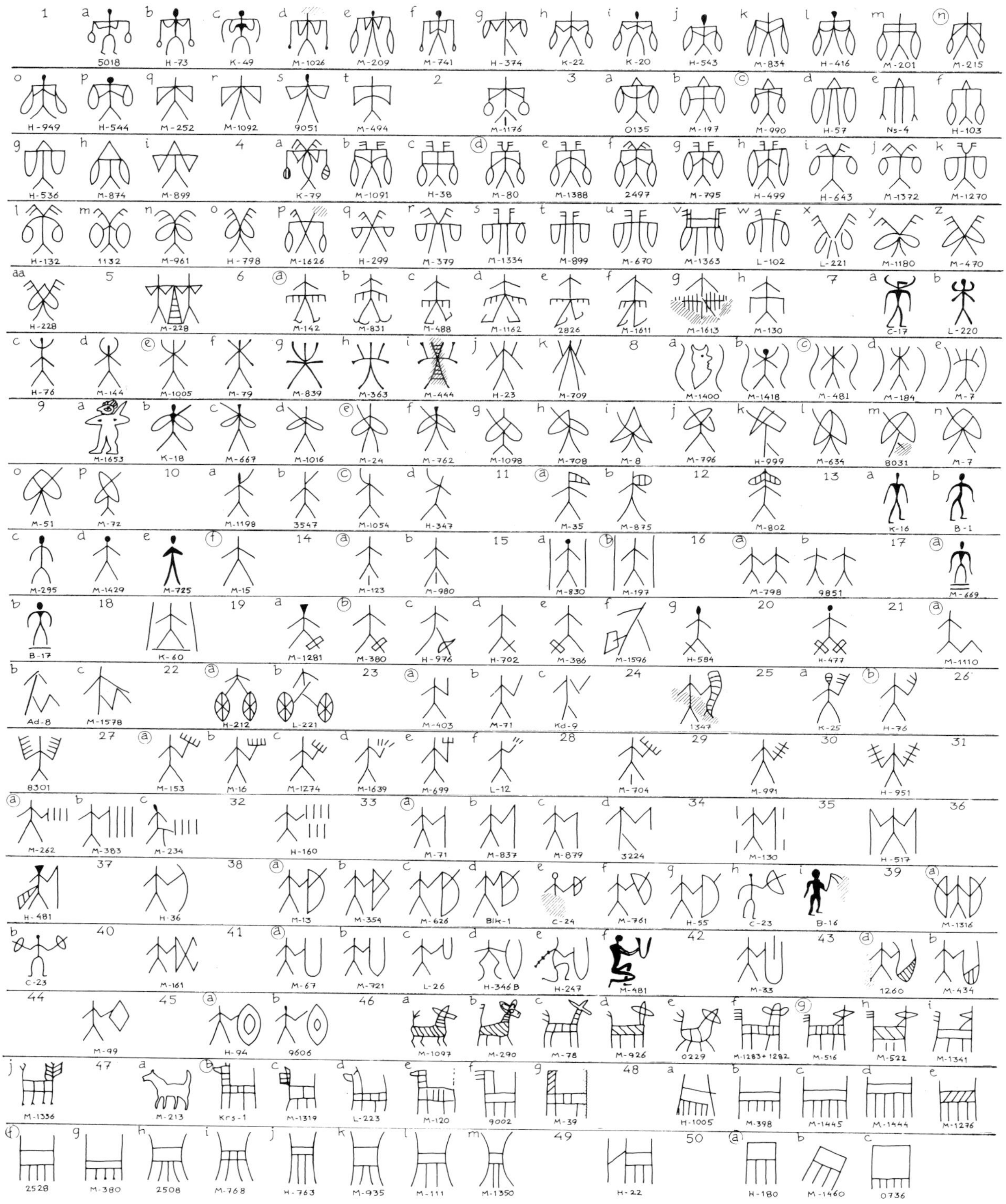

Fig. 5.1. A sign list of the Indus script, with principal graphic variants (each with one reference).

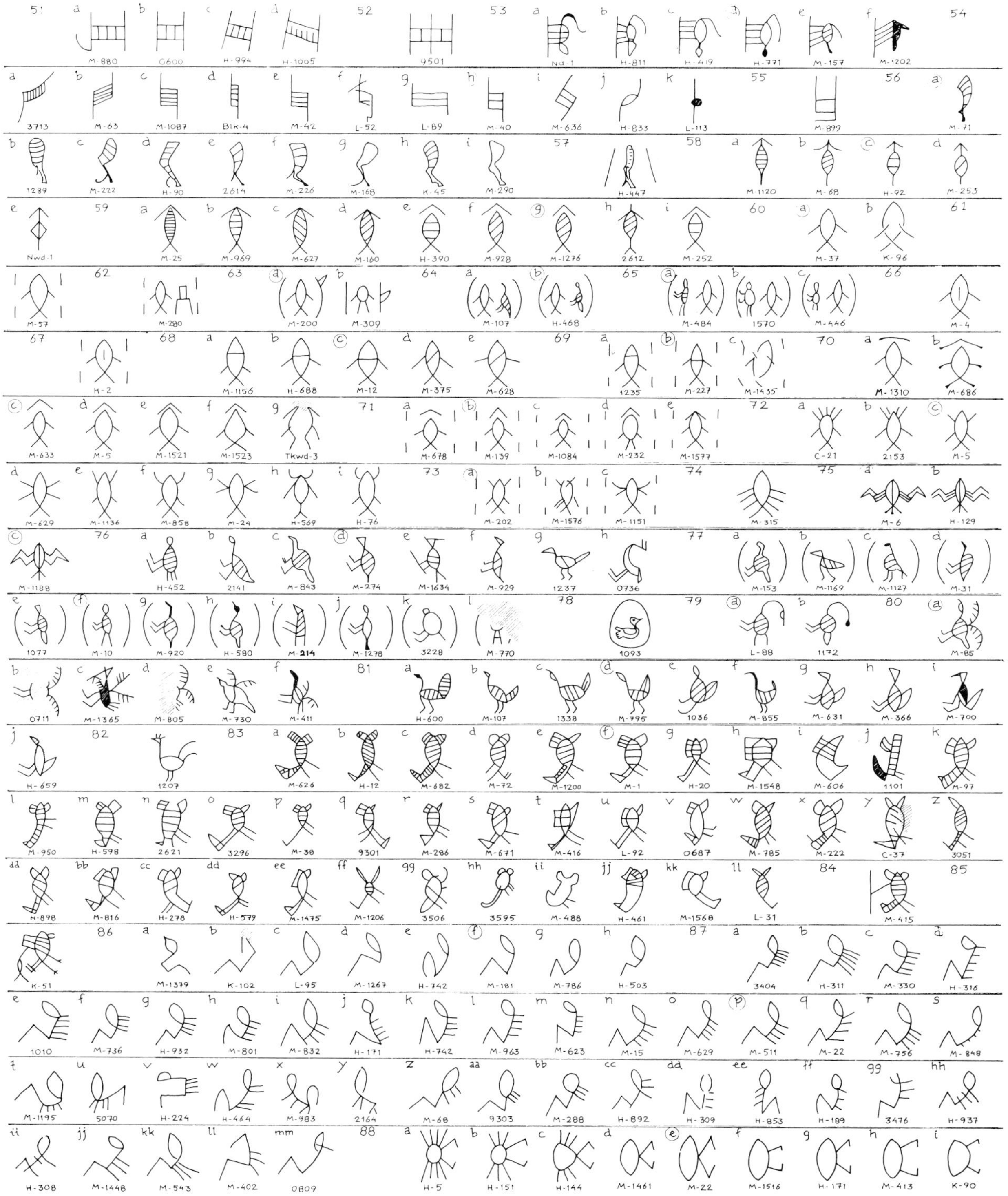

Fig. 5.1. (*cont.*)

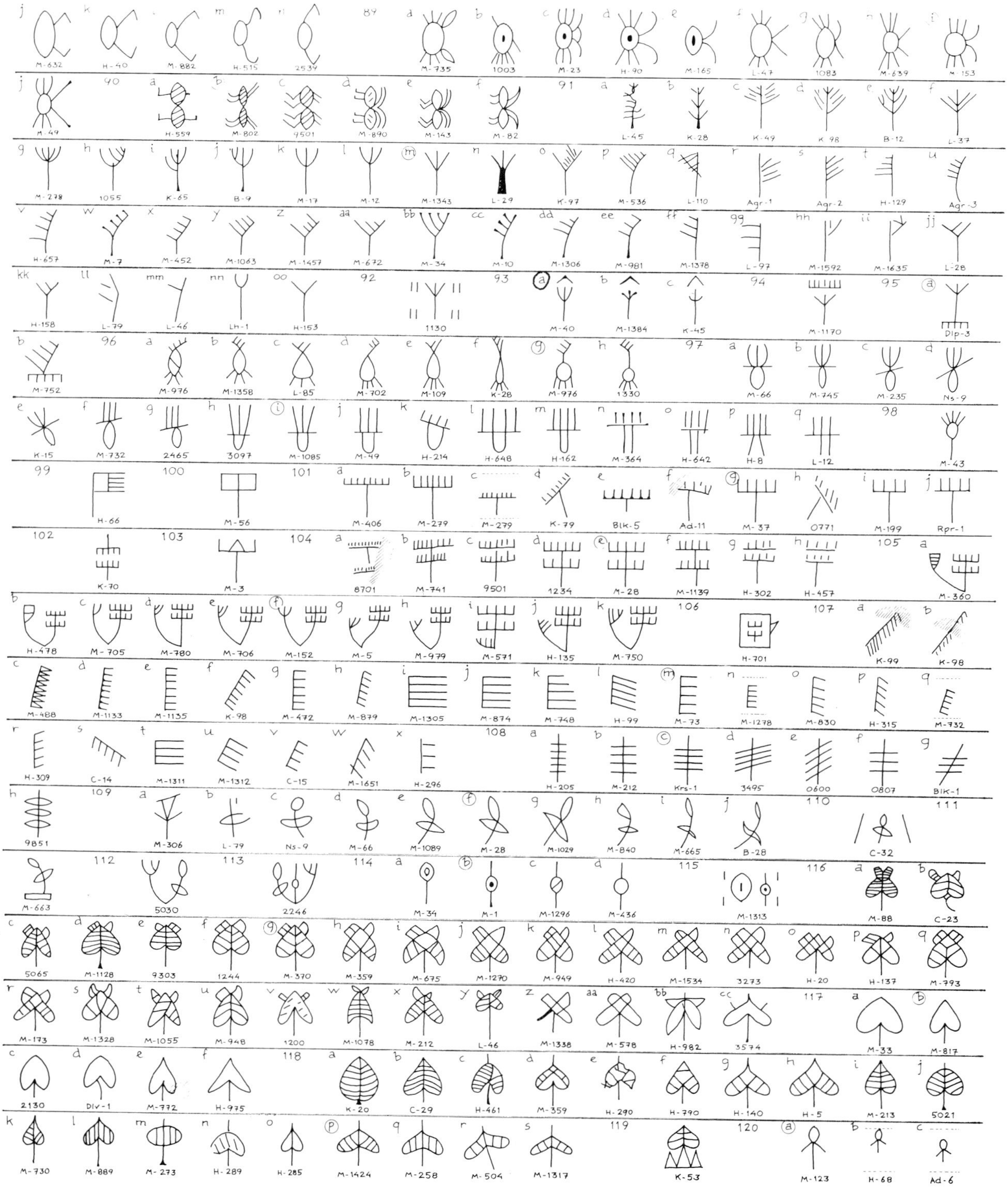

Fig. 5.1. (cont.)

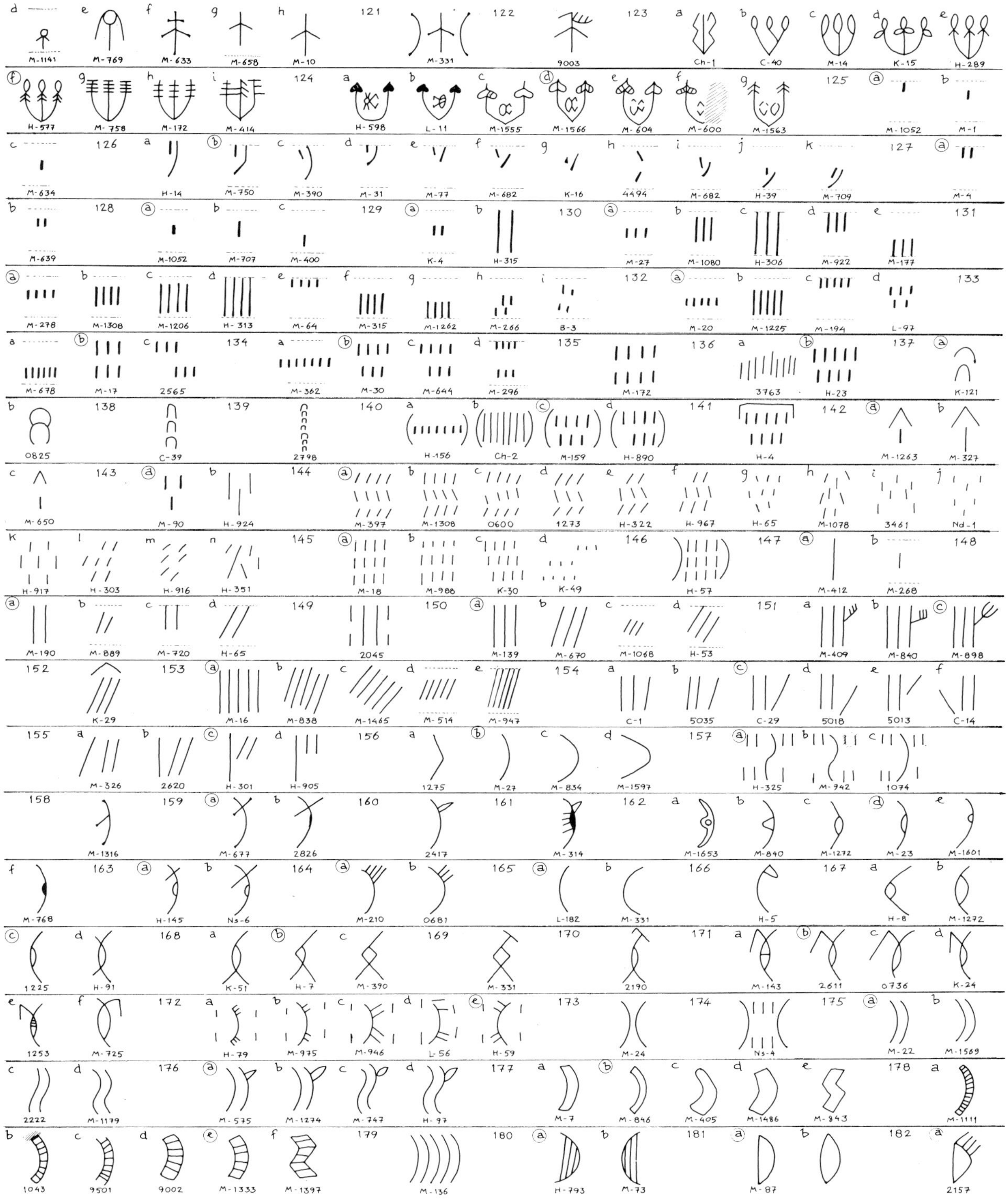

Fig. 5.1. (*cont.*)

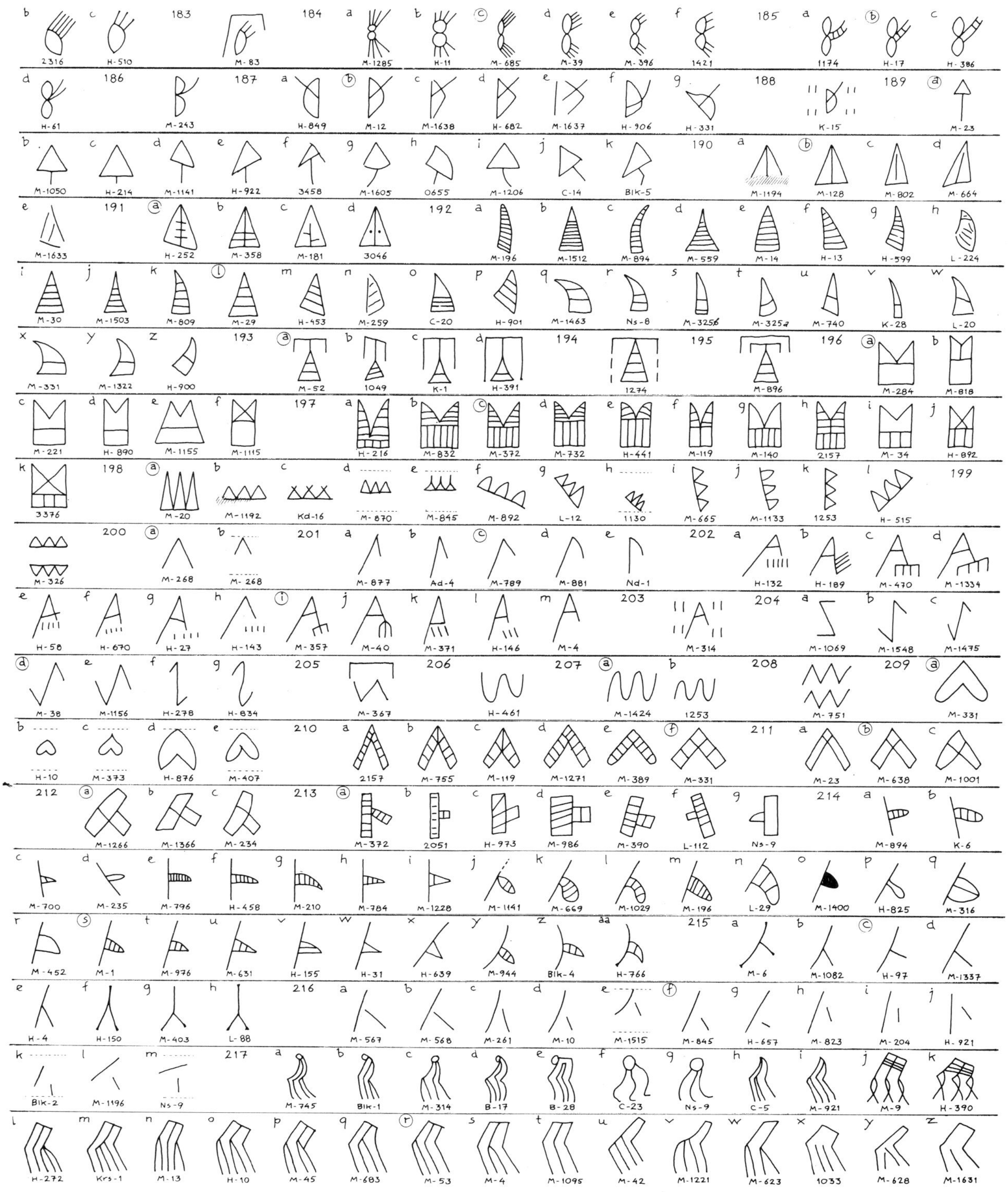

Fig. 5.1. (*cont.*)

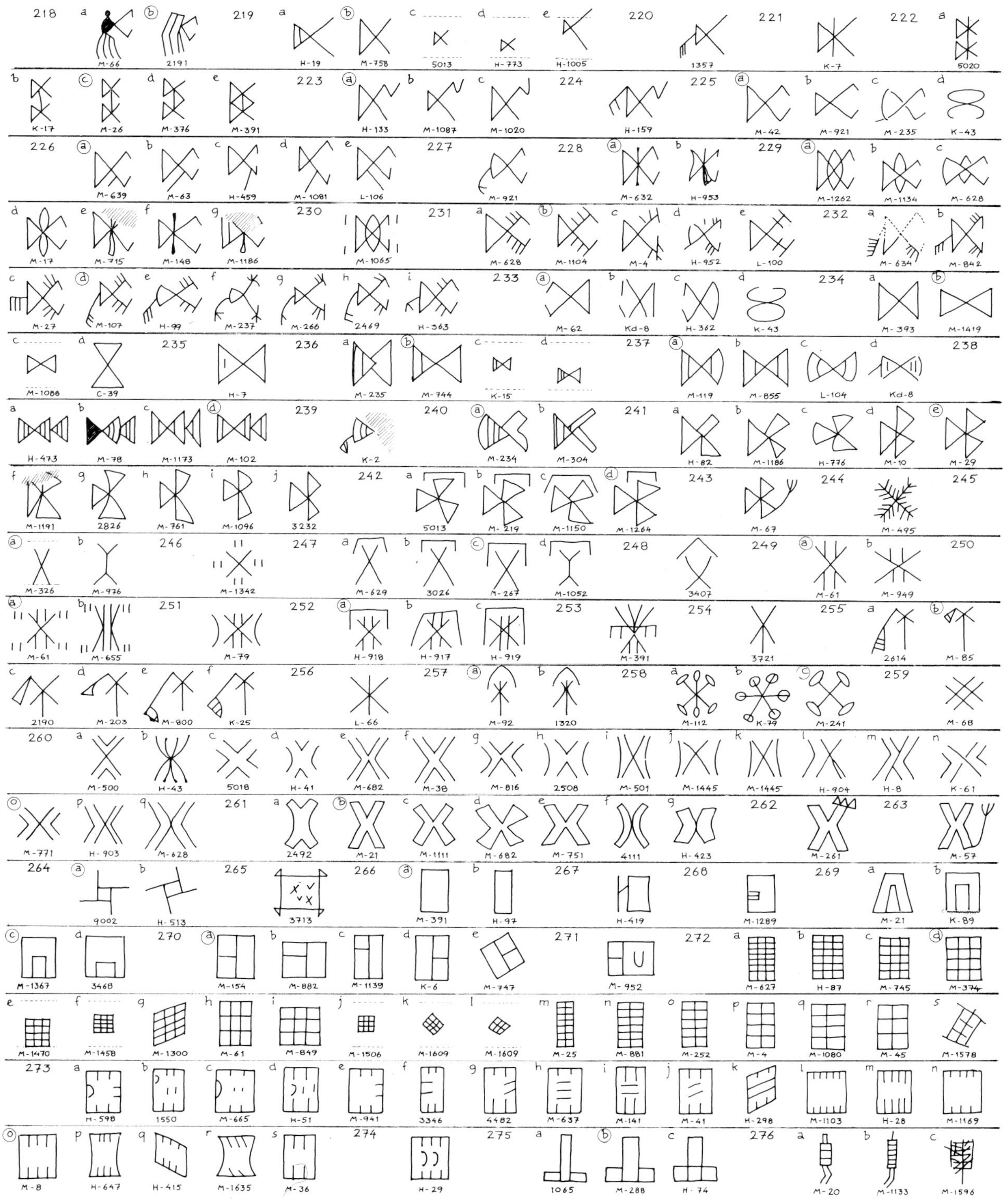

Fig. 5.1. (*cont.*)

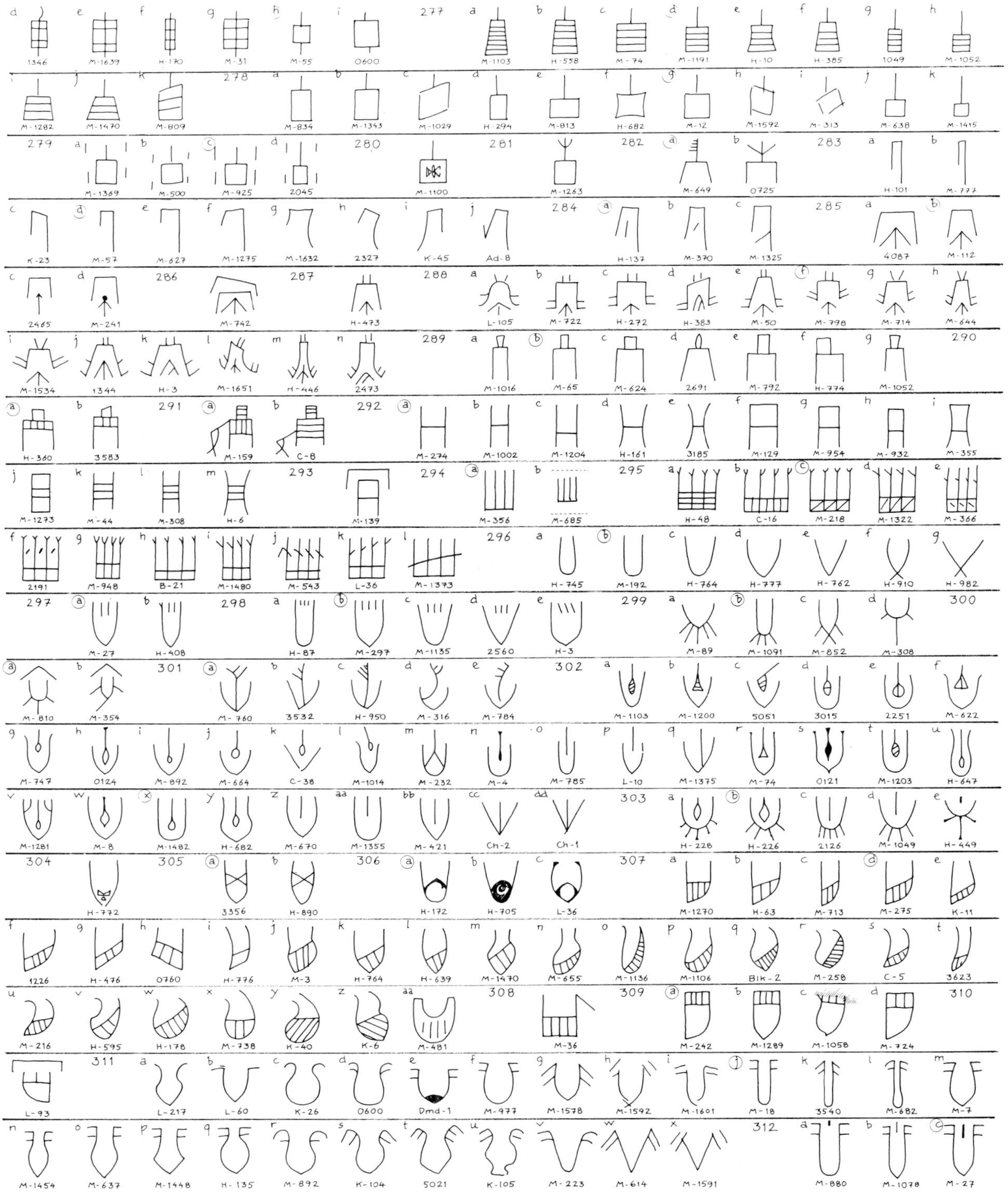

Fig. 5.1. (*cont.*)

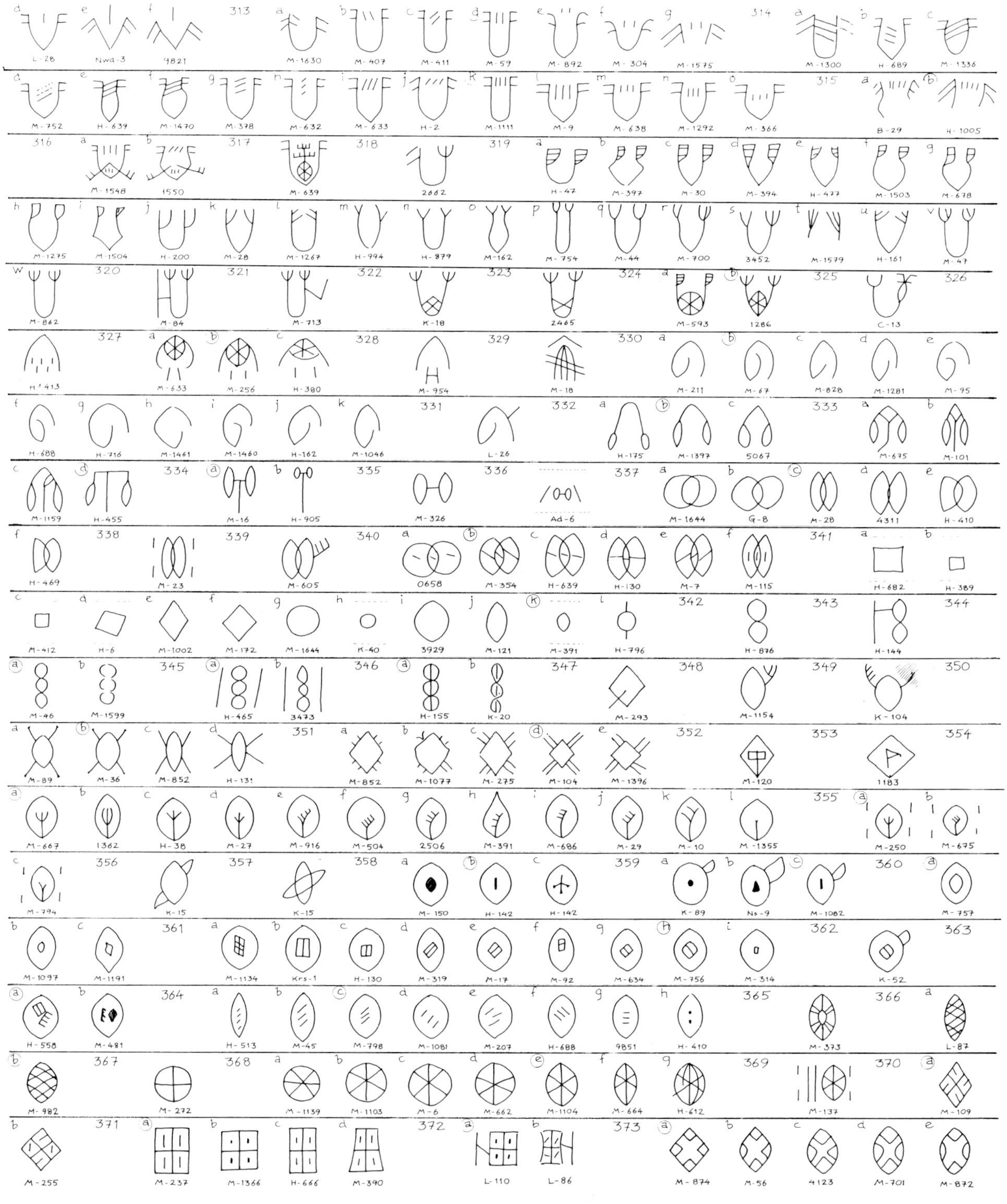

Fig. 5.1. (*cont.*)

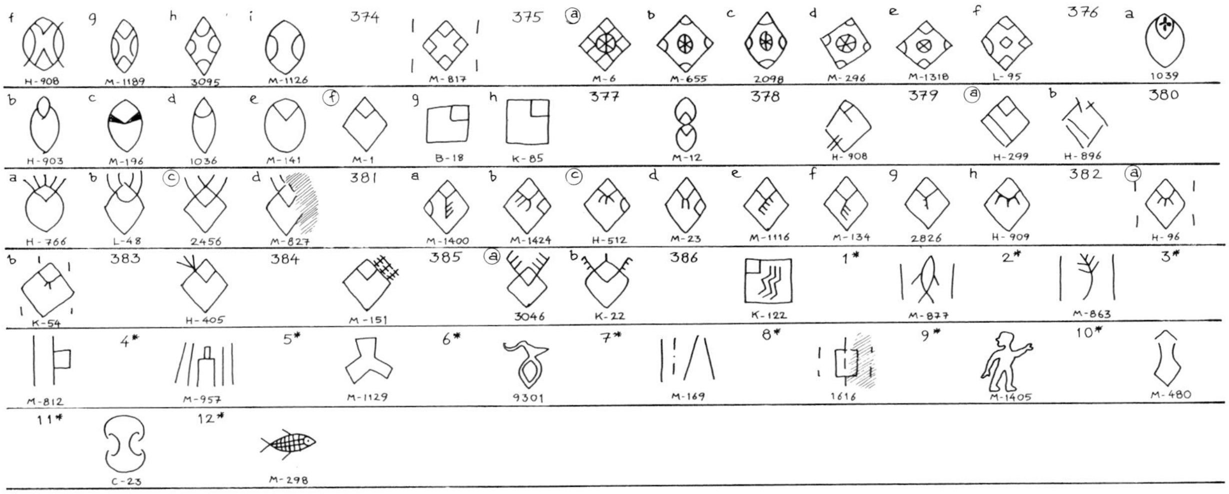

Fig. 5.1. (*cont.*)

Table 5.1. *Frequency distribution of the 417 graphemes distinguished in his corpus of the Indus inscriptions by I. Mahadevan*

Frequency range	No. of signs	Total sign occurrences	Percentage (of total occurrences)
1000 or more	1	1395	10.43
999–500	1	649	4.85
499–100	31	6344	47.44
99–50	34	2381	17.81
49–10	86	1833	13.71
9–2	152	658	4.92
Only once	112	112	0.84
Total	417	13372	100.00

After Mahadevan 1977: 17 (cf. figures in Parpola et al. 1969a: 9).

their meaning is close to the sign ↑ that is often found in this position (fig. 6.6).

Graphemes, once distinguished, must be arranged in a sign list. The order should be such that the position of a sign within the list can easily be located and remembered. While progress in the interpretation of the archaic Sumerian script has made it possible to arrange its new sign list according to phonetic values, the outer form of the Indus signs is the only possible basis for organizing the signs at present. In the accompanying sign list (fig. 5.1), the signs that look like men come first, then those that look like animals or their body parts, then the signs that look like plants, and finally the various classes of more abstract geometrical shapes (vertical strokes, curved vertical strokes and semicircles, cones, crosses, squares, U-shapes, circles). (The pictorial interpretation of any sign in these terms may be wrong – one placed among 'plants' may not be intended to represent a plant. But that does not really matter.) The sign list proper includes only complete and clearly distinguished characters occurring in texts that unmistakably represent the Indus script; graffiti with singly occurring signs that might be just potter's marks or ownership marks are excluded. All the principal sign variants encountered in the texts are included (their range of variation is indispensable to understanding their pictorial meaning: see §7.2); they are marked with letters (a, b...) or (after z) with doubled letters (aa...); a circle is drawn around the letter for the form chosen as the standard to be used in normalized texts. The short supplementary list (with numbers followed by an asterisk) includes some problematic signs: do the components in 'signs' 1* to 4* and 7* belong to one or several graphemes? Are the 'signs' 9* to 12* script or iconography?

It is not always possible to distinguish allographs and graphemes. Incomplete preservation may make it impossible to decide whether a given sign resembles this or that grapheme. Potential allographs (and other signs that might be confused) are placed as close to each other as possible in the sign list, even if this means deviation from the order suggested by outward appearance. In uncertain cases it is better to keep the signs distinct rather than to merge them, and these deviations from the formal order ensure that the signs suspected of being related to each other appear in close proximity in the concordance and other lists.

A primary function of the sign list is to define a sequential order of the graphemes so as to make the construction of various indexes, concordances and the like possible. (To use the term 'alphabetical order' might create the impression that the Indus script is an alphabetic writing system.) At present, each sign is listed only once. This means that composite signs put together from two or more signs cannot be placed near all of their component signs, but near only one of them. At the moment it seems best to treat all composite signs systematically as single graphemes while processing the material for statistical and linguistic analysis. If we could be certain that each of their components represents a linguistic entity, to be read one after the other in linguistic order, it would be advisable to try to dissolve the composite signs consistently for linguistic analysis. However, as in other early writing systems, a component of a composite sign may be just an auxiliary sign, not to be pronounced at all. In such cases splitting a composite sign into two or more successive graphemes would distort the linguistic analysis.

The provisional sign list of the Indus script contains 386 (+12?) graphemes. This figure is subject to various reservations. In the first place, not all the allographs may have been distinguished; in the most extreme case, the grapheme count might be as low as 350. On the other hand, only a small proportion of Indus texts has been preserved. The total range of signs once present in the Indus script is certain to have been greater than is observable now, for new signs have kept turning up in new inscriptions. The rate of discovery has been fairly low, though, and the new signs have more often been ligatures of two or more signs already known as separate graphemes than entirely new signs.

When the number of signs in the Indus script is being estimated, therefore, it seems useful to distinguish between 'simple signs' and 'composite signs' or ligatures. Allowing a maximum margin for various judgements (including what is and what is not an allograph), there are some 170 to 220 simple signs and elements of composite signs not occurring as independent signs, and some 170 to 200 composite signs. In the archaic Sumerian writing system, the formation of ligatures by combining simple signs was one of the most effective ways of reducing the number of signs and making writing more economical (§ 2.2).

5.2 Composite signs

Alternative spellings constituted precious clues to the interrelationships of signs in the decipherment of the Linear B script. Likewise, pairs of nearly identical Indus inscriptions such as

2146 / 2326

1018 / 2353

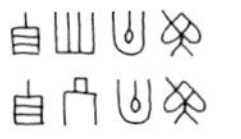

are valuable in suggesting the likelihood of some semantic or phonetic similarity between the variant signs (here ≈ and ≈). All such instances of near-identical texts in which only one or two signs differ must be carefully collected.

The significance of such parallels is enhanced if the variable signs also resemble each other in form. This applies specifically to the composite signs, which are examined in this section. But before proceeding any further, let us define our terminology. 'Ligature' and 'composite sign' are here synonyms, used for signs formed by combining two or more 'elements' or 'components'. One component may be placed inside another, as in = + , or above another, as in = + . If the component parts are placed beside one another, they may be tied together with a connecting line, so as to indicate that a ligature and not a sequence of signs is meant: = + .

Not all elements of ligatures occur singly as 'free graphemes': some elements are 'bound graphemes'. (These terms parallel the free and bound morphemes used in linguistics: the word *boys* contains a free morph *boy* and a bound morph *-s*.) For example, the 'diacritical' or distinguishing mark is added to the simple sign to form the ligature . A sign looking like a pedestal is found only in the ligatures and , where it has been placed beneath the simple signs and . Both the simple 'man' sign and the 'man'+'pedestal' ligature are combined with the sign to form further ligatures: and .

How can context help us in the interpretation of ligatures? The closely similar texts 2456 and 6022 suggest that the sequences and may be synonymous and the signs and may be variant spellings. The sign looks like a ligature of the independently occurring signs and . If these hypotheses hold good, then the sign is redundant: it may have been added to the sign to ensure its correct reading. This would imply that the sign has several different meanings, and that in this particular case its reading may be ambiguous without such an auxiliary sign. As a phonetic or semantic determinative, the added sign would represent either a close homophone or a close synonym of the main component of the ligature, or indicate the major semantic class to which the latter belongs.

Some bound graphemes occur as elements in numerous ligatures. One looks like the 'sky' sign of Egyptian hieroglyphs, placed above a corresponding free grapheme:

ligature
free grapheme

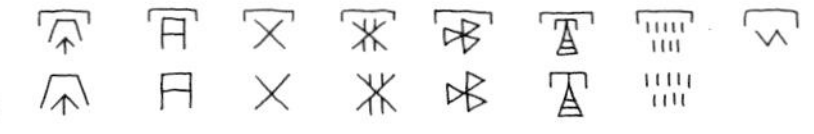

The ligature may replace the corresponding free grapheme in a parallel sequence (here the similarity of the context is restricted to the respective sign's being the first of an inscription and its being followed by an identical sign or two):

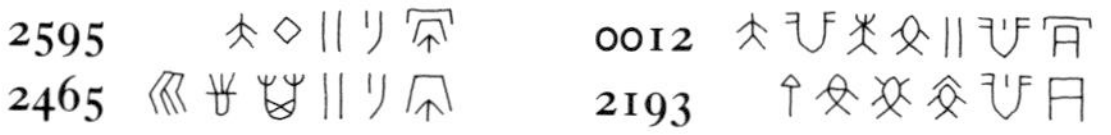

The free grapheme itself can already be a ligature, like the sign , composed of and . This sign forms a component in several other complex ligatures in turn: . The symmetrically drawn bound grapheme is to be distinguished from the asymmetrical sign , which both occurs as a free grapheme and forms a component of a ligature: .

In the following examples, the ligatures formed with the sign correspond to the respective simple signs in similar contexts:

In the above inscriptions, the similarity of the context again suggests near-identity of meaning. The ligatured sign , therefore, appears to be redundant, and may be a determinative. The same may be said of the plain sign prefixed to many different sign sequences, which occur without this prefixed sign in other texts (fig. 5.2). (Formally and functionally the sign could be compared to the single vertical wedge signifying number 'one', which in the cuneiform script of the first millennium BC was prefixed to proper names as their determinative.)

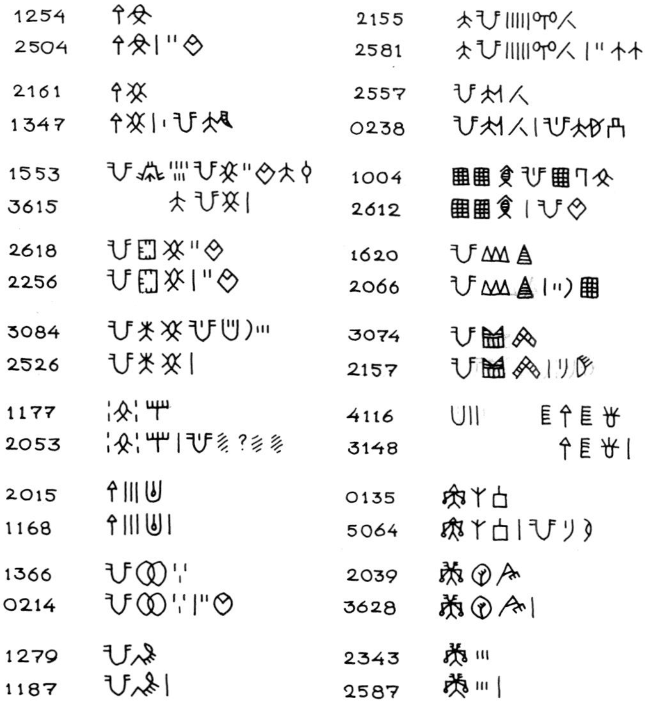

Fig. 5.2. Variation between absence and presence of the sign at the beginning of 18 parallel sign sequences.

It is not always possible to identify the different components of a ligature with certainty. For example, one of the components in the ligature is clearly but the other one could be either or . Seals 2340 and 1048 end in an identical sequence, so the ligature opening one inscription may have the same meaning as the initial sequence in the other. In that case, however, one would have expected the order of the components in the ligature to be reversed: instead of .

Many scholars have interpreted the following signs as ideograms:

	= 'a man holding a bow and arrow'	= 'archer' or 'soldier'
	= 'a man holding a mortar and pestle'	= 'miller'
	= 'a man holding a long stick or sceptre'	= 'overseer' or 'master'

The analysis of these signs as ligatures has sometimes been expressly condemned as far-fetched. It must be admitted that all too often Indus signs have been overanalysed (§ 4.2) and that some of the 'man' ligatures may well be ideograms (§§ 7.2–3). However, a number of features suggest that these and other similar signs are ligatures. In the first place, the other elements in the 'man' ligatures occur as separate signs in the Indus script. In the second, the components are usually tied together with a connecting line like other ligatures. Thirdly, several 'man' ligatures occupy the same position as their corresponding 'manless' component signs, the contexts being fully or nearly identical (fig. 5.3a).

This parallel function of the component sign and its 'man' ligature suggests that the 'man' component may be optional, and that the information may lie mainly in the other component. The 'man' component may function as a semantic determinative of occupational titles (such a determinative is commonly used in the cuneiform script), or it could be part of a compound like *policeman*, which may be replaced by mere *police*. A 'man' ligature that forms a complete inscription (fig. 5.4) is likely to denote an official title. That the various 'man' ligatures form a semantically coherent group is suggested not only by their common 'man' component, but also by their sharing some identical contexts, e.g. seal inscriptions 1070 and 2061 . (The parallelism of the signs and after the same rare sequence in 1402 and 1404 suggests that they are allographs.)

'A man holding a bow and arrow in *both* hands' hardly qualifies as a picture of an 'archer'. The existence of such 'double ligatures' is yet another argument against a purely iconic interpretation of many 'man' ligatures. In several cases

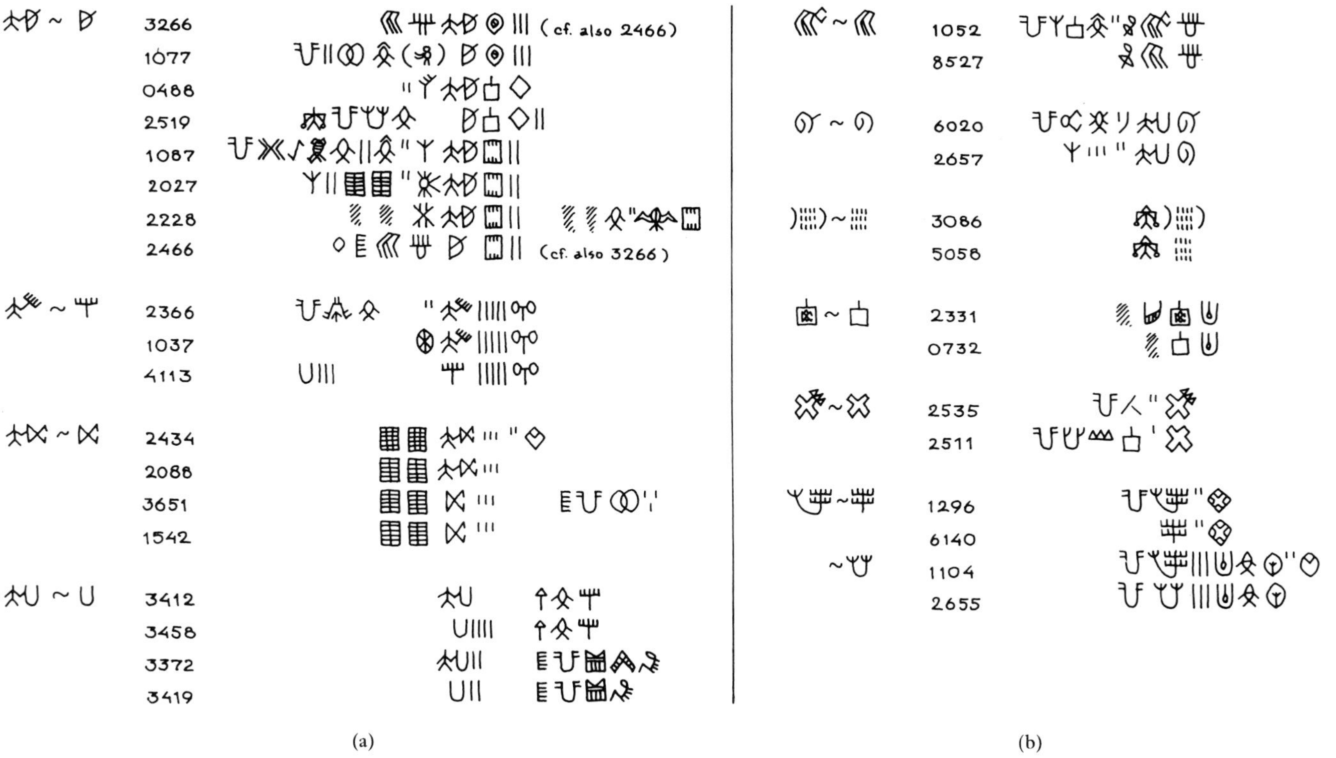

Fig. 5.3. Comparisons of texts with partially identical sequences showing a functional correspondence between ligatures and their component signs: (a) 'man' ligatures; (b) other signs.

a simple sign, a single ligature and a double ligature form functionally related sign sets:

That the double ligature is close in meaning to the single ligature can be seen from the similarity of their contexts in the inscriptions 9201 and 1142 (in each case the sign we are comparing starts the inscription and is followed by the same second sign). Both the single and the double ligature may occur in one and the same inscription: 5076 .

This 'mirror image' arrangement of the double ligature is also found without an intervening 'man' sign: . The particular sequence occurs in contexts similar to those of the corresponding simple sign and its 'man' ligature: compare text 2486 with the texts given in fig. 5.3. But it is difficult to decide whether the sequence is one grapheme (a ligature) or two separate signs, and . Both and also occur separately, and in seal 0118 the two mirrored signs are separated by one other sign, possibly a determinative, if this three-sign sequence too is a ligature.

In the mirror image sign pairs, the axis of reflection lies not only vertically but also horizontally: , , . Significantly, the sequences , , , and do not occur, although other signs are often repeated: , (§ 10.4), , , , , , , , , , , , , (§ 8.2), , (§ 12.1), (§ 7.4).

A few signs occur with three- or fourfold repetition: , , , . Of these signs, only and are preceded (in other texts) by groups of strokes, which evidently denote numbers. The sequence occurs on the reverse sides of some of the miniature tablets from Harappa (fig. 7.10), which normally show the sequences , , or (fig. 7.9). The sequence in the broken seal inscription 1165 is paralleled by the sequence on the reverse of tablet H-247 (fig. 7.11). The sequences and form the entire inscriptions of two ivory sticks (2795 and 2803), but a third ivory stick (2792) bears the inscription . It therefore seems safe to regard and as alternative ways to write '3 '.

Many ancient scripts represent numbers as groups of vertical strokes, and the Indus script appears to be no exception. But not all such groups are numerals; the sign , for example, appears not to be. In addition to looking like a numeral, a sign must replace other numerals in otherwise similar contexts – in front of the 'fish' sign, for instance: , , , (§ 10.4). There can be no doubt that these

Fig. 5.4. A seal from Harappa (H-94) with a single 'man' ligature.

sign pairs form coherent sequences wherever they occur; on one seal, the entire inscription consists of just the two signs, '7' and 'fish': ⚝‖‖ (fig. 10.24). Groups of small semicircles, ⌒, ⌒⌒, ⌒⌒⌒, which occur together with the stroke-numbers on pottery and on bronze objects (fig. 7.8b, d), very likely stand for 'tens'.

Numbers seem to be represented by repeated long vertical strokes only in the early inscriptions (the miniature tablets of Harappa). In the mature script, the smaller numbers (ones) are written exclusively with short strokes (in one or two tiers), while the long strokes have some other meaning. This can be concluded from the fact that the number of short strokes varies in front of specific pictograms (especially ⚝, ⅄ and ∪), while the number of long strokes does not (to any significant degree), except in the early texts. Moreover, the long strokes in the later inscriptions do not cover all the numbers represented by the short strokes, and they occur much less often, mainly in a few predictable sequences.

Most of the double repetitions do not lend themselves to numerical interpretation, because there are no triple or quadruple repetitions. In some cases, though, double repetition could be a purely graphic means of expressing a collective concept, as in archaic Chinese 𣎴 𣎴 'trees' = 'grove, forest'. The frequency of double repetition suggests instead a counterpart in the underlying language. The doubled signs could represent a repeated syllable or morpheme. They could alternatively reflect a grammatical feature, such as the plural, as in Sumerian (*kur-kur* 'mountains') or Indonesian (*buku-buku* 'books'). In many Indian languages, the repetition of a word either intensifies its meaning (e.g., Hindi *bahut bahut* 'very much', or Tamil *pala pala* 'very many') or expresses distribution (e.g. Sanskrit *dine dine* 'every day'). The repeated Indus signs could also parallel such determinative compounds as Sanskrit *rāja-rāja* 'king of kings'.

5.3 Segmentation of texts

A structural and distributional study of the Indus inscriptions requires a decision on the unit of analysis. In the cuneiform texts of Mesopotamia, including the seal inscriptions, conceptual units have been clearly distinguished from one another by being placed in framed 'fields' or 'boxes' (figs. 2.4 and 14.20–2). In the Indus texts, however, there is no such device, nor, as we shall see, have the word boundaries been marked by means of 'word dividers'. Therefore the only warranted procedure is to begin by basing the study on the physically observable divisions. These are: the inscribed object as a whole; its different inscribed sides; and its various lines of text, irrespective of the side.

The line is a good unit of analysis for studying the direction of writing, which may vary from one line to another. But in a structural and distributional study this choice could lead to distortions. In cases like seal M-892 (fig. 4.13), where the second line is clearly intended to continue the first line without a break, the connection between the last sign of the first line and the first sign of the second line would be missed, and these signs would be erroneously recorded as occupying the final and initial position respectively.

It is, however, useful to take the line division into account as an important clue to the segmentation of continuous sequences into smaller units; in most cases the line division does coincide with other evidence for junctures. For example, apart from a small difference in the first line, to be discussed later, each of the three lines on a seal from Harappa (H-103, fig. 4.10) is also found as a one-line inscription on three other seals:

first line	∪⩛⚝ᄑ⊕	2605	∪⩛⚝ᄑ
second line	⅄⫽⫽∪	2015	⅄‖‖∪
third line	⚝⼁大⼁	2371	⚝⼁大⼁

The two lines of another seal (5012) can be similarly matched:

| first line | "◇ | 8523 | "◇ |
| second line | ∪冏✕ | 2502 | ∪冏✕ |

These parallels clearly indicate that the one-line seal text 2618 ∪冏✕"◇ is to be segmented into two distinct subsets. Many other texts consisting of a single line can be segmented into smaller units by the use of similar comparisons.

The example just quoted suggests that when the text on any one side of an inscribed object is divided into two or more lines, each line is likely to be a separate unit, while together the lines make up a larger syntactically coherent unit, an 'utterance'. But is there a syntactic integrity between inscriptions on different sides of an object? If such an integrity is assumed, in which order are the sides to be read? In many cases this will remain uncertain, though precious hints are

Fig. 5.5. Impression of the longest continuous Indus inscription, a seal from Mohenjo-daro (M-314).

given by some very rare texts that unite into a single line sequences that normally appear on different sides of a tablet, e.g. 4512 '' (cf. 3665 reverse , obverse ''). It seems wisest, then, to adopt the side of an object as the basic unit for linguistic analysis of the text corpus and to posit a major syntactic boundary at either end of it. But even if the other inscribed sides may not be taken as parts of the same syntactic unit, they provide additional contextual information that may be at least semantically revealing; this information must be preserved by listing all the sides of an inscribed object together.

The longest Indus text, preserved in two identical moulded tablets (M-494 and M-495), has 26 signs divided among the three sides of a triangular prism:

The longest text on a single side is seal M-314, where 17 signs have been divided into three lines (fig. 5.5).

The longest one-line inscriptions comprise 14 signs each:

0104
2654

Most texts, however, are considerably shorter; some consist of only a single sign (fig. 5.4). The average length of an inscription is five signs, and such five-sign inscriptions are also the ones that occur most frequently. Five signs could constitute a word, but it is unlikely that 14 signs would do so in a non-alphabetic script. How do we therefore go about establishing the Indus word division?

The signs ' and '' are similar in their outward appearance to word dividers in some other ancient scripts, such as Linear B, Hittite hieroglyphic and Persian cuneiform. At first glance the suggestion that these signs have a comparable function in the Indus script seems plausible, if one compares, for instance, the following parallel sequences: 1229 '' and 4452 . A good example of the sign ' as a potential word divider is seal 1418 ' , for the sequences on either side are attested as complete texts in other inscriptions: cf. 1453 and 1040 .

But there are cases where two potential word dividers (' and '') occur one after the other:

1436
3282

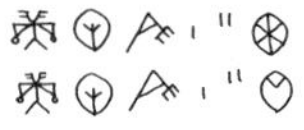

The sign ' is in fact found more or less regularly before the sequence (which forms an independent phrase in seal 0682):

2170
3297
2023
4061

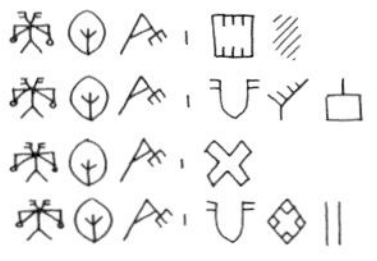

If the sign ' is really a word divider, it is difficult to understand why the sign should be so frequent in a very limited number of contexts like this, but omitted from the vast majority of word boundaries. And why should a word divider occur at the end of an inscription, as both ' and '' often do? If they mark the end of a word, the end of an inscription is the place where such a marker is least needed. And why should a word divider mostly occur after the very first sign of an inscription? And finally, the earliest certain examples of word dividers are from the Old Assyrian cuneiform texts in Cappadocia, dated to *c.* the eighteenth century BC, when the Indus Civilization had already collapsed.

In the absence of a securely identified word divider, other means of segmentation have to be established. This is a crucial task, not only for establishing the average word length – a criterion of the type of writing the script belongs to – but also for isolating inflection (if it is marked at all) and syntactic patterns.

The only reliable basis for the segmentation of the texts is provided by known junctures (beginnings and ends of complete texts). If two segments of a longer text each coincide with shorter complete inscriptions, it can safely be assumed that there is a juncture between those segments. From such examples we may deduce rules to be applied where exact parallels are not available.

We have already seen that three parallel shorter texts could help break the inscription on seal H-103 (fig. 4.10) into three major phrases corresponding to the three lines. The first line is not matched by an identical short text, but one where the first sign is missing:

First line of H-103
2605

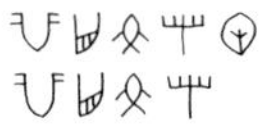

This variation in the presence and absence of the 'prefix'-like sign ⊙ characterizes other parallel texts as well:

| 1224 | ∪ ⟩ ⊙ | 2589 | ⇑ ⦀ ∪ ⊙ |
| 1005 | ∪ ⟩ | 2015 | ⇑ ⦀ ∪ |

Or consider a longer sequence:

3281	⇑ ⦀ ∪ ♉ ✸ ⊙ " ⊗
1065	⇑ ⦀ ∪ ♉ ✸ " ⬚ ⚹⊳ ‖
3135	" ⬚ ⚹⊳ ‖

The first half of seal 1065 is exactly paralleled by seal 3135, while the second half matches part of seal 3281, where it is preceded by the 'prefix'-like sign ⊙. Pursuing this method, one would hope to see the sequence " ⊗ from seal 3281 forming an entire inscription, and this may be the case on seal 2554 " ⊕ , if the unique sign ⊕ is an allograph of the sign ⊗ . Otherwise, a less direct indication of a major boundary between ⊙ and " ⊗ in text 3281 is provided by the analogy of other texts which can be broken into parts by this means:

1114	∪ ⟩ ♉ ‖ " ⊗
1082	‖ ∪ ⟩ ♉ ‖ " ○
1120	∪ ⟩ ♉ ‖	8523	" ◇

The 'prefix' is found before the sequence ♉ ‖ , too, for example in texts 2227 ∪ ⦀ ✸ ♉ ‖ ⊙ and 205 | ○ ⊗ ¦ ♉ ¦ ♉ ‖ ⊙ " ⊗ .

The positional distribution of signs, too, can be helpful in locating boundaries in the texts. The sign before a boundary is expected to occur often at the end of inscriptions, and the sign after a boundary at the beginning of inscriptions. In fact, a few signs are indeed found mostly at the end of inscriptions, notably ∪ and ⇑, and they are major aids in the segmentation of texts. The sign ∪ is by far the most common sign of the Indus script, representing about 10 per cent of all sign occurrences. About one-third of all inscriptions end with this sign. Apart from ligatures, where it is modified by the addition of other graphs, and the few cases where it is the sole sign, ∪ is never found at the beginning of inscriptions.

When the sign ∪ occurs in the middle of a sequence, one can often demonstrate that it belongs to the previous sign or group of signs and that a syntactic boundary is to be posited after it, while the opposite is hard to demonstrate. For instance, in seal 1553 ∪ ⚹ ⦀ ∪ ✸ " ◇ ♦ ♦ , a 'word' boundary can be placed at least on either side of the sequence ∪ ✸ . The last three signs, ∪ ⚹ ⦀ , form the entire inscription in seal 2214. Moreover, the sequence ∪ ✸ is known to occur 15 times, while the sequence ⦀ ∪ is known from seal 1553 alone. Further, although the sequence ∪ ✸ is not found as a separate text, it is found, among other texts, in 3026 ⋈ ∪ ✸ ⟩ ⋈ , surrounded by signs which elsewhere constitute complete inscriptions: 5031 ⋈ and 3561 ⟩ ⋈ .

Inscriptions with shared sequences which occur in a variable order supplement and confirm the evidence for segmentation provided by this method:

1293	○	3307	∪ ✸ ♉	3091	⊞ ⦀
0382		○ ∪ ✸ ♉ ⊞ ⦀
2395	⊞ ⦀ ' ✸ ♉ ⊞ △
3091	⊞ ⦀	3307	∪ ✸ ♉	1597	∪ ⊞ △

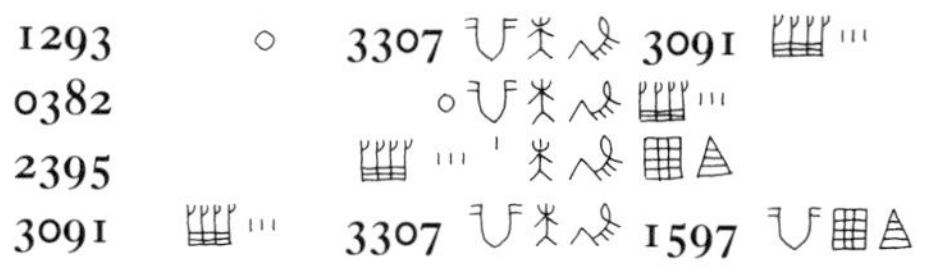

In the above example, text 0382 can be divided into three component parts by comparing it with the texts shown above it (only one side of seal 1293 is quoted here; the sign ○, which occurs alone on that side, occupies a separate line in seals 1325, 0204, 1135 and 2466). Now text 2395 has two of these three components, but in an order different from that of 0382, the first segment of 0382 here coming after and not before the second segment. The first component of 2395 may be compared with text 1597. The sequence ⊞ ⦀ mainly occurs at the end of inscriptions, and is never followed by the usual 'end' sign ∪. The sequences ✸ ♉ and ⊞ △, on the other hand, are often followed by the 'end' sign ∪, but may occur without it in the middle of an inscription, as in 2395.

In sections 5.1 to 5.3, we have analysed the graphemes and segmentation of the Indus inscriptions. We are now ready to deal with the question of the type of the writing system, which is important for the further analysis of the script and for its decipherment in general (§§ 3.3 and 7.1).

5.4 The type of writing system

Is the Indus script logo-syllabic (morphemic), syllabic or alphabetic (phonemic)? Theories of writing (chapter 2) and decipherment (chapter 3) provide us with several criteria by which to judge this.

Table 5.2. *Basic types of writing system and the Indus script*

Referent of the sign	Oldest examples (country)	Age	Number of distinct signs
Word	Sumer (Iraq) Elam (Iran) Egypt	3200 BC	*c.*700–450
Word or syllable	Mesopotamia (Iraq) Egypt	3000 BC	
Syllable	Elam (Iran) Greece	2250 BC	less than 200 (90% of the texts 100–50)
Phoneme	Syria	1600 BC	less than 50
?	Indus	*c.*2600 BC	*c.*450

After Parpola 1988a: 128, fig. 1a.

The number of distinct signs (graphemes) is one such criterion. Widely different estimates have been given, ranging from about 400 to 450, which is the figure most commonly quoted, to the unacceptably low figure of just 52. The reasons for such a discrepancy are twofold. First, the same sign may appear in several variants (allographs). Secondly, many signs are clearly composed of two or more elements, and it can be difficult to decide whether a given sign is composite or not. Nevertheless, we can certainly identify at least 200 basic signs, a fact which immediately precludes an alphabetic script or a purely syllabic script. On the other hand, 200 or even 450 signs are too few for a purely 'logographic' script like the most archaic Sumerian. Thus the Indus script is likely to be logo-syllabic.

However, not all logo-syllabic scripts are alike. According to D. O. Edzard (1990), the number of different signs in a corpus of 271 Old Akkadian seal inscriptions is *c.*185; this number is unlikely to exceed 200 even if the corpus were increased so as to match in size the corpus of Indus seals. From the fact that the Indus script uses about 400 signs where the Akkadian cuneiform manages with about 200, Edzard is inclined to draw these conclusions: the Indus script may have used more logograms (word signs) than the cuneiform; the use of a given sign to express several meanings was probably much less widespread in the Indus script than in cuneiform.

'Word' length is another criterion of script typology. Many Indus texts consist of just one sign, which should represent a 'word'. Most Indus texts can, in addition, be divided into phrases of one to three signs by internal comparison. Thus it looks as if the Indus script may be the same kind of writing as the Sumerian script of Early Dynastic times, in which only the lexical meaning of the word is expressed and all or most of the grammatical affixes are omitted and understood from the context. Edzard also points out that, while the average length of the Indus seal inscriptions is about five signs, it is about eight in the Old Akkadian seals: this again suggests that the former used fewer syllabic signs than the latter.

These indications, based on the number of graphemes and 'word' length, concur with the suggested date of the invention of the script. We have seen that the Indus script is likely to have been created about the early half of the twenty-sixth century BC (§ 4.1). At that time writing systems used only a logo-syllabic script, in which each sign stands for a word or morpheme of one or more syllables. The oldest syllabic scripts (Eblaite cuneiform and Linear Elamite) date from the twenty-fourth and twenty-third centuries BC, while alphabetic writing did not appear until around 1600 BC (table 1.1 and § 2.3).

It seems more than likely, therefore, that the Indus script is a logo-syllabic script.

6 Internal evidence for the structure of the Indus language

6.1 Typological linguistics as a tool in decipherment

From the internal evidence relating to the type of the Indus script we can now turn to the internal evidence for the structure of the Indus language or languages. (The question of whether one or more languages are involved will be dealt with in § 8.1.) At the outset, it will be useful to ask what are we trying to find out, and why.

The main objectives in the linguistic analysis of the Indus inscriptions are to determine grammatical features that can help us to understand the grammatical structure of the texts and determine the affinity of the Indus language(s) to documented natural languages. A valuable tool for this task is provided by typological linguistics.

In the nineteenth and early twentieth centuries, the main concern of typological linguistics was the global classification of the world's languages on the basis of one single parameter, the morphological structure of the words. In its refined current version, this morphological classification usually distinguishes between three major types:

(1) Isolating languages (such as Chinese and Vietnamese) have no or very few morphological markers and express grammatical relationships by means of the word order, which therefore has very strict rules.

(2) Agglutinative languages (such as Finnish, Turkish and Tamil) typically 'glue' grammatical affixes into a transparently segmentable sequence of morphemes, each of which expresses just one grammatical meaning: an example is the Finnish plural inessive *talo-i-ssa-mme* 'in (*-ssa*) our (*-mme*: cf. *me* 'we') houses (*talo* 'house' + plural marker *-i-*)'. It is also characteristic of agglutinative languages that they have just one set of case suffixes for all nouns, which are the same in the singular and plural (compare the singular inessive of the above-mentioned Finnish word, *talo-ssa-mme* 'in our house').

(3) Inflecting (or rather fusional) languages (for example the Semitic and early Indo-European languages) show grammatical relationships by changing the internal structure

of the words, both by root modification (compare ancient Greek present *leípō* 'I leave' with the aorist *élipon* 'I left'), in which it is not possible mechanically to separate the root from the affix, and by inflection, in which the endings may carry several meanings at once (in Latin *amō* 'I love', for example, the suffix *-ō* simultaneously expresses the first person singular, present tense, active and indicative). Moreover, languages that inflect often have different sets of suffixes for different nominal stems and different suffixes for the singular and plural (Latin *puella* 'girl', dat. sg. *puellae*, dat. pl. *puellis*; *nox* 'night', dat. sg. *nocti*, dat. pl. *noctibus*).

These three morphological types are hardly ever found in a pure form, however. Although most languages contain a mixture, one can nevertheless speak of trends. Moreover, languages can and do gradually change their type.

Typological linguistics as a way of examining cross-linguistic patterns started in earnest in 1960 with the publication of Joseph H. Greenberg's researches in 'word order' phenomena. Language typology in this modern sense attempts to uncover similarities and differences in the structure of natural languages. The similarities found between languages lead us to further investigation and postulation of 'language universals', whereas differences between languages lead us to further investigation of the reason for the range of possible structures available to languages.

For example, an important distinction between different types of languages is made on the basis of the natural or favoured order of three basic functional constituents of a declarative sentence, S(ubject), O(bject) and V(erb):

SVO Man eats food. (English, Hausa, Vietnamese, modern Hebrew, etc.)
SOV Man food eats. (Japanese, Tibetan, Dravidian, Amharic, etc.)
VSO Eats man food. (Welsh, Tongan, classical Hebrew, etc.)
VOS Eats food man. (Malagasy, Tzotzil, etc.)
OVS Food eats man. (Some Amazon languages only)
OSV Food man eats. (Jamamadi, Apurina, etc.)

The first two types, SVO and SOV, cover over 75 per cent of languages, and the first three about 90 per cent. In addition to these six basic types come non-basic ones, including 'free word order' (Latin, Quechua, Navajo, etc.), and some mixed types like German with SVO in main clauses but SOV in subordinate clauses. All six orders can occur in Russian, for instance, but only SVO is stylistically neutral: the alternative orders mark diverse emphases, the chief device for such emphasis being initial position. Other word-order patterns, too, are subject to such occasional changes for the sake of emphasis.

As the examples in parentheses show, languages from different parts of the world can be typologically similar, while cognate languages or even different phases of the same language can in some respects be typologically different from each other. Moreover, languages which in this particular classification belong to the same type may be quite different in respect of some other structural feature.

Many typological features, however, tend to correlate with certain others. Research pertaining to 'word order' phenomena in fact has led to the formulation of various 'implicational universals' of language. These take the general form: 'If a language exhibits property X (and Y...), then it will in all likelihood (or perhaps universally) exhibit the property Z.' Implicational universals established by an investigation of genetically and geographically divergent languages throughout the world converge on the simplification of the above word-order classification into two basic types, VO and OV languages. (Subject is left out of consideration, because subjects almost always precede objects, and because the SO / OS order, unlike the VO / OV order, does not correlate or harmonize with other typological patterns.) Typological features that harmonize with these two basic types of languages are listed in table 6.1.

The correlation of these two sets of typological features, consisting of various preferences for specific word orders, must be understood only as a general tendency. Very few languages are exclusive and consistent in their adherence to one of these patterns. As has already been mentioned, languages often undergo typological change, and this causes deviations from the expected pattern. Thus English, which is an SVO language, has the feature Adj + N, which does not conform with the pattern of VO languages (N + Adj); however, this is a feature of Proto-Germanic, an SOV language out of which English has developed.

In spite of such restrictions on their validity, implicational universals provide us with a powerful tool for the decipherment of languages such as that of the Indus inscriptions, for, if we can establish some specific feature of the structure of a particular language, we can deduce the probable existence of further features from such implicational universals. Thus implicational universals can enlarge the scope of individual conclusions in somewhat the same way as the phonetic grid elaborated by Alice Kober and Michael Ventris in the decipherment of Linear B (§ 3.2).

The Indus inscriptions are very short and thus can hardly be expected typically to contain complete sentences with all the basic constituents. They may be nothing but noun phrases, and even then finer distinctions are probably impossible to achieve.

But how can a word order analysis be carried out, if nothing is known about the meaning of the words? The numerals, which can be securely identified (§ 5.2), provide one starting-point, suggesting that the Indus language had the OV pattern

Table 6.1. *Implicational universals of language*

Feature	VO language	OV language
O(bject) : V(erb)	VO	OV
Adposition[1]	*Prep(osition) + N(oun)*	*N + Postp(osition)*
G(enitive)	*N + G*	*G + N*
Poss(essive)	*N + Poss*	*Poss + N*
Dem(onstrative)	*N + Dem*	*Dem + N*
Num(eral)	*N + Num*	*Num + N*
Rel(ative clause)	N + Rel	Rel + N
Adj(ective)	*N + Adj*	*Adj + N*
Adv(erb) : Adj(ective)	Adj + Adv	Adv + Adj
Comparison	Adj(ective) + M(arker)/P(ivot) + St(andard)	St + M/P + Adj
Aux(iliaries) : (Main) V(erb)	Aux + V	V + Aux
Inter(rogative particle)	Inter + Sentence	Sentence + Inter

[1] Features that appear to be particularly relevant for the study of the Indus script are in italics.
Based on Croft 1990: 56, table 3.1, and Andersen 1983: 16ff.

Num + N. In each case, where there is clearly an alternation between different numbers in otherwise identical or nearly identical contexts, it can be shown that the number forms a noun phrase with the following sign, which apparently represents its head word (for examples, see fig. 7.21, I). This definition leaves out of account such repeatedly occurring sign sequences as , which always involve just one specific number (7 in this case), for it is not certain that the number has a numeral value in such sequences (it may have been used as a rebus, for example: see the end of § 14.1). Another objection that D. O. Edzard (1990) has made against the use of the numeral for defining the linguistic type of the Indus language is that the written sequence of the numeral and its head word need not correspond with the spoken sequence; he refers to modern parallels like $30 = 'thirty dollars' and points out that in Sumerian accounts the numeral was for optical and practical reasons placed before the symbol for the thing counted, against the actual word order of the Sumerian language. This objection, too, can be invalidated, for the Indus inscriptions are not accounts but mostly seal texts: sequences that can securely be interpreted as representing Num + N always follow this order whenever they occur in the middle of a longer inscription (short inscriptions with just the two signs could be examples of inverted writing direction).

Edzard is right, of course, in reminding us that the word order of Num + N does not necessarily also imply the word order Adj + N: in French, for example, the adjective can be placed either before or after the noun, but the numeral only before the noun. Typology suggests, however, that if the Indus language had Num + N, it most probably also had Adj + N. We shall revert to the word order of the attribute in §§ 6.2–3.

6.2 A positional analysis of phrases

Identifiable numerals may provide an opening into the structure of the Indus language. But can the hypothesis of an OV language based on this clue be verified? How, for example, can one distinguish between attributes and their nominal head words in order to find out what their order is?

The attributive elements may be recognized from their optionality, for in a syntactic string, the total construction consisting of a modifier plus the head word, or the head word plus a modifier, has the same distributional characteristics as the head constituent. In the following example, the two *head words* that cannot be omitted retain their relative positions irrespective of the number of modifiers:

All these three *texts*	contain	very long *accounts* of those interesting events.
These three *texts*	contain	long *accounts* of those events.
These *texts*	contain	*accounts* of events.
Texts	contain	*accounts*.

The optionality of certain phrase constituents can be spotted if the Indus texts are arranged into a 'grid' (fig. 6.1), but that is by no means all that can be learnt from such an arrangement. The grid used here differs slightly from the computer-processed concordance lists (fig. 4.7), where the key sign(s) in different inscriptions appear in the same

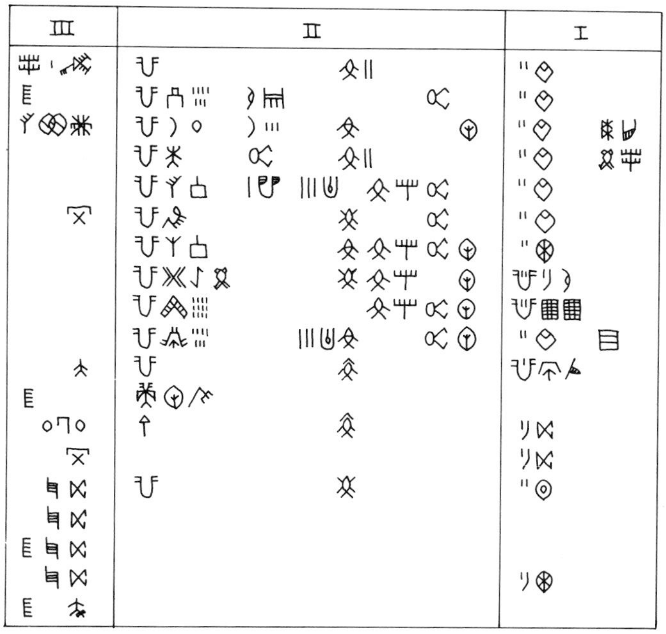

Fig. 6.1. A 'grid' analysis of some Indus inscriptions illustrating the positional slots I–III.

column, unlike the signs forming the context, which are quoted continuously (except for gaps indicating a shift of line or side) in each inscription. In the grid, the context signs too are keyed, so that similar or analogical signs and phrases in different inscriptions form columns; in this arrangement gaps are left in the rows as and when required, because one or more intermediate elements appearing in any one inscription may be missing in others.

The rows and columns of the grid correlate the syntagmatic and paradigmatic relationships of single signs and sign sequences. The word *syntagm(a)* means 'a string of elements forming a syntactic unit', coming (like the word *syntax* 'sentence structure and its rules or study') from the Greek verb *syn-* 'together' + *tassein* 'to arrange' = 'to put together, to put in (linear) order'. A *paradigmatic* relationship is 'the relationship of substitution between one linguistic unit and other comparable units at a particular place in a structure'; the term comes from *paradigm* 'set of all the inflectional forms of a word' (< Greek *paradeigma* 'pattern, model'), since different inflectional forms of a given word often alternate with each other paradigmatically. In the syntagms ***I** saw a bird* and ***We** saw a bird*, the subjects *I* and *we* stay in a paradigmatic relation to each other. To quote an example of the phonetic level of relationships, the initial consonants in ***m**ake*, ***t**ake*, ***b**ake* are paradigmatically related.

The syntagmatic relationships that can be determined from such grids give us relevant information concerning (a) the combination(s) of signs and sign sequences, i.e. which signs (or sign sequences) are combined with which other signs (or sign sequences), and (b) the linear (word) order of these signs or sign sequences, i.e. the distribution of signs and sign sequences in longer texts. The paradigmatic relationships that can be determined from such grids give us relevant information concerning (a) which signs or sign sequences are mutually exclusive within a particular syntagmatic 'position', and (b) the extent or possibilities of variation within a particular syntagmatic 'position'. In other words, the investigation of the syntagmatic relationships determined from these grids leads to the establishment of particular 'functional' or 'grammatical' units, whereas the investigation of paradigmatic relationships leads to the establishment of the range and structure of these particular 'functional' or 'grammatical' units.

Even a cursory examination of such grids will show that particular signs and phrases which recur in many inscriptions tend to be in the same linear order. It is true that occasionally cases of differing 'word order' are to be found (confirming the division of a longer sequence into several independently occurring segments or phrases; see § 5.3); but on the whole, the syntagmatic order of units seems to remain fairly constant. This raises the question of the extent to which it will be possible to correlate the order of the written units with the order of the linguistic units in the language of the inscriptions.

Several constraints must be noted here. The linguistic elements that are expected to correspond to the signs are morphemes rather than phonemes (§ 5.4). Secondly, all of the morphemes pronounced in the spoken Indus language may not, and are not even likely to, have a counterpart in its written form (§§ 2.2 and 5.4). In the third place, all preserved Indus inscriptions are very short, appearing on objects like seals, which are not so likely to contain even normal sentences, with such basic constituents as a verbal predicate or an object, let alone complex sentences.

Nevertheless, by means of a comparative analysis of the Indus 'sentences' it is possible to construct a general model for their linear structure, consisting of a series of slots which may or may not be filled. Signs and phrases occupying the same positional slot would either represent the same grammatical category or share the same semantic meaning. As word order varies from language to language (§ 6.1), we can hardly expect dramatic results before the genetic affinity of the Indus language has been identified. But in the decipherment of the Maya script, where long inscriptions containing full sentences are available and the language of the inscriptions is known, this method of 'positional schematism' has played a major role (§ 3.4). In addition to the language, however, we must also be acquainted with the 'routine formulae' of the specific textual categories (§§ 7.3–5).

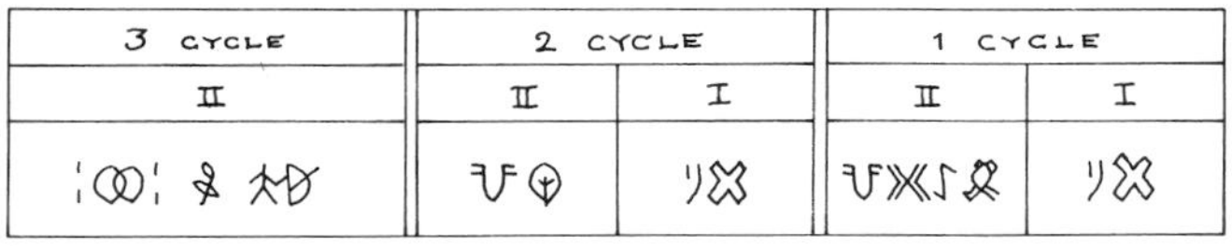

(a)

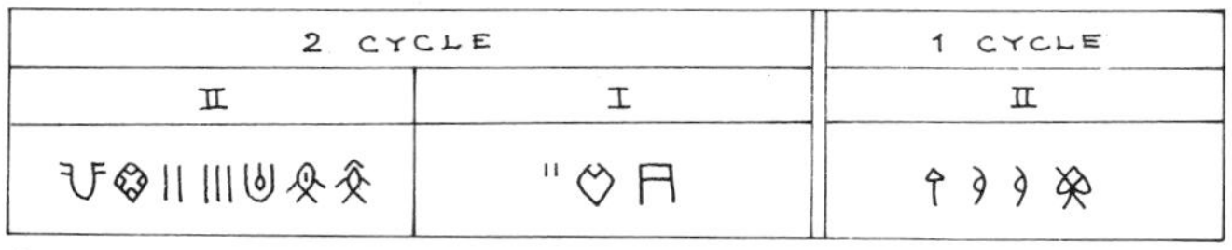

(b)

Fig. 6.2. Two unusually long texts with sequences representing more than one 'cycle' of positions I–III: (a) 1012; (b) 2654.

Until the grid analysis has been computerized, it seems practical to concentrate on a few easily recognized constituents. In the following, I distinguish 'cycles' with three major 'positions', numbered I to III (fig. 6.1), each with further subslots. The criteria on which the grid analysis is based consist of the results of the segmental analysis (§ 5.3) and the occurrence of repeated and statistically significant patterns at the beginning and end of the positions. All the positions need not be filled in any particular inscription; a cycle may be realized with signs belonging to position I alone, or position II alone (this is very common), or position III alone, or we may have combination I + II or I + III or II + III. Some unusually long texts contain two or more such cycles; a major syntactic boundary is likely to occur between the cycles (fig. 6.2).

Position I

A phrase that belongs to this position, unless it has been omitted, usually starts the inscription and often consists of just two signs; compare the following six pairs and one set of four parallel inscriptions:

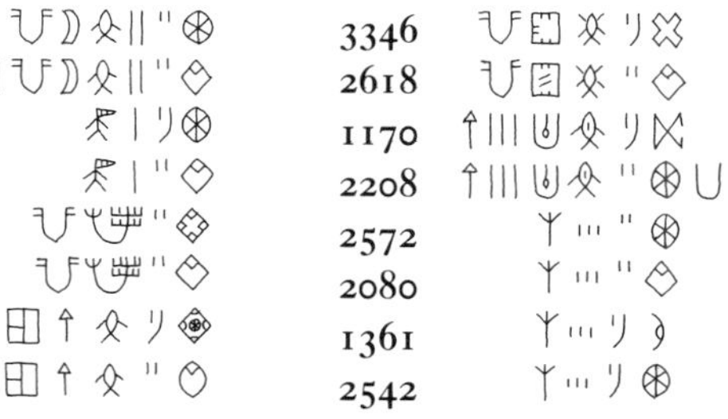

1114, 1082, 1189, 6044, 1294, 2102, 1387, 1554; 3346, 2618, 1170, 2208, 2572, 2080, 1361, 2542

A position I phrase is usually easily recognized by the signs that typically occur at its beginning and end. In the above examples, seven particularly diagnostic signs alternate with each other at the beginning. These and other signs which are usually found in the initial position may sometimes be preceded by either (1) one or two (possibly attributive) signs, or (2) a phrase found in position II of another cycle, or (3) both.

Among the signs that end a position I phrase, two paradigmatic sets are particularly prominent: (1) ', '' and [sign], and (2) [signs]. These two sets differ from each other in some respects. Thus a sign belonging to set 2 can occur after a sign belonging to set 1:

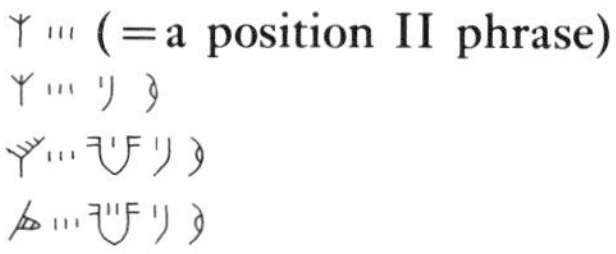

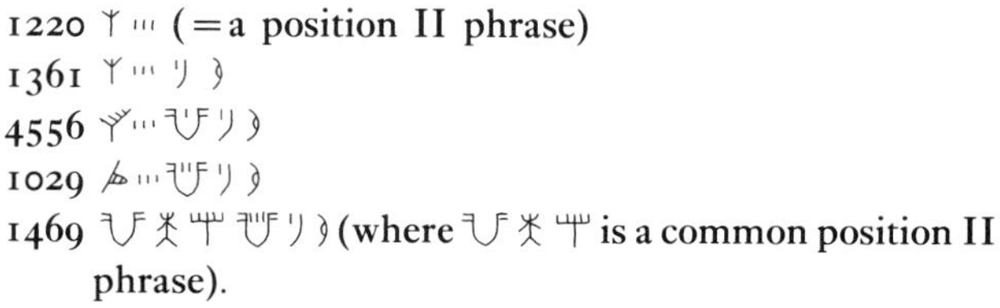

1220 (= a position II phrase)
1361
4556
1029
1469 (where [signs] is a common position II phrase).

Secondly, the signs of set 2 can start an inscription, while the signs of set 1 cannot:

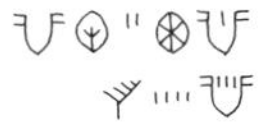

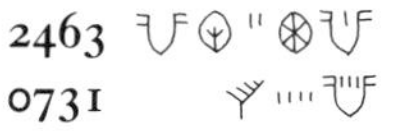

2463
0731

The plain sign [sign], which usually ends a position II phrase and consequently the whole inscription in most cases, sometimes ends the position I phrase, e.g., in C-12 [signs], but normally the sequence [signs] is followed by [signs]. The following two sets of inscriptions suggest that the plain sign [sign] is closely related to (though not interchangeable with) the signs [signs]:

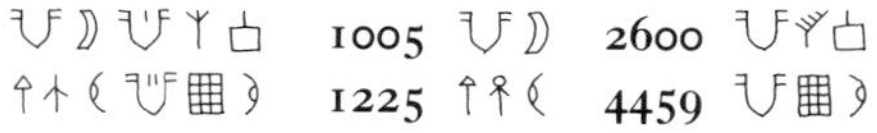

2300, 1005, 2600
1457, 1225, 4459

Thus the signs [signs] may well be ligatures of the plain sign [sign]. The other components of these ligatures would then most likely be the signs ' and '', as these usually conclude a normal position I phrase. This explanation fits the distribution of some of the signs that typically begin position I, like [signs]. Though relatively infrequently, they also tend to occur at the end of an inscription, which is the normal place for [sign]. *There* these signs are normally *not* followed by the signs ', '' and [sign]:

2176, 1338, 2474

The fact that the ligatures [signs] and the plain sign [sign] may both be dropped (§ 6.3) strengthens the case for a connection between them:

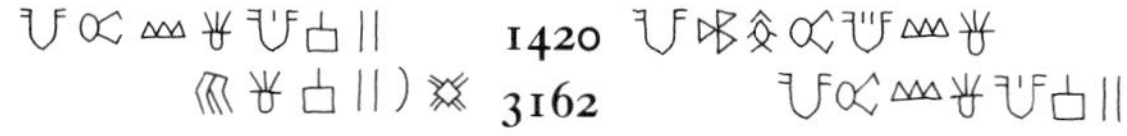

3162, 1420
2415, 3162

All the evidence therefore suggests that the signs ', '' and [sign] are special markers required by the structure of the inscriptions in position I.

(a) (b) (c)

Fig. 6.3. (a–c) The three sides of an amulet from Harappa (3305), each side showing a deity and the same single Indus sign. The god with bull's legs and a raised club (cf. fig. 14.12b) compares directly with the sign (fig. 5.1 no. 9).

On each of the three sides of amulet 3305 (fig. 6.3), the sign occurs alone. Here at least, this sign cannot be a bound morphological marker, but must be a distinct word, probably the name of the deity depicted on the amulet, or a title applied to gods, such as 'Lord' in English. Should this really be the case, then the same might be assumed to be true for the plain sign at the end of position II, especially in the light of the evidence of seals 2300, etc., quoted above. In this respect we must notice that in (S)OV languages titles generally follow names:

(S)VO	(S)OV
Mr Jones	Jōns avarkaḷ (Tamil)
King Asoka	aśoko rājā (Sanskrit)

There is one circumstance that suggests that the phrase in position I may be a title. The obverse of seals M-318 and H-102 bears a text consisting of phrases in positions I and II, while the knob on the reverse side repeats simply the respective position I phrase (fig. 6.4a–d). For example, some occasions may have required a stamp indicating just the person's official title, while on other occasions he may have given both his title and his proper name in the seal impression. From these exceptional seals we may assume that individuals may have possessed two (or more) separate seals, corresponding to the two sides of these seals. In seal M-1203, only the second of the first two signs on the obverse is repeated on the reverse (fig. 6.4e–f). The first sign, which could be omitted, may express an attribute of the indispensable title rendered by the second sign: 'man with a raised club' (fig. 6.3) = 'strong, mighty'?

Position II

There may be one or more phrases in position II; in the longer sequences, the following components (each of which may be omitted) can be distinguished, starting from the beginning and moving towards the end:

(1) signs preceding 'fish' signs (as their attributes?), usually one (, , ,) or two ( ), rarely more, but in such cases always following each other in a fixed order;

(2) a sequence of one, two or three successive signs whose basic shape looks like a fish (including both 'fish' ligatures and recurring compound-like sequences like + the plain 'fish' sign, or + the plain 'fish' sign), plus or minus some specific sequences like (these follow the 'fish' signs, if there are any, but may also occur without them. The signs belonging to this group of 'fish' signs are numerically very significant in the Indus inscriptions – approximately 10 per cent of all occurrences – and they occupy a focal position in the attempt at decipherment to which this book is devoted (§§ 10.1ff.));

(3) a series of one or more sequences, each consisting of one or several signs, with a large number of alternatives.

The phrase(s) in position II conclude(s) either (a) in the sign or (b) in the sign or (c) in some other sign. Most Indus inscriptions end with the phrase(s) in position II, so that this threefold classification of the final sign often applies to the inscription as a whole. But it must be borne in mind that not infrequently the position II phrase is followed by a position III one, so a distinction must be made according to whether the inscription-final 'other sign(s)' belong to position II or position III. For examples, see fig. 6.1.

Fig. 6.4. Three seals with an inscription on the knob of the reverse repeating (in the case of f only partly) the initial portion of the inscription on the obverse: (a–b) H-102 from Harappa; (c–d) M-318; (e–f) M-1203 from Mohenjo-daro.

In the unusually long texts with two or more cycles (fig. 6.2), phrases with a IIa ending and a IIb ending occur side by side. *If* both relate to one and the same person, i.e. the owner of the object, they are complementary in meaning. In that case, individual Harappans may have owned several seals, with inscriptions ending in IIa, IIb, IIc or III, just as they are likely to have had separate seals containing nothing but a position I phrase.

Position III

Position III is initially defined by the occurrence of a phrase or two after signs and ending a position II phrase, which is normally the case. But such a phrase or phrases can also occur after a position II phrase ending in some other sign (IIc), or alone (position III forming then the entire inscription), or directly after a phrase in position I.

One configuration connected with the final phrases of the inscriptions seems quite significant in this connection. When a position III phrase occurs after a position II phrase ending in , the sign which immediately precedes this IIa-final sign usually belongs to the group of 'fish' signs (II-2 above). It is one of these same 'fish' signs that most often precedes the IIb-final sign . The 'fish' signs occur also in inscriptions ending with IIc, i.e. with no position III phrase following, but in that case there is usually one or more signs belonging to the II-3 group between the IIa-final sign and the 'fish' sign(s) (see figs. 6.5, 6.6). A possible explanation of this structural pattern will be proposed at the end of section 7.5.

After this very provisional syntagmatic analysis we turn to the paradigmatic patterns.

6.3 The problem of inflection

The recognition of inflectional paradigms in systematic sign alternations at the end of words played a major role in the decipherment of Linear B. It enabled not only the building up

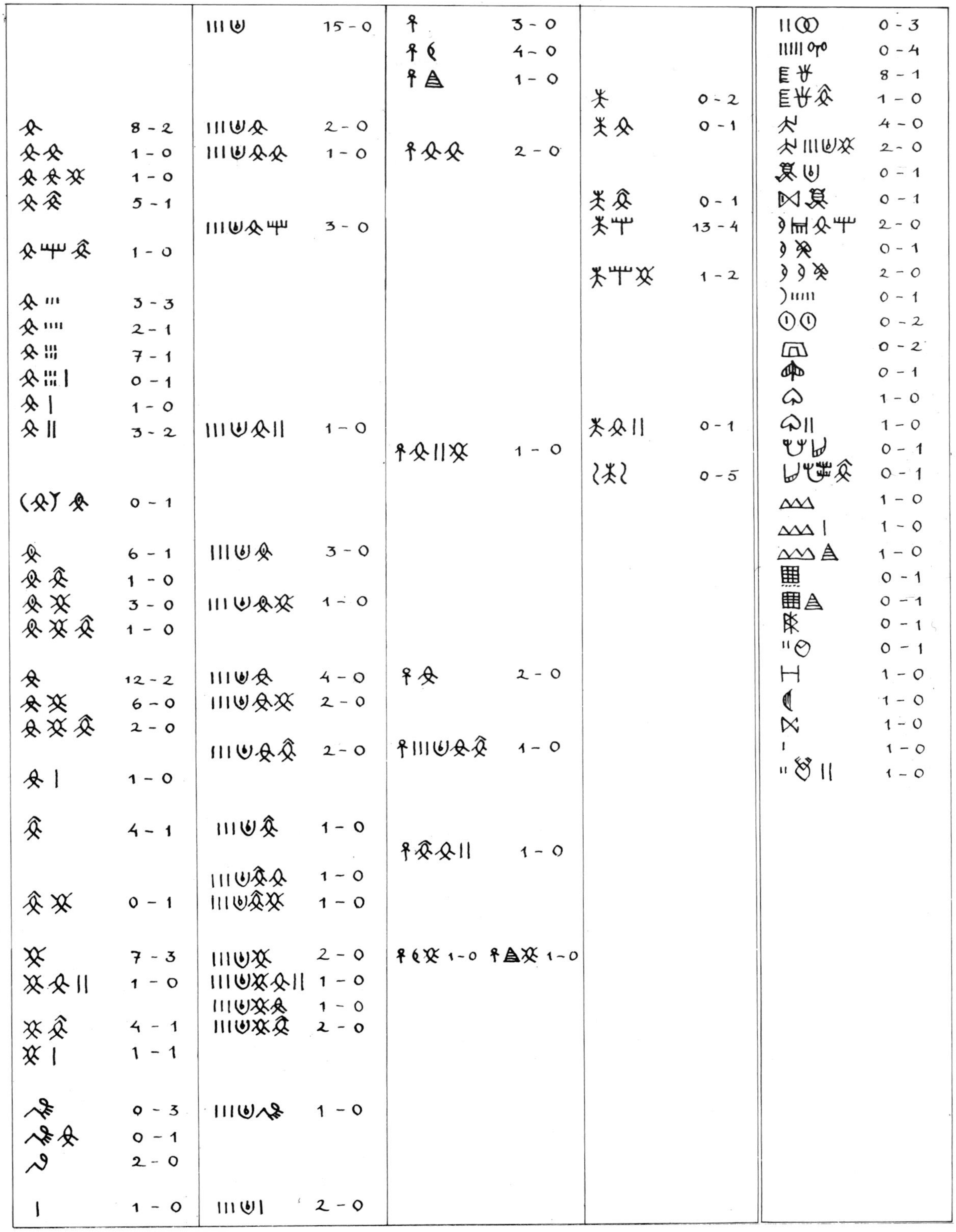

Fig. 6.5. Integral sign sequences occurring immediately before the sign and the sequence , classified and with their respective frequencies of occurrence (ignoring identical inscriptions). The majority of these signs belong to the 'fish' group (column I), often followed by the sequence (column II).

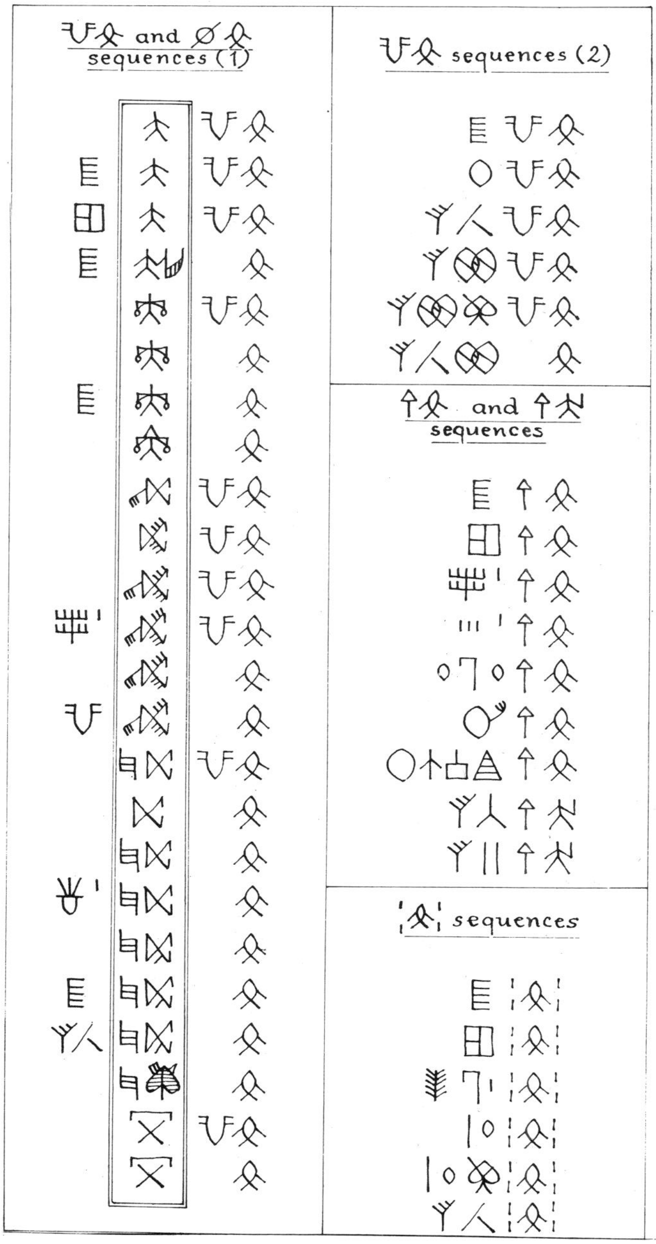

Fig. 6.6. A simplified analysis of the 'final phrases' (in position III) that occur after the different 'fish' signs (and the sign , which provides supplementary data). In this figure, the plain 'fish' sign stands for any one of the various 'fish' signs, and all the signs preceding this 'fish' sign are ignored. The table lists the signs occurring immediately after the sequences ≈ (see § 6.3 for the variation between the sign and zero represented by an empty space in this position) as well as those occurring after the sequences ≈ (see § 5.1 for their probable functional similarity). The signs and sign sequences in position III appear to fall into two groups: (1) 'man' and other signs framed in this figure: they are found only after (or its zero variant), and (2) another group of signs, which occurs *both* after (or its zero variant), *and* , , *as well as* after the signs of the framed group.

Fig. 6.7. Paradigmatic alternation at the end of some recurring sequences of Indus signs.

of a phonetic grid but also a rough grammatical analysis of the texts (§ 3.2). Can we discover evidence for inflection in the Indus inscriptions?

Many scholars have concluded that the signs and are likely to represent inflectional suffixes. These signs usually occur at the end of inscriptions, are very frequent, and can be postfixed to a large number of different signs; they are mutually exclusive (one never being found before or after the other), and seem to alternate after many recurring sequences, e.g. vs. , or vs. . This paradigmatic alternation can sometimes involve other signs too (fig. 6.7).

The sign is evidently a ligature of the signs and , and probably a ligature of the signs and (though is theoretically also possible; however, this sign never occurs as the final sign nor does it figure in alternations of the kind illustrated above). The signs , and are not as frequent as and , but they occur relatively often, and almost always at the end of an inscription. Whenever these signs occur in the middle of an inscription, it is usually possible to show that they belong to the preceding rather than the following sequence. Except for a couple of doubtful cases, they are not found at the beginning of an inscription. On these grounds the signs appear to form a coherent system, and in 1969 our Finnish team set up the following hypothetical paradigm of inflectional suffixes (fig. 6.8):

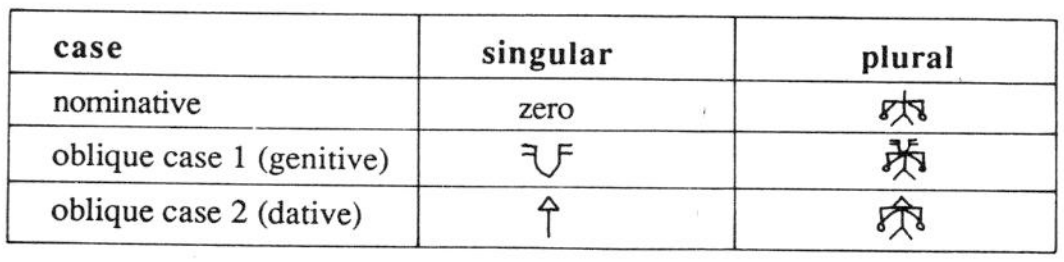

Fig. 6.8. Indus language inflection pattern proposed (and abandoned) by the Finnish team in 1969. Cf. Parpola et al. 1969a: 18–23; 1969b: 6–8.

This paradigm has been found to be untenable, however. Although the hypothesis fits most of the material, there are a few texts that refute it. Seals like 5061 and 6172

⟨signs⟩ have sequences which should be impossible if the paradigm is right. It could be supposed, of course, that the ligature ⟨sign⟩ may occasionally be written in a different way, by placing its two components one after the other, but in that case their order would be wrong. Since the case governs the entire noun (phrase) – including the categories for number (i.e. singular [unmarked] and plural [marked]) – it should follow both the noun and the plural. Moreover, in inscription 2472 ⟨signs⟩, even such a 'variant spelling' hypothesis is impossible, especially in the light of the fact that the signs ⟨sign⟩ and ⟨sign⟩ are mutually exclusive (the sequences ⟨signs⟩ and ⟨signs⟩ never occur).

A first step towards a different explanation is the observation that the three texts just mentioned are matched by inscriptions where the last sign is missing:

5061 ⟨signs⟩	6172 ⟨signs⟩	2472 ⟨signs⟩
3497 ⟨signs⟩	2818 ⟨signs⟩	5021 ⟨signs⟩
2526 ⟨signs⟩		

Moreover, there is a further set of parallels in which ⟨sign⟩ is dropped:

2375 ⟨signs⟩	5061 ⟨signs⟩	2519 ⟨signs⟩ ⟨signs⟩
3617 ⟨signs⟩	6048 ⟨signs⟩	3073 ⟨signs⟩

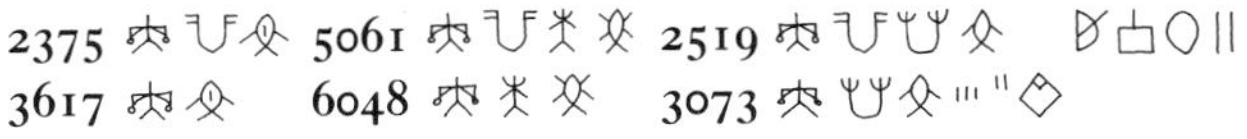

In this latter set, the alternative phrases may represent two ways of expressing the same thing, i.e. the presence of the sign ⟨sign⟩ could be optional. In any case, this alternation of the sign ⟨sign⟩ with zero (i.e. its absence) is confirmed by a large number of parallel cases. The zero option is clearly the preferred alternative in medial occurrences, while at the end of an inscription the presence of the sign ⟨sign⟩ seems to be the norm. This pattern does not conflict with (but neither does it prove) the hypothesis that it is an inflectional suffix, more particularly that of the genitive.

In order to show that ⟨sign⟩ and ⟨sign⟩ are separate words and not suffixes, one would need inscriptions containing nothing but these signs. With one uncertain exception (the broken potsherd H–374), such inscriptions are lacking, probably for semantic reasons: it may not have made sense to write simply 'carrier' (or the like), without specifying (for example) what is being carried. But an indirect hint is supplied by other signs occupying the same position, such as the 'man' sign, which will be studied more closely. Compare, for instance, the following:

5035 ⟨signs⟩	3442 (rev.) ⟨sign⟩ (obv.) ⟨signs⟩	
2344 ⟨signs⟩	1109	⟨signs⟩

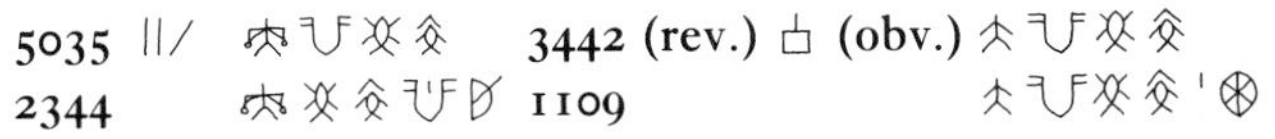

Inscriptions ending in the 'man' sign are very similar to others without it, as was the case with the 'yoke carrier' sign (⟨signs⟩ vs. ⟨signs⟩):

7031 ⟨signs⟩	1376 ⟨signs⟩	
2775 ⟨signs⟩	2380 ⟨signs⟩	
1536 ⟨signs⟩	3306 ⟨signs⟩	
3143 ⟨signs⟩	3289 ⟨signs⟩	
1115 ⟨signs⟩	1181 ⟨signs⟩	
2177 ⟨signs⟩	2580 ⟨signs⟩	
2074 ⟨signs⟩	5020 ⟨signs⟩	
3037 ⟨signs⟩	5021 ⟨signs⟩	

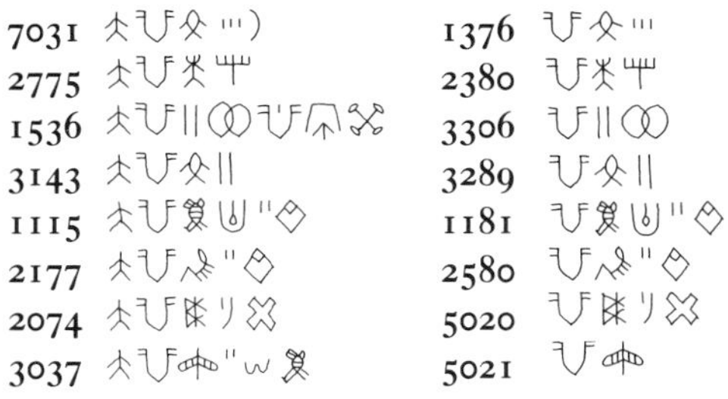

Similarly, the sign ⟨sign⟩, which follows the sign ⟨sign⟩ in seal 0003 ⟨signs⟩, is seen after the 'man' sign in a number of inscriptions resembling those cited above:

3164 ⟨signs⟩	7031 ⟨signs⟩	
3325 ⟨signs⟩	2775 ⟨signs⟩	
2404 ⟨signs⟩	2155 ⟨signs⟩	
1227 (obv.) ⟨signs⟩	1536 ⟨signs⟩	

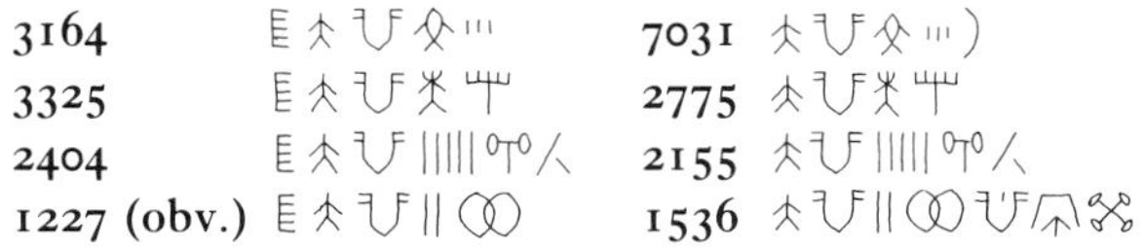

We can now take a series of three inscriptions for comparison:

2380	⟨signs⟩
2775	⟨signs⟩
3325	⟨signs⟩

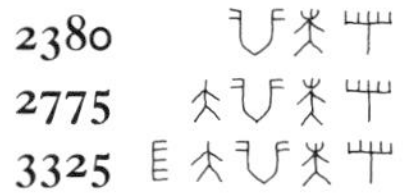

There seem to be two possibilities: either ⟨sign⟩ and ⟨signs⟩ are separate 'words' forming one 'phrase' with the preceding sequence which forms an integral whole in 2380, or they (or at least ⟨sign⟩) are inflectional 'suffixes' added to the preceding sequence.

The following complete inscriptions endorse the first alternative: 0206 ⟨sign⟩, 3235 ⟨signs⟩, 3414 ⟨signs⟩. In all these cases, the 'man' sign is modified by the addition of diacritics, which undoubtedly give it a special meaning. On the other hand, the plain 'man' sign and the parallel sequence ⟨signs⟩ do not occur alone, again (like the 'yoke carrier' signs) probably for semantic reasons: for if the sign ⟨sign⟩ means just 'man', as is suggested by its form, it would be meaningless without a closer specification. This specification of the plain 'man' sign could be a genitive attribute, for example. Perhaps such a construction demands the presence of the ⟨sign⟩ sign in front of the 'man' sign, for ⟨sign⟩ never seems to be dropped in this context.

The sign ⟨sign⟩ repeatedly occurs in contexts parallel to those of the 'man' sign:

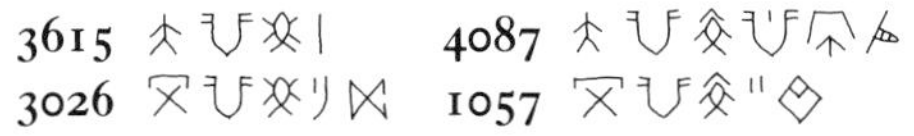

3615 ⟨signs⟩	4087 ⟨signs⟩	
3026 ⟨signs⟩	1057 ⟨signs⟩	

As the ligature ⟨sign⟩ is the only sign on seal 5031, it should represent a word there, not merely a suffix. It seems likely that it is a 'word', not a 'suffix' even in texts 3026 and 1057.

As in front of the various 'yoke carrier' signs, the sign ⟨sign⟩ alternates with zero also in front of other signs or sequences which usually end the inscription, including the one we have just been discussing (but not the 'man' sign, as noted above):

1053		2281	
4160		1096	
5031		2244	

In these cases, the final sign or sequence is one that can occur as an integral phrase.

The existence of a 'word' boundary between or and in inscriptions like those above runs counter to the Soviet team's findings regarding inflection in the Indus inscriptions. Analysing the Indus texts into 'blocks' corresponding to linguistic units by means of their recurrence (but without due regard to the boundaries suggested by the parallel texts), the Soviet scholars distinguish between (1) 'attributive semivariables', which may appear before 'constant' signs, (2) 'constant' signs, one or two forming a sequence which remains the same in all contexts, (3) 'semivariable' signs (above all and), which immediately follow the 'constant' signs and always precede the 'variable' signs (if they are present), and (4) 'variable' signs occurring at the end of the blocks.

Chiefly on the basis of their position and stability, the 'constant' signs are equated with 'roots' (said to consist of one sign in morphemic and of two in syllabic spelling), the 'semivariables' with derivational or stem-forming suffixes, and the 'variables' with such morphological markers as gender and case suffixes. Thus, in the opinion of the Soviet scholars, the following sequences form a 'micro-paradigm of variable signs' (fig. 6.9):

Indus sequences (4) (3) (2) (1)	Dravidian reading	English translation
	per amma	great lady
	ñanṭu per amma-at(tu)	the ruling great lady's (power)
	per amma-at(tu)-kā	belonging to the great lady (poss. dat.)
	ke per amma-at(tu)-āṉ	he of the red great lady
	per amma-at(tu)-āṉ-kā	to him of the great lady

Fig. 6.9. Indus language inflection pattern proposed by the Soviet team in 1968–81. Cf. Knorozov [1968] 1976: 103; Knorozov et al. 1981: 10ff., 28ff.

In the sequence , the sign is interpreted, according to the Soviet reconstruction, as the Proto-Dravidian formant of the oblique stem **-at(tu)*, which can function in the genitive case as well, the sign is said to be **-āṉ*, the marker of the masculine gender (however, the assumed Proto-Dravidian **-at(tu)-āṉ* is hardly the origin of Tamil *-tt-āṉ*, to which it is compared), and the sign is said to be the marker of the dative case, **-kā* in Proto-Dravidian (but **-(k)ku* according to Zvelebil 1977a: 33). This construction obviously collapses as an inflectional paradigm if and are in reality separate 'words'.

The Soviet scholars think that the 'semivariables' (1), which may or may not precede the 'constant' signs (2), are attributive. This seems a plausible hypothesis.

We have seen (in § 5.3) that such 'prefix'-like signs as and appear to be optional (singly or as a sequence) in front of recurring sequences. That these signs are probably not grammatical prefixes is suggested by the following features of the sequences. In a non-final position the signs and normally do not take 'suffices', but at the end of an inscription they are followed by the sign (e.g. 1217 or 3726). Occasionally this happens even in the middle of an inscription, so that there is an alternation between the sign and zero:

2555
2539

On this basis, the 'prefix'-like signs or (in the Soviet terminology) 'attributive semivariables' are like the recurrent sequences (or 'constant' signs) preceding the 'yoke carrier' and 'man' signs when the latter occur in the inscription-final position. One possibility for interpreting this common group of prefixed phrases is to see them as genitive attributes (see pp. 96–7).

In the Indus script, the attribute often consists of a single sign, prefixed without any explicitly written morphological marker; but this does not necessarily mean that the attributes were indeclinable in the Indus language, because such markers could have been omitted in the script. Similarly, from the point of view of linguistic structure it would be important if we could establish the presence or absence of prefixes, but the early Sumerian example quoted in section 2.2 reminds us that such grammatical finesses as prefixes or infixes could be omitted altogether in early scripts, even if they were present in the spoken language.

Let us now summarize what we know about the possibility of inflection in the Indus language. If the short Indus texts consist mainly of noun phrases, as seems most probable, the cases most likely to occur may be expected to be the nominative (often zero-marked), genitive and dative cases. The assumption of an 'accusative' case for marking 'objects' becomes relevant only if the Indus texts are thought to have contained verbs as well, and even then this is not necessary because there are languages without an overt marking for the accusative case.

The occurrence of complete sentences with finite verbs remains a possibility, of course. The position of the finite verb varies in different languages according to the word order typology. If the Indus language represents the (S)OV language type, for example (§ 6.1), a good candidate for a verb would be something found at the end of longer texts that does not occur in shorter ones (i.e. the signs in position III in § 6.2). In any case, we must bear in mind that non-finite verb forms (especially participles), with objects in the accusative and other complements, are by no means unlikely to occur among the nominal attributes of noun phrases.

The most likely candidates for inflectional markers are the two signs  and  mentioned at the beginning of this section. They occur with a high frequency, are juxtaposed with many different signs, and are generally word-final; in those instances where other signs follow them in the text, it is often possible to show that there is a word boundary between these signs and the following ones. This also indicates that the signs that follow them are themselves 'words' and not other markers for different grammatical categories.

Assuming that these signs are attached to nouns or noun phrases, it seems reasonable to regard them as representing some type of grammatical category compatible with noun phrases, one likely candidate being 'case' markers. This is supported by the fact that, excluding some texts of dubious nature, the signs in question do not occur separately and are in some instances optionally employed. In many languages, case relations can be expressed either with or without explicit case markers (in English, for example, *the table of / in the hall = the hall table*).

If premodification is preferred in the Indus language (§§ 6.1–2), one would expect to find that not only 'adjectives' but also 'genitives' modifying noun phrases should be placed in front of the noun phrases they modify. One would also expect to find that a marker for the genitive case is employed with two separate noun phrases, i.e. the modified (which would be unmarked for case) and the modifying noun (which would be marked for the genitive case), as in most phrases filling positions II + III. Having numerous instances of the sign  employed with only a single noun in a short text, and rather frequently in text-final position, therefore either indicates (a) that the sign is not, strictly speaking, a sign for the genitive case being employed exclusively as a modifier of another noun phrase, or (b) that the 'genitive case' has a much more general function, e.g. possession. Something stamped with a seal ending in this sign would then be labelled as 'the possession of X', while in other contexts the same sign could function as a genitive marker. In South Dravidian languages, for example, these two functions fuse in the possessive case marker that has (relatively recently) developed from a postfixed noun meaning 'possession, property, wealth' (*uṭay*).

Other interpretations cannot be excluded, however. Particularly important is the suggested functional connection between the plain sign  of position II with the ligatured signs  and  in position I. In the three-sided amulet illustrated in fig. 6.3, the sign  occurs alone and therefore is hardly a morphological marker, but rather a distinct word, probably referring to the deity depicted on the amulet. Thus the sign  could be a title of respect commonly added to proper names, whether human or divine. This hypothesis does not necessarily exclude that of the possessive marker, for South Asian languages provide several examples of titles formed from nouns meaning 'possession, property', e.g. Tamil *uṭaiyavaṉ* 'owner, possessor of wealth, master, lord, husband, ruler' (cf. *uṭai* 'possession'), or the synonymous Sanskrit *svāmin* (cf. *sva-* 'one's own'). Perhaps the diacritics like '' served to distinguish between such different meanings, possibly by expressing derivational suffixes.

We must conclude by frankly admitting our present inability to identify morphological markers with any certainty.

6.4 A computerized syntactic analysis

This section describes a method of analysing the Indus inscriptions with the help of a computer. It has been developed by Seppo Koskenniemi, Kimmo Koskenniemi and Päivikki Parpola with the following assumptions as the starting-point: (1) the Indus script is a morphemic writing system and (2) the correspondence between signs and morphemes may not be one to one, that is, not all morphemes need be indicated in the script, but what is redundant in a context may be omitted.

These assumptions imply that similarities in the distribution of signs and systematic replacements of signs in similar contexts cannot be expected systematically to reflect phonological similarities (e.g. shared phonological components, as in the grid worked out for Linear B by Kober and Ventris, fig. 3.3). Replacements and similar distributions must be interpreted in terms of the distribution of morphemes or morpheme clusters, and this is the domain of syntax (or syntax and morphology together).

The findings and hypotheses of the distributional analysis are to be expressed in terms of a *formal grammar* (based on the outward formal structure of the language, as opposed to a *notional grammar*, whose terms rely on extralinguistic notions). Any set of strings with a meaningful syntax, such as the corpus of Indus inscriptions, can be described by a formal grammar. Among the different types of formal grammars, context-free grammars (i.e. grammars ignoring the non-linguistic situations in which language is used) are the simplest, with sufficient power to produce some kind of description of a natural language. They are also the most complex of the grammars that can be managed with a relatively easy formalism.

It has proved impossible to infer a context-free grammar correctly from a text if no information additional to the sign distributions is available. In order to collect the necessary additional information, the method described here analyses the combinatorial properties of the strings. This is not sufficient for a complete, uniquely correct grammar, but in this case the grammar need not be complete. The purpose of the present procedure is simply to find structural features of the strings that describe the properties and relationships of the signs.

Information for forming context-free rules can be collected in several different ways. The approaches used here are syntagmatic, paradigmatic (for these terms, see § 6.2) and the 'Harris' approach' (pp. 98–9). These are all three based on the assumption that the set of strings has a reasonable syntax, which means that not all sequences of signs are possible. This is characteristic of natural languages. 'Sign' here refers to the unit to be analysed. In the Indus script it is a grapheme probably standing for a morpheme, but in the analysis of an English text it might be a word, represented in writing by several characters (letters).

Word boundaries are not indicated in the Indus script. The preceding sections have described conventional methods purporting first to segment the continuous texts into 'words' and then to analyse and classify the segments. The method outlined here does not separate these two operations but unifies them within a single syntactic analysis.

If we study sentences (or utterances) as sequences of morphemes, and not as sequences of phonological units, we notice that there are no formal criteria for distinguishing between attributes and affixes, or between postpositions and inflectional endings. We should therefore not hurry to make such distinctions early on. The stability of patterns and their freedom of occurrence will perhaps provide sufficient evidence for decisions of this nature to be taken at a later stage. Furthermore, we do not know in advance whether the language of the texts is analytic (having just one morpheme per word) or synthetic (having more than one morpheme per word). The computerized syntactic analysis described here can handle both cases.

The *syntagmatic approach* studies the probabilities of sign co-occurrence. Some of the signs are more frequent than others; some may be extremely rare. The accidental co-occurrence of two frequent signs side by side is probable, whereas for two rare signs it would be a surprising coincidence, especially if it were repeated. The strength of a syntactic connection between two successive signs is approximated by comparing the actual frequency of the pair to its statistically expected frequency. If the actual frequency is significantly greater than the expected, the syntactic connection is supposed to be strong. On the other hand, an observed frequency that is near the expected frequency indicates the probability of a major syntactic boundary. When we have the approximations for the syntactic strengths of the joints, we can draw an approximate syntax tree for the inscription by joining adjacent signs or constituents in descending order of their joint strength (fig. 6.10).

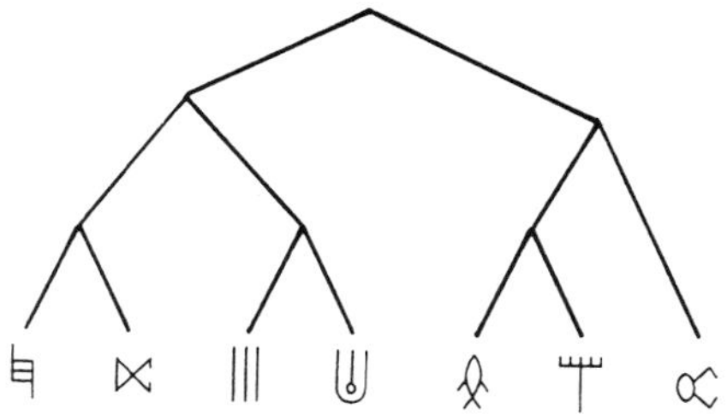

The observed frequency of the pair	62	5	155	12	80	24
The expected frequency of the pair	1	1	4	6	4	1
Approximation to the strength of the linkage	69	3	75	2	38	21

Fig. 6.10. An Indus text (2541) analysed syntagmatically according to the pairwise frequencies of its signs. After Koskenniemi 1981: 128, fig. 1 (as in Parpola 1986a: 409, fig. 3).

The *'Harris' approach* is based on the method for discovering morpheme boundaries from sentence-forming phoneme sequences developed by Zellig Harris in the 1950s. It considers sentences with identical openings, counting the number of alternative continuations after each phoneme. The continuous differentiation of alternatives can be presented by a tree structure, as in the following English example (fig. 6.11):

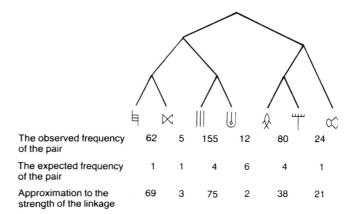

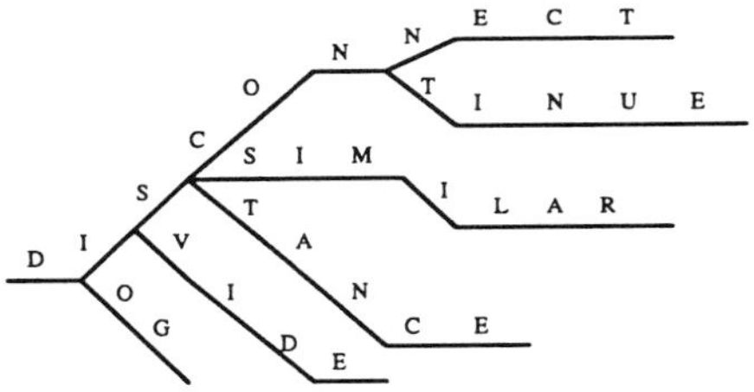

Fig. 6.11. Branching of alternative continuations after each phoneme in English words beginning in the same way. After P. Parpola 1987: 4, based on Harris 1968.

Within a morpheme the number of alternatives decreases gradually, while on a morph boundary it suddenly increases, as illustrated by a phonetically written English sentence in figure 6.12.

The coordinate points connected with lines represent the number of possible continuations after each phoneme. It can be seen that the peaks of the graph match the morpheme boundaries marked with dots. In cases where the beginning of a morpheme is identical with some complete morpheme (e.g. *dis-*, *di-*), the boundary is often misplaced. The error can in most cases be corrected by doing the analysis in the reverse direction (i.e. for sentences ending similarly). This type of

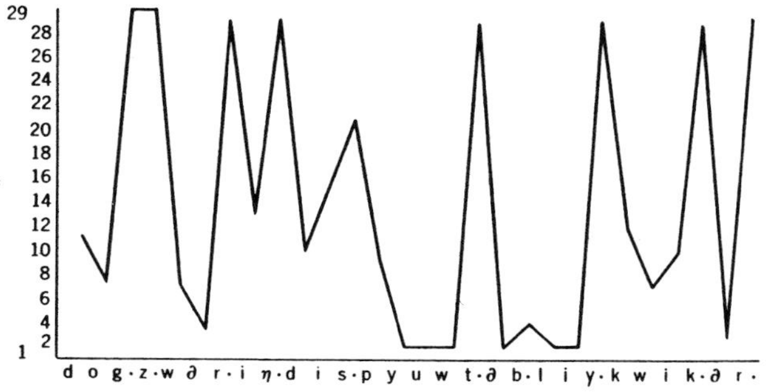

Fig. 6.12. Syntactic morph boundaries and the number of possible continuations after each phoneme in the English sentence 'Dogs were indisputably quicker.' The coordinate points connected with lines describe the number of possible continuations after each phoneme. The peaks of the graph correspond to the syntactic morph boundaries marked with dots in the phonetic transcription of the sentence. After Harris 1968: 25, fig. 1.3.

analysis is made possible by the redundancy built into natural languages.

Harris's method was developed for finding morphological boundaries in phoneme sequences, but it can be applied to morpheme sequences as well. The method has to be slightly modified, however, because the cohesion between morphemes is much looser than between phonemes (in connected speech, adjacent sounds frequently assimilate to each other). A syntax tree for a morpheme sequence can be formed by counting the texts that are identical up to each node, and by counting the possible continuations. The number of different signs that can follow is expected to rise at a major syntactic boundary (fig. 6.13).

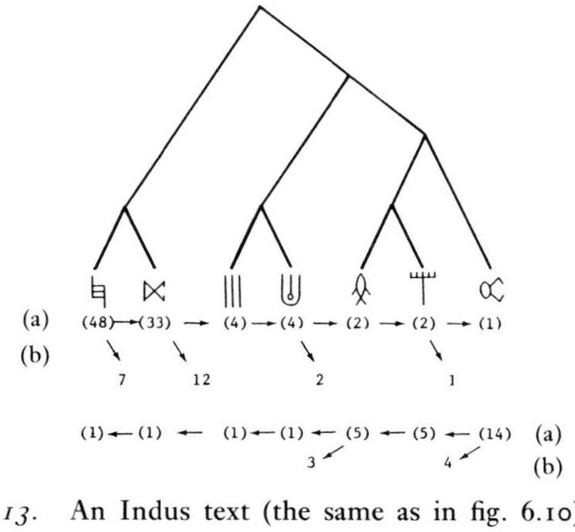

Fig. 6.13. An Indus text (the same as in fig. 6.10) analysed according to the 'Harris method'. After Koskenniemi 1981: 129, fig. 2. (a) = number of inscriptions identical up to this sign. (b) = number of different next signs.

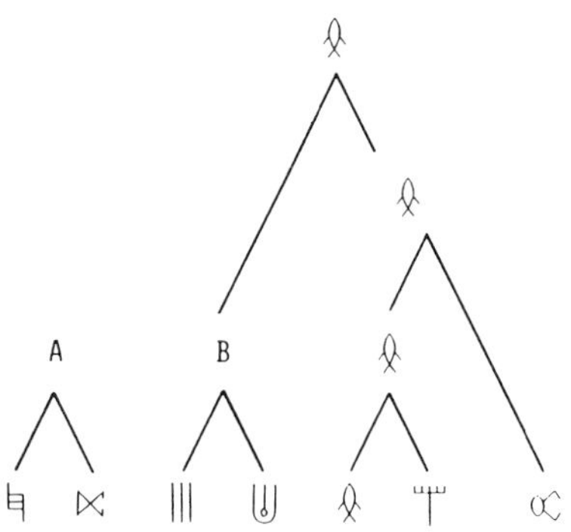

Fig. 6.14. Nodes of a syntactic tree that govern both an obligatory and an optional element can be labelled according to the obligatory constituent. After Koskenniemi 1981: 130, fig. 3.

Figure 6.13 gives a syntax tree for the same Indus text that was syntagmatically analysed in figure 6.10. It has been constructed by using texts in the corpus that have an identical beginning or ending. These two syntax trees have been constructed according to different criteria, but they are remarkably similar. Only the two highest nodes have changed their order; all lower-level constituents are identical.

The syntax trees in figures 6.10 and 6.13 are unlabelled. Even a preliminary study of the paradigmatic relations shows that certain elements are optional, that is, one can find inscriptions containing a particular element and others without it that are otherwise identical. Nodes that govern both an obligatory and an optional element can be labelled according to the obligatory constituent, as in figure 6.14. The problems with the segmentation can now be seen if we look at the three signs that are furthest to the right in the sample inscription. Should there be one, two or three segments? None of these alternatives would seem adequately to reflect the relations between these signs.

The proposed formal descriptive grammar for the Indus corpus is to have (at least) two levels of categories: subcategories for signs or sign pairs with very similar distribution, and broader categories for collecting similarly functioning subcategories together. These broader categories would also cover whatever constructions are discovered (for instance, attribute + noun that functions like a single noun). The direction of synthesis is from the bottom up, starting from the lowest level of the syntax tree.

In the *paradigmatic approach*, the degree of similarity between two different signs (T, R) is computed on the basis of their distributions; that is, how often they occur next to specific signs on the left (S_1) and on the right (S_2). A similarity index is calculated for each pair of signs. Two signs with a high similarity are distributed very similarly and are expected to have syntactic properties that resemble each other. Such

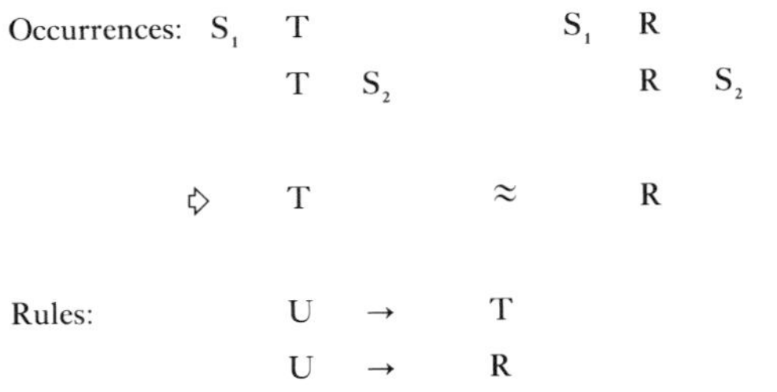

Fig. 6.15. Rule-forming in the paradigmatic approach. After P. Parpola 1987: 3.

signs might be words belonging to the same part of speech, for instance. In a grammar, this could be presented by rules which produce these signs from the same non-terminal symbol (U) (fig. 6.15).

The paradigmatic approach can take the syntagmatic analysis a stage further, by discovering whether the distribution of a sign pair with a strong syntactic connection is similar to the distribution of either of the signs occurring in it. Only occurrences outside the pair are taken as representatives of the individual signs. For instance, if TR is a pair with a particularly strong syntactic connection, either the rule T →TR, the rule R →TR or the rule U →TR (where U is a new non-terminal) is recommended according to the distributions of the signs and the entire sequence.

The formal grammar is developed stepwise, through repeated statistical analysis. The grammar grows gradually as the work proceeds. Each addition or correction to the current version of the grammar is based on the statistics and lists that have been computed using the information in the current grammar. Thus every iteration of the program produces a number of possible rules, out of which the user chooses the ones to be added to the grammar. Between iterations the original set of strings is always replaced with one obtained by partially parsing the original set according to the current version of the grammar. This is repeated until the user is satisfied with the grammar (fig. 6.16).

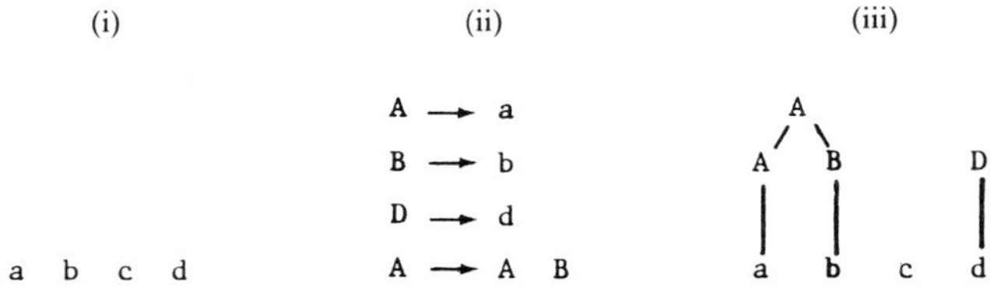

Fig. 6.16. Parsing a string according to an intermediate grammar. The sentence to be parsed is on the left (i), a fraction of an intermediate grammar in the middle (ii), and the partial parse induced by this grammar on the right (iii). The next analysis would be performed on the string AcD. After Koskenniemi 1981: 131.

Table 6.2. *The first ten pairs of words most similar to each other in an English text, obtained by means of the paradigmatic analysis on the first iteration*

similarity index	$sign_1$	$sign_2$	$freq._1$	$freq._2$
0.77	south	north	25	21
0.76	Pacific	Atlantic	7	6
0.76	Mark	Juan	57	60
0.56	looked	look	6	8
0.47	happening	going	6	8
0.44	Europe	Asia	8	7
0.40	said	asked	110	37
0.36	ground	earth	7	31
0.36	learn	find	7	11
0.34	right	left	9	7

Based on P. Parpola 1987.

How do we know that we are going in the right direction as we add new rules to the grammar? The addition of correct rules is expected to produce grammars in which the broad categories stay well apart from each other, while that of incorrect ones tends to produce a single dummy category that covers anything.

The method has been tested by running the program with English text material (table 6.2). The amount of material is about the same as that in the Indus corpus, though the sentences are longer. Each word form ('sign') occurring in the text has been replaced by a given number. Initially only signs occurring five times or more in the texts were included in the analysis. (The minimum absolute frequency of occurrence of any sign can be built into the program.)

The meaning of the signs in this English example is known, so the analysis suggests the terms in which the discovered similarity between the signs may be interpreted: both signs in each pair normally belong to the same word class and are semantically close to each other (being usually synonyms or antonyms); sometimes they share the same grammatical form or are different forms of the same word.

The same analysis has been run with the Indus material (figs. 6.17–18). Confidence in the results is increased by the fact that the program correctly identifies the numeral signs as similar to each other without the clues provided by their visual form (§ 5.2).

The grid constructed for the decipherment of Linear B indicated identical initial segments of the signs in each row and identical final segments in each column (fig. 3.3). The grid did not give any actual values for these segments, but any value guessed for any one sign would automatically imply the same first segment for the whole row, and the same final

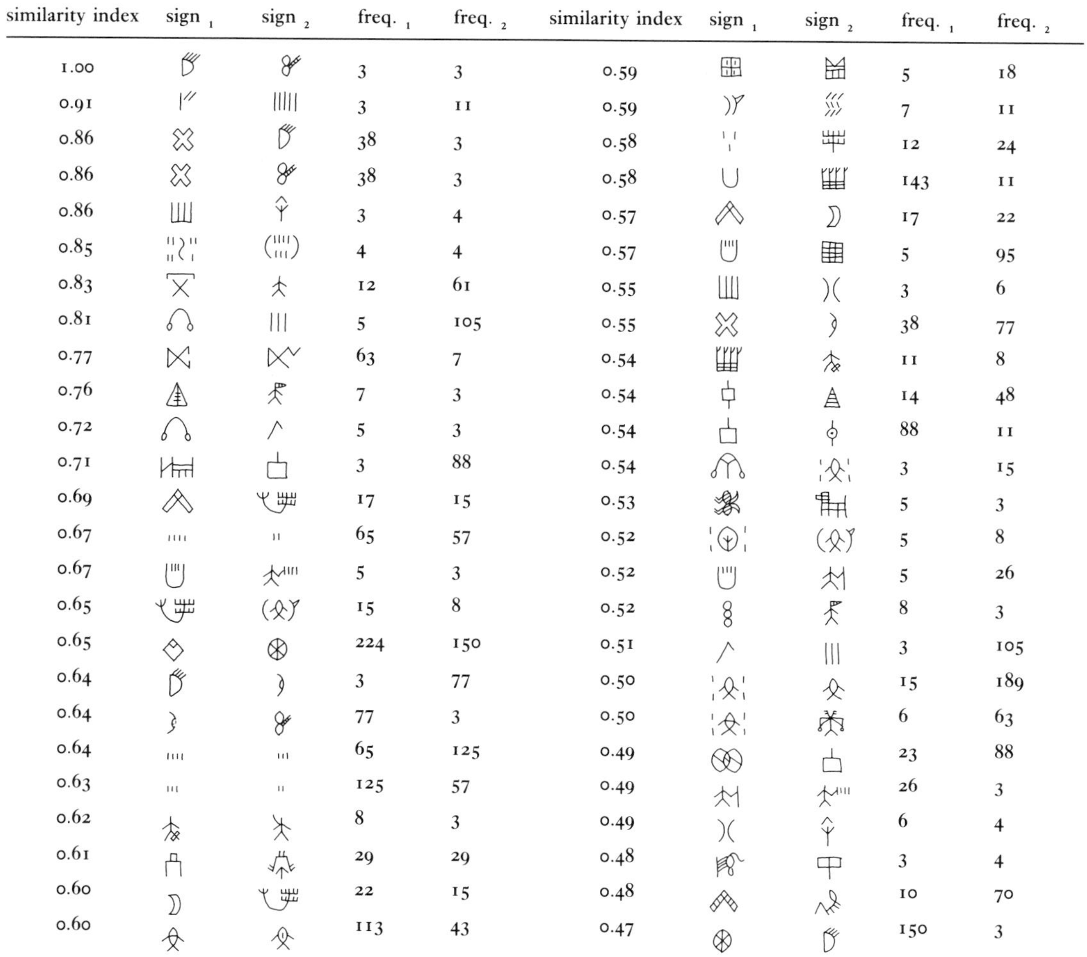

similarity index	sign 1	sign 2	freq. 1	freq. 2	similarity index	sign 1	sign 2	freq. 1	freq. 2
1.00			3	3	0.59			5	18
0.91			3	11	0.59			7	11
0.86			38	3	0.58			12	24
0.86			38	3	0.58			143	11
0.86			3	4	0.57			17	22
0.85			4	4	0.57			5	95
0.83			12	61	0.55			3	6
0.81			5	105	0.55			38	77
0.77			63	7	0.54			11	8
0.76			7	3	0.54			14	48
0.72			5	3	0.54			88	11
0.71			3	88	0.54			3	15
0.69			17	15	0.53			5	3
0.67			65	57	0.52			5	8
0.67			5	3	0.52			5	26
0.65			15	8	0.52			8	3
0.65			224	150	0.51			3	105
0.64			3	77	0.50			15	189
0.64			77	3	0.50			6	63
0.64			65	125	0.49			23	88
0.63			125	57	0.49			26	3
0.62			8	3	0.49			6	4
0.61			29	29	0.48			3	4
0.60			22	15	0.48			10	70
0.60			113	43	0.47			150	3

Fig. 6.17. The first 50 pairs of signs most similar to each other in the Indus corpus, obtained by means of paradigmatic analysis on the first iteration. The method used is exactly the same as that used for computing table 6.2. Based on P. Parpola 1987.

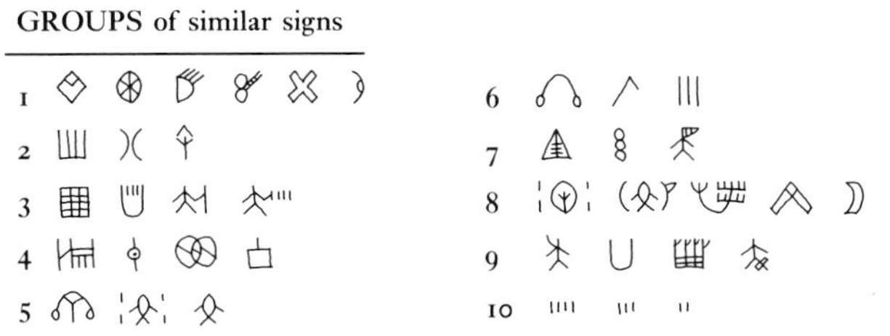

Fig. 6.18. List of the first ten groups of similar signs in the Indus corpus obtained after several iterations. Note that the last group consists of numbers only. Based on P. Parpola 1987.

segment for the whole column. Thus the positive (or negative) effect of any guess was greatly amplified, and this led to a solution.

Assuming the Indus script to be a logo-syllabic writing system, we are not trying to establish similar phonological grids. What we are endeavouring to create instead is a formal grammar of the corpus that indicates the paradigmatic and syntagmatic relations of the signs and sign sequences. The stricter categories are expected to indicate both syntactic and semantic similarity, the broader categories plainly syntactic similarity. A guess concerning the value of a single sign will imply a syntactically and semantically similar value for all other signs within the same strict category, and a syntactically similar function for all signs in the broad category. In this way, we can hope to reach a similar amplification of the consequences of guesses as in the decipherment of Linear B, but the similarity is in the levels of syntax and semantics rather than in the phonological level.

The formal grammar of the Indus inscriptions, which is in preparation, will thus be useful in limiting the range of guesswork when a breakthrough is achieved. But the breakthrough itself cannot be achieved by this method.

7 External clues to the Indus script

7.1 Basic methodology for deciphering the Indus script

Logo-syllabic scripts, unlike alphabetic and syllabic scripts, cannot be deciphered at a stroke. In an alphabetic or syllabic script, each sign has only one value as a rule, and these values are all phonetic and interrelated, forming a closed system. Once the phonetic values of a few signs have been correctly determined, their contexts will suggest the values of the remaining signs. Logo-syllabic scripts are open systems; their signs may have several values and represent larger linguistic units with interrelationships that are not nearly so clearly defined. Nevertheless, if the Indus script is logo-syllabic or morphemic writing, we can devise a basic methodology for deciphering it.

The earliest logo-syllabic scripts are based on the rebus principle. Many of the signs were originally pictures denoting the objects they represented. But in order to express things impossible to represent by pictures in a simple and unambiguous manner, the meaning of a pictogram was extended from the word for the depicted object to all its homophones, that is, words with a similar phonetic shape but a different meaning. For example, in the Sumerian script the drawing of an arrow meant 'arrow' but also 'life' and 'rib', because all three words were pronounced alike in the Sumerian language: *ti*.

Homophones are language-specific: they do not normally translate. This does not prevent aetiological myths based on homophony from travelling like any other myths and stories. Why, for example, was Eve created from Adam's rib? The Biblical story is made comprehensible by the older Sumerian paradise myth, in which the goddess *Nin-ti* 'Mistress Life' healed the rib of the sick god Enki. This myth relies on the identical sounds of the Sumerian words for 'life' and 'rib'. The Hebrew name of Eve, *Ḥawwā*, also means 'life'; but it bears no resemblance to the Hebrew word for 'rib', *ṣēlaᶜ*.

The use of the rebus principle may therefore help us to

identify an ancient language and to decipher parts of its script, but only if four conditions are simultaneously fulfilled: (1) the object depicted in a given pictogram can be recognized; (2) the pictogram has been used phonetically for a word with the same sound as, but a meaning different from, the object it represents; (3) this intended meaning (expressed by the pun) can be deduced from the context; and (4) a linguistically satisfactory homophony with these two meanings exists in a likely language.

If an opening can be effected, the order of the operations can be permuted.

7.2 The iconic meaning of the signs

The pictorial nature of some Indus signs constitutes one of the chief keys to their interpretation. If a sign has been used in its ideographic (iconic) meaning, that meaning may be roughly understood directly, irrespective of how any word corresponding to the sign was pronounced in the language of the Indus texts.

The problem is that the pictorial meaning of most Indus signs is not clear. As in many other scripts, the demand for fluency in writing led to a radical simplification of the shapes. The signs were reduced to the barest essentials. This tendency has not gone as far as in the Sumerian script, where the recognizable shapes of the earliest phase soon gave way to cuneiform symbols; but the student of the Indus script certainly envies the intelligibility of the Egyptian hieroglyphs.

Nevertheless, individual inscriptions may contain naturalistic variants revealing the pictorial meaning of a sign. For example, from seal Nd-1 (fig. 7.1a) it appears that the sign  represents the five-striped palm squirrel (*Funambulus pennanti* Wroughton), 'the commonest and most familiar of all Indian wild animals' (Prater 1971: 201), which is found in cities and villages throughout the Indus plains, and is represented among the Harappan animal figurines (fig. 7.1b). The creators of the Indus script have tried to secure the identification by depicting the animal in its typical pose (fig. 7.1c): 'In cool weather, the squirrels ... have been seen to hang head down in the sun on the vertical trunk of a tree for considerable periods' (Roberts 1977: 228). This habit has given the palm squirrel its Sanskrit name *vr̥kṣa-śāyikā* 'sleeping in the tree' (Suśruta, 1,46,76). An interpretation of this sign is attempted in § 13.1.

A comparative study of the allographs provides one important means of identifying the iconic meaning of even fairly abstract shapes. The proposed interpretation must fit all the allographs. The following long parallel inscriptions suggest that the signs  and  may represent one and the same grapheme:

(a)

(b)

(c)

Fig. 7.1. (a) An Indus sign probably depicting the palm squirrel (sleeping head downwards on a tree): the first sign on the left in the inscription of a seal stamp (Nd-1) from Nindowari-damb. (b) Two faience figurines of the palm squirrel from Mohenjo-daro. After During Caspers 1985c: pl. 1 a. (c) The five-striped palm squirrel (*Funambulus pennanti* Wroughton) in typical pose. After Roberts 1977: 227 (ill. 66).

```
2436        ⇡⇡⟡⟡"◇⊟⇡⟩⟩⊗
2654     ⋃◇‖‖‖⋃⟡⟡"◇⊟⇡⟩⟩⊗
```

As there are very few signs that occur immediately before the sequence "◇, it is almost certain that the sign ⊟, also occurring in this position, is an allograph of ⊢and ⊟. Another less certain allograph, ⊟, can be added to this list, which forms a continuum: ⊢⊟⊟⊟. Taken together, these signs can be understood as pictures of a single object, namely, 'steps, staircase, or ladder'; taken individually, such a conclusion would hardly be possible.

The fact that ligatured signs may be attached to different parts of the body in the 'man' component is significant. Where the added sign was placed in each case seems to have depended on its (pictorial) meaning. Thus the graphic variant ⋏ suggests that the horizontal element in the sign ⋏ might depict a beak, and this interpretation is supported by the attachment of this element to the head in the ligature ⋏.

Provided one abstains from unlikely conclusions about the genetic relationship between different writing systems and from assigning phonetic values to Indus signs on this basis (§ 4.2), similar-looking pictograms in other ancient scripts can be valuable clues to the pictorial meaning of the Indus signs (fig. 4.6). For example, the Indus signs ⟩ and ⟨, which may have been turned 90° in order to save space, have parallels in the Egyptian hieroglyph ⌢ for the sickle moon and the Sumerian pictogram ⌣, which is assumed to depict the sun rising among the eastern mountains. The Sumerian sign later came to mean 'sun, sun-god, day, daylight, white'; combined with various diacritics and numerals, it is assumed to have expressed divisions of time (days, months and years) in the Uruk texts. It is noteworthy that the Indus signs too are modified with diacritics.

Essential hints of pictorial meanings are given by the archaeological remains of the Indus Civilization and the antecedent Early Harappan cultures, which are close to the date of creation of the Indus script. Clues may be found in architecture, in tools and weapons, and in art. Art on painted pottery (figs. 10.20, 13.16) and in the motifs of seals and tablets (figs. 7.12, 10.1) is of special significance as it reveals the native Harappan way of representation. Comparisons should also be sought in quite unrelated ancient civilizations and in ethnology; the latter can suggest, for example, the shapes of wooden tools which the Harappans may have used but which have not survived (fig. 7.2).

Simplification is likely often to have obscured the pictorial meaning. A prime example is the most frequent Indus sign ⋃, whose importance calls for some discussion. It has been suggested that the sign depicts a jar or a fig tree. These meanings, however, suit other Indus signs better (§ 7.3 and §§ 13.3–14.1). Moreover, the former explanation, which

derives it from 'a tall vase with a slightly concavo-convex profile and narrow base' (Lal 1975b: 176) fails to account for the characteristic extensions at the top. The hypothesis (based on Sumerian and Egyptian parallels) that these are the lip and handles of a jar is not corroborated by the archaeological evidence, for no such jar can be found in the inventory of Harappan vessel types (Dales and Kenoyer 1986). Many Indus signs have variant forms, and if the sign ⋃ depicts a fig tree, then it is strange that more than two 'branches' are hardly ever shown (the only exception is ⋃ in seal 5021). There are three branches on each side of the tree in the 'fig deity' seal (fig. 14.35), which is the basis of this interpretation. The similarity of the sign ⋃ to a motif on Iranian and Early Harappan painted pottery (fig. 7.3) has made me think of such iconic meanings as 'bird', 'eagle', 'wing' or 'to fly', but this explanation, too, suffers from the absence of variants showing more than two 'feathers' on either side.

The best explanation I can offer is that the sign ⋃ may have developed from a frontal picture of a cow's head, the two projections on either side representing a pair of horns and a pair of ears. Closely similar cow head motifs have in fact been found painted on Early Harappan pottery from Rahman Dheri (fig. 7.4c–i). Comparable animal heads can be found in Near Eastern glyptics (fig. 7.4a–b). A simplified boucranium has been a popular motif in many places.

Techniques of writing and engraving, style, and considerations of space have undoubtedly all influenced the shape of many Indus signs. Thus the early variant ⋔ of the sign ⋿(§ 4.1) can be explained as representing an intermediate stage in the process of turning this sign into a vertical position in order to save space: the Harappan pottery with its 'comb' motifs suggests that this sign was originally lying in a horizontal position. The sign ⊘◇, which resembles Harappan ladles made of conch shell, appears in both a round and an angular variant. The original form of the Indus sign ⊕ seems to have been circular, as in some of its graphic variants – ⊕ – and to have become elliptical later for reasons of space.

In its round form the sign ⊕ is strikingly similar to some prominent symbols of kingship in Near Eastern as well as in later Indian iconography and religion (fig. 7.5). Of course such analogies may be purely coincidental. Given the discontinuity between the Indus script and the earliest historical writing of India (§ 4.1), one may well ask how much credence can be placed on later Indian parallels, particularly those transmitted in Sanskrit and other Indo-Aryan languages. There is some concrete evidence suggesting that the later South Asian tradition has preserved genuine Harappan survivals (figs. 4.6, 1.9–10). In the field of religion such a link is particularly likely, and the 'wheel' symbol can be traced back to times not far removed from the Indus Civilization. Nevertheless, purely iconic interpretations

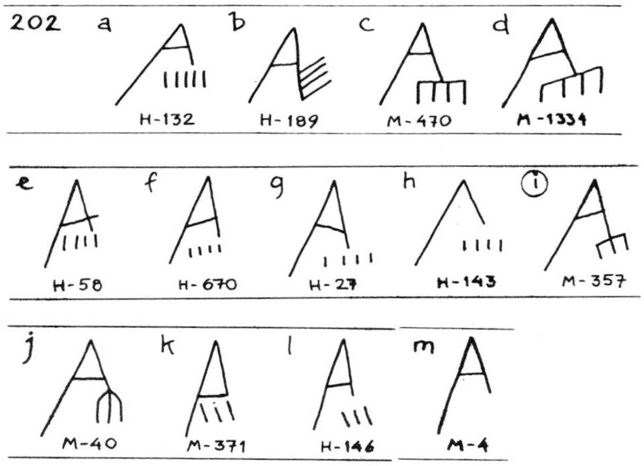

(a)

(b)

Fig. 7.2. (a) Graphic variants of an Indus sign that may be interpreted as different representations of 'hoe' or 'hoeing'. (b) A man hoeing a field in the wall painting from the tomb of Nakht at Thebes, Egypt, *c.*1420 BC (now in the Metropolitan Museum of Art, New York). Cf. Parpola 1975a: 189, fig. 7.

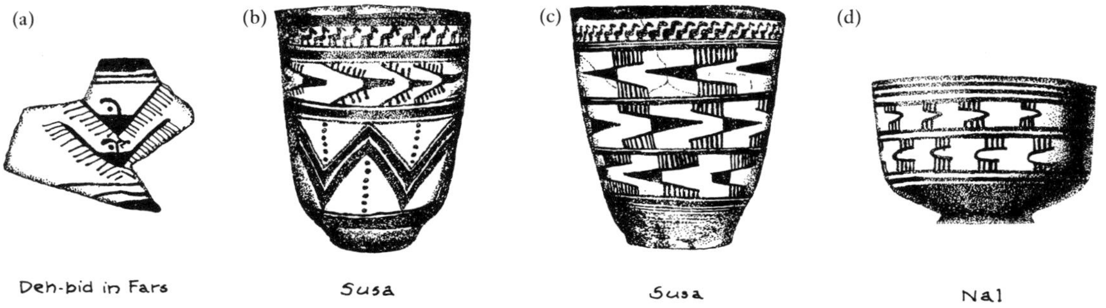

Fig. 7.3. The motif of a 'flying bird' on the painted pottery from Iran and Baluchistan. (a) Deh-bid in Fars, Iran. Drawn after Starr 1941: 50, no. 72. (b–c) Susa I (*c.*4100–3500 BC) in Iran. Drawn after Marshall 1931a: III, pl. 93: 4s and 6s. (d) Nal in Baluchistan (*c.*2600 BC). Drawn after Marshall 1931a, III, pl. 93: 5n.

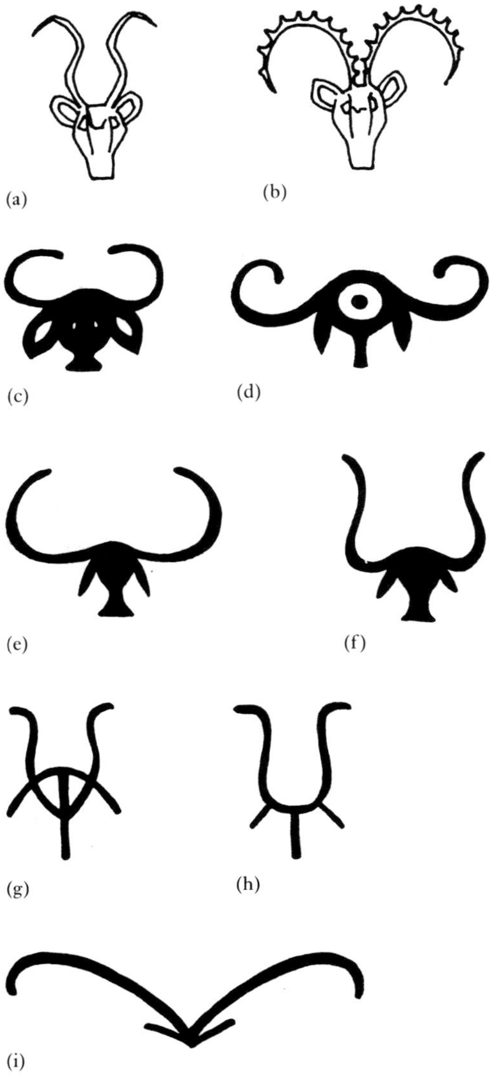

Fig. 7.4. Frontal images of animal heads with horns and ears. (a, b) An Early Dynastic A–B (probably Proto-Elamite) seal from Iran. Drawn after Collon 1987: no. 55. (c–i) Painted potsherds from Rahman Dheri. Drawn after *CISI* 2: 372ff.: (c) Rhd-241, (d) Rhd-242, (e) Rhd-243, (f) Rhd-240, (g) Rhd-246, (h) Rhd-245, (i) Rhd-249.

Fig. 7.5. The solar 'wheel' of cosmic law or righteousness (*dharmacakra*) was one of the foremost symbols of royalty in ancient India. Here it distinguishes the universal emperor (*cakravartin*) who, protected by the royal parasol and surrounded by his chief queen, his chief minister and the crown prince, stands in a heavenly shower of gold. (According to Kālidāsa's Raghuvaṁśa, 5.29–33, even the miracle of a rain of gold, filling the royal treasury, can take place when the monarch abides by his duty.) At his feet are the imperial elephant and horse. A relief from the stupa at Jaggayyapeṭa on the lower Kistna river, Andhra Pradesh, *c.* first century BC. After V. S. Agrawala 1969: 93, fig. 44.

mostly remain hard to corroborate and cannot alone amount to a decipherment of the script.

7.3 Inscribed objects other than seals

The function of an object on which an Indus inscription occurs can be an important clue to the meaning of its signs. Weapons found in the ancient Near East carry texts identifying the owner, for instance (fig. 7.6). A bronze axe dated to *c.*2200 BC bears the inscription, 'Šu-Turul, the mighty, king of Akkad'. Five inscribed bronze axes provided the starting-point for the decipherment of the Ugaritic script (fig. 7.7). Charles Virolleaud (1929) guessed that their inscriptions might be analogous to later Phoenician arrow-heads inscribed 'the arrow of N. N.'. He then assumed that the first word on one axe meant 'axe', and suspected that the second word, found alone on the other four axes, denoted the owner. This hypothesis seemed to be supported by the occurrence of the second word at the beginning of a clay tablet, preceded by a single sign. Akkadian letters of the time normally begin with the preposition *ana* 'to', followed by the name of the addressee. Virolleaud now guessed, correctly, that the first word on the Ugaritic clay tablet was the West Semitic preposition *la* 'to'.

The owner of the Ugaritic axes was found to be the 'head priest'. The 'head priest' or 'king' could well be the owner of two copper axe blades found at Mohenjo-daro, which bear a distinctive sequence of seven pictograms; for this very same

Fig. 7.6. A votive shaft-hole axe made of silver and electrum and ornamented with the figure of a boar and the head of a lion. 5.9 × 12.5 cm. From the temple of the goddess Kiririsha at Tchoga-Zanbil (near Susa in southwestern Iran), capital of king Untash-Napirisha. *c.*1250 BC. The cuneiform inscription on the blade is in the Middle Elamite language and means: 'Me, Untash-Napirisha.' Musée du Louvre / *AO* (sb 3972). After *Naissance de l'écriture* 1982: 103, no. 60.

Fig. 7.7. An inscribed axe-adze from Ras Shamra (ancient Ugarit) in Syria. The text written in cuneiform alphabet reads *ḫrṣn rb khnm* 'axe of the high priest'. Thirteenth century BC. Bronze. Height of the shaft: 4.5 cm; length: 23 cm; max. width: 5 cm. Musée du Louvre / *AO* 11 611. After *Naissance de l'écriture* 1982: 178, no. 117.

sequence is also found on a fragmentary seal discovered nearby and in a clay impression of another, large seal (fig. 7.8).

There are numbers, too, on copper weapons or tools: series of short vertical strokes for numbers 1 to 9 and semicircles probably standing for tens. Are they inventory numbers, or do they record the weight of the precious objects on which they are inscribed? If the original weight can be determined with fair accuracy, this alternative can be tested.

In the case of pots, most of the graffiti scratched on the rims after firing, or sometimes on the body of the pot, are bare numbers. Signs incised in the wet clay before the firing are much less frequent; still rarer are script signs painted on pots, though there are a number of stamped seal impressions on pottery vessels. But did an inscription or seal indicate the potter or the person or institution for whom the pot was made? A similar question may be asked of the large storage jars, which have inscriptions raised in relief on their bases, formed by negative incisions in the open mould where they were manufactured.

Clues to the meaning of these inscriptions may again be sought among comparable texts that can be read. A number of Mesopotamian pots have inscriptions indicating their capacity: e.g. a large jar of 180 litres from Nippur in the Ur III period has written on both rim and shoulder '$175\frac{5}{6}$ sila'. Other vessels, usually made of expensive materials such as alabaster or bronze, carry the owner's name or dedications to divinities. In India, in later times, earthen pots bear almost exclusively proper names, apparently of the owners. Inscriptions on vessels made of other materials record dedications to temples or other religious institutions.

The few inscriptions on the early Chinese pots of the Shang dynasty at An-yang (second millennium BC) are single characters: either numbers or the name of the owner. 'A very unusual case is the large character *ssu* [= Pinyin *si*], "sacrifice", written with ink and brush on a potsherd' (Tsien 1962: 58). Later Chinese pottery inscriptions, mostly seal impressions, 'generally include names of makers or owners, official titles, places, dates of vessels and their manufacture' (ibid.: 60).

A major category of Indus texts consists of small 'tablets' in various forms and materials; they have text, and occasionally pictorial motifs, on one, two, three, four or six sides. Among the oldest examples of the Indus script are the 'miniature tablets' from the lower levels of Harappa, incised flat plates of steatite. Engraved copper tablets are known from Mohenjo-daro only, a few cast copper tablets from both Mohenjo-daro and Harappa. In addition, terracotta or faience tablets were mass-produced in moulds; their texts are in relief. Sometimes large numbers of identical tablets have been found together, or in places close to one another. This has suggested that the tablets may have been tokens of votive offerings to temples, or amulets. Historical parallels may exist in the large numbers of identical seal impressions belonging to Hindu temples and mentioning the name of the deity. They are supposed to have been distributed by the priests to devotees visiting the shrine. The Chinese pilgrim Yi-jing remarks that seal impressions inscribed with the Buddhist creed, if placed in the stupas, were sources of great blessing. Such clay sealings were often returned to the worshippers, who kept them as potent objects of worship.

The inscriptions on the Indus tablets point to a religious purpose. Many have on one side a U-shaped sign which looks like a pot drawn in profile, preceded by between zero and four vertical strokes that clearly stand for numbers (fig. 7.9). Three identical tablets (fig. 7.10) have the sequence UUU (which occurs also in the longest Indus text; see § 5.3): this may be another way of writing the sequence U||| that occurs on numerous tablets and may mean 'three pots' (§ 5.2). Sometimes, the U-shaped sign on the reverse of the tablets is

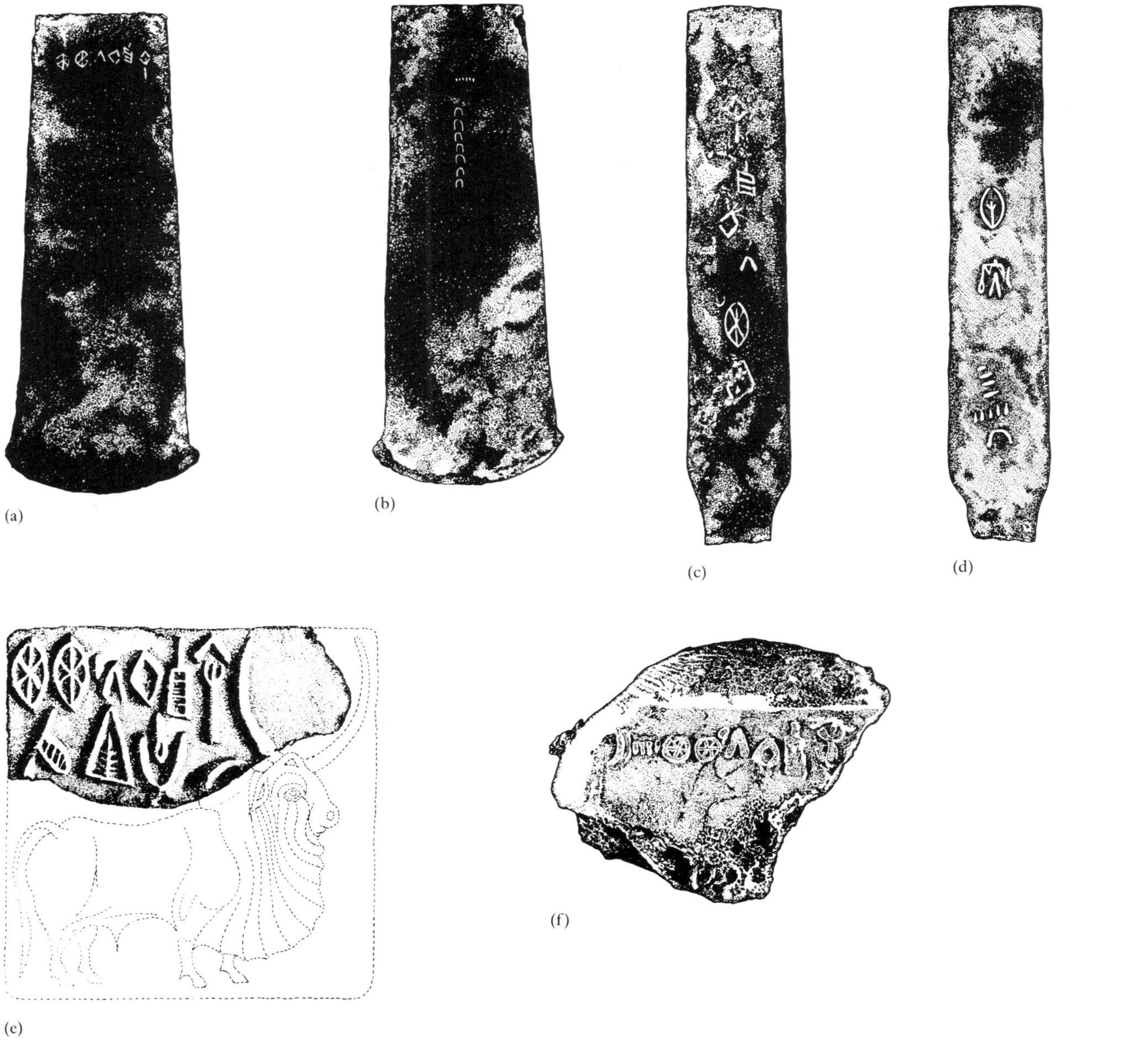

Fig. 7.8. Recurrence of a distinctive sequence of seven Indus signs (possibly ending in a royal title) on copper axes and seals found at Mohenjo-daro. Obverse (a, c) and reverse (b, d) of two axe blades (2798 = DK 7856 and 2796 = DK 7535) found (as part of a hoard of many copper objects) in room 15, house I, block 12A, G section, DK area. (e) A fragmentary seal (2119) from room 5, house I, block 26, G section, DK area. (f) Impression of a large seal (*c*.4.5 × 4.5 cm) on a clay tag found in the drain 124, house X, block 8, HR-B area. Drawn after Mackay 1938: II, pl. 126: 5 and pl. 131: 35–6; Photo Archive of the ASI, Sind vol. 17, p. 79: 400 (= a–b); Mackay 1938: II, pl. 126: 2; pl. 131: 31; Sind vol. 17, p. 80: 403–4 (= c–d); Mackay 1938: II, pl. 85: 119 (= e); *CISI* 2: 183, M-1384 (= f). See also pp. 116–17.

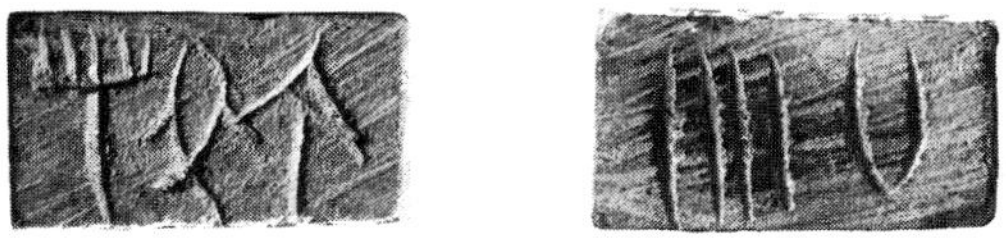

(a) (b)

Fig. 7.9. (a) Obverse and (b) reverse of a typical 'miniature tablet' (3458) from the lower levels of Harappa. The writing is reversed (cf. p. 64). See also fig. 13.1.

Fig. 7.10. The reverse of a moulded tablet (H-764) from Harappa.

Fig. 7.11. The reverse of a miniature tablet from Harappa (H-247) showing a kneeling man who holds the 'vessel' sign U preceded by the sign || = 'number two'.

Fig. 7.12. 'Sacrificial vessel' in the iconography and text of a moulded tablet (M-478) from Mohenjo-daro.

held in the hand of a kneeling or standing 'man' sign (fig. 7.11). On one particular moulded tablet (existing in several identical copies), we see an anthropomorphic deity sitting on a low dais, flanked on either side by a kneeling man and a snake; one of these supplicant men has both his hands raised in worship, while the other is giving what looks like a sacrificial vessel to the deity (fig. 13.2b). Another moulded tablet (again available in several copies) has a similar offering scene, except that here the kneeling worshipper holds out the pot towards a tree (fig. 7.12, right-hand side). On both tablets the sacrificial vessel looks exactly like the U-formed Indus sign, but on the second the iconographic motif is accompanied by the text E |大| U ''''. It seems evident that the tree is sacred and that the sacrificing person (possibly expressed by the phrase E |大|) has presented four pots (= the sequence U '''') to its deity (another possible meaning of the phrase E |大|) as an offering. This most important tablet also suggests that some of the pot inscriptions may be of a dedicatory nature.

The interpretation is supported by other considerations as well. The Egyptian hieroglyph [hieroglyph] depicting 'forearm with hand holding bowl' functions as a determinative with the meaning 'offer, present'. In South India, offerings of various kinds (milk, sugar, honey, flowers, fruits, fish, even snakes) are traditionally brought in pots to the Tamil god Murukaṉ, who is identified with the North Indian war-god Skanda (§ 13.1); these sacrificial vessels are carried on the shoulders with a ceremonial carrying yoke (*kāvaṭi*). This custom can be traced back to very early North Indian sources. According to Vedic descriptions of a sacrifice called Tryambakahoma (ŚB 2,6,2,17; KŚS 5,10,21; ĀpŚS 8,18,9), 'baskets' or 'bundles' (*mūṭa*) with cakes (*apūpa*) for Rudra (the dreaded Vedic predecessor of Skanda) are to be fixed on a carrying pole (*vīvadha* or *veṇu-yaṣṭi* 'bamboo stick'); this shoulder yoke with its baskets is then carried northwards and hung on a tree, a dry stump, a bamboo or a termite hill, so high that a cow cannot reach it, with this mantra: 'This, O Rudra, is your part; with this provision go over to the other side of the Mūjavat mountain, dressed in skin, with the Pināka weapon in your hand, and with your bow unstrung.' (For Rudra and his bow see § 13.4.)

In the longest Indus inscription (§ 5.3), the sequence of 'three sacrificial vessels' (the 'vessel' sign repeated three times) occurs next to the sign [sign] that without a doubt represents 'a man carrying pots by means of a shoulder yoke' (compare the graphic variants in fig. 5.1, no. 1). This co-occurrence recurs elsewhere in significant contexts. One is tablet 1532 from Mohenjo-daro with an inscription closely parallel to that of fig. 7.12: [sign] |大| U|||. The sequence '3' + 'vessel' (i.e. 'three vessels') follows after the 'yoke carrier' sign on one side of a tablet from Harappa (fig. 7.13a), while the reverse side of this tablet shows a person kneeling with uplifted arms in front of an anthropomorphic deity within a sacred fig tree (fig. 7.13b). The Āśvalāyana-Gṛhyasūtra (1,12,1–3) also contains a rare reference to the non-Vedic *caitya* cult well known from Buddhist and Jaina texts: if the caitya shrine (often a sacred tree with or without a railing or some more elaborate building) happens to be far off, one may send one's sacrificial offering (*bali*) in the baskets of a shoulder

(a)

(b)

Fig. 7.13. (a) The 'sacrificial vessel' and 'yoke carrier' signs in an inscription on the obverse of a faience tablet from Harappa (H-177). (b) The reverse shows worship of the 'fig deity' (§§ 14.3–4 and fig. 14.35).

yoke by a middleman. In Tamil, *kāvaṭi* 'carrying yoke' is also the name of a subcaste of the *Kuṟavar*, Gypsy-like wandering mountaineers and worshippers of Murukaṉ; the duties of this subcaste consist in bringing offerings to the god on a carrying yoke, and of carrying the god himself in religious processions. Thus the 'yoke carrier' sign of the Indus script may well refer to an individual worshipper or to a priestly officer bearing sacrificial offerings.

The shoulder yoke has been used to carry offerings in ancient China as well, for the pictogram [sign], which according to Bernhard Karlgren (1957: no. 740) probably depicts 'a man with a carrying pole on the shoulder', is used to write the word meaning 'sacrifice to the spirits of the four quarters'. This parallel gives occasion to note that it must have some special significance that the number connected with the 'vessel' sign on the Indus tablets never exceeds four. One explanation could be that a given sacrifice relates to one or another of the four quarters of space, another that a sacrifice relates to one or another of the four quarters of the year defined by the equinoxes and solstices (§ 11.2). The first alternative may be exemplified by the spring festival of the North Dravidian-speaking Oraons of Central India. The priest and his assistants, each carrying two pots on a carrying yoke, bring four pots full of water to a sacred grove. With one end of the carrying yoke, the priest traces out four grooves on the ground so as to make a rectangle. The pots are then placed in the four corners and left standing overnight. If any one of them has less water in the morning, this indicates that the rains will be less abundant in that direction.

These rare cases where inscription and iconographic motif clearly are related to each other (see also fig. 6.3) are extremely valuable clues to the meaning of the Indus signs: one can even consider them 'pictorial bilinguals'. The incised copper tablets from Mohenjo-daro, analysed in fig. 7.14, display this relationship. There are many groups of identical tablets, and the inscription on the obverse side always corresponds to a specific iconographic motif (normally an animal figure) or a short text on the reverse side. The mythical nature of the animals is suggested by the fact that many of them consist of parts belonging to different creatures. Sometimes, an identical inscription on the obverse connects two tablet groups whose reverse sides are different; interestingly, the iconographic motif on the reverse of one group often corresponds to a single script sign (usually a ligature) on the reverse of the other group. Supposing that they denote the same deity, I shall later (in §§ 13.3–5) try to interpret one ligature (on the reverse side of the tablets of group C6) and the corresponding picture of an archer, anthropomorphic except for his horns and tail (on the reverse side of the tablets of group B19).

Inscriptions have also been found on about two dozen short bone or ivory sticks decorated with geometrical motifs. Their function is unknown, but the occurrence of various numbers of concentric circles on different sides suggests that the sticks may have been used as dice or as mantic sticks; calendrical interpretations have been proposed too.

The number of inscribed bangles (fig. 13.5) has been increased to 40 by recent surface surveys at Mohenjo-daro. Just a few years ago they were almost unknown.

Miscellaneous objects with inscriptions include terracotta cones, a terracotta drainpipe, a shell ladle, a carved ivory plaque, a cubic ivory die (with the text [signs]), and small stone balls. With the possible addition of one broken stone slab from Harappa (3599), there is only one object that could be characterized as a monumental royal inscription. This 3-metre-long text was discovered near the city gate of Dholavira in 1990 (fig. 7.15). The ten large signs are to be read from left to right; in the following, however, the direction of writing has been normalized, so that the text reads from right to left thus: [signs]. The recurrence of the 'wheel' sign, possibly denoting 'king' (§§ 7.2 and 7.5), is noteworthy, as is the recurrence of a significantly long sequence of five signs in other contexts suggesting nobility (see fig. 7.8).

Finally, a terracotta bull figurine from Allahdino deserves special mention. It is probably a votive object representing a fertility-god, whose name may have been mentioned in the unfortunately fragmentary inscription [. . .] [sign]. The initial sign, which alone has been preserved, occurs chiefly in the sequences [signs] and [signs] in the other Indus texts, so the inscription on the bull may with some degree of probability be assumed to have consisted of one or the other of them.

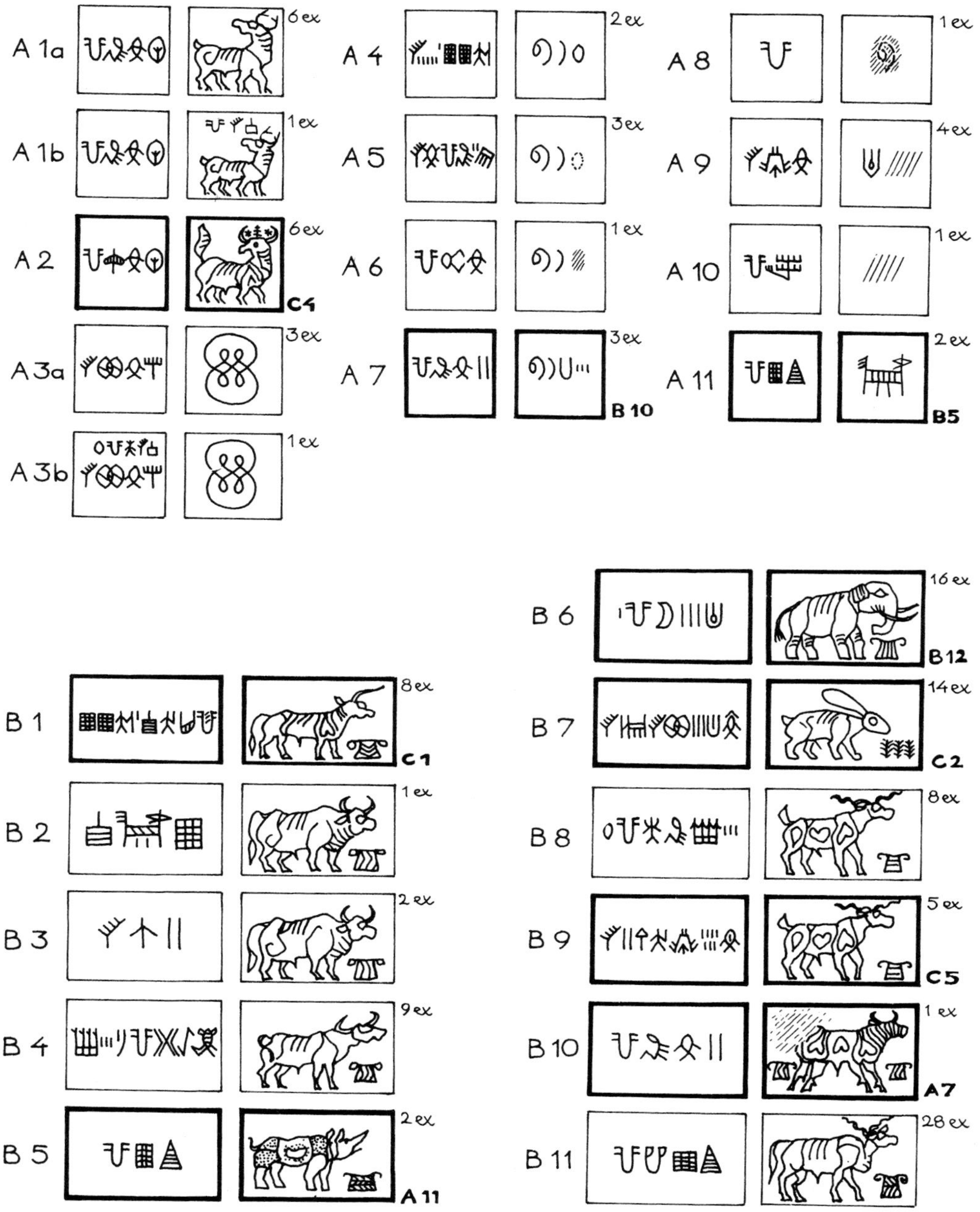

Fig. 7.14. A typological analysis of the copper tablets from Mohenjo-daro. After Parpola in press, c. Instead of showing each extant tablet in its present state of preservation, the figure records only the different prototypal tablets (with their original texts ± iconographic motifs reconstructed by comparing all the extant examples); the number in the upper right corner indicates how many (originally) identical tablets belonging to each group have been found. Uncertain reconstructions have been drawn with broken lines, and tablets too poorly preserved to allow classification have been excluded, together with the completely illegible ones.

The 46 tablet groups have been sorted first according to their shapes: A = square (34 tablets), B = rectangular (144 tablets) and C = long and narrow (rectangular) (39 tablets). Their average sizes are (A) 2.66 × 2.65 × 0.35 cm, (B) 3.38 × 2.65 × 0.35 cm, and (C) 3.30 × 2.40 × 0.30 cm. The next criterion of classification is the iconographic motif or inscription on the reverse side. The inscription on the obverse is the third distinguishing criterion. The addition of another (upper) line of inscription on either the obverse (as in A3, B15 and B17) or on the reverse (as in A1; cf. also B12), or the reversed direction of writing in the inscription(s) (as in C4 and C5) distinguish subgroups. The frames of certain (prototypal) tablets are drawn with a thicker line than the others. Each of these tablet groups is linked to another tablet group (referred to in bold face in the lower right corner) by an identical inscription, normally the inscription on the

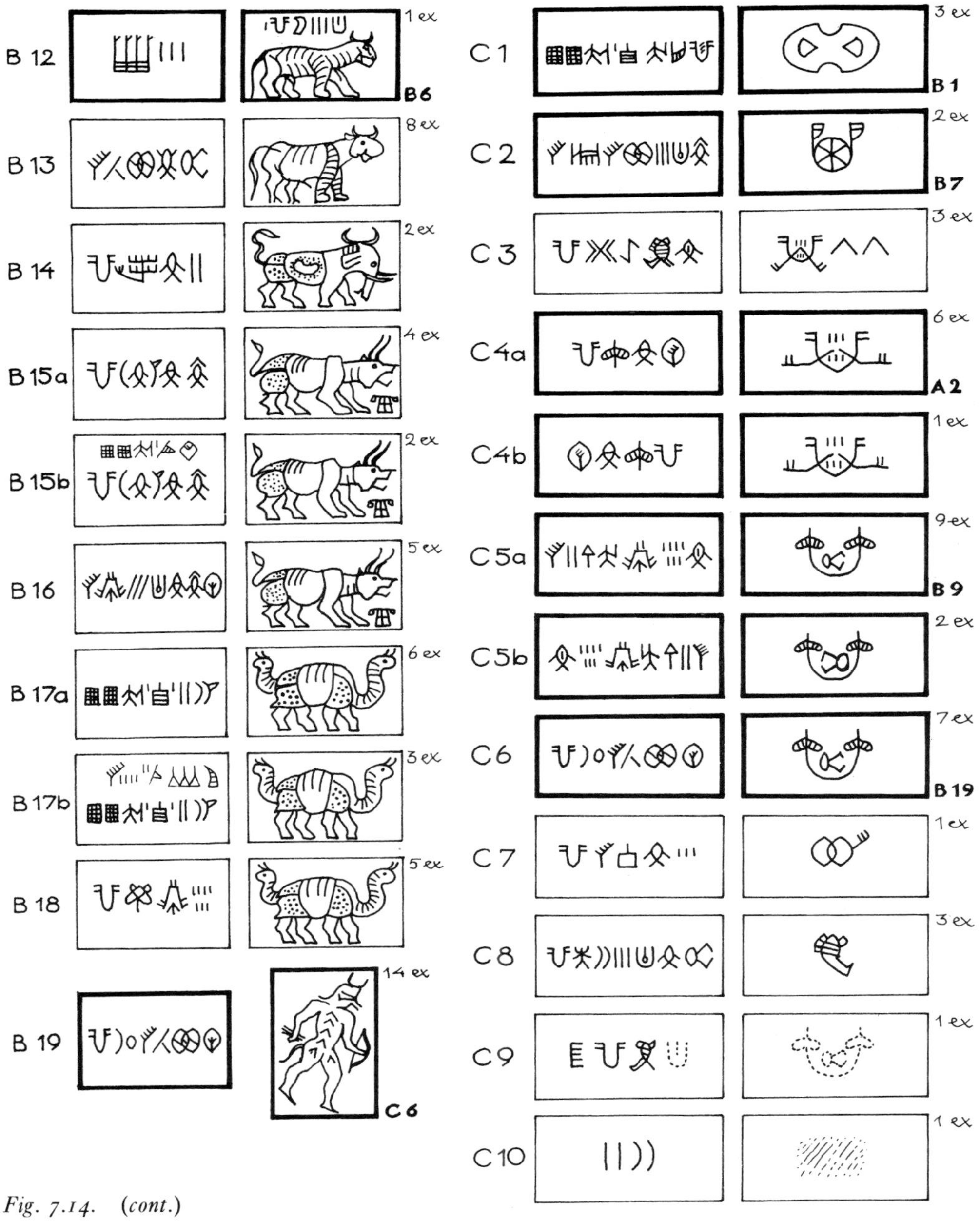

Fig. 7.14. (*cont.*)

obverse consisting of at least three but often many more signs. Group B12 is exceptional in that here it is the inscription on the reverse that connects this group with B6; this is also the only case in which tablet groups of the rectangular (B) shape are interrelated in this way. In all other cases the identical inscriptions connect an iconographic motif on the reverse of one group (A2, B1, B5, B7, B9, B10 and B19) with an inscription on the reverse side of another (C4, C1, A11, C2, C5, A7 and C6 respectively). Usually the inscription on the reverse side, which is thus linked with a particular iconographic motif, consists of a single Indus pictogram (B5, C2, C4, C5 and C6), rarely a longer sequence (A7, C3); one of the single pictograms (that occurring in both C5 and C6) is connected with two different iconographic motifs, the markhor goat (B9) and the horned archer (B19). In these cases, the iconographic motifs appear to express pictorially the same thing as the corresponding Indus signs express in writing: both seem to symbolize particular Harappan divinities.

Mackay (1931a: 401) plausibly thought that the copper tablets 'were probably used as amulets, wrapped up in some material and worn round the neck or wrist, or sewn to the clothing. This would account for the rough finish of some of them, for if worn in this way they would not have been exposed to view. It is possible that the possession of one of these amulets placed the wearer under the special protection of the deity whose particular animal was engraved upon it.'

(a)

(b)

Fig. 7.15. (a) A unique monumental inscription from the city of Dholavira in Kutch, Gujarat, found on the floor of the western chamber in the northern gate complex of the citadel. There are traces suggesting that the ten signs, each about 37 cm high and made of pieces of crystalline rock, were once inlaid in a wooden plank about 3 metres long; see the close-up (b) of the three first signs on the left. In a letter of 17 January 1993 the excavator, Dr R. S. Bisht, supposes that the inscription may have been sported on the façade of the gate so that it commanded the entire cityscape. In the poor conditions of Late Harappan times, the inscription may have been in danger of falling down and therefore removed to its present location.

(a)

(b)

Fig. 7.16. A clay tag from Umma, Iraq. (a) Obverse bearing an impression of a typically Harappan square stamp seal with Indus script and the 'unicorn' bull. (b) Reverse with an impression of cloth. Department of the Ancient Near East (accession no. 1931.120), Ashmolean Museum, Oxford.

7.4 Seals

Approximately 60 per cent of the Indus texts are inscriptions carved on seal stones intended for stamping wet clay. About 10 per cent of these seals are rectangular and show nothing but text, and a few have other shapes. Normally, the seals are square, with a line of text at the top of one face and beneath it an iconographic motif, most often the 'unicorn' bull facing an unidentified cult object (figs. 7.16a and 8.5).

The proportion of Indus inscriptions found on seals is further increased by the considerable number of ancient seal impressions that have survived. Those on pottery have already been mentioned. The vast majority are on tags once attached to bales of goods, for their reverse sides usually show traces of packing materials such as woven cloth or reed matting. One such impression comes from Umma in Mesopotamia (fig. 7.16). Of special significance in understanding Harappan bureaucracy is the corpus of nearly a hundred clay labels from the burnt-down warehouse or granary at Lothal; there all the tags were in use simultaneously and the seal impressions are interrelated (fig. 7.17).

In ancient Mesopotamia, seals were impressed upon clay labels fixed on the knots of ropes with which bales of goods were tied, after they had been wrapped in packing materials (fig. 7.18). The packets were sealed above all in order to protect their contents against pilfering. On the arrival of goods at their destination, the seals were broken open and the contents weighed and checked, in the presence of witnesses. Cuneiform texts show that it was considered a crime to open a sealed packet in transit:

frequency of occurrence			reference numbers of the tags with multiple impressions		6067	6079	6092	6158	6178	6065	6176	6180	6149	6167	6152	6175	6185	6187
total	on tags with one impression	on tags with many impressions	number of seal impressions per tag		4	4	3	3	3	2	2	2	2	2	2	2	2	2
			text	iconography	order (A = uppermost, etc.)													
15	7	8	[Indus script text]	unicorn	D	C	B	A	A			B	A	A				
9	4	5	[Indus script text]	unicorn	A	D				B	B							B
8	2	6	[Indus script text]	?	C		A		C		A	A			B			
7	2	5	[Indus script text]	unicorn	B		C			A			B	B				
6	3	3	[Indus script text]	unicorn											A	B	A	
3	1	2	[Indus script text]	unicorn												A	B	
1	0	1	[Indus script text]	unicorn				B										
1	0	1	[Indus script text]	unicorn					B									
1	0	1	[Indus script text]	?														A
3	2	1	indistinct	unicorn				C										
3	2	1	indistinct	?		A												
1	0	1	indistinct	?		B												

Fig. 7.17. An analysis of the seal impressions on clay tags from the burnt-down warehouse at Lothal, showing interconnected inscriptions. Of the 77 tags analysed, 21 bear two, three or four seal impressions. As many as 14 of these 21 tags are interconnected, linked with each other by shared seal impressions. Of the nine different seal texts that can be read on these 14 tags, six recur also on tags with single seal impressions, the text with the highest total frequency appearing on 15 different tags. Altogether, the 14 tags with multiple sealings and the related tags with single impressions shown in the figure comprise 37 tags, i.e. nearly 50 per cent of the total of 77. The remaining inscriptions (including those on the five other tags with multiple seal impressions: 6034, 6001, 6151, 6195, 6077) occur once only, with a few exceptions: two tags, each bearing a double impression of one seal (different in each case: 6058, 6184); one text recurring twice on tags with single impressions (6155, 6170), and, strikingly, one seal text, [Indus script text] (pictorial motif: elephant), which is repeated 11 times (more than any other text) on tags with single impressions, but not once on tags with multiple seal impressions. After Parpola 1986a: 401f. (More material from Lothal, made available after this analysis was completed, has been published in *CISI* 1.)

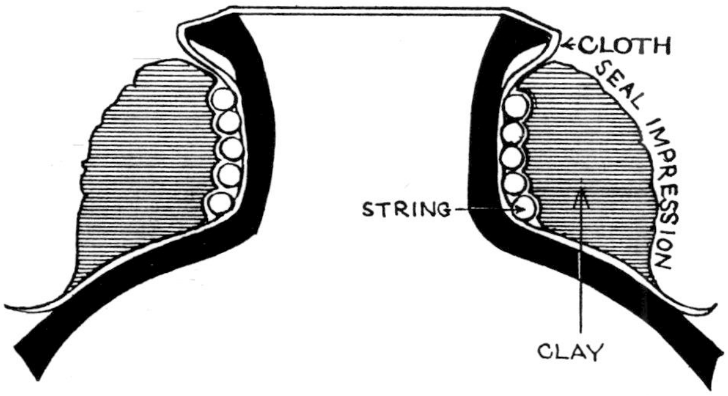

Fig. 7.18. The method of securing the integrity of a commodity container in third millennium Mesopotamia. After Frankfort 1939: 2, text-fig. 1.

From the merchandise transported by Īlī-ašranni 6 $\frac{1}{3}$ minas of tin and $\frac{1}{2}$ textile are under the custody of Īlabrātbāni. He acted high-handedly and broke open my *šuqlum* [i.e. pack of merchandise of standard size or weight] and took my tin. Like a criminal he himself took my own tin! (*TC* 2,3,4–11, trans. Veenhof 1972: 32)

In the Indus cities, seals have been found occasionally in close association with weights (cf. Vats 1940: II, pl. 22a). This demands comparison with the ancient customs house convincingly identified on the island of Bahrain in the Gulf (fig. 7.19). Gulf seals and stone weights of the Harappan type were found in remarkable numbers in the houses right next to the city gate, where a well and a trough served as a halting place for pack animals. They indicate that the incoming and / or outgoing goods were weighed and stamped by customs.

Seals were later central to the control of trade in classical Indian civilization according to the Arthaśāstra, the handbook of polity and statecraft ascribed to Kauṭilya, the prime

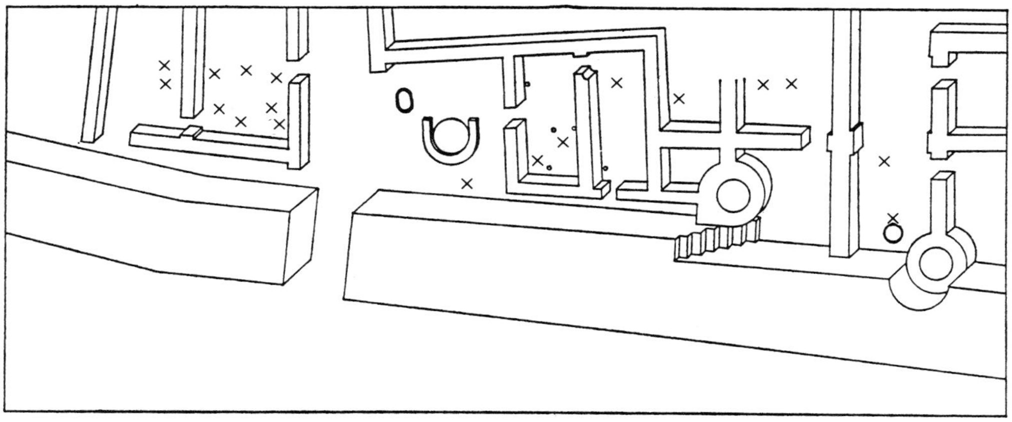

Fig. 7.19. An ancient customs house in Bahrain. Isometric view of the City II area within the north wall at Qala'at al-Bahrain. To the right is the cul-de-sac, and to the left the city gate, and between them the guard-room with its well and staircase to the ramparts. Find spots of seals (x) and weights (o) are marked, showing their preponderance in the rooms on either side of the gate. After Bibby 1972: 368.

minister of Emperor Candragupta Maurya (late fourth century BC):

2, 21, 1. The Collector of Customs and Tolls should establish the customs house and the flag facing the east or the north in the vicinity of the big gates (of the city). 2. The receivers of duty, four or five in number, should record in writing (details about) traders who have arrived in a caravan, who they are, from what place, with how much merchandise and where the identity-pass (was issued) or the stamping was made. 3. For (goods) without the stamp the penalty is double the dues. 4. For those with a forged stamp, the fine is eight times the duty. 5. For those with broken stamps, the penalty is distraint in the warehouse... 16. And for goods that have passed beyond the foot of the flag without the duty being paid, the fine is eight times the duty. 17. Secret agents operating on roads and in places without roads should find out such (evasion). (trans. Kangle 1972: II, 141–3)

One important purpose of sealing bales of goods is to identify their owners. A number of phrases in the cuneiform documents relate to this. The following examples are from texts dealing with the Old Assyrian textile trade (Veenhof 1972: 41f.):

Four bags with x *kutānū*-textiles, with the seals of A.
X+1 bags A, son of B, took; they are with C under his seal.
If... my textiles come down (from the palace), mark them with my seal.
Mark the textiles with your seal... so that we can entrust them to a commission agent.
Six textiles of good quality, with my seals, which are marked with the name of A as A's property.

The last text, together with some others not mentioned, suggests the use of more than one seal at a time:

We have to assume that the clay bullas attached to the bag or the textiles themselves carried not only a seal impression of the person who had packed and sent them, but also the name of the merchant or owner involved, or even the name of the recipient or consignee of the lot. (Veenhof 1972: 42)

A few clay bullae with the impression of an Indus seal have a rounded back carefully smoothed with the fingers. They may have been identification passes, qualifying their carrier as the legal representative of the owner of the seal. According to the Arthaśāstra (2,34,1–5), such identification stamps were used in the control of road traffic.

The use of the seal impressions with a smoothed back as 'sealed passes' is not their only possible use. They may have had a religious use too, analogous to that of the moulded and incised tablets (§ 7.3). Seven of them, each bearing a partial impression of a single 'unicorn' seal, were recovered from the southern part of the acropolis of Kalibangan, where sacrificial rituals were performed (§ 12.2).

The iconography of Indus seals might well be expected to provide clues to the meaning of their inscriptions. Many scholars have nevertheless asserted that this relationship is purely coincidental. They point to the fact that a single motif (e.g. the 'unicorn') is found with a large number of different inscriptions. Moreover, one and the same inscription may be accompanied by different motifs:

Seals 1388 ('unicorn') and 2280 (zebu)
both have the text 
Seals 2693 ('unicorn') and 3230 (elephant)
both have the text 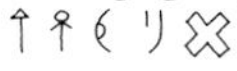
Seals 2560 ('unicorn') and 3240 (buffalo)
both have the text 
Seals 1169 ('unicorn') and 3246 (tiger)
both have the text 

Seal M-324 even has the same inscription on both sides, accompanied by different motifs ('unicorn' and 'composite animal'). A parallel case is seal 2636; here the same inscription occurs with both the zebu and the 'composite animal'. Clearly the seal owner needed different motifs for different purposes. That the animal itself had less relevance in identifying the seal owner than the inscription had is apparent from the care taken to secure a good impression of the inscription, but not of the iconographic motif. Often the horn is the only part of the 'unicorn' visible in the tags.

However, the idea that there is no connection between an Indus text and the accompanying iconography has rightly been questioned. Other scholars have proposed that the inscription indicated the individual name and / or title of the owner, and the animal motif his or her wider social position, such as the caste, for even today many Indian tribes and castes have clans linked with certain animals and totemic observances and taboos. The disproportionately large number of 'unicorn' seals does not support this assumption. Later Indian seals offer an alternative explanation. In these, the image of the zebu, representing Śiva's bull Nandin, marked the owner as a worshipper of Śiva. Such a religious motif could also refer to specific social groups. Thus the Gaja-Lakṣmī motif, in which two elephants sprinkle water over the goddess of welfare, was popular in the seals of state officials of the Gupta period.

A few Indus seals are hollowed out and provided with a lid so that something – probably a magic charm – could be kept inside. The seal would then have been worn as a talisman, a suggestion supported by the hole pierced through the boss on the back, used for suspending the seal from a string. Further evidence comes from the ancient Near East, where statues of divinities wear seals as ornaments on a necklace. In the royal tombs of Ur, around 2400 BC, cylinder seals were usually suspended from a pin, which fastened the robe on the right shoulder. A protective function for the seal is suggested, too, by the clearly religious nature of the iconographic motifs. In medieval Europe, amulet-seals were usually inscribed with both the name of the protecting deity and the name of the seal owner to be protected, e.g. 'O Christ, protect Charles, the king of the Franks!'

In Mesopotamia, the seal worn visibly on the owner's person seems to have been a status symbol too. The best quality seals could be afforded only by the wealthy and powerful. The cheapest seals were mass-produced, carelessly carved out of coarse material. They are in sharp contrast to the magnificently carved seals dedicated to the gods by kings. Such votive seals are also much larger. This was also true in classical India and in medieval Europe, where the king had the largest and most magnificent seal.

The quality of an Indus seal usually increases with its size. Moreover, large seals often display unusual iconography, such as those depicting the 'Proto-Śiva' (fig. 10.18) and the 'fig deity' (fig. 14.35). Large size, high quality and impressive or unusual iconography are features that, especially in combination, point to a high official or to a royal or divine personage as the owner. We can test this hypothesis by seeing whether the inscriptions on such seals are distinctive and coherent. If they are, the 'royal' connection will help us in interpreting them. In fact, they do seem to form classes of their own. The formulae of texts in the 'Proto-Śiva' and 'fig deity' seals, for example, closely agree, and can be interpreted as priestly titles (§§ 7.5, 10.2, 14.4).

7.5 Seal inscriptions

In scanning through the uncommonly large Indus seals, one is struck by the recurrence of certain pictographic signs and sign sequences, which might well be royal titles. An example is the rare sign  alone on the second row, found in several large seals, whose iconographic motifs, too, support the 'royal' hypothesis:

0233 (zebu)  [upper line(s) broken off]
1001 (broken bovid: zebu?) 
1016 ('unicorn' bull) 
1332 (zebu) 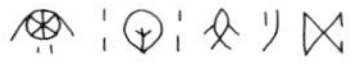
2431 (zebu) 

The zebu, or humped Brahmani bull (*Bos indicus*), is magnificently carved on most of the relatively few (and therefore élite) Indus seals where it appears, and suggests the owner of the seal had majestic status. A relationship between the motif and the inscription on the zebu seals is suggested also by the fact that the zebu recurs on all three seals (1628, 2366 and 3626) which contain the sequence 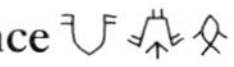.

The sign  can be regarded as a ligature. The 'arch' over it and the two short strokes beneath it can be compared to the sign  (although here three more strokes are placed in the middle). A further component of the ligature is the sign , whose similarity in form with the Mesopotamian and Indian symbols of royalty was discussed in section 7.2. In three *large* seals, the position of the sign  is unusual (§ 6.2):

2422 
3003 
3010 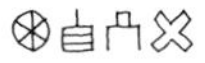

In these seals, the sign  ends the inscription, without being followed by any suffix-like sign(s). This suggests that it may refer to a 'king' as the owner of the seal. In the vast majority of seals, which are smaller in size and possibly indicate lower social status, the sign  begins the inscription and is followed by the suffix-like signs ', '' and). In these ordinary seals, the sign  may have an attributive function and refer to the 'king' as the lord of the seal owner.

The threefold repetition of the sign  in the first part of the inscription in the large seal 2069  reminds one of the elaborate royal titles of ancient Western Asiatic rulers, such as Darius the Great: 'I am Darius the Great King, King of Kings, King in Persia, King of Countries ...' The sign  is often doubled in the sequence , which might mean 'king of kings'. Interestingly, this sequence  *ends* the first line in the carefully carved inscription found on the fragment of the large seal 2119 (fig. 7.8e). The motif on this seal had undoubtedly once been the zebu bull, though its left horn and hump alone survive. The first line is an integral whole, for it recurs on two inscribed bronze axes; the analogy of inscribed Near Eastern axes also suggests royal ownership (§ 7.3).

Similarly, the inscription , found on a curved bronze dagger (3795) and (fragmentarily) on a bronze axe blade (3796), ends in the sign . Both these weapons are part of a large hoard of copper tools and weapons found at Harappa in a copper jar containing 20 axes of different kinds, 9 daggers, 14 spearheads, 1 macehead, 10 chisels, 2 saws, etc. Their owner must have been a mighty person.

Many North Indian seals of the early historical period (last quarter of the first millennium BC) contain proper names ending in the genitive suffix (Prakrit *-sa*, Sanskrit *-sya*), conveying that the seal and its impression belonged to the person named. These later seals have been quoted in support of the hypothesis that the Indus sign  which ends the majority of the Indus seals may be a genitive suffix (§ 6.3). However, there is no unbroken bureaucratic tradition connecting the Indus seals with the later Indian seals nor is the Indus script related to the later Kharoṣṭhī and Brahmi scripts. The historical seals with their genitive endings may indeed follow the Greek tradition introduced by Alexander's coinage.

Given the fact that Indus seals and Mesopotamian seals both served to control administration and trade, and that there was a historical contact, it is likely that Indus seal inscriptions are analogous to contemporaneous Mesopotamian ones, which can of course be read and understood. Mesopotamian seal inscriptions of the period 2600–1600 BC will therefore be exemplified in this section, based on Ignace J. Gelb's typological survey (1977). The relative frequencies given for the main types of inscriptions are based on their representation in a collection of 272 Old Akkadian seal inscriptions (Edzard 1968).

The great majority of the Mesopotamian inscriptions simply identify the seal owner or user. The most common type (62/272) consists of nothing but a proper name. A large number of seals (78/272) append to the name only the profession of the owner or his office:

Urani the scribe. (Early Dynastic III)
Dudu the incantation priest. (Old Akkadian?)

'Scribe' is by far the most frequent professional title in the early seals (45/272). After the establishment of scribal schools in the Ur III period, 'scribe' became an honorific of graduates, to be placed between the name and the professional title.

Other occupations mentioned include different kinds of priests for specific gods and temples (usually particularized), various kinds of foremen ('foreman of millers', 'foreman of the house', etc.), cupbearers (including 'the highest cupbearer of the city of Adab'), merchants, judges, policemen, granary-keepers, porters, builders, couriers, barbers, washermen, stone-cutters, smiths, cooks and musicians. All the urban occupations seem to be represented. There were no restrictions on ownership. Even slaves could acquire a seal. Herodotus (1,195) says of the Babylonians that 'every one carries a seal'.

Of the 2,000 or so seals found in the partially excavated city of Mohenjo-daro alone, one or two have been found in almost every exposed room, in addition to those recovered from streets. It therefore seems likely that in the Indus Valley, too, every person or head of a family engaged in a profession had a seal.

The profession of a seal owner might possibly be elucidated by the find spot of his seal. Unfortunately, according to Ernest Mackay (1938: 1, 41), 'it is well-nigh impossible to determine the use of a building with any certainty from the antiquities found in it'. Nevertheless, room 85 in house IX of the HR area in Mohenjo-daro was probably occupied by a shell-cutter; for in one corner of it 'a mass of shell-inlay was found ... along with ... many waste pieces of sea-shells' (Mackay 1931a: 1, 195). Five square 'unicorn' seals (one broken) were recovered from this room. Another example concerns the 'citadel' area, assumed to be the seat of higher authority. Seals 1158  and 1057 , which share the same three initial pictograms, were both found north of the Stupa mound in the acropolis at Mohenjo-daro. Figure 7.20 illustrates the find spots of 12 seals recovered from one house in the HR area of the same city.

The distribution of sites, too, may provide clues to the seal inscriptions. In Dravidian-speaking South India today, the name of the ancestral village often forms the first element of a person's proper name. Such a place-name, of course, serves the purpose of interregional identification. It is not impossible that place-names were used for this purpose in the Indus seals. Minoan-Mycenaean place-names surviving to historical times played a central role in the decipherment of Linear B

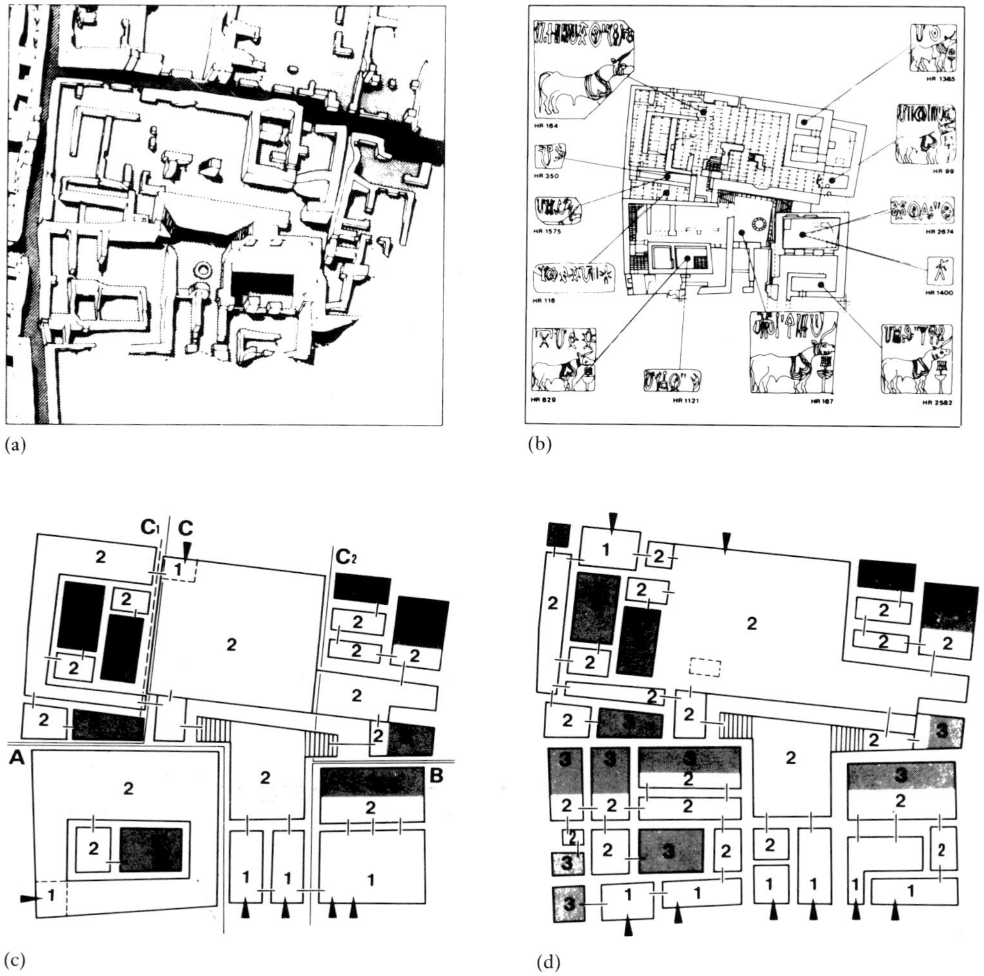

Fig. 7.20. Michael Jansen's analysis of house I, HR-A area, Mohenjo-daro: (a) isometry, (b) find spots of seals, (c) reconstruction of the original structure, (d) reconstruction of the final structure. The numbers in (c) and (d) refer to: 1: rooms immediately adjacent to the exit, 2: transit rooms having more than one door, 3: terminal rooms with just one door. The number of seals found in this house is unusually high, and the presence of many prestige objects suggests that it was not just an ordinary residence; Sir Mortimer Wheeler assumed that it was a temple. After Jansen 1986: 200f., fig. 125.

(§ 3.2). A similar survival of Harappan place-names in the Greater Indus Valley is not at all unlikely (§ 9.4). But how can potential place-names in Indus inscriptions be isolated?

A fundamental condition is that the sign or sign sequence suspected to represent a toponym should be peculiar to inscriptions from a single place. The likelihood that a sign known from one site only represents the ancient name of that site increases with the frequency of the sign. As toponyms can hardly be expected to be a regular component of all seal inscriptions, they should stand out from the more usual contents and be placed at either the beginning or end of the text, perhaps even clearly apart from other signs.

Following these criteria, at least one Harappan toponym can be isolated with a fair amount of confidence. Altogether 70 Indus inscriptions have been recovered from Chanhujo-daro. Eleven of them contain the sign ||/, which is not known from any of the thousands of Indus inscriptions found at other sites. This sign starts texts twice (5018, 5036) and ends them eight times, just one of its occurrences being medial (5033). In five of the final occurrences, it occupies the whole of the second line of the inscription alone, suggesting that it forms a separate phrase. That the remaining part of the inscription, too, forms an integral whole, not necessarily requiring the addition of the sign ||/, is shown by parallel inscriptions (in the following examples from Mohenjo-daro) which lack the sign ||/, characteristic of inscriptions from Chanhujo-daro:

5024 0413  5035 2375 

After this digression on the clues provided by the archaeological context, we return to those given by Mesopotamian seals. Many of them (26/272) add the name of the owner's father to that of the owner:

Ur-Lamma son of Urgar. (Ur III)

An indication of descent such as this also served to show that the owner was a free citizen. On the seals of women, which are relatively rare, we find 'daughter of' and 'wife of'.

Different combinations of these most simple and most frequent types of seal inscriptions occur, and the father's profession or office is often indicated too:

Abu-ṭaāb, son of Lu-Inanna the merchant. (Old Akkadian)
En-miussa, the anointing priest of the E'e, son of Lu'lu. (Ur III)
Lugal-engardu the scribe, son of Ur-meme the prefect of the temple of the goddess Inanna. (Ur III)
Adda, son of Lugal-Eriduše the cupbearer of the god Ba'u. (Ur III)
Ahumma, son of Dingir-amu the shepherd of the fatted sheep. (Ur III)

Many inscriptions (52/272) further identify the rank of the owner by mentioning the higher authority on whose behalf he acts. Dependants style themselves 'servants' or 'slaves' of their masters, just as their masters are 'servants' or 'slaves' of the king, the king in turn being the 'servant' or 'slave' to a deity. Temples are also referred to:

Šarkališarri the king of Akkad, Kirbanum the scribe (is) his servant. (Old Akkadian)
Šulgi the great man, the king of Ur, Naram-ili the messenger (and) doorkeeper (is) your servant. (Ur III)
Amar-Suena the strong man, the king of Ur, the king of the four quarters, Lugal-itida the scribe, son of Ur-Dumuzida (is) your servant. (Ur III)
Sin-muštal son of Sin-mangir, servant of (king) Rim-Sin. (Old Babylonian)
Tišpak, the hero, my god, Puzrum the scribe (is) your servant. (Old Akkadian)
Eli-eressa daughter of Ilšu-ibnišu, maid servant of the gods Zababa and Ba'u. (Old Babylonian)
Nanna-mansi the diviner, servant of the god Nanna (and) (king) Nur-Adad. (Old Babylonian)

About 20 Neo-Sumerian and early Old Babylonian inscriptions record that the king has presented the seal to a relative or to a high official on his appointment:

Nurahaum, beloved of the god Tišpak, king of Ešnunna, has presented (this seal) to Ušašum his son-in-law, son of Abda-El, *rabiān Amurrim*. (*c*.2000 BC)

Other seals mention just the name of one or two divinities, with or without attributes:

The divine mistress of (the city) Isin. (Old Akkadian)
The god Ninurta, the goddess Nin-Nibrua [i.e. the chief deities of the city of Nippur]. (Old Babylonian)
Amurru the son of Anu, the deity whose lustration is pure [i.e. cleansing]. (Old Babylonian)

Such seals, notably ones bearing the names of the divine pair 'Šamaš and Aya', are found in great numbers, and their poor quality is typical of mass-production in the Old Babylonian period. The omission of a personal name implies that different persons could use such a seal in some routine action. Impressions of them have been found on documents recording transactions. In the Indus Valley, seals without text and only simple iconography, such as the many identical swastika seals, probably belonged to institutions where several individuals were authorized to use them in lower ranking tasks.

Votive seals, a minor category in Mesopotamia, may have been put to such a functional use, rather than being mere ornaments. (There are, however, votive seals with positive inscriptions which were obviously never meant to be impressed.) Their inscriptions identify the donor and the divinity:

To divine Bēlat-iškun, Ilak-nu''id the stone-cutter has donated (this seal). (Old Akkadian)

Chinese seals of the Han dynasty and the earliest Egyptian seals differ rather radically from the Mesopotamian seals in containing very few proper names of individuals. Most of them display nothing but official titles or names of institutions. Official seals of this kind might exist among the Indus seals too, along with the larger number of seals bearing proper names. The appearance of numerous institutional seals in historical India reinforces this possibility. But how can one distinguish between these two categories if one cannot read the script? The fact that institutional or official seals tend frequently to repeat themselves can be a clue (fig. 7.21).

However, duplicated inscriptions are in a minority among the Harappan seal texts. The majority are likely to follow the Mesopotamian analogy and bear proper names. Although the Assyriologist D. O. Edzard (1990) agrees on this point, the conclusion does not, in his opinion, give rise to any kind of optimism: if we are dealing with proper names, then the difficulties of decipherment become practically insurmountable. For one thing, the names may, but need not, be in the language in which the texts are written, whatever it be: in the Old Akkadian seal inscriptions, we find both Sumerian and Akkadian proper names. This is undoubtedly a correct observation, and we shall see that it is valid in the case of the Indus seal inscriptions too (§ 8.2).

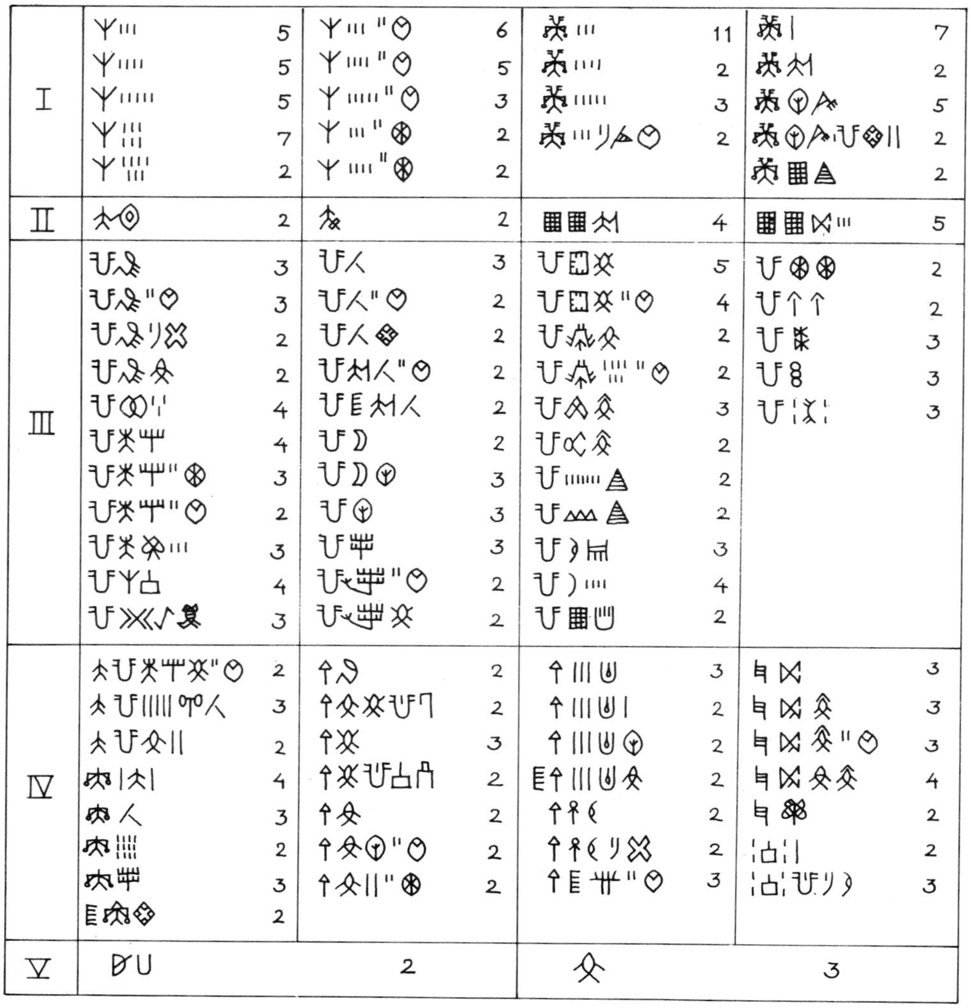

Fig. 7.21. Seal inscriptions that appear more than once, arranged in five major groups by final signs. The first group stands out by its high incidence of duplicates. This group consists of two series, ending in and respectively. The sign is always and in some cases preceded by a varying number. That these two series are interrelated is suggested by seal 2322 , where the sequence equals (§ 5.2). Two seals belonging to this group were found in a single house in Kalibangan, the one with the text being a cylinder seal (fig. 14.25), the other, reading , a square stamp seal (fig. 14.26), and displaying a rare iconographic motif. On the basis of the Kalibangan seals, this group of officials may have been of a military nature, either soldiers or guards, for the motif may be interpreted as a deity of war (§ 14.2).

The second group of duplicated seal inscriptions includes two that might well be official titles, given their form (ligatures ending in the 'man' sign) and their brevity (just one sign: fig. 5.4); the other two texts also contain or imply (fig. 5.3) a 'man' ligature. The third group comprises inscriptions ending in the sign , which closes the great majority of all the inscriptions. It may include common personal names, but short and frequent texts are likely to be names of deities, especially as some sequences like , or are shared with inscriptions on the tablets (§ 7.3). For the fourth group, see § 6.2. The fifth group is simply what remains.

Onomastics, the study of names, clearly provides one of the most useful and relevant types of external evidence that can be brought to bear upon the study of the Indus seals. A brief note on the structure of Sumerian and Akkadian proper names is therefore in order. Like the names of most other ancient oriental peoples, including the Egyptians, Syrians, etc., they were to a large extent theophoric, i.e. they contained names of deities. For example, during the Ur III dynasty, Sumerian proper names which included the god Enlil comprised three main types (cf. Limet 1968: 126f.):

1 The genitive construction (the final syllable, containing the genitive suffix *-lá*, is often omitted): *Lú- / Ur- / Gemé- / Ir*$_{11}$*-* / ^{d}*En-líl-lá* 'Man / Dog / Slave-girl / Servant / of Enlil'; ^{d}*En-líl-lá* '(He is) Enlil's own'.
2 Names with a predicative construction: 'Enlil (is) great', 'Enlil (is) learned', 'Enlil (is) an encouragement', 'Enlil (is) a hero', 'Enlil (is) favourable', 'Enlil (is) your god' (words of the father addressing his son), 'The father (is) Enlil', 'Amar-Su'ena is the farmer of Enlil'.
3 Other constructions: 'Enlil knows', 'Enlil is gratified', 'Would there be a town without Enlil?' (the name resembles the wording of a hymn), 'Ibbi-Sin who has confidence in Enlil', 'In the presence of Enlil', 'To Enlil I have explained', 'Let Enlil make live', 'The speech of Enlil (is sure)'.

In the Mesopotamian seals, names of divinities are also found outside proper names of individuals, especially in priestly titles, and in the 'beloved of the god N. N.' formula. The divine names that were native to Mesopotamia were nearly always preceded by the determinative sign *dingir* 'god'. Thus names of divinities or the word 'god' can be expected to occur often in the inscriptions of the Indus seals, in positions suiting both proper names and priestly titles.

The cultic scenes on the famous 'Proto-Śiva' (fig. 10.18) and 'fig deity' (fig. 14.35) seals suggest that these large and finely carved seals belonged to the high priests of the depicted deities. On the latter seal, a person wearing a horned head-dress similar to that of the anthropomorphic god inside the fig tree is kneeling in front of the sacred tree and raising his hands in worship. In the ancient Near East, the king was often portrayed as the high priest and representative ('governor') of the chief divinity of the country. Can we interpret the closely comparable inscriptions of the 'Proto-Śiva' and 'fig deity' seals as priestly titles in line with similar Mesopotamian seals? Both texts end in the plain 'man' sign, preceded by a 'fish' sign plus the normally final sign :

M-304 ('Proto-Śiva') 
M-1186 ('fig deity') (1st line) 
(2nd line) 

The rough meaning of those three similar final signs could in both cases well be 'The man (i.e. servant) of god N. N.'; the initial signs could stand for epithets of the respective deity.

This hypothesis implies that the large group of signs having the basic appearance of 'fish' (and others sharing the same position in the inscriptions; fig. 6.5) denote divinities. It is not improbable that 'fish', the ideographic meaning of the 'fish' signs, should be found in inscriptions of a river-borne civilization having fish as a major component of the diet. In fact, there are Harappan texts where this meaning appears to occur, and they will be discussed in detail later (§§ 10.2–3). But if the Indus inscriptions are assumed to be mainly proper names and titles, the 'fish' signs are most likely to involve a phonetic transfer through rebus. This could serve as a starting-point for a linguistic decipherment. Assuming the iconic meaning to be 'fish' and the intended meaning to be 'god', the question is: are these meanings linked by homophony in any historically plausible language? Before replying to this question (in § 10.1) we must consider the problem of the Indus language.

Part III

The linguistic context

8 In search of the Indus language

8.1 Restriction of the search

The Indus script can be deciphered only if its language can be identified as one belonging to a family sufficiently well known from other sources (§ 3.3). But how can we find out whether the Harappan language is a member of any known language family? Or did the Harappans speak several languages? There are different kinds of evidence, some of them quite complex, which must all be taken into account:

1. the linguistic patterns revealed by the distributions of signs in Indus texts;
2. the best-informed reconstructions of the early linguistic history of the area;
3. the configurations of archaeological cultures and historical circumstances.

The area of the Indus Civilization is quite extensive and is likely to have included many languages. In the area of the Mesopotamian Civilization several literary languages were used, Sumerian and Akkadian often side by side in one and the same city. The Indus inscriptions, however, suggest that only one 'official' language was used across the vast Harappan realm and throughout its entire duration. The evidence for this consists in the syntactic uniformity of the texts, the same characteristic sign sequences being repeated everywhere. (The validity of this argument is supported by the entirely different sequences on many Indus seals from the Near East, discussed in the next section.) Regional dialects of this 'official' language, which undoubtedly existed, are very difficult to recognize in a morphemic script. This is illustrated by the situation in modern China, where speakers of different dialects of the Chinese language may not understand each other's speech, but can read the sole Chinese script.

The Indus inscriptions have also yielded some evidence of the structure of the Indus language. These typological features can be compared to those of various real languages, which can thus be identified as likely and unlikely candidates. The Indus language appears to prefer premodification, because the optional elements usually precede the head word of the phrase (§§ 6.1–3). This is quite clearly the case with the numeral qualifiers, which can be recognized on the basis of their outward appearance and distribution (§ 5.2). This word order excludes, for example, the Tibeto-Burman languages, in which the order is N+Num. The likelihood that the Harappan language has agglutinative morphology is much less certain.

These few typological features that seem to characterize the Indus language are not very helpful if we have to match them against all the 6,000 languages of the world. But the languages of Easter Island and Mesoamerica, for instance, hardly qualify as historically likely cognates of the Indus language, so efforts spent in such comparisons are wasted. This consideration applies to even closer regions. Thus some scholars have noted that the so-called 'Altaic' languages fit the typological characteristics of the Indus inscriptions, implying that they should be taken into account as serious candidates. Historically, however, these languages, originally restricted to Siberia, are a remote possibility. The Turkic- and Mongolian-speaking peoples became mobile and started expanding westwards only after they had adopted horsemanship from Iranian-speaking nomads in the first millennium BC. Typological parallels between the 'Altaic' languages and the language of the Indus texts simply cannot be used in and of themselves for the establishment of any genetic relationship between these languages. What alternatives, then, can be considered reasonable possibilities? If we set some limits, we can proceed more effectively, examining arguments for and against the various candidates.

The archaeological evidence defines fairly exactly the extent of the Indus Civilization and the related Early and Late Harappan cultures. Obviously this area, with its immediate surroundings, is the most likely place to look for possible descendants or cognates of the Harappan language. To be on the safe side, the search may be extended from the Indo-Iranian borderlands to Central Asia and the whole of the Indo-Pakistani subcontinent. These languages will be considered more closely in sections 8.3ff. We also know the Harappans' spheres of commercial and cultural interaction. Another area where cognates of the Harappan language may be sought on this basis is the ancient Near East, for there is no doubt about the contacts of the Indus Civilization with Western Asia, chiefly the Gulf and Mesopotamia.

Many languages are known to have died out during the past few hundred years. Obviously numerous languages spoken in the ancient Near East and the area of the Indus Civilization in the third millennium BC are likely to have disappeared without any recognizable trace. Could the Indus language have vanished in this way? We will have something more to say about this possibility in sections 9.2–3. But first we turn to the ancient Near East and the Iranian plateau.

8.2 Languages of the ancient Near East and the Iranian plateau

A number of languages existed in the ancient Near East (fig. 8.1). We shall start with a quick survey of them, going from north to south, then consider our typological criteria and finally discuss other pertinent evidence.

Anatolia was in constant contact with Syria and Mesopotamia and may be included in the survey, even if it can be considered less relevant to the Harappan problem on account of its greater distance. Anatolian is the oldest known, and an archaic, branch of the Indo-European family, supposed to have arrived via the Balkans *c.*2700–2600 BC (§ 8.4). It consists of several closely related languages. Hittite, documented *c.*1800–1200 BC in cuneiform script, was spoken in central Anatolia, from where the Hittites ruled their empire (fig. 8.16). The contemporary Palaic was spoken by their vassals in the north, and Luvian by their rivals in western and southern Anatolia. Luvian was written both in cuneiform (*c.*1400–1200 BC) and in the Hittite hieroglyphic script (*c.*1300–700 BC); it survives in later Lycian and Lydian (attested *c.*500–300 BC in the Greek alphabet) and probably also Carian (seventh century BC in a script of its own). Armenian, spoken in northeastern Anatolia, represents another branch of Indo-European, which arrived somewhat later. The Hittite cuneiform documents of the second millennium BC have preserved considerable evidence of Ḫattic, the isolated language of the earliest population in northern central Anatolia. Ancient tradition recorded by Herodotus (1,94) and inscriptions from the island of Lemnos suggest that the isolated language of Etruscan (see § 3.3), too, was originally an Anatolian language.

Another branch of Indo-European, which early found its way to Western Asia, is the Proto-Indo-Aryan spoken by the rulers of the Mitanni kingdom in northern Syria *c.*1500 BC (fig. 8.16), to be discussed in more detail in section 8.4. Within the next two centuries, these Aryan nobles became linguistically assimilated to their subjects, who spoke Hurrian. Hurrian, recorded for 2,000 years from the third millennium BC, was related to the Urartian of the Lake Van area, known from the ninth to the sixth centuries BC. Recently these two languages have been shown to belong to the Caucasian family.

The Kassites, who ruled the Middle Babylonian kingdom *c.*1730–1155 BC (fig. 8.16), are usually thought to have come from the mountains on the border of Iran, but the first king to bear a Kassite name, Kaštiliaš, ruled at Hana (near Mari) on

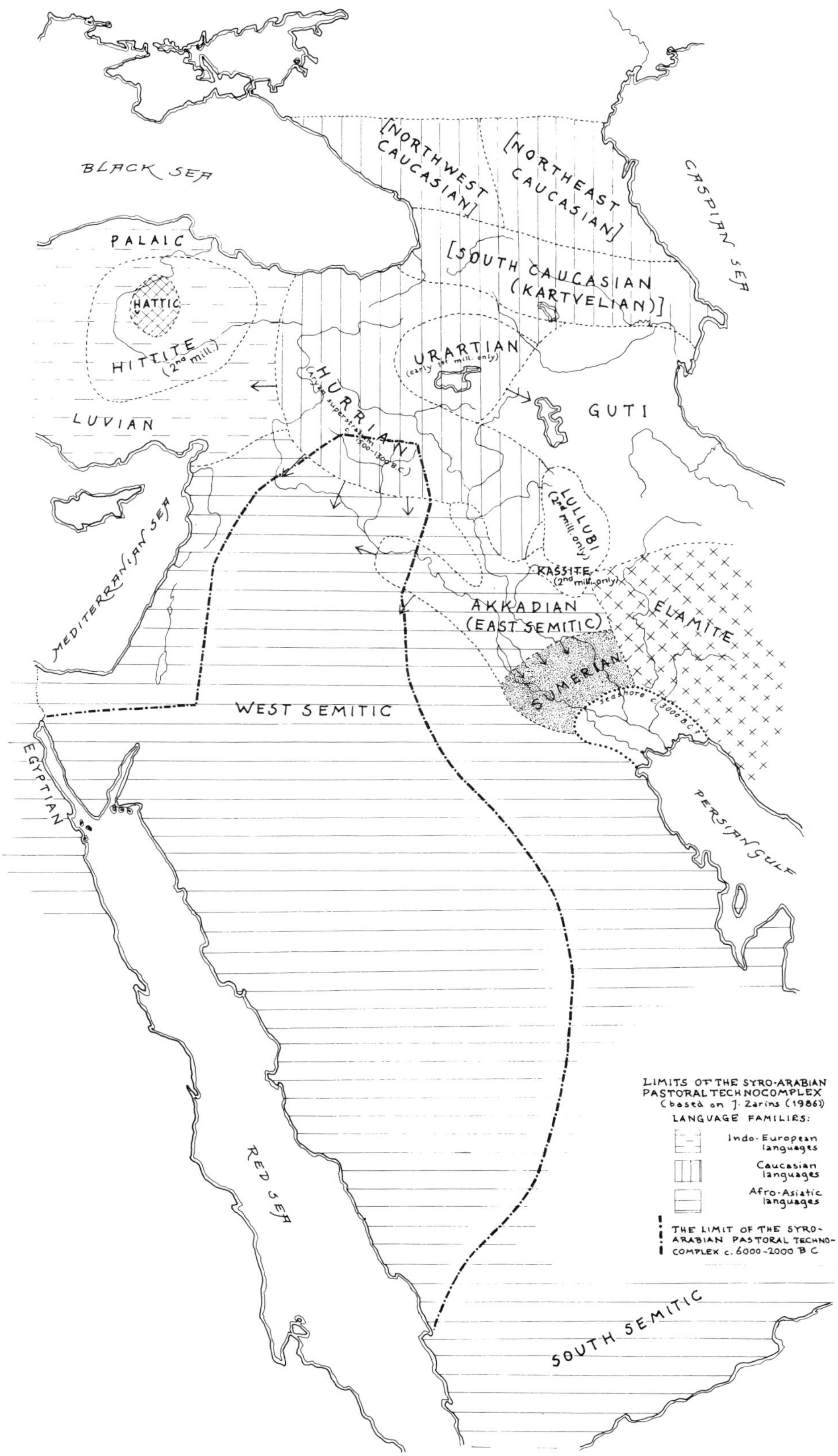

Fig. 8.1. Languages spoken in the ancient Near East. The map mainly reflects the situation in the third and second millennia BC. The Hurrians of Mitanni were ruled by Proto-Indo-Aryan-speaking nobles *c.*1500–1300 BC (fig. 8.16). The recently discovered 'Syro-Arabian pastoral technocomplex', dated to *c.*6000–2000 BC, may in its older stage (*c.*6000–4000 BC) represent speakers of the Proto-Semitic language. This map has been adapted from an unpublished one by Gene Gragg (1979), with the borders of the Syro-Arabian pastoral technocomplex added after Zarins 1986: 237, fig. 68.

the middle Euphrates. The Kassites started speaking Babylonian and their original language is only very poorly known from a few Kassite–Akkadian lists of words, gods and names. From these samples it appears to be an isolated language. Only the name *Šu-ri-ya-áš*, equated with that of the Akkadian sun-god *Šamaš*, is clearly Aryan (Sanskrit *sūrya* 'sun'), which undoubtedly reflects the influence of the neighbouring contemporary Mitanni rulers. Guti (in the third millennium BC) and Lullubi (second millennium) are other very little-known languages spoken in the western end of the Iranian plateau.

The Semitic languages were dominant in the ancient Near East from at least 3000 BC. They form the Afroasiatic family together with the distantly related 'Hamitic' languages of North Africa, which do not form a coherent branch but comprise several independent groups: ancient Egyptian (documented from 3000 BC, surviving now only as a liturgical language in Coptic), the Berber languages of North Africa (including Tuareg), the modern Cushitic languages of Ethiopia and Somalia (including Somali), and the modern Chadic languages spoken around northern Nigeria. Proto-Afroasiatic is supposed to have been located in North Africa, possibly in the area of the present Sahara desert.

The original home of the Semitic languages is thought to have been in either the Arabian peninsula or the Horn of Africa. The Semitic languages are divided into two major branches, East Semitic and West Semitic. East Semitic comprises the ancient language of Mesopotamia, Akkadian, which is documented from the twenty-seventh century BC to the first century AD. Its two later branches reflect the political division: Assyrian in the north and Babylonian in the south.

West Semitic has two sub-branches, Northwest (or Central) Semitic and South Semitic. Northwest Semitic comprises (1) Aramaic, originally spoken in Syria and documented from about 1000 BC (it was used as the official language of the Persian empire from Egypt to the Indus Valley, and still survives as Syriac); and (2) Canaanite, whose ancient form is known from Byblos (*c.*1600–1400 BC) and probably also comprises Eblaitic in northern Syria (twenty-fourth century BC), the poorly attested Amorite (*c.*2000–1500 BC), and Ugaritic (documented at Ras Shamra in Syria, *c.*1400–1200 BC); more recent forms of Canaanite are Phoenician, originally spoken in Lebanon but carried by seafaring merchants all over the Mediterranean (documented *c.*1200 BC to AD 500), and Hebrew (documented from *c.*1200 BC). Traditionally, Arabic (documented from the sixth century AD) has been classified as South Semitic, but recent research suggests that it too belongs to Northwest Semitic.

The South Semitic sub-branch comprises the non-Arabic Semitic languages of south Arabia (attested from the ninth century BC) and Ethiopian Semitic (including modern Amharic), imported from south Arabia around 500 BC and attested from the fourth century AD.

In its phonology, syntax and vocabulary, Akkadian was heavily influenced by Sumerian, an isolated language that was spoken in the alluvial plains of southern Mesopotamia until about 1900 BC, when Sumerian died out as a spoken language, although it continued to be used as a classical language in the cuneiform documents. It was most probably the Sumerians who created the cuneiform script in the Uruk IV period, *c.*3300 BC (§§ 2.1–2). There is no solid evidence for Proto-Euphratic, a hypothetical substratum language that Sumerian is often supposed to have replaced.

The principal neighbours of the Mesopotamians to the east lived on the alluvial plain of Susiana at the foot of the Zagros mountains. In the Late Uruk period the 'Proto-Elamites' of Susa seem to have adopted the art of writing from the Sumerians, using the same materials and devices, but adapting the script to their own apparently different language and using pictograms of their own (fig. 2.2). Among the languages of the ancient Near East, Proto-Elamite may be singled out as the most probable candidate for being the Indus language, because archaeological evidence (tablets inscribed with the Proto-Elamite script and Proto-Elamite seals) suggests that it penetrated as far east as Shahr-i Sokhta in Iranian Seistan.

Unfortunately, the Proto-Elamite script (*c.*3100–2900 BC) is very poorly understood, and it is not certain (though it is likely) that it represents the same Elamite language as that known from cuneiform texts (*c.* twenty-third to fifth century BC) and from the Linear Elamite script used in the twenty-third century in Susa (§ 2.3). In any case, Elamite is the only reasonably well-documented non-Indo-European language that is known to have been spoken in ancient times in the vast area separating Mesopotamia from the Indus Valley (fig. 1.12). The only other non-Indo-European language of this area, but known from much more recent times, is Brahui. Brahui belongs to the Dravidian family, spoken today at the eastern end of the plateau, from Baluchistan to the Indus Valley (§ 9.1). Elamite has generally been considered to be an isolated language. In recent years, however, it has been claimed as a distant relative of the Dravidian family; the evidence is provocative, but inconclusive.

The vast area between the Near East and the Indo-Pakistani subcontinent has for the past three millennia been occupied mainly by speakers of the Iranian branch of the Aryan or Indo-Iranian languages (fig. 8.2). Iranian proper names and place-names start being mentioned in the cuneiform documents of Assyria and Babylonia in the ninth century BC. Median, spoken by the tribes who founded the first Iranian empire (*c.*673–549 BC), is only scantily and indirectly known. The first major monuments of Iranian

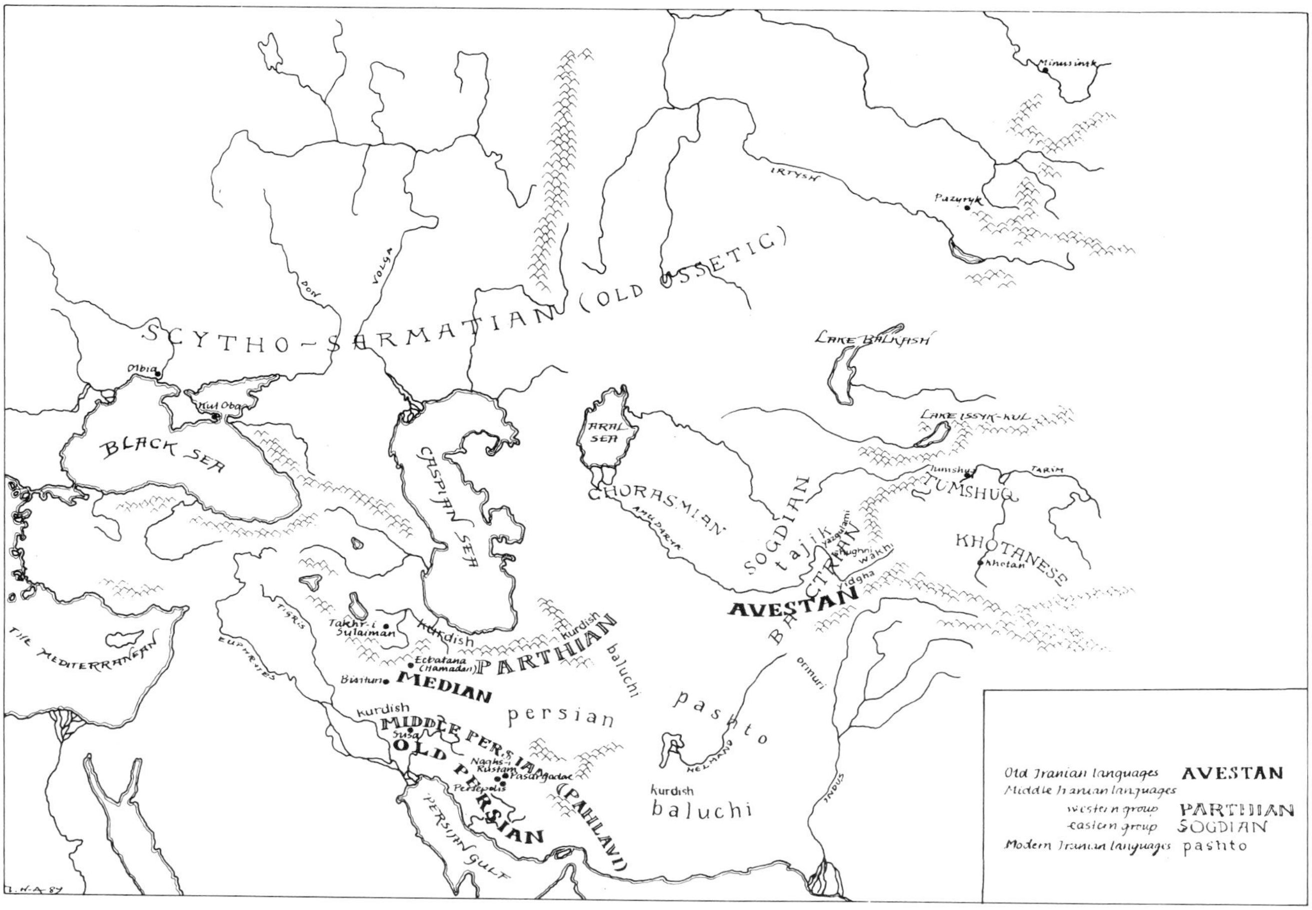

Fig. 8.2. Approximate distribution of the Iranian languages.

languages that have been directly preserved are the royal edicts of the Achaemenid kings who ruled Iran *c.*549–331 BC. These inscriptions are in Old Persian, the language of Persis or the modern province of Fars. A different variety of Old Iranian (which is a more comprehensive term than Old Persian) is represented by Avestan, the language of the Avesta, the collection of sacred texts of the Zarathustran religion composed in southern Central Asia or in the eastern part of the Iranian plateau. The dichotomy of West Iranian and East Iranian is continued in the Middle and Neo-Iranian phases. Middle Iranian is dated roughly between the fall of the Achaemenid empire and the Arab conquest of Iran, and documented in Iran and Central Asia in several forms (West Iranian: Middle Persian or Pahlavi in the south, and Parthian in the north; East Iranian: Sogdian, Chorasmian, Saka, Bactrian, all in Central Asia, plus mainly onomastic traces of Sarmatian, Alanian, and some other languages spoken in the Eurasian steppes). Scarce inscriptions show that Iranian languages were spoken also by the Kuṣāṇas and Śakas, whose realm extended from Central Asia to northwestern and partly even western India between *c.*100 BC and AD 300. The more than 20 Neo-Iranian languages also comprise a western group, including modern Persian with its many dialects, Kurdish, Baluchi and others, and an eastern group from Ossetic, spoken in the Caucasus, to the archaic Pamir languages (Shughni, Sarikoli, Yazgulami, Wakhi, Ishkashmi, Munjani, Yidgha) and Pashto, the language of the Pathans of Afghanistan and Pakistan. The relevance of the Iranian languages for the Indus Civilization will be discussed later (§§ 8.4–5; cf. also § 12.2).

In the Gulf, the eastern shores of Arabia were occupied by people with a distinct local culture (including burial customs) and probably a language of their own, at least from the late fourth millennium BC. At the same time, the Gulf became a meeting place of various peoples coming from different directions. Archaeological and textual evidence attests to Sumerian visits from *c.*3300 BC onwards (cf. below and § 1.4). Akkadian merchants, too, regularly sailed to the Gulf. Harappans had been trading in the Gulf since at least Akkadian times until the early centuries of the second millennium BC. The Indus people exerted a particularly strong influence (possibly involving immigration of Harappan merchants) in Ur III times, about 2050–2000 BC, when Bahrain replaced the eastern province of Saudi Arabia as the centre of Dilmun. While trade was carried on between Dilmun and Syro-Anatolia from the twenty-fourth century BC to the second century AD, a drastic change in this relationship took place around 2000 BC. The iconography and style of the stamp seals, among other things, suggests new northwestern influences in the Gulf, probably in the form of immigration and even take-over of the political power. From this time onwards, a sizeable portion of the Dilmunites appear to have been speakers of West Semitic.

Between *c.*2500 and 1950 BC, the Mesopotamian texts refer to 'westerners' (*MAR*-TU in Sumerian, *amurru* in Akkadian), usually called Amorites in scholarly literature. Their language belongs to the West Semitic group, and they are described as bedouin-like pastoral nomads living in the vast open steppes west of the Euphrates river and extending from northern Syria all the way to south Arabia. Material remains (structures, including homesteads and cattle pens, lithics, rare ceramics and rock art) of a homogeneous pastoral techno-complex have been found at various sites in this huge area, dating from 6000 to 2000 BC. Its older phase, *c.*6000–4000 BC, might well represent the Proto-Semitic speakers (fig. 8.1). Arid periods peaking around 3000 and 2000 BC drove these nomads eastwards, to Mesopotamia and to Dilmun and Makan on the Gulf. At first the Amorites infiltrated the Mesopotamian cities peacefully, but they became increasingly aggressive. In 2034 BC, King Šu-Sin of Ur built a wall to keep the 'westerners' away. Yet his son Ibbi-Sin had great difficulties with them.

In the early twentieth century BC an Amorite dynasty ruled the city of Larsa. The city of Ur, which had become a dependency of Larsa, served as a port for foreign trade. At least 60 Amorite names occur in economic texts of this period at Ur, among them Zubabum, Mi-il-ku-da-nu-um, Mi-li-ik-i-li-a and Alazum, who acted as traders sailing to Dilmun. A mercantile agreement dated 1923 BC and bearing the impression of a Gulf seal (fig. 15.1) mentions as the obligated partner Ha-tin-ILI-iba-nu-um, son of Ap-ka-lu-um, both of which are Amorite names. Another contemporary tablet from Susa, again with the stamp of a circular Gulf seal, mentions several persons with Amorite names, among them Mi-il-ki-il, son of Te-im-^{d}En-za-ak. The father's name contains the name of Inzak, the tutelary god of Dilmun. A text from Ur mentions a person with the Amorite name Me-a-ti-a-num as an inhabitant of Dilmun. Some Amorites living in Dilmun were associated with (sea) fishing. Several inscriptions found at Failaka contain Amorite names, and so does the small cuneiform tablet found in association with a round Indus seal in Bahrain (§ 1.4).

Meagre though they are, the typological clues of the Indus texts discussed in the last chapter help in eliminating some of the principal candidates among the Near Eastern languages. Semitic languages are inflecting, Sumerian and Hurrian agglutinative languages. In all three, the attribute (adjective attribute as well as genitive attribute) is placed after the head word; this word order differs from that of the Indus language, if our inferences about the word order are correct (§§ 6.1–2). Thus in Semitic Akkadian (which also employs prepositions), we have *ana* ('to') *šarri* ('the king') *rabî* ('great'); and in Sumerian *lu-gal* 'king', lit. 'man great', *e-gal* 'palace', lit. 'house great'; *dumu ninsun-ak* 'son of Ninsun'. In Elamite, the attribute also has the same 'personal' suffix as the head word. Thus the animate class nominal suffix *-k*, *-t*, *-r* or *-p* is postfixed to the genitive attribute *sunki-me* meaning 'of the kingdom' (formed with the inanimate class nominal suffix *-m*, which in the Middle Elamite period replaced the older inanimate suffixes *-t* and *-n*), depending on whether it follows the first, second or third person or the plural form of the noun *sunki* 'king': *sunki-k sunki-me-k* '(I), the king of the kingdom' vs. *sunki-r sunki-me-r* '(he,) the king of the kingdom' vs. *sunki-p sunki-me-p* 'the kings of the kingdom'.

Some other considerations support the elimination of the Near Eastern languages. The fact that a completely new script was created for writing the Harappan language makes it unlikely to be either Sumerian or Proto-Elamite, both of which had an earlier writing system at their disposal. Of course it might be argued that Sumerian or Proto-Elamite colonists could have forgotten their own script on the way and devised a new one.

It must be emphasized that not a single object of clearly Mesopotamian origin has been recovered from the Early or Mature Harappan sites of the fourth and third millennia BC. (Even from Iran and the Gulf there are only a few stray objects in the Indus Valley, undoubtedly items of trade.) This contrasts with the situation in the Gulf, where the Mesopotamians were after the rich copper deposits of Oman. Imported 'Ubaid pottery (found at many sites in Bahrain, Qatar and the eastern province of Saudi Arabia) attests to the presence of seafaring visitors from southern Mesopotamia in the sixth and fifth millennia BC, as does the Jemdet Nasr pottery (found in the United Arab Emirates) again in the early third millennium BC.

When sea contacts finally developed between the Indus Valley and Mesopotamia in the Akkadian period, the cuneiform documents for the first time mention by name the

Fig. 8.3. A squarish Indus-style stamp seal from Ur (U.7683; BM 120573), with a cuneiform inscription. (a) Impression. (b) Reverse. Cf. Mitchell 1986: 280–1 no. 7 and fig. 111.

country of Meluḫḫa as the most distant participant in the flourishing sea trade (§ 1.5). Given the probability that Meluḫḫa at least partially refers to the Indus Civilization, the discovery of foreign words expressly designated as Meluḫḫan in third millennium cuneiform documents would be of considerable significance in settling the linguistic affinity of the Harappans. Unfortunately no such words, excepting of course the name Meluḫḫa itself (considered in § 9.4), have yet turned up. (The 'Meluḫḫan' words of later lexicographic lists pertain to the later Meluḫḫa located in Africa; see § 1.5.) The cuneiform tablets, it is true, do mention by name several Meluḫḫans, but all these personal names are exclusively Sumerian and therefore not directly useful to the identification of the Harappan language.

One squarish stamp seal with the image of a bison and a cuneiform inscription was found at Ur (fig. 8.3). The form and iconography of this clearly locally made seal suggest Harappan affinity. Unfortunately the three signs are sketchily carved and therefore not legible with certainty. In order of likelihood, the signs may be read as (1) *sak* or *ka*, (2) *ku* or *ma*, and (3) *ši* or *ba*. The meaning of this text remains obscure; it may contain a foreign name or an unusual Sumerian name, such as *ka* / *inim-dab*$_5$*-ba* '(His) mouth is "seized"' (referring to one unable to speak properly), or *sag-ma-*BA (cf. the proper name *sag-ma*).

An Akkadian cylinder seal inscribed 'Šu-ilišu, Meluḫḫa interpreter' (fig. 8.4) is highly significant in showing that the language of Meluḫḫa differed so fundamentally from the contemporaneous languages of the ancient Near East that an official interpreter was needed. This is in agreement with the archaeological evidence, which shows that the Indus Civilization evolved independently of Mesopotamia.

Twelve cuneiform texts, dated between 2062 and 2028 BC, suggest that by Ur III times people associated with Meluḫḫa were fully integrated in Mesopotamian society. This, of course, is only to be expected after they had been present in the country for several generations. Meluḫḫa appears now as the name of a person and as the name of a village near Tellō, whose inhabitants had purely Sumerian names.

A partial acculturation of the Harappan merchants operating in the Near East has been independently suggested by their adaptation to local conventions. Both cylinder seals of the Mesopotamian type and round stamp seals of the Gulf type have been found bearing the Indus script and / or Harappan iconography (with animals native to India but not to Mesopotamia, such as the rhinoceros: fig. 1.6).

G. R. Hunter has made an important observation concerning the texts on the Indus seals coming from the Near East:

> The four examples of round seals found in Mohenjo-daro show well-supported sequences, whereas the three from Mesopotamia show sequences of signs not paralleled elsewhere in the Indus script. But the ordinary square seals found in Mesopotamia show the normal Mohenjo-daro sequences. In other words, *the square seals are in the Indus language, and were probably imported in the course of the trade; while the circular seals, though in the Indus script, are in a different language, and were probably manufactured in Mesopotamia for a Sumerian- or Semitic-speaking person of Indus descent.* (Hunter 1932: 469, with emphasis added)

During the 60 years that have passed since Hunter wrote this, more Indus seals have been found both in the Indus Valley and in the Near East, but the new finds have not invalidated his conclusions. On the contrary, a careful examination of the Near Eastern Indus seals with the help of a concordance to all Indus inscriptions makes the difference between seals from Pakistan or India and those from Mesopotamia stand out even more markedly than before. Two examples may serve to illustrate this point.

A square stamp seal found at Kish bearing the figure of a 'unicorn' and a cult object (fig. 8.5a) is identical with the most common type of seal from the Indus Valley in both its form and its iconography. Its inscription, , recurs in that form on two seals from Mohenjo-daro (one in fig. 8.5b) and 20 times as a part of longer inscriptions from the Indus Valley.

One circular seal from Mesopotamia (fig. 8.6) has a five-sign Indus inscription reading 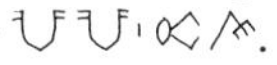. All its signs are among the most common ones in the Indus script, one appearing over 40 times, others well over 100 times. Yet none of the juxtapositions of signs occurring in this inscription are attested elsewhere. Most striking is the fact that the sign  is doubled only here, although its occurrences constitute about 10 per cent of the sign total of all Indus inscriptions.

The most natural explanation for such strange sign sequences on Indus seals with a Near Eastern form would

Fig. 8.4. Impression of an Akkadian cylinder seal that, according to its inscription, belonged to 'Šu-ilišu, Meluḫḫa interpreter'. Musée du Louvre / *AO* 22 310, Collection De Clercq. In a letter dated 16 May 1990, Dr Dominique Collon comments on the iconography as follows:

The seal depicts a seated figure, identifiable by her long hair as feminine and by her horned head-dress (chipped) as a deity. The flounced robe is also generally an indication of divinity. The child on her lap could be the owner of the seal but is more likely to be an attribute of the goddess. The figures approaching the goddess are probably the owner of the seal and his wife although it is possible that these are priestly figures. Several centuries later, in Old Babylonian times, it is the king who almost always carries the animal offering but he is probably seeking favourable omens and the deities he approaches are those particularly connected with omens (see Collon 1986: III, 37). On these later, Old Babylonian seals, the figure carrying a situla or bucket is generally a priest but here it is clearly a woman and there is nothing to indicate that she is a priestess or a queen. Both wear Akkadian dress and nothing distinguishes them as foreigners. The significance of the kneeling male figure and the pots behind is difficult to interpret: they could be an attribute of the goddess, and the large pots on stands are used even today for water – perhaps an additional reference to the goddess' fertility aspect. Among the seals illustrated by R. M. Boehmer (1965) seals 549 and 555 make clear that some sort of drink is involved. Boehmer's plate 47 also shows that the scene belongs to a well-established iconographical group and was not specifically created for the Meluḫḫan interpreter – indeed it was probably chosen from a range of ready-cut seals in a seal-cutter's workshop and the inscription was added. This would account for the fact that the figures overlap the inscription frame on both sides. Boehmer attributes the seal to his Akkadisch III period – i.e. from Naramsin onwards.

(a) (b)

Fig. 8.5. Two square stamp seals with 'unicorn' and an identical sequence of Indus signs. (a) From Kish (IM 1822); cf. Mackay 1925. (b) From Mohenjo-daro (M-228).

Fig. 8.6. Impression of a round stamp seal (BM 120228) probably found in Mesopotamia, engraved with very common Indus signs which, however, are arranged in a unique order. Cf. Gadd 1932: no. 17.

seem to be that these seals belonged to merchants of Harappan origin who lived in Mesopotamia or the Gulf and had adopted local names but still maintained connections with their home country or visiting native Harappan merchants. Such people could have functioned as commercial agents monopolizing the Indus–Mesopotamian trade. The total dissimilarity of the native Harappan language and the local language, which are thus both used in the Indus seals found in the Near East, leads to the same conclusion as that suggested by the seal of the 'Meluḫḫa interpreter' quoted earlier, and makes Sumerian, Akkadian and West Semitic, quite unlikely candidates for the language of the Indus Civilization.

On the other hand, the hybrid inscriptions of the Near Eastern Indus seals constitute an important potential clue and a way of testing the decipherment of the Indus script. After a large enough number of Indus signs has been confidently interpreted, it should become possible, by the application of the phonetic values thus established, to read Near Eastern names (and titles?) on these foreign Indus seals.

8.3 Languages of South Asia

Turning from the Near East and the Iranian plateau to South Asia, we face the difficulty that nothing is directly known from any written sources about the linguistic situation in these areas during the third and early second millennia BC. This, of course, is one of the reasons why the decipherment of the Indus script has posed such a great problem. The different language families will now be surveyed in chronological order according to the age of their oldest sources. First comes the Aryan or Indo-Iranian branch of the Indo-European family in its Iranian and Indo-Aryan sub-branches, then the various non-Aryan families.

Iranian languages – already surveyed in section 8.2 (fig. 8.2) – have been spoken around the northwestern border of the Indian subcontinent continuously since approximately 1000 BC, when the ancestors of the various East Iranian languages are thought to have arrived. East Iranian languages spoken today in Afghanistan and Pakistan include Pashto and many less widely spoken languages of an archaic character, like Wakhi. The Old Persian kings ruled the Indus Valley from the late sixth to late fourth century BC. The Indo-Scythian dynasties of Śakas, Kuṣāṇas and Parthians (Pahlavas) extended their rule to the Indo-Gangetic divide and western India between the first century BC and the third century AD. The Baluchis, who speak a West Iranian language, are thought to have arrived in Baluchistan around the tenth century AD (§ 9.1).

For a period of a thousand years, from the late second to the late first millennium BC, literary records available from South Asia are exclusively in Indo-Aryan languages. The earliest texts, the hymns of the Ṛgveda, are assumed to have come into being during the latter half of the second millennium BC, but it has not been possible to date their composition exactly; their final redaction, however, took place only about 700 BC. These documents, recording an archaic form of Old Indo-Aryan, are limited to the northwest of the subcontinent. During the early first millennium BC, the younger Vedic texts covered ever-widening areas of north India (fig. 8.22). Their dialects were gradually approaching Classical Sanskrit, that variety of Old Indo-Aryan which was spoken in the northwest around 400 BC, when it was described by Pāṇini in his marvellous grammar. Classical Sanskrit is close to the Epic Sanskrit of the bardic tradition which composed the core of the great epic Mahābhārata, perhaps in the fifth century BC, and thereafter continued to extend and elaborate it until about AD 400.

Middle Indo-Aryan represents a stage of linguistic development that presupposes Old Indo-Aryan, which it replaced as spoken language by the third century BC. *Saṁskṛta-bhāṣā* 'refined or perfected speech' continued to be cultivated by the learned Brahmins only. Middle Indo-Aryan is represented by various dialects called in the sources by the term *prākṛta-bhāṣā* or Prakrit, which denotes either 'natural speech', 'vulgar speech' or 'speech derived (from Sanskrit)'. It must be noted, however, that Middle Indo-Aryan has, to some extent at least, coexisted with Old Indo-Aryan as early as the times of the Ṛgveda, whose language has been penetrated by some typically Prakritic features.

The sociolinguistic position of Sanskrit as a prestige language is illustrated by the convention adopted in the dramatic literature, the earliest examples of which date from the first century AD. In the dramas, the king and the Brahmins speak Sanskrit, while women, children and all members of the lower castes speak different Prakrits. This is a clear historical antecedent of the present-day social stratification in South Asia, where there is great linguistic diversity. The various Prakrits spoken in the dramas are named after specific regions: thus Māgadhī is the eastern Prakrit of Magadha, Śaurasenī the Prakrit spoken in the country of the Śūrasenas around Mathurā, and Mahārāṣṭrī the western Prakrit of Maharashtra.

Gautama Buddha and Mahāvīra Jina, who lived between the sixth and fourth centuries BC in eastern India, taught in the local language of the common people, the Māgadhī Prakrit. The early texts redacted after the death of these religious leaders were adapted to the appropriate regional languages when Buddhism and Jainism spread westwards from Magadha. Thus birch-bark manuscripts of the Buddhist text Dharmapada found in the sandy deserts of eastern Turkestan have preserved evidence of Gāndhārī, the Prakrit spoken in ancient Gandhāra in the northwestern Indus Valley. Pali, which became the koine or link language of

Theravāda Buddhism, is a mixture of several dialects, but seems to have represented originally the Prakrit of Vidiśā in western central India, the place from which Asoka's son Mahinda is said to have brought Buddhism to Sri Lanka. Only a few characteristically eastern features survive in the 'Magadhisms' of Pali, limited to one or two fixed phrases of the Buddha. Ardha-Māgadhī, 'half-Māgadhī, used in the early parts of the Jaina canon of the Śvetāmbara school, has characteristics of eastern as well as western dialects.

Around 250 BC, King Asoka issued edicts and had them carved on rocks and pillars in different parts of his large empire, from Afghanistan and northern Pakistan all over North India and as far south as Karnataka. After the Indus texts, these inscriptions are the earliest directly preserved literary sources of South Asia. They are also the first texts that can be dated fairly exactly. The value of Asoka's edicts is further enhanced by the fact that they have been redacted in the local dialects, even if the bureaucratic procedures involved affect the authenticity of the Middle Indo-Aryan forms recorded in them. Their importance for the history of Indo-Aryan can hardly be exaggerated.

The decline of Buddhism and Jainism and the revival of Brahmanism in the second century BC coincided with an increasing diversification of the Prakrits, which became mutually incomprehensible. As the only supra-regional vehicle of communication, Sanskrit became a link language that could be understood all over South Asia. This led to the renaissance of Sanskrit, which started being used in inscriptions and in literature, even among the Buddhists of North India with their Buddhist Hybrid Sanskrit.

Between the sixth and tenth century AD, Middle Indo-Aryan went through its last phase called *apabhraṁśa* 'downfall, corruption'. Wide-ranging change, especially in morphology and syntax, initiated the Neo-Indo-Aryan stage. Sinhalese spoken on Sri Lanka developed in isolation from the other Neo-Indo-Aryan languages; its evolution can be followed in an uninterrupted series of inscriptions and literary texts. It has not been possible to establish a reliable genealogical tree diagram for the evolution of the various Neo-Indo-Aryan languages (fig. 8.7). There is a universal tendency for peripheral dialects to be more conservative than those in the centre, and this may partly explain the contrast between Hindi and its dialects and the nearly related Panjabi on the one hand, and the surrounding languages on the other, particularly Sindhi, Gujarati and Marathi, and Assamese, Bengali and Oriya.

Moreover, isolated dialects tend to preserve older forms than dialects in more accessible areas. The Dardic languages, spoken in the mountainous regions of the northwest from the Hindu Kush to Kashmir, are examples of this tendency, being the only modern languages to retain the augment, for instance; their ancestral forms seem to have more or less skipped the Middle Indo-Aryan phase. The Dardic languages (comprising Kalāšā, Khowār, Damelī, Gawar-bati, Šumaṣṭī, Pašaī, Baškarīk, Tōrwālī, Maiyā̃, Woṭapūrī, Tirāhī, Ṣiṇā, Phalūṛa, Ḍumākī and Kashmiri) clearly belong to the Indo-Aryan group. The 'Kafir' or Nuristani languages (Katī, Tregami, Waigalī, Prasun, Aškun), spoken by fewer than 100,000 people immediately west of the Dardic languages in the Hindu Kush mountains (fig. 8.7), form a peculiar group of Aryan languages resistant to classification as either Indo-Aryan or Iranian (see § 8.4).

The first of the non-Aryan languages of South Asia to be recorded is Tamil, known from inscriptions and literature that go back to the last centuries preceding the Christian era. Telugu, Kannaḍa and Malayāḷam, the other principal Dravidian languages of South India, have been recorded from the middle or second half of the first millennium AD. The rest of the Dravidian family (to be discussed in greater detail in chapter 9) consists of some 20 tribal languages noted down for the first time by modern researchers (fig. 8.8). The same applies to all the other non-Aryan languages of the sub-continent, which will be discussed in this section. Exceptions are Tibetan (written since AD 632), Newari (in Nepal), Lepcha (in Sikkim) and Manipuri (in Manipur), all of which have their own script systems of Indian origin, as well as Burmese (written since AD 1113); these languages belong to the Tibeto-Burman branch of the large Sino-Tibetan family (fig. 8.13).

The Muslim conquest of Sind in AD 712 marked the beginning of Perso-Arabic influence on South Asian languages. It has led, among other things, to the formation of Urdu, a variety of Hindi written in the Arabic script and having a large proportion of Perso-Arabic vocabulary. The sea trade initiated by Vasco da Gama in 1498 brought European languages to South Asia. Portuguese and English have been especially influential.

Some language families of South Asia have not been mentioned so far to avoid repetition. We shall now proceed with the elimination of irrelevant candidates in our search for the Indus language, paying attention to the archaeological as well as the linguistic evidence. Although archaeology constitutes one of the few sources of information about the prehistory of unwritten languages, it has been badly neglected in this connection. We must be clearly aware of the speculative nature of the information, however. Some methodological problems are, therefore, considered here.

Archaeological data, textual sources and linguistic evidence have preserved different aspects of antiquity. Each of these sources requires its own special methods of study, and yields a limited reconstruction of the past. The various reconstruc-

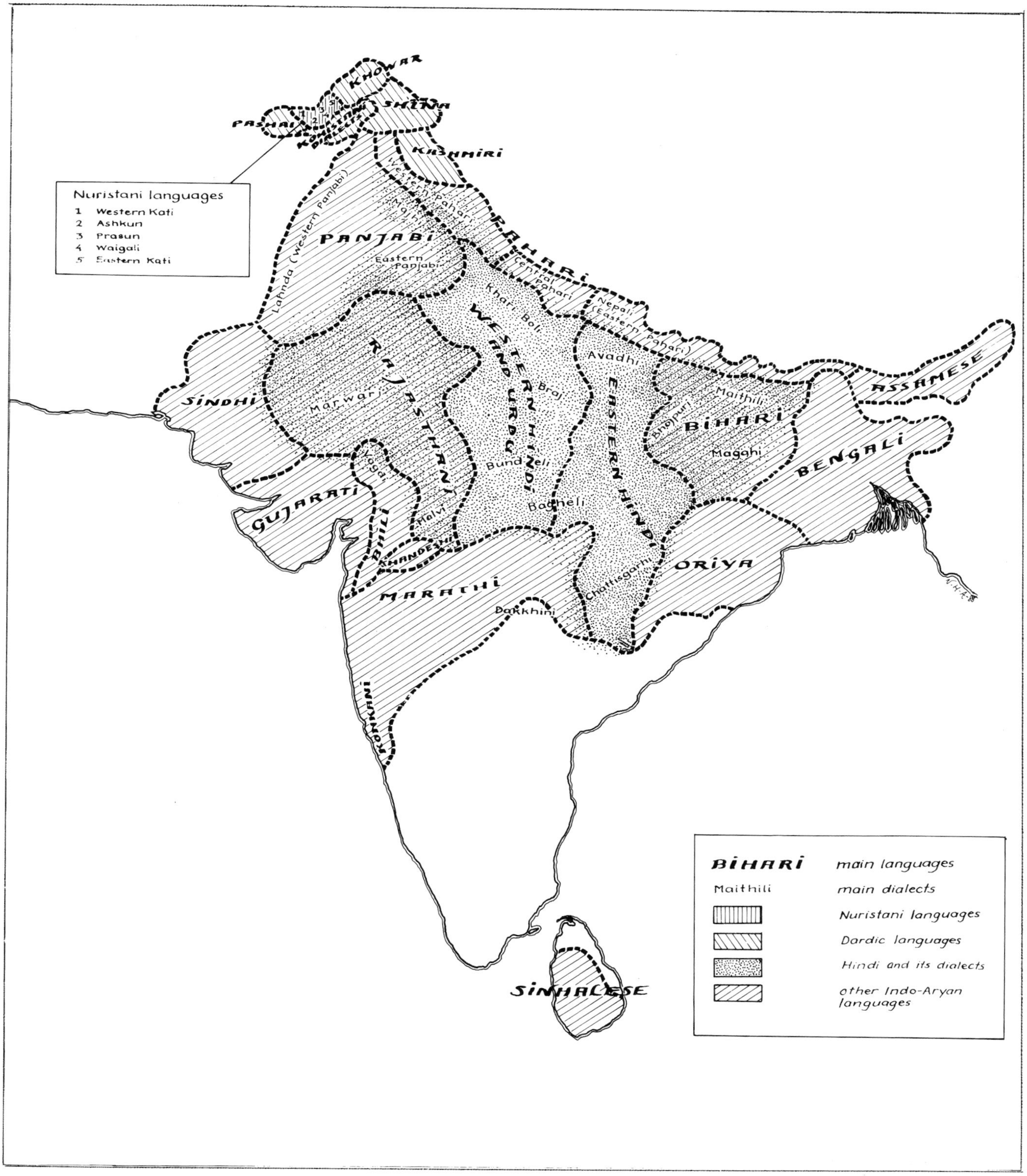

Fig. 8.7. Modern Indo-Aryan and Nuristani languages.

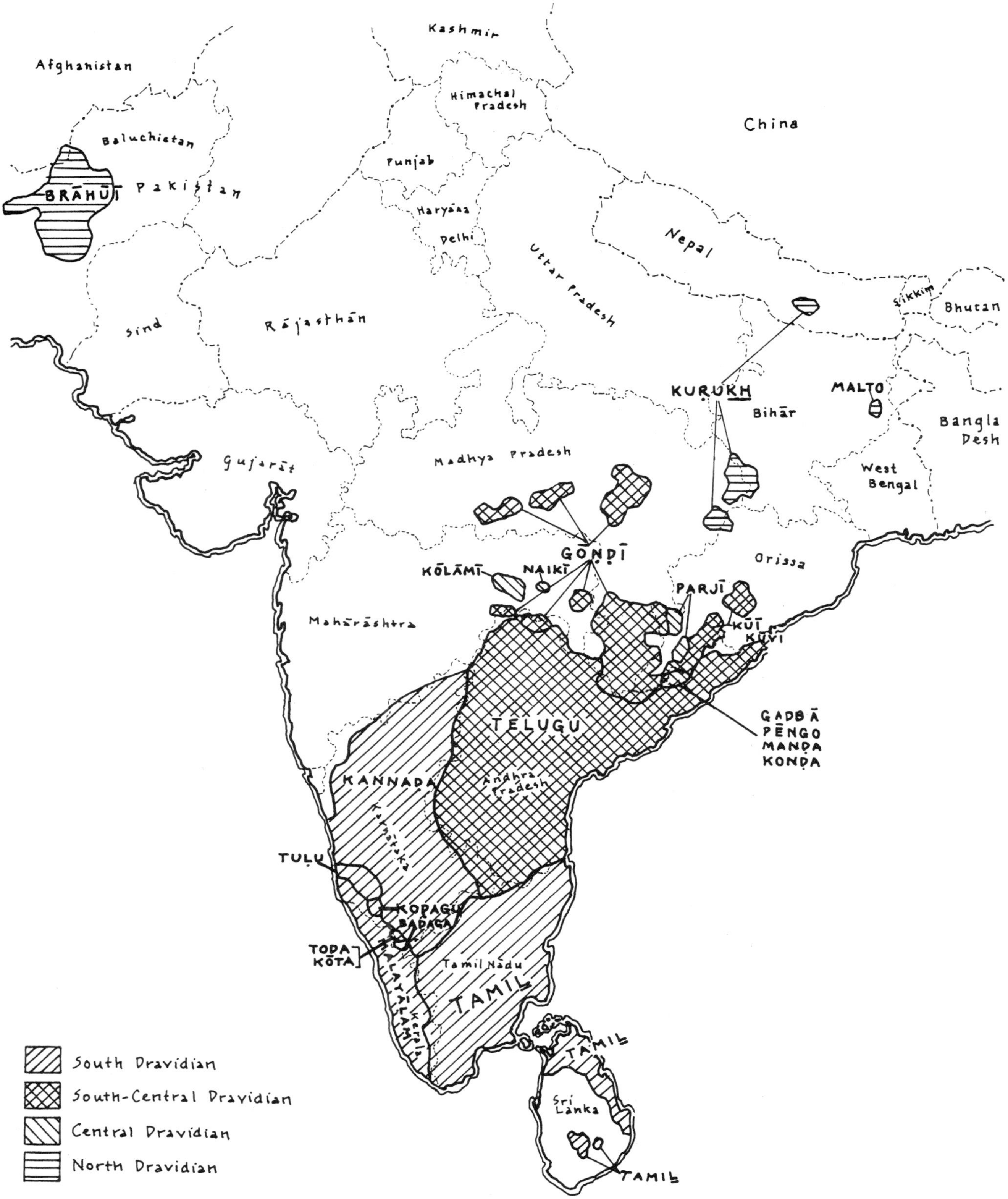

Fig. 8.8. Present-day distribution of the Dravidian languages.

tions may overlap in one or more basic aspects: time, space, content and external relationships. These partial overlaps may be sufficient for accurate correlations. As different sources usually provide complementary information, their integration, when it is verifiable, can produce new insights. It may become possible to date and locate texts and languages with the help of archaeology, and to interpret material remains with the help of texts.

Unfortunately, the correlation of textual-linguistic and archaeological data is complicated by a variety of factors. A language, like a material culture, can be adopted, and both can give and take loans in the form of isolated words and isolated material characteristics. The correspondence between language and culture is not always one to one: the culture of ancient Mesopotamia, for example, was shared by peoples speaking completely different languages. A number of languages are likely to have vanished without leaving any recognizable traces, and the archaeological record is often quite lacunary. The usefulness of a comparison naturally diminishes with the increase in the distance between the archaeological culture and the linguistic documentation that are being compared. Historical parallels show that the linguistic constellations of any given region can change fundamentally in 500 years.

Difficulties like these have often led to conflicting speculations, and critical scholars have been unwilling to accept hypotheses resting on such unsafe foundations. But if the chances are reasonable, hyper-scepticism should not deter us from suggesting an integrated hypothesis that best fits and explains the evidence. An uncertain but possible hypothesis is better than no hypothesis. No such higher level reconstruction can ever claim finality, so it must be revised continuously. New excavations and analyses are constantly refining our understanding of archaeological cultures; changes are likewise being brought about by newly discovered texts, languages, etymologies, and so forth.

The reconstructions achieved separately by archaeology, linguistics, philology and anthropology through the critical application of their own special methodologies should be taken as the basis for a working hypothesis. Secondly, one should try to match the entire spectrum of the archaeological cultures of an area with the whole range of languages and dialects known from historical linguistics, instead of operating with isolated cultures and languages. Each of the different cultures and languages has its own real or assumed temporal and spatial range and is related to other cultures or languages in a particular way. The individual pieces are thus tested against an overall pattern.

The Mesolithic hunter-gatherers of South Asia and the primitive Neolithic farmer-pastoralists of the northern plains and peninsular India must have spoken hundreds of languages, as the aboriginal tribes of Australia and New Zealand did until recently. The differences between their cultures entitle us to assume that their languages, too, were quite dissimilar from those used in the advanced Neolithic cultures of Baluchistan which started spreading to the Indus Valley and beyond in the fourth millennium BC (§ 1.6). This eastward migration led to a population explosion and to the permanent settlement of large areas. Ethnographic parallels from present-day India suggest some degree of symbiosis between the nomadic and settled populations, based on an exchange of goods and services.

Over the millennia, contacts of this nature have led to bilingualism and the gradual assimilation and extinction of many local languages. Such dead languages are likely to be the source of words for indigenous plants and animals that have no etymology in the known language families. It has been estimated that as much as one-third of the agricultural vocabulary of Hindi is of unknown origin. In less accessible and less hospitable areas the earlier inhabitants have undoubtedly preserved their original languages for a long time. The isolated Andamanese of the Andaman Islands is spoken even today, if only by a few hundred people. A few other hunter-gatherer tribes and primitive farmers have preserved in their languages some (mainly lexical) remnants of otherwise unknown languages; these include the Nahāli in western Madhya Pradesh, the Iruḷa in the Nilagiris of Tamil Nadu, and the now extinct Vedda and Rodiya in Sri Lanka (fig. 8.9).

The Austro-Asiatic languages of India were spoken by about 5 million people in 1951. This made them the third largest linguistic family after Indo-European and Dravidian. Until the nineteenth century, they had been unwritten tribal languages. The Munda languages of central and eastern India (including Mundari and Santali) form the westernmost branch of the Austro-Asiatic family. Khasi (spoken in Assam) and Nicobarese of the Nicobar Islands link the western branch with the much larger eastern branch of this great language family spoken in Southeast Asia (fig. 8.10).

The distribution of the Austro-Asiatic family best agrees with that of the Eastern Neolithic culture of India. The Eastern Neolithic, known in several variants, dates from *c.*2000 BC. Its characteristic tool is the shouldered and faceted ground stone axe, widely distributed in Bihar, Orissa, Assam and Bengal. These axes have parallels in Southeast Asia and South China (fig. 8.11).

Austro-Asiatic loanwords or other influences on the oldest phase of Indo-Aryan in the northwest have not been demonstrated with any certainty. Among the most likely candidates is the Vedic word for 'rice', *vrīhi* < **vrīźhi*, because rice cultivation seems to have spread from the Ganges Valley to Swat, to Pirak in the Kachi plain and to Gujarat in the first

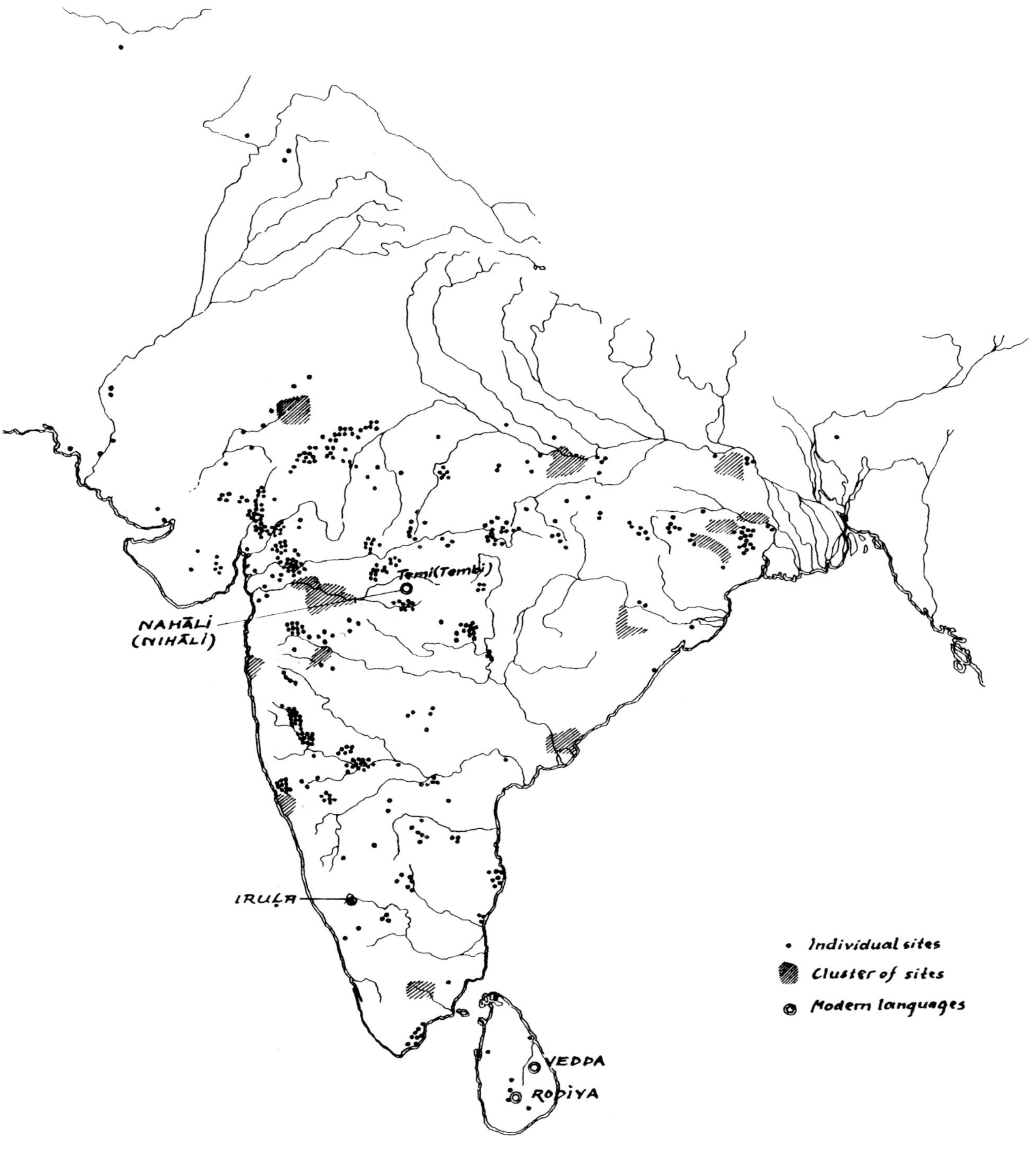

Fig. 8.9. Microlithic sites in South Asia (according to Schwartzberg 1978) and the areas in which the relict languages Nahāli, Iruḷa, Vedda and Rodiya are or were spoken.

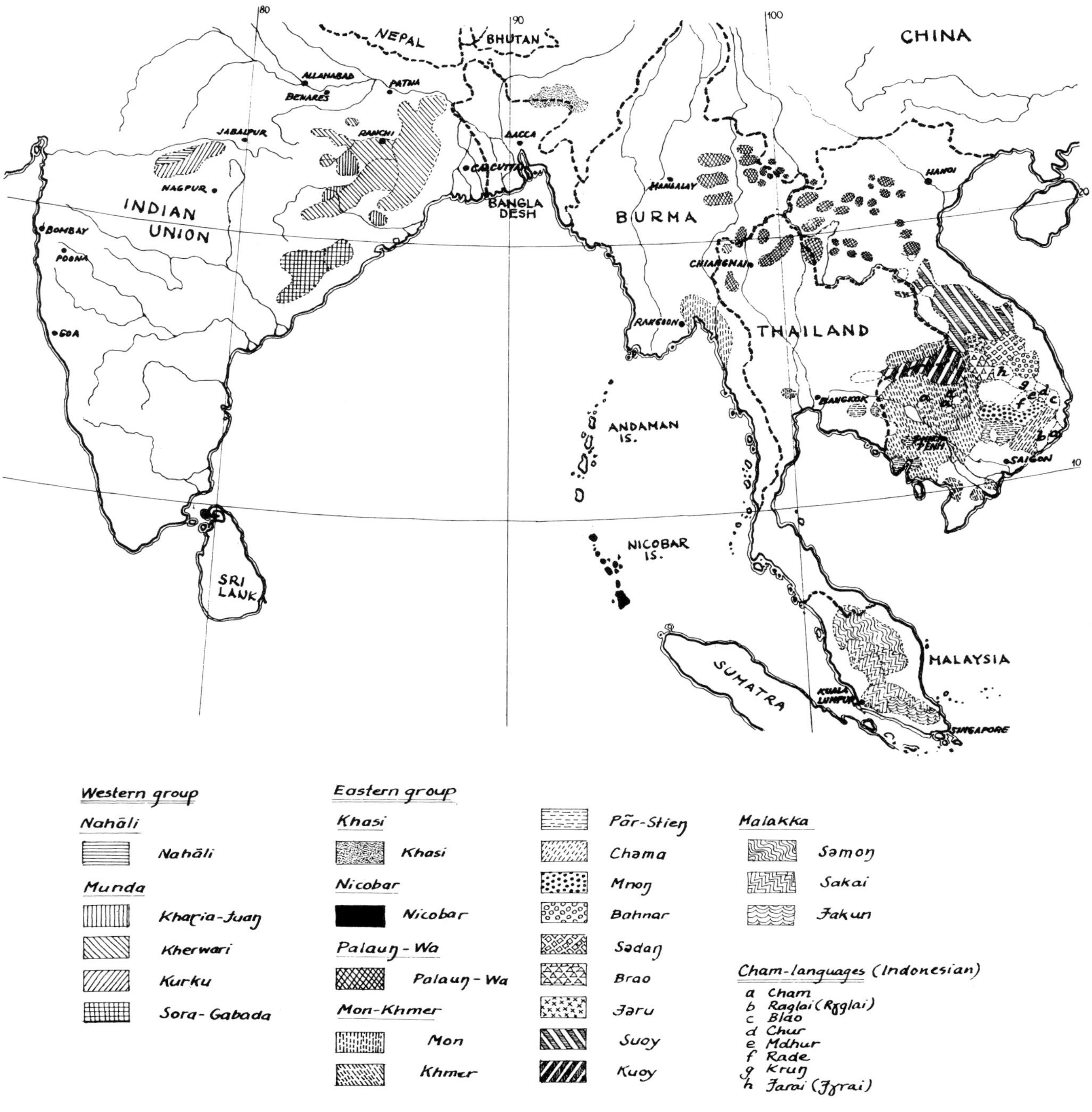

Fig. 8.10. Distribution of the Austro-Asiatic languages. Redrawn from Pinnow 1959.

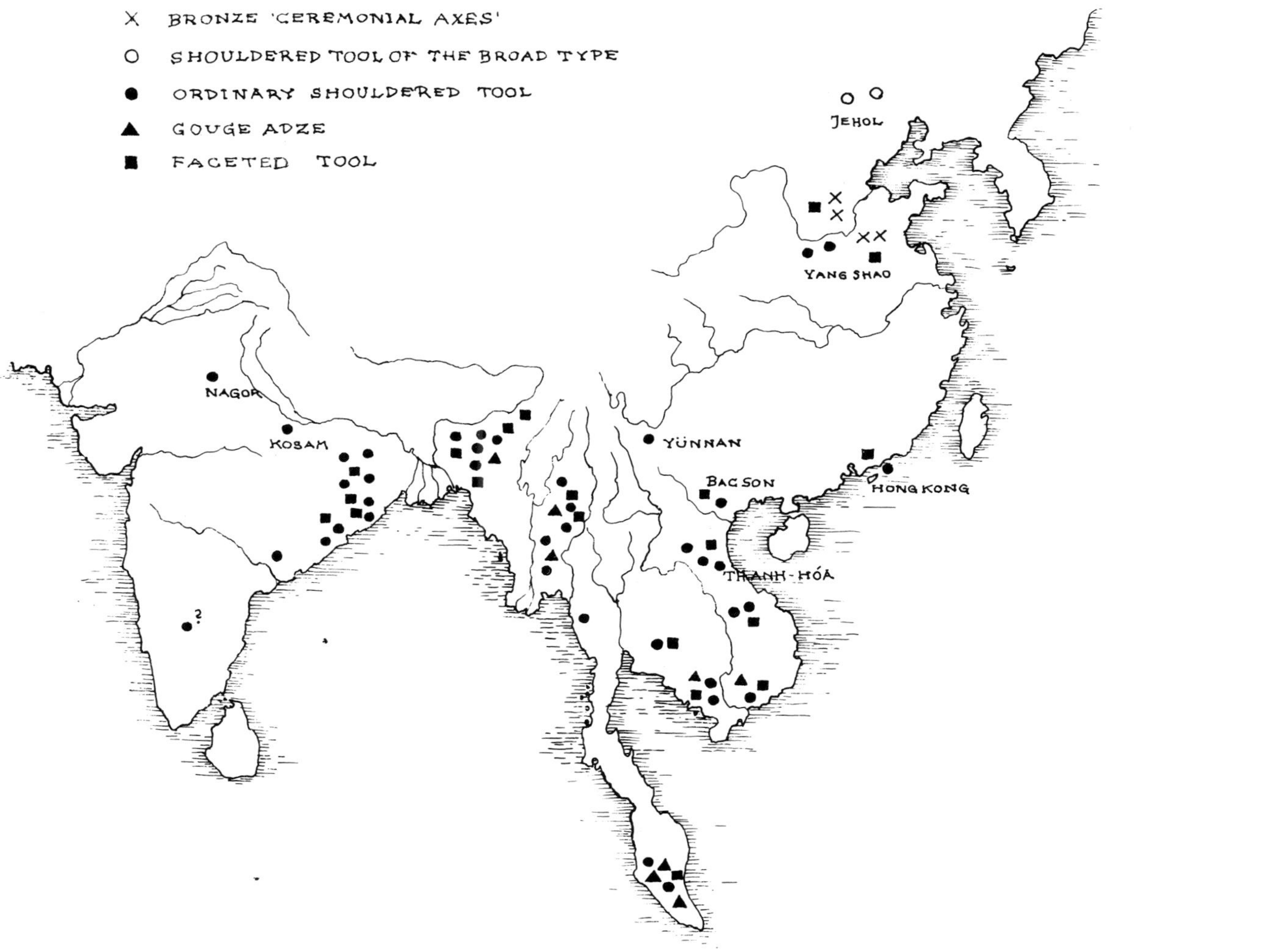

Fig. 8.11. Distribution of Eastern Neolithic cultures of South Asia and their external relationships. Redrawn from Dani 1960: map 8.

quarter of the second millennium BC. Tamil *arici* and related Dravidian words for 'rice' may go back to the same source. However, the etymology of the Vedic word has remained unclear, and does not tally with the Proto-Austro-Asiatic words for 'rice' (**bak / *bah*, and reduplicated **ba(k)bak*; **pɛG / *piG*) or their historical developments. The earliest evidence for domesticated rice in India comes from the Neolithic site of Koldihwa on the Belan river near Allahabad in the middle Ganges Valley. The radiocarbon dates place these finds *c.*7000–4000 BC, and they may well predate the arrival of the Austro-Asiatic speakers to the subcontinent from the east. It does not seem very likely, therefore, that the Austro-Asiatic languages would have been spoken in the Indus Valley in the third millennium BC.

Further evidence to this effect is supplied by areal linguistics (§ 9.2). Retroflex phonemes are absent from the eastern Austro-Asiatic languages and are less completely represented in the Munda languages than in Indo-Aryan and Dravidian. This situation is best explained by assuming that the Munda languages came into contact with Indo-Aryan and Dravidian relatively late, which again suggests that Austro-Asiatic speakers were even in early times mainly confined to central and eastern India; the Ganges–Yamunā doab may have been their westernmost border. The proper name of one of the principal enemies of the early Aryans, *Śambara*, is often quoted as evidence for Austro-Asiatic substratum in the R̥gveda; but this name can be better explained otherwise (§ 8.4).

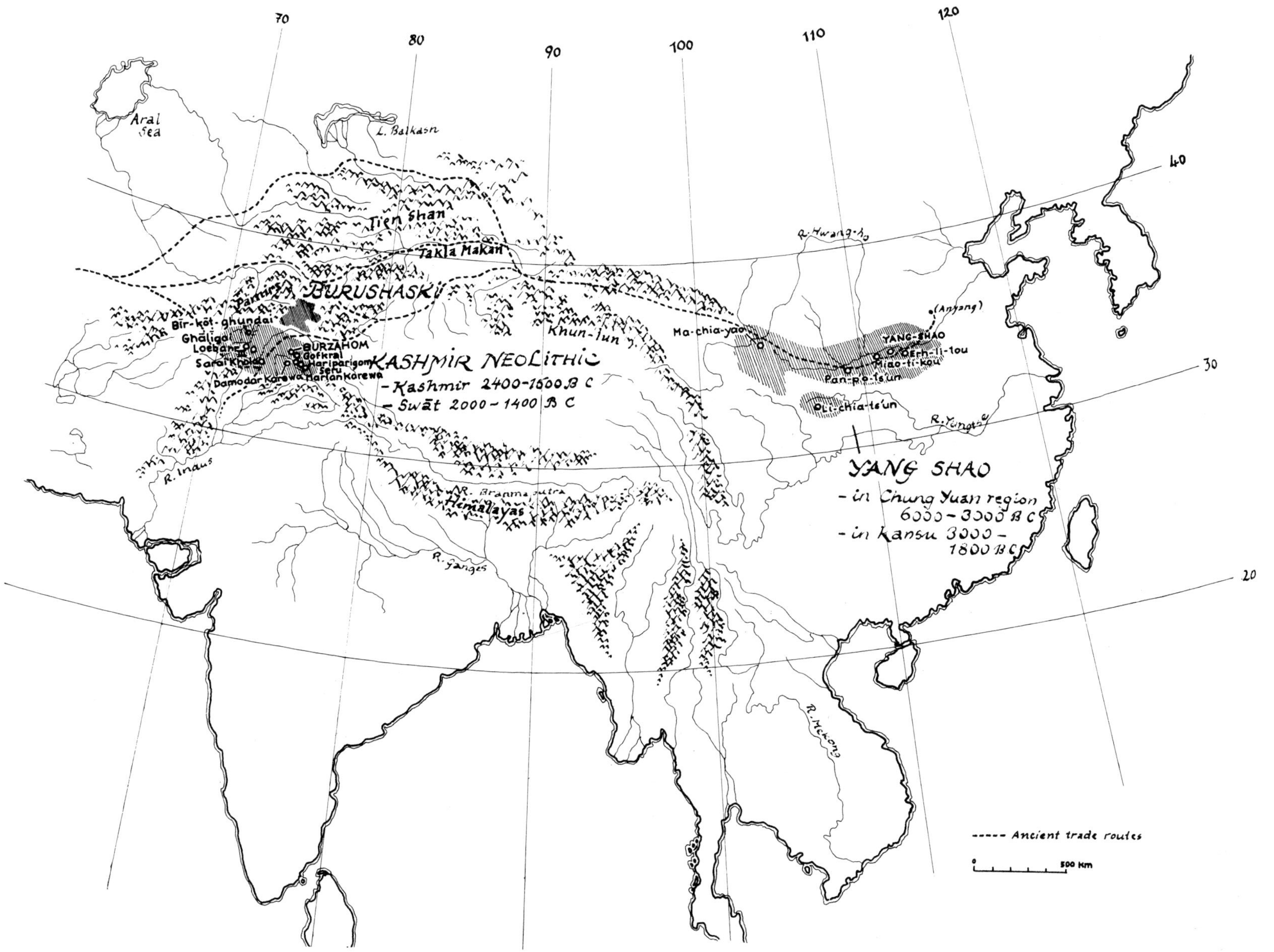

Fig. 8.12. Area in which the Burushaski language is spoken today; the Northern Neolithic of South Asia; the Yang Shao Neolithic of China; and ancient trade routes in Inner Asia.

The isolated language of Burushaski is spoken high in the Karakorum mountains, in the valleys of Yasin, Hunza and Nagir (fig. 8.12). Burushaski has strong areal ties with the neighbouring languages Shina and Khowar (belonging to the Dardic group of Indo-Aryan), Wakhi (East Iranian) and Balti (Tibetan). Outside this rather small area its influence has been minimal or relatively recent. For instance in Kashmiri there appears to be little trace of Burushaski. It is therefore difficult to link it with the Northern Neolithic found in Kashmir (Burzahom), the Potwar plateau (Sarai Khola I) and in the valley of Swat (Ghalegay I). Rather, it seems likely that the earliest speakers of Burushaski entered their present homeland from the north after the inception of the Northern Neolithic, and have never gone much further. Are the Burusho perhaps to be connected with the evidence of some recently discovered petroglyphs in Chilas in the Hindu Kush, suggesting connections with the Tazmin culture that flourished in south Siberia *c.*3000–2500 BC? Such speculation cannot be soundly based until there has been archaeological excavation in the Hunza Valley.

The Northern Neolithic of the third and second millennia BC is considered to be genetically related to the Yang Shao Neolithic cultures of northern China and Mongolia, with which it shares a number of traits (fig. 8.12). These shared traits include the burial of dogs with their masters, distinctive rectangular stone knives with two holes at one edge, and underground houses which provided shelter against the cold of the winter and the heat of the summer. Somewhat comparable pit houses are still constructed along the Yellow River in China. Nephrite beads found at Loebanr in Swat also point to trade with Khotan.

The language (assuming there was only one) spoken by the people of the Northern Neolithic may have died out, but not without influencing the later languages of the regions. The many phonological and syntactic peculiarities of Indo-Aryan Kashmiri, which set it apart from the rest of the Dardic group, point to an extinct substratum language. Whatever the affinity of that language was, it has not much relevance for the study of the Indus Civilization, because the contacts between the Northern Neolithic and the Harappans were very limited. Among the few artefacts testifying to this infrequent intercourse is an Early Harappan pot of the Kot Dijian type found at Burzahom in Kashmir (fig. 14.19d).

One possible candidate for the Northern Neolithic seems worth further consideration, however. The Tibeto-Burman languages belonging to the great Sino-Tibetan family occupy the mountain ranges bordering the Indian subcontinent on the north and the east (fig. 8.13). The Tibetic branch consists of Tibetan in its different varieties and the Himalayan languages (including, for example, Kanauri on the upper Sutlej river and Gurung spoken in Nepal, Sikkim and Assam). While Tibetan is thought to have come to Tibet from the northeast, the difference between the Tibetan and Himalayan languages allows the assumption that the latter may have arrived by a different route, from the northwest, and thus the Northern Neolithic may have been Proto-Himalayan-speaking. This is suggested also by the fact that a manuscript relating to the Bon religion of western Tibet has been discovered in Dun Huang, written in the extinct Zhang Zhung language, which appears to have been closely related to Kanauri.

Exactly when the Tibeto-Burman languages arrived in their present areas is unknown, but their location and external contacts make them rather unlikely candidates for being related to the literary language of the Indus Civilization:

> This linguistic family has always remained essentially external to India proper. Furthermore it appears that on the eastern frontiers of India these peoples have displaced earlier Austro-Asiatic populations and that their contact is not very ancient. It is possible that a few Sanskrit words may eventually be traced to this origin, but at present no satisfactory evidence of such influence is available. (Burrow 1973a: 376).

There is no permanent bond between race and language: one language can be changed for another. But language does play a role in the preservation of ethnic identity. It is a fact that most of the people speaking Tibeto-Burman languages belong to the Mongoloid racial type, and have done so for a long time. It used to be maintained that the skeletal remains from Harappa attest to the presence of a few Mongoloids there, but this conclusion has not withstood the re-examination of the evidence by the Italian anthropologist Mario Cappieri. A typological characteristic of Tibeto-Burman (the word order N + Num) which is contrary to the Indus evidence has been mentioned already (§§ 6.1 and 8.1).

We have thus concluded our preliminary survey of the languages spoken in South Asia. The peoples of these areas nowadays mainly speak Aryan and Dravidian languages. Some decades ago, the speakers of Indo-Aryan constituted about three-quarters of the population of the Indian subcontinent and the speakers of Dravidian about one-quarter, but with the rapid increase in population the proportion of the Indo-Aryan speakers has increased further. There has also been an extensive literature in the Indo-Aryan and Dravidian languages from early times. These two families have emerged as the main contenders for a genetic relationship with the Indus language, and the problems of their prehistory will be discussed at some length in what follows.

8.4 The coming of the Aryans

The Aryan or Indo-Iranian branch of the Indo-European (= IE) language family is classified into three distinct groups:

Fig. 8.13. Distribution of the Sino-Tibetan languages. The Daic / Tai / Thai languages are not Sino-Tibetan, but seem to contain a layer of a Sino-Tibetan superstratum. Based on Shafer 1974: xvi and Egerod 1974: 722, fig. 24.

Indo-Aryan, Iranian and Nuristani. The Indo-Aryan languages, spoken mainly on the Indian subcontinent, have had a continuous literary tradition since the second millennium BC, when the hymns of the Ṛgveda are supposed to have been composed in the northwest of Pakistan and India. The earliest directly preserved texts are the Middle Indo-Aryan inscriptions of King Asoka belonging to the third century BC. The Iranian languages, spoken in historical times on the Iranian plateau and the Eurasian steppes, have their earliest directly preserved monuments in the Old Persian inscriptions of the Achaemenid kings (sixth to fourth century BC). The songs of Zarathustra, the most ancient parts of the holy texts of Avesta, may be either just a little or considerably older, and are thought to have been composed in the northeast of the Iranian plateau. The Nuristani languages spoken in the Hindu Kush mountains are known from modern times only.

Both philologists and archaeologists have long tried to solve the questions of where and when the Aryan branch came into

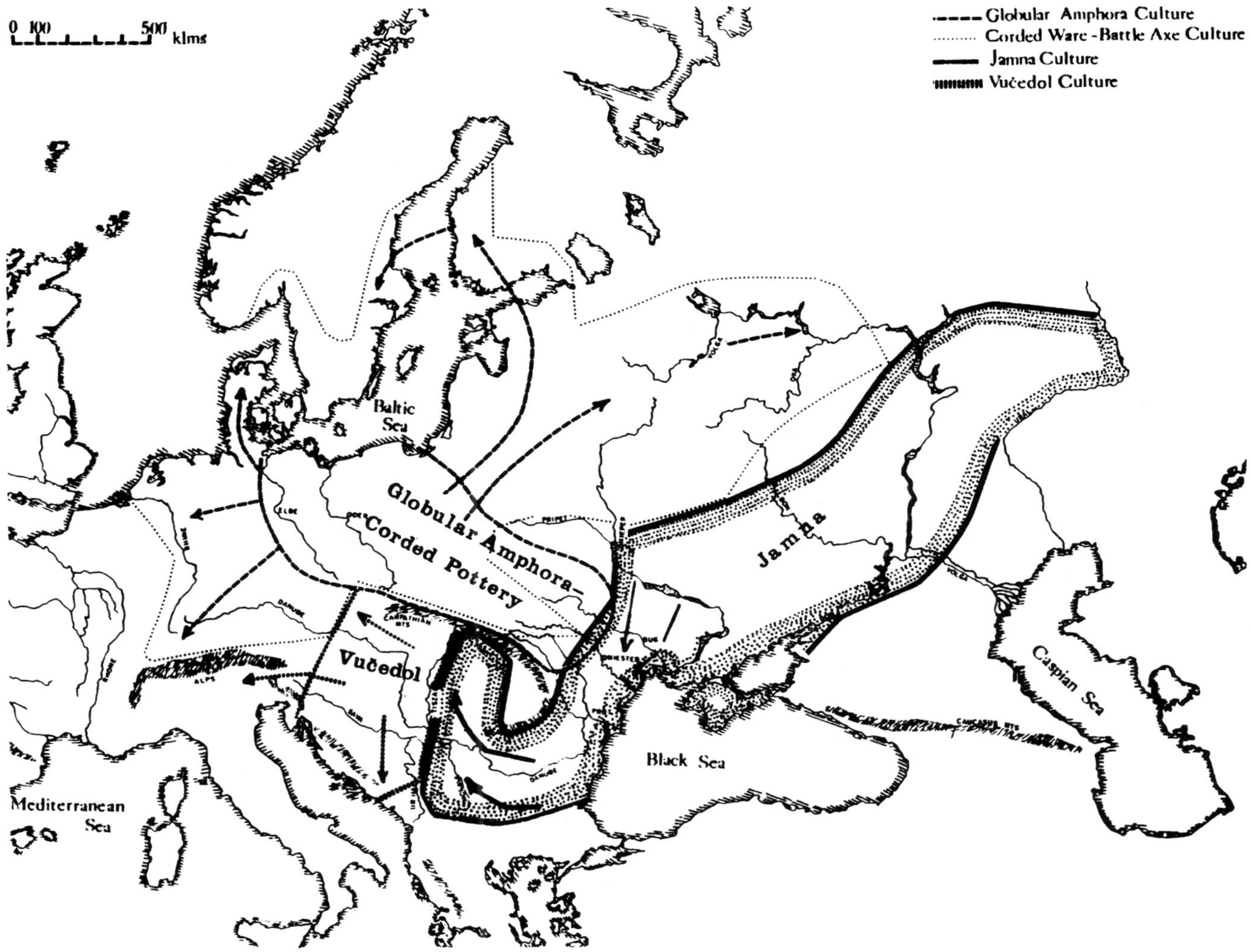

Fig. 8.14. The spread of the Proto-Indo-European language *c.*3000–2800 BC according to Marija Gimbutas: primarily from the Pit Grave (Yamna) culture of the Pontic-Caspian steppes and secondarily through the Globular Amphora / Corded Ware horizons. After Gimbutas 1986: 8, fig. 2.

being, how exactly the Proto-Aryan language disintegrated and when and by which routes the various Aryan groups came to the Near East, Iran and India. Hundreds of hypotheses have been proposed, based on different kinds of source material. Although the research so far has not been able to produce definitive answers, recent discussions have defined many aspects of the Aryan problem more clearly and thus brought it closer to a solution. The startling discoveries in Central Asia made lately by Soviet archaeologists have provided fresh evidence in the light of which the pieces of the puzzle may now be reassembled.

The Pit Grave (in Russian, Yamna) culture which flourished in the Pontic-Caspian steppe *c.*3500–2800 BC was first thought to represent the Proto-Indo-European speakers by Gordon Childe in 1926. This idea has been elaborated since the 1950s by Marija Gimbutas, who has spoken of the 'Kurgan (i.e. barrow) culture' (fig. 8.14). In 1989, J. P. Mallory published a well-informed and many-sided synthesis of the relevant evidence endorsing this hypothesis, which has been the one most favoured by Indo-Europeanists in recent times. In regard to its contents, location and chronology, the Pit Grave culture compares well with those of the Proto-Indo-European speech community, whose disintegration can be dated towards the end of the fourth millennium BC (§ 8.5). There are some parallel traits, but as yet no convincing link, between the Pit Grave culture and the Corded Ware horizon of central and northern Europe, which is most likely to have been associated with the early spread of the Indo-European language into these regions (fig. 8.14).

The Indo-Iranian languages share with Greek and

Armenian certain innovations. The forefathers of Proto-Greeks, Proto-Armenians and Proto-Aryans may therefore have lived in contact with each other for some time in the steppes north of the Black Sea early in the third millennium. They separated, however, before the IE palatal gutturals became affricated in the Satəm group of languages. In addition to the Aryan languages, the Satəm language group included Baltic, Slavic, Albanian and Armenian. Their protoforms were spoken in the centre of the IE area, while the Centum languages preserving the original gutturals were spoken on the periphery. Hittite and related dialects in Anatolia, the oldest known Indo-European languages written in early second millennium BC (§ 8.2), belong to the Centum group, which is otherwise found mainly in western Europe. The presence of an isolated Centum language called Tocharian in Chinese Turkestan is difficult to explain archaeologically unless it was carried eastwards as early as *c*.3000 BC by an early Pit Grave offshoot in south Siberia, the Afanasievo culture. This is a good example of how expansions from the Pontic-Caspian region can account for the dispersion of the Indo-European languages.

Baltic and Slavic, which share a number of linguistic features with Germanic, also have idiosyncrasies in common with Indo-Iranian, and were their closest neighbours in the Satəm period. If Proto-Baltic and Proto-Slavic were spoken near their earliest historically attested areas, Proto-Aryan is likely to have been spoken in the Pontic-Caspian steppes. This hypothesis is supported by other considerations.

The Uralic languages contain a number of loanwords borrowed from neighbouring Indo-European languages, datable by linguistic criteria from Pre-Indo-European to the present day. The Uralic protolanguage is nowadays thought to have disintegrated by *c*.4000 BC; the succeeding phases of its Finnic branch are dated as follows: Proto-Finno-Ugrian *c*.4000–3000 BC, Proto-Finno-Permic *c*.3000–2000 BC, and Proto-Volga-Finnic *c*.2000–1500 BC. The early Uralic speakers are commonly identified with the hunters and fishers of the forest zone stretching from northeastern Europe to western Siberia and associated with the Comb- and Pit-marked Pottery tradition. Archaeological evidence for early Indo-European contact with this northern tradition is provided by the Eneolithic Samara culture in the middle Volga forest-steppe.

Some of the Aryan loanwords in Uralic languages go back to protoforms that are so close to Proto-Indo-European that they can be recognized as being (Pre-)Aryan in origin only from their exclusively Aryan distribution on the Indo-European side from which they were taken.

An example is the etymon meaning 'spindle', found in all the languages of the Baltic-Finnic branch (Finnish *kehrä*, etc.) and also in languages of the Volgaic branch (Mordvin E *št'eŕe*, *štšeŕe*, M *kšt'iŕ*, Cheremis *š°δ°r*, *šüδ°r*). The internal Finno-Ugric evidence yields a reconstructed protoform *kesträ / *kesträ (possibly < *keṭṣträ) 'spindle' that goes back at least to the Volga-Finnic period but is likely to be as old as Proto-Finno-Ugric. On the Indo-European side, the etymon is attested in the Aryan branch alone, in both Iranian and Indo-Aryan, including Sanskrit *cāttra-* and *cattra-* 'spindle', of which the latter corresponds to Pashto *cāṣ̌ai* 'spindle' < Old Iranian *cas-tra- < Proto-Aryan *ket^{s}tro-. The Proto-Aryan reconstructions seem to represent the Proto-Indo-European stage: *ket^{s}tro- < *kēt^{s}tro- < *kert^{s}tro- < *kert-tro- < *kert- > Sanskrit *kr̥t-kr̥ṇátti* 'spins', *karttr̥* 'spinner'. (Koivulehto 1979, summarized)

In addition to such very early Proto-Aryan loanwords, Uralic languages also have some younger loanwords, which already have a distinctly Proto-Aryan form. A well-known example is the numeral '100', Finnish *sata*, Veps and Estonian *sada*, Livonian *sadà*; Lapp N *čuotte* / *čuode*; Mordvin E *śado*, M *śada*; Cheremis (Mari) *šüδə*; Votyak *śu*; Zyrian *śo*; Vogul *śāt*, *sēt*, *sāt*; Ostyak *sot*; Hungarian *száz*. The reconstructed protoform presupposed by these words is *śata, traditionally considered to go back to the Proto-Finno-Ugric period. But in spite of its wide distribution on the Finno-Ugric side, Proto-Aryan *ćatám / śatám (not Proto-Iranian *satam or PIE *(d)km̥tóm) 'hundred' is now thought to have been borrowed only after the Proto-Finno-Ugric period. Still other loanwords in Uralic languages reflect Proto- or later Iranian, which is in agreement with the archaeological model suggesting an unbroken cultural continuity from the Eneolithic to the Iron Age in the Pontic-Caspian steppes.

The late phase of the Pit Grave culture, known as the Hut Grave culture and dated to *c*.2800–2000 BC, is most likely to represent the Proto-Aryan-speaking community. The Pit Grave and Hut Grave cultures were succeeded without break by the Timber Grave (in Russian, Srubnaya) culture, which flourished *c*.2000–800 BC in the Pontic-Caspian steppes, and by the related Andronovo cultures, which covered an enormous area of the steppes from the southern Urals over Kazakhstan to southern Siberia *c*.1800–900 BC (fig. 8.15). The Timber Grave and Andronovo cultures in their turn were the direct ancestors of the Iron Age cultures of the Iranian-speaking Scythians and Sakas.

The earliest directly preserved written evidence of an Aryan language is found in documents relating to the kingdom of Mitanni in northern Syria, dated *c*.1500–1300 BC (fig. 8.16). While the majority of the Mitanni population spoke the local Hurrian language, the ruling aristocracy had Aryan names and invoked Aryan gods as oath deities in their treaties. A Hittite text on horse-training and chariotry written by a Mitannian called Kikkuli employs a number of technical terms which are of Aryan etymology.

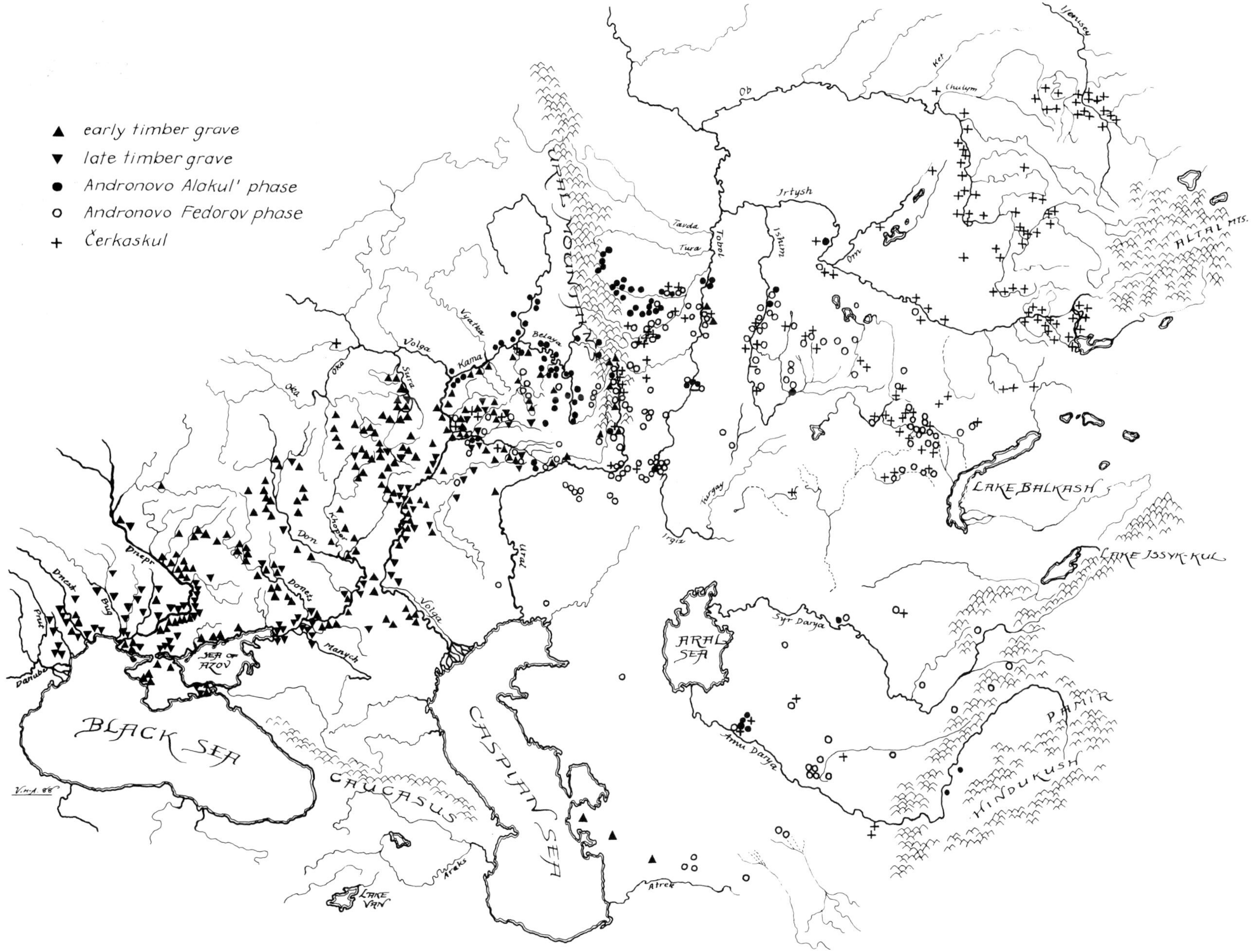

Fig. 8.15. Distribution of the Timber Grave and Andronovo cultures. Based on Chlenova 1984: map facing page 100.

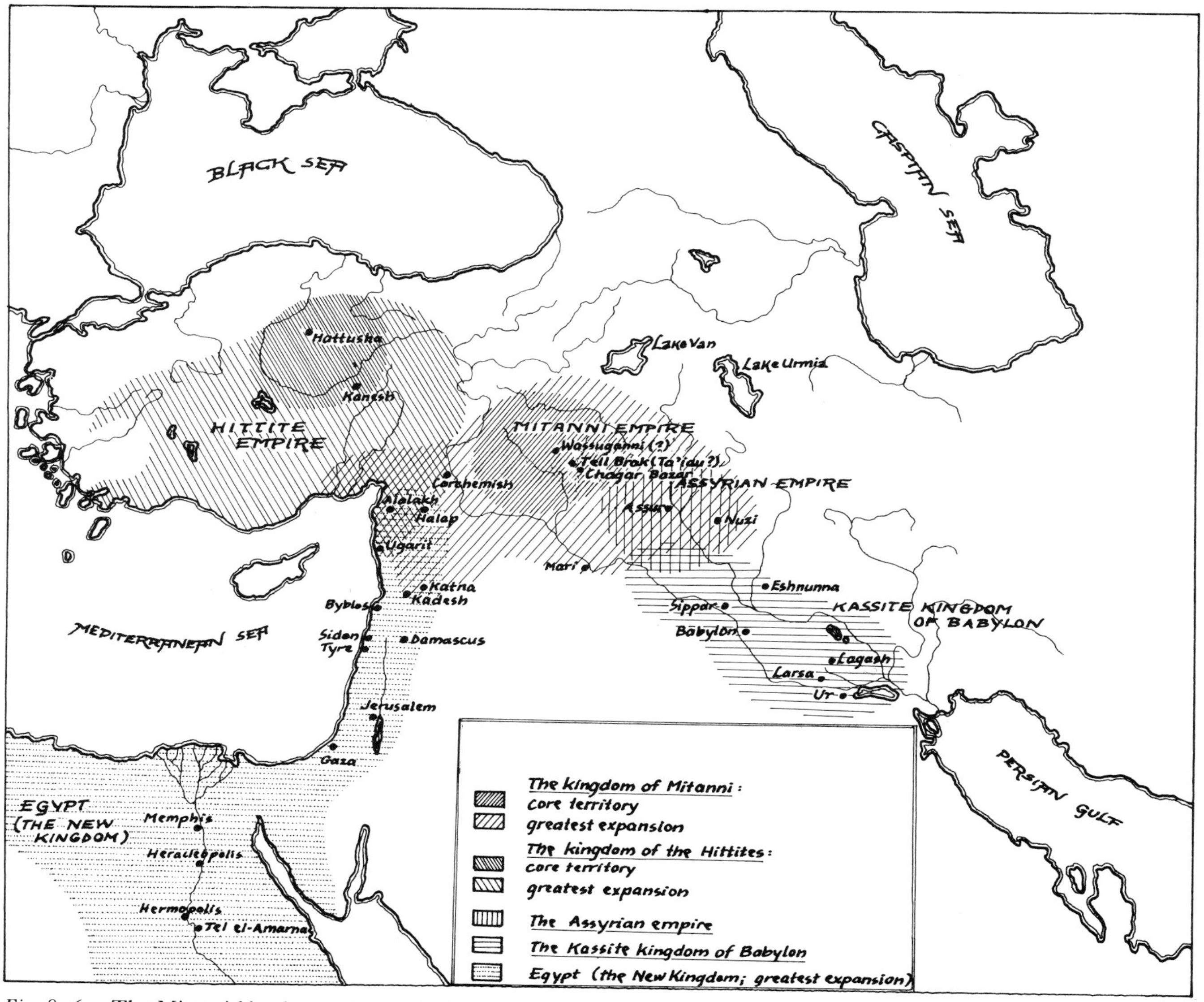

Fig. 8.16. The Mitanni kingdom and its neighbours.

It is now generally agreed that Mitanni Aryan is related to the Indo-Aryan rather than the Iranian or Nuristani branch. Here the linguistic evidence is not as conclusive as the oath deities mentioned in the Mitanni treaties. Paul Thieme (1960) has shown that the cuneiform renderings correspond to the Vedic deities Mitrā-Varuṇā (dual form for a pair), Indra and Nāsatyā (= Aśvinau, dual). All these gods are invoked as protectors of treaties in the R̥gveda, and in one stanza they are mentioned together and in the same order (R̥S 10,125,1bc). Only Mitra, whose name originally means 'contract, treaty', is common to both the Vedic and the Zarathustran religions, while Varuṇa is known from the Veda alone. Indra, the chief god of the Vedic pantheon, is mentioned in the Avesta only twice (Vīdevdāt 10,9 and 19,43), both times as a bad 'demon' together with Saurva (Vedic Śarva) and Nāŋhaiθya (Vedic Nāsatya). The Avestan word for 'demon', *daēva*, goes back to **daiva*, the earlier form of the Vedic word for 'god', *deva*, while the Avestan and (Proto-Iranian) word for 'god' is *baga* (related to Old Slavonic *bogŭ* 'god').

The Mitanni Aryans in the west (Syria) and the Indo-Aryans in the east (India) are both assumed to have come from a Proto-Indo-Aryan 'homeland' that was situated in the middle of these two peripheral areas, somewhere in southern Central Asia or the eastern parts of the Iranian plateau. After the arrival of Proto-Iranians from the northern steppes, Zarathustra, who was born in that country, instituted a religious reform, condemning the cult of the *daēvas* (cf. Yašt 13,89–90) which had continued until his times. Worshippers of *daēvas* seem to have existed even in Māzandarān, between the Caspian Sea and the Elburz mountains, on the route to Mitanni.

It is thought that the Proto-Indo-Aryan language associated with the Mitanni nobles was practically dead by 1500–1300 BC, as its speakers had largely adopted the local Hurrian language. Roman Ghirshman (1977) has proposed that the symbiosis between the Mitanni Aryans and the Hurrians may have started earlier and further east. In any case, Proto-Indo-Aryan, having already clearly diverged from Proto-Iranian, must have existed around 1600 BC; Thomas Burrow (1973a) has estimated that the separation of these two Aryan branches had started by 2000 BC at the latest.

Ghirshman thought that the Mitanni Aryans had come from the Gurgan plain at the southeastern corner of the Caspian Sea. One of his arguments was the similarity between the dark luxury ceramics of the Mitanni palaces and the Gurgan Grey Ware of the Tepe Hissar IIIc horizon. The similarity is not very close, however. On the other hand, Cuyler Young (1985; in press), a leading authority on early Iranian archaeology, is inclined to see the Early West Iranian Grey Ware that suddenly appears in great quantities all along the Elburz mountains, in Azerbaijan and around Lake Urmia *c.*1500 BC as an evolved form of Gurgan Grey Ware; in addition, there are linkages in the metallurgy. This major break, represented by Early West Iranian Grey Ware in the archaeological record of Iran, cannot yet signal the arrival of the Medes and the Persians, who are first mentioned as being in the Zagros area in the Neo-Assyrian textual sources *c.*850 BC. Their coming is linked with the appearance in the ninth century of Late West Iranian Buff Ware, entirely new pottery in every respect, which is clearly ancestral to Achaemenid ceramics and is probably derived from the buff wares that appear in the Gurgan region around the eleventh century BC.

Ghirshman thought that the horsemanship for which the Mitannians were so famous had its origins in the regions southeast of the Caspian Sea. A cylinder seal from Tepe Hissar IIIb bears what has been claimed to be the earliest known representation of a horse-drawn chariot (fig. 8.17). The chariot has two cross-bar wheels, which represent a transitional stage between solid wheels and spoked wheels. Miniature models of trumpets, made of gold and silver, have been found at Tepe Hissar IIIc (and probably at Tureng Tepe, too) in Gurgan; as Ghirshman pointed out, trumpets were needed for directing chariots in battle, and an Egyptian bas-relief of Ramses III (early twelfth century BC, soon after intensive Egyptian contacts with Mitanni) shows that trumpets were used in training horses.

Fig. 8.17. A horse-drawn two-wheeled chariot on an alabaster cylinder seal from Tepe Hissar IIIb in northern Iran. After Littauer and Crouwel 1977: pl. 9b.

Close similarities in a wide variety of characteristic cultural traits connect the Gurgan assemblage of northern Iran (Tepe Hissar IIIc) and the intervening piedmont of the Kopet Dagh mountains (Namazga VI) further east with Margiana (modern Merv), comprising the delta oases of the Murghab river, and with Bactria (northern Afghanistan). The excavations of Viktor Sarianidi and other Soviet archaeologists have revealed in these regions a previously unknown Bronze Age civilization now called the 'Bactria and Margiana Archaeological Complex' or BMAC (fig. 1.17). Recent (1990–1) calibrated radiocarbon dates place the two continuous phases of BMAC I and II at *c.*1900–1700 and 1700–1500 BC, corresponding to the Namazga VI phase in the Kopet Dagh area. Very typical of the BMAC are 'miniature columns', which apparently had a ritual function (35 such columns were found *in situ* in Togolok-21), and magnificent weapons, seals, vessels of stone and precious metal, and toilet objects (pins, antimony bottles and mirrors), all usually decorated with animal and mythological motifs. Flexed burials with nearby cenotaphs also distinguish the BMAC. According to the continuing research of C. C. Lamberg-Karlovsky and Fred Hiebert, the assemblages at the Gurgan and Kopet Dagh sites represent diffusion from Margiana and Bactria rather than vice versa, as was earlier thought. The BMAC spread to Seistan, too (Godar-i Shah and Shahr-i Sokhta). A strongly stratified society is implied by the abundance of luxury goods, as well as the construction and maintenance of an elaborate irrigation system, which was the economic basis of the culture, and monumental architecture with strong fortifications.

In Bactria, the BMAC appeared at about the time when the Mature Harappan colony of Shortugai on the Oxus river ceased to be occupied. An abundance of many kinds of weapons, especially shaft-hole axes impressively decorated with animal and mythological motifs, are characteristic of the Bactrian variant of the BMAC. The horse is represented in these weapons (figs. 8.25–8.26), and miniature trumpets similar to those from the Gurgan sites have been found.

Together they suggest that the ruling élite engaged in chariot warfare. A bronze statuette from the plundered tombs of Bactria even shows a horse with a naked, ithyphallic rider, who presses his bent legs backwards beneath the horse, without stirrups (Bothmer 1990: 43, no. 29).

An important argument in favour of the hypothesis that the warring élite of the Bactrian culture spoke Proto-Indo-Aryan has emerged from the excavations directed by Jean-François Jarrige during the past two decades. The French archaeologists have been digging at a strategically important point along one of the main routes that lead from Baluchistan to Sind, at the entrance to the Bolan Pass. At Mehrgarh-7, at Sibri, and between Mehrgarh and Nausharo, there are cemeteries with typically BMAC graves and cenotaphs: the grave goods include pottery whose shapes are quite similar to those of the pottery found in Bactria and Margiana, and a wide variety of artefacts characteristic of the BMAC. A very rich BMAC hoard with 'miniature columns', a gold vessel with four wolves in relief, and other prestige objects was found at Quetta in 1985. At Nausharo, the Mature Harappan phase is succeeded by the BMAC; there is no evidence here of the Jhukar culture, which in Sind now initiates the Late Harappan phase (*c.*1900–1800 BC). On the other hand, while the Jhukar culture clearly continues predominantly Harappan traditions, it has a number of new elements that can be traced back to the BMAC, such as the steatite whorls very common in Central Asia. There is thus good evidence for the presence of the entire BMAC in Baluchistan and for its significant interaction with the Indus Civilization at the end of the Mature Harappan period. The population movement that is implied coincides with the distintegration of the Indus Civilization (§ 1.6).

A locally made cylinder seal known from an impression on a potsherd from Taip-depe in Margiana was divided into two registers by means of a plait. This is a device that was inaugurated in Syria in the eighteenth century BC. At this time Assyria was trading with Cappadocia and importing tin from the east. The source of this tin may have been in central and northern Afghanistan (Kandahar and Badakshan), where the Harappans and the Bactrians appear to have obtained their tin. On the other hand, from the eighteenth century BC onwards, north Syrian seals show such a typically Central Asian motif as the two-humped Bactrian camel. There are also a number of other parallels; e.g. the copper mirrors with anthropomorphic handles that have been found in Bactria and Baluchistan go back to Egyptian prototypes via Syria. All this evidence for cultural contacts supports the suggested Central Asian origin for the Mitanni Aryans.

Viktor Sarianidi's recent excavations in Margiana have contributed a new argument in support of the hypothesis that the Aryans of Mitanni and the Indo-Aryans who composed the early hymns of the Ṛgveda came from Bactria and Margiana. The most popular god of the Ṛgveda is Indra, also invoked at Mitanni, but a demon for Zarathustra. A central element in the cult of Indra was a drink originally called **Sauma*: Vedic *Soma* corresponds to Avestan *Haoma*, the cultic drink of Zoroastrianism. The botanical identity of this plant has been debated for a long time, but most specialists nowadays opt for *Ephedra*. Evidence for *Ephedra* has been discovered in residues of liquid contained in ritual vessels placed on shelves on the walls, and actual plant remains have survived under successive layers of plaster coating on these shelves. The vessels and shelves were in special rooms in the temple-forts of Togolok-21 and Gonur-1, dating from the BMAC II phase (*c.*1700–1500 BC).

So far everything has suggested a straightforward identification of the nobility in the BMAC with Proto-Indo-Aryan speakers. The textual evidence of the Ṛgveda, however, forces us to restrict this identification to the later phase of the Bactria-Margiana culture. It seems that the Proto-Indo-Aryans came into being around the eighteenth century BC, during the period of transition between BMAC I and II, when two distinct, successive Aryan tribes seem to have fused together, with a concomitant restructuring of religion. A parallel process was the later amalgamation of the Proto-Indo-Aryans of Central Asia and of Proto-Iranians in Zarathustra's reform, which reinstituted Ahura < *Asura in place of Indra and other *daēvas*. Let us first consider the textual evidence relating to the postulated fusion.

Important clues to an archaeological identification of the Ṛgvedic invasion are provided by the references to the enemies of the Ṛgvedic Aryans. Indra and his protégés, the earliest Ṛgvedic kings, are said to have destroyed the strongholds of these enemies, who are called *Dāsa*, *Dasyu* and *Paṇi*. When Sir Mortimer Wheeler unearthed the huge defensive walls of Harappa in 1946, he identified the Dāsa forts as the fortified cities of the Indus Civilization. This hypothesis was widely accepted until 1976, when Wilhelm Rau published his study of the relevant Vedic passages. Rau showed that, unlike the square layout of the Indus cities, the Dāsa forts had circular and often multiple, concentric walls. Moreover, the Dāsa forts were not regularly inhabited cities but functioned as only temporary shelters.

I have proposed identifying the Dāsa forts with the hundreds of fortified villages that have been discovered in Bronze Age Bactria and Margiana. This is precisely the region where the Dāsas, Dasyus and Paṇis had been placed a hundred years ago on the basis of Old Persian, Greek and Latin sources. In Old Persian inscriptions, *Daha* (< **Dasa*) is the name of a people and (in the plural) of a province situated next to that of the Sakas (fig. 1.1). According to Q. Curtius Rufus (8,3) and Ptolemy's Geography (6,10,2), the people

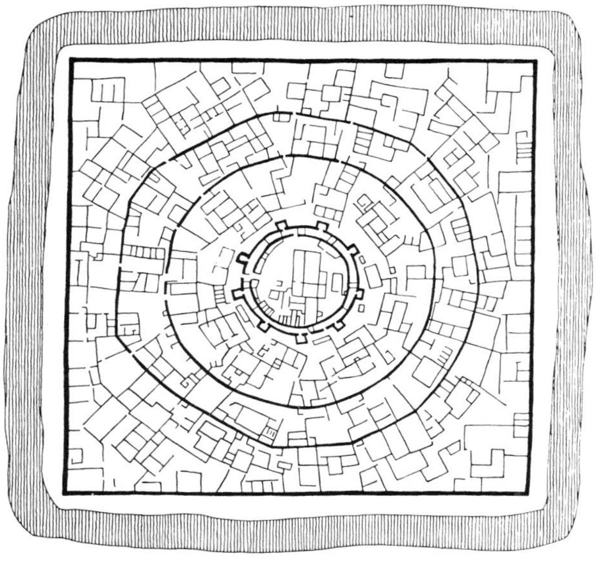

Fig. 8.18. Ground-plan of the 'temple-fort' at Dashly-3 in Bactria (north Afghanistan), with three concentric circular walls. *c.*1900–1700 BC. About 150 × 150 m. After Sarianidi 1986a: 59.

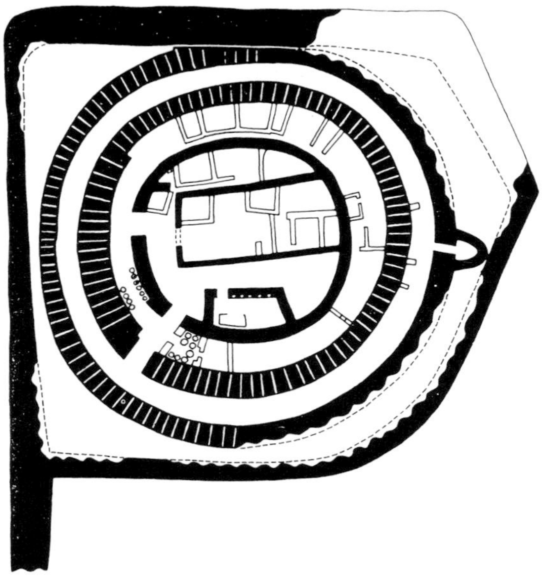

Fig. 8.19. Ground-plan of the Achaemenid fortress at Kutlug-Tepe in Bactria. About 40 × 40 m. After Sarianidi 1986a: 73.

called Daha lived on the lower course of the river Margos (modern Murghab), that is, in Margiana, while Pomponius Mela (3,42), based on Eratosthenes, says that the river Oxus bends towards the northwest near the Dahas. Strabo (11,9,2) informs us that a people called Parnoi was one of the Da(h)a tribes and that they had previously lived along the Okhos river (modern Tejend in Margiana). Vedic *Paṇi* is best explained as derived from **Pr̥ṇi*, a low-grade variant of *Parnoi*; this ethnicon and the name of the Dāsa king *Pipru* may both go back to the Aryan verbal root *pr̥-* (present *piparti* or *pr̥ṇāti*) 'to bring over, rescue, protect, excel, be able'.

A fortified ceremonial centre with three concentric circular walls was found in the BMAC I settlement in the oasis of Dashly-3 in north Afghanistan (fig. 8.18). The tradition of building forts with three concentric walls survived in Bactria until Achaemenid times (fig. 8.19). The form of these forts agrees with the description of a 'threefold fort' (*tripura*) in the Śatapatha-Brāhmaṇa (6,3,3,24–5). In later Vedic and Hindu mythology, *tripura* is usually the abode of Asuras, 'demons', opposed to Devas, 'gods'. The R̥gveda speaks of 'a hundred forts' of the Dāsas, while the Aryans themselves are never said to have had anything but fire or river as their 'fort'. The later Vedic texts confirm this by stating that when the Asuras and Devas were fighting, the Asuras always won in the beginning, because they alone had forts. This suggests that the earliest R̥gvedic Aryans were newcomers in Margiana and Bactria, whose hundreds of fortified villages they must in any case have passed on their way to northwest India. The R̥gvedic Aryans describe their enemies as rich and powerful, defending their cattle, gold and wonderful treasures with sharp weapons, horses and chariots. This description fits the first phase of the BMAC in Bactria, with its finely ornamented golden cups and weapons, and animal figures including the horse (figs. 8.25–6).

The difference in the skin colour between the fair Aryans and the dark Dāsas, emphasized in the R̥gveda, points to the same conclusion. Darkness of skin is a very relative concept, however, and need not mean more than a very slight difference in complexion: compare *mustalainen* 'black man' as the Finnish name for the local Gypsies. Nevertheless, it has been one reason why the Dāsas are still commonly thought to have been the non-Aryan aboriginals of India. Another reason is the later meaning of the word *dāsa* 'slave' in Sanskrit. This meaning, however, is due to the fact that people with the ethnic name Dāsa were taken captive in war, just as the English word *slave* originally denoted a captive *Slav* or the Finnish word *orja* 'slave' a captive *Aryan*. Many peoples call themselves by their native word for man or human being. The tribal name *Daha* (from earlier *Dasa*, possibly related to Mycenaean Greek *doero* < **doselos* 'slave') appears to be originally a noun meaning 'male person, man, hero', which survives as such in Khotanese Saka *daha*. The Wakhi word *dāi*, *δayək* has the same meaning; it goes back to Old Iranian *dahyu* from earlier *dasyu*. These are East Iranian languages later spoken in the Dāsa area. The Dāsas, Dasyus and Paṇis could therefore actually have spoken an Aryan language, though one dialectally different from that of the R̥gvedic Aryans.

One of the main reasons why the Dāsas, Dasyus and Paṇis are still commonly thought to have been non-Aryan speakers is the apparently foreign look of many of their proper names, even if *Varcin* and *Pipru* do make the opposite impression. Most important in this respect is the name *Śambara*, which so far has been considered to be of Austro-Asiatic origin, being connected with the tribe of the Austro-Asiatic-speaking *Sora* (<*Śabara*) in the state of Orissa in eastern India. The Mahābhārata, however, has preserved several variants of Śambara as the name of an enemy of Indra, one of them being *Saṁvara*. This suggests that Śambara is a Proto-Māgadhī-like variant of a noun meaning 'protector, defender', from the root *vr̥-* 'to surround, cover, protect'. The etymology agrees well with the meaning 'fort(ification)', which *śambara* as a neuter noun appears to have in the R̥gveda (2,24,2), and with Karl Jettmar's comparison of the Dashly-3 fort with Avestan *var* 'fort'. It would also explain the variation between a form with the nasal and one without it, *Śambara : Śabara*; rather than providing evidence for Austro-Asiatic infixation, it can be evoked as evidence for different ablaut grades, paralleled by the alternation in the Sanskrit prefix *sam- : sa-*, the latter going back to the reduced grade **sm̥-*. The alternation of palatal and dental sibilants, one of the most characteristic features of eastern Indo-Aryan, is attested (in Vedic, Epic and Middle Indo-Aryan texts) also for the word *dāsa* itself.

The R̥gvedic Aryans make it clear that the rituals of the Dāsas differed greatly from the Aryans' own worship of Indra with the cultic drink Soma. The enemies and their evil gods possessed 'magic power', *māyā*. The Dāsas worshipped gods called Asuras, while the Aryan gods were called Devas. It is true that, after the fusion of the Aryans and Dāsas, even Aryan gods like Indra are occasionally called Asura, through Indra originally has the title 'slayer of Asuras'. The foremost Asura is Varuṇa, often paired with Mitra; as the universal ruler (*sam-rāj*) Varuṇa upholds the cosmic order (*r̥ta*) 'with the magic power of Asura'. In the Avesta, Varuṇa is not mentioned but has an exact counterpart in Ahura (Mazdāh) 'the (wise) Lord', whom Zarathustra re-established as the highest god in eastern Iran instead of the *daēva* Indra, whom he condemned as a demon: the Avestan compound *Miθra-Ahura* corresponds to the (secondary) Vedic and Mitanni compound *Mitrā-Varuṇā*, the Avestan Ahura guards *aša* (<**r̥ta*) and is *hu-māyā* 'endowed with good māyā'. Varuṇa's name is probably derived from the root *vr̥-* 'to surround, protect' and may be just a variant of the Dāsa name *Śambara* = *Saṁ-vara*. The word *saṁ-varaṇa*, which usually means 'enclosure' (for keeping and defending cattle), occurs as a proper name in R̥gveda 5,33,10; in the Avesta, the cognate word *hąm-varᵊtay-* means '(manly) courage' and is also a divinity (Yašt 10,66; 11,2, etc.).

R̥gvedic hymns indicate that some Aryan kings entered into alliances with the irreligious enemy, and that some rich Dāsa kings like Balbūtha Tarukṣa started worshipping Indra. Apparently in order to secure the loyalty of their newly won Dāsa subjects, early Aryan kings made a compromise and adopted the cult of Varuṇa, the principal god of the former enemy. Thus in the R̥gvedic hymn 4,42, addressed to both Indra and Varuṇa on behalf of Trasadasyu, Varuṇa first says, 'I, Varuṇa, am the sovereign; it was I who was first destined to be Asura. The gods follow the advice of Varuṇa', but then he admits that Indra is the unparalleled god of war, insuperable in his fury created by Soma. In R̥gveda 10,124,5, Indra invites Varuṇa to join the ranks of the devas as a king after the defeat of the Asuras. Because *both* Indra *and* Varuṇa are invoked in the Mitanni oath of 1380 BC, the Mitanni Aryans must have come from Bactria and Margiana *after* this amalgamation of early R̥gvedic Aryans and Dāsas had taken place.

If the R̥gvedic Aryans conquered southern Central Asia and northwest India as newcomers, we would expect them to have arrived from the northern steppes, the original Aryan homeland. The coming of the steppe nomads was indeed once thought to be a possible reason for the sudden decline of wealth in the BMAC at the shift between its phases I and II (now dated to *c.*1700 BC). However, this hypothesis has not been so popular with archaeologists in recent years, because no traces of violent destruction have been found. Moreover, the vestiges of a southward expansion of the Andronovo culture from the steppes of Kazakhstan (fig. 8.15) have been dated mainly to the latter part of the second millennium BC. However, this Soviet chronology of the steppe cultures, chiefly based on typology, is suspected to be too low.

Early Andronovo cemeteries in the southern Urals, such as that on the Sintashta river dated (by Soviet scholars) to *c.*1600 BC, also favour the invasion hypothesis. The horse-chariots buried with their owners in the Sintashta cemetery had two wheels with ten spokes each (fig. 8.20). In the ancient Near East, most chariots continued to have only four spokes until about 1400 BC. Thus the chariotry of the early Andronovo of the northern steppes was more advanced and had the potential to introduce new chariot technology into the ancient Near East, where the Mitanni Aryans appear as masters in chariotry by the sixteenth century BC (§ 8.5). In fact, one Syrian seal dated between 1750 and 1600 BC shows a war-chariot with two eight-spoked wheels.

If the Sauma Aryans were originally steppe nomads representing the early Andronovo culture, who became the rulers of the BMAC *c.*1700 BC, what about the Dāsas? The BMAC I emerged with the second phase of occupation in Margiana. The form of the rectangular fortified settlements is a continuation of that of the first phase but their proportions are monumental, with walls over 100 metres long and 4 metres wide. The continuity with the ceramics of the earlier phase is

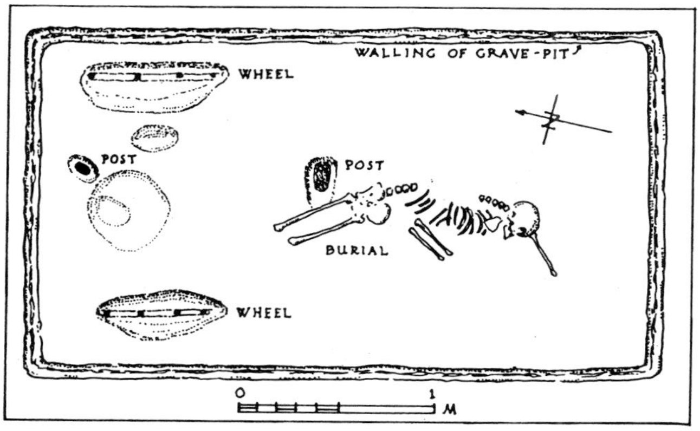

Fig. 8.20. A chariot burial at the Sintashta river cemetery near Chelyabinsk in the southern Urals. Early Andronovo culture, dated to *c*.1600 BC. After Piggott 1983: 92, fig. 47.

extremely close, but the small finds exhibit a drastic change, with a sudden explosion in luxury goods. These prestige objects clearly betray an ultimately Near Eastern, more particularly Elamite, influence. The distance to Elam is bridged by Shahdad in Kerman, where a great number of comparable objects has been found. It has also recently become clear that, for example, the compartmented metal seals of Bactria go back to the traditions of the Early Harappan period in Baluchistan. Margiana was first occupied during the late Namazga V period (*c*.2100–1900 BC) by settlers coming from the piedmont region immediately to the west, the assemblage being closely similar to that of Anau and Namazga in everything but architecture. In other words, the BMAC essentially continues the local, undoubtedly pre-Aryan traditions, just as the Gurgan Grey Ware to the west goes back to earlier local painted pottery.

The only possible connection of the BMAC I or the Hissar IIIb horizon with the Dāsas would be for a small wave of Aryan-speaking nomads to have taken over the leadership in southern Central Asia around 2000 BC and totally adopted the local culture, yet retained their own language. There is some very scant evidence for the presence of such nomads in the discovery in 1991 of a few sherds of Poltavka-type ceramics on BMAC I floors at Togolok-1 in Margiana, linked with the lower Volga steppes (fig. 8.24a). As the Dāsa religion did not include the cult of Sauma, this would imply that drinking the extract of the *Ephedra* plant as a way of increasing fighting powers was an innovation of the early Andronovo culture, where advanced chariot technology had also been developed in the meantime (fig. 8.24b).

After their assumed conquest of the Dāsa forts in Margiana and Bactria around 1700 BC (which may have taken place more peacefully than the texts suggest), the Sauma Aryans too would have largely adopted the earlier local culture, thereby transforming the cult of the Asura-worshipping Dāsas into the pre-Zarathustran Daiva cult (involving the *Sauma drink). Immediately after this second cultural fusion had taken place, one group of the resulting acculturated Proto-Indo-Aryans branched westwards to Gurgan, and from there to northern Syria, becoming the rulers of the Mitanni kingdom, while another faction continued (at least partly via Seistan) eastwards to Swat, founding there the Proto-R̥gvedic (= Proto-Dardic) culture of the Gandhara Grave culture (Ghalegay IV period) (fig. 8.24b).

The pottery of the intrusive Ghalegay IV culture of Swat, which flourished from the eighteenth to the fifteenth century BC, bears some resemblance to (but is not identical with) the BMAC pottery of Bactria. Ghalegay IV is the first cultural assemblage of Swat to have the horse, and its area of distribution largely coincides with that of the Dardic languages, which are the only ones to preserve some distinctly R̥gvedic dialectal variants such as the gerund formed with the suffix *-tvī*. The spread of the Ghalegay IV culture to the Punjab in the sixteenth century BC, with its concomitant acculturation, agrees with textual evidence that attests to battles in the plains and to the intrusion of new dialectal forms and subject-matter into the R̥gveda.

The culture of Pirak I, dating from the eighteenth century BC, is the first culture in Sind certainly in possession of the horse and the camel. This intrusive culture differs from the BMAC tradition and may represent in an unacculturated form the steppe nomads whom we have assumed to have taken over the BMAC about this time. Their arrival marks the introduction of agricultural innovations, for the cultivation of rice was introduced in Sind, as it was in Swat, in the Ghalegay IV phase. In both cases the rice undoubtedly came from the Ganges Valley, suggesting a new level of mobility in North India. Even the terracotta stamp seals of Pirak and the only seal of the Ghalegay IV period so far found in Swat resemble each other.

The succeeding Ghalegay V phase in Swat, dated to *c*.1400–800 BC, is thought to have analogies with the early Iron Age cultures of western Iran, such as Hasanlu V. Some of the recently discovered petroglyphs in the upper Indus Valley at Chilas also have west Iranian parallels of this same period. This prompts one to consider the old problem posed by the Nuristani languages from a new perspective. The Nuristani disaspiration is an important isogloss with the Iranian languages, though the development is identical only with regard to the voiced aspirates. Their position on the western edge of the Dardic languages certainly suggests that the Nuristani languages arrived from the west later than the Dardic languages, and not vice versa, as is generally assumed.

A few archaeological links have been recorded between the Ghalegay V culture of Swat and the Painted Grey Ware

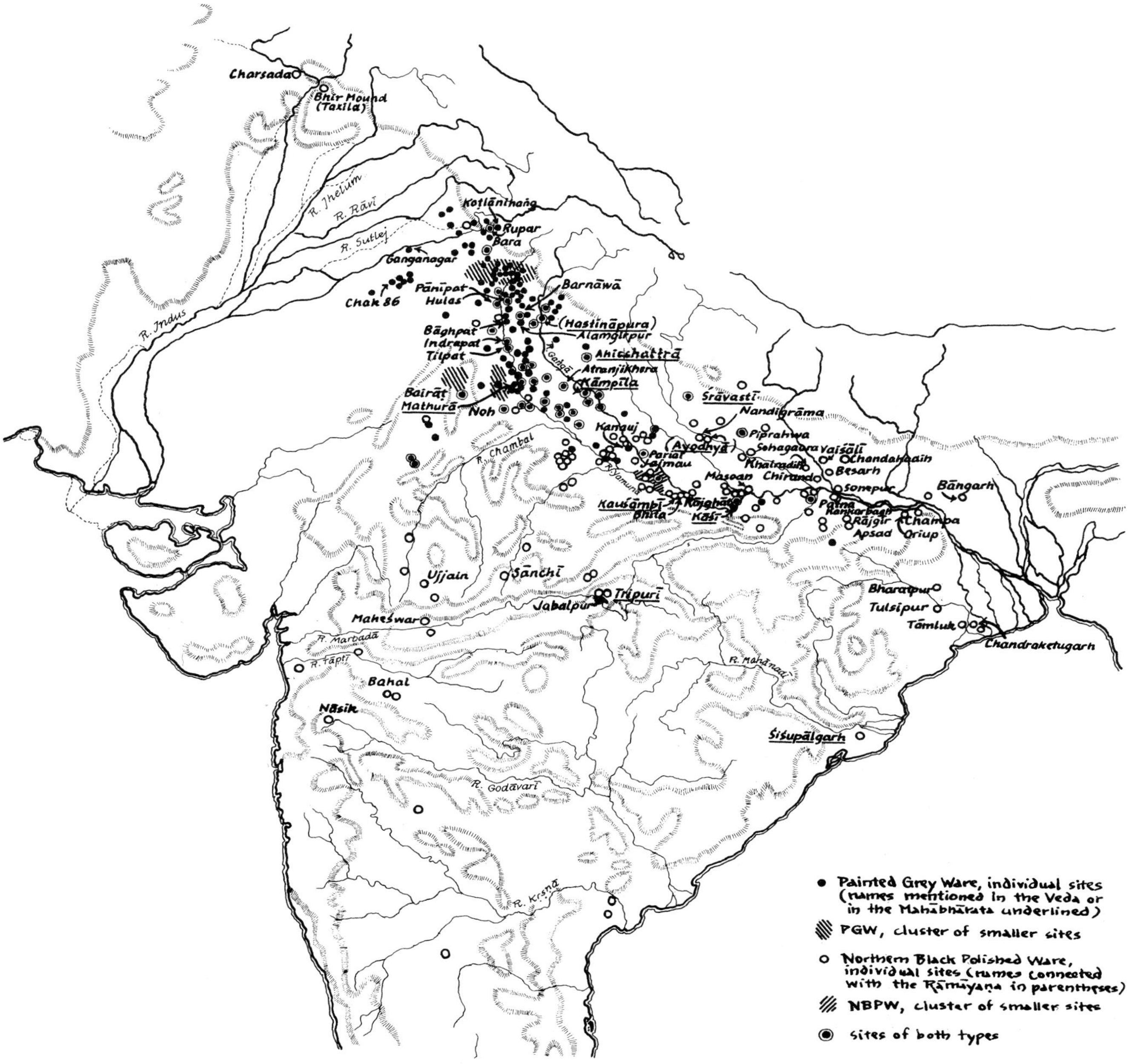

Fig. 8.21. Distribution of Painted Grey Ware (*c.*1100–350 BC) and Northern Black Polished Ware (*c.*700–100 BC) in northern South Asia.

culture (fig. 8.21) of the Madhyadeśa, the 'middle region' of the North Indian plains, but after this, the culture of the northwest developed in relative isolation. The pattern agrees with the Vedic culture (fig. 8.22), which started in the northwest, but in the middle and late Vedic period had little contact with that region. With their spread from Swat to the plains, the Ghalegay IV–V cultures seem to offer the best counterpart to the early Vedic culture. Apart from the latest phase, during which some iron was used, these cultures belong to the Chalcolithic period, and inhumation and cremation exist side by side, as in the Ṛgveda. The Painted Grey Ware culture, in its turn, flourishing between 1100 and 350 BC in the Madhyadeśa (fig. 8.21), provides a close parallel with the middle and late Vedic culture (fig. 8.22) temporally, spatially and in terms of cultural content.

Before the expansion of the Gandhara Grave culture, the Harappan or (in the case of OCP) Early Harappan traditions were continued in the Late Harappan Chalcolithic cultures

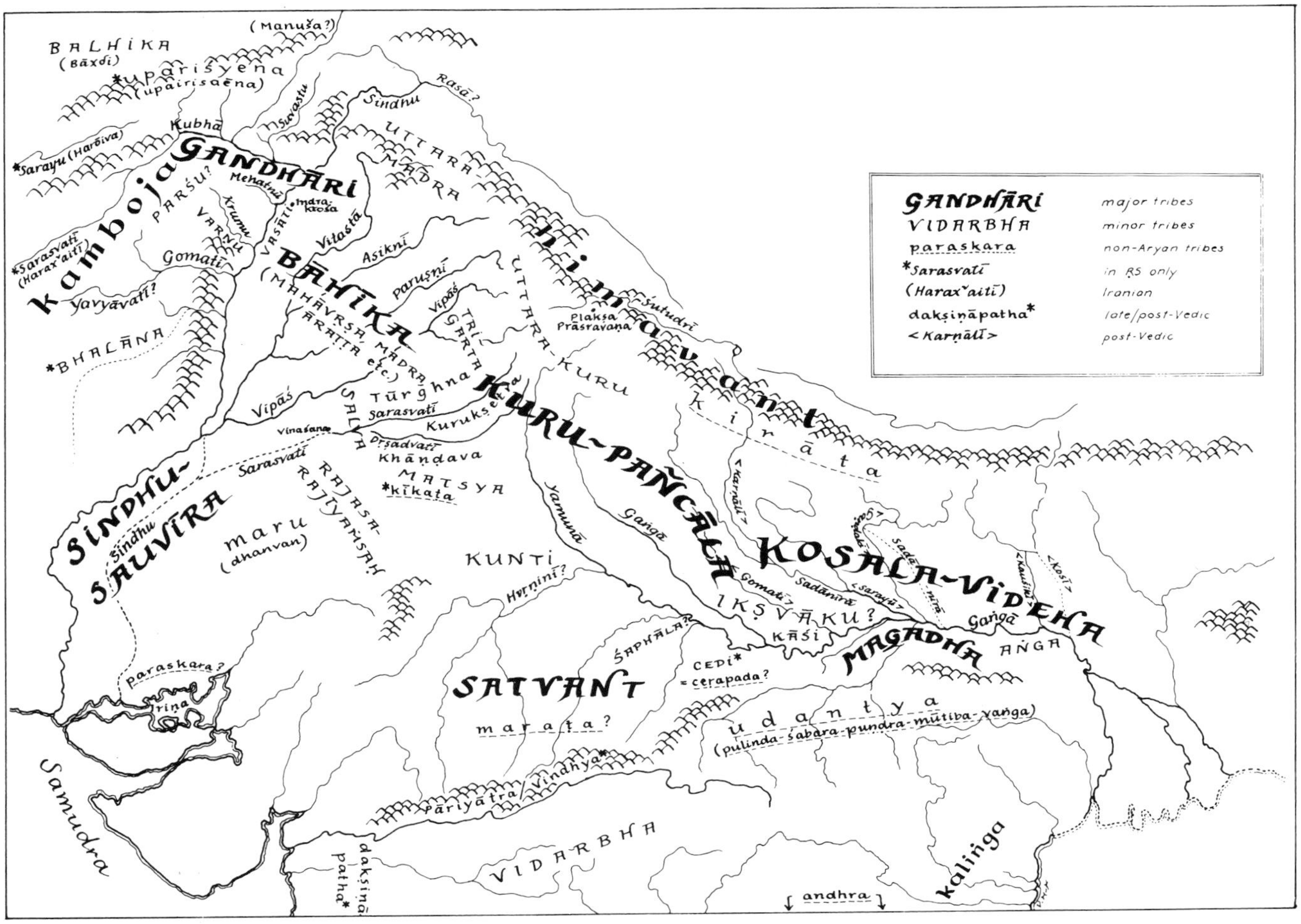

Fig. 8.22. Places and peoples mentioned in the Vedic texts, *c.*1500–500 BC. Incomplete with regard to the earliest period. Redrawn from Witzel 1987: 210.

that occupied the plains of northwest India (fig. 1.17): the Cemetery H culture of the Punjab, the Jhukar culture of Sind, and the Ochre Coloured Pottery (OCP) culture of the Ganges–Yamuna doab (around modern Delhi). On the other hand, some unmistakably intrusive traits appear in these cultural complexes. A major source of these new features is undoubtedly the BMAC, which arrived in South Asia via Baluchistan around the nineteenth century BC (see pp. 148f.). These early 'Indian Dāsas', are likely to have become the ruling élite of the Late Harappan cultures. It is their tradition that probably developed the complex fire-altar ritual, which is not mentioned at all in the Ṛgveda, but is suddenly incorporated in the Vedic ritual at the beginning of the middle Vedic phase, that is, when the Punjab had already become the focus of the Vedic culture and the earliest Yajurvedic texts were compiled (fig. 8.24a).

An antennae-hilted sword coming from extensive illicit digs in Bactria is closely similar to comparable swords from Fatehgarh near Delhi (fig. 8.23). This suggests that 'Indian Dāsas' may have introduced some artefact types found in the Copper Hoards of the upper Ganges Valley. On the other hand, the 'fish' symbol incised on one of the 'anthropomorphs' typical of the Copper Hoards (fig. 4.2), and the discovery of one such anthropomorph in Harappan layers at Lothal, point to some Harappan influence. However, the main tradition behind the Gangetic Copper Hoards seems to be the local OCP assemblage (possibly related to the Early Harappan Sothi Ware complex), which has been encountered at one or two sites that have yielded Copper Hoards. The introduction of swords may mark a Dāsa infiltration leading to élite dominance. When the Vedic culture penetrated the Gangetic Valley to the east in the middle Vedic period, the Vedic Aryans had to fight with 'barbarians' who worshipped Asuras and spoke a language that has been identified (on the basis of the sample in Śatapatha-Brāhmaṇa 3,2,1,23) as akin to the easternmost branch of the later Middle Indo-Aryan

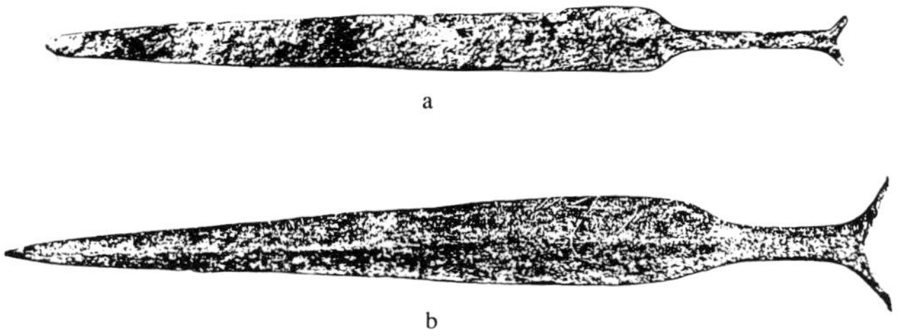

Fig. 8.23. Antennae-hilted copper swords. (a) From Bactria in northern Afghanistan, representing the BMAC. Length 52 cm. (b) From Fatehgarh in Uttar Pradesh, India, representing the Gangetic Copper Hoards. Length 63.5 cm. After Parpola 1988b: 285, fig. 10, based on (a) Sarianidi 1986a: fig. 75, and (b) Gordon 1960: pl. 27b.

languages, Māgadhī. Magadhans are mentioned as a hostile tribe living in the east as early as the Atharvaveda. The hypothesis that Māgadhī is descended from an earlier wave of Aryan immigrants (the Dāsas) is also in agreement with the age-and-area model of cultural anthropology.

The use of iron and a grey ceramic ware in the Painted Grey Ware phase may have spread to India from Central Asia and the Iranian plateau mainly through Baluchistan. This event appears to be documented at Pirak III (*c.*1100 BC), and is perhaps connected with the arrival of the East Iranian speakers to the Indo-Iranian borderlands.

The hypotheses concerning the formation of the Aryan branch of Indo-European, as proposed in this section, are summarized in fig. 8.24.

8.5 The horse argument

The view that an early form of Indo-Aryan was spoken by the Indus people continues to have its supporters. It is therefore necessary to emphasize in conclusion one important reason why the Harappan people are unlikely to have been Indo-European- or Aryan-speakers. This is the complete absence of the horse (*Equus caballus*) among the many wild and domesticated animals that have been identified at a large number of Early and Mature Harappan sites (table 8.1).

Because the horse issue is so very central and conflicting reports exist, it seems advisable to quote a fairly up-to-date authoritative report:

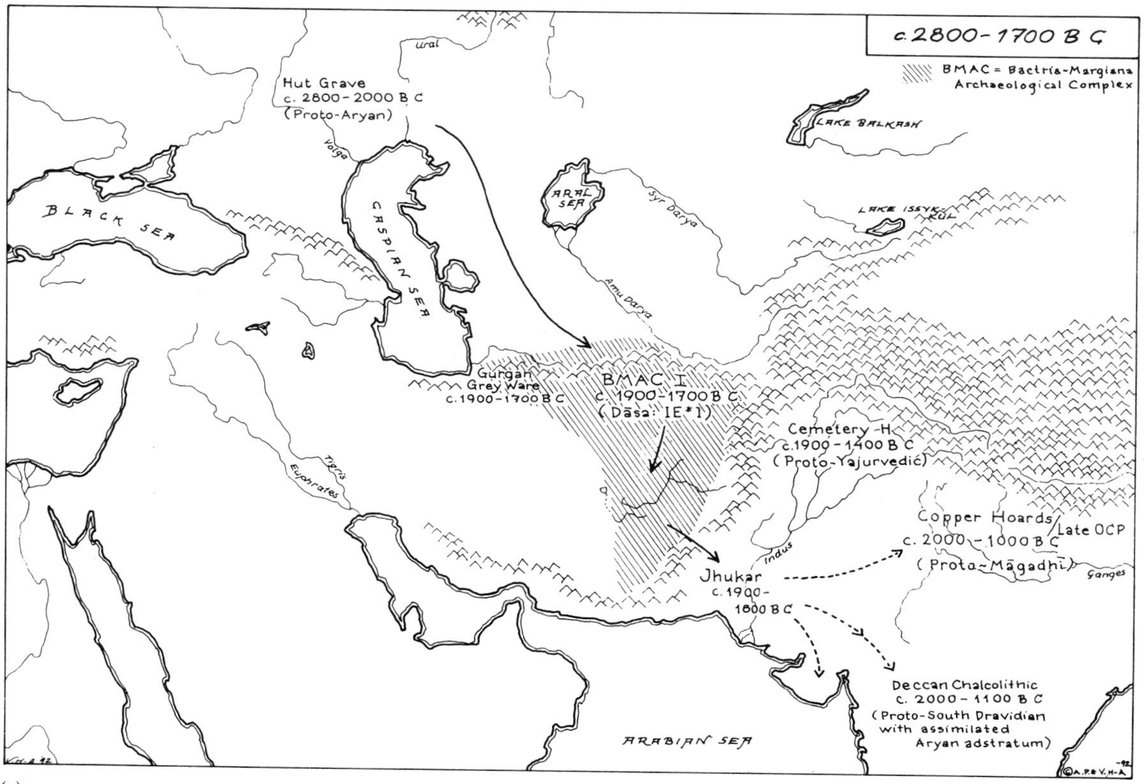

(a)

Fig. 8.24. Formation of the Aryan branch of Indo-European in three hypothetical stages: (a) *c.*2800–1700 BC, (b) *c.*1700–1400 BC, (c) *c.*1400–700 BC.

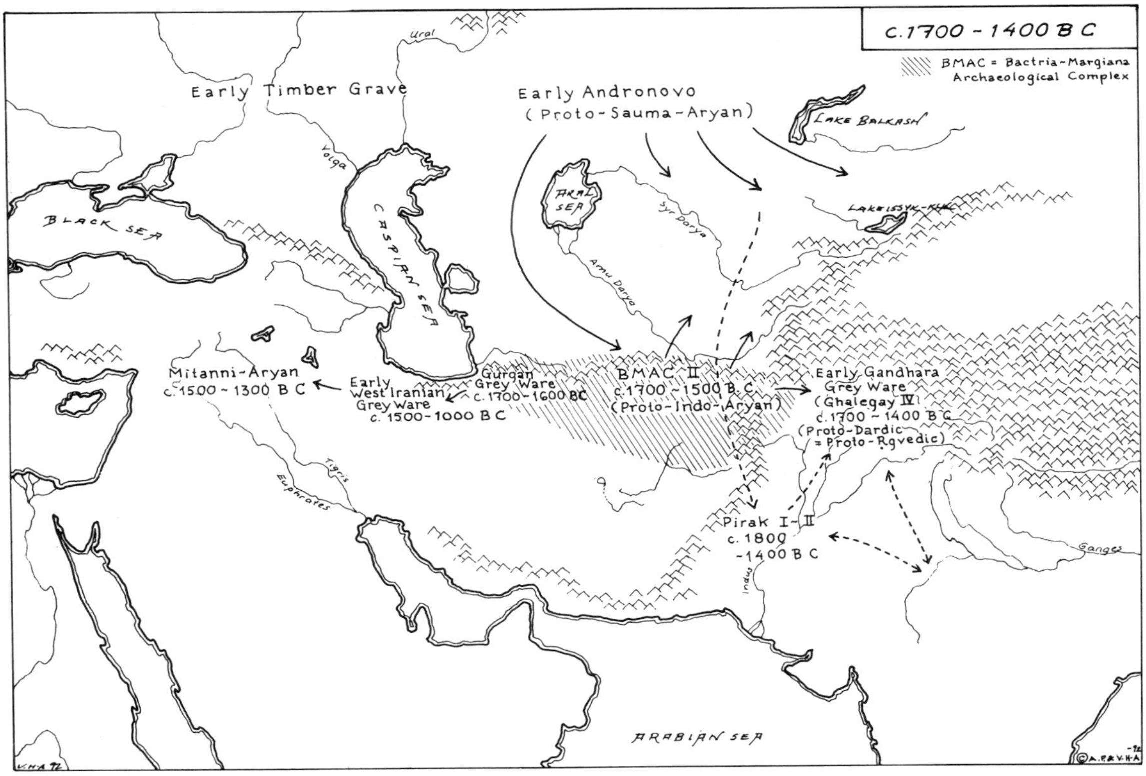

(b)

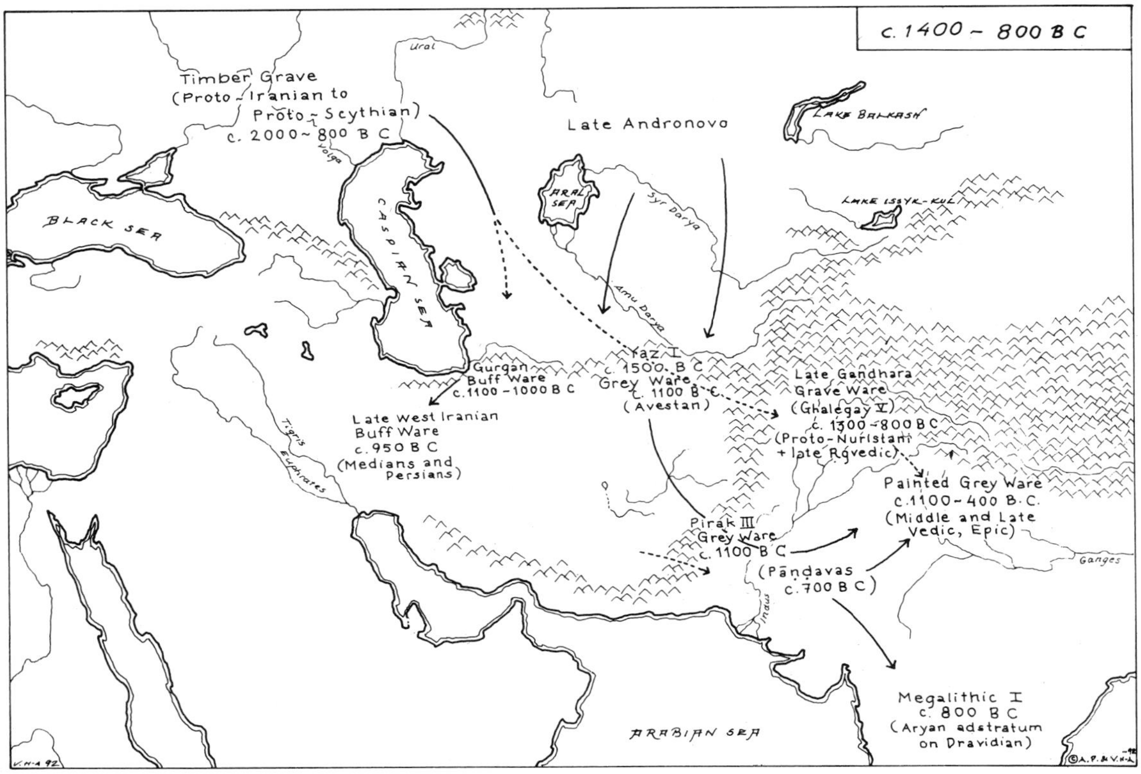

(c)

Fig. 8.24. (*cont.*)

Table 8.1. *Ungulates represented by faunal remains at sites in the Greater Indus Valley*

	Mehrgarh I	Mehrgarh II	Mehrgarh III–VII	Balakot	Jalilpur	Nausharo	Harappa	Mohenjo-daro	Sibri	Pirak
Wild										
Elaphas maximus (Indian elephant)	?	+					+	+		?
Rhinoceros unicornis (one-horned rhinoceros)						+	+			
Equus hemionus (khur, onager)	+	+	+	+		+	?	?	+	+
Sus scrofa (wild boar)	+	+	+	+		+	+	+	+	+
Axis axis (chital, spotted deer)	+	?					+	+		
Axis porcinus (hog deer)							+	+		
Cervus duvauceli (barasingha, swamp deer)	+	+	+				+			?
Boselaphus tragocamelus (nilgai, blue bull)	+	+		+			+			
Bos primigenius (wild cattle)	+	+								
Bubalus arnee (wild water buffalo)	+		?	?			?	?		
Antilope cervicapra (blackbuck)	+	+	+				+			
Gazella bennetti (chinkara, gazelle)	+	+	+	+	+	+	+	+	+	+
Capra aegagrus (wild goat)	+	+		?		?				
Ovis orientalis (urial, wild sheep)	+	+	?	?		+				
Domestic										
Equus caballus (horse)										+
Equus asinus (donkey)										+
Camelus bactrianus (two-humped camel)							?	?		+
Bos indicus (zebu, humped cattle)	+	+	+	+	+	+	+	+	+	+
Bos taurus (non-humped cattle)				?		?	+	?		?
Bubalus bubalis (domestic water buffalo)			?	?		?	?	?		
Capra hircus (domestic goat)	+	+	+	+	+	+	+	+	+	+
Ovis aries (domestic sheep)	+	+	+	+	+	+	+	+	+	+

After Meadow 1991: 55, table 2.

There are, as yet, no convincing reports of horse remains from archaeological sites in South Asia before the end of the second millennium BC. Many claims have been made (e.g., Sewell 1931; Nath 1962, 1968; Sharma 1974) but few have been documented with sufficient measurements, drawings, and photographs to permit other analysts to judge for themselves. An additional complication is that some specimens come from archaeological deposits which could be considerably younger than the main body of material at the site (e.g., Mohenjo-daro and Harappa). Identifications, no matter how firm, are not particularly useful if the bones on which they are based come from poorly defined contexts.

Northwestern South Asia is the home of *Equus hemionus khur*, a subspecies of 'onager' or Asiatic wild ass (Groves and Mazák 1967). This animal, before the present century, was distributed throughout the alluvial plains of the northwestern portion of the subcontinent and in Baluchistan (Roberts 1977), intergrading with the Persian onager (*E.h. onager*) in eastern Iran. Today, a relict population finds refuge in the Rann of Kutch. The wild relatives of the horse (*E. caballus*) and donkey (*E. asinus*) are not native to the Iranian plateau and South Asia, the domesticated animals having been brought into the area probably from the west and north. It is the date and circumstances of the introduction of these domesticated forms which is at issue. (Meadow 1987: 908f.)

Why should the horse be such a strong indicator of the Aryan and Indo-European culture? The first strong evidence for horse domestication comes from Dereivka on the Dnieper river, a site belonging to the Ukrainian Srednij Stog culture, which flourished about 4200–3500 BC. During the following Pit Grave culture (*c.*3500–2800 BC), widely considered as Proto-Indo-European-speaking, full-scale pastoral technology, including the domesticated horse, wheeled vehicles, stockbreeding and limited horticulture, spread from the Ukraine eastwards over the vast grasslands.

The Proto-Aryan word for 'horse', **áśva-* (retained in

Vedic but in Avestan already changed into *aspa-*), is clearly a Proto-Indo-European inheritance. It has undergone the sound change *ḱ > *ć > *ś, assumed to have taken place dialectally in the late Satəm phase of the Indo-European period. Like its cognates, Old Irish *ech*, Latin *equus*, Old English *eoh*, Gothic *aíhwa-*, Tocharian *yakwe*, Proto-Aryan **áśva-* is derived from Proto-Indo-European *(H_1)*éḱwos* 'horse' (Lithuanian further has *ešva*, *ašva* 'mare'). This word is thought to date from the early phase of Proto-Indo-European, because it is almost certainly related to the adjective *(H_1)*ōḱus* 'swift' (whence Greek *ōkús* and Sanskrit *āśú-*) and because these two words are linked by derivational processes no longer operative in the late phase of Proto-Indo-European.

Various terms associated with the wheeled vehicle represent the most recent technological concept solidly reconstructed for Proto-Indo-European from most of the Indo-European languages and therefore are temporally most diagnostic for the maintenance of Proto-Indo-European linguistic unity. Archaeological evidence suggests a rapid dispersal of wheeled vehicles from the Near East through Transcaucasia and the Pontic steppe to central and northwestern Europe within a few centuries in the late fourth millennium BC. This again fits with the idea that the carriers of the Pit Grave culture spoke a late form of Indo-European.

Among the earliest textual evidence relating to the Aryans is the name of the Mitanni king *Tu(i)š(e)ratta*, corresponding to the Vedic attribute *tveṣá-ratha-* (< **tvaišá-ratha-*) 'having an impetuous chariot' (R̥S 5,61,13). The textbook on the training of chariot horses written in Hittite by a Mitannian called Kikkuli contains several technical terms that have unanimously been considered to be of Aryan etymology.

When the R̥gvedic tribes invaded northwestern India, they drove (*vah-*) in war-chariots (*ratha-*) with two wheels (*cakra-*), an axle (*akṣa-*) and a thill (*īṣā-*), and drawn by horses (*aśva-*). All these terms have a good Indo-European etymology and thus indicate that the Vedic chariotry had its roots firmly in the Proto-Indo-European heritage. In the middle Vedic period, the horse was the principal victim in the most magnificent royal sacrifice.

The horse and chariot can thus with good reasons be expected to be physically and ideologically present in the archaeological cultures identified as Aryan. This is the case in the Gurgan culture of northern Iran, with the chariot seal of Tepe Hissar IIIb (fig. 8.17), in the Bactria and Margiana Archaeological Complex (figs. 8.25–8.26), and in the Late Harappan or Post-Harappan cultures of the Indian subcontinent. At Pirak I and II (*c.*1800–1300 BC), the horse has been found only in the form of equid figurines with a forelock, a characteristic feature of the domestic horse, while the first bones definitely attributable to the horse come only

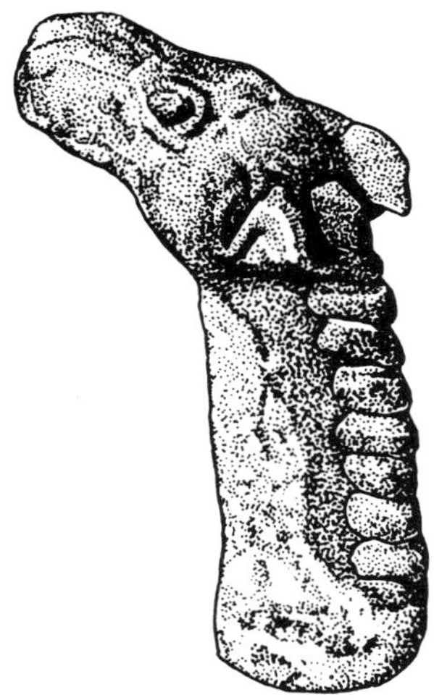

Fig. 8.25. A horse-headed macehead from plunder excavations in northern Afghanistan. Copper. After Sarianidi 1986a: 211.

Fig. 8.26. Shaft-hole axe with horse head. Afghanistan, early second millennium BC. Copper alloy. Height 7.9 cm, width 14.9 cm. Metropolitan Museum of Art, New York, 1989.281.39 (gift of Norbert Schimmel Trust, 1989). After Pittman 1984: 70, fig. 32.

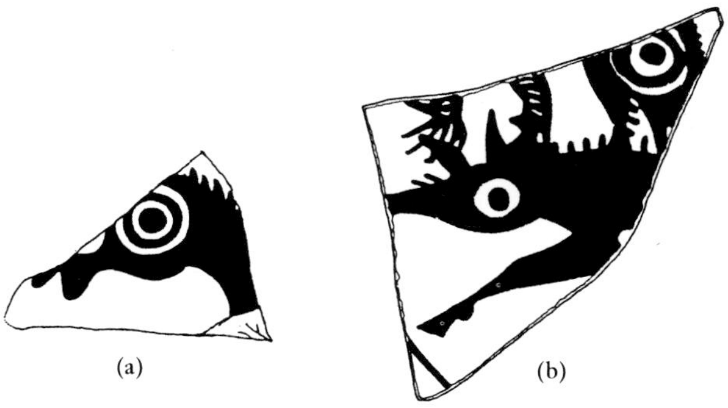

Fig. 8.27. (a, b) Representations of the horse on black-on-red painted pottery from Bīr-kōṭ-ghwaṇḍai, Swat Valley, northern Pakistan. Latter half of the Ghalegay IV period (*c.*1700–1400 BC). After Stacul 1987: fig. 46: f (=a), h (=b).

from Period III (*c.*1300–800 BC). In the Swat Valley, the horse is present in the Ghalegay IV period (*c.*1700–1400 BC) at Bīr-kōṭ-ghwaṇḍai, both in the motifs of painted pottery (fig. 8.27) and osteologically: out of 158 equid bones, 13 have been identified as those of *Equus caballus*.

The picture is totally different when we turn to the Indus Civilization. There is no evidence of the horse whatsoever, either osteological (table 8.1) or representational. The horse is never depicted in the Harappan seals, amulets or statuettes, although many other animals are. It is the image of the 'unicorn' bull that dominates in the seals, and the Harappan deities wear the buffalo's horns as their crowns. This evidence does not prove that Aryans never visited the Indus Valley in the third millennium – a few probably did – but it does suggest that the Indus Civilization in general and its rulers were non-Aryans.

9 Dravidian languages and the Harappan culture

9.1 The Brahui problem and North Dravidian

A Dravidian language, Brahui, is spoken by several hundred thousand people in the mountain valleys and plateaux of Baluchistan and Afghanistan, a core area of the Early Harappan Neolithic cultures. Its presence there is an anomaly referred to as the 'Brahui problem', which Sir Denys Bray defined as follows in his pioneering description of the Brahui language:

Then there is his alien, and to the ears of his neighbours barbarous, language, an island of Dravidian utterly severed from its kin by many hundreds of miles of surrounding Indian and Iranian languages and possibly by far more hundred years of isolation... Who are these strange, Dravidian-speaking tribesmen?... And if the racial riddle of such a commixture of people is unanswerable, what of their language? Polyglot in vocabulary, it is sheer Dravidian in structure. Is it indigenous to Baluchistan or immigrant? If immigrant, whence and when did it wander in? And if it is indigenous, when and why and how did its kin wander forth beyond its utmost ken? (Bray 1934: II, 41)

Bray himself was very much inclined to see the key to the Brahui problem in the Indus Civilization and the contemporary Bronze Age cultures of Baluchistan. He also thought that doubts arising from the great contrast 'between the highly developed city-civilization of Mohenjo-daro and the wandering tent-life of the hill Brahuis' could be resolved:

Sir Aurel Stein [1931] faces the difficulty with imaginative candour. In the Brahuis he sees not indeed the descendants of the ancient settled race who founded the civilisation, but descendants of the semi-barbarous peoples on the fringe, its poor relations as it were. And he points to the Brahui hills above the plains about Mohenjo-daro, bleak, barren, affording the invader neither attraction nor room for settlement, as just the ground where a nomadic fringe of the city-civilisation might be left undisturbed throughout the ages, long after the cities had been blotted out. Real or imaginary, the picture Sir Aurel draws is true to life; how true no one perhaps can feel who has not himself wandered in those unkind hills and seen the wilder Brahuis

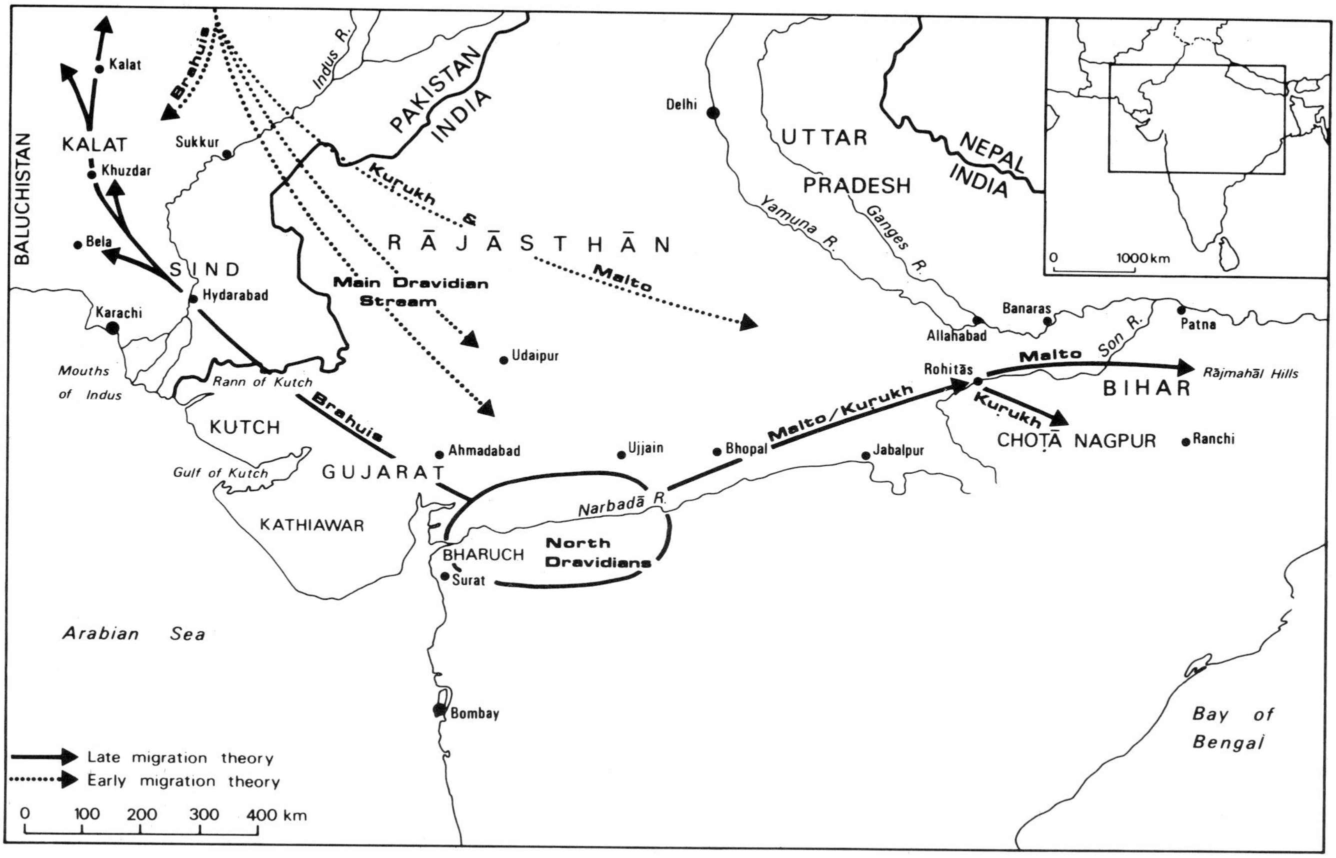

Fig. 9.1. Two views of the formation of North Dravidian. After Elfenbein 1987: 216.

encamping for the night in their goats' hair tents. (Bray 1934: II, 42)

Sir John Marshall had already pointed out in 1924 that the presence of Brahui in Baluchistan suggests that the Dravidian languages entered India through this area. The most impressive attempts to find linguistic relatives for the Dravidian language family, indeed, have connected it with the Elamite language once spoken in southwestern Iran, with the Uralic family in northern Eurasia, and with the 'Altaic' languages that have spread from Siberia and Mongolia. However, none of these long-range comparisons can be considered as proven or generally accepted.

In recent decades, Marshall's view has been essentially endorsed by leading Dravidologists including M. S. Andronov and Kamil V. Zvelebil, who have seen the Brahuis as the first group that broke off from the mainstream of Dravidian languages when they entered the Indian subcontinent around the fourth millennium BC. Marshall's hypothesis was, however, opposed from its inception in 1924, when Jules Bloch suggested that the Brahuis had come to Baluchistan quite recently from South or Central India, where the other Dravidian languages are spoken. Georg Morgenstierne disputed Bloch's hypothesis in 1932, while Murray B. Emeneau, in his important studies on Brahui published in the 1960s, was hesitant. In a recent paper, Josef Elfenbein (1987) has strongly argued along the same lines as Bloch (fig. 9.1).

As the prehistory of Brahui is of considerable relevance to the issue concerning the language of the Indus Civilization, the evidence relating to it must be examined carefully. We shall first deal with Brahui's relationship with Baluchi and the known history of the tribes speaking these two languages. This will be followed by an examination of the relationship of Brahui to the other Dravidian languages. In addition to purely linguistic evidence, we shall deal with the evidence of ethnic names as well, because these have figured in the discussion. In conclusion, I shall argue that the truth may lie somewhere between the two rival hypotheses mentioned above.

Brahui has been spoken in very much the same areas as Baluchi (or Balochi), an archaic Iranian language: broadly, from southeastern Iran (the province of Sistan-va-Baluchestan) over southwestern Afghanistan to western

Pakistan, where the province of Baluchistan is their core area. Baluchi is a Northwest Iranian language. Its Middle Iranian ancestor was close to the Parthian spoken to the southeast of the Caspian Sea. The Baluch are assumed to have migrated from that region towards the southeast in several successive waves, starting around the seventh century and reaching the borders of Sind and west Punjab by about the twelfth century. According to Sir Harold Bailey (supported by Elfenbein), the name *Balōč* may come (via **Wardauč*) from the ancient name for eastern Baluchistan, Old Iranian **Vadravatī* '(land) with underground water channels', Greek *Gedrosia*. If the Baluch acquired their present name only after settling in their present habitats, this would explain why they are not mentioned by this name in any sources earlier than the tenth century.

According to the 1961 census of Pakistan, 363,000 people spoke Brahui as their primary language (151,000 in the Kalat region of Baluchistan), and 87,000 people as their second language. The Brahui are traditionally nomadic tribesmen. During the winter season, they used to take their flocks from the cold highlands of Baluchistan to the lowlands of Sind, migrating back again for the summer season. They have started staying in Sind permanently only in relatively recent times, from the end of the eighteenth century onwards; this has increased their contact with the Indo-Aryan languages of Sindhi and Siraiki (or Lahnda). Estimates of the numbers of Brahui speakers living in southeast Afghanistan vary between 50,000 and 200,000 (Elfenbein thinks the latter figure may be a mistake for 100,000); the majority are tenant farmers or hired herders working for Baluchi or Pathan khans, and most of them also speak either Pashto or Baluchi or both. Elfenbein (1987) estimates the grand total of Brahui *speakers* now to be around 500,000, of whom perhaps only about 100,000 are primary speakers.

During the past decades, the numbers of Brahui speakers have been declining somewhat in favour of Baluchi speakers, who nowadays number around 3,500,000 in all. The tribesmen calling themselves Brahui in Iranian and Afghan Seistan have ceased to speak Brahui; they adopted Baluchi about two generations ago.

The Brahui tribes are mentioned for the first time in Persian chronicles referring to a 'Brahui Confederation' established in Baluchistan in the sixteenth century; in 1660 Mīr Ahmad, belonging to the Brahui Mīrwārī, established the Khanate in Kalat. In the course of its history, the Brahui Confederation made alliances with the surrounding tribes (mainly Baluchi, but also Pathans, Sindhis and others), who then became full members of the confederation. Many of the tribes have changed their language. Today, there are 24 Brahui tribes in Pakistani Baluchistan. Sixteen are said to be of non-Brahui origin, but six of these speak Brahui as their first language, while of the eight tribes said to be Brahui in origin, only three remain Brahui speakers; the rest are either bilingual with Baluchi as their first and Brahui as their second language, or have completely given up Brahui in favour of Baluchi.

As the Brahui themselves explain, their ethnic name in all probability denotes just one branch of the Baluchi tribe:

> The word 'Brāhūī' (older 'Brāhōī') is almost certainly a modern term, taken from the Siraiki ('Jaṭki') *brāhō*, the local form of *ibrāhīm*, to which the Balochi *-ī* adj. suffix has been added, as is usual, to form an ethnicon. As far as is known, this ethnicon was first used in the 16th C. to refer to a now vanished tribe of Baloch, the Ibrāhīmī, who dwelt amongst the Jaṭṭs of Awārān in Pakistani Makran. (Elfenbein 1987: 223)

Brahui and Baluchi have for very many centuries been in close contact with each other. While the numerically fewer Brahuis had earlier enjoyed higher social prestige, the situation has been reversed since about 1750. The symbiosis of the Brahui and Baluchi speakers has resulted in an extensive bilingualism of a rare, bilateral type (normally the minority alone is bilingual):

> Amongst bilaterally bilingual speakers ... Brahui tribal matters between equals are discussed in Brahui; in group conversation between 3 or more persons, an inferior speaks to a superior in Brahui, who answers in Balochi; equals may use either language indifferently; in formal discussion, Balochi is used regardless of rank. For extra-tribal matters of an official kind, Urdu is used if possible with Government officials. Within a family context, an elder son speaks to his father in Balochi, a younger in Brahui; a father speaks to his son in Brahui if the mother is Brahui-speaking; in Balochi if the mother is Balochi-speaking. The language used between brothers and sisters depends on the language of the mother, in a polygamous society, and depends on status. A husband speaks to a wife in her language, a wife to a husband in his – but this depends also on status. (Elfenbein 1987: 222f.)

Brahui is assumed to have been in close and continuous contact with Baluchi since at least the fourteenth century, and probably a few centuries longer. During this long period Baluchi has exercised such a profound and pervasive influence on Brahui that it has been completely changed, not only lexically but also in phonology, morphology and syntax.

> The main Balochi influences on Brahui are: (1) Brahui has largely adopted the Balochi phonological system; (2) the loss of gender in Brahui; (3) Brahui has taken the imperfective prefix *a-* from Balochi; (4) Brahui has a present-continuative tense formed as a calque on its Balochi model; (5) the Brahui use of the conjunction *ki* is taken from Balochi; (6) Brahui uses suffixed pronouns after a Balochi model; (7) the Brahui verbal stem *kan-* 'to do' is borrowed from Balochi; (8) Brahui has an *-ā* case, used as loc., from Balochi; (9) Brahui employs Balochi word order, and (10) approximately 20 percent of the Brahui lexicon are loanwords from Balochi. (Elfenbein 1989: 360)

Brahui has been able to retain only its own Dravidian morphology and a small proportion of its original Dravidian lexicon (constituting perhaps 15 per cent of its vocabulary). Thus, only the first three numerals are Dravidian, while the rest are Baluchi. The influence of Brahui on Baluchi, on the other hand, has been mainly lexical, and the number of Brahui loanwords in Baluchi is very small.

The overwhelming majority (more than 95 per cent) of the Brahuis and Baluchis are Sunni Muslims, and about one-third of their vocabulary consists of Persian and Arabic loanwords. But both Brahui and Baluchi also have a large number of Indo-Aryan loanwords, perhaps a quarter of the vocabulary. These words come from Sindhi and from southern Siraiki (or Lahnda), known in Baluchi as Jaṭkī or Jaḍ-gālī, i.e. the language of the Jaṭṭ people. The ethnicon *Jaṭṭ* comes from Middle Indo-Aryan *Jaṭṭa*, from Old Indo-Aryan **Jarta*, known from the Mahābhārata in the form *Jartika* as the name of a people living in the northern Indus Valley. Five Brahui and several Baluchi tribes claim Jaṭṭ origin, and the Hindu Sewā rulers of Kalat before the sixteenth century were Jaṭṭs. The Jaḍ-gālī speakers of Iranian Baluchistan apparently migrated from the east several centuries ago, and they arrived in Makran as early as the fourth century AD. Indo-Aryan loanwords have spread far to the west also through frequent reverse migrations of the Baluch and Brahui from the borders of Sind westwards into Iran and Afghanistan. According to Elfenbein, Baluchi has got the retroflex consonants *ṭ ḍ ṛ* from Indo-Aryan: 'Their presence is most marked in Eastern Hill Balochi (which has probably also the greatest number of Jaṭkī loanwords), lessening as one moves westwards, and in Iran they tend to be assimilated to *t d r*, respectively' (Elfenbein 1989: 358f.). However, a more likely source would seem to be Brahui, which likewise has three retroflexes *ṭ ḍ ṛ*, all of Proto-Dravidian origin.

But although Sindhi and Siraiki have exerted a very strong influence on Brahui vocabulary, 'there is no real evidence for any deeper, structural influence from Indo-Aryan on Brahui . . . "Linguistic aggression" against Brahui has been almost entirely by Balochi until quite recent times, when Urdu has taken over as chief aggressor, together with Sindhi and Siraiki for those Brahui-speakers who live in Sind' (Elfenbein 1982: 79f.).

The absence of any deeper structural influence of Indo-Aryan upon Brahui would seem to rule out the possibility that Brahui has arrived from the plains of India in relatively recent times. In 1962, Murray Emeneau had reservations in this respect, because some structural changes in Brahui were ambiguous and could potentially be due to Indo-Aryan influence. Now these doubtful items have been removed by Josef Elfenbein, who has shown the source to be Baluchi here too. The conclusion can therefore be drawn that Brahui has certainly been spoken in Baluchistan ever since the Baluch arrived there perhaps a thousand years ago. The only controversial issue is whether the Brahui were living in Baluchistan before that time. The answer to this question can be sought in Brahui's relationship with the other Dravidian languages.

Since M. B. Emeneau's study (1962a), it has generally been agreed that no dialectal features connect Brahui specifically with any of the Central or South Dravidian languages; in contrast, Brahui belongs to a separate North Dravidian subgroup with Kurukh and Malto, by virtue of several shared innovations:

1 Most important among these innovations is the fricativization of the Proto-Dravidian word-initial velar stop (**k- > χ-*) before vowels other than the high vowels **i*, **ī* and **u*, **ū*, in which position it remains unchanged (*k-*).
2 The change of Proto-Dravidian word-initial **c-* into *k-* before **u*, **ū*, **e* and **ē* in a few etyma.
3 The change of Proto-Dravidian **v-* into *b-*. It is possible that this is not a shared innovation in the two branches of North Dravidian but a separate development. A parallel change has taken place in Eastern Indo-Aryan and the Kurukh-Malto change may have been induced by it.
4 The use of a velar suffix **-k-* in the formation of the past tense.
5 Seven words not found in other Dravidian languages.

The Kurukh language is nowadays spoken by about 1,300,000 people from Nepal and Madhya Pradesh to Bihar, Orissa, Bengal and Assam. Most of the Kurukh speakers live in the Choṭā-Nāgpur plateau, the greatest concentration being in the Ranchi District of Bihar and the neighbouring Raigarh District of Madhya Pradesh. Kurukh has remained a relatively uniform language, so its spread over vast areas in North India is fairly recent. It is also closely related to Malto, which is restricted to the Rājmahāl hills in Bihar and West Bengal and spoken by about 90,000 people.

In their folk narratives, the Kurukh speak of the Azamgarh region (about midway between Lucknow and Patna) as their original home, from which they migrated in ancient times to a (not certainly identifiable) place called Hardiban, and later, along the Narbadā river, to Gujarat. The invasions of the Gurjaras (in the fifth and sixth centuries AD) and the Muslims (from the eighth century) into the Daybāl-Broach-Ujjain area, however, forced the Kurukhs to retreat eastwards towards Bihar and back to Rohtas near the Son river, where they split into two groups: the Malto went northeast to the Rājmahāl hills, and the Kurukh to the Choṭā-Nāgpur plateau (fig. 9.1).

These Kurukh legends about their migration to Gujarat and back have been referred to as a possible bridge to South India. The name *Kurukh* (phonemically */kuṛχ/*, phonetically

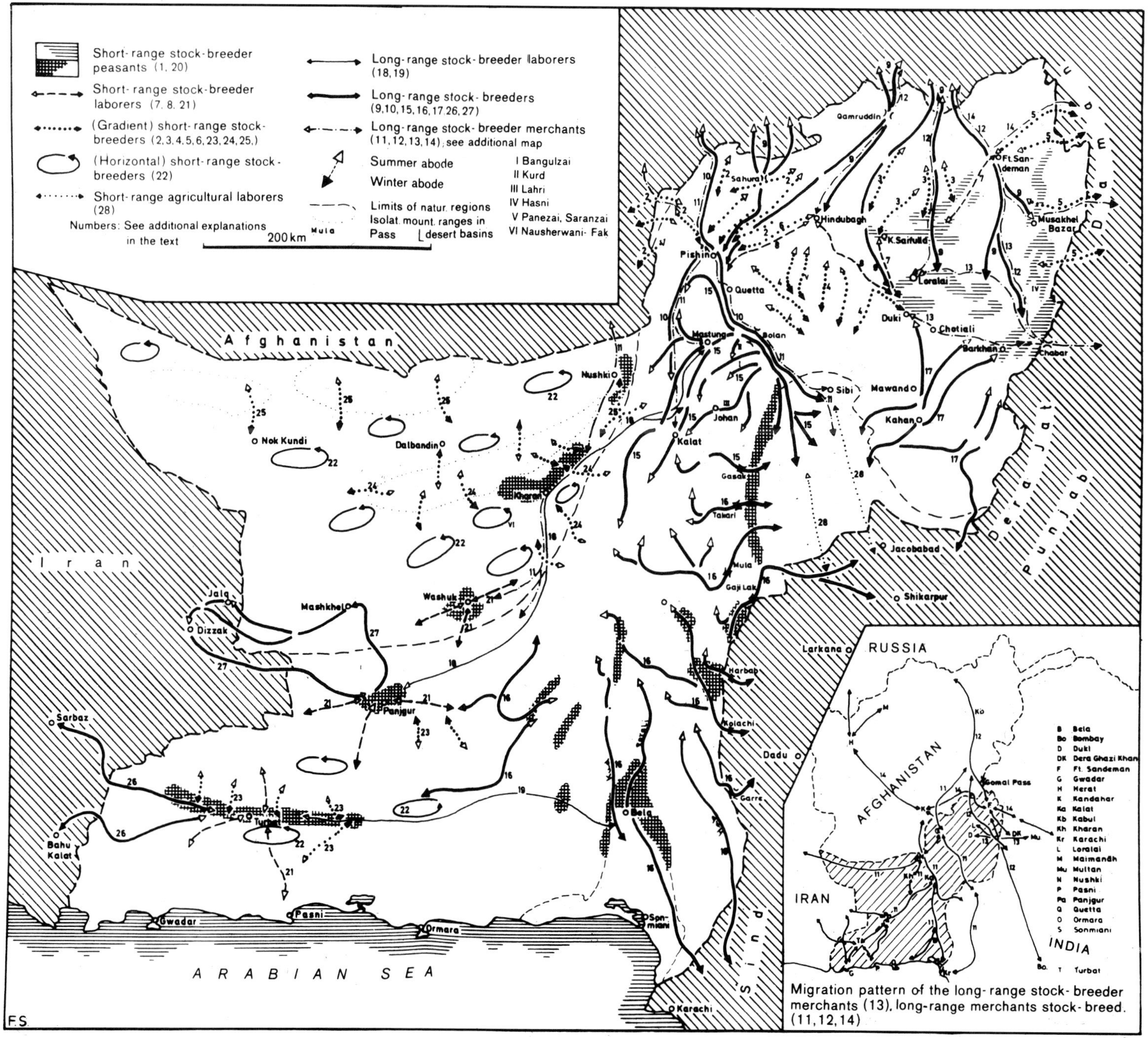

Fig. 9.2. Migration pattern of nomadic people in Baluchistan at the end of the nineteenth century. After Scholz 1983: fig. 5.

[*kúṛuχ*]) has been etymologically connected with *Koḍagu*, the name of a Dravidian people and language in Karnataka. However,

> because of Tamil *kuṭakku* 'west', the PDr root reconstructed here [**kuṭ-V-k-*] may originally have denoted the point of the compass, and only later on came to be used as the name of a people. In this case it would not be necessary to assume a direct relationship between *Koḍagu* and *Kuṛux* (or between the speakers of these languages), for such a geographical designation [i.e. 'westerners'] may have been used for quite different ethnical groups. (Pfeiffer 1972: 64)

The Tamil word *kuṭa* 'setting sun' indeed suggests that the ultimate etymology of these words may be the Proto-Dravidian verb *kiṭa* 'to lie down, rest, fall down', for the change *i* > *u* before retroflexes is common in Dravidian.

What is more important, no grammatical features of Koḍagu link it with North Dravidian. On the other hand, D. N. Shankara Bhat (1968, 1971) has claimed that the Koragas of South Kanara speak (besides Tulu) a separate Dravidian language which shares several grammatical features with North Dravidian and Kurukh in particular. However, the evidence presented so far is in many respects uncertain, and such authorities as Martin Pfeiffer (personal communication) and P. S. Subrahmanyam (1983) have reserved their judgement.

On the present evidence, then, the North Dravidian branch consists of just two sub-branches, Brahui and Kurukh-Malto. Brahui, of course, has diverged from Kurukh and Malto much more than they have from each other. Thus more than half (108 etyma) of Brahui's relatively small Dravidian vocabulary (202 etyma) is not represented in Kurukh-Malto. Nevertheless, I am inclined to think that the split within North Dravidian is much more likely to have occurred in the first millennium AD (as suggested by Elfenbein) than the second millennium BC, and that it may well have been caused by the Gurjara and Muslim invasions.

On the other hand, the linguistic separation of North Dravidian from the rest of Dravidian must be much older. As Thomas Burrow pointed out in 1943, the change of Proto-Dravidian **k-* into Proto-North Dravidian **χ-* is absent from the numerous loanwords which Brahui, Kurukh and Malto have borrowed from Indo-Aryan, the very few exceptions being mostly reborrowings of Dravidian borrowings in Indo-Aryan. The only notable exception is Brahui *χōlum* 'wheat' < Sanskrit *gōdhūma* 'wheat, *Triticum sativum*' (first attested in the Yajurveda; the Sanskrit word is also the source of Proto-Nuristani **gōdūma*). If this etymology is correct (and the Brahui word is not rather related to Tamil *kūlam* and Central Dravidian *kūli*, *kūḍi* 'grain, paddy', as recently suggested by Burrow and Emeneau), it would imply that the North Dravidian sound change was still productive at the very beginning of the Indo-Aryan influence. Burrow's argument implies that the sound change had already taken place and was no longer productive in North Dravidian when it came into contact with Indo-Aryan languages. On the other hand, Sanskrit *khala-* 'threshing-floor', a loanword from Dravidian attested as early as the Ṛgveda (*c.*1000 BC), starts with an aspirated velar stop, apparently reflecting the North Dravidian fricativization of Proto-Dravidian **k-* (cf. Tamil *kaḷam* 'threshing-floor' vs. Kurukh *χall* 'field'); compare Ṛgvedic Sanskrit *múkham* 'mouth' < Proto-Dravidian *mukam* 'face, mouth', reflecting the lenition of **-k-* in intervocalic position.

On the basis of the Kurukh legends, Elfenbein locates the North Dravidian homeland on the Narbada river. He concludes that Proto-Brahui speakers migrated through Gujarat and Sind to their present home around Kalat in Baluchistan about 1,000 years ago, and became absorbed early into the Baluch tribal system (fig. 9.1). There is little doubt about this early absorption and its occurrence in Baluchistan. I disagree with Elfenbein, however, about the location of the North Dravidian homeland. In my opinion it was in Baluchistan rather than in 'Central West India', which means that the Proto-Brahui speakers were already in Baluchistan when the Baluch came, rather than vice versa.

Baluchistan was hardly uninhabited when the Baluch arrived there, as there is archaeological evidence of more or less continuous occupation from the seventh millennium BC. All this time nomadic people have migrated seasonally between highlands and lowlands, spending the hot summers in the coolness of the hills and the cold winters in the mildness of the plains (§ 1.6). In 1901, 60 per cent of the Brahuis were nomadic and 13 per cent semi-nomadic. Since that time, these figures have been drastically decreasing, but in former times seasonal migrations brought large numbers of Brahui and Baluchi nomads annually to Sind (fig. 9.2). Many groups extended their winter wanderings to Gujarat and Rajasthan. It is easy to imagine that the Kurukh and Malto represent one such nomadic tribe which continued its migration to the hills of central and eastern India when once its way back to Baluchistan had become blocked. It is more difficult to imagine that people of the plains forced their way into the rugged mountains of Baluchistan, especially if those mountains were already occupied by such hardy tribes as the Baluch. And would the Baluch have accepted such plains people into their fold, respecting them as much as or even more than themselves? If the Brahuis were not the indigenous inhabitants of Baluchistan, who were? Certainly not the Baluch, who came from northern Iran in the tenth century AD or later.

The conclusion that the Brahui and Kurukh-Malto represent remnants of the language spoken by the

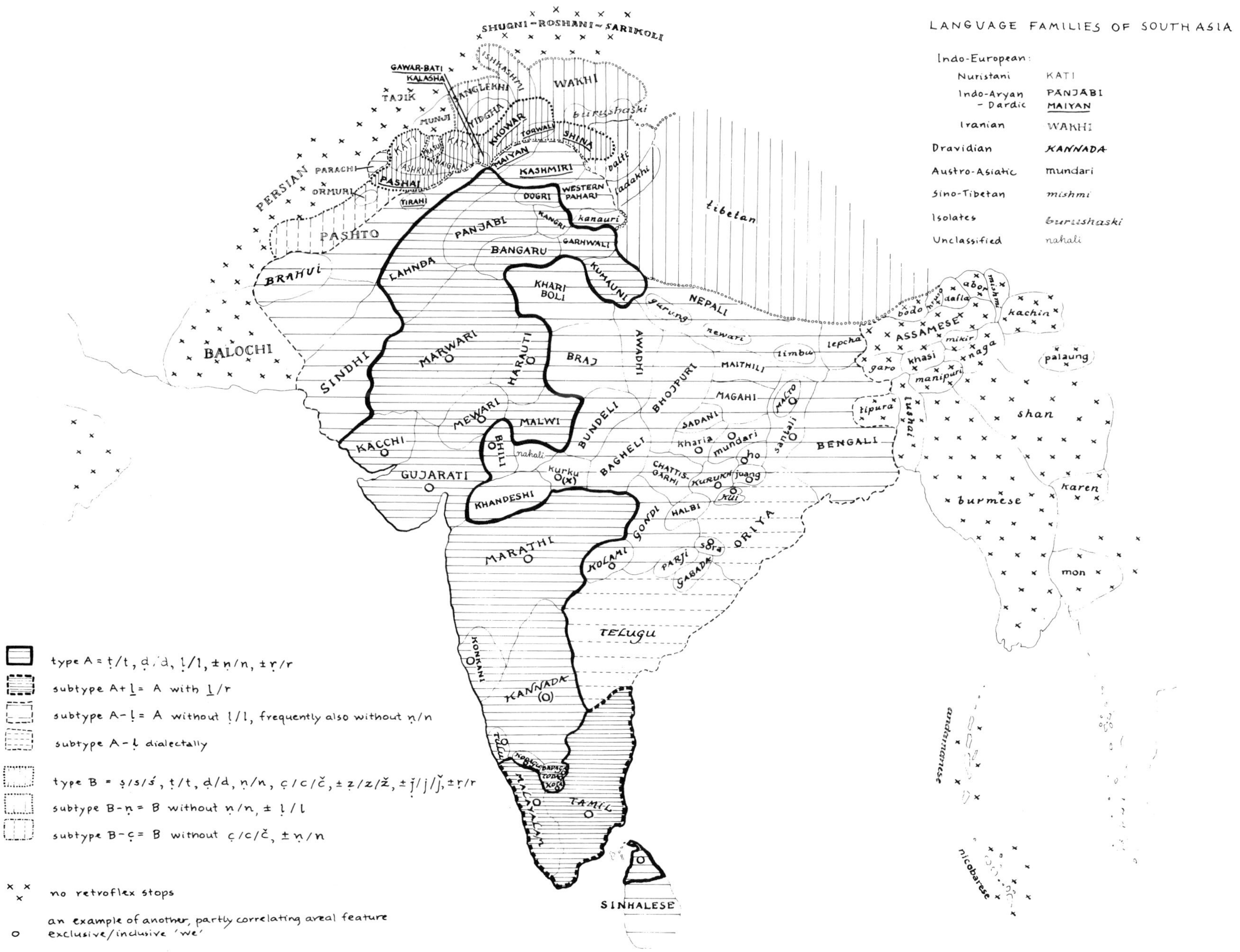

Fig. 9.3. Major linguistic areas in South Asia as defined by the retroflex systems; also, the distribution of the inclusive / exclusive distinction in the pronoun of the first person plural. Based on the ongoing researches of Bertil Tikkanen.

descendants of the Early Harappan population of Baluchistan is supported by the evidence of Old Indo-Aryan, to which I shall turn in § 9.3, after considering areal linguistics in a broader perspective.

9.2 Linguistic convergence in South Asia

Many language families and individual languages spoken in South Asia lack ancient written sources. Areal linguistics provides evidence that is indispensable in charting their prehistory and thus also in determining which language was spoken by the Harappans. Some of this evidence has already been hinted at here and there.

The way in which a person speaks a second or third language is influenced by his or her mother tongue and vice versa. Linguistic transferences mediated by bilingual individuals gradually lead to borrowings and structural resemblances between contiguous languages. Areal isoglosses (that is, geographical lines that separate neighbouring regions according to distinct linguistic features) cut across the boundaries set by the genetic relationships.

Some peoples have been able to maintain their language through millennia; others have yielded to social, political or cultural pressures and changed their language. But even if a language has died out, it may be possible to determine its earlier presence in the area from loanwords and from the structural influences it has exerted on the remaining languages. The term 'adstratum' refers to a living language exerting influence on another language, 'substratum' to an older local language that has died out but influenced the language that has replaced it, while 'superstratum' refers to the opposite, a language which newcomers have given up in favour of the local language, which they have adopted, adding to it their own 'accent' and other peculiarities.

The mapping of isoglosses thus makes it possible to ascertain the former extent of different language families to some degree. Historically significant patterns emerge when several isoglosses cluster into isogloss bundles with approximately the same boundaries, and when the origin of a given linguistic feature and the direction of its diffusion can be established. Here it is important to establish whether the feature can be attributed to the reconstruction of the protolanguage of the family or branch involved, and whether it is present in the cognate languages outside South Asia.

It goes beyond the scope of the present book to present a comprehensive and up-to-date summary of the major areal isoglosses in South Asia. However, figure 9.3 charts the most important conclusion that Dr Bertil Tikkanen has drawn from his ongoing (and so far mostly unpublished) analysis and synthesis of the currently available evidence. It concentrates on the only linguistic feature that demarcates South Asia as a linguistic area in Asia, namely the presence of retroflex or (post)alveolar versus dental stops. Other retroflex consonants, such as sonorants, sibilants and affricates, have either a narrower or a broader distribution. It is possible to distinguish between two basic retroflex typologies (A and B) and subtypes within each of them. There is a convergence along the contact areas towards the less marked types (A). This retroflex typology correlates to some extent with other areal isoglosses. For the sake of clarity, however, these other areal features have not been indicated on the map, excepting just one isogloss most relevant for the theme of this book, namely the distinction between forms excluding and including the addressee in the pronoun of the first person plural, 'we'.

Tikkanen's analysis suggests that Dravidian had once been spoken also in all those parts of the type A retroflex system area which are Indo-Aryan-speaking now. This distribution makes Dravidian the most likely language to have been spoken by the Harappans.

9.3 Dravidian substratum influence on Old Indo-Aryan

Recent analysis of extensive cranial and dental material suggests two major biological discontinuities in the population of the Greater Indus Valley, the first between 6000 and 4500 BC, and the second between 1750 / 800 and 200 BC:

> The results of this research do not support Renfrew's Neolithic Arya Hypothesis [which] ... calls for introduction of Indo-European speakers with the development of agriculture ... The Harappan Civilization does indeed represent an indigenous development within the Indus Valley, but this does not indicate isolation extending back to neolithic time. Rather, this development represents internal continuity for only 2000 years, combined with interactions with the West and specifically with the Iranian Plateau ... The second biological discontinuity ... indicate[s] a change during the millennium following the end of the Harappan Civilization. This latter difference could be interpreted as support for Renfrew's 'Mounted Nomads of the Steppe' hypothesis ... [which postulates] a movement of Indo-European speakers into South Asia after the end of the Harappan Civilization but before composition of the Hymns of the Rigveda [i.e.] ... after 1750 BC but before 1000 BC. (Hemphill et al. 1992: 173–4, with the order of the quotations changed)

The Aryan-speaking nomads thus seem to have started coming to the Indian subcontinent at the beginning of the second millennium BC (§§ 8.4–5). Initially their numbers must have been very small in comparison to the population living in the cities and villages of the Indus Civilization, estimated to have been at least a million. All the Harappan people could not possibly have been killed or driven away. Archaeological evidence also shows that the Harappan traditions continued without a break, becoming transformed gradually into the various Late Harappan cultures (§ 1.6). The new elements appearing at this level, such as the Jhukar seals which have parallels in the Bronze Age culture of Margiana and Bactria, are likely to represent the incoming minority who formed a dominating élite speaking an Aryan language (§§ 8.4–5).

Nor could the Harappan language(s) have disappeared overnight. In the course of centuries and through gradually increasing bilingualism, the earlier population eventually adopted the Aryan languages. An analogy closer to our time may illustrate this process. After Caesar's legions had conquered the Gauls, the originally Celtic-speaking tribes of what is now France gradually adopted the Latin language. Such a process of linguistic assimilation leaves evidence of the disappearing substratum language in the structure and vocabulary of the surviving language: the way in which a person speaks a second language is affected by his or her mother tongue. Modern French has developed from a vulgar Latin that was rather different from the Latin on which modern Italian is based. Less than a millennium separates the Indus Civilization from the earliest preserved literary sources, the hymns of the R̥gveda, so the chances of finding some trace of Harappan substratum influence in them look fair.

Geographical references and cultural content suggest the Ghalegay IV culture of Swat (*c.*1700–1400 BC) as the milieu of the most ancient Indian hymns of the R̥gveda (§ 8.4). But were there any Harappans in Swat before the arrival of the R̥gvedic Aryans? The earliest inhabitants of the Swat Valley had a Neolithic culture with a pebble-tool industry, Ghalegay I (*c.*3000–2500 BC), which was comparable to that of Neolithic sites in Himachal Pradesh and, north of the Hindu Kush and Pamir mountains, in south Tadzhikistan and in China. There is nothing to connect them with the Early Harappans. But the culture of the Ghalegay II period (*c.*2500–2000 BC), contemporaneous with the Indus Civilization, is very different. Its fine wheel-made and painted pottery is similar to that of Hathial I and Sarai Khola II near Taxila, a regional variety of the Early Harappan Kot Diji-style pottery. The scarcity of structural remains and domestic articles in Ghalegay II Swat contrasts with the abundance of the pottery, suggesting a periodic rather than continuous occupation. Giorgio Stacul (1987: 117) plausibly suggests that this reflects Harappan exploitation of Swat's rich coniferous forests, evidenced by the fact that some Harappan houses were built of deodar cedars. Until recently, this wood has been transported from Swat by floating it down the river.

The next period, Ghalegay III (*c.*2000–1700 BC), is characterized by the almost complete disappearance of the Harappan-related wheel-made pottery and by the reappearance of the pebble-tool industry, accompanied by a coarse pottery similar to that of the Northern Neolithic at Sarai Khola I near Taxila and at Burzahom in Kashmir (fig. 8.12). This culture persisted as a minor component during the following Ghalegay IV period (*c.*1700–1400 BC), which may represent the early R̥gvedic culture. The potter's wheel and the related traditions of period II did not entirely disappear during period III, however, for they reappear little by little in period IV.

This cultural background would account for the paucity of Dravidian substratum influence upon the early R̥gvedic language. Still, few though they are, some Dravidian loanwords can be recognized in the R̥gveda, including *phálam* '(ripe) fruit' (cf. PDr *paḻam* 'ripe fruit') as well as *múkham* 'mouth' and *khála-* 'threshing-floor' (§ 9.1). The Harappans used a plough, and the R̥gvedic word for 'plough', *lāṅgala*, is probably derived from Proto-Dravidian **ñāṅgal* / **nāṅgal* (there are other examples of the replacement of Proto-Dravidian **ñ-* with *l-* in Indo-Aryan, cf. § 12.2), even if the etymon may ultimately go back to Austro-Asiatic.

The number of Dravidian loanwords increases dramatically in post-R̥gvedic literature. Thomas Burrow has presented a list of 85 'words in Sanskrit which can be traced either with certainty or with a high degree of probability to a Dravidian origin'. The great majority of these appear in the later Vedic texts, the earliest classical Sanskrit texts like Pāṇini's grammar, and in Pali, between *c.*700 and 300 BC.

> This is significant from the point of view of locality where the influence took place. It is not possible that at this period such influence could have been exercised by the Dravidian languages of the South. There were no intensive contacts with South India before the Maurya period by which time the majority of these words had already been adopted by Indo-Aryan. If the influence took place in the central Gangetic plain and the classical Madhyadeśa the assumption that the pre-Aryan population of this area contained a considerable element of Dravidian speakers would best account for the Dravidian words in Sanskrit. (Burrow 1973a: 386)

The R̥gveda is assumed to contain not only Dravidian loanwords but also phonological and syntactic Dravidisms, in particular the development of (1) retroflex phonemes, (2) the gerund, and (3) the quotative and (4) onomatopoeic constructions, all of which are absent from the closely related Iranian branch of Aryan languages. In each case, however, alternative explanations are possible and have been suggested: a spontaneous internal development or the influence of some other language family, including unknown substrata. But the cumulative evidence weighs heavily in the balance. One further reason why some scholars have been unwilling to accept these structural features as Dravidisms, in addition to the small number of Dravidian loanwords (which are also called into question), is their early and sudden appearance. This, however, is exactly what can be expected if the

Dravidisms were adopted indirectly, through another Aryan language that had been subject to direct substratum influence of Dravidian for a longer time. We must bear in mind that the Ṛgveda was largely composed in the plains of the Punjab relatively late, and redacted even later. The language, as well as the contents, of the Yajurveda reflects an entirely different tradition, which probably evolved in the Punjab and was incorporated in the Veda only during the acculturation that may be assumed to have taken place after the descent of the Ṛgvedic tradition from the Swat Valley. Epic Sanskrit, which contains a larger number of Dravidian loanwords than the Vedic texts, is likely to go back to the same 'Proto-Yajurvedic' dialect of Old Indo-Aryan. Prakritization, which eventually led to a radical simplification of the complex Indo-Aryan syllable structure through assimilation and intrusive vowels, is best explained as an adjustment to the phonology of a Dravidian substratum.

9.4 Archaeological identification of Proto-Dravidian speakers

In the third millennium, when the Aryan languages had probably not yet arrived and the Gangetic Valley had not yet become intensively cultivated (it is thought that this became possible only with the arrival of iron *c.*1000 BC), and with the south only sparsely populated, speakers of the Harappan languages are likely to have formed the majority of the South Asian population. As far as numbers of speakers are concerned, the Dravidian family is the best match for Harappan among the known non-Aryan language families of long standing in South Asia. After Indo-Aryan, the Dravidian languages make the second largest linguistic family: until recently, about one-quarter of the entire population spoke Dravidian. Speakers of the third largest linguistic family, Austro-Asiatic, number just a few per cent.

In 1965, Kamil Zvelebil, one of the leading Dravidologists, linked the carriers of the cultures characterized by the heterogeneous Black-and-Red Ware (=BRW) with the speakers of Dravidian languages, because both 'once inhabited the *whole* of India', and because the interaction between the culture marked by the Painted Grey Ware (identified with the Vedic culture) and the surrounding BRW cultures around 500 BC coincides with the period of a massive influx of Dravidian words into Sanskrit. There is certainly a lot to be said for this identification, provided it is not made too exclusive. An exclusively Dravidian identification of the BRW cultures would leave little room for non-Vedic Indo-Aryan, including Proto-Māgadhī, which is known to have been spoken east of the Vedic area in the Brāhmaṇa period (§ 8.4). Since the BRW is ultimately of Harappan origin and makes an early appearance in Late Harappan cultures with intrusive elements, a more balanced view is to see it as a ceramic style which became fashionable among both native Dravidians and the earliest wave(s) of Indo-Aryans who interacted with them.

The identifications made in section 8.3 onwards leave only one major archaeological complex that can be aligned with Proto-Dravidian: the Harappan culture with its Early Harappan background. In fact, this is by far the most satisfying match both temporally and geographically, particularly in view of areal linguistics (§ 9.2) and also the distribution of the North Dravidian branch and the dating of its principal innovation (the spirantization of PDr **k-*) to the very beginning of its contact with Indo-Aryan languages (§ 9.1). There are other arguments, too, supporting this equation.

A provisional analysis of the Indus inscriptions has given us a few hints of the typological characteristics of the Harappan language, notably the hypothesis that different sorts of attributes (including the adjective and genitive attributes as well as numerals) precede the head word (§§ 6.1–3). Proto-Dravidian matches perfectly these characteristics, Dravidian languages being the only ones in the Indian subcontinent with a consistent ordering of modifier before modified.

Some cultural traits of the Indus Civilization have linguistic implications. Its standardized weights reveal that the numeral system was a mixed one, binary or octonary plus decimal. The smaller ratios weigh $\frac{1}{2}$, $\frac{1}{4}$, $\frac{1}{6}$, $\frac{1}{8}$ and $\frac{1}{16}$ of the basic unit (13.625 grams), the bigger ratios 2, 4, 10, 12.5, 20, 40, 100, 200, 400, 500, 800 times the basic unit. This agrees with the traditions of classical India, where $8 \times 8 = 64$, and $10 \times 10 = 100$, were considered 'round numbers', not to mention the former division of the monetary unit, the rupee, into 16 annas. There is evidence in the numeral system of Proto-Dravidian for both a decimal and an octonary system. The numerals for both 'ten' (**pak̲tu*) and 'hundred' (**nūr̲u*) can be reconstructed for Proto-Dravidian. On the other hand, in Proto-Dravidian the root for 'eight' (**eṇ*) also means 'number' and 'to count', suggesting that this was the original turning-point in counting (once apparently performed with the help of fingers but excluding the thumbs).

Based on palaeobotanical evidence, D. Bedigian (1985) has suggested that sesame may have come to Mesopotamia from India with the Indus trade, and in this connection called attention to the similarity between Akkadian *ellu / ūlu* 'sesame oil' and Sumerian *ilu / ili* on the one hand, and South Dravidian *eḷ*, *eḷḷu* '*Sesamum indicum*' on the other. This argument is not fully satisfactory, however: (1) according to most recent research, sesame is an originally African cultivar; (2) the evidence for sesame in the Indus Civilization is rather poor; and (3) the quoted Dravidian word can be reconstructed only for Proto-South Dravidian, not for Proto-Dravidian.

The most important single piece of actual linguistic evidence relating to the Indus Civilization is the toponym *Meluḫḫa*, mentioned as a distant foreign country engaged in sea trade in the cuneiform sources of the Akkadian through Old Babylonian times (§ 1.5). In 1960, C. J. Gadd (in Leemans 1960: 164) hazarded the guess that this toponym might be etymologically related to Sanskrit *mlēccha*, a word that signifies a 'stranger speaking a language unintelligible to the Vedic Aryans'. It must be noted, however, that the earliest occurrence of Sanskrit *mlēccha* (in ŚB 3,2,1,18ff.) refers to people living rather a long way from the Harappan area, namely, the 'Asuras' of the east, who moreover spoke a Māgadhī-like Middle Indo-Aryan language. Even so, *mlēccha* might preserve a Harappan ethnic name, as these Mlecchas appear to be descended from the 'Indian Dāsas' who, upon their entry into Sind, evidently mixed with Indus people (§ 8.4).

The cognate Pali word *milakkha* 'barbarian' suggests that Sanskrit *mlēccha* goes back to **mlēkṣa*, which in turn may, as Sir Harold Bailey has pointed out, represent **mlēχa-*, where χ stands for a velar spirant not found in Indo-Aryan. With the metathesis characteristic of Central Dravidian and with the normal (Proto-)Dravidian spirantization of **-k-* in the intervocalic position, this word could go back to Proto-Dravidian **Mēl-akam* 'highland'. This compound, however, is not known from any Dravidian language. The second element does figure in the Old Tamil toponym *Tamiḻakam* 'Tamil country'; the question of a possible relationship between this toponym and *Meluḫḫa* is bound up with the problem concerning the etymology of the ethnic name *Tamiḻ* and its Sanskrit form *Draviḍa* or *Dramila*.

In early cuneiform texts, *Meluḫḫa* can also be read *Melaḫḫa* (*me-làḫ-ḫa*), which is closer to **Mēlakam* or even *(Ta)miḻakam*. The meaning 'high country' would be in agreement with the Sumerian characterization of *Meluḫḫa* as 'highland' (§ 1.5); this meaning would fit Baluchistan, the original home of the Early Harappans (§ 1.6). In fact John Hansman (1973) has tried to connect *Meluḫḫa* with the ethnic name *Baluch* (for a different etymology, see § 9.1); Hansman's bridge is the Neo-Assyrian word *^{riq}baluḫḫu* 'galbanum', an extract of a tree growing in eastern Iran and Afghanistan (a timber called *^{is}si-in-da-a* in the same Neo-Assyrian text probably denotes 'wood from Sind').

The place-names of the Harappan area provide one more potential source of clues to identifying the Harappan language (see also § 7.4). Settlement names are particularly relevant, because they may go back to the Early Harappan period but not further. Among the elements which denote 'village' or 'town' in the Harappan area there are several of common occurrence that are of non-Aryan etymology, and all of these have a Dravidian origin and occur frequently in South Indian place-names. They include *nagára* (cf. *Binagára* in Sind on Ptolemy's map [7,61] = *Minnagára* in Periplous 38 = *Min Nagar* near Bahmanabad in a thirteenth-century Sindhi chronicle; *Minagára* in Saurashtra in Ptolemy 7,63 = *Minnagára* in Periplous 41, exporting much cotton; *Nagára* in Afghanistan in Ptolemy 7,43, etc.); *palli* 'village' (whence *valli* and modern *-oli*, *-ol* in Gujarat), corresponding to South Dravidian *paḷḷi*; and *pāṭa(ka)* or *pāṭi* (whence *-vāṭa*, *-vāṭi*, etc., modern *-vāḍā*, *vāḍ*, etc. in Gujarat) as well as *paṭṭana* (Gujarati *paṭṭan*), all originally 'pastoral village' from the Dravidian root *paṭu* 'to lie down to sleep'. The word *kōṭṭa* 'fort' (generally considered to be of Dravidian origin) is of particular interest, because its distribution in North India is mainly limited to the Harappan area and the northwest. Most of the Harappan settlements were fortified.

In addition to place-names, other linguistic evidence suggests that Dravidian was formerly spoken in Maharashtra, Gujarat and, less evidently, Sind, all of which belonged to the Harappan realm. It includes Dravidian structural features in the local Indo-Aryan languages Marathi, Gujarati and Sindhi, such as the distinction between two forms of the personal pronoun of the first person plural, indicating whether the speaker includes the addressee(s) in the concept 'we' or not (fig. 9.3). Dravidian loanwords are conspicuously numerous in the lower-class dialects of Marathi.

Further evidence for the former presence of Dravidian speakers in Maharashtra and Gujarat is supplied by the Dravidian kinship system. The kinship systems prevalent in Dravidian-speaking South India today can be shown to be descended from a common system, which distinguishes between marriageable cross-cousins (children of opposite-sex siblings, a brother and a sister) and unmarriageable parallel cousins (children of same-sex siblings). The Proto-Dravidian kinship terminology is logically dependent on the rule of cross-cousin marriage as an ordering principle. The cross-cousin marriage has two effects which have been prohibited in the Indo-Aryan kinship systems by rules of marriage: the exchange of sisters in marriage, and the perpetuation of affinity between two lineages (fig. 9.4). 'Thus sharp contrasts between the Dravidian and the Indo-Aryan kinship systems exist at every level: concepts (kinship terms), rules, behavior' (Trautmann 1981: 25).

Thomas Trautmann has carefully analysed stories in Sanskrit, Prakrit and Pali texts where Dravidian cross-cousin marriage is placed in North Indian settings. Most of these tales, however, turned out to have been written in South India or Sri Lanka, reflecting conditions prevalent there and not in North India. Nevertheless, their testimony is valuable in authenticating the antiquity of cross-cousin marriage in South India. But the Jaina literature composed in Maharashtra, Gujarat and Saurashtra also contains examples

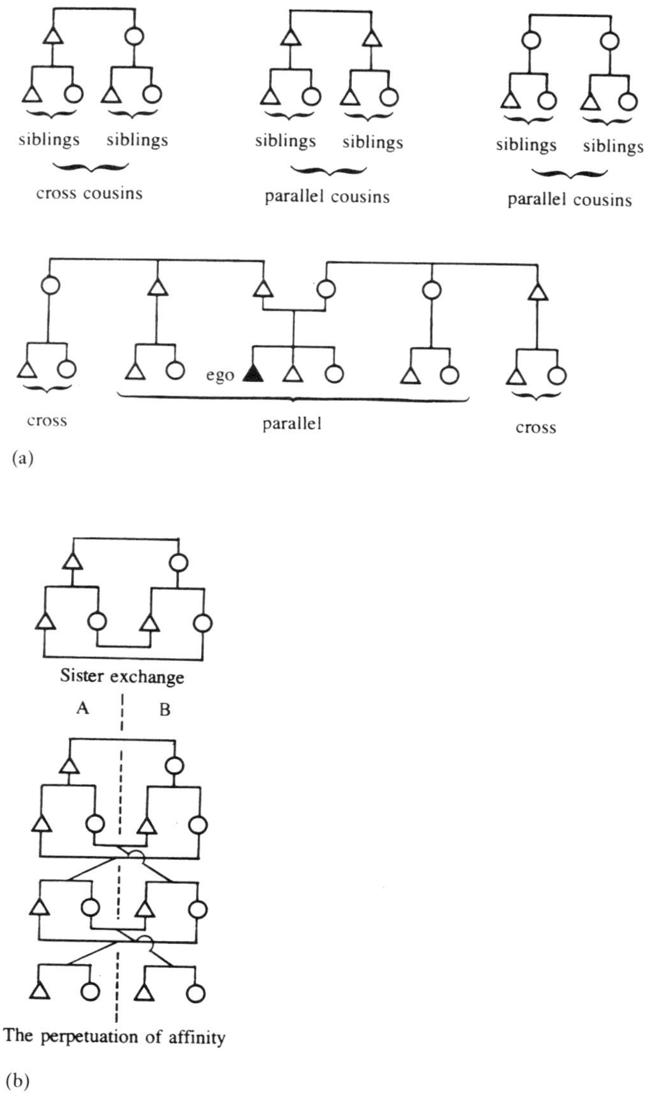

Fig. 9.4. The Dravidian kinship system based on cross-cousin marriage. (a) Cross cousins and parallel cousins. (b) Synchronic and diachronic effects of cross-cousin marriage. After Trautmann 1981: 23, fig. 1.5 and 25, fig. 1.7.

of cross-cousin marriage. These undoubtedly reflect local marriage norms, for 'though the languages of this area are Indo-Aryan, many of its castes are Dravidian in their kinship terminology, and for them the contemporary practice or the memory, preserved in proverbs and folklore, of cross cousin marriage is reported in the ethnography' (Trautmann 1981: 337).

9.5 South Dravidian and the archaeology of peninsular India

The Tamil language is spoken in the extreme south of India. Protected from Indo-Aryan influence by surrounding Dravidian languages and conserved by an ancient literary tradition of two millennia, Tamil has remained surprisingly close to Proto-Dravidian in its phonetic structure. The substantial corpus of bardic poetry in Old Tamil is also a unique source for ancient Dravidian culture and religion. The poems were composed and collected between about the first century BC and the sixth century AD. In the earlier parts of this literature, there is relatively little North Indian influence. The poetic conventions are original, Indo-Aryan loanwords scarce, and deities, officiants and other aspects of the cult have native names. Obviously the Old Tamil traditions constitute a most important source in any attempt to decipher the Indus script based on the hypothesis of a Dravidian affinity for the Indus language. But is there any historical relationship between the Tamil culture of the extreme south and the Indus Civilization of the northwest? How did the Tamil culture arise and when and where did the Tamil language come from? These questions should be answered, not only to legitimize the use of Old Tamil sources, but also in order to evaluate them better.

One of the most widely supported hypotheses was proposed in 1953 by Christoph von Fürer-Haimendorf. He suggested that the Dravidian languages came to India from the west through Iran about 700 BC with the carriers of the Megalithic culture, which is distributed all over South India including Tamil Nadu and which persisted there well into the early centuries of the Christian era. The isolated Megalithic stone cists near Karachi would explain the presence of the Brahui speakers in Baluchistan.

The last phase of the Megalithic culture (*c.*300–100 BC) does overlap the period of Old Tamil literature (*c.*100 BC – AD 600), which in its militaristic idealization of warfare (including such elements as the horse and iron weapons) closely resembles the martial character of the Megalithic culture (in which weapons were regular grave goods). Though cremation (cf. Puṟam 363) had by this time been imported from North India, Megalithic burial customs, too, were occasionally referred to (cf. Maṇimēkalai 6,66–7; Puṟam 231, 228, 256). It is indeed very probable that, during the last few centuries BC, the carriers of the Megalithic culture spoke Dravidian, at least in the extreme south. But this does not necessarily imply that the people who brought the Megalithic culture to South Asia also introduced the Dravidian languages there.

The earliest Iron Age period in South India, *c.*1100–800 BC, is essentially a continuation of the preceding Chalcolithic culture, with the addition of the iron daggers and arrowheads that appear in the graves. As in the Chalcolithic period, the graves are simple pits, which may have a ring of stones around them, and which may be covered by stone slabs or a mound. The burials are always complete inhumations. With the arrival of the Megalithic culture around 800 BC, however, a completely new mode of disposing of the dead was introduced. From now on, burial in ossuaries of bones that have previously been exposed for excarnation and then broken gradually becomes predominant.

A recent typological study by Jane R. McIntosh (1985) has established several temporally distinct types of megaliths, which have spread from north to south, starting *c.*800 BC (fig. 9.5). The earliest sites are in ancient Vidarbha, in northeastern Maharashtra. The settlement pattern consists of a habitation mound surrounded by megalithic stone circles with burials. There is evidence of advanced metal technology including iron-smelting. Important finds are copper ornaments for the face and flanks of horses, which have parallels at early Scythian sites. Horses fully equipped with such ornaments and trappings, and with iron bits, were buried together with the dead (some of whom had met a violent death) in almost all megalithic circles. The excellent carpentry tools fit in with the discovery of postholes for habitation huts 2 metres in diameter, with a semicircular hearth of clay inside. These dwellings recall the yurts of the Central and East Asian nomads.

To the first Megalithic phase (*c.*800–550 BC) belong also the cists made of stone slabs, usually with a porthole in the eastern slab. Temporally and geographically the nearest large group of porthole megaliths are the cemeteries in the Kuban region east of the Black Sea and in the Caucasus, dated to the early centuries of the first millennium BC. They are linked with South India by porthole megaliths at the Sialk B necropolis (*c.*1000–800 BC) in northwestern Iran and at Las Bela in South Baluchistan. These burials are of broken bones, and the grave goods include horse furniture and iron weapons. The Megalithic cairns of Moghul Ghundai in Baluchistan have been compared with Sialk B, which is supposed to reflect the coming of Iranian tribes from the steppes north of the Caucasus.

All this evidence suggests the introduction of the Megalithic culture into India by horse-riding and warring nomads, probably speaking an Aryan language that belonged to the Iranian branch. In India, the invaders adopted the local Black-and-Red Ware (§ 9.4), which is the characteristic ceramic of the Megalithic culture. Like the Iranian Śakas, who later ruled western India, the Megalithic invaders, too, were comparatively few in relation to the earlier inhabitants and are likely to have quickly become linguistically assimilated.

The Megalithic invasion into the Deccan was followed about two centuries later by raids from North India. The introduction of cremation to Maharashtra heralds the arrival of northern influences in the late sixth century BC. It was followed by the full-scale conquest of Maharashtra around 400 BC. This was probably when Mahārāṣṭrī, known as a literary language from the early centuries AD, was introduced into the Deccan. The North Indian expansion continued until it reached its maximum extent in Asoka's empire *c.*250 BC. The Mauryan political influence probably reached Karnataka around the end of the fourth century BC, when the Digambara Jainas are traditionally supposed to have moved there. The Paraśu-Rāma legend derives the Brahmanical culture of the west coast, down to Kerala, from the Pañcāla area in Uttar Pradesh via Malwa, the Narmada river and Śūrpāraka. The early Tamil-Brāhmī inscriptions of the second and first centuries BC record gifts to Jaina and Buddhist monks and nuns, and the Paraśu-Rāma legend (cf. Akam 220) and Vedic sacrifices are referred to in the earliest Old Tamil poems from around the beginning of the Christian era.

The Megalithic culture seems to have expanded explosively over the previously sparsely settled Kerala and Tamil Nadu around the fourth century BC. (The popular guardian deity of Tamil villages, the horse-riding *Ayyaṉār*, is likely to reflect these Megalithic traditions; the name of the god is derived from Prakrit *ayya* corresponding to Sanskrit *ārya*). While the similarity of artefacts suggests a southward migration from Maharashtra and Karnataka, many cultural traits seem to have spread from Gujarat via sea traffic to Sri Lanka and Tamil Nadu during the fifth to third centuries BC. Among such probably seaborne importations are swords, inurned cremation, and the irrigation agriculture of rice, which greatly contributed to the prosperity of these regions. The palaeography of the Tamil-Brāhmī script also suggests its derivation from Gujarat. In the time of the Old Tamil literature, sea trade flourished, and there were Graeco-Roman trading stations on the western as well as the eastern coast of South India.

That the Dravidians could not have arrived in India as late as the Megalithic culture is clear from the fact that there is evidence in the Vedic texts for the presence of Dravidian languages in the Punjab already in the second millennium BC (§ 9.3). Bridget and Raymond Allchin (1982: 353) have therefore opted for the alternative that the Neolithic herdsmen of South India already spoke Dravidian languages. While the unbroken continuity of some very basic aspects of the material culture in the villages (including the construction of the huts) of the Southern Neolithic with the subsequent cultures up to the present day may be advanced as an argument in favour of its Dravidian linguistic affinity, there is little to suggest any connection with the Harappan tradition of

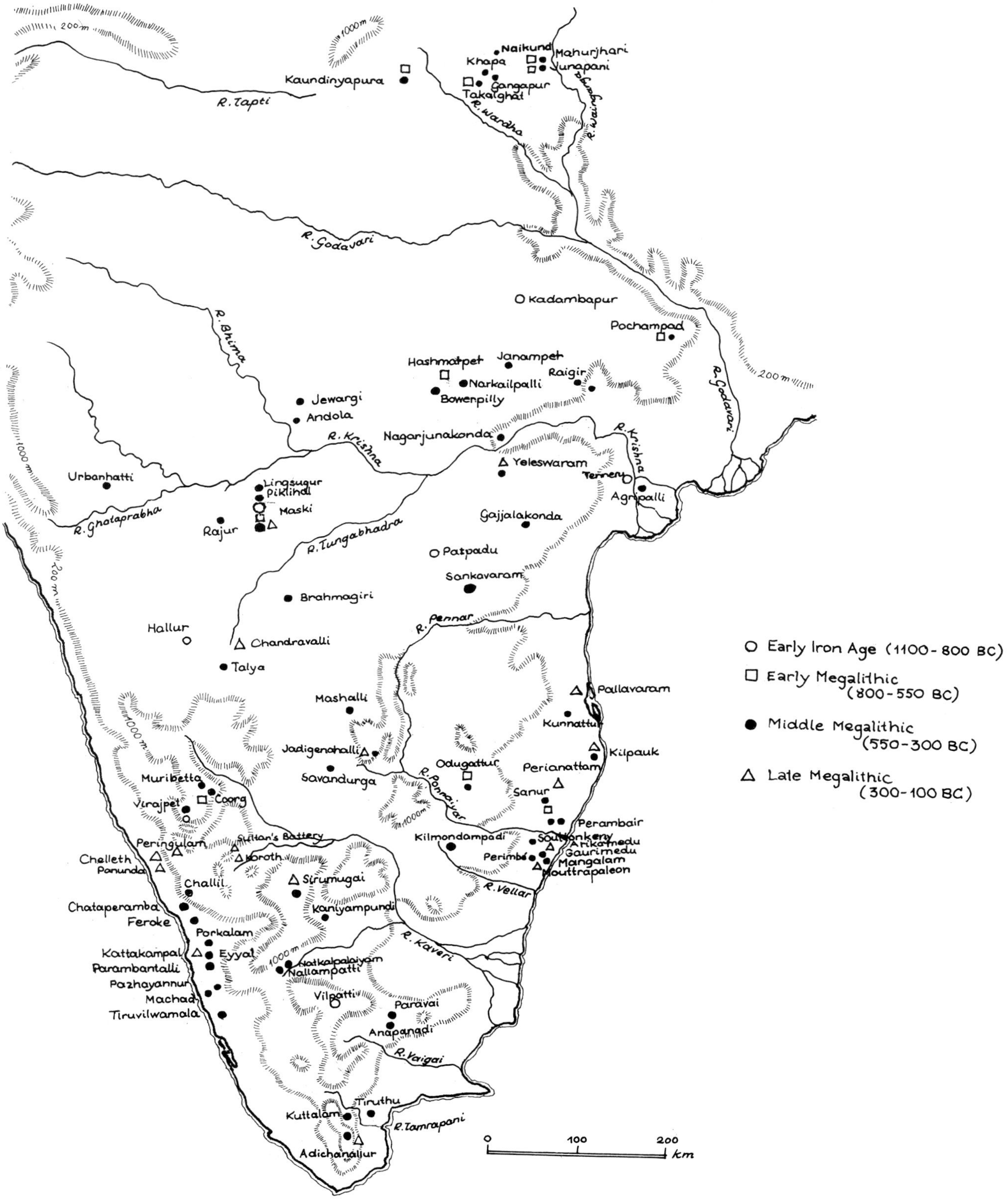

Fig. 9.5. Principal Megalithic sites, like Mahurjhari, in peninsular India. Redrawn from McIntosh 1985 (MS).

the northwest. This impression is supported by the absence of any metal. About 2100–1700 BC, permanent settlements with circular huts of wattle and daub on wooden frames were built on the tops and slopes of granite hills. Some changes in the pottery and a few copper implements suggest the beginning of contact with the north.

It is the subsequent Chalcolithic phase, *c.*1700–1050 BC, falling between the Neolithic and Megalithic cultures, that offers a third and so far overlooked possibility of explaining the coming of the Dravidian languages to South India. This fully agricultural period was introduced by an invasion into Karnataka from the northern Deccan. The copper tools and weapons are similar to those of Malwa and Maharashtra. The antennae swords found at Kallur resemble those of the Gangetic copper hoards and the sword from the clandestine excavations of Bactria (fig. 8.23), which probably is the ultimate source. The wheel-thrown pottery is related to the Jorwe Ware of Maharashtra. A bone of the horse (*Equus caballus*) found at Hallur belongs to the beginning of this period. At the same time, there is remarkable continuity with the earlier periods, whose settlements and material culture, including stone axes as the commonest tools, continue without a break.

The more northerly zone of peninsular India that they came from, including Maharashtra, Malwa, Rajasthan and Gujarat, seems to have been controlled from about 1900 BC by a warring élite, apparently of the same ultimately Bactrian parentage as the seal owners of the Jhukar culture in Sind (fig. 1.17). In spite of the new elements, the Mature Harappan culture continued considerably longer in Gujarat than in the Indus Valley, and the last known examples of the Indus script come from Daimabad in Maharashtra, dated to *c.*1700 BC (§ 4.1). This suggests that the Harappan language survived for a long time in Gujarat and Maharashtra, and that the incoming, originally Aryan-speaking élite adopted the local Dravidian speech, just as the Aryan rulers of Mitanni adopted the local Hurrian language (§ 8.4). Even today, Gujarati and especially Marathi have a high percentage of Dravidian loan-words.

The oldest Tamil poems of the *puṟam* category are heroic war lyrics, and derive their spirit from a military society dedicated to war and raids. Moreover, it has been shown that, while the poetic conventions of the Old Tamil bards were quite different from those of the Sanskrit poetry of North India, they are fairly closely paralleled by the earliest popular poems in Mahārāṣṭrī, Hāla's Sattasaī, and that Kālidāsa, who lived in Malwa, was also influenced by this South Indian poetic tradition. The immediate context of the Old Tamil heroic poetry dating from the centuries around the beginning of the Christian era naturally seems to be the Megalithic culture, but its affinity with Sattasaī rather suggests a Proto-South Dravidian origin for this bardic tradition in the second millennium Chalcolithic culture.

We have seen that Brahui, Kurukh and Malto make a separate North Dravidian branch (§ 9.1). If the hypothesis sketched above concerning the formation of South Dravidian is accepted, the origins of the remaining Central and Central-South Dravidian branches (to be discussed in § 9.6) may be sought in the early Chalcolithic cultures of Malwa and the Choṭā-Nāgpur plateau, as these appear to be related to the Chalcolithic cultures of the Deccan.

9.6 Dravidian and decipherment of the Indus script

In the second part of this book I came to the conclusion that the Indus script was probably of the logo-syllabic type (§ 5.4); the conclusion of this third part is that the Harappan language is most likely to have belonged to the Dravidian family. Once these two conclusions are accepted as working hypotheses, we must also agree upon how Dravidian linguistic material may be used in the decipherment of the Indus script.

Whether the Indus signs were used iconically, as ideograms, or phonetically, by taking advantage of the rebus principle, the signs may be expected to stand primarily for Dravidian root syllables, which all seem to have been monosyllabic originally. In Dravidian languages, the bare root often has both a verbal meaning and a nominal meaning. Furthermore, in Proto-Dravidian (as in modern Tamil, for example) the bare stem could stand for inflected forms, and, as the meaning could be understood from the context, endings could be dropped. It may therefore not have been necessary to mark the case endings in the Indus script. In fact, they are mostly left out in the archaic Sumerian script (§ 2.2). Hence we are mainly operating with roots only. Fortunately this procedure is methodologically justified, for the reconstruction of non-root morphemes is much more difficult and uncertain in the present state of Dravidology.

About 25 Dravidian languages are known today (fig. 8.8). Several other languages once spoken in North India have died out, but the Proto-Dravidian mother tongue of all these languages can be reconstructed by the comparative method to a large extent and with a fair degree of certainty. On the one hand, the divergences between the different Dravidian languages are not too great, and on the other hand, the parent language branched off into three or four major subgroups so early that the reconstructed form reaches back to a very early time. There is little disagreement about the North Dravidian and South Dravidian groups now (excepting the position of Tulu), but whether what was until recently called Central Dravidian consists of the Kolami-Parji group alone or includes (as was earlier thought) the Telugu-Kuwi group too, and whether the Telugu-Kuwi is an independent branch or an

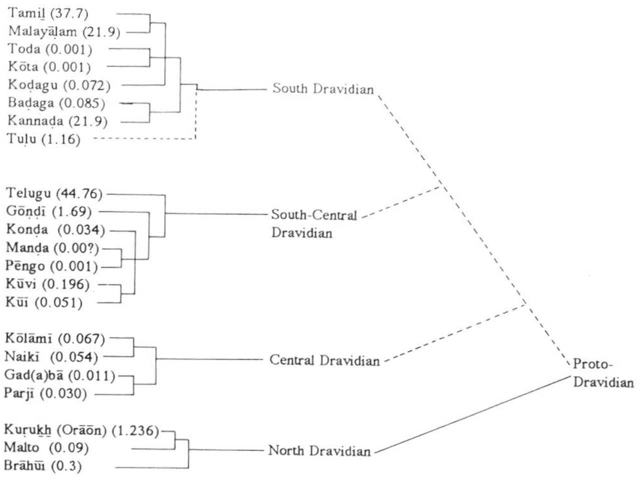

Fig. 9.6. Provisional family tree of the principal Dravidian languages, with the number of their speakers (in millions) in 1971. Based on Zvelebil 1990: xiv, 55–8.

early offshoot of South Dravidian is still being debated. These uncertainties are expressed by broken lines in the family tree in figure 9.6.

Effective comparative study of the long-neglected Dravidian languages became possible only a few decades ago with the publication of a good etymological dictionary by Thomas Burrow and Murray B. Emeneau in 1961, augmented and revised in 1968 and 1984.

In principle, only words and forms reconstructable for Proto-Dravidian are acceptable for the decipherment of the Indus script, and in their reconstruction one must follow strictly the rules established by comparative linguistics. Ideally, an etymon should be attested in at least two major branches. Etyma that appear only in a few languages within one sub-branch are suspect. In the case of two contiguous branches, the possibility of borrowing is always at hand, especially between Tamil-Kannada and Telugu.

An important methodological question is how much variation may be allowed between homophones. Most languages have a fairly large number of words that are pronounced identically, although they have a widely different meaning, and often also a different origin. But no language, not even Dravidian languages, which are usually rich in homophones, possesses them in such quantities that it would be possible to compile an effectively functioning logo-syllabic script in which all rebus puns are based on perfect homophones, especially as these homophones should moreover express concrete objects or actions that can be easily identified in the written signs.

In examining other early scripts, we noted that the limitations of homophony were overcome in various ways. The Egyptian and Semitic scripts, for example, ignored differences in vocalization (§ 2.3). But the method requires great rigour: rebus equations are the more convincing the closer the homophones are to each other. We cannot be as liberal as the ancient priestly 'etymologists' in the Vedic Brāhmaṇa texts, who, for example, equated the Sanskrit word *ulūkhala-* with *urukara-* (ŚB 7,4,1,13). Only alternations actually attested within single Dravidian etyma, which can be presumed to have prevailed in the Proto-Dravidian also, may in principle be allowed between the posited homophones. It is necessary to allow for variation between short and long vowels and between short and long consonants, but these modest liberties are in line with the morphophonemic rules governing the Proto-Dravidian roots.

Part IV

Interpretations of Indus pictograms

10 The 'fish' signs of the Indus script

10.1 Fish = star: astral divinities

An early form of Dravidian has emerged from this examination of the evidence as the language most probably spoken by the Indus people. Assuming that this was indeed the case, we may now turn to the 'fish' signs, which we found to be a good starting-point for testing our basic methodology for deciphering the script (p. 121). As in other early logo-syllabic scripts, a sign may be expected to express (1) a pictorial meaning (here: 'fish') and (2) a phonetic meaning based on rebus (here: any homophone of the word for 'fish' in the language of the Indus script). The 'fish' signs fulfil one basic requirement of decipherment by being pictorially recognizable. But the iconic meaning, which is directly comprehensible, is not so helpful in the identification of the Indus language. From the point of view of decipherment, the 'fish' signs seem to have this advantage over other iconically transparent signs that most of their occurrences are likely to have a rebus meaning, and a meaning that can perhaps be approximately determined from the context.

The pictorial interpretation of the basic sign  as 'fish' has been called into question. For example, it has been suggested that what look like the fins of a fish are just diacritic modifications of the basic sign , which depicts a loop or twist. It is true that a sign  occurs on three potsherds coming from Harappa and Kalibangan (though these singly occurring graffiti are not necessarily script: they may well be just potter's marks), and that there is an Egyptian hieroglyph 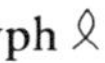 depicting a loop of cord; but if 'loop' was meant, it would be odd to modify it almost everywhere so that it resembles a 'fish' so strongly that the overwhelming majority of people who have commented on this sign in print have considered it to depict 'fish'. The vertical position, which seems unnatural for a fish, can be understood as a means of saving writing space.

In fact, the identification of the sign  as 'fish' can hardly be doubted, for in the iconography of Indus amulets an identically drawn fish is shown in the mouth of the fish-eating

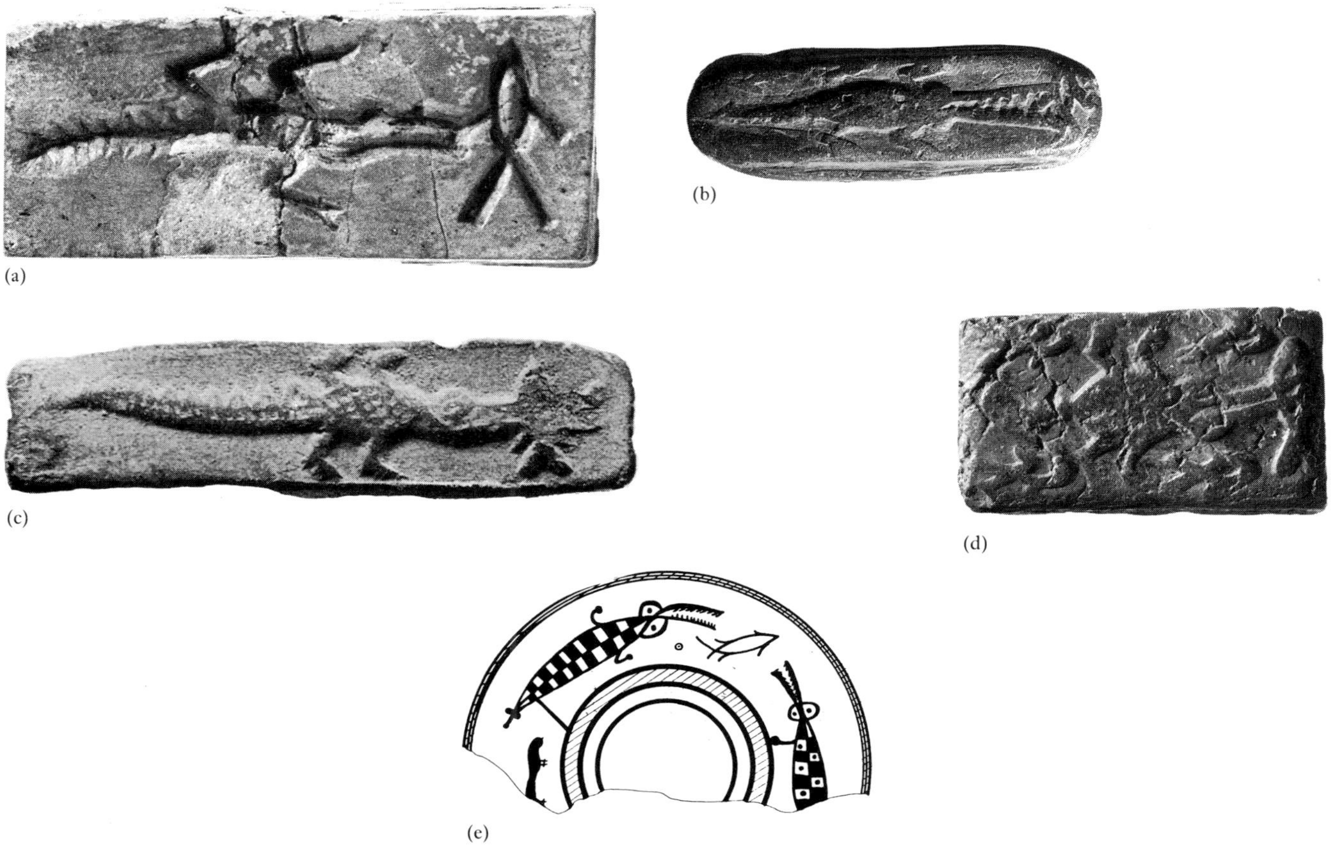

Fig. 10.1. Examples of the fish-eating alligator (gavial) in Harappan art. (a) An Indus seal from Mohenjo-daro (M-410). (b) The reverse side of an amulet from Mohenjo-daro (M-482). (c) One side of a moulded terracotta amulet in the form of a triangular prism from Mohenjo-daro (M-1429). Length 4.6 cm. (For the two other sides, see figs. 1.10 and 12.7.) After Dales 1968: 39. (d) Reverse side of an Indus tablet from Harappa (H-172). (e) A Harappan painted pot from Amri IIIA. After Casal 1964: II, fig. 75: 323.

alligator, called gharial or gavial (fig. 10.1), which in one case is surrounded by four more fish swimming around it (fig. 10.1d). A Harappan painted pot from Amri IIIA (fig. 10.1e) shows the same motif of alligator and fish, but in this case the fish has two pairs of fins (instead of just one pair in the simplified Indus sign) like most of the more naturalistic representations of fish on Early Harappan ceramics (fig. 10.20). In one exceptional seal from Mohenjo-daro, a very naturalistically depicted fish with eye and scales is placed horizontally above a two-headed animal, a bison-and-'unicorn' (fig. 10.2); it is paralleled by two Indus-style cylinder seals from the Near East, one from Tell as-Sulema, showing a bird over a 'unicorn' and a fish (horizontally) over a bison (fig. 10.3), the other from Ur, with a fish (horizontally) over and (vertically) in front of a 'unicorn' bull (fig. 10.4).

There are, as we shall see (§§ 10.2–3), some contexts where the plain 'fish' sign was most probably used in its primary pictorial meaning. However, the 'fish' signs are far too numerous to denote 'fish' whenever they occur: roughly every tenth sign occurring in the Indus inscriptions is a 'fish' sign. Seal texts in particular are unlikely to discuss fish very often. Mesopotamian parallels rather suggest that the Indus seals mainly contain proper names and official (priestly) titles. The 'fish' signs may therefore well stand for the names of divinities, which are basic elements of proper names both in the ancient Near East and in classical India (§ 7.5). The task now is to see whether the two assumed meanings, 'fish' and 'god', can be linked through a homophony in the historically and typologically most likely language, Proto-Dravidian.

In most Dravidian languages the usual word for 'fish' is *mīn* (table 10.1). This phonetic shape can be reconstructed also for the mother language, Proto-Dravidian. (Sanskrit *mīna* 'fish', which has no convincing Indo-European etymology, is clearly a loanword from Dravidian, for it is not attested in the oldest Indo-Aryan texts, i.e. in the Veda, but is known only from the epics and Manu onwards, and it has no cognate in Iranian; nor

Fig. 10.2. A naturalistically depicted fish placed above the Harappan iconographic motif of joined animals. Impression of a seal (M-298) from Mohenjo-daro.

Fig. 10.3. A bird over a 'unicorn' bull and a fish over a bison. Impression of an Indus-style cylinder seal (IM 87798) from Tell as-Sulema (2: 662 / 236) in Mesopotamia, level IV (Akkadian to Early Old Babylonian). Gypsum. Length 2.6 cm, diameter 1.6 cm. Drawing by Lamia Al-Gailani Werr. Cf. Collon 1987: 143, no. 609.

Fig. 10.4. A fish in front of and above a 'unicorn' bull. Impression of an Indus-style cylinder seal (IM 8028) from Ur in Mesopotamia. White shell. Height 1.7 cm, diameter 0.9 cm. Cf. Mitchell 1986: 280–1, no. 8 and fig. 112.

is the word found in any Neo-Indo-Aryan language with the exception of Sinhalese.) A homophone *mīn* denoting 'star' likewise occurs in many Dravidian languages and can be reconstructed for Proto-Dravidian (table 10.1). The relationship obtaining between Proto-Dravidian **min* 'to glitter, shine' and Proto-Dravidian **mīn* 'star' illustrates a common Dravidian grammatical process which uses alternation of vowel quantity to derive root nouns from root verbs and vice versa. Another example of this process that can also be reconstructed for Proto-Dravidian is **kaṇ* 'eye': **kāṇ* 'to see'. It does not seem impossible that even 'fish' as a glittering thing could have its ultimate etymology in the root **min* 'to glitter, to sparkle' (but this hypothesis is in no way necessary for our argument):

> Who that has seen the phosphorescence flashing from every movement of the fish in tropical seas or lagoons at night, can doubt the appropriateness of denoting the fish that dart and sparkle through the waters, as well as the stars that sparkle in the midnight sky, by one and the same word – viz., a word signifying that which glows or sparkles? (Caldwell 1913: 573f.)

The conception of stars as fish swimming in the waters of the night sky is attested in the Old Tamil text Paripāṭal (16,36–8), where the river Vaiyai is compared to the heavenly Ganges with its *mīṉ*. The Ganges, the holiest river of India, is so sacred because it is believed to have descended from heaven: the Sanskrit name of the ecliptic, the course which the planets travel through the sky, is *ākāśa-gaṅgā* 'heavenly Ganges'. While explaining the background of the R̥gvedic hymn 8,67, the Br̥haddevatā (6,88–90) speaks of fishes rising to the sky:

> Fishermen, having by chance seen fish in the water of the Sarasvatī, cast a net, caught them, and threw them upon the dry land out of water. And they [the fishes], frightened by the fall of their bodies, praised the sons of Aditi. And they (the Ādityas) then released them, and graciously conversed with them (the fishermen [and the fish]), (saying) 'O fishermen, be not afraid of hunger', and 'Ye shall obtain heaven.' (trans. Macdonell 1904: II, 233; that the latter phrase is addressed to the fish is suggested by the close parallel of JB 3,193–4. According to MBh 13,51,39f., 'the Niṣādas went to heaven with the fishes'.)

In Pañcatantra (Tantrākhyāyika I, verse 95), on the other hand, a goose dives for the reflection of a star in the night, thinking it a fish (and in disappointment abandons fishing efforts even in daytime).

The art of the Indus Civilization reflects its ideological concepts. It seems significant that painted Mature Harappan potsherds from Amri IIIA and C combine the motifs of 'fish' and 'star' (fig. 10.5). These potsherds suggest that the Indus people associated the two concepts and thereby support the hypothesis that the Harappans spoke a Dravidian language, where one and the same word is used for both of these things.

Table 10.1. Representation of the etyma **mīn* 'fish' and **mīn / *vīṇ / *vīṇt-V-kk-* 'star', **min / *vin / *miṇ / *viṇ* 'to glitter, shine, flash' in Dravidian languages (for the sigilla of Gondi and Kuwi dialects and sources, see *DEDR*: xxviii–xxx). As the words for 'star' and 'firefly' are the same in the Maṛia dialect of Gondi, the word for 'firefly' is given in parentheses in the absence of 'star'. As Dravidian loanwords, Indo-Aryan has Sanskrit *mīna* 'fish' (the oldest attestations are post-Vedic, in Manu and the epics), Prakrit *mīṇa* 'fish' and Sinhalese *min* 'fish'; and possibly the only lexically attested Sanskrit *miñj-* 'to shine'.

Language	'fish' (pl.)	'star' ('firefly')	'to glitter, shine, flash (of lighting)'
Tamiḻ	mīṉ	mīṉ	miṉ, miṉṉu, miṉuṅku
Malayāḷam	mīn	mīn	minnuka
Kota	mīn	mīn	minc- (past tense: minc-)
Toda	mīn	mīn	mic- (mič-)
Kannaḍa	mīn	mīn	minuku, mirnugu, miṇaku, miṇuku, miñcu
Koḍagu	mīnï		minn- (minni-)
Tuḷu	mīnu̥	(meṇkoḷi, menkōri)	miṇ(u)kuni, meṇ(u̥)kuni, minukuni, meñcuni, miñcuni
Telugu	mīnu	(miṇũgu, miḍũgu)	miṇuku, min(u)ku, miñcu
Parji	mīni (mīnul)		(minnal 'spark')
Gadba	mīn (mīnil)	(munake)	
Gondi (A.)	mīn (mīnk)		miṛc-
Gondi (ASu.)			miṛc-
Gondi (SR.)			miḍcānā
Gondi (Tr.)	mīn (mīnk)	mīnkō	miḍstānā
Gondi (Ch. D.)	mīn (mīnk)		
Gondi (W.)	mīn (mīnk)	(minko)	miṛsānā
Gondi (Ph.)	mīn	(minko)	miṛsīlnā, mirsīltānā
Gondi (Mu.)	mīn (mīnk)	miṛkom	
Gondi (Ma.)	mīn (mīnk)	minˀkonj(i) (pl. minˀkosku)	miṛs-
Gondi (L.)		miḍkos	mīḍsā, mīrcā
Gondi (M.)		miṛko	miṛkānā
Gondi (S.)	mīn (mīnku)		
Gondi (Ko.)		(miṛko)	
Gondi (KoB.)		miṛko	
Gondi (LuS.)			meershinta
Konḍa	mīn (mīnga)		mirs-
Pengo	min (minku)		
Manḍa	min (minke)		
Kui	mīnu (mīnga)		
Kuwi (F.)	mīnu (mrīka)		
Kuwi (S.)	mīnu (mīnka)		mrih'nai
Kuwi (Su.)	mīnu (mṇīka)		miṇs-, mṇih- (mṇist-)
Kuwi (P.)	mīnu (mṇīka)		
Kuwi (Mah.)			miṇig-
Kuwi (Isr.)	m(ṇ)īnu (mṇīka)		mṇīh- (mṇīst-)
Kuṛuk͟h		bīnkō	
Malto	mīnu	bīnḍke	

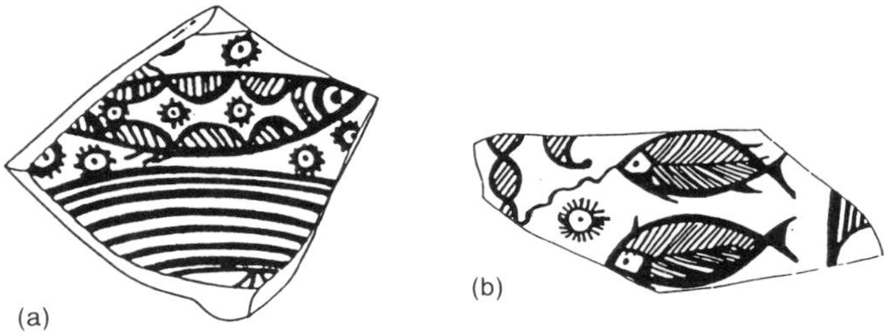

Fig. 10.5. 'Fish' and 'star' motifs combined on Mature Harappan pottery from Amri: (a) period IIIA, (b) period IIIC. After Casal 1964: II, fig. 92: no. 487 (=a) and fig. 78: no. 343 (=b).

Fig. 10.6. A monochrome goblet painted with three 'star' symbols, discovered among 143 in a storage room (locus 118) at Mehrgarh, period VII, *c.*3000–2600 BC. After Santoni 1989: 183, fig. 8: 21; cf. ibid. 181–5.

Fig. 10.7. A water carrier with a star on either side of the head. Impression of an Indus-inspired round Dilmun seal from Ur (U.16747). After Porada 1971: pl. 9, fig. 5.

One side edge of seal L-66 from Lothal bears the single sign of 'plain fish', ⚲, while another edge has the single sign ⚹. This latter sign is attested just this one time and, apart from it, the Indus inscriptions proper do not contain a pictogram of 'star' comparable to archaic Sumerian ✳ *an* 'sky', and ⁎⁎⁎ *mul* 'constellation'. Yet the Early and Mature Harappan pot-marks and painted motifs include symbols that can be interpreted as denoting 'stars' (fig. 10.6). This suggests that the meaning 'star' was expressed punningly in the Indus script, through the rebus principle, just as in Egyptian ★ *sb3* 'star' was also used to write the words *sb3* 'door' and *sb* 'to teach'.

But the assumed phonetic meaning of the 'fish' sign in the Indus seals was 'god', not 'star'. However, the 'fish' signs can be interpreted as denoting gods, if stars were used as symbols of deities. This would indeed seem quite possible. In India, the worship of planetary deities has been popular for the past two millennia at least, and each of the planets has one of the principal gods of Hinduism as its overlord. We shall soon consider more closely the textual evidence which suggests that this cult and some important astral myths go back to the Indus Civilization (chapter 11).

On the other hand, the Harappans were in contact with the Mesopotamians, who early on associated their divinities with specific heavenly bodies. For example, Inanna-Ishtar, the goddess of love and war, was symbolized by the planet Venus. In the cuneiform script, the sign ✳ depicting a star has the meaning *dingir* 'god', and this sign is usually prefixed to every god's name as a determinative of divinity (§ 2.2 and fig. 2.3).

In the ancient Near East, the 'star' sign marked divinities in art, too. The following examples all concern deities who seem to be related to the Harappan 'Proto-Śiva' (§ 14.2). Thus in the Early Dynastic serpentine bowl from Khafajeh, a rosette-shaped star is placed beside the head of both of the anthropomorphic deities depicted (fig. 14.13b–c). These stars resemble the rosette-flowers which are set, in early Iranian and Sumerian fashion, into the loops of the huge horns worn by a buffalo-deity on a pot from Kot Diji (fig. 14.19a), an Early Harappan predecessor of the Indus 'Proto-Śiva' (fig. 10.18). Intermediate parallels have been found between the Indus Valley and Mesopotamia. The sitting 'deity' on the seal on a potsherd from Tepe Yahya IVA in southeastern Iran (fig. 14.17) has a circle beside its head; there was probably another such circle on the other side, which has broken off. The Harappan-inspired water carrier depicted on a Gulf seal from Ur likewise has a star on either side of his head (fig. 10.7). Edith Porada has compared this water carrier with an approximately eighteenth-century BC Syrian cylinder seal, which represents a man with streams of water flowing from his shoulders in the fashion of the Sumerian water-god Enki (fig. 10.8). According to Porada, the two stars beside his head distinguish the man from mortals or lesser supernatural beings.

A most important parallel to these and other similar

Fig. 10.8. A naked anthropomorphic figure with streams of water flowing from his shoulders and a star on either side of his head. Note the fish beside the stream. Impression of a Syrian-style cylinder seal in the Pierpont Morgan Library, New York City, dated to *c.* eighteenth century BC. Cf. Porada 1971.

examples is provided by a native Harappan seal from Mohenjo-daro. The buffalo-horned god sitting in the 'yogic' posture has a star on either side of his head, in the loops of the horns (fig. 10.9). In other examples, such stars surround the buffalo in its animal form but with the addition of a peculiar head-dress (Mackay 1938: II, pl. 103.8), a mythical composite animal (fig. 7.14: A2); and a fig tree around a deity (fig. 14.5). It would thus appear, independently of the suggested readings of the 'fish' pictograms, that the Indus gods, like the Near Eastern deities, had an astral aspect.

10.2 Fish as an emblem of 'Proto-Śiva', Enki, Varuṇa and Kāma

If stars functioned as emblems of divinity for the Indus people, as was suggested in section 10.1, why did the Harappans not express the meaning 'star' directly with a 'star' pictogram in their script, as the ancient Egyptians did? Why did they resort to the more complicated rebus principle and use a 'fish' pictogram? One answer is that, though this method may appear more complicated to us, it probably did not appear so to the Indus scribes, in whose language the same word denoted both 'fish' and 'star'. But there is also another answer to this question.

In the Sumerian script, the 'star' pictogram means not only *dingir* 'god' but also *an* 'sky'. It has been assumed that the 'star' pictogram originally was the exclusive symbol and attribute of the sky-god An. And because An was the leading divinity of the Sumerian pantheon, his symbol came to mean also 'godhead', and then 'god' in general. The reason why the Harappan scribes selected 'fish' and not 'star' to represent the concept of 'god' may have been somewhat parallel. Fish, the aquatic animal *par excellence*, is one of the most popular motifs of the Early Harappan painted pottery (fig. 10.20). It seems that in the (Early) Harappan religion, the god of waters and fertility, having the fish as his emblem and symbol, occupied a central position. We shall be discussing in some detail the relationship between the fish and the 'Proto-Śiva', whose importance in the Harappan pantheon is indicated by his popularity in the Indus iconography. Attention will be paid to both Mesopotamian and later Indian parallels, which can shed light on the nature of this deity and his symbols.

In a cylinder seal that comes from the Near East but is engraved in Indus style (fig. 10.10), a buffalo-horned anthropomorphic deity sitting on a throne is flanked on either side by what looks exactly like the plain 'fish' sign of the Indus script. In this case, however, the 'fish' do not seem to represent writing, but 'a pair of fish' which are emblems of the deity, who is surrounded also by a pair of horned snakes and a pair of water buffaloes. If this seal of foreign provenance were the only one to contain such a motif, its validity for the Indus religion and script could be called in question. But in a moulded triangular terracotta prism from Mohenjo-daro the same deity, squatting in the same 'yogic' posture as the famous 'Proto-Śiva', is flanked on either side by a fish, an alligator and a snake (fig. 10.11).

As the preserved coins and other evidence show, the 'fish' emblem of the Tamil kings of the Pāṇḍya dynasty usually consisted of two carp. In Tamil, this pair of carp is called *iṇai-kayal* or *puṇar-mīṉ*. Both *iṇai* and *puṇar* mean 'pair, couple' as well as 'copulation, sexual intercourse', just like Sanskrit *mithuna*, which occurs in the corresponding Sanskrit term for the symbol of 'a pair of fishes', *mīna-mithuna* (= *matsya-yuga*). This is one of the ancient Indian 'auspicious symbols', shared by the Hindus, Buddhists and Jains, and considered to represent fertility (fig. 10.12). Thus the Digambara Jainas have 'a pair of fish playing in a lake' as the sixteenth and last of the dreams seen by Triśalā when she conceived Mahāvīra, indicating that her son was destined to become a worldly or spiritual emperor. Fish still figure prominently in the Indian marriage ceremony (see also § 14.4). The following is reported from Orissa:

> The fish is a symbol of auspiciousness. People also say that the fish means that the woman is not a widow since widows cannot eat fish. When the bride first goes to her husband's house after the marriage, a fish goes ahead of her. At wedding ceremonies, the painters (*citrakāra*) are called to draw auspicious paintings around the entrance door. The most common motifs are young women holding plantain trees, fishes and *pūrṇa kumbha*, a brass pot full of water covered with mango leaves and topped by a coconut . . . The fish is the 'fruit' of the water. (Marglin 1985: 56)

The 'fish pair' symbol can be traced back even to what appear to be pre-Vedic elements of Indian origin in the Vedic ritual. The obscene dialogue, which accompanies the simulated sexual union of the dead victim and the chief queen in the Vedic horse sacrifice, compares a pair of *śakula* fish to the labia of the female organ (AS 20,136,1; VS 23,28; etc.).

Fig. 10.9. Indus signs (including 'fish' signs) and a deity sitting in a 'yogic' posture on a fragmentary seal from Mohenjo-daro (M-305). There is a star in both loops of the buffalo's horns worn by the deity in the head-dress, which also bears a fig branch.

Fig. 10.10. Impression of an Indus-style cylinder seal of unknown Near Eastern origin. Musée du Louvre / *AO* (Collection De Clercq 1.26). One of the two anthropomorphic figures carved on this seal wears a crown of water buffalo horns with the leafed branch of a fig and sits on a throne with hoofed legs, surrounded by a pair of horned snakes, a pair of fishes and a pair of water buffaloes. The other figure stands, fighting two tigers, and surrounded by trees, a markhor goat and a vulture above a rhinoceros.

Fig. 10.11. One side of a triangular terracotta amulet (MD 013) found from the surface at Mohenjo-daro in 1936, showing a horned deity sitting in 'yogic' posture on a throne with hoofed legs, surrounded by fishes, gavials and snakes. Department of Eastern Art, Ashmolean Museum, Oxford.

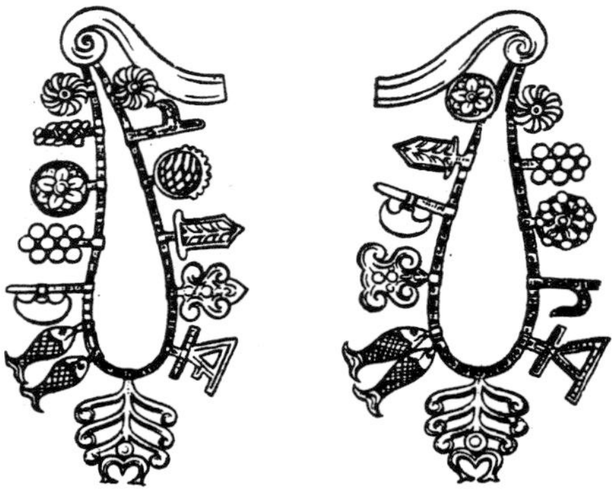

(a) (b)

Fig. 10.12. The symbol of 'two fish' among Buddhist auspicious signs (*maṅgalaka*) in necklaces depicted on a pillar of a gateway (*toraṇa*) at the stupa of Sāñcī, Central India, first century BC. After V. S. Agrawala 1969: fig. 62.

The symbol of 'a pair of fishes' is to be found in the ancient Near East as well (fig. 10.13). In the glyptic art of Mesopotamia, fish are brought for the ceremonial repast by a nude attendant or two 'carrying a big vessel in one hand, while from his other hand two fishes hang from a cord threaded through their gills... Amulets in the shape of two fishes strung together were found at Uruk in the E-anna precinct, in Temple VI at Khafajah and elsewhere' (Buren 1948: 106). In a cylinder seal of the Early Dynastic III period, portraying an enthroned divine couple, 'two fishes are placed tail to tail so that they point in opposite directions, for the footstool beneath the god's feet' (ibid.: 108).

On very early Iranian seals from Susa B, a water-god holding in his hands streams of water is flanked on either side by a fish (fig. 10.14); in Proto-Elamite glyptics, fish are depicted as swimming in a stream (fig. 10.15). In comparable fashion, the Mesopotamian water-god Enki (also called Ea) has fish in or around the rivers flowing out of his shoulders (fig. 10.16). In some representations, the rivers are left out and it is merely the fish that distinguish Enki (fig. 10.17), so that he

Fig. 10.13. A man carries two fishes in either hand. Detail of the middle row in the mosaic 'Peace' panel from Ur. Early Dynastic III period, *c.* twenty-fifth century BC (BM). Cf. Woolley, *Ur excavations* II, pl. 91.

Fig. 10.14. Fish and the water-god in an early Iranian seal from Susa B (Protoliterate period, *c.*3500–3300 BC). After Amiet 1980a: pl. 6, no. 117.

Fig. 10.15. Fish swimming in a river. A Proto-Elamite seal, *c.*3100–2900 BC. After Amiet 1980a: pl. 35, no. 547.

Fig. 10.16. The Mesopotamian water-god Enki (Ea), depicted with fish swimming in the streams of water that issue from his shoulders. Impression of an Akkadian cylinder seal (BM 89115). Greenstone, 3.9 × 2.55 cm. The inscription reads: 'Adda, scribe'.

Fig. 10.17. Five fishes surround the water-god Enki, to whom a captive bird-man is brought and announced by the two-faced attendant Usimu, another god following. An Akkadian cylinder seal (AS. 32: 593) from house IVa (locus K 19: 10) at Tell Asmar. Black stone, 3.4 × 2 cm. After Frankfort 1955: no. 619.

Fig. 10.18. The 'Proto-Śiva' seal from Mohenjo-daro (M-304). The deity wears the horns of the water buffalo and sits in a 'yogic' posture on a drum (?)-legged throne, surrounded by a tiger, an elephant, a rhinoceros and a water buffalo.

comes to correspond very closely to the Harappan deity flanked by a pair of fish (figs. 10.10–11). In one cylinder seal of the Akkadian period, Enki has, in addition, a big fish as his footstool, and this is thought to have developed into the 'goat-fish', which in the Neo-Sumerian period became Enki's distinctive attribute. Enki is the god of the *apsû* 'deep water, sea', the cosmic subterranean water which is the source and outlet of rivers and the place where fish live.

In the famous 'Proto-Śiva' seal itself (fig. 10.18), the god wears the horns of a water buffalo. A water buffalo is also depicted above the god along with a tiger, an elephant and a rhinoceros. All these animals are noted for their ferocity and virility, being prominent symbols of war, death and fertility in South Asian religions. While the fish is absent from the iconographic scene, it figures in the accompanying inscription, where the divinity seems to be represented by the plain 'fish' sign. This text is largely parallel to that of the 'fig deity' seal (§ 14.4), and the last three signs  may be read tentatively as *mīn-ā āḷ* 'the man (or servant) of (the god represented by) *mīn*' (§ 7.5). The 'man'-shaped sign can be read in Dravidian as *āḷ* / *āṇ* 'man, manly person, warrior, husband, servant'; in Tamil this word also means 'devotee (of a deity)'. The sign , which may in this context be the marker of the possessive case (§§ 6.3 and 7.3), is read as the Proto-Dravidian possessive case suffix **-ā* / **-a* (Zvelebil 1977a: 31f.); interpretation of the iconic form of the sign as 'bull's head' (§ 7.2) allows this suffix **-ā* to be expressed through its Proto-Dravidian homophone **ā* 'cow'. In most other seal texts, I am inclined to interpret the 'fish' signs as names of stars on the basis of the Dravidian homophony *mīn* 'fish' = *mīn* 'star'. In this case, however, it seems that we have to give preference to the meaning 'fish'. (And yet the astral meaning is not excluded, either; cf. § 10.4.) The interpretation of the plain 'fish' sign of the 'Proto-Śiva' seal is (along with that of the 'fig deity' seal to be discussed in § 14.4) actually crucial for understanding why the Harappans chose 'fish' rather than 'star' as their pictorial symbol of divinity, even if they mostly used this picture of 'fish' as a rebus for 'star'.

In the early Indian pantheon, the animal manifestations of the Harappan 'Proto-Śiva' as revealed by the seals and amulets mentioned above resemble most of all those associated with the god Varuṇa. In the Brāhmaṇa texts of the Veda, Varuṇa is the only god who received buffaloes in sacrifice (MS 3,14,10; VS 24,28); in later Hinduism (as well as in Lamaist Buddhism), the buffalo is best known as the vehicle of Yama (fig. 14.33), the god of death, a partial doublet of Varuṇa (§ 12.1). Starting with the Ṛgveda, Varuṇa is 'the lord (and husband) of waters' (*apāṁ patiḥ*) and he is identified with the Ocean (MS 4,7,8) and with waters (MS 4,8,5; KS 13,2). In the post-Vedic mythology, Varuṇa becomes almost exclusively the god of waters, who possesses the rivers and has his abode in the ocean. He is often called 'the lord of aquatic creatures' (*yādasāṁ pati* or *ambhasāṁ pati*) in the Mahābhārata; as sea monsters that are 'Varuṇa's creatures', the epic (13,86,25) lists *timi*, *timiṅgila*, *makara*, *jhaṣa*, *kūrma* and *grāha*. The Vedic texts associate such creatures not only with Varuṇa but also with other deities related to him. Thus according to VSM 24,21 and MS3, 14,2 crocodiles (*śiśumāra*) are sacrificed to the Ocean, fishes (*matsya*) to the Water, and crocodiles (*nākra*) to Varuṇa. TS 5,5,13, MS 3,14,16 and VS 24,35 assign the *jhaṣa*, the crocodile (*nākra*) and the *makara* to Apāṁ Naptṛ 'the son of waters'.

The word *mīṉ* 'fish' is used in Tamil also in the meaning of *mīṉ ēṟu*, literally 'fish-male' or 'fish-bull', i.e. 'a sea monster' or 'shark' (*cuṟā mīṉ*). This may be what is meant when it is said that the water-god Varuṇa has the *mīṉ* for his mount (Tamil *mīṉ-ūrti*), because Varuṇa is also said to ride a *makara*, and 'shark' is the meaning recorded for the Prakrit and Sinhalese cognates of *makara* 'aquatic monster'. Portuguese *marraxo*, derived from Sanskrit **makaraśa*, is likewise used of a 'shark' of the man-eating variety. According to the Bhagavad-gītā (10,31), *makara* is the foremost among the *jhaṣas*. In the Indian flood myth, the 'large fish' or *jhaṣa* had a horn (*śṛṅga*), to which Manu tied his ark. The exact meaning of the term *jhaṣa* in the Vedic texts remains unclear, but in the

Vādhūlasūtra (4,19a), the *rohita* fish and the *caṣa* (=*jhaṣa*) fish form a pair of a 'domestic' and a 'wild' animal related to each other, like the pair of the domestic goat (*aja*) and the wild markhor goat (*śarabha*). In Old Tamil literature, *kōṭṭu mīṉ* 'horn-fish' is the name of the shark, which is worshipped as sacred to Varuṇa, the god of the ocean.

Varuṇa is not the only god in Indian religions to be associated with the fish and other aquatic creatures. However, in most cases there seems to be a historical connection between these deities, in the sense that one and the same god may appear with different names in different traditions. Thus we have seen that the Vedic god Varuṇa appears to continue the earlier (Indus-influenced) traditions of Bactria associated with the Dāsa god Śambara (§ 8.4). In the non-Vedic religion of the Tantras, Śambara is a terrifying and erotic manifestation of Śiva in the form of a buffalo. In the Śākta tradition, again, Śambara has a counterpart in Mahiṣa Asura, the Buffalo demon, who is the antagonist / lover-husband of the goddess Durgā (§ 14.2). According to the Rāmāyaṇa (2,8,12 Gorr.; 2,44,11 Schl.), Śambara has a great fish in his flag (*timi-dhvaja*). In AS 11,2,24–5, the crocodiles (*śiṁśumāra*), *jhaṣas* and fishes (*matsya*) are said to be sacred to Rudra, the Vedic predecessor of the Hindu gods Śiva and Skanda. In the Skanda-Purāṇa (Māheśvara Khaṇḍa 17), Śiva is called 'Fish' (*mīna*) or 'the Lord of the Fish'. Indeed,

> the connection of fish with Śiva is well-known. Both the Śaiva, the Krama and Kaula schools considered Matsyendra, Macchendra 'the lord of the fish' as one of the transmitters of the revelation of the secret doctrine. How Matsyendra came to hear that revelation, while he was in the belly of a gigantic fish, is narrated in the Skandapurāṇa, Nāgarakhaṇḍa chapter 263 (Baṅgabaśī edn). Here Śiva is said to have descended on the top of a mountain in the Śvetadīpa and then to have taught Pārvatī the Jñānayoga. Then continuing on their journey they saw in the ocean a big fish and Śiva requested it to say who it was. The fish or rather the man inside the fish (Matsyodara) related how he had overheard the talk between the god and the goddess, and how he had then acquired Jñānayoga.
>
> The Krama school, which is said to have prospered in the Uḍḍiyānapīṭha, that is Swat, is considered to have been revealed in the four yuga ... by four nāthas. These being the revealers cannot be but forms of Śiva, the last being Matsyendra, Macchinda: they all have names of animals... Macchinda (Kaliyuga) the revealer in the shape of a fish (Mahānayaprakāśa p. 46, v. 12)... Thus the terms Śiva, water, fish occur together. If Matsyendranātha became later an initiatic name and matsya was taken to mean 'senses' in the paribhāṣā, the technical terms, used in the esoteric schools, this usage came no doubt at a later date. (Tucci 1963: 170f.)

Fish is also associated with Kāma, the god of love, who likewise has a connection with Varuṇa. Thus in the Viṣṇudharmottara-Purāṇa (3,52), Pradyumna as the reborn god of love Kāma is equated with Varuṇa. Like Varuṇa, Kāma is represented as riding the fish (being therefore called *mīṉ-ūrti* in Tamil). *Makara*, another mount of Varuṇa in addition to the fish, was also the ensign of Pradyumna (Harivaṁśa 10639, 10882; Mahābhārata 3,18,11) as well as of Kāma, the god of love (Mahābhārata 3,281,27; 13,11,3). The shrine at Besnagar dedicated to Pradyumna was marked by a *makara-dhvaja* as early as the second century BC. Another aquatic animal in Kāma's flag is the *jhaṣa*, again one of Varuṇa's animals.

The association of the fish with the god of love and sexuality is natural, for the fish, which increase rapidly and have a phallic appearance, represent the power of reproduction:

> Fish are also revered in connexion with cults or as types of fertility. At Tungnāth by the lower Himalaya in the Sarasvatī pool there is a linga in the centre, and a large fish appears on the 14th day of the dark fortnight of every month, oblations to it ensuring that every wish will be accomplished ... another fish cures impotency; the patient strips off his clothes ... rubs vermilion on its [the fish's] head and says: 'O fish! I am changing my state for yours.' (Crooke, 1926: 378)

Fish-broth (*matsya-yūṣa* or *matsya-sūpa*) is among the foremost aphrodisiacs both in Kṣemendra's handbook for courtesans (Samayamātṛkā 2,25; 71; etc.) and in Kalhaṇa's Rājataraṅginī 7,522: 'Though he disported himself daily with many women, his strength did not fail him, on account of [the use of] fish-broth and other aphrodisiacs' (trans. Stein 1900: 310). In the Buddhist tradition, food prepared from *rohita* fish is a royal dish craved by the queen (Jātaka 292); after eating such a dish, the queen is supposed to conceive a son, who will become a universal monarch (cf. the parallel story of Jātaka 281). The *śakula* and *rohita* fish are eaten as aphrodisiacs in the orgiastic cult of the Goddess (§ 14.4). As we have seen, fish figure prominently in the Indian marriage ceremony as well.

The Mesopotamian water-god Enki – distinguished by the fish emblem – is the principal 'god of creation (^{d}*nu-dím-mud* = *ša nab-ni-ti*)'. The myth of 'Enki and Ninḫursag' recounts Enki's sexual exploits, and here water fecundating the soil is equated with male semen (in Sumerian, one word stands for both):

> The one who was alone, the cunning one, in front of
> Nintu, mother of the land,
> Enki, the cunning one, in front of Nintu, mother of the
> land,
> has his phallus fill the ditches full with semen,
> has his phallus glut the reeds with an overflow of sperm,
> has his phallus tear away the noble cloth that covers the
> lap.
> (Enki and Ninḫursag, lines 65–9, trans. Kramer and Maier 1989: 24)

Discussing Enki as 'the power to fecundate', Jacobsen (1976: 111) notes that 'another connection between productivity and water is the "birth water" which precedes and announces birth'.

The character of the Sumerian water-god Enki comes quite close to that of Vedic Varuṇa in many respects. Thus Varuṇa too is a phallic god (§ 12.2) and associated with the womb and amniotic sac (§ 12.1). Varuṇa is the overseer of physical and moral order, who 'grasps' evil-doers and punishes them with disease and death; in this capacity he is also the principal oath-god, and is associated with the bath that cleanses away sin (§ 12.1). Similarly Enki, as the god of the cleansing waters, is the deity of ritual lustration and purification from polluting evil. As the god of the holy water, Enki is further the main deity of the oath ritual, 'the lord of the oath formula' (*bêl šipti*).

Varuṇa is omniscient and beholds all the secret things that have been or shall be done (R̥S 1,25,7; 9; 11); he is the possessor of the 'magic craft' or 'occult power' (*māyā*) of the Asura. Enki, in his turn, was the Sumerian god of cunning and wisdom, 'the wise one among the gods'. He masters all branches of knowledge, and has established the laws, taught people to write, to build houses and cities, to cultivate land, to sail ships, to heal diseases, as well as to practise arts and crafts of every kind.

The Sumerian word *apkallu* (or *abgal*) meaning 'wise man, expert', and used as the title of a priest, exorcist or diviner, is an epithet of Enki. It refers to mythological sages, too, especially the seven antediluvian sages: the cuneiform texts speak of 'an oral tradition of the [seven] ancient sages from before the flood', and 'the seven sages of the *apsû*, the sacred *purādu*-fish, who like their lord, Ea, have been endowed with sublime wisdom'. These servants of Enki are represented in the art as half-fish, half-man (fig. 10.19).

Indian mythology, too, knows Seven Sages, who are equated with the stars of Ursa Major (§§ 10.4; 11.3: 12.2; 14.1), and they, too, are connected with fish (§ 10.5). There may indeed be an ancient connection between the Mesopotamian and Indian mythologies here, for the Mahābhārata (3,185,1–54) and Agni-Purāṇa (2,3ff.) likewise connect the Seven Sages with the flood myth: they are said to have been in the boat with Manu, the first man. In the older Vedic version of the flood myth, told in ŚB 1,8,1, Manu is the sole survivor. In both cases, Manu's boat is saved from the flood by a great fish (*matsya*, *jhaṣa*) which Manu had first saved and protected by keeping it in a jar and then in a pond, before taking it to the ocean. In the R̥gveda, the 'seven sacrificers' (i.e. the Seven Sages) assist Manu in his performance of the first sacrifice (§ 12.2). Manu 'man' is a multi-form of Yama, the first man and first mortal, and hence the king of the dead, and in later Hinduism, the god of death. Yama in his turn is a partial duplicate of Varuṇa, the righteous king (§ 12.1). Like Manu, Varuṇa sails in a ship (R̥S 7,88,3). As we have seen, Varuṇa is also the god of waters associated with aquatic animals, including the fish. In the Sumerian flood myth, on the other hand, it was the water-god Enki who warned Ziusudra of the coming flood.

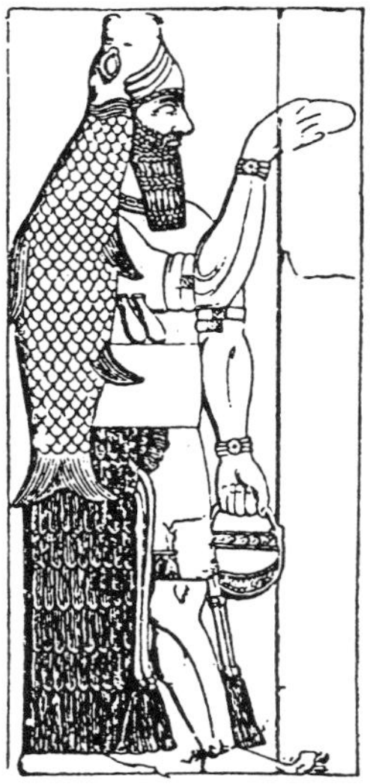

Fig. 10.19. A priest masked as Enki, half-fish and half-man, in a relief of Assurnasirpal II (883–859 BC) from Calah. Gypsum. Height *c.*2.5 m. After Jeremias 1929: 353, fig. 183.

10.3 Fish offerings

The 'fish in the jar' motif of the Indian flood myth discussed in the preceding section has its counterpart in the cult. In the ceremony of *matsya-dvādaśī-vrata*, a golden fish image of Viṣṇu (with whom the fish of the flood myth is identified in the late versions of the Purāṇas) is placed in the middle of four jars filled with water, said to represent the four oceans. The performer asks Viṣṇu to save him, as the god saved the Vedas from the nether world in the flood myth (Varāha-Purāṇa 39,26–77).

The 'fish in the jar' also reminds one of the Early Harappan painted pots with very realistic pictures of fish (fig. 10.20). It is not uncommon for the fish or pairs of fish to be depicted even now on water vessels in India. The motif of 'a libation jar flanked by two fishes' occurs in Mesopotamian seals, where it is connected with the ritual of the ceremonial meal: a nude attendant carries a big vessel in one hand and two fishes in the other (§ 10.2).

In the early 'miniature tablets' of Harappa, the plain 'fish' pictogram is seen to occur in close association with the U sign, which apparently denotes 'sacrificial vessel' (fig. 7.12). These occurrences indeed suggest that 'fish' may have been the material offered in at least some of these sacrificial pots, for the 'fish' sign may be placed not only after the 'numeral (2–4) + U' sequence, but even in the middle of it (fig. 10.21). Some of the 'miniature tablets' of Harappa are in the shape of a fish (fig. 10.22). In present-day South India, the offerings that devotees bring to the god Murukaṉ by means of a shoulder yoke include pots full of fish (Tamil and Malayalam *mīṉ-kāvaṭi*, *macca-k-kāvaṭi*). On several two-, three- or four-sided Indus tablets, the plain 'fish' sign occurs alone on one side (H-288; H-350; H-366; H-849 to H-851; H-884; H-885; H-973; H-976; H-977), as does the picture of an alligator on one side of other similar tablets (H-287; H-846 to H-848; H-879 to H-883; H-974; H-975). In some cases the other sides of these 'fish' (H-973) and 'alligator' (H-827) tablets share identical inscriptions. Bearing in mind the Harappan representations of alligators devouring fish (fig. 10.1) and the fact that in later Indian religion the alligator is the vehicle and symbol of Varuṇa (the god of waters) and Kāma (the god of love / desire), it seems possible that the Indus people offered potfuls of fish in sacrifice to holy alligators. Until recently, goats were sacrificed to greedy crocodiles kept as sacred by native Hindu castes in a pool called Muggur Pir near Karachi; and the crocodile continues to be worshipped as a god by tribal people in Gujarat.

Harappan fish offerings are made likely by the Mesopotamian parallel:

Fish were an important item of food, not for men only, but also for the gods. Fishermen in the service of the larger temples were charged to deliver stated quantities of fish of different species, and it was clearly indicated whether the fish should be fresh, roasted or dried. The quantities required were enormous, so much so, indeed, that, although in the case of the rarer species the number of the fish to be brought was stated, the more ordinary varieties were delivered by the bundle or basketful. These abundant supplies served not only for the daily repasts of the divinities and the temple personnel, but also for sacrifices on special occasions. We do not know when these fish-sacrifices were instituted, but it must have been at a very remote period. In the sacrificial lists almost every divinity received *1 ḫa kešda (du)*, 'one basketful of fish'. (Buren 1948: 102f.)

Excavations at Eridu, the chief site of Enki's cult, have shown that, from *c*.5000 to *c*.3200 BC, fish were offered in fires in the temple. Great heaps of ash were recovered in specific rooms, mixed with vast quantities of fish bones. From the Jemdet Nasr period onwards no burnt offerings of fish were made. Instead, fishes were placed on top of the remains from the preceding ceremony outside the temple in a separate place within the sacred precinct, and were left to decay. Many tiny miniature models of fish supposed to be dedicated memorials of fish offerings have been found in temples (e.g. the Moon temple at Khafajeh). The scenes carved on seals also depict sacred meals where fish were served and libation jars. In the first millennium BC, King Sennacherib, offering 'pure sacrifices' to Enki, 'cast into the sea a gold fish and a gold tortoise' along with 'a ship of gold'.

Besides Enki, the Mesopotamians worshipped especially the goddess Inanna-Ishtar with fish offerings:

There were also a few divinities for whom the sacrifices appointed consisted entirely of fish in portentous quantities, as the little group of clay tablets recording fish-offerings brought to the goddess Ninni or Inanna prove. These divinities do not seem to have been exclusively those who had some connexion with water, but were usually those associated with fertility. (Buren 1948: 103)

In the second century AD, the goddess Atargatis (who had a son called 'Fish') received similar fish offerings in the Syrian city of Hierapolis:

Mnaseas in the second book of his work on Asia says: 'In my opinion, Atargatis was a cruel Queen and ruled the people harshly, even to the extent of forbidding them by law to eat fish; on the contrary, they must bring them to her because of her fondness for that food. For this reason the custom still holds that whenever they pray to the Goddess, they bring her offerings of fish made of silver and gold; but the priests bring to the Goddess every day real fish which they have fancily dressed and served on the table. They are broiled or baked, and the priests of the Goddess, of course, consume the fish themselves.' Proceeding a little further, he again says: 'Atargatis ... with her son Ichthys ["Fish"], was sunk in the Lake of Ashkelon because of her outrageous conduct and eaten up by the fish.' (Athenaios, Deipnosophistae 8, 346–7, trans. C. B. Gullick, IV: 68–71, quoted from Wright 1991: 37)

These Near Eastern fish offerings to the Goddess demand comparison with the consumption of fish and intoxicants in the orgiastic feasts of the Indian goddess Durgā (§§ 14.2ff.), whose cult images are drowned in water at the conclusion of her festival. Fish (*matsya*), especially the red carp (*rohita-matsya*), and alligator or crocodile (*grāha*) are also specified as sacrificial victims which give special joy to the Goddess along with certain other virile male animals, including all those that are depicted in the 'Proto-Śiva' seal: the buffalo (*mahiṣa*), rhinoceros (*khaḍga*), elephant (*hastin*), tiger (*śārdūla*, *vyāghra*) and man (*nara*) (cf. Kālikā-Purāṇa 55 [= 57 in the translation], 1–6; 67,3ff.). These animals represent, it seems, the decapitated (or castrated) and afterwards 'resurrected' 'fertility demon', the adversary and simultaneously the father-son-lover-husband of the Goddess (§ 14.2).

A fish-offering plays a central part in a resuscitation ritual performed nowadays in rural Bengal:

The death and resurrection theme also finds expression in the ritual of an actual dead body which is connected with the popular [Bengali] *gājana* and *caḍaka* festivals of Dharma. In this ritual a

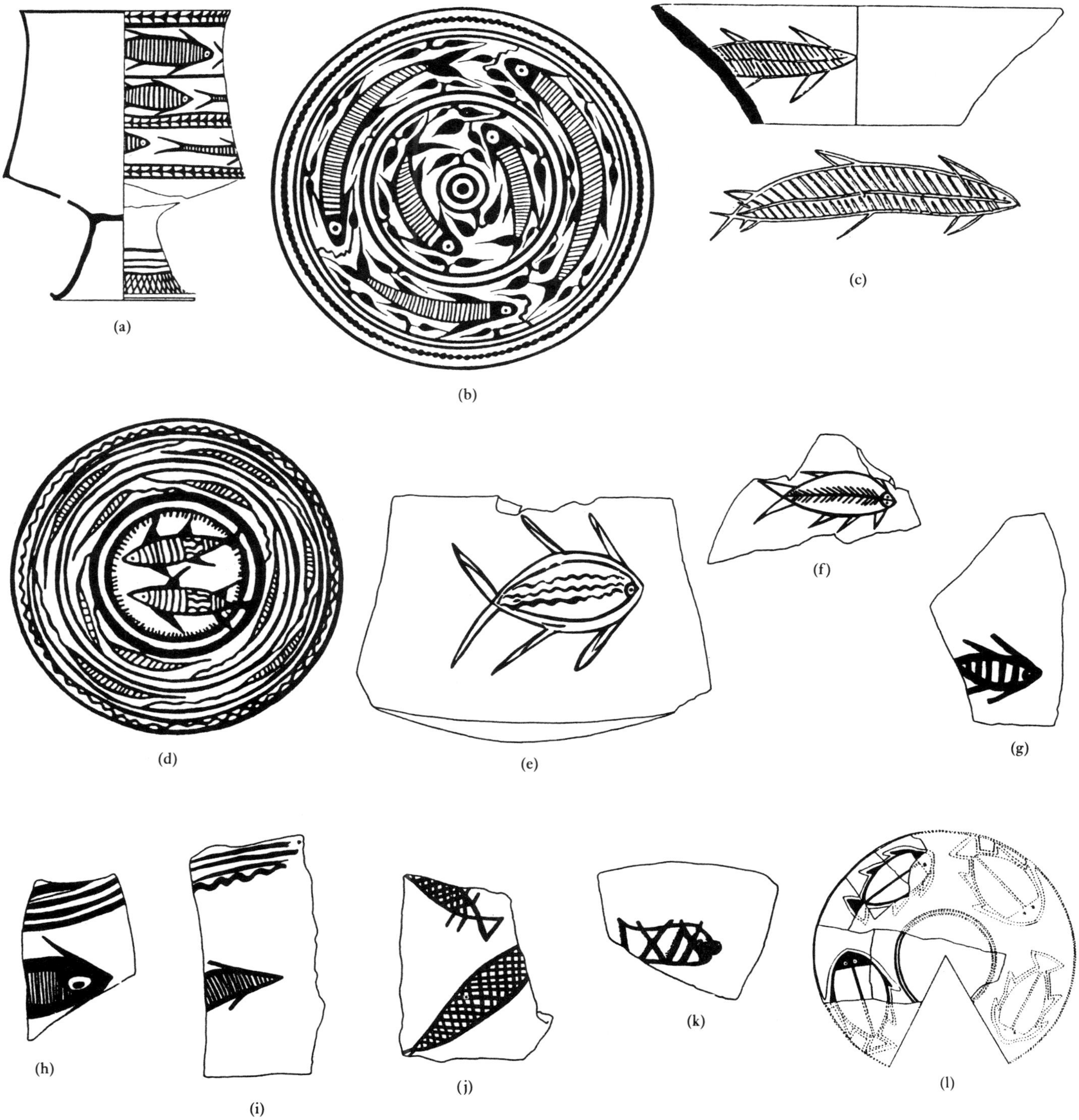

Fig. 10.20. Painted and incised fish motifs on pottery from the Greater Indus Valley in Early and Mature Harappan periods.
(a–c) Mehrgarh, Kachi plain, Baluchistan, *c.*3200–2600 BC: (a) period VI, pedestal goblet of Faiz Mohammad Grey Ware, type 3; after Jarrige and Lechevallier 1979: 506, fig. 24: 5; (b) period VII, shallow open bowl of Faiz Mohammad Grey Ware, type 2; after Wright 1984: 105, fig. 3.12; (c) period VII, incised pottery bowl from locus 113; after Santoni 1989: 183, fig. 8: 1.
(d) Shahr-i Sokhta, Seistan, Iran, *c.*3000–2600 BC. A unique black-on-grey bowl from grave IUP 731–36, probably an imitation of Faiz Mohammad ceramics made at Shahr-i Sokhta. The form is typical of the local Emir ceramics, and while the fish motif is characteristic of

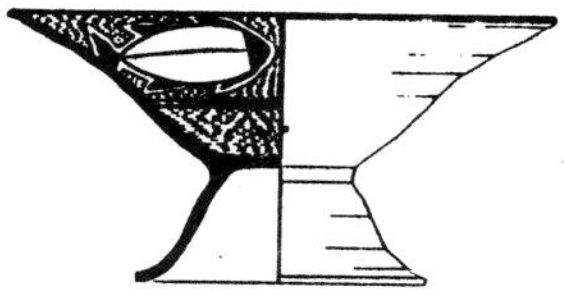

(l)

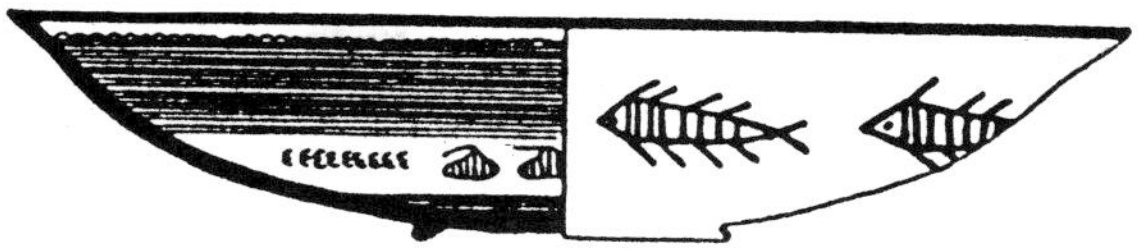

(m)

(n)

(o)

(p)

(q)

(r)

(s)

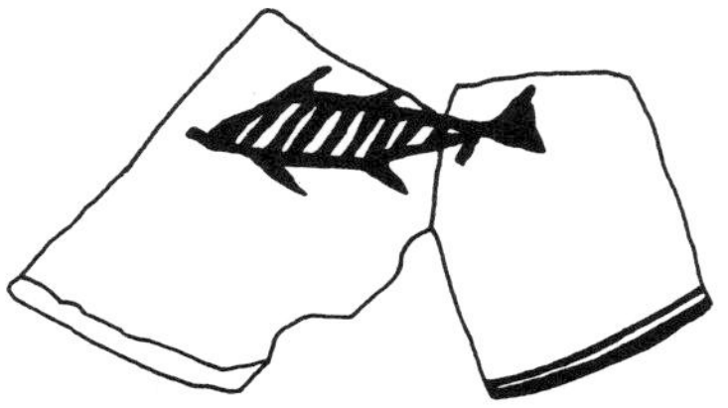

(t)

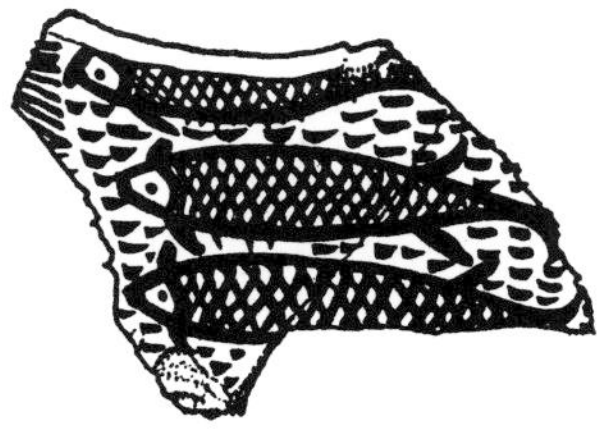

(u)

the Faiz Mohammad tradition, the Faiz Mohammad conventions of combining designs are not followed. After inv. (drawing no.) 7539 in Wright 1984 (cf. p. 147, n. 3).
(e–k) Rahman Dheri, Northwest Frontier Province, *c.*3200–2300 BC: (e–f) period I, polychrome cups, (g–k) periods II–III (?). Drawn after *CISI* 2: 373, 376f., Rhd-260 (=e), Rhd-259 (=f), Rhd-254 (=g), Rhd-255 (=h), Rhd-253 (=i), Rhd-256 (=j), Rhd-224 (=k).
(l) Lewan, Bannu Basin, Northwest Frontier Province, *c.*3200–2600 BC. An open bowl on a hollow-footed stand, with a frieze of four fish, their black outlines filled with red, over an interior covered with a white slip. After Allchin et al. 1986: 215.
(m–n) Quetta Valley, Baluchistan, *c.*3200–3000 BC: shallow open bowls of Faiz Mohammad Ware, type 1. After Fairservis 1956: 264, fig. 55B (=m), and 309, design 450 (=n). Cf. Wright 1984: 85–97.
(o–p) Nal, south Baluchistan, *c.*3200–2600 BC: Nal-style polychrome pottery. Drawn after Hargreaves 1929: pl. 20b (=o), and Gordon 1960: pl. 6a (=p).
(q–s) Mehi, Maskai Valley, south Baluchistan, third millennium BC. Red ware with black paint. After Possehl 1986: 24–5, fig. 6, Mehi III.4.6 and Mehi III.3.4; 45, fig. 17, Mehi I (based on Stein 1931: pl. 29 and 27).
(t) Kalibangan, northern Rajasthan, *c.*2600 BC: period I, painted pottery, fabric E. Drawn after Allchin and Allchin 1982: fig. 6.29.
(u) Harappa, *c.*2500 BC: a sherd of Mature Harappan painted pottery from the earthen make-up of the 'rampart' and platform. Drawing of Diana Holmes ('after the original in the Moenjo-daro Museum') in Piggott 1961: 247, fig. 11. Cf. Wheeler 1947a: 44, 7.

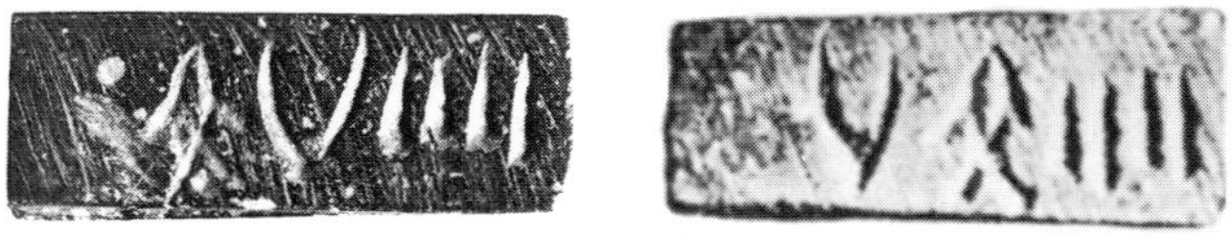
(a) (b)

Fig. 10.21. Possible recording of fish offerings in 'miniature tablets' from the lower Mature Harappan layers at Harappa: (a) H-302 ('four pots fish') and (b) 3452 ('four fish-pots'); after Vats 1940: II, 452 B.

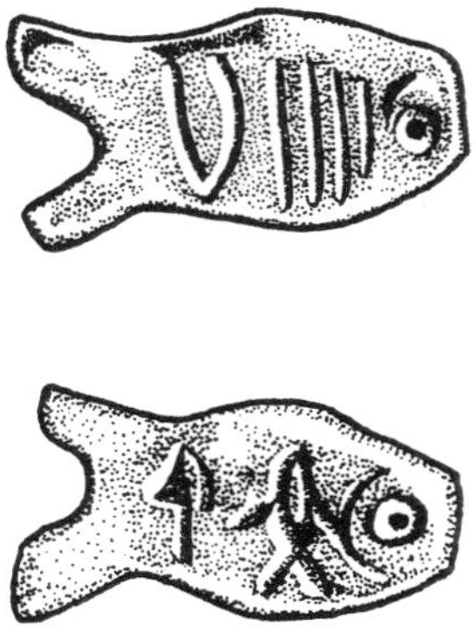

Fig. 10.22. A fish-shaped tablet (3428) from Harappa, incised with an Indus inscription. Note the eye consisting of a dot-in-a-circle. Drawn after Vats 1940: II, pl. 95, no. 428.

game is played with the head of a dead person . . . The concluding function of the *caḍaka* ritual is the resuscitation of the dead. The chief devotee cooks a *sol* [i.e. *śakula*] fish, roasting it in embers. Some parboiled and husked rice is also cooked and rice-wine is poured on the fish and the rice, which are placed in an earthen pot. These are taken at midday to a tree standing in some lonely meadow, and the food is placed on a plantain leaf and left for the ghosts to devour. This offering is sometimes made in the meadow where the village dead are cremated. (Bhattacharyya 1982: 140f.)

In Nepal, during the Dasaĩ ('tenth day of victory') feast in honour of the goddess Durgā, low-caste gardeners masked as the Nine Durgās dance orgiastic dances and drink the blood of animals sacrificed to them, as well as alcohol from a human skull. One of the gardeners holds in his hands a vase containing a fish. Another dancer, representing Bhairava, tries to empty a basket of fish on the heads of the spectators.

According to the Harappan amulets, too, sacrificial pots represented by the U sign were offered to sacred trees (fig. 7.12). From the time of the earliest written records, such trees have been the favourite abodes of fertility spirits (male or female, usually called *yakṣa* or *yakṣī*). In ancient India (and still today at least in Bengal), 'fish-water' (i.e. water with fish or parts of fish in it) as well as 'flesh-water' (i.e. water with pieces of raw flesh in it) was poured at the roots of cultivated trees (such as the mango, the tree of the god of love) in order to make them grow and bear fruit (Agni-Purāṇa 247,28 = 282,13 = Śukranīti 4,4,109). The more rotten the fish or flesh put under the tree and the more it stinks, the better (Varāhamihira's Bṛhatsaṁhitā 55,20f.).

In the Harappan amulets, human worshippers offer sacrificial vessels also to anthropomorphic deities who resemble the 'Proto-Śiva' and who are attended by serpents (fig. 13.2b). Strong drinks and fish were also integral parts of sacrifices to fertility spirits (*yakṣa*) and serpent gods (*nāga*) in the early popular religion of North India:

In those days a festival was proclaimed in Benares, and the people resolved to sacrifice to the ogres (*yakkha*). So they strewed fish and meat about courtyards, and streets, and other places and set great pots of strong drink. . . . where just before certain persons had been offering to the Nāgas a sacrifice of milk, and rice and fish and meat and strong drink and the like. (Jātaka 113 and 146)

10.4 The sign sequences of 'number' + 'fish'

Fish bones, fish hooks, and representations of fishing nets found at Harappan sites attest the importance of fish in the diet of the Indus people. People of ancient Mesopotamia, too, caught and ate fish. Amounts of fish are quantified in the archaic Sumerian texts from Uruk, which contain numerals in association with 'fish' pictograms probably used in their iconic meaning (fig. 10.23). Yet it is difficult to accept the suggestion made by the Assyriologist James Kinnier Wilson that the sequences of Indus signs consisting of Num + 'fish' denote rations of fish. The Uruk tablets are *administrative texts*, while the Indus texts are mainly *seals*, and fish are not quantified on Mesopotamian seals. Moreover, the numbers actually attested before the 'fish' sign in the Indus inscriptions are restricted to 3, 4, 6 and 7. The hypothesis of a Dravidian pun offers an alternative which explains this restriction and better suits the seal contexts.

The most frequent sequence corresponds to the native name of the Pleiades in Old Tamil (e.g. Akanāṉūṟu 141): *aṟu-mīṉ*, literally '(the constellation consisting of) six (visible) stars'. The Pleiades occupy the first position in the ancient Indian star calendar and they figure prominently in astral myths (§§ 11.2–3).

The sequence, which is next in frequency of occurrence, yields in Dravidian *mu-m-mīṉ* '(constellation of) three stars', which is actually attested in Piṅkala-Nikaṇṭu (243) as the Old Tamil name of the Mṛgaśīrṣa asterism. (In this compound, *mu-* is the monomorphemic adjective form of the numeral '3' before a noun starting with a consonant, and *-m-* represents the automatic doubling of the following consonant.) A comparative study of the Indus inscriptions

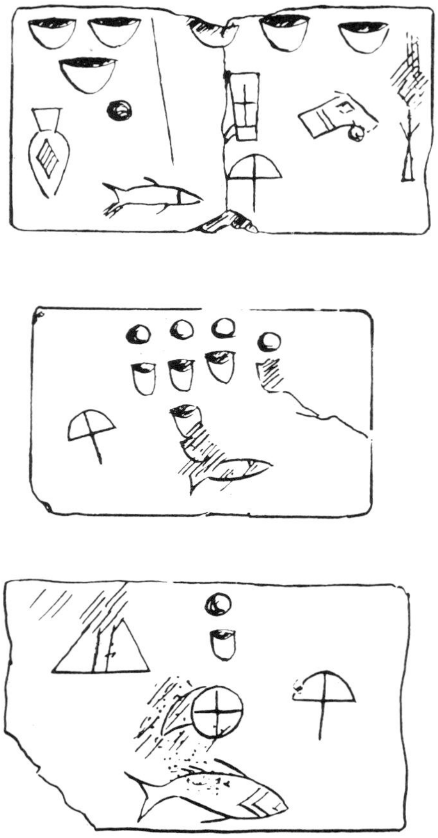

(a)

(b)

(c)

Fig. 10.23. (a, b, c). Archaic Sumerian tablets from Uruk with numbers and fish signs. Drawn by J. V. Kinnier Wilson (1987: 43, fig. 2) after photographs in Falkenstein 1936: texts 256 (=a), 68 (=b) and 336, reverse (=c).

Fig. 10.24. Inscription consisting of just the signs '7' + 'fish' on an Indus seal from Harappa (H-9).

suggests that the sequences Num + 'fish' belong together syntactically; this conclusion is supported by a large and finely carved seal with the sole text '7' + 'fish', ⋉‖‖‖ (fig. 10.24). The latter sequence gives in Dravidian *eḻu-mīn* '(constellation of) seven stars', which is the Old Tamil name of the Ursa Major (e.g. in Naṟṟiṇai 231), again a most important asterism in ancient Indian cult and mythology (§§ 10.2; 11.3; 12.2; 14.1).

Vasiṣṭha is the chief among the Seven Sages associated with the seven stars of Ursa Major. Ṛgveda 7,33,7–13 gives a remarkable account of the birth of Vasiṣṭha and Agastya or Māna, the latter known in later Hindu mythology as the 'pot-born' sage of the southern direction connected with the bright star Canopus. Bṛhaddevatā (5,149–55) explains that when the gods Mitra and Varuṇa saw the beautiful water nymph Urvaśī, they emitted seed. Falling on earth, into a sacrificial pot and into water, the seed became respectively Vasiṣṭha, Agastya and a 'greatly shining fish' (*matsyo mahādyutiḥ*). Here a fish is expressly identified as a luminous object and placed side by side with sages connected with

well-known stars. 'Fish' and 'star' are not phonetically or semantically associated in Indo-Aryan (in fact, fish is exceedingly seldom mentioned in the Ṛgveda), so this tradition is likely to reflect ancient Dravidian mythology.

The plain 'fish' sign is doubled in contexts where this sequence, ⋉⋉, clearly forms a syntactic whole and occupies a position similar to Num + 'fish' and other similar combinations supposed to denote a deity (3232 ⇑⋉⋉" ◯ and 2875 ⇑‖‖ Ⓤ⋉⋉" ◇). This could reflect the intensifying reduplication of the root, which is typical of the Dravidian languages, and which is attested in several languages also for the root *min*: Tamil *miṉṉi miṉuṅku* 'to twinkle (of stars)', *miṉu-miṉukkam* 'twinkling (of stars)'; Kannada *mini-minisu*, *minu-minisu* 'to shine brightly'; Tulu *miṇi-miṇi* 'twinkling, glistening, dimly shining'; Telugu *mina-mina* 'glitter, shining'. Thus the juxtaposed two plain 'fish' signs could mean 'the brightly shining one' or 'the shining star' or 'the shining fish' in Dravidian. But they could also be interpreted as meaning 'a pair of fish', an important symbol in historical India and apparently in the Indus Civilization, too (see § 10.2).

10.5 The planets Mercury and Saturn

Even though these interpretations of the plain 'fish' sign strongly support the Dravidian hypothesis, it might still be possible to propose quite different but also reasonable explanations for sequences like ⋉‖‖ and ⋉⋉. And while puns are language-specific, surprisingly a pair of homophonous words meaning 'fish' and 'star' can also be found outside Dravidian, namely in one Caucasian language called Lezgi (formerly Kürin), where both words have the phonetic shape *γed*. But in this case only the word for 'star' seems to be ancient (it has cognates in Tabasaran *χæž*, Aγul *had*, Rutul *χædei*, Caxor *χare*), so the homophony may not necessarily go back to Proto-Caucasian. The 'visual pun' provided by the possible derivation of both 'fish' and 'star' from the root meaning 'to sparkle, glitter' in Dravidian is also missing here.

It is therefore necessary to examine further this tentative interpretation of the 'fish' pictograms. One crucially important way of doing so is to study Indus signs that occur in combination with the 'fish' pictograms. The task now is to test whether any of these signs can be interpreted by applying the same methods and hypotheses in such a manner that what emerges is reasonable.

A structural analysis of the Indus inscriptions shows that the 'fish' pictograms often form syntactically coherent sequences with the immediately preceding signs, such as the numbers discussed above. Moreover, many of the 'fish' signs themselves are composite signs (ligatures) consisting of the basic 'fish' pictogram and various diacritic marks, that is, differentiating or modifying additions. It is most likely that such compound and diacritic signs in the Indus script have had the same function as in the deciphered writing systems of ancient Sumer and Egypt, where they have been used either to express words compounded with the basic sign or to clarify its meaning by specifying one of its homophones or synonyms.

In contrast to the plain 'fish' signs, the ligatured 'fish' signs are never doubled or preceded by numbers. This prevents them from representing different sorts of fish because, if that were the case, they too would be quantifiable. On the other hand, their general distributions as well as outward appearances are so close to the plain 'fish' sign that their meanings should be closely similar. The question now is whether the signs that are combined with the basic 'fish' sign can be interpreted systematically and in such a way that they fit their context and the assumed reading of the 'fish' sign. If so, are the emerging compounds actually attested in Dravidian languages? In this case we would expect to find native Dravidian astral terms. Here, the scanty remains of such native vocabulary surviving in the Old Tamil texts written around the beginning of the Christian era are of crucial importance. Although the names of the months used in these texts have all been borrowed from Indo-Aryan-speaking North India,

> the use of terms quite unrelated to the northern ones for many of the asterisms and the planets suggests . . . that the Tamils had their own names for some constellations and planets before they imported the northern system. The northern system must have been imported long before the time of the anthologies, for the Sanskrit terms have been changed radically to conform to Tamil phonetics . . . and the system had been so completely assimilated in Tamilnad that it was used to determine the dates of most festivals and marriages . . . Northern astrologers must have been brought by kings and others at a very early date, perhaps before Kannada and Tamil split apart, but in any case probably before the Brāhmī script was adopted. (Hart 1975: 77)

Unfortunately most of the Indus signs are so stylized and simplified that their original pictorial meaning cannot be recognized unambiguously. This means that most of the pictorial interpretations are bound to remain subjective guesses. There are, however, a few whose pictorial meaning can be reasonably explained.

One of the diacritic signs in the 'fish' ligatures is drawn either directly or obliquely across the body of the basic 'fish' pictogram: , . It could express the idea of 'halving' or 'dividing'. Dividing a fish is a popular motif of South Asian folklore. Thus Jātaka 400 tells of two otters who had managed to catch a great fish together but could not divide it. The jackal, whom they asked to be the arbitrator, gave the head to one and tail to the other, taking for himself the middle portion as his pay. The Proto-Dravidian root **pacu* 'to halve, to divide into two parts', is homophonous with Proto-Dravidian **pacu* 'green'. The resulting compound, **pacu-mīn* at once 'halved fish' and 'green star', is not known as such from Dravidian languages, but *Tamil Lexicon* records *pacu-v-ā-mīṉ* in the sense of a 'rose-coloured fish', deriving *pacu* from *pacumai* 'greenness, greenish yellow' (cf. also *paca* 'to be golden, like the sky in the evening') and *-ā-* from the root *ā-* 'to be(come), be like' (the intervening *-v-* is an automatic glide); *ā-* may have been added to prevent the most immediate modern Tamil interpretation of the compound from *pacu* 'cow' < Sanskrit *paśu* 'cow'. Moreover, in Old Tamil the word *paccai* literally meaning 'greenness' is attested as the name of the planet Mercury. The name seems to be due to the fact that Mercury is visible only shortly before sunrise or shortly after sunset (cf. Tamil *paccai-veyil* 'evening sun'). *Paccai* is also the name of the green-hued god Kṛṣṇa-Viṣṇu, who (as Nārāyaṇa) is the presiding deity of the planet Mercury in Jaiminīya-Gṛhyasūtra 2,9.

The concepts 'green', 'the planet Mercury' and 'the god Kṛṣṇa-Viṣṇu' are associated with each other in other sources as well. Thus greenish-yellow is the colour of the planet Mercury not only according to Tamil texts but also according to Sanskrit texts. The green emerald is the stone of Mercury among the 'nine gems' (*nava-maṇi*) connected with the 'nine planets', and Kṛṣṇa-Viṣṇu is called *marakata-mēniyaṉ* 'emerald-coloured' in Tamil. One of the principal Old Tamil names of Viṣṇu, *māl* 'darkness', is also the name of the planet Mercury. Similarly, one of Mercury's Sanskrit names is *śyāmāṅga* 'dark-limbed' or *śyāma* 'dark', also used of Kṛṣṇa-Viṣṇu.

Derived from the Dravidian root **pacu* '(to be) green, fresh, young', which was used in the above interpretation, appears to be the Proto-Dravidian word meaning 'boy, child' (Tamil *pacal*, *paiyaṉ*, etc.), which recalls the fact of Kṛṣṇa's being a child-god; such a connotation can be seen as symbolically agreeing with the sign of 'halved fish' (boy = half-adult). The hypothesis that the planet Mercury (which could be seen only for a short time near the rising or setting sun) represented a child-god does not seem far-fetched in the light of a Canaanite parallel. It has been suggested that the bright morning star, the star of the war-god 'Aṯtar worshipped as the divine king (*mlk*, whence Moloch of the Old Testament) of the city of Tyrus, was understood to be the king of the stars whose fate it was to die young, at the appearance of the sun, the great fire: it would have been in imitation of this fate that 'Aṯtar was offered children who perished in fire.

Another relatively unambiguous diacritical mark is one that has been placed over the 'fish' sign and looks like a 'roof': . Roofs having such a shape can be seen, for example, in some of the monolithic temples built by the Pallava kings in Māmallapuram in the seventh century AD, and in the traditional houses of the Toda tribe, who in their isolation in the Nilagiri mountains of South India have preserved many archaic customs. The most widespread root from which words denoting 'roof' are derived in the various Dravidian languages is **vay* / **vey* / **mey* 'to cover a house with a thatched roof', in which etymon the phonetic alternations **v-* / **m-* and **-ay-* / **-ey-* can be reconstructed for Proto-Dravidian. Thus in Proto-Dravidian the root **vey* / **mey* '(to) roof' was partially homophonous with the root **may* 'black'. The sequence of the pictograms for 'roof' and 'fish' in the Indus script can be read in Proto-Dravidian as **mey-mīn* in the sense of **may-mīn* 'black star'. What makes this reading really significant is that the last-mentioned compound is factually attested as the name of the planet Saturn in the earliest poems written in Old Tamil (Puṟanāṉūṟu 117).

This Old Tamil name *mai-m-mīṉ* is indeed a fitting name for Saturn, which is a dim planet most of the time. The Dravidian root **may* (Tamil *mai*) means not only 'to be or become black' but also 'to be dim'. According to the oldest Sanskrit texts dealing with the worship of the planets, Saturn's complexion and his garments are black. They further mention Yama and Prajāpati, the Hindu gods of death and creation, as the main and subsidiary deities presiding over this dark planet. In fact, many things suggest that Saturn is the astral aspect of the god of death. The name of Yama is used for the planet Saturn in both Sanskrit and Tamil tradition. Mars and Saturn are much feared as angry and ominous planets.

Black is the colour of darkness, night and death. Yama is associated with the colour black in the Brāhmaṇa texts of the Veda (e.g. MS 3,14,11). In classical Hinduism, Yama as the god of death has black as his colour and the dark water buffalo, a lethally dangerous beast, as his vehicle. The planet Saturn, too, is said to ride the water buffalo in several texts, while others mention the crow and 'black vulture' as his vehicles; these black birds are also most intimately associated with death as eaters of carrions, and the crow also as the consumer of the rice-cakes offered to the dead.

Saturn is not only a dark but also a slow planet. For this reason it is called 'slowly-going' (Sanskrit *śani* or *śanaiścara*) or 'lame' (Sanskrit *paṅgu*, Tamil *muṭavaṉ*), and in the images his left foot is usually distorted. The iconographic manuals of the Buddhists and the Jains mention the turtle (*kacchapa*, *kūrma*, *kamaṭha*) as the mount or draught-animal of the planet Saturn. This is an animal whose slowness is proverbial: in the Old Tamil text Akanāṉūṟu 256, the slow movement of the turtle (*yāmai*) is compared to a drunkard's walk. It is conceivable that this association of the planet Saturn with the turtle may go back to Harappan times: the compound Indus sign depicting a fish with a roof over it could, then, symbolize the deified planet Saturn even pictorially through his vehicle, for the turtle is an aquatic animal (i.e. a kind of 'fish') covered with a shell (i.e. a kind of roof).

11 The astronomical and astrological background

11.1 Planetary worship in India

Before we continue along the line begun in chapter 10 and interpret other Indus signs as names of stars and planets, it seems advisable to take a good look at the sources and ask: Is such an astral approach warranted? How likely is it that the heavenly bodies played a major role in the Harappan life, religion and name-giving? We begin with planetary worship in India and its origins.

The worship of the planets occupies a prominent position in the religious life of India today. Many diseases and other troubles of earthly existence are ascribed to the malign influence of angered planetary deities, whose wrath is to be pacified. In South India, one of the most frequented places in practically every Śiva temple is a small shrine to the planetary gods (fig. 11.1). The images stand on a circular or square platform as a group, the sun in the centre and the others at eight points around it. Any one of the 'planets' may be the object of special attention, to be worshipped on a particular day of the week, or at other appropriate times. According to the Vaikhānasa-Gṛhyasūtra (4,13), written in Sanskrit influenced by Tamil in South India in the first centuries of the Christian era, the 'propitiation of the nine planets' (*nava-graha-śānti*) should precede all religious rites. The planetary maṇḍala can be made of metal, with the symbols of the planets carved on it, or of more temporary material, and worshipped at home (fig. 11.2).

Monumental representations of planets start appearing in North India in the Gupta period (*c.* fifth century AD), spread to central and western India in the eighth century, and to South India in the eleventh century. They correspond to the iconographic descriptions of such texts as the Agni-Purāṇa (51; 120; 301) and the Viṣṇudharmottara-Purāṇa (1,106), whose ancient parts date from around the sixth and seventh century. In the early examples, the 'nine planets' (Sanskrit *nava-graha*) are usually in a row arranged according to the order of the days of the week, sculptured on a rectangular

Fig. 11.1. Worship of the planet Saturn at 6.30 p.m. on 10 January 1985, in the Nava-graha hall of the Śiva Vaidyanātha temple in Tiṭṭaguḍi, South Arcot, Tamil Nadu, South India.

stone relief forming a lintel of the temple door. But Viṣṇudharmottara-Purāṇa (3,86,52) describes a temple of 'eight planets' (excluding Ketu), which function as 'guardians of the directions'. The antiquity of the group of eight planets is supported by its mention in the Mahābhārata (5,187,31). The group of five planets is at least as old: it is likewise attested in the Mahābhārata (6,96,35–6), which compares the main heroes, the five Pāṇḍava brothers, to the five planets (*grahāḥ*) which oppress the sun and the moon at the twilight of aeons.

The group of nine 'planets' comprises the five true planets visible to the naked eye, the sun and the moon, plus Rāhu and Ketu. Rāhu is the name of the eclipse demon. According to the well-known and popular Hindu myth told in the Mahābhārata (1,17,4–8) and many other sources, the demon Rāhu drank of the nectar of immortality, which was produced at the churning of the milk ocean and reserved for the gods alone. He was, however, found out by the sun and the moon, and decapitated by Viṣṇu. As Rāhu had not yet completely swallowed the nectar, only his head became immortal. The eclipses are caused because the head of the avenging Rāhu eternally swallows the sun and the moon. Early Vedic texts, starting with the Ṛgveda (e.g. 5,40,5–9), ascribe the eclipse of the sun to the magic (*māyā*) of the demoniac (*āsura*, punningly also 'sunless') Svarbhānu 'having the light of the sun'. Stephanie Jamison (1991) has identified Svarbhānu as the god of fire (Agni = Rudra), whose smoke hides the sun with darkness.

Ketu originally seems to refer to smoke as the heaven-reaching banner (*ketu*) of the fire-god Agni (e.g. ṚS 5,11,3). It also denotes the 'tailed' meteor or comet: the plural *ketavaḥ* appears in the early Vedic texts, and continues to do so in later times. In the sixth century AD, however, Varāhamihira interpreted Ketu as the tail of Rāhu, said to have the form of a snake, and connected Rāhu and Ketu with the ascending and descending nodes of the moon.

In today's North India, planetary worship is regularly performed on a temporary altar as part of domestic ritual. According to a Kumaoni Paddhati, it is a lengthy ritual which,

Fig. 11.2. A traditional metal plate made *c.* 1985 in Thanjavur, Tamil Nadu, South India, with images and symbols of the nine planets arranged in a gridiron representing nine directions. In the centre: the sun with a circle (*vṛtta*); clockwise from the upper left corner: Mercury with an arrow (*bāṇa*) in the northeast, Venus with a pentagon (*pañcakoṇa*) in the east, the moon with a square (*caturaśra*) in the southeast, Mars with a triangle (*trikoṇa*) in the south, Rāhu with a winnowing basket (*śūrpa*) in the southwest, Saturn with a bow (*dhanus*) in the west, Ketu with a flag (*dhvaja* [= *ketu*]) in the northwest, and Jupiter with a rectangle (*dīrghacaturaśra*) in the north. The directions and symbols of the planets follow exactly the prescriptions of the late Vedic texts (Baudhāyana-Gṛhya-Pariśeṣa-Sūtra 1,16,12–15 and Jaiminīya-Gṛhyasūtra 2,9).

together with the initiation, takes the greater part of the day, but is abbreviated on other occasions, such as the marriage ceremonies:

> First, an eight-petalled lotus is drawn upon an altar of about 18″ square. Then each of the petals is smeared with the appropriate colour of the planet to which it is assigned. The celebrant now places on the lotus figure in the proper order either images of the planets or pieces of metal etc., stamped with appropriate symbols, pieces of coloured cloth, and small heaps of rice mixed with curds. Each of the planetary symbols is first washed with the 'nectar of five ingredients' to the accompaniment of mantras, then set up while reciting the 'mystic words'; next the attendant deities are addressed and placed on the right and left of each planet. Then follows meditation on the form and symbolism of each planet. Finally, each of the planets is offered special food with appropriate mantras, burning special fuel gathered for each of the planets. (Kaye 1920: 73)

This ritual of the nine 'planets' is virtually identical to that of the first detailed descriptions dating from the beginning of the Christian era, in the Yājñavalkya-Smṛti (1,290–303) and in the latest parts of the Vedic literature (e.g. Jaiminīya-Gṛhyasūtra 2,9). 'Those desirous of prosperity or desirous of peace should worship the planets. For rain, for long life, for nourishment, act in the same way.' The texts describe the geometric and other symbols for the different planets, as well as specify their orientations (fig. 11.2); then come the kinds of wood used as fuel, the kinds of porridge offered, the mantras that accompany the oblations, the kinds of sacrificial fee to the priest, and the kinds of good qualities one may expect to acquire: all these differ with the different planets, whose colours (or coloured material sacred to them, especially metals and precious stones) are also mentioned in some of these texts. Others mention a presiding and a sub-presiding deity for each of the planets; their names figure as the key words of the mantras used in offering to the planets.

All these texts already enumerate the planets in the order of the seven-day week adopted from the Near East (sun, moon, Mars, Mercury, Jupiter, Venus, Saturn), followed by Rāhu and Ketu. But like the iconographic descriptions of the Buddhist and Jaina texts, which attest to the popularity and antiquity of the planetary deities in India, these texts are completely different from, and independent of, the Hellenistic tradition. In contrast, the description of the planets in the voluminous Sanskrit texts on astrology is full of Hellenistic influence. It is clear, then, that the roots of the *nava-graha* worship lie deep in the pre-Hellenistic traditions of India.

There are references to the planets in Vedic texts, but they are surprisingly few. Most explicit are those of the relatively late Maitrāyaṇī Upaniṣad, which associates the stars, the moon, Venus (*śukra*), Saturn (*śani*), Rāhu and Ketu with various compass directions (7,1–6) and then speaks of Jupiter (*bṛhaspati*) and Venus (*śukra*) as the teachers of the gods and demons respectively (7,9). The earlier Atharvaveda (19,9,7 and 10) speaks of the sun, moon, Rāhu and Mṛtyu Dhūmaketu ('Death with the apparition of smoke'), and 'seizers travelling in the sky' (*divicarā grahāḥ*). *Graha*, 'seizer', is later the principal word for 'planet'. This expression seems to have a Harappan-Dravidian background, and will be discussed in detail later (§ 13.3).

The popularity of planetary worship from late Vedic times onwards is in strong contrast with the almost complete absence of the planets in the Veda. Many scholars have even maintained that the Vedic Aryans did not know the planets at all in the early period. This, however, is quite unlikely. How could people who used a stellar calendar and habitually observed lunar asterisms fail to notice the planets, which are distinguished from all other luminaries of the sky by their motion and brightness? There must be a special reason for the early Vedic silence regarding the planets. This reason may have been the prevalence of planetary worship among the rivals and enemies of the Vedic Aryans, from whom it was finally adopted wholesale even by the orthodox Brahmans.

11.2 The Vedic star calendar

The orientation of the Harappan cities according to the cardinal directions (figs. 1.4 and 1.8; Wanzke 1987) provides irrefutable proof for the practice of astronomy by the Indus people. The origins of ancient Indian astronomy and time-reckoning is a complex and controversial issue, but of the greatest importance for the study of the Indus Civilization. As the question of a Harappan and Dravidian background here is vital for the astral interpretations of the 'fish' signs, we must touch all essential issues, including the possible role of Mesopotamian astronomy and time-reckoning.

The seven-day week and zodiac of twelve signs (Sanskrit *rāśi*) were borrowed into India from the West rather late, with Hellenistic astrology and astronomy. Mentions of days of the week and zodiacal signs are conspicuously absent in the Veda and even in the Mahābhārata, although the latter contains many references to portents arising from the positions of the planets in relation to the asterisms.

The Indian star calendar based on 27 or 28 constellations (Sanskrit *nakṣatra*) (fig. 11.3) is much older. Convincing references to these marking stars are found in the tenth book of the Ṛgveda, which was in existence by about 1000 BC. The nakṣatras are all listed slightly later (TS 4,4,10,1–3; MS 2,13,20; KS 39,13; AS 19,7,2–5). Time-reckoning is at the basis of the complex ritual of the fire-altar: the 10,800 bricks of the altar, including circularly placed nakṣatra bricks, symbolize the 10,800 moments of the year (360 days of 30 moments each). This elaborate ritual is unknown to the Ṛgveda, but appears suddenly and fully developed in the oldest Yajurvedic texts. It probably had a long prehistory in northwest India.

It is generally agreed that the Vedic nakṣatra calendar is of the same origin as the closely similar calendars of the Chinese and Arabs, which consist of 28 *xiu* 'mansions' and 28 *manāzil* (*al-kamar*) 'mansions (of the moon)' respectively. The Indian derivation of the Arabic calendar is hardly disputed, but there has been much controversy about whether the Vedic calendar is based on the Chinese or vice versa. (The Chinese calendar is probably first attested in the oracle bones of the Shang dynasty, *c.*1500 BC.) In either case Mesopotamia, famous for its ancient astronomy and astrology, has been vaguely assumed to be the ultimate source. Since much of this debate took place before the discovery of the Indus Civilization, the latter is hardly mentioned in this context. In fact, however, many things point to a Harappan origin of the nakṣatra calendar. Knowledge of it could have reached China through the mediation of the Harappan-influenced Bactria and

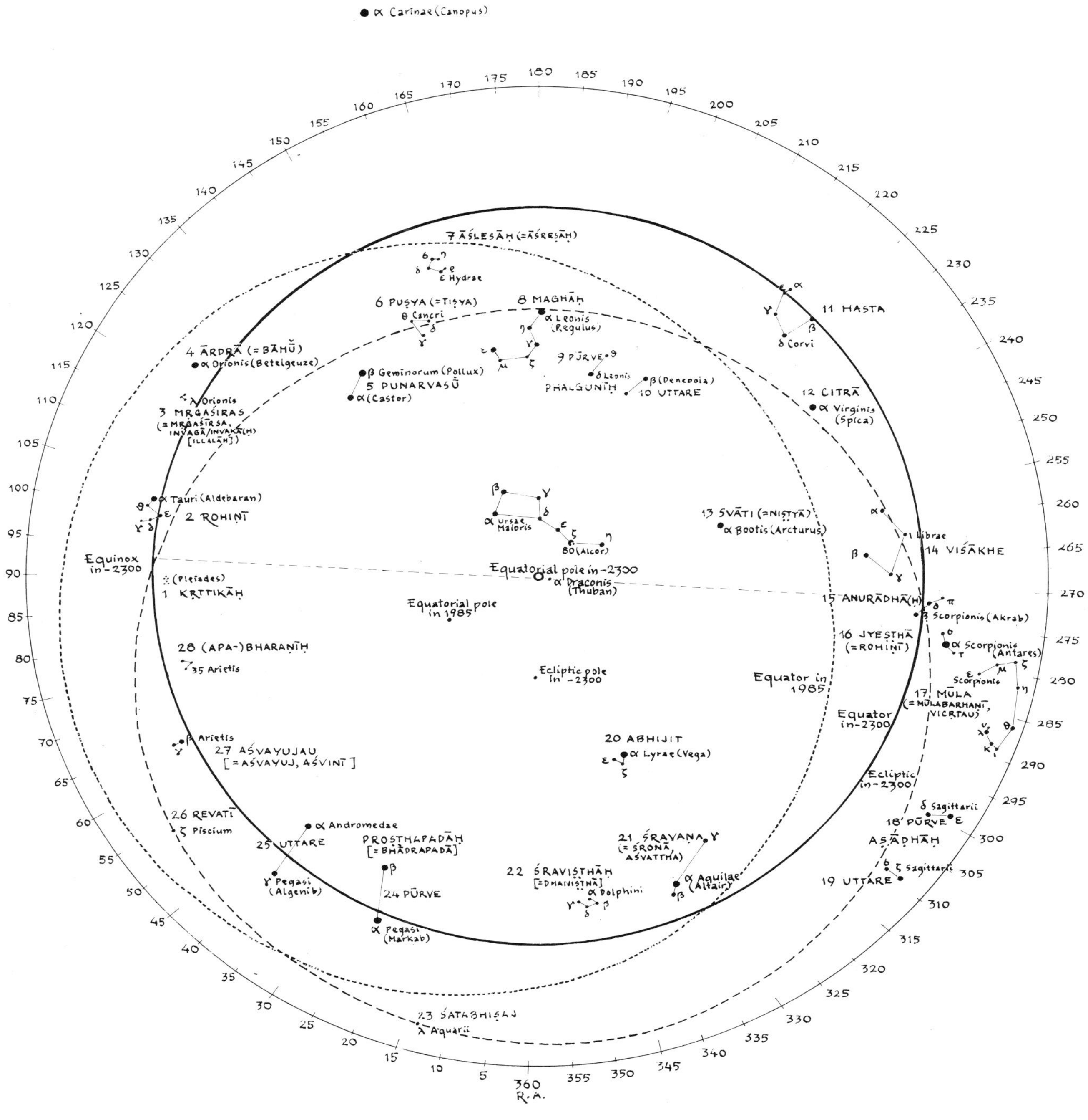

Fig. 11.3. Map of the calendrical stars of the Veda in 2250 BC. Based on the diagram of Kaye (1924), but rearranged in the form adopted in the map of the Chinese marking stars by Needham (1959), and with the positions of the stars computed by Professor K. A. Hämeen-Anttila, Department of Astronomy, University of Oulu.

Margiana Archaeological Complex (fig. 1.17 and § 8.4), whose seals have been discovered as far east as the Ordos region of China.

That the nakṣatra calendar was adopted by the Ṛgvedic Aryans from the earlier inhabitants of northwest India is suggested by the absence of any clear reference to it in the old 'family books' of the Ṛgveda and in the oldest Iranian documents. Exact time-reckoning is not a vital requirement for pastoral nomads. On the other hand, the correlation of lunar and solar time-reckoning was a necessary component of the urbanization process of the early agricultural societies (§ 1.6).

From Palaeolithic markings on bones we know that the earliest time-reckoning was in the easily observed synodic lunar months (each lasting *c.*$29^{d}\ 12^{h}\ 44^{m}\ 3^{s}$), during which the moon completes one series of successive phases. The solar year is roughly 365 days, and 12 lunar months make roughly 354 days, so a purely lunar time-reckoning is out of step with the seasons, which are determined by the yearly course of the sun. The chief interest of the Neolithic and Chalcolithic astronomers therefore undoubtedly concentrated on fixing the course of the sun in relation to the fixed stars, and on correlating the solar and lunar time-reckonings. A lunisolar calendar was an essential instrument in administration and religion: it enabled the co-ordination of trade and agricultural activities (forecasting yearly monsoons and floods) and the celebration of seasonal feasts at the proper time.

A five-year co-ordination period (*yuga*) was employed in Vedic religion to correlate solar and lunar time-reckoning. The solar year was calculated as comprising 12 months of 30 days = 360 days. Five times 360 days + one intercalary month of 30 days makes 1,830 days, giving a length of 366 days for a solar year. (This is about $\frac{3}{4}$ of a day more than the actual length.) The lunar time was reckoned in synodic lunar months. In ritualistic practice, one of each two successive months contained 30 and the other 29 days. Twelve times $29\frac{1}{2}$ makes 354 days (the actual synodic lunar year lasts about 354.3671 days). The difference from the solar year was corrected by intercalating a month of 30 days at the end of the third and the fifth year. The five-year period thus comprised three synodic-lunar years with 12 months and two with 13 months, or 30 months of 29 days and 32 months of 30 days, making altogether 1,830 days.

The solar year is divided into four quarters by the equinoxes and solstices. The vernal and autumnal equinoxes are the two points of time, six months apart (about 21 March and 22 September), when the day and night are of equal length in all parts of the earth. The winter and summer solstices (around 21 December and June respectively) are the year's shortest and longest days. At the equinoxes the sun rises due east and sets due west, but from the vernal equinox to the autumnal equinox the sun rises north of due east, and from the autumnal equinox to the vernal equinox it rises south of due east. The solstices are the times when the sun has reached the extreme northern and southern points in its rising from the horizon.

The shifts in the position of the points of sunrise and sunset against the contours of the horizon were carefully noted by the ancient stargazers. In India as elsewhere, astronomical observations were made primarily at those two moments. Thus Manu (2,101) prescribes: 'Let him stand during the morning twilight, muttering the *sāvitrī* until the sun appears, but (let him recite it) seated in the evening until the constellations can be seen distinctly.' As the earth is constantly revolving, the heavenly bodies seem to rise from the eastern horizon and to wander over the sky until they set in the western horizon.

To pass from one equinox or solstice to the same point takes the sun about $365^{d}\ 5^{h}\ 48^{m}\ 46^{s}$. This 'solar year' is about 20^{m} 23^{s} shorter than the 'sidereal year', $365^{d}\ 6^{h}\ 9^{m}\ 10^{s}$, the time during which the earth makes one revolution around the sun with reference to the fixed stars. As the cycle repeats itself almost identically from one year to another, a given seasonal point can be fixed fairly exactly by reference to the date on which a star first becomes visible at dawn. In ancient Egypt, for example, the flooding of the Nile was announced by the heliacal rising of Sirius.

However, the brightness of the rising sun makes the stars fade and their heliacal observation difficult. In the Indian star calendar the asterisms have been chosen so that they form diametrically opposing pairs; sometimes bright stars have been rejected as markers in favour of stars that are dimmer but more precisely located. This arrangement exploits the opposition of the sun and the full moon: the sun's position among the asterisms can be ascertained from their easily observed conjunctions with the full moon.

This principle, which the Indian calendar shares with the Chinese and Arabic calendars, differs fundamentally from the simpler principle of the contiguity of the sun and the marker star, on which the Egyptian and Mesopotamian star calendars are based. It is true that the opposition of the sun and the full moon was utilized in Mesopotamia, too, but not as the basis of the regular calendar: from about 1100 BC, there is evidence of the use of 26 culmination stars, called after *ziqpu* 'zenith', which were distributed at regular intervals and used for the determination of lunar eclipses and related phenomena. Their number is close to but not identical with the number of nakṣatras (originally 24, then 27 or 28). Moreover, this is a late phenomenon in Mesopotamian astronomy: the texts listing all the nakṣatras date from about the same time.

Apart from scanty and ambiguous data in the earlier texts, the oldest Mesopotamian sources on astronomy are star lists, probably going back to the time of the Third Dynasty of Ur, *c*.2000 BC. Most of the star names are Sumerian. At least from the Fara period (mid-third millennium BC) onwards, the year was reckoned in lunar months of 29 or 30 days, from one first appearance of the sickle of the new moon at the sunset to its next first appearance. The lunar time-reckoning had to be correlated with the solar year, which began around the vernal equinox. Until the first millennium BC, however, there was great irregularity in the intercalation of the thirteenth month, which could be added after either the sixth or the twelfth month of the year. This irregularity has led to the belief that in early times the solar year was determined on the basis of fluctuating seasonal changes (such as the rise of the water in the rivers in the spring) rather than of astronomical observations.

From about 1500 BC onwards, the Mesopotamians had circular astrolabes listing 36 stars, whose heliacal rise divided the year into 12 months. The 36 stars were divided among three concentric circles corresponding to a zone south of, upon, and north of the heavenly equator: each month had the star of the god Ea (Enki) in the outer circle, the star of the god An in the middle circle, and the star of the god Enlil in the innermost circle. The reason for this arrangement was that all the heavenly zones were not visible during the whole year: in the summer, the stars rise north of due east, in the winter south of it, and in the spring and autumn they rise in the 'middle zone'. This threefold division goes back at least to Old Babylonian times (early second millennium BC).

Heliacal observations of calendrical asterisms were certainly made in Vedic times (TB 1,5,2,1). The nakṣatra calendar contains evidence suggesting that it was originally created to determine the 12 solar months. Of the 27 asterisms commonly used, only 24 have a distinct name, and in the Veda, the year is divided into 24 half-months. In China, too, there were originally 24 (later 28) *xiu*. From late Vedic times until the present day, the solar months have names derived from 12 nakṣatras (the *kārttika* month, for example, is the one in which the moon is full in the Pleiades or *kṛttikāḥ*). The solar calendar was then refined by 'lunarizing' it. Three of the asterisms were split into two (called 'former X' and 'latter X'). Thus the moon got a separate 'house' for each night of its sidereal revolution (the period it takes the moon to return to a given point in its orbit, or sidereal lunar month, $27^{d}\ 7^{h}\ 43^{m}\ 11^{s}$). It is now possible to determine each day of the month: one said, for example, 'today is Puṣya', when the moon was in the Puṣya asterism (Pāṇini 4,2,4). The daily conjunctions of the moon were also keenly observed by those in charge of the rituals in order to determine whether the day was auspicious or not, for this varied according to the individual asterisms.

The time when the nakṣatra calendar was compiled can be ascertained from astronomical evidence. Some scholars have denied such a possibility, and indeed many quite unreliable speculations have been put forward. It is easy to understand the scepticism that even acceptable astronomical datings have met, if one remembers that those who presented them did not distinguish between the age of the calendar and the age of the Vedic texts, but actually sought to determine the antiquity of the Vedas by this means. However, a critical sifting of the data leaves two kinds of evidence that can be confidently used.

The path plotted in the sky by the stars chosen as calendrical asterisms and exactly described by later astronomers (in partial agreement with the Chinese tradition) agrees best with the celestial horizon of the twenty-fourth century BC (fig. 11.3). This date agrees remarkably well with another, independent, temporal indicator for the origin of the nakṣatra calendar. All the earliest Vedic lists of the lunar marking stars begin with the constellation Pleiades, and TB 1,2,1,2 emphatically affirms that 'The Pleiades, forsooth, are the beginning of the calendrical asterisms'. (The Arabic star list also begins with the Pleiades; in China, the Pleiades head one of the quadrants into which the celestial circle is divided.) It seems fair to suppose that there was a special reason for starting the list with a given star, and that the reason was that the star marked the beginning of the year. In the following section we shall review the Vedic evidence showing that originally the new year began with the vernal equinox, as it did in ancient Mesopotamia. The nakṣatra calendar seems to have been compiled around the time when the Pleiades rose heliacally at the vernal equinox. The time when the Pleiades was exactly in the equinoctial point was *c*.2240 BC, and it was the asterism closest to the equinoctial point *c*.2720–1760 BC.

The points at which the sun crosses the celestial equator on the equinoxes slowly keep moving westwards along the ecliptic (the apparent path of the sun, moon and the planets among the fixed stars). This precession of the equinoxes causes the equinoxes to occur slightly earlier in each successive sidereal year. Since the time of the compilation of the nakṣatra calendar, the sun's position at the vernal equinox has gradually altered. In the fifth or sixth century AD, the Indian astronomer Brahmagupta reported that in his time the asterism Revatī (δ Piscium) 'had no longitude, being situated precisely at the close of the asterism and commencement of the following one, Aśvinī, without latitude or declination, exactly in the equinoctial point'. The calendrical list was therefore revised by shifting the two last constellations of the earlier list to the beginning of a new list, which is still in use. There is evidence suggesting that Aldebaran (Sanskrit *rohiṇī*) was the original star to be designated the new year star and that the Vedic star list beginning with the Pleiades results from a similar calendrical revision made by the Harappan astronomers around the middle of the third millennium (§§ 14.1 and 14.4). In MUL. APIN, the cuneiform text summarizing astronomical knowledge in Mesopotamia *c.*700 BC, the list of the (17) stars in the path of the moon starts with the Pleiades (^{MUL}MUL).

A serious objection raised against this dating of the nakṣatra calendar is that solar rather than lunar conjunction is assumed to have been the basis of the calendar even at the time of its creation. Ancient calendrical myths, however, preserve a tradition, according to which the new year star was originally the wife of the sun, but was then robbed by the moon (§ 14.4). Another issue critical to this dating of the nakṣatra calendar will be considered in the next section: the Vedic texts are somewhat contradictory as far as the beginning point of the new year is concerned.

11.3 Vernal equinox, due east and the asterism of the new year

The number of seasons in the Vedic texts varies from three to six (spring, summer, rains, autumn, winter and dewy season), but whenever the seasons are enumerated, they begin with spring. On that account, spring is called 'the head' or 'the door' of the year, or 'the mouth' of seasons. As the beginning of the yearly cycle, spring corresponds to the new moon (the beginning of the monthly cycle) and to the sunrise (the beginning of the daily cycle). This is evident from ŚB 2,1,3,3–5 correlating the two halves of the year, the two halves of the month, and day and night with the gods and the ancestors respectively. TB 1,5,2,6–9 specifies that the first 14 nakṣatras, from the Pleiades (*kr̥ttikāḥ*) to the *viśākhe*, are the asterisms of the gods and pass across the southern heavens: it is under these asterisms that one should perform sacrificial rites. The remaining nakṣatras belong to Yama, the king of the dead, and pass across the northern heavens.

The division of the year into two opposing halves, the sun's 'northern course' and 'southern course', is mirrored in the Vedic year-long sacrifice of 360 days, divided into two halves of 180 days in 'forward' and 'reversed' arrangement. The turning-points at the middle and end of the sacrificial year were marked with ten-day festivals ending in days called *viṣuvat* and *mahāvrata* respectively. *Viṣuvat* is the term used of 'equinox' in Sanskrit, and its derivatives in modern Indian languages (e.g. Malayalam *viṣu*) denote the festival of the vernal equinox. If the viṣuvat was celebrated when the sun was in conjunction with the Pleiades (*kr̥ttikāḥ*) at the vernal equinox, then the mahāvrata, with its 'sacred marriage' rituals (§ 14.2), took place when the moon was full in the Pleiades at the autumnal equinox, at the end of the rainy season. This is suggested also by the names of the individual stars making up the Pleiades (enumerated, e.g., in KS 40,4), for several of them relate either to rain (*varṣayantī*) or to rain clouds (*abhrayantī*, *meghayantī*).

However, several Vedic texts clearly attest to a different (and undoubtedly secondary) scheme of celebrating the viṣuvat and mahāvrata festivals during the summer and winter solstice respectively (cf. AB 18,8). In this case the sacrificial year started at the winter solstice with the new moon (and the sun) in the asterism of *maghāḥ* (cf. KB 19,3), or in the next asterism of *phalgunī(ḥ)* (cf. e.g. KB 4,4; 5,1). According to R̥S 10,85,13, this was the time when the marriage of Soma (the moon) and the sun-maid Sūryā was celebrated, while the Rāmāyaṇa (1,70,24; 1,71,12) connects it with the marriage of Rāma and Sītā. Even in this scheme, the vernal equinox coincided with the Pleiades: for when the asterisms *kr̥ttikāḥ* and *viśākhe* defined the equinoxes, the asterisms *maghāḥ* (also called *aghāḥ*) and *śraviṣṭhāḥ* (also called *dhaniṣṭhā*) defined the solstices. The Buddhist texts Mahāvastu (3,305–10) and Lalitavistara (24) also single out these very asterisms: they head the four groups of nakṣatras allotted to the four cardinal directions.

According to ŚB 2,1,3,5, the sacred fires may be set up during the auspicious half of the year when the sun moves northwards, and more specifically, a Brahman (as a member of the first-ranking social class) should set up his fires in the spring, a kṣatriya in the summer, and a vaiśya in the rainy season. The Pleiades are mentioned first among the several nakṣatras under which the fires may be set up (2,1,2,1ff.). In this context it is stated that the Pleiades 'do not move away from the eastern quarter, whilst the other asterisms do move from the eastern quarter'. Jean Filliozat (1962) has interpreted this to mean that while the east is defined by the sun's rising above the horizon in the east, due east or the east *par excellence* is defined by the sun's double rising at the vernal equinox: the sun rises into the northern hemisphere as well.

The dictum, 'The Pleiades do not forsake the eastern direction', is cited also in Baudhāyana's Śrautasūtra (25,5). This is the earliest Vedic text to deal with the methods of orientation (*c.*700 BC); it prescribes that the measuring (of the sacrificial hut with the eastward-oriented beam) is to be done on the appearance of the Pleiades in the horizon. Here and in the Mānava-Śulbasūtra (10,1,1,3) other asterisms are mentioned as alternatives.

It is most likely that this method was being used by the Harappans before this period. The axes of Mohenjo-daro diverge by 1° to 2° clockwise from the cardinal points. Holger Wanzke (1987: 37) has explained this divergence by assuming that the axes were oriented towards the setting point of the Pleiades and the star Aldebaran, which could be observed on the horizon.

The Vedic texts do mention another simple method of orientation. Kātyāyana-Śulbasūtra (2) prescribes:

Driving a peg (i.e. the gnomon) into a levelled (ground), and drawing a circle with a rope whose length is equal to the (length of) the (gnomon) peg, one drives two (other) pegs at the two (points on the circular) line where the shadow of the tip of the (gnomon) peg falls (in the forenoon and in the afternoon when it is coming into, and going out of, the circle). This (i.e. the straight line between the two pegs) is the east(–west line).

One of the favourite Harappan decorative motifs on the painted pottery is the 'intersecting circles', which suggests that this common orientation method was also known at the time of the Indus Civilization.

But let us return to the establishment of the sacred fires. The divinity presiding over the Pleiades is the fire-god Agni, and this is one reason why the sacred fires are to be set up under this particular asterism. ŚB 2,1,2,4–5 explains that originally the Pleiades were the wives of the Seven Sages, but are now precluded from intercourse with their husbands, as the Seven Sages (the stars of the Ursa Major) rise in the north, but the Pleiades in the east. Now the Pleiades have Agni as their mate, and it is with Agni that they have intercourse.

This fragmentary account is one of the earliest versions of the famous Hindu myth of the birth of the war-god Skanda, whose metronym *Kārttikeya* connects him with the Pleiades (*kṛttikāḥ*). According to the fuller epic versions, Agni (or Śiva) seduced the Pleiades in the absence of their husbands, the Seven Sages. Only Arundhatī, the faithful wife of sage Vasiṣṭha, could not be seduced, and was allowed to remain as the star Alcor together with her husband, in the asterism of the Great Bear; the other wives were divorced. In some variants, the six Pleiades were bathing in the Ganges river (i.e. the heavenly river of ecliptic), where the fiery seed of Agni or Śiva fell down. They became pregnant by the seed, or nursed the child instantly born of the seed. In order to suck all his nurses simultaneously, Skanda developed six faces. Skanda evidently symbolizes the new year (with its six seasons), i.e. the (re)born sun.

We shall return to this ancient myth many times. In this connection, I would like to emphasize the dominant position occupied by its central figures in the nakṣatra calendar and its creation. The calendar starts with the Pleiades, which marked the beginning of the new year (i.e. the birth of the sun). All the stars of the ecliptic are not simultaneously visible in the sky; some of them are under the horizon. Therefore the choice of stellar oppositions, which is the basis of the nakṣatra calendar, must have been achieved by means of clearly recognizable circumpolar stars, such as the Ursa Major: only stars close enough to the pole of the rotating heavens never go beneath the horizon and are available for taking bearings at all times.

The great Holi festival around the vernal equinox is celebrated by burning bonfires in many places in India; this custom is connected with the burning of the god of love and with the birth of Skanda (§ 12.2). Another name for Holi is *āvīrotsava*, 'the feast of red dust', which is flung at and daubed on all people, and explained as representing 'the vermilion hue of the dawn or rising sun' (Wayman 1965: 304). (For the red colour and Skanda, see § 13.4.)

This myth connects the birth of the Hindu war-god Skanda with the Pleiades. Many other Vedic texts, starting with the Ṛgveda, relate another myth which connects the birth of the Vedic war-god Rudra with the star *Rohiṇī*, the red star Aldebaran. According to the Aitareya-Brāhmaṇa (3,33), the creator-god 'Prajāpati felt love towards his own daughter, the sky some say, Uṣas [the Dawn] others. Having become a stag he approached her in the form of a red she-antelope (*rohit*) ... [which] is *Rohiṇī* "the red (star)".' In order to punish Prajāpati for his incest, the gods created a killer, Rudra, out of their own most dread forms. Rudra, who shot Prajāpati, is in a parallel version (KB 6,1) represented as the son of Prajāpati. The different versions of this myth allow a naturalistic interpretation: Rudra is the rising sun, who with his arrow-like rays kills his father, the moon (impersonating also the night), the paramour of the calendrical star (identified with the dawn, the time of its heliacal rise).

The moon is specifically connected with the asterism Rohiṇī also in different myths, to be discussed later (§ 14.4), together with other evidence suggesting that originally it was not the Pleiades but Aldebaran that started the nakṣatra calendar. Aldebaran's heliacal rise at the vernal equinox, *c*.3054 BC, would date the beginnings of Indian astronomy in the times of the Early Harappan (Kot Dijian) culture. This is in agreement with the development of astronomy and writing in Mesopotamia and other early civilizations before the era corresponding to the Mature Harappan phase (§ 1.6).

The hypothesis of a Harappan or even Early Harappan origin of the nakṣatra calendar is supported by a Dravidian etymology for an obsolete name of the nakṣatras, no longer understood in Vedic times. In a mantra used in the fire-altar ritual, it is said: 'The most blessed sun-rayed moon is the gandharva (i.e. fertility spirit); his apsarases (i.e. mistresses) are the stars, *bhēkuri* by name' (VS 18,42). The Śatapatha-Brāhmaṇa (9,4,1,9), commenting on the name, explains: '*bhākuri* these, indeed, are called, for the stars make light (*bhāṁ hi nakṣatrāṇi kurvanti*)'. This Sanskrit etymology cannot be right, for parallel texts have handed down the name in the form *bēkuri* (KS 18,14; MS 2,12,2) or *vēkuri* (KapS 29,3). In another mantra, this ancient word for star appears in the form *bēkurā* (PB 1,3,1; 6,7,6; LŚS 1,11,9) or *vēkurā* (JB 1,82). It is invoked as the name of the goddess Vāc, who is further identified with the goddess Sarasvatī. Both Vāc and

Sarasvatī appear as goddesses of war and victory in the Veda, anticipating the later Hindu goddess Durgā (§ 14.2), whose intimate connection with the morning star and specifically Rohiṇī we shall discuss later (§ 14.4).

A suitable Dravidian etymology is offered by the word *vaikuṟu mīṉ* 'morning star' occurring in several Old Tamil texts (Akam 17,21; Perumpāṇ. 318; Naṟṟiṇai 48,4); cf. also *vaikal mīṉ* 'morning star' (Maturaikkāñci 108). Related words meaning 'morning star' are found also in Gondi (*viyā sukum*) and Kui (*vēgam boḍuri*). Tamil *vaikuṟu* 'daybreak' is derived from the Proto-Dravidian roots **vay-k-* / **vey-k-* 'to halt, dwell, stay the night, pass the night, protract till dawn, to dawn; to cohabit', and **uṟu* / **uṯ V* 'to be near, be joined, come in contact with, dwell, abide, have sexual intercourse with'. The meanings of both roots agree with those of the Sanskrit root *vas-* 'to dwell, stay overnight, have sexual intercourse', which is used of the moon in connection with a nakṣatra (ŚB 10,5,4,17 *candramā nakṣatre vasati*), and with the Vedic notion that 'King Soma (i.e. the moon) cohabits with all the nakṣatras, for Soma is the seed-layer' (ṢB 3,12). The changes **v-* > *b-* and **ay* / **ey* > *ē* are both characteristic of North Dravidian. There are other examples for Proto-Dravidian intervocalic **-ṯ-* > Sanskrit *-r-* and for PDr **-k-* > Skt *-k-*.

These two sections have therefore shown that there is substantial evidence to the effect that the Vedic nakṣatra calendar was devised by the Harappans or even Early Harappans, and that its original language was Dravidian.

11.4 Astral proper names in India

The interpretation of the 'fish' signs of the Indus seals in terms of stars and the planets implies that the Indus people had astral proper names (§§ 7.5 and 10.1). To what extent is this hypothesis warranted by later Indian onomastics and name-giving practices? This section maintains that the habit of naming the child according to its birth star was adopted by Vedic Aryans from the earlier inhabitants of India along with the astral calendar.

The Vedic Gṛhyasūtras contain the earliest systematic expositions of ancient Indian name-giving. The specifications concerning the name of the child are usually given in connection with the name-giving ceremony proper (celebrated on the tenth or twelfth day after the birth), but in some texts in connection with the birth ritual. Gobhila distinguishes between the secret (*guhyam*) name mentioned at the birth (2,7,15–16), the name given at the name-giving ceremony (2,8,14–16), and the name used in formal addresses, chosen by the teacher at the time of the initiation (2,10,23–5); this last name is derived either from the child's birth nakṣatra or from its presiding deity, or from the clan name.

In Āpastamba-Gṛhyasūtra 6,15,2–3, the father mentions the child's nakṣatra name at the birth, and this is the secret (*rahasyam*) name. Bhavatrāta (on Jaiminīya-Śrautasūtra 1,7,5) calls the nakṣatra name 'the god-given name' of the newborn. Jaiminīya-Gṛhyasūtra 1,9, dealing with the name-giving ceremony, prescribes that the name should be formed after the nakṣatra (of the child's birth), after the deity (presiding over the birth nakṣatra) or after the names current in the child's family; and in the name-giving ritual as well as on the birthdays of the boy, the father should make a sacrificial libation of ghee to the nakṣatra, to the deity of the nakṣatra, and to the lunar day (of the boy's birth). According to Āgniveśya-Gṛhyasūtra 2,2,1, the birthday is celebrated on the day of the birth nakṣatra every year, every six months, every four months, every season, or every month.

But do we actually have any evidence that the nakṣatra names are earlier than the Gṛhyasūtras and that they are intrusions in the Vedic tradition from non-Vedic circles? In connection with the name-giving, the Gṛhyasūtras quote early Brāhmaṇa texts, which explain why a Brahman should have two names and, more specifically, why one of these names should be the nakṣatra name. Thus the Śatapatha-Brāhmaṇa (3,6,2,24) says of the seven *dhiṣṇya* hearths (§ 12.2) of the sacrificial area (fig. 12.15), which it identifies with the mythical Gandharvas, that they

> have two names; for, in truth, they themselves insisted thereon, saying, 'We have not prospered with these names, since Soma has been taken away from us; well, then, let us take each a second name!' They took each a second name, and therewith prospered, inasmuch as they from whom the Soma-draught had been taken away had a share in the sacrifice assigned to them; hence they have two names. Wherefore let a Brāhman, if he prosper not, take a second name, for verily he prospers, whosoever, knowing this, takes a second name.

The Soma drink is identified with the moon and the dhiṣṇya fireplaces with the Gandharvas, who once guarded the Soma in the sky. In ŚB 5,1,4,8, the Gandharvas are said to be 27 in number, which clearly associates them with the 27 lunar asterisms. On the human level, the Gandharvas appear to represent the hostile earlier inhabitants of the northwest, the habitat of the Soma plant, whose sap the Aryans sacrificed to Indra and other gods. The gods (i.e. the Aryans) forcefully took the Soma away from the Gandharvas, but allowed them a subsidiary share in the Soma sacrifice: they now guard the Soma on the earth even as they formerly did in the sky. This myth seems to reflect the conquest of non-Vedic people practising a fire cult and having astral names, who adopted new Vedic names after becoming (inferior) members of the Vedic society.

Furthermore, a number of proper names derived from the names of the lunar asterisms *Aṣāḍhāḥ*, *Rohiṇī* and *Citrā* are known from the Brāhmaṇa texts: Aṣāḍha Kaiśin, Āṣāḍhi Sauśromateya, Aṣāḍha Sāvayasa, Aṣāḍha Bhāllabeya, Gaireya Āṣāḍhi, and Aṣāḍha Uttara Pārāśarya; Rauhiṇa Vāsiṣṭha and Rauhiṇāyana; and Citra Gāṅgyāyani. Other nakṣatra names are found in the teacher genealogies of the late Vaṁśa-Brāhmaṇa: Śravaṇa-datta, Puṣya-yaśas and Mūla-mitra.

The Vedic texts comprise hundreds of proper names, but the number of nakṣatra names and names derived from deities (presiding over the nakṣatras) is very small. V. S. Agrawala (1963: 182) has even mistakenly claimed that no names of this kind are found in the Veda, suggesting that 'such naming came into vogue in much later times with a change in religious beliefs'. Around the fifth century BC the situation is radically different, for the grammarian Pāṇini (4,3,34–7; 8,3,100) gives elaborate rules concerning the formation of proper names from the names of asterisms. Astral names are frequent in early Buddhist texts, too. P. V. Kane explains this change in this way: 'In the times of the Brāhmaṇas nakṣatra names were secret and so not met with. Gradually however nakṣatra names ceased to be secret and became common' (Kane 1941: II.1, 248).

Even today there is secrecy in Indian name-giving. Knowledge of the name gives power over a thing or person (cf. AS 7,12,2; 19,48,6; SVB 2,5), so keeping the name secret protects its owner against sorcery (cf. Devapāla on KāṭhGS 36,4; Nārāyaṇa on GGS 2,7,15). According to some Gṛhyasūtras, the secret name of the child was known by the parents only until the initiation, that is, until the second birth into adulthood, when the dangers of childhood were essentially over.

Secret names derived from the names of calendrical asterisms certainly existed as early as the Brāhmaṇa period:

> He may also set up his fires under the Phalgunīs. They, the Phalgunīs, are Indra's asterism, and even correspond to him in name; for indeed Indra is also called Arjuna, this being his secret name (*guhyaṁ nāma*); and they (the Phalgunīs) are also called Arjunīs [cf. ṚS 10,85,13]. Hence he overtly calls them Phalgunīs, for who dares to use his (the god's) secret name? (ŚB 2,1,2,11)

Another likely reason for the scarcity of nakṣatra names in Vedic texts is the non-Vedic origin of this tradition. Those that are found were probably adopted as a result of mixed marriages. Manu (3,9) among others prohibits marriage with a girl 'named after a constellation, a tree, or a river, one bearing the name of a low caste, or of a mountain, or one named after a bird, a snake, or a slave, or one whose name inspires terror'. Such prohibitions of astral names, contradictory to the express prescriptions to give the child a name after its birth asterism, have been explained as follows:

> Whatever convention the pre-Aryans may have followed in naming their children, it is now lost ... But much can be learned of the general tendency among non-Aryans in an indirect way from the prohibitions imposed on Aryans in this matter, since the early Aryans could not very well adopt the practice current among their despised subjects. Thus Vedic Aryans avoided personal names from the vocabulary of divine or religious nomenclature ... The custom of giving names of deities may have been common among non-Aryans, if we are to judge from its prevalence in South India even to the present day ... The names of stars, constellations, planets, sun, moon, asterisms, were also avoided in Vedic times by the Aryans, as was the use of names taken from nature e.g. of mountains, hills, rivers, forests ... since nature names were current among the non-Aryans ... In course of time the Aryans themselves adopted the native convention which became quite common. (Walker 1968: II, 116f.)

The inclusion of girls with names denoting low castes and foreign tribes in the list of unacceptable brides indeed makes this explanation likely, and thus speaks strongly for a pre-Vedic Indian origin of the nakṣatra names.

The very late Vaikhānasa-Gṛhyasūtra (3,14) is the only one to speak of the planets in connection with the birth ritual. According to this text, the father should ascertain the position of the planets and stars in his son's natal horoscope at the precise moment when the tip of the nose emerges from the womb. Ever since those times, casting such a birth horoscope has been a most important affair in India. It is a vital document at the time of marriage, for the horoscopes of the bride and the groom have to match. It is true that the planetary astronomy used in casting this horoscope is of Babylonian and Greek origin and came to India from the West only around AD 200. But the birth asterism of the child was anxiously observed long before this, in early Vedic times. This is shown by the Atharvavedic hymn 6,110, which was recited as an expiatory charm if the child was born under an unlucky star.

Planetary proper names can be found in Vedic texts predating any Babylonian influence, though they are still rarer than nakṣatra names. Thus the names of *Saurāyaṇi* Gārgya (Praśna-Upaniṣad 1,1), *Sūrya-datta* (ŚĀ 7,4) and Gotama *Rāhūgaṇa* (ŚB 11,4,3,20) are derived from the sun (*sūrya*) and the eclipse demon (*rāhu*) respectively. The name of King *Hariścandra* in AB 7,13 means 'the yellow moon'. The name *Budha Saumāyana* in PB 24,18,6 agrees with that of the planet Mercury (*budha*), the son of the moon (*soma*). *Baudhāyana*, the name of an early Yajurvedic Sūtra author, is likewise derived from *Budha* (Mercury).

Outside the Vedic area, such names are more frequent and fairly early. Among the oldest examples is the name given by the Buddha to his son, *Rāhula*, i.e. *Rāhu-datta* 'given by the eclipse demon Rāhu', i.e. born at the time of an eclipse. Another well-known name is *Candra-gupta*, 'protected by the moon', the founder of the Maurya dynasty of Magadha in the fourth century BC. According to an inscription dated AD 150, the brother-in-law of the emperor Candragupta was called *Puṣya-gupta*, 'protected by the lunar asterism Puṣya'.

Among the clearly planetary names of the Mahābhārata (12,29,81–2) is that of King *Aṅgāra* 'live coal, the planet Mars'. According to Harivaṁśa (23,130–2), a king called *Aṅgāra* or *Aṅgāra-setu* has given his name to a large part of Gandhāra. This area originally belonged to the Harappan culture and remained outside the sphere of the classical Vedic culture, as did the Madra country of the upper Indus Valley, where a king was called *Aṅgāra-prabha* 'having the brilliance of Mars'. The name of his son, *Candra-prabha* 'having the brilliance of the moon', leaves no doubt about the planetary reference (Kathāsaritsāgara 8,1,17). The planet Mars is also called *aṅgāraka*, and in Mahābhārata 3,249,10 a prince named *Aṅgāraka* is localized in Sauvīra, i.e. the region of Sindh and Gujarat. Early historical sources on this core area of the Indus Civilization are scanty, so it is difficult to be certain how representative such isolated names are. But this particular name certainly suggests a continuity in Sindhi name-giving from the times of the epics until the present day.

More recently it has been possible to study Sindhi personal names systematically. Planetary names, such as *Maṅgala-dāsu* 'devotee of Mars', 'were very common among males during prepartition days' (Gidwani 1981). The sun, the moon, stars (e.g. male name *Tārā-candu* 'moon in conjunction with a star', female name *Tārā*), constellations (e.g. male name *Mūl-candu*) and the dawn are other astral terms commonly occurring as the first part of a Sindhi name. Other words occurring in this position denote rivers, flowers and trees, animals (including birds), gems, metals, seashells and ornaments, human qualities, and names of gods and mythical heroes, as well as words related to protective magic. In their semantic content, then, the Sindhi names conform closely to those name types which, as we have seen, were considered as inadmissible for prospective brides by the orthodox Brahmanical lawgivers more than two millennia ago.

Planetary names are current also among some Dravidian-speaking peoples, such as the Koragas of South Canara, or the Koṇḍa Dora and the Bison-horn Maria Gondis of Andhra Pradesh. But in all these cases, the names of the planets are derived from their Sanskrit names as they appear in the names of the days of the week, for nowadays planetary names are usually given on the basis of the day of the week on which the child is born. But we have seen that the worship of the planets in India predates the introduction of the seven-day week and that a few planetary names also date from this early period. A pre-Aryan planetary name may have survived among the isolated tribe of the Todas in the Nilgiris of South India. The Todas speak a Dravidian language which separated from Tamil in the third century BC or earlier. One of the male personal names of the Todas is *Kwïṭnaṣpiḷy*, which has purely Dravidian components meaning 'the planet Venus (*piḷy*), beautiful (*naṣ*) with a lock of hair (*kwïṭ*)'.

We started interpreting the 'fish' signs of the Indus script according to these premisses:

1 The inscriptions of the Indus seals record mainly proper names and official titles.
2 The proper names are probably mostly theophoric, i.e. contain names of divinities as components. Priestly titles, too, are likely to mention divine names.
3 The gods' names may have been expressed through the 'fish' signs, which have a suitable frequency and distribution.
4 Reading these signs in Dravidian implies that deities were represented by stars.

We have seen that the Gṛhyasūtras prescribe two kinds of proper names which the Vedic people are likely to have adopted from the earlier inhabitants of India: names derived from stars and names derived from deities. In the latter case, the deity is that presiding over the child's birth star, as is made plain by several Vedic texts (GGS 2,10,24; MGS 1,18,2; BaudhGS 2,1,28; JGS 1,9).

The nakṣatra names are derived from the asterism under which a person was born. Likewise, the planetary names are nowadays derived from the planet which rules the day of the week coinciding with the child's birth. In the Harappan inscriptions, the 'fish' signs interpretable as designations of stars or planets do not always occur singly, but may form a string of two or three consecutive 'fish' signs. In personal names, such a collection of 'fish' signs might represent the stellar conjunction at the moment of birth. But other kinds of astronomical, astrological or mythological relationships between the different heavenly bodies are also conceivable. For instance, the planets Jupiter and Venus are often (at least eight times) mentioned together in the Mahābhārata, because they are the mythical teachers and court priests of the gods and demons respectively. Mercury and Venus are both seen only in connection with the sunrise and the sunset; there are at least three comparisons in the epic mentioning them together. There are dual and even triadic deities in both the Vedic and Hindu religions, and in Indian personal names the names of several gods may be combined (e.g. Rādhā-Kṛṣṇa, Rāma-Kṛṣṇa, etc.).

In contrast to early Vedic texts, where names derived from the names of deities are rarely met with, theophoric names predominate in post-Vedic India, as they do in ancient Mesopotamia. Such names express the conviction that the child has been given – or is protected or owned – by the god mentioned in the name: 'The Brahmans and her father gave her the name of Sāvitrī, for she had been given by (the goddess) Sāvitrī when she was pleased with the oblations he had offered with the *sāvitrī* formula' (Mahābhārata 3,277,24). The manuals of religious sects, such as the Jayākhya-Saṁhitā of the Vaiṣṇavas (5,127), prescribe that initiated members should be given names not only mentioning the name of their god but also expressing his 'lordship', 'ownership', or the like. The late Vedic Mānava-Gṛhyasūtra (1,18,2), while prescribing that the child should be given a name derived either from its birth star or from the deity (of that star), actually forbids giving the child the actual name of the god. Thus it was possible to call a child *Rudra-datta* 'given by Rudra', but not just *Rudra*. Yet such names do occur – apparently they are abbreviated pet-names – and are now very common.

12 The trefoil motif: further evidence for astral religion

12.1 Indus bull figurines and dresses

The 'fish' pictograms of the Indus script are not the only indications of the possibility that stars and planets may have played an important role in the Harappan religion. In 1931, C. J. Gadd (in Mackay 1931a: I, 356f., n. 2) assumed an astral symbolism for the trefoil decoration of the garment worn by the statue of the 'priest-king', one of the best known and most cited examples of Harappan art (fig. 12.1). In this chapter we shall take a closer look at this hypothesis, concentrating on the symbolism of the 'trefoil'.

The designation 'priest-king' goes back to Sir John Marshall (1931a: I, 54), who thought that 'probably it is the statue of a priest or maybe of a king-priest, since it lacks the horns which would naturally be expected if it were a figure of the deity himself'. Marshall's argument is invalid, however. The two holes drilled just beneath the ears and the flat circular patch on the crown of the head suggest that interchangeable head-dresses could be secured there with metal hooks. The buffalo-horned crown of the 'Proto-Śiva' is a likely possibility. The 'Proto-Śiva' (fig. 10.18) squats with the knees bent and hands on his knees. The 'priest-king' was probably represented in a seated position, which is an expression of senior status and authority: it shares many features with other seated statues from Mohenjo-daro, and the right arm is bent forwards, evidently for the hand to rest on the knee.

The 'priest-king's' cloak is decorated all over with a design of trefoils in relief. There is a shallow pitting in the middle of each trefoil roundel, suggesting that it had been made by the point of a drill. Two linked concentric circles or 'figures-of-eight' are seen at the top of the back. There are also single circles with a dot. All these designs were once filled in with red pigment, traces of which remain here and there.

Trefoils and occasionally quatrefoils, cut into the stone surface and originally inlaid with lapis lazuli and carnelian, are found on several small amulets from Sumer which are in the shape of reclining bulls; they come from Uruk and are dated

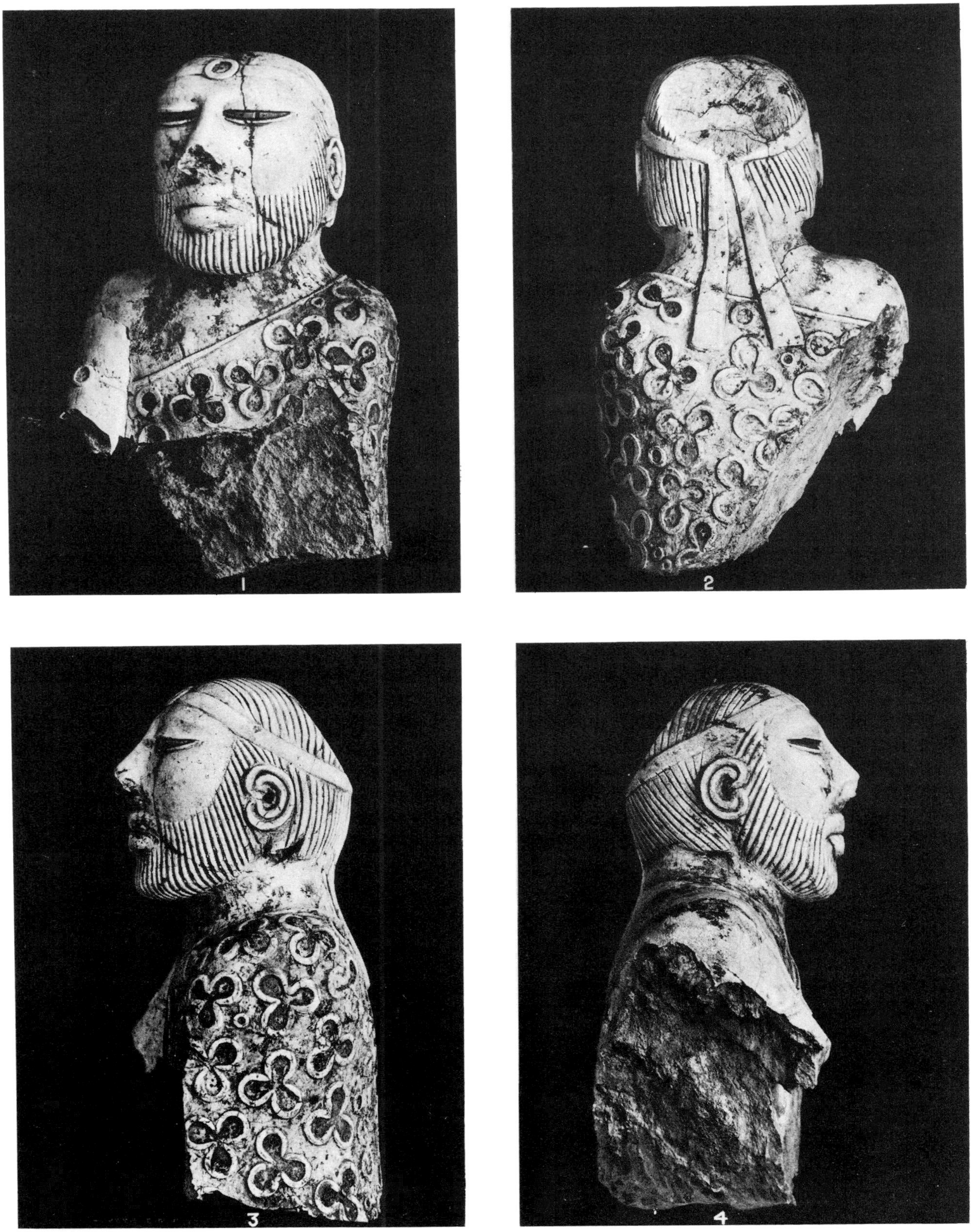

Fig. 12.1. The 'priest-king' statue from Mohenjo-daro (DK 1909), viewed from different sides. White steatite, with remnants of red paste inside the trefoils of the robe. Height (after repair) 17 cm. National Museum of Pakistan, Karachi. After Marshall 1931a: pl. 98.

Fig. 12.2. A bull statuette with trefoil inlays from Uruk (w 16017), *c.*3000 BC. Shell mass with inlays of lapis lazuli. Length 5.3 cm. Vorderasiatisches Museum, Berlin.

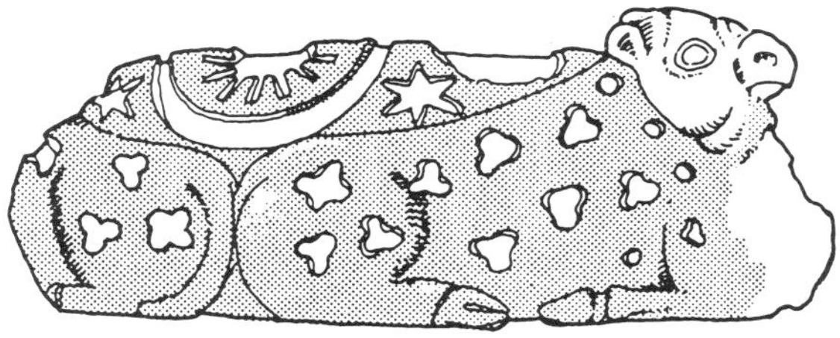

Fig. 12.3. A bull incumbent and decorated with trefoils. Fragment of a steatite bowl from Ur (U.239), *c.* twenty-first century BC. The explicitly astral symbols of the sun, the (sickle of) moon, and stars, which have been added to this later image of a reclining bull, suggest that trefoils and quatrefoils, which alone appear in the older statuettes (fig. 12.2), had a similar meaning. They could at the same time represent hair-whorls in the animal's hide. After Ardeleanu-Jansen 1989: 205, fig. 19. Cf. Woolley 1955: 52 and pl. 35; Hartner 1965: 4 and pl. 6, fig. 12.

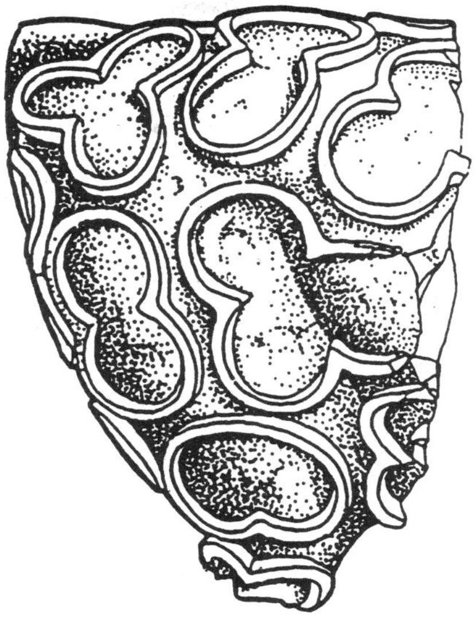

Fig. 12.4. Trefoil-decorated bull. Fragment of a steatite statuette from Mohenjo-daro (SD 767). Traces of red pigment remain inside the trefoils. After Ardeleanu-Jansen 1989: 196, fig. 1.

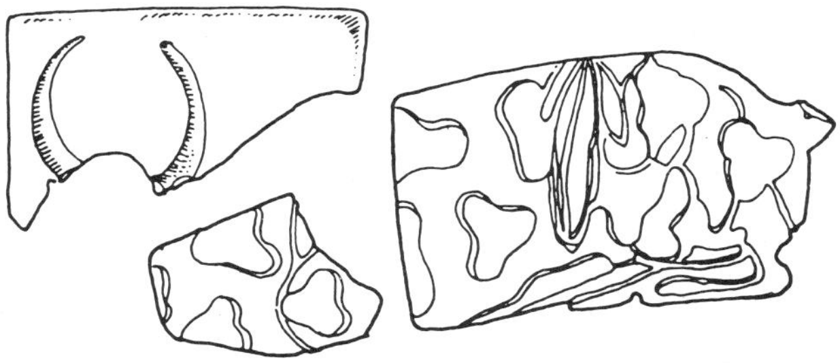

Fig. 12.5. Fragments of alabaster mosaic in the form of a bull ornamented with trefoils. From the 'palace' of Dashly-3 in north Afghanistan, *c.*1800 BC. After Ardeleanu-Jansen 1989: 205, fig. 20.

to the Jemdet Nasr period (*c.*3100–2900 BC) (fig. 12.2). In the time of Gudea and the Third Dynasty of Ur (*c.*2100–2000 BC), trefoils decorate a couple of small stone reclining bulls with a bearded human head from Tello and similar bulls surround a bowl from Ur (fig. 12.3). C. J. Gadd's suggestion quoted at the beginning of this chapter was based on the assumption that the Sumerian bulls with trefoils are 'representations of the "Bull of Heaven" (a Babylonian name for one of the constellations [i.e. Taurus]) and therefore the trefoils represent stars'.

The Harappans, too, associated the trefoil pattern with cattle. A steatite fragment from Mohenjo-daro represents an animal decorated all over with trefoils, with some red pigment still visible inside the trefoils. Though the head and feet are missing, the animal may be identified as a bull (fig. 12.4). An alabaster mosaic representing humped bulls decorated with trefoils has been found at Dashly-3 in north Afghanistan (fig. 12.5). The treasure found at Quetta in 1985, culturally related to Dashly, included a large number of trefoils shown in outline and made of ivory. These discoveries show that Harappan traditions, apparently with all their associated symbolism, were taken over by the Bronze Age culture of Bactria and brought back to the Indus Valley around the nineteenth century BC. This warrants the expectation that relevant information may have survived in the later Aryan sources of India and Central Asia.

In 1949, A. Leo Oppenheim analysed the cuneiform texts and monumental evidence relating to 'the golden garments of the gods' and divine kings. Numerous Neo-Babylonian texts of the seventh century BC refer to the making of splendid festive garments reserved for divine beings alone. The Neo-Babylonian documents provide ample evidence for attaching golden ornaments described as rosettes, stars (*mul.guškin*), discs, rings and lions. Although these texts are rather late, sporadic textual references testify to the existence of such 'golden garments' as early as around 2000 BC. Such a

Fig. 12.6. A gold rosette with four holes for fixing it on clothing. From an Uruk period tomb at Tepe Gawra, late fourth millennium BC. After Mallowan in Piggott 1961: fig. 43.

use has now been attested also in Ebla around the twenty-fourth century BC. The oldest archaeological evidence for 'golden garments' comes from the twelfth stratum of Tepe Gawra representing the Uruk period (*c.*3500–3200 BC): it consists of thin gold rosettes which have 'four small holes (arranged approximately in a rectangle) near the center and were therefore obviously destined to be sewed onto some fabric' (fig. 12.6). This prompted Oppenheim to suggest that the trefoils in the garment of the Harappan 'priest-king' 'could be interpreted as representing some kind of appliqué work of metal or cut-out materials of contrasting texture and/or colour to decorate a monochrome garment' (1949: 188). In fact, Mackay (1931a: I, 362), while discussing the shawl of the 'priest-king', had already found that 'the prominence of the design suggests that the trefoils and circles were sewn or fastened on in some way instead of being woven in the material'.

What do the Near Eastern sources tell us about the ideological implications of these decorative ornaments? In his report to the king, a Babylonian astrologer quotes some ritual text as follows:

The sixteenth (and) seventeenth day a bull shall be slaughtered ... before Nabū, the eighteenth day he (the god) shall be clad in AN.MA.

The logograms *AN.MA* (as well as their Akkadian gloss *nalbaš šamê*) literally denote 'garment of the sky'. In Oppenheim's opinion (1949: 180f.), this text evidently refers to 'vestment of the image of Nabū, decorated with stars sewed on'. This seems to be confirmed by Nonnos (Dionysiaca 40,367-416), who in the fifth century AD described Dionysus' visit to the temple of the 'Starclad God' (*Bēl astrokhítōn*), the guardian deity of the Syrian city of Tyrus. The cult image was 'clad in a patterned robe like the sky, an image of the universe', and Dionysus in his hymn of praise states: 'Be thou called the Starclad, since by night starry mantles illuminate the sky.'

But the phrase *nalbaš šamê* has another meaning too, for in a lexical text it is identified with *erpētu* (*ur-pi-ti*) 'clouds', which cover the sky like a garment. In this latter meaning it is attested twice in the great astrological text Enuma Anu ^{d}Enlil.

Clouds and stars are thus placed in a relationship which is difficult for us to appreciate and to grasp, which, however, on a different level of artistic expression, is patently paralleled by the comparative ease with which stars and rosettes are seen in hair whirls. (Oppenheim 1949: 187, n. 25)

One may speculate that the special value of stars in the divine garments may be due to the fact that star was the symbol of divinity in Mesopotamia (§§ 2.2; 10.1–2).

The Near Eastern data relating to the Harappan 'priest-king's' garment have some striking but so far overlooked parallels in the Indian tradition, starting with the hymns of the Ṛgveda. Significantly, these Indian parallels are intimately associated with Varuṇa, the divine king *par excellence*, who as the chief Asura appears originally to have been the principal god of the Dāsas, the probable rulers of Bronze Age Bactria (§ 8.4). Varuṇa is the guardian of the cosmic order and truth, but also the god of waters (§ 10.2). As the lord of the heavenly waters he naturally controls rain, and is in numerous hymns implored to send rain: 'Wet our pastures with (gushes of) melted butter!' 'Grant in abundance lovely heavenly water!' In ṚS 7,64,1, 'clothes of ghee' are attributed to Varuṇa and Mitra who in the following verse are asked to send rain down from heaven. 'Ghee' here stands for rain, and the garments of Varuṇa and Mitra for rainclouds.

According to ṚS 1,25,13, King 'Varuṇa bearing a golden mantle dons a shining dress, while his spies sit around him'. It is likely that the rainclouds were not the only model for Varuṇa's 'shining' dress. In the description of Varuṇa's hall in the waters Mahābhārata 2,9,6 says that Varuṇa 'wears celestial jewellery and attire, adorned with celestial ornaments'. A clue to the nature of Varuṇa's bejewelled attire is provided by a comparison in Mahābhārata 10,1,25: 'Adorned with planets, constellations and stars that have been scattered all over, the night sky, like a festal garment, shines everywhere beautiful to the view.' In the Avesta, the stars are explicitly mentioned as ornaments of Ahura Mazda's sky-garment: 'The sky ... which the Wise one is wearing as his garment, is decorated with stars, made of a heavenly substance' (Yašt 13,3). It is generally accepted that Ahura Mazda, the chief deity of the Zarathustran pantheon, corresponds to Varuṇa, the greatest Asura in the Ṛgveda.

The Brāhmaṇa texts appear to connect Varuṇa with the nocturnal heaven. On the one hand, this world is said to be Mitra and that (celestial) world Varuṇa (ŚB 12,9,2,12). On the other hand, the day belongs to Mitra and the night to Varuṇa (TS 2,1,7,4). In fact Varuṇa is often directly equated with the night (e.g. KS 22,6). The colour black is characteristic of the night and darkness (MS 2,5,7, etc.) and 'whatever is black belongs to Varuṇa' (ŚB 5,2,5,17).

Stars and blackness are among the principal characteristics of the night sky and there is general agreement that the stars are meant in R̥S 10,127,1, where the goddess Night is said to have arrived, looked in many places (or directions) with her many eyes, and to have put upon herself all her splendid ornaments (or royal insignia). In R̥S 7,34,10, Varuṇa is thousand-eyed. Why? Varuṇa is the righteous king of the universe, whose duty it is to see that the eternal laws are followed and to punish wrongdoers. For this reason, Varuṇa vigilantly watches everything that is secret, every deed done and to be done. Like an earthly king, Varuṇa (with or without Mitra) is surrounded by spies, who are trustworthy and wise. Abel Bergaigne suggested that 'in the purely naturalistic order of the world the spies of Varuṇa, of the god who chiefly rules over darkness, might here represent the stars, the "eyes" of night'. He pointed out that in R̥S 1,33,8 'the spies whom Indra "envelops" (causes to disappear) in (a ray of) the sun ... appear definitely to be stars' (Bergaigne 1978: III, 172).

Unwinking vigilance is, according to Amarakośa (3,218), a quality shared only by gods and fishes. Fish are actually unable to close their eyes, and the fact that 'when the fish sleeps it does not close its eyes' was noticed by ancient Indians. While the 'fish' sign seems to have stood for both 'fish' and 'star' = 'god' in the Indus script, the dots-in-circles, figures-of-eight and trefoils on the 'priest-king's' garment seem to symbolize both stars and eyes (on the 'third eye' implied by the trefoil, see § 14.4).

I would like to suggest that the sign ⊙ of the Indus script is the stylized 'dot-in-circle' eye of the fish-shaped Harappan amulets (fig. 10.22) and that it is to be read in Dravidian as *kaṇ* 'eye', a basic word attested in all Dravidian languages and related to the Proto-Dravidian verbal root *kāṇ* 'to see'. The repetition of the 'eye' sign ⊙⊙ corresponds to the 'figure-of-eight' sign found on the Harappan 'priest-king's' cloak, and suggests a pair of eyes. The reduplication is meaningful in Dravidian: in Tamil we have the word *kaṇ-kāṇi* 'overseer'. This would be a fitting epithet for Varuṇa, who is probably meant in R̥S 10,129,7, which speaks of an 'overseer (*ádhyakṣa*) of this (world) in the highest heaven'. Varuṇa is the 'thousand-eyed' guardian of the cosmic order, and looks down on the earth with the eye of the sun. In the R̥gveda, the sun is the eye of Mitra and Varuṇa, of Varuṇa alone, of the sun-god Svar or Sūrya, of Agni, or of the gods in general; in other

Fig. 12.7. Inscription on a moulded terracotta amulet from Mohenjo-daro (M-1429). After Dales 1968: 39. The two other sides of this triangular prism show a fish-eating alligator (fig. 10.1c) and a ship (fig. 1.10).

Vedic texts, the sun and moon are the eyes of the highest Brahma.

The sequence U⊙⊙ forms the entire text of one ordinary seal (2582) and of one pottery stamp (2877): these inscriptions may well have referred to quite mundane 'overseers'. But at the end of an inscription on a three-sided terracotta amulet from Mohenjo-daro (fig. 12.7), the same sequence is followed by the 'man' sign, possibly meaning 'Servant (or devotee) of the Overseer ...' The two other sides of the amulet suggest that the text relates to the water-god of the Harappans: one has the picture of a boat, the other an alligator. Both designs refer to water, which is the realm of the god Varuṇa. Varuṇa is the 'lord of aquatic animals', including the crocodile (§ 10.2), and the boat is explicitly connected with Varuṇa in R̥gveda 7,88,3.

In Mesopotamia, the starry garments of the gods were worn not only by their images (to which the Harappan 'priest-king' can be compared) but also by their human representatives, the priest-kings. The garment of the divine king Varuṇa, too, has a counterpart in the Vedic ritual – the garment called *tārpya*, intimately associated with kingship and with Varuṇa. Thus the tārpya garment is among the essential paraphernalia of the royal consecration (*rājasūya*) which is also called *Varuṇa-sava* 'Varuṇa's sacrifice'. The waters, being the specific dominion of Varuṇa, have a special place in this consecration: 'the waters are of Varuṇa's nature, anointing him (the king) with the waters he has made him (identical with) Varuṇa' (MS 4,49,17).

The tārpya garment is not mentioned in the R̥gveda. In fact, KS 12,3 relates that the tārpya garment originally belonged to the Asuras, the rivals and enemies of the Vedic gods. Yet it must be a very ancient dress, because there is uncertainty about the meaning of the name *tārpya* even in the oldest Śrautasūtras. Baudhāyana's Karmāntasūtra (25,34) is the first to record different explanations of the word *tārpya*, repeated by later commentators. One reads: 'this is a cloth satiated (*tr̥p-*) with melted butter'. The numerous R̥gvedic references to Varuṇa's (and Mitra's) 'fatty garment' suggest that this is the correct interpretation.

The investment of the sacrificer for the unction ceremony

of the royal consecration is explained in the Śatapatha-Brāhmaṇa (5,3,5,20–4) as follows: 'He then makes him (the king) put on garments. There is that one called *tārpya*; therein are wrought all forms of sacrifice: that he makes him put on, (with the mantra VS 10,8) "Thou art the inner caul of knighthood."' A more accurate description of the figures sewn into it is given in connection with the three-day rite of Garga. According to ĀpŚS 22,16,3 and HŚS 17,6,31, 'in the tārpya garment is tied the form of the fireplaces (*dhiṣṇiyānāṁ rūpam*)'. J. C. Heesterman (1957: 92) understands this to mean that the tārpya garment 'is decorated with images of the *dhiṣṇiyas* ... (i.e. probably a series of circles)'. This would match well the devices on the Harappan 'priest-king's' cloak, which consist of combinations of one to three 'dots-in-circles'. In order to understand the symbolism of these images, we must subject the term *dhiṣṇ(i)ya* to a closer scrutiny.

In the Vedic ritual, the word *dhiṣṇ(i)ya* in the strict sense denotes the fireplaces of seven priests officiating in a Soma sacrifice; six of these are built in a row in the sitting-hall; the seventh (belonging to the *agnīdh* or fire-kindler) is in a separate shed on the northern edge of the sacrificial area (fig. 12.15).

If the circles on the 'priest-king's' garment represent fireplaces, it becomes clear why they have been filled with a red paste – the colour of fire – and why the trefoil pattern even elsewhere is associated with the colour red. Two sherds of Harappan polychrome pottery and Mackay's commentary on them underline this most important fact and its significance:

> They are decorated with irregularly placed red trefoils with white borders on an apple-green ground ... The red colouring of the lobes also suggests that this pattern is not derived from the clover leaf, for otherwise the painter of the jar would surely have painted them green. That red was the recognised colour for this motif is clear from the fact that in no instance has a trefoil of any other colour been found at Mohenjo-Daro. (Mackay 1938: I, 227f.)

But why should a fireplace be represented by a trefoil? Traditionally, the fireplace in an Indian kitchen consists of three stones set in a triangle so that the kettles and other utensils can be placed firmly over the fire. Sometimes a mud wall is plastered around the three stones, so as to prevent the ashes from spreading about; such an arrangement comes close to the trefoil motif. Definite evidence for a fireplace with three stones comes from the Late Harappan (Jhukar) levels at Chanhujo-daro.

On the basis of references to Varuṇa's starred dress and the Mesopotamian parallels, however, we would have expected the embroidered patterns of the tārpya garment to represent stars and not fireplaces. In fact, the word *dhiṣṇ(i)ya*, used of the embroidered decorations and of the ritual fireplaces, is occasionally used with the meaning 'star' in later astronomical texts (e.g. Sūrya-Siddhānta 8,1; Vasiṣṭha-Saṁhitā 37,27). A striking explanation of this double symbolism is found in the epic description of Arjuna's journey to the heavenly world of Indra (Mahābhārata 3,43). Arjuna flies upwards into the sky in a divine car driven by Indra's charioteer, Mātali:

> While becoming invisible to the mortals who walk on earth, he saw wondrous airborne chariots by the thousands. No sun shone there, or moon, or fire, but they shone with a light of their own acquired by their merits. These lights that are seen as the stars look tiny like oil flames because of the distance, but they are very large. The Pāṇḍava saw them bright and beautiful, burning on their own hearths (*dhiṣṇya*) with a fire of their own. There are the perfected royal seers, the heroes cut down in war, who, having won heaven with their austerities, gather in hundreds of groups. So do thousands of Gandharvas with a glow like the sun's or the fire's and of Guhyakas and seers and the hosts of Apsaras ... (Mātali) said ... 'Those are men of saintly deeds, ablaze on their own hearths, whom you saw there, my lord, looking like stars from the earth below.' (trans. Buitenen 1975: II, 308)

This is not the only such instance in the Mahābhārata. Thus in 3,290,20, Princess Kuntī, given divine eyesight by the sun-god, 'saw all the thirty gods, who stood in the sky upon their own hearths'.

The association of the dhiṣṇya-fireplaces with the stars can be directly traced back to early Vedic texts. That the stars in the sky were understood to be the heavenly abodes of holy people is explicitly stated in TS 5,4,1,3–4 (the passage deals with the piling of bricks upon the fire-altar):

> He puts down the constellation bricks; these are the lights of the sky; verily he wins them; the Nakṣatras are the lights of the doers of good deeds; verily he wins them; verily also he makes these lights into a reflection to light up the world of heaven.

The Śatapatha-Brāhmaṇa also refers to the stars as the lights of holy people (6,5,4,8). All these references agree that it is ancient sacrificers who shine in the sky upon their own hearths. MS 1,8,6 is most explicit in connecting the stars with ancient sacrificers: 'If someone, after having given much (as sacrificial gifts or as alms) and having sacrificed much, removes (i.e. gives up, or rather, has to give up) his fires, this (i.e. the fruit of his giving up and sacrificing) is not lost for him. The virtuous who have offered this reach yonder world. They are these stars.'

The dhiṣṇyas as decorations of the tārpya garment thus represent not only fireplaces but also stars. In Mesopotamia, where the trefoil motif also seems to have astral symbolism, the word *mul* 'constellation' was written with a pictogram consisting of a group of three stars. Could the trefoil refer to some particular three-star asterism?

Post-Vedic sources describe the asterisms as having the shape of specific objects. The object connected with the three-starred asterism of (Apa-)Bharaṇī strikingly fits with the inference concerning the relation beween the dhiṣṇya hearths and the 'trefoil' motif. The Digambara Jainas explain the Bharaṇī asterism as having the form of a 'fireplace consisting of three stones'. The words used are *cullī-pāṣāṇa* and *dṛṣac-cullī*, where *pāṣāṇa* and *dṛṣad* both mean '(large) stone'. The Digambara tradition of South India is in agreement with the Tamil tradition, for one of the Tamil names of the Bharaṇī nakṣatra in Piṅkala's Nikaṇṭu is *mu-k-kūṭṭu* 'oven, as formed of three stones or lumps of earth placed triangularly'. In Burushaski, spoken in the extreme north, the word *śi* denoting 'fireplace of three stones' is likewise the name of a three-starred asterism. On the other hand, the three stars of (Apa-)Bharaṇī are pictured as forming the pubic triangle: the Śvetāmbara Jainas speak of the 'vulva' (*bhaga*) and the late Vedic texts of the 'womb' (*yoni*). This symbolism is inherent in the Dravidian etymology that may be proposed for the word *cullī* in the Digambara sources.

The word *cullī* is the most common word for the traditional Indian fireplace, which consists of three stones serving as a stand on which vessels can be placed above the fire. This etymon is attested in practically all of the Indo-Aryan languages. In Sanskrit, however, the word *cullī* is not attested until the Laws of Manu (3,68), around 300 BC, and it has no Indo-European etymology. It is generally held to be of Dravidian origin, being derived from Tamil *cuḷḷai*, *cūḷai* 'potter's kiln, furnace, funeral pile', and its cognate in Malayalam. While this is plausible both semantically and phonologically (as Proto-Dravidian **ḷ* and **l* have merged in North and Central Dravidian), it is strange that a word belonging to the basic household vocabulary should have survived only in these two southernmost languages on the Dravidian side. In South Dravidian, Proto-Dravidian **c-* has frequently been dropped. Therefore, the Indo-Aryan words are rather to be connected with an etymon for 'fireplace' found in 16 Dravidian languages, including Tamil *ulai*, Kannada and Koḍagu *ole*, Manḍa *huli*, Pengo *hol*, Kuwi *hollu*, *holu*, Konḍa *solu*, Parji *colngel* (with *kel* 'stone').

On the basis of the regular morphophonemic rules governing Proto-Dravidian, **cul-ay* / **cull-V* 'fireplace, hearth' may be assumed to have had a variant **cūl*, homophonous with Proto-Dravidian **cūl* 'to become pregnant; pregnancy, pregnant'. This Dravidian homophony may be reflected in the double image of the (Apa-)Bharaṇī asterism as 'fireplace' and 'womb'. The idea that the 'fireplace' is a 'womb' is also fundamental to Vedic religious thinking, starting with the Ṛgveda, where the three sacred fires are said to be the 'wombs of Agni' (ṚS 2,36,4). According to the Brāhmaṇa texts, the fireplace is the womb of the sun, who 'dies' in the evening and passes the night in the fireplace in the condition of an embryo, to be reborn in the morning (JB 1,8; 1,9; 1,11; etc.).

The Apabharaṇī nakṣatra is connected with the god of death, Yama, and its three stars are identified with the 'womb' as well as the 'hearth of three stones'. This could therefore be the asterism denoted by the trefoil on the 'priest-king's' garment and by the images of 'fireplaces / stars' on the Vedic tārpya garment, the nightly robe of Varuṇa, which itself is replete with womb symbolism. We have already seen that the tārpya garment is called 'the embryonic cover of kingship'. 'Varuṇa, assuredly, is the womb,' states the Śatapatha-Brāhmaṇa (12,9,1,17). Darkness, which the JUB (3,2,4,2) associates with the womb, is in other Vedic texts connected with the colour black, sin or evil and death. Moreover, the colour black is said to be 'the symbol (or form, colour) of rain' or symbol of waters. Varuṇa is the god of waters and rain as well as of night. The Apabharaṇī nakṣatra ruled by Yama could thus be the asterism *par excellence* of King Varuṇa and the asterism primarily represented by the trefoils of the Harappan 'priest-king'. This is suggested also by the ideas associated with the Apabharaṇī nakṣatra.

The name *apabharaṇīḥ* (later shortened to *bharaṇī*) means 'those (waters) which carry away'. Apabharaṇī is the very last asterism of the old nakṣatra cycle, and thus understandably connected with death and Yama, the king of the dead: 'Let the Bharaṇīs carry away (our) evil, let the venerable king Yama perceive that; for he is the great king of a great world, let him make the path easy to go and fearless for us!' (TB 3,1,2,11). Apabharaṇī is synonymous with *avabhṛtha*, the name of the expiatory bath of the Vedic sacrifice. The two words are close to each other even etymologically and are likely to have referred originally to one and the same thing. The Apabharaṇī asterism marks the close of the year, and the avabhṛtha bath is taken at the end of the sacrifice (according to ŚB 6,2,2,38, 'the purificatory bath is the completion'). Both aim at getting rid of evil.

There is a most intimate connection between the avabhṛtha bath and Varuṇa:

> 10. Where there is a standing pool of flowing water, there let him (the sacrificer) descend into water – for whatsoever parts of flowing water flow not, these are holden by Varuṇa; and the expiatory bath belongs to Varuṇa – to free himself from Varuṇa. But if he does not find such, he may descend into any water. 11. While he makes him descend into water, he bids him say, 'Homage be to Varuṇa: downtrodden is Varuṇa's snare!' Thus he delivers him from every fetter of Varuṇa, from everything pertaining to Varuṇa . . . 23. Thereupon both (the sacrificer and his wife) having descended, bathe, and wash each other's back. Having wrapped themselves in fresh garments they step out: even as a snake is delivered from its skin, so he is delivered from all evil. There is not in him even as much sin as there is in a toothless child. (ŚB 4,4,5,10–23; trans. adapted from Eggeling 1885: II, 381, 385)

Reference is here made to the 'fetter' or 'noose' of disease and death, which is an attribute of Varuṇa, the god of avabhṛtha bath, as well as of Yama, the god of the Apabharaṇī asterism. *Pāpman* 'evil', from which one is to be delivered, is likewise connected with both Varuṇa and Yama. *Pāpman* refers to all kinds of evils but especially to death; it occurs as a synonym as well as an attribute to Mṛtyu 'Death'. The avabhṛtha symbolizes both death and rebirth. We have seen that the Brāhmaṇa texts identify Varuṇa with the night, darkness, the colour black and the womb. The Vedic texts speak of the removal of the darkness from the sun in the same terms as of the removal of the embryonic cover from a newborn baby.

While discussing the avabhṛtha bath of the sautrāmaṇī sacrifice, ŚB 12,9,2,7 connects the shedding of evil with the shedding of the garment of consecration. Here the discarded cloth is equated with sin and darkness, while the very next paragraph (ibid.: 8) likens the clean sacrificer in his fresh garment to the sun rising in the sky. There cannot be any doubt that the dark garment which is discarded in the waters of the avabhṛtha bath represents the black cloak of night. In other words, the black garment of which the rising sun divests himself is the star-decorated mantle of night and death. In the royal unction, this discarded garment of consecration is the tārpya garment of King Varuṇa, whose symbolism and probable connection with the Harappan 'priest-king's' trefoil-decorated robe we have discussed above.

The three-starred Apabharaṇī asterism may have been meant by the sequence of 'three' + 'fish' = Dravidian *mu-m-mīn* 'three-star(red asterism)' (attested in a Medieval Tamil lexicon as the name of another asterism with three stars, the Mṛgaśīrṣa). This compound occurs on the three-sided terracotta amulet from Mohenjo-daro (fig. 12.7), which shows an alligator (fig. 10.1c) and a boat (fig. 1.10) on the other two sides. We have already assumed that this amulet was associated with the water-god Varuṇa, and that Varuṇa may have been meant by the sequence of repeated 'eye' motifs, ⊙⊙, which follows (perhaps as an apposition) the sequence of '3' + 'fish' (both sequences end in the hypothetical 'genitive suffix'). Both the external and the internal context, then, suggest that the compound '3' + 'fish' stands for an asterism of Varuṇa.

12.2 'Liṅga stands': the Seven Sages and the Great Bear

The initial working hypothesis concerning the Harappan 'priest-king's' garment examined in the preceding section was that its trefoil motif had an astral meaning. We have seen that its Vedic counterpart, the royal tārpya garment of the god Varuṇa, was decorated with images of fireplaces equated with the stars. It was thought that the trefoil represented for the Indus Civilization one particular asterism, the three-starred Apabharaṇī. In the Vedic religion, the fireplace, the Apabharaṇī star and the tārpya garment all symbolize the womb or the female organ. A find from Mohenjo-daro seems to give substance to the hypothesis that this 'womb' symbolism was shared by the trefoil motif in the Harappan religion.

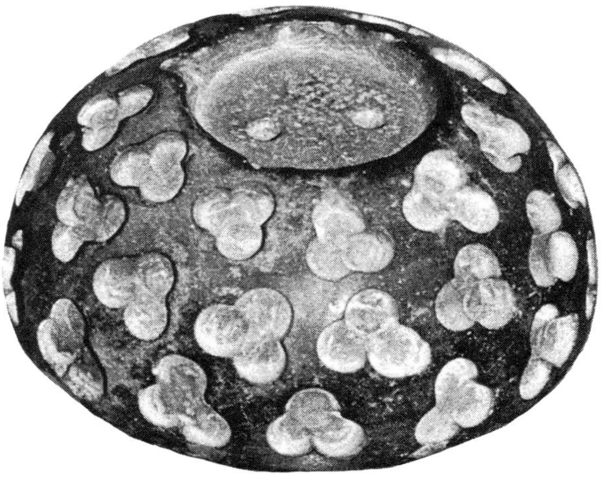

Fig. 12.8. A 'liṅga stand' from Mohenjo-daro (DK 4480), made of finely polished red stone and decorated with 'trefoil' inlays. National Museum of Pakistan, Karachi. For a section drawing, see Mackay 1938: II, pl. 107: 35.

The trefoil pattern has been incised at regular intervals on the surface of a carefully smoothed and partially polished pedestal of dark red stone (fig. 12.8). Its extraordinary workmanship indicates that this stand must have been an object of great importance. Altogether ten such stands have been described from Mohenjo-daro, and they have been compared to the round stand of the later Hindu *liṅgas* (images of Śiva's phallus) representing the *yoni* (the 'vulva' or 'womb' of the Goddess): 'They are invariably carefully made . . . The exact purpose of these stands is problematical, but . . . some of them may, in fact, be the bases of liṅgas' (Mackay 1938: I, 411).

In recent years both archaeologists and art historians have seriously questioned the sexual interpretation of conical and circular stones from Indus sites:

> Where then is the evidence to support published statements such as 'Phallic worship was an important element of Harappan religion' (Basham 1954: 24)? With the single exception of the unidentified photograph of a realistic phallic object in Marshall's report (pl. 13, 3), there is no archaeological evidence to support claims of special sexually-oriented aspects of Harappan religion. (Dales 1984: 115)

Fig. 12.9. A standing human couple in sexual intercourse (*a tergo*) on one of the three sides of a moulded tablet from Mohenjo-daro (M-489B). The other motifs include two goats eating leaves from a tree; a cock or hen (?); and a three-headed animal.

Fig. 12.10. A standing human couple in sexual intercourse (*a tergo*) on an Early Dynastic seal from Ur. After Amiet 1980a: pl. 63, no. 850.

It is true that Marshall's and Mackay's hypotheses of a Harappan worship of the liṅga and yoni rested on rather slender grounds. However, some pieces of evidence for a Harappan sexual cult appear undeniable.

George Dales, the author of the critical article quoted above, himself finds one of the conical stone objects mentioned by Marshall 'very convincingly phallic-shaped' and another 'possible'. The difficulty in accepting them as proofs of phallism 'is that, apart from a general mention that these objects belong to the Indus civilization, no information is published concerning where they were found'. After a study (in 1975) of the photographic archives of the Archaeological Survey of India, I can to some extent supply the missing data. The latter object was found at Mohenjo-daro in 1925–6, and the more important one, of terracotta, at Mohenjo-daro in 1927–8. But we still lack the excavation numbers and the exact provenance.

That these cones are phallic in nature is made likely by the existence of ithyphallic male statuettes. In addition to the two from Chanhujo-daro and (as a Harappan import) from Nippur, which have been considered ithyphallic by Dales (1968), there are several further clear examples from Mohenjo-daro (Parpola 1985b: fig. 27). It is not difficult to find parallels for these ithyphallic statuettes in later Indian religions.

Even more important evidence of Harappan sexual rites is provided by a three-faced terracotta amulet from Mohenjo-daro (fig. 12.9). One of its motifs, interpreted as 'a man driving a goat' in the excavation report, actually seems to depict sexual intercourse between a human couple: a woman bends forward in front of a standing ithyphallic man. Comparable scenes are found on Mesopotamian (fig. 12.10) and Gulf seals (fig. 12.11). A round stamp seal with Indus script presumably coming from Mesopotamia represents a bull in the act of mating with a cow (fig. 12.12).

In addition, a scene engraved on a seal from Chanhujo-daro appears to depict an Indian bison (gaur) bull mating with a nude human priestess lying on the ground (fig. 14.32). This motif may be compared to the Vedic horse sacrifice with its

Fig. 12.11. A standing human couple in sexual intercourse (*a tergo*) on a Dilmun seal from Failaka island in the Gulf. After Kjærum 1983: no. 269.

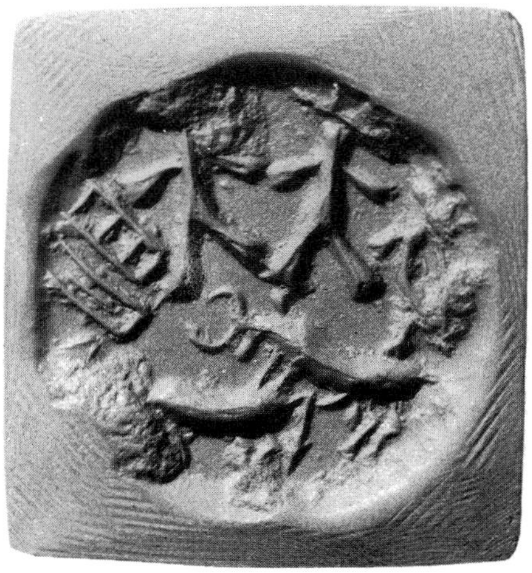

Fig. 12.12. Indus script and the motif of a bull mating with a cow. Impression of a round stamp seal (BM 123059), which comes from an antique dealer in Baghdad. Cf. Gadd 1932: no. 18.

simulated sexual intercourse between the chief queen (*mahiṣī*, literally 'great female', but also 'buffalo cow') and the horse-victim (which probably substitutes a pre-Aryan buffalo-victim, *mahiṣa* 'the great male, buffalo bull', to match the queen's title). We can further compare the copulation of

Fig. 12.13. Worship of Śiva's liṅga with trefoil bilva leaves. Fragmentary roof painting at the Śiva Vaidyanātha temple in Tiṭṭaguḍi, South Arcot District, Tamil Nadu.

Yama's buffalo with an old or dead woman in the Lamaist iconography (fig. 14.33), and the marriage of the Goddess and the Buffalo demon in the South Indian village religion (§ 14.2).

We must conclude that there is direct archaeological evidence for sexual cults in the Harappan religion. This permits us to take up the old hypothesis of Harappan 'liṅga stands' for serious consideration. Additional support for this hypothesis is provided by the fact that the trefoil is also found on a small moulded 'gamesman' or 'phallus' made of paste.

In classical Hinduism, the liṅga and yoni symbolize male and female genital organs united in sexual intercourse. They are cult objects and an integral part of their worship consists of throwing leaves of the bilva tree upon them (fig. 12.13). The bilva or 'wood-apple' tree (*Aegle marmelos*) 'is one of the most sacred of Indian trees, cultivated near temples and dedicated to Śiva, whose worship cannot be complete without its leaves'. The leaves of bilva are trifoliate, so the trefoils depicted on one of the Harappan liṅga stands may represent bilva leaves actually thrown on such an object in the cult.

Significantly, the Sanskrit name of the tree, *bilva*, is generally considered to be of Dravidian etymology, being compared to Tamil *veḷḷil* and its cognates. This word is closely homophonous with the Proto-Dravidian root *veḷ* 'to be(come) white or bright, shine' and its derivative *veḷḷi* 'star, Venus', also 'semen' (both being white). If the bilva leaves symbolize drops of semen, one can understand why they are thrown on the liṅga and yoni in the cult.

Ernest Mackay (1938: I, 411) observed that though no liṅga stones have been found fixed to such Harappan 'yoni' stands, this absence can be explained by assuming that they were of wood. However, because in the historical period 'the *liṅga* is invariably made of stone', Mackay thought it likely that this was so in Harappan times as well. But Mackay's rather categorical statement is not true: in Puri in Orissa, for example, pillars expressly identified as Śiva's liṅga are made of wood.

The hypothesis of a Harappan origin of the liṅga cult has been objected to because (1) there is no archaeological evidence for a liṅga cult after the Indus Civilization and before the second or first century BC, and because (2) the earliest historical liṅgas are realistic and contrast with the abstract form of the Harappan conical stones. The first point is true, but it applies to most other stone structures as well. Secondly, realistic and highly stylized liṅgas seem to have existed side by side in the Indus Civilization itself. The earliest sculptures of the historical period similarly comprise not only anatomically realistic liṅgas but also columns with abstract shapes – the famous pillars (*stambha*) of Asoka and his predecessors: 'The association between cosmic pillar and phallus is explicit in Mahābhārata X.17.8ff. where Śiva pulls off his own penis and sets it up as a sacred pillar' (Irwin 1980: 259 n. 18).

In Goddess worship in Kaṉṉapuram, a South Indian village, the tree-trunk (called in Tamil *kampam* from Sanskrit *skambha* 'pillar') in front of which the sacrificial victims to the Goddess are decapitated is said to be the husband of the Goddess. At the end of the yearly marriage rite, when the last victim is slaughtered, the trunk is uprooted and the Goddess is divested of her ornaments like a widow. The pillar and its uprooting correspond to Śiva's phallus and its castration. The sacrificial post used to be burnt in South India after the marriage feasts of the Goddess. In a story about the origin of the tree-trunk (*kampam*), Pārvatī is said to have implanted herself in the womb of a Brahman woman and been born as a girl. An untouchable Paṟaiya boy fell in love with her and obtained her parents' consent to their marriage, the fact that he was an untouchable being discovered only later. Pārvatī was so angry that, with a look, she engulfed her husband in flames and from his ashes caused a margosa tree to grow. In this form her husband was to stand forever outside her house.

Some of the stories describing how Śiva burnt Kāma (erotic desire) in a fit of anger, further mention that the object of his wrath took the form of a tree. The myths also link this burning of desire to the use of ashes in ritual. Hence the ashes on Śiva's ascetic body are said to be those of the burnt Kāma. Many local myths, in parallel, insist that when Māriyamman burnt her outcaste lover, she turned him into ashes. A description of a festival celebrated by Tamil workers in Sri Lanka explicitly reenacts this myth of Śiva's burning of Kāma. In that festival Kāma is not only impersonated, but also burnt in his form as a post (*kampam*). (Beck 1981: 121 n. 60)

In Central and South India, the spring festival Holi (around the time of the vernal equinox, § 11.3) is celebrated to commemorate the death and resurrection of Kāma with a big bonfire. The Mannewārs make human figures representing Kāma and his wife Rati ('Sexual pleasure'), and throw the male figure into the fire. In Maharashtra, people walk around the fire shouting words for female genitals, and dances imitating copulation are performed. In Kumaon, each clan celebrates the Holi by planting a pole in the ground, dancing around it, singing songs in honour of the amorous cowherd-god Kṛṣṇa and his milkmaids, and burning the pole on the last day of the festival.

The sacrificial stakes (*yūpa*) of the Vedic ritual to which the victims were tied were made of wood. They symbolized the primeval cosmic tree on the navel of the earth upholding the sky and thus leading to heaven (AS 10,7,35 'the *skambha* sustains both heaven-and-earth here'). 'It is through the sacrificial stake that the offerings go to the heavenly world', says MS 4,8,8. After a Vedic animal sacrifice the post was either left standing or thrown into the sacred fire. The burning of the sacrificial stake is explained by the notion that the fireplace is the womb of the gods, and the sacrificer will be born in heaven with a body of gold (AB 2,3).

That the (partially burnt) sacrificial post had a phallic connotation even in the Veda is evident from the Vedic rite of *puṁsavana* 'causing the birth of a male child'. Here various symbols of the male generative organ are used, such as two beans (for testicles) together with a barleycorn (for the phallus), a shoot of the banyan tree with a fruit on either side, and an aerial root of the banyan (JGS 1,5; HGS 2,1,2,2–4; GGS 2,6,9–11; PGS 1,14,3). The banyan shoots and air roots are pounded with millstones (an activity symbolizing sexual intercourse) and the husband inserts the resulting paste into the right nostril of his wife. Among the other things that may be mixed with this potent paste expressly equated with sperm is 'a splinter of a sacrificial post . . . exposed to the fire' (HGS 2,1,2,6).

The deity prayed to in the puṁsavana ritual is Prajāpati 'the lord of offspring'; but the means used in it, barley and beans (KS 36,6; MS 1,10,12), as well as the banyan tree (GGS 4,7,24), are all said to belong to Varuṇa. According to AB 7,14,1, Varuṇa is also the deity to approach to get a son. This underlines the phallic nature of Varuṇa and his relationship with Prajāpati and with Śiva, the god of the liṅga in later Hinduism.

We can conclude that wooden sacrificial pillars representing the phallus were burnt to ashes at the end of their ritual use, both in Vedic times and later. Such burnt pillars seem to me to have been the prototypes of Śiva's famous 'flaming liṅga pillar' in Hindu mythology. If this is correct, it becomes clear why the missing liṅga of the trefoil-decorated pedestal from Mohenjo-daro was made of wood, and why the stand itself was made of red stone: like the trefoil motif, which is always red in Harappan art (§ 12.1), the pedestal represents the fireplace; and the fireplace was in Vedic times conceived to be a womb (§ 12.1). A comparison with the later yoni stand does not appear to be far-fetched.

In the context of the Harappan 'liṅga stands' and the myth of 'Śiva's flaming liṅga', the finds in the 'citadel' of Kalibangan assume great importance. The southern rhomb of this bipartite structure contained no residential buildings, but at least five (and probably once eight or nine) ceremonial platforms built of mud-brick. A flight of steps led to these platforms from the streets that separated them from each other. On the top of one of the platforms was 'a row of seven "fire-altars"' (Thapar 1985: 55), partly damaged clay-lined pits containing ash, charcoal, the remains of a clay stele and terracotta cakes (fig. 12.14). Fire-altars with a clay stele in the middle are known also from the Lower Town of Kalibangan, where one room of many of the dwellings was set aside to house one. Better preserved clay stelae from the Lower Town were cylindrical or slightly faceted and 30–40 cm high.

At Lothal, too, ritual fireplaces have been discovered in Mature Harappan layers, from the earliest (IIA) to the latest (IV). 'A terracotta ladle found in close proximity to the altar in street 9 and bearing smoke-marks . . . suggests that it was used in pouring a liquid into the fire' (Rao 1979: 1, 216–18). The 'posthole' discovered in this altar suggests the use of wooden parallels for the clay stele at Kalibangan. The libation of liquid on such a heated stake recalls the ablutions of Śiva's liṅga with the five products of the cow (milk, sour milk, melted butter, urine and dung) and sacred water mixed with bilva leaves in the present-day Hindu cult.

The Vedic ritual provides an even more striking parallel in the milk poured as an offering into the fire (in the daily ritual) or into a heated vessel (in the pravargya sacrifice). The heated milk is the sun or the sun's seed poured into the womb: 'Sūrya (the sun) and Agni (the fire) were in the same receptacle [*yoni* 'womb']. Thereupon Sūrya rose upwards. He lost his seed. Agni received it . . . he transferred it to the cow. It (became) this milk' (KS 6,3).

The seven 'fire-altars' at Kalibangan are closely paralleled by the dhiṣṇya hearths of the Vedic Soma sacrifice (fig. 12.15). Six of these hearths are in a north–south row inside the

Fig. 12.14. Seven fire-altars in a row on the top of a ceremonial platform in the Mature Harappan period 'citadel' at Kalibangan. After Thapar 1985: 59, fig. 27.

'sitting-hall' (the priests sit to the west of them, facing east, as at Kalibangan). They belong to six priests, while one more priest (the 'fire-kindler') has a fireplace of his own to the north of the others, on the border of the sacrificial area. The seven officiating priests who have a special dhiṣṇya are also known as 'the seven sacrificers' (*sapta hotrāḥ*).

In ancient India, the stars were conceived as ancient sacrificers standing in heaven on their own fireplaces, dhiṣṇyas (§ 12.1). Almost all the Brāhmaṇa texts equate the dhiṣṇya hearths of the sacrificial area with the Gandharvas, mythical beings who guard Soma (Indra's sacred drink and the Moon) in the heavenly world (§ 11.4). In Vedic texts, the number of these Gandharvas is 27, the number of the lunar asterisms, or, when identified with the ritual fireplaces, seven.

There are many references to the 'first divine or heavenly sacrificers', seven in number; they are undoubtedly the 'seven divine sages' in R̥S 10,130,7, apparently identified with the 'human sages, our forefathers' who were the first to perform a sacrifice (§ 10.2). They are said to be the sages who won the world of heaven with ascetic practices. JUB 4,26,12 makes it quite clear that the Seven Sages are the circumpolar stars of Ursa Major by stating that 'the centre of heaven is where the Seven Sages are'. These Seven Sages are involved in the myths concerning the origin of the liṅga worship, which deserve a closer scrutiny.

The Śatapatha-Brāhmaṇa (2,1,2,4) states that 'the Seven Sages (*sapta r̥ṣayaḥ*) were formerly called "Bears" (*r̥kṣāḥ*)'. The latter is an old Indo-European appellation of Ursa Major, for Homer (Iliad 18,487–9 = Odyssey 5,273–5) speaks of a single circumpolar asterism called 'She-Bear' (*árktos*) 'that circles ever in her place . . . and alone has no part in the baths of the Ocean'. But since the times of the late R̥gveda (R̥S 10,82,2), this constellation is almost exclusively called 'the Seven Sages'; as the younger name does not differ very much phonetically from the older one, it looks like a transformation based on an earlier Indian name for the asterism.

A most important piece of evidence relating to the early symbolism of the constellation of Ursa Major and its connection with the phallic liṅga cult is given by the Avestan name of this asterism. Avestan *haptō-iringa-* 'Ursa Major' corresponds to **sapta-liṅga-* 'having seven liṅgas' in Sanskrit, though such a compound is not known from the Indian texts. The Sanskrit word *liṅga* is first attested in late Vedic and epic texts, and its basic meaning is 'characteristic mark, sign'; in Śiva's liṅga and other contexts, it has the meaning of 'penis, phallus' as the 'characteristic mark' of the male sex. Avestan *iringa-* has been explained as having the basic meaning of 'mark, sign'. While this explanation naturally remains valid and possible, the seven fireplaces of Kalibangan with clay 'liṅgas', corresponding to the Vedic dhiṣṇya fireplaces, in turn associated with the 'Seven Sacrificers' (= Ursa Major), do suggest that the Avestan name *haptō-iringa-* may be understood to imply the meaning 'phallus' too.

A fairly frequently occurring sequence of two Indus signs

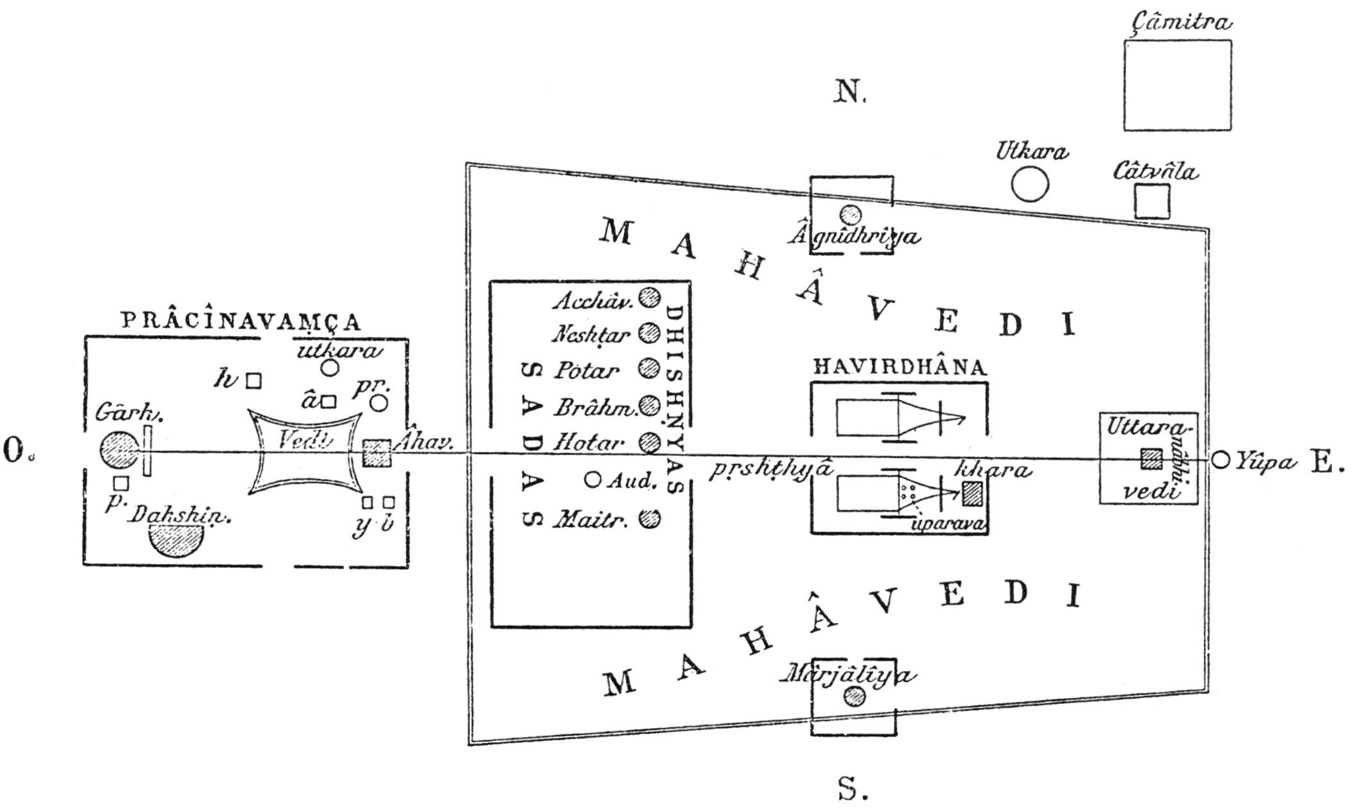

Fig. 12.15. The fireplaces (*dhiṣṇya*) of the 'seven sacrificial priests' in the Vedic Soma sacrifice. After Caland and Henry 1906: 1, pl. 4.

may or may not be relevant here, . Number '7' is followed by a sign resembling the Sumerian pictogram for 'phallus', . It is noteworthy that in Proto-Dravidian, the word for 'seven', **eḻu*, happens to be homophonous with the root **eḻu* 'to rise, ascend (as a heavenly body), to be high, to be roused or excited, inflame (as passions), to grow, to swell (as breasts)', meanings that fit both Ursa Major and the phallus. That the sign possibly depicting 'phallus' had an astral meaning is suggested by the sign sequence (§ 5.1).

The etymology of the word *liṅga* is an open question. Because it is not found in the oldest Sanskrit texts, because it is so central to the terminology of the non-Aryan phallic cult, and because none of the proposed Indo-European etymologies is convincing, many scholars have opted for a non-Aryan origin. We know that the Aryans had a different Indo-European name for the constellation Ursa Major, while 'seven liṅgas' is in agreement with the seven fireplaces with a clay stele in their midst at Kalibangan. A translation loan is not excluded, but in view of the Harappan influence on the Bactria and Margiana Archaeological Complex (figs. 12.4–5), which could be the source of the Avestan term, it looks more likely that *liṅga* is a Dravidian loanword. If this is the case, it should be possible to find a solution. Moreover, since Avestan, like the Ṛgvedic language, was characterized by rhotacism (merger of *l* and *r* into *r*), while classical Sanskrit has preserved the distinction between *l* and *r*, *liṅga* may be closer to the original than **ringa*.

Proto-Dravidian seems to have had no word-initial *l*- or *r*-, but a number of etyma in Kannaḍa, Telugu and some Central Dravidian and North Dravidian languages beginning with *l*- originally had **n*- initially. There are also

> a few words in Sanskrit of Dravidian origin which show initial *l*- as opposed or *n*- or *ñ*- in Dravidian. A fluctuation between *l*- and *n*- occurs sporadically in Indo-Aryan at all periods... Consequently it is not surprising to find *l*- for *n*- in Sanskrit words, even in cases where no form with initial *l*- is found in Dravidian. (Burrow 1943–6c: 615)

On this basis, Sanskrit *liṅga* can be derived from the Proto-Dravidian root **niṅg*- / **nig*- 'to rise, become erect, stand upright, be extended'. Such a derivation agrees well with the meanings 'phallus' and 'erected post' for *liṅga*. The meaning 'mark, sign' can be understood to have developed from '(out)standing object' > '(land)mark'.

Hindu mythology associates the liṅga cult with the Seven Sages and therefore also with Ursa Major, thus endorsing the suggested interpretations of the Kalibangan fire-altars and of Avestan *haptō-iringa-*. In many well-known myths, the Seven Sages and their wives are, in one way or another, specifically associated with sexual intercourse and with Śiva's liṅga or seed. It was in the hermitage of the Seven Sages that Śiva broke his vow of chastity and had intercourse with the wives of the Seven Sages:

The sages cursed Śiva's liṅga to fall to the earth, and it burnt everything before it like a fire... Brahmā said 'As long as the liṅga is not still, there will be nothing auspicious in the universe. You must propitiate Devī so that she will take the form of the yoni, and then the liṅga will become still.'... Thus liṅga-worship was established. (Śiva-Purāṇa 4,12,17–52, summarized by O'Flaherty 1973: 257)

It was suggested above that Śiva's mythical 'fiery liṅga' may correspond to the burning of the sacrificial stake in rituals, and the uprooting of the stake to which the husband-victim is bound to the castration of Śiva in the myth. The establishment of the liṅga cult by the Seven Sages and the burning of Śiva's liṅga fit with the seven fire-heated 'liṅgas' of the Kalibangan ritual hearths.

The specific relationship between the liṅga cult and the Seven Sages becomes clear if the Pole Star (surrounded by the stars of Ursa Major) was understood as Śiva's or Varuṇa's liṅga. This is quite likely, for the Pole Star is called the 'pillar' (*methī*) of the universe (§ 14.1). In PB 13,9,17, *methī* is used of the post to which the milch cow and its calf are tethered. Usually, however, the word denotes the pillar in the middle of the threshing ground, to which oxen walking round it are bound, and in this sense the Bhāgavata-Purāṇa 4,9,20ff. connects it with the mythical Dhruva, who is to become the Pole Star. The Pole Star was also conceived in this way in ancient Rome (where Ursa Major was called *septem triones* 'the seven threshing oxen') and among the Turkic and Chukchi nomads of Central Asia and northeast Siberia (who think of the Pole Star as a post to which horses or reindeer are tethered). In India, as in ancient China, the Pole Star as the firm centre around which everything else whirls is a symbol of royalty (Mahābhārata 14,15). The Pole Star as the 'pillar' of the universe accordingly belongs to Varuṇa and is invoked in the royal consecration (§ 14.1).

The asceticism (*tapas*, literally 'fiery heat, glow') of the Seven Sages is seemingly in conflict with sexuality, but actually purports to heighten their powers of creation: in Hinduism the Seven Sages are the mental sons of the creator-god Brahmā who actually carry out the creation of the world. Indeed this same paradox 'asceticism and eroticism' is central to the mythology of Śiva and his liṅga: Śiva is 'permanently ithyphallic, yet perpetually chaste' (O'Flaherty 1973). The seed is synonymous with creative powers: spilling it means loss of power and energy; restraining it means accumulation of power.

In the epic versions of the myth, as in the Śatapatha-Brāhmaṇa, the Seven Sages forsake their beautiful wives, the Pleiades, because they all had intercourse with Agni (the Fire) or Śiva, excepting Arundhatī, the faithful wife of Vasiṣṭha, who could not be seduced. In some variants, the Pleiades (*kṛttikāḥ*) bathe in the river Ganges at the spot where the fiery seed falls down; the Pleiades become pregnant by it, or nurse the child who is instantly born of the seed, the warrior-god Skanda-Kārttikeya. Note the parallelism between the falling down of the fiery seed and the falling down of the fiery phallus: we are dealing with two variants of one and the same mythic complex.

This myth of *kumāra-saṁbhava* 'the birth of the male child (the war-god Rudra, Skanda, Kārttikeya)' – as it is called in the title of Kālidāsa's celebrated poem – is one of the very oldest and most central myths in the entire Vedic and Hindu mythology. Its antiquity is demonstrated above all by its connection with the Seven Sages and their wives: these mythological figures can be traced back to Harappan seals and fireplaces, and they are centrally connected with the nakṣatra calendar and its creation *c.*2300 BC (§ 11.3). In the next chapter we shall deal with various aspects of this myth.

13 Evidence for Harappan worship of the god Muruku

13.1 Murukaṉ and the bangle cult

If the Harappan language is Dravidian, the oldest available sources in Dravidian assume great importance in the study of the Indus texts. The literature composed in South India two thousand years ago in Old Tamil is the only source that will grant us glimpses into the religion and ideology that prevailed among Dravidian speakers before the language had been much contaminated with Indo-Aryan (§ 9.5).

The principal native deity of the early Tamils was a youthful god of war and love, in many respects resembling the North Indian war-god Skanda (Vedic Rudra) and soon explicitly identified with him. This god has various native Dravidian names; perhaps the most important of them is *Muruku* or (with the suffix *-aṉ*, the rational masculine marker) *Murukaṉ*, which means 'youth, young man'. To the present day, Murukaṉ has remained the 'national god' of the Tamils; his names, including the Sanskrit synonyms, such as Skanda and Subrahmaṇya, figure most prominently in the male proper names of South India. Couples desiring the birth of a male child often make a pilgrimage to a famous shrine of Murukaṉ and, after the birth, name their son after the god, who is usually depicted as a beautiful young boy.

In ŚB 6,1,3,1ff., the newborn Rudra is above all the crying infant (Sanskrit *rud-* means 'to cry'); in this connection Rudra is called in Sanskrit *Kumāra*, 'young boy, young man', which remains one of the principal names of the war-god. In traditional Indian medicine, Āyurveda, Skanda is intimately connected with infants and human fertility (§§ 13.4–5).

According to the ancient myth, the Pleiades (Sanskrit *kṛttikāḥ*) were the mothers of Skanda, whose metronym therefore is *Kārttikeya*; in Old and Medieval Tamil, he is called *aṟu-mīṉ kātalaṉ* 'son of the Pleiades'. We have seen that this myth is inextricably linked with the creation of the Indian star calendar around the twenty-third century BC, which suggests a Harappan origin for it (§§ 11.2–3).

(a)

(b)

Fig. 13.1. An incised 'miniature tablet' from Harappa (H-306) with the Indus sign of 'intersecting circles'. (a) Obverse. (b) Reverse.

(a)

(b)

Fig. 13.2. (a) An Indus inscription containing the sign sequence on the obverse of a moulded faience tablet from Mohenjo-daro (M-453). (b) The reverse shows a deity sitting in a 'yogic' posture on a low throne, flanked by erect cobras and worshippers (one extending a vessel of offerings, one raising arms).

It therefore seems most likely that Murukan̠ and Rudra-Skanda are both descended from one of the principal deities of the Proto-Dravidians, and that his name or names occur in the Indus inscriptions. But how to identify these names? The most reliable clue seems to be his association with the Pleiades, because the Pleiades can be spotted in the Indus texts: their Old Tamil name *ar̠u-mīn̠* 'six-star' corresponds to the sign sequence '6' + 'fish' (§ 10.4). One of the many contexts where this sequence occurs is seal M-112. The first three signs of this seal, possibly denoting an epithet, recur in this same order in just one other context, namely seal M-241 (the first sign has a variant form here). Because the two first signs both have a very low frequency, their co-occurrence makes the parallelism significant and suggests that the sign sequence may be a name of Skanda, because it corresponds to a sequence involving the name of the Pleiades.

The sign sequence occurs very frequently in the Indus inscriptions (fig. 13.1), and some contexts strongly support the hypothesis that it refers to a deity. Thus the text is repeated on several identical moulded tablets, probably amulets, whose reverse sides show an anthropomorphic deity sitting on a throne and surrounded by a kneeling worshipper and a snake on either side (fig. 13.2). In South India, Murukan̠ is associated with the snake cult. In Tamil Nadu,

the serpent's association with Subrahmaṇya is a strange one. It is virtually ubiquitous; for at most shrines and temples of Murukan̠ serpent icons can be found at some point. The snake is also commonly depicted clutched in the talons of the peacock [which is Murukan̠'s vehicle]. Yet seldom is the snake shown on or near the person of the god as is so common with both Śiva and Viṣṇu. And even more striking, there is a remarkable paucity of myths and even references to the snake in the officially recognized mythology of the god. The snake's significance seems to be more implicit than explicit. (Clothey 1978: 187).

Yet the devotees of Murukan̠ may bring living snakes as offerings to their god with the ceremonial carrying pole (*carppa-k-kāvaṭi*). In Tamil Nadu, as everywhere in South India, women also walk round stone images of snakes (often represented in the act of copulation) in the hope of getting a child. In Karnataka, Subrahmaṇya is directly identified with the snake and worshipped as such for getting offspring. The myth connected with this cult is known also in Kerala:

When Murukan̠ imprisoned Brahmā for the older god's ignorance of spiritual truth, Brahmā cursed the playful child to become a snake. Unable to find their child anywhere Śiva and Pārvatī, as they continued their search, prayed and fasted that he be returned to them. Years passed; the world became darker and darker, and the gods more terrified. At last Śiva learned from Brahmā that Subrahmaṇya was a snake. Therewith Śiva touched the head of the snake and Subrahmaṇya emerged from within its skin. Immediately, the world became light again and order was restored. (Clothey 1978: 187)

This myth may be compared with the conception of the rising sun as a serpent that creeps upwards, found in Vedic texts (AB 7,20). Rudra-Skanda represents, among other things, the vernal and rising sun (§§ 11.3; 13.3–5; 14.4).

Another Harappan tablet is inscribed with simply this sign sequence on both sides, one of which shows in addition a row of five swastikas facing alternate ways, the other a man in front of a tiger (fig. 13.3). In the Veda, the tiger is 'the king of the wild beasts' (ŚB 12,7,1,8; AB 8,6,1), an epithet that connects it with Rudra (TS 4,5,3 e). The tiger symbolizes the king and the warrior (a war-chariot was covered with the tiger's skin: JB 2,103), and is also identified with the Fire (ŚB 3,1,3,28; TS 6,2,5,5), all of which are associated with Rudra. In classical Hinduism, the tiger is the

(a)

(b)

Fig. 13.3. A tablet from Harappa (H-182). (a) The obverse bears an Indus inscription consisting of the sign sequence ᒍ||ↀ and the motif of 'a man (drummer?) in front of a tiger'. (b) The same text accompanies a row of swastikas on the reverse.

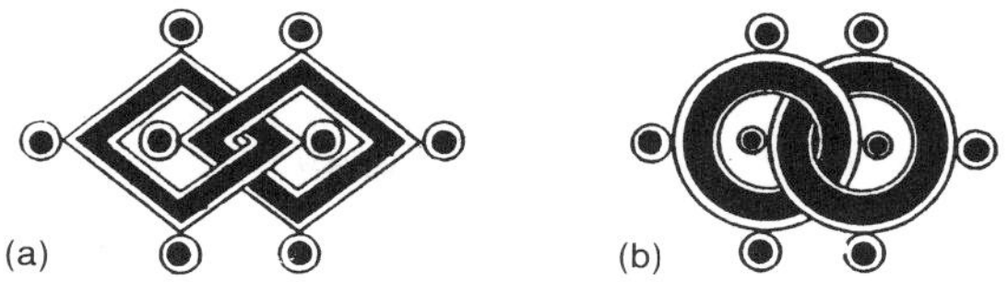

(a) (b)

Fig. 13.4. 'Intersecting circles' in traditional Lamaistic art: auspicious symbols representing the ear-rings of the king (a) and the queen (b). After Maydar 1981: 111.

vehicle of Durgā, the virginal goddess of victory, the female counterpart (Kumārī) of the war-god Rudra-Skanda (Kumāra).

These considerations allow the hypothesis that the sign of 'two intersecting circles', ↀ, might express an ancient Dravidian name for Skanda, or part of it. The most obvious choice is his Old Tamil name *muruku*, which has cognates in many South and Central Dravidian languages, warranting its Proto-Dravidian origin and the meaning 'young man' (besides 'young of an animal'). Does this word have any ancient homophone, whose meaning could explain the form of the pictogram involved?

There is, in fact, an exact and ancient Dravidian homophone which provides an excellent rebus, namely **muruku*, meaning 'ring', a derivative of the verbal root **murV* 'to bend, to be bent, to twist'; the specific meanings 'ear-ring', 'nose-ring' and 'bangle' are variously attested in the South and Central Dravidian languages, from which this etymon is known. The idea of 'ring', of course, could be expressed by means of a single circle, but this would remain slightly ambiguous, since it could be interpreted in various other ways as well. Ear-rings, however, are usually worn in pairs, one in each ear, and the Old Tamil epic Cilappatikāram, for instance, has a *pair* of anklets (*cilampu*) as one of its central themes. Ear-rings and anklets occur regularly in both the Mahābhārata and Old Tamil literature as accoutrements of warriors, making them an appropriate symbol for Skanda as god of war.

A symbol identical with the Harappan pictogram of 'intersecting circles' is part of the traditional repertory of the notoriously conservative Lamaist art (fig. 13.4), where it represents royal ear-rings.

But besides 'ear-ring', the word *muruku* in Dravidian languages also denotes 'arm-ring, bangle'. That the sign of 'two intersecting circles' indeed means 'bangle' seems to be confirmed by the fact that it has a disproportionately high frequency on the 40 or more inscribed Harappan 'stoneware' bangles. Several of these bangle inscriptions contain nothing but the sign of 'two intersecting circles' (fig. 13.5). Recent work at Mohenjo-daro has revealed that they were manufactured by means of a highly sophisticated technique involving firing in saggars at a temperature of 1200°C. These very smooth, even, heavy bracelets, which ring like metal when they are struck, must have been highly prized, for the coated saggar jars have been carefully sealed to prevent their unauthorized opening. The inscriptions have been traced on the bracelets with a very sharply pointed tool before firing.

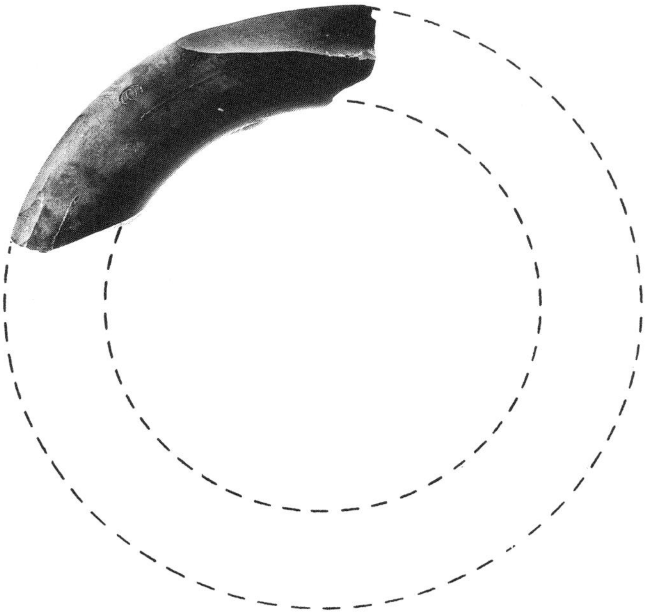

Fig. 13.5. The Indus sign of 'intersecting circles' on a Harappan stoneware bangle from Mohenjo-daro (M-1644).

It is not unusual that ancient inscriptions carved on various objects mention the name of the object, though one would normally expect the name of the owner to be added as a genitive attribute. On the other hand, objects are often

Fig. 13.6. The signs of 'fireplace' and 'intersecting circles' in the impression of a seal from Harappa (H-147).

inscribed when they are given as votive offerings. In this context, therefore, the pictogram of 'two intersecting circles' could be understood to denote the Dravidian word *muruku* not only in the sense of 'bangle' but also in the sense of a 'boy child' wished for by the donor of the votive bangle. The homonymy would make a bangle an appropriate gift in sympathetic fertility magic. Can this hypothesis be further substantiated?

A sign which consists of 'three short strokes forming a triangle', ∵, is connected with the sign of 'two intersecting circles', occurring almost exclusively in the frequently occurring sign sequence ⚭ ∵ (fig. 13.6). The pictogram ∵ might represent the 'fireplace consisting of three stones placed in a triangle' and its Proto-Dravidian name **cullV / *cūl*, which also means 'pregnancy, womb' (§ 12.1). The interpretation of the sign ∵ as **cullV / *cūl* 'fireplace / pregnancy, womb' makes good sense, as the fireplace is conceived to be the womb of the sun or the fire (§ 12.1), and Rudra (or Skanda) is said to be the son of Fire (Agni); Rudra is also often directly equated with the fire-god Agni in the Veda (e.g. ŚB 6,1,3,10). In the Ṛgveda (5,2,1–2; 10,79,3), Agni is called *kumāra* 'boy child'. In ṚS 5,2,2, Agni is an 'embryo' (*garbha*), who is cherished by his mother in secret (*guhā*); *Guha* 'secret, hidden', is one of Skanda's later names. In AS 5,25,7, Agni, the embryo, is asked to place an embryo in the womb.

On the other hand, it is a fact that the bangle has a strong association with pregnancy in many parts of India (fig. 13.7). During pregnancy and childbirth, the mother and baby are both in great danger of being attacked by demons. In Tamil Nadu, for example, in the fifth or seventh month after conception, the expectant mother is ritually 'adorned with bangles and blessed by older women. The bangles symbolize an enclosed circle of protection, containing the creative power within her.' These bangles are called *cūl kāppu*, where the word *cūl* means 'pregnancy' and *kāppu* means (primarily) 'protection' and (secondarily) 'bangle'. The Tamils customarily provide the newborn baby, too, with bangles and anklets on the fifth, seventh or ninth day after its birth.

In many places in India, 'persons desirous of being rid of sins or sickness creep, or are passed, through [stones pierced by a hole] for that purpose' (Hartland 1920: 865). Passing

Fig. 13.7. Gisèle Krauskopff's drawing of a domestic sanctuary among the Tharu people of Nepal. The pair of glass bangles (E), suspended from a nail driven into the silo wall, represents Curinyā, the spirit of a woman who died in childbed. She menaces children and pregnant women, and is therefore venerated in many Tharu houses. After Krauskopff 1989: 101, fig. 29.

through a hole naturally symbolizes birth and renewal. But people creep through perforated stones also in order to become pregnant or sexually potent (Meyer 1937: III, 171). Likewise, bangles and rings are connected with pregnancy not only as protective amulets but also as charms bringing about reproduction.

Frequently, the bangles are of green glass and are hung on a sacred tree. Thus at Allahabad, near the tomb of Musa Sohag is

> a very old, large Champa tree (*Michelia champaka*), the branches of which are hung with glass bangles. 'Those anxious to have children come and offer the saint bangles, 7, 11, 13, 21, 29, or 126, according to their means and importunity. If the saint favours their wish, the Champa tree snatches up the bangles and wears them on its arms.' (Crooke 1926: 417)

In Karnataka, green glass bangles are similarly offered to the goddess Ellamma (a form of Durgā) by women wishing to become pregnant. In two shrines at Vijayanagar, for instance, the bangles are inserted in sticks projecting from the walls of the shrine just outside the *garbhagṛha*, or hung on the branches of a tree standing in front of the shrine.

This widespread folk custom may well go back to Harappan traditions, for green faience bangles are known also from the Indus Civilization. Moreover, the deity standing inside the fig tree in the famous seal from Mohenjo-daro (fig. 14.35) wears bangles on both arms. The seven anthropomorphic figures at the bottom of this seal are likely to be female and to represent the 'Seven Mothers' (§§ 11.3; 14.3),

Fig. 13.8. A sacred tree with railing, in a moulded tablet from Harappa (H-188).

Fig. 13.9. Worship of a sacred Bodhi tree. Vedikā medallion from the Buddhist stupa of Bhārhut, second century BC. The Indian Museum, Calcutta.

famous as ambivalently child-granting and child-killing goddesses like their son Skanda (§ 13.5).

In fact, whenever the Harappan deities are represented in an anthropomorphic form, they are usually shown wearing bangles. Often, although the deity is not actually within a tree, he or she can nevertheless be recognized as a tree spirit from the leafy branch worn in the horn crown. Some of the Harappan deities are clearly wearing fig leaves in their horn crowns (figs. 10.10; 14.16), others the branches of other trees (figs. 14.24–5), as do the tree spirits of early historical India, usually called Yakṣa and (in feminine) Yakṣī or Yakṣiṇī. The fertility spirits, the Gandharvas and Apsarases, are associated with fig trees in the Veda (§ 14.3). In Bengal, the 'forest' form of the goddess Ṣaṣṭhī, who presides over childbirth, is worshipped under the banyan fig in the form of a cat made of rice paste, and bangles made of rice paste are presented to the cat.

The bangles and leaf crowns, then, suggest that the Harappan deities were, among other things, tree spirits worshipped for offspring. Several tablets actually illustrate worshippers kneeling with an offering jar in their hands in front of a tree (fig. 7.12). Worship of trees, especially to obtain children, was an important part of early Indian folk religion:

At Sāvatthī, we are told, lived a householder named Great-Wealth, Mahā-Suvaṇṇa. He was rich, possessed of great wealth, possessed of ample means of enjoyment, but at the same time he was childless. One day, as he was on his way home from bathing at a *ghāṭ*, he saw by the roadside a large forest tree with spreading branches. Thought he, 'This tree must be tenanted by a powerful tree-spirit.' So he caused the ground under the tree to be cleared, the tree itself to be enclosed with a wall (*pākāra*), and sand to be spread within the enclosure. And having decked the tree with flags and banners, he made the following vow: 'Should I obtain a son or a daughter, I will pay you great honor.' Having done so, he went on his way. (Dhammapada Atthakathā, trans. Burlingame 1921: I, 146, quoted from Coomaraswamy 1928: I, 22)

A number of Indus tablets (fig. 13.8) depict trees with railings (*prākāra* or *vedikā*) of the kind mentioned in this story and illustrated in early Buddhist art (fig. 13.9). It is obvious that this tree cult has continued in an unbroken tradition in South Asia from Harappan times right to the present day.

The tree spirits have been and continue to be among the principal divinities approached for getting children. The fact that bangles are offered to them for this purpose strongly supports the interpretation that the sign of 'two intersecting circles' engraved on many Harappan bangles denotes the Dravidian word *muruku*, which means both 'bangle' and 'son, boy child', and is also the proper name of the child-granting divinity and divine child.

In seal M-1202, the sign of 'two intersecting circles' starts the inscription and is followed by the sign  identified as depicting the five-striped palm squirrel in § 7.2 (fig. 7.1). In Tamil, the striped palm squirrel is called *aṇil* or *aṇiṟ piḷḷai*. In the latter expression, the word *piḷḷai* (which is of Proto-Dravidian origin) means 'child, infant, son, youth, lad, boy' as well as 'young of mammals (excepting the dog), birds and trees', being used particularly of animals living in trees. In the case of some small animals like the squirrel, parrot (*kiḷi*) and mongoose (*kīri*), the word *piḷḷai* is added to form an affectionate diminutive, and can also alone refer to the animal concerned; thus *Maturai-t tamiḻ pēr akarāti* (1956) records *piḷḷai* in the meaning of *aṇil* 'squirrel'. This usage goes back to Proto-Dravidian, for in the Parji language, *piṛca* (with *ṛ* from **ḷ*) means 'squirrel' and in the dialects of Gondi, *warcē* and *verce* 'small striped squirrel'. The word *piḷḷai* is similarly added to the various names of the god Muruku to form affectionate variants that are popular as male proper names in Tamil: *Muruku-p-piḷḷai*, *Kanta-p-piḷḷai* (where *Kanta* is from Sanskrit *Skanda*), or *Vēlu-p-piḷḷai*. (The word *piḷḷai*, being synonymous with *muruku* 'youth, young one', is also used alone, usually in the honorific plural form *Piḷḷaiyār*, to denote the deity: the *Tamil Lexicon* records it in the meanings Bhairava, Gaṇeśa and Skanda = *Muruka-k-kaṭavuḷ* 'god Murukaṉ'.) The whole inscription on one side of tablet H-771 consists of the sequence || , where  appears to be a variant of the plain , since the three signs correspond to the more common sequence || . We can turn now to the sign || in this sequence, which at the beginning of this section was assumed to relate to the god Skanda.

13.2 Murukaṉ's name and the planet Venus: a case for cross-checking

At the beginning of the last section it was argued that the sign sequence ||  is likely to be one of the names of Murukaṉ in the Indus inscriptions. The proposed interpretation for the sign  as Dravidian *muruku* '(pair of) ear-rings, bangles' *and* 'young boy, youth, god Muruku' (§ 13.1) could be further verified if we could interpret the sign || with which it apparently forms a compound. The sign || offers the opportunity of a double cross-check, for there can be little doubt that it also forms a compound with another sign for which we have a very probable reading; namely, it precedes the sign of 'plain fish' in the frequently occurring sequence  ||.

How are we to read the pictogram consisting of 'two long vertical strokes'? Such a simplified symbol can be pictorially interpreted in many different ways. For example, it could be assumed to denote 'two', or 'pair', or 'path', or 'parallel'. In the absence of any clue about the intended meaning, it would be difficult to decide which, if any, of these possible interpretations is correct. However, the suggested readings for the signs of 'two intersecting circles' and 'fish' make it possible to approach the problem from an altogether different angle. We can scan through the various indexes to Old Tamil literature collecting (1) all actually attested composite names of the god Murukaṉ that start with the word *muruku-*, and (2) all actually attested compounds denoting either stars or fish which end in the word *-mīṉ*. We are looking for two compounds in which the missing part X (*muruku-X* and *X-mīṉ*) is the same. If such a shared second member should be found in these two relatively limited groups of compounds, the hypothesis can be tested by asking whether the meaning(s) of that common second member will adequately explain the pictorial form of the sign ||.

A successful completion of this and other similar tasks requires good lexicons. Fortunately, there is a comprehensive index to the words occurring in Old Tamil texts, supplemented by special vocabularies to individual texts. Beyond these, the *Tamil Lexicon* in seven volumes is an indispensable tool that covers fairly well the voluminous medieval literature and the modern dialects; in addition, thanks to my friends (see preface), I have had access to an unpublished index to the non-initially occurring members of compounds in the *Tamil Lexicon*.

To start with the names of the Tamil war-god, the best match for the sequence is the compound *muruka-vēḷ* (in the colophon of Paripāṭal 14; in the commentary on Paṭṭiṉappālai 158; in an anonymous medieval stanza quoted by Mu. Irākavaiyaṅkār as fragment 98 of Peruntokai; and in Kantapurāṇam 1,16,6; 5,1,24). The component *vēḷ* corresponding to the sign || occurs in the same position in several other names of Murukaṉ as well: besides *Kanta-vēḷ* (with *Kanta* from Sanskrit *Skanda*) and *Kumara-vēḷ* (where *Kumara* corresponds to Sanskrit *Kumāra* 'youth, Skanda'), Murukaṉ is often called *Ce-v-vēḷ* (e.g. in Paripāṭal), where the first word means 'red'. *Vēḷ* also occurs alone, as the name of Murukaṉ in Old Tamil (e.g. in Tirumurukāṟṟuppaṭai 273).

The word *vēḷ* in Murukaṉ's name can be explained in several ways. A Proto-Dravidian etymon of this shape meaning 'chief, king, illustrious or great man, hero' can be posited by comparing Tamil *vēḷ* (pl. *vēḷir*), which has all these meanings, with North Dravidian (Kurukh) *bēlas* 'king, god'; this would suit well the god of war, but the reconstruction suffers from the word being attested in so few languages.

But Murukaṉ is not only the god of war in Old Tamil texts; he is connected with love and sex as well. *Vēḷ* in Old Tamil denotes both Murukaṉ and Kāma, the ancient Hindu god of sexual desire and lust. In Kuriñcippāṭṭu 208–10, *Kāma-vēḷ* is an aspect of Murukaṉ presiding over the marriage. A case can be made for the identity of the god of war and the god of love (see also § 13.5): Ishtar and Durgā are examples of divinities with exactly this kind of double nature. The Atharvaveda speaks of Kāma as a crusher of foes (AS 9,2) and refers to his weapons:

The arrow, winged with longing, barbed with love, whose shaft is unswerving desire, with that, well-aimed, Kāma shall pierce thee in the heart, in order that thou shalt be at my bidding, shalt follow my thought. (AS 3,25,2, trans. Bloomfield 1899: 70)

In Kāma's name (and according to Kamil Zvelebil in Murukan̲'s name too), the word *vēḷ* means 'desire'; the corresponding verb, *vēḷ* 'to desire, want, wish, ask, beg, require', belongs to the most basic Proto-Dravidian vocabulary, being much used as an auxiliary ('be required or necessary, must'). A homophonous verb *vēḷ* 'to offer sacrifices in fire, to worship (god), to marry' in South Dravidian and Telugu is likely to be derived from it, and the ultimate etymology may be Proto-Dravidian *vē* 'to burn, to be hot, to glow, also with anger or desire'. These connotations agree very well with Murukan̲ as the wrathful (*cin̲a-miku*) god of war and as the god of love and marriage.

From Murukan̲'s name we can now turn to astronomical terms. The word for 'white' that has the widest distribution in the Dravidian language family is *vel*, a close homophone of Murukan̲'s name *Vēḷ*. The compound *ven̲-mīn̲* (< *veḷ* + *mīn̲*) 'white (or bright) star' is known from Old Tamil as the name of the planet Venus, that brightest star of the morning and evening sky; and the noun *veḷḷi*, derived from the same verbal root *veḷ* 'to be(come) white or bright', denotes 'the planet Venus' in a number of Dravidian languages; *veḷḷi-mīn̲* 'Venus' is also known from Tamil.

Now that the phonetic shape *veḷ* / *vēḷ* has emerged as the shared component *X* in the compounds *Muruku-X* and *X-mīn* that we set out to find, the next question is whether this intended meaning enables us to retrieve the rebus and understand the pictorial meaning of the sign ||. There is in fact a Proto-Dravidian homophone, *veḷi* 'enclosed or intervening space, open or public space, outside', whose meaning could conceivably be expressed pictorially by 'two long vertical strokes', especially in the light of the ligature of the signs || + 人 (§ 5.2), |人|, where a 'man' is placed in the space between the two long vertical strokes (cf. Tamil *vēḷ-āḷan̲* / *vēḷvi-y-āḷan̲* 'munificent person, sacrificer', and fig. 7.12).

The semantics of the word *veḷḷi* offer yet another possibility of cross-checking this interpretation of the sign ||. In Tamil, at least, *veḷḷi* is used not only in the meaning of 'the planet Venus', but in the general meaning of 'star' as well, e.g. in the following sentences:

iravil vāṉattil veḷḷikaḷ kāṇappaṭum: 'In the night, stars are seen in the sky.' (Jotimuttu 1965: 184)

vāṉattil uḷḷa veḷḷiyai kaṇakkiṭa muṭiyumā? 'Is it possible to count the stars in the sky?' (*TL*)

The first two renderings for 'star' in Chidambaranatha Chettiar's *English–Tamil dictionary* (1965: 993b) are *viṇ-mīn̲* and *vān̲-veḷḷi* (both *viṇ* and *vān̲* mean 'sky': these attributes are added to avoid confusion with the homonym *mīn̲* 'fish'; § 10.1). The word *veḷḷi* is found in this meaning even in compounds, as a synonym of *mīn̲*. Thus both *viṭi-veḷḷi* and *viṭi-mīn̲* are used in Tamil with the meaning 'the star of the dawn, Venus' (*veṭi* / *viṭi* means 'to dawn, break as the day'). In view of this double meaning of the word *veḷḷi*, it is striking that the sign || is used in the Indus script not only as an *attribute* of the 'fish' pictogram (in the compound read above as *veḷ* + *mīn* 'white star' = 'Venus') but also as its *synonym*.

The sign || is attested as a synonym of the plain 'fish' sign in the following pair of inscriptions:

M-172 (fig. 13.10)
H-6 (fig. 13.11)

Fig. 13.10. The sign sequence 'fig tree' + 'fish' in an impression of an Indus seal from Mohenjo-daro (M-172). After Marshall 1931a: III pl. 106, 71.

Fig. 13.11. The sign sequence 'fig tree' + 'two long vertical strokes' in an impression of a seal from Harappa (H-6).

The two signs, the plain 'fish' and ||, both occur as the second member of a compound sharing one and the same grapheme as its first member. Identity of meaning is suggested by the fact that both compounds are embedded in the same context, which includes the preceding as well as the following sign. The matter is complicated by the fact that all three identical graphemes in this continuous sequence of four signs are represented by variant forms (allographs) in the two inscriptions:

Evidence supporting the equation of these three sign pairs as allographs cannot be presented here, but it can be checked by consulting a concordance to the Indus inscriptions (Koskenniemi and Parpola 1982: 84–6, 72–3, 185–67).

In §§ 13.4–5 and 14.1, we shall attempt an interpretation of the sign which forms the first member in these two compounds ending in || and 'fish'. This sign, which appears to depict 'a fig tree' (§§ 13.4 and 14.1), has in fact even more graphic variants than the ones we have discussed. In addition, it seems to form part of the ligature . We shall start with this ligature in § 13.4, because it is used in semantically revealing contexts. But before that, it is necessary to discuss the other component of this ligature, namely, the sign .

13.3 The 'seizer'

The hypothesis that the 'fish' signs symbolize Harappan deities in their astral aspect is supported by another very common sign, whose shape is not that of a fish. It occurs more than 125 times in the Indus texts, often immediately before or after the 'fish' signs (or compound-like sequences ending in the plain 'fish' sign). The variant forms of this pictogram suggest that it represents a 'crab', which is sometimes shown as having feet, but which mostly consists of nothing but the body and the claws;

That the signs with feet really are allographs of those without feet is indicated by the presence of this variation in ligatures where the 'crab' sign is placed inside a sign depicting a 'fig tree' (§§ 13.3–14.1): the identity of these ligatures and is suggested by the fact that the two following signs are identical in the two inscriptions, one from Lothal, the other from Harappa (fig. 13.12).

The claws are clearly emphasized in the 'crab' sign. It is, therefore, quite feasible that it expresses the concept of 'grasping' or 'seizing'. 'Crab' with its 'claws' would be a perfect symbol for this concept, because 'grasping' is consistently associated with the crab in Indian folklore. In the Buddhist Baka-Jātaka a crab addresses a crane that has promised to carry it away from a dried-up pond:

(a)

(b)

Fig. 13.12. The ligature composed of the 'fig tree' and 'crab' signs in two variant forms, occurring in texts with parallel sequences: (a) impression of a seal from Harappa (H-598); (b) impression of a seal from Lothal (L-11).

'You'd never be able to hold me tight enough, friend crane; whereas we crabs have got an astonishingly tight grip [the Pali word used in the original is *su-gahaṇam*, corresponding to Sanskrit *su-grahaṇam*] . . .' With his claws the crab gripped hold of the crane's neck as with the pincers of a smith. (trans. R. Chalmers, in Cowell 1895: I, 97).

The same comparison is found in the Kakkaṭa-Jātaka, where a giant crab catches an elephant's foot 'tight in his claw, like a smith seizes a lump of iron in a huge pair of tongs'. Likewise, a proverb quoted in the Pañcatantra (1,10) says that 'the crab has just one grip (*karkaṭasya . . . eko grahaḥ*)', i.e. it will never let go what it has once grasped. This concept appears to be pan-Indian, for the Old Tamil text Perumpāṇāṟṟuppaṭai (verses 206–8) also compares the claws of the crab to the pincers of the blacksmith. The verbal root *koḷ* 'to seize, grasp, take' is in Old Tamil texts used of the crab's 'seizing' with its claws (Naṟṟiṇai 35; Aiṅkuṟunūṟu 27).

The planets are firmly believed to 'seize' people and afflict them with ills. In his 'Adventures of the ten princes' (*c.* AD 700), Daṇḍin speaks of the 'terrifying stars and planets' (*caṇḍa-tārā-grahāḥ*), which the magicians try to control with magical diagrams and other means. Abbé J. A. Dubois, for 40 years a keen observer of the *Hindu manners, customs and ceremonies* in the eighteenth century, relates in detail on the role of the planets in incantations:

> Brahma, Vishnu and Śiva themselves are subject to the commands of the magicians. There are, however, certain divinities who are invoked by preference. Among these the planets occupy the first place. The term *graha*, by which they are designated, signifies the *act of seizing*, that is, of laying hold of those whom they are enjoined by the magical enchantments to torment ... The magician sometimes repeats ... mantrams in a humble and supplicatory manner, loading with praises the god whom he invokes; but he quickly resumes his imperious tone, and exclaims as though in a vehement rage, 'Grasp it! Grasp it!' ... No sooner is this done that the *grahas* or planets take possession of the person against whom such incantations are directed, and afflict him with a thousand ills. (Dubois 1906: 387ff.)

Because the contexts – vicinity of the 'fish' signs assumed to denote stars and planets – would suit well the meaning 'planet', the 'crab' sign may stand for Proto-Dravidian *kōḷ* 'seizure', in Tamil also 'planet', from the verbal root *koḷ* 'to seize'. The Sanskrit word *graha*, from the verbal root *grah-* <*grabh-* 'to grab, seize', has exactly the same meanings, 'seizure' as well as 'planet'. Since there is clear evidence for the practice of astronomy by the Harappans, while experts have debated whether the Vedic Aryans knew the planets at all, and since the related Indo-European languages do not have a noun meaning 'planet' derived from this verbal root, Sanskrit *graha* is more likely to be a translation loan from Dravidian than *kōḷ* is to be a calque on Sanskrit *graha*. It is true that on the Dravidian side the meaning 'planet' for *kōḷ* is known from Tamil only, but this is not surprising, as Sanskrit astronomical terms have almost everywhere in India replaced the original native terms in non-Aryan languages.

The word *kōḷ* 'planet' is, however, already found in the oldest literature in Old Tamil dating from the beginning of the Christian era. Here it refers to eclipse demons. Thus Puṟanāṉūṟu 260 speaks of 'the full moon that has escaped the sharp teeth of the snake (*pāmpu*) that had coiled in order to make the world to suffer, after it had let go its seizure (*kōḷ*)'. The oldest certain occurrence of the Sanskrit word *graha* in an astral sense is in the Atharvaveda (19,9,7 and 10), which prays for the appeasement of 'seizers wandering in the sky' (*divícarā gráhāḥ*) [Sāyaṇa's commentary: Mars etc.] and of 'lunar and solar seizures (*grahāḥ*) by Rāhu'. The eclipse demon's name *Rāhú-* appears to be a synonym of the word *graha*, for it is most probably derived from **rābhú-*, from the root *rabh-* 'to take hold of, grasp'. Eclipse demons may be meant also in JUB 3,1,1,1ff.; Kauśikasūtra 99,1 discusses the occasion 'when the darkness grasps (*gr̥hṇāti*) the sun'. The first really unambiguous reference for the word *graha* in the meaning 'planet' is in the Maitrāyaṇī Upaniṣad (§ 11.1).

Instead of *kōḷ* 'planet', a synonymous compound, *kōṉ-mīṉ* (with *ḷ* changed into *ṉ* before the following *m*) 'seizing star', is used in the Old Tamil text Ciṟupāṇāṟṟuppaṭai (242–4): 'In golden plates, that ridicule the young-rayed (morning) sun surrounded by the seizing stars in the bright sky, he will serve the many dishes suited to your taste.' Another Old Tamil text, Puṟanāṉūṟu, also compares a golden vessel to a 'seizing star' (392,17 *kōṉmīṉaṉṉa polaṅ kalat taḷaii*). Paṭṭiṉappālai 67–8 speaks of the wrestling-grounds where fishermen mingle in fight, 'as in the dark-blue sky the seizing stars which mingle with the day-stars that turn to the right when they rise'. In this text, *kōṉ-mīṉ* is contrasted with *nāṉ-mīṉ* 'calendrical fixed star'; the first member in the latter compound is *nāḷ* 'day, early dawn, tomorrow', each day of the month being calendrically defined by a fixed star (§ 11.2). It is remarkable that not only does the sign combination 'crab' + 'fish' (corresponding to the Tamil compound *kōṉ-mīṉ*) occur three times in the Indus inscriptions, but the identity of the following sequence in two parallel inscriptions suggests that this combination, 'crab' + 'fish', is actually synonymous with the plain 'crab' sign, as is Tamil *kōḷ* with *kōṉ-mīṉ*:

M-387
M-57

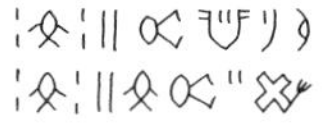

13.4 The name of Rudra

The interpretation of the 'crab' sign can be further checked by examining the ligature mentioned at the end of § 13.2, , where it forms one of the two components. One particular context in which this ligature occurs, in the copper tablets of Mohenjo-daro, is exceptionally favourable for establishing its intended meaning. It is among the few Indus signs for which the copper tablets function as 'semi-bilinguals', mediating the meaning of these signs visually, through an iconographic image.

We have seen in § 7.3 that the copper tablets constitute a rare category of objects with a clear interdependence between the inscription on the obverse and the iconographic motif on the reverse. This is certified by the existence of numerous duplicates, forming sets of identical tablets. In some sets, an isolated ligature on the reverse has the same inscription on the obverse as an iconographic motif in another set. This seems to mean that the ligature stands for the name of the deity or mythological hero depicted pictorially through the iconographic motif (fig. 7.14).

Thus an identical inscription on the obverse side of two sets of copper tablets equates the ligature with a male figure armed with bow and arrows, anthropomorphic apart from having a bull's horns and tail, and with long eyes (fig. 13.13). A male deity having similar long eyes and bull's horns, but a goat's beard in addition, is known from several terracotta masks and terracotta statuettes (fig. 13.14). The Harappan art depicts also the markhor (wild mountain goat) with a human face which has similar long eyes and a goat's beard (fig. 14.35).

As we have seen, the ligature has variant forms, showing the 'crab' sign with or without 'legs' (fig. 13.12). The other component of the ligature is a sign which also has several allographs in the Indus texts (fig. 13.15). Comparison with a motif occurring on Early, Mature and Late Harappan painted pottery from various parts of the Greater Indus Valley (fig. 13.16) suggests that this pictogram represents a fig tree, either the pipal (*Ficus religiosa*) or the banyan (*Ficus indica* = *Ficus bengalensis*). Except when it is combined with the 'crab' sign, the tree is shown as three-branched on a single stem, just as in the pottery motif. In the seals depicted in fig. 13.12, one of the three branches of the 'fig tree' sign has been left out in order to accommodate the 'crab' sign inserted in the middle, but the remaining two branches end in the fig leaf, just as on the painted pots. In the other variants the branches seem to produce either figs or hanging aerial roots (figs. 14.1–2) or both; for the schematic representation of the air roots, compare the hatchings on both sides of the middlemost branch of the fig tree on a pot coming from Nausharo ID (fig. 13.16e). The 'fruit' variants come close to the 'fig' ideograms in the Cretan hieroglyphic and Linear B scripts (,).

If the 'crab' sign in this ligature is assumed to function as a phonetic determinative, then the combination of the 'crab' and 'fig' signs into one ligature produces a satisfying explanation from the vocabulary of the Dravidian languages. In § 13.3, the 'crab' sign was read as *kōḷ* 'seizer, planet'. A close homophone with an eminently suitable meaning is *kōḷi* 'banyan, pipal, all kinds of fig trees which bear fruit without outwardly blossoming, epidendron, grasping plant (some figs are of this nature)'. This word is found already in Old Tamil (Puṟam 58,2; 254,7), and it has cognates in other South Dravidian languages and Tulu. The meaning 'grasping plant' suggests that it is a derivative of the Proto-Dravidian root *koḷ* 'to grasp, seize'.

But we still have to explain how the word *kōḷi* can be connected with the Harappan archer-god depicted on the copper tablets. In the Ṛgvedic hymns and especially in the Brāhmaṇa texts, the god Rudra is described as a cruel hunter and raider, who with the bow, his characteristic weapon, shoots arrows at cattle and people, arrows which are also metaphorically understood to mean fever and disease (ṚS 2,33,10–11; 5,42,11; 10,125,6; ŚB 9,1,1,6 and 14). The number of Ṛgvedic hymns addressed to Rudra, praying him to desist from shooting, is small in the light of his importance in the following period, and this has generally been taken as an indication of his intrusion into the Vedic pantheon at a late stage and thus of his pre-Ṛgvedic Indian origin. Rudra is the Vedic predecessor of the Hindu god Śiva (the adjective *śiva* 'kind' being a euphemistic attribute of Rudra in the Veda) and also of Śiva's 'son' (i.e. youthful aspect), the Hindu war-god Skanda. As an archer, Rudra appears as the punisher of his incestuous father Prajāpati in the famous myth of his own birth, which is associated with the origins of the Indian star calendar and datable to the third millennium BC (§§ 11.3; 12.2; 14.4). There are some distinctive features in the mythology of Rudra that compare closely with concepts implied by the Dravidian words *kōḷ* and *kōḷi* and their close homophones.

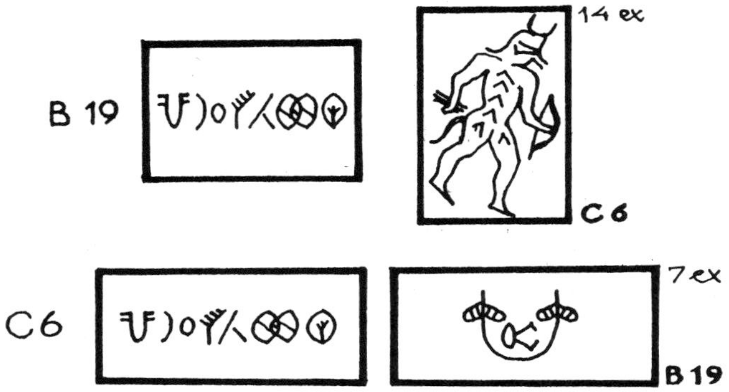

Fig. 13.13. The ligature of 'fig tree' + 'crab' signs corresponding to the motif of 'horned archer' in two sets of copper tablets from Mohenjo-daro (cf. § 7.3 and fig. 7.14).

In the first place, Śiva is often called *Hara* 'seizer, taker, robber', and this name is used already of his Vedic predecessor Rudra (Āśvalāyana-Gṛhyasūtra 4,8,19), and, even as early as Kaṭha-Saṁhitā (8,2), of Agni, the god of fire, who is often identified with Rudra (e.g. ṚS 2,1,2; TS 5,5,7). In fact, from the later Vedic texts it is evident that Rudra was the prototypal robber and raider (VS 16,20–2), just as Skanda or Kumāra in Hinduism is not only the divine leader of the army but also the god of thieves and robbers (e.g. Śūdraka's Mṛcchakaṭika 3,13–15). This sense is implied in the meaning of 'grasping epiphytic fig' for *kōḷi*, which strangles its host trees, and especially in the word *kōḷ* 'seizure, taking, pillage, plunder, robbery' and the Proto-Dravidian verbal root from which it is derived, *koḷ* 'to seize, take, rob'. A Proto-Dravidian verbal root fully homophonous with (and possibly also derived from) this, *koḷ*, means 'to strike, hurt, hit, beat, shoot with bow, kill', and its derivative *kōḷ* means 'killing, murder, hitting, wound, damage'.

Fig. 13.14. A Harappan male deity whose human face has elongated eyes, horns of a bull and a goat's beard: (a–c) three views of a terracotta mask from Mohenjo-daro (DK 13013).

Secondly, in South Dravidian, Tulu and Telugu the word **kōḷ* denotes 'sound of howling, lamenting, wailing, loud outcry'. This reminds one of the numerous passages in the Vedic texts where Rudra's name is associated with the Sanskrit root *rud-* 'to cry, weep, lament' (ŚB 6,1,3,7f.; 9,1,1,6; 11,6,3,7; TS 1,5,1,1; MS 4,2,12). A unique passage in the Vādhūlasūtra (3,94) dealing with horse sacrifice suggests that Rudra, or Kumāra 'young man, boy', as he is also called, was the Indian counterpart of the Near Eastern Tammuz, the youthful husband of the Goddess, whose death was greatly lamented: his human representative was sacrificially beheaded (Parpola 1983: 52ff.).

There must have been some such deep religious reason to stress Rudra's association with 'crying, lamenting', since it has apparently led to such an 'etymological' change in his name as this. The desire to link *Rudra* with the verb *rud-* and possibly the analogy of another god's name, Indra, which ends in *-dra*, would satisfactorily explain the irregular disaspiration ($d < dh$) that may be assumed to have taken place in his name. There is every reason to believe that Rudra's name originally was **Rudhra*, an Indo-European word meaning 'red' (cf. Greek *e-ruthrós* 'red' and Sanskrit *rudhira* 'red; blood'). A number of different epithets all meaning 'red, reddish brown' (*aruṣa*, *babhru*, *babhluśa*, *tāmra*, *aruṇa*, *vilohita*) are applied to Rudra in the R̥gveda (e.g. 1,114,5; 2,33,5 and 9) and later Vedic texts (e.g. VS 16,7). Not only is Rudra associated with blood (which he sheds as the god of war; see also § 13.5), but he is also frequently identified with fire, and said to shine like the sun or gold (R̥S 1,43,5).

The counterpart of Rudra-Skanda in Old Tamil texts is the youthful war-god Murukaṉ, who is likewise connected with the colour red. Murukaṉ's complexion and garments are red. As the god of the hunting hillmen,

> Murukaṉ is also typically associated with the colours of the hills, especially with the red colour of the foliage; he is compared to the sun rising above the hills and setting beyond the mountains. His weaponry drips blood; Murukaṉ's elephant has tusks covered with blood; his cock is red; the blood of the ram (*kaṭā*) used in the sacrifice is red. The blossoms of the *kaṭampu* tree (*Nauclea cadamba*) which he wears as his garland, are red. His earliest names – Cevvēḷ, Ceyyōṉ, Cevvēl – all contain the [word] 'red'. (Zvelebil 1977b: 232)

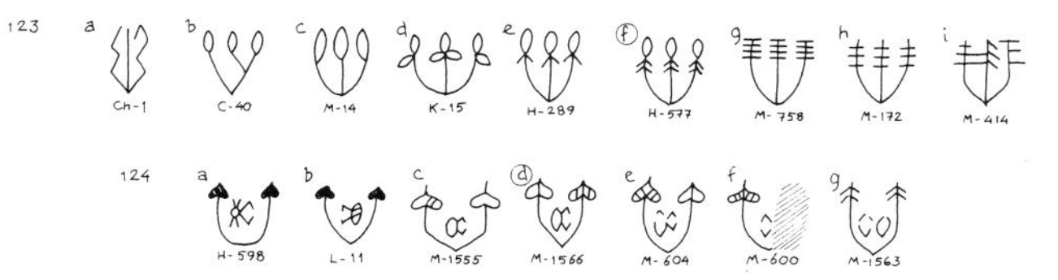

Fig. 13.15. Allographs of the Indus sign representing a three-branched 'fig tree' and of its ligature with the 'crab' sign, where the middlemost branch has been omitted to accommodate the inserted 'crab' sign.

Fig. 13.16. 'Three-branched fig tree with a single stem' as a motif on Early, Mature and Late Harappan pottery.
(a–c) Mundigak IV,1, eastern Afghanistan, *c.*2600 BC. After Casal 1961: II, fig. 64, nos. 167 (a), 169 (b), 171 (c).
(d) Rahman Dheri III (late Kot Diji period), *c.*2600–2300 BC. After Durrani and Wright 1992: 151, fig. 2b.
(e) Nausharo ID, transitional phase between the Early and Mature Harappan periods, *c.*2600–2550 BC. Goblet painted in black on a red slip from structure II. Locus 3. After Samzun 1992: 250, fig. 29.4 no. 2.
(f) Amri IIIA, Sind, early phase of Mature Harappan, *c.*2500–2300 BC. After Casal 1964: II, fig. 78: 338.
(g) Cemetery R37 at Harappa, Punjab. Mature Harappan period, second half of the third millennium BC. Drawn by VHA after Wheeler 1947a: pl. 46: 6; cf. Wheeler 1947a: 107.
(h) Bīr-kōṭ-ghwaṇḍai, Swat Valley, northern Pakistan. Late Harappan black-on-red pottery from the latter half of the Ghalegay IV period (*c.*1700–1400 BC). After a drawing of Giorgio Stacul.
(i) Late Harappan Cemetery H pottery from Harappa, Punjab. Drawn after Tyulyaev 1988: 55, fig. 47.

In Tamil, Murukaṉ's names *Cēy*, *Cēyōṉ*, *Ceyyōṉ*, *Ceyyavaṉ*, all derived from Proto-Dravidian **ke-* / **kē-* 'red', also means 'young son, child', since the infant is conceived to be red in colour. Red is often said to be the colour of the newborn baby in the Mahābhārata, too, also specifically in connection with the newborn baby Skanda (3,224,14316–8). In ŚB 6,1,3,1ff. Rudra is a crying (*rud-*) baby (*kumāra*); and in traditional medicine, Skanda is the principal disease demon (*graha*) attacking the newborn baby and thirsting for its blood. Skanda is also associated with blood as the presiding deity of the red planet Mars, one name of which is *Rudhira*: this Sanskrit word means 'red' as well as 'blood'.

According to the Aitareya-Brāhmaṇa (7,13ff.), King Hariścandra ('yellow moon') had a thousand wives (i.e. the stars), but could not get a son. On the advice of sage Nārada, Hariścandra had recourse to King Varuṇa, asked for the birth of a son, and promised to sacrifice him to Varuṇa. The boy, called *Rohita* 'red', was demanded by Varuṇa after his birth, but the father got the sacrifice postponed until Rohita was 16 years old and fit to bear arms. At this point, however, Rohita refused to become the victim, took his bow and disappeared into the forest.

In this myth Rohita was to be sacrificed as a human victim at 16, the age of initiation for young soldiers and the age of the war-god Skanda, the 'eternal youth'. Like the lamented young bard of the horse sacrifice mentioned above, he appears to impersonate the Vedic war-god Rudra. This is suggested also by his name. The 13th book of the Atharvaveda extols Rohita as the red god of the rising (*ruh-*) sun: 'Rohita has climbed the heights, he has ascended them' (AS 13,1,4). Rohita is the god of war, for he 'conquers wealth, conquers cattle, and conquers booty' (AS 13,1,37).

13.5 The goat-faced god

We must examine the mythology of Rudra and Skanda a little further in order to explain the goat's beard worn by his assumed predecessor in the Harappan terracotta masks and statuettes (fig. 13.14). This male god also has the same elongated eyes as the archer-god of the copper tablets (fig. 13.13) and the human-faced markhor in the 'fig deity' seal (fig. 14.35). As we shall see, this goat-faced god is intimately associated with the fig tree, as implied by the sign  = *kōḷi* 'grasping fig', which has been interpreted as standing for his name and as corresponding to Rudra in § 13.4.

In the Vedic texts, Rudra is often directly identified with Agni, the god of fire, whose animal form is the goat and its wild counterpart, the markhor (AS 4,14,1; 9,5,7 and 9; VS 13,51). In post-Vedic texts, too, Agni's vehicle is the goat (e.g. Matsya-Purāṇa 260,11) or the ram (Skanda-Purāṇa 1,2,16,53ff.), while Rudra's successor in Hindu mythology, Skanda, is said to have as one of his six heads that of the goat (Mahābhārata 3,217,12). A special goat-faced form or 'son' of Skanda is the young hero Viśākha, 'branched', born from the right side of Skanda, where Indra had hurled his thunderbolt. In Tantrākhyāyika 1,44 it is asked: 'Do the pious not worship Viṣṇu in the shape of a boar . . . and the six-headed (Skanda) in the shape of the goat?'

Rudra's doublet Rohita, the red rising sun, is also called 'the one-footed goat' (*aja ekapād*) (AS 13,1,6) who 'has risen in the east' (TB 3,1,2,8). The red-coloured, youthful and beautiful Skanda is directly compared with the red rising sun (e.g. Mahābhārata 3,214,19). Sunrise and sunset are critical moments of liminality, open to attacks by demonic forces. The Sanskrit word for 'the ray of sun', *raśmi*, primarily means 'rope'. According to ŚB 4,6,5,1ff., the rising and setting sun is a disease demon, which seizes beings:

> Now the Seizer (*graha*), forsooth, is he that burns yonder, since by him all these creatures are seized (*gr̥hītāḥ*). Hence they say . . . 'They walk, seized by the grahas.' He approaches either the rising or the setting sun, thinking, 'Thou art the seizer, seize thou N.N. by such and such a disease!' (naming) him whom he hates.

The term *graha* 'seizer' is used in its sense of 'the planets', specifically of the two most ominous planets, Mars and Saturn, which are thought to be demoniac gods, attacking people and 'seizing' them with invisible nooses of illness. The planets are usually referred to as a group of 'nine seizers' (*nava-graha*) (§ 11.1). In classical Indian medicine, there is a group of nine demons of sickness, also called 'nine seizers' (*nava-graha*), which attack newborn babies and their mothers, but if properly propitiated and worshipped, protect them and also grant children.

Most dangerous among these godlings, all of them clearly multiforms of one and the same deity, is *Skanda-graha*, who sucks the blood of the infants. There can be little doubt about the identity of Skanda-graha with the red planet Mars, who is presided over by Skanda, and who is called, among other names, Rudhira 'red' (also 'blood'). We have seen that Rudra, too, was feared for his fiery arrows that caused fever, and that blood is associated with Rudra. And the Vedic texts dealing with the birth rituals already prescribe fumigation and formulae for averting the attacks of demons on children; the long list of their names in PGS 1,16,23–5 includes that of *Kumāra* 'young boy, infant', which is one of the important names of Rudra and Skanda (cf. also HGS 2,1,3,4–7).

Suśruta-Saṁhitā, one of the basic works on Indian medicine, confirms the identity of the disease demon Skanda with the war-god Skanda in chapter 6,37 dealing with the origin of 'the nine presiding deities, namely, Skanda and others, of the nine diseases of infant life'. They are said to be all 'possessed of ethereal frames and divine effulgence', and created together with the war-god Skanda:

Fig. 13.17. The goat-headed fertility-god Naigameṣa is illustrated more than a dozen times in the early Jaina art of Mathurā, Uttar Pradesh, *c.* AD 100. This relief, found on a railing fragment from the Vodva stupa at the Kankālī Ṭīlā site, is the most notable example. 'Lord Nemeṣa' (*bhagavā nemeso*), called so in the inscription beneath the deity, is shown enthroned and flanked by child and female attendants. Red sandstone, 25 × 55 cm. Lucknow Museum (J 626).

They were created by the gods Agni, Mahādeva (Śiva) and the goddesses Kṛttikā and Umā for guarding the new-born Guha (i.e. Rudra-Skanda) ... The Naigameṣa Graha who has a ram's face was created by the goddess Pārvatī as the friend and protector of the young god Guha; he was as dear to him as his own self. Skandāpasmāra ... was created by Agni. He is as bright as fire itself and is a constant companion of the god Skanda, and is also known by the name of Viśākha. The god Skanda, the tutelary divinity of the disease of that denomination, was begotten by the almighty Destroyer of Tripura (Śiva) and is otherwise known by the name of Kumāra. (trans. Kunjalal Bhishagratna 1963: III, 161)

The ram and he-goat associated with Skanda are prominent symbols of virility (AS 4,4,8). The potent goat-headed, ram-headed (*meṣānana*) child-demon *Naigameṣa* mentioned in the passage quoted above is known as a son-granting deity called *Nejameṣa* as early as the apocryphal verses (Khila 30,1) of the Ṛgveda (inserted after ṚS 10,184, a hymn to be recited by the husband at the time of cohabitation; cf. ĀpGS 8,13). Of the three stanzas intended to form a hymn probably only the first one was originally addressed to Nejameṣa:

O Nejameṣa! Fly away, and fly hither again bringing a beautiful son; to me here who is longing for a son grant thou an embryo, and that a male one. (trans. Winternitz 1895: 150–1)

The verses are to be uttered, after touching her generative organs, by a woman who does not conceive (according to Ṛgvidhāna 4,23,2–3). They are also recited at the ceremony for safe delivery (ŚGS 1,22,7; ĀśvGS 1,14,3) and at cohabitation (ĀpGS 8,13). The BaudhGS (2,1,18) prescribes an offering after childbirth to the 'not terrible' (*aghora*) *Nejameya* on the leaves of the pipal fig (*aśvatthaparṇeṣu*) in the cow shed. In the Mahābhārata, *Naigameya* is one of the names of Skanda (3,232,14634), or a form or son of Skanda, born from his back; Fire is also said to have become the goat-faced Naigameya, who has many children, and to have played with the newborn Skanda (3,226,14367). Iconographically, the identity of Naigameṣa and Skanda is confirmed by a statue excavated at Mandhal near Nagpur in 1975–6. This ram-headed, ithyphallic icon, dated to the fifth century AD, holds in its right hand the spear typical of Skanda.

The Jaina religion, too, knew a goat-faced male deity called *Prajāpati Naigameṣa* or *Naigameṣin*, who supervised conception and childbirth, and who was propitiated to obtain offspring (fig. 13.17). According to the Śvetāmbara Kalpasūtra, the commander of the celestial armies (i.e. a duplicate of Hindu Skanda), called *Hari-Ṇegameṣin*, transferred the embryo of Mahāvīra Jina from one womb to another. In the seventh chapter of Neminātha Carita, this same god plays a central role in the conception and birth. In the Jaina tradition Naigameṣa's vehicle is the peacock, again a feature he shares with the Hindu god Skanda. On the other hand, the epithet Prajāpati 'Lord of Offspring' links the Jaina Naigameṣa with one of the principal deities of the Vedic Brāhmaṇa literature, the creator-god Prajāpati. That both ultimately are really one and the same is made very likely by the fact that Prajāpati, too, is closely connected with childbirth and, in that connection, with the banyan fig (§ 12.2).

In ŚB 2,4,4,1–2, the Vedic Prajāpati is identified with Dakṣa, who, desirous of offspring, first performed the

Dākṣāyaṇa sacrifice. In the post-Vedic literature, Dakṣa is famous for his sacrifice, to which he did not invite Śiva. In one account, Dakṣa was beheaded, and a goat's head, evidently one that had been severed in the sacrifice, was exchanged for his own. Śiva-Purāṇa 2,6,2–32 derives Skanda's goat vehicle from a sacrificial victim. It appears that the victim was identified with Skanda (§ 14.3).

In § 13.4, the ligature , read as *kōḷi* 'grasping fig', was interpreted as the name of the Harappan predecessor of Rudra-Skanda, depicted as an anthropomorphic hunter, often with a goat's beard. Suśruta-Saṁhitā 2,36 discusses rites in which the goat-faced god Naigameṣa is invoked for the protection of infants and in which the banyan tree figures prominently. Thus the infant should wear as a charm a *jaṭilā* 'an aerial root of the banyan tree'; the plant called 'goat's delight' should be used to fumigate the child's body; and the child should be bathed under a banyan tree (*vaṭa-vr̥kṣa*) on the sixth lunar day (six being the holy number of Skanda, the six-headed son of the six Pleiades), and a *bali* offering should be made at the foot of the banyan tree 'to the Ram, the father of children' (*kumārapitr̥meṣa*), using this mantra: 'May the far-famed god Naigameṣa, the father of children (*bāla-pitā*), who has a goat's face (*ajānanaḥ*) with moving brows and rolling eyes (*calākṣibhrūḥ*) and who can assume different forms at will, protect the child!'

Naigameṣa appears to have a Harappan predecessor. One Indus tablet shows a horned deity, long arms covered in bangles, whose head seems to be that of a ram and who stands inside a fig tree (fig. 13.18). It is likely that this is the same deity as the caprine-eyed archer-god of the copper tablets. In the Vedic texts, Rudra has a bow as the god of war and robbery; and the rays of the red sun are arrows of fever. But the god of war is also the god of love (§ 13.2), and the bow and arrow are connected with sex and fertility too. The missiles of love and desire (*Kā́ma*) are painful (AS 3,25); the male member is asked to become taut like a bow (AS 4,4,6–7); and a male foetus is asked to come to the womb, as an arrow to a quiver (AS 3,23,2).

The Dravidian word *kōḷi*, interpreted as the name of the Harappan archer-god (expressed by the 'crab' + 'fig' ligature), means 'all kinds of fig trees which bear fruit without outwardly blossoming, epidendron, grasping fig'. This word seems to be a derivative of the root *koḷ* 'to take', which is used also in the sense of 'receiving, acquiring, getting'; cf. Old Tamil *kōḷ* 'the act of bearing fruit' (Akam 2,1; 162,19; 335,14; 382,10; 399,14), and in Sanskrit, *óṣadhayaḥ phálaṁ gr̥bhṇanti* 'the plants get (lit. 'take': from the same verbal root as *graha*) fruit', *gr̥bhītá-* 'fructified, fruit-bearing', lit. 'taken' (said of the wood-apple tree in AB 2,1), and *garbha* 'fruit, embryo'.

Fig. 13.18. A ram-faced deity with long arms full of bangles, standing inside a fig tree. A moulded tablet from Harappa (H-178 B).

The ligature of 'crab' + 'fig tree' thus seems also to express the deity iconically: the 'seizing' / 'fructifying' deity or his 'embryo' is placed inside the fig tree, just as the anthropomorphic deities are often depicted inside fig trees in the Indus glyptics (figs. 13.18; 14.35).

The pipal fig has leaves resembling the flame, and it was used both as the kindling stick and as fuel in Vedic sacrifices. The 'father' and 'mother' of the Fire (Agni) are two pieces of wood, either from an *aśvattha* (masculine) and a *śamī* (feminine, *Prosopis spicigera*) tree, or both pieces from an aśvattha that has grown on a śamī. In the Veda, the igniting of a fire is compared to sexual intercourse. According to Kauśikasūtra 35,8, one should recite the hymn Atharvaveda 6,11 in the rite performed for the conception of a son. The first verse of this hymn refers to the firewood: 'The aśvattha (has) mounted upon the *śamī*; there is made the generation of a male; that verily is the obtainment of a son; that we bring into women.' Agni, Fire, is contained in the kindling sticks like an embryo (R̥S 3,29,2); he is the embryo in the wood (R̥S 2,10,3). The pipal is said to be the abode of Agni (cf. TS 1,1,3,9; KS 8,2) or to have the brilliance of the newborn Agni (MS 1,6,5), and Agni is often equated with Rudra: 'Agni is Rudra.'

14 Evidence for Harappan worship of the Goddess

14.1 The North Star

In sections 13.3–5 we have assumed that the 'crab' sign was ligatured with the 'fig' sign as a phonetic (and also as a semantic) determinative, so as to indicate that the 'fig' sign in this particular case is to be read with a phonetic value similar to that of the 'crab' sign = *kōḷ* 'seizure' (§ 13.3), namely *kōḷi*. If this is indeed so, then the normal phonetic value of the 'fig' sign may be expected to have been different. There are several reasons to think that this ordinary reading of the 'fig' sign was *vaṭa* 'banyan tree, the Indian fig, *Ficus indica* L.', which is also among the meanings of the word *kōḷi* (§ 13.4).

One of the reasons is a striking visual parallel offered by the living tradition of India. The Early Harappan pottery motif with its three fig leaves (fig. 13.16), from which the 'fig' sign of the Indus script appears to be derived, is virtually identical with the three-leaved fig-symbol carried upon her head and in her hand by Sāvitrī, the model of marital faithfulness, in a drawing (based on traditional models) which illustrates her connection with the banyan tree (fig. 14.1).

Sāvitrī, often called *pati-vratā* 'devoted to her husband, chaste', is one of the most famous examples of conjugal fidelity in Sanskrit literature. The myth of Sāvitrī, told in the Mahābhārata (3,293–9) and many Purāṇas, seems to be quite ancient and to go back to the marriage hymn of the R̥gveda (R̥S 10,85), where Sāvitrī appears as the divine bride of Soma (§ 14.4). A shrine of the goddess Sāvitrī existed in Mūlasthāna (present Multan) in the Indus Valley (Skanda-Purāṇa 7,4,14,14–18), in the heartland of the Harappan culture, while the Sāvitrī-vrata is said to have been performed in ancient times at a *vaṭa* tree called *Bodhi-nyagrodha* at Avantī in Malwa (Bhaviṣya-Purāṇa, Uttara-khaṇḍa 102,86).

In the myth, the goddess Sāvitrī is pleased with King Aśvapati after he has fasted and performed sacrifice for 18 years, pronouncing the Sāvitrī mantra a hundred thousand times. In response to the king's wish for offspring a princess named Sāvitrī is born to him. On her coming of age, she

Fig. 14.1. Vaṭa-Sāvitrī in a picture drawn after traditional models by Mrs Gupte about 1905. After Gupte 1906, plate: nos. 15, 22, 40. The dying Satyavat, shown beneath a banyan fig, holds one of the air roots of the tree, while his faithful wife Sāvitrī holds another air root in her right hand. In her left hand and over her head, Sāvitrī has a miniature banyan with three branches, each ending in a single leaf; this is identical with the 'three-branched fig tree' motif of Harappan pottery (see fig. 13.16). Leafed branches (including fig branches) on the head distinguish Harappan gods (cf. figs. 10.9–10; 14.16; 14.18; 14.35) as well as tree spirits of later Hinduism (§ 13.1).

chooses to marry prince Satyavat ('truthful') in spite of the prophecy that Satyavat will die one year after their marriage. On the appointed hour, Satyavat dies under a banyan fig (§ 14.3), and Yama, the god of death, seizes him with his noose; but Satyavat is revived and blessed with many children when his faithful wife, through her persistent devotion to her husband, wins these favours from Yama.

A ritual, called *Vaṭa-sāvitrī-vrata*, is performed even today in many parts of India by women whose husbands are living and who want to get children and avoid widowhood. Like Sāvitrī, the women observe their vow of complete fasting for three days. These three days seem to represent the period during which the moon is not visible before the sickle of the new moon appears: the moon dies but is reborn after three days. Rebirth of the sun also seems to be involved. The texts identify the goddess Sāvitrī with the sacred verse *sāvitrī* pronounced at the sunrise. Moreover, the vrata is performed from the 13th day of the bright half of the Jyeṣṭha month until the 15th or full moon day, and the conjunction of the full moon with the Jyeṣṭhā star appears originally to have coincided with the vernal equinox and the beginning of the new year, which symbolizes the death and rebirth of the sun (§§ 11.2–3; 14.4). The women observing the Vaṭa-sāvitrī-vrata sprinkle water at the root of the banyan tree, embrace it and wrap cotton thread around it; in the marriage ritual, the bride and groom are bound together with cotton thread. According to Hemādri, a woman performing the Vaṭa-sāvitrī-vrata rite should also look at the star Arundhatī and worship it as the faithful wife of sage Vasiṣṭha; this is another element of the marriage ritual, which we shall soon examine more closely. Finally, the women worship the banyan tree and, beneath it, images of Sāvitrī and Satyavat, the goddess Sāvitrī (dressed in red clothes) and her husband Brahmā (dressed in white) and Yama (Skanda-Purāṇa 7,1,166,77ff.; Bhaviṣya-Purāṇa, Uttara-khaṇḍa 102,66–86; Agni-Purāṇa 194,5–8; Brahmavaivarta-Purāṇa, Prakr̥ti-khaṇḍa 23,42ff.; Padma-Purāṇa, Sr̥ṣṭi-khaṇḍa 7,10–23; Hemādri, Caturvarga-cintāmaṇi, Vrata-khaṇḍa 21).

It is true that the word *vaṭa* 'banyan' has been considered an Indo-Aryan word, a 'Prakritic' form derived from Sanskrit *vr̥ta* 'circular' or (via **vaṭṭa*) from *vr̥tta* 'turned'. However, these Sanskrit words are not used with the meaning 'banyan tree'. Secondly, the Aryan nomads did not bring this tree to the subcontinent, but first encountered it there, so their adoption of the tree's earlier native name would have been a natural thing to do. A non-Aryan origin is likely also because the word *vaṭa* is not known from the Vedic texts but only from the Mahābhārata onwards. The banyan tree is called *vaṭam* in a number of Dravidian languages, and this name seems to be ultimately derived from the Proto-Dravidian word **vaṭam* / **vaṭi* 'rope, cord'. The rope-like hanging aerial roots are characteristic of the Indian fig tree (fig. 14.2), and it would be natural to call it in Proto-Dravidian (as in Tamil) *vaṭa-maram* 'rope-tree' (and in Sanskrit *vaṭa-vr̥kṣa*, *vaṭa-druma*, in Pali *vaṭa-rukkha*), whence *vaṭam* for short. In a somewhat comparable manner, the Portuguese named it *albero de laiz* 'root tree'.

The Dravidian explanation of the Indian fig's name *vaṭa* as 'rope-tree' makes it possible to find a Dravidian homophone eminently fitting the astral context assumed in the Indus texts where the 'fig' pictogram is followed either by the 'fish' sign, read as *mīṉ* 'fish' *and* 'star' (fig. 14.3), or by its synonym || = *veḷḷi* 'star' (§ 13.2 and fig. 13.11). In Dravidian, the word *vaṭa* also means 'north', and in Old Tamil literature the compound *vaṭa-mīṉ* 'star of the north' occurs many times (e.g. Puṟanāṉūṟu 122,8) as the symbol of conjugal fidelity (*kaṟpu* or *tiṟam*).

The Śatapatha-Brāhmaṇa (2,1,2,3–4) states that the six Pleiades were separated from their husbands, the seven stars of the Great Bear, on account of their infidelity (§§ 11.3; 12.2). Other texts specify that only one of the seven wives, Arundhatī, remained faithful and was therefore allowed to stay with her husband Vasiṣṭha (§ 11.3): she is identified with the small star Alcor in the Great Bear, next to Mizar, the central star of the tail, or ζ Ursae Maioris, which represents Vasiṣṭha (fig. 14.4). This myth is known as early as the Kaṭha-Saṁhitā (8,1) and the Maitrāyaṇī Saṁhitā (1,6,9),

Fig. 14.2. The banyan tree (*Ficus indica* L. = *F. bengalensis* L.) with its characteristic aerial roots.

Fig. 14.3. The sequence 'fig tree' + 'fish' in the inscription of a seal from Mohenjo-daro (M-414).

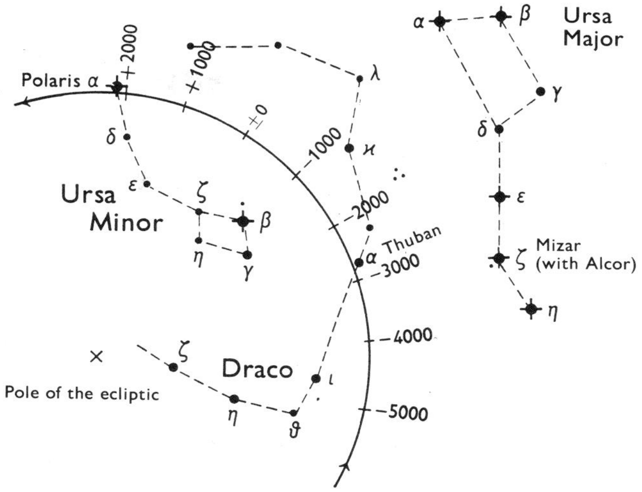

Fig. 14.4. Circumpolar stars and the celestial pole between 5000 BC and AD 2000. The semicircle marks the path of the gradually shifting celestial pole. After Liebert 1969: 168.

which speak of 'the seven Pleiades', including Arundhatī. They are likely to be the seven human and evidently female figures represented in a row in Harappan seals and amulets (fig. 14.35 and § 14.3).

The ancient commentators on the Old Tamil texts unanimously identify *vaṭa-mīṉ* with Arundhatī, the chaste wife of the sage Vasiṣṭha. According to the first canto of Cilappatikāram, *vaṭa-mīṉ* was pointed out to brides by grooms some 1,500 years ago, as is still done in South India. In the Vedic marriage ritual, the groom similarly shows the Arundhatī star to the bride, after having first shown her the star called *dhruva* 'steadfast, firm, fixed', i.e. the Pole Star. According to later explanations, the Pole Star is shown to the bride first because it is easier to see than the small star Alcor; it has become an example of 'maxim' (*nyāya*) of 'gradual instruction' (Śankara on UMS 1,1,8 and 12). However, some Gṛhyasūtras indicate that only the Pole Star should be shown (PGS 1,8,19; ŚGS 1,17,3–4), as does Kālidāsa (Kumārasaṁbhava 7,85); other texts prescribe that, in addition to the Pole Star and Arundhatī (just these two in GGS 2,3,8–12), other stars should also be shown, especially the Seven Sages (JGS 1,21; ĀśvGS 1,8,22; HGS 1,22,14). There can be no doubt that both Arundhatī and the Pole Star are here models for the wife:

> To the Pole Star she addresses, looking at it, the formula: 'Thou art the Pole Star (*dhruva*, firm), may I become firm (i.e. fixed) in the house of my husband So-and-so', uttering the name of her husband (instead of 'So-and-so'), and at the end of the formula her own name in the nominative case. On Arundhatī she looks with the formula: 'Arundhatī, may I be held fast [*ruddhā*] by my husband So-and-so', uttering the name of her husband and at the end of the formula her own name. (JGS 1,21, trans. Caland 1922: 39)

It would seem logical to assume that originally there was just one star symbolizing marital faithfulness, and that it was the 'steadfast' Pole Star. In 2780 BC, the star Thuban (α Draconis) was only 0·6° distant from the heavenly Pole. Thuban is the only star that could really be called 'unmoving' or 'fixed' (*dhruva*) before our own Pole Star Polaris (fig. 14.4). Many scholars have therefore drawn the conclusion that the notion of a 'fixed' Pole Star in India must date from the third millennium. This date links it with the Harappan tradition.

At the very earliest stage of the nakṣatra calendar, the new year star seems to have been Rohiṇī (Aldebaran) (§ 11.3); as the 'faithful wife' of the sun and the moon (§ 14.4), it was apparently identified with the 'steadfast' Pole Star. Because of precession, the beginning of the year shifted to the next asterism towards the end of the third millennium, and the myth of the Pleiades as the mothers of the young sun came into being (§ 11.3). At this later stage, the stars of the Pleiades were conceived as the wives of the Seven Sages, six of them separated from their husbands because of their unfaithfulness; thus Alcor became the 'faithful' wife of Vasiṣṭha, and remained with her husband. The following passage in Mahābhārata 1,188,14 seems to relate to the earlier phase and to the Pole Star. In reply to King Drupada's question, 'How can one woman be the wife of many men and yet the Law be not broken?' Yudhiṣṭhira defends the polyandrous marriage of the Pāṇḍavas by mentioning this precedent: 'We hear in the ancient Lore that a Gautamī by the name of *Jaṭilā* lay with the Seven Seers.'

The name *Jaṭilā* for the common wife of the Seven Sages, probably the Pole Star, is significant, for the Sanskrit word *jaṭila* means 'wearing the hair in twisted locks'. As this is the traditional hairstyle of ascetics, the name is well suited to Arundhatī, leading an ascetic life in the forest hermitage of the Seven Sages. But the word also has another meaning not recorded in dictionaries, 'possessing aerial roots (*jaṭā*)', used with reference to the banyan and plakṣa figs in Hemacandra's Triṣaṣṭiśalākāpuruṣacarita (1,5,559; 1,6,405; 1,3,128) and punningly in Kālidāsa's Raghuvaṁśa 13,71:

The old ministers had a change in their appearance produced by the growth of their beards [unshaven during Rāma's fourteen years of absence] and had matted hair (*jaṭila*) and thus were like *plakṣa* trees which are full of aerial roots (*jaṭila*) because of the shoots (from their branches). (trans. Emeneau 1949: 363.)

This association between Arundhatī and the banyan tree in the name *Jaṭilā* is doubled in the proper name *Arundhatī-vaṭa*, mentioned as a place of pilgrimage in the Mahābhārata (3,84,8019).

Many sacred localities (including Allahabad and Bodh Gaya) have had an *akṣaya-vaṭa* 'eternal banyan'. Banyan trees are extremely long-lived, but this epithet obviously also has a cosmic dimension, for the Kaṭha-Upaniṣad (6,1), the Taittirīya-Āraṇyaka (1,11,5), the Maitrī Upaniṣad (6,4) and the Bhagavad-Gītā (15,1) speak of a heavenly pipal fig (*aśvattha*) which is 'eternal'. According to AS 5,4,3 a pipal fig is the seat of the gods in the third heaven from here. That the fig tree had an astral aspect in the Harappan religion is suggested by an Indus tablet from Harappa, where a star is depicted on either side of a fig tree inhabited by an anthropomorphic deity; these stars are placed in the loops of the tree (fig. 14.5; cf. § 10.1).

Their association with *both* conjugal fidelity *and* the banyan tree suggests a mythical identity for Arundhatī and Rohiṇī. There is other evidence to support this hypothesis. In Indian poetry, creeper plants that wind themselves around trees are prominent symbols of loving wives. In the Atharvaveda, the word *arundhatī* denotes a climbing creeper with healing properties due to its red lac; the red colour is indicated also in the first syllable (*aru-* means 'red, sun'). The redness and ascent of the *arundhatī* plant are punningly referred to in words associating it with Rohiṇī: *róhaṇy asi rohiṇi* 'you are a grower, o red one!'(AS 4,12,1). Among the many Sanskrit names of the banyan tree (*vaṭa*) are *rohin*, *rohiṇa* and *rauhiṇa*, which associate it with both Arundhatī and Rohiṇī.

Besides *vaṭa-mīṉ*, Arundhatī is called *cem-mīṉ* in Old Tamil (Patiṟṟuppattu 31,28). *Cem-mīṉ* means both 'the star of straightness or propriety (i.e. conjugal fidelity)' and 'the red star'. In the latter meaning, which is undoubtedly primary for a star, *cem-mīṉ* is a synonym of *Rohiṇī* 'red' and is appropriate for Aldebaran, but not for Alcor. Another consideration points to the same conclusion. According to an old Indian dictum, 'He who does not smell the odour of an outblown lamp, hear the words of a friend, or see Arundhatī, is about to die' (Rāmāyaṇa 3,59,16). This belief concerning Arundhatī (found as early as LŚS 3,3,6–7) implies that the star was normally easily visible; this is certainly true of Aldebaran, but

Fig. 14.5. An anthropomorphic deity within a fig tree on a moulded terracotta tablet from Harappa (H-179). The stars on either side of the fig, placed in its horn-like loops (cf. fig. 10.9) at the bottom, suggest a 'heavenly' nature for the fig tree (§ 10.1).

not of Alcor. Arundhatī's brilliance is emphasized in a myth preserved in the Skanda-Purāṇa (7,1,129,5–33): During a drought, the Vedic sages asked a low-caste Cāṇḍāla for food. The Cāṇḍāla gave food after the chief sage Vasiṣṭha had married his daughter called Akṣamālā ('garland of dice / eyes'). She practised austerity and became so brilliant that her lustre obstructed the sun (*arkabimbam arundhata*), whence her new name Arundhatī.

In the myth and cult of Sāvitrī, the banyan tree is connected with Sāvitrī, as it is with that other model of chastity, Arundhatī. But the banyan tree is also associated with death and with Yama, the god of death, who likewise figures in the Sāvitrī legend. ṚS 10,135,1 speaks of 'a tree with good or beautiful leaves' (*vṛkṣé supalāśé*) where Yama drinks with the gods (in Rāmāyaṇa 3,35–6, a banyan tree is characterized by 'beautiful leaves': *suparṇaḳṛtalakṣaṇaṁ* ... *nyagrodham*), while AS 5,4,3 is more specific in saying that the gods abide in an *aśvattha* fig in the third heaven. I have proposed that Yama is partly identical with Varuṇa (§§ 10.2; 12.1), who is, as we shall soon see, likewise associated with a heavenly fig tree (the banyan). But why should the god of death have a special relationship to the banyan tree? In very early times, it seems, the dead were disposed of by suspending them from trees to expose them; this could well be meant in AS 18,2,34, which states that the dead are burnt, buried, cast out and 'put up'; later texts like Vetāla-Pañcaviṁśatikā actually speak of the dead hanging from trees in cemeteries. A special reason for connecting the banyan tree with death is that in Indian narrative literature people committing suicide often hang themselves by the aerial roots of this tree. They are likely to be the reality behind Yama's mythical 'noose' with which he seizes the dying like Satyavat. (In the Ṛgveda, it is Varuṇa who seizes evildoers with his noose.)

As early as the Ṛgveda (1,24,7), mention is made of an Indian fig in the middle of the sky: 'King Varuṇa holds up the crown of the (heavenly banyan) tree in the bottomless space; those (branches) which hang down have (their) roots above: may these beams of light (*ketavaḥ*) be fixed on us!' In heavenly contexts, the word *ketu* usually denotes 'beam of light, meteor or comet', but here the meaning 'aerial root' of banyan is also implied. In Dravidian, such an association has a linguistic motivation: from the root *viḻu* 'to fall down, descend', there is both *viḻutu*, *vīḻal* 'aerial root of the banyan, falling roots of a fig tree' and (in Tamil) *viḻu-mīṉ* 'meteor'. In the passage at hand, the aerial roots of the banyan correspond to beams of light that bring vital energy to living beings. Such an idea is expressed in ŚB 2,3,3,7–8, where the rays (*raśmi*) of the sun are conceived as ropes (*raśmi*) that both bring and take life: '7. Now yonder burning (sun) doubtless is no other than Death ... It is by the rays (or reins, thongs, *raśmi*) of that (sun) that all these creatures are attached to the vital airs (breaths or life), and therefore the rays extend down to the vital airs. 8. And the breath of whomsoever he (the sun) wishes he takes and rises, and that one dies' (trans. Eggeling 1882: 1, 343). The very next verse of the Ṛgvedic hymn quoted above, 1,24,8, indeed refers to the rising sun: 'For King Varuṇa has made a wide path for the sun to follow.'

Later cosmological descriptions in the Purāṇas answer the question of why the stars remain in the sky and do not fall down by explaining that the stars and planets are fixed to the Pole Star with invisible 'ropes of wind' (*vāta-raśmi*) (cf. e.g. Viṣṇu-Purāṇa 2,9 and 12; Matsya-Purāṇa 127,12–14; Bhartṛhari 3,91).

The oldest certain reference for invisible 'cords of wind' holding up stars seems to be Maitrī Upaniṣad 1,4, where 'the wandering of the Pole Star and the tearing of the windcords' (*vāta-rajju*) are among the cosmic catastrophes enumerated. However, even the Ṛgveda speaks of 'ascetics having ropes of the wind' (*múnayo vāta-raśanāḥ*), who 'dress in reddish dirt' and 'go along the movement of the wind' (10,136,2), saying: 'we have ascended the wind: you mortals see only our bodies' (3); 'through the air flies the ascetic, looking down on all the forms' (4). The traditional index of the Ṛgveda identifies these flying ascetics with the Seven Sages (i.e. Ursa Major), while in TĀ 1,23ff. 'sages having ropes of the wind' (*vāta-raśanā ṛṣayaḥ*) are identified with 'red beams of light' (*aruṇāḥ ketavaḥ*), which came into being together with the sun and rule the cardinal directions.

The idea that the stars are bound to the Pole Star seems to be implied as early as the Ṛgveda, which states that 'those stars, which, being fixed from above (*níhitāsa uccā*), were to be seen in the night, have gone somewhere in daytime' (ṚS 1,24,10). As this same hymn speaks of the heavenly fig tree and of its air roots as beams of light, it does not seem far-fetched to think that the poet linked this banyan tree with the Pole Star.

Proto-Dravidian homophony, linking *vaṭa* 'rope', *vaṭa* 'Indian fig' and *vaṭa* 'north', provides a natural explanation for such a cosmological conception. It is worth noting that Tamil *vaṭa-mīṉ* cannot be a translation from Sanskrit, for the Sanskrit sources do not have a term meaning 'northern star'. But the Sanskrit tradition has preserved another conception, which seems relevant here and which can be understood against the Dravidian linguistic background. According to the Purāṇa texts, four mountains arise in the four cardinal directions around the golden mount Meru in the centre, and on the top of each mountain grows an enormous tree, different in each direction. The tree growing in the north is the banyan fig (called *vaṭa* in most sources, e.g. Viṣṇu-Purāṇa 2,2; Agni-Purāṇa 108, 11–12; Matsya-Purāṇa 113,47; 264,15–16; *nyagrodha* in other texts).

Important religious symbols often have many meanings. In the marriage ceremony, the steadfast Pole Star is the model of the bride, as is the faithful Arundhatī, who is associated with the banyan tree. In the Ṛgveda, however, the heavenly banyan tree belongs to King Varuṇa (also in GGS 4,7,24, 'the banyan is Varuṇa's tree'), and apparently the Pole Star, too, belongs to Varuṇa (for the Pole Star's probable connection with the sacrificial stake and liṅga, see § 12.2). Some Gṛhyasūtras (e.g. HGS 1,22,14–1,23,1) prescribe that the groom (and not the bride) should address a long mantra to the Pole Star; some parts of this mantra are worth quoting, because they support the above interpretation of ṚS 1,24,7 and 10, and because they link the Pole Star with Varuṇa:

> Then he worships the Pole Star with (the formula), 'Firm dwelling, firm origin. The firm one art thou, standing on the side of firmness. Thou art the pillar of the stars; thus protect me against the adversary.
>
> . . . . .
>
> I know thee as the nave of the universe. May I become the nave of this country.
> I know thee as the centre of the universe. May I become the centre of this country.
> I know thee as the string that holds the universe. May I become the string that holds this country.
> I know thee as the pillar of the universe. May I become the pillar of this country.
> I know thee as the navel of the universe. May I become as the navel of this country.

The Pole Star as the 'firm dwelling' demands comparison with ṚS 8,41,9: 'Fixed is Varuṇa's dwelling-place (*váruṇasya dhruvám sádaḥ*); (there) he governs the seven.' The wording of the rest clearly indicates that the original context of these mantras is the royal consecration, which is 'Varuṇa's sacrifice' (§ 12.1); also the formula R̥S 10,173,4 that GGS 2,3,12 prescribes should be uttered by the bridegroom after the bride has addressed the Pole Star originally relates to the establishment of kingship. The connection between Varuṇa and the Pole Star and its characterization as 'the string that holds the universe' supports an interpretation of Varuṇa's heavenly banyan tree that is in accordance with the Purāṇic cosmology and the Dravidian homophony of *vaṭa* 'rope' = 'banyan fig' = 'north'.

The Dravidian interpretation of the sequence  as *vaṭa-mīn* is thus not only in agreement with relevant terminology and ideas in later Indian cosmology, but also enables us to understand this tradition. External evidence in the form of Harappan painted pottery (fig. 13.16) and Indian folk-art (fig. 14.1) has been adduced to justify the pictorial interpretation of the 'fig tree' pictogram. Further external and internal support for this interpretation is given by two identical Indus amulets (fig. 14.6).

One side of each amulet shows nothing but a clearly recognizable fig leaf, suggesting that the message on the other side relates to fig trees. The other side shows a short inscription of three pictograms, the middlemost being that read as *vaṭa*. The last (rightmost) of the three signs is not so significant, since most Indus texts end in it. But the first (leftmost) sign is important for two reasons: because it can be assumed either to be an attribute of the word expressed by the 'Indian fig tree' sign or to form a compound with it, and because its pictorial shape can be interpreted with minimal ambiguity.

There can be no reasonable doubt that this attributive sign represents the numeral '4' by its four short vertical strokes (§ 5.2). Read in Dravidian, does it make any sense in this context? 'Four' was **nāl* in Proto-Dravidian, and there is a closely homophonous Proto-Dravidian (or at least Proto-South Dravidian) root **ñāl* meaning 'to hang, be suspended', used among other things with reference to hanging ropes and vines (cf. Malayalam *ñāli* 'a hanging tendril of the pepper- or betel-vine, a branch-root', Tulu *nēla* 'a hanging rope'). Thus the compound formed by the two pictograms '4' + 'fig' would yield **nāl-vaṭa*, meaning '(tree characterized by) hanging ropes', like Tamil *nāl-vāy* '(animal characterized by) a hanging mouth, elephant' or *nāṉūl* '(sacred) thread hanging (from the shoulder)'. This is a fitting description of the tree, which is called in Sanskrit *nyag-rodha* 'downwards grower' (ŚB 13,2,7,3 *nyañco nyagrodhā rohanti*). The meaning 'to hang oneself' for *ñāl* also demands comparison with the references to suicides on the branch-roots of the banyan tree in Indian narrative literature (e.g. KSS 13).

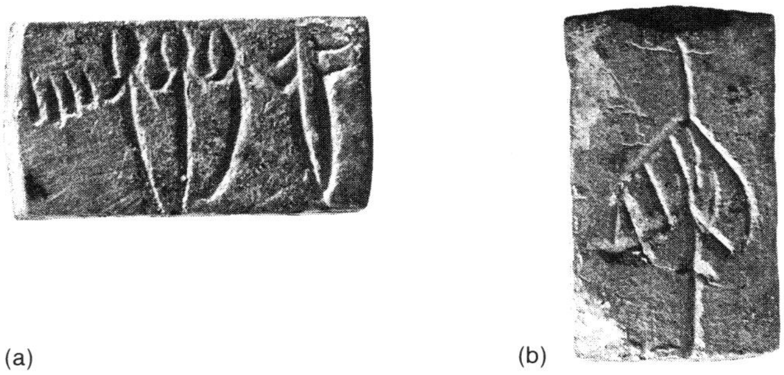

(a) (b)

Fig. 14.6. An incised 'miniature tablet' from Harappa (H-289). (a) The inscription on the obverse contains the sequence '4' + 'fig tree'. (b) The reverse shows a sign (or iconographic motif?) that represents a 'fig leaf'. The direction of writing is, exceptionally, from left to right.

I have not been able to trace the reconstructed compound **nāl-vaṭa* in any Dravidian language. However, there is something else that increases the likelihood of this interpretation. The generally assumed phonetic alternation between *ñ-*, *n-* and *ф-* (loss of the nasal) in Proto-Dravidian makes *ñāl* 'to hang' fully homophonous with *nāl* '4'. But this alternation also enables one to suggest a new etymology for one of the principal Dravidian names of the Indian fig tree, namely *āl* or *āla-maram*. If it is derived from *ñāl* 'to hang; hanging rope', the compound **(ñ)āl-maram* would mean 'tree with hanging ropes', which I have assumed to be the original meaning of *vaṭa-maram*, too. It must be observed, however, that there is nothing wrong with the traditional etymology which derives the word from the Proto-Dravidian root *akal* (contracted into *āl*) 'to spread', for the branches of the tree do indeed spread widely.

In this section we have interpreted an Indus sign that appears to depict a banyan fig, exploring various symbolic associations with this sacred tree. It figures prominently in the glyptics of one of the most famous Harappan seals, the 'fig deity' seal, which seems to offer an unusually large number of clues to its interpretation. But before we can examine the iconography of this seal, we must explore a little the relationship prevailing between the Harappan and Near Eastern glyptic art, since the latter constitutes one of the few relevant sources for understanding the former.

14.2 The 'contest' motif and Durgā's fight with the Buffalo demon

The 'contest' motif is one of the most convincing and widely accepted parallels between Harappan and Near Eastern glyptic art. A considerable number of Harappan seals depict a manly hero, each hand grasping a tiger by the throat (e.g. fig. 14.7). In Mesopotamian art, the fight with lions and / or bulls

Fig. 14.7. The 'contest' motif in the Indus Valley: a nude hero with six locks of hair holds back two tigers. Impression of a seal from Mohenjo-daro (M-308).

is the most popular motif. The Harappan substitution of tigers for lions merely reconciles the scene with the fauna of the Indus Valley. In early Elamite and Sumerian art (fig. 14.8) and occasionally later (figs. 14.9–11), the hero is fighting alone with two lions in a way similar to that on the Harappan seals. The six dots around the head of the Harappan hero (fig. 14.7) are a significant detail, since they may be compared to the six locks of hair characteristic of the Mesopotamian hero, from Jemdet Nasr to Akkadian times (fig. 14.11).

In Proto-Elamite art, the 'contest' motif is represented in a very distinctive style, showing animals in human attitudes. Here the two adversaries are the lion and the bull. In carefully balanced engravings, they are depicted symmetrically as winners and losers in turn (fig. 14.12). Pierre Amiet (1956) has proposed that these scenes represent the endless struggle between the dualistic forces of nature, manifested especially in the alternating succession of day and night, or summer and winter.

Indeed, the golden-skinned hairy lion is an archetypal symbol for the golden-rayed sun (cf. Aelianus 12,7), the lord of the day, whose appearance kills the god of the night. The night is equally well represented by the bull, whose horns connect it with the crescent of the moon, the ruler of the night sky. As sun and moon, or day and night, the lion and the bull could at the same time personify other antithetical cosmic forces, such as heat and cold, fire and water, light and darkness, life and death.

Fig. 14.8. The 'contest' motif on the ivory handle of a flint-bladed knife, found at Gebel el-ʿAraq in Upper Egypt. Carved in Egypt in the Sumerian style of the Jemdet Nasr period, *c.*3000 BC. Drawn after Pritchard 1969b: 90, no. 290.

Fig. 14.9. An Early Dynastic III cylinder seal from Susa with the 'contest' motif. After Legrain 1921: 252.

An Early Dynastic serpentine bowl from Khafajeh in Mesopotamia, comparable to those manufactured at Tepe Yahya in Iran (fig. 1.16), is linked to the 'contest' theme by a scene where a lion is killing a zebu bull (fig. 14.13a). The two other scenes on this bowl show anthropomorphic deities associated with these two animals. The man sitting upon two zebu bulls, with his legs bent underneath in the fashion of the Proto-Elamite bull, is apparently a god of water and fertility,

Fig. 14.10. The 'contest' motif on an Early Dynastic II votive plaque from the temple of the goddess Inanna at Nippur. The lower register with its two 'unicorn' bulls around a tree is stylistically similar to Harappan. Drawn after Pritchard 1969b: 356, no. 646.

for he holds in his hands streams of water and is surrounded by ears of corn. He is linked to the moon and the night by the crescent beside his head (fig. 14.13b). The other deity stands upon two lionesses and grips a snake on either side (fig. 14.13c). Snakes are often associated with demoniac powers and death, and these again with night. The distinction made on this bowl between the sitting and standing posture may be compared to the Vedic worship of the rising and setting sun, performed standing and sitting respectively (Manu 2,101; Gautama-Dharmasūtra 2,11).

In the Proto-Elamite seals, the bull keeps its legs bent double beneath it while squatting. In this posture, the bull is usually shown in profile (fig. 14.14a), but sometimes it is also viewed from the front when the legs are both bent double beneath it and turned away from each other (fig. 14.14b). Some Proto-Elamite seals (fig. 14.15) seem to be the model for that 'yogic' posture so distinctive of the 'Proto-Śiva' (fig. 10.18) and other squatting anthropomorphic deities of the Indus Civilization (fig. 14.16). A sealed potsherd showing a very similar male figure with hoofed legs found at Tepe Yahya, half-way between Susa and the Indus Valley, gives even more credibility to this parallelism (fig. 14.17). The sherd comes from a post-Proto-Elamite stratum (IVA), which is partly contemporaneous with the Indus Civilization and has also produced a potsherd with the impression of a seal that seems to bear Indus script.

The Harappan 'Proto-Śiva' (fig. 10.18) wears the horns of a water buffalo, a formidable beast which is the natural enemy of the tiger. Both tiger and buffalo are among the wild animals which are depicted on the 'Proto-Śiva' seal, actually opposing each other. The substitution of the water buffalo for the bull or bison of Elam is again obviously conditioned by the local fauna (fig. 14.18). Early Harappan pots depicting the head of the water buffalo from Sind, the northern Indus Valley and Kashmir (fig. 14.19) make it evident that the buffalo-horned 'Proto-Śiva' has a long local prehistory. In later India, the buffalo was the vehicle of Yama, the god of death (fig. 14.33); it was also connected with Varuṇa, who in one of his aspects is the god of waters (§10.2).

The water buffalo is native to North India, but not to Mesopotamia, where it first appears in the last third of the reign of Sargon the Great (2334–2279 BC). Sargon himself says that boats from Meluḫḫa came to Akkad (§ 1.5) and brought him gifts. In the ancient Orient, rare and exotic animals were royal gifts. According to the cuneiform texts, a limited number of water buffaloes were kept in royal parks

Fig. 14.11. A hero with six locks of hair checks two bulls, while a bull-man checks two lions. An Early Dynastic II / III cylinder seal from Fara (BM 89538), *c.*2650 BC.

Fig. 14.12. (a, b) The 'contest' of lion and bull on Proto-Elamite seals from Susa, *c.*3100–2900 BC. After Amiet 1980a: pl. 38, no. 585 (=a) and no. 591 (=b). See also fig. 6.3.

(a)

Fig. 14.13. An 'intercultural-style' steatite bowl from Khafajeh, Mesopotamia. Early Dynastic period, *c.*2600 BC. Height 11.5 cm. BM 128887. The bowl has three scenes:
(a) 'Contest' between a lion and a bull. The victorious lion is assisted by a bird of prey. The bull is lying on its back, and there is a scorpion in front of its head, while behind its hind legs, a small bear (?) stands facing a palm tree that is placed under the hind legs of the lion. There are ears of corn (or trees) in the background.

(b)

(c)

(b) A deity sits, with his legs bent underneath, upon two humped bulls. He holds in his hands streams of water and there is the sickle moon and a rosette-formed star in front of his head. In the background, there are ears of corn (or trees).
(c) A deity stands upon two lionesses or other felines and holds attacking serpents in his hands. In front of his head is a rosette-shaped star.

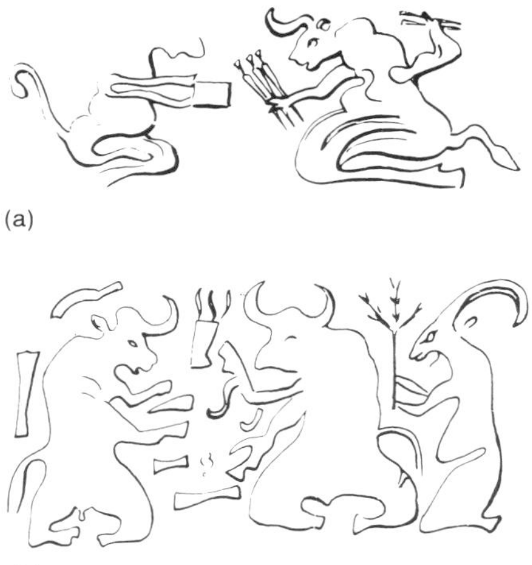

(a) (b)

Fig. 14.14. Proto-Elamite seals from Susa Cc-Da, *c.*3000–2750 BC. Bulls and other animals are represented in sitting posture, both (a) in profile and (b) also as seen from the front with their legs turned to either side. After Amiet 1980a: pl. 37, no. 570 (= a) and 569 (= b).

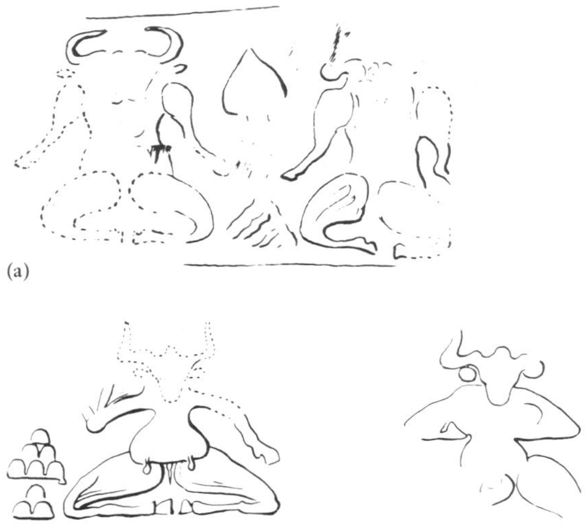

(a) (b) (c)

Fig. 14.15. Proto-Elamite seals from Susa Cc-Da, *c.*3000–2750 BC. (a–c) Bulls sitting with legs bent double and fully turned to either side, seen from the front. After Amiet 1972: pl. 25, no. 1017 (= a); and Amiet 1980a: pl. 38, nos. 581–2 (= b, c).

Fig. 14.16. A seal from Mohenjo-daro (M-1181) with a multifaced anthropomorphic god squatting on a throne that has hoofed legs. This so-called 'yoga' posture may simply imitate the Proto-Elamite way of representing seated bulls (fig. 14.15). The deity's arms are both full of bangles; the crown on the head has buffalo horns and a fig branch.

Fig. 14.17. A seated male deity with hoofed legs bent double beneath and turned out to either side, seen from the front. There is a dot beside the head (originally presumably one on either side). Seal impression on a potsherd found in 1975 at Tepe Yahya in Kerman, southeastern Iran. Period IVA, *c.*2200–1800 BC.

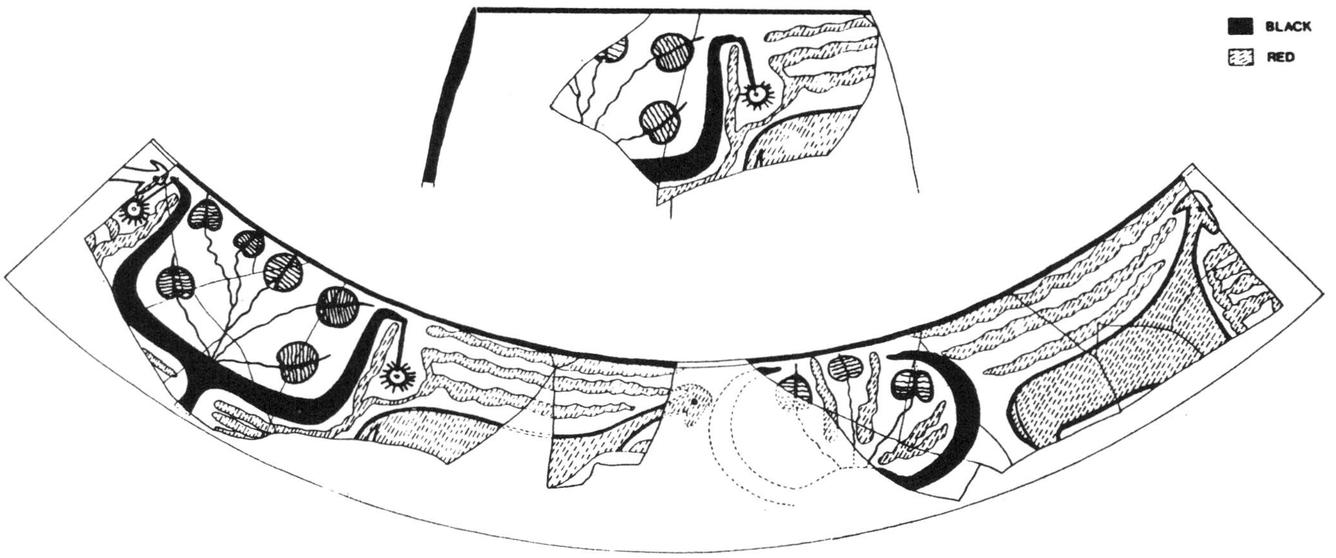

Fig. 14.18. A painted pot excavated at Lewan Dheri in the Bannu Valley, Northwest Frontier Province, Pakistan. Kot Dijian period, *c.*3000–2600 BC. After R. and B. Allchin 1982: 165, fig. 6.32. The motifs comprise two goats and the heads of a buffalo and a zebu. The fig leaves rising from the head between the horns of both the buffalo and the zebu connect them with the Indus deities (fig. 14.16) and suggest their association with vegetation and fertility. The two may form a contrasting pair. The water buffalo has a dark skin and bathes daily in water; it may thus be compared to the bull in the Proto-Elamite version of the 'contest' motif (fig. 14.12), which appears to represent water, night and death. The zebu usually has a light-coloured skin, and may symbolize the cosmic force of the 'day'. This interpretation is supported by the pompoms hanging from its horns here; they have a parallel in the single 'sun' symbol placed between the horns of a zebu's head in the painted pottery of the nearby Early Harappan site of Rahman Dheri (RHD-247).

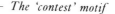

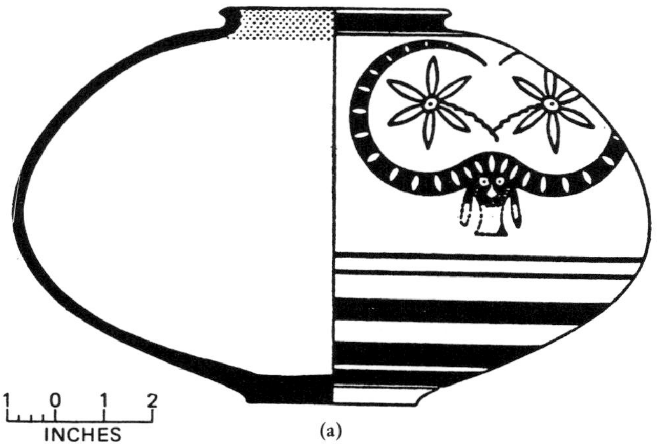

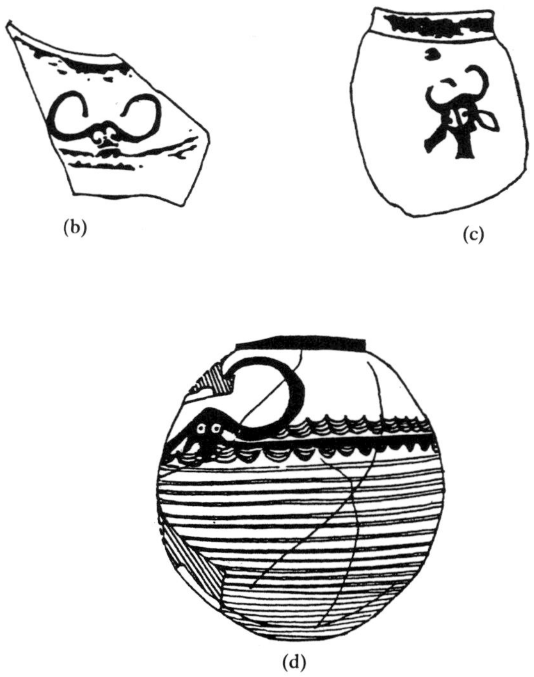

Fig. 14.19. The water buffalo in Kot Dijian painted pottery. Early Harappan period, *c.*3000–2600 BC. (a) From Kot Diji, Sind. (b, c) From Gumla, Northwest Frontier Province. For the nearby site of Rahman Dheri, see fig. 7.4c–i. (d) A Kot Dijian-style pot from Burzahom, a Northern Neolithic site in Kashmir. After Sankalia 1974: 354, fig. 88: k (=a), b (=b), c (=c), e (=d).

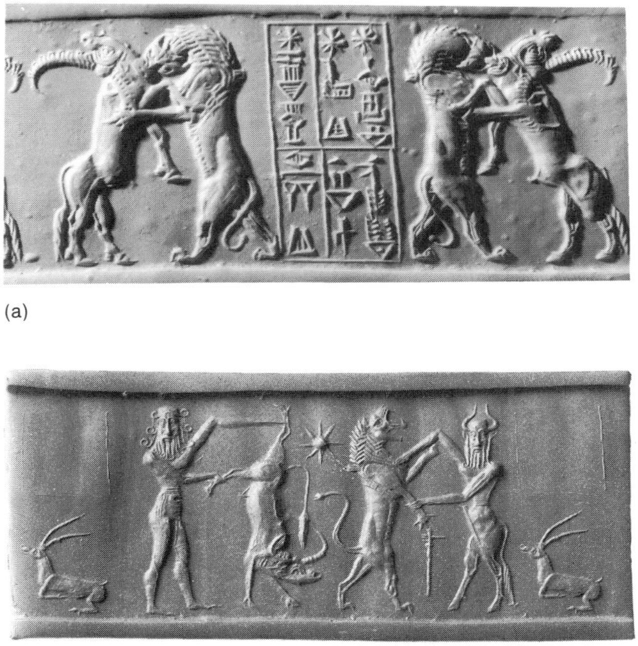

(a)

(b)

Fig. 14.20. Water buffalo on late Akkadian cylinder seals with the 'contest' motif:
(a) The fight between lion and buffalo. The inscription reads, 'Naram-Sin of Akkad: Ukin-Ulmash his son'. The 'Sarre cylinder', Collection Othmar Keel, Fribourg; cf. Collon 1987: no. 528. (b) A hero with six locks of hair fights a water buffalo and a bull-man fights a lion. The Oriental Institute of the University of Chicago (AS. 33: 113). After Boehmer 1965: no. 230.

Fig. 14.21. The hero with six locks of hair slakes the thirst of the buffalo with water flowing from the pot of Enki. Inscribed 'Šargališarri, king of Akkad: Ibnišarrum, the scribe, (is) your servant'. A late Akkadian cylinder seal, *c.*2200 BC. Musée du Louvre / *AO* 22303 (Collection De Clercq). After Boehmer 1965: no. 232. Cf. Collon 1987: no. 529.

Fig. 14.22. The water-god Enki sits between two water buffaloes subdued by two six-locked heroes. Each hero places a foot on the head of one of the subdued beasts. A late Akkadian cylinder seal. After Boehmer 1965: no. 223.

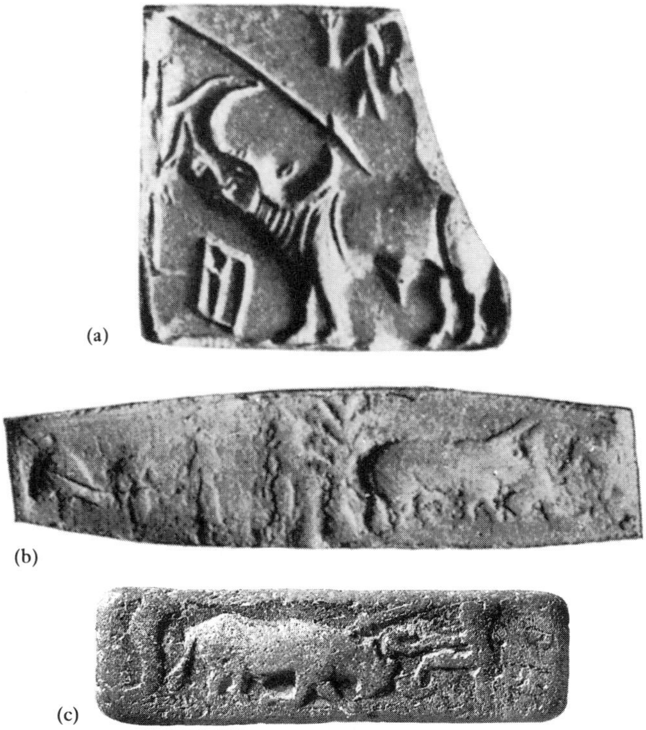

(a)

(b)

(c)

Fig. 14.23. The water buffalo being speared, apparently in sacrifice, by a naked man who lifts one of his feet onto the head (or horn) of the animal. This motif recurs several times in Harappan glyptic art.
(a) Impression of an Indus seal from Mohenjo-daro (DK 8165). After Mackay 1938: pl. 88, no. 279.
(b) A moulded terracotta tablet from Mohenjo-daro (DK 4547). The buffalo sacrifice appears to take place in front of a sacred tree. After Mackay 1938: pl. 92: 11b.
(c) One side of a moulded tablet in the shape of a triangular prism from Mohenjo-daro (M-492 C). Behind the slaughtered buffalo is a cobra with its hood expanded, possibly representing the deity to whom the offering was due.

Fig. 14.24. Durgā, the Hindu goddess of victory riding on a lion, defeats the Buffalo demon Mahiṣa Asura. Rock-cut granite relief in Mamallapuram, South India. Pallava period, *c.* AD 650. After Kramrisch 1954: pl. 86.

Fig. 14.25. Impression of a Harappan cylinder seal from Kalibangan (K-65). Two warriors, distinguished by the hair worn in a divided bun at the back of the head, are spearing each other, while they are both being held by the hand by a goddess wearing a head-dress with a long pendant (comparable to the ones decorated with cowry shells and turquoise that are worn by the women of Ladakh and Chitral), bangles on the arms, and a skirt. Next to the combat scene (where space appears to have prevented the depiction of these details), her body merges with that of the tiger (later the vehicle of the Hindu goddess of war) and her head-dress is elaborated with animal horns and a tree branch.

Fig. 14.26. A square stamp seal from Kalibangan (K-50). ASI. This seal with the tiger-bodied goddess (here her horns are those of the markhor goat) was found in the same room as the cylinder seal shown in fig. 14.25.

Fig. 14.27. Sumerian electrum helmet (U.10000) from the Royal Cemetery at Ur (tomb PG/755). Early Dynastic III period, *c.*2400 BC. After Pritchard 1969b: 49, no. 160.

and used as sacrificial animals. After Sargon's time, the mighty beast starts to be substituted for the bull or bison in the 'contest' scene (fig. 14.20). The buffalo was closely associated with the water-god Enki, whose six-locked servant hero not only subdues the buffalo, but also slakes its proverbial thirst with water streaming from the pot of Enki (fig. 14.21). Enki is himself also represented in the 'contest' scenes (fig. 14.22). Around 2000 BC, however, the buffalo disappeared from Mesopotamian art, and no new buffaloes were imported.

There is a new detail in the composition of the 'contest' scenes of the late Akkadian glyptics: the hero places his foot upon the head of the buffalo (fig. 14.22). This device is without parallel in earlier Mesopotamian art, but is characteristic of the Harappan seals and tablets where a naked man spears a buffalo to death (fig. 14.23). The correspondence cannot be a mere coincidence.

In Hinduism until quite recently, the water buffalo was one of the principal sacrificial animals offered to Durgā, the goddess of victory, who rides a lion or tiger. Such offerings were made especially at the end of the rainy season, at the principal festival of the goddess celebrating Durgā's victory over the Buffalo demon, Mahiṣa Asura (fig. 14.24). The earliest images of Durgā as the killer of the Buffalo demon (*mahiṣāsura-mardinī*) date from early Kuṣāṇa times, about the beginning of the Christian era. The most important full account of the myth is that of the Devī-Māhātmya, forming chapters 79–80 of the Mārkaṇḍeya-Purāṇa. Probably none of the textual versions is older than the fifth century AD. The cult of Durgā and her fight with the buffalo – a variant of the archetypal contest between lion and bull – are thus known only from sources almost two millennia younger than the Indus Civilization. Nevertheless, there is some evidence suggesting that the Harappans may already have worshipped a predecessor of Durgā.

Fig. 14.28. Ishtar as the goddess of war with her foot on the back of a lion, a worshipper and a five-line inscription. A late Akkadian cylinder seal of unknown provenance. Black stone, height 4.2 cm, diameter 2.5 cm. The Oriental Institute of the University of Chicago. Cf. Pritchard 1969b: 177 no. 526.

(a)

(b)

Fig. 14.29. A golden seal with a winged goddess and lions from Bactria. (a) Obverse. (b) Reverse. After Ligabue and Salvatori n.d. [1989]: figs. 58–9.

A goddess of war riding a tiger is seen in a cylinder seal from Kalibangan. Here she holds two men by the hand while they are spearing each other; next to this scene, she is shown with a tiger's body (fig. 14.25). The non-Harappan form of the Kalibangan cylinder seal points to western contacts. But the goddess herself cannot be labelled non-Harappan, for she is depicted also on native square Indus seals (fig. 14.26); even on the Kalibangan cylinder seal, the style is Harappan. The warriors of the Kalibangan seal are wearing their hair in a divided bun at the back of the head (fig. 14.25). There are several other examples of this hairstyle in Harappan art, including a steatite plaque from Banawali (B-26), which shows two pugilists fighting with each other. The model for this hairstyle comes from Early Dynastic III period Mesopotamia, where it is reproduced upon royal helmets (fig. 14.27).

In the Akkadian seals, Ishtar as the goddess of war is associated with the lion (fig. 14.28). Inanna-Ishtar is just one among the many similar goddesses of war and fertility connected with felines, whose cult appears to have spread all over the ancient Near East (and the Aegean) from Neolithic

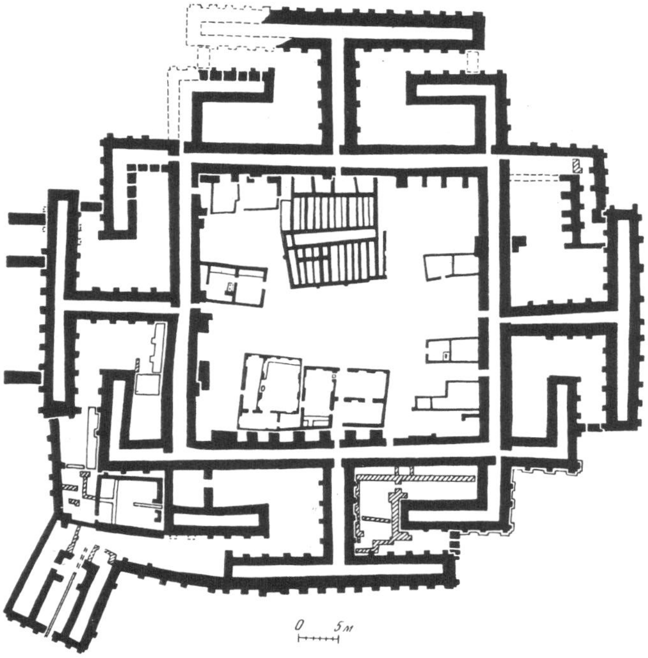

Fig. 14.30. Ground-plan of the 'palace' in Dashly-3, Bactria, northern Afghanistan. First phase of the Bactria and Margiana Archaeological Complex, *c.*1900–1700 BC. After Sarianidi 1986a: 53.

Fig. 14.31. Example of a Tantric maṇḍala: the maṇḍala of Mahākālī. After Preston in Parpola 1985b: fig. 24.

Fig. 14.32. A bison bull (*Bos gaurus*) about to have intercourse with a priestess lying on the ground. Impression of a seal from Chanhujo-daro. After Mackay 1943: pl. 51: 13.

Anatolia, and from Western Asia towards the Iranian plateau and the Greater Indus Valley in the third millennium BC. A goddess associated with the lion appears also on several seals of the Bronze Age culture of Bactria dated to *c.*1900–1700 BC (fig. 14.29).

This comparison of Near Eastern and Harappan glyptics has caused me to re-examine the prehistory of the cult of Durgā in the light of the Near Eastern, Harappan, Bactrian and Vedic evidence. It would take us too far from the purpose of this book to go into this in any detail, so a brief summary of the principal theses will have to suffice. In the Near Eastern and the Mediterranean tradition, the goddess and her guarding lions are specifically connected with the city walls. This is another link with the Indian goddess, many of whose names (Durgā, Tripurā, Koṭṭavī, Aparājitā, Śāradā) can be connected with expressions denoting 'fortress, stronghold' (*durga*, *tripura*, *koṭṭa*, *aparājitā pur*, *śāradī pur*). Citadels were characteristic of all Harappan settlements, but the name Tripurā specifically points to the strongholds of the Asura-worshipping Dāsas mentioned in the Veda, and identified above (in § 8.4) with the temple-forts of Bronze Age Bactria, exemplified by that in Dashly-3 (fig. 8.18). The 'palace' at Dashly-3, connected with the Harappan tradition by its bull-mosaic (fig. 12.5), links Bactria historically with the later Tantric tradition of India, as its ground-plan (fig. 14.30) evidently is the prototype of the Tantric maṇḍala, supposed to represent the royal palace as the abode of divinity (fig. 14.31).

The royal and Tantric cults connected with the worship of Durgā in historical times, especially those of the *navarātri* festivals around the vernal and autumnal equinoxes, culminate in the orgiastic celebration of the 'tenth day of victory'. In my opinion, they are directly related to the so-called *vrātya* rituals of the Veda, especially the *vrātya-stomas*, the *mahāvrata* and the horse / human sacrifice. The vrātya-stomas were lustrations connected with raiding expeditions like the 'tenth day of victory'. These 'pre-classical' rituals of the Veda, moreover, link the esoteric sexual 'circle worship' of the later Śākta Tantrism with the 'sacred marriage' rituals of the Mesopotamian, Harappan and Bactrian cultures (see also figs. 12.9–12). The carnal union of the sacrificed horse and the queen in the Veda is paralleled by the intercourse between a bison and a prostrate priestess or queen in an Indus seal from Chanhujo-daro (fig. 14.32) and that between Yama's buffalo and an old woman in Lamaist iconography (fig. 14.33). The 'pairing of (different) beings' (Aitareya-Āraṇyaka 5,1,5) at the Vedic mahāvrata is likewise matched by a Bactrian cylinder seal depicting human and animal couples mating (fig. 14.34).

14.3 Iconography of the 'fig deity' seal

The famous 'fig deity' seal from Mohenjo-daro (fig. 14.35) is of great interest to the history of Indian religions and the study of the Indus script. If the iconographic scene and inscription on this seal each convey essentially the same message (as assumed in § 7.5), we can first try to understand the pictorial part of this rare 'bilingual', and then use the results as a key to the inscription.

A search for parallels in the Near Eastern and later Indian traditions which can be assumed to be historically related to the Harappan forms the basis of the iconographic approach. Several alternative interpretations are possible, of course, but a solution that integrates all the different motifs is most likely to be correct, since they may be assumed to make a mythically and cultically coherent whole.

An anthropomorphic figure has knelt in front of a fig tree, with hands raised in respectful salutation, prayer or worship.

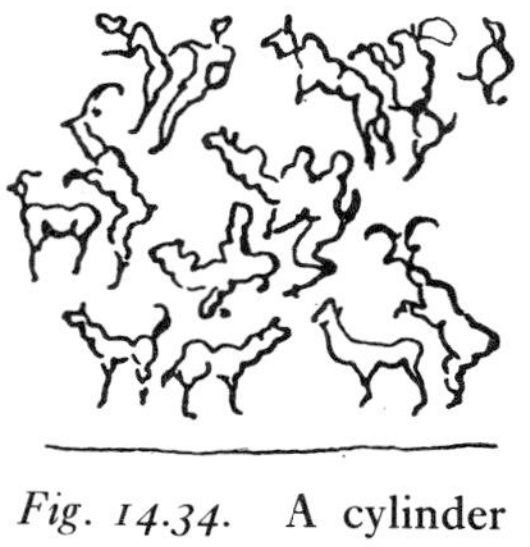

Fig. 14.34. A cylinder seal from southern Bactria with the motif of mating couples of different beings, human and animal. The Bactria and Margiana Archaeological Complex, *c.*1900–1500 BC. After Amiet 1986a: 322, fig. 191b.

Fig. 14.33. A Lamaist *thang-ka* showing ithyphallic Yama, the god of death, riding a buffalo which mates with an old woman. E. M. Scratton Collection, Department of Eastern Art, Ashmolean Museum, Oxford. Cf. Mallmann 1975: 463.

This reverence suggests the divinity of its object, another anthropomorphic figure standing inside the fig tree. In the ancient Near East, the gods and goddesses, as well as their earthly representatives, the divine kings and queens functioning as high priests and priestesses, were distinguished by a horned crown. A similar crown is worn by the two anthropomorphic figures on the 'fig deity' seal. Among various tribal peoples of India, horned head-dresses are worn by priests on sacrificial occasions.

The divinity of the standing figure is also suggested by the fig leaves that issue from the top of the worshipper's head-dress (such fig leaves adorn the deity's crown in figs. 10.9–10 and 14.16; cf. also fig. 14.18). In historical times, the spirits inhabiting sacred trees were represented as having human form, with leaves of the tree on the crowns of their heads (§ 13.1). The long, broad 'tail-pendant' which starts from the top of the head and hangs down the back is part of the head-dress in some other examples of Harappan art as well. In a seal from Mohenjo-daro (1357), such a head-dress is worn by an anthropomorphic figure with bovine legs and distinctly female breasts; this mythical creature is associated with a horned tiger. The tiger-bodied war-goddess on the cylinder seal of Kalibangan, compared above with the later goddess Durgā, also has such a pendant as part of her head-dress (fig. 14.25).

One of the main clues to the identity of the divine figure represented in this seal is the fig tree. All the principal varieties of fig are worshipped as sacred in India: the banyan (*Ficus indica* L. = *Ficus bengalensis* L., in Sanskrit *vaṭa* or *nyagrodha*), the pipal (*Ficus religiosa*, in Sanskrit *aśvattha* or *pippala*), the country fig (*Ficus glomerata*, in Sanskrit *udumbara*) and the wavy-leaf fig (*Ficus infectoria*, in Sanskrit *plakṣa*). To judge from the shape of its leaves, the tree on the 'fig deity' seal is most probably either the pipal or the banyan (fig. 14.1). The various fig trees often have the same symbolism and are interchangeable in the cult, particularly the two principal ones, the pipal and the banyan.

The fig trees have a special relationship with kingship. Thus in AB 7,27–34, all four principal varieties of fig trees (nyagrodha, aśvattha, udumbara and plakṣa) are most emphatically associated with kingship. To judge from the horned crown, similar to that of the deity, the 'worshipper' of the 'fig deity' seal is likely to have been royal. According to the Old Tamil literature, the ancient kings of South India carefully maintained a 'tutelary tree' in the courtyard of their palaces or in some other safe place. This tree (which could but need not be a fig tree) was a totemic symbol associated with the ruling dynasty from ancient times and was believed to have the power to protect the town. Its destruction was a most ominous event for the king and the state, and a victorious ruler often cut the tutelary tree of his vanquished enemy.

The same custom was prevalent at the other end of the Indian subcontinent. The Kashmirian text Kathāsaritsāgara (90) relates that Jīmūtavāhana, the prince of the mythical Vidyādharas, had in his palace garden a wishing-tree, a family heirloom, called 'the granter of desires'. When Jīmūtavāhana was made crown prince, his father's ministers advised him: 'Prince, you must continually worship this wishing-tree, unapproachable by any creature, which grants all our desires. For, as long as we have this, not even Indra could injure us, much less any other enemy.' When Jīmūtavāhana renounced this tree in favour of the whole world, it flew off to heaven, showering blessings on the earth, but Jīmūtavāhana soon lost his kingdom. The epithet of the tree, *adhṛṣya* 'unapproachable, invincible', reminds one of *durga* 'unapproachable place, fort', associated with the goddess Durgā.

The important theme of 'fig trees and fertility' has already been touched on on several occasions. In many Buddhist stories of the Jātaka collection, the child-granting tree is specified as the banyan (e.g. Jātaka 509), worshipped with bloody offerings, even with human sacrifices (cf. Jākata 50). But so far we have mainly spoken of the fig tree's connection with male gods of fertility, especially Skanda (chapter 13) and Varuṇa (§§ 12.2 and 14.1). However, the connections of the fig tree with female deities of fertility are equally strong and important. For one thing, all fig trees are laticiferous, and their milky sap naturally associates them with the milk-giving mother. According to the Mahābhārata, 'people desiring sons should worship the man-eating divine women called dryads (*vṛkṣikāḥ*) born in trees' (3,220,16).

To take a more specific example, in Bengal

> the Vaṭa (*Ficus indica*) is associated with *Ṣaṣṭhī*. The tree bears numerous fruits, so it is symbolized as the seat of Ṣaṣṭhī, the deity of fertility and many children. It is believed that the tree is the abode of the deity and the deity is worshipped under the tree. (Mahapatra 1972: 144)

Like most fertility spirits, Ṣaṣṭhī has an ambivalent nature: in her benevolent aspect, she grants and protects children, but, if she is not properly pacified, she is a demoness harassing newborn babies and their mothers. Ṣaṣṭhī is associated with the cat (§ 13.1), which identifies her as a form of Durgā. Her name, 'the Sixth', refers to the sixth day after birth (often critical for the mother), when she is worshipped in the lying-in chamber. The sixth lunar day is also the birthday of Skanda, the six-headed youthful Hindu god of war, whose wife Ṣaṣṭhī is said to be.

Similarly at Prabhāsa (in Saurashtra), a terrible goddess called Bhūtamātā 'mother of ghosts' (comparable to Durgā as *bhūta-priyā* 'fond of ghosts'), said to be benevolent towards children, lives in an old tree: she is to be worshipped by women lest she enter their houses to harm them, among other things by worshipping a banyan tree (*vaṭa*) and planting its branch (Skanda-Purāṇa 7,1,167,74). Eka-parṇā or Eka-pāṭalā is the name of a goddess, daughter of the Himalayan mountains like Pārvatī, who subsists by eating daily one leaf of the banyan tree (Brahma-Purāṇa 34,81–92). Lakṣmī, the goddess of good fortune, is said to dwell in the pipal fig every Saturday, while on the other days of the week the tree is occupied by her elder sister Alakṣmī, the goddess of misfortune (Padma-Purāṇa, Uttarakhaṇḍa 118, 24–7). The pipal tree is also called *śrī-vṛkṣa* 'the tree of Śrī, the goddess of good fortune'.

The pipal fig is a female divinity in Matsya-Purāṇa 178,69, which mentions a 'mother' goddess called Aśvatthā, while one of the 108 forms of the goddess, called Vandanīyā ('to be praised'), lives in the aśvattha tree (MP 13,51). According to the Rajput tradition, Āśāpūrṇā ('fill of wishes'), the tutelary goddess of the Bundi state, appeared out of an aśvattha tree in order to protect the queen. According to Bhaviṣya-Purāṇa (Uttarakhaṇḍa 138,33), the idol of the goddess Durgā worshipped during the autumnal navarātri festival is to be established on an altar having the shape of the female organ or the pipal leaf (*yonyaśvatthadalābhayā*).

The Brahmavaivarta-Purāṇa (Śrīkṛṣṇakhaṇḍa 16,177) prescribes the worship of the goddess Caṇḍikā (i.e. Durgā as the goddess of victory) at the root of the banyan tree. The Skanda-Purāṇa (5,1,70,41ff.) speaks of goddesses called *vaṭa-mātaraḥ* 'mothers of the banyan fig'; in addition to one called Vaṭa-yakṣiṇī, this group contains multiforms of Durgā such as Brahmāṇī, Kaumārī, etc. They were created to kill the demon Andhaka ('darkness') near a banyan tree (5,1,37,24). In the Kālī-nautch festival of Bengal, the goddess is worshipped under a banyan tree at midnight.

In Bengal, many kinds of trees including the sheora (*Trophis aspera*) and aśvattha are worshipped as the abode of the goddess Vana-Durgā or 'sylvan Durgā'. Goats, sheep and buffaloes are sacrificed to Vana-Durgā and her twelve sons near the tree on Tuesday or Friday. Once a year during the navarātri festival, the women of the village worship the tree of Vana-Durgā. After the pūjā, expectant mothers, and young mothers whose children have died shortly after birth, tie pieces of new cloth dyed in turmeric to the branches of the tree to ensure the long life of their coming children.

In eastern Bengal, a goddess of victory called Jaya-Durgā is worshipped in the form of an earthen pitcher filled with water that is 'placed either at the root of a tree or in some waste place unfrequented by human beings'. Her non-Brahmin priests

> strip themselves naked and dance before the pitcher and thereby invoke her . . . Then twenty-nine diagrams of mystic significance are drawn with powdered rice . . . On each of these diagrams are placed oblations of boiled rice and roasted fish for the goddessling Jaya Durgā. Last of all, beasts . . . are sacrificed and Homa ceremony is performed. (Mitra 1931: 970–1)

Fig trees were also instrumental in securing victory in war. Thus in the Atharvavedic hymn 3,6 (cf. also 8,8,3) repeated invocations to crush the foes are addressed to the pipal fig (*aśvattha*). According to GGS 4,7,23, the banyan tree presages war. Two ancient descriptions of royal fig worship for the sake of victory are of special importance for the interpretation of the 'fig deity' seal.

In Rāmāyaṇa, the righteous-minded demon Vibhīṣaṇa has deserted his evil-minded brother Rāvaṇa, the demon king of Sri Lanka, and joined the forces of Rāma. Vibhīṣaṇa reveals to his ally that the greatest hero of the demons, Rāvaṇa's son Indrajit, will perform a sacrifice at a shrine (*caitya*) called Nikumbhilā (6,71,13); this sacrifice makes him invincible in battle (verse 14 uses the term *durādharṣa*, verse 22 its synonym *adhṛṣya* 'unapproachable, invincible' that we saw applied to the tutelary tree in Kathāsaritsāgara 90). Vibhīṣaṇa therefore advises Rāma that Lakṣmaṇa should kill Indrajit at the moment when he is returning from the battle to renew his sacrifice, because Indrajit can be slain when he has not yet completed his ritual (6,71,13–22). Vibhīṣaṇa then personally guides Lakṣmaṇa to a great forest not far from Laṅkā, showing him the place where the ritual is observed (6,74,2): 'a terrible-looking banyan-tree (*nyagrodha*) which has the appearance of a dark blue thundercloud' (3); 'it is after bringing an offering to the ghosts (*bhūta*) living here that Rāvaṇa's mighty son thereafter betakes himself to the battle' (4). Another son of Rāvaṇa, Meghanāda, is also said to have obtained many miraculous weapons of war through his sacrifices at 'the great forest of Laṅkā called Nikumbhilā' (7,25,2ff.).

Nikumbhilā appears to be the name of a goddess of war, for the demonesses of Laṅkā refer to drinking alcohol (*surā*), eating human flesh, and dancing (5,22,41) as ways of worshipping her and the commentaries identify her as 'the goddess Bhadrakālī who dwells at the western gate of Laṅkā'. Nikumbhilā is the feminine gender counterpart of Nikumbha, attested as the name of several demons, of a Kuru warrior and a warrior in the army of Skanda, the god of war. It may be a variant of Niśumbha, the name of a demoniac adversary of Durgā as well as a noun meaning 'killing, murder'.

In the Buddhist Dhonasākha Jātaka (no. 353), a king who wanted to conquer the city of Taxila (in the northern Indus Valley) settled under a big banyan tree. His priest advised the king to sacrifice a thousand captured princes to the deity of the tree in order to obtain victory: 'And surrounding the tree with a rimmed circumference let us fill it with blood five inches deep. And so shall the victory soon be ours.' (The tree of the 'fig deity' seal seems to have a rimmed circumference – many other sacred trees shown on moulded tablets from Harappa have a railing: fig. 13.8.)

The next motif on the 'fig deity' seal that I shall discuss is

Fig. 14.35. The 'fig deity' seal from Mohenjo-daro (M-1186). The iconography of this seal is discussed in § 14.3. For a simpler variant of the same ritual scene see fig. 7.13b.

the human head placed on a throne or sacrificial altar beneath the fig tree. The hair on this head is bound at the back into a double bun, like the hair of the two soldiers who spear each other on the cylinder seal from Kalibangan (fig. 14.25) and the hair in the electrum helmet from the Royal Cemetery at Ur (fig. 14.27). This suggests that the human head on the 'fig deity' seal belonged to a warrior.

Beheading a victim in sacrifice used to be central to the cult of Durgā, the Hindu goddess of victory. A severed human head (or a garland made of such heads) is among her iconographic attributes and cult objects (e.g. KP 67,86). In ancient South India, brave warriors won the favour of Durgā by cutting off their own heads: thus they tried to make her grant victory to the king they served. Up to the early years of British rule in Karnataka, human sacrifice was a regular part of the yearly navarātri festival of the goddess, initiating war expeditions. In the myth of Durgā's main feat, the slaying of the Mahiṣa Asura, celebrated at the culmination of this festival, the final form which the decapitated demon-victim assumes is that of a manly hero.

That the human head on the 'fig deity' seal is the result of a sacrifice is suggested by the pictogram 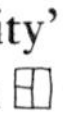 placed nearby, apart from the rest of the inscription. This sign appears to be in some way related to sacrifice, because it occurs, similarly detached from the main inscription, beside the victim in a seal that depicts the spearing of a buffalo (fig. 14.23a). Hunting of wild buffalo (a most ferocious beast) is less likely than sacrifice in this scene, because the spearman is repeatedly shown as having placed one of his feet on the head of the brute (fig. 14.23). Buffalo sacrifice is one indication of the cult of Proto-Durgā in the Indus Civilization. In one other seal (M-952), the sign 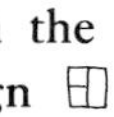 encloses another pictogram: 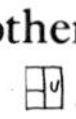. The inserted sign 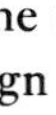 is likely to mean 'pot containing sacrificial offering', because in some moulded tablets an inscription containing this sign is accompanied by a scene in which a kneeling man holds such a pot in his hands, which are extended towards a tree (fig. 7.12), while in other tablets worshippers extend the pot towards an anthropomorphic figure sitting on a throne and wearing a horned head-dress (fig. 13.2b). These scenes also remind us of the Bengali worship of Jaya-Durgā with pots offered to trees (quoted above); the sign  may represent a magic diagram upon which the pot is placed, with its offerings.

The markhor goat is yet another detail in the 'fig deity' seal that supports the interpretation in terms of Durgā's cult. The half-human, half-caprine face of the markhor is likely to have belonged to the Harappan predecessor of the goat-faced Hindu god Skanda, connected with virility, fertility and the banyan tree (§§ 13.4–5). According to the Vaikhānasa Āgama, the planet Mars (a manifestation of the war-god Skanda, the presiding deity of this planet), is depicted as having the markhor in his flag (*śarabha-dhvaja*). One meaning of the Sanskrit word *skanda* is 'the leaper', and the markhor is famed for being able to jump to 'inaccessible places' (AS 9,5,9; Kālidāsa's Meghadūta 55): the word for 'inaccessible place' used in this connection, *durga*, also means 'fort' and connects the beast with the goddess Durgā. According to the Kālikā-Purāṇa (57,5–6), the wild markhor goat (called *śarabha* in Sanskrit) is, next to man and the water buffalo, most highly esteemed by the goddess as a sacrificial animal. These victims are at the top of a long list of male sacrificial animals, which may be compared to the various manly forms assumed by Mahiṣa Asura in his combat with Durgā, all killed by the goddess (§ 10.3). The most common animal victim is the goat, which is in many ways associated with Skanda (§ 13.5).

The last motif on the 'fig deity' seal to be examined is the row of seven anthropomorphic figures at the bottom. They wear their hair in a single long plait, as did women in ancient times in the Near East, a style still followed today in South Asia. This motif also points to Skanda and to the goddess of victory. As the leader of the divine army, Skanda is accompanied by the dread goddesses of destruction and illness, called 'mothers', usually seven in number. These 'seven mothers' are aspects of Durgā, the goddess of war and victory; at the same time, they are the wives of the Seven Sages (the asterism of the Great Bear). Six of them (the stars of the Pleiades) are the 'mothers' or wet-nurses of the war-god Rudra-Skanda in the Vedic as well as in the Hindu religions (§§ 11.3; 12.2; 13.1).

The seven anthropomorphic figures are dressed in skirts. If they are female, then why does the 'fig deity' not also wear a skirt, if she too is female? Perhaps because the goddess is naked (according to KP 66,86–90, for example, the goddess Tripurā is naked; for Kōṭṭavī, dictionaries give the meaning 'naked woman'; compare also the naked or 'self-denuding' goddess of northern Syria and Mesopotamia in the first half of the second millennium BC).

14.4 The inscription on the 'fig deity' seal: the star of the Goddess, the carp and the red dot on the forehead

We are now ready to turn to the main inscription on the 'fig deity' seal. The preceding discussion has suggested that the seal probably belonged to the high priest or priestess of a goddess, who was a predecessor of the later Durgā. We have also assumed that the message of the seal was conveyed in two different ways: (1) pictorially on the iconographic scene and (2) in writing in the inscription. Structurally, the inscription is identical with that of the famous 'Proto-Śiva' seal (§ 7.5). In both cases (reading the impression from right to left) the final sign is , which depicts 'man'. It can be read in Dravidian as *āḷ* / *āṇ* 'man, manly person, warrior, husband, servant'; in Tamil this word also means 'devotee (of a deity)'. The immediately preceding sign may in contexts like this represent the Proto-Dravidian genitive suffix **-ā* (§ 10.2). The sign before that one, fish-shaped in both these seals, would express the name of the deity, preceded by other signs that probably express epithets.

We have seen that the fish signs of the Indus script can be interpreted as the Dravidian names of stars and planets (§§ 10.1; 10.4–5; 12.2; 13.2–3; 14.1; fig. 15.2), used as symbols of divinities and in this capacity also as the building blocks of proper names (§ 11.4). In the inscription on the 'fig deity' seal, the sign  'fish with a dot inside' is likely to represent the deity depicted on the seal. Pictorially, the 'dot' or 'single short vertical line' inside the fish sign is somewhat ambiguous; it might denote 'number one' (§ 5.2), but other meanings, too, are conceivable (e.g. 'hole', 'drop', 'dot'). This problem of iconic interpretation may be solved, however, if we approach it from a different angle. For if the iconographic and religious considerations presented in § 14.3 are correct and the divinity of the 'fig deity' seal was the goddess of victory and fertility, we can take the star of the goddess as the starting-point.

The first question to be asked is: Which star was most likely to be associated with the protoform of Durgā in India in most ancient times? If a satisfactory answer can be found, the next task is to discover whether any native Dravidian name for the heavenly body concerned has survived in our sources; generally speaking, the prospects are not very good, because relatively few of the original Dravidian star-names have survived, most having been replaced by the corresponding names in Sanskrit and related Indo-Aryan languages in the course of the millennia. Should we succeed in this second task as well, there will be an important test of the candidate: we shall see whether it has or does not have the power to explain the pictorial shape of the 'fish with a dot' sign.

Venus is one obvious possibility, for all over the ancient Near East, the goddess of war and sexual love was associated with this planet. In Mesopotamia, for example, Venus as the morning star represented Inanna-Ishtar as the goddess of war; as the evening star, Venus represented her as the goddess of love, and this association between the Goddess and the planet Venus can be traced back to the archaic texts of the fourth millennium BC (fig. 2.3). A statue of the Elamite goddess Narunde discovered at Susa and dated to *c*.2220 BC shows her with two lions and a star as her attributes: the star is undoubtedly Venus (fig. 14.36). The Bactrian goddess riding the lion (fig. 14.29) was probably also associated with the planet Venus, because her iconography is heavily influenced by the art of Mesopotamia and Elam. Moreover, the Old Iranian goddess of waters, fertility and victory, Anāhitā, was identified with Venus, for in the later Zarathustran literature the name of the goddess, Anāhīd, usually denotes the planet Venus.

The Indian goddess Durgā or Kālī, too, is connected with Venus. For example, until 1835, before the British stopped the practice, a young boy was sacrificed to the goddess in the principal Kālī temple of Calcutta every Friday, the day of the planet Venus, and the same practice is reported concerning the Kālī shrine of the Bṛhadīśvara temple at Thanjavus in South India. However, the seven-day week and, with it, the connection between Friday and Venus, are comparatively recent in India, having come from the West in Hellenistic times, so we cannot be satisfied with this evidence. We must look for more ancient data relating to the astral aspect of the Indian goddess.

Fig. 14.36. Statue of Narunde, the Elamite goddess of victory, with lions and the star symbol of Venus. From her temple at Susa, *c*.2220 BC. Musée du Louvre / *AO* (SB 54–6617). After *Naissance de l'écriture* 1982: 220, no. 162.

Tārā, whose name denotes 'star', is worshipped as a popular tutelary goddess in Tibetan Buddhism. Traditionally, her name is taken to mean 'saviouress' (from Sanskrit verb *tārayati* 'takes across, saves, protects'), but the astral meaning (*tārā* < **stārā*- < Indo-European **ster*-) is implied in the earliest known reference to this Buddhist deity, Subandhu's Vāsavadattā (*c*.650 AD):

> 'The Lady Twilight was seen, devoted to the stars and clad in red sky, as a Buddhist nun [is devoted to Tārā and is clad in red garments.]' The pun centers on the ambivalence of two words: *tārā* as either 'star' or 'Tārā', and *ambara* as either 'sky' or 'garment'. (Beyer 1973: 7)

It is also clear that this goddess has been taken over by Buddhism from Hinduism, where an astral goddess called Tārā is known from a widely attested Puranic myth (e.g., Viṣṇu-Purāṇa 4,6):

> Soma, the moon, performed the Vedic rite of royal consecration. He became arrogant and abducted Tārā, the wife of Bṛhaspati, the priest and teacher of the gods, who is identified with the planet Jupiter. The gods declared the war of stars, in which the Asuras (demons) and their teacher Uśanas Kāvya, identified with the planet Venus, fought on the side of the moon. After Tārā was restored to her husband, she was found to be pregnant. At first, Bṛhaspati wished to have the child abandoned, but after the birth of a splendid son, the planet Mercury, both Bṛhaspati and Soma claimed paternity. When Tārā, threatened by her son, finally declared Soma to be the father, the moon named the child Budha, 'wise'.

This myth is very ancient, being referred to as early as the Ṛgveda (10,109), around 1000 BC. But which star was Tārā? Another myth of Soma's love affairs is known from the oldest Brāhmaṇas (KS 11,3; MS 2,2,7; TS 2,3,5). The moon was married to the nakṣatras, the lunar marker stars, but he favoured only one of them, the red star Aldebaran, called *Rohiṇī* 'the red female'; the others, neglected, returned home.

Soma went after them, but their father Prajāpati did not return them until Soma had promised to treat them equally. Because the moon again favoured only Rohiṇī, he was punished with the disease of consumption that causes him to wane.

The first asterism of the Vedic star calendar is the Pleiades, whose heliacal rise at the vernal equinox took place *c*.2240 BC. The myths of Rohiṇī as the favoured mate of the moon probably refer to a still earlier time, when Rohiṇī was not the second but the first nakṣatra, i.e., when Aldebaran rose with the sun at the vernal equinox, *c*.3054 BC. This would take us to Early Harappan times (§ 11.3). The Mahābhārata (3,219,10) in fact speaks of the time before the Pleiades rose to the heavens, when 'Rohiṇī was the first'. In the Rāmāyaṇa (5,31,5 ed. Gorresio), too, Rohiṇī is called 'the first of the stars' (*jyotiṣām agryā*). Albrecht Weber (1862) has pointed to a structural feature in the calendar that seems to bear out this interpretation: one variant of the oldest nakṣatra list (in TS 4,4,10,1–3; cf. also TB 1,5,1,4) contains *two* lunar houses, both called *rohiṇī*, the 2nd and the 16th (in other lists, this *rohiṇī* is called *jyeṣṭhā* 'the oldest': § 14.1); from the fact that these two stars are diametrically opposed to each other, Weber concluded that the two halves of the calendrical cycle had once begun with the same name.

Rohiṇī, then, was probably the oldest marking star of both the vernal and the autumnal equinox. The two great feasts of Durgā are celebrated around these two dates, in the spring and in the autumn (§§ 11.3; 14.3). Before starting out on a war expedition on the 'tenth day of victory' that concludes the autumnal navarātri festival, the Rajput king traditionally lustrates his army. On the appearance of the first star (Biardeau 1981b: 226), he parades to worship the goddess of victory and her tree (śamī, a hard tree used together with the pipal fig in the kindling of fire). According to Dharmasindhu, the king is to go to the northeast and to pray: 'May Aparājitā ... bestow victory on me!' Northeast is the 'invincible (*aparājitā*) direction' (AB 1, 14) of the dawn and the rising star.

In the earliest phase of Indian astronomy, the beginning of the new year would have been observed from the *heliacal rise* of Rohiṇī (§ 11.2), at that time more or less the only calendrical star of importance. The later shift to lunar observation (the star's conjunction with the full moon) appears to be reflected in the story of Rohiṇī's being the favoured mate of the moon, for Tārā is said to have been the wife of Bṛhaspati before she was appropriated by Soma (the moon). Bṛhaspati later becomes the golden planet Jupiter, but in this myth he is undoubtedly the rising sun. In the JUB (4,27), Savitṛ (the sun) and his mate Sāvitrī form the archetypal 'couple' (*mithuna*); the later state of affairs is reflected in the marriage hymn of the Ṛgveda (ṚS 10,85), where Sāvitrī is the bride of the moon (Soma's identity with the moon is clear from verse 2, where it is said to be 'in the lap of these [calendrical] stars'). The Atharvaveda (13,1,22), too, supports this hypothesis by making the goddess Rohiṇī the mate of the rising sun and, significantly, a goddess of war: 'Devoted to Rohita is Rohiṇī his mistress, with beautiful colour (complexion), great, and lustrous: through her may we conquer booty of every description, through her win every battle!' (trans. Bloomfield 1897: 210). Rohiṇī 'the ruddy one' of course refers to the dawn (the sun's daily bride) as well as to the star Aldebaran (his yearly bride). In most versions of the myth of Prajāpati's incest, his daughter is expressly said to be Uṣas 'Dawn'.

According to the Skanda-Purāṇa (5,3,108,12), Rohiṇī won the love of her husband after propitiating the goddess who killed the Buffalo demon. That Rohiṇī is the star of Durgā is also suggested by the fact that Tārā (who we have seen denotes Rohiṇī in the Veda) remains one of Durgā's names: 'The wise seers call her Ugra-tārā, for Ambikā always protects her devotees against danger, however terrible it may be' (KP 63,61). Sāvitrī, too, is associated with Durgā and Tārā by her epithet *durga-taraṇī* 'she who saves from difficulties or dangers' (Mahābhārata 2,11,34 B); this is significant, as the cult of Sāvitrī is connected with the banyan fig (§ 14.1).

We can now return to the 'fish' sign on the 'fig deity' seal. If we are right in assuming that the 'fig deity' is the goddess of victory and fertility and that she is expressed through the 'fish with a dot' sign in the inscription of this seal, then the star represented by that sign is in all likelihood Rohiṇī, 'the red (female)'. How can we utilize this hypothesis for interpreting the sign? Can we find a pictorial interpretation that would connect it with the Rohiṇī star? Let us, first of all, examine what the Indian astronomical texts have to say about the symbolic shape of Rohiṇī.

According to later astronomical Sanskrit texts (such as Jyotiṣaratnamālā 6,74ff. or Brahmasiddhānta's Śākalya-saṁhitā 272ff.), the Rohiṇī asterism is symbolized by a cart (*śakaṭa*). We shall return to this symbol later. But Kālidāsa's Rātrilagnanirūpaṇa mentions the *śakula* fish as the symbol of Rohiṇī. *Śakula* is the carnivorous catfish called 'snakehead, or murrel (*Ophiocephalus striatus* Bloch or *Channa striatus* Bloch)' (fig. 14.37); 'a kind of carp', however, is recorded as a meaning for the Hindi word *saurī* or *saur*, which is derived from Sanskrit *śakula*. This confusion is curious, as the snakeheads and carps look quite different, although they belong to the same order of Cypriniformes; on the other hand, both are very common and great delicacies, and both play a prominent role in the cult of the Goddess. Thus *śāla* (contracted from *śakula*) 'snakehead' and *rohita* 'carp (*Cyprinus rohita* or *Labeo rohita* Hamilton)' (fig. 14.38) are among the three best kinds of fish specified by the Tantric texts as fit to be offered to the Goddess, the fish (*matsya*) being

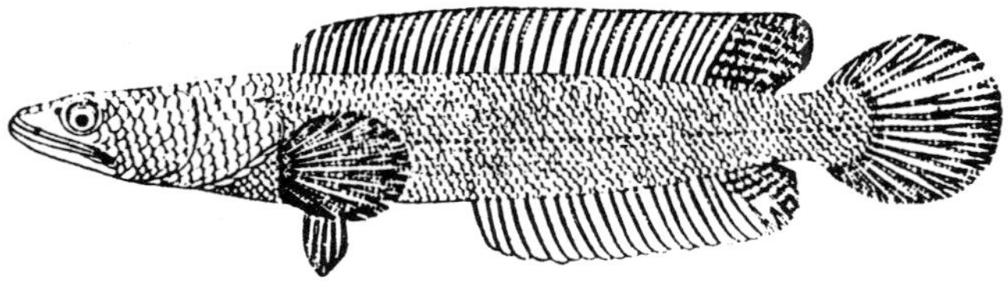

Fig. 14.37. The 'snakehead' fish, *Ophiocephalus striatus* Bloch (Sanskrit *śakula*, *śāla*). After Hora 1952, pl. 1: 5.

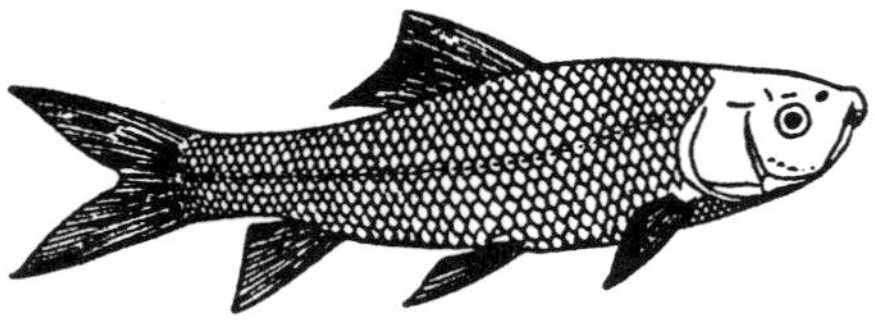

Fig. 14.38. The carp, *Cyprinus rohita* Hamilton, alias *Labeo rohita* Hamilton (Sanskrit *rohita*). After Hora 1955: 4, fig. 2 b.

one of the five essential components of the infamous 'circle worship' of the Goddess:

There are three sorts of the best kind of fish: *śāla*, *pāṭhīna* [*Silurus pelorius*], and *rohita*. The middling sort are the ones without bones, and the worst are the ones that have lots of bones – though these, too, may be offered to the Goddess if they are very well roasted or fried. (Mahānirvāṇa-Tantra 6, 1–20, trans. O'Flaherty et al. 1988: 133)

The 'left-hand' orgies of the Goddess, in which fish is eaten as an aphrodisiac (§ 10.2), are practised particularly on the 'tenth day of victory', and they have a close parallel in two archaic Vedic rituals that appear to have pre-Vedic roots in India, namely the new year rite mahāvrata and the horse sacrifice (§ 14.2). Interestingly, in the obscene dialogue accompanying the simulated sexual union of the dead victim and the chief queen in the horse sacrifice, a pair of *śakula* fish is mentioned (this being almost the only occurrence of the word in the Veda: AS 20,136,1; VS 23,28; etc.). Here the *śakula* are compared to the labia of the female organ. Even this symbolism the *śakula* shares with the *rohita* fish, for a pair of carp is a well-known symbol of fertility in ancient India (§§ 10.2–3); as a fertility symbol it is also associated with the goddess of Durgā (fig. 14.42). *Rohita* has 'scales with orange to reddish centre', and is therefore a more appropriate symbol for the Rohiṇī asterism than *śakula*, which is without scales. Its very name is the same Sanskrit word for 'red' as that of the star – the difference being that the gender of *rohita* is masculine, while that of *rohiṇī* is feminine. Carps (Cyprinidae and *Labeo* spp.) are also significantly represented among the fish remains unearthed at Harappa (Belcher 1992: 113).

If the 'fish with a dot' sign stands for the *rohita* fish as a symbol of the star Rohiṇī, how can we read it? The sign can be broken into two components: (1) the basic 'fish' sign, and (2) a single short stroke or 'dot' or 'point' placed in its middle. It is the 'dot' inside that must make the expected meaning 'red fish, carp' explicit. There is one 'dot' or 'point' (*bindu*) that is most important in the Hindu cult and that moreover happens to be usually red, namely the dot which is painted on the forehead. In many South and Central Dravidian languages, this is called **poṭṭu* 'dot, spot, round (red) mark on the forehead, drop of water'. In Central Dravidian languages there is a perfect homophone **poṭṭu* meaning 'a kind of fish', and in Gondi at least, specifically '*rohita* fish'; from Pengo this word is, moreover, known compounded with the word for 'fish' as *boṭu mīn*. The etymon appears to go back to Proto-Dravidian, as cognates seem to exist in South Dravidian as well (Tamil *poṭṭu-k-kārai* 'a kind of fish'; Malayalam *poṭṭan* 'a fish'). That we have here indeed hit upon the right pictorial interpretation of the Indus sign assumed to stand for the asterism of Rohiṇī is suggested by the little-known fact that the red forehead mark is directly connected with the Rohiṇī star in the Hindu tradition.

The red forehead mark is called by many names, the Dravidian word mentioned above being current mainly in South India. In North India, among the most common terms are Sanskrit *tilaka* 'mark on the forehead; small mole on the skin' (from *tila* 'sesamum seed, small particle'), and the unexplained *ṭīkā*, to which we shall return a little later. In its most common function, it is an indispensable attribute of a married Hindu woman whose husband is alive. Texts like Tryambakayajvan's Strīdharma-Paddhati, which details the duties of the 'perfect wife', prescribe putting the auspicious tilaka mark on the forehead as a necessary part of the wife's daily toilette. The traditional verses quoted in this connection stress that this should not be forgotten by the devoted wife (*pati-vratā*) who wishes her husband to live long:

The sectarian marks so important for men are deemed irrelevant to their wives ... The ... references to tilaka have no relation to either Viṣṇu or Śiva. The mark is made with ... [saffron or reddish paste, called] *kuṅkuma*, the sign of a woman's marital happiness or *saubhāgya*. For the tilaka is the visible symbol of a woman's religious allegiance as distinct from that of men. It declares first that her husband is her deity; secondly, that he is still alive to receive her daily service and worship. As we have seen, the bulk of the rulings on a woman's appearance carry the same message: her husband lives; all religious devotion must be directed to him alone. A man without his sectarian mark is a man without a god; a woman without her tilaka is one whose god is dead. (Leslie 1989: 96–101)

The wife devoted to her husband has Sāvitrī and Rohiṇī as her models; if the dot on her forehead symbolizes her

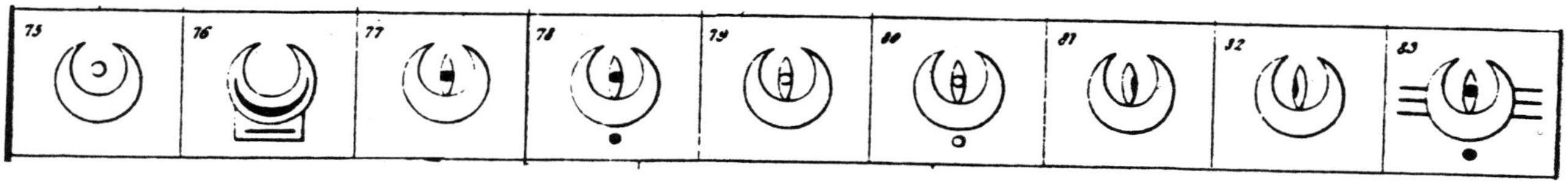

Fig. 14.39. Some Hindu forehead marks. After Moor 1810: pl. 2, nos. 75–83.

husband, then it should depict the sun, because Savitṛ and Rohita, as the husbands of Sāvitrī and Rohiṇī respectively, both represent the sun-god. This is, indeed, in agreement with the red and circular form of the mark and the testimony of C. D. Maclean, whose *Glossary of the Madras Presidency* (1893), under the word 'Pottoo (*boṭṭu*, Telugu; *poṭṭu*, Tamil)', records that 'the dot is the mark of the sun'. The Rāmāyaṇa (3,22,8) compares the northern direction, which is without the sun, to a woman who lacks the tilaka.

One of the most extensive and detailed collections of Hindu forehead marks was published by Edward Moor in his book *The Hindu pantheon* in 1810. The astral nature of the 'crescents, variously accompanied' in nos. 75–83 of Moor's catalogue (reproduced in fig. 14.39) is clear from his comments:

> This lunar hieroglyphic seems exclusively the distinction of MAHADEVA and his family: I do not, in this instance, find any exception. Nos. 75 and 76 ... the *Shivanites* paint ... on the forehead in yellow, as emblems of ŚIVA and PARVATI – the Sun and Moon. In all my pictures the crescents are white. (Moor 1810: 408)

This interpretation agrees with classical Hindu mythology, according to which Śiva has the crescent of the moon as a diadem on his forehead, and a sun-like third eye on his brow.

But if the 'eye' above the crescent is the sun (and the sun is the 'eye' of various Vedic gods already: § 12.1), what is the dot beneath the crescent in nos. 78, 80 and 83 (and in fig. 14.42)? We find an explanation in B. A. Gupte's article 'Notes on female tattoo designs in India', published in 1902:

> 1. *The mole* is a well-known protection from the Evil Eye. It is also an emblem of the *Chāndani*, corresponding to Venus, whose approach to the Moon, a personified *male* (as distinguished from the female of the West) is a natural phenomenon held to represent the meeting of a loving pair. The Moon is called Rāktīpati or Tārāgaṇapati, 'King of the Night', 'Husband of the Stars'.
>
> 2. *Rohiṇī* is his favourite wife, and she is represented thus •, while a crescent shows the Moon. A dot between the horns  represents the face of the Moon, which is often, however, drawn like the human face in profile  with another dot below it to represent his loving consort. It is an emblem of conjugal happiness.

Here Gupte does not specify the placement of these tattoo marks, but other reports do: 'Both men and women of the Korava class wear tattoo marks of circular or semicircular form on their foreheads and forearms' (P. Paupa Rao Naidu, *History of railway thieves*, 1900, quoted in Thurston 1906: 377). 'Many Pulayan men in Travancore are tattooed on the forehead with a crescent and circular spot' (Thurston 1906: 378). Thus the red dot on the forehead, with or without the lunar crescent, seems to have denoted both 'the sun' and 'the star Rohiṇī'.

The star Rohiṇī is praised as the best of all women: this goddess stays not even a second in the sky without the Moon, her husband (Rāmāyaṇa 3,3,11, ed. Gorresio); the preceding verse lauds Sāvitrī and Arundhatī (discussed § 14.1) for their marital faithfulness, through which they have reached the heavens (also Rāmāyaṇa 5,31,5–6). In the cultic ritual, too, the Rohiṇī star is worshipped together with the moon. Thus a vow called *rohiṇī-candra-śayana-vrata* is celebrated on the fifth day of the bright half-month that falls on a Monday, or on a full-moon day that falls on the Rohiṇī asterism (Matsya-Purāṇa 57). It includes the votive offering of a bed (*śayana*), given with a prayer for a happy married life.

In many Gṛhyasūtras (BaudhGS 1,1,20; MGS 1,7,5; KāṭhGS 14,10) Rohiṇī is mentioned first among the nakṣatras of marriage. According to the Old Tamil poem preserved in Akanāṉūṟu 136, the marriage took place 'as omens fell together favorably, as the broad sky shone with clear light, and as there was an unjeopardized conjunction of the moon and *cakaṭam* [=the asterism of Rohiṇī]' (trans. Hart 1975: 72). In Akanāṉūṟu 86,5–7, too, the moon and 'the faultless [Rohiṇī] star of excellent fame' are connected with marriage.

Like the Rohiṇī star, the red dot on the forehead is one of the foremost symbols of marital fidelity. As such it plays a central role in Indian marriage ceremonies. The rite of applying red powder to the bride's forehead and the parting of her hair (*sindūra-dāna*) is, in North India, sometimes the only marriage rite, and often the binding part of the ritual, after which the marriage cannot be annulled. Even the Brahuis of Baluchistan, though they have been Muslims for many centuries, have the bride's forehead painted with red, green and yellow. 'Then all the ladies who have daughters of their own yet unmarried, come forward and do worship to the *ṭik*, or bridal markings, on the bride's forehead' (Bray 1913: 64).

The Gṛhyasūtras, the Vedic manuals on domestic ceremonies, do not enjoin the marking of the bride's forehead with red powder. This strongly suggests that the ritual is of

(a)

(b)

Fig. 14.40. Women wearing a forehead mark in the early historical art of India. (a) Woman with a mirror in left hand, preparing her forehead ornament. Medallion on a balustrade of the Bhārhut stupa, second century BC. After Naudou 1966: 76, fig. 1. (b) A court attendant. Ajaṇṭā, Cave 10, *c.*100 BC. After Alkazi 1983: 61, fig. 8.

non-Aryan origin. That it nevertheless did exist in the Vedic period is shown by the Kauśikasūtra, the erratic Gṛhyasūtra of the 'unorthodox' Atharvaveda, which alone prescribes (in 76,12) the fixing of gold (*hiraṇya*) on the forehead (*lalāṭa*) of the bride.

The earliest female figures of Indian art wear on their foreheads either large round golden ornaments, as in the Bhārhut stupa of the second century BC (fig. 14.40a), or what look like tilakas, as in Cave 10 at Ajaṇṭā *c.*100 BC (fig. 14.40b). The earliest clear references to tilakas made with red powder on the forehead are in the Rāmāyaṇa, dating from around the beginning of the Christian era. Already around the fifth century BC, however, Pāṇini (4.3.65) mentions *lalāṭikā* 'ornament of the forehead (*lalāṭa*)'. It seems that *ṭikā* or *ṭīkā*, one of the principal expressions used nowadays for the 'forehead mark', which has been an etymological problem, can be explained from this word. It appears that later, when the Persian word *lālā* 'bright, shining; red' had entered Indo-Aryan, the variant form *lālāṭikā* was falsely understood to be a compound of two separate words.

The *sindūra-dāna* as the culmination of North Indian marriage has as its counterpart in South Indian marriage the tying of a string with an auspicious ornament (called *tāli* in Tamil) around the neck of the bride. That this marriage badge was originally tied on the forehead and that it thus corresponds to the red dot painted on the bride's forehead in North India is suggested by the fact that in Tamil the word *poṭṭu* denotes both 'a spot of sandal paste or other stuff put on the forehead' and 'a round plate of gold, the matrimonial token worn by Telugu women, *tāli-p-poṭṭu*' (Fabricius 1972: 745). The Harappan 'priest-king' statue wears a circular ornament on his forehead, kept there by a fillet (fig. 12.1). The male gender of the wearer is no obstacle to identifying this as a *poṭṭu*; among the Jāṭ tribes of the northern Punjab, for example, it is the bridegroom who is given the red dot in the wedding ceremonies:

> About five days before the wedding ... the [genealogist] then brings a ram (*chatra*, whence the name of the rite itself), cuts its ear, and with his thumb imprints a mark (*ṭīkā*) of its blood on the youth's forehead, and on those of all present. He gets the ram and a rupee as his vail. The youth then bathes, and boiled wheat is distributed. He is oiled, and a red tape is tied round his forehead. Thenceforward he must keep a knife or sword in his hand till the wedding day. (Rose 1914: 490b)

The vermilion used for the *sindūra-dāna* ritual in the North Indian wedding is, at least in eastern India, often kept in fish-shaped metal containers. This fish-shaped box is not the only link between the fish and the dot on the forehead, which appears to be represented by the 'dot' in the 'fish' pictogram of the 'fig deity' seal:

> The fish as a symbol of fertility has an important part in the marriage rites. The Brahmans of Kanara take the married pair to a pond and make them throw rice into the water and catch a few minnows [i.e. carp]. They let all go, save one, with whose scales they mark their brows. If there be no pond near, the rite is done by making a fish of wheat flour, dropping it into a vessel of water, taking it out and marking their foreheads with the paste. (Crooke 1906: 222)

Significantly, this custom is not restricted to South India:

> The Emperor Jahangir, before undertaking a journey, used to have a huge carp brought into his presence, followed by a dish of starch, into which he plunged his fingers and rubbed them between the eyes of the fish and then on his own forehead. He probably got the idea from the Kashmiri ladies of his harem; at any rate, Mr Val Prinsep describes the Maharaja of Kashmir doing exactly the same rite a few years ago. (Crooke 1906: 222)

The time of celebration and the dot made on the forehead are not the only connections that the star Rohiṇī has with brides and marriage. The Sanskrit word *rohiṇī* also denotes a marriageable young virgin, according to Parāśara-Smṛti 7,7,4, one who is nine years old. The Gṛhyāsaṁgraha (2,18) in turn defines *rohiṇī*: 'the girl is "red" (*rohiṇī*) after she has attained menstruation.' This meaning is connected with that of 'the Rohiṇī star' in a Vedic myth narrated in the Aitareya-Brāhmaṇa (3,33), where the star Rohiṇī is the first-born daughter of the creator-god Prajāpati. In a primeval act of incest, Rohiṇī was approached by her own father, but the father was killed in punishment for his sinful behaviour. One function of this myth seems to have been to warn of the dire consequences of incest and to enforce the sacred law which states: 'Out of fear of the appearance of the menses let the father marry his daughter while she still runs about naked. For if she stays (in the house) after the age of puberty, sin falls on the father' (Vāsiṣṭha-Dharmaśāstra 17,70).

In this connection, the expression 'red one' (*rohiṇī*) appears to get its meaning from the fertile red blood (*rohita*) in her womb. The following considerations lead to the same conclusion. Unmarried girls traditionally have a black forehead mark, the red mark being reserved for married women. Moreover, a woman is not to wear the auspicious red mark on her forehead when she has menses, but is supposed to put a black mark instead on three days. During this time, sexual intercourse is prohibited. On the fourth day she is again available to her husband, and puts on the red mark. (It is undoubtedly this custom that is reflected in giving the goddess Durgā her forehead mark on the *fourth* day of the yearly navarātri festival.) If a woman becomes a widow or her husband is away, she is not entitled to wear the red tilaka mark.

The menstrual blood (*rohita*) in the womb of the sexually mature girl (*rohiṇī*) corresponds to the icon of 'a dot *inside* a fish' in the Indus pictogram that we have supposed to signify the star Rohiṇī. Of course purely practical reasons speak against placing the 'dot' sign *in front* of the 'fish' sign. For although this latter alternative is conceivable for a compound consisting of words that mean 'dot' and 'fish', it would have caused ambiguity, because a single short stroke in front of the plain 'fish' sign could have been understood to denote 'number one' (§§ 5.2; 10.4). But there seem to have been strong symbolic reasons for placing the 'dot' inside the 'fish' as well. The fish-shaped vermilion box with its contents, the red powder, is another instance of such a correspondence of image with the Indus sign we are interpreting, as the 'dot' *inside* the 'fish' pictogram appears to stand for **poṭṭu*, the dot made with the red powder. This word **poṭṭu* has some connotations and homophones in Dravidian languages, apparently going back to Proto-Dravidian, which support the placement of the 'dot' *in the belly or womb* of the 'fish' in the Indus pictogram. To start with the homophones, there is the word **poṭṭV* 'belly, stomach, womb, pregnancy'.

Among the connotations of the word **poṭṭu* in the sense of 'dot, forehead mark' is the meaning 'drop (of water or other liquid)', which it shares with the Sanskrit word *bindu* 'drop', and also 'dot, spot' and (lexically) 'a coloured mark made on the forehead between the eyebrows'; compare with the last-mentioned sense the name *candra-bindu* for the graphic sign of nasalization over letters, consisting of an upward-opening crescent moon (*candra*) and a dot above it. An etymon found only in Middle and New Indo-Aryan has the same semantic range: Prakrit *ṭippī* 'spot on forehead', Sindhi *ṭipo* 'dot placed over letters', Hindi *ṭipkā* 'drop', Oriya *ṭip-ṭip* 'dripping', and so forth; here the primary meaning is clearly the onomatopoeic sound of dripping or dropping (cf. *tippua* 'to drip', *tippa* 'drop' in the unrelated Finnish language); this is shown by the existence of related words with vowel variation, for example (with *-a-*) Bengali *ṭap* 'sound of dropping', Awadhi *ṭapa-ṭapa* 'patter of drops', Oriya *sindūra-ṭapā* 'dot made with vermilion on the forehead of married women', and (with *-o-*) Oriya *ṭopā* 'raindrop', *ṭopī* 'small spot on forehead'. This parallel suggests that the ultimate etymology of the word **poṭṭu* 'drop, dot' might well be the Proto-Dravidian onomatopoeic root **poṭṭu* 'to burst noisily', **poṭu-poṭu* 'onomatopoeic expression signifying the falling of fruits or stones one after another'.

We have seen that the 'dot on the forehead' is associated with the sexual maturity of women. The North Dravidian-speaking Oraons believe that the forehead mark is the seat of a demon who can interfere with the fertility of women; this demon is exorcized so as to be transferred from a barren woman to her forehead mark, which is thereafter carefully disposed of. The conception of fertility is very much associated with the concept of 'drop': water fructifies, so a drop of water symbolizes seed. In Bengal, the ceremonial bathing of the god Dharma (identified with the sun) is the most important festival in his annual worship. Barren women throng to get the 'first drop' of water on their heads when the basket in which the god's image has been immersed is raised from the water: it is firmly believed that she who gets it will conceive.

In the Ṛgveda, the Sanskrit word for 'drop', *drapsa*, refers to 'seed'. In ṚS 7,33,11–13, the sage Vasiṣṭha is said to have been born from the drop of seed (*drapsa*) that 'jumped' (*skand-*) from the gods Mitra and Varuṇa when they saw the heavenly nymph (*apsaras*) Urvaśī. We have met Vasiṣṭha as the most famous of the Seven Sages who shine as the stars of the Ursa Major; he is the husband of Arundhatī, the paragon of marital faithfulness. This astral myth of the Veda has an interesting parallel in a later myth, in which the Apsaras has the form of a fish. The Mahābhārata (1,57) tells how seed 'jumped' (*skand-*) from the Cedi king Vasu during a hunting expedition. The king sent his spilt seed on a leaf carried by a bird to his wife, but it dropped into the Yamunā river. There it was eaten by a heavenly nymph (*apsaras*) who had been cursed into the form of a fish (*mīna*). She conceived, and the fisherman who caught her found twins in her womb. The boy was adopted by the king and became King Matsya ('fish'). People called Matsya 'fish' were the neighbours of the Cedis. The female fish of heavenly origin, from whom their eponymous king Matsya was born, is likely to stand for the star Rohiṇī, the daughter of the creator-god Prajāpati. Rohiṇī the daughter of Prajāpati is also called *Virāṭ*, meaning both 'widely shining' and 'widely ruling' (TB 1,1,10,6; 1,2,1,27); another name of King Matsya is *Virāṭa*. In this legend a 'drop' of seed got into the belly of a 'fish', again reminding us of the 'dot' *inside* the 'fish' in the Indus pictogram  supposed to represent the star Rohiṇī.

The myth of the creator-god Prajāpati's incest with his virginal daughter Rohiṇī has many variants. In the Vedic texts, Prajāpati's fiery seed spilt on this incestuous occasion becomes the fierce god Rudra, who kills his own father with arrows to punish him. In the epic versions of this same myth, either the fire-god Agni or Śiva sees the stars of the Pleiades as beautiful nymphs (*apsaras*) bathing in the heavenly river. Then the god spills his seed, which falls into the Ganges and becomes the war-god Skanda, nursed by the Pleiades. The shift from Rohiṇī to the Pleiades as the 'mother(s)' of Rudra-Skanda can be understood in terms of the astronomical shift that took place in the third millennium BC: instead of Rohiṇī, the Pleiades became the asterism of the new year in which the sun rose at the vernal equinox (§ 11.3). We have discussed Rudra's identity with Rohita, the 'red' rising sun, whose rays may be conceived as arrows killing the demon of the night. Rudra's variant name *Skanda* connects him with the 'jumping' (*skand-*) seed-drop.

Before we continue with this theme, the repeated motif of men becoming excited by the sight of bathing women calls for comment. Women are supposed to stand up and take their bath early in the morning, before the sunrise, and before the men rise and bathe. Immediately after the bath they put the red dot on their forehead. As the faithful wife of Rohita, the Rohiṇī star (or the goddess of dawn, with whom she is equated in AB 3,33) also rises before her husband, the red sun, and bathes in the ecliptic, i.e. the heavenly Ganges. However, the rising sun is not only the husband but also the son of Rohiṇī, the 'golden embryo', to whom she gives birth at sunrise, the 'dot' in the 'womb' of the 'fish' swimming in the heavenly river.

The Ṛgvedic verse 10,17,11 starting with the catchwords, 'The drop jumped (*drapsaś caskanda*)', is recited in a cosmogonic episode while the Vedic fire-altar is being constructed. A circular gold plate equated with the sun is placed upon a lotus leaf, which is identified with the waters, the earth and the womb. A golden man (*puruṣa*) is then laid on the golden plate with the mantra, 'The golden embryo (*hiraṇya-garbha*) came first into existence' (ṚS 10,121,1). Then comes the verse 'The drop jumped', which ŚB 7,4,1,20 comments on by stating that 'the drop is yonder sun'. This agrees with the conception of Rohita, the 'red' rising sun, as an embryo (AS 13,1,4 and § 13.5). In section 13.5 we discussed Skanda, another hypostasis of the rising sun, as one of the foremost godlings associated with embryos and childbirth. These conceptions seem thus to have been implied when the Indus scribes have placed the 'drop' or 'dot' (i.e. the forehead mark representing the sun) in the womb of the 'fish' sign.

The Ṛgvedic verse 10,17,11, starting with 'The drop jumped', is also recited in the Vedic Soma sacrifice. Here the verse accompanies the libations that the priests pour in expiation for drops of Soma spilled during the morning service. Interestingly, the chanter-priests use for this same purpose another mantra, which pays homage to the goddess Vāc with the words, 'You are Bekurā by name' (JB 1,82). This seems to imply a connection between the 'drop that jumped' and Bekurā. According to Albrecht Weber (1862: 274f.), *bekurā* originally meant 'calendrical asterism', a word that was already obsolete in Vedic times. It has been argued (in § 11.3) that it may be a borrowing from Dravidian, corresponding to Old Tamil *vaikuṟu-mīṉ* 'morning star'. That Bekurā should be identified with Rohiṇī as the asterism *par excellence* is suggested by Bekurā being here the name of the Vedic goddess Vāc: the names and epithets used of Vāc, 'invincible' (*aṣāḍhā*) and 'conquering' (*sahamānā*) (VS 13,26 and ŚB 7,4,2,32–9) and 'a lioness overcoming the enemies' (VS 5,10; 5,12; TS 6,2,7,2–8,1) suggest that she is an early form of Durgā.

So far we have seen that the forehead mark, the carp and the Rohiṇī asterism are all associated with one another and that they are important symbols of fertility. The other, martial aspect of the goddess that has emerged as an important theme in the iconographic study of the 'fig deity' seal we have so far met only in the invocation to Rohiṇī in AS 13,1,22: 'through her may we conquer booty of every description, through her win every battle!' There is, however, much more to be said about this dimension. Thus the star Rohiṇī and the Moon are worshipped as a couple on the birthday of Kṛṣṇa, who is identified with the moon and said to have been born under Rohiṇī. This day is particularly auspicious if it happens to fall on Rohiṇī, when it is called *jayantī* 'victorious' (Padma-Purāṇa, Uttara-khaṇḍa 32, 41–8; Agni-Purāṇa 183,14). This parallel, too, suggests that the original star of Durgā's 'tenth day of victory' was Rohiṇī.

The Vedic text TS 2,1,3,1 states that offering a sacrificial victim with a spot on the forehead to the angry god of war guarantees victory. A red cow, whose name connects it with the star Rohiṇī, similarly destroys an enemy:

> The blood (*lohitam*) which fell Rudra seized (*grah-*); it became a fierce (*raudrī*) red (*rohiṇī*) cow... He who practises witchcraft should offer a red (cow) to Rudra; verily he has recourse to Rudra with his own share; verily he cuts him down to him; swiftly he reaches destruction; it is red, for it has Rudra as its deity. (TS 2,1,7,2 and 7, trans. Keith 1914: I, 140f.)

In South India, it is still the routine practice to put a red dot (*poṭṭu*) on the forehead of sacrificial victims (in earlier periods including human victims). The dot marks the victim as the bridegroom of the goddess (§ 12.2). Since the buffalo is one of the principal victims offered to the goddess, one is immediately reminded of the prominent 'third eye' on the forehead of the buffalo-headed, angry portrayal of the god of death in Lamaist art (fig. 14.33). A terracotta statuette of a bull found at Harappa has four 'dots-in-circles' painted on its forehead (Vats 1940: II, pl. 79 no. 73). Bull figurines with a star on the forehead come from the excavations of Mehrgarh (period VII) and Nausharo (period ID) and from the Quetta Valley (fig. 14.41), dating from the transition from the Early to the Mature Harappan phase, *c.*2550 BC; there is a triangle between the horns of the bull in the Kulli pot shown in fig. 1.15. Several roughly contemporaneous star-headed terracotta bulls are known from Shahr-i Sokhta. Many Mesopotamian bull statuettes have inlays of various shapes (triangles, quatrefoils) suggestive of a star on their foreheads.

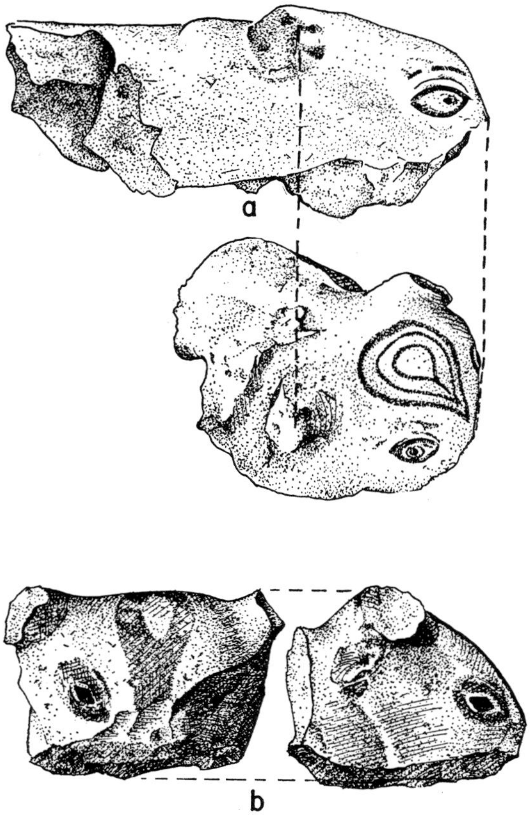

Fig. 14.41. (a, b) A 'third eye' on two bull figurines from the Quetta Valley, Baluchistan: Site Q8, Damb Sadaat III levels (*c.*2600 BC). After Fairservis 1956: 226, fig. 18: a, b.

Several scholars have identified the trefoil-ornamented bulls as images of the constellation Taurus (§ 12.1); Willy Hartner (1965: 4) speaks in this connection of the horned head of this celestial bull, which is 'dominated by the very bright star Aldebaran [=Rohiṇī] as the bull's eye'.

Vedic texts state that the sacrificial horse must have on its forehead a spotted mark (*lalāma*) (TS 7,3,17: KS 5,3,7). What is more, the White Yajurveda expressly links this spotted mark on the forehead with the star of the new year by calling it 'the mark of the Pleiades' (ŚB 13,4,2,4; KŚS 20,1,34). The commentators explain this as meaning 'a mark (*puṇḍram*: later used of the sectarian marks on the forehead) which has the form of the cart (*śakaṭa*) of the Pleiades'. According to the Mahābhārata (3,219,11), too, 'the Pleiades now twinkle as a constellation in the form of a cart (*śakaṭa*)'. Astronomical Sanskrit texts, however, mention only razor (*kṣurā*), razor's edge (*kṣura-dhārā*), or fan (*vyajana*) as the form of the Pleiades, whose Sanskrit name *Kṛttikāḥ* can be associated with the root *kṛt-* 'to cut', while cart (*śakaṭa*) is mentioned only as the form of Rohiṇī. In Tamil, too, Rohiṇī has many names meaning 'cart', some borrowed from Indo-Aryan, some native Dravidian. The latter include *uruḷ* and *uruḷi*, which literally mean 'anything circular, circle, ball, wheel'. Sanskrit *śakaṭa* 'cart' might therefore well be short for *śakaṭacakrākṣa* 'an eye like the wheel of a cart', an expression occurring in Vāmana-Purāṇa 9,18. It agrees perfectly with the description of the forehead mark of the sacrificial horse, for the Śatapatha-Brāhmaṇa equates it with the pupil of the eye. We have seen that the circular dot on the forehead is in many ways associated with the Rohiṇī star, and this suggests that the cart too was originally the symbol of Rohiṇī, as it is in the astronomical texts. When the White Yajurveda associates it with the Pleiades, this seems to result from the calendrical shift that took place in the third millennium, making the Pleiades the asterism of the new year instead of Rohiṇī (§ 11.3).

According to the Kālikā-Purāṇa (60,15–24), one should, after worshipping the goddess Durgā, make a tilaka on one's forehead, either with powder used for drawing her magic diagram, or with blood from the sword used for beheading the victim sacrificed to her. While putting the mark on the forehead, one should pronounce the 'all-subduing formula', which runs as follows: 'Whomever I touch with my foot, whomever I see with my eye, he must come into my power, even if he be equal to Indra; *Oṁ aiṁ hrīṁ śrīṁ*, 'O lady greatly excited by sexual passion, hail!' The text states that then the whole world will be in one's power. Nṛsiṁha Bhaṭṭa's Vidhānamālā (79,1ff.), too, assures victory over the enemy for one who has put a 'tilaka of battle' (*raṇa-tilaka*) on his forehead. According to the twelfth-century Tamil poet Oṭṭakkuttār (Takkayāka-p-paraṇi, verse 100), followers of the Goddess take blood from the intestines of fallen heroes on the battlefield to put on their own foreheads.

A red forehead mark is specific to men of the warrior class. According to Padma-Purāṇa (25, 26) and other texts, the priestly class of Brahmans should have a white tilaka mark, the warrior class of Kṣatriyas red, the merchant and artisan class of Vaiśyas yellowish, and the servile class of Śūdras black. White contributes to salvation, red is for controlling others, yellowish for wealth and black for peace (Padma-Purāṇa, Uttara-khaṇḍa 253,40). Thus the red tilaka, by means of which one is able to subdue kings, proud women and dangerous beasts (cf. also Lakṣmaṇa's Śāradā-tilaka 11,65–70) is the prerogative of warriors. Tilakas of the four social classes differ in their shape as well. Mitramiśra (in his seventeenth-century commentary on Yājñavalkya-Smṛti 1,22) quotes a text called Vāmana-Paddhati to the effect that the Kṣatriyas wear on their forehead a fish-shaped (*mīnākāraṁ*) tilaka. Fish as a mark of the warrior may seem odd, but in fact 'the fish is a symbol of violence in Hindu culture: *matsyanyāya*, the law of the fish, is a common term for anarchy (the larger fish devouring the smaller)' (Shulman 1980: 399).

Mīnākṣī 'fish-eyed', the guardian goddess of the South Indian city of Madurai, was according to the local legend a princess trained in martial arts who conquered the whole world. Her connection with the asterism Rohiṇī (approached by her own father in AB 3,33) is also suggested by what Megasthenes (*c*.300 BC) says about her:

As Herakles could find no other husband worthy of his daughter Pandaiē, he himself had, shortly before his death, incestuous intercourse with her, thus originating a race of kings (i.e. the Pāṇḍya kings of Madurai). Pandaiē was then only seven years old, but that is the age when women become marriageable in that part of India. (Arrian, Indike 8–9)

Mīnākṣī's Tamil name *Aṅ-kayaṟ-kaṇṇ-ammaiyār* means 'the goddess with beautiful eyes that are like the carp (i.e. the red rohita fish)'. Old Tamil literature frequently compares the 'long eyes' of a flirting maiden to the 'red carp' (Cilapp. 4,53 *ceṅ-kaya-ṉeṭuṅ-kaṇ*). The red carp frisking in the water has not only erotic but also martial connotations, being likened to spears (Puṟam 249,6) and arrows (Perumpāṇ. 269f.). This connection of the red carp with eyes of the goddess demands comparison between the iconic similarity of the Indus sign  'dot-in-fish' and the sign  'dot-in-circle' identified as an image of the eye (§ 12.1).

The three magic syllables *aiṁ hrīṁ śrīṁ*, pronounced in the 'all-subduing mantra' while the tilaka is being put on the forehead, constitute the so-called 'eye-seed' (*netra-bīja*) formulae of Durgā, connected with her three eyes; she is said to have emerged from these seeds to kill the Buffalo demon (KP 61,2–11). Durgā is indeed described as having three eyes (fig. 14.42):

The Goddess stood on the lion, flaming violently with her three eyes which were of the colour of blood, constantly piercing Mahiṣa with her trident. (KP 62,60–1)

The early Mesopotamian religion offers an interesting parallel to Durgā's connection with the fish (§ 10.3; note also that *triśūla* 'a trident spear', is a common weapon of Durgā):

It is . . . interesting to note how often a fish is placed close to Ištar in warlike aspect, and holding her tripartite sceptre; there is even a curious scene in which the goddess does not appear in person, but is symbolised by her great tripartite sceptre, beside which a fish is placed, while a short-clad attendant and a divinity leading a female worshipper draw near to pay homage. (Buren 1948: 101)

Let us summarize some of the main arguments of the investigation. The Indus sign  was assumed to stand for a Proto-Dravidian name of the asterism Rohiṇī in the inscription of the 'fig deity' seal: this star appeared most likely

Fig. 14.42. A traditional brass mask representing the goddess Durgā, made in Varanasi around 1967. Hand-repoussé work, height 51 cm, width 45 cm. Private collection of Oppi Untracht. Note the 'dot' beneath the 'sickle of moon' and 'the third eye' on the forehead, and the pair of carp on either side of the face. The peacock is the traditional vehicle of the war-god Skanda as well as of the goddess Sarasvatī, an ancient doublet of Durgā (Parpola, in press d). The mask is worn by a man impersonating the Goddess in a religious drama performed during the autumnal navarātri festival.

to stand for the ancient Indian goddess of victory and fertility, who was assumed to be represented in the iconography of this seal. Consisting of a 'dot' or 'drop' (*poṭṭu*) in the 'stomach' (*poṭṭu*) of a 'fish' (*mīn*), the sign yields the Dravidian compound *poṭṭu-mīn*, which has been recorded as occurring with the meaning of '*rohita* fish', i.e., the carp, whose red scales are sometimes used for making the forehead mark in marriage ceremonies, while the red powder normally employed for this purpose is kept in fish-shaped containers. *Rohita* is the masculine form of the same word for 'red' that occurs in the feminine in the name *Rohiṇī*, so the *rohita* fish is assumed to have originally symbolized the red star Rohiṇī rather than the *śakula* fish mentioned as such a symbol in one astronomical text. The star Rohiṇī is spoken of as a goddess of victory in the Artharvaveda, and the 'red dot put on the forehead' (*poṭṭu*) has a central role in the cult of the goddess of victory. The goddess has eyes shaped like the red carp, which is also implied by the shape of the Indus sign. The red forehead mark of a warrior, too, should have the form of a fish (*mīna*). The warrior killed in battle demands comparison with the warrior-shaped Buffalo demon slaughtered by the Goddess, and the sacrificial animals wearing the *poṭṭu* mark on their forehead. While the star on the forehead of the Mesopotamian bull figurines may be the star Aldebaran (=Rohiṇī) as the eye of the constellation Taurus, Vedic and epic texts connect the forehead mark directly with the Pleiades and the eye, and indirectly with the Rohiṇī asterism. The dot on the forehead of the bride and of married Hindu women symbolizes the red rising sun, Rohita, as the husband of the Rohiṇī star, the exemplar of marriageable maidens (*rohiṇī*) and the faithful wife *par excellence*. The sun, however, is also the embryo carried in its womb by this fertile heavenly maiden. In folktales, she may assume the form of a fish (*mīna*) and become pregnant from a 'drop' (*drapsa* = Dravidian *poṭṭu*) of seed. Thus the interpretation of the Indus sign of a 'dot or drop inside a fish' agrees in every respect with the suggested iconographic interpretation of the 'fig deity' as a 'Proto-Durgā', the goddess of victory and fertility, and with the symbolism of the forehead mark, the *rohita* fish, and the Rohiṇī star.

What has been presented above has by no means exhausted the meanings of these rich symbols. Enough has been said, however, to make the point that they are all inextricably intertwined and touch some of the most central aspects of ancient Indian religion. Thus the Indus sign turns out to be not simply a phonetically used grapheme, but a highly condensed religious symbol, which suggests, for example, that the still surviving ancient Hindu habit of making a red mark on the forehead probably goes back to the third millennium BC.

15 Epilogue

It is by no means impossible that one day the archaeologists may find a bilingual with an Indus text and its translation into a known language and script. Such a happy find is most likely to be made in the Near East, and would probably take the form of a cuneiform tablet with a trade contract, mentioning the name of a Harappan merchant who had stamped the document with his Indus seal. A similar contract bearing the impression of a Dilmun seal (§ 1.4) has already been found (fig. 15.1).

Until some such find is made, we must try to manage without it. Historically known proper names of people and places in inscriptions are not necessarily the only possible clues in the absence of bilinguals (chapter 3). In the case of the Indus script, the cultural and religious context supplies a lot of clues.

The problem of the Indus script is in many respects like a crossword puzzle. As long as there is no bilingual, we cannot be absolutely sure whether the script or a sign belonging to it has been deciphered correctly, just as the solution to a puzzle or an individual clue will remain a matter of probability until it can be verified by the official published version. In both cases, however, the probability of correctness increases with the number of interlocking solutions, provided that they comply with the rules of the game and other conditions. In the puzzle, for instance, only genuine words and names may be used, and the words must be written horizontally and vertically without leaving any gaps. In the Indus script, the interpretations have to be in agreement with the theories of writing and decipherment. In the puzzle, the word guesses must fit the available space and the clues to their meaning. In the Indus script, the interpretations must be in line with the historical context, including the vocabulary of the languages involved, and with the clues offered by the inscribed objects.

In both cases, some guesses will fit the available evidence better than others. An incorrect solution blocks progress, while a correct one allows further solutions. Only very experienced puzzle-solvers will arrive at the correct solutions

Fig. 15.1. (a–e) A cuneiform tablet (Yale Babylonian Collection 5447) dated in its inscription to the tenth year of Gungunum, king of Larsa, i.e. 1923 BC (according to the most commonly accepted 'middle chronology'). The tablet has an impression of a Dilmun seal and mentions Amorite proper names (§ 8.2). See Buchanan 1967.

right away. Usually some guesses have to be revised in the light of other guesses: the solutions are tested against each other, because the words in the rows and columns cross each other within a matrix and therefore have to fit together. Similarly, in the decipherment of the Indus script, we must continually check the hypotheses against all relevant material until the results are fully satisfactory. Among the best indirect proofs we can get are interlocking solutions, especially of ligatures and compounded signs.

Although bilinguals in the narrow meaning of the word are missing, we have something approaching these external tests in a few 'pictorial bilinguals' (like the Linear B tablet in fig. 3.4), such as the 'fig deity' seal (§§ 14.3–4), the copper tablets (fig. 7.14 and §§ 13.3–5), and some other objects like the stoneware bangles (§ 13.1) or tablets depicting offerings with vessels (figs. 7.12 and 13.2b). Clues can be sought in the Indus signs themselves, too. It seems that the creators of the script were at pains to invent symbols whose pictorial and phonetic messages would be in harmony with each other. Witness, for example, the 'roofed fish' (pictorial message) as the rebus for the 'black star' (phonetic message), which can both be understood to represent the slow and dark planet Saturn, conceived in later times as a deity riding a turtle (= an aquatic animal with a cover, i.e. a kind of 'fish' with a 'roof'), or the unbelievably rich symbolism that can be seen in the 'dot-in-fish' sign dealt with in § 14.4. Such semantic webs of interconnected symbols and meanings constitute one of the few tests that can be used in the decipherment of the Indus script: the likelihood that an interpretation is correct increases with the complexity of its match with the tradition.

A number of systematic, interlocking interpretations of individual Harappan signs have been presented; they are summarized in fig. 15.2. They suggest that the Indus script is essentially similar to the other pictographic scripts that were created before the middle of the third millennium BC, that the language of the Indus people belonged to the Dravidian family, and that they professed a religion that was genetically related to the religions of both ancient Western Asia and later

No.	Sign or sequence	Pictorial meaning	Shared phonetic shape in Dravidian	Intended meaning	Literary attestation of the compound in Dravidian, associated ideas, and other notes
1		fish	*mīn*	(1) fish (2) star	Fish is the emblem and symbol of the god of water and fertility in India and in Mesopotamia. The heavenly bodies (conceived of as fish swimming in the ocean of heaven) represent gods.
2		fish + fish	*mīn* + *mīn* *min* + *min*		Intensifying repetition (cf. no. 10) exists for the Drav. root *min* 'to shine'. Contexts suggest a deity is meant, but the exact intention remains unclear. Cf. the 'greatly shining fish' born along with astral sages (Bṛhaddevatā), and the auspicious 'fish pair'.
3		3 + fish	*mu(m)* + *mīn*	three stars	The asterism of Mṛgaśiras has this name in Tamil.
4		6 + fish	*(*c)aṟu* + *mīn*	six stars	The new year asterism Pleiades has this name in Tamil. In myth the wives of the Seven Sages and mothers or wet nurses of the god of war (: the vernal sun).
5		7 + fish	*eḻu* + *mīn*	seven stars	In Tamil, this is the name of Ursa Major = the 'Seven Sages' in India (cf. 7 fish-shaped sages in Sumer).
6		roof + fish	*mey/may* + *mīn*	black star	Saturn's name in Tamil. Saturn rides a turtle (= a 'fish' with a 'roof') and represents 'black' Death.
7		halving + fish	*pacu* + *mīn*	green star	Cf. Tamil *paccai* 'greenness, the planet Mercury'. Mercury (which rises only a little over the horizon) represents the green-hued child god Kṛṣṇa.
8		dot/drop + fish	*poṭṭu* + *mīn*	(1) carp fish (= Skt *rohita* 'red') (2) star or red dot or blood drop (= Skt *rohiṇī* 'red')	The red dot painted on the forehead at marriage = the 'third' eye of the Heavenly Bull = alpha Tauri = the ancient star of the new year (marriage of Sun + the heavenly bride: *rohiṇī* 'menstruating'), represented by the red fish (scales as tilaka mark).
9		dot-in-circle = eye	*kaṇ*		Cf. nos. 8 ('dot' = 'eye') and 10 (repetition). The intended meaning remains to be determined.
10		eye + eye	*kaṇ* + *kāṇ(i)*	overseer	In an Indus amulet with a ship and alligator: Veda associates these with Varuṇa, the 'overseer'. Cf. no. 2. Other contexts (pot-stamps) suggest a profane title.

Fig. 15.2. Interpretations of (partially interconnected) Indus signs and sign sequences.

No.	Sign or sequence	Pictorial meaning	Shared phonetic shape in Dravidian	Intended meaning	Literary attestation of the compound in Dravidian, associated ideas, and other notes
11		ring(s)/bangle(s)	*muruku*	boy, youth, Muruku (the youthful god of love and war)	The sign signifies 'royal ear-rings' in Lamaism. The sign recurs, sometimes alone, on Indus stone bangles; Indus tree-gods wear bangles; in later folk religion, bangles are offered to sacred trees with prayers for offspring (cf. *muruku* 'boy').
12		hearth of three stones + ring(s)/bangles(s)	*cūl + muruku*	pregnancy bangle(s)	Cf. Tamil *cūl-kāppu* 'pregnancy bangle'. Perhaps a possessive compound: name of a deity?
13		ring(s)/bangle(s) + palm squirrel	*muruku pil̤l̤ay*	Muruku-p-pil̤l̤ay	In Tamil onomastics, *pil̤l̤ai* 'young one' is added to names of divinities to form affectionate diminutives.
14		rings(s)/bangle(s) + intermediate space	*muruku + vēl̤(i)*	Muruku-Vēl̤	Both *Muruka-Vēl̤* 'Youth-Desire' and *Vēl̤* 'Desire' are Old Tamil names of the god Muruku (no. 11).
15		intermediate space + fish	*vēl̤(i) + mīn*	white star	*Vel̤-mīn* and *Vel̤l̤i* both mean 'Venus' in Tamil. Cf. no. 17.
16		fig tree + fish	*vaṭa + mīn*	North Star	*Vaṭa-mīn* is the 'star Alcor', orig. prob. Thuban. 'Banyan fig' is the tree of 'ropes' (*vaṭa*): stars do not fall, because they are fixed to the North Star (in Dr. also 'fig / rope star') by means of invisible ropes.
17		fig tree + intermediate space	*vaṭa + vēl̤(i)*	North Star	In Tamil, *vel̤l̤i* means both (1) 'the planet Venus' (cf. no. 15) and (2) 'star (= *mīn*)': cf. no. 15.
18		4 + fig tree	*nāl + vaṭa*	hanging rope	Banyan as '(the tree) possessed of hanging ropes': *ñāl / nāl / āl* 'to hang down' seems to be the etymology for *āl(a-maram)* 'banyan tree'. Indus tablets with '4 + fig' have a solitary fig leaf on the reverse.
19		fig tree + grasping	*kōl̤i (kōl̤)*	'grasping fig / robber'	In copper tablets, the ligature (where the inner sign is a phonetic determinator) replaces the 'Archer'; Vedic Rudra is an archer and a robber, called also *Hara* 'grasper', and he is associated with fig trees.
20		grasping (crab's claws)	*kōl̤*	grasper	In Old Tamil, *kōl̤* 'grasper' means both 'eclipse demon' and 'planet', as does Skt *graha* 'grasper'.

Fig. 15.2. (*cont.*)

No.	Sign or sequence	Pictorial meaning	Shared phonetic shape in Dravidian	Intended meaning	Literary attestation of the compound in Dravidian, associated ideas, and other notes
21		grasping + fish	*kōḷ + mīn*	grasping star	In Old Tamil, 'planet' is called both 'grasping star' and 'grasper'; in two parallel Indus texts,  = 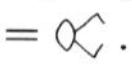.
22		pot		pot (containing offerings)	'Pictorial bilinguals' clarify the intended meaning; there is no rebus to determine the phonetic shape.
23		man	*āḷ / āṇ*	man, servant	The remarks in no. 22 apply here too. The sign occurs in priestly titles paralleling Mesopotamian titles 'Man / Servant (of the god X)'; and the most common Dr. word for 'man' also means 'servant'.
24		(head of) cow	*ā (±-tu)*	possessive suffix	The interpretation of this important sign remains open; this is just a suggestion that needs testing.

Fig. 15.2. (*cont.*)

India. While these results are not unexpected, the interpretations are integrated in a detailed and coherent historical reconstruction, and they have, in addition, suggested reasonable new solutions to a number of old problems. The statistical probability of such a convergence emerging from purely accidental coincidences is very small.

It is symptomatic of the present state of decipherment that, although several scholars have been working on the Indus script with largely similar methodology and basic assumptions (including the Dravidian hypothesis) in recent years, there is, as yet, little consensus on individual interpretations. Notable exceptions are the readings of the 'fish' sign and its combinations with the numeral signs. It was first suggested by Henry Heras that '6' + 'fish' stands for the indigenous Dravidian name of the Pleiades, and, along with other similar cases ('7' + 'fish', '3' + 'fish'), this interpretation is included in the solutions proposed by the Soviet scholars as well as in the present attempt (§ 10.4). These readings are also accepted by Mahadevan. The 'sacrificial vessel' (§§ 7.3 and 10.3) is another interpretation that is accepted by many scholars, including Hrozný.

I think these agreements have to be taken seriously. There is an obvious reason why few people have yet done so. Any really significant interpretations have been obscured by an overwhelming number of other proposals that have been either highly implausible or at least subjective and insufficiently established. This is most clearly demonstrated by the work of Hrozný, which utterly fails to carry conviction and yet appears to contain some grains of truth. The judgement passed by Maurice Pope (1975: 68) on Thomas Young's contribution to the decipherment of the Egyptian script is even more valid here: his 'few positively correct suggestions of detail . . . were accompanied by a much larger mass of incorrect suggestions, and there was no way to tell which was which.' It was this situation that Chadwick (as quoted in the preface) wanted to have remedied in 1969.

Although there are considerable differences between the Indus script and the Maya script, the materials available for their decipherment, and the historical circumstances relating to them (including the linguistic history of their respective areas), there are also remarkable similarities. Both scripts have pictorial signs and are apparently of logo-syllabic nature. In both cases, the survival of languages closely related to those used in the two scripts is an absolute precondition for the decipherment. While extensive 'pictorial bilinguals' exist for the Maya script, such clues are not entirely lacking in the case of the Indus script. To some extent, their meagreness and the almost complete lack of historical information in the case of the Indus script are compensated by the wealth of information that we have on the ancient Indian and Mesopotamian religions: this can profitably be used once a beginning has been made in unravelling the Harappan religion.

The methodology of the present approach is close to that followed in the Maya decipherment. The interlocking of phonetic decipherments of several sign sequences and their simultaneous agreement with external evidence have been the basis for a broad acceptance of Knorozov's pioneering work. Evidence of a similar nature has been offered here. If any more general agreement on the methodological and historical framework as well as on some specific readings can be reached, it will be possible to join forces on a frontal attack, as has happened in Maya studies. I therefore look forward to a fruitful debate on the issues raised in the present book.

There is still much scope for further research in this field. Some grave limitations must be noted, however. Many of the signs of the Indus script are so simplified and schematic that it is very difficult to understand their pictorial meaning unambiguously and objectively. Another drawback is the scantiness of the material. Numerous signs occur only once or twice, and it is difficult to ascertain or check their intended meaning from the contexts with any confidence. For these reasons it looks most unlikely that the Indus script will ever be deciphered fully, unless radically different source material becomes available. That, however, must not deter us from trying.

Appendix

Compounds ending in the word *mīṉ* in *Tamil Lexicon*

The various ligatures and compounds having the 'fish' sign as their basic element constitute one of the principal clues to the Indus script. As long as all of them have not been satisfactorily explained, they are likely to remain among the principal targets of further research. In this search for new solutions, an exhaustive list of all compounds ending in the word *mīṉ* ('fish' as well as 'star') that actually occur in the Dravidian languages would be an ideal tool to suggest various possible lines of enquiry. The following list naturally falls short of such an ideal; similar lists covering other Dravidian languages would contain entries not found here (compare, for example, Pengo *boṭu min* 'a kind of fish' quoted in § 14.4 from *DEDR* 4498, and Malayalam *kōlā-mīn* 'needle-fish' in *DEDR* 2241). The basis of the present list is the unpublished reverse index to the entries in *Tamil Lexicon* compiled by Eric Grinstead et al. (see Preface). The list contains 34 compounds denoting stars and 65 compounds denoting fish, prefixed with the codes S (=star) and F (=fish) for ready reference (codes in parentheses register meanings attested for the first part of the compound, without the addition of the word *mīṉ*); several compounds belong to both groups. The information given in *Tamil Lexicon* (including the Tamil glosses, quotations of source texts [with the compounds split into their components by means of hyphenation], and secondary compounds) is supplemented, if possible, with the literal meaning of the first member(s) of the compound (with references to *DEDR*) and with cross-references (including references to sections of the present book). Some compounds not found as entries in *Tamil Lexicon* have been added, including *kuḷa-mīṉ* and *mu-m-mīṉ*, which are attested in Old Tamil, and others given as Tamil glosses on the entry words. Note that the ordinal numbers of the lunar asterisms are those given in *Tamil Lexicon* and valid today, not those of the early Vedic calendar: the Pleiades, for example, are the third (and not the first) nakṣatra (§ 11.2). The list follows the order of the Tamil alphabet.

F *aṟakkuḷā-mīṉ* = *arkkuḷā* 'seer-fish', bluish above, silvery below, attaining 4 inches in length, *Cybium commersonii*; *kaṭal-mīṉ-vakai* ['kind of sea-fish'].

S *aṟu-mīṉ* [*aṟu-* '6', *DEDR* 2485] 'Pleiades, as containing six stars; *kārttikai*' (Piṅkala-nikaṇṭu). [See § 10.4.]

aṟu-mīṉ-kātalaṉ 'Skanda, being one brought up by the goddesses of the Pleiades; *muruka-k-kaṭavuḷ* ['god Murukaṉ']' (Cēntaṉ Tivākaraṉ). [Cf. § 13.1]

S *āti-mīṉ* [*āti* < Sanskrit *ādi* 'beginning'] 'the first nakṣatra; *acuvini* (< Sanskrit *aśvinī*)': *āti-mīṉ ṟōṇi yiṟu* (Cētu-purāṇam by Nirampavaḻakiya Tēcikar, Kantamā. 17).

S *āṟā-mīṉ* [*āṟu* 'six', *DEDR* 2485; *ā* 'to be(come)', *DEDR* 333] 'Pleiades, as containing six stars; *kārttikai*'.
āṟā-mīṉ-aṟa-v-ōttu 'passage of the sun through the segment of the zodiac occupied by Pleiades, regarded by seamen as a period when rough weather is to be anticipated; *kārttikaiyil cūriyaṉ piravēcikkuṅ kālam* ['the time of the sun's entering the Pleiades']' (Winslow 1862 [hereafter simply Winslow]).

F *āṟṟu-mīṉ* [*āṟu* 'river', *DEDR* 5159] 'fresh-water fish': as Tamil gloss on *noy-m-mīṉ*.

F *āṉai-mīṉ* [*āṉai* 'elephant', *DEDR* 5161][= *yāṉai-mīṉ*, q.v.] 'a huge fish; *peru-mīṉ-vakai* ['a kind of large fish']' (Cūṭāmaṇi-nikaṇṭu). [Cf. *āṉai-y-arkkuḷā* 'a marine fish' (local usage).]

F *iṭi-mīṉ* 'a fish'; *mīṉ-vakai* ['a kind of fish'] (Pondicherry usage). [*TL*, Suppl.]

S *uttara-mīṉ* [*uttara-* < Sanskrit *uttara-* 'northern'] 'the star Arundhatī in Ursa Major, the smaller of the two in Mizar, the central star in the tail; *aruntati naṭcattiram: uttara-mīṉiṉ koṉkaṉ* (Cētu-purāṇam by Nirampavaḻakiya Tēcikar, Tuttama. 6) [the very late Tamil word *uttara-mīṉ* is a synonym of Old Tamil *vaṭa-mīṉ*, with Sanskrit *uttara* 'northern' for Tamil *vaṭa* 'northern'; note that *uttara-* in the meaning 'northern' is not known to the Sanskrit dictionaries of Böhtlingk and Roth; Monier Williams, etc., in star names; cf. § 14.1].

F *etir-mīṉ* [*etir* 'to oppose; that which is opposite or contrary', *DEDR* 795] 'fish that goes against the current; *nīr-p-pāy-c-calai etirttu-c cellum mīṉ*'.

S *eḻu-mīṉ* [*eḻu-* 'seven', *DEDR* 910] 'the seven principal stars of Ursa Major, Charles's Wain; *capta-riṣi-maṇṭalam* ['the sphere of the Seven Sages']': *kai-toḻu marapiṉ eḻu-mīṉ pōla* (Naṟṟiṇai 231). [See § 10.4.]

S *ai-m-mīṉ* [*ai-* 'five' < Proto-Drav. **cay-*, *DEDR* 2826, possibly < < **kay* / **key* 'hand', *DEDR* 2023] (1) 'the thirteenth nakṣatra, so called because of its five principal stars; *attam* [< Sanskrit *hasta-* 'hand']' (Piṅkala-nikaṇṭu) [cf. *kai-m-mīṉ*]; (2) 'the fourth nakṣatra; *urōkiṇi* [< Sanskrit *rohiṇī-*]' (Vīmēcura-v-uḷḷamuṭaiyāṉ, Madras 1917).

F *ōṭṭu-mīṉ* [*ōṭu* 'shell', *DEDR* 1042] 'crustacean; shellfish; *mīṉ-vakai*'.

F *kaṭaṉākku-mīṉ* [*kaṭal* 'sea', *DEDR* 1118; *nākku* 'tongue', *DEDR* 3633] 'flat fish, brownish or purplish black, attaining at least 16 inches in length, *Pleuronecter erumei; erumai nākkumīṉ*'. [Cf. *nākku-mīṉ*.]

F *kaṭiccai-mīṉ* [*kaṭiccai*, ? < *kaṭi* 'speed, sharpness, pungency', *DEDR* 1135] 'a sea-fish, greyish, with black bloches on its sides, attaining 16 inches in length, *Pristipoma maculatum*; *kaṭal-mīṉ-vakai*'. (Winslow.)

F *kaṭu-mīṉ* [*kaṭu* 'severe, cruel, harsh', *DEDR* 1135] 'ferocious fish, as shark; *curā-mutaliyaṉa* ['shark, etc.']': *kaṭu-mīṉ kalippiṉum* (Akanāṉūṟu 50).

S *kaṭai-mīṉ* [*kaṭai* 'end, limit', *DEDR* 1109] 'the twenty-seventh nakṣatra, i.e. the last of the asterisms, the end-star; *irēvati* [< Sanskrit *revatī*]' (Cēntaṉ Tivākaraṉ).

F *kallu-k-kōḻi-mīṉ* [*kallu* 'stone', *DEDR* 1298; *kōḻi* 'cock, fowl', *DEDR* 2248] 'a sea-fish, bluish, *Holocanthus imperator*; *kaṭal-mīṉ-vakai*.' [Cf. *kōḻi-mīṉ*.]

F *kaḻi-mīṉ* [*kaḻi* 'backwater, shallow sea-waters, salt river', *DEDR* 1359] 'salt-water fish': as Tamil gloss on *koḻu-mīṉ*.

F *kaṉ-mīṉ* [*kal* 'stone', *DEDR* 1298] 'bride-fish, purplish-yellow, attaining 16 inches in length, *Lutjanus marginatus*; *oru-vakai-k kaṭal-mīṉ* ['one kind of sea-fish']'.

F *kākkāy-mīṉ* [*kākkāy* 'crow', *DEDR* 1425] 'a kind of fish; *mīṉ-vakai*'.

F *kiḷi-mīṉ* [*kiḷi* 'parrot', *DEDR* 1548] 'a sea-fish, green, *Pseudoscarus chrysopoma*; *kaṭal-mīṉ-vakai*'.

F *kīrai-mīṉ* [*kīrai* 'greens, pot-herbs, vegetables', *DEDR* 1617] 'a small kind of fish; *oru-vakai ciṟiya mīṉ*'.

F *kuttuvā-mīṉ* [*kuttuvā* 'herring'] 'a herring, golden, glossed with purple, *Pellona brachysoma*; *kaṭal-mīṉ-vakai*'.

F *kutirai-mīṉ* [*kutirai* 'horse', *DEDR* 1711a] 'a kind of fish; *mīṉ-vakai*': *kutirai-mīṉōṭ āṉai-mīṉ* (Kurukūrppaḷḷu by Caṭakōpa-p Pulavar, p. 7). (*TL*, Suppl.)

S *kula-mīṉ* [*kulam* < Sanskrit *kula-* '(noble) family'] 'Arundhatī; *aruntati*': *kula-mīṉ arukiya kaṟpum* (Kallāṭam 73,1). [Cf. Sanskrit *kula-nakṣatra* 'an asterism distinguished above others', including Rohiṇī, Puṣya, Maghā, Uttaraphalgunī, Citrā, Viśākhā, Jyeṣṭhā, Pūrvāṣāḍhā, Śravaṇā, Uttarabhādrapada and Bharaṇī: thus Radhakanta's Śabdakalpadruma, quoting a verse from Tantrasāra: *vāruṇārdrābhijinmūlaṁ kulākulam udāhṛtam / kulāni samadhiṣṭhyāni śeṣāṇi cākulāni ca //*; cf. Böhtlingk and Roth 1858: II, 353.]

F *kuḻi-mīṉ* [*kuḻi* 'hole, hollow', *DEDR* 1818] 'conger eel, olive, attaining more than 10 feet in length, *Muraenesox talabon*; *pāmpu-vaṭi-v-āṉa mīṉ-vakai*'.

S *kuḷa-mīṉ* [*kuḷam* 'tank, pond, lake', *DEDR* 1828] 'a certain star' [probably the twentieth (Sanskrit *pūrvāṣāḍhā*) or the twenty-first nakṣatra (Sanskrit *uttarāṣāḍhā*) called in Tamil *muṟ-kuḷam* 'first tank' or *uṭai-kuḷam* 'breached tank' and *kaṭai-k-kuḷam* 'last tank' respectively; note that the Digambara Jaina explanation of the shape of the latter asterism as being like that of a breached tank (*bhagna-vāpī*, *khāta-vāpī*) agrees with the Tamil name *uṭai-kulam* of the former, while according to the Śvetāmbara Jainas, the twenty-second nakṣatra *śravaṇa* has the shape of a tank (*kāsāra*); cf. Kirfel 1920; N. Subrahmanian (1966a: 302) identifies *kuḷa-mīṉ* with the *kārttikai* star, the third nakṣatra, Hart (1975: 73–4) with the seventh nakṣatra, Sanskrit *punarvasu*]: *kuḷa-mīṉoṭun tāṭ pukaiyiṉum* (Puṟanāṉūṟu 395,35) [quoted in *TL* III: 1855a *s.v. tāḷ*[1] (11) 'comet'].

F *kuṟu-mīṉ* [*kuṟu* 'short, small', *DEDR* 1851] 'a kind of fish; *mīṉ-vakai*'. (Winslow.)

S *kai-m-mīṉ* [*kai* 'hand', *DEDR* 2023] 'the thirteenth nakṣatra; *attam* [< Sanskrit *hasta-* 'hand']' (Cēntaṉ Tivākaraṉ). [Cf. *ai-m-mīṉ*.]

F(S) *kokku-mīṉ* [*kokku* 'crane, stork', *DEDR* 2125; 'the nineteenth lunar asterism, *mūlam*': *kokku-c-cōti* (Vitāṉamālai by Nārāyaṇacuvāmikaḷ, Kuṇākuṇa. 12.)] 'a long-nosed marine fish, yellowish green, *Belone strongylura*; *ūci-k-kaḻutti* ['needle-necked']' (Maclean 1893: 203a).

F *koy-mīṉ* [= *koy* 'a fresh-water fish, rifle-green, attaining 8.5 inches in length, *Anabas scandens*; *eṭṭarai aṅkulam nīḷam uḷḷatum naṉ-ṉīril vāḻvatum paciya niṟattatum āṉa mīṉ-vakai*': *cempuṉal koyyaṉaittuṅ koṉarum* (Tēvāram 196,3)] 'a kind of fish; *mīṉ-vakai*': *koy-mīṉ ceppali* (Kurucūrppaḷḷu by Caṭakōpa-p Pulavar, p. 20). (*TL*, Suppl.) [Cf. Turner 1966 no. 2959 (and Watt 1890: III, 370): Sanskrit *kavayī-*, *kavikā-* f. 'the fish *Cojus cobojus*' lex., Assamese *kāwai* (Watt: *koi*) 'the fish Anabus', Bengali *kaï*, *kai*, *kayī*, *koi* 'the climbing fish', Oriya *kaï*, *kaü* (Watt: *koi*) 'the fish *Anabus scandens*' (Watt: Singhalese *kavaya*).]

F *koḻu-mīn* [cf. Malayalam *koḻu-mīn* 'porpoise' (Gundert 1871: I, 312b); *koḻu* 'fat', *DEDR* 2146] 'a salt-water fish; *kaḷi-mīṉ-vakai*': *iruṅ-kaḻivāyk koḻu-mīṉ uṇṭa vaṉṉaṅkaḷē* (Tirukkōvaiyār by Māṇikkavācakar, 188).

F *kōṭṭu-mīṉ* [*kōṭu* 'horn, tusk', *DEDR* 2200] 'shark; *cuṟā*': *kōṭṭu-mīṉ eṟinta v-uvakaiyār* (Naṟṟiṇai 49). [Cf. *makara-mīṉ*, and see § 10.3.]

S *kōṉ-mīṉ* [*kōḷ* 'seizure', *DEDR* 2151]: 'planet, distinguished from *nāṉ-mīṉ*; *kirakam* [< Sanskrit *graha* 'seizure; planet']': *vāṉ iṟa vicumpiṟ kōṉ-mīṉ* (Ciṟupāṇāṟṟuppaṭai 242). [See § 13.3.]

F *kōḻi-mīṉ* [*kōḻi* 'cock, fowl', *DEDR* 2248] 'sturgeon, blackish-brown, attaining 18 inches in length, *Achanthurus gahm*; *patiṉeṭṭ' aṅkula nīḷamum karu-niṟamum uḷḷa kaṭal-mīṉ- vakai*'. [Cf. *kallu-k-kōḻi-mīṉ*; *mañcaṭ-kōḻi-mīṉ*.]

F *cippi-mīṉ* [*cippi* 'shell', *DEDR* 2535] 'oyster, cockle, shellfish' (as the Tamil gloss on *maṭṭi*: see *maṭṭi-mīṉ*).

F *ciṟaki-mīṉ* [*ciṟaki* 'common teal; *kiḷuvai*'; *ciṟaku* 'wing', *DEDR* 2591] 'a flying fish, *Exocoetus*; *paṟavai-mīṉ* ['bird-fish']'. (Winslow.)

SF *ciṟu-mīṉ* [*ciṟu* 'small', *DEDR* 1594] (1) 'the star Arundhatī; *aruntati*': *ciṟumīṉ puraiyuṅ kaṟpiṉ aṟunutal* (Perumpāṇāṟṟuppaṭai 303); (2) 'loach, sandy colour, *Cobitio thermalis*; *ayirai* (Piṅkala-nikaṇṭu), *noy-m-mīṉ*'. Cf. also the Tamil gloss on *pittaḷai-k-kācu-mīṉ*.

F *curumpu-mīṉ* [*curumpu* 'bee', *DEDR* 2689] 'sea-fish, lead colour, attaining 10 inches in length, *Lactarius delicatulus*; *cāmpaṉiṟamum 10-aṅkula nīḷamum uṭaiya kaṭal-mīṉ-vakai*'.

SF *cem-mīṉ* [*ce*(*m*)- 'red', *DEDR* 1931] (1) 'the star Arundhatī; *aruntati*': *cemmīṉ aṉaiyaṉiṉ ṟoṉṉakar-c celvi* (Patiṟṟuppattu 31,28); (2) 'Mars; *cevvāy*': *cemmīṉ imaikkum āka vicumpiṉ* (Puṟanāṉūṟu 60,2); (3) 'the sixth nakṣatra; *tiruvātirai* [< Sanskrit *ārdrā*]' (Puṟanāṉūṟu 60,2, urai); (4) 'sperm whale, *Euphysetes macrocephalus*; *peruntalai-t timiṅkilam*' (Maclean 1893: 345). [Cf. *rōkita-mīṉ*: Hart 1975: 76; and see §§ 14.1 and 14.4.]

cem-mīṉ-vayiram 'ambergis, as found in the intestines of the sperm whale; [*cemmīṉ vayiṟṟiṟ kāṇappaṭuvatu*] *mīṉampar eṉṟum maruntu-p paṇṭam*'. (Winslow.)

F *taḷappaṟṟu-mīṉ* [*taḷappaṟṟu* (< Sanskrit *tāla-pattra*) 'palm leaf'] 'a kind of sea-fish; *kaṭal-mīṉ-vakai*' (Yāḻppāṇattu Māṉippāyakarāti by Cantiracēkarap Pulavar).

F *tūḷ-mīṉ* [*tūḷ* 'dust, powder, particle; anything small collectively, as fish, stones, roots, etc., *DEDR* 3283] 'small fish; *poṭi-mīṉ*' (Jaffna usage).

F *tūṟu-mīṉ* 'a kind of fish; *mīṉ-vakai*' (Periyamāṭṭuvākaṭam 101). (*TL*, Suppl.)

F *nakara-mīṉ* [*nakara* < Sanskrit *nakhara* 'nail, talon, claw'] 'ring worn on the little toe by Parava women, one of *ai-varṇam*, q.v.; *parava-makaḷiratu ai-varṇa-v-aṇiyuḷ kāliṉ kaṇṭu-viraliṟ pūṇum aṇi-vakai*' (Parava usage). Cf. *mīṉ-pīli* 'fish-shaped ring worn on the little toe; *kāṟ ciṟu-viralil aṇiyum mīṉ-uru-v-āṉa mōtiram*'. (Winslow.)

F *naṉ-ṉīr-mīṉ* [*nal* 'good', *DEDR* 3610; *nīr* 'water', *DEDR* 3690a] 'fresh-water fish': as Tamil gloss on *paṉai-mīṉ*.

F *nākku-mīṉ* [*nākku* 'tongue', *DEDR* 3633] [= Malayalam *nākku-mīn*, Telugu *nāluka cēpa*] (1) 'Indian sole, *Pleuronectidae solea*; *kaṭalmīṉ vakai*'; (2) 'flat fish, brownish and purplish black, attaining 16 inches in length, *Psettodes erumier*; *patiṉāṟu aṅkulam vaḷarvatum karu-niṟam uḷḷatum āṉa vārai y-eṉṉum mīṉ-vakai*'.

S *nāṉ-mīṉ* [*nāḷ* 'day, early dawn', *DEDR* 3656] 'the lunar asterism; *acuvati* [< Sanskrit *aśvinī*] *mutaliya naṭcattirap-potu*: *nāṉ-mīṉ vāy cūḻnta mati pōl* (Kalittokai 104,27).

F *nāy-mīṉ* [*nāy* 'dog', *DEDR* 3650] 'parrot wrasse, olivaceous, *Pseudoscarus aeruginosus*; *kaṭal-mīṉ-vakai*'.

SF *ney-m-mīṉ* [*ney* 'oil, ghee, fat', *DEDR* 3746] (1) = *ney-vāṉ-mīṉ* (Piṅkala-nikaṇṭu); (2) 'white prawn; *vel-l-iṟal*', (Winslow.)

S *ney-vāṉ-mīṉ* [*ney* 'oil, fat', *DEDR* 3746; *vāṉ* 'sky', *DEDR* 5381] 'the fourteenth nakṣatra; *cittirai-nāḷ* [< Sanskrit *citrā*]' (Cēntaṉ Tivākaraṉ).

F *noy-m-mīṉ* [*noy* 'grits, smallness, minuteness', *DEDR* 3779] 'fresh-water fish, sandy in colour, *Lepido cephalichthys thermalis*; *maṇal-niṟam uḷḷa āṟṟu-mīṉ-vakai*' (Piṅkala-nikaṇṭu). Cf. *ciṟu-mīṉ* (2).

F *pacu-v-ā-mīṉ* [*pacu* 'green, greenish, yellow, yellow, golden', *DEDR* 3821; *ā* 'to be(come)', *DEDR* 333] 'a sea-fish, rose-coloured, *Priacanthus holocentrum*; *rōjā-niṟam uḷḷa kaṭal-mīṉ-vakai*'. [Cf. § 10.5.]

F *para-veṭṭi-mīṉ* 'mud-skipper, brownish, attaining 9 inches in length, *Periophthalmus schlosseri*; *ney-veṭṭi*'.

F *paṟavai-mīṉ* [*paṟavai* 'bird', *DEDR* 4020] 'a flying fish, *Exocoetus*' (as Tamil gloss on *ciṟaki-mīṉ*).

F *paṉṟi-mīṉ* [*paṉṟi* 'pig, hog', *DEDR* 4039] [cf. Kannaḍa *pandi-mīn* 'a sort of fish' (Kittel 1970: III, 994b, quoting Rājaśekharaviḷāsa 5, 115)] (1) 'cock-up, greyish, attaining 2 feet in length, *Cromileptes altivelis*; *paṉṟi-c-cēttaṉ*'; (2) 'cock-up, grey, attaining 5 feet in length, *Lates calcarifer*; *paṉṟi-c-cēttaṉ*'; (3) 'sea-fish, yellowish, attaining a large size, *Serranus lanceolatus*; *mañcaḷ-niṟam āṉatum neṭitāy vaḷ-aruvatum āṉa kaṭal-mīṉ-vakai*'; (4) 'sea-fish, brownish, attaining 7 feet in length and weighing 300 pounds, *Serranus pantherinus*; *paḷuppu-niṟam uḷḷatum ēḻ aṭi vaḷarvatum āṉa kaṭal-mīṉ-vakai*'.

F(S) *paṉai-mīṉ* [*paṉai* 'palmyra palm', *DEDR* 4037; 'the seventeenth nakṣatra; *aṉuṭam* (Sanskrit *anurādhā*)': *oṅkum paṉai tuḷaṅk' oḷi puraṭṭāti* (Ilakkaṇa viḷakkam by Vaittiyanāta Tēcikar, 791); cf. also Hart 1975: 74] (1) 'a fresh-water fish, rifle-green, attaining 3 inches in length, *Polyacanthus cupanus*; *mūṉṟ' aṅkulam vaḷarvatum karuppu-niṟam uḷḷatum āṉa naṉ-ṉīr-mīṉ-vakai*': *cuṉaiyiṟ paṉai-mīṉ* (Kampa-Rāmāyaṇam kaṭaṟāvu. 50); (2) 'climbing fish, rifle-green, attaining 8.5 inches in length, *Anabas scandens*; *eṭṭ' aṟai aṅkula vaḷarcciyum karuppu-niṟamum uḷḷa mīṉ-vakai*': *paṉai-mīṉ vaḷaṅkum vaḷaimēy parappiṉ* (Maturaikkāñci 375).

F *pāl-mīṉ* [*pāl* 'milk', *DEDR* 4096] 'milk-fish, brilliant glossy blue, attaining 3 feet in length, *Chanos salmoneus*; *nīla-niṟam uḷḷatum mūṉṟu aṭi vaḷarvatum āṉa veḷḷai-mīṉ-vakai*'. (Winslow.)

F *pittaḷai-k-kācu-mīṉ* [*pittaḷai* < Sanskrit *pittalā* 'brass, copper'; *kācu* 'coin', *DEDR* 1431] 'a small fresh-water fish, *Etroplus maculatus*; *naṉ-ṉīril vāḻum ciṟu-mīṉ-vakai*'.

F *puṇar-mīṉ* [*puṇar* 'to join, unite, copulate', *DEDR* 4160b] 'brace of carp in gold or silver, an auspicious object carried before kings or other great personages, one of *aṭṭa-maṅkalam* [< Sanskrit *aṣṭa-maṅgalam* 'eight auspicious objects']; *iṇai-k-kayal*' (Cūṭāmaṇi-nikaṇṭu by Maṇṭalapuruṭaṉ). [See § 10.2.]

F *puḷi-mīṉ* [*puḷi* 'sour, acid; tamarind', *DEDR* 4322] 'fish soured with tamarind juice and eaten as a relish; *puḷi-y-iṭṭa mīṉ kaṟi*'. (Winslow.)

F *puḷi-vār-iṭṭa mīṉ* [*puḷi* 'sour; tamarind', *DEDR* 4322; *vār* 'to pour', *DEDR* 5356; *iṭu* 'to put', *DEDR* 442] = *puḷi-mīṉ*. (Winslow.)

F *pū-mīṉ-keṇṭai* [*pū* 'flower', *DEDR* 4345; 'gill of a fish; *mīṉiṉ kuvācakkaruvi*'; *keṇṭai* 'carp fish', *DEDR* 1947] 'mahsir, silvery, weighing 100 to 150 pounds, *Barbus tor*, the great fresh-water game-fish of India; *naṉ-ṉīril vāḻum peru-mīṉ-vakai*'. [See also *poṉ-mīṉ*.]

F *peru-mīṉ* [*peru* 'big', *DEDR* 4411] 'a kind of large fish; *yāṉai-mīṉ*' (Cēntaṉ Tivākaraṉ).

F *poṭi-mīṉ* [*poṭi* 'dust, powder, particle', *DEDR* 4481] 'small fish' (as the Tamil gloss on *tūl-mīṉ*, see above).

F(S) *poṉ-mīṉ* [*poṉ* 'gold', *DEDR* 4570; 'planet Jupiter; *viyāḻaṉ*: *poṉṉoṭu veḷḷiyum ... irukkai yīyavē* (Kampa-Rāmāyaṇam Mārīca. 16)] 'mahsir; *pū-mīṉ-keṇṭai*' (local usage).

F *makara-mīṉ* [*makaram* 'shark, crocodile' < Sanskrit *makara-* 'water monster, crocodile'] 'shark; *cuṟā*' (Piṅkala-nikaṇṭu). [See also *kōṭṭu-mīṉ* and § 10.2.]

F *mañcaṭ-kōḻi-mīṉ* [*mañcaḷ* 'yellow; turmeric', *DEDR* 4635; *kōḻi* 'cock, fowl', *DEDR* 2248] 'a sea-fish, buff, vertically banded, *Chaetodon octofasciatus*; *kaṭal-mīṉ-vakai*'. [Cf. *kallu-k-kōḻi-mīṉ*; *kōḻi-mīṉ*.]

F *maṭṭi-mīṉ* [*maṭṭi* 'oyster, cockle, shellfish; *cippi-mīṉ*' (Winslow); *maṭṭi-c-cippi* 'oyster shell; *cippi-mīṉ-ōṭu*' (Winslow); *maṭṭi-vāy* (1) 'gaping mouth; *tiṟant' akaṉṟa vāy*'; (2) 'a sea-fish, silvery grey, attaining 18 inches in length, *Chrysophrys datnia*; *patiṉeṭṭ' aṅkulam vaḷarvatum cāmpa-niṟam uḷḷatum āṉa kaṭal-mīṉ-vakai*'; (3) 'a sea-fish, pale dull red, attaining one foot in length, *Scolopsis vosmerii*; *maṅkiya civappu-niṟam uḷḷatum ōr aṭi vaḷarvatum āṉa kaṭal-mīṉ-vakai*'; *maṭṭi-vāyaṉ* (1) 'one who has a gaping mouth; *tiṟant' akaṉṟa vāyai y-uṭaiyavaṉ*'; (2) 'black rock-cod, silvery grey, attaining 30 inches in length, *Sparus berda*; *muppatu aṅkulam vaḷarak kūṭiyatum cāmpal-niṟam uḷḷatum āṉa mīṉ-vakai*'; (3) = *maṭṭi-vāy* (2)] 'a kind of fish; *mīṉ-vakai*: *paruntu-vāyaṉ maṭṭi-mīṉ pāra-k-keṇṭai* (Paṟāḷaivināyakar paḷḷu by C. V. Jampuliṅkam Piḷḷai, 15).

F *maṭavā-mīṉ* 'grey mullet, silvery, *Mugil oligolepe*; *veṇ-ṇiṟam uḷḷa mīṉ-vakai*' (Yāḻppāṇattu māṉippāyakarāti, by Cantiracēkarap Pulavar, Jaffna 1842) = *maṭavai* (this meaning in Patārttakuṇa cintāmaṇi 932); the latter word also means 'post; oar, paddle; whirling-nut'. Cf. also *maṭavai-k-keṇṭai* 'a species of carp; *mīṉ-vakai*' (Yāḻ. aka.).

F *maṇalai-mīṉ* = *maṇalai* [*maṇal* 'sand', *DEDR* 4666b] 'a sea-fish, purple-red, attaining at least 16 inches in length, *Upeneus indicus*; *kal-navarai*' [*kal* 'stone, gravel', *DEDR* 1298; *navarai* 'red mullet, *Upeneoides sulphurens*'] (Winslow.)

F *mayil-mīṉ* [*mayil* 'peacock', *DEDR* 4642] (1) 'sail-fish, bluish grey, attaining 9 feet in length, *Histiophorus gladius*; *oṉpat' aṭi nīlam vaḷarvatum maṅkiṉa nīla-niṟam uṭaiyatum āṉa kaṭal-mīṉ-vakai*'; (2) 'peacock-fish, grey, *Histiophorus immaculatus*; *ēmaṅ-kōlā*' (= *iyamaṅ-kōlā* 'flying fish of Yama, the god of death', Maclean 1893: 672).

S *mu-m-mīṉ* [*mu-* 'three', *DEDR* 5052] 'the fifth nakṣatra; *mirukacīriṣam* (< Sanskrit *mṛgaśīrṣa*) (Piṅkala-nikaṇṭu). [See § 10.4.]

S *mai-m-mīṉ* [*mai* 'black, dark', *DEDR* 5101] 'the planet Saturn, as black in colour; *caṉi*': *maimmīṉ pukaiyiṉum* (Puṟanāṉūṟu 117). [Cf. Hart 1975: 76; see § 10.5.]

S *mōṭṭu-mīṉ* [*mōṭu* < *mukaṭu* 'height, high position, hill, eminence, top of house, etc.', *DEDR* 4888] 'star; *naṭcattiram*': *mōṭṭu-mīṉ kuḷāttiṉ* (Cīvakacintāmaṇi 2325).

F *yaṉai-mīṉ* [*yāṉai* 'elephant', *DEDR* 5161] [= *āṉai-mīṉ*, q.v.] (1) 'a very large fish; *peru-mīṉ-vakai*' (Piṅkala-nikaṇṭu); (2) 'a kind of whale; *timiṅkila-vakai*' (Takkayākaparaṇi 384, urai). [See also *peru-mīṉ*.]

F(S) *rōkita-mīṉ* [*rōkita* < Sanskrit *rohita* 'red; carp with reddish scales, *Labeo rohita*'] 'a kind of fish; *oru-vakai mīṉ*'. [Cf. *cem-mīṉ*, and see § 14.4.]

S *vaṭa-mīṉ* [*vaṭa* 'northern', *DEDR* 5218] (1) 'the scarcely visible star Alcor of the Great Bear, supposed to be Arundhatī transformed; *aruntati naṭcattiram*'; (2) 'Arundhatī, the wife of Vasiṣṭha, considered a paragon of chastity; *vaciṣṭar maṉaivi*': *vaṭa-mīṉ puraiyuṅ kaṟpiṉ maṭa-moḻi* (Puṟanāṉūṟu 122). [Cf. *uttara-mīṉ*; Hart 1975: 76; and see § 14.1.]

S *vaya-mīṉ* [*TL*: probably *vayam* 'state of subjugation' < Sanskrit *vaśa* 'power, control'] 'the fourth nakṣatra; *urōkiṇi* [< Sanskrit *rohiṇī*]'. [Cf. § 14.4.]

F *vavvāl-mīṉ* [*vavvāl* (< *vāval*) 'bat', *DEDR* 5370; in Tamil also = *vavvāl-mīṉ*] 'pomfret, sea-fish, *Stromateus paru*; *mīṉ-vakai*' (Yāḻ. aka., by Cantiracēkarap Pulavar, Jaffna 1842).

F *vaṉ-mīṉ* [< *val* 'strong, powerful', *DEDR* 5276] 'crocodile; *mutalai*' (Piṅkala-nikaṇṭu): *miṭaintu vaṉmīṉ uyir kavara* (Piramōttirakkāṇṭam, by Varatuṅkarāmapāṇṭiyaṉ, 6,35).

S *vāl-mīṉ* [*vāl* 'tail' < Sanskrit *vāla-* 'tail, hair', *DEDR* App. 57] 'comet; *vāl-naṭcattiram*' (Winslow).

F *vāḷ-mīṉ* [*vāḷ* 'sword', *DEDR* 5376] 'swordfish; *ēmaṅ-kōlā*'.

S (1) *vāṉ-mīṉ* [*vāṉ* 'sky', *DEDR* 5381] 'star; *naṭcattiram*' (Puṟanāṉūṟu Arum.). Cf. *ney-vāṉ-mīṉ*.

S (2) *vāṉ-mīṉ* [*vāl* 'tail' < Sanskrit *vāla-* 'hair, tail', *DEDR* App. 57] 'comet' = *vāl-mīṉ* (Piṅkala-nikaṇṭu).

S *viṭi-mīṉ* [*viṭi* 'to dawn, break as the day', *DEDR* 5475] 'Venus, as the morning star; *viṭi-veḷḷi*' (Winslow): *viṭi-mīṉ muḷaitta tāḷam* (Kallāṭam 17,12).

S *viṇ-mīṉ* [*viṇ* 'sky', *DEDR* 5396] 'star; *naṭcattiram*' (Cūṭāmaṇi). See § 13.2.

S (1) *viḻu-mīṉ* [*viḻu* 'to fall', *DEDR* 5430] 'meteor; *viṇ-vīḻ-koḷḷi*'. [= *vīḻ-mīṉ*. Cf. § 14.1.]

F (2) *viḻu-mīṉ* 'hilsa, silvery shot with gold and purple, *Clupea ilisha*; *ullam*'.

S *vīḻmīṉ* [*vīḻ* 'to fall', *DEDR* 5430] 'meteor; *viṇ-vīḻ-koḷḷi*' (Tolkāppiyam, Poruḷatikāram 91, urai). [= *viḻu-mīṉ*. Cf. § 14.1.]

S *veṉ-mīṉ* [*veḷ* 'white, bright', *DEDR* 5496a] 'Venus; *cukkiraṉ*': *veṉ-mīṉ ticai tiruntu teṟk' ēkiṉum* (Paṭṭinappālai 14). [= *veḷḷi-mīṉ*. See § 13.2.]

S *veḷḷi-mīṉ* [*veḷḷi* 'silver; Venus', *DEDR* 5496a] 'Venus; *cukkiraṉ*': *veḷḷi-mīṉai y-orukaikkuṭ piṭittu* (Koṇṭal viṭu tūtu 191). [= *veṉ-mīṉ*. See § 13.2.]

F *veḷḷai-mīṉ* [*veḷḷai* 'whiteness', *DEDR* 5496a] 'white fish' (as the Tamil gloss on *pāl-mīṉ*, see above).

S *vaikuṟu-mīṉ* [*vaikuṟu* 'daybreak', *DEDR* 5554] 'morning star; *viṭi-veḷḷi*': *vaikuṟu-mīṉiṉ ṟōṉṟum* (Akanāṉūṟu 17). [See §§ 11.3; 14.4.]

Bibliographical notes

These notes are meant (1) to document the sources used and the earlier versions of this work and (2) to provide the reader with references for further reading on particular topics. The references are selective, particularly in section 4.2. The arrangement of the *topics* broadly follows the order in which they have been presented in the text, while the references themselves are in alphabetic order. Occasionally quotations and information supplementary to the text have been given in the notes.

Preface

Early phases of the Finnish approach: (1) Aalto 1974; Parpola 1970; Parpola et al. 1966; 1969a; 1969b; 1970; *criticism*: Berger 1970; Burrow 1969; Brice 1970a; 1970b; Casal 1969b; Clauson and Chadwick 1969; Conway 1985: 54–9, 92–106; Joseph 1970; Emeneau 1971; Filliozat 1972; Friedrich 1969; Gurov and Knorozov 1969; 1970; Kalyanaraman 1969; Kamal 1969; Lal 1970; Leemans 1970a; 1970b; Lienhard 1969; 1974; Mahalingam 1969; B. K. Majumdar 1968–9; Mallowan 1969 (1971): 291; Marr 1971; Mayrhofer 1970; Pande 1972; Pandit 1969; Pisani 1969; Saint-Blanquat 1970; Schmid 1969; Shevoroshkin 1973; Sircar 1969; R. Thapar 1969; W. Thomas 1970–1; Trautmann 1970; Tucci 1972; Vacek 1970; Zide and Zvelebil 1970a; 1970b; Zvelebil 1973c; 1985a; 1990: 89–91. (2) S. Koskenniemi et al. 1973; *criticism*: Brice 1976; Carruba 1976; Emeneau 1975; Knorozov and Probst 1976; Krick 1975; Mahadevan 1977: 21, 26; Marr 1975; Pande 1974a; B. Pottier 1974; Rau 1978; Schmitt 1974; Vacek 1975.

Chapter 1

Summaries and expositions of the Indus Civilization and its contexts: Agrawal 1982; Agrawal and Chakrabarti 1979; Allchin and Allchin 1982; Casal 1969a; Chakrabarti 1980; Childe 1934: 204–27, 312; 1950; Dani 1981; 1988; Fairservis 1961; 1967; 1975; Fentress 1976; Ghosh 1965; 1989b; Gordon 1960; Jansen 1979; 1986; Jansen and Urban 1984–7; Jansen et al. 1991; Kenoyer 1989; Lal 1975d; 1989a; Lal and Gupta 1984; Lambrick 1964: 70–99; 1973: 1–66; *Les Cités . . .* 1988; Mackay 1938; 1943; 1948; Marshall 1931a: I, 1–112; Meadow 1992; Mode 1959; Piggott 1952: 132–213; Possehl 1979; 1980; 1982a;

1992a; Rao 1973; 1991; *SAA* 1971–91; Sankalia 1974: 313–97; B.K. Thapar 1985; Vats 1940; *Vergessene Städte* ... 1987; Wheeler 1947; 1959: 93–117, 184–5; 1961; 1968.

Bibliographies: *ABIA* I–XXIII, 1928–84 (careful, complete, annotated); Anderson 1967 (continuation of Heras 1953: covers the years 1954–66; 233 items); Brunswig 1974 (*c.*800 items, subdivisions, many inaccuracies); Dandekar 1946: 281–303, 363–6 (210 items, annotations); 1961: 655–85, 719 (206 items, annotated); 1973: 928–82 (432 items, annotated); 1985 (*c.*3416 items in 10 subdivisions, annotated, author index); 1987; Franke-Vogt 1991 (1992): xix–xlix; E. von Fürer-Haimendorf 1958: 25–55, 292–3, 314–15, 326–7; 1964: II, 23–43, 168–9, 182–3, 194–5; E. von Fürer-Haimendorf and Kanitkar 1970: III, 25–43, 194–7, 208–11; Heras 1953: I, xxxviii–cix (1,014 items, many irrelevant, annotated); Jansen et al. 1991: 240–58; Kanitkar and E. von Fürer-Haimendorf 1976; Pande and Ramachandran 1971 (*c.*1,120 items, many inaccuracies); Possehl 1979b (*c.*1,600 items); Regamey 1934 (1935) (234 annotated items arranged chronologically: 1856–1934, covering also relevant linguistic and other non-archaeological items); Renou 1931: 140–1 (21 items); Roy and Gidwani 1982; Sankalia 1974: 569–82.

§ 1.1

Earlier versions: Parpola 1975a: 178–80; 1981a (1984a): § 3; Conway 1985: 3–5.

Difficulties / pessimistic judgements about the chances of deciphering the Indus script: Burrow 1969: 274; Casal 1969a: 137; Dales 1967; Dani 1963: 14; Doblhofer 1973: 304; Friedrich 1939: 5–6 ('Wo jede Möglichkeit der Anknüpfung fehlt, wie einstweilen bei der Indusschrift ... kann nur der Dilettant und Phantast auf Erfolg hoffen'); 1966: 135, 145; 1969: 493; Meriggi 1934: 198; Vacek 1970: 198–200; Wheeler 1968: 108; Zide [1968] 1970: 8; 1973: 348.

Scientific / scholarly research: Bunge 1967.

Cultural background and decipherment: Gelb 1974: 309 ('Frequently the key to a decipherment has been provided by a source external to the writing under study ... Therefore, before doing any work on the decipherment of a specific writing or language, a would-be decipherer must become acquainted with the historical-geographical background of the area from which it comes. One should remember Champollion, who spent years in familiarizing himself with the history, geography, religion, and languages of Egypt as preserved in the Classical sources or by tradition.'); Marshall 1931a: I, ix (Effective interpretation 'can only be accomplished, now or in the future, by specialists conversant with the subject in all its bearings. I cannot refrain from stressing this point here, because the antiquities from Mohenjo-daro and Harappā ... have been made the subject of much nonsensical writing, which can be nothing but a hindrance in the way of useful research.').

South Asian history and civilization: Basham 1954; 1975; Bechert and Simson 1979; Patterson 1982; Renou and Filliozat 1947–53; Smith 1958.

§ 1.2

The strategic position of the Indus Valley: Brown 1953: 131f.; Emeneau 1954: 283f.

Achaemenids and the Persian empire: Gershevitch 1985.

Sindhu / Hindu / Indus: Mayrhofer 1976: III, 468.

Arma(ka): Burrow 1963; 1977; Falk 1981; Rau 1976: 42–50.

Early Graeco-Indian contacts: Jong 1973; Karttunen 1989.

Aristoboulos: Lévi 1925.

Burnes: Burnes 1834 (III, 137f. on Harappa); Duarte n.d.: 89–98.

Other early visitors of Harappa: James Lewis's visit in 1827 (Duarte n.d.: 65–75; Masson [pseud.] 1842: I, 452–4 ['Harípah']; Whitteridge 1986; Windisch 1917–20: 100–1); Private Wakefield's visit in 1849 (Swinson and Scott 1968: 118–19).

Brunton: Brunton 1939: 82f., 98, 112, 117–25, 159; Piggott 1952: 13f.

History of Indology: Windisch 1917–20 (22–6: Jones; 98–112: Prinsep).

ASI: Ghosh 1953; Roy 1953.

Discovery of the Indus Civilization: Conway 1985: 11–36; Cunningham 1875; Dames 1886; Fleet 1912a; Franke-Vogt 1991 (1992): 13–14; Jansen 1986; Marshall 1922: 617f. and pl. 11: 22f.; 1923: 15–17; 1924; 1926a: 47–54 and pl. 19; 1926b; 1928; 1931a; Mode 1959: 7–17; Pande 1982; Possehl 1982a; 1992b; Urban 1991.

§ 1.3 See under chapter 1.

Distribution (with catalogues) and size of Indus settlements: Bhan 1989; Chakrabarti 1979; Fairservis 1975; Jansen 1979: 298–306; Joshi et al. 1984; Mughal 1981; 1990a; 1990d; 1992b; 1992c; Rao 1991: 359–77.

Town-planning and architecture: Fentress 1976; Jansen 1979; 1991a; in press; Sarcina 1979a; 1979b.

Banawali and Dholavira: Bisht 1982; 1984; 1987; 1989; 1991.

Mesopotamian parallels for the Great Bath: Barton 1928: 80 (Lagash); Gropp 1992 (Elam).

Criticism of the 'granary' interpretations: Fentress 1976: 159–67; 1984; but cf. the granaries of Mehrgarh (§ 1.6).

Reflections on the social structure: Franke-Vogt 1991 (1992): 161–2; Jacobson 1986b; Kenoyer 1989b; D. Miller 1985.

Statue of urial ram: F.R. Allchin, in press.

Animals, plants and agriculture: Costantini 1990; Meadow 1987; 1989; 1991; 1992b; Miller 1992; Weber 1991; 1992.

Fuel: Lambrick 1964.

Climate: Misra 1984.

River changes: Holmes 1968; Lambrick 1967; Misra 1984; Mughal 1982; Pal et al. 1984; Stein 1988; Wilhelmy 1966; 1968; 1969.

Fishing: Belcher 1992.

§ 1.4

Indus Civilization and ancient Near East, including the Gulf (see also under § 1.5): Al Khalifa and Rice 1986; Asthana 1976; Bibby 1958; 1972; Buchanan 1965; 1967; Cardi 1989; Chakrabarti 1977; 1990; Cleuziou and Tosi 1986; 1987; 1989; Dales

1962a; 1962b; During Caspers 1970–1; 1972a; 1976; 1979; 1982; 1983; Frankfort 1932; 1933; 1934; Frifelt 1975; Højlund 1989; in press; Kjærum 1983; 1986; Lamberg-Karlovsky 1972b; Mackay 1931b; Méry 1991; Mode 1944; Nissen 1988; 1991; 1992a; Potts 1990a; 1990b; Ratnagar 1981; Reade 1986; in press; Reade and Méry 1987; Schmökel 1966; Tosi 1991; in press.

Lothal: Leshnik 1968; Possehl 1976; S. R. Rao 1963; 1965; 1973; 1979–85; 1986; 1988; 1991; Yule 1982.

Indus seals / inscriptions in the Near East: Al-Gailani Werr 1982; Bissing 1927; Brunswig et al. 1983; Chakrabarti 1978a; 1978b; 1990; Cleuziou and Tosi 1989; Collon 1987: 142–4; in press, a; Corbiau 1936; Franke-Vogt 1991 (1992): 7, n. 5; Frankfort 1933: 50–3; Gadd 1932; Genouillac 1930; Gibson 1977; Hunter 1932: 468–9, 484; Langdon 1931a: 424–6; 1931b; 1932; Mackay 1925; Meriggi 1937b; Mitchell 1986; Potts 1990a; Scheil 1900: 129, fig. 8; 1916; 1925; Speiser 1935: I, 163–4; Thureau-Dangin 1925; Weisgerber 1984; Wheeler 1968: 114–19; Wyatt 1983.

Gulf / Dilmun seals: Bibby 1958; Kjærum 1983; 1986.

Fuchsite: Mackay 1938: I, 159; II, pl. 116, 2; Wheeler 1968: 80.

Carnelian beads: Beck 1933; Chakrabarti 1982; During Caspers 1972b; Inizan, in press; Mackay 1931b; 1938; Reade 1979; Tosi 1986a; 1991.

Ancient bead industry and its survival: Karanth 1992; Mackay 1937; Possehl 1981.

§ 1.5 See under § 1.4.

Dilmun, Makan and Meluḫḫa: Edzard et al. 1977; Gelb 1970; Glassner in press; Hansman 1973; 1975; Leemans: 1960 (Meluḫḫa: 159–66); 1968a; 1968b; Mallowan 1965; Oppenheim 1954; Pettinato 1972; Sollberger 1970; *different opinion*: R. Thapar 1975.

Dilmun: Amiet 1986b; Bibby 1970; 1972; 1986a; 1986b; Cornwall 1946; MacAdam 1990; Nissen 1986b; Potts 1981b; 1983a; 1983b; 1985; 1986; 1990; 1991; *different opinion*: Kramer 1963a; 1964; (now withdrawn) Kramer and Maier 1989: 217 n. 43.

Makan: Bailey 1982; Gershevitch 1957 and 1978 (sissoo); Maxwell-Hyslop 1983 (sissoo); Potts 1981b; Weisgerber 1980; 1981; 1984.

Meluḫḫa: Bernhardt and Kramer 1960 (Enki and the world order); Grayson and Sollberger 1976: 115 (rebellion against Naram-Sin); Mallowan 1969 (1971): 291 n. 3 (Meluḫḫa bird as the peacock); A. and S. Parpola 1975; S. Parpola et al. 1977; Potts 1982b; 1990.

Bāveru-Jātaka and the 'direction-crow' (fig. 1.10): Cowell 1895: III, 83–4; Heras 1953: 196 with n. 3; Srivastava 1977.

§ 1.6

The early 'Indo-Sumerian' hypothesis: Franke-Vogt 1991 (1992): 7; see also under § 4.2.

Deep diggings at Mohenjo-daro: Dales 1965a; Mackay 1938: I, 223f.; Wheeler 1968: 119f.

Amri: Casal 1964; Majumdar 1934: 24–8.

Chronology (table 1.1): Amiet 1986a: 12–13; Aurenche et al. 1987; Brinkman 1964; Dyson 1987; Ehrich 1965; 1992; Franke-Vogt 1991 (1992): I, 9 n. 19 (survey of earlier datings of the Indus Civilization), 21–6 (Mohenjo-daro); Jansen et al. 1991: xii; Jarrige 1987b; 1991; *Naissance de l'écriture* 1982: 38–42; Nissen 1987a; 1987b; Possehl 1990b; in press, b; Possehl and Rissman 1992; Potts 1993; Shaffer 1986: table 3; 1992; Voigt 1987; Voigt and Dyson, in press.

Indo-Iranian borderlands, Baluchistan (including Mehrgarh and Nausharo) and Early Harappan: Asthana 1985; Cardi 1964; 1965; 1970; 1983; 1984; Fairservis 1956; 1959; 1961a; 1961b; 1967; Hargreaves 1929; Jansen 1992; Jarrige 1977; 1979; 1982; 1985c; 1986; 1988a; 1988b; 1989 (1991); 1991a; Jarrige and Lechevallier 1979; Jarriage and Meadow 1980; 1992; Joshi 1989; Konishi 1984; Marshall 1931a: I, 96–101; Mughal 1970; 1972; 1973; 1974; 1977; 1981; 1988; 1990b; 1990d; 1990e; 1991; 1992b; 1992c; Piggott 1952: 66–131; Ross 1946 (Rana Ghundai); Samzun 1992; Shaffer 1978; 1986; 1992; Stein 1905; 1929; 1931; 1934; 1937; Wheeler 1968: 9–24 (p. 135: foreign inspiration of urbanization).

Shahr-i Sokhta: Lamberg-Karlovsky and Tosi 1973; Tosi 1977; 1979; 1983; 1986; Tucci 1977.

Proto-Elamite / Elam and Tepe Yahya: Alden 1982; Amiet 1966a; 1972; 1979; 1986; Carter and Stolper 1984; Dyson 1987; Hinz 1964; Kohl 1978; Lamberg-Karlovsky 1970; 1971; 1972a; 1973a; 1975; 1977; 1978; 1986; Lamberg-Karlovsky and Tosi 1973; 1989; Potts 1977; 1980.

Mundigak: Casal 1961.

Rahman Dheri: Durrani 1981a; 1981b; 1984; 1986; 1988.

Kot Diji: F. A. Khan 1965; Mughal 1970: 50ff.

Kulli: Casal 1966; Possehl 1986.

Intercultural-style stone vessels: Burkholder 1971; Kohl 1975; 1978; 1979; Lamberg-Karlovsky 1988; Mackay 1932.

'Cult object' of the 'unicorn' seals (cf. fig. 1.15): During Caspers 1985d: 68–70; Franke-Vogt 1991 [1992]: I, 105–6, 115–16, 183–4; II, table 44; Mahadevan 1984.

Altyn Tepe seals: Masson 1981.

Ra's al-Junayz: Cleuziou and Tosi 1986; 1987; Tosi 1991; in press.

Ra's al-Hadd: Reade and Méry 1987.

Wadi Asimah: Vogt, in press.

Chemical, typological and contextual analysis of Harappan pottery found in Oman: Méry 1991.

Comparison of early civilizations: Bernal 1969; Steward 1955; Steward et al. 1955.

Militarism: Jacobson 1986b: 160–2.

Harappan 'cultural uniformity': Fentress 1976; Franke-Vogt 1991 (1992): 8; Kenoyer 1989.

Criticism of early excavations: Wheeler 1947b.

Recent work at Mohenjo-daro: Alcock 1952; Dales 1964; 1965a; 1965b; 1965d; 1966; 1967; 1976; Dales and Kenoyer 1986; Franke-Vogt 1991 (1992): 14–16; Jansen and Urban 1984–7; Urban and Jansen 1983; Wheeler 1950a; 1950b; 1950c.

Recent work at Harappa: Dales et al. 1992; Meadow 1992a; Possehl 1992b.

Late and Post-Harappan (see also § 8.4): Agrawal 1982: 188–95; Allchin and Allchin 1982: 229ff.; Dales 1964; 1965; 1966; Dikshit 1989; Fairservis 1967; Kennedy 1982; 1984; Mackay 1943; Mughal 1981; 1984; 1990c; 1990f; 1992a; 1992b; 1992c; Piggott 1948; Possehl 1967; 1977; Raikes 1964; Raikes and Dales 1977; Wheeler 1968: 126–34.

BMAC (§ 8.4) and the Kachi plain: Franke-Vogt 1991 (1992): I, 86 n. 231; Jarrige 1985a; 1985b; 1987; 1991b; Jarrige and Hassan 1989; Santoni 1980; 1984; 1988.

Harappan culture in Gujarat: Dhavalikar and Possehl 1992; Possehl 1980; Possehl and Raval 1989.

Chapter 2

'The scholars who are familiar with the handling of hieroglyphic and pictorial writings are obviously best prepared for tackling a new species of apparently the same genus. Investigators not familiar with such early modes of writing can hardly even realize the nature of the task or the possibilities and impossibilities involved' (Thomas 1932: 461): Claiborn 1974; Cohen 1958; Coulmas 1989; DeFrancis 1989; Diringer 1968; Driver 1976; Friedrich 1966b; Gelb 1963; Harris 1986; Hill 1967; Jensen 1969; *Naissance*... 1982; Pettersson 1991; Sampson 1985; Senner 1989.

Bibliographies: Cohen 1958: II, 1–29 (annotated survey of all principal works up to 1957); Sattler and Selle 1935 (3,010 items, up to 1930); *linguistic bibliography for the years 1939–1947* and the subsequent yearly issues (section 'script, alphabets, orthography', fairly exhaustive).

§ **2.1** (see also under chapter 2)

Importance and function of writing: Coulmas 1989: 3–16.

Prehistory of writing: Friedrich 1966b: 15–24; Leonard 1973; Steensberg 1989.

Evolution of language: Greenberg 1968: chapter 1; Lieberman 1975.

Markings on Palaeolithic and Mesolithic artefacts, etc.: Chollot-Varagnac 1980; Marshack 1972; 1979.

Pot-marks in Susiana: Dollfus and Encrevé 1982.

Tokens, bullae, tablets and seals: Amiet 1966b; 1986: 55, 78–86, ills. 23ff.; Charvat 1988; Jasim and Oates 1986; Schmandt-Besserat 1978; 1992; Vallat 1986: 335–8.

Cylinder seal: Collon 1987.

§ **2.2** (see also under chapter 2)

The Sumerian writing system: Civil 1973; Civil and Biggs 1966 (12f.: 'nuclear writing', with the quoted example of the Fara period); Coulmas 1989: 72–84; Damerow and Englund 1987; Damerow et al. 1988a; 1988b; DeFrancis 1989: 69–89; Diakonoff 1975; Edzard 1969; 1980; Englund 1987; 1988; Englund and Gregoire, in press; Falkenstein 1936; Green 1980; 1981; 1989; Green and Nissen 1987 (new sign list of archaic Sumerian); Labat 1948; Lieberman 1980; Mallowan 1961; Nissen 1986a; Nissen et al. 1990; Powell 1981; Vaiman 1974.

Homophony in primitive communication, religion and folklore: Bertholet 1940; Gelb 1963: 4–5; Haas 1957; see also under § 9.6.

§ **2.3** (see also under chapter 2)

Proto-Elamite: Brice 1962; Damerow and Englund 1987; Ghirshman 1938: 65–8, pl. 31, 92–3; Lamberg-Karlovsky and Tosi 1989; Le Brun and Vallat 1978; Mecquenem 1949; 1959; Meriggi 1971–4; 1975; Scheil 1905; 1923; 1935; Vallat 1971; 1986.

Linear Elamite: Amiet 1979: 197; 1986: 144f.; Hinz 1962; 1964: 25–34; 1969a; 1969b: chapter 1; 1975; Vallat 1986.

Egyptian: Brunner 1969; Coulmas 1989: 57–71; DeFrancis 1989: 151–64; Gardiner 1957; Ray 1986; Schott 1951; Westendorf 1969.

West Semitic and Greek alphabets: Coulmas 1989: 137–78; DeFrancis 1989: 164–86; Garbini 1988; Millard 1986; Naveh 1987; Röllig 1969; Sass 1988.

Brahmi: see under § 4.1.

Chinese: Boltz 1986; Coulmas 1989: 91–110; DeFrancis 1989; Reischaer and Fairbank 1960: 40–4; Tsien 1962; *sign lists of archaic Chinese*: Grinstead 1972; Karlgren 1957.

Classification and evolution of writing systems according to their way of recording the entities of language (discourse, sentence, phrase, word, morpheme, phoneme): Coulmas 1989: 17–90; DeFrancis 1989: 47–69, 211–69; Hill 1967; Sampson 1985.

Chapter 3

Aalto 1945; Barber 1974 (recommended further reading); Doblhofer 1957; 1973; Friedrich 1966a; Gelb 1973; 1974; 1975; Gordon 1971; Leclant 1975; Pope 1975; Voegelin and Voegelin 1963; Zide 1973.

§ **3.1** (see also under chapter 3)

Egyptian: Åkerblad 1802; Andrews 1981; Champollion 1822; 1824; Erman 1922; Gardiner 1957: 10–18; Hartleben 1906; Pope 1975: 60–84; de Sacy 1802; 1811; Young 1823; *sign lists*: Erman and Grapow 1926–53; Gardiner 1957: 438–548; Petrie 1927.

Cuneiform: Booth 1902; Budge 1925; Grotefend 1802; 1837; Hincks 1850; Kent 1953; Löwenstern 1845; Messerschmidt 1910; Niebuhr 1778: II; Pallis 1956: 94–187; Pope 1975: 85–122; Rask 1823; 1826a; 1826b; G. Rawlinson 1898; H. C. Rawlinson 1846/7–9; 1850a; 1850b; 1851; H. Rawlinson et al. 1857; de Sacy 1787; 1792; *sign list*: Labat 1948.

Hittite: Forrer 1932; Friedrich 1939; Gelb 1931–42; D. Hawkins 1986; Hrozný 1915; 1917; Knudtzon 1902; Ménant 1890; Meriggi 1929; Pope 1975: 136–45; Sayce 1876; 1880a; 1880b; 1903; *sign lists*: Laroche 1960; Meriggi 1962.

§ **3.2** (see also under chapter 3)

Cypriot script: Pope 1975: 123–35; Schmidt 1874; Smith 1871.

Linear B: Barber 1974: 11–12, 15–16, 27–33; Chadwick 1960; Cowley 1927; Evans 1935: IV, 666–763; Hooker 1980; Kober

1946; 1948; 1949; Olivier 1986; Pope 1975: 146–79; Ventris 1954; Ventris and Chadwick 1956; 1973.

§ 3.3 (see also under chapter 3)
Etruscan: Pallottino 1955; 1968; Pfiffig 1969; 1972.
Role of linguistics in decipherment: Barber 1974: 3–79, esp. 21–8.
Comparative linguistics: Anttila 1972; Hock 1991.
'Nostratic': Cavalli-Sforza 1991; Cavalli-Sforza et al. 1988; Illich-Svitych 1971–84; Kaiser and Shevoroshkin 1988; Shevoroshkin 1989.
Criticism of 'distant relationship': Doerfer 1973.
Uralic: Janhunen 1981; Korhonen 1981; Sinor 1988.
'Altaic': Poppe 1965 (125–56: 'Altaic theory'); Ramstedt 1952–66.
Typology of decipherments: Barber 1974: 13–19; Friedrich 1939: 5–6; 1966a: 135; Gelb 1973: 268–71; 1974: 303–8; 1975: 96–8; Gordon 1971: 19–29.
Ugaritic cuneiform alphabet: Bauer 1930; 1932; Corré 1966; Virolleaud 1929; 1931.

§ 3.4
The Maya script and its decipherment: Barthel 1969: 161–6; Berlin 1958; Brasseur de Bourbourg 1861–4; 1869–70; Coe 1987: 161–87; 1992; Culbert 1991; Förstemann 1880; 1904; 1906; Houston 1989; Justeson 1986; Kelley 1976 (245–8: methods of decipherment); Knorozov 1958; 1963; [1963] 1967; Landa 1566; Proskouriakoff 1960; Robinson 1990; Schele 1981; Schele and Freidel 1990; Stuart and Houston 1989; Thompson 1950; Villacorta and Villacorta 1977; *sign lists*: Thompson 1962; Zimmermann 1956.

Chapter 4

Bibliographies on the Indus script (see also under chapter 1 and § 4.2): Dandekar 1987: 178–249; Kalyanaraman 1988 (many mistakes); Mahadevan 1988: 22 n. 2; Mahadevan and Rangarao 1986; Zvelebil 1990: 144–5.

§ 4.1
Earlier versions: Parpola 1986a: 403–7.
Early Harappan pot-marks: CISI 2: 352–78 (Rahman Dheri), 389 (Amri), 393–7 (Gumla, Hissam-dheri, Kot Diji), 410–11 (Periano-ghundai, Sarai Khola), 414 (Tarakai Qila); Casal 1961 (Mundigak); 1964 (Amri); Dales 1974: 16ff. (Bala-kot); Durrani 1981a; 1986: fig. 1 (Rahman Dheri); Fairservis 1956: 328–35 and pl. 14 (Quetta Valley); 1959: 359 and fig. 59 (Periano-ghundai); Halim 1972: 95–9 with table 11 (Sarai Khola); Quivron 1980 (Mehrgarh); *comparisons with the Indus script*: Agrawal 1968: 248; Durrani 1981a; 1986: fig. 1; Fairservis 1975: 279–82; Lal 1975b: 173f.; 1992b; Parpola 1986a: 404–6; Potts 1981a; 1982a.
Vinča: Winn 1981.
Origins of the Indus script / Proto-Elamite comparisons: Fairservis 1976: 44–6; Hertz 1937: 393; Hunter 1932: 483, 485; 1934: 1, 21, 45–9; Parpola 1975: 188; 1986a: 403–6; in press c; Potts 1981a; 1982a.
Mesopotamian origins of the Egyptian script: Ray 1986; *evidence for Protoliterate Sumerian or Elamite presence in late Pre-Dynastic (Nagada II) Upper Egypt:* Amiet 1980b: 38–9; 1986: 89; Boehmer 1974a; 1974b; Drower 1968–9; Frankfort 1951: 100–11; Kantor 1942; 1944; 1952; 1965: 10–15; Nissen 1987a: 613; Scharff 1942.
Little diachronic change in the Indus script: Wheeler 1968: 107.
Harappan writing materials / lost records: Casal 1969a: 137; Gelb 1973: 254–8; Hunter 1934: 18–19; Konishi 1987; Marshall 1931a: I, 40; Mode 1959: 39; *later India*: Gopal 1989; cf. Tsien 1962: 90–1.
'Late Harappan script' (Rangpur): S. R. Rao 1962–3, esp. pl. 25ff.; 1973: 329; 1982; *criticism*: Mahadevan 1981–2.
Discontinuation of the Indus script: Sarma 1967: 37–8 (the script was known only to a selected few in Harappan times, and was confined to city-dwellers and businessmen. When the Harappan empire fell, there was no longer any need of a script).
'Anthropomorph' with a 'fish' from Sheorajpur: Yule 1985b: 43 and pl. A and 23: no. 348; *anthropomorphs in general*: R. C. Agrawala 1985; Yule 1985b: 105; 1985c.
Daimabad: Sali 1986.
Graffiti of the Deccan and South India: Asthana 1989; Conway 1985: 34–6; Fairservis 1977: 43 and fig. 16b–g; Gurumurthy 1986; Lal 1960; 1974a; Sarma 1967: 38 (critical); Thomas 1932: 459; Vacek 1970: 202 n. 22; Yazdani 1917: 63; Zvelebil 1965; 1970: 23.
Early Indian punch-mark coins: Bhatia 1989; Cribb 1985; Gupta and Hardaker 1985; M. Mitchiner 1975–6; *comparison with the Indus script*: Aravamuthan 1942; Bongard-Levin 1957; 1960; Fábri 1935; Naster 1944 (Indo-Greek coins: argues for their connection with Indus seals on the basis of their non-Hellenic square form and Indian animals); *criticism*: Dani 1963: 20–2; Gonda 1965: 26–7.
Semi-permanent auspicious designs (Sanskrit raṅgavalli, Tamil kōlam, Bengali alpanā): Archana n.d.; Gode 1969: III, 87–102; Konishi 1991; *'endless knot':* Heras 1953: li, no. 181; Sarkar and Pande 1969–70.
Other traditional Indian symbols as possible Harappan survivals: Mahadevan 1972: 4 ('iconographic elements and other religious symbols, royal insignia, emblems on coins and seals, heraldic signs of nobility, corporate symbols, totem signs of clans and tribes, etc.').
Brahmi script: Bühler 1896; 1898; Coulmas 1989: 181ff.; Dani 1963; Gelb 1963: 147ff.; Gopal and Verma 1989; Gupta and Ramachandran 1979; Hinüber 1990; Masica 1991: 133–51; Salomon 1982; Wackernagel and Renou 1957: 32–4, 109–12 (n. 488–511); *Tamil Brahmi*: Mahadevan 1968; 1971; Panneerselvam 1972.
Comparison of the Indus and Brahmi scripts: Cunningham 1877: 61 and pl. 38; Fairservis 1977: 43–4; Hunter 1932: 483, 485–9; 1934: 1, 17, 22, 44–5, 90ff. (pp. 73, 75, 77 on 'fish signs'); Jayaswal 1913; Kak 1987; Langdon 1931a: 423, 426–7, 431, 433 (comparative table); Meriggi 1935: 543; J. Mitchiner 1978: 11–12; Paranavitana 1961; Ray 1963; 1965; 1966; Zide and Zvelebil 1970: 964; and many others; *criticism*: Aalto 1975: 19–21; Burrows 1936; Conway 1985: 12–24 (on Cunningham);

Hertz 1937: 397–8; Jaritz 1981: 120 and fig. 3 (comparative table); Marshall 1931a: I, 39ff.; Printz 1933: 137–9; Sarma 1967: 37; Strauss 1932: 648 (referring to [oral?] comments of Heinrich Lüders and Sten Konow); Thomas 1932: 464; Vacek 1970: 201–4.

§ 4.2

'Es ist kein Geheimnis, dass alle bisherigen Versuche, die Indusschrift zu entziffern (zum Teil erstaunliche Curiosa), jeweils nur ihre eigenen Urheber zu überzeugen vermochten' (Rau 1978: 75).

Overviews of some of the (more than 50) attempts at decipherment (see also under chapter 4): Aalto 1975; Abegg 1940; Basham 1949: 143–4; Conway 1985: 6–137; Dales 1967; Dani 1963: 13–14; 1973; Fábri 1934; Gurov 1972; Heras 1953: I, 29–60; Jaritz 1981; Jensen 1969: 344–51; Khan 1978; 1990; J. Mitchiner 1978: 1–5; Mode 1959: 39–40; O'Flaherty 1972: 292–6; E. Otto 1936; Pande 1989; Parpola 1979; 1981c; 1986a: 407f.; 1991; Rau 1979; Vacek 1970; Zide 1968; Zvelebil 1985a; 1990: 84–98.

Comparison with Lolo writing: Lacouperie 1882: 118; 1885: 440 ('the stone seal of Setchuen or Shuh writing, which was found a few years ago in the ruins of Harapa'); *criticism*: Conway 1965: 24–7; Wüst 1927: 269.

Comparison with Proto-Elamite: Sayce 1924.

Comparison with Easter Island tablets: Heine-Geldern 1934; 1938; 1950; 1956; Hevesy 1933a; 1933b; 1934; 1938; Jeffreys 1947; Langdon in Hunter 1934: ix; Paranavitana 1979; and many others; *criticism*: Mackay 1934: 253; Métraux 1938; 1946; 1969; see also Barthel 1958; 1963; 1968; 1969; 1971; Conway 1985: 27–8; Gelb 1973: 267–8 ('Easter Island script' not writing).

Comparison with Etruscan: Piccoli 1933.

Comparison with Egyptian: Petrie 1932.

'Indus language might be Indonesian': Ross 1938: 30; *criticism*: Bloch 1939; Conway 1985: 47–8; Gonda 1939.

Maldives: Heyerdahl 1986; Sabaratnam 1982; *criticism*: Forbes 1983.

'Indo-Mexican' hypothesis: Barthel 1979; 1981; 1984.

Sindhi approach: Memon 1964; *criticism*: Khubchandani 1969: 218.

Brahmi approach: see under § 4.1.

'Indo-Sumerian' hypothesis: Gadd and Smith 1924; Waddell 1925; *criticism*: Barton 1926–7 (1928); 1929: 264–8; Charpentier 1925; Ipsen 1929.

Sumerian: Kinnier Wilson 1974; 1984; 1986; 1987; *criticism*: Burrow 1975b; Sollberger 1976; Zvelebil 1977d.

Harappans = Asuras of the Veda = Assyrians: Shendge 1977; *criticism*: Rau 1979.

Some of the many 'Aryan' decipherments: Mitchiner 1978; Paranavitana 1961; Krishna Rao 1969; 1982; S. R. Rao 1971; 1973a: 125–34; 1973b; 1979: I, 170–211, 261–5; 1982; S. K. Ray 1963; 1965; 1966; *criticism*: Bright 1982; Cohen 1981; Conway 1985: 107–9; Gurov 1970: 17–20, 44–6; Lal 1969; 1970; 1983; Mahadevan 1981–2; Norman 1984.

'Tantric code' (varṇabījakoṣa): Goudriaan and Gupta 1981: 160–1; Raghu Vira and Taki 1938; Vidyāratna 1913; *comparisons with the Indus script*: Barua 1946; Sankarananda 1944: II, 43–104; 1955; *criticism*: Gurov 1972: 13–16; Heine-Geldern 1957; Vacek 1970: 204–5.

'Indo-Hittite' hypothesis: Hrozný 1939; 1941–2; 1943; *criticism*: Gonda 1960: I, 6 n. 2; Gurov 1970: 20–3; W. Otto 1941; Quintana Vives 1946; Ryckmans 1944; cf. also Meriggi 1934: 214 (similarities with Hittite hieroglyphs too systematic to be coincidental; but p. 200: historical connection hardly possible); 1937a; *criticism*: Gurov 1970: 28–30.

Dravidian decipherments: (a) Henry Heras: Heras 1953 (with a bibliography of the author's earlier papers: lvii–lix, nos. 250–84; summarized by Quintana Vives 1946); 1990; *criticism*: Brown 1939: 37–8; Conway 1985: 50–4; Emeneau 1954: 282–4 (1980: 86ff.); Gurov 1970: 23–5; Heine-Geldern 1955; Joseph 1964; 1970; Vacek 1970: 205–6; Zvelebil 1970: 23.

(b) Soviet team (earlier Soviet interest in the Indus script following Hrozný: Benediktov 1954; Struve 1947): Al'bedil' 1986; Al'bedil' et al. 1982; Alekseev 1965; [1965] 1976; Bongard-Levin and Gurov 1981; Gurov 1970a; 1970b; 1972a; 1972b; 1975a; 1975b; [1968] 1976; Gurov and Katenina 1967; Knorozov 1965; 1970a; 1970b; 1972; 1975; [1965] 1976; [1968] 1976; 1981; 1986; Knorozov et al. 1981; 1984; Kondratov 1965; [1965] 1976; Misyugin 1972; 1975; *Predvaritel'noe* ... 1965; Probst 1965; [1965] 1976; *Proto-Indica*: 1968; 1970; 1972; 1979 (1981); Volchok 1965; 1970a; 1970b; 1972a; 1972b; 1975; [1968] 1976; 1981; 1986; *criticism*: Conway 1985: 59–84; Knižková 1966; Knyazeva 1980; Vacek 1970: 206–7; Zide and Zvelebil 1970; 1976.

(c) Finnish team: see under preface.

(d) Schrapel 1969; *criticism*: Vacek 1970: 210.

(e) Mahadevan 1970; 1973; 1979; 1980; 1981; 1982; 1986a; *criticism*: Conway 1985: 109–11; Lal 1974b; Zvelebil 1990: 94f.

(f) Fairservis 1977; 1983; 1984; 1992; *criticism*: Bright 1986; Conway 1985: 111–37; McAlpin 1979; Zvelebil 1990: 92–4.

Borrowing of sign forms and their values from one script to another: Barber 1974: 97–8; Friedrich 1966a: 139; Gelb 1963: 143–4; 1973: 272–3; Hertz 1937: 391–2.

Earlier versions of fig. 4.7: Parpola 1975: 189, fig. 8; 1979: 171.

§ 4.3

Earlier versions: K. Koskenniemi and A. Parpola 1979: 7–17; 1980; 1982: 1–17; Parpola 1975a: 180–2; 1986a: 400.

Preparatory work, statistics: Gelb 1973: 273–6.

Use of computer: Barber 1974: 69–83, 101–11, 171–7; Gelb 1973: 280–1; *computer graphics*: Conway 1985: 225ff.; Damerow and Englund 1989.

Early editions and / or concordances / sign lists of Indus texts: Barton 1928–9 (1930); Barua 1946: pl. 3–4 (a list of 177 signs, with many non-existent signs and with allographs as distinct graphemes); Dani 1963: 12–22, pl. 1–2; Gadd and Smith 1931 (*criticism*: Hunter 1932: 477; Marshall 1931a: I, 40); Hunter 1932: 494–503; 1934 (*criticism*: Burrows 1936; K. Koskenniemi and A. Parpola 1982: 8; Mackay 1934; Meriggi 1935);

Langdon 1931a: 434–55 (*criticism*: Printz 1933: 137–8); Vats 1940: II, pl. 105–16.

Recent computer editions / concordances (with sign lists): K. Koskenniemi and A. Parpola 1979; 1980 (duplicates collected); 1982 (*criticism*: Vacek 1986); S. Koskenniemi et al. 1973 (*criticism*: see under preface); Mahadevan 1977 (*criticism*: K. Koskenniemi and A. Parpola 1979: 8–17; 1982: 8–13); 1988: 12–13, pl. 2–3, 8; cf. Mahadevan and Visvanathan 1973; Rangarao and Mahadevan 1986.

Other sign lists: Conway 1985: 247–52; Fairservis 1992: 149–88.

New photographic edition: CISI 1 = Joshi and Parpola 1987; *CISI* 2 = Shah and Parpola 1991.

Other documentation of the inscribed objects from Mohenjo-daro: Franke-Vogt 1991 (1992): I, 16–29; II, 231–434 (catalogue); Jansen and Urban 1985.

Little-reported excavations: ASI, Annual Report for the years 1930–1, 1931–2, 1932–3 and 1933–4 (1936): I, 70–2 (excavations at Mohenjo-daro in 1931–2 and 1933–4 by Q. M. Moneer; according to oral information from the late Justice Feroz Nana, Karachi, Mr Moneer's diary, unknown to Urban 1987: 23, should be still extant and with his son); 1934–5 (1937): 31–3 and pl. 9–11 (excavations at Harappa in 1934–5 by M. Nazim); 1935–6 (1938): 35–6 (excavations at Harappa in 1935–6 by Mohammad Hamid Kuraishi); 1936–7 (1940): 39–41 (excavations at Harappa in 1936–7 by H. L. Srivastava), 41 (excavations at Mohenjo-daro, DK-i area, in 1936–7 by K. N. Puri; cf. Puri 1938); Dales 1982: 99; Franke-Vogt 1991 (1992): I, 14–19; Jansen 1984: 77–9; Mahadevan 1977: 4; Parpola 1972; Possehl 1992b: 8; K. N. Sastri 1965: II, xii, I, 39–53 (excavations at Harappa in 1937–41 by K. N. Sastri).

§ 4.4

Establishing the direction of writing: Barber 1974: 99f.

Direction of writing in archaic Sumerian: Edzard 1969: 216–17; Falkenstein 1936: 9–12, 36; Gelb 1968.

Direction of writing in the Egyptian script: Gardiner 1957: 25; Gelb 1963: 73–4.

Direction of writing in the Greek script: Woodhead 1959: 24–7.

Direction of writing in the Indus script: Alekseev [1965] 1976: 18–20; Dani 1963: 16; Gadd and Smith 1931: II, 409–11; Hunter 1932: 466, 472, 482; 1934: 19–20, 37–43; Kinnier Wilson 1974: 30–3; Knorozov 1968: 7–8; Lal 1966; 1967–8; 1975a; 1975b; Langdon 1931a: 427–8, 431; Lüders 1934 ('nur soviel scheint sicher, dass diese Bilderschrift von rechts nach links gegangen ist'); Mahadevan 1972: 293; 1977: 10–14; 1988: 6–8, pl. 4; Marshall 1931a: I, 40–1; Meriggi 1934: 202; Parpola 1975: 182; Parpola et al. 1969: 18; Raman 1986; Ross 1938: 4, 10–11; 1939: 556–8; Thaplyal 1972; 1973: 342–3; Zide and Zvelebil 1976: 20–1.

Chapter 5 Many of the observations on the Indus signs and textual comparisons are made for the first time here; others, with similar or different conclusions, have been published earlier.

§ 5.1

Earlier versions: K. Koskenniemi and A. Parpola 1979: 12–15.

Graphemic analysis / sign boundaries: Alekseev [1965] 1976: 17–18; Barber 1974: 87–92; Conway 1985: 102–6, 117–18, 159–224; Edzard 1990; Gadd and Smith 1931; Hunter 1932: 486–7; 1934; Mahadevan 1977: 14–18 (text 1218 as an example); 1988: 6, 8–10, pl. 1; Ross 1938: 11–12.

Sign list: see under § 4.3. Fig. 5.1 is a new list.

Round and angular variants of signs: Jaritz 1981: 117–18 and 129, fig. 2; *vertical variants*: Hrozný 1941: 220 n. 1 (the example given is erroneous); *style of carving signs with 'expanded ends'*: Heras 1953: 221–2.

'Enclosure' ligatures: Gadd and Smith 1931: 409; Hunter 1932: 476, 480; Jaritz 1981: 118; Meriggi 1934: 208–13.

The 'frame' of four dots: Hunter 1932: 478, 485, 488; 1934: 67, 99–101; Meriggi 1934: 208–10; 1935: 544; Parpola et al. 1970: 25; Rauff 1985; 1988; Zide and Zvelebil 1976: 21–2.

§ 5.2

Earlier versions: Parpola 1975a: 183; Parpola et al. 1969a: 24–7, 45f., 63–5.

Composite signs: Barber 1974: 145–9; Conway 1985: 102–6, 117–18, 120–1, 159–224; Fairservis 1977: 26–8; Mahadevan 1977: 14–18; 1988: 13–15.

Seals 2340 and 1048: Hrozný 1942: 6–7.

'Man' ligatures: Dani 1963: 17; Gurov and Knorozov 1970: 7; Hrozný 1942: 24–5, 66, 74 (no. 351), 86, 88; Hunter 1934: 106–9, 203; Meriggi 1934: 213–14, 219–20, 225, 229 n. 1, 231; Parpola et al. 1969a: 29ff., 64–5; Vacek 1970: 207–8 ('archer' with two bows hardly realistic).

Overanalysis of Indus signs: e.g. Heras 1953: 81ff., 92ff.; S. R. Rao 1973: 323–7.

Sign repetition: Gadd and Smith 1931: 421; Heras 1953: 87, 150–4; Hunter 1934: 117, 125; Jaritz 1981: 119; Mahadevan 1977: 16; Meriggi 1934: 222; Parpola et al. 1969a: 23f.; Zide and Zvelebil 1970: 957.

Numerals: Gadd and Smith 1931: 412–13, 419; Hunter 1932: 478–81; 1934: 95–101, 204; Knorozov [1968] 1976: 103–4; Mackay 1934: 254; Mahadevan 1988: pl. 7(1); Meriggi 1934: 230–1; Ross 1938 (*criticism*: Conway 1985: 37–50; Gonda 1939; Parpola et al. 1969a: 58); Zide and Zvelebil 1976: 110–11.

§ 5.3

Earlier versions: Parpola 1975a: 182f.; 1981a (1984a): § 5; Parpola et al. 1969: 11f.; K. Koskenniemi and A. Parpola 1980; S. Koskenniemi et al. 1973: xi–xii.

Segmentation: Barber 1974: 85–7, 113–43; Hunter 1932: 483, 491–2 (this list of 'words' is misleading, cf. Parpola et al. 1969a: 11); 1934: 42–3, 125–8; Kondratov [1965] 1976; Mahadevan 1977: 7–10; 1988: 10–13, pl. 5–6; Meriggi 1934: 203; Rauff 1987: 73ff.; Siromoney and Huq 1982; 1988.

'Word dividers': Edzard 1990: 130f.; Meriggi 1934: 203–7; *function of these signs*: see under § 6.2.

§ 5.4

Earlier versions: K. Koskenniemi and A. Parpola 1982: 10–11; Parpola 1986a: 408f.; 1988a: 115f.

Type of writing system: Barber 1974: 93–8; Brice 1970b: 222; Chadwick in Clauson and Chadwick 1969: 204–5; Edzard 1990; Gelb 1973: 261, 266 ('Proto-Indic' one of the seven original and fully developed logo-syllabic systems); Gurov and Knorozov 1970: 1; Jaritz 1981: 117–19; Mahadevan 1988: 2–5, 12, 18; Marshall 1931a: 1, 39–41; Meriggi 1934a: 202; 1935: 543; Rauff 1987: 71–2; Shevoroshkin 1973: 85; Wüst 1927: 268–9; Zide 1973: 352; Zide and Zvelebil 1970: 955–9.

Number of graphemes or 'basic signs': Fairservis 1992: 149–52 (230 graphemes); Gadd and Smith 1931: 407 (*c.*396 graphemes); Hunter 1932 (149 graphemes); 1934: 49 ('roughly 250'); Mahadevan 1977 (419 graphemes); Meriggi 1934: 202 (around 275 graphemes); S. R. Rao 1979: 1, 170; 1982 (62 basic signs in the Mature Indus script, 20 in the 'Late Indus script'); Trautmann 1970: 716 ('The rebus principle at least doubles the number of meanings ... But it is likely that the relative fewness of known signs of the Indus script is a function of the smallness of our sample ... we may expect new signs to be added to this number as more inscriptions are brought to light'); Wüst 1927: 269 n. 1 (110 graphemes in the 59 texts published then).

Chapter 6

§ 6.1

Earlier versions: K. Koskenniemi and A. Parpola 1982: 11–12; Parpola 1975a: 190.

Language typology and universals: Andersen 1983: 16–18; Croft 1990: 27–63; Crystal 1987: 84f., 98f.; Greenberg 1966a; 1966b; 1978; J. Hawkins 1983; Knorozov 1970; [1965] 1976; [1968] 1976; Masica 1976: 13–39.

Typological-universalist study of writing systems: Justeson 1977; Justeson and Stephens, in preparation; Stephens and Justeson 1978; *application to the study of the Indus script*: Edzard 1990: 128–30; Knorozov et al. 1981: 13ff.; Ross 1938: 13 (numerals).

§ 6.2

Earlier versions: Parpola 1975a: 183; 1981a (1984a): § 6; Parpola et al. 1969a: 62.

Positional analysis (and inflection: § 6.3): Barber 1974: 145–70; Barthel 1968: 173 (grid in the structural analysis of undeciphered Maya texts); Conway 1985: 123–5; Fairservis 1977: 6–8 and fig. 1; 1983: 47–51; 1984: 154f.; 1986: 112f. and fig. 3 (a grid of 14 positions each hypothetically associated with a particular word class; but the rigidity of the grid may force functionally similar signs into different slots); Gadd and Smith 1931: 415–21; Hunter 1934: 65 ('fish' signs as prefixes); Meriggi 1934: 199 note (space added between 'words' in analyses); Rauff 1987 (our positional slots I, II and III correspond to Rauff's P, M, F; Rauff discusses also the 'fish' signs and their ordering); Ray 1965: 52–3 (grid).

Function of the 'grammatical' strokes / 'word dividers' / 'accents' (see also § 5.3): Hunter 1932; 478–80; 1934: 57–8; 60–1 (significance of the object shown in our fig. 6.3), 81–2, 90–3, 101–2; Jaritz 1981: 125–6; Langdon 1931a: 428ff.; Meriggi 1935: 543–4; Thomas 1932: 464.

Seals with part of the inscription repeated on the boss of the reverse side (fig. 6.4): Hunter 1932: 482.

§ 6.3

Earlier versions: Parpola 1975a: 183; 1981a (1984a): §§ 6, 11; 1981b: 74–9; Parpola et al. 1969a: 18–23, 41f. (zero alternation); 1969b: 6–8.

Inflection (see also under § 6.2): Gadd and Smith 1931: 421–2; Gurov 1968; 1970a: 61–3; 1970b; 1972b; Hunter 1934: 27, 55–62, 116–17; Knorozov et al. 1981: 7–15; Mahadevan 1982a; 1986b; 1988: 15f.; Meriggi 1934: 216–18; 1935: 544; J. Mitchiner 1978: 30f., 47f., 66ff.; Pandit 1969; Vacek 1970; Zide and Zvelebil 1970: 954ff.; 1976.

§ 6.4

Earlier versions: K. Koskenniemi 1981; P. Parpola 1988; see also S. Koskenniemi et al., 1970; P. Parpola 1987.

Method: Harris 1951; 1954; 1968; *with application to Linear B*: Barber 1974: 113–43.

Another parallel automatic approach to the analysis of Indus texts: Huq 1988; Siromoney and Huq 1986. Cf. also Cohen 1982.

Automatic methods to determine the type of script, classify the signs into different functional classes, and divide the texts into syntactic units: Knorozov and Gurov 1970; Kondratov 1965; [1965] 1976; Probst 1965; [1965] 1976; *criticism*: Conway 1985: 64–71; Shevoroshkin 1973: 84; Zide and Zvelebil 1976: 37, 49–53.

Chapter 7

§ 7.1

Earlier versions: Parpola 1975a: 188; 1976; 1981a (1984a): § 4; 1986a: 409f.; Parpola et al. 1969a: 8–10. Cf. Gelb 1973: 272–9; Petrie 1932: 33–4; Thomas 1932: 463.

The Sumerian myth of Enki's rib: Kramer 1963b: 149; Kramer and Maier 1989: 12–13, 22–30.

§ 7.2

Earlier versions: Parpola 1975a: 187–90; 1981b; 1986a: 406f., 410; 1986b; 1988a: 116f.; Parpola et al. 1969a: 10, 24; 1969b: 20f. Cf. Conway 1985.

Some suggested pictorial meanings of Indus signs (often not convincing): Bongard Levin 1960; Fairservis 1976: 146–95; 1977: fig. 14; 1992: 27–114, 153–88; Gadd and Smith 1931: 407–9; Knorozov [1968] 1976: 104–5 (*criticism*: Zide and Zvelebil 1976: 111); Knorozov et al. 1981: 71–108; Mackay 1934: 254 ('The horned figure amongst the signs, which he [i.e. Dr Hunter] identifies as the sign for a deity, is comparable with the horned figurines of pottery that are so frequently found at Mohenjo-daro'); Nagaswamy 1986; Pande 1974b; 1985; Sankarananda 1963: 107–19; 1967: III (1), 46–52 (these two lists contain many non-existent signs and quite fanciful explanations, but also a few possible suggestions).

Pictorial identification of the 'squirrel' sign: cf. Heras 1953: 114 ('squirrels', without further explanation: understood to refer to an alleged non-Aryan tribe); Jaritz (1981: 121) and Meriggi (1934: 238) see in the sign a 'monkey'.

Comparable signs in other pictographic scripts: see sign lists in references on chapters 2 and 3; *actual comparisons (most rather unsatifactory):* Barton 1926–7 (1928): 82ff.; 1928–9 (1930); Fairservis 1992: 228–9; Heras 1953: 76–8, 251–77; Hunter 1934: 201–10 (*criticism*: Mackay 1934: 252–3; Meriggi 1935: 542–3); Jaritz 1981: 119–25, 130–1; Langdon 1931a: 427, 434–55; Meriggi 1934: 214; Petrie 1932: 34–6; Ray 1965: 36–41; Thomas 1932; *'mountain' signs (fig. 4.7)*: Jaritz 1981: 123; Parpola 1975: 189, fig. 8; 1979: 171; 1988a: 128, fig. 1b.

Archaeological remains and sign forms: Scharff 1942 (comparative study of object and sign forms even enables dating the latter).

The most frequent sign, as 'jar with lip and handles': Barton 1926–7 (1928): 84; 1928–9 (1930): 86; Fairservis 1992: 44f.; Hunter 1934: 55, 210 (Egyptian and Sumerian parallels); Lal 1974; 1975: 176 and pl. 3; 1979b; Mahadevan 1970: 173; *as pipal tree*: Knorozov 1968: 15; Knorozov et al. 1981: 73; Parpola 1981a (1984a): § 11; *criticism*: Lal 1979b; *as 'ship' (Sumerian parallels)*: Parpola et al. 1969a: 21–2; *criticism*: Lal 1969; 1970; 1979b; *as ox head*: Kenoyer (1992, orally); Ray 1965: 37; 1966: 4, fig. 2; Parpola 1992a.

Wheel as a symbol of royalty: Gonda 1954: 96f.; 1969: 123ff.; Mahadevan 1979: 264–5; Parpola 1986b; Parpola et al. 1969b: 20–1.

§ 7.3

Earlier versions: Joshi and Parpola 1987: xv–xvi, xxviii–xxx; Parpola 1975a: 184–5, 196–9; 1981b; 1986a: 402f.; in press, c; Parpola et al. 1969a: 12–15.

The relationship between an inscription and the object upon which it has been written as quasi-bilingual information: Forrer 1932; Gelb 1973: 276–7; Meriggi 1934: 199–200.

Object typology: Al'bedil' 1986; Conway 1985: 140ff.; Dales 1967; Fentress 1976: 208–17, 326–8; Franke-Vogt 1991; 1991 (1992): I, 34–5, 43–57; II, table 7; 1992; Joshi and Parpola 1987: xxviii–xxx, 365; Knorozov 1968: 4–7 (Zide and Zvelebil 1976: 97–9); 1975; K. Koskenniemi and A. Parpola 1980: 17f.; S. Koskenniemi et al. 1973: xviiiff.; Mackay 1931a; 1938; Mahadevan 1977: 6f.; Vats 1940.

Inscribed weapons from ancient Near East: Calmayer 1969: Dossin 1962; Driver 1976: 106; Gelb 1963: 287 n. 21; *Naissance*... 1982: 103, 178, 180; Pritchard 1969b: nos. 261, 805; Virolleaud 1929; *from Harappan sites*: Franke-Vogt 1991 (1992): I, 55–6; II, table 21: nos. 114–16; Knorozov 1975: 14–15.

Comparison of inscriptions on Indus weapons and seals (fig. 7.8): Franke-Vogt 1989: 237, 242–5; 1991 (1992): 56 n. 102; Parpola 1975: 185, fig. 3.

Numbers on bronze weapons or tools: John Sören Pettersson (letter).

Inscriptions on Harappan pottery: Franke-Vogt 1991 (1992): I, 54–5; II, table 20; Mackay 1938: I, 182f., 187; Marshall 1931a: I, 291f., 317; Pande 1972–3; Vats 1940: I, 286f; Wheeler 1947: 120; 1968: 94.

Inscriptions on Mesopotamian pottery: Gelb 1982; Nies and Keiser 1920: 15ff.; Salonen 1966: II, tables 166–9, no. 1.

Inscriptions on Phoenician pottery: Driver 1976: 114.

Inscriptions on later Indian pottery: Lal 1954–5: 99, pl. 57; 1970: 200; Sircar 1965: 77ff.

Inscriptions on Chinese pottery: Tsien 1962: 58–61.

Indus tablets: Conway 1985: 143–4; Franke-Vogt 1991 (1992): I, 50–2; II, tables 11–13; Hunter 1932: 473; Joshi and Parpola 1987: xvi, xxix; Knorozov [1968] 1976: 105–7; Mackay 1931a: II, 397–8; 1938: I, 349ff.; 1948: 70; Shendge 1985 (an inadmissible comparison with the Proto-Elamite accounting tablets); Vats 1940: I, 31ff., 195f., 324f.; Wheeler 1968: 106f.

The 'pot' sign and offering to tree (see also § 10.3): Franke-Vogt 1991 (1992): I, 82; Hrozný 1942: 36, 39–40 (including comparison with the Hieroglyphic Hittite sign for 'pot', of a kind in which the Hittite offered sacrifices to ancestors), 57; Hunter 1934: 310 no. 4; Knorozov [1968] 1976: 105–7; Knorozov et al. 1981: 44, 106; Parpola 1981b: 81–3.

Egyptian sign of 'arm with hand holding a pot': Gardiner 1957: 454 no. D39.

The 'yoke carrier' sign compared to Indian and Chinese parallels: Parpola 1981b: 82–9.

Kāvaṭi subcaste: Thurston 1909.

Oraon omen ritual with four pots: Roy 1972: 144–5.

Copper tablets: Conway 1985: 208–9; Franke-Vogt 1991 (1992): I, 52–4, 149–56 (found especially in the Great Bath, C and DKB areas and in the 'Late Period'), 180–1, 215; II, tables 14–19; 1992; Hunter 1932: 473–4; 1934: 26–8 and pl. 3–4: 24–61; Mackay 1931a: II, 398–401 and Marshall 1931a: III, pl. 117: 1–6 and pl. 118: 1–6; Mackay 1934: 253–4; 1938: I, 363–9; II, pl. 93: 1–14; pl. 103: 1–7, 12; Pande 1973; Parpola 1975a: 196–9; in press, c; Yule 1985a: 32–45, tables 17–26 (nos. 331–474).

Ivory sticks: Fairservis 1977: 9ff. ('calendars'); Franke-Vogt 1991 (1992): I, 56; II, table 21: no. 117; Mackay 1931a: II, 563; 1938: I, 561ff.

Inscribed bangles: see under § 13.1.

Monumental inscription from Dholavira: Lal 1992a: 2; S. R. Rao 1991: pl. 54C (the whole inscription cannot be clearly seen).

Bull figurine from Allahdino: Ad-11 in *CISI* 2: 388.

§ 7.4

Earlier versions: Parpola 1975a: 184–6; 1986b: 400–2; 1988a: 117.

Seals in general: Berchem 1918; Collon, in press; Ewald 1914; Kittel 1970.

Seals in the ancient Near East: Collon 1987; Frankfort 1939; 1955; Gibson and Biggs 1977; Nissen 1977; *their administrative use*: Charvat 1988; Ferioli et al. 1979; Fiandra 1981; Fiandra and Ferioli 1984; Gibson and Biggs 1977; Mariani and Tosi 1987; Veenhof 1972: 30ff., 41ff.; Zettler 1987.

Indus seals and sealings (typology, manufacture, use, iconography); Conway 1985: 140–58; Fairservis 1976; 1992: 189–223, 227; Franke-Vogt 1991; 1991 (1992): I, 43–50; II, 467–93, tables

8–10; (iconography, inc. tablets) I, 61–124; II, 435–466, 495–504, tables 22–44; 1992; Hunter 1934: 471; Joshi and Parpola 1987: xii ff.; K. Koskenniemi and A. Parpola 1980: 17f.; S. Koskenniemi et al. 1973: xvii ff.; Lal 1975: 146; Mackay 1931a: II, 370ff.; 1938: I, 325ff., 346f.; 1948: 70; Mahadevan 1977: 7–9, 793ff.; Rissman 1989; Sharif 1990; F. W. Thomas 1932: 460; Vats 1940: I, 317ff.; Wheeler 1968: 101; *text rather than iconography impressed*: Hunter 1932: 472; Mackay 1931a: II, 394, 397; *relationship between iconography and inscription*: Franke-Vogt 1991 (1992): I, 110; Hunter 1932: 470; Lal 1975: 147f.; *seals with a case for an amulet*: Mackay 1931a: II, 380; 1938: I, 343f.; Wheeler 1968: 108.

Sealings of Lothal: Parpola 1986a: 400–2; S. R. Rao 1979: I, 111ff.; Yule 1982.

Chinese seals: Lai 1976; Tsien 1962: 54–8; Wagner, in press.

System of naming offices by the number of officials: Petrie 1932: 34 (Egypt; Cappadocia; Rome: *duumviri*, *triumviri*, *quattuorviri*, *septemviri*, *decemviri*, *quindecimviri*).

Size and quality of Mesopotamian seals: Nissen 1977; Porada 1977.

Size and quality of Indus seals: Franke-Vogt 1991 (1992): I, 43–8, 117–21, 141–7, 171ff.; Parpola 1986b.

§ 7.5

Earlier versions: Parpola 1975a: 184–7; 1975b; 1981a (1984a): §§ 8, 16, 26; Parpola et al. 1969a: 13; 1969b: 12–14, 41.

High quality of zebu seals: Franke-Vogt 1991 (1992): I, 66, 120.

Jar 277 from Harappa with copper objects: Vats 1940: I, 85ff., 287.

Inscriptions of Indian seals of the historical period: V. S. Agrawala 1984; *IAR*, *passim*; Thaplyal 1972; 1989; *compared to Indus seals*: Heras 1953: 60, 66f.; Thaplyal 1973; 1981.

Inscriptions on early Indian coins: Allan 1936; M. Mitchiner 1975–6.

Inscriptions on Near Eastern seals: Edzard 1968; 1990; Gelb 1977; Hallo 1981; *compared to those on the Indus seals*: Gadd and Smith 1931: 412; Hunter 1934: 23.

Archaeological context of the Indus seals and their vertical and horizontal distribution: Fentress 1976: 211, 218–32, 336–84; Franke-Vogt 1991 (1992): I, 16–26, 125–56, 194–227; II, 505–40, tables 45–57 (Mohenjo-daro); Hunter 1932: 471–2 ('Their find spots suggest that every family in Mohenjo-daro possessed a seal'); Kenoyer 1992: 50–7 (Harappa); Mahadevan and Rangarao 1987; Siromoney 1980.

Isolation of Harappan place-names in Indus inscriptions; Parpola 1975b.

Inscriptions on Chinese seals: Tsien 1962: 54–8.

Sumerian and Akkadian proper names: Kramer 1963b: 118; Limet 1968; 1971; Tallquist 1914.

'High priest' seal hypothesis: Parpola et al. 1969b: 12–14 (also some further examples with parallel inscriptions).

Chapter 8

Earlier versions of chapters 8 and 9: Parpola 1974; 1975a: 190–2; 1981a (1984a): § 9; 1986a: 410–12; 1988b.

§ 8.1

Summary listing of the languages of the world: Crystal 1987: 436–44.

The problem of the Harappan language (general considerations and restriction of search): Bloch 1965: 322–4; Burrow 1969: 274–5; Dales 1967: 34 (we do not know); Emeneau 1954: 282–4; Gelb 1973: 277–8; Hertz 1937: 396–7; Hunter 1934: 12–13, 17; Knorozov 1976; Marshall 1924: 548; 1926: 398; 1931a: I, 42, 107–12; J. Mitchiner 1978: 5–11; Piggott 1950: 180–1; Wüst 1927: 270–5.

Several ethnic groups in the Greater Indus Valley in the third and second millennia BC: Shaffer and Lichtenstein 1989.

Altaic alternative: Zide and Zvelebil 1970a: 961; Zvelebil 1985: 152–3.

'Altaic' homeland in Jehol or Manchuria: Ramstedt 1957: I, 14–16; cf. Poppe 1965: 144–5.

Adoption of mounted nomadism by peoples speaking 'Altaic' languages in the first millennium BC: Jettmar 1966: 65–7, 74, 90.

'Proto-Turks' assumed to come to Altai from the east in the fifth century AD: Jettmar 1966: 77–9; Spuler 1966b: 125–6.

Huns (in Chinese: Hsiung-nu) mobile since the second century BC: Jettmar 1966: 77–9; Reischauer and Fairbank 1960: 99.

§ 8.2

Languages of the ancient Near East in general: Benveniste 1952; Gragg 1979; *Yazyki . . .* 1957–67.

Anatolia: Friedrich et al. 1969; Kammenhuber 1975.

Hittite and other Indo-European languages: see under § 8.4.

Hurro-Urartian: Diakonoff and Starostin 1986.

Afroasiatic and Semitic: Hetzron 1987a; 1987b; Hodge 1970; Ullendorff 1970.

Sumerian: Falkenstein 1949–50; 1959; Thomsen 1984.

Elamite: Grillot 1987; Hinz and Koch 1987; Reiner 1969.

Iranian languages (see also § 8.4–5): Diakonoff 1985b; Hoffmann 1958; Kellens 1989; Kent 1953; Mayrhofer 1973; 1989; Morgenstierne 1926; 1932; 1958; 1973; Payne 1987; Pirart 1989; Schlerath 1968; Schmitt 1989a–f; Skjærvø 1989.

Gulf and Amorites: Brunswig et al. 1983; Højlund, in press; Kjærum 1986; Potts 1986; 1990; Zarins 1986.

Sumerian Jemdet Nasr pottery in the Gulf: Frifelt 1979; Oates 1986.

The 'Indus' seal with cuneiform inscription: Gadd 1932: 193f.; Gadd and Smith 1931: 413; S. Jaritz 1981: 114, 129 (fig. 1 shows the proper forms of the cuneiform signs SAG.KU.ŠI in Akkadian ductus); Parpola et al. 1977: 156, n. 30.

Seal of the 'Meluḫḫa interpreter': Collon 1987: 142, 147 (no. 637); Lamberg-Karlovsky 1981.

'Meluḫḫa village' in Sumer: S. Parpola et al. 1977.

Sequences of the Indus seals from the Near East: Brunswig et al. 1983; Hunter 1932: 469; S. Parpola et al. 1977: 155–9.

§ 8.3

South Asian languages in general: Breton 1976; Burrow 1958; Emeneau 1954; Grierson 1903–28; Maloney 1974; Sebeok 1969; Shapiro and Schiffman 1981; Zograph 1982.

Iranian: see under § 8.2.
Indo-Aryan languages: Bechert 1980; Bloch 1963; 1965; Burrow 1973a; 1973b; 1975a; Caillat 1989a; 1989b; Cardona 1987a; 1987b; Cardona and Emmerick 1974; Elizarenkova 1989; Emeneau 1966; Gonda 1971; Hinüber 1986; Hock and Pandharipande 1976; Hoernle 1880; Jha 1967; Lamotte 1958: 607–57; Masica 1990; Mayrhofer 1956–80; 1986–92; Morgenstierne 1926; 1930; 1932; 1957; 1958; 1973; Norman 1980; Pischel 1900; Salomon 1989; Thieme 1938; Turner 1966; 1975; Wackernagel 1896; Wackernagel and Renou 1957; Witzel 1987; 1989.
Nuristani languages and culture: Edelberg and Jones 1979; Fussman 1972; Jettmar 1975; 1986; Morgenstierne 1945; 1973: 298–343; Nelson 1986; Tikkanen 1988b.
Dravidian: see under chapter 9.
Combining archaeology, texts and linguistics: Bright 1986; Ehret 1976; 1988; Fairservis 1986; Möhlig 1989; Parpola 1974; 1981a (1984a): § 9; Renfrew 1987 and its many reviews.
Mesolithic and Neolithic South Asia: Misra 1989; B. K. Thapar et al. 1989.
Neolithic cultures of the upper Ganges Valley: Sharma 1980; Sharma et al. 1980.
Eastern Neolithic: Dani 1960.
Agricultural terms of non-Aryan origin in North Indian languages: Masica 1979; Southworth 1976b; 1988; 1992; Zide and Zide 1976.
Austro-Asiatic languages: S. Bhattacharya 1975; Burrow 1958; Jenner et al. 1976; Konow 1906; Kuiper 1948; Pinnow 1959; 1963; Shorto 1963; Zide 1966; Zide and Zide 1976.
Burushaski language: Berger 1974; in press; Lorimer 1935–8; 1937; Morgenstierne 1935; 1947; Tikkanen 1988a.
Northern Neolithic: Stacul 1992; B.K. Thapar 1985; B.K. Thapar et al. 1989.
Yang Shao culture of China: Chang 1977.
Petroglyphs of northern Pakistan: Jettmar 1985; Jettmar and Thewalt 1987.
Sino-Tibetan: Benedict 1972; Egerod 1974; R. A. Miller 1969; Shafer 1957–63; 1974.
Distribution of the mongoloid man: Reischauer and Fairbank 1960: 4 (map), 13–15.
Physical anthropology of the Indus people: see under § 9.3.

§ 8.4

Earlier more extensive and fully documented version of this section: Parpola 1988b (revised summary: Parpola, in press, b; earlier sketches: Parpola 1973; 1974; 1976b); *criticism*: Falk 1991; Norman 1990; Renfrew 1991; Sethna 1992: 204–420.
Other more general recent studies of the 'Aryan problem': F.R. Allchin 1981; Allchin and Allchin 1982: 298–308; Burrow 1975a; *Ethnic problems...* 1981; Ghirshman 1977; Mallory 1989; Renfrew 1987: 178–210; Witzel 1989.
Indo-European languages and Proto-Indo-European: Baldi 1987; Benveniste 1973; Birnbaum and Puhvel 1966; Buck 1949; Cowgill 1974; 1986; Lehmann 1990; Mayrhofer 1986a; 1986b (102ff.: Centum vs. Satəm); Pokorny 1959; Szemerényi 1989.
Archaeological identification of the Proto-Indo-European speakers and the Pit Grave / Kurgan culture: Anthony 1986; 1990; 1991; Anthony and Wailes 1988; Cardona, Hoenigswald and Senn 1970; Childe 1926; Coleman 1988; Diakonoff 1985a; Gamkrelidze and Ivanov 1984; 1985a; 1985b; 1985c; 1987; 1990; Gimbutas 1956; 1965a; 1965b; 1970; 1973; 1977; 1979; 1980; 1985; 1988; Jettmar 1983b; Mallory 1976a; 1976b; 1977; 1988; 1989 (*criticism*: Lehmann 1990b); Markey and Greppin 1990; Polomé 1982; Renfrew 1987; 1990; Scherer 1968; Skomal and Polomé 1987; Thomas 1982.
Proto-Indo-European / Proto-Aryan loanwords in Uralic languages: Janhunen 1983; Joki 1973; Koivulehto 1979; 1991; Makkay 1990; Rédei 1983; 1986.
Bronze and Iron Age cultures of the northern steppes (Timber Grave, Andronovo, Scythians / Sarmatians): Chernikov 1960; Chlenova 1984; Francfort 1992a; Gening 1977; 1979; Grjasnow 1970; Jettmar 1972; 1983a; 1983b; Kuz'mina 1985a; 1985b; 1986a; 1988b; Kuz'mina and Vinogradova 1983; Mandel'shtam 1968; Phillips 1961; Rolle 1980; Sinor 1990; Smirnov and Kuz'mina 1977; Trippett 1974.
Mitanni Aryans: Burrow 1973b; Diakonoff 1972; Ghirshman 1977; Mayrhofer 1966; 1969; 1974; Thieme 1960.
Archaeology of Iran relating to the early Aryans (see also under BMAC, below): Dyson 1973; Frye 1984; Ghirshman 1964; 1977; Matheson 1976; Young 1967; 1985; in press.
BMAC (see also under § 1.6): Amiet 1986; 1989a; 1989b; *L'Archéologie de la Bactriane...* 1985; *L'Asie centrale...* 1988; Biscione 1977; Brentjes 1981; 1983; 1987; 1989; Dales 1992b; Francfort 1984b; 1985a; 1985b; 1987; 1989; 1992a; 1992b; Francfort and Pottier 1978; Hiebert, in press; Hiebert and Lamberg-Karlovsky, in press; Jettmar 1981; Kohl 1981; 1984; Lamberg-Karlovsky 1989; *Le Plateau iranien...* 1977; Ligabue and Salvatori 1989; Lyonnet 1988; Masson 1987; Masson and Sarianidi 1972; Pittman 1984; P'jankova / Pyankova 1986; 1989; Pottier 1980; 1984; Sarianidi 1977a; 1977b; 1979; 1981a; 1981b; 1985; 1986a; 1986b; 1986c; 1987; 1988; 1989a; 1989b; 1989c; 1989d; 1990; [1992]; Schmidt 1937; Tosi 1986; 1989.
Indra: Benveniste and Renou 1934; Gonda 1960; Macdonell 1897; Oldenberg 1917; Rau 1966.
Soma: Brough 1971; Falk 1989; Flattery and Schwartz 1989; Gershevitch 1974; Nyberg, in press; Wasson 1971.
Zarathustra: Boyce 1979; Duchesne-Guillemin 1962; Gnoli 1980; Hinz 1961.
The fortresses (pur) in the Ṛgveda: Basham 1949: 142–3; Burrow 1977; Parpola 1988b: 211–17; Rau 1976; Wheeler 1947: 82.
Dāsa / Daha: Bailey 1960; 1979; Hale 1986: 146–69; Hillebrandt 1891: I, 83–116; 1902: III, 255–9, 267–93; Keith 1925; Konow 1912; Macdonell 1897: 62–4, 156–62; Muir 1874: II, 358–96; Parpola 1988b: 208–29; Tomaschek 1901; Zimmer 1879: 100–18.
Śambara / Saṁvara: Hopkins 1915; Mallmann 1975; Parpola 1988b: 260–2.
Varuṇa and Asura: Bergaigne 1978; Brereton 1981; Heesterman 1957; Hopkins 1915; Johansson 1917; Kuiper 1979; Lüders

1951–9; Macdonell 1897; Parpola 1983; 1988b: 227–9; 1992b; Rodhe 1946; Rönnow 1929: 113.

Gandhara Grave culture / Ghalegay sequence of Swat: Dani 1967; Stacul 1969; 1970; 1971; 1976; 1979; 1980; 1987; 1992; Stacul and Tusa 1977; Tusa 1979.

Indo-Aryan and Nuristani languages: see under § 8.3.

Vedic religion and material culture: Dandekar 1946–85; Gonda 1960; 1975 (traditional chronology: 22f., 360f.); 1977; 1980a; Heesterman 1957; 1962; 1987; Hillebrandt 1897; Keith 1925; Kuiper 1991; Rau 1957; 1972, 1974; 1976; 1977; 1983; Renou 1931; Staal 1983; Weber 1868–73; Witzel 1987; 1989; Zimmer 1879.

Aryans and Indian archaeology: Allchin and Allchin 1982: 298–308; Lal 1981a; 1981b; Leshnik 1972: 152–4; Thapar 1965; 1970.

PGW: Agrawal 1982; Allchin and Allchin 1982: 316–24; Gaur 1981; Lal 1954–5; 1981a; 1981b; 1982; 1989b; Tripathi 1976.

Pirak: Jarrrige and Santoni 1979.

Late Harappan (Cemetery H, Jhukar): see under § 1.6.

OCP and Copper Hoards: R. C. Agrawala 1985; Gaur 1973; 1989; S. P. Gupta 1989; Lal 1972; Yule 1985b; 1985c; 1989.

Ahar / Banas: Dhavalikar et al. 1989; Hooja 1988; Misra 1969.

§ 8.5

'Indus people spoke Indo-European / Aryan': Renfrew 1987: 178–210; Sethna 1992; Shaffer 1984; *contra, pregnantly*: Lüders 1934: *23* ('Dass diese alte Kultur nicht indogermanisch-arisch sein kann, ergibt sich aus folgenden [fünf] Gesichtspunkten: ... 3. Der Indus-Kultur fehlt trotz der grossen Zahl ihrer Haustiere das Pferd, das bei den Indern seit indogermanischer Zeit Haustier ist'); Marshall 1931a: I, 110–12.

Horse domestication and the Indo-Europeans: Anthony 1986; Bökönyi 1978; Hamp 1990; Koppers 1936; Kuz'mina 1977; Levine 1990; Mallory 1981; 1989; Telegin 1986.

Proto- / Early Indo-European vocabulary connected with horses and wheeled vehicles: Anthony and Wailes 1988: 442; Buck 1949: 167–8; Coleman 1988: 450; Mallory 1976a: 51; Mayrhofer 1987: I, 140; Pokorny 1959: I, 301–2.

Horsemanship of the Mitanni Aryans: Kammenhuber 1961; 1968; Mayrhofer 1974.

The horse in Old Iranian proper names: Schwartz 1985.

Earliest wheeled vehicles: Littauer and Crouwel 1977; 1979; 1980; Moorey 1986; Piggott 1952; 1968; 1974; 1975; 1983; Shaughnessy 1988; Singh 1965; Sparreboom 1983; Treue 1986.

The horse in South Asia: Jarrige and Santoni 1979: I, 404f., 408; Meadow 1987; 1991; *unacceptable claims of earlier appearance:* Badam 1989: 4f.; Sethna 1992: 247–53.

Chapter 9

Dravidian languages and culture: Burrow 1968; Burrow and Emeneau 1984; Caldwell 1856; 1913; Emeneau 1967a; 1967b; 1969; 1988; Emeneau and Burrow 1962; Hart 1975; Gundert 1871–2; Kittel 1968–71; Konow 1906; Krishnamurti 1961; 1969; 1985; Lehmann and Malten 1992; Marr 1975; Pfeiffer 1972; Rajam 1992; Shanmugam 1971; Southworth 1976a; Steever 1987; Subrahmanian 1966a; 1966b; Subrahmanyam 1969; 1971; 1983; 1988; *TL*; Zvelebil 1970; 1972a; 1972b; 1973a; 1974a; 1974b; 1975; 1977a; 1990.

§ 9.1

Elamite and Dravidian: McAlpin 1974; 1975; 1979; 1981; *criticism*: in McAlpin 1975; Zvelebil 1985; 1990: 104–15.

Dravidian and Uralic: Bouda 1955–6; Burrow 1943–6b; Schrader 1925; Tyler 1968.

Dravidian and 'Altaic': Bouda 1955–6; Menges 1977; Vacek 1987; *criticism*: Zvelebil 1990: 99–103.

Brahui and North Dravidian: Andronov 1980; Bray 1907–34; Burrow 1943–6a; Elfenbein 1982; 1983a; 1983b; 1987; Emeneau 1962a; 1962b; 1974b; 1980; Parkin 1989; Pfeiffer 1972; Pinnow 1964; Rossi 1979; Subrahmanyam 1983; Zvelebil 1972a.

Baluch(i): Bailey 1973; Elfenbein 1966; 1989; Frye 1961; Rossi 1979; Scholz 1983; Trumpp 1880.

North Dravidian fricativization and 'wheat': Burrow 1943–6a; *DEDR* 1906; Emeneau 1962a: 54; Mayrhofer 1990: I (7), 498f.; Rossi 1979: 155; Subrahmanyam 1983: 300.

Migrations of the Kurukh: Burrow 1968: 329; Elfenbein 1987: 230; Grignard 1909: 12–15; Pfeiffer 1972: 2–3; Roy 1915: 17.

§ 9.2

Areal linguistics: Chambers and Trudgill 1980; Weinrich 1968; *in South Asia*: S. Bhattacharya 1975; Bloch 1963; 1965: 322–4; Breton 1976; Emeneau 1954; 1956; 1962b; 1971; 1974a; 1978b; 1980; Fairservis and Southworth 1989; Fussman 1972; Heston 1980; 1981; Hock 1975; 1979; 1982; 1984; 1991; Krishnamurti 1986; Kuiper 1967; Masica 1976; Ramanujan and Masica 1969; Tikkanen, 1987; 1988a; 1992; Vermeer 1969; Zvelebil 1990: 60–83.

§ 9.3

Estimates of Harappan population: Kenneth A. R. Kennedy, orally in 1991 (1 million); McEvedy and Jones 1978: 182 (5 million).

Physical anthropology: Cappieri 1965; Hemphill et al. 1992.

Swat: see under § 8.4.

Dravidian substratum influence on Indo-Aryan: Bloch 1924; Burrow 1958; 1973a; Deshpande 1979; Emeneau 1954; 1956; 1962b; 1971; 1974; 1980; Hock 1975; 1979; 1982; 1984; Kuiper 1955; 1976; Meenakshi 1986; Southworth 1974; 1979; in press; Tikkanen 1987; Zvelebil 1990: 70–83.

§ 9.4

BRW: Ghosh 1989c; Singh 1982.

Dravidian and BRW: Converse 1974: 82; Zvelebil 1965: 65; *criticism*: Parpola 1973: 20–2.

Indus Civilization and Dravidian: Casal 1969: 210–11; Fairservis and Southworth 1989; Marshall 1924: 548; 1926: 398; 1931a: I, 42, 107–12; Meriggi 1934: 198–9; 1937; Parpola 1974; Thomas 1932: 459; Zvelebil 1977e: 213–14.

Harappan weights: Agrawal 1982: 146; Hemmy 1931–8; Hendrickx-Baudot 1972; Mackay 1948: 103; J. Mitchiner 1978: 14–15; Piggott 1952: 181; Venkatachalam 1986; Wheeler 1968: 83.

Octaval number system: Collins 1926; Parpola et al. 1969a: 25; 1969b: 37; Zvelebil in: Zide and Zvelebil 1976: 110 n. 3.

Sesamum: Bedigian 1985; Southworth 1992: 83; Weber 1991: 26, 176.

Meluḫḫa / Mleccha: Bailey 1973; Hansman 1973; 1975; A. and S. Parpola 1975; Zide and Zvelebil 1970a: 966–7.

Toponyms: Parpola, in press, a; Southworth, in press.

Dravidian kinship system: Parkin 1989; Trautmann 1981.

§ 9.5

Archaeology and early history of South India: Allchin and Allchin 1982: 121–4, 262–97, 325–46; Begley 1986; Maloney 1970; 1975.

Old Tamil Sangam literature: Hart 1975; Lehmann and Malten 1992; Rajam 1992.

South Indian megaliths: Allchin and Allchin 1982: 325–45; S. P. Gupta et al. 1989; Leshnik, 1972; 1974; McIntosh 1985.

Megaliths and Dravidians: Fürer-Haimendorf 1953; *criticism*: Emeneau 1954: 286–7 and n. 23; Parpola 1973: 1–20.

Megaliths and the Aryans: Parpola 1984c.

Tamil Brahmi: see under § 4.1.

Neolithic cultures of South India: F.R. Allchin 1963; B.K. Thapar et al. 1989.

South Dravidian: Emeneau 1967b.

Malwa and Jorwe: Dhavalikar et al. 1989; Miller 1984; Sankalia 1955; 1963; Sankalia et al. 1971; Shinde 1989.

§ 9.6

Use of Dravidian in decipherment: Burrow 1969; Parpola 1976: 129–33.

Dravidian languages and their subgrouping: Zvelebil 1990: xiii–xiv, 46–59; and literature quoted under chapter 9.

Use of homophony in early scripts: Gelb 1963: 69–72, 75–81; *homophony in Brāhmaṇa etymologies*: Gonda 1955–6; see also under § 2.2.

Chapter 10

§ 10.1

Earlier versions: Parpola 1975a: 192–4; 1976: 132f.; 1980a: 24, 31–2, 37; 1981a (1984a): § 17; 1984b; 1986a: 413; 1988a: 118f.; Parpola et al. 1969a: 40–4.

Identification as 'fish': e.g. Barton 1928–9 (1930); Barua 1946: 20; Casal 1969a: 137; Dani 1963; Fábri 1935: 311–12; Fairservis 1975: 279; Filliozat 1972: 78 ('l'image du poisson est aisément reconnaissable'); Heras 1953: 70, 99–100; Hunter 1934: 209; Ipsen 1929: 93; Jaritz 1981: 121 (comparing a similar Chinese sign for 'fish'); Jayaswal 1913 ('fish-picture letters'); Marshall 1926: 50 ('It is manifest from the formation of the characters themselves that originally the writing was a pictographic one, one of the commonest characters for example on our Indian seals bearing still the obvious likeness of a fish'); Printz 1933: 138f.; Ray 1965: 39; Sankarananda 1944: II, 99; 1967: III (1), 48; Thomas 1932: 463 n. 1; *doubt about 'fish'*: Brice 1970a: 26; Fairservis 1984: 156, 158; 1992: 50–8 (rather 'loop'); Gadd and Smith 1931: 408 ('The suggested "fish" signs are more puzzling, since the modifications to which the original (?) [plain "fish" sign] is subjected are not particularly natural as indicating different kinds of fish, and it is by no means certain that a fish is intended at all, but the comparison suggests itself at once, and it is hard to find a better').

Alligator with fish in mouth (establishing the pictorial meaning of the 'fish' sign): Conway 1985: 121–2, 131–5; Fábri 1935: 308–9 (compares later Indian punch-marked coins that show a crocodile with a fish in its mouth); Franke-Vogt 1991 (1992): I, 73, 87–8; Heras 1953: 376–7 (with a photograph (fig. 244) of a later Indian parallel: a vertical fish between two crocodiles facing it, carved on stone walls of the Mātsi Buruj of the bathing ghat in front of Ahilyabai's palace at Maheshwar in Madhya Pradesh); Hunter 1932: 475; 1934: 33.

'Fish' sign = Dravidian mīn: Gurov [1968] 1976: 123; Heras 1953: 84–8, 97–100, 108, 150f., 155–7, 166, 174f., 179, 261; Knorozov [1965] 1976: 59; Mahadevan 1970: 182ff.; Parpola et al. 1969a: 43; Schrapel 1969: 25.

*Proto-Dravidian *mīn 'fish' (table 10.1): DEDR* 4885.

Indo-Aryan loanwords (Sanskrit mīna, etc.): Mayrhofer 1963: II, 643f.; Turner 1966, no. 10140a.

*Proto-Dravidian *vin / *min, *viṇ / *miṇ 'to glitter', *mīn / *vīṇ / *vīṇṭ-V-kk- 'star': DEDR* 4876; Pfeiffer 1972: 69 no. 421; 109–10 no. 826 ('especially Malt. *bīṇḍke* suggests a PDr form **vīṇṭ-* and not **vīṇ-*. An older form **biiṇḍko*, in which **-ḍ-* between consonants was elided, can also explain why the nasal was not assimilated to the following velar stop'); 98 no. 723 ('m- which prevails in the SDr and CDr languages, might be due to the influence of medial nasal'); Krishnamurti 1961: 460 no. 984 reconstructs for PSDr and PCDr **min- / *miṯ-*; cf. Zvelebil 1970: 132: 'In PDr, **-n-* (>**-ṉ-*) seems to have also alternated with **-ṯ-* (>**-ṟ-*)'; for the unusual PDr **-ṇ- / *-n-* alternation, cf. Pfeiffer 1972: 109 no. 825. Sanskrit *miñj-* 'to shine': Dhātupāṭha 33,83 (omitted by some authorities: Böhtlingk and Roth 1868: 5, 767); Gurov 1970: 87 n. 23.

Possible etymological connection between Proto-Dravidian mīn 'fish' and mīn 'star' / min 'glitter': Caldwell 1856: 446f.; 1913: 573f.; Gurov 1970: 74; Heras 1953: 274; Ramaswami Aiyar 1950; Singaravelu 1966: 106; *criticism*: Burrow and Emeneau 1984: xvii; Zide and Zvelebil 1976: 56 n. 6; from the point of view of the decipherment, the two etyma need not *really* be related to each other; what is relevant is that the ancients seem to have associated them.

Proto-Dravidian min: mīn: Zvelebil 1970: 184f.; 1973a: 42.

Stars as 'fish' of heavenly ocean in Tamil: cf. also Kittel 1970: III, 1328a; and Francken 1735: XXIV, 1027 (8 October 1726): 'Einen ieden Stern *a part* nennen sie *Mīn*, das ist, Fisch: als schwuemmen gleichsam die Sterne in der Luft wie *Wünmīngöl* oder Luft-Fische' [*viṇ* 'sky' is often prefixed to *mīn* in Tamil when 'star' is meant: Singaravelu 1966: 106].

Heavenly river: Stietencron 1972: 63, 77.
Goose dives for star, thinking it a fish: Bødker 1957: 94 no. 951.
Absence of a 'star' sign from the Indus script: Brice 1970a: 28.
The Sumerian 'star' sign: Driver 1976: 37.
Star as distinguishing feature of god in Near Eastern art: Porada 1971.
Star as distinguishing feature of god in Harappan art: Parpola 1984; cf. Franke-Vogt 1991 (1992): 1, 78.

§ 10.2

Earlier versions: Parpola 1980a: 34; 1984b; 1988a: 119f.
Star originally the attribute of An: Ebeling 1932.
The Harappan style cylinder seal with 'Proto-Śiva': Corbiau 1936; *prism from Mohenjo-daro*: Franke-Vogt 1991 (1992): 1, 89–90.
Fish pair on Tamil coins: Kiruṣṇamūrtti 1986; *in Indian religions*: Höltker 1944: 16–17; Liebert 1976: 176.
Enki: Ebeling 1938; Jacobsen 1970; 1976; Kramer and Maier 1989.
'Proto-Śiva': V. S. Agrawala 1984b: 60; Aiyappan 1939; Banerjea 1956: 159–60; During Caspers 1985d: 70–2; 1989; Eliade 1969: 355–6; Franke-Vogt 1991 (1992): 1, 78–82; Gonda 1965: 28–9; Hiltebeitel 1978; Hopkins and Hiltebeitel 1987: 221–3; Jayakar 1980: 50; Mackay 1938: 1, 334–9; Marshall 1931b: 52–6; Schrader 1934; Srinivasan 1975–6; 1983; 1984; Sullivan 1964: 119–20.
'Man' sign: Parpola 1981a (1984a): § 26; Parpola et al. 1970: 12f.
*Proto-Dravidian *āḷ / *āṇ: DEDR* 399; Pfeiffer 1972: 23 no. 91; *TL* 1: 254a; Zvelebil 1970: 134–5 (PDr **ḷ / *ṇ* alternation).
Varuṇa: see under § 8.4.
Makara / nākra / śi(ṁ)śumāra: Artola 1977: 1–12; Coomaraswamy 1931: II, 47–56; Darian 1976; Edgerton 1959; Hoffmann 1975: 1, 107f.; Lüders 1942: 61–81; Zimmer 1879: 96f.
Matsyendranātha: Eliade 1969: 307–18, 421–2; Locke 1980; Tucci 1963 (thanks to A. Padoux for this reference).
Pradyumna shrine at Besnagar: Thapliyal 1983: 74.
Fish as a symbol of fertility: Pischel 1905.
The seven apkallus of Mesopotamia and the Seven Sages of India: Mitchiner 1982: 268–9; Reiner 1961.
Fish and the deluge myth in India and Mesopotamia: Heras 1953: 411–39; Kramer 1969: 42–4; Kramer and Maier 1989: 128–34, 159–69; Mitchiner 1982: 72, 303; Shastri 1950; Winternitz 1901: 268–9.

§ 10.3

Earlier versions: Parpola 1980a: 35–7; 1981a (1984a): § 30; Parpola et al. 1969a: 43 (fish and pot).
Harappan tablets and the hypothesis of fish offerings, possibly to the alligator: Hrozný 1942: 52–3.
Tank of sacred crocodiles near Karachi: Brunton 1939: 103–4; *crocodile as a tribal god in south Gujarat*: Fischer and Shah 1971.
Mesopotamian fish offerings: Buren 1948; Civil 1961; Ebeling 1957; Salonen 1970; Unger 1938; Wright 1991.
Nepali rituals of the goddess Durgā involving fish in a vase or basket: Toffin 1981: 65–6.
Trees and 'fish water': Meyer 1933.

§ 10.4

Earlier versions: Parpola 1975a; 1976a; 1980a 24–5; 1981a (1984a): § 17; 1986a: 413f.; 1988a: 123f.; Parpola et al. 1969a: 44; 1969b: 35.
Fish in Harappan economy: Belcher 1992.
Hypothesis of fish rations: Kinnier Wilson 1974; 1984; 1986; 1987; *criticism*: Burrow 1975b; Sollberger 1976; Zvelebil 1977d; cf. also Gadd and Smith 1931: 412; Thomas 1932: 460 ('despite the numerals abundant on them they [the Indus seals] were not labels denoting particular substances and amounts as is proved by the fact that they were for the most part elaborately carved on stone').
Astral interpretations of the 'number' + 'fish' signs (see also chapter 15): Gurov 1968: 34; 1970: 63f., 80; Gurov and Katenina 1967: 176f.; Heras 1953: 84, 100, 127f.; Knorozov in: *Predvaritel'noe* 1965: 51 (in English: Zide and Zvelebil 1976: 59); Knorozov et al. 1981: 93; Mahadevan 1970: 179ff., 255f.; *Proto-Indica*: 1968: 34; Shevoroshkin 1973: 86–7.
Doubled 'fish' sign and Proto-Dravidian min-min: DEDR 4876; Gurov 1968: 43f.; Shevoroshkin 1973: 87; Zide and Zvelebil 1970b: 957.

§ 10.5

Earlier versions: Parpola 1975a: 194; 1981a (1984a): § 18; 1988a: 120f.; Parpola et al. 1969b: 19f.; 1970: 20; cf. Shevoroshkin 1973: 87.
Caucasian 'fish' = 'star': Bouda 1955–6: 142 no. 13; *Lezgi:* Talibov and Gadžiev 1966; I thank Sir Harold Bailey for kindly checking the Caucasian evidence.
Jackal divides the fish caught by two otters: Bødker 1957: 39 no. 297.
*Proto-Dravidian *pacV (*payV) 'to divide': DEDR* 3936; Zvelebil 1970: 115; *'green': DEDR* 3821; Janert and Subramanian 1973: 142; Zvelebil 1970: 70; 1973a: 42; *'boy, child': DEDR* 3939; Zvelebil 1970: 70.
Canaanite child offerings and the morning star: Maag 1961: 583f.
'Roof' interpretation: Brown 1959: pl. 8 (roof types in early historical India); Hrozný 1941: 225 ('Dachlein'); Jaritz 1981: 118 ('eine Art Zirkumflex in Form eines Firstdaches'); Meriggi 1934: 215 ('Dach').
*Proto-Dravidian *vay- / *vey- / *mey- 'roof':* DEDR 5532; Krishnamurti 1961: 497; Parpola 1988a: 124 n. 3; Pfeiffer 1972: 50 no. 308, 98 no. 725, 114 no. 912.
*Proto-Dravidian *may- 'black': DEDR* 5101; Janert and Subramanian 1973: 146; Pfeiffer 1972: 58 no. 365.
*Proto-Dravidian *v- / *m- alternation:* Pfeiffer 1972: 114; Zvelebil 1970: 125–8, 157.
*Proto-Dravidian *-a- / *-e- alternation before *-y:* Pfeiffer 1972: 45 no. 277; Zvelebil 1970: 71f.
Saturn and turtle: Gail 1980; Pal and Bhattacharyya 1969: 47, 67.
Ominous character of Saturn: Negelein 1928: 245f.

Chapter 11

Astronomy in ancient civilizations: Bernal 1969; Bray 1968: 163ff.; Ginzel 1906; Hodson 1974; Nilsson 1920; Leach 1954; Steward 1955: 194ff.

§ 11.1

Earlier versions: Parpola 1975a: 194f.; 1980a: 26–7; Parpola et al. 1969b: 8–20.

Planetary worship in South Asia: Banerjea 1956: 429, 443–5; Bhattacharya 1974: 117–21; Th. Bloch 1896: 4–7; Burgess 1904; Diehl 1956: 197–211, 289–304; Eilers 1976; Fleet 1912b; Gail 1980; Gopinatha Rao 1914: I (2), 318–22; Kane 1958: 5 (1): 493–5, 525, 569ff.; 1962: 5 (2): 748–56; Kaye 1920 (p. 73: the Kumaoni Paddhati quoted); 1924: 103–17; Kirfel 1920: 33, 141f., 278ff.; Mallmann 1963: 81–94, 234; Mitra 1965; Pal and Bhattacharyya 1969; Pingree 1965; Renou and Filliozat 1947: I, 491; Scherer 1953: 84–8; Tucci 1929.

§ 11.2

Earlier versions: Parpola 1975a: 195; 1980a: 27–8; 1988a: 119, 123f.

Assumption of Harappan astronomy: Ashfaque 1977; 1989; Maula 1984 (the identification of 'calendar stones' is controversial); Ruben 1952: 130; 1954: 66–8; 1971: IV, 24ff.; Wanzke 1987.

Orientation of Mohenjo-daro: Wanzke 1987.

Indian stellar astronomy and time-reckoning: T. Bhattacharyya 1953–5; Deppert 1976: 174ff.; Faddegon 1926; Filliozat 1962; Ginzel 1906: I, 70–7, 310–402; Jacobi 1895; 1896; 1909; 1910; Kane 1958: 5 (1), 463–718; Kaye 1924; Kirfel 1920: 33–6, 138–41, 190, 280ff.; Krick 1982: 9–47; Lenz 1939; Macdonell and Keith 1912: I, 409–31; Merrey 1982; Needham 1959: 246ff.; Oldenberg 1894; 1895; Pingree 1981; 1982; Renou and Filliozat 1953: II, 177–94, 720–38; Scherer 1953: 149ff.; Thibaut 1899; Weber 1861–2 (fundamental work); 1863; 1865–8; 1888; Whitney 1864; 1874b; 1896.

Vedic fire-altar of bricks: Converse 1974; Krick 1982; Staal 1983; Weber 1873.

Chinese astronomy and its relation to Indian: Ginzel 1906: I, 70–7, 450–97; Needham 1959: III, 246ff.; 1974; Saussure 1922: 265ff.

BMAC and Ordos seals: Amiet 1986; Biscione 1985; Jettmar 1983c.

Mesopotamian astronomy and time-reckoning: Englund 1988; Ginzel 1906: I, 78–85, 107–49; Hunger 1977; Jeremias 1929: 270ff.; Pingree 1982; Waerden 1968 (64–79: MUL.APIN); Weidner 1957–71.

§ 11.3

Sacred fires, asterisms, spring and due east: Filliozat 1962; Krick 1982: 9–47; Wayman 1965.

Viṣuvat as summer solstice: e.g. Jamison 1991: 278–80.

Vedic orientation methods: Pingree 1981: 6, 52; Yano 1986: 17–18, 28.

The Indus art motif of intersecting circles: Dumarçay 1966.

The birth of Kārttikeya: P.K. Agrawala 1967: 4, 26–7, 54; Deppert 1976: 174ff.; Kramrisch 1981: 40–3, 370–4; O'Flaherty 1973.

Bekurā: Parpola 1979: 179; 1981a (1984a): § 20; Weber 1862: 274–5.

Old Tamil vaikuṟu-mīṉ: Akam 17 (*TL* 6: 3850b); Burrow and Emeneau 1984: nos. 5554 (PDr **vay-* / **vey-*: Pfeiffer 1972: 30, no. 148) and 710 (PDr **uṯV*; Proto-Dravidian **-ṯ-*: Zvelebil 1970: 94ff.); Singaravelu 1966: 106 (*vaikal-mīṉ*).

§ 11.4

More extensive and fully documented earlier version of this section: Parpola 1990a (cf. also 1980a: 26).

Indian onomastics: V. S. Agrawala 1963: 182–93; Emeneau 1978; Gonda 1970b; 1980a: 374f.; Hilka 1910; Hillebrandt 1897: 45ff.; Kane 1938; 1941: 2 (1), 238–54; Pandey 1969: 78–85; Velze 1938; Walker 1968: II, 116–21.

Natal horoscope: Hilka 1910: 39f., 42ff.; Kane 1958: 5 (1), 627ff.

Sindhi proper names: Gidwani 1981.

Combinations of planets in the Mahābhārata: Sörensen 1925: 38, 168f.

Dual deities and divine triads in the Veda: Gonda 1974; 1976.

Chapter 12

More extensive and fully documented earlier version of this chapter: Parpola 1985b (partly summarized in Parpola 1985a; earlier version: Parpola 1980a: 33–4).

§ 12.1

Trefoil: During Caspers 1970–1: 114–16; 1971; C. J. Gadd and E. Mackay in Marshall 1931a: I, 356f., n. 2: Parpola et al. 1969a: 44; Wheeler 1968: 87.

The 'priest-king' and other Indus human statuettes (see also under § 14.4): Ardeleanu-Jansen 1984; 1991; During Caspers 1985a; 1985b.

Indus bull with trefoils: Ardeleanu-Jansen 1989.

Mesopotamian 'sky garment' of the gods and kings: Eisler 1910; Oppenheim 1949.

Varuṇa: see under § 8.4.

Tārpya garment: Parpola 1985: 44–75, 91–100.

Evil: darkness: death: Varuṇa's fetters: embryonic covers and their removal: Jamison 1991: 183–211; Rodhe 1946.

*Proto-Dravidian *cul-ay / *cull-V / *cūl 'fireplace made of (three) stones': DEDR* 2857; Turner 1966: no. 4879; Zvelebil 1970: 52 (PDr **uCay*>**oCay*).

VCC: V̄C in Proto-Dravidian roots: Zvelebil 1970: 184ff.; 1973a: 45.

*Proto-Dravidian *cūl 'pregnancy': DEDR* 2733.

Burushaski śi: Lorimer 1938: III, s.v.

§ 12.2

Hypothesis of Harappan phallic cult: During Caspers 1987; Marshall 1931a: I; *criticism*: Dales 1968; 1984; S. R. Rao 1991: 306; Srinivasan 1975–6; 1983; 1984.

Sexual intercourse on the amulet from Mohenjo-daro (fig. 12.9): Franke-Vogt 1991 (1992): 96; Parpola 1985: 102–3.

Liṅga cult and the sacrificial pillar: Beck 1981: Biardeau 1989a;

1989b; Briggs 1938 (124 and pl. 11: wooden liṅgas of Puri); Hiltebeitel 1991: chapters 5–6; Kramrisch 1977; 1981: 119–22, 153–96 (pillar of flames: 158–60), 241–9; Mitterwallner 1984; O'Flaherty 1973; Parpola 1985: 101–40, 158–62; Srinivasan 1984; Wayman 1987.

Bilva: Gonda 1970: 112; Gupta 1971: 21ff.; Majupuria and Joshi 1989: 85–92.

Holi: Crooke 1914.

Ritual fireplaces, in Kalibangan: Lal 1979a; 1984: 57–8; B.K. Thapar 1973; 1975; 1985; *in Lothal:* S. R. Rao 1979: I, 216–18.

Seven Sages: Mitchiner 1982.

Ursa Major, the Pole Star, and pillar: Brereton 1991; Scherer 1953: 134–6.

l- vs. ñ- / n-: Burrow 1943–6c: 615; Zvelebil 1970: 143.

*Proto-Dravidian *ñi(ṅ)g- / *ni(ṅ)g- (intr.) 'to rise, become erect' / *ñikk- / *nikk- (tr.) 'to raise, erect': DEDR* 2922, 3662, 3665, 3730.

Chapter 13

Earlier versions (with documentation): Parpola 1975a; 1990b.

Further evidence not touched upon here (kinnara): Parpola 1983; cf. also 1988b: 251–63; 1992b.

Murukaṉ / Skanda: P.K. Agrawala 1967; V. S. Agrawala 1970: 69–103; Chatterjee 1970; Clothey 1978; Filliozat 1973; Gros 1968; Hopkins 1915; Zvelebil 1973; 1976; 1977b; 1977c; 1981; 1984.

§ 13.1

Earlier versions: Parpola 1976a: 150f.; 1990b; Parpola et al. 1970: 27.

Old Tamil literature: Hart 1975; Subrahmanian 1966a; 1966b; Zvelebil 1973b; 1974b; 1975.

Proto-Dravidian muruku 'youth': DEDR 4978.

Proto-Dravidian muruku 'ring, bangle': DEDR 4979 (evidently from Proto-Dravidian **mur-V* 'to curve, bend, turn round, twist', *DEDR* 4977).

Pictorial identification of *as 'two rings':* Zide 1973: 353 (as an example of rebus, to express English 'touring').

Folk religion relating to bangles and pierced stones: Crooke 1896; 1920; 1926; Hartland 1920.

Tibetan symbol of royal ear-rings: Dagyab 1977: II, 30.

Harappan inscribed stoneware bangles: Dales 1992a: 67–8; Franke 1984; Franke-Vogt 1989; 1991 (1992): I, 55; II, table 20: 112–13; Halim and Vidale 1984; Hunter 1932: 482 (the sign depicted is in fact that of 'intersecting circles'); Vidale 1990.

Harappan bangle types and their use: Kenoyer 1991.

Possible temple with a railing for a sacred tree in Mohenjo-daro: During Caspers 1990; Jansen 1985.

Fireplace of three human heads connected with the worship of the Goddess (cf. §§ 14.3–4): Silva 1955: 580–1.

*Proto-Dravidian *peḷḷ- / *piḷḷ- 'young, child': DEDR* 4198; Pfeiffer 1972: 45–6 no. 281.

Parji pirca 'squirrel': DEDR 4189.

§ 13.2

Earlier versions: Parpola 1976a: 142, 155f.; 1981b: 82–3; 1988a: 121f.

Complete concordance to Old Tamil Caṅkam literature: Lehmann and Malten 1992.

*Proto-Dravidian (?) *vēḷ 'king, god': DEDR* 5545; Pfeiffer 1972: 47 no. 290.

*Proto-Dravidian *vēḷ / *vēṇ '(to) desire': DEDR* 5528; Krishnamurti 1961: 496–7 no. 1201; Zvelebil 1970: 134–5 (PDr *ḷ / *ṇ alternation).

Tamil Vēḷ 'Desire' = Muruku: Zvelebil 1977b: 229.

*Proto-Dravidian *vēḷ 'to offer, to marry': DEDR* 5544; Krishnamurti 1961: 497 no. 1203 (< **vē-ḷ-*, from **vē-* 'to burn, boil').

*Proto-Dravidian *veḷ 'white': DEDR* 5496; Janert and Subramanian 1973: 144–5; Krishnamurti 1961: 449 no. 922, 495–6 nos. 1192–3, 1195–6; 1963: 560; Pfeiffer 1972: 28–9 no. 142.

*Proto-Dravidian *veḷi 'outside; (intervening) space': DEDR* 5498; Krishnamurti 1961: 495 nos. 1193–4.

§ 13.3

Earlier versions: Parpola 1975a: 196; 1976a: 138f.; 1981a (1984a): § 21; Parpola et al. 1969a: 44; 1969b: 28; 1970: 39f.

Pictorial identification of the 'crab' sign: e.g. Jaritz 1981: 121; Knorozov 1976: 105.

Planets 'seize' people with invisible nooses of sickness: Negelein 1928: 271.

Graha: Böhtlingk and Roth, s.v.; Macdonell and Keith 1912, s.v.

*Proto-Dravidian *kōḷ 'seizure', *koḷ / *koṇṭ- < *koḷ-nt- 'to seize, take': DEDR* 2151; Gurov 1970: 78, Krishnamurti 1961: 337 no. 320; Pfeiffer 1972: 52 no. 319; Zvelebil 1970: 134–5 (PDr *ḷ / *ṇ alternation).

Rāhu: Caland 1926.

§ 13.4

Earlier versions: Parpola 1975a: 199–202; 1976a: 138f.; 1981a (1984a): § 22.

Horned archer: During Caspers 1989; Franke-Vogt 1991 (1992): I, 83; Mackay 1931a: II, 399; 1938: I, 366.

Harappan horned masks of a male god: During Caspers 1985c: 277–8 and pl. 6–7; 1985d: 67; 1989: 228–30; cf. also the horned figurines and the 'horned man' of the Indus script (fig. 5.1 no. 7; Mackay 1934: 254, quoted under § 7.2).

*Proto-South Dravidian *kōḷi 'grasping fig': DEDR* 2254.

*Proto-Dravidian *koḷ 'to take, seize' (see under § 13.3) and 'to hit, shoot, kill': DEDR* 2152.

*Proto-South Dravidian (?) *kōḷ 'lamenting': DEDR* 2252.

Rudra: Arbman 1922; Charpentier 1909; Dandekar 1953; Deppert 1977; Gonda 1960; 1970; 1980b; Kramrisch 1981 (archer: 27–50, 511–12); Wüst 1955.

Śatarudriya; Rudra-Skanda as the god of robbers: P. K. Agrawala 1967: 8–10, 18–22, 73f.; George 1991; Gonda 1979.

*Rudra < *Rudhra:* Mayrhofer 1965: III, 66f.

Redness of Murukaṉ: Janert and Subramanian 1973: 150; Zvelebil 1977d: 5–6, 11.

§ 13.5

Earlier version: Parpola 1990b.

Skanda-graha: Filliozat 1937.

Goat-faced Skanda / Naigameṣa: P. K. Agrawala 1967: 15f., 34, 50–2; V. S. Agrawala 1937; 1970: 72, 78; A. K. Bhattacharyya 1953; Chatterjee 1970: 5f.; Deglurkar 1988–9; Dresden 1941: 173–4; Filliozat 1937; Rolland 1975 (1977): 26; Winternitz 1895.

Chapter 14 In this chapter are incorporated parts of a forthcoming larger study on the origins of the cult of Durgā / Śākta Tantrism in South Asia; its early version (Parpola 1984d) has been partially published in Parpola 1988b: 258–60 and in Parpola 1992b.

Harappan goddess worship: Hopkins and Hiltebeitel 1987; Kinsley 1986: 212–20; Marshall 1931a: I, 48ff.

§ 14.1

Earlier versions: Parpola 1975a: 202f.; 1976a: 139–44; 1980b; 1981a (1984a): § 23; 1988a: 122–4.

Sāvitrī legend and vrata: A. H. Allen 1901; Brough 1951: 22–69; Buitenen 1975: II, 760–78; Crooke 1926: 407; Dange 1987: 59–66; Gupte 1906; Hauer 1927: 238f.; Kane 1958: 5 (1): 91–4.

Sanskrit (and Dr) vaṭa 'banyan': <Dr vaṭam 'rope' (*DEDR* 5220) also in Masica 1991: 38; cf. Uhlenbeck in Mayrhofer 1976: III, 129 (reference to the air roots); Turner 1966: 654 nos. 11211–12. Maclean (1893: 72a) derives *vaṭa* 'banyan' <Sanskrit *vr̥ta-* 'round; circle' ('from its circumference'). Tedesco (1947: 90–1) derives *vaṭa-* 'rope' and Pāli *vaṭa-rukkha* 'banyan as the *turned* tree' from Prakrit **vaṭṭa-* <Sanskrit past participle *vr̥tta-* 'turned, twisted'. But in Marathi, *baṭa* means 'a quantity of fibres of hemp etc. as clotted together, or as lying in preparation for being rolled into yarn. Hence applied to a disorderly tress or a clotted lock of hair' (Molesworth 1857: 561b); thus *vaṭa* parallels Sanskrit *rajju* and *jaṭā*, which both mean 'air root of banyan' and 'clotted lock of hair of an ascetic'; the banyan tree with its air roots is compared to Śiva as the great ascetic with clotted locks of hair.

*Proto-(South) Dravidian *vaṭa 'north': DEDR* 5218.

Marriage rituals (inclusive of showing the Pole Star and / or Arundhatī, and of the application of the forehead mark discussed in § 14.4): Chatterjee 1978; Gonda 1980; Pandey 1969; Saraswati 1977; Winternitz 1892: 77–9.

Pole Star as 'firm': Liebert 1969.

Jaṭilā: Hopkins 1915: 182; Negelein 1926: 905.

Air roots of the banyan; figs and their cult (also for § 14.3): Bosch 1960: 65–75 (the celestial fig); Charpentier 1930 (banyan and human sacrifices); Chaṭṭopādhyāya 1930; Chaudhuri 1943; Coomaraswamy 1938; Emeneau 1949 (jaṭila and jaṭā: 363f.); Geldner 1889 (banyan in R̥S 1,24); Maclean 1893: III, 72f.; Majupuria and Joshi 1989: 72–84; Volchok [1965] 1976: 74–6; Walker 1968: II, 357–8; *sacred figs in places of pilgrimage:* Ensink 1974 (1975): 63; Gode 1961: I, 374–83.

Ketu and Ketavaḥ: Jamison 1991; Negelein 1928.

Tree of the north: Kirfel 1920: 93f., 175.

*Proto-Dravidian *nāl '4': DEDR* 3655; Shanmugam 1971: 151–4.

*Proto-(South) Dravidian *ñāl 'to hang': DEDR* 2912.

Proto-Dravidian ñ- / n- / ø- alternation: Burrow 1943–6c; Zvelebil 1970: 135ff.

*Proto-Dravidian *āl 'banyan': DEDR* 382.

*Proto-Dravidian *akal 'to spread': DEDR* 8; Krishnamurti 1961: 277 no. 1 (**ay-al-*).

**Akal as etymology of āl 'banyan':* Maclean 1893: III, 72b; *TL* I: 246a.

§ 14.2

Earlier versions: Parpola 1980a: 28–32; 1984b; 1988b: 251–64; 1992b.

Contest motif / lion–bull combat: Amiet 1956; 1972; 1980a; Boehmer 1965; Collon 1987; During Caspers 1970–1: 111–12; Franke-Vogt 1991 (1992): I, 90–1; Hartner 1965; Kuz'mina 1987.

Khafajeh bowl (fig. 14.13): Smith 1937.

'Proto-Śiva' and buffalo: Aiyappan 1939; Hiltebeitel 1978; 1980.

Harappan buffalo-god: Franke-Vogt 1991 (1992): I, 57 n. 113, 80 n. 194, 82; Pathak 1992; Shinde 1991a; 1991b; 1992.

Vessel from Lewan (fig. 14.18): Allchin and Knox 1981: 243.

Water buffalo in Mesopotamia: Boehmer 1965; 1975; Collon 1982; Franke-Vogt 1991 (1992): I, 68.

Harappan buffalo sacrifice: Fábri 1937; Franke-Vogt 1991 (1992): I, 91–2; Hiltebeitel 1978.

Durgā Mahiṣāsuramardinī and her cult: P. K. Agrawala 1984; Biardeau 1981a; 1981b; 1989; Divakaran 1984; Erndl 1987; Harle 1963; Hiltebeitel 1978; 1988–91; Jacobi 1912; Kane 1958: 5 (1), 154–94; Kinsley 1986; Kooij 1972; Shulman 1976; 1980; Sircar 1967; Stietencron 1983; Tiwari 1985; Toffin 1981.

Kalibangan cylinder seal and Durgā / Kālī: Franke-Vogt 1991 (1992): I, 95–6; Parpola 1970: 94 (last paragraph); cf. Hiltebeitel 1978: 777; *archaeological context of the seal:* Lal 1975a: 147–8.

Harappan hairstyle: During Caspers 1979: 133–5; Franke-Vogt 1991 (1992): I, 78 n. 175, 95.

Inanna-Ishtar: Balz-Cochois 1992; Hörig 1979; Wolkstein and Kramer 1983.

'Maṇḍala' of Dashly-3: Brentjes 1981; 1983.

Śākta Tantrism: Banerji 1978; Bharati 1965; Bhattacharyya 1974; 1977; Dehejia 1986; Goudriaan and Gupta 1981; Nagaswamy 1982; Rawson 1973; Snellgrove 1987.

Vrātyas, Vrātyastomas, Mahāvrata, horse sacrifice: Bhawe 1939; Biswas 1955; Charpentier 1909; Dumont 1927; Falk 1986; Fišer 1966; Hauer 1927; Heesterman 1962; Horsch 1966; O'Flaherty 1980; Parpola 1973: 34–58; 1976b; 1983; 1988b: 251–64; 1992b; Rolland 1973.

Chanhujo-daro seal with bison and priestess (fig. 14.32): F. R. Allchin 1985; Franke-Vogt 1991 (1992): I, 96 n. 302; Mode 1959: 69–71; Parpola 1980a: 69–70; 1983: 56; 1992b: 300; S. Parpola et al. 1977: 162–3.

§ 14.3

Earlier versions: Parpola 1980a: 10, 70; 1985b: 215f.; 1992a; 1992b: 290.

'Fig deity' seal and its variants: Franke-Vogt 1991 (1992): I, 96–8; Hiltebeitel 1978: 779–80, 789; Jayakar 1980: 55–6; Mackay 1938: I, 39, 232, 335–9; II, 94 no. 430; 1948: 58–9.

Harappan hairstyle: see under § 14.2.

Harappan and later Indian tree cult (on figs specifically see under § 14.1): Coomaraswamy 1928–31; Fergusson 1873; Franke-Vogt 1991 (1992): I, 102–5; Majupuria and Joshi 1989; Viennot 1954.

Tutelary tree of Old Tamil kings: Hart 1975: 15–17; Singaravelu 1966: 89ff., 161; Subrahmanian 1966b: 85, 131ff.

Yakṣiṇīs, Yoginīs, Ḍākinīs and 'mothers' as epiphanies of Durgā dwelling in trees: Coomaraswamy 1928: I, 9–10; Dange 1987: II, 686ff.; Eliade 1969: 345–8.

Ṣaṣṭhī: V. S. Agrawala 1970: 77ff., 90–5; Härtel 1987; Mahapatra 1972: 144.

Bana-Durgā and Jaya-Durgā: Chakravarti 1930; Chaudhuri 1945; Dange 1986–90; Eliade 1969: 387–8; Mitra 1922; 1931.

Kālī worship under the banyan in Bengal: Majumdar 1923.

Altar under the sacred tree: Coomaraswamy 1928: I, 17; Eliade 1969: 345–6.

Human sacrifice to Durgā: Silva 1955: 579–83; Vogel 1930–2.

Śarabha-dhvaja of the planet Mars: Gopinatha Rao 1914: I (2), app. A; Thapliyal 1983: 74.

Markhor of the 'fig deity' seal as a sacrificial animal: Fairservis 1975: 275; Hiltebeitel 1978: 780; Mackay 1938: I, 63–4.

Seven mothers: Dhavalikar 1963; Harper 1977; Jayakar 1980: 55–6; Volchok 1970: 42–4.

§ 14.4

Earlier version: Parpola 1992a.

'Dot-in-fish' sign of the 'fig deity' seal: cf. Jayakar 1980: 55 ('A fish forming part of the script is sharply defined . . . The size of the fish is out of proportion to the rest of the script and within the fish is a dot, the *bindu*. The fish is a recurrent female symbol in the Indian tradition of the aphrodisiacal and was later identified with *bhaga* [i.e. the female organ], as the sexual, the female divinity; the *bindu*, the dot within the fish is the *yoni*, the eye of love, the mark of the Goddess, a symbol of the female generative organ, the doorway to the secret places, to the mysteries of creation.')

Venus as the star of the Goddess: see refs. on Inanna-Ishtar under § 14.2.

Tārā: Beyer 1973; Kinsley 1986: 165–72; Sircar 1967: 105–68; cf. also Erndl 1987: 161–217 ('Story of Queen Tārā' related during an all-night vigil while worshipping the Goddess in the form of a flame).

Rohiṇī star: T. Bhattacharyya 1953–5; Deppert 1977: 186ff., 265ff.; Kirfel 1920: 35–6, 138, 281; Krick 1982: 22–7; O'Flaherty 1973: 93ff.; Weber 1862: II, 276ff., 368–9.

Army worships the Goddess at the rise of the first star on the vijayadaśamī day: Biardeau 1981b: 226; *Dharmasindhu*: Kane 1958: 5 (1), 190; Kinsley 1986: 107; *northeast*: also Varāhamihira, Bṛhatsaṁhitā 44,3; cf. also Silva 1955: 579 (lights burned through the whole night following the 10th day of Durgā's yearly feast as a sign for the warriors to assemble), and Erndl as quoted above (on Tārā).

The sun as the original husband of Rohiṇī (Tārā): cf. also Jamison's (1991: 288–300) forceful identification of the myth of Prajāpati's incest and punishment with that of the sun's punishment by Svarbhānu (= Agni = Rudra). The latter myth explains the origin of sunspots and (*pace* Jamison) of solar eclipse as resulting from a sin committed by the sun.

The śakula / śāla and rohita fishes: Chandy 1989; Hora 1952: 1955.

*Proto-Dravidian *poṭṭu 'drop, spot, round mark worn on the forehead': DEDR* 4492.

*Proto-Dravidian *poṭṭu 'a kind of fish' (Gondi: 'rohita fish'): DEDR* 4498 + *TL* 5: 2915a (Tamil *poṭṭu-k-kārai* 'a kind of fish'); Gundert 1871–2: II, 710b (Malayalam *poṭṭan* 'a fish').

Forehead mark: Ayyar 1925: 4–6; Bray 1913 (Brahui marriage); Dubois 1906: 333–5 (*inter alia, poṭṭu*); Kane 1941: II (1), 672–5; Leslie 1989: 96–101; Moor 1810; Roy 1972 (Oraon); Shah n.d.

Marriage rituals: see under § 14.1.

The forehead ornament of the Harappan priest-king: cf. Oppenheim 1949: 173 n. 4 (a large golden 'front rosette' (*aiar pāni*) was held by means of a fillet above the forehead of the divine beings and kings in ancient Mesopotamia); *Mediterranean (Greek) parallels to the 'third eye on the forehead' of Indian gods:* Kirfel 1955: 173; cf. also Sarma and Singh 1967: 783–4 (a male human head of terracotta from Kalibangan: 'the receding forehead contains two roughly incised horizontal lines probably depicting the wrinkles of the forehead or "Vibhuti" marks (i.e. the horizontal lines made with sacred ashes, constituting the Śaiva forehead mark)').

Fishes in marriage: Crooke 1926; Marglin 1985.

Rohiṇī as virgin coming of age: see also M. R. Allen 1986: 67–8.

*Proto-Dravidian *poṭṭV 'belly, stomach, womb, pregnancy': DEDR* 4494.

*Indo-Aryan *ṭVp- 'drop, spot on the forehead':* Marglin 1985: 53 (Oriya *sindūra-ṭapā* 'dot made with vermilion on the forehead of married ladies'); Turner 1966, no. 5444.

*Proto-Dravidian *poṭṭu 'to burst or fall noisily': DEDR* 4490.

Fructifying first drop in Bengal: Mahapatra 1972: 111–12.

Fish-shaped Apsaras: Meyer 1930: 223–4.

Expiation for spilled drops of Soma: Caland and Henry 1906: I, 169–70 § 134b.

Forehead mark of the sacrificial victim: Biardeau 1989b: 24 (*poṭṭu*); Silva 1955: 582–3, 587.

Forehead mark on bull figurines: Fairservis 1956: 226 and fig. 18 (Quetta Valley, Site Q8, DS III Levels); C. Jarrige: personal communication 1991 (Mehrgarh VII; Nausharo ID); Santini 1990: 443 and figs. 20–2 (Shahr-i Sokhta).

Taurus and Aldebaran: Hartner 1965.

Forehead mark made of the blood of the human victim by warriors on the 10th day of Durgā's yearly festival: Kane 1958: 5 (1), 166–7; Silva 1955: 579.

Mitramiśra's quotation from Vāmana-Paddhati: Khiste and Hośinga 1930: 53.

Mīnākṣī: Brown 1947; Shulman 1980: 206ff.

Subjugation (vaśīkaraṇa): Goudriaan 1978: 310–33 (311–12: 'names of female divine powers as personifications of subjugation', 317ff.: by means of the forehead mark); Kooij 1972: 92–3.

Religious symbol as multireferential: Turner 1967.

Chapter 15

Earlier versions: Parpola 1981a (1984a): § 1; 1986a: 414; 1988a: 124 and 132, fig. 5.

Cuneiform tablet with impression of a Dilmun seal (fig. 15.1): Buchanan 1965; 1967; Hallo and Buchanan 1965. There is a possibility that 'the Sumerians, with their highly philological tendencies, have left somewhere a vocabulary [of the Indus language] or a bilingual' (Thomas 1932: 461, paraphrasing Gadd and Smith 1931: 406; cf. also Fábri 1934: 56; Langdon in Hunter 1934: xi–xii).

Scientific problem compared to a crossword puzzle: Bunge 1967: 1, 196–7; *decipherment in particular*: Gordon 1971: 25 ('Guesses . . . are necessary, but they cannot be off the top of one's head; to be successful, they must reckon with the realities, or at least probabilities, of the text to be deciphered. Even then most guesses are wrong, so that a prime quality in the crypt-analyst or decipherer is flexibility. Wrong guesses are usually exposed as incorrect by the fact that they lead to impossible combinations when applied elsewhere in the texts to be deciphered. But it is also necessary to follow through with the truth if a successful decipherment is to be achieved').

South Asian cultural history: see under § 1.1.

Agreement on 'fish' signs: Shevoroshkin 1973: 86–7.

References

Ancient authors and works

With the exception of some references to authors listed under 'Modern authors' (mainly relating to the translations quoted), the editions and translations of the ancient texts will not be described; the reader is referred to bibliographical information available in Emeneau 1935 for most of the texts marked (in parentheses) as being written in 'Sanskrit' or 'Prakrit'; in Dandekar 1946–85, Gonda 1975–7 and Renou 1931 for texts characterized as 'Sanskrit: Veda'; in Rocher 1986 for 'Sanskrit: Purāṇa' texts; in Goudriaan and Gupta 1981 for 'Sanskrit: Tantra' texts; in *TL* and Zvelebil 1974 and 1975 for 'Tamil' texts (NB also relatively modern Tamil texts cited after *TL* in the appendix are listed here rather than in the following section); in Schlerath 1968 for 'Avesta' texts; and in Karttunen 1989, Lesky 1963 and Ziegler and Sontheimer 1975 for 'Greek' and 'Latin' texts. Texts better known by their titles are entered under these rather than under their authors.

Aelianus (Ailianós), *De natura animalium* (*Perì zṓiōn idiótētos*) (Greek)

Agni-Purāṇa (Sanskrit: Purāṇa)

Aiṅkuṟunūṟu (Tamil)

Aitareya-Āraṇyaka = AĀ (Sanskrit: Veda)

Aitareya Brāhmaṇa = AB (Sanskrit: Veda)

Akanāṉūṟu = Akam (Tamil)

Amara-kośa (Sanskrit)

Arrian (Arrianós), *Anabasis Alexandri et Indica* (Greek), ed. and trans. Brunt 1983

Atharvaveda(-Saṁhitā) = AS (Sanskrit: Veda), trans. Bloomfield 1897; Whitney 1905

Baudhāyana-Gṛhya-Pariśeṣa-Sūtra (Sanskrit: Veda)

Baudhāyana-Karmāntasūtra (Sanskrit: Veda)

Bhagavad-gītā (Sanskrit)

Bhāgavata-Purāṇa (Sanskrit: Purāṇa)

Bhartṛhari, *Śatakatrayam* (Sanskrit)

Bhaviṣya-Purāṇa (Sanskrit: Purāṇa)

Brahma-Purāṇa (Sanskrit: Purāṇa)

Brahmasiddhānta, *Śākalyasaṁhitā* (Sanskrit)

Brahmavaivarta-Purāṇa (Sanskrit: Purāṇa)

Bṛhad-Āraṇyaka-Upaniṣad = BĀU (Sanskrit: Veda)

Br̥haddevatā attributed to Śaunaka (Sanskrit: Veda), ed. and trans. Macdonell 1904
Cēntaṉ Tivākaram by Maṇṭalapuruṭar (alias Tivākaraṉ) (Tamil)
Cētu-purāṇa by Nirampa-v-aḻakiya Tēcikar (Tamil)
Cilappatikāram by Iḷaṅkō-v-aṭikaḷ (Tamil)
Ciṟupāṇāṟṟuppaṭai by Nattattaṉār (Tamil)
Cīvakacintāmaṇi by Tiruttakkatēvar (Tamil)
Curtius Rufus, Quintus, *History of Alexander* (Latin), ed. and trans. J. C. Rolfe. 2 vols. (Loeb Classical Library) London 1946
Cūṭāmaṇi-nikaṇṭu by Maṇṭalapuruṭaṉ (Tamil)
Daṇḍin, *Daśakumāracarita* (Sanskrit)
*Devī-Māhātmya (*in *Mārkeṇḍeya-Purāṇa)* (Sanskrit: Purāṇa)
Gobhila-Gr̥hyasūtra = GGS (Sanskrit: Veda)
Gopatha-Brāhmaṇa = GB (Sanskrit: Veda)
Gr̥hyāsaṁgraha (Sanskrit: Veda)
Hāla, *Sattasaī* (Prakrit)
Harivaṁśa (Sanskrit)
Hemacandra, *Triṣaṣṭiśalākāpuruṣacarita* (Sanskrit)
Hemādri, *Caturvargacintāmaṇi* (Sanskrit)
Hiraṇyakeśi-Gr̥hyasūtra = HGS (Sanskrit: Veda)
Hiraṇyakeśi-Śrautasūtra = HŚS (Sanskrit: Veda)
Homer (Hómēros), *Iliad (Iliás)* (Greek)
Odyssey (Odusseía) (Greek)
Ilakkaṇa viḷakkam by Vaittiyanāta Tēcikar (Tamil)
Jaiminīya-Brāhmaṇa = JB (Sanskrit: Veda)
Jaiminīya-Gr̥hyasūtra = JGS (Sanskrit: Veda), ed. and trans. Caland 1922
Jaiminīya-Śrautasūtra = JŚS (Sanskrit: Veda)
Jaiminīya-Upaniṣad-Brāhmaṇa = JUB (Sanskrit: Veda)
Jātaka (Prakrit), trans. Cowell 1895–1913
Jayākhya-Saṁhitā (Sanskrit)
Jyotiṣaratnamālā (Sanskrit)
Kalhaṇa, *Rājataraṅginī* (Sanskrit), trans. Stein 1900
Kālidāsa (1), *Kumārasaṁbhava* (Sanskrit)
Meghadūta (Sanskrit), ed. De 1957
Raghuvaṁśa (Sanskrit)
Kālidāsa (2), *Rātrilagnanirūpaṇa* (Sanskrit), cited after Böhtlingk and Roth 1852–75
Kālikā-Purāṇa = KP (Sanskrit: Tantra / Purāṇa), trans. (in part) Kooij 1972
Kalittokai (Tamil)
Kallāṭam by Kallāṭaṉār (Tamil)
Kalpasūtra (Kappasutta) by Bhadrabāhu (Prakrit)
Kampa-Rāmāyaṇam (Tamil)
Kantapurāṇam by Kacciyappa Civācārya (Tamil)
Kapiṣṭhala-Kaṭha-Saṁhitā = KapS (Sanskrit: Veda)
Kāṭhaka-Gr̥hyasūtra = KāṭhGS (Sanskrit: Veda)
Kaṭha-Saṁhitā = KS (Sanskrit: Veda)
Kathāsaritsāgara by Somadeva = KSS (Sanskrit)
Kātyāyana-Śrautasūtra = KŚS (Sanskrit: Veda)
Kātyāyana-Śulbasūtra (Sanskrit: Veda)
Kauśikasūtra (Sanskrit: Veda)
Kauṣītaki-Brāhmaṇa = KB (Sanskrit: Veda)
Kauṭilya, *Arthaśāstra* (Sanskrit), trans. Kangle 1965–72
Koṇṭal viṭu tūtu (Tamil)
Kṣemendra, *Samayamātr̥kā* (Sanskrit)
Kuriñcippāṭṭu by Kapilar (Tamil)
Kurukūrppaḷḷu by Catakōpa-p Pulavar (Tamil)
Lalitavistara (Sanskrit)
Lāṭyāyana-Śrautasūtra = LŚS (Sanskrit: Veda)
Mahābhārata = MBh (Sanskrit), crit. ed. Sukthankar et al. 1933–59; partial trans. Buitenen 1973–8
Mahānirvāṇa-Tantra (Sanskrit: Tantra)
Mahāvastu (Sanskrit)
Maitrāyaṇī Saṁhitā = MS (Sanskrit: Veda)
Maitrāyaṇī (= Maitrī) Upaniṣad (Sanskrit: Veda)
Mānava-Gr̥hyasūtra = MGS (Sanskrit: Veda), trans. Dresden 1941
Mānava-Śulbasūtra (Sanskrit: Veda)
Māṇikkavācakar, *Tirukkōvaiyār* (Tamil)
Maṇimēkalai by Cāttaṉār (Tamil)
Manu (= Manu-Smr̥ti = Mānava-Dharmaśātra) (Sanskrit), trans. Bühler 1886
Mārkaṇḍeya-Purāṇa (Sanskrit: Purāṇa)
Matsya-Purāṇa (Sanskrit: Purāṇa)
Maturaikkāñci by Māṅkuṭi Marutaṉār (Tamil)
Mitra Miśra, *Vīramitrodaya* (Sanskrit), ed. Pant 1913
Vitāṉamālai by Nārāyaṇacuvāmikaḷ (Tamil)
Naṟṟiṇai (Tamil)
Neminātha-carita (Nemināha-cariu) by Haribhadra (Prakrit)
Nonnos, *Dionysiaca* (Greek), ed. and trans. Rouse 1956–63
Nr̥siṁha Bhaṭṭa, *Vidhānamālā*, cited after Shah n.d.
Oṭṭakkuttār, *Takkayāka-p-paraṇi* (Tamil)
Padma-Purāṇa (Sanskrit: Purāṇa)
Pañcatantra (Sanskrit)
Pañcaviṁśa-Brāhmaṇa = PB (Sanskrit: Veda)
Pāṇini, *Aṣṭādhyāyī* (Sanskrit)
Paṟāḷaivināyakar paḷḷu by C. V. Jampuliṅkam Piḷḷai (Tamil)
Parāśara-Smr̥ti (Sanskrit)
Pāraskara-Gr̥hyasūtra = PGS (Sanskrit: Veda)
Paripāṭal (Tamil), ed. and trans. Gros 1968
Patārttakuṇa cintāmaṇi (Tamil)
Patiṟṟuppattu (Tamil)
Paṭṭiṉappālai by Kaṭiyalūr Uruttiraṅkaṇṇaṉār (Tamil)
Periyamāṭṭuvākaṭam (Tamil)
Perumpāṇāṟṟuppaṭai by Kaṭiyalūr Uruttiraṅkaṇṇaṉār (Tamil)
Piṅkala-Nikaṇṭu (Tamil)
Piramōttirakkāṇṭam by Varatuṅkarāmapāṇṭiyaṉ (Tamil)
Pomponius Mela, *De Chorographia* (Latin)
Praśna-Upaniṣad (Sanskrit: Veda)
Ptolemy (Klaúdios Ptolemaîos), *Geography (Geōgraphías huphḗgēsis)* (Greek), partial ed. Renou 1925
Puṟanāṉūṟu = Puṟam (Tamil)
Rājaśekharavilāsa (Kannaḍa), cited after Kittel 1970
Rāmāyaṇa (Sanskrit): in addition to the critical edition also those of Gorr(esio) and Schl(egel)
R̥gveda(-Saṁhitā) = R̥S (= RV) (Sanskrit: Veda), ed. Aufrecht 1877, trans. Geldner 1951–7; Renou 1955–66
R̥gvidhāna (Sanskrit: Veda)

Ṣaḍviṁśa-Brāhmaṇa = ṢB (Sanskrit: Veda)
Sāmavidhāna-Brāhmaṇa = SVB (Sanskrit: Veda)
Śāṅkhāyana-Āraṇyaka = ŚĀ (Sanskrit: Veda)
Śāṅkhāyana-Gṛhyasūtra = ŚGS (Sanskrit: Veda)
Śāṅkhāyana-Śrautasūtra = ŚŚS (Sanskrit: Veda)
Śatapatha-Brāhmaṇa = ŚB (Sanskrit: Veda), trans. Eggeling 1882–1900
Śiva-Purāṇa (Sanskrit: Purāṇa)
Skanda-Purāṇa (Sanskrit: Purāṇa)
Somadeva: see *Kathāsaritsāgara* = KSS (Sanskrit)
Strabo (Strábōn), *Geography (Geōgraphiká)* (Greek), ed. and trans. H. L. Jones, 8 vols. (Loeb Classical Library) London 1949–54
Subandhu, *Vāsavadattā* (Sanskrit)
Śukranīti (Sanskrit)
Sūrya-Siddhānta (Sanskrit)
Suśruta-Saṁhitā (Sanskrit), trans. Kunjalal Bhishagratna 1963
Taittirīya-Āraṇyaka = TĀ (Sanskrit: Veda)
Taittirīya-Brāhmaṇa = TB (Sanskrit: Veda)
Taittirīya-Saṁhitā = TS (Sanskrit: Veda)
Tirumurukāṟṟuppaṭai by Nakkīrar (Tamil), ed. and trans. Filliozat 1973
Tolkāppiyam (Tamil)
Tryambakayajvan, *Strīdharma-Paddhati* (Sanskrit): see Leslie 1989
Uttaramīmāṁsāsūtra (= Brahmasūtra = Vedāntasūtra) = UMS (Sanskrit)
Vādhūlasūtra (Sanskrit: Veda), partial ed. and trans. Caland 1926–8
Vaikhānasa Āgama (Sanskrit)
Vaikhānasa-Gṛhyasūtra (Sanskrit: Veda)
Vājasaneyi-Saṁhitā (Mādhyandina-śākhā) = VS(M) (Sanskrit: Veda)
Vārāha-Gṛhyasūtra (Sanskrit: Veda)
Varāhamihira, *Bṛhatsaṁhitā* (Sanskrit)
Varāha-Purāṇa (Sanskrit: Purāṇa)
Vāsiṣṭha-Dharmasūtra (Sanskrit)
Vasiṣṭha-Saṁhitā (Sanskrit)
Vetāla-Pañcaviṁśatikā (Sanskrit)
Vīdēvdāt (= Vendidad) (Avesta)
Vīmēcura-v-uḷḷamuṭaiyāṉ (Tamil)
Viṣṇudharmottara-Purāṇa (Sanskrit: Purāṇa)
Viṣṇu-Purāṇa (Sanskrit: Purāṇa)
White Yajurveda: mainly VS + ŚB + BĀU + KŚS + PGS
Yājñavalkya-Smṛti (Sanskrit)
Yāḻppāṇattu māṉipāy akarāti (= Yāḻ. aka.) by Cantiracēkarap Pulavar (Tamil)
Yašt (Avesta)

Modern authors

Aalto, Pentti, 1945. Notes on methods of decipherment of unknown writings and languages. *SO* 11 (4): 1–26.
1974. Deciphering the Indus script, methods and results. *Anantapāraṁ kila śabdaśāstram: księga pamiątkowa ku czci Eugeniusza Słuszkiewicza*: 21–7. Warsaw.
1975. Indus script and Dravidian. *Studies in Indian Epigraphy* 2: 16–31. Also in: *SO* 55 (1984): 411–26.
Abegg, Emil, 1940. Die Indusschrift entziffert? [Review of Hrozný 1939.] *Neue Zürcher Zeitung*, 29 September 1940: 1402.
Agrawal, D. P., 1968. An integrated study of the copper-bronze technology in the light of chronological and ecological factors. (Ph.D. thesis, Banaras Hindu University.) Tata Institute of Fundamental Research, Bombay.
1982. *The archaeology of India*. (Scandinavian Institute of Asian Studies, Monograph Series, 46.) London.
Agrawal, D. P. and Dilip K. Chakrabarti (eds.), 1979. *Essays in Indian protohistory*. (Indian Society for Prehistoric and Quaternary Studies, History and Archaeology Series, 5.) Delhi.
Agrawal, D. P. and A. Ghosh (eds.), 1973. *Radiocarbon and Indian archaeology*. Bombay.
Agrawala, Prithvi Kumar, 1967. *Skanda-Kārttikeya: a study in the origin and development*. (Monographs of the Department of Ancient Indian History, Culture and Archaeology, 3.) Varanasi.
1984. *Goddesses in ancient India*. New Delhi.
Agrawala, R. C., 1985. Indian copper anthropomorphs: a review. In: Gnoli and Lanciotti 1985: 1, 3–8.
Agrawala, V. S., 1937. The presiding deity of childbirth amongst the ancient Jainas, with special reference to figures in the Mathurā Museum. *The Jaina Antiquary* 2 (4): 75–9.
1963. *India as known to Pāṇini*. 2nd edn. Varanasi.
1969. *The deeds of Harsha (being a cultural study of Bāṇa's Harshacharita)*. Redacted and edited by P. K. Agrawala. Varanasi.
1970. *Ancient Indian folk cults*. (Indian Civilisation Series, 7.) Varanasi.
1984a. *Varanasi seals and sealings*. Edited with supplementary notes by Prithvi K. Agrawala. (Indian Civilisation Series, 28.) Varanasi.
1984b. *Śiva Mahādeva, the Great God (an exposition of the symbolism of Śiva)*. 2nd edn. Varanasi.
Aiyappan, A., 1939. Śiva-seal of Mohenjo-daro. *JRASB* 5: 401–6.
Åkerblad, J. D., 1802. *Lettre sur l'inscription égyptienne de Rosette, adressée au citoyen Silvestre de Sacy*. Paris.
Al'bedil', M. F., 1986. Tipy protoindijskikh nadpisej. In: Knorozov 1986: 36–68.
Al'bedil', M. F., B. Ya. Volchok and Yu. V. Knorozov, 1982. Issledovaniya protoindijskikh nadpisej. In: *Zabytye sistemy pis'ma: Ostrov Paskhi, Velikoe Lyao, Indiya. Materialy po deshifrovke*: 240–95. Moscow. [Russian version of Knorozov et al. 1981.]
Alcock, Leslie, 1952. Exploring Pakistan's past: the first year's work. *Pakistan Quarterly* 2 (1): 12–16.
Alden, John R., 1982. Trade and politics in Proto-Elamite Iran. *CA* 23 (6): 613–40.

Alekseev, G. V., 1965. Kharakteristika protoindijskogo pis'ma. In: *Predvaritel'noe* 1965: 6–10. [English translations: Alekseev [1965] 1976; Alekseev et al. 1969.]

[1965] 1976. The characteristics of the Proto-Indian script. In: Zide and Zvelebil 1976: 17–20 ['commentary' by the translators: 20–2].

Alekseev, G. V., Yu. V. Knorozov, A. M. Kondratov and B. Ya. Volchok, 1969. *Soviet studies on Harappan script*. Translated by Hem Chandra Pande, edited by Henry Field and Edith M. Laird. (Field Research Projects, Occasional Paper 6.) Coconut Grove, Fla. [Original text in Russian: *Predvarit'elnoe* 1965.]

Al-Gailani Werr, Lamia, 1982. Catalogue of the cylinder seals from Tell Suliemieh-Himrin. *Sumer* 38: 68–88.

Alkazi, Roshen, 1983. *Ancient Indian costume*. New Delhi.

Al Khalifa, Shaikha Haya Ali and Michael Rice (eds.), 1986. *Bahrain through the ages: the archaeology*. London.

Allan, John, 1936. *Catalogue of the coins of ancient India in the British Museum*. London.

Allchin, Bridget (ed.), 1984. *South Asian Archaeology 1981*. (University of Cambridge Oriental Publications, 35.) Cambridge.

Allchin, Bridget and Raymond Allchin, 1968. *The birth of Indian civilization: India and Pakistan before 500* BC. (Pelican Books, A 950.) Harmondsworth.

1982. *The rise of civilization in India and Pakistan*. Cambridge.

Allchin, F. R., 1963. *Neolithic cattle-keepers of South India: a study of the Deccan ashmounds*. (University of Cambridge Oriental Publications, 9.) Cambridge.

1981. Archaeological and language-historical evidence for the movement of Indo-Aryan speaking peoples into South Asia. In: *Ethnic problems 1981*: 336–49.

1985. The interpretation of a seal from Chanhudaro and its significance for the religion of the Indus Civilization. *SAA 1983*: 369–84.

in press. On a Harappan stone statue of a urial ram that has recently turned up in the antique trade. *Proceedings of the Second International Symposium on Moenjo-daro held at Karachi and Moenjo-daro on 24–27 February 1992*. Karachi.

Allchin, F. R., B. Allchin, F. A. Durrani and M. F. Khan (eds.), 1986. *Lewan and the Bannu basin: excavation and survey of sites and environments in north west Pakistan*. (BAR International Series, 310.) Oxford.

Allchin, F. R. and J. Robert Knox, 1981. Preliminary report on excavations at Lewan (1977–78). *SAA 1979*: 241–4.

Allen, Albert Henry, 1901. The Vaṭa-sāvitrī-vrata, according to Hemādri and the Vratārka. *JAOS* 21 (2): 53–66.

Allen, Michael R., 1986. *The cult of Kumari: virgin worship in Nepal*. 2nd edn. Kathmandu.

Amiet, Pierre, 1956. Le symbolisme cosmique du répertoire animalier en Mésopotamie. *RA* 50: 125–6.

1966a. *Elam*. Auvers-sur-Oise.

1966b. Il y a 5000 ans, les Elamites inventaient l'écriture. *Archeologia* 12: 20–2.

1972. *Glyptique susienne*, I–II. (Mémoires de la Mission Archéologique en Iran, Mission de Susiane, 43.) Paris.

1979. Archaeological discontinuity and ethnic duality in Elam. *Antiquity* 53: 195–204.

1980a. *La Glyptique mesopotamienne archaïque*. 2nd edn. Paris.

1980b. *Art of the ancient Near East*. New York.

1986a. *L'Age des échanges inter-iraniens 3500–1700 avant J.-C.* (Notes et Documents des Musées de France, 11.) Paris.

1986b. Susa and the Dilmun culture. In: Al Khalifa and Rice 1986: 262–8.

1988. La vallée de l'Indus et le monde de l'Iran. In: *Les Cités oubliées de l'Indus*: 194–202.

1989a. Elam and Bactria. In: Ligabue and Salvatori n.d.: 125–40.

1989b. Antiquities of Bactria and Outer Iran in the Louvre collection. In: Ligabue and Salvatori n.d.: 159–80.

Ammer, Karl, 1948. Die L-Formen im Ṛgveda. *WZKM* 51 (1–2): 116–37.

Andersen, P. K., 1983. *Word order typology and comparative constructions*. (Amsterdam Studies in the Theory and History of Linguistic Science, IV: Current Issues in Linguistic Theory, 25.) Amsterdam.

Anderson, Bernard, 1967. Indus Valley Civilization: a bibliography 1954–1966. *Indica* 4 (2): 107–24.

Andrews, Carol, 1981. *The Rosetta Stone*. (British Museum Publications.) London.

Andronov, M. S., 1980. *The Brahui language*. Moscow.

Anquetil Duperron, Abraham-Hyacinthe, 1771. *Zend-Avesta, ouvrage de Zoroastre*, I–III. Paris.

Anthony, David W., 1986. The 'Kurgan culture', Indo-European origins, and the domestication of the horse: a reconsideration. *CA* 27 (4): 291–313.

1990. Migration in archaeology: the baby and the bathwater. *AA* 92: 895–914.

1991. The archaeology of Indo-European origins. *JIES* 19 (3–4): 193–222.

Anthony, David W. and Bernard Wailes, 1988. [Review of Renfrew 1987.] *CA* 29 (3): 441–5.

Anttila, Raimo, 1972. *An introduction to historical and comparative linguistics*. New York.

Aravamuthan, T. G., 1942. *Some survivals of the Harappa culture*. Bombay.

Arbman, Ernst, 1922. *Rudra. Untersuchungen zum altindischen Glauben und Kultus*. (Uppsala Universitets Årsskrift 1922: Filosofi, Språkvetenskap och Historiska Vetenskaper, 2.) Uppsala.

Archana, (Ms), n.d. *The language of symbols: a project on South Indian ritual decorations of a semi-permanent nature*. Madras.

Ardeleanu-Jansen, Alexandra, 1984. Stone sculptures from Mohenjo-Daro. In: Jansen and Urban 1984: 139–57.

1989. A short note on a steatite sculpture from Mohenjo-Daro. *SAA 1985*: 196–210.

1991. The sculptural art of the Harappa culture. In: Jansen et al. 1991: 166–78.

Artola, George T., 1977. *The banner of Kāmadeva and other topics of Sanskrit literature and Indian culture*. (Monographs of the Department of Sanskrit and Indian Studies, University of Toronto, 3.) Bombay.

Arutyunov, S. A. and N. N. Cheboksarov, 1972. Protoindijskaya tsivilizatsiya i sovremennye dravidy. In: *Proto-Indica: 1972*: I, 153–64.

Ashfaque, Syed M., 1977. Astronomy in the Indus Valley Civilization: a survey of the problems and possibilities of the ancient Indian astronomy and cosmology in the light of Indus script decipherment by the Finnish scholars. *Centaurus* 21 (2): 149–93.

1989. Primitive astronomy in the Indus Civilization. In: Kenoyer 1989a: 207–15.

Asthana, Shashi P., 1976. *History and archaeology of India's contacts with other countries from earliest times to 300* BC. New Delhi.

1985. *Pre-Harappan cultures of India and the Borderlands*. New Delhi.

1989. Graffiti on pottery. In: Ghosh 1989a: 359.

Aufrecht, Theodor, 1877. *Die Hymnen des Rigveda*, I–II. 2nd edn. Bonn.

Aurenche, Olivier, Jacques Evin and Francis Hours, 1987. *Chronologies du Proche Orient / Chronologies in the Near East: relative chronologies and absolute chronology 16,000–4,000* BP, I–II. (BAR International Series 379.) Oxford.

Ayyar, P. V. Jagadisa, 1925. *South Indian customs*. Madras.

Badam, G. L., 1989. Domestication of animals. In: Ghosh 1989a: I, 1–5.

Bailey, H. W., 1960. Iranian *Arya-* and *Daha-*. *TPS* 1959: 71–115.

1973. Mleccha-, Balōč, and Gadrōsia. *BSOAS* 36 (3): 584–7.

1979. *Dictionary of Khotan Saka*. Cambridge.

1982. Maka. *JRAS* 1982 (1): 10–13.

Baldi, Philip, 1987. Indo-European languages. In: Comrie 1987a: 31–67.

Balz-Cochois, Helgard, 1992. *Inanna: Wesensbild und Kult einer unmütterlichen Göttin*. (Studien zum Verstehen fremder Religionen, 4.) Gütersloh.

Banerjea, J. N., 1956. *The development of Hindu iconography*. 2nd edn. Calcutta.

Banerji, S. C., 1978. *Tantra in Bengal*. Calcutta.

Barber, Elisabeth J. W., 1974. *Archaeological decipherment: a handbook*. Princeton.

Barthel, Thomas S., 1958. *Grundlagen zur Entzifferung der Osterinselschrift*. (University of Hamburg, Abhandlungen aus dem Gebiet der Auslandskunde, 64–B 36.) Hamburg.

1963. Rongorongo-Studien. *Anthropos* 58: 372–436.

1968. Writing systems [of South America and Mexico]. In: Sebeok 1968: IV, 275–301.

1969. Entzifferung früher Schriftsysteme in Alt-Amerika und Polynesien. In: *Frühe Schriftzeugnisse der Menschheit*: 151–76. Göttingen.

1971. Pre-contact writing in Oceania. In: Sebeok 1971: VIII, 1165–86.

1979. Enigmatisches im Codex Vaticanus 3773: Kosmogramm und Eschatologie. Ein Beitrag zur Indo-Mexikanistik. *Tribus* 28: 83–122.

1981. Planetary series in ancient India and prehispanic Mexico: an analysis of their relations to each other. *Tribus* 30: 203–30.

1984. Von Mexico zum Indus. *Tribus* 33: 75–9.

Bartholomae, Christian, 1904. *Altiranisches Wörterbuch*. Strasburg.

Barton, George A., 1926–7 (1928). On the so-called Sumero-Indian seals. *AASOR* 8:79–85.

1928–9 (1930). A comparative list of all the signs in the so-called Indo-Sumerian seals. *AASOR* 10: 75–94.

1929. Whence came the Sumerians? *JAOS* 49: 263–8.

Barua, D. M., 1946. Indus script and Tantric code. In: D. R. Bhandarkar and P. K. Gode (eds.), *Dr B. C. Law volume*: II, 461–7. Calcutta. Reprinted in: *Indo-Iranica* 1 (1946): 15–21.

Basham, A. L., 1949. Recent work on the Indus Civilization. *BSOAS* 13 (1):140–5.

1954. *The wonder that was India: a survey of the culture of the Indian subcontinent before the coming of the Muslims*. London.

(ed.), 1975. *A cultural history of India*. Oxford.

Bauer, Hans, 1930. *Entzifferung der Keilinschriften von Ras Shamra*. Halle.

1932. *Das Alphabet von Ras Shamra*. Halle.

Bechert, Heinz (ed.), 1980. *Die Sprache der ältesten buddhistischen Überlieferung*. (Abhandlungen der Akademie der Wissenschaften in Göttingen, Philologisch-historische Klasse, 3rd series, 117.) Göttingen.

Bechert, Heinz and Georg von Simson (eds.), 1979. *Einführung in die Indologie: Stand, Methoden, Aufgaben*. Darmstadt.

Beck, Brenda E. F., 1981. The goddess and the demon: a local South Indian festival and its wider context. In: Biardeau 1981a: 83–136.

Beck, Horace C., 1933. Etched carnelian beads. *The Antiquaries Journal* 13: 384–98.

Bedigian, Dorothea, 1985. Še-giš-ì sesame or flax. *Bulletin on Sumerian Agriculture* 2: 159–78.

Begley, Vimala, 1986. From Iron Age to early historical in South Indian archaeology. In: Jacobson 1986a: 297–319.

Belcher, William R., 1992. Fish resources in an early urban context at Harappa. In: Meadow 1992a: 107–20.

Benedict, Paul K., 1972. *Sino-Tibetan: a conspectus*. Cambridge.

Benediktov, A. A., 1954. K vopruso o rasshifrovke protoindijskoj pis'mennosti. *Uchenye zapiski, Filologicheskaya seriya* 5: 77–97. Stalinabad.

Benveniste, Emile, 1952. Langues asianiques et méditerranéennes. In: A. Meillet and M. Cohen (eds.), *Les Langues du monde*, 2nd edn: 183–225. Paris.

1973. *Indo-European language and society*. Coral Gables, Fla.

Benveniste, Emile and Louis Renou, 1934. *Vṛtra et vṛθragna: étude de mythologie indo-iranienne*. (Cahiers de la Société Asiatique, 3.) Paris.

Berchem, Egon von, 1918. *Siegel*. (Bibliothek für Kunst- und Antiquitätensammler, 11.) Berlin.

Bergaigne, Abel, 1978. *Vedic religion*, I–IV. Translated by V. G. Paranjpe. Delhi.

Berger, Hermann, 1970. [Review of Parpola et al. 1969a and 1969b.] *ZDMG* 120 (2): 420–1.

1974. *Das Yasin-Burushaski (Werchikwar): Grammatik, Texte, Wörterbuch.* (Neuindische Studien, 3.) Wiesbaden.

in press. *Die Burushaski-Sprache von Hunza und Nagir*, I: *Grammatik.*

Berlin, Heinrich, 1958. El glifo 'emblema' en las inscripciones mayas. *Journal de la Société des Americanistes* NS 47: 111–19.

Bernal, J. D., 1969. *Science in history*, 1. (Pelican Book A 994.) Harmondsworth.

Bernhardt, Inez and Samuel Noah Kramer, 1960. Enki und Weltordnung. *Wissenschaftliche Zeitschrift der Friedrich-Schiller-Universität Jena, Gesellschafts- und sprachwissenschaftliche Reihe* 9 (1–2): 231–56 and tables 1–18.

Bertholet, Alfred, 1940. *Wortlanklang und Volksetymologie in ihrer Wirkung auf religiösen Glauben und Brauch.* (Abhandlungen der Preussischen Akademie der Wissenschaften, Phil.-hist. Klasse, 1940: 6.) Berlin.

Beyer, Dominique, 1989. Un nouveau témoin des relations entre Mari et le monde iranien au IIIème millénaire. *Iranica Antiqua* 24: 109–20.

Beyer, Stephen, 1973. *The cult of Tārā.* Berkeley.

Bhan, Kuldeep K., 1989. Late Harappan settlements of western India, with specific reference to Gujarat. In: Kenoyer 1989a: 219–42.

Bharati, Agehananda, 1965. *The Tantric tradition.* London.

Bhatia, P., 1989. Coins. In: Ghosh 1989a: 1, 10–14.

Bhattacharya, Brindavan Chandra, 1974. *The Jaina iconography.* 2nd edn. Delhi.

Bhattacharya, S., 1975. Linguistic convergence in the Dravido-Munda culture area. *IJDL* 4: 199–214.

Bhattacharyya, Asoke Kumar, 1953. Iconography of some minor deities in Jainism. *IHQ* 29 (4): 332–9.

Bhattacharyya, N. N., 1974. *History of the Śākta religion.* Delhi.

1975. *Ancient Indian rituals and their social contents.* Delhi.

1977. *The Indian mother goddess.* 2nd edn. New Delhi.

1982. *History of the Tantric religion (a historical, ritualistic and philosophical study).* New Delhi.

Bhattacharyya, Tarakeshwar, 1953–5. A forgotten chapter of the history of ancient Indian astronomy. *Journal of the Ganganatha Jha Research Institute* 11–12 (1–4): 11–54.

Bhawe, Shrikrishna S., 1939. *Die Yajus' des Aśvamedha.* (Bonner Orientalistische Studien 25.) Stuttgart.

Biardeau, Madeleine, 1976. Le sacrifice dans l'hindouisme. In: Biardeau and Malamoud 1976: 7–154.

(ed.), 1981a. *Autour de la déesse hindoue.* (Puruṣārtha, 5.) Paris.

1981b. L'arbre śamī et le buffle sacrificiel. In: Biardeau 1981a: 215–43.

1989a. *Histoires de poteaux: variations védiques autour de la déesse hindoue.* (PEFEO 154.) Paris.

1989b. Brahmans and meat-eating gods. In: Hiltebeitel 1989: 19–33.

Biardeau, M. and Charles Malamoud, 1976. *Le Sacrifice dans l'Inde ancienne.* (Bibliothèque de l'Ecole des Hautes Etudes, Sciences Religieuses, 79.) Paris.

Bibby, Geoffrey, 1958. The 'ancient Indian style' seals from Bahrain. *Antiquity* 32: 243–6 and pl. 26–7.

1970. '... efter Dilmun norm' ('... according to the standard of Dilmun'). *Kuml* 1970: 345–53.

1972. *Looking for Dilmun.* Harmondsworth.

1986a. The origins of the Dilmun Civilization. In: Al Khalifa and Rice 1986: 108–15.

1986b. 'The land of Dilmun is holy ...' In Al Khalifa and Rice 1986: 192–4.

Birnbaum, Henrik and Jaan Puhvel (eds.), 1966. *Ancient Indo-European dialects.* Berkeley.

Biscione, Raffaele, 1977. The crisis of Central Asian urbanization in II millennium BC and villages as an alternative system. In: *Le Plateau iranien* 1977: 113–27.

1985. The so-called 'Nestorian seals': connections between Ordos and Middle Asia in Middle–Late Bronze Age. In: Gnoli and Lanciotti 1985: 1, 109.

Bisht, R. S., 1982. Excavations at Banawali: 1974–77. In: Possehl 1982a: 113–24.

1984. Structural remains and town-planning of Banawali. In: Lal and Gupta 1984: 89–97.

1987. Further excavation at Banawali: 1983–84. In: B. M. Pande and B. D. Chattopadhyaya (eds.), *Archaeology and history: essays in memory of Shri A. Ghosh*, 1: 135–55. Delhi.

1989. A new model of the Harappan town planning as revealed at Dholavira in Kutch: a surface study of its plan and architecture. In: Bhaskar Chatterjee (ed.), *History and archaeology: Prof. H. D. Sankalia felicitation volume*: 397–408. Delhi.

1991. Dholavira: a new horizon of the Indus Civilization. *Purātattva* 20: 71–82.

Bissing, Friedrich Wilhelm von, 1927. Ein vor etwa 15 Jahren erworbenes 'Harappa-Siegel'. *Archiv für Orientforschung* 4 (1): 21–2.

Biswas, S. N., 1955. Die Vrātyas und die Vrātyastomas. (Ph.D. dissertation, Free University, Berlin.)

Bloch, Jules, 1924. Sanskrit et dravidien. *BSL* 25: 1–21.

1939. [Review of Ross 1938.] *BSL* 40: 34.

1963. *Application de la cartographie à l'histoire de l'indo-aryen.* (Cahiers de la Société Asiatique, 13.) Paris.

1965. *Indo-Aryan from the Vedas to modern times.* Revised edn, trans. by Alfred Master. Paris.

Bloch, Theodor, 1896. *Über das Gṛhya- und Dharmasūtra der Vaikhānasa.* Leipzig.

Bloomfield, Maurice (trans.), 1897. *Hymns of the Atharva-Veda.* (SBE, 42.) Oxford.

1899. *The Atharva-Veda and the Gopatha Brāhmaṇa.* (Grundriss II.1.B.) Strasburg.

Bødker, Laurits, 1957. *Indian animal tales: a preliminary survey.* (FF Communications 170.) Helsinki.

Boehmer, R. M., 1965. *Die Entwicklung der Glyptik während der*

Akkad-Zeit. (Untersuchungen zur Assyriologie und vorderasiatischen Archäologie, 4.) Berlin.

1974a. Orientalische Einflüsse auf verzierten Messergriffen aus dem prädynastischen Ägypten. *Archäologische Mitteilungen aus Iran* NS 7: 15–40.

1974b. Das Rollsiegel im prädynastischen Ägypten. *Archäologischer Anzeiger* 1974: 495–514.

1975. Das Auftreten des Wasserbüffels in Mesopotamien in historischer Zeit und seine sumerische Bezeichnung. *ZA* 64: 1–19.

Böhtlingk, Otto and Rudolph Roth, 1852–75. *Sanskrit-Wörterbuch*, I–VII. St Petersburg.

Bökönyi, Sandor, 1978. The earliest waves of domestic horse in East Europe. *JIES* 6: 17–76.

Boltz, William G., 1986. Early Chinese writing. *WA* 17 (3): 420–36.

Bongard-Levin, G. M., 1957. Izobrazheniya khranilishcha dlya zerna na pechatyakh Mokhendzho-daro i Kharappy. *Sovetskoe Vostokovedenie* 1957 (6): 119–22. [English translation: Bongard-Levin 1960.]

1960. Symbols of granary on the seals of Mohenjo-daro and Harappa. *Indian Studies Past and Present* 1 (2): 377–9.

Bongard-Levin, G. M. and N. V. Gurov, 1981. Deshifrovka protoindijskoj pis'mennosti: osnovnye napravleniya i itogi rabot. *Vestnik Akademii Nauk SSSR* 1981 (3): 126–38.

Bosch, F. D. K., 1960. *The golden germ: an introduction to Indian symbolism*. (Indo-Iranian Monographs, 2.) The Hague.

Bothmer, Dietrich von (ed.), 1990. *Glories of the past: ancient art from the Shelby White and Leon Levy Collection*. New York.

Bouda, Karl, 1955–6. Dravidisch und Uralaltaisch. *Lingua* 5 (2): 129–44.

Boyce, Mary, 1979. *Zoroastrians: their religious beliefs and practices*. London.

Brasseur de Bourbourg, Charles Etienne, 1861–2–4. *Collection de documents dans les langues indigènes, pour servir à l'étude de l'histoire et de la philologie de l'Amerique ancienne*: I. Popol Vuh. II. Gramatica de la lengua Quiché [et Rabinal-Achi, drame indigène avec sa musique originale]. III. Relation des choses de Yucatan par Diego de Landa: texte espagnol et traduction français. Paris.

Bray, Denys De S., 1907–34. *The Brahui language*, I–III. Calcutta and Delhi.

1913. *The life-history of a Brāhūī*. (Prize Publication Fund, 4.) London.

Bray, Warwick, 1968. *Everyday life of the Aztecs*. London and New York.

Brentjes, Burchard, 1981. *Die Stadt des Yima. Weltbilder in der Architektur*. Leipzig.

1983. Das 'Ur-Mandala' (?) von Daschly-3. *Iranica Antiqua* 18: 25–49 and table 1.

1987. Probleme der baktrischen Bronzezeit. *Iranica Antiqua* 22: 117–58 and pl. 1–5.

1989. Stempel und Rollsiegel aus Baktrien und Chorasan. *Baghdader Mitteilungen* 20: 315–35.

Brereton, Joel P., 1981. *The Ṛgvedic Ādityas*. (American Oriental Series, 63.) New Haven, Conn.

1991. Cosmographic images in the Bṛhadāraṇyaka Upaniṣad. *IIJ* 34 (1): 1–17.

Breton, Roland J.-L., 1976. *Atlas géographique des langues et des ethnies de l'Inde et du subcontinent: Bangladesh, Pakistan, Sri Lanka, Népal, Bhoutan, Sikkim*. (Travaux du Centre International de Recherche sur le Bilinguisme, A-10.) Quebec.

Brice, W. C., 1962. The writing system of the Proto-Elamite account tablets of Susa. *Bulletin of John Ryland's Library* 45 (1): 15–39.

1967. The structure of Linear A with some Proto-Elamite and Proto-Indic comparisons. In: W. C. Brice (ed.), *Europa. Festschrift E. Grumach*: 32–41. Berlin.

1970a. The Copenhagen decipherment of the Proto-Indic script. *Kadmos* 9 (1): 22–8.

1970b. [Review of Parpola et al. 1969a and 1969b.] *JRAS* 1970 (2): 221–3.

1976. [Review of S. Koskenniemi et al. 1973.] *JRAS* 1976 (2): 161.

Briggs, George Weston, 1938. *Gorakhnāth and the Kānphaṭa Yogīs*. Calcutta.

Bright, William, 1982. [Review of Mitchiner 1978.] *JAOS* 102: 233–5. Reprinted with modifications and the title 'How not to decipher the Indus Valley inscriptions' in Bright 1990: 118–23.

1986. Archaeology, linguistics, and ancient Dravidian. In: Bh. Krishnamurti (ed.), *South Asian languages: structure, convergence and diglossia*: 108–12. Delhi. Reprinted in Bright 1990: 124–9.

1990. *Language variation in South Asia*. New York.

Brinkman, J. A., 1964. Mesopotamian chronology of the historical period. In: Oppenheim 1964: 335–52.

Brough, John, 1951. *Selections from classical Sanskrit literature with English translation and notes*. London.

1971. Soma and Amanita muscaria. *BSOAS* 34: 331–62.

Brown, Percy, 1959. *Indian architecture (Buddhist and Hindu periods)*. Bombay.

Brown, W. Norman, 1939. The beginnings of civilization in India. *JAOS* 59, Supplement 4: 32–44.

1947. The name of the goddess Mīnākṣī, 'Fish-eye'. *JAOS* 67: 209–14.

1953. *The United States and India and Pakistan*. Cambridge, Mass.

Brunner, Hellmut, 1969. Die Schrift der Ägypter. In: Hausmann 1969: 208–13.

Brunswig, Robert H., Jr, 1974. A comprehensive bibliography of the Indus Civilization and related subjects and areas. *Asian Perspectives* 16 (1): 75–111.

Brunswig, Robert H., Jr, Asko Parpola and Daniel Potts, 1983. New Indus and related seals from the Near East. In: Daniel T. Potts (ed.), *Dilmun* (Berliner Beiträge zum Vorderen Orient, 2): 101–15 and pl. 1–3. Berlin.

Brunt, P. A. (ed. and trans.), 1983. Arrian, *Anabasis Alexandri & Indica*, I–II. (The Loeb Classical Library, 236, 269.) Cambridge, Mass., and London.

Brunton, John, 1939. *John Brunton's book*. Edited by J. H. Clapham. Cambridge.

Buchanan, Briggs, 1965. A dated 'Persian Gulf' seal and its implications. In: Hallo and Buchanan 1965: 204–9.

1967. A dated seal impression connecting Babylonia and ancient India. *Archaeology* 20 (2): 104–7. Reprinted in: Possehl 1979a: 145–7.

1981. *Early Near Eastern seals in the Yale Babylonian collection*. Introduction and seal inscriptions by William W. Hallo. Edited by Ulla Kasten. New Haven, Conn.

Buck, C. D., 1949. *A dictionary of selected synonyms in the principal Indo-European languages*. Chicago.

Bühler, Georg (trans.), 1886. *The Laws of Manu*. (SBE, 25.) Oxford.

1896. *Indische Palaeographie von circa 350 a. Chr. – circa 1300 p. Chr.* (Grundriss 1:11.) Strasburg.

1898. *On the origin of the Indian Brāhma alphabet*. 2nd edn. Strasburg.

Buitenen, J. A. B. van (trans.), 1973–8. *The Mahābhārata*, I–III. Chicago.

Bunge, Mario, 1967. *Scientific research*, I–II. (Studies in the Foundations, Methodology and Philosophy of Science, 3.) Berlin, Heidelberg and New York.

Buren, E. Douglas Van, 1948. Fish-offerings in ancient Mesopotamia. *Iraq* 10: 101–21.

Burgess, J., 1904. The Navagraha or nine planets and their names. *IA* 33: 61–6.

Burkholder, G., 1971. Steatite carvings from Saudi Arabia. *Artibus Asiae* 33: 306–23.

Burlingame, E. W. (trans.), 1921. *Buddhist legends*, I. (Harvard Oriental Series, 28.) Cambridge, Mass.

Burnes, Alexander, 1834. *Travels into Bokhara; being the account of a journey from India to Cabool, Tartary, and Persia; also, Narrative of a voyage on the Indus, from the sea to Lahore, with presents from the King of Great Britain; performed under the orders of the supreme Government of India, in the years 1831, 1832, and 1833*, I–III. London.

Burrow, Thomas, 1943–6a. Dravidian studies III: two developments of initial *k-* in Dravidian. *BSOAS* 11: 122–39. Reprinted in Burrow 1968: 32–64.

1943–6b. Dravidian studies IV: the body in Dravidian and Uralian. *BSOAS* 11: 328–56. Reprinted in Burrow 1968: 65–112.

1943–6c. Dravidian studies V: initial *y-* and *ñ-* in Dravidian. *BSOAS* 11: 595–616. Reprinted in Burrow 1968: 113–49.

1958. Sanskrit and the pre-Aryan tribes and languages. *Bulletin of the Ramakrishna Mission Institute of Culture*, February 1958. Reprinted in: Burrow 1968: 319–40.

1963. On the significance of the term *arma-*, *armaka-* in early Sanskrit literature. *Journal of Indian History* 41 (1–3): 159–66.

1968. *Collected papers on Dravidian linguistics*. (Annamalai University, Department of Linguistics, Publication 13.) Annamalainagar.

1969. Dravidian and the decipherment of the Indus script. *Antiquity* 43 (172): 274–8. Reprinted in 1970 in *JTS* 2 (1): 149–56.

1973a. *The Sanskrit language*. 3rd edn. London.

1973b. The Proto-Indoaryans. *JRAS* 1973 (2): 123–40.

1975a. The early Āryans. In: Basham 1975: 20–9.

1975b. [Review of Kinnier Wilson 1974.] *Antiquity* 49 (194): 151–3.

1977. [Review of Rau 1976.] *Kratylos* 21 (1976): 72–6.

Burrow, Thomas and M. B. Emeneau, 1961. *A Dravidian etymological dictionary*. Oxford. (= *DED*)

1984. *A Dravidian etymological dictionary*. 2nd edn. Oxford. (= *DEDR*)

Burrows, E., 1936. [Review of Hunter 1934.] *JRAS* 1936: 331–2.

Caillat, Colette (ed.), 1989a. *Dialectes dans les littératures indo-aryennes*. (Publications de l'Institut de Civilisation Indienne, Série in-8°, 55.) Paris.

1989b. Sur l'authenticité linguistique des édits d'Asoka. In: Caillat 1989a: 413–32.

Caland, W. (ed. and trans.), 1922. *The Jaiminigṛhyasūtra*. (Punjab Sanskrit Series, 2.) Lahore.

1926. Rāhu im Veda. In: W. Kirfel (ed.), *Beiträge zur Literaturwissenschaft und Geistesgeschichte Indiens; Festgabe Hermann Jacobi*: 240–1. Bonn.

1926–8. Eine dritte / vierte Mitteilung über das Vādhūlasūtra. *AO* 4 (1): 1–41; (2): 161–213; 6 (2–3): 97–241.

Caland, W. and V. Henry, 1906–7. *L'Agniṣṭoma: description complète de la forme normale du sacrifice de soma dans le culte védique*, I–II. Paris.

Caldwell, R., 1856. *A comparative grammar of the Dravidian or South Indian family of languages*. London. 1913, 3rd edn, revised by J. L. Wyatt and T. Ramakrishna Pillai. London.

Calmayer, P., 1969. *Datierbare Bronzen aus Luristan und Kirmanshah*. (Untersuchungen zur Assyriologie und Vorderasiatischen Archäologie, 5.) Berlin.

Cappieri, Mario, 1965. Ist die Indus-Kultur und ihre Bevölkerung wirklich verschwunden? *Anthropos* 60: 719–62.

1970. *The population of the Indus Civilization*. (Field Research Projects, Occasional Paper 11.) Coconut Grove, Fla.

Cardi, Beatrice de, 1964. British expeditions to Kalat, 1948 and 1957. *PA* 1: 20–9.

1965. Excavations and reconnaissance in Kalat, West Pakistan: the prehistoric sequence in the Surab region. *PA* 2: 86–182 and pl. 1–9.

1970. *Excavations at Bampur, a third millennium settlement in Persian Baluchistan, 1966*. (APAMNH, 51: 3.) New York.

1983. *Archaeological surveys in Baluchistan, 1948 and 1957*. (University of London, Institute of Archaeology, Occasional Publications, 8.) London.

1984. Some third and fourth millennium sites in Sarawan and Jhalawan, Baluchistan, in relation to the Mehrgarh sequence. *SAA 1981*: 61–8.

1989. Harappan finds from Tomb 6 at Shimal, Ras al-Khaimah, United Arab Emirates. *SAA 1985*: 9–13.

Cardona, George, 1987a. Indo-Aryan languages. In: Comrie 1987a: 440–7.

1987b. Sanskrit. In: Comrie 1987a: 448–69.

Cardona, George and R. E. Emmerick, 1974. Indo-Aryan languages. In: *The New Encyclopaedia Britannica*. 15th edn, *Macropaedia* 9: 439b–57a. Chicago.

Cardona, George, Henry M. Hoenigswald and A. Senn (eds.), 1970. *Indo-European and Indo-Europeans*. Philadelphia.

Carruba, Onofrio, 1976. [Review of S. Koskenniemi et al. 1973.] *WZKM* 68: 278–80.

Carter, E. and M. Stolper, 1984. *Elam: surveys of political history and archaeology*. (University of California Publications, Near Eastern Studies, 25.) Berkeley.

Casal, Jean-Marie, 1961. *Fouilles de Mundigak*, I–II. (Mémoires de la Délégation Archéologique Française en Afghanistan, 17.) Paris.

1964. *Fouilles d'Amri*, I–II. (Publications de la Commission des Fouilles Archéologiques: Fouilles du Pakistan.) Paris.

1966. Nindowari: a Chalcolithic site in South Baluchistan. *PA* 3: 10–21, pl. 5–17.

1968. Nindo Damb. *PA* 5: 51–5.

1969a. *De la Mésopotamie à l'Inde: la civilisation de l'Indus et ses énigmes*. Paris.

1969b. Une méconnue et une inconnue: la civilisation de l'Indus et son écriture. *Science, Progrès, Decouverte* 3415: 423–7.

Cavalli-Sforza, Luigi Luca, 1991. Genes, people and languages. *Scientific American* 265 (5): 72–8 / 104–10.

Cavalli-Sforza, L. L., A. Piazza, P. Menozzi and J. L. Mountain, 1988. Reconstruction of human evolution: bringing together genetic, archaeological and linguistic data. *Proceedings of the National Academy of Sciences* 85 (16): 6002–6.

Chadwick, John, 1960. *The decipherment of Linear B*. 2nd edn. Cambridge.

Chakrabarti, Dilip K., 1977. India and West Asia: an alternative approach. *ME* 1: 25–38.

1978a. Seals as an evidence of Indus–West Asia interrelations. In: Debiprasad Chattopadhyaya (ed.), *History and society: essays in honour of Prof. Niharranjan Ray*: 93–116. Calcutta.

1978b. The Nippur seal and Indus chronology. *ME* 2: 88–90.

1979. Size of the Harappan settlements. In: Agrawal and Chakrabarti 1979: 205–15.

1980. Early agriculture and the development of towns in India. In: Andrew Sherratt (ed.), *The Cambridge encyclopedia of archaeology*: 162–7. Cambridge.

1982. 'Long barrel-cylinder' beads and the issue of pre-Sargonic contact between the Harappan Civilization and Mesopotamia. In: Possehl 1982a: 265–70.

1989. Iron Age. In: Ghosh 1989a: I, 108–10.

1990. *The external trade of the Indus Civilization*. New Delhi.

Chakravarti, Chintaharan, 1930. The cult of Bāro Bhāiyā of eastern Bengal. *JRASB* 26: 379–88.

Chambers, J. K. and P. Trudgill, 1980. *Dialectology*. Cambridge.

Champollion le Jeune, Jean François, 1822. *Lettre à M. Dacier, secrétaire perpétuel de l'Academie Royal des Inscriptions et Belles-Lettres, relative à l'alphabet des hiéroglyphes phonetiques employés par les égyptiens pour inscrire sur leur monuments les titres, les noms et les surnoms des souverains grecs et romains*. Paris.

1824. *Précis du système hiéroglyphique des anciens égyptiens, ou recherches sur les éléments premiers de cette écriture sacrée*. Paris.

Chandy, Mary, 1989. *Fishes*. Revised edn. (India – The Land and the People.) New Delhi.

Chang Kwang Chih, 1977. *The archaeology of ancient China*. 3rd edn. New Haven, Conn.

Charpentier, Jarl, 1909. Über Rudra-Śiva. *WZKM* 23: 151–79.

1925. [Review of Waddell 1925.] *JRAS* 1925: 797–9.

1930. Naicasakha. *JRAS* 1930: 335–45.

Charvat, P., 1988. Archaeology and social history: the Susa sealings, ca. 4000–2340 BC. *Paléorient* 14 (1): 57–63.

Chatterjee, Asim Kumar, 1970. *The cult of Skanda-Kārttikeya in ancient India*. Calcutta.

Chatterjee, Chanchal Kumar, 1978. *Studies in the rites and rituals of Hindu marriage in ancient India*. Calcutta.

Chaṭṭopādhyāya, K., 1930. Naicasakha. *JRAS* 1930: 894–7.

Chaudhuri, Nanimadhab, 1943. A pre-historic tree cult. *IHQ* 19 (4): 318–29.

1945. The cult of Vana-Durgā, a tree-deity. *JRASB*, 3rd series, 11: 75–84.

Chernikov, S. S., 1960. *Vostochnyj Kazakhstan v èpokhu bronzy*. (Materialy i Issledovaniya po Arkheologii SSSR, 88.) Moscow.

Chettiar, A. Chidambaranatha, 1965. *English–Tamil dictionary*. Madras.

Childe, V. Gordon, 1926. *The Aryans*. London.

1934. *New light on the most ancient East: the oriental prelude to European prehistory*. London.

1950. The urban revolution. *Town Planning Review* 21 (1): 3–17. Reprinted in: Possehl 1979a: 12–17.

Chlenova, N. L., 1984. Arkheologicheskie materialy k voprosu ob irantsakh doskifskoj èpokhi i indo-irantsakh. *SA* 1984 (1): 88–103.

Chollot-Varagnac, Marthe, 1980. *Les Origines du graphisme symbolique: essai d'analyse des écritures primitives en préhistoire*. Paris.

Civil, Miguel, 1961. The home of the fish: a new Sumerian literary composition. *Iraq* 23: 154–75.

1973. The Sumerian writing system: some problems. *Orientalia* NS 42: 21–34.

Civil, Miguel and R. D. Biggs, 1966. Notes sur des textes sumériens archaïques. *RA* 60: 1–16.

Claiborn, Robert, 1974. *The birth of writing*. (The Emergence of Man.) New York.

Clauson, Gerard and John Chadwick, 1969. The Indus script deciphered? [Review of Parpola et al. 1969a.] *Antiquity* 43 (171): 200–7.

Cleuziou, Serge and Maurizio Tosi (eds.), 1986. *The Joint Hadd*

Project: summary report on the first season December 1985. Rome.

(eds.), 1987. *The Joint Hadd Project: summary report on the second season November 1986–January 1987*. [Rome.]

1989. The south-eastern frontier of the ancient Near East. *SAA 1985*: 14–47.

Clothey, Fred W., 1978. *The many faces of Murukan: the history and meaning of a South Indian god*. The Hague.

Coe, Michael D., 1987. *The Maya*. 4th edn. (Ancient Peoples and Places.) London.

1992. *Breaking the Maya code*. London.

Cohen, M., 1958. *La Grande Invention de l'écriture et son évolution*, I–III. Paris.

Cohen, Richard J., 1981. [Review of J. Mitchiner 1978.] *JAS* 40 (3).

1982. Graphemic distribution and redundancy in the Indus script. Paper presented at the annual meeting of the American Oriental Society held at the University of Texas, Austin, 28–31 March 1982.

Coleman, Robert, 1988. [Review of Renfrew 1987.] *CA* 29 (3): 449–53.

Collins, Mark, 1926. *On the octaval system of reckoning in India*. (University of Madras, Dravidic Studies, 4.) Madras.

Collon, Dominique, 1982. Water-buffaloes in ancient Mesopotamia. *Ur* 2–3: 123–5.

1986. *Catalogue of the Western Asiatic seals in the British Museum*, III. London.

1987. *First impressions: cylinder seals in the ancient Near East*. London.

in press, a. Mesopotamia and the Indus: the evidence of the seals. In: Julian Reade (ed.), *The Indian Ocean in antiquity*. London.

(ed.), in press, b. *Seals of the world*. London.

Comrie, Bernard (ed.), 1987a. *The world's major languages*. London and Sydney.

1987b. Introduction. In: Comrie 1987a: 1–29.

Converse, H. S., 1974. The agnicayana rite: indigenous origins? *History of Religions* 14(2): 81–95.

Conway, John Richard, 1985. Visual analysis in cultural and linguistic interpretation of the Indus Valley or Harappan script. (Ph.D. dissertation, University of Texas at Austin.) Ann Arbor.

Coomaraswamy, Ananda K., 1928–31. *Yakṣas*, I–II. (Smithsonian Institution Publications 2926, 3059.) Washington D.C.

1938. The inverted tree. *QJMS* 29 (2): 111–49.

Corbiau, Simone, 1936. An Indo-Sumerian cylinder. *Iraq* 3: 100–3.

Cornwall, Peter B., 1946. On the location of Dilmun. *BASOR* 103: 3–11. Reprinted in: Possehl 1979a: 164–7.

Corré, Alan D., 1966. Anatomy of a decipherment. *Wisconsin Academy of Sciences, Arts and Letters* 55: 11–20.

Costantini, Lorenzo, 1990. Harappan agriculture in Pakistan: the evidence of Nausharo. *SAA 1987*: I, 321–32.

Coulmas, Florian, 1989. *The writing systems of the world*. Oxford.

Cowell, E. B. (ed.), 1895–1913. *The Jātaka; or, stories of the Buddha's former births, translated from the Pali by various hands*, I–VII. Cambridge.

Cowgill, Warren, 1974. Indo-European languages. In: *The New Encyclopaedia Britannica*. 15th edn, *Macropaedia* 9: 431–8. Chicago.

1986. I: Einleitung. Ins Deutsche übersetzt und bibliographisch bearbeitet von Alfred Bammesberger und Martin Peters. In: Mayrhofer 1986: I, 9–71. Heidelberg.

Cowley, A. E., 1927. A note on Minoan writing. In: S. Casson (ed.), *Essays in Aegean archaeology presented to Sir A. Evans*: 5–7. Oxford.

Cribb, Joe, 1985. Dating India's earliest coins. *SAA 1983*: 535–54.

Croft, William, 1990. *Typology and universals*. (Cambridge Textbooks in Linguistics.) Cambridge.

Crooke, William, 1896. *The popular religion and folklore of northern India*, I–II. Westminster.

1906. *Things Indian, being discursive notes on various subjects connected with India*. London.

1914. The Holi: a vernal festival of the Hindus. *Folk-Lore* 25: 55–83.

1920. Stones: Indian. In: *ERE* 11: 871–6.

1926. *The religion and folklore of northern India*. Prepared for the press by R. E. Enthoven. Oxford.

Crystal, David, 1987. *The Cambridge encyclopedia of language*. Cambridge.

Culbert, T. Patrick (ed.), 1991. *Classic Maya political history: hieroglyphic and archaeological evidence*. (School of American Research Advanced Seminar Series.) Cambridge, Mass.

Cunningham, Alexander, 1875. Harappa. In: *Archaeological Survey of India, report for the year 1872–73*, V: 105–8 and pl. 32–3. Calcutta. Reprinted in: Possehl 1979a: 102–4.

1877. *Corpus inscriptionum Indicarum*, I: *Inscriptions of Aśoka*. Calcutta.

Dagyab, Loden Sherap, 1977. *Tibetan religious art*, I–II. (Asiatische Forschungen, 52.) Wiesbaden.

Dahlquist, Allan, 1962. *Megasthenes and Indian religion*. Stockholm.

Dales, George F., Jr, 1962a. Harappan outposts on the Makran coast. *Antiquity* 36: 86–92 and pl. 12–15.

1962b. A search for ancient seaports. *Expedition* 4 (2): 2–10, 44.

1964. The mythical massacre at Mohenjo-Daro. *Expedition* 6 (3): 36–43. Reprinted in: Possehl 1979a: 293–6.

1965a. New investigations at Mohenjo-Daro. *Archaeology* 18 (2): 145–50. Reprinted in: Possehl 1979a: 192–5.

1965b. Civilization and floods in the Indus Valley. *Expedition* 7 (4): 10–19.

1965c. A suggested chronology for Afghanistan, Baluchistan, and the Indus Valley. In: Ehrich 1965: 257–84.

1965d. Re-opening Mohenjo-Daro excavations. *ILN*, 29 May 1965: 25–7.

1966. The decline of the Harappans. *Scientific American* 214 (5): 92–100. Reprinted in: Possehl 1979a: 307–12.

1967. South Asia's earliest writing – still undeciphered. *Expedition* 9 (2): 30–7.
1968. Of dice and men. *JAOS* 88 (1): 14–23. Reprinted in: Possehl 1979a: 138–44.
1973. Archaeological and radiocarbon chronologies for protohistoric South Asia. *SAA 1971*: 157–69. Reprinted in: Possehl 1979a: 332–8.
1974. Excavations at Balakot, Pakistan, 1973. *Journal of Field Archaeology* 1 (1–2): 3–22.
1976. New inscriptions from Moenjo-Daro, Pakistan. In: Barry L. Eichler (ed.), *Kramer anniversary volume: cuneiform studies in honor of Samuel Noah Kramer* (Alter Orient und Altes Testament, 25): 111–23. Kevelaer and Neukirchen-Vlyun.
1979. The Balakot project: summary of four years' excavations in Pakistan. *SAA 1977*: I, 241–74.
1982. Mohenjo-daro miscellany: some unpublished, forgotten, or misinterpreted features. In: Possehl 1982a: 97–106.
1984. Sex and stone at Mohenjo-daro. In: Lal and Gupta 1984: 109–15.
1991. The phenomenon of the Indus Civilization. In: Jansen, Mulloy and Urban 1991: 129–44.
1992a. Some specialized ceramic studies at Harappa. In: Meadow 1992a: 61–9.
1992b. A line in the sand: explorations in Afghan Seistan. In: Possehl 1992c: 19–32.
Dales, George F. and J. Mark Kenoyer, 1986. *Excavations at Mohenjo-Daro Pakistan: the pottery*. (University Museum Monograph 53.) Philadelphia.
1992. Harappa 1989: summary of the fourth season. *SAA 1989*: I, 57–68.
Dales, George F., Jonathan Mark Kenoyer and the staff of the Harappa Project, 1992. Summaries of five seasons of research at Harappa (District Sahiwal, Punjab, Pakistan), 1986–1990. In: Meadow 1992a: 185–262.
Dales, George F. and R. L. Raikes, 1968. The Mohenjo-daro floods: a rejoinder. *AA* 70 (5): 957–61.
Damerow, Peter and Robert K. Englund, 1987. Die Zahlzeichensysteme der archaischen Texte aus Uruk. In: Green and Nissen 1987: 117–66 and tables 54–60.
1989. *The Proto-Elamite texts from Tepe Yahya*. With an introduction by C. C. Lamberg-Karlovsky. (The American School of Prehistoric Research, Bulletin 39.) Cambridge, Mass.
Damerow, Peter, Robert K. Englund and Hans J. Nissen, 1988a. Die Entstehung der Schrift. *Spektrum der Wissenschaft*, February 1988: 74–85.
1988b. Die ersten Zahldarstellungen und die Entwicklung des Zahlbegriffes. *Spektrum der Wissenschaft*, March 1988: 46–55.
Dames, M. Longworth, 1886. Old seals found at Harappa. *IA* 15 (179): 1.
Dandekar, R. N., 1946–85. *Vedic bibliography*, I–IV. Poona.
1953. Rudra in the Veda. *Journal of the University of Poona, Humanities Section*, 1: 94–148.
1987. *Harappan bibliography*. (Government Oriental Series, B 15.) Poona.
Dange, Sadashiv Ambadas, 1983. Indus Civilization and the Vedic culture: re-examination of the problem. *QJMS* 74 (1): 49–82.
1986–90. *Encyclopaedia of Puranic beliefs and practices*, I–V. New Delhi.
1987. *Glimpses of Puranic myth and culture*. Delhi.
Dani, A. H., 1960. *Prehistory and protohistory of eastern India*. Calcutta.
1963. *Indian palaeography*. Oxford.
1967. Timargarha and Gandhara Grave culture. *Ancient Pakistan* 3: 1–407.
1970–1. Excavations in the Gomal Valley. *Ancient Pakistan* 5: 1–177.
1973. Mystery script of the Indus Valley: one of the world's oldest writing systems still resists the efforts of scholars. *Unesco Courier* 26 (12): 28–30.
(ed.), 1981. *Indus Civilization – new perspectives*. Islamabad.
1988. *Recent archaeological discoveries in Pakistan*. Paris and Tokyo.
Darian, Steven, 1976. The other face of the makara. *Artibus Asiae* 38 (1): 29–36.
De, Sushil Kumar, 1957. *The Megha-dūta of Kālidāsa, critically edited*. New Delhi.
DeFrancis, John, 1989. *Visible speech. The diverse oneness of writing systems*. Honolulu.
Deglurkar, G. B., 1988–9. Naigameṣa, emerging as Kārtikeya: the iconographic record. *BDCRI* 47–8: 57–9.
Dehejia, Vidya, 1986. *Yoginī cult and temples: a Tantric tradition*. New Delhi.
Deppert, Joachim, 1977. *Rudras Geburt: systematische Untersuchungen zum Inzest in der Mythologie der Brāhmaṇas*. (Beiträge zur Südasienforschung, 28.) Wiesbaden.
de Sacy, A. I. Silvestre, 1878. Sur les inscriptions de Nakshi Roustam. Paper read at the Académie des Inscriptions. Printed in: de Sacy 1793.
1793. *Mémoires sur diverses antiquités de la Perse*. Paris.
1802. *Lettre au citoyen Chaptal ... au sujet de l'inscription égyptienne du monument trouvé à Rosette*. Paris.
1811. [Review of Etienne Quatremère, *Mémoires géographiques et historiques sur l'Egypte*, Paris 1811.] *Magasin Encyclopédique* 1811 (4): 177ff.
Deshpande, Madhav M., 1979. Genesis of Rigvedic retroflexion: a historical and sociolinguistic investigation. In: Deshpande and Hook 1979: 235–315.
Deshpande, Madhav M. and Peter Edwin Hook (eds.), 1979. *Aryan and non-Aryan in India*. (Michigan Papers on South and Southeast Asia, 14.) Ann Arbor.
Dhavalikar, M. K., 1963. The origin of the Saptamatrikas. *BDCRI* 21: 19–26.
1992. Kuntasi: a Harappan port in western India. *SAA 1989*: I, 73–82.
Dhavalikar, M. K., V. N. Misra, S. R. Roy, K. P. Gupta, A. Ray, S. B. Deo, M. N. Deshpande, S. A. Sali, H. Sarkar and

K. S. Ramachandran, 1989. Chalcolithic. In: Ghosh 1989a: I, 95–107.

Dhavalikar, M. K. and Gregory L. Possehl, 1992. The Pre-Harappan period at Prabhas Patan and the Pre-Harappan phase in Gujarat. *ME* 17 (1): 71–8.

Diakanoff (D'yakonov), Igor M., 1972. Die Arier im Vorderen Orient: Ende eines Mythos. (Zur Methodik der Erforschung verschollener Sprachen.) *Orientalia* NS 41: 91–120.

1975. Ancient writing and ancient written language: pitfalls and peculiarities in the study of Sumerian. In: Stephen J. Lieberman (ed.), *Sumerological studies in honor of Thorkild Jakobsen on his seventieth birthday, June 7, 1974*: 99–127. Chicago.

1985a. On the original home of the speakers of Indo-European. *JIES* 13 (1–2): 92–174.

1985b. Media. In: Gershevitch 1985: 36–148.

Diakonoff, I. M. and S. A Starostin, 1986. *Hurro-Urartian as an Eastern Caucasian language*. (Studien zur Sprach-wissenschaft, Supplement 12.) Munich.

Diehl, Carl Gustav, 1956. *Instrument and purpose: studies on rites and rituals in South India*. Lund.

Dikshit, K. N., 1989. Late Harappa. In Ghosh 1989a: I, 89–91.

Diringer, David, 1968. *Writing: a key to the history of mankind*, I–II. 3rd edn. London.

Divakaran, Odile, 1984. Durgā the great goddess: meanings and forms in the early period. In: Meister 1984: 271–88.

Doblhofer, Ernst, 1957. *Zeichen und Wunder*. Vienna.

1973. *Voices in stone: the decipherment of ancient scripts and writings*. Translated by Mervyn Savill. London and New York.

Doerfer, Gerhard, 1973. *Lautgesetz und Zufall: Betrachtungen zum Omnicomparatismus*. Innsbruck.

Dollfus, G. and P. Encrevé, 1982. Marques sur poteries dans la Susiane du Ve millénaire: réflexions et comparaisons. *Paléorient* 8 (1): 107–15.

Dossin, G., 1962. Bronzes inscrits du Luristan de la collection Foroughi. *Iranica Antiqua* 2: 149–64 and 21 pl.

Dresden, Mark Jan (trans.), 1941. *Mānavagṛhyasūtra: a Vedic manual of domestic rites. Translation, commentary and preface*. Groningen.

Driver, G. R., 1976. *Semitic writing: from pictograph to alphabet*. 3rd edn, revised by S. A. Hopkins. London.

Drower, M. S., 1968–9. Early connections between Sumer and Egypt. *Bulletin of the Institute of Classical Studies, University of London*, 8–9: 243–7.

Duarte, Adriana, n.d. [*c*.1974]. *The beggar saint of Sehwan and other sketches of Sind*. Edited by S. Khan. Karachi.

Dubois, Jean Antoine, [1815] 1906. *Hindu manners, customs and ceremonies*. Translated by Henry K. Beauchamp. 3rd edn. Oxford.

Duchesne-Guillemin, J., 1962. *La Religion de l'Iran ancien*. Paris.

Dumarçay, Jacques, 1966. Décors à base de cercles sécants dans la céramique harapéenne et leur construction. *Arts Asiatiques* 14: 41–4.

Dumont, Paul-Emile, 1927. *L'Aśvamedha: description du sacrifice solennel du cheval dans le culte védique*. Paris and Louvain.

Duperron. See Anquetil Duperron.

During Caspers, E. C. L., 1970–1. Some motifs as evidence for maritime contact between Sumer and the Indus Valley. *Persica* 5: 107–18 and pl. 8–11.

1971. New archaeological evidence for maritime trade in the Persian Gulf during the late Protoliterate period. *EW* NS 21: 9–20.

1972a. Harappan trade in the Arabian Gulf in the third millennium BC. *Mesopotamia* 7: 167–91.

1972b. Etched cornelian beads. *BIA* 10: 83–98.

1976. Cultural concepts in the Arabian Gulf and the Indian Ocean: transmissions in the third millennium and their significance. *Proceedings of the Seminar for Arabian Studies* 6: 8–39.

1979. Sumer, coastal Arabia and the Indus Valley in Protoliterate and Early Dynastic eras: supporting evidence for a cultural linkage. *JESHO* 22 (2): 121–35.

1982. Sumerian traders and businessmen residing in the Indus Valley cities: a critical assessment of the archaeological evidence. *AIUON* 42: 337–79.

1983. Triangular stamp seals from the Arabian Gulf and their Indus Valley connections. *AIUON* 43 (4): 661–70.

1985a. The 'priest king' from Moenjo-daro: an iconographic assessment. *AIUON* 45: 19–24 and pl. 1–4.

1985b. More on the stone sculpture from Moenjo-daro. *AIUON* 45: 409–26 and pl. 1–6.

1985c. Sundry technical aspects of the manufacture of Indus Valley terracotta art. In: Gnoli and Lanciotti 1985: I, 267–85 and pl. 1–12.

1985d. Hindu mythology and Harappan religion: selected aspects. *Itihas Patrika* 5 (3): 66–73. Thane, Maharastra.

1987. Of linga stones and gaming boards. *AIUON* 47 (1): 67–74 and pl. 1–8.

1989. Magic hunting practices in Harappan times. *SAA 1985*: 227–336.

1990. Harappan temples – fact or fallacy? *SAA 1987*: 245–61.

Durrani, F. A., 1981a. Indus Civilization: evidence west of Indus. In: Dani 1981: 133–8 and pl. 1–19.

1981b. Rahman Dheri and the birth of civilization in Pakistan. *BIA* 18: 191–207.

1984. Some Early Harappan sites in Gomal and Bannu Valleys: In: Lal and Gupta 1984: 505–10.

1986. Rehman Dheri and the origins of Indus Civilization, I–II. (Ph.D. dissertation, Temple University. UMI 86–27444.) Ann Arbor.

1988. Excavations in the Gomal Valley: Rehman Dheri excavation report, no. 1. *Ancient Pakistan* 6: 1–232. Peshawar.

Durrani, Farzand A. and Rita P. Wright, 1992. Excavation at Rehman Dheri: the pottery typology and technology. In: Possehl 1992c: 145–62.

Dyson, Robert H., Jr, 1973. The archaeological evidence of the second millennium BC on the Persian plateau. In: I. E. S. Edwards, C. J. Gadd, N. G. L. Hammond and E. Sollberger (eds.), *The Cambridge ancient history*, 3rd edn, II.I: 686–715. Cambridge.

1987. The relative and absolute chronology of Hissar II and the Proto-Elamite horizon of northern Iran. In: Aurenche et al. 1987: II, 647–78.

Ebeling, Erich, 1932. An. In: *RLA* I: 115–17.

1938: Enki (Ea). In: *RLA* II: 374–81.

1957. Fisch. In: *RLA* III: 66–7.

Edelberg, Lennart and Schuyler Jones, 1979. *Nuristan*. Graz.

Edgerton, Franklin, 1959. Śiśumāra, and other alleged Indic derivatives of IE. al- 'nourish'. *JAOS* 79: 43–5.

Edzard, Dietz Otto, 1968. Die Inschriften der altakkadischen Rollsiegel. *Archiv für Orientforschung* 22: 12–20.

1969. Die Keilschrift. In: Hausmann 1969: 214–21.

1980. Keilschrift. In: *RLA* V: 544–68.

1986. [Review of Parpola 1985b.] *ZA* 76 (1): 160.

1990. Indusschrift aus der Sicht des Assyriologen: Rezensions-artikel zu *Corpus of Indus Seals and Inscriptions*, vol. 1, von J. P. Joshi und A. Parpola. *ZA* 80 (1): 124–34.

Edzard, Dietz Otto, Gertrud Farber and Edmond Sollberger, 1977. *Répertoire géographique des textes cuneiformes*, I: *Die Orts- und Gewässernamen der präsargonischen und sargonischen Zeit*. (Beihefte zum Tübinger Atlas des Vorderen Orients, B 7/1.) Wiesbaden.

Egerod, Søren Christian, 1974. Languages of the world: Sino-Tibetan languages. In: *The New Encyclopaedia Britannica*, 15th edn, *Macropaedia*, 22: 721–31.

Eggeling, J. (trans.), 1882–1900. *The Śatapatha-Brāhmaṇa*, I–V. (SBE, 12, 26, 41, 43, 44.) Oxford.

Ehret, Christopher, 1976. Linguistic evidence and its correlation with archaeology. *WA* 8 (1): 5–18.

1988. Language change and the material correlates of language and ethnic shift. *Antiquity* 62 (236): 564–74.

Ehrich, Robert W. (ed.), 1965. *Chronologies in Old World archaeology*. Chicago.

(ed.), 1992 *Chronologies in Old World archaeology*. 3rd edn. I–II. Chicago.

Eilers, Wilhelm, 1976. *Sinn und Herkunft der Planetennamen*. (Bayerische Akademie der Wissenschaften, Philos.-historische Klasse, Sitzungsberichte, 1975: 5.) Munich.

Eisler, R., 1910. *Weltenmantel und Himmelszelt*, I–II. Munich.

Elfenbein, J. H., 1966. *The Baluchi language: a dialectology with texts*. (Royal Asiatic Society Monographs, 27.) London.

1982. Notes on the Balochi–Brahui linguistic commensality. *TPS* 1982: 77–98.

1983a. The Brahui problem again. *IIJ* 25: 103–25.

1983b. A Brahui supplementary vocabulary. *IIJ* 25: 191–209.

1987. A periplous of the 'Brahui problem'. *Studia Iranica* 16: 215–33.

1989. Balōčī. In: Schmitt 1989a: 350–62.

Eliade, Mircea, 1969. *Yoga: immortality and freedom*. Translated by W. R. Trask. 2nd edn. (Bollingen Series, 56.) Princeton.

(ed.), 1987. *The encyclopedia of religion*, I–XVI. New York.

Elizarenkova, T. Ya., 1989. About traces of a Prakrit dialectal basis in the language of the R̥gveda. In: Caillat 1989a: 1–17.

Elmore, Wilber Theodore, 1915. *Dravidian gods in modern Hinduism: a study of the local and village deities of southern India*. (The University Studies of the University of Nebraska, 15: 1.) Lincoln, Nebr.

Elwin, Verrier, 1951. *The tribal art of Middle India: a personal record*. London.

Emeneau, Murray B., 1935. *A union list of printed Indic texts and translations in American libraries*. (American Oriental Series, 7.) New Haven, Conn.

1949. The strangling figs in Sanskrit literature. *University of California Publications in Classical Philology* 13: 345–70. Berkeley.

1954. Linguistic prehistory of India. *PAPS* 98 (4): 282–92. Reprinted in Emeneau 1980: 85–104.

1956. India as a linguistic area. *Language* 32: 3–16. Reprinted in Emeneau 1980: 105–25.

1962a. *Brahui and Dravidian comparative grammar*. (University of California Publications in Linguistics, 27.) Berkeley. Chapters 2 (7–20), 4 (47–61) and 5 (62–70) reprinted with modifications and the titles 'Brahui vowels' (329–32), 'Iranian and Indo-Aryan influence on Brahui' (333–49) and 'The position of Brahui in the Dravidian family' (320–8) in Emeneau 1980.

1962b. Bilingualism and structural borrowing. *PAPS* 106: 430–42. Reprinted in Emeneau 1980: 38–65.

1966. The dialects of Old Indo-Aryan. In: Birnbaum and Puhvel 1966: 123–38.

1967a. *Dravidian linguistics, ethnology and folktales: collected papers*. (Annamalai University, Department of Linguistics, Publication 8.) Annamalainagar.

1967b. The South Dravidian languages. *JAOS* 87: 365–413.

1969. The non-literary Dravidian languages. In: Sebeok 1969: V, 334–42.

1971a. Dravidian and Indo-Aryan: the Indian linguistic area. In: A. F. Sjoberg (ed.), *Symposium on Dravidian Civilization*: 33–68. Austin. Reprinted in Emeneau 1980: 167–96.

1971b. [Review of *Proto-Indica: 1968*; Parpola et al. 1969a; 1969b; 1970; Schrapel 1969.] *JAOS* 91 (4): 541–2.

1974a. The Indian linguistic area revisited. *IJDL* 3: 92–134. Reprinted in Emeneau 1980: 197–249.

1974b. [Review of Pfeiffer 1972.] *Language* 50 (4): 755–8.

1975. [Review of S. Koskenniemi et al. 1973.] *JAOS* 95 (1): 138–9.

1978a. Towards an onomastics of South Asia. *JAOS* 98: 113–30.

1978b. [Review of Masica 1976.] *Language* 54: 201–10.

1980. *Language and linguistic area: essays*. Selected and introduced by Anwar S. Dil. Stanford.

1988. Proto-Dravidian **c-* and its developments. *JAOS* 108: 239–68.

Emeneau, M. B. and T. Burrow, 1962. *Dravidian borrowings from Indo-Aryan*. (University of California Publications in Linguistics, 26.) Berkeley.

Englund, R. K., 1987. Liste der zusätzlichen Zeichen der Texte der 33. und 34. Kampagne. In: Green and Nissen 1987: 347–50.

1988. Administrative timekeeping in ancient Mesopotamia. *JESHO* 31: 121–85.

Englund, Robert K. and J.-P. Gregoire (eds.), in press. *Proto-cuneiform texts from Jemdet Nasr*, I: *Copies, transliterations and glossary*. With a contribution by R. J. Matthews. (Materialien zu den frühen Schriftzeugnissen des Vorderen Orients, I.) Berlin.

Ensink, Jacob, 1974 (1975). Problems of the study of pilgrimage in India. *IT* 2: 57–79.

Erman, Adolf, 1922. *Die Entzifferung der Hieroglyphen*. (Sitzungsberichte der Preussischen Akademie der Wissenschaften, Phil.-hist. Klasse, 1922.) Berlin.

Erman, Adolf and Hermann Grapow (eds.), 1926–53. *Wörterbuch der ägyptischen Sprache*, I–XIII. Leipzig and Berlin.

Erndl, Kathleen Marie, 1987. Victory to the Mother: the goddess cult of northwest India. (Ph.D. dissertation, University of Wisconsin, Madison. University Microfilms International NEZ 87–20457.) Ann Arbor.

Ethnic problems of the history of Central Asia in the early period (second millennium BC*)*. Moscow 1981.

Evans, A. J., 1935. *The palace of Minos at Knossos*, IV. London.

Ewald, Wilhelm, 1914. *Siegelkunde*. (Handbuch der mittelalterlichen und neueren Geschichte, IV.) Munich.

Fábri, C. L., 1934. Latest attempts to read the Indus script: a summary. *Indian Culture* 1: 51–6.

1935. The punch-marked coins: a survival of the Indus Civilization. *JRAS* 1935 (2): 307–18.

1937. The Cretan bull-grappling sports and the bull-sacrifice in the Indus Valley Civilization. *Archaeological Survey of India, Annual Report for 1934–35*: 93–101.

Fabricius, Johann Philip, 1972. *Tamil and English dictionary*. 4th edn. Tranquebar.

Faddegon, B., 1926. The thirteenth month in ancient Hindu chronology. *AO* 4: 124–33.

Fairservis, Walter A., Jr, 1956. *Excavations in the Quetta Valley, West Pakistan*. (APAMNH 45 (2): 169–402.) New York.

1959. *Archaeological surveys in the Zhob and Loralai Districts, West Pakistan*. (APAMNH 47 (2): 277–448.) New York.

1961a. *The Harappan Civilization – new evidence and more theory*. (American Museum Novitates, 2055.) New York. Reprinted in: Possehl 1979a: 49–65.

1961b. *Archaeological studies in the Seistan basin of south-western Afghanistan and eastern Iran*. (APAMNH 48 (1): 1–128.) New York.

1967. *The origin, character, and decline of an early civilization*. (American Museum Novitates, 2302.) New York. Reprinted in: Possehl 1979a: 66–89.

1975. *The roots of ancient India: the archaeology of an early Indian civilization*. 2nd edn. (Phoenix Book 636.) Chicago.

1976. *Excavations at the Harappan site of Allahdino*, I: *The seals and other inscribed material*. (Papers of the Allahdino Expedition, 1.) New York.

1977. *Excavations at the Harappan site of Allahdino*, III: *The graffiti. A model in the decipherment of the Harappan script*. (Ibid., 3.) New York.

1983. The script of the Indus Valley Civilization. *Scientific American* 248 (3): 44–52.

1984. Harappan Civilization according to its writing. *SAA 1981*: 154–61.

1986. A review of the archaeological evidence in connection with the identity of the language of the Harappan script. In: Jacobson 1986a: 175–93.

1992. *The Harappan Civilization and its writing: a model for the decipherment of the Indus script*. New Delhi.

Fairservis, Walter A. and F. C. Southworth, 1989. Linguistic archaeology and the Indus Valley culture. In: Kenoyer 1989a: 133–41.

Falk, Harry, 1981. Vedisch *árma*. *ZDMG* 131 (1): 160–71.

1986. *Bruderschaft und Würfelspiel: Untersuchungen zur Entwicklungsgeschichte des vedischen Opfers*. Freiburg.

1989. Soma I and II. *BSOAS* 52 (1): 77–90.

1991. [Review of Parpola 1988b.] *IIJ* 34 (1): 57–60.

Falkenstein, Adam, 1936. *Archaische Texte aus Uruk, bearbeitet und herausgegeben*. (Ausgrabungen der Deutschen Forschungsgemeinschaft in Uruk / Warka, 2.) Berlin.

1949–50. *Grammatik der Sprache Gudeas von Lagaš*, I–II. Rome.

1959. *Das Sumerische*. (Handbuch der Orientalistik I: 1: 1–2: 1.) Leiden.

Fedorova, I. K., 1965. K voprosu o lingvisticheskoj prinadlezhnosti protoindijskogo yazyka. In: *Predvaritel'noe* 1965: 52–5. [English translations: Alekseev et al. 1969; Fedorova [1965] 1976.]

[1965] 1976. On the question of the linguistic affinity of the Proto-Indian texts. In: Zide and Zvelebil 1976: 63–6 [with 'commentary' by the translators: 66–71].

Fentress, Marcia Antoinette, 1976. Resource access, exchange systems, and regional interaction in the Indus Valley: an investigation of archaeological variability at Harappa and Moenjodaro. (Ph.D. dissertation, University of Pennsylvania. University Microfilms International 77–10,163.) Ann Arbor.

1984. The Indus 'granaries': illusion, imagination and archaeological reconstruction. In: Kennedy and Possehl 1984: 89–98.

Fergusson, James, 1973. *Tree and serpent worship*. 2nd edn. London.

Ferioli, P., E. Fiandra and S. Tusa, 1979. Stamp seals and functional analysis of their sealings at Shahr-i Sokhta II–III (2700–2200 BC). *SAA 1975*: 7–26 and pl. 3–8.

Fiandra, Enrica, 1981. The connection between clay sealings and tablets in administration. *SAA 1979*: 29–43.

Fiandra, E. and P. Ferioli, 1984. A proposal for a multi-stage approach to research on clay sealings in protohistorical administrative procedures. *SAA 1981*: 124–7.

Filliozat, Jean, 1937. *Etude de démonologie indienne. Le Kumāratantra de Rāvaṇa et les textes parallèles indiens,*

tibétains, chinois, cambodgiens et arabes. (Cahiers de la Société Asiatique, 4.) Paris.
1962. Notes d'astronomie ancienne de l'Iran et de l'Inde. *JA* 250: 325–50.
1972. [Review of *Proto-India: 1968*; Parpola et al. 1969a; 1969b; 1970; Schrapel (1969).] *BSL* 67 (2): 76–9.
1973. *Un texte de la religion kaumāra: le Tirumurukāṟṟuppaṭai*. (Publications de l'Institut Français d'Indologie, 49.) Pondicherry.
Fischer, Eberhard and Haku Shah, 1971. *Mogra Dev, tribal crocodile gods: wooden crocodile images of Chodri, Gamit and Vasava tribes, south Gujarat (India)*. (Art for Tribal Rituals in South Gujarat, 1.) Ahmedabad.
Fišer, Ivo, 1966. *Indian erotics of the oldest period*. (Acta Universitatis Carolinae, Philologica Monographia, 14.) Prague.
Flattery, David Stophlet and Martin Schwartz, 1989. *Haoma and harmaline: the botanical identity of the Indo-Iranian sacred hallucinogen 'Soma' and its legacy in religion, language, and Middle Eastern folklore*. (University of California Publications: Near Eastern Studies, 21.) Berkeley.
Fleet, J. F., 1912a. Seals from Harappa. *JRAS* 1912: 699–701.
1912b. The use of the planetary names of the days of the week in India. *JRAS* 1912: 1039–46.
Forbes, Andrew, 1984. Wrong footed. *Guardian*, 31 August 1984: 8.
Forrer, Emil O., 1932. *Die hethitische Bilderschrift*. (Studies in Ancient Oriental Civilization, 3.) Chicago.
Förstemann, Ernst (ed.), 1880. *Die Mayahandschrift der Königlichen öffentlichen Bibliothek zu Dresden*. Leipzig.
1904. Aids to the deciphering of the Maya manuscript [and other essays]. In: Eduard Saler, E. Förstemann, Paul Schellhas, Carl Sapper and E. P. Dieseldorf, *Mexican and Central American antiquities, calendar systems and history: twenty-four papers*, translated from the German under the supervision of Charles P. Bowditch. (Smithsonian Institution, Bureau of American Ethnology, Bulletin 28.) Washington, D.C.
1906. *Commentary on the Maya manuscript in the Royal Public Library of Dresden*. Translated by Selma Wesselhoeft and A. M. Parker, translation revised by the author. (Papers of the Peabody Museum of American Archaeology and Ethnology, 4: II: 53–267.) Cambridge, Mass.
Francfort, Henri-Paul, 1984a. The Harappan settlement of Shortughai. In: Lal and Gupta 1984: 301–10.
1984b. The early periods of Shortughai (Harappan) and the western Bactrian culture of Dashly. *SAA 1981*: 170–5.
1985a. Towns in the Bronze Age. In: *The world atlas of archaeology*: 228–9. London.
1985b. Fortifications et sociétés en Asie centrale protohistorique. In: Huot et al. 1985: 379–88.
1987. La civilisation de l'Indus aux rives de l'Oxus. *Archeologia* 227: 44–55.
1989. *Fouilles de Shortughaï: recherches sur l'Asie centrale protohistorique*, I–II. (Mémoires de la Mission Archéologique Française en Asie Centrale, II.) Paris.
1992a. New data illustrating the early contacts between Central Asia and northwest India. *SAA 1989*: I, 97–102.
1992b. Dungeons and dragons: reflections on the system of iconography in Protohistoric Bactria and Margiana. In: Possehl 1992c: 179–208.
Francfort, H.-P. and M.-H. Pottier, 1978. Sondage préliminaire sur l'établissement protohistorique harappéen et post-harappéen de Shortugaï (Afghanistan du N.-E.). *Arts Asiatiques* 34: 29–79 and pl. 1–7.
Francken, A. G. (ed.), 1735. *Der Königl. Dänischen Missionarien aus Ost-Indien eingesandter Ausfuehrlichen Berichten Anderer Theil, Von der XIII. bis XXIV. Continuation*. Halle.
Franke, Judith A., 1977. Presentation seals of the Ur III / Isin-Larsa period. In: Gibson and Biggs 1977: 61–6.
Franke, Ute, 1984. A selection of inscribed objects recovered from Mohenjo-Daro. In: Jansen and Urban 1984: I, 117–38.
Franke-Vogt, Ute, 1989. Inscribed bangles: an enquiry into their relevance. *SAA 1985*: 237–46.
1991. The glyptic art of the Harappa culture. In: Jansen et al. 1991: 179–87.
1991 (1992). *Die Glyptik aus Mohenjo-Daro. Uniformität und Variabilität in der Induskultur: Untersuchungen zur Typologie, Ikonographie und räumlichen Verteilung*, I–II. (Baghdader Forschungen, 13.) Mainz.
1992. Inscribed objects from Mohenjo-daro: some remarks on stylistic variability and distribution patterns. *SAA 1989*: I, 103–12.
Frankfort, H., 1932. Early days in Babylonia: intercourse with India (new evidence). *The Times*, 26 March 1932: 15.
1933. *Tell Asmar, Khafaje, and Khorsabad: second preliminary report of the Iraq Expedition*. (Oriental Institute of the University of Chicago Communications, 16.) Chicago.
1934. The Indus Civilization and the Near East. *ABIA* 7: 1–12.
1939. *Cylinder seals*. London.
1951. *The birth of civilization in the Near East*. Bloomington, Ind.
1955. *Stratified cylinder seals from the Diyala region*. (The University of Chicago Oriental Institute Publications, 72.) Chicago.
Friedrich, Johannes, 1939. *Entzifferungsgeschichte der hethitischen Hieroglyphenschrift*. (Die Welt als Geschichte, Sonderheft 3.) Stuttgart.
1966a. *Entzifferung verschollener Schriften und Sprachen*. 2nd edn. (Verständliche Wissenschaft, 51.) Berlin.
1966b. *Geschichte der Schrift, unter besonderer Berücksichtigung ihrer geistigen Entwicklung*. Heidelberg.
1969. [Review of Parpola et al. 1969a; Schrapel 1969.] *Orientalia* NS 38: 493–4.
Friedrich, J., E. Reiner, A. Kammenhuber, G. Neumann and A. Heubeck, 1969. *Altkleinasiatische Sprachen [und Elamisch]*. (Handbuch der Orientalistik I: I: 1–2: 2.) Leiden.
Frifelt, Karen, 1975. On prehistoric settlement and chronology of the Oman peninsula. *EW* NS 25 (3–4): 359–424.

1979. The Umm an-Nar and Jemdet Nasr of Oman and their relations abroad. *SAA 1975*: 43–57 and pl. 22–5.

Frifelt, Karen and Per Sørensen (eds.), 1989. *South Asian Archaeology 1985*. (Scandinavian Institute of Asian Studies, Occasional Papers, 4.) London.

Frye, Richard N., 1961. Remarks on Baluchi history. *Central Asiatic Journal* 6: 44–50.

1966. *The heritage of Persia*. (Mentor Books MQ662.) New York.

1984. *The history of ancient Iran*. (Handbuch der Altertumswissenschaft III: 7.) Munich.

Fürer-Haimendorf, C. von, 1953. New aspects of the Dravidian problem. *TC* 2 (2): 127–35.

Fürer-Haimendorf, Elizabeth von, 1958–64. *An anthropological bibliography of South Asia, together with a directory of recent anthropological field work*, [I]–II. (Le Monde d'Outre-mer Passé et Présent, 4th series: Bibliographies, 3–4.) Paris and The Hague.

Fürer-Haimendorf, Elizabeth von and Helen Kanitkar, 1970. *An anthropological bibliography of South Asia, together with a directory of recent anthropological field work*, III. (Le Monde d'Outre-mer Passé et Présent, 4th series: Bibliographies, 8.) Paris and The Hague.

Fussman, Gérard, 1972. *Atlas linguistique des parlers dardes et kafirs*, I–II. (PEFEO 86.) Paris.

Gadd, C. J., 1932. Seals of ancient Indian style found at Ur. *Proceedings of the British Academy* 18: 191–210 and pl. 1–3. Reprinted in: Possehl 1979a: 115–22 and pl. 6–8.

Gadd, C. J. and Sidney Smith, 1924. The new links between Indian and Babylonian civilizations. *ILN*, 4 October 1924: 614–16. Reprinted in: Possehl 1979a: 109–10.

1931. Sign list of early Indus script. In: Marshall 1931a: II, 406–22 and III: pl. 119–29.

Gail, Adalbert J., 1980. Planets and pseudoplanets in Indian literature and art with special reference to Nepal. *EW* NS 30 (1–4): 133–46 and 19 figs.

(ed.), in press. *South Asian Archaeology 1991*.

Gamkrelidze, T. V. and V. V. Ivanov, 1984. *Indoevropejskie yazyki i indoevropejtsy*, I–II. Tbilisi.

1985a. The ancient Near East and the Indo-European question: temporal and territorial characteristics of Proto-Indo-European based on linguistic and historico-cultural data. *JIES* 13 (1–2): 3–48.

1985b. The migrations of tribes speaking the Indo-European dialects from their original homeland in the Near East to their historical habitations in Eurasia. *JIES* 13 (1–2): 49–91.

1985c. The problem of the original home of the speakers of Indo-European languages (in response to I. M. Diakonoff's articles in *Vestnik Drevnej Istorii*, 1982, nos. 2 and 3). *JIES* 13 (1–2): 175–84.

1987. *Indo-European and the Indo-Europeans*, I. (Trends in Linguistics, Studies and Monographs.) The Hague and Berlin.

1990. The early history of Indo-European languages. *Scientific American* 262 (3): 82–9.

Garbini, Giovanni, 1988. The question of the alphabet. In: Sabatino Moscati (ed.), *The Phoenicians*: 86–103. Milan.

Gardiner, Alan, 1957. *Egyptian grammar*. 3rd edn. London.

Gaur, R. C., 1973. Lal Qila excavation and the OCP problem. In: Agrawal and Ghosh 1973: 154–62.

1981. The Painted Grey Ware and the Aryan problem. In: *Ethnic problems* 1981: 326–35.

1989. Ochre-coloured Ware (OCW). In: Ghosh 1989a: I, 93–4.

Gelb, Ignace J., 1931; 1935; 1942. *Hittite hieroglyphs*, I–III. (Studies in Ancient Oriental Civilization, 2; 14; 21.) Chicago.

1963. *A study of writing*. Revised edn. Chicago and London.

1970. Makkan and Meluḫḫa in early Mesopotamian sources. *RA* 64 (1): 1–8.

1973. Written records and decipherment. In: Sebeok 1973: XI, 253–84.

1974. Records, writing, decipherment. *Visible Language* 8 (4): 293–318.

1975. Methods of decipherment. *JRAS* 1975 (2): 95–104.

1977. Typology of Mesopotamian seal inscriptions. In: Gibson and Biggs 1977: 107–26.

1982. Measures of dry and liquid capacity. *JAOS* 102 (4): 585–90.

Geldner, Karl F., 1889. Ficus indica in RV. 1,24,7. In: Pischel and Geldner 1889: I, 113–15.

(trans.), 1951–7. *Der Rigveda*, I–IV. (Harvard Oriental Series, 33–6.) Cambridge, Mass.

Gening, V. F., 1977. Mogil'nik Sintashta i problema rannykh indoiranskikh plemen. *SA* 1977 (4): 53–73.

1979. The cemetery at Sintashta and the early Indo-Iranian peoples. *JIES* 7 (1–2): 1–29.

Genouillac, H. de, 1930. Rapport sur les travaux de la Mission de Tello, IIᵉ campagne: 1929–1930. *RA* 27 (4): 169–86.

George, Dieter, 1991. *Ṣaṇmukhakalpa: ein Lehrbuch der Zauberei und Diebeskunst aus dem indischen Mittelalter*. (Monographien zur indischen Archäologie, Kunst und Philologie, 7.) Berlin.

Gershevitch, Ilya, 1957. Sissoo at Susa (OPers. *yakā-* = *Dalbergia Sissoo* Roxb.). *BSOAS* 19: 317–20.

1974. An Iranianist's view of the Soma controversy. In: Ph. Gignoux and A. Tafazzoli (eds.), *Mémorial Jean de Menasce*: 45–75. Louvain.

1978. Ad Sissoo at Susa. *BSOAS* 21: 174.

(ed.), 1985. *The Cambridge history of Iran*, II: *The Median and Achaemenian periods*. Cambridge.

Ghirshman, Roman, 1938. *Fouilles de Sialk près de Kashan 1933, 1934, 1937*, I. (Musée du Louvre, Département des Antiquités Orientales, Série archéologique, 4.) Paris.

1964. *The arts of ancient Iran, from its origins to the time of Alexander the Great*. Translated by Stuart Gilbert and James Emmons. New York.

1977. *L'Iran et la migration des Indo-Aryens et des Iraniens*. Leiden.

Ghosh, A., 1953. Fifty years of the Archaeological Survey of

India. *AI* 9: 29–52.
1965. The Indus Civilization: its origins, authors, extent and chronology. In: Misra and Mate 1965: 113–36.
(ed.), 1989a. *An encyclopaedia of Indian archaeology*, I–II. New Delhi.
1989b. Copper / Bronze Age. In: Ghosh 1989a: I, 69–75.
1989c. Black-and-Red Ware – upper Ganga valley. In: Ghosh 1989a: I, 94–5.
Gibson, M., 1977. An Indus Valley stamp seal from Nippur, Iraq. *ME* I: 67.
Gibson, McGuire and Robert D. Biggs (eds.), 1977. *Seals and sealing in the ancient Near East*. (Bibliotheca Mesopotamica, 6.) Malibu.
Gidwani, Parso J., 1981. A preliminary study of Sindhi personal names. *BDCRI* 40: 202–6.
Gimbutas, Marija, 1956. *The prehistory of eastern Europe*, I. (American School of Prehistoric Research, Peabody Museum, Harvard University, Bulletin 20.) Cambridge, Mass.
1965a. The relative chronology of Neolithic and Chalcolithic cultures in eastern Europe north of the Balkan peninsula and the Black Sea. In: Ehrich 1965: 459–502.
1965b. *Bronze Age cultures in Central and Eastern Europe*. The Hague.
1970. Proto-Indo-European culture: the Kurgan culture during the fifth, fourth and third millennia BC. In: Cardona et al. 1970: 155–97.
1973. The beginning of the Bronze Age in Europe and the Indo-Europeans: 3500–2500 BC. *JIES* I (2): 163–214.
1977. The first wave of Eurasian steppe pastoralists into Copper Age Europe. *JIES* 5 (4): 277–337.
1979. The three waves of the Kurgan people into Old Europe, 4500–2500 BC. *Archives Suisses d'Anthropologie Générale* 43 (2): 113–37.
1980. The Kurgan wave 2 (*c*.3400–3200 BC) into Europe and the following transformation of culture. *JIES* 8: 273–315.
1985. Primary and secondary homeland of the Indo-Europeans. Comments on Gamkrelidze–Ivanov articles. *JIES* 13 (1–2): 185–202.
1986. Remarks on the ethnogenesis of the Indo-Europeans in Europe. In: Bernhard and Kandler-Pálsson (eds.), *Ethnogenese europäischer Völker*: 5–20. Stuttgart.
1988. [Review of Renfrew 1987.] *CA* 29 (3): 453–6.
Ginzel, F. K., 1906. *Handbuch der mathematischen und technischen Chronologie: das Zeitrechnungswesen der Völker*, I. Leipzig.
Glassner, J.-J., in press. The cuneiform evidence for early Gulf trade. In: Julian E. Reade (ed.), *The Indian Ocean in antiquity*. London.
Gnoli, Gherardo, 1980. *Zoroaster's time and homeland: a study on the origins of Mazdeism and related problems*. (Istituto Universitario Orientale, Seminario di Studi Asiatici, Series minor, 7.) Naples.
Gnoli, Gherardo and Lionello Lanciotti (eds.), 1985; 1987; 1988. *Orientalia Iosephi Tucci memoriae dicata*, I–III. (Serie Orientale Roma, 56.1–3.) Rome.
Gode, P. K., 1961–9. *Studies in Indian cultural history*, I–III. (Vishveshvaranand Indological Series, 9.) Hoshiarpur.
Gonda, Jan, 1939. [Review of Ross 1938.] *Tijdschrift voor Indische Taal-, Land- en Volkenkunde* 79: 456–9.
(trans.), 1950. *The Ṛgvidhāna*. Utrecht.
1954. *Aspects of early Viṣṇuism*. Utrecht.
1955–6. The etymologies in the ancient Indian Brāhmaṇas. *Lingua* 5: 61–86.
1960. *Die Religionen Indiens*, I: *Veda und älterer Hinduismus*. (Die Religionen der Menschheit, 11.) Stuttgart.
1965. *Change and continuity in Indian religion*. (Disputationes Rheno-Traiectinae, 9.) The Hague.
1969. *Ancient Indian kingship from the religious point of view*. Leiden.
1970a. *Viṣṇuism and Śivaism: a comparison*. London.
1970b. *Notes on names and the name of god in ancient India*. (VKAW, NS 75:4.) Amsterdam.
1971. *Old Indian*. (Handbuch der Orientalistik, II. I. I.) Leiden and Cologne.
1974. *Dual deities in the religion of the Veda*. (VKAW, NS 81.) Amsterdam.
1975. *Vedic literature (Saṃhitās and Brāhmaṇas)*. (A History of Indian Literature, I: I.) Wiesbaden.
1976. *Triads in the Veda*. (VKAW, NS 91.) Amsterdam.
1977. *The ritual Sūtras*. (A History of Indian Literature, I: 2.) Wiesbaden.
1979. The Śatarudriya. In: M. Nagatomi, B. K. Matilal and J. M. Masson (eds.), *Sanskrit and Indian studies: essays in honor of Daniel H. H. Ingalls* (Studies of Classical India, 2): 75–91. Dordrecht.
1980. *Vedic ritual: the non-solemn rites*. (Handbuch der Orientalistik, II: 4: I.) Leiden.
Gopal, L., 1989. Materials [of writing]. In: Ghosh 1989a: 360–1.
Gopal, L. and T. P. Verma, 1989. Brāhmī and its derivatives. In: Ghosh 1989a: 365–8.
Gopinatha Rao, T. A., 1914–16. *Elements of Hindu iconography*, I–II. Madras.
Gordon, Cyrus H., 1971. *Forgotten scripts: the story of their decipherment*. Revised edn. (Pelican Books.) Harmondsworth.
Gordon, D. H., 1960. *The prehistoric background of Indian culture*. 2nd edn. Bombay.
Gorham, A., *s.a. Indian mason's marks in the Moghul dynasty*. London.
Goudriaan, Teun, 1978. *Māyā divine and human*. New Delhi.
Goudriaan, Teun and Sanjukta Gupta, 1981. *Hindu Tantric and Śākta literature*. (A History of Indian Literature, II: 2.) Wiesbaden.
Gragg, Gene B. (co-ordinator), 1979. Non-Semitic, non-Indo-european languages of ancient Western Asia: a typological and areal survey. Unpublished course organized at the Oriental Institute of the University of Chicago.

Grayson, A. K. and E. Sollberger, 1976. L'insurrection général contre Narâm-Suen. *RA* 70: 103–28.

Green, Margret W., 1980. Animal husbandry at Uruk in the Archaic period. *JNES* 39 (1): 1–35.

1981. The construction and implementation of the cuneiform writing system. *Visible Language* 15 (4): 345–72.

1989. Early cuneiform. In: Senner 1989: 43–57.

Green, Margret W. and Hans J. Nissen, 1987. *Zeichenliste der archaischen Texte aus Uruk*, in collaboration with P. Damerow and R. K. Englund. (Ausgrabungen der Deutschen Forschungsgemeinschaft in Uruk / Warka, 2.) Berlin.

Greenberg, Joseph H. (ed.), 1966a. *Universals of language*. 2nd edn. Cambridge, Mass.

1966b. Some universals of grammar with particular reference to the order of meaningful elements. In: Greenberg 1966a: 73–113.

1968. *Anthropological linguistics: an introduction*. (Random House Studies in Anthropology, AS8.) New York.

1971. *Language, culture and communication: essays*. Selected and introduced by Anwar S. Dil. Stanford.

(ed.), 1978. *Universals of human language*, I–IV. Stanford.

Grierson, George A. (comp. and ed.), 1903–28. *Linguistic survey of India*, I–XI. Calcutta.

Grignard, A., 1909. The Oraons and Mundas from the time of their settlement in India. *Anthropos* 4: 1–19.

Grillot, Françoise, 1987. Mécanismes de l'ancien structure nominale en élamite. *Studia Iranica* 16: 163–72.

Grinstead, Eric, 1972. *Guide to the archaic Chinese script*. Characters drawn by Gordon To. (Scandinavian Institute of Asian Studies Monograph Series, 11.) Lund.

Grjasnow, Michail, 1970. *Südsibirien*. (Archaeologia Mundi.) Genf.

Gropp, Gerd, 1992. A 'Great Bath' in Elam. *SAA 1989*: I, 113–18.

Gros, François, 1968. *Le Paripāṭal: texte tamoul. Introduction, traduction et notes*. (Publications de l'Institut Français d'Indologie, 35.) Pondicherry.

Grotefend, Georg Friedrich, 1802. *Praevia de cuneatis quas vocant inscriptionibus Persepolitanis legendis et explicandis relatio*. Paper presented at a meeting of the Göttingen Academy on 4 September 1802, reviewed by Th. Chr. Tychsen in *Göttingische Gelehrte Anzeigen* III (149), 1802: 1481–7, and published only by Wilhelm Meyer in: *Nachrichten von der Königlichen Gesellschaft der Wissenschaften zu Göttingen*, 1893: no. 14.

1837. *Neue Beiträge zur Erläuterung der persepolitanischen Keilschrift nebst einem Anhange über die Vollkommenheit der ersten Art derselben*. Hanover.

Gundert, Hermann, 1871–2. *A Malayalam and English dictionary*, I–II. Mangalore.

Gupta, P. L. and T. R. Hardaker, 1985. *Indian silver punch-marked coins: Magadha-Maurya Karshapana Series*. (Indian Institute of Research in Numismatic Studies, Monograph 1.) Anjaneri, Nashik, Maharashtra.

Gupta, S. M., 1971. *Plant myths and traditions in India*. Leiden.

Gupta, S. P., 1989. Copper Hoard. In: Ghosh 1989a: I, 91–3.

Gupta, S. P. and K. S. Ramachandran (eds.), 1979. *The origin of Brahmi script*. Delhi.

Gupta, S. P., K. S. Ramachandran, B. M. Pande, P. C. Pant, S. C. Ray, T. C. Sharma, S. B. Deo, H. Sarkar, A. Sundara, K. V. Soundara Rajan and Y. D. Sharma, 1989. Megalithic. In: Ghosh 1989a: I, 110–30.

Gupte, B. A., 1902. Notes on female tattoo designs in India. *IA* 31: 293–8.

1906. The symbolism of the Sāvitrī-vrata. *IA* 35: 116–19 and pl.

Gurov, N. V., 1968. Prospects for the linguistic interpretation of the Proto-Indian texts (on the basis of the Dravidian languages). In: *Proto-Indica: 1968*: 28–50. Reprinted with the editors' critical comments in: Gurov [1968] 1976; and with some modifications in: Gurov 1970a.

1970a. Towards the linguistic interpretation of the Proto-Indian texts. *JTS* 2 (1): 53–87. [See Gurov 1968.]

1970b. Morfologicheskaya struktura protoindijskikh nadpisej. In: *Proto-Indica: 1970*: 43–100.

1972a. Izuchenie protoindijskikh tekstov (kratkij obzor). In: *Proto-Indica: 1972*: I, 5–51.

1972b. Imennoe sklonenie v dravidijskikh yazykakh i mikroparadigma protoindijskikh tekstov (opyt sopostavleniya). In: *Proto-Indica: 1972*: I, 52–152.

1975a. Protoindijskij blok nazvaniya prazdnika. In: *Proto-Indica: 1973*: 52–3.

1975b. K voprosu o poiskhozhdenii drevneindijskogo pyatiletnego tsikla. In: *Proto-Indica: 1973*: 54–64.

[1968] 1976. Prospects for the linguistic interpretation of the Proto-Indian texts (on the basis of the Dravidian languages). In: Zide and Zvelebil 1976: 119–33 [with 'commentary' by the editors: 133–8]. Reprint of Gurov 1968.

Gurov, N. V. and T. E. Katenina, 1967. Novyj ètap v izuchenii protoindijskikh nadpisej. *SÈ* 1967 (2): 171–8.

Gurov, N. V. and Yu. V. Knorozov, 1969. [Review of Parpola et al. 1969a.] *SÈ* 1969 (6): 151–8. [English translation: Gurov and Knorozov 1970.]

1970. *Finnish decipherment of Proto-Indian inscriptions*. Translated by Hem Chandra Pande, edited by Henry Field. (Field Research Projects, Study 42.) Coconut Grove, Fla. [Russian original: Gurov and Knorozov 1969.]

Gurumurthy, S., 1986. The Indus script and Iron Age graffiti of South India. *Tamil Civilization* 4 (3–4): 9–14.

Haarmann, Harald, 1990. *Universalgeschichte der Schrift*. Frankfurt.

Haas, Mary L., 1957. Thai word games. *Journal of American Folklore* 70 (276): 173–5.

Hale, W. E., 1986. *Asura in early Vedic religion*. New Delhi.

Halim, M. A., 1971–2. Excavations at Sarai Khola, I–II. *PA* 7: 23–89; 8: 1–112.

Halim, M. A. and Massimo Vidale, 1984. Kilns, bangles and coated vessels: ceramic production in closed containers at Moenjodaro. In: Jansen and Urban 1984: I, 63–97.

Hallo, William W., 1981. Seal inscriptions. In: Buchanan 1981: 440–62.

Hallo, William W. and Briggs Buchanan, 1965. A 'Persian Gulf' seal on an Old Babylonian mercantile agreement. In: *Studies in honor of Benno Landsberger on his seventy-fifth birthday April 21, 1965* (The Oriental Institute of the University of Chicago, Assyriological Studies, 16): 199–209.

Hamlin, Carol, 1971. The Ḫabur Ware ceramic assemblage of northern Mesopotamia: an analysis of its distribution. (Ph.D. thesis, University of Pennsylvania.) Ann Arbor.

Hammond, Norman (ed.), 1973. *South Asian Archaeology [1971]*. London.

Hamp, Eric P., 1990. The Indo-European horse. In: Markey and Greppin 1990: 211–26.

Hansman, John, 1973. Periplous of Magan and Meluḫḫa. *BSOAS* 36 (3): 554–84.

1975. A further note on Magan and Meluḫḫa. *BSOAS* 38 (3): 609–10.

Hargreaves, H., 1929. *Excavations in Baluchistan, 1925: Sampur Mound, Mastung and Sohr Damb, Nāl.* (MASI, 35.) Calcutta.

Harle, James C., 1963. Durgā, goddess of victory. *Artibus Asiae* 26: 237–46.

Harper, Katherine Anne, 1977. An iconological study on the origins and development of the Saptamātṛkās. (Ph.D. dissertation, University of California at Los Angeles.) Ann Arbor.

Harris, Roy, 1986. *The origin of writing*. London.

Harris, Zellig, 1951. *Methods in structural linguistics*. Chicago.

1954. Distributional structure. *Word* 10 (2): 146–62.

1968. *Mathematical structures of language*. New York.

Hart, George L., III, 1975. *The poems of ancient Tamil: their milieu and their Sanskrit counterparts*. Berkeley.

Härtel, Herbert (ed.), 1981. *South Asian Archaeology 1979*. Berlin.

1987. Die Kuṣāṇa-Göttin Ṣaṣṭhī. In: Harry Falk (ed.), *Hinduismus und Buddhismus. Festschrift für Ulrich Schneider*: 152–62. Freiburg.

Hartland, E. S., 1920. Stones: introductory and primitive. In: *ERE* XI: 864–9.

Hartleben, H., 1906. *Champollion: sein Leben und sein Werk*, I–II. Berlin.

Hartner, Willy, 1965. The earliest history of the constellations in the Near East and the motif of the lion–bull combat. *JNES* 24 (1–2): 1–16 and pl. 1–6.

Hastings, James (ed.), 1908–26. *Encyclopaedia of religion and ethics*, I–XII and index. Edinburgh. (= *ERE*)

Hatch, W. J., 1928. *The land pirates of India*. London.

Hauer, J. W., 1927. *Der Vrātya: Untersuchungen über die nichtbrahmanische Religion Altindiens*, I. Stuttgart.

Hausmann, Ulrich (ed.), 1969. *Allgemeine Grundlagen der Archäologie*. Munich.

Haussig, H. W. (ed.), 1984. *Wörterbuch der Mythologie*, I (5): *Götter und Mythen des indischen Subkontinents*. Stuttgart.

Hawkins, David, 1986. Writing in Anatolia: imported and indigenous systems. *WA* 17 (3): 363–76.

Hawkins, John A., 1983. *Word order universals*. (Quantitative Analyses of Linguistic Structure.) San Diego.

Hawley, John Stratton and Donna Marie Wulff (eds.), 1982. *The divine consort: Rādhā and the goddesses of India*. Berkeley.

Heesterman, J. C., 1957. *The ancient Indian royal consecration*. (Disputationes Rheno-Traiectinae, 2.) The Hague.

1962. Vrātya and sacrifice. *IIJ* 6 (1): 1–37.

1987. Vedism and Brahmanism. In: Eliade 1987: XV, 217–42.

Heine-Geldern, Robert, 1934. Osterinsel, China und Indien. *Congrès international des sciences anthropologiques et ethnologiques, compte-rendu de la première session, Londres, 1934*: 197–8. London.

1938. Die Osterinselschrift. *Anthropos* 33: 815–909.

1950. China, die ostkaspische Kultur und die Herkunft der Schrift. *Paideuma* 4: 51–92.

1955. [Review of Heras 1953.] *Anthropos* 50: 990–2.

1956. The origin of ancient civilizations and Toynbee's theories. *Diogenes* 13: 81–99.

1957. [Review of Sankarananda 1955.] *Artibus Asiae* 20 (2–3): 229–30.

Hemmy, A. S., 1931–8. System of weights at Mohenjo-daro [I–II]. In: Marshall 1931a: II, 589–97 and Mackay 1938: I, 601–12.

Hemphill, Brian E., John R. Lukacs and K. A. R. Kennedy, 1992. Biological adaptations and affinities of Bronze Age Harappans. In: Meadow 1992a: 137–82.

Hendrickx-Baudot, M. P., 1972. The weights of the Harappa-culture. *Orientalia Lovanensia Periodica* 3: 5–34.

Heras, Henry, 1953. *Studies in Proto-Indo-Mediterranean culture*, I. (Studies in Indian History of the Indian Historical Research Institute, St Xavier's College, 19.) Bombay.

1990. *Indological studies*. Edited by Bernard Anderson et al. New Delhi.

Hertz, Amelja, 1937. The origin of the Proto-Indian and the Brāhmī scripts. *IHQ* 13 (3): 389–99.

Heston, W. L., 1980. Some areal features: Indian or Irano-Indian? *IJDL* 9: 141–57.

1981. [Review of Masica 1976.] *IL* 10: 180–7.

Hetzron, Robert, 1987a. Afroasiatic languages. In: Comrie 1987a: 645–53.

1987b. Semitic languages. In: Comrie 1987a: 654–63.

Hévesy, Guillaume de, 1933a. Sur une écriture océanienne paraissant d'origine néolithique. *Bulletin de la Société Préhistorique Française* 30 (7–8): 434–49. Le Mans.

1933b. Océanie et Inde préaryenne: Mohenjo-daro et l'Ile de Pâques. *Bulletin de l'Association Française des Amis de l'Orient* 14–15: 29–50. Paris.

1938. The Easter Island and the Indus Valley scripts. *Anthropos* 33: 808–14.

Hevesy, Wilhelm von, 1934. Osterinselschrift und Indusschrift. *OLZ* 37 (11): 666–74.

Heyerdahl, Thor, 1986. *The Maldive mystery*. London.

Hiebert, Fredrik T., in press. Chronology of Margiana and radiocarbon dates. *IASCCAIB*.

Hiebert, Fredrik T. and C.C. Lamberg-Karlovsky, in press. Khurab and its Central Asian connections. *SAA 1991*.

Hilka, Alfons, 1910. *Beiträge zur Kenntnis der indischen Namengebung: die altindischen Personennamen*. (Indische Forschungen, 3.) Breslau.

Hill, Archibald A., 1967. The typology of writing systems. In: W.M. Austin (ed.), *Papers in linguistics in honor of Léon Dostert*: 92–9. The Hague.

Hillebrandt, Alfred, 1891–1902. *Vedische Mythologie*, I–III. Breslau.

1897. *Ritual-Litteratur. Vedische Opfer und Zauber*. (Grundriss III: 2.) Strasburg.

Hiltebeitel, Alf, 1978. The Indus Valley 'Proto-Śiva', reexamined through reflections on the goddess, the buffalo and the symbolism of the *vāhanas*. *Anthropos* 73: 767–97.

1980. Rāma and Gilgamesh: the sacrifices of the water buffalo and the bull of heaven. *History of Religions* 19: 187–223.

1988–91. *The cult of Draupadī*, I–II. Chicago.

(ed.), 1989. *Criminal gods and demon devotees: essays on the guardians of popular Hinduism*. Albany, N.Y.

Hincks, Edward, 1850. On the Khorsabad inscriptions. *Transactions of the Royal Irish Academy* 22 (2), *Polite Literature*: 3–72.

Hinüber, Oskar von, 1986. *Das ältere Mittelindisch im Überblick*. (SÖAW 467.) Vienna.

1990. *Der Beginn der Schrift und frühe Schriftlichkeit in Indien*. (Akademie der Wissenschaften und der Literatur, Abhandlungen der Geistes- und sozialwissenschaftlichen Klasse, 1989: 11.) Mainz.

Hinz, Walther, 1961. *Zarathustra*. Stuttgart.

1962. Zur Entzifferung der elamischen Strichschrift. *Iranica Antiqua* 2: 1–21.

1964. *Das Reich Elam*. (Urban-Bücher, 82.) Stuttgart.

1969a. *Altiranische Funde und Forschungen*. Berlin.

1969b. Die Schrift der Elamer. In: Hausmann 1969: 222–7.

1975. Problems of Linear Elamite. *JRAS* 1975 (2): 106–15.

Hinz, Walther and Heidemarie Koch, 1987. *Elamisches Wörterbuch*, I–II. (Archäologische Mitteilungen aus Iran, Supplement 17.) Berlin.

Hock, Hans Henrich, 1975. Substratum influence on (Rig-Vedic) Sanskrit? *SLS* 5 (2): 76–125.

1979. Retroflexion rules in Sanskrit. *South Asian Languages Analysis* 1: 47–62.

1982. The Sanskrit quotative: a historical and comparative study. *SLS* 12 (2): 39–85.

1984. (Pre-)Rig-Vedic convergence of Indo-Aryan with Dravidian? Another look at the evidence. *SLS* 14 (1): 89–108.

1991. *Principles of historical linguistics*. 2nd edn. Berlin.

Hock, Hans Henrich and Rajeshwari Pandharipande, 1976. The sociolinguistic position of Sanskrit in pre-Muslim South Asia. *Studies in Language Learning* 1 (2): 106–38.

Hodge, Carleton T., 1970. Afroasiatic: an overview. In: Sebeok 1970: VI, 237–54.

Hodson, F.R. (ed.), 1974. *The place of astronomy in the ancient world*. (Philosophical Transactions of the Royal Society, A 276.) London.

Hoernle, A.F.R., 1880. *A comparative grammar of the Gaudian languages*. London.

Hoffmann, Karl, 1958. Altiranisch. In: *Iranistik*, 1: *Linguistik* (Handbuch der Orientalistik I: 4: 1): 1–19. Leiden.

1975. *Aufsätze zur Indoiranistik*, I–II. Edited by Johanna Narten. Wiesbaden.

Højlund, Flemming, 1989. Some new evidence of Harappan influence in the Arabian Gulf. *SAA 1985*: 49–53.

in press. The ethnic composition of the population of Dilmun. *Proceedings of the Seminar for Arabian Studies 1992*.

Holmes, D.A., 1968. The recent history of the Indus. *GJ* 134: 367–82.

Holst, Staffan, 1973. Into the Indus script. *Orientalia Suecana* 22: 122–6.

Höltker, Georg, 1944. Das herz- oder nierenförmige Ornament auf einer Vase von Mohenjo-daro. *Ethnos* 9 (1): 1–34.

Hooja, R., 1988. *The Ahar culture and beyond: settlement and frontiers in 'Mesolithic' and early agricultural sites in south-eastern Rajasthan ca. 3rd–2nd millennium* BC. (BAR International Series, 412.) Oxford.

Hooker, J.T., 1980. *Linear B: an introduction*. Bristol.

Hopkins, E.W., 1915. *Epic mythology*. (Grundriss 3.1.B.) Strasburg.

Hopkins, Thomas A. and Alf Hiltebeitel, 1987. Indus Valley religion. In: Eliade 1987: VII, 215–23.

Hora, Sunder Lal, 1952. Fish in the Rāmāyaṇa. *JASB* 18 (2): 63–9 and pl. 1.

1955. Fish in the Jātaka sculpture. *JASB* 21 (1): 1–13 and pl. 1–5.

Hörig, Monika, 1979. *Dea Syria*. (Alter Orient und Altes Testament, 208.) Kevelaer and Neukirchen-Vluyn.

Hornell, James, 1944. The ancient village gods of South India. *Antiquity* 18 (70): 78–87.

Horsch, Paul, 1966. *Die vedische Gāthā- und Śloka-Literatur*. Berne.

Houston, S.D., 1989. *Maya glyphs*. (Reading the Past.) London.

Hrozný, Bedřich, 1915. Die Lösung des hethitischen Problems. *Mitteilungen der Altorientalischen Gesellschaft* 56: 17–50.

1917. *Die Sprache der Hethiter*. Leipzig.

1939. *Die älteste Völkerwanderung und die proto-indische Zivilisation*. Prague.

1941–2. Inschriften und Kultur der Proto-Inder von Mohenjo-daro und Harappa (*c*.2500–2200 v. Chr.). Ein Entzifferungsversuch. *Archiv Orientální* 12: 192–259 and 13: 1–102.

1943. *Die älteste Geschichte Vorderasiens und Indiens*. 2nd edn. Prague.

Hunger, H., 1977. Kalender. In: *RLA* V (3–4): 297–303.

Hunter, G.R., 1932. Mohenjo-daro – Indus epigraphy. *JRAS* 1932: 466–503.

1934. *The script of Harappa and Mohenjo-daro and its connection with other scripts.* (Studies in the History of Culture, 1.) London.

1938. [Letter to G. de Hévesy dated 1 June 1938.] In: Hévesy 1938: 809–10.

Huot, J.-L., M. Yon and Y. Calvet (eds.), 1985. *De l'Indus aux Balkans: recueil à la mémoire de Jean Deshayes.* Paris.

Huq, Abdul, 1988. Computer analysis of the Indus script. (Ph.D. thesis, University of Madras.)

Illich-Svitych, Vladislav M., 1971–84. *Opyt sravneniya nostraticheskikh yazykov (semito-khamitskij, kartvelskij, indoevropejskij, ural'skij, dravidskij, altajskij)*, I–III. Moscow.

In the image of man: the Indian perception of the universe through 2000 years of painting and sculpture. London 1982.

Inizan, Marie-Louise, in press. The dawn of trade: carnelian from India to Mesopotamia in the third millennium. *SAA 1991*.

Ipsen, G., 1929. [Review of Waddell 1925.] *OLZ* 32 (2): 91–4.

Irākavaiyaṅkār, Mu., 1935–6. *Peruntokai*, I–II. Maturai.

Irwin, John, 1980. The axis mundi and the phallus: some unrecognized east–west parallels. In: V. J. Newall (ed.), *Folklore studies in the twentieth century*: 250–9. Woodbridge.

Jacobi, Hermann, 1895. Der vedische Kalender und das Alter des Veda. *ZDMG* 49: 218–30.

1896. Nochmals das Alter des Veda. *ZDMG* 50: 69–83.

1909. On the antiquity of Vedic culture. *JRAS* 1909: 721–6.

1910. The antiquity of Vedic culture. *JRAS* 1910: 456–64.

1912. Durgā. In: *ERE* V, 117–19.

Jacobsen, Thorkild, 1970. *Toward the image of Tammuz and other essays on Mesopotamian history and culture.* Cambridge, Mass.

1976. *The treasures of darkness.* New Haven, Conn.

Jacobson, Jerome (ed.), 1986a. *Studies in the archaeology of India and Pakistan.* New Delhi.

1986b. The Harappan Civilization: an early state. In: Jacobson 1986a: 137–73.

Jamison, Stephanie W., 1991. *The ravenous hyenas and the wounded sun: myth and ritual in ancient India.* (Myth and Poetics.) Ithaca, N.Y.

Janert, Klaus Ludwig and P. Rajagopal Subramanian, 1973. Colours in early Tamil: a study based on Cilappadikaram. *IJDL* 2 (1): 141–50.

Janhunen, Juha, 1981. Uralilaisen kantakielen sanastosta. (Zusammenfassung: Über den Wortschatz des Protouralischen.) *JSFOu* 77 (9): 219–74.

1983. On early Indo-European-Samoyed contacts. In: *Symposium saeculare Societatis Fenno-Ugricae* (MSFOu 185): 115–27. Helsinki.

Jansen, Michael, 1979. *Architektur in der Harappakultur.* (Veröffentlichungen des Seminars für orientalische Kunstgeschichte an der Universität Bonn, 2.) Bonn.

1984. Architectural remains in Mohenjo-daro. In: Lal and Gupta 1984: 75–88.

1985. Mohenjo-daro, HR-A, House I, a temple? Analysis of an architectural structure. *SAA 1983*: I, 157–206.

1986. *Die Indus-Zivilisation: Wiederentdeckung einer frühen Hochkultur.* Cologne.

1991a. Mohenjo-daro – a city on the Indus. In: Jansen et al. 1991: 145–65.

1991b. Save Mohenjo-daro! In: Jansen et al. 1991: 220–34.

1992. Non-contemporaneity of the contemporaneous in the Indus culture. In: Possehl 1992c: 209–22.

in press. (Paper on the evolution of Mohenjo-daro.) *Proceedings of the Second International Symposium on Moenjo-daro, held at Karachi and Moenjo-daro on 24–27 February 1992.* Karachi.

Jansen, Michael, Máire Mulloy and Günter Urban (eds.), 1991. *Forgotten cities on the Indus: early civilization in Pakistan from the 8th to the 2nd millennium* BC. Mainz.

Jansen, M. and G. Urban (eds.), 1984–7. *Interim reports*, I–II: Reports on field work carried out at Mohenjo-Daro, Pakistan, 1982–83 [and] 1983–84 by the IsMEO–Aachen University Mission. Aachen and Rome.

(eds.), 1985. *Mohenjo-Daro: data collection*, I: *Fieldbooks and concordance of HR area.* Leiden.

Jaritz, Kurt, 1981. Zum Problem der Indusschrift. In: Roswitha G. Stiegner (ed.), *Al-Hudhud: Festschrift Maria Höfner zum 80. Geburtstag*: 113–31. Graz.

Jarrige, Catherine (ed.), 1992. *South Asian Archaeology 1989.* (Monographs in World Archaeology, 14.) Madison, Wis.

Jarrige, Jean-François, 1977. Nouvelles recherches archéologiques au Baluchistan: les fouilles de Mehrgarh. In: *Le Plateau iranien* 1977: 79–94.

1979. Excavations at Mehrgarh–Pakistan. *SAA 1975*: 76–87, pl. 30–44.

1982. Excavations at Mehrgarh: their significance for understanding the background of the Harappan Civilization. In: Possehl 1982a: 79–84.

1985a. Les relations entre l'Asie centrale méridionale, le Baluchistan et la vallée de l'Indus à la fin du 3e et au début du 2e millénaire. In: *L'Archéologie de la Bactriane ancienne*: 105–18. Paris.

1985b. Continuity and change in the north Kachi plain (Baluchistan, Pakistan) at the beginning of the second millennium BC. *SAA 1983*: I, 35–68.

1985c. The Indian world. In: *The world atlas of archaeology*: 238–47. London.

1986. Excavations at Mehrgarh-Nausharo. *PA* 10–22: 63–131.

1987a. A prehistoric élite burial in Quetta. *NBS* 4: 3–9.

1987b. Problèmes de datation du site néolithique de Mehrgarh, Baluchistan, Pakistan. In: Aurenche et al. 1987: I, 381–6.

1988a. Introduction. In: *Les Cités oubliées de l'Indus*: 13–38.

1988b. Excavations at Nausharo: 1986–87. *PA* 23: 149–203.

1989 (1991). Excavations at Nausharo: 1987–88. *PA* 24: 21–67.

1991a. Mehrgarh: its place in the development of ancient cultures in Pakistan. In: Jansen et al. 1991: 34–50.

1991b. The cultural complex of Mehrgarh (period VIII) and Sibri. The 'Quetta hoard'. In: Jansen et al. 1991: 94–103.
Jarrige, Jean-François and M. Usman Hassan, 1989. Funerary complexes in Baluchistan at the end of the third millennium in the light of recent discoveries at Mehrgarh and Quetta. *SAA 1985*: 150–66.
Jarrige, Jean-François and M. Lechevallier, 1979. Excavations at Mehrgarh, Baluchistan: their significance in the prehistorical context of the Indo-Pakistani borderlands. *SAA 1977*: 463–535.
Jarrige, Jean-François and Richard H. Meadow, 1980. The antecedents of civilization in the Indus Valley. *Scientific American* 243 (8): 102–10.
1992. Mélanges Fairservis: a discourse on relations between Kachi and Sindh in prehistory. In: Possehl 1992c: 163–78e.
Jarrige, Jean-François and Marielle Santoni, 1979. *Fouilles de Pirak*, I–II. (Publications de la Commission des Fouilles Archéologiques, Fouilles du Pakistan, 2.) Paris.
Jasim, Sabah Abboud and Joan Oates, 1986. Early tokens and tablets in Mesopotamia: new information from Tell Abada and Tell Brak. *WA* 17 (3): 348–62.
Jayakar, Pupul, [1980]. *The earthen drum: an introduction to the ritual arts of rural India*. New Delhi.
Jayaswal, K. P., 1913. The Harappa seals. *IA* 42: 203.
Jeffreys, M. D. W., 1947. Mohenjo-daro and Easter Island. *Man* 47 (73): 67–8.
Jenner, P. N., L. C. Thompson and S. Starosta (eds.), 1976. *Austroasiatic studies*, I–II. (Oceanic Linguistics, Special Publication 13.) Honolulu.
Jensen, Hans, 1969. *Die Schrift in Vergangenheit und Gegenwart*. 3rd edn. Berlin.
Jeremias, Alfred, 1929. *Handbuch der altorientalischen Geisteskultur*. 2nd edn. Berlin.
Jettmar, Karl, 1966. Mittelasien und Sibirien in vortürkischer Zeit. In: Spuler 1966a: 1–105.
1972. Die Steppenkulturen und die Indoiranier des Plateaus. *Iranica Antiqua* 9: 65–93.
1975. *Die Religionen des Hindukusch*. With contributions from Schuyler Jones and Max Klimburg. (Die Religionen der Menschheit 4,1.) Stuttgart.
1981. Fortified 'ceremonial centres' of the Indo-Iranians. In: *Ethnic problems*: 220–9.
1983a. Geschichte der Archäologie in Sibirien und im asiatischen Steppenraum. *BAVA* 5: 187–226.
1983b. 'Frühe Nomaden' und 'nördliche Nomaden'. *MAGW* 113: 33–43.
1983c. The origins of Chinese civilization: Soviet views. In: David N. Keightley (ed.), *The origins of Chinese civilization* (Studies on China, 1): 217–36. Berkeley.
1985. Non-Buddhist traditions in the petroglyphs of the Indus Valley. *SAA 1983*: II, 751–77.
1986. *The religions of the Hindukush*, I: *The religion of the Kafirs. The pre-Islamic heritage of Afghan Nuristan*. Translated by Adam Nayyar. With contributions from Schuyler Jones and Max Klimburg and a glossary by Peter S. C. Parkes. London.
Jettmar, Karl and Volker Thewalt, 1987. *Between Gandhāra and the silk roads: rock-carvings along the Karakorum Highway. Discoveries by German–Pakistani expeditions 1979–1984*. Mainz.
Jha, Munishwar, 1967. *Māgadhī and its formation*. (Calcutta Sanskrit College Research Series, 60.) Calcutta.
Johansson, K. F., 1917. *Über die altindische Göttin Dhiṣáṇā und Verwandtes: Beiträge zum Fruchtbarkeitskultus in Indien*. (Skrifter utgifna af K. Humanistiska Vetenskaps-Samfundet i Uppsala, 20: 1.) Uppsala.
Joki, Aulis J., 1973. *Uralier und Indogermanen: die älteren Berührungen zwischen den uralischen und indogermanischen Sprachen*. (MSFOu, 151.) Helsinki.
Jones, H. L. (ed. and trans.), 1928, 1930. *The geography of Strabo*, V and VII. (The Loeb Classical Library, 211, 241.) Cambridge, Mass., and London.
Jong, J. W. de, 1973. The discovery of India by the Greeks. *Asiatische Studien* 27 (2): 115–42.
Joseph, P., 1964. The Harappa script: a tragedy in timing. *TC* 11 (4): 295–307.
1970. Harappa script decipherment: Fr. Heras and his successors. *JTS* 2 (1): 111–34.
Joshi, J. P., 1989. Pre-Harappa. In: Ghosh 1989a: I, 75–9.
Joshi, J. P., Madhu Bala and Jassu Ram, 1984. The Indus Civilization: a reconsideration on the basis of distribution maps. In: Lal and Gupta 1984: 511–30.
Joshi, Jagat Pati and Asko Parpola (eds.), 1987. *Corpus of Indus Seals and Inscriptions*, I: *Collections in India*. (AASF, B 239 and MASI, 86.) Helsinki. (= *CISI* 1.)
Jotimuttu, P., 1970. *A guide to Tamil by the direct method*. 3rd edn. Madras.
Justeson, John S., 1977. Universals of language and universals of writing. In: Alphonse Juilland, Andrew M. Devine and Laurence D. Stephens (eds.), *Linguistic studies offered to Joseph Greenberg on the occasion of his sixtieth birthday*: I, 57–94. Saratoga, Calif.
1986. The origin of writing systems: Preclassic Mesoamerica. *WA* 17 (3): 437–58.
Justeson, John S. and Laurence D. Stephens, in preparation. *Writing systems: structure and development*.
Kailasapathy, K., 1968. *Tamil heroic poetry*. Oxford.
Kaiser, Mark and V. V. Shevoroshkin, 1988. Nostratic. *Annual Review of Anthropology* 17: 309–29.
Kak, Subhash C., 1987. The study of the Indus script: general considerations. *Cryptologia* 11 (3): 182–91.
Kalyanaraman, A., 1969. [Review of Parpola et al. 1969a.] *ALB* 33: 419–22.
Kalyanaraman, S., 1988. Indus script – a bibliography. Manila.
Kamal, Mahr, 1969. Indus Valley script deciphered! [Review of Parpola et al. 1969a.] *Perspective* 3 (2): 65–7. Karachi.
Kammenhuber, Annelies, 1961. *Hippologica Hethica*. Wiesbaden.
1968. *Die Arier im Vorderen Orient*. Heidelberg.

1975. The linguistic situation of the 2nd millennium BC in ancient Anatolia. *JRAS* 1975 (2): 116–20.
Kane, P. V., 1938. Naming a child or person. *IHQ* 14: 224–44.
1941–58. *History of Dharmaśāstra*, I–V. (Government Oriental Series, B6.) Vol. I in 2nd edn. Poona.
Kangle, R. P. (ed. and trans.), 1965–72. *The Kauṭilīya Arthaśāstra*, I–III. Bombay.
Kanitkar, Helen and Elizabeth von Fürer-Haimendorf, 1976. *An anthropological bibliography of South Asia, together with a directory of recent anthropological field work*. New series, I. The Hague and Paris.
Kantor, Helene J., 1942. The early relations of Egypt with Asia. *JNES* 1: 174–213.
1944. The final phase of the Predynastic culture. *JNES* 3: 110–36.
1952. Further evidence for early Mesopotamian relations with Egypt. *JNES* 11: 239–50.
1965. The relative chronology of Egypt and its foreign correlations before the late Bronze Age. In: Ehrich 1965: 1–46.
Karanth, R. V., 1992. The ancient gem industry in Cambay. *ME* 17 (1): 61–70.
Karashima, Noboru (ed.), 1985. *Indus Valley to Mekong delta: explorations in epigraphy*. Madras.
Karlgren, Bernhard, 1957. Grammata Serica recensa. *The Museum of Far Eastern Antiquities, Stockholm, Bulletin* 29: 1–332.
Karttunen, Klaus, 1989. *India in early Greek literature*. (SO 65.) Helsinki.
Kaye, G. R., 1920. Hindu astronomical deities. *JASB* NS 16 (1): 57–75 and pl. 7–11. Reprinted as appendix II (pp. 103–17) in Kaye 1924.
1924. *Hindu astronomy*. (MASI, 18.) Calcutta.
Keith, Arthur Berriedale (trans.), 1914. *The Veda of the Black Yajus school entitled Taittirīya Sanhitā*, I–II. (Harvard Oriental Series, 18–19.) Cambridge, Mass.
1925. *The religion and philosophy of the Veda and Upanishads*, I–II. (Harvard Oriental Series, 31–2.) Cambridge, Mass.
Kellens, Jean, 1989. Avestique. In: Schmitt 1989a: 32–55. Wiesbaden.
Kelley, D. H., 1976. *Deciphering the Maya script*. Austin, Tex.
Kennedy, Kenneth A. R., 1982. Skulls, Aryans and flowing drains: the interface of archaeology and skeletal biology in the study of the Harappan Civilization. In: Possehl 1982a: 289–95.
1984. Trauma and disease in the ancient Harappans. In: Lal and Gupta 1984: 425–36.
Kennedy, K. A. R. and Gregory L. Possehl (eds.), 1976. *Ecological backgrounds of South Asian prehistory*. (South Asia Occasional Papers and Theses, 4.) Ithaca, N.Y.
(eds.), 1984. *Studies in the archaeology and palaeoanthropology of South Asia*. New Delhi.
Kenoyer, Jonathan Mark (ed.), 1989a. *Old problems and new perspectives in the archaeology of South Asia*. (Wisconsin Archaeological Reports, 2.) Madison, Wis.
1989b. Socio-economic structures of the Indus Civilization as reflected in specialized crafts and the question of ritual segregation. In: Kenoyer 1989a: 183–92.
1991a. Shell-working in the Indus Civilization. In: Jansen et al. 1991: 216–19.
1991b. Ornament styles of the Indus Valley tradition: evidence from recent excavations at Harappa, Pakistan. *Paléorient* 17 (2): 79–98.
1992. Urban process in the Indus tradition: a preliminary model from Harappa. In: Meadow 1992a: 29–60.
in press. Excavations on Mound E, Harappa: a systematic approach to the study of Indus urbanism. In: *SAA 1991*.
Kent, Roland G., 1953. *Old Persian: grammar, texts, lexicon*. 2nd edn. (American Oriental Series, 33.) New Haven, Conn.
Khan, Ahmad Nabi, 1978. The Indus Valley script: a survey of the attempts at its decipherment. *Studies in South Asian Culture* 7: 116–21.
1990. The Indus Valley script: a survey of attempts for its decipherment. *The Archaeology* 2 (2): 108–15. Karachi.
Khan, F. A., 1965. Excavations at Kot Diji. *PA* 2: 11–85.
Khiste, Nārāyaṇa Śāstrī and Jagannātha Śāstrī Hośinga (eds.), 1930. *The Yājñavalkya Smṛti with Viramitrodaya, the commentary of Mitra Misra, and Mitaksara, the commentary of Vijnanesvara*. (The Chowkhamba Sanskrit Series, 62.) Varanasi.
Khubchandani, Lachman M., 1969. Sindhi. In: Sebeok 1969: V, 201–34.
Kinnier Wilson, J. V., 1974. *Indo-Sumerian: a new approach to the problems of the Indus script*. Oxford.
1984. The case for accountancy. In: Lal and Gupta 1984: 173–8.
1986. The case for accountancy in the Indus script, with a restatement on the meaning and theory of 'Indo-Sumerian'. *Tamil Civilization* 4 (3–4): 204–13.
1987. Fish rations and the Indus script: some new arguments in the case for accountancy. *South Asian Studies* 3: 41–6.
Kinsley, David, 1986. *Hindu goddesses: visions of the divine feminine in the Hindu religious tradition*. Berkeley.
Kirfel, W., 1920. *Die Kosmographie der Inder nach den Quellen dargestellt*. Bonn.
1955. Die vorgeschichtliche Besiedelung Indiens und seine kulturellen Parallelen zum alten Mittelmeerraum. *Saeculum* 6: 166–79.
Kiruṣṇamūrtti, Irā, 1986. *Canka kālac cōḻar nāṇayankaḷ*. Madras.
Kittel, Erich, 1970. *Siegel*. (Bibliothek für Kunst- und Antiquitätenfreunde, 11.) Braunschweig.
Kittel, Ferdinand, 1968–71. *Kannaḍa–English dictionary*, I–IV. Revised by M. Mariappa Bhat. Madras.
Kjærum, Poul, 1983. *Failaka / Dilmun: the second millennium settlements*, 1.1: *The stamp and cylinder seals*. (Jutland Archaeological Society Publications, 17.1.) Aarhus.
1986. The Dilmun seals as evidence of long distance relations in the early second millennium BC. In: Al Khalifa and Rice 1986: 269–77.

Knižková, H., 1966. One more step towards the deciphering of the Proto-Indian script. *New Orient* 5 (5): 139–40.

Knorozov, Yuri V., 1958. The problem of the study of the Maya hieroglyphic writing. *American Antiquity* 23 (3): 284–91.

1963. *Pis'mennost' indejtsev Majya*. Moscow and Leningrad.

1965. Kharakteristika yazyka protoindijskikh nadpisej. In: *Predvaritel'noe* 1965: 46–51. [English translations: Alekseev et al. 1969; Knorozov [1965] 1976.]

[1963] 1967. *Selected chapters* [i.e. 1, 6, 7 and 9] *from 'The writing of the Maya Indians'*. Translated by Sophie Coe. Collaborating editor Tatiana Proskouriakoff. (Peabody Museum of Archaeology and Ethnology, Harvard University, Russian Translation Series, 4.) Cambridge, Mass. [Russian original: Knorozov 1963.]

1968. The formal analysis of the Proto-Indian texts. In: *Proto-Indica: 1968*: 4–19. Reprinted in: Knorozov [1968] 1976, and with some modifications in: Knorozov 1970b.

1970a. Klassifikatsiya protoindijskikh blokov. In: *Proto-Indica: 1970*: 3–14.

1970b. The formal analysis of the Proto-Indian texts. *JTS* 2 (1): 13–25. [Reprint, with some modifications, of Knorozov 1968.]

1972. Formal'noe opisanie protoindijskikh izobrazhenij. In: *Proto-Indica: 1972*: II, 178–245.

1975. Klassifikatsiya protoindijskikh nadpisej. In: *Proto-Indica: 1973*: 4–15.

[1965] 1976. The characteristics of the language of the Proto-Indian inscriptions. In: Zide and Zvelebil 1976: 55–9 [with 'commentary' by the translators: 59–62].

[1968] 1976. The formal analysis of the Proto-Indian texts. In: Zide and Zvelebil 1976: 97–107 [with 'commentary' by the editors: 107–12].

1981. Protoindijskie nadpisi. (K problemam deshifrovki.) *SÈ* 1981 (5): 47–71.

(ed.), 1986. *Ètnicheskaya semiotika: drevnie sistemy pis'ma*. Moscow.

Knorozov, Yu. V., M. F. Al'bedil' and B. Ya. Volchok, 1981. *Proto-Indica: 1979. Report on the investigation of the Proto-Indian texts*. Moscow. [English version of Al'bedil' et al. 1982.]

Knorozov, Yu. V. and M. A. Probst, 1976. [Review of Koskenniemi et al. 1973.] *IIJ* 17 (1–2): 83–8.

Knorozov, Yu., B. Volchok and N. Gurov, 1984. Some groups of proto-religious inscriptions of the Harappans. In: Lal and Gupta 1984: 169–71.

Knudtzon, J. A., 1902. *Die zwei Arzawa-Briefe, die ältesten Urkunden in indogermanischer Sprache*. Leipzig.

Knyazeva, O., 1980. Zagadka schitalas' nerazreshimoj... Sovetskie uchenye prochli drevneindijskie pis'mena. *Izvestiya* 26 (19396), 30 January 1980: 6.

Kober, Alice, 1946. Inflection in Linear Class B: 1. Declension. *AJA* 50: 268–76.

1948. The Minoan scripts: fact and theory. *AJA* 52 (1): 82–103.

1949. 'Total' in Minoan Linear Class B. *Archiv Orientální* 17 (1): 286–98.

Kohl, Philip, 1975. Carved chlorite vessels: a trade in finished commodities in the mid-third millennium. *Expedition* 18 (1): 18–31.

1978. The balance of trade in Southwestern Asia in the mid-third millennium BC. *CA* 19 (3): 436–92 (476–85: comments by 15 scholars).

1979. The 'world economy' of West Asia in the third millennium BC. *SAA 1977*: I, 55–85.

(ed.), 1981. *The Bronze Age civilization of Central Asia: recent Soviet discoveries*. Armonk, N.Y.

(ed.), 1984. *Central Asia: Palaeolithic beginnings to the Iron Age*. Paris.

Koivulehto, Jorma, 1979. Phonotaktik als Wegweiser in der Lehnwortforschung: die ostfi. *-str-*Wörter. *Finnisch-ugrische Forschungen* 43: 67–79. Helsinki.

1991. *Uralische Evidenz für Laryngaltheorie*. (SÖAW 566.) Vienna.

Kondratov, A. M., 1965. Pozitsionno-statisticheskij analiz protoindijskikh tekstov. In: *Predvaritel'noe* 1965: 31–45. [English translations: Alekseev et al. 1969; Kondratov [1965] 1976.]

[1965] 1976. The positional-statistical analysis of the Proto-Indian texts. In: Zide and Zvelebil 1976: 39–48 [with 'commentary' by the translators: 49–53].

Konishi, Masatoshi, 1984. 'Pre-' or 'Early' Harappan culture: a conceptual battle. In: Lal and Gupta 1984: 37–42.

1987. Writing materials during the Harappan period. In: B. M. Pande and B. D. Chattopadhyaya (eds.), *Archaeology and history: essays in memory of Shri A. Ghosh*: 213–. Delhi.

1991. Zur Symbolik der bengalischen Bodenmalerei: die Alpanās des Māghmaṇḍala-Rituals. *Zeitschrift für Semiotik* 13 (1–2): 43–53.

Konow, Sten, 1906. *Muṇḍā and Dravidian languages*. (Linguistic Survey of India, IV.) Calcutta.

1912. Vedic *'dasyu'*, Toxri *'dahā'*. In: *Festschrift Vilhelm Thomsen zur Vollendung des siebzigsten Lebensjahres*: 96–7. Leipzig.

Kooij, K. R. van, 1972. *Worship of the Goddess according to the Kālikāpurāṇa*, I. (Orientalia Rheno-Traiectina, 14.) Leiden.

Koppers, Wilhelm, 1936. Pferdeopfer und Pferdekult der Indogermanen. In: *Die Indogermanen- und Germanenfrage* (Weiner Beiträge zur Kulturgeschichte und Linguistik 4): 279–411. Salzburg.

Korhonen, Mikko, 1981. *Johdatus lapin kielen historiaan*. Helsinki.

Koskenniemi, Kimmo, 1981. Syntactic methods in the study of the Indus script. *SO* 50: 125–36.

Koskenniemi, Kimmo and Asko Parpola, 1979. *Corpus of texts in the Indus script*. (Department of Asian and African Studies, University of Helsinki, Research Reports, 1.) Helsinki.

1980. *Documentation and duplicates of the texts in the Indus script*. (Ibid., 2.) Helsinki.

1982. *A concordance to the texts in the Indus script*. (Ibid., 3.) Helsinki.

Koskenniemi, Seppo, Asko Parpola and Simo Parpola, 1970. A method to classify characters of unknown ancient scripts. *Linguistics* 61: 65–91.

1973. *Materials for the study of the Indus script*, I: *A concordance to the Indus inscriptions*. (AASF B 185.) Helsinki.

Kramer, Samuel Noah, 1963a. Dilmun: quest for paradise. *Antiquity* 37: 111–15.

1963b. *The Sumerians: their history, culture, and character*. Chicago.

1964. The Indus Civilization and Dilmun, the Sumerian paradise land. *Expedition* 6 (3): 44–52. Reprinted in: Possehl 1979a: 168–73.

1969. Sumerian myths and epic tales. In: Pritchard 1969a: 37–59.

Kramer, Samuel Noah and John Maier, 1989. *Myths of Enki, the crafty god*. New York.

Kramrisch, Stella, 1954. *The art of India*. London.

1977. Linga. In: *Beiträge zur Indienforschung Ernst Waldschmidt zum 80. Geburtstag gewidmet* (Veröffentlichungen des Museums für Indische Kunst Berlin, 4): 256–66. Berlin.

1981. *The presence of Śiva*. Princeton.

Krauskopff, Gisèle, 1989. *Maîtres et possédés: les rites et l'ordre social chez les Tharu (Népal)*. Paris.

Krick, Hertha, 1974. [Review of S. Koskenniemi et al. 1973.] *WZKS* 18: 217–18.

1982. *Das Ritual der Feuergründung (Agnyādheya)*. (SÖAW 399). Vienna.

Krishna Deva and Donald E. McCown, 1949. Further exploration in Sind: 1938. *AI* 5: 12–30 and pl. 1–7.

Krishnamurti, Bh., 1961. *Telugu verbal bases: a comparative and descriptive study*. (University of California Publications in Linguistics, 24.) Berkeley.

1963. [Review of *DED*.] *Language* 39 (3): 556–64.

1969. Comparative Dravidian studies. In: Sebeok 1969: v, 309–33.

1985. An overview of comparative Dravidian studies since *Current Trends 5* (1969). In: V. Z. Acson and R. L. Leed (eds.), *For Gordon H. Fairbanks* (Oceanic Linguistics Special Publication, 20): 212–31. Honolulu.

(ed.) 1986. *South Asian languages: structure, convergence and diglossia*. Delhi.

Krishna Rao, M. V. N., 1969. The Indus script. Krishna Rao's solution. *Hindustan Times Weekly Review*, 30 March 1969: i, iii.

1982. *Indus script deciphered*. Delhi.

Kuiper, F. B. J., 1948. *Proto-Munda words in Sanskrit*. (VKAW, NS 51: 3.) Amsterdam.

1955. Rigvedic loanwords. In: Otto Spies (ed.), *Studia Indologica: Festschrift für Willibald Kirfel*: 137–85. Bonn.

1976. The genesis of a linguistic area. *IIJ* 10 (2–3): 81–102.

1979. *Varuṇa und Vidūṣaka*. (VKAW, NS 100.) Amsterdam.

1991. *Aryans in the Rigveda*. (Leiden Studies in Indo-European, 1.) Amsterdam.

Kunjalal Bhishagratna (trans.), 1963. *An English translation of the Sushruta Samhita based on original Sanskrit text*, I–III. 2nd edn. (The Chowkhamba Sanskrit Studies, 30.) Varanasi.

Kuz'mina, E. E., 1977. Rasprostranenie konevodstva i kulta konya u iranoyazychnykh plemen Srednej Azii i drugikh narodov starovogo sveta. In: *Srednyaya Aziya v drevnosti i srednevekove*: 28–52. Moscow.

1985a. Les contacts entre les peuples de la steppe et les agriculteurs et le problème de l'iranisation de la Bactriane ancienne. In: *L'Archéologie de la Bactriane ancienne*: 289–90. Paris.

1985b. Classification and periodisation of Andronovo cultural community sites. *IASCCAIB* 9: 23–46.

1987. The motif of the lion–bull combat in the art of Iran, Scythia, and Central Asia and its semantics. In: Gnoli and Lanciotti 1987: II, 729–45.

1988. Kul'turnaya i ètnicheskaya atributsiya pastusheskikh plemen Kazakhstana i Srednej Azii èpokhi bronzy. *Vestnik Drevnej Istorii* 1988 (2): 35–59.

Kuz'mina, E. E. and N. M. Vinogradova, 1983. Beziehungen zwischen bronzezeitlichen Steppen- und Oasenkulturen in Mittelasien. *BAVA* 5: 35–55.

Labat, R., 1948. *Manuel d'épigraphie akkadienne (signes, syllabaire, idéogrammes)*. Paris.

Lacouperie, Terrien de, 1882. On a Lolo Ms. written on satin. *JRAS* 14: 118.

1885. Beginnings of writing in and around Tibet. *JRAS* 17: 415–41.

Lai, T. C., 1976. *Chinese seals*. Seattle.

Lal, B. B., 1954–5. Excavations in Hastināpura and other explorations in the upper Gangā and Sutlej basins 1950–52. *AI* 10 and 11: 5–151.

1960. From the Megalithic to the Harappan: tracing back the graffiti on the pottery. *AI* 16: 4–24 and pl. 1–34.

1966. The direction of writing in the Harappan script. *Antiquity* 40 (157): 52–5 and pl. 12–13. [Reprinted with slight changes in: Lal 1970: 189–95.]

1967–8. A further note on the direction of writing in the Harappan script. *Purātattva* 1: 15–16 and pl. 1.

1969. The Indus script: inconsistencies in claims of decipherment. [Review of Parpola et al. 1969a; and Krishna Rao 1969.] *Hindustan Times Weekly Review*, 6 April 1969: 14. [Reprinted with slight changes in Lal 1970: 195–202.]

1970. Some observations on Harappan script. In: *India's contribution to world thought and culture (Vivekananda commemoration volume)*: 189–202. Madras. [See Lal 1966; 1969.]

1972. The Copper Hoard culture of the Ganga Valley. *Antiquity* 45 (184): 282–7.

1974a. Some aspects of the archaeological evidence relating to the Indus script. *Purātattva* 7: 20–4, pl. 3–6.

1974b. Has the Indus script been deciphered? An assessment of two recent claims. [Review of Mahadevan 1972 and S. R. Rao 1971; 1973b.] Paper read at the 29th International

Congress of Orientalists, Paris 1973. (Indian Institute of Advanced Study, Reprint Series.) Simla.

1975a. Archaeological evidence for the Indus script. In: Leclant 1975: 145–9.

1975b. The Indus script: some observations based on archaeology. *JRAS* 1975 (2): 173–7.

1975c. The Indus Civilization. In: Basham 1975: 11–19.

1979a. Kalibangan and the Indus Civilization. In: Agrawal and Chakrabarti 1979: 65–97.

1979b. On the most frequently used symbol in the Indus script. *EW* NS 29 (1–4): 27–35.

1981a. The Indo-Aryan hypothesis *vis-à-vis* Indian archaeology. In: *Ethnic problems* 1981: 280–94.

1981b. The two Indian epics *vis-à-vis* archaeology. *Antiquity* 55: 27–34 and pl. 2–3.

1982. West was west and east was east, but when and how did the twain meet? The role of Bhagwanpura as a bridge between certain stages of the Indus and Ganges Civilizations. In: Possehl 1982a: 335–8.

1983. Reading the Indus script. [Review of S. R. Rao 1982.] *Indian and Foreign Review*, 15 April 1983: 33–6.

1984. Some reflections on the structural remains at Kalibangan. In: Lal and Gupta 1984: 55–62.

1989a. Harappa. In: Ghosh 1989a: I, 79–89.

1989b. Painted Grey Ware (PGW). In: Ghosh 1989a: I, 107–8.

1992a. We archaeologists and society. *ME* 17 (1): 1–6.

1992b. Antecedents of the signs used in the Indus script: a discussion. In: Possehl 1992c: 45–55.

Lal, B. B. and S. P. Gupta (eds.), 1984. *Frontiers of the Indus Civilization: Sir Mortimer Wheeler commemoration volume.* New Delhi.

Lamberg-Karlovsky, C. C., 1970. *Excavations at Tepe Yahya 1967–69. Progress report*, I. (American Schools of Prehistoric Research, Bulletin 27.) Cambridge, Mass.

1971. The Proto-Elamite settlement at Tepe Yaḥyā. *Iran* 9: 87–96.

1972a. Tepe Yaḥyā 1971: Mesopotamia and the Indo-Iranian borderlands. *Iran* 10: 89–100.

1972b. Trade mechanisms in Indus–Mesopotamian interrelations. *JAOS* 92 (2): 222–30. Reprinted in: Possehl 1979a: 130–7.

1973a. Urban interaction on the Iranian plateau: excavations at Tepe Yahya 1967–1973. *Proceedings of the British Academy* 59: 5–43.

1973b. Prehistoric Central Asia: a review. *Antiquity* 47 (185): 42–8.

1975. The third millennium modes of exchange and modes of production. In: Sabloff and Lamberg-Karlovsky 1975: 341–68.

1977. Foreign relations in the third millennium at Tepe Yahya. In: *Le Plateau iranien* 1977: 33–43.

1978. The Proto-Elamites on the Iranian plateau. *Antiquity* 52 (205): 114–20.

1981. Afterword. In: Kohl 1981: 386–97.

1982. Sumer, Elam and the Indus: three urban processes equal one structure? In: Possehl 1982a: 61–8.

1986. Third millennium structure and process: from the Euphrates to the Indus and the Oxus to the Indian Ocean. *Oriens Antiquus* 25 (3–4): 189–219.

1988. The 'Intercultural style' carved vessels. *Iranica Antiqua* 23: 45–95, with 4 figs. and 10 pl.

1989. The Bronze Age of Bactria. In: Ligabue and Salvatori n.d.: 13–21.

Lamberg-Karlovsky, C. C. and Maurizio Tosi, 1973. Shahr-i Sokhta and Tepe Yahya: tracks on the earliest history of the Iranian plateau. *EW* NS 23 (1–2): 21–57, 151 figs.

1989. The Proto-Elamite community at Tepe Yahya: tools of administration and social order. *SAA 1985*: 104–13.

Lambrick, H. T., 1964. *Sind: a general introduction.* (History of Sind Series, 1.) Hyderabad (Sind).

1967. The Indus flood plain and the 'Indus' Civilization. *GJ* 133 (4): 483–95. Reprinted in: Possehl 1979a: 313–22.

1973. *Sind before the Muslim conquest.* (History of Sind Series, 2.) Hyderabad (Sind).

Lamotte, Etienne, 1958. *Histoire du bouddhisme indien: des origines à l'ère Śaka.* (Bibliothèque du Muséon, 43.) Louvain.

Landa, Diego de, 1566. Relación de las Cosas de Yucatán. (Manuscript.) [Ed. and trans. Brasseur de Bourbourg 1864; trans. Tozzer 1941.]

Langdon, Stephen, 1931a. The Indus script. In: Marshall 1931a: II, 423–55.

1931b. A new factor in the problem of Sumerian origins. *JRAS* 1931: 593–6.

1932. Another Indus Valley seal. *JRAS* 1932: 47–8.

L'Archéologie de la Bactriane ancienne. Paris 1985.

Laroche, E., 1960. *Les Hiéroglyphes hittites*, I: *L'Ecriture.* Paris.

L'Asie centrale et ses rapports avec les civilisations orientales des origines à l'âge du fer. Actes du colloque franco-soviétique, Paris, 19–26 novembre 1985. (Mémoires de la Mission Archéologique Française en Asie Centrale, 1.) Paris 1988.

Leach, E. R., 1954. Primitive time-reckoning. In: Charles Singer, E. J. Holmyard and A. R. Hall (eds.), *A history of technology*, I: 110–27. Oxford.

Le Brun, Alain and François Vallat, 1978. L'origine de l'écriture à Suse. *Cahiers de la Délégation Archéologique Française en Iran* 8: 11–59.

Leclant, Jean (ed.), 1975. *Le Déchiffrement des écritures et des langues. Colloque du XXIXe Congrès International des Orientalistes.* Paris.

Leemans, W. F., 1960. *Foreign trade in the Old Babylonian period, as revealed by texts from southern Mesopotamia.* (Studia et Documenta ad Iura Orientis Antiqui Pertinentia, 6.) Leiden.

1968a. Old Babylonian letters and economic history: a review article with a digression on foreign trade. *JESHO* 11: 171–226.

1968b. Additional evidence for the Persian Gulf trade and Meluḫḫa. *JESHO* 11 (2): 215–26.

1970a. De betrekkingen tussen Mesopotamië en het Indus-gebied en de ontcijfering van het oude indische scrift. *Phoenix* 15 (2): 248–67.

1970b. [Review of Parpola et al. 1969a.] *Bibliotheca Orientalis* 27 (5–6): 422.

Legrain, L., 1921. *Empreintes de cachets élamites.* (Mémoires de la Mission Archéologique de Perse, 16.) Paris.

Lehmann, Thomas and Thomas Malten, 1992. *A word index of Old Tamil Caṅkam literature.* (Beiträge zur Südasienforschung, 147.) Stuttgart.

Lehmann, Winfred P., 1990a. The current thrust of Indo-European studies. *General Linguistics* 30: 1–52.

1990b. [Review of Mallory 1989.] *Diachronica* 7 (1): 101–16.

Lentz, Wolfgang, 1939. *Zeitrechnung in Nuristan und am Pamir.* (Abhandlungen der Preussischen Akademie der Wissenschaften zu Berlin, 1938: 7.) Berlin.

Leonard, Jonathan Norton and the editors of Time-Life Books, 1973. *The first farmers.* (The Emergence of Man.) Alexandria, Va.

Le Plateau iranien et l'Asie centrale des origines à la conquête islamique: leur relations à la lumière des documents archéologiques. (Actes du Colloque International du CNRS, 567.) Paris 1977.

Les Cités oubliées de l'Indus: archéologie du Pakistan. Paris 1988.

Leshnik, Lawrence S., 1968. The Harappan 'port' at Lothal: another view. *AA* 70 (5): 911–22. Reprinted in: Possehl 1979a: 203–11.

1972. Pastoral nomadism in the archeology of India and Pakistan. *WA* 4 (2): 150–66.

1974. *The Pandukal complex: South Indian 'Megalithic' burials.* Wiesbaden.

Lesky, Albin, 1963. *Geschichte der griechischen Literatur.* 2nd edn. Berne.

Leslie, I. Julia, 1989. *The perfect wife: the orthodox Hindu woman according to the Strīdharmapaddhati of Tryambakayajvan.* (Oxford University South Asian Studies Series.) Delhi.

Lévi, Sylvain, 1925. [Untitled note in the proceedings of the Société Asiatique: session of 13 February 1925.] *JA* 206 (2): 371–2.

Levine, Marsha A., 1990. Dereivka and the problem of horse domestication. *Antiquity* 64: 727–40.

Lieberman, Philip, 1975. *On the origins of language: an introduction to the evolution of human speech.* (Macmillan Series in Physical Anthropology.) New York.

Lieberman, Stephen J., 1980. Of clay pebbles, hollow clay balls, and writing: a Sumerian view. *AJA* 84: 339–58.

Liebert, Gösta, 1969. Beitrag zur Frage des Polarsterns in der altindischen Literatur. *Orientalia Suecana* 17 (1968): 155–70.

1976. *Iconographic dictionary of the Indian religions: Hinduism, Buddhism, Jainism.* Leiden.

Lienhard, Siegfried, 1969. Finska forskare tyder Indusskriften. [Review of Parpola et al. 1969a.] *Orientaliska Studier* 1: 4–7. Stockholm.

1974. [Review of Parpola et al. 1969a.] *OLZ* 69 (5–6): 283–5.

Ligabue, Giancarlo and Sandro Salvatori (eds.), [1989]. *Bactria: an ancient oasis civilization from the sands of Afghanistan.* Venice.

Limet, Henri, 1968. *L'Anthroponymie sumerienne dans les documents de la 3e dynastie d'Ur.* (Bibliothèque de la Faculté de Philosophie et Lettres de l'Université de Liège, 180.) Paris.

1971. *Les Légendes des sceaux cassites.* (Académie Royale de Belgique, Classe des Lettres et des Sciences Morales et Politiques, Mémoires, 60.2.) Brussels.

Linguistic bibliography.

Littauer, M. A. and J. H. Crouwel, 1977. Origin and diffusion of the cross-bar wheel? *Antiquity* 51: 95–105.

1979. *Wheeled vehicles and ridden animals in the ancient Near East.* (Handbuch der Orientalistik, 7.1.2.B.1.) Leiden.

1980. Kampfwagen (Streitwagen): B. Archäologisch. *RLA* 5 (5–6): 344–51.

Locke, John K., 1980. *Karunamaya: the cult of Avalokitesvara-Matsyendranath in the Valley of Nepal.* Kathmandu.

Lorimer, D. L. R., 1935–8. *The Burushaski language,* I–III. (Instituttet for sammenlignende kulturforskning, Series B: 29: 1–3.) Oslo.

1937. Burushaski and its alien neighbours: problems in linguistic contagion. *TPS* 1937: 63–98.

Löwenstern, Isidore, 1845. *Essai de déchiffrement de l'écriture assyrienne.* Paris.

Lüders, Heinrich, 1934. Die Ausgrabungen von Mohenjodaro. *ZDMG* 88 (NS 13): *22*–*23*.

1942. Von indischen Tieren. *ZDMG* 96: 23–81.

1951–9. *Varuṇa,* I–II. Aus dem Nachlass, ed. by L. Alsdorf. Göttingen.

Ludwig, Alfred, 1878. *Der Rigveda, übersetzt,* III. Prague and Leipzig.

Lyonnet, Bertille, 1988. Les relations de la Bactriane orientale avec le monde indo-baluche à partir des données céramicoloques, du 3e au 2e millénaires avant notre ère. In: *L'Asie centrale* 1988: 143–51.

Maag, Victor, 1961. Syrien – Palästina. In: Hartmut Schmökel (ed.), *Kulturgeschichte des Alten Orients* (Kröners Taschenausgabe, 298): 448–604. Stuttgart.

MacAdam, Henry Innes, 1990. Dilmun revisited. *Arabian Archaeology and Epigraphy* 1 (2–3): 49–87.

McAlpin, David W., 1974. Elamite and Dravidian: the morphological evidence. *IJDL* 3: 343–58.

1975. Elamite and Dravidian: further evidence of relationship. (With comments by seven scholars.) *CA* 16 (1): 105–15.

1979a. Linguistic prehistory: the Dravidian situation. In: Deshpande and Hook 1979: 175–88.

1979b. [Review of Fairservis 1977.] *JAOS* 99 (2): 353–4.

1981. *Proto-Elamo-Dravidian: the evidence and its implications.* (Transactions of the American Philosophical Society, 71: 3.) Philadelphia.

Macdonell, A. A., 1897. *Vedic mythology.* (Grundriss III.1.A.) Strasburg.

(ed. and trans.), 1904. *The Bṛhad-Devatā attributed to*

Śaunaka: a summary of the deities and myths of the Rig-Veda, I–II. (Harvard Oriental Series, 5–6.) Cambridge, Mass.

Macdonell, A. A. and A. B. Keith, 1912. *Vedic index of names and subjects*, I–II. London.

McEvedy, Colin and Richard Jones, 1978. *Atlas of world population history*. (Pelican Books.) Harmondsworth.

McIntosh, Jane R., 1985. Dating the South Indian megaliths. *SAA 1983*: II, 467–93.

Mackay, Ernest J. H., 1925. Sumerian connections with ancient India. *JRAS* 1925: 697–701.

1931a. Chapters 10–11, 15–21, 24, 25/2–28. In: Marshall 1931a: I: 131–75, 233–364; II: 365–405, 459–80, 488–588.

1931b. Further links between ancient Sind, Sumer and elsewhere. *Antiquity* 5: 459–73. Reprinted in: Possehl 1979a: 123–9 and pl. 9.

1932. An important link between ancient India and Elam. *Antiquity* 6 (23): 356–7.

1934. [Review of Hunter 1934.] *Antiquity* 8 (30): 252–4.

1937. Bead making in ancient Sind. *JAOS* 57: 1–15.

1938. *Further excavations at Mohenjo-daro*, I–II. Delhi.

1943. *Chanhu-daro excavations, 1935–36*. (American Oriental Series, 20.) New Haven, Conn.

1948. *Early Indus civilizations*. 2nd edn, revised by Dorothy Mackay. London.

Maclean, C. D. (ed.), 1893. *Manual of the administration of the Madras Presidency*, III: *Glossary of the Madras Presidency*. Madras.

Mahadevan, Iravatham, 1968. Corpus of the Tamil–Brahmi inscriptions. In: R. Nagaswamy (ed.), *Seminar on inscriptions, 1966*: 57–73. Madras.

1970. Dravidian parallels in Proto-Indian script. *JTS* 2 (1): 157–276.

1971. Tamil–Brahmi inscriptions of the Sangam age. In: R. E. Asher (ed.), *Proceedings of the Second International Conference Seminar of Tamil Studies, Madras, India, January 1968*, I: 73–106. Madras.

1973. Method of parallelisms in the interpretation of the Proto-Indian script. *International Association of Tamil Research, Proceedings of the Third International Conference Seminar, Paris 1970* (PIFI, 50): 44–55. Pondicherry.

1977. *The Indus script: texts, concordance and tables*. (MASI, 77.) New Delhi.

1979. Study of the Indus script through bi-lingual parallels. (Paper read at the Second All-India Conference of Dravidian Linguists, Sri Venkateswara University, 1972.) In: Possehl 1979a: 261–7.

1980. Recent advances in the study of the Indus script. *Purātattva* 9: 34–42.

1981. Place signs in the Indus script. *Proceedings of the Fifth International Conference-Seminar of Tamil Studies, Madurai, India, 5–10 January 1981*, I (2): 91–. Madras.

1981–2. S. R. Rao's decipherment of the Indus script. *Indian Historical Review* 8 (1–2): 58–73.

1982. Terminal ideograms in the Indus script. In: Possehl 1982a: 311–17.

1984. The cult object on unicorn seals: a sacred filter? *Puratattva* 13–14: 165–86. Reprinted in: Karashima 1985: 219–58.

1986a. Study of the Indus script: a bi-lingual approach. In: Krishnamurti 1986: 113–19.

1986b. Towards a grammar of the Indus texts: 'intelligible to the eye, if not to the ears'. *Tamil Civilization* 4 (3–4): 15–30.

1986c. Dravidian models of decipherment of the Indus script: a case study. *Tamil Civilization* 4 (3–4): 133–43.

1988. What do we know about the Indus script? *Neti neti* ('Not this nor that'). Presidential address, section 5, Indian History Congress, 49th session, Dharwar, 2–4 November 1988. Madras.

Mahadevan, Iravatham and Mythili Rangarao, 1986. The Indus script and related subjects: a bibliography of recent studies (1960–86). *Tamil Civilization* 4 (3–4): 214–37.

1987. Archaeological context of Indus texts at Mohenjodaro. *Journal of the Institute of Asian Studies* 4 (2): 25–56.

Mahadevan, I. and K. Visvanathan, 1973. Computer concordance of Proto-Indian signs. In: Agrawal and Ghosh 1973: 291–304.

Mahalingam, T. V., 1969. The Indus script. [Review of Parpola et al. 1969a; 1969b.] *The Hindu*, 20 November 1969: 6. Madras.

Mahapatra, P. K., 1972. *The folk cults of Bengal*. Calcutta.

Majumdar, B. K., 1968–9. [Review of Parpola et al. 1969a.] *The Quarterly Review of Historical Studies* 8 (4): 268–9.

Majumdar, Dhirendra Nath, 1923. Notes on Kālī-nautch in the district of Dacca in eastern Bengal. *Man in India* 3: 202–5.

Majumdar, N. G., 1934. *Explorations in Sind*. (MASI, 48.) Delhi.

Majupuria, Trilok Chandra and D. P. Joshi, 1989. *Religious and useful plants of Nepal and India*. Lashkar, Gwalior.

Makkay, J., 1990. New aspects of the PIE and the PU / PFU homelands: contacts and frontiers between the Baltic and the Urals in the Neolithic. In: *Congressus Septimus Internationalis Fenno-Ugristarum*, IA: *Sessiones plenares*: 55–83. Debrecen.

Mallmann, Marie-Thérèse de, 1963. *Les Enseignements iconographiques de l'Agni-Purāṇa*. (Annales du Musée Guimet, Bibliothèque d'Etudes, 67.) Paris.

1975. *Introduction à l'iconographie du tântrisme bouddhique*. Paris.

Mallory, J. P., 1976a. Time perspective and proto-Indo-European culture. *WA* 8 (1): 44–56.

1976b. The chronology of the early Kurgan tradition (Part 1). *JIES* 4: 257–94.

1977. The chronology of the early Kurgan tradition (Part 2). *JIES* 5: 339–68.

1981. The ritual treatment of the horse in the early Kurgan tradition. *JIES* 9: 205–26.

1988. [Review of Renfrew 1987.] *Antiquity* 62 (236): 607–9.

1989. *In search of the Indo-Europeans: language, archaeology and myth.* London.
Mallowan, Max E. L., 1961. The birth of written history. In: Piggott 1961: 65–96.
1965. The mechanics of ancient trade in Western Asia: reflections on the location of Magan and Meluhha. *Iran* 3: 1–7.
1969 (1971). Elamite problems. *Proceedings of the British Academy* 55: 255–92.
Maloney, Clarence, 1970. The beginnings of civilization in South India. *JAS* 29 (3): 603–16.
1974. *Peoples of South Asia.* New York.
1975. Archaeology in South India: accomplishments and prospects. In: Burton Stein (ed.), *Essays on South India* (Asian Studies at Hawaii, 15): 1–40. Honolulu.
Mandel'shtam, A. M., 1968. *Pamyatniki èpokhi bronzy v yuzhnom Tadzhikistane.* (Materialy i Issledovaniya po Arkheologii SSSR, 145.) Leningrad.
Marglin, Frédérique Apffel, 1985. *Wives of the god-king: the rituals of the devadasis of Puri.* Delhi.
Mariani, Luca and Maurizio Tosi, 1987. L'universo familiare a Shahr-i Sokhta attraverso le attività domestiche e le strutture residenziali. In: Gnoli and Lanciotti 1987: II, 853–79.
Markey, T. L. and John A. C. Greppin (eds.), 1990. *When worlds collide: Indo-Europeans and Pre-Indo-Europeans. The Rockefeller Foundation's Bellagio study and conference.* (Linguistica Extranea, Studia 19.) Ann Arbor.
Marr, John R., 1971. [Review of Parpola et al. 1969a; 1969b; 1970.] *BSOAS* 34 (1): 160–4.
1975a. Early Dravidians. In: Basham 1975: 30–7.
1975b. [Review of S. Koskenniemi et al. 1973.] *BSOAS* 38 (3): 709.
Marshack, Alexander, 1972. *The roots of civilization: the cognitive beginnings of man's first art, symbol, and notation.* New York.
1979. Upper Paleolithic symbol systems of the Russian plain: cognitive and comparative analysis. *CA* 20 (2): 271–311.
Marshall, John, 1922. The monuments of ancient India. In: E. J. Rapson (ed.), *The Cambridge history of India*, I: chapter 25. Cambridge.
1923. *Annual Report of the Director-General of Archaeology in India 1920–21.* Calcutta.
1924. First light on a long-forgotten civilization. *ILN* 20 September 1924: 528–32, 548. Reprinted in: Possehl 1979a: 105–7.
1926a. Harappa and Mohenjo Daro. *Annual Report of the Archaeological Survey of India, 1923–24*: 47–54. Calcutta. Reprinted in: Possehl 1979a: 181–6.
1926b. Unveiling the prehistoric civilisation in India: discoveries in Sind, the Punjab, and Baluchistan – cities older than Abraham. *ILN* 27 February and 6 March 1926: 346–9, 398–400.
1928. A new chapter in archaeology: prehistoric civilisation of the Indus. *ILN* 7 and 14 January 1928: 12–15, 42–5, 78.
(ed.), 1931a. *Mohenjo-daro and the Indus civilization*, I–III. London.
1931b. Religion. In: Marshall 1931a, I: 48–78.
Masica, Colin P., 1976. *Defining a linguistic area: South Asia.* Chicago.
1979. Aryan and non-Aryan elements in North Indian agriculture. In: Deshpande and Hook 1979: 55–151.
1990. *The Indo-Aryan languages.* (Cambridge Language Surveys.) Cambridge.
Masson, Charles [pseudonym of James Lewis], 1842. *Narrative of various journeys in Balochistan, Afghanistan, and the Panjab; including a residence in those countries from 1826 to 1838*, I–III. London.
Masson, V. M., 1981. Seals of a Proto-Indian type from Altyn-depe. In: Kohl 1981: 149–62.
1987. *Das Land der tausend Städte: Baktrien, Choresmien, Margiane, Parthien, Sogdien. Ausgrabungen in der südlichen Sowjetunion.* Wiesbaden and Berlin.
Masson, V. M. and V. I. Sarianidi, 1972. *Central Asia: Turkmenia before the Achaemenids.* (Ancient Peoples and Places.) London.
Matheson, Sylvia, 1976. *Persia: an archaeological guide.* 2nd edn. London.
Maturai-t tamil pēr akarāti. 2nd edn. Maturai 1956.
Maula, Erkka, 1984. The calendar stones from Moenjo-Daro. In: Jansen and Urban 1984: 159–70.
Maxwell-Hyslop, K. R., 1983. *Dalbergia sissoo* Roxburgh. *Anatolian Studies* 33: 67–72 and pl. 23.
Maydar, D., 1981. *Pamyatniki istorii i kultury Mongolii*, VIII. Moscow.
Mayrhofer, Manfred, 1956–80. *Kurzgefasstes etymologisches Wörterbuch des Altindischen*, I–IV. Heidelberg.
1966. *Die Indo-Arier im alten Vorderasien. Mit einer analytischen Bibliographie.* Wiesbaden.
1969. Die vorderasiatischen Arier. *Asiatische Studien* 23: 139–54.
1970. [Review of Parpola et al. 1969a; 1969b.] *Die Sprache* 16: 91–2.
1973. *Onomastica Persepolitana: das altiranische Namengut der Persepolis-Täfelchen.* (SÖAW 286.) Vienna.
1974. *Die Arier im Vorderen Orient – ein Mythos? Mit einem bibliographischen Supplement.* (SÖAW 294: 3.) Vienna.
(ed.), 1986a. *Indogermanische Grammatik*, I. Heidelberg.
1986b. 2: Lautlehre. In: Mayrhofer 1986a: I, 73–181.
1986–92. *Etymologisches Wörterbuch des Altindoarischen*, I. Heidelberg.
1989. Vorgeschichte der iranischen Sprachen; Uriranisch. In: Schmitt 1989a: 4–24.
Meadow, Richard H., 1987. Faunal exploitation patterns in eastern Iran and Baluchistan: a review of recent investigations. In: Gnoli and Lanciotti 1987: II, 881–916.
1989. Continuity and change in the agriculture of the Greater Indus Valley: the paleoethnobotanical and zooarchaeological evidence. In: Kenoyer 1989a: 61–74.
1991. The domestication and exploitation of plants and

animals in the Greater Indus Valley, 7th–2nd millennium BC. In: Jansen et al. 1991: 51–8.
(ed.), 1992a. *Harappa excavations 1986–1990: a multidisciplinary approach to third millennium urbanism.* (Monographs in World Archaeology, 3.) Madison, Wis.
1992b. Faunal remains and urbanism at Harappa. In: Meadow 1992a: 89–106.
Mecquenem, R. de, 1949. *Epigraphie proto-élamite.* (Mémoires de la Mission Archéologique en Iran, 31.) Paris.
1956. Notes proto-élamites. *RA* 50: 200–4.
Meenakshi, K., 1986. The quotative in Indo-Aryan. In: Krishnamurti 1986: 209–18.
Meister, Michael W. (ed.), 1984. *Discourses on Śiva.* Bombay.
Memon, Siraj ul-Haque, 1964. *Sindhī boli.* Hyderabad, Sind.
Ménant, Joachim, 1890. Etudes hétéennes. *Recueil de Travaux Relatifs à la Philologie et Archéologie Égyptiennes et Assyriennes* 13: 26–47 and 131–45.
Menges, Karl H., 1977. Dravidian and Altaic. *Anthropos* 72 (1–2): 129–79.
Meriggi, Piero, 1930. Die hethitische Hieroglyphenschrift. (Eine Vorstudie zur Entzifferung.) *ZA* 39 (NS 5): 165–212.
1934. Zur Indus-Schrift. *ZDMG* 87 (NS 12): 198–241.
1935. [Review of Hunter 1934.] *OLZ* 38 (8–9): 542–4.
1937a. Die Hieroglyphenschrift der Induskultur. *Geistige Arbeit* 4 (5): 9–10. Berlin.
1937b. Über weitere Industiegel aus Vorderasien. *OLZ* 40 (10): 593–6.
1962. *Hieroglyphisch-Hethitisches Glossar.* 2nd edn. Wiesbaden.
1971–4. *La scrittura proto-elamica,* I–III. Rome.
1975. Der Stand der Erforschung des Proto-elamischen. (Abstract.) *JRAS* 1975 (2): 105.
Merrey, Karen L., 1982. The Hindu festival calendar. In: Guy R. Welbon and Glenn E. Yocum (eds.), *Religious festivals in South India and Sri Lanka*: 1–25. New Delhi.
Méry, Sophie, 1991. Origine et production des récipients de terre cuite dans la péninsule d'Oman à l'âge du bronze. *Paléorient* 17 (2): 51–78.
Métraux, Alfred, 1938. The Proto-Indian script and the Easter Island tablets: a critical study. *Anthropos* 33: 218–39.
1946. Mohenjodaro and Easter Island again. *Man* 46: 70–1.
1969. The mysterious hieroglyphs of Easter Island. *Unesco Courier* 22: 16–17.
Meyer, Johann Jakob, 1930. *Sexual life in ancient India: a study in the comparative history of Indian culture.* London.
1933. Die Baumzuchtkapitel des Agnipurāṇa in textgeschichtlicher Beleuchtung. In: Otto Stein and Wilhelm Gampert (eds.), *Festschrift Moriz Winternitz*: 56–65. Leipzig.
1937. *Trilogie altindischer Mächte und Feste der Vegetation,* I–III. Zurich.
Millard, A. R., 1986. The infancy of the alphabet. *WA* 17 (3): 390–8.
Miller, Daniel, 1984. 'Malwa' and 'Jorwe' in the Chalcolithic of India. *SAA 1981*: 213–20.
1985. Ideology and the Harappan Civilization. *Journal of Anthropological Archaeology* 4: 34–71.
Miller, Heather Margaret-Louise, 1992. Urban palaeoethnobotany at Harappa. In: Meadow 1992a: 121–6.
Miller, Roy Andrew, 1969. The Tibeto-Burman languages of South Asia. In: Sebeok 1969: V, 431–49.
Misra, V. N., 1969. Early village communities of the Banas basin, Rajasthan. In: M. C. Pradhan, R. D. Singh, P. K. Misra and D. B. Sastry (eds.), *Anthropology and archaeology: essays in commemoration of Verrier Elwin, 1902–64*: 296–310 and pl. 1–12. Bombay.
1984. Climate, a factor in the rise and fall of the Indus Civilization: evidence from Rajasthan and beyond. In: Lal and Gupta 1984: 461–89.
1989. Mesolithic. In: Ghosh 1989a: I, 37–43.
Misra, V. N. and M. S. Mate (eds.), 1965. *Indian prehistory: 1964.* Poona.
Misyugin, V. M., 1972. K voprosu o proiskhozhdenii moreplavaniya i sudostroeniya na Indijskom okeane. In: *Proto-Indica: 1972*: I, 165–77.
1975. O vozmozhnosti drevnego moreplavaniya vdol' zapadnogo berega Indii. In: *Proto-Indica: 1973*: 65–70.
Mitchell, T. C., 1986. Indus and Gulf type seals from Ur. In: Al Khalifa and Rice 1986: 278–85.
Mitchiner, John E., 1978. *Studies in the Indus Valley inscriptions.* New Delhi.
1982. *Traditions of the Seven Ṛṣis.* Delhi.
Mitchiner, Michael, 1975–6. *Indo-Greek and Indo-Scythian coinage,* I–IX. London.
Mitra, Debala, 1965. A study of some *graha*-images of India and their possible bearing on the *Nava-Devās* of Cambodia. *JASB*, 4th series, 7 (1–2): 13–37 and pl. 1–18.
Mitra, Sarat Chandra, 1922. On the cult of the tree-goddess in eastern Bengal. *Man in India* 2: 230–40.
1931. Notes on a few village deities of the Faridpur District in eastern Bengal. *The Journal of the Anthropological Society of Bombay* 14 (8): 969–74.
Mitterwallner, Gritli von, 1984. Evolution of the *liṅga*. In: Meister 1984: 12–31.
Mode, Heinz, 1944. *Indische Frühkulturen und ihre Beziehungen zum Westen.* Basle.
1959. *Das frühe Indien.* (Grosse Kulturen der Frühzeit.) Stuttgart.
Möhlig, Wilhelm J. G., 1989. Sprachgeschichte, Kulturgeschichte und Archäologie: die Kongruenz der Forschungsergebnisse als methodologisches Problem. *Paideuma* 35: 189–96.
Molesworth, James T., 1857. *A dictionary, Maráṭhí and English.* Assisted by George and Thomas Candy. 2nd edn. Bombay.
Moneer, Q. M., 1936. Work during 1933–34 [at the DK-I section of Mohenjo-Daro]. *Annual Report of the Archaeological Survey of India 1930–34*: 72.
Moor, Edward, 1810. *The Hindu pantheon.* London.
Moorey, P. R. S., 1986. The emergence of the light, horse-drawn

chariot in the Near East *c.*2000–1500 BC. *WA* 18 (2): 196–215.

Morgenstierne, Georg, 1926. *Report on a linguistic mission to Afghanistan.* (Instituttet for sammenlignende kulturforskning, Series C, I: 2.) Oslo.

1930. Notes on Torwali. *AO* 8: 294–310.

1932. *Report on a linguistic mission to north-western India.* (Instituttet for sammenlignende kulturforskning, Series C, III: 1.) Oslo.

1935. Preface. In: Lorimer 1935: I, vii–xxx.

1945. Indo-European *k'* in Kafiri. *Norsk Tidsskrift for Sprogvidenskap* 13: 225–38.

1947. Notes on Burushaski phonology. *Norsk Tidsskrift for Sprogvidenskap* 14: 61–95.

1957. Sanskritic words in Khowar. In: *Felicitation volume presented to S. K. Belvalkar*: 84–98. Varanasi.

1958. Neu-iranische Sprachen. In: *Iranistik*, I: *Linguistik* (Handbuch der Orientalistik I, 4, 1): 155–78. Leiden and Cologne.

1973. *Irano-Dardica.* (Beiträge zur Iranistik, 5.) Wiesbaden.

Moses, S. T., 1923. Fish and religion in South India. *QJMS* 13: 549–54.

Mughal, M. Rafique, 1970. The Early Harappan period in the Greater Indus Valley and northern Baluchistan (*c.*3000–2400 BC). (Ph.D. dissertation, University of Pennsylvania, Philadelphia.) Ann Arbor.

1972. Explorations in northern Baluchistan. *PA* 8: 137–51.

1973. *Present state of research on the Indus Valley Civilization.* Karachi. Reprinted in: Possehl 1979a: 90–8.

1974. New evidence of the Early Harappan culture from Jalilpur, Pakistan. *Archaeology* 27 (2): 106–13.

1977. Cultural links between Pakistan and Iran during the pre-historic period (5000–1000 BC). In: *Iran–Pakistan: a common culture*: 33–82. Islamabad.

1981. New archaeological evidence from Bahawalpur. In: Dani 1981: 33–41, with a map and 22 pl.

1982. Recent archaeological research in the Cholistan desert. In: Possehl 1982a: 85–95.

1984. The Post-Harappan phase in Bahawalpur distt., Pakistan. In: Lal and Gupta 1984: 499–503.

1988. Genesis of the Indus Valley Civilization. *LMB* 1 (1): 45–54.

1990a. The Harappan 'twin capitals' and reality. *Journal of Central Asia* 13 (1): 155–62.

1990b. Further evidence of the Early Harappan culture in the Greater Indus Valley: 1971–90. *South Asian Studies* 6: 175–99.

1990c. The protohistoric settlement patterns in the Cholistan desert. In: *SAA 1987*: I, 143–56.

1990d. The Harappan settlement systems and patterns in the Greater Indus Valley (*circa* 3500–1500 BC). *PA* 25: 1–62.

1990e. Archaeological field research in Pakistan since independence: an overview. *BDCPGRI* 49 (H.D. Sankalia Memorial Volume): 261–78.

1990f. The decline of the Indus Civilization and the Late Harappan period in the Indus Valley. *LMB* 3 (2): 1–17 and 8 figs.

1991. The rise of the Indus Civilization. In: Jansen et al. 1991: 104–10.

1992a. Jhukar and the Late Harappan cultural mosaic of the Greater Indus Valley. *SAA 1989*: I, 213–22.

1992b. The geographical extent of the Indus Civilization during the Early, Mature and Late Harappan times. In: Possehl 1992c: 123–43.

1992c. The consequences of river changes for the Harappan settlements in Cholistan. *The Eastern Anthropologist* 45 (1–2): 105–16.

Muir, John, 1872–4. *Original Sanskrit texts on the origin and history of the people of India, their religion and institutions, collected, translated and illustrated*, I–V. 2nd and 3rd edns. London.

Münter, Frederik, 1801. Undersögelser om de persepolitanske inscriptioner. *Det Kongelige Danske Videnskabers-Selskabs Skrivter for aar 1800*, I (1): 251–92; (2): 293–348. Copenhagen.

Nagaswamy, R., 1982. *Tantric cult of South India.* Delhi.

1986. Architectural roots of some Harappan symbols. *Tamil Civilization* 4 (3–4): 31–4.

Naissance de l'écriture: cuneiformes et hiéroglyphes. Paris 1982.

Naster, P., 1944. Des sceaux de Mohenjo-daro aux monnaies indo-grecques: une survivance. *Le Muséon* 57: 157–62 and pl. 1.

Naudou, Jean, 1966. Symbolisme du miroir dans l'Inde. *Arts Asiatiques* 13: 59–82.

Naveh, Joseph, 1987. *Early history of the alphabet: an introduction to West Semitic epigraphy and palaeography.* 2nd edn. Jerusalem.

Needham, Joseph, 1959. *Science and civilization in China*, III: *Mathematics and the sciences of the heavens and the earth.* Cambridge.

1974. Astronomy in ancient and medieval China. In: Hodson 1974: 67–82.

Negelein, Julius von, 1926. Zum kosmologischen System in der ältesten indischen Literatur. *OLZ* 29 (10): 903–7.

1928. Die Wahrzeichen des Himmels in der indischen Mantik. *Archiv für Religionswissenschaft* 26: 241–95.

Nelson, David Niles, 1986. The historical development of the Nuristani languages. (Ph.D. dissertation, University of Minnesota.) Ann Arbor.

Niebuhr, Carsten, 1778. *Reisebeschreibung nach Arabien und andern umliegenden Ländern*, II. Copenhagen.

Nies, James B. and Clarence E. Keiser, 1920. *Historical, religious and economic texts and antiquities.* (Babylonian inscriptions in the collection of James B. Nies, 2.) New Haven, Conn.

Nilsson, Martin P., 1920. *Primitive time-reckoning.* (Skrifter utgivna av Kungl. Humanistiska Vetensskapssamfundet i Lund, 1.) Lund.

1950. *The Minoan-Mycenaean religion and its survival in Greek religion.* 2nd edn. (Ibid., 9.) Lund.

Nissen, Hans J., 1977. Aspects of the development of early cylinder seals. In: Gibson and Biggs 1977: 15–24.
1986a. The archaic texts from Uruk. *WA* 17 (3): 317–34.
1986b. The occurrence of Dilmun in the oldest texts of Mesopotamia. In: Al Khalifa and Rice 1986: 335–9.
1987a. The chronology of the proto- and early historic periods in Mesopotamia and Susiana. In: Aurenche et al. 1987: II, 607–14.
1987b. Introduction and summary of the session: la chronologie de 6.000 à 4.000 BP. In: Aurenche et al. 1987: II, 679–80.
1988. *The early history of the ancient Near East: 9000–2000 BC.* Translation by Elizabeth Lutzeier, with Kenneth J. Northcott. Chicago.
1991. Early civilizations in the Near and Middle East. In: Jansen et al. 1991: 27–33.
Nissen, Hans J., Peter Damerov and Robert K. Englund, 1990. *Frühe Schrift und Techniken der Wissenschaftsverwaltung im alten Vorderen Orient. Informationsspeicherung und – verarbeitung vor 5000 Jahren.* Berlin.
Norman, K. R., 1980. The dialects in which the Buddha preached. In: Bechert 1980: 61–77. Göttingen.
1984. The decipherment of the Indus Valley script. [Review of Mitchiner 1978, Krishna Rao 1982, and Rao 1982.] *Lingua* 63: 313–24.
1988. [Review of Renfrew 1987.] *Lingua* 76: 91–114.
1989. Dialect forms in Pali. In: Caillat 1989a: 369–92.
1990. [Review of Parpola 1988b]. *AO* 51: 288–96.
Nyberg, Harri, in press. The problem of the Aryans and the soma: botanical evidence. In: George Erdosy (ed.), *Ethnicity in ancient South Asia.*
Oates, Joan, 1986. The Gulf in prehistory. In: Al Khalifa and Rice 1986: 79–86.
O'Flaherty, Wendy Doniger, 1972. Disregarded scholars: a survey of Russian Indology. *South Asian Review* 5 (4): 289–304.
1973. *Asceticism and eroticism in the mythology of Śiva.* London.
O'Flaherty, Wendy Doniger, with Daniel Gold, David Haberman and David Shulman (eds. and trans.), 1988. *Textual sources for the study of Hinduism.* Manchester.
Oldenberg, Hermann, 1894. Der vedische Kalender und das Alter des Veda. *ZDMG* 48: 629–48.
1895. Noch einmal der vedische Kalender und das Alter des Veda. *ZDMG* 49: 470–80.
1917. *Die Religion des Veda.* 2nd edn. Stuttgart.
Olivier, J.-P., 1986. Cretan writing in the second millennium BC. *WA* 17 (3): 377–89.
Oppenheim, A. Leo, 1949. The golden garments of the gods. *JNES* 8: 172–93.
1954. The seafaring merchants of Ur. *JAOS* 74: 6–17. Reprinted in: Possehl 1979a: 155–63.
1964. *Ancient Mesopotamia: portrait of a dead civilization.* Chicago.
Otto, E., 1936. Die Indusschrift: ihre Entzifferungs- und Einordnungsversuche. *Zentralblatt für Bibliothekswesen* 53 (3): 109–14.
Otto, Walter, 1941. *Die älteste Geschichte Vorderasiens. Kritische Bemerkungen zu B. Hrozný's gleichnamigem Werk.* (Sitzungsberichte der Bayerischen Akademie der Wissenschaften, Philosophisch-historische Abteilung, 1941, II: 3.) Munich.
Pal, Pratapaditya and Dipak Chandra Bhattacharyya, 1969. *The astral divinities of Nepal.* (Indian Civilization Series, 9.) Varanasi.
Pal, Y., B. Sahai, R. K. Sood and D. P. Agrawal, 1984. Remote sensing of the 'lost' Sarasvati river. In: Lal and Gupta 1984: 491–7.
Pallis, Svend Aage, 1956. *The antiquity of Iraq: a handbook of Assyriology.* Copenhagen.
Pallottino, Massimo, 1955. *The Etruscans.* (Pelican Book A 310.) Harmondsworth.
1968. *Testimonia linguae Etruscae.* 2nd edn. Florence.
Pande, B. M., 1972. Siṁdhu lipi: rahasyodghāṭan kī diśā meṁ. *Dinmān*, 29 October 1972: 25–7. Delhi.
1972–3. Inscribed Harappan potsherds from Chandigarh. *Purātattva* 6: 52–5.
1973. Inscribed copper tablets from Mohenjo-daro: a preliminary analysis. In: Agrawal and Ghosh 1973: 305–22. Bombay. Reprinted in: Possehl 1979a: 268–83.
1974a. Siṁdhu lipi: ek anbujh pahelī. *Dinmān*, 13 October 1974: 24–5. Delhi.
1974b. On the origin of the Harappan sign 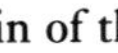. *Purātattva* 7: 25–33.
1982. History of research on the Harappan culture. In: Possehl 1982a: 395–403.
1985. On the origin of certain Harappan signs. In: Karashima 1985: 205–13.
1989. Indus script. In: Ghosh 1989a: I, 360–5.
Pande, B. M. and K. S. Ramachandran, 1971. *Bibliography of the Harappan culture.* (Field Research Projects, Study 56.) Miami, Fla.
Pandey, Raj Bali, 1969. *Hindu saṁskāras: socio-religious study of the Hindu sacraments.* 2nd edn. Delhi.
Pandit, Prabodh B., 1969. Cracking the code: a linguist looks at the problems of deciphering the script. *Hindustan Times Weekly Review*, 30 March 1969: ii–iii. Delhi.
Panneerselvam, R., 1972. A critical study of Tamil Brahmi inscriptions. *Acta Orientalia* 34: 163–97.
Pant, Pārvatīya Nityānanda (ed.), 1913. *Mitra Miśra's Vīramitrodaya*, I–III. (The Chowkhamba Sanskrit Series, 30.) Varanasi.
Paranavitana, S., 1961. A proposed decipherment of the Indus script. In: *International Conference on Asian Archaeology, Summaries of Papers*: 42–4. New Delhi.
1979. Stepping-stones in the migration of the Indus script to Easter Island. Paper submitted to the Second International Conference-Seminar on Asian Archaeology, Colombo 1969. *Ancient Ceylon* 3: 237–42.
Parkin, Robert, 1989. Some comments on Brahui kinship terminology. *IIJ* 32: 37–43.

Parpola, Asko, 1970a. The Indus script decipherment: the situation at the end of 1969. *JTS* 2 (1): 89–109.

1970b. Computer techniques in the study of the Indus script. *Kadmos* 10 (1): 10–15.

1972. [Report on research carried out in Pakistan and India in 1971.] *Newsletter of the Scandinavian Institute of Asian Studies* 5: 12–14. Copenhagen.

1973. *Arguments for an Aryan origin of the South Indian megaliths.* (Tamil Nadu Department of Archaeology, Publication 32.) Madras.

1974. On the protohistory of the Indian languages in the light of archaeological, linguistic and religious evidence: an attempt at integration. *SAA 1973*: 90–100.

1975a. Tasks, methods and results in the study of the Indus script. *JRAS* 1975 (2): 178–209.

1975b. Isolation and tentative interpretation of a toponym in the Harappan inscriptions. In: Leclant 1975: 121–43.

1976a. Interpreting the Indus script, II. *SO* 45: 125–60.

1976b. The encounter of religions in India 2000–1000 BC: methods of analysis. *Temenos* 12: 21–36.

1978. India's name in early foreign sources. *Sri Venkateswara University Oriental Journal* 18 (1–2), 1975: 9–19. Tirupati.

1979. The problem of the Indus script. In: Agrawal and Chakrabarti 1979: 163–86.

1980a. *Från Indusreligion till Veda: studier i de äldsta indiska religionerna.* (Populärvetenskapliga skrifter utgivna av Finska Orient-Sällskapet, Svensk serie, 6.) Copenhagen.

1980b. [Review of Buitenen 1973–5.] *AO* 41: 85–95.

1981a. Interpreting the Indus script [I]. In: Dani 1981: 117–31. [≈ Parpola 1984a.]

1981b. On the Harappan 'yoke-carrier' pictogram and the kāvaḍi worship. In: M. Arunachalam (ed.), *Proceedings of the Fifth International Conference-Seminar of Tamil Studies, Madurai – Tamilnadu – India, January 1981*, I: 2.73–89. Madras.

1981c. Recent developments in the study of the Indus script. In: Hamida Khuhro (ed.), *Sind through the centuries (proceedings of an international seminar held in Karachi in spring 1975 by the Department of Culture, Government of Sind)*: 71–86. Karachi.

1983. The pre-Vedic Indian background of the Śrauta rituals. In: Staal 1983, II: 41–75.

1984a. Interpreting the Indus script [I]. In: Lal and Gupta 1984: 179–91. [≈ Parpola 1981a.]

1984b. New correspondences between Harappan and Near Eastern glyptic art. *SAA 1981*: 176–95.

1984c. On the Jaiminīya and Vādhūla traditions of South India and the Pāṇḍu / Pāṇḍava problem. *SO* 55: 429–68.

1984d. From Ištar to Durgā: sketch of a prehistory of India's feline-riding and buffalo-slaying goddess of victory. Unpublished manuscript. Partially published in Parpola 1988b: 258–60; 1992b; and in press, d.

1985a. The Harappan 'Priest-king's' robe and the Vedic tārpya garment: their interrelation and symbolism (astral and procreative). *SAA 1983*: 385–403.

1985b. *The sky-garment. A study of the Harappan religion and its relation to the Mesopotamian and later Indian religions.* (SO 57.) Helsinki.

1986a. The Indus script: a challenging puzzle. *WA* 17 (3): 399–419.

1986b. The size and quality of the Indus seals and other clues to the royal titles of the Harappans. *Tamil Civilization* 4 (3–4): 144–56.

1987. Zur Entzifferung der Indus-Schrift. In: *Vergessene Städte am Indus*: 196–205.

1988a. Religion reflected in the iconic signs of the Indus script: penetrating into long-forgotten picto+graphic messages. *Visible Religion* 6: 114–35.

1988b. The coming of the Aryans to Iran and India and the cultural and ethnic identity of the Dāsas. *SO* 64: 195–302. (Unauthorized partial reprint: *IJDL* 17 (2), 1988: 85–229.)

1990a. Astral proper names in India: an analysis of the oldest sources, with argumentation of an ultimately Harappan origin. *ALB* 53: 1–53.

1990b. Bangles, sacred trees and fertility: interpretations of the Indus script related to the cult of Skanda-Kumāra. *SAA 1987*: I, 263–84.

1991. On deciphering the Indus script. In: Jansen et al.: 188–97.

1992a. The 'fig deity seal' from Mohenjo-daro: its iconography and inscription. *SAA 1989*: I, 227–36.

1992b. The metamorphoses of Mahiṣa Asura and Prajāpati. In: A. W. van den Hoek, D. H. A. Kolff and M. S. Oort (eds.), *Ritual, state and history in South Asia: essays in honour of J. C. Heesterman* (Memoirs of the Kern Institute, 5): 275–308. Leiden.

in press, a. Toponymic evidence for the Dravidian identity of the Harappan language. In: S. Arasaratnam et al. (eds.), *Felicitation volume in honour of Father X. S. Thani Nayagam.*

in press, b. Margiana and the Aryan problem. *IASCCAIB*.

in press, c. Copper tablets from Mohenjo-daro and the study of the Indus script. In: *Proceedings of the Second International Symposium on Moenjo-daro held at Karachi and Moenjo-daro on 24–27 February 1992.* Karachi.

in press, d. The use of sound as a ritual means: Why is the goddess of victory called Vāc in the Veda? In: K. K. A. Venkatachari (ed.), *Upāsanā by the religious and areligious. Proceedings of an international Indological seminar held at Somaiya Vidyavihar, Bombay, 27–30 December 1992.* Bombay.

Parpola, Asko, Seppo Koskenniemi, Simo Parpola and Pentti Aalto, 1969a. *Decipherment of the Proto-Dravidian inscriptions of the Indus Civilization: a first announcement.* (The Scandinavian Institute of Asian Studies, Special Publications, 1.) Copenhagen.

1969b. *Progress in the decipherment of the Proto-Dravidian Indus script.* (Ibid., 2.) Copenhagen.

1970. *Further progress in the Indus script decipherment.* (Ibid., 3.) Copenhagen.

Parpola, Asko and Simo Parpola, 1975. On the relationship of the Sumerian toponym *Meluḫḫa* and Sanskrit *mleccha*. *SO* 46: 205–38.

Parpola, Asko, Simo Parpola and Seppo Koskenniemi, 1966. Computing approach to Proto-Indian, 1965: an interim report. (Cyclostyled.) Helsinki.

Parpola, Päivikki, 1987. Väline merkkijonojoukkoa kuvaavan kieliopin löytämiseksi askelittain. (M.Sc. thesis, University of Helsinki.)

1988. On the synthesis of context-free grammars. In: Matti Mäkelä, Seppo Linnainmaa and Esko Ukkonen (eds.), *STeP-88 (Finnish artificial intelligence symposium, University of Helsinki, August 15–18, 1988)*, I: 133–41. Helsinki.

Parpola, Simo, Asko Parpola and Robert H. Brunswig, Jr, 1977. The Meluḫḫa village: evidence of acculturation of Harappan traders in late third millennium Mesopotamia? *JESHO* 20 (2): 129–65.

Pathak, V. S., 1992. Buffalo-horned human figure on the Harappan jar at Padri: a note. *ME* 17 (1): 87–9.

Patterson, Maureen L. P., 1982. South Asian civilization: a bibliographic synthesis. Chicago.

Payne, J. R., 1987. Iranian languages. In: Comrie 1987a: 514–22.

Petrie, Hilda, 1927. *Egyptian hieroglyphs of the First and Second Dynasties*. London.

Petrie, W. M. Flinders, 1932. Mohenjo-daro. *Ancient Egypt* 1932: II, 33–40.

Pettersson, John Sören, 1991. *Critique of evolutionary accounts of writing*. (Reports from Uppsala University: Linguistics, 21.) Uppsala.

Pettinato, Giovanni, 1972. Il commercio con l'estero della Mesopotamia meridionale nel 3. millennio av. Cr. alla luce delle fonti letterarie e lessicali sumeriche. *Mesopotamia* 7: 43–166.

Pfeiffer, Martin, 1972. *Elements of Kuṛux historical phonology*. (Indologia Berolinensis, 3.) Leiden.

Pfiffig, Ambros Josef, 1969. *Die etruskische Sprache: Versuch einer Gesamtdarstellung*. Graz.

1972. *Einführung in die Etruskologie: Probleme, Methoden, Ergebnisse*. Darmstadt.

Phillips, E. D., 1961. The royal hordes: the nomad peoples of the steppes. In: Piggott 1961: 301–28.

Piccoli, Giuseppe, 1933. A comparison between signs of the 'Indus script' and signs in the Corpus Inscriptionum Etruscarum. *IA* 62: 213–15, 2 pl.

Piggott, Stuart, 1948. Notes on certain metal pins and a mace-head in the Harappa culture. *AI* 4: 26–40.

1952. *Prehistoric India to 1000 BC*. (Pelican Books, A205.) Harmondsworth.

(ed.), 1961. *The dawn of civilization*. London.

1968. The earliest wheeled vehicles and the Caucasian evidence. *Proceedings of the Prehistoric Society* 34: 266–318.

1974. Chariots in the Caucasus and in China. *Antiquity* 48: 16–24 and pl. 3–5.

1975. Bronze Age chariot burials in the Urals. *Antiquity* 49: 289–90.

1983. *The earliest wheeled transport: from the Atlantic coast to the Caspian Sea*. London.

Pingree, David, 1965. Representations of the planets in Indian astrology. *IIJ* 8 (4): 249–67.

1981. *Jyotiḥśāstra: astral and mathematical literature*. (A History of Indian Literature, 6: 4.) Wiesbaden.

1982. Mesopotamian astronomy and astral omens in other civilizations. In: Hans-Jörg Nissen and Johannes Renger (eds.), *Mesopotamien und seine Nachbarn: XXV. Rencontre Assyriologique Internationale Berlin 3. bis 7. Juli 1978* (Berliner Beiträge zum Vorderen Orient, 1): II, 613–31.

Pinnow, Heinz-Jürgen, 1959. *Versuch einer historischen Lautlehre der Kharia-Sprache*. Wiesbaden.

1963. The position of the Munda languages within the Austroasiatic language family. In: Shorto 1963: 140–55.

1964. Bemerkungen zur Phonetik und Phonemik des Kurukh. *IIJ* 8 (1): 32–59.

Pirart, Eric, 1989. Avestique et dialectologie ṛgvédique. In: Caillat 1989a: 19–33.

Pisani, Vittore, 1969. Approcci alla decifracione delle iscrizioni della Valle dell' Indo. [Review of Parpola et al. 1969a; 1969b; Schrapel 1969.] *Paideia* 24 (3–6): 209–12.

Pischel, R., 1900. *Grammatik der Prakrit-Sprachen*. (Grundriss I: 8.) Strasburg.

1905. Der Ursprung des christlichen Fischsymbols. *Sitzungsberichte der Königlich Preussischen Akademie der Wissenschaften, Philosophisch-historische Classe*, 25: 506–32.

Pischel, Richard and Karl F. Geldner, 1889–1901. *Vedische Studien*, I–III. Stuttgart.

Pittman, Holly, 1984. *Art of the Bronze Age – southeastern Iran, western Central Asia and the Indus Valley*. New York.

P'jankova, L. T. (see also Pyankova, L. T.), 1986. *Jungbronzezeitliche Gräberfelder im Vachš-Tal, Süd-Tadžikistan*. (Materialien zur Allgemeinen und Vergleichenden Archäologie, 36.) Munich.

Pokorny, Julius, 1959. *Indogermanisches etymologisches Wörterbuch*, I. Berne.

Polomé, Edgar C. (ed.), 1982. *The Indo-Europeans in the fourth and third millennia*. (Linguistica Extranea, Studia 14.) Ann Arbor.

Pope, Maurice, 1975. *The story of decipherment: from Egyptian Hieroglyphic to Linear B*. London.

Poppe, Nicholas, 1965. *Introduction to Altaic linguistics*. (Ural-Altaische Bibliothek, 14.) Wiesbaden.

Porada, Edith, 1971. Remarks on seals found in the Gulf states. *Artibus Asiae* 33 (4): 331–7.

1977. Of professional sealcutters and nonprofessionally made seals. In: Gibson and Biggs 1977: 7–14.

Possehl, Gregory L., 1967. The Mohenjo-daro floods: a reply. *AA* 69 (1): 32–40.

1976. Lothal: a gateway settlement of the Harappan Civilization. In: Kennedy and Possehl 1976: 198–201. Reprinted in: Possehl 1979a: 212–18.

1977. The end of a state and continuity of a tradition: a discussion of the Late Harappan. In: Richard G. Fox (ed.),

Realm and region in traditional India: 234–54. New Delhi.
(ed.), 1979a. *Ancient cities of the Indus*. New Delhi.
1979b. An extensive bibliography of the Indus Civilization. In: Possehl 1979a: 361–422.
1980. *Indus Civilization in Saurashtra*. New Delhi.
1981. Cambay bead-making. *Expedition* 23: 39–47.
(ed.), 1982a. *Harappan Civilization: a contemporary perspective*. New Delhi.
1982b. Discovering ancient India's earliest cities: the first phase of research. In: Possehl 1982a: 405–13.
1986. *Kulli: an exploration of an ancient civilization in South Asia*. (Centers of Civilization, 1.) Durham, N.C.
1990a. Revolution in the urban revolution: the emergence of Indus urbanization. *Annual Review of Anthropology* 19: 261–82.
1990b. *Radiocarbon dates for South Asian archaeology*. Philadelphia.
1992a. The Harappan cultural mosaic: ecology revisited. *SAA 1989*: I, 237–44.
1992b. A short history of archaeological discovery at Harappa. In: Meadow 1992a: 5–11.
(ed.), 1992c. *South Asian archaeology studies*. New Delhi.
in press, a. Harappan and Post-Harappan maritime interests. In: Reade, in press.
in press, b. The date of the early Indus urbanization: a proposed chronology for the Pre-Urban and Urban phases. In: *SAA 1991*.
Possehl, Gregory L. and M. H. Raval, 1989. *Harappan Civilization and Rojdi*. New Delhi.
Possehl, Gregory L. and Paul C. Rissman, 1992. The chronology of prehistoric India: from earliest times to the Iron Age. In: Ehrich 1992: I, 465–90 and II, 447–74.
Pottier, B., 1974. [Review of S. Koskenniemi et al. 1973.] *BSL* 69 (2): 299.
Pottier, Marie-Hélène, 1980. Un cachet en argent de Bactriane. *Iranica Antiqua* 15: 167–74 and pl. I.
1984. *Matériel funéraire de la Bactriane méridional de l'âge du bronze*. Drawings by Guy Samoun. (Recherche sur les Civilisations, Mémoire 36.) Paris.
Potts, Daniel, 1977. Tepe Yahya and the end of the fourth millennium on the Iranian plateau. In: *Le Plateau iranien* 1977: 23–31.
1980. Tradition and transformation: Tepe Yahya and the Iranian plateau during the third millennium. (Ph.D. dissertation, Harvard University.) Ann Arbor.
1981a. The potter's marks of Tepe Yahya. *Paléorient* 7 (1): 107–22.
1981b. Towards an integrated history of culture change in the Arabian Gulf area: notes on Dilmun, Makkan and the economy of ancient Sumer. *Journal of Oman Studies* 4 (1978): 29–51.
1982a. The role of the Indo-Iranian borderlands in the formation of the Harappan writing system. *AIUON* 42: 513–19.
1982b. The road to Meluḫḫa. *JNES* 41 (4): 279–88.
(ed.), 1983a. *Dilmun: new studies in the archaeology and early history of Bahrain*. (Berliner Beiträge zum Vorderen Orient, 2.) Berlin.
1983b. Dilmun: where and when? *Dilmun: Journal of the Bahrain Historical and Archaeological Society* 11: 15–19.
1985. Reflections on the history and archaeology of Bahrain. *JAOS* 105 (4): 675–710.
1986. Dilmun's further relations: the Syro-Anatolian evidence from the third and second millennia BC. In: Al Khalifa and Rice 1986: 389–98.
1990. *The Arabian Gulf in antiquity*, I–II. Oxford.
1993. The late prehistoric, protohistoric, and early historic periods in eastern Arabia (ca. 5000–1200 B.C.). *Journal of World Prehistory* 7 (2): 163–212.
Potts, D. T., R. Dalongeville and A. Prieur, 1990. *A prehistoric mound in the Emirate of Umm al-Qaiwain, UAE: excavations at Tell Abraq in 1989*. Copenhagen.
Powell, Marvin A., 1981. Three problems in the history of cuneiform writing: origins, direction of script, literacy. *Visible Language* 15 (4): 419–40.
Prater, S. H., 1971. *The book of Indian animals*. 3rd edn. Bombay.
Predvaritel'noe soobshchenie ob issledovanii protoindijskikh tekstov. Moscow 1965. [See Alekseev 1965; Fedorova 1965; Knorozov 1965; Kondratov 1965; Probst 1965; Volchok 1965. English translation: Alekseev et al. 1969; another English translation, with critical comments by the translators: Zide and Zvelebil 1976: 11–90.]
Preston, J. J., 1980. *Cult of the goddess: social and religious change in a Hindu temple*. Delhi.
Printz, Wilhelm, 1933. [Review of Marshall 1931a.] *ZDMG* 86 (NS 11): 135–9.
Pritchard, James, 1969a. *Ancient Near Eastern texts, relating to the Old Testament*. 3rd edn. Princeton.
1969b. *The ancient Near East in pictures, relating to the Old Testament*. 2nd edn. Princeton.
Probst, M. A., 1965. Mashinnye metody issledovaniya protoindijskikh tekstov. In: *Predvaritel'noe* 1965: 11–30. [English translations: Probst [1965] 1976; Alekseev et al. 1969.]
[1965] 1976. Machine methods of investigation of the Proto-Indian texts. In: Zide and Zvelebil 1976: 23–37f. [with 'commentary' by the translators: 37].
Proskouriakoff, Tatiana, 1960. Historical implications of a pattern of dates at Piedras Negras, Guatemala. *American Antiquity* 25 (4): 454–75.
Proto-Indica: 1968. Brief report on the investigation of the Proto-Indian texts. Moscow 1968. [Presented at the VIII International Congress of Anthropological and Ethnographical Sciences, Tokyo, September 1968. See Gurov 1968; Knorozov 1968; Volchok 1968. Reprinted, with critical comments by the editors, in: Zide and Zvelebil 1976: 91–140.]
Proto-Indica: 1970. Soobshchenie ob issledovanii protoindijskikh tekstov. Moscow 1970. [See Gurov 1970b; Knorozov 1970; Volchok 1970b.]
Proto-Indica: 1972. Soobshchenie ob issledovanii protoindijskikh

tekstov, I–II. Moscow 1972. [See Arutyunov and Cheboksarov 1972; Gurov 1972a; 1972b; Knorozov 1972; Misyugin 1972; Vasil'kov 1972; Volchok 1972a; 1972b.]

Proto-Indica: 1979. See Knorozov et al. 1981.

Pulavar, Cantiracēkara, 1842. *Yāḻppāṇattu māṉippāy akarāti*. Jaffna.

Puri, Kidar Nath, 1938. *La Civilisation de Mohen-jo-daro*. (Thesis, Paris.) Paris.

Pyankova, L. T. (see also P'jankova, L. T.), 1989. Pottery complexes of Bronze-Age Margiana (Gonur and Togolok 21). *IASCCAIB* 16: 27–54.

Quintana Vives, Jorge, 1946. *Aportaciones a la interpretación de la escritura proto-india* (Consejo Superior de Investigationes Cientificas, Instituto Arias Montero, Series C, 2.) Madrid and Barcelona.

Quivron, Gonzague, 1980. Les marques incisées sur les poteries de Mehrgarh au Baluchistan, du milieu du IVe millénaire à la première moitie du IIIe millénaire. *Paléorient* 6: 269–80.

1991. The Neolithic settlement at Mehrgarh: architecture from the beginning of the 7th to the first half of the 6th millennium BC. In: Jansen et al. 1991: 59–72.

Raghu Vira and Shodo Taki (eds.), 1938. *Dakṣiṇāmūrti's Uddhāra-kośa: a dictionary of the secret Tantric syllabic code. Text, introduction, appendices and exegetical notes*. Reprinted, New Delhi, 1978.

Raikes, Robert L., 1964. The end of the ancient cities of the Indus. *AA* 66 (2): 284–99. Reprinted in: Possehl 1979a: 297–306.

Raikes, Robert L. and George F. Dales, 1977. The Mohenjo-Daro floods reconsidered. *Journal of the Palaeontological Society of India* 20: 251–60.

Rajam, V. S., 1992. *A reference grammar of classical Tamil poetry*. (Memoirs of the American Philosophical Society, 199.) Philadelphia.

Raman, B. S., 1986. Direction of writing in the Indus script: a new approach. *Tamil Civilization* 4 (3–4): 35–45.

Ramanujan, A. K. and Colin Masica, 1969. Toward a phonological typology of the Indian linguistic area. In: Sebeok 1969: v, 543–77.

Ramaswami Aiyar, L. V., 1950. Dravidic word-studies: I. Dravidic 'fish', 'star', 'sky'. *IL* 11 (2–4): 1–10.

Ramstedt, G. J., 1952–66. *Einführung in die altaische Sprachwissenschaft*, I–III. Edited and published by Pentti Aalto. (MSFOu 104: 1–3.) Helsinki.

Rangarao, Mythili and Iravatham Mahadevan, 1986. Database for the Indus script: a computerised concordance of the Indus texts. *Tamil Civilization* 4 (3–4): 46–61.

Rao, S. R., 1962–3. Excavations at Rangpur and other explorations in Gujarat. *AI* 18–19: 5–207.

1963. A 'Persian Gulf' seal from Lothal. *Antiquity* 37: 96–9 and pl. 9–11. Reprinted in: Possehl 1979a: 148–50 and pl. 10.

1965. Shipping and maritime trade of the Indus people. *Expedition* 7 (3): 30–7.

1971. Indus script deciphered. *Illustrated Weekly of India*, 12 December 1971: 21–5.

1973a. *Lothal and the Indus Civilization*. Bombay.

1973b. The Indus script: methodology and language. In: Agrawal and Ghosh 1973: 323–40.

1979–85. *Lothal, a Harappan port town (1955–62)*, I–II. (MASI 78.) New Delhi.

1982. *The decipherment of the Indus script*. Bombay.

1986. Trade and cultural contacts between Bahrain and India in the third and second millennia BC. In: Al Khalifa and Rice 1986: 376–82.

(ed.), 1988. *Marine archaeology of Indian Ocean countries: Proceedings of the First Indian Conference on Marine Archaeology of Indian Ocean Countries 1987*, I–II. Dona Pala, Goa.

1991. *Dawn and devolution of the Indus Civilization*. New Delhi.

Rask, Rasmus, 1823. [Letter communicated to Silvestre de Sacy by Frederik Münter.] *JA* 2: 143–50.

1826a. *Om Zendsprogets og Zendavestas ælde og ægthed*. (Det Skandinaviske Litteraturselskabs Skrifter 21: 231–74.) Copenhagen.

1826b. *Über das Alter und die Echtheit der Zend-Sprache*. Trans. into German by H. von der Hagen. Berlin.

Ratnagar, Shereen, 1981. *Encounters: the westerly trade of the Harappa Civilization*. Delhi.

Rau, Wilhelm, 1957. *Staat und Gesellschaft im alten Indien, nach den Brāhmaṇa-Texten dargestellt*. Wiesbaden.

1966. Fünfzehn Indra-Geschichten übersetzt. *Asiatische Studien* 20: 72–100.

1972. *Töpferei und Tongeschirr im vedischen Indien*. (AMAW, 1972: 10.) Mainz.

1974. *Metalle und Metallgeräte im vedischen Indien*. (AMAW, 1973: 8.) Mainz.

1976. *The meaning of* pur *in Vedic literature*. (Abhandlungen der Marburger Gelehrten Gesellschaft, 1973: 1.) Munich.

1977. Ist vedische Archäologie möglich? *XIX. Deutscher Orientalistentag 1975 in Freiburg im Breisgau, Vorträge* (Zeitschrift der Deutschen Morgenländischen Gesellschaft, Supplement III.1): 83–100.

1978. [Review of S. Koskenniemi et al. 1973.] *OLZ* 73 (1): 75–7.

1979. [Review of Shendge 1978.] *IIJ* 21 (4): 281–2.

1983. *Zur vedischen Altertumskunde*. (AMAW, 1983:1.) Mainz.

Rauff, James V., 1985. A structural function of the 'cage' in the Harappan writing system. *JTS* 28: 1–3.

1987. Some structural aspects of the Indus script. *JTS* 31: 69–88.

Rawlinson, G., 1898. *A memoir of Major-General Henry Creswicke Rawlinson*. London.

Rawlinson, H. C., 1846/7–9. The Persian cuneiform inscription at Behistun, decyphered and translated; with a memoir on Persian cuneiform inscriptions in general and on that of Behistun in particular. *JRAS* 10: i–lxxi, 1–349 (chapters

1–5); 11 (1) (chapter 6: Vocabulary of the ancient Persian language).

1850a. Note on the Persian inscriptions at Behistun. *JRAS* 12: i–xxi.

1850b. On the inscriptions of Assyria and Babylonia. *JRAS* 12: 401–83.

1851. Memoir on the Babylonian and Assyrian inscriptions. *JRAS* 14 (1): 1–32, i–cvi, pl. 1–17.

Rawlinson, Henry, et al., 1857. *Inscription of Tiglath Pileser I, King of Assyria, BC 1150, as translated by Sir Henry Rawlinson, Fox Talbot Esq., Dr Hincks and Dr Oppert.* London.

Rawson, Philip, 1973. *Tantra: the Indian cult of ecstasy.* London.

Ray, John D., 1986. The emergence of writing in Egypt. *WA* 17 (3): 307–16.

Ray, Sudhansu Kumar, 1963. *Indus script.* (Memorandum 1.) New Delhi.

1965. *Indus script.* (Memorandum 2.) New Delhi.

1966. *Indus script: methods of my study.* New Delhi.

Reade, Julian, 1979. *Early etched beads and the Indus–Mesopotamia trade.* (British Museum, Occasional Papers, 2.) London.

1986. Commerce or conquest: variations in the Mesopotamia–Dilmun relationship. In: Al Khalifa and Rice 1986: 325–34.

(ed.), in press. *The Indian Ocean in antiquity.* London.

Reade, Julian and Sophie Méry, 1987. A Bronze Age site at Ra's al-Hadd. In: Cleuziou and Tosi 1987: 75.

Rédei, Károly, 1983. Die ältesten indogermanischen Lehnwörter der uralischen Sprachen. In: *Symposium saeculare Societatis Fenno-Ugricae* (MSFOu 185): 201–33. Helsinki.

1986. *Zu den indogermanisch-uralischen Sprachkontakten.* (SÖAW 468.) Vienna.

Regamey, Constantin, 1934 (1935). Bibliographie analytique des travaux relatifs aux éléments anaryens dans la civilisation et les langues de l'Inde. *BEFEO* 34: 429–566.

Reiner, Erica, 1961. The etiological myth of the Seven Sages. *Orientalia* NS 30: 1–11.

1969. The Elamite languages. In: Friedrich et al. 1969: 54–118.

Reischauer, Edwin O. and John K. Fairbank, 1960. *East Asia: the great tradition.* (A History of East Asian Civilization, 1.) London.

Renfrew, Colin, 1987. *Archaeology and language: the puzzle of Indo-European origins.* London.

1990. Archaeology and linguistics: some preliminary issues. In: Markey and Greppin 1990: 15–24.

1991. [Review of Parpola 1988b.] *JRAS*, 3rd series, 1 (1): 106–9.

Renou, Louis, 1925. *La Géographie de Ptolémée (VII, 1–4), texte établi.* Paris.

1931. *Bibliographie védique.* Paris.

1955–66. *Etudes védiques et pāṇinéennes*, I–XV. (Publications de l'Institut de Civilisation Indienne, Série in-8°, 1, 2, 4, 6, 9, 10, 12, 14, 16–18, 20, 22, 23, 26.) Paris.

Renou, Louis and Jean Filliozat, 1947–53. *L'Inde classique: manuel des études indiennes*, I–II. Paris.

Rissman, Paul C., 1989. The organization of seal production in the Harappan Civilization. In: Kenoyer 1989a: 159–69.

Roaf, Michael, 1982. Weights of the Dilmun standard. *Iraq* 44: 137–41.

Roberts, T. J., 1977. *The mammals of Pakistan.* London.

Robinson, Andrew, 1990. The writing that was murdered. (Unpublished manuscript for a TV programme on the Maya script by Brian Lapping Associates, London.)

Rocher, Ludo, 1986. *The Purāṇas.* (A History of Indian Literature, II: 3.) Wiesbaden.

Rodhe, S., 1946. *Deliver us from evil: studies on the Vedic ideas of salvation.* (Skrifter utgivna av Svenska sällskapet för missionsforskning, 2.) Lund and Copenhagen.

Rolland, Pierre, 1973. Le Mahāvrata. *Nachrichten der Akademie der Wissenschaften in Göttingen, Philologisch-historische Klasse*, 1973: 51–79. Göttingen.

1975 (1977). *Compléments au rituel domestique védique: le Vārāhagṛhyapuruṣa.* (Etudes Indiennes, 3.) Aix-en-Provence.

Rolle, Renate, 1980. *Die Welt der Skythen.* Lucerne and Frankfurt-on-Main.

Röllig, Wolfgang, 1969. *Die Alphabetschrift.* In: Hausmann 1969: 289–302.

Rönnow, Kasten, 1929. Zur Erklärung des Pravargya, des Agnicayana und der Sautrāmaṇī. *Le Monde Oriental* 23: 69–173.

Rose, H. A., 1914. Jāṭ. In: *ERE* VII, 489–91.

Ross, Alan S. C., 1938. *The 'numeral signs' of the Mohenjo-daro script.* (MASI 57.) Delhi.

1939. The direction of the Mohenjo-daro script. *The New Indian Antiquary*, Extra Series 2: 554–8.

Ross, E. J., 1946. A Chalcolithic site in northern Baluchistan. With prefatory remarks by D. E. McCown. *JNES* 5: 284–316.

Rossi, Adriano V., 1979. *Iranian lexical elements in Brāhūī.* (Istituto Universitario Orientale, Seminario di Studi Asiatici, Series Minor, 8.) Naples.

Rouse, W. H. D. (ed. and trans.), 1956–63. *Dionysiaca of Nonnos.* (Loeb Classical Library.) London and Cambridge, Mass.

Roy, Ashim Kumar and N. N. Gidwani, 1982. *Indus Valley Civilization: a bibliographic essay.* New Delhi.

Roy, Sarat Chandra, 1915. *The Oraons of Chōtānāgpur: their history, economic life and social organization.* Ranchi.

1972. *Oraon religion and customs.* Reprint of the 1928 edn. Calcutta.

Roy, Sourindranath, 1953. Indian archaeology from Jones to Marshall (1784–1902). *AI* 9: 4–28.

Ruben, Walter, 1952. *Über die Literatur der vorarischen Stämme Indiens.* (Deutsche Akademie der Wissenschaften zu Berlin, Veröffentlichungen des Instituts für Orientforschung, 15.) Berlin.

1954. *Einführung in die Indienkunde: ein Überblick über die historische Entwicklung Indiens.* Berlin.

1967–71. *Die gesellschaftliche Entwicklung im alten Indien*, I–IV.

(Deutsche Akademie der Wissenschaften, Veröffentlichungen des Instituts für Orientforschung, 67: 1–4.) Berlin.
Ryckmans, G., 1944. [Review of Hrozný 1943.] *Le Muséon* 57: 181–4.
Sabaratnam, T., 1982. Links with Indus Valley history? Thor Heyerdahl uncovers the ancient Maldives. *Ceylon Daily News*, 22 November 1982.
Sabloff, Jeremy A. and C. C. Lamberg-Karlovsky (eds.), 1975. *Ancient civilization and trade*. Albuquerque, N. Mex.
Saint-Blanquat, Henri de, 1970. [Review of Parpola et al. 1969a.] *Science et Avenir*, January 1970: 61–7.
Sali, S. A., 1986. *Daimabad 1973–79*. (MASI, 83.) New Delhi.
Salomon, Richard, 1982. [Review of Gupta and Ramachandran 1979.] *JAOS* 102: 553–5.
1989. Linguistic variability in post-Vedic Sanskrit. In: Caillat 1989a: 275–94.
Salonen, Armas, 1966. *Die Hausgeräte der alten Mesopotamier*, II: *Gefässe*. (AASF, B 144.) Helsinki.
1970. *Die Fischerei im alten Mesopotamien nach sumerisch-akkadische Quellen*. (AASF, B 166.) Helsinki.
Sampson, Geoffrey, 1985. *Writing systems: a linguistic introduction*. London.
Samzun, Anaïck, 1992. Observations on the characteristics of the Pre-Harappan remains, pottery, and artifacts at Nausharo, Pakistan (2700–2500 BC). *SAA 1989*: I, 245–52.
Sankalia, H. D., 1955. Spouted vessels from Navdāṭoli (Madhya Bharat) and Iran. *Antiquity* 29: 112–15.
1963. New light on the Indo-Iranian or Western Asiatic relations between 1700 BC–1200 BC. *Artibus Asiae* 26 (3–4): 312–32.
1972–3. The 'Cemetery H' culture. *Purātattva* 6: 12–19. Reprinted in: Possehl 1979a: 323–7.
1974. *The prehistory and protohistory of India and Pakistan*. 2nd edn. Poona.
1986. The problem of the Indus script. *Tamil Civilization* 4 (3–4): 7–8.
Sankalia, H. D., S. B. Deo and Z. D. Ansari, 1971. *Chalcolithic Navdatoli: the excavations at Navdatoli, 1957–59*. Poona.
Sankarananda, Swami, 1944–73. *The Rigvedic culture of the prehistoric Indus*, I–III. Calcutta.
1955. *The Indus people speak*. Calcutta.
1963. *The dictionary of Indian hieroglyphs*. Calcutta.
Santini, Geraldina, 1990. A preliminary note on animal figurines from Shahr-i Sokhta. *SAA 1987*: I, 427–51.
Santoni, Marielle, 1980. Un site de l'âge du fer dans la plaine de Kachi, Baluchistan, Pakistan. *Paléorient* 6: 287–302.
1984. Sibri and the south cemetery of Mehrgarh: third millennium connections between the northern Kachi plain (Pakistan) and Central Asia. *SAA 1981*: 52–60.
1988. Aspects matériels des cultures de Sibri et de Mehrgarh VIII (plaine de Kachi, Baluchistan, Pakistan) à la fin du troisième et au début de deuxième millénaires. In: *L'Asie centrale* 1988: 135–41.
1989. Potters and pottery at Mehrgarh during the third millennium BC (periods VI and VII). *SAA 1985*: 176–85.
Saraswati, Baidyanath, 1977. *Brahmanic ritual traditions in the crucible of time*. (Studies in Indian and Asian Civilizations.) Simla.
Sarcina, Anna, 1979a. The private house in Mohenjo-daro. *SAA 1977*: II, 433–62.
1979b. A statistical assessment of house patterns at Mohenjo-daro. *Mesopotamia* 13–14: 155–99.
Sarianidi, Viktor I., 1977a. *Drevnie zemledel'tsy Afganistana: materialy Sovetsko-Afganskoj èkspeditsii 1969–1974 gg*. Moscow.
1977b. Bactrian centre of ancient art. *Mesopotamia* 12: 97–110.
1979. New finds in Bactria and Indo-Iranian connections. *SAA 1977*: II, 643–59.
1981a. Margiana in the Bronze Age. In: Kohl 1981: 165–93.
1981b. Seal-amulets of the Murghab style. In: Kohl 1981: 221–55.
1985. Monumental architecture of Bactria. In: Huot et al. 1985: 417–32.
1986a. *Die Kunst des alten Afghanistan*. Leipzig.
1986b. The Bactrian pantheon. *IASCCAIB* 10: 5–20.
1986c. Le complexe culturel de Togolok-21 en Margiane. *Arts Asiatiques* 41: 5–21.
1987. South-west Asia: migrations, the Aryans and Zoroastrians. *IASCCAIB* 13: 44–56.
1988. Cult symbolism of Bactrian and Margiana amulets. In: Gnoli and Lanciotti 1988: III, 1281–94.
1989a. Soviet excavations in Bactria: the Bronze Age. In: Ligabue and Salvatori n.d.: 107–23.
1989b. Protozoroastrijskij khram v Margiane i problema vozniknoveniya Zoroastrizma. *Vestnik Drevnej Istorii* 1989, 1: 152–69.
1989c. *Khram i nekropol' Tillyatepe*. Moscow.
1989d. Siro-khettskie bozhestva v baktrijsko-margianskom panteone. (Syro-Hittite deities in Bactria and Margiana.) *SA* 1989 (4): 17–24.
1990. *Drevnosti strany Margush*. Askhabad.
[1992]. *I zdes' govoril Zaratushtra*. (*Sine loco*.)
Sarkar, H. and B. M. Pande, 1969–70. A note on a knot design from Mohenjo-Daro and its occurrence in later times. *Purātattva* 3: 44–8.
Sarma, I. Karthikeya, 1967. The origins of Indian scripts. *IA*, 3rd series, 2 (1): 34–9.
Sarma, I. Karthikeya and B. P. Singh, 1967. Terracotta art of protohistoric India. *Journal of Indian History* 45 (3): 773–98.
Sass, Benjamin, 1988. *The genesis of the alphabet and its development in the second millennium BC*. (Ägypten und Altes Testament, 13.) Wiesbaden.
Sastri, K. N., 1957–65. *New light on the Indus Civilization*, I–II. New Delhi.
Sattler, Paul and Götz von Selle, 1935. *Bibliographie zur Geschichte der Schrift bis in das Jahr 1930*. (Archiv für Bibliographie, Supplement 17.) Linz a.D.
Saussure, Léopolde de, 1922. Les origins de l'astronomie

chinoise, I: Le zodiaque lunaire (1re partie). *T'oung Pao* 21: 251–318.
Sayce, A. H., 1876. The Hamathite inscriptions. *TSBA* 5: 22–32.
1880a. The monuments of the Hittites. *TSBA* 7: 248–93.
1880b. The bilingual Hittite and cuneiform inscription of Tarkondimos. *TSBA* 7: 294–308.
1903. The decipherment of the Hittite inscriptions. *Proceedings of the Society of Biblical Archaeology* 25: 141ff., 347ff.
1924. Remarkable discoveries in India. *ILN*, 27 September 1924: 526. Reprinted in: Possehl 1979a: 108.
Scharff, A., 1942. *Archäologische Beiträge zur Frage der Entstehung der Hieroglyphenschrift*. (Sitzungsberichte der Bayerischen Akademie der Wissenschaften, Philos.-hist. Abt., 1942: 3.) Munich.
Scheil, Vincent, 1900. *Textes élamites-sémitiques*. (Mémoires de la Délégation en Perse, 2.) Paris.
1905. *Documents en écriture proto-élamite*. (Mémoires de la Délégation en Perse, 6.) Paris.
1916. Cylindres et légends inédits. *RA* 13: 5–26.
1923. *Textes de comptibilité proto-élamites (nouvelle série)*. (Mémoires de la Mission Archéologique de Perse, Mission de Susiane, 17.) Paris.
1925. Un nouveau sceau hindou pseudo-sumérien. *RA* 22 (2): 55–6.
1935. *Textes de comptabilité proto-élamites (troisième série)*. (Mémoires de la Mission Archéologique de Perse, 26.) Paris.
Schele, Linda, 1981. *Notebook for the Maya hieroglyphic writing workshop at Texas*. Austin, Tex.
Schele, Linda and David Freidel, 1990. *A forest of kings: the untold story of the ancient Maya*. New York.
Scherer, A., 1953. *Gestirnamen bei den indogermanischen Völkern*. (Indogermanische Bibliothek, 3.1.) Heidelberg.
(ed.), 1968. *Die Urheimat der Indogermanen*. Darmstadt.
Schlerath, Bernfried, 1968. *Awesta-Wörterbuch, Vorarbeiten*, II: *Konkordanz*. Wiesbaden.
Schmandt-Besserat, Denise, 1978. The earliest precursor of writing. *Scientific American* 238 (6): 50–9.
1992. *Before writing*, I–II. Austin, Tex.
Schmid, Wolfgang P., 1969. [Review of Parpola et al. 1969a; 1969b.] *Indogermanische Forschungen* 74: 212–20.
Schmidt, Erich F., 1937. *Excavations at Tepe Hissar, Damghan*. Philadelphia.
Schmidt, Moriz, 1874. *Die Inschrift von Idalion und das kyprische Syllabar*. Jena.
Schmitt, Rüdiger, 1974. [Review of S. Koskenniemi et al. 1973.] *Kratylos* 19: 203–5.
(ed.), 1989a. *Compendium linguarum Iranicarum*. Wiesbaden.
1989b. Iranische Sprachen: Begriff und Name. In: Schmitt 1989a: 1–3.
1989c. Die altiranischen Sprachen im Überblick. In: Schmitt 1989a: 25–31.
1989d. Altpersisch. In: Schmitt 1989a: 56–85.
1989e. Andere altiranische Dialekte. In: Schmitt 1989a: 86–94.
1989f. Die mitteliranischen Sprachen im Überblick. In: Schmitt 1989a: 95–105.
Schmökel, Hartmut, 1966. Zwischen Ur und Lothal: die Seehandelsroute von Altmesopotamien zur Induskultur. *Forschungen und Fortschritte* 40: 143–7.
Schoff, V. (trans.), 1912. *The Periplous of the Erythraean Sea*. London.
Scholz, Fred, 1983. Baluchistan: a brief introduction to the geography of Pakistan's mountainous province. *NBS* 1: 13–8.
Schotsmans, Janine and Maurizio Taddei (eds.), 1985. *South Asian Archaeology 1983*, I–II. (Istituto Universitario Orientale, Seminario di Studi Asiatici, Series Minor, 23.) Naples.
Schott, Siegfried, 1951. *Hieroglyphen: Untersuchungen zum Ursprung der Schrift*. (AMAW, 1950: 24.) Mainz.
Schrader, F. Otto, 1925. Dravidisch und Uralisch. *Zeitschrift für Indologie und Iranistik* 3: 81–112.
1934. Indische Beziehungen eines nordischen Fundes. *ZDMG* 88 (NS 13): 185–93.
Schrapel, Dieter, [1969]. *Die Entzifferung des Yatischen*. [Marburg.]
Schwartz, Martin, 1985. The Old Eastern Iranian world view according to the Avesta. In: Gershevitch 1985: 640–63.
Schwartzberg, Joseph E. (ed.), 1978. *A historical atlas of South Asia*. Chicago.
Sebeok, Thomas A. (ed.), 1968–73. *Current trends in linguistics*, IV–XI. The Hague.
Senner, Wayne M. (ed.), 1989. *The origins of writing*. Lincoln, Nebr.
Sethna, K. D., 1992. *The problem of Aryan origins from an Indian point of view*. 2nd edn. New Delhi.
Shafer, Robert, 1957–63. *Bibliography of Sino-Tibetan languages*, I–II. Wiesbaden.
1974. *Introduction to Sino-Tibetan*. Wiesbaden.
Shaffer, Jim G., 1978. *Prehistoric Baluchistan*. New Delhi.
1984. The Indo-Aryan invasions: cultural myth and archaeological reality. In: John R. Lukacs (ed.), *The people of South Asia: the biological anthropology of India, Pakistan and Nepal*: 77–90. New York.
1986. The archaeology of Baluchistan: a review. *NBS* 3: 63–111.
1992. The Indus Valley, Baluchistan and Helmand traditions: Neolithic through Bronze Age. In: Ehrich in press, I: 441–64.
Shaffer, Jim G. and Diane A. Lichtenstein, 1989. Ethnicity and change in the Indus Valley cultural tradition. In: Kenoyer 1989a: 117–26.
Shah, Priyabala, n.d. (1985?) *Tilaka: Hindu marks on the forehead*. Ahmedabad.
Shah, Sayid Ghulam Mustafa and Asko Parpola (eds.), 1991. *Corpus of Indus Seals and Inscriptions*, 2: *Collections in Pakistan*. (AASF B 240 and Memoirs of the Department of

Archaeology and Museums, Government of Pakistan, 5.) Helsinki. (= *CISI* 2.)
Shankara Bhat, D. N., 1968. The Koraga language. In: Bhadriraju Krishnamurti (ed.), *Studies in Indian linguistics*: 290–5. Annamalainagar.
1971. *The Koraga language.* (Linguistic Survey of India Series, 7.) Poona.
Shanmugam, S. V., 1971. *Dravidian nouns: a comparative study.* (Annamalai University Department of Linguistics, Publication 25.) Annamalainagar.
Shapiro, Michael C. and Harold F. Schiffman, 1981. *Language and society in South Asia.* Delhi.
Sharif, Mohammad, 1990. Some new seals from Mohenjo-daro and the evidence of seal-making. *LMB* 3 (1): 15–18, pl. 1–3.
Sharma, G. R., 1980. *History of prehistory: archaeology of the Vindhyas and the Ganga Valley.* Allahabad.
Sharma, G. R., V. D. Misra, D. Mandal, B. B. Misra and J. N. Pal, 1980. *Beginnings of agriculture: from hunting and food gathering to domestication of plants and animals (Epi-Palaeolithic to Neolithic: excavations at Chopani-Mando, Mahadaha and Mahagara).* (Studies in History, Culture and Archaeology, 4.) Allahabad.
Shastri, Suryakanta, 1950. *The flood legend in Sanskrit literature.* Delhi.
Shaughnessy, Edward L., 1988. Historical perspectives on the introduction of the chariot into China. *Harvard Journal of Asiatic Studies* 48 (1): 189–237.
Shendge, Malati J., 1977. *The civilized demons: the Harappans in Ṛgveda.* New Delhi.
1983. The use of seals and the invention of writing. *JESHO* 26 (2): 113–36.
1985. The inscribed calculi and the invention of writing: the Indus view. *JESHO* 28 (1): 50–80.
Shevoroshkin, Vitaly V., 1973. [Review of Parpola et al. 1969a; 1969b; 1970.] *Linguistics* 107: 82–95.
(ed.), 1989. *Reconstructing languages and cultures. Abstracts and materials from the first International Interdisciplinary Symposium on Language and Prehistory, Ann Arbor, November 8–12, 1988.* (Bochum Publications in Evolutionary Cultural Semiotics, 20.) Bochum.
Shinde, Vasant, 1989. New light on the origin, settlement system and decline of the Jorwe culture in the Deccan, India. *South Asian Studies* 5: 59–72.
1991a. A horn-headed human figure on a Harappan jar from Padri, Gujarat. *ME* 16 (2): 87–9.
1991b. Harappan horned deity: the evidence from Padri in western India. *Purātattva* 21: 79–81.
1992. Excavations at Padri – 1990–91: a preliminary report. *ME* 17 (1): 79–86.
Shorto, H. L. (ed.), 1963. *Linguistic comparison in South East Asia and the Pacific.* London.
Shulman, D. D., 1976. The murderous bride: Tamil versions of the myth of Devi and the Buffalo demon. *History of Religions* 16 (2): 120–47.
1980. *Tamil temple myths: sacrifice and divine marriage in the South Indian Śaiva tradition.* Princeton.
Silva, Severine, 1955. Traces of human sacrifice in Kanara. *Anthropos* 50: 577–92.
Singaravelu, S., 1966. *Social life of the Tamils: the classical period.* Kuala Lumpur.
Singh, H. N., 1982. *History and archaeology of Black-and-Red Ware (Chalcolithic period).* Delhi.
Singh, Sarva Daman, 1965. *Ancient Indian warfare with special reference to the Vedic period.* Leiden.
Sinor, Denis (ed.), 1988. *The Uralic languages: description, history and foreign influences.* (Handbuch der Orientalistik VIII: 1: 1.) Leiden.
(ed.), 1990. *The Cambridge history of early Inner Asia.* Cambridge.
Sircar, D. C., 1965. *Indian epigraphy.* Delhi.
(ed.), 1967. *The Śakti cult and Tārā.* Calcutta.
1969. [Review of Parpola et al. 1969a.] *Journal of the Oriental Institute, M. S. University of Baroda* 19 (1–2): 176–8.
Siromoney, Gift, 1980. *Classification of frequently occurring inscriptions of Indus Civilization in relation to metropolitan centers.* (Madras Christian College, Scientific Report 45.) Madras.
Siromoney, Gift and Abdul Huq, 1981. Cluster analysis of Indus signs: a computer approach. In: M. Arunachalam (ed.), *Proceedings of the Fifth International Conference-Seminar of Tamil Studies, Madurai – Tamil Nadu – India, January 1981*, 1 (2): 15–23. Madras.
1982. Segmentation of unusually long texts of Indus writings: a mathematical approach. *Journal of the Epigraphical Society of India* 9: 68ff.
1986. Measurement of affinity and antiaffinity between signs of the Indus script. *Tamil Civilization* 4 (3–4): 62–94.
1988: Segmentation of Indus texts: a dynamic programming approach. *Computers and the Humanities* 22: 11–21.
Skjærvø, Prods O., 1989. Modern East Iranian languages. In: Schmitt 1989a: 370–83.
Skomal, S. N. and E. Polomé (eds.), 1987. *Proto-Indo-European: the archaeology of a linguistic problem.* Washington, D.C.
Sluşanski, Dan, 1971. [Review of Parpola et al. 1969b.] *Revue Romaine de Linguistique* 16 (3): 269–72.
Smirnov, K. F. and E. E. Kuz'mina, 1977. *Proiskhozhdenie indoirantsev v svete novejshikh arkheologicheskikh otkrytij.* Moscow.
Smith, George, 1871. On the reading of the Cypriote inscriptions. *TSBA* 1: 129–44.
Smith, Sidney, 1937. Early sculptures from Iraq. *The British Museum Quarterly* 11 (3): 116–21 and pl. 31–2.
Smith, Vincent A., 1958. *The Oxford history of India.* 3rd edn, edited by Percival Spear. Oxford.
Snellgrove, David L., 1987. *Indo-Tibetan Buddhism.* London.
Sollberger, Edmond, 1970. The problem of Magan and Meluḫḫa. *BIA* 8–9: 247–50.
1976. [Review of Kinnier Wilson 1974.] *BSOAS* 39 (1): 183–4.

Southworth, F. C., 1974. Linguistic stratigraphy of North India. *IJDL* 3 (2): 201–23.
1976a. On subgroups in Dravidian. *IJDL* 5: 114–37.
1976b. Cereals in South Asian prehistory: a look at the linguistic evidence. In: Kennedy and Possehl 1976: 52–75.
1979. Lexical evidence for early contacts between Indo-Aryan and Dravidian. In: Deshpande and Hook 1979: 191–233.
1988. Ancient economic plants of South Asia: linguistic archaeology and early agriculture. In: M. A. Jazayery and W. Winter (eds.), *Languages and cultures: studies in honor of Edgar C. Polomé* (Trends in Linguistics, Studies and Monographs, 36): 649–86. New York.
1990. The reconstruction of prehistoric South Asian language contact. In: E. H. Benedict (ed.), *The uses of linguistics* (The New York Academy of Sciences, Annals 583). New York.
1992. Linguistics and archaeology: prehistoric implications of some South Asian plant names. In: Possehl 1992c: 81–5.
in press. Reconstructing social context from language: Indo-Aryan and Dravidian prehistory. Paper read at an international conference on 'Archaeological and linguistic approaches to ethnicity in South Asia', held at the University of Toronto, 4–6 October 1991. (To be edited by George Erdosy.)
Sparreboom, Marcus, 1983. Chariots in the Veda. (Ph.D. dissertation, University of Leiden.)
Speiser, E. A., 1935. *Excavations at Tepe Gawra*, I. Philadelphia.
Sprockhoff, J., 1981. Āraṇyaka und Vānaprastha in der vedischen Literatur. *WZKS* 25: 19–90.
Spuler, Bertold (ed.), 1966a. *Geschichte Mittelasiens.* (Handbuch der Orientalistik, I, 5: 5.) Leiden.
1966b. Geschichte Mittelasiens seit dem Auftreten der Türken. In: Spuler 1966a: 123–310.
Srinivasan, D., 1975–6. The so-called Proto-Śiva from Mohenjo-Daro: an iconological assessment. *Archives of Asian Art* 29: 47–58.
1983. Vedic Rudra-Śiva. *JAOS* 103 (3): 543–56.
1984a. Unhinging Śiva from the Indus Civilization. *JRAS* 1984 (1): 77–89 and 7 pl.
1984b. Significance and scope of pre-Kuṣāṇa Śaivite iconography. In: Meister 1984: 32–46.
Srivastava, Balram, 1977. Dishakaka on a terracotta amulet from Mohenjo-Daro. In: Summaries of Papers, Seminar 'Indus Civilization: problems and issues'. Simla. Cf. *ME* 2 (1978): 122f.
Srivastava, H. L., 1940. Excavation at Harappa. *Archaeological Survey of India, Annual Report for 1936–37*: 39–41. Calcutta.
Staal, Frits (ed.), 1983. *Agni: the Vedic ritual of the fire altar*, I–II. Berkeley.
Stacul, Giorgio, 1969. Excavation near Ghālīgai (1968) and chronological sequence of protohistorical cultures in the Swāt Valley. *EW* NS 19 (1–2): 44–91.
1970. The Gray Pottery in the Swāt Valley and the Indo-Iranian connections (ca. 1500–300 BC). *EW* NS 20 (1–2): 92–102.
1971. Cremation graves in northwest Pakistan and their Eurasian connections: remarks and hypotheses. *EW* NS 21 (1–2): 9–19.
1976. Excavation at Loebanr III (Swat, Pakistan). *EW* NS 26: 13–20.
1979. The sequence of the proto-historical periods at Aligrāma (Swāt, Pakistan). *SAA 1975*: 88–90 and pl. 45–51.
1980. Loebanr III (Swat, Pakistan): 1979 excavation report. *EW* NS 30: 67–76.
1987. *Prehistoric and protohistoric Swāt, Pakistan (c.3000–1400 BC).* (IsMEO, Reports and Memoirs, 20.) Rome.
1992a. Swāt, Pirak, and connected problems (mid-2nd millennium BC). *SAA 1989*: 1, 267–70.
1992b. Further evidence for 'The Inner Asia Complex' from Swat. In: Possehl 1992c: 111–22.
Stacul, Giorgio and S. Tusa, 1977. Report on the excavations at Aligrama (Swat, Pakistan), 1974. *EW* NS 27: 151–204.
Starr, Richard F. S., 1941. *Indus Valley painted pottery: a comparative study of the designs on the painted wares of the Harappa culture.* (Princeton Oriental Texts, 8.) Princeton.
Steensberg, Axel, 1989. *Hard grains, irrigation, numerals and script in the rise of civilisations.* Copenhagen.
Steever, Sanford B., 1987. Tamil and the Dravidian languages. In: Comrie 1987a: 725–46.
Stein, M. Aurel (trans.), 1900. *Kalhaṇa's Rājataraṅgiṇī: a chronicle of the kings of Kashmir*, I–II. London.
1905. *Report of archaeological survey work in the North-West Frontier Province and Baluchistan, 1904–05.* Peshawar.
1929. *An archaeological tour in Wazīristān and northern Balūchistān.* (MASI, 37.) Calcutta.
1931. *An archaeological tour in Gedrosia.* (MASI, 43.) Calcutta.
1934. The Indo-Iranian borderlands: their prehistory in the light of geography and of recent excavations. *Journal of the Royal Anthropological Institute of Great Britain and Ireland* 64: 179–202.
1937. *Archaeological reconnaissances in north-western India and south-eastern Iran.* London.
1988. *An archaeological tour along the Ghaggar-Hakra river.* Other contributors: A. Ghosh, M. Rafique Mughal, V. N. Misra, Yash Pal, Baldev Sahai, R. K. Sood. Edited by S. P. Gupta. (Kusumanjali Indian History Monographs, 1.) Meerut.
Stephens, Laurence and John S. Justeson, 1978. Reconstructing 'Minoan' phonology: the approach from universals of language and universals of writing systems. *Transactions of the American Philological Association* 108: 271–84.
Steward, Julian H., 1955. *Theory of culture change: the methodology of multilinear evolution.* Urbana, Ill.
Steward, Julian H., Robert M. Adams, Donald Collier, Angel Palerm, Karl A. Wittfogel and Ralph L. Beals, 1955. *Irrigation civilizations: a comparative study.* (Social Science Monographs, 1.) Washington, D.C.
Stietencron, Heinrich von, 1972. *Gangā und Yamunā: zur symbolischen Bedeutung der Flussgöttinnen an indischen Tempeln.* (Freiburger Beiträge zur Indologie, 5.) Wiesbaden.

1983. Die Göttin Durgā Mahiṣāsuramardinī: Mythos, Darstellung und geschichtliche Rolle bei der Hinduisierung Indiens. *Visible Religion* 2: 118–66.

Strauss, Otto, 1932. Frühgeschichtliche Induskultur. [Review of Marshall 1931a.] *OLZ* 35 (10): 641–53.

Struve, V. V., 1947. Deshifrovka protoindijskikh pis'men. *Vestik Akademii Nauk SSSR* 1947 (8): 51–8.

Stuart, David and Stephen D. Houston, 1989. Maya writing. *Scientific American*, August 1989: 70–7.

Subrahmanian, N., 1966a. *Pre-Pallavan Tamil index*. (Madras University Historical Series, 23.) Madras.

1966b. *Sangam polity*. Madras.

Subrahmanyam, P. S., 1969. The Central Dravidian languages. *JAOS* 89: 739–50.

1971. *Dravidian verb morphology*. (Annamalai University Department of Linguistics, Publication 24.) Annamalainagar.

1983. *Dravidian comparative phonology*. (Ibid., 74.) Annamalainagar.

1988. Comparative Dravidian studies since 1980. *IJDL* 17 (1): 59–71.

Sukthankar, V. S., S. K. Belvalkar and P. L. Vaidya (eds.), 1933–59. *The Mahābhārata, critically edited*. I–XIX, Poona.

Sullivan, H. P., 1964. A re-examination of the religion of the Indus Civilization. *History of Religions* 4 (1): 115–25.

Swinson, A. and D. Scott (eds.), 1968. *The memoirs of Private Wakefield, soldier in Her Majesty's 32nd Regiment of Foot, Duke of Cornwall's Light Infantry, 1842–1857*. London.

Szemerényi, Oswald, 1989. *Einführung in die vergleichende Sprachwissenschaft*. 3rd edn. Darmstadt.

Taddei, Maurizio (ed.), 1979. *South Asian Archaeology 1977*, I–II. (Istituto Universitario Orientale, Seminario di Studi Asiatici, Series Minor, 6.) Naples.

Taddei, Maurizio (ed.), with the assistance of Pierfrancesco Callieri, 1990. *South Asian Archaeology 1987*, I–II. (Serie Orientale Roma, 66: 1–2.) Rome.

Talibov, B. and M. Gadžiev, 1966. *Lezginsko-russkij slovar'*. Moscow.

Tallqvist, Knut, 1914. *Assyrian personal names*. (Acta Societatis Scientiarum Fennicae, 43: 1.) Helsingfors.

Tamil Lexicon, I–VI and Supplement. Published under the authority of the University of Madras. Madras 1924–39. (= *TL*)

Tedesco, P., 1947. Sanskrit *mālā-* 'wreath'. *JAOS* 67: 85–106.

Telegin, Dmitriy Yakolevich, 1986. *Dereivka: a settlement and cemetery of Copper Age horse keepers on the Middle Dnieper*. Translated by V. K. Pyatkovskiy, edited by J. P. Mallory. (BAR International Series, 287.) Oxford.

Thapar, B. K., 1965. Relationship of the Indian Chalcolithic cultures with West Asia. In: Misra and Mate 1965: 157–76.

1970. The Aryans: a reappraisal of the problem. In: *India's contribution to world thought and culture (Vivekananda commemoration volume)*: 147–64. Madras.

1973. New traits of the Indus Civilization at Kalibangan: an appraisal. *SAA 1971*: 85–104.

1975. Kalibangan: a Harappan metropolis beyond the Indus Valley. *Expedition* 17 (2): 19–32. Reprinted in: Possehl 1979a: 196–202.

1985. *Recent archaeological discoveries in India*. Paris and Tokyo.

Thapar, B. K., K. S. Ramachandran, G. C. Mohapatra, K. V. Soundara Rajan, A. K. Ghosh, D. Sen, T. C. Sharma and H. Sarkar, 1989. Neolithic. In: Ghosh 1989a: I, 43–69.

Thapar, Romila, 1969. Indus script: Romila Thapar's view. *Hindustan Times Weekly Review*, 30 March 1969: i–ii. Delhi.

1975. A possible identification of Meluḫḫa, Dilmun and Makan. *JESHO* 18 (1): 1–42.

Thapliyal, U. P., 1983. *The Dhvaja (standards and flags of India – a study)*. Delhi.

Thaplyal, K. K., 1972. *Studies in ancient Indian seals. A study of North Indian seals and sealings from* circa *third century BC to mid-seventh century AD*. Lucknow.

1973. Probable nature of Harappan seal-inscriptions. In: Agrawal and Ghosh 1973: 341–6.

1981. Some observations on Harappan and early historical seals. In: M. S. Nagaraja Rao (ed.), *Madhu: recent researches in Indian archaeology and art history. M. N. Deshpande felicitation volume*: 37–40. Delhi.

1989. Seals and sealings. In: Ghosh 1989a: I, 14–15.

Thibaut, G., 1899. *Astronomie, Astrologie und Mathematik*. (Grundriss III. 9.) Strasburg.

Thieme, Paul, 1938. *Der Fremdling im Ṛgveda*. (Abhandlungen für die Kunde des Morgenlandes, 23.2.) Leipzig.

1955. [Review of Burrow 1955.] *Language* 31: 428–48.

1960. The Aryan gods of the Mitanni treaties. *JAOS* 80: 301–17.

Thomas, F. W., 1932. [Review of Marshall 1931a.] *JRAS* 1932: 453–66.

Thomas, Homer L., 1982. Archaeological evidence for the migrations of the Indo-Europeans. In: Polomé 1982: 61–85.

Thomas, Werner, 1970–1. [Review of Parpola et al. 1969a; 1969b.] *Oriens* 23–4: 614–15.

Thompson, J. Eric S., 1950. *Maya hieroglyphic writing: introduction*. (Carnegie Institution of Washington, Publication 589.) Washington, D.C.

1962. *A catalog of Maya hieroglyphs*. Norman, Okla.

Thomsen, Marie-Louise, 1984. *The Sumerian language: an introduction to its history and grammatical structure*. (Mesopotamia, 10.) Copenhagen.

Thureau-Dangin, F., 1925. Sceaux de Tello et sceaux de Harappa. *RA* 22 (3): 99–101.

Thurston, Edgar, 1906. *Ethnographic notes in southern India*. Madras.

1909. *Castes and tribes of South India*, I–VII. Madras.

Tikkanen, Bertil, 1987. *The Sanskrit gerund: a synchronic, diachronic and typological analysis*. (SO 62.) Helsinki.

1988a. On Burushaski and other ancient substrata in northwestern South Asia. *SO* 64: 303–25.

1988b. [Review of Nelson 1986.] *SO* 64: 407–10.

1992. Etelä-Aasian areaalilingvistiikka. [Areal linguistics of South Asia, in Finnish.] Manuscript. Helsinki.

Tiwari, J. N., 1985. *Goddess cults in ancient India*. Delhi.

Toffin, Gérard, 1981. Culte des déesses et fête du Dasaĩ chez les Néwar (Népal). In: Biardeau 1981a: 55–81.

Tomaschek, W., 1901. Daai. In: Georg Wissowa (ed.), *Paulys Real-Encyclopädie der Classischen Altertumswissenschaft*. Revised edn, IV: 1945–6. Stuttgart.

Tosi, Maurizio, 1977. The archaeological evidence for protostate structures in eastern Iran and Central Asia at the end of the 3rd millennium BC. In: *Le Plateau iranien* 1977: 45–66.

1979. The proto-urban cultures of eastern Iran and the Indus Civilization. *SAA 1977*: I, 149–71.

(ed.), 1983. *Prehistoric Sīstān*, I. Rome.

1986a. Early maritime cultures of the Arabian Gulf and the Indian Ocean. In: Al Khalifa and Rice 1986: 94–107.

1986b. The archaeology of early states in Middle Asia. *Oriens Antiquus* 25 (3–4): 153–87 and tables 11–13.

1989. The origins of early Bactrian Civilization. In: Ligabue and Salvatori n.d.: 41–72.

1991. The Indus Civilization beyond the Indian subcontinent. In: Jansen et al. 1991: 111–28.

in press. Natural resources of the Indian Ocean littoral: trade as a subsistence strategy. In: Reade in press.

Tozzer, Alfred M., 1941. *Landa's Relación de las cosas de Yucatán: a translation edited with notes*. (Peabody Museum of American Archaeology and Ethnology, Harvard University Papers, 18.) Cambridge, Mass.

Trautmann, Thomas R., 1970. [Review of Parpola et al. 1969a.] *JAS* 29 (3): 714–16.

1981. *Dravidian kinship*. Cambridge.

Treue, W. (ed.), 1986. *Achse, Rad und Wagen: fünftausend Jahre Kultur- und Technikgeschichte*. Göttingen.

Tripathi, Vibha, 1976. *The Painted Grey Ware: an Iron Age culture of northern India*. Delhi.

Trippett, Frank, 1974. *The first horsemen*. (The Emergence of Man.) Alexandra, Va.

Trumpp, Ernest, 1880. *Grammatische Untersuchungen über die Sprache der Brāhūis*. (Sitzungsberichte der philosophisch-philologischen und historischen Classe der königl. bayerischen Akademie der Wissenschaften zu München 1880, Supplement 6.) Munich.

Tsien, Tsuen-hsuin, 1962. *Written on bamboo and silk*. Chicago.

Tucci, Giuseppe, 1929. A visit to an 'astronomical' temple in India. *JRAS* 1929: 247–58.

1963. Oriental notes II: an image of a devī discovered in Swat and some connected problems. *EW* NS 14 (3–4): 146–82.

1972. [Review of Parpola et al. 1969a.] *EW* NS 22 (3–4): 340.

(ed.), [1977]. *La città bruciata del deserto salato*. Venice.

Turner, R. L., 1966. *A comparative dictionary of the Indo-Aryan languages*. London.

1975. *Collected papers, 1912–1973*. London.

Turner, Victor W., 1967. *The forest of symbols: aspects of Ndembu ritual*. Ithaca, N.Y.

Tusa, Sebastiano, 1979. The Swāt valley in the 2nd and 1st millennia BC: a question of marginality. *SAA 1977*: II, 675–95.

Tyler, Stephen A., 1968. Dravidian and Uralian: the lexical evidence. *Language* 44: 798–812.

Tyulyaev, C. I., 1988. *Iskusstvo Indii III-e tysyacheletie do n.è. – VII vek n.è.* Moscow.

Ullendorff, Edward, 1970. Comparative Semitics. In: Sebeok 1970: VI, 261–73.

Unger, Eckkard, 1938. Eridu. In: *RLA* II: 464–70.

Urban, Günter, 1991. The Indus Civilization: the story of a discovery. In: Jansen et al. 1991: 18–26.

Urban, G. and M. Jansen (eds.), 1983. *Mohenjo-daro: Dokumentation in der Archäologie: Techniken, Methoden, Analysen*. Aachen.

Urban, Thomas, 1987. State of research on the architecture in 'Moneer' area, Mohenjo-Daro. In: Jansen and Urban 1987: 23–32.

Vacek, Jaroslav, 1970. The problem of the Indus script. *Archiv Orientální* 38: 198–212.

1975. [Review of S. Koskenniemi et al. 1973.] *Archiv Orientální* 43: 370–1.

1986. Progress in the analysis of the Indus script. [Review of K. Koskenniemi and Parpola 1982.] *Archiv Orientální* 54: 92–4.

1987. The Dravido-Altaic relationship. (Some views and future prospects.) *Archiv Orientální* 55: 134–49.

Vaiman, A. A., 1974. Über die protosumerische Schrift. *Acta Antiqua Academiae Scientiarum Hungaricae* 22 (1–4): 15–27.

Vallat, François, 1971. *Les Documents épigraphiques de l'acropole (1969–1971)*. (Cahiers de la Délégation Archéologique Française en Iran, 1.) Paris.

1986. The most ancient scripts of Iran: the current situation. *WA* 17 (3): 335–47.

Van Buren. See Buren.

van Lohuizen-de Leeuw, J. E. (ed.), 1979. *South Asian Archaeology 1975*. Leiden.

van Lohuizen-de Leeuw, J. E. and J. M. M. Ubaghs (eds.), 1974. *South Asian Archaeology 1973*. Leiden.

Vasil'kov, Ya. V., 1972. 12-letnij tsikl v drevnej Indii. *Proto-Indica: 1972*: II, 313–37.

Vats, M. S., 1940. *Excavations at Harappa*, I–II. Delhi.

Veenhof, Klaas Roelof, 1972. *Aspects of Old Assyrian trade and its terminology*. Leiden.

Velze, J. A. van, 1938. *Names of persons in early Sanscrit literature*. Utrecht.

Venkatachalam, K., 1986. A study of the weights and measures of the Indus Valley Civilization. *Tamil Civilization* 4 (3–4): 95–102.

Ventris, Michael, 1951–2. Work notes on Minoan language research, I–XX. [Privately distributed.]

1954. King Nestor's four-handled cups: Greek inventories in the Minoan script. *Archaeology* 7 (1): 15–21.

Ventris, Michael and John Chadwick, 1956. *Documents in Mycenaean Greek*. 2nd edn by John Chadwick, 1973. Cambridge.

Vergessene Städte am Indus: frühe Kulturen in Pakistan vom 8. – 2. Jahrtausend v. Chr. Mainz 1987.

Vermeer, H. J., 1969. *Untersuchungen zum Bau Zentral-Süd-Asiatischer Sprachen.* (Wissenschaftliche Bibliothek, 9.) Heidelberg.

Vidale, Massimo, 1990. Stoneware industries of the Indus Civilization. In: D. Kingery (ed.), *Ceramics and civilization*, 5: 231–56. Westerville, Ohio.

Vidyāratna, Tārānātha (ed.), 1913. *Tantrābhidhāna with Vījanighaṇṭu and Mudrānighaṇṭu.* (Tantrik Texts, 1.) Calcutta and London.

Viennot, Odette, 1954. *Le Culte de l'arbre dans l'Inde ancienne.* (Annales du Musée Guimet, Bibliothèque d'Etudes, 59.) Paris.

Villacorta, J. Antonio C. and Carlos A. Villacorta, 1977. *Codices Mayas reproducidos y desarrollados.* 2nd edn. Guatemala.

Virolleaud, Charles, 1929. Les inscriptions cunéiformes de Ras Shamra. *Syria* 10: 304–10.

1931. Le déchiffrement des tablettes alphabétiques de Ras Shamra. *Syria* 12: 15–23.

Voegelin, C. F. and F. M. Voegelin, 1963. Patterns of discovery in the decipherment of different types of alphabets. *AA* 65: 1231–53.

Vogel, J. Ph., 1930–2. The head-offering to the Goddess in Pallava sculpture. *BSO(A)S* 6: 539–43.

Vogt, B., in press. The impact of Bronze Age maritime trade in the Oman mountains. In: Reade in press.

Voigt, Mary, 1987. Relative and absolute chronologies for Iran between 6500 and 3500 cal BC. In: Aurenche et al. 1987: II, 615–46.

Voigt, M. M. and R. H. Dyson, Jr, in press. The chronology of Iran, ca. 8000–2000 BC. In: Ehrich, in press.

Volchok, B[erta] Ya., 1965. Izobrazheniya na ob"ektakh s protoindijskimi nadpisyami. In: *Predvarit'elnoe* 1965: 56–68. [English translation: Volchok [1965] 1976.]

1968. Towards an interpretation of the Proto-Indian figures. *Proto-Indica: 1968*: 19–27. [Reprinted in: Volchok [1968] 1976, and with some modifications in: Volchok 1970a.]

1970a. Towards an interpretation of the Proto-Indian pictures. *JTS* 2 (1): 29–51. [See Volchok 1968.]

1970b. K interpretatsii nekotorykh protoindijskikh izobrazhenij. *Proto-Indica: 1970*: 15–42.

1972a. Protoindijskie bozhestva. *Proto-Indica: 1972*: II, 246–304.

1972b. Protoindijskie paralleli k mifu o Skande. *Proto-Indica: 1972*: II, 305–12.

1975. Traditsii protoindijskogo kalendarya i khronologii v indijskoj kul'ture. *Proto-Indica: 1973*: 16–51.

[1965] 1976. Images on objects with Proto-Indian inscriptions. In: Zide and Zvelebil 1976: 73–84 [with 'commentary' by the translators: 84–7]. See Volchok 1965.

[1968] 1976. Towards an interpretation of the Proto-Indian figures. In: Zide and Zvelebil 1976: 113–18 [with 'commentary' by the editors: 118]. See Volchok 1968.

1981. Proto-Indian writings deciphered. *National Herald*, 27 December 1981. [Cf. Knyazeva 1980.]

1986. Protoindijskij bog razliva. In: Knorozov 1986: 69–106.

Wackernagel, Jakob, 1896. *Altindische Grammatik*, I. Göttingen.

Wackernagel, Jakob and Louis Renou, 1957. *Altindische Grammatik: introduction générale.* New edition of the text published in 1896, by Louis Renou. Göttingen.

Waddell, L. A., 1925. *The Indo-Sumerian seals deciphered: discovering Sumerians of the Indus Valley as Phoenicians, Barats, Goths, and famous Vedic Aryans, 3100 to 2300 BC.* London.

Waerden, B. L. van der, 1968. *Erwachende Wissenschaft*, II: *Die Anfänge der Astronomie.* (Wissenschaft und Kultur, 23.) Basle.

Wagner, Lother, in press. Seals of China. In: Collon, in press.

Walker, Benjamin, 1968. *Hindu world: an encyclopedic survey of Hinduism*, I–II. London.

Wanzke, Holger, 1987. Axis systems and orientation at Mohenjo-Daro. In: Jansen and Urban 1987: II, 33–44.

Wasson, R. Gordon, 1971. The Soma of the Rig Veda: what was it? *JAOS* 91: 169–87.

Watt, G., 1889–93. *A dictionary of the economic products of India*, I–VI. Calcutta.

Wayman, Alex, 1965. Climactic times in Indian mythology and religion. *History of Religions* 4 (2): 295–318.

1987. O, that liṅga! *Annals of the Bhandarkar Oriental Research Institute* 68: 15–54.

Weber, Albrecht, 1861–2. Die vedischen Nachrichten von den *naxatra* (Mondstationen). *Abhandlungen der Königlichen Akademie der Wissenschaften zu Berlin, aus dem Jahre 1860*: 282–332 and *1861*: 267–400. Berlin.

1863. Über den Vedakalender, Namens *Jyotisham. Abhandlungen der Königlichen Akademie der Wissenschaften zu Berlin, aus dem Jahre 1862*: 1–130. Berlin.

1865–8. Zur Frage über die nakshatra. *IS* 9: 424–59; 10: 213–53.

1868–73. Zur Kenntniss des vedischen Opferrituals. *IS* 10: 321–96; 13: 217–92.

1888. Über alt-irânische Sternnamen. *Sitzungsberichte der Königlich Preussischen Akademie der Wissenschaften zu Berlin*, 1888: I, 3–14.

Weber, Steven A., 1991. *Plants and Harappan subsistence: an example of stability and change from Rojdi.* New Delhi.

1992. South Asian archaeobotanical variability. *SAA 1989*: I, 283–90.

Weidner, Ernst, 1957–71. Fixsterne. In: *RLA* III: 72–82.

Weinreich, Uriel, 1968. *Languages in contact: findings and problems.* The Hague.

Weisgerber, Gerd, 1980. '... und Kupfer in Oman'. Das Oman-Projekt des Deutschen Bergbau-Museums. *Der Anschnitt* 32 (2–3): 62–110.

1981. Mehr als Kupfer in Oman: Ergebnisse der Expedition 1981. *Der Anschnitt* 33 (5–6): 174–263.

1984. Makan and Meluḫḫa – third millennium BC copper production in Oman and the evidence of contact with the Indus Valley. *SAA 1981*: 196–201.

Westendorf, Wolfhart, 1969. Die Anfänge der altägyptischen Hieroglyphen. In: *Frühe Schriftzeugnisse der Menschheit*: 56–87. Göttingen.

Wheeler, Mortimer, 1947a. Harappa 1946: the defences and Cemetery R 37. *AI* 3: 58–130 and pl. 15–60. Partially (78–82: Harappan chronology and the Rig Veda) reprinted in: Possehl 1979a: 289–92.

1947b. The recording of archaeological strata. *AI* 3: 143–50.

1950a. Newly found at Mohenjo-daro: a huge 4000-year-old granary. *ILN*, 20 May 1950: 782–3.

1950b. New light on the Indus Civilization: the Mohenjo-daro granary. *ILN*, 27 May 1950: 813–16.

1950c. Man in 4000-year-old Mohenjo-daro: grotesque and savage human figurines. *ILN*, 3 June 1950: 854–5.

1959. *Early India and Pakistan to Asoka*. London.

1961. Ancient India. In: Piggott 1961: 229–52.

1968. *The Indus Civilization*. 3rd edn. Cambridge.

Whitehead, Henry, 1921. *The village gods of South India*. 2nd edn. Calcutta.

Whitney, W. D., 1864. On the views of Biot and Weber, respecting the relations of the Hindu and Chinese systems of asterisms, with an addition on Müller's views respecting the same subject. *JAOS* 8: 1–94 and 382–98.

1874a. *Oriental and linguistic studies*, I–II. New York.

1874b. On the lunar zodiac of India, Arabia, and China. In: Whitney 1874a: II, 341–421 and chart.

1896. On a recent attempt, by Jacobi and Tilak, to determine on astronomical evidence the date of the earliest Vedic period as 4000 BC. *JAOS* 16: lxxxii–xciv.

(trans.), 1905. *Atharva-Veda-Saṁhitā*, I–II. (Harvard Oriental Series, 7–8.) Cambridge, Mass.

Whitteridge, Gordon, 1986. *Charles Masson of Afghanistan: explorer, archaeologist, numismatist and intelligence agent*. Warminster.

Widengren, Geo, 1965. *Die Religionen Irans*. (Die Religionen der Menschheit, 14.) Stuttgart.

Wilhelmy, Herbert, 1966. Das 'wandernde' Strom. Studien zur Talgeschichte des Indus. *Erdkunde* 20: 265–76.

1968. Verschollene Städte im Indusdelta. *Geographische Zeitschrift* 56 (4): 256–94.

1969. Das Urstromtal am Ostrand der Indusebene und das 'Sarasvati-Problem'. In: *Zeitschrift für Geomorphologie*, Supplement 8: 76–93.

Windisch, Ernst, 1917–20. *Geschichte der Sanskrit-Philologie und der indischen Altertumskunde*, I–II. (Grundriss I.I.B.) Strasburg.

Winn, Shan M. M., 1981. *Pre-writing in southeastern Europe: the sign system of the Vinča culture ca 4000 BC*. Calgary, Alberta.

Winslow, Miron, 1862. *A comprehensive Tamil–English dictionary*. Madras.

Winternitz, Moriz, 1892. *Das altindische Hochzeitsrituell nach dem Āpastamba-Gṛhyasūtra und einigen anderen verwandten Werken*. (Denkschriften der Kaiserlichen Akademie der Wissenschaften in Wien, Philos.-hist. Classe, 40: 1.) Vienna.

1895. Nejamesha, Naigamesha, Nemeso. *JRAS* 1895: 149–55.

1901. Die Flutsagen des Alterthums und der Naturvölker. *MAGW* 31: 305–33.

Witzel, Michael, 1987. On the localisation of Vedic texts and schools. In: Gilbert Pollet (ed.), *India and the ancient world* (Orientalia Lovanensia Analecta, 25): 173–213. Leuven.

1989. Tracing the Vedic dialects. In: Caillat 1989a: 97–265.

Wolkstein, Diane and Samuel Noah Kramer, 1983. *Inanna: queen of heaven and earth*. New York.

Woodhead, A. G., 1959. *The study of Greek inscriptions*. Cambridge.

Woolley, C. L., 1923. Excavations at Ur of the Chaldees. *The Antiquaries Journal* 3 (4): 311–33.

1934. *Ur excavations*, II: *The Royal Cemetery*. London.

1955. *Ur excavations*, IV: *The early periods*. London.

Wright, G. R. H., 1991. Of fishes and men: fish symbols in ancient religion. *Journal of Prehistoric Religion* 3–4: 30–44.

Wright, Rita, 1984. Technology, style and craft specialization: spheres of interaction and exchange in the Indo-Iranian Borderlands, third millennium BC. (Ph.D. dissertation, Harvard University.) Ann Arbor.

Wüst, Walther, 1927. Über die neuesten Ausgrabungen im nordwestlichen Indien. *ZDMG* 81 (NS 6): 259–77.

1955. *Rudrá, m.N.pr.* (Wortkundliche Beiträge zur arischen Kulturgeschichte und Weltanschauung, 3.) Munich.

Wyatt, N., 1983. A press-seal, possibly of Indus type, found in Iraq. *JRAS* 1983: 3–6.

Yano, M., 1986. Knowledge of astronomy in Sanskrit texts of architecture (orientation methods in the Īśānaśivagurudevapaddhati). *IIJ* 29: 17–29.

Yazdani, G., 1917. Megalithic remains of the Deccan: a new feature of them. *Journal of the Hyderabad Archaeological Society* 1917: 56–79.

Yazyki drevnej Perednej Azii, I–III. Moscow 1957–67.

Young, Thomas, 1823. *An account of some recent discoveries in hieroglyphical literature, and Egyptian antiquities, including the author's original alphabet as extended by M. Champollion*. London.

Young, T. Cuyler, Jr, 1967. The Iranian migration into the Zagros. *Iran* 5: 11–34.

1985. Early Iron Age Iran revisited: preliminary suggestions for the re-analysis of old constructs. In: Huot et al. 1985: 361–77.

in press. The Iranians: Medes and Persians. Paper read at an international conference on 'Archaeological and linguistic approaches to ethnicity in South Asia', held at the University of Toronto, 4–6 October 1991. (To be edited by George Erdosy.)

Yule, Paul, 1982. *Lothal: Stadt der Harappa-Kultur*. (AVA-Materialien, 9.) Munich.

1985a. *Figuren, Schmuckformen und Täfelchen der Harappa-Kultur*. (Prähistorische Bronzefunde, I: 6.) Munich.

1985b. *Metalwork of the Bronze Age in India*. (Prähistorische Bronzefunde, XX: 8.) Munich.

1985c. On the function of prehistoric Copper Hoards of the Indian subcontinent. *SAA 1983*: 467–94.

1989. The Copper Hoards of the Indian subcontinent: preliminaries for an interpretation, with appendix I and II by Andreas Hauptmann and Michael J. Hughes. *Jahrbuch des Römisch-Germanischen Zentralmuseums* 36: 193–275. Mainz.

Zarins, Juris, 1986. MAR-TU and the land of Dilmun. In: Al Khalifa and Rice 1986: 233–50.

Zettler, Richard L., 1987. Sealings as artifacts of institutional administration in ancient Mesopotamia. *Journal of Cuneiform Studies* 39 (2): 187–240.

Zide, Arlene R. K., 1968. A brief survey of work to date on the Indus Valley script. *Papers from the 4th regional meeting, Chicago Linguistic Society, April 19–20, 1968*: 225–37. Chicago. Reprinted in: *JTS* 2 (1), 1970: 1–12 and in: Possehl 1979a: 256–60.

1973. How to decipher a script (and how not to). In: Agrawal and Ghosh 1973: 347–58.

Zide, Arlene R. K. and Norman H. Zide, 1976. Proto-Munda cultural vocabulary: evidence for early agriculture. In: Jenner et al. 1976: II, 1295–334.

Zide, Arlene R. K. and Kamil V. Zvelebil, 1970a. [Review of *Predvaritel'noe* 1965; *Proto-Indica: 1968*; Parpola et al. 1969a; 1969b.] *Language* 46 (4): 952–68.

1970b. [Review of Parpola et al. 1969a, b.] *IIJ* 12 (2): 126–34.

(eds.), 1976. *The Soviet decipherment of the Indus Valley script: translation and critique.* (Janua Linguarum, Series Practica, 156.) The Hague and Paris.

Zide, N. H. (ed.), 1966. *Studies in comparative Austro-Asiatic linguistics.* (Indo-Iranian Monographs, 5.) The Hague.

Ziegler, Konrat and Walther Sontheimer (eds.), 1975. *Der kleine Pauly: Lexikon der Antike*, I–V. Munich.

Zimmer, Heinrich, 1879. *Altindisches Leben: die Cultur der vedischen Arier nach den Saṁhitā dargestellt.* Berlin.

Zimmermann, G., 1956. *Die Hieroglyphen der Maya-Handschriften.* (Abhandlungen aus dem Gebiet der Auslandskunde, 62 B 34.) Hamburg.

Zograph, G. A., 1982. *Languages of South Asia: a guide.* Translated by G. L. Campbell. (Languages of Asia and Africa, 3.) London.

Zvelebil, Kamil V., 1965. Harappa and the Dravidians: an old mystery in a new light. *New Orient* 4 (3): 65–9.

1970. *Comparative Dravidian phonology.* (Janua Linguarum, Series Practica, 80.) The Hague.

1972a. The descent of the Dravidians. *IJDL* 1 (2): 57–63.

1972b. Dravidian case-suffixes: attempt at a reconstruction. *JAOS* 92 (2): 272–6.

1973a. Problèmes fondamentaux de phonologie et morphologie des langues dravidiennes. *BEFEO* 60: 1–48.

1973b. *The smile of Murugan: on Tamil literature of South India.* Leiden.

1973c. The so-called 'Dravidian' of the Indus inscriptions. *International Association of Tamil Research, Proceedings of the Third International Conference Seminar, Paris 1970* (Publications de l'Institut Français d'Indologie, 50): 32–41. Pondicherry.

1974a. Dravidian languages. In: *The New Encyclopaedia Britannica.* 15th edn, 989–92.

1974b. *Tamil literature.* (A History of Indian Literature, X: 1.) Wiesbaden.

1975. *Tamil literature.* (Handbuch der Orientalistik, II. 2. 1.) Leiden.

1977a. *A sketch of comparative Dravidian morphology*, I. (Janua Linguarum, Series Practica, 180.) The Hague.

1977b. The beginnings of *bhakti* in South India. *Temenos* 13: 223–57.

1977c. Vaḷḷi and Murugan: a Dravidian myth. *IIJ* 19: 227–46.

1977d. A guide to Murukaṉ. *JTS* 9: 1–22.

1977e. [Review of Kinnier Wilson 1974.] *JRAS* 1977 (2): 211–14.

1981. *Tiru Murugan.* Madras.

1983. Beginnings of the history of Dravidian civilization in South India. *JTS* 23: 17–25.

1984. Mythologie der Tamilen und anderer Drawidisch sprechenden Völker. In: Haussig 1984: 825–950 and pl. 1–8.

1985a. Recent attempts at the decipherment of the Indus Valley script and language (1965–1980): a critique. In: Karashima 1985: 151–87.

1985b. [Review of McAlpin 1981.] *JAOS* 105: 364–72.

1990. *Dravidian linguistics: an introduction.* (Pondicherry Institute of Linguistics and Culture, Publication 3.) Pondicherry.

Index of Indus signs and sign sequences

This index to (1) individual signs and (2) sign sequences of the Indus script follows the order of the sign list (fig. 5.1) which is not included in the index. Italicized numbers refer to figures, including their captions (tables are treated as text); the same page number is not repeated in roman if the matter occurs in the text in addition to an illustration.

 56, 61, 69, *94*, 95, 109, *110*, *120*, 292

 61, *94*, 95

 56, 61, *94*, *101*, *120*

 69, *93*, 110, 291, 299

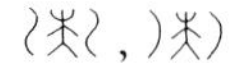 69, *93*

 *91f.*, 117

 95, *101*

 *101*, 104

 69, 79, 81, *89*, *93f.*, 95f., *101*, *120*, 121, *188*, 215, 231, *260*, 261, 277, 297

 69, 79, *109*, *120*, 231

 79

 79

 81, *89*, 95, *101*, *120*

 81

 *93f.*

 81

 81

 80, *81*

 69, *101*

 80f., *101*

 81

61, 80, *81*

80f., *113*, 290

81

63, *81*, *109*

80

82, 115, *120*

101

101

101, *103*, 229f., *276*, 291

56, 59, 64, 79, 81f., 91, *93*, *101*, *120*, 121, 179f., 183f., *185*, *188*, 190f., *194f.*, 196, *215*, 218, 223, 226, 230, *231*, 232f., 241, *243*, 246, *275–7*, 296

69, *94*, *101*

69

101

69

69

56, 59f., *93*, *101*, 121, *250*, *260*, 261–4, 267f., 270, 272, 274, *275*, 301

56, *63*, 79, *93*, 96, *101*, *120*, 196f., *275*

101

56, *93*, 117, *120*, 197, 274, *275*, 297

56, *59f.*, 67, *93*, 96, *120*

69

64

64, 81

80, *243*

80

59, *93*

59, 64, *93*, *101*

66, *89*, 91, 96, *98f.*, 131, 232–4, *235*, 239f., *276f.*, 299

81

101

66, 69, 80–2, *120*, *253f.*

101, *108*

81, *101*, 110, *113*

64, *65*, 69, *81*, 91, 110, *120*

81

81

81, *94*, *101*

67, *81*, *101*

54, 64, 81, *89*, *94*, 95f., 104, *109*

69, 79

79

69

69, *101*

110, *113*, *120*

61

81, *93*

54, *231*, 232, 234, *235*, 239–41, *243*, 246, *276*

112, *232*, 233, *234f.*, 237, 239f., *276*

83, 90, *94*, 116f., 131, *231*, 232, 291

90, 116f., 291

66, 83f., 90, 97, 116f., 291

67, *101*

67, 69, 81, 84, *101*, *120*, 194, *253*, *275*, 277

69, 81, *101*, *109*, *120*, 194, *246*, *254*, *276*

81, 194f., 226, *275*, 277

64, 79, 81f., 88, *195*, 223, *275*, 277

79

82

82

82

101, *114*

79

81

101, *120*, *228*, *276*

101

81, 91

81

69, 79, *80*, 91, *92f.*

60, 69, 79f., 91, *109*, *226f.*, 230–3, 241, *276*

81, *101*

81, *109*

101

95, 118f., *256*, 293

101

79

79, *101*

81, 90, *101*, 104

104

101

69

101

79, *101*

101

101

81

53f., 61, 64, 78, 84, 91f., *93f*, 95–7

101

88, *101*

79

79

101

58, 81, 292

81

94

101

105, 131

79

81

101

101

61, *104*

81

81

59

101

59, *81*, *89*, 90, *94*, 96, *98f.*, *101*, *120*

94, 117, *120*

94

94

94

59, 81

79

79

60, 79f.

59, 79, 84, *89*, *94*, 95f., *101*, 117

60, 79f.

80

80

79

80, *89*

183

95, 226

80, *81*, 90, *101*

81

80, 233

81

94, *252*, *260*, 261

260

81, *101*

66, 82, *92*, *120*, 131, *132*

101

81, *108*

66f., 69, *81*, *101*

81

80f.

80

79f.

79f.

81, *101*, 116, *120*

63, 69, 79, *89*, *92*, *101*, 223

79f., 89, *90*, 103f., *219*

79f.

79, *92*, *101*

84, *101*, *111f.*

81, 82, *101*, 107, *109–11*, 190f., 260, *277*, 292

101

92

53, *55*, 56, 60f., 64–7, 69, 81, 84, 90–3, *94*, 95–7, 104, 110, *111f.*, *114*, 116f., 119, *120*, 121, 131, *188*, *215*, 218, *226–8*, *232*, *234*, *246*, *250*, *260*, 261, *277*, 292

56, 90, 97

56, 90, *91*, 97, 121, *188*, *260*

56, 80, 90

56

69, 79f., *81*

79f.

116

116f.

81

81

101

101

53, *226–8*, 229f., *276*, 299

101

84, *231*, 232

101, *120*

69, 81–4, 89, 91, 96, *215*

101

81, *93*, *215*, 218, 270, *275*

84

66, 69, 81, 84, 90, *101*, 104, *108*, 110, *113*, 116f., 292

101

61, 69, 90

69, 90

61, 66, 81, 90, *101*, 104

81

66, 79

66

94, 290

79f.

179

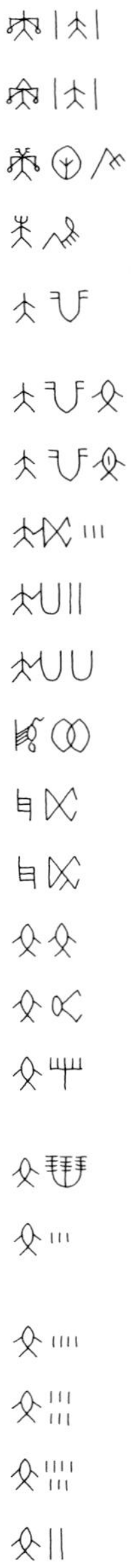

69, *94*, 109
65, 82, *94*
83, *89*, *120*
84, *111*
93f., 95, *96*, *114*, *120*, 121, *188*, *215*, 260
121, *188*
121, *260*, 261
81
81, *109*
63, 81
230, *276*
89, *94*, 96, *98f.*, *120*
94, 117, *120*
81, 93, 195, *275*, 297
233, *277*
64f., 69, *81*, 82, *89*, 90f., *93*, *98f.*, *109*, 110, 117
231, 232, 241, *243*, 246, *276*
65, 69, 81, *93*, 194, *215*, 218, *275*, 277
81, *93*
81, *93*, 194f., 226, *275*, 277
81, *195*, *275*, 277
69, 84, *89*, 91, *93*, 94, *120*, 230f., *276*

63, 69, 223
190, *194*
69, *80*
69
69, 233

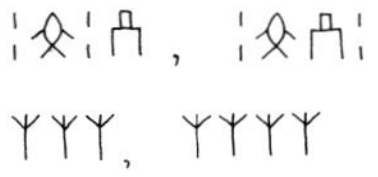

69
81, *120*

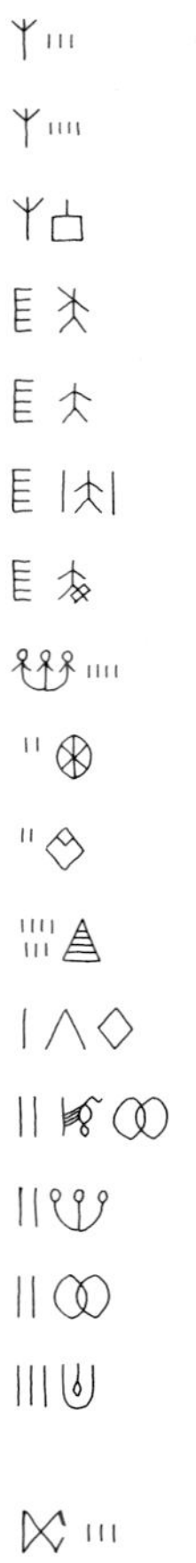

90, *92*, *120*, *253*
81, 83, 90, *113*, *120*, *254*
63, *66*, 69, 83, *89*, 90, *94*, *114*, *120*
95
94, 95, *96*
109
89, 95
246, *276*
66, 84, 89
66, 82, *89*, *93*, 104
88, *120*
108, 110, *113*
230
231, 232, 241, *276*
63, 83, *93*, 95, *226f.*, 230, *276*
63, *65*, *80*, 82, 84, *89*, 91, *93*, *98f.*, *120*, 195
81, *120*

81
81
81
84, *93f.*, *111*, *120*
89, 223
190, *194*
81
81, 107, 109f.
81, *109*, *194*
81, 83, 107, *109*
84, 89
64, *80*, *94*, *120*
66, 90
114
82, *92*, *120*, 131, *132*, *232*
116, 120
84
81, 131, *132*
95, 226
92
80f., *120*, *228*, *276*
81, *93*, *215*, 218, *275*
81, *108*, 110, *113*, 117, *120*

Index

Italicized numbers refer to figures, including their captions (tables are treated as text); the same page number is not repeated in roman if the matter occurs in the text in addition to an illustration.

AĀ 256
Aachen xix, 24
AB 205f., 208, 221, 226, 237, 239, 258, 263, 267f., 270
Abbasids 41
abbreviation of names 210
ablaut 150f., 158
aboriginal 150
absence, *see* omission
abstract: notion 33; shape of liṅga 220; of sign(s) 32, 35, 38, 50, 278
'accents' 291
acceptance of a decipherment 3, 41f., 49f., 61
account, accounting 29f., 43f., 88
acculturation 131, 151f., 169
accusative 96f.
aceramic 15
Achaemenid 4, *5*, 13f., 18, 38, 41f., 56, 129, 133, 143, 148, *150*, 285
acrophony 36, 58
acropolis (citadel) 6, *8*, 11, *12*, 21f., *58*, 61, *113*, 115, 117, 221, *222*, 256; *see also* fort(ification)
Adam and Eve 102
adaptation 38
addressing 207
adjective 51, 60, *88*, 97, 130, 169, 194
administration (bureaucracy) 6, 9, 17, 24, 26, 30, 54, 56, 60–2, 113–17, 119, 134, 194, 203, 292; *see also* official
adposition *88*
adstratum language *155f.*, 167
adverb *88*
Aegean 255; scripts 38, 43
Aegle marmelos 220
Aelianus 247
aerial root, *see* root
Afanasievo 145
affix 34, 38, 50, 87, 98
affricate, affrication 145
Afghanistan 15–17, 22–3, 129, 133f., *136*, 148f., *150*, *155f.*, *158*, 160–3, *164*, 170, *213*, *236*, *255*
Africa 46, 128, 130, 169
Afroasiatic 35f., 46, 128, 293
Agastya 195
agate 11
age 45, 267, 270; age 16 237; *see also* dating
age-and-area 155; *see also* centre, periphery
agent 30, 110, 133; secret 115
Agni 199, 206, 215, 217, 221, 224, 226, 228, 234, 237–9, 268, 301; *see also* fire; fire-altar
Agnīdh (Āgnīdhra), Āgnīdhrīya 216, *223*
Agni-Purāṇa 190, 194, 198, 241, 245, 269
ĀgniveśyaGS 207
Agrawala, V. S. *106*, *186*, 208
agriculture 4, 9, 15, 17, 24, 30, 43, 54, 136, 152, 172, 174, 190, 203, 285, 294
Aγul *had* 196
Ahar (culture) *25*
Ahura (Mazdāh) 149, 151, 214
Aiṅkuṟunūṟu 232
air root, *see* root
Ajanta *266*
Akam 172, 194, 197, 207, 239, 265
Åkerblad, J. D. 40
Akkad 13, 106, 119, 248, *252*
Akkadian: cuneiform 18, 34, *35*, 43, 85; dynasty 14; empire 54; letters 106; names 119, 121, 293; people and language 34, *35*, 43, 199, 121, 125, *127*, 128f., 133: *amurru* 130; *ana* 106; *ana šarri rabi* 130; *bêl šipti* 190; *ellu/ūlu* 169; *erpētu* 214; *nalbaš šamê* 214; *šadû, -dānu, -dāni* 44; *Šamaš* 128; *sāmtu* 14; *ša nab-ni-ti* 189; *ziqpu* 203; period 9, 18, 117, 119, 129–31, *132*,

170, *181*, 188, 247, *252*, *254*, 255; seals and inscriptions xvi, 85, 117, 119, 131, *132*, *187*, 188, *252*, *254*, 255
Akṣamālā 244
alabaster 107, *213*
Alakṣmī 259
Alamgirpur *7*, *10*, *153*
Alanian 129
Albanian 145
alcohol, *see* intoxicant
Alcor *202*, 206, 241, *243*, 244, *276*
Aldebaran *202*, 204–6, 244, 262f., 269, 272, 301; = Rohiṇī, q.v.
Alexander the Great 5, 117
Allahabad *139*, 140, 228, 244
Allahdino *7*, *10*, 110, 292
Allchin, B. 172
Allchin F. R. 172
alligator (gavial, gharial) and crocodile *11*, *180*, 184, *186*, *215*, 218, *275*, 296f.
alliteration 33
allograph (graphic variant, sign variant) 33, 54, 59, 68f., *70–8*, 78f., 85, 103f., *105*, 226, *232*, 234, 290
alphabet(ic script)(s): Canaanite Linear 38; consonantal 36, *37*, 38, 56; Etruscan 45; Greek 18, 35f., *37*, 38, 40f., 58, 126, 287, 290; 'hieroglyphic' 36; Indian, *see* Brāhmī; Kharoṣṭhī; Italic 45; Latin 45, 58; 'Maya' *49*, 50; Phoenician *37*, 38; Proto-Canaanite 38; Proto-Sinaitic 38; Roman, *see* Latin; 'syllabic' 56; Ugaritic cuneiform 18, 38, 48, 106, *107*, 288; (West) Semitic 18, 36, *37*, 38, 56, *84*, 174, 287
alphabetic writing 18, 36–9, *37*, 41, 48f., 84f., 102
'Altaic' 46f., 126, 161, 288, 293, 295
altar 199f., *228*, 259f., 301
alternation (paradigmatic) 44, 79, *80*, 81f., 88–92, *93f.*, 95, *96*, 97–8, *99f.*, *120*, 181, 223, 246, 267, 300
Altin (Altyn) Tepe *10*, *16*, 22, *26*, 286
Amarakośa 215
ambiguity 3, 34, 38, 67, 79, 102, 227, 231, 246, 261f., 267, 278
Ambikā 263
Amharic 87, 128
Amiet, P. 247
Amnisos 45
Amorite 11, 128, 130, *274*, 293
Amri *7*, *10*, 15, *16*, 17, *20*, 21f., 24, *25*, 52, *180*, 181, *183*, *236*, 286; Amrian Ware and culture *20*, 21, 52
amulet 3, *14*, 64, *91*, 97, 107, *112*, 116, *180*, 184, *186*, 194, 211, *215*, 218, 228, 243, 246, *252*, *275*, 297f.
An *32*, 184, 204, 297; *see also* sky
Anāhīd, Anāhitā 262
analogy 46, 235
analysis of texts 47
Anatolia 42f., 45, 83, 126, *127*, 130, 145, 256, 293
Anatolian branch of Indo-European 126, 145, 293
Anau 152
ancestors 205, 222; *see also* dead
Andamanese 137, *166*
Andaman Islands 137, *139*
Andhaka 259
Andhra Pradesh *105*, *136*, 209
Andronov, M. S. 161
Andronovo 145, *146*, 151, *152*, *156*, 294
Aṅgāra(ka) 209
Aṅgāra-prabha 209
Aṅgāra-setu 209
anger, angry 197f., 220, 231, 269f.
animal 3, 9, *11*, 15, 17, 21, 32, 44, 49–51, 59, 64, 69, *91f.*, *103*, 104, *106*, 110, *111f.*, 114–16, 131, *132*, 137, 148, 150, 155, 157, *181*, 188, 191, 194, 197, 209, *213*, 215, *219*, 221, 227, 230, 232, 235, 237f., *247–57*, 259, 261, 270, 272, 274, 285, 288; composite (mythical) 110, *111f.*, 116, 180, *181*, 184; domestic 9, 15, 189; wild 9, 15, 189, 226, 247f.
anklet 227
annals, *see* history
Annio of Viterbo 45
Anquetil Duperron, A. H. 41f.
anthill 109
antelope 206
antennae-hilted sword 154, *155*, 174
anthropology, physical, 142, 167
'anthropomorph' 54, *55*, 288
anthropomorphic (human) being 3, 50, 150, 234, 247, *250*, 258, 261; *see also* man
antimony bottle 148
antonym 100
anvil 11
An-yang 107, *141*
Apabharaṇī(ḥ) (Bharaṇī) *202*, 216–18
Apabhraṃśa 134
Apāṃ Naptṛ 188
Aparājitā 256, 263
ĀpGS 207, 238
aphrodisiacs 189, 264, 301
appeasement, *see* propitiation
appliqué work 214, 216
apposition 218
Apsaras 206, 216, 229, 301
ĀpŚS 109, 216
Arabia 13, 128–30
Arabian Gulf, *see* Gulf
Arabian Sea *10*, 15
Arabic tradition and language, 128f., 134, 163, 201, 203f.; *'ain* 36; *manāzil (al kamar)* 201
Aramaic: language 128; script 38, 56
archaeology, archaeological context / evidence xvi, 4, 47, 64, 104, 117–19, 125f., 134, 137, 143–5, 157, 168f., 171–4, 218, 220, 273, 293–6, 300; and linguistic evidence xvi, 134, 137
Archaeological Survey of India 6, 62, 219, 285
Archaic Sumerian, *see* Sumerian
archer 80, 110, *112*, *234*, 237, 239, *276*, 299
architecture 24, 50, 104, 152, 285; monumental 21f., 148, 151
archives (recording, registering) 30, 32, 43, 62, 115; *see also* inventory
Ardha-Māgadhī 133
areal linguistics/relationship xvi, 140, 142, 162f., *166*, 167, 169, 295
Aristoboulos 5, 285
Arjuna 208, 216
Arjunīs 208
arm(s) 36, *37*, 109, *110*, 211, *226*, 227f., *239*, *250*, *253*, *260*; *see also* hand
Armenian 126, 145
army, *see* war(rior)
Arrian 270
Arthaśāstra, *see* Kauṭilya
arrow 61, 102, 106, *112*, 172, *200*, 206, 231, 234, 237, 239, 268, 270
arsenic 9
art 4, 9, 24, 32, 35f., 47, 51, 53, 55–7, 60, 62, 104, *180*, 181, 183, 186, 211, 221, *238*, 246f., 254, 258, 262, *266*, 269, 297f.
Arundhatī 206, 224, 241, 243–5, 265, 268, 300
Arundhatī-vaṭa 244
Aryan xvi, 4, 6, 126, *127*, 128, 133f., *135*, 140, 142–59, *155f.*, 167f., 174, 207f., 213, 223, 241, 294–6; decipherments of Indus script 58f., 289; *see also* Indo-Aryan; Proto-Aryan
Arzawa 43
AS 155, 184, 189, 201, 208, 221, 228, 230f., 233, 237–9, 244, 259, 261, 263f., 268f., 272
Aṣāḍha, Āṣāḍhi 208
Aṣāḍhāḥ *202*, 207
Āśāpūrṇā 259
ascetic(ism) 221f., 224, 243–5, 300
ash 11, 191, 216, 220f., 301
Ashkelon 191
Ashkun 134, *135*, *166*
Asiatic Society 5
Asoka (Aśoka) 5f., 38, 56, 134, 143, 172, 220
aspirate 152
ass, Asiatic wild, 157
Assam 137, 142, 163
Assamese 134, *135*, *166*
assimilation 46, 98, *155*, 168f., 172
association 44f.
Assurnasirpal *190*
Assyria 128, *147*, 149
Assyrian 83, 128; ^{na4}*baluḫḫu* 170; ^{iš}*si-in-da-a* 170; Assyrians as Asuras 289; *see also* Neo-Assyrian period
Assyriology xv, 42, 58
asterisk 47, 78
asterism (constellation, nakṣatra) 183, 194–6, 201, *202*, 203–9, 213f., 216–18, 222–4, 233, 241, 261–5, 267–70, 272, *275*, 298; first 194, 204f., 263, 301; *see also* star, star calendar
astrolabe 204
astrologer, astrology 196, 198–201, 205–10, 214
astronomy, astronomer xvi, 24, 49, 201–8, 216, 231, 233, 263, 268–70, 272, 298
Asura 149–52, 154, 170, 190, 214f., 256, 262, 294; as Assyrian 289; *see also* demon; Mahiṣa Asura
Aśvapati 240
aśvattha, *see* pipal
Aśvatthā 259
ĀśvGS 109, 234, 238, 243
Aśvin 147
Aśvinī *202*, 204
Atargatis 191
Atharvaveda 266; *see also* AS
Athenaios 191
'Aṭṭar 197
attribute (epithet; grammatical) 88, 90f., 95–9, 117, 119, 121, 126, 130, 169, 215, 226f., 231, 234f., 244, 246, 258, 260–4, 268f., 297; *see also* emblem
auspiciousness 55, *56f.*, 57, 184, *186*, 204f., 224, *227*, 264, 266f., 269, *275*, 288; inauspiciousness 209
Austro-Asiatic 137, *139*, 140, 142, 151, *166*, 168f., 294; *bak/bah/ba(k)bak* 140; *pεG/piG* 140
autumn(al) 9, 204f., 256, 259, 263, *271*
auxiliary sign, *see* determinative
auxiliary verb *88*, 231
avabhṛtha 217f
Avantī 240
Avesta 41, 129, 143, 147f., 151, 203, 213f.
Avestan language 41f., *129*, *154*, *156*, 223; *ahura* 151; *anāhitā* 262; *aša* 151; *aspa* 158; *baga* 147; *daēva* 147–9, 151; *dahyu* 150; *hąm-var*^{ə}*tay-* 151; *haoma* 149; *haptō-iringa* 222, 224; *hu-māyā* 151; *iringa* 222f.; *Miθra* 151; *Nāŋhaiθya* 147; *r* 223; *Saurva* 147; *var* 151
Awadhi *135*, *166*; *ṭapa-ṭapa* 267
Awan *35*
Awārān 162
axe 8, 13, 15, *57*, 106, *107f.*, 117, 137, *140*, 148, *158*, 174
axle 158
Āyurveda, *see* medicine
Ayyaṉār 172
Azamgarh 163
Aztec 39, 54

Bābiruš *5*, 14
Bābilu 14
Babur 9
Babylon(ian) 14, *147*, 208, 214, language 14, 58, 128: *Bābilu* 14; *see also* Middle/Neo-/Old Babylonian
Bactria *10*, *25*, 26, 148f., *150*, 151f., 154, *155f.*, 158, 174, 189, 213f., *255f.*, 262; *see also* BMAC
Bactrian (language) *129*
Badakshan 149
Baḍaga *166*, *175*
Bahmanabad 170
Bahrain *10*, 11–13, 114, *115*, 130
Bailey, H. W. 162, 170
Bala-kot *7*, *10*, *16*, *20*, 52, *53*, 157
Balbūtha Tarukṣa 151
bale (of goods), *see* package
Balkans 126
ball, inscribed, 110
Balti 142, *166*
Baltic 145
Baltic-Finnic 145
Baluchi (Balochi) *129*, 133, 161–3, *164*, 165, *166*, 295; *Balōč* 162, 170; *-ī* 162; *ki* 162
Baluchistan 14–24, *25*, 26, 53, 59, *105*, 128, 133, *136*, 137, 149, 152, 154, *155f.*, 157, 160, *161*, 162f., *164*, 165, 170–2, *192f.*, 265, *269*, 286
bamboo 11, 109
Bampur *17*, *23*
Banas river, Banas culture *25*
Banawali *7*, *10*, *20*, 62, 255, 285
Banerjee, R. D. 6
bangle 9, 227, *228*, 229f., *239*, *250*, *253*, *260*, *276*, 299; inscribed 110, *227*, 274, 292, 299
banner, *see* flag
Bannu *192f.*, *251*
banyan (*Ficus bengalensis*, *Ficus indica*, nyagrodha, vaṭa) 221, 234, 238–40, *241f.*, 244–6, 258f., 261, 263, *276*, 300f.; eternal 244, 300; *see also* fig tree
barber 177
Baric *143*
bark-paper 49
barley 8f., 15, 221
barrenness 268
barrow culture 144
Basham, A. L. 218
Baškarīk 134
basket 15, 109, 191, 194, *200*, 297; *see also* pot
bath(ing) 56, 190, 206, 217f., 222, 224, 229, 239, *251*, 268, 296
Bath, Great (Mohenjo-daro) 6, *8*, 285
battle, *see* contest; war
Battle Axe culture *144*
Baudhāyana 208
BaudhGPS *200*
BaudhGS 209, 238, 265
BaudhŚS 205, 215
Bauer, H. 48
Bāveru *14*, 286
bazaar 6
bead 8f., 11, *12*, 14, 17, 22, 142, 286
'beak' 104
bean 221
bear 222, *249*
beard 14, 234, *235*, 237, 239, 244
Becanus, G. 57
Beck, B. E. F. 221
Bedigian, D. 169
bedouin 130
beer 33
beginning of text/time period/word 32, 42f., 45, 48, 50, 58, 65f., 69, *80*, 82–4, 87, 90f., *92*, 94, *98*, 100, 106, 116–18, 121, 204–6, 241, 243, 263; *see also* first
beheading, *see* decapitation
Belan 140
Belcher, W. R. 264
belly (stomach) 189, 267, 272, 301
'bending' 227, 299
benevolence, *see* kindness
Bengal *136*, 137, 163, 191, 194, 229, 259, 268, 301
Bengali 134, *135*, *166*; *alpanā* 288; *caḍaka* 191, 194; *gājana* 191; *sol* 194; *ṭap* 267
Berber 128
Bergaigne, A. 215
Berlin, H. 50
Besnagar 189, 297
Beyer, S. 262
Bhadrakālī 159
Bhagavad-Gītā 188, 244
Bhāgavata-Purāṇa 224
Bhairava 194, 230
Bharaṇī, *see* Apabharaṇī(ḥ)
Bharata 61
Bharhut *229*, *266*
Bhartṛhari 245
Bharuch (Broach) *161*, 163
Bhattacharyya, N. N. 194
Bhavatrāta 207
Bhaviṣya-Purāṇa 240f., 259
Bhīlī *135*, *166*
Bhūtamātā 258
Biardeau, M. 263
Bible 42, 102, 197
bibliography 285, 287f.
bichrome pottery 17
Bihar *136*, 137, *161*, 163
Bihari *135*
bilingual(ism) 3, 31, *35*, 40, 43–5, *46*, 48f., 60, 137, 162; bilateral 167f., 273f., 302; pictorial *46*, 49, *50*, *109–12*, 256, 274, *277*; quasi-bilingual 43, 47, 292; semi-bilingual 45, 233
bilva 220f., 299
Binágara 170
binary system 169
binding, *see* tying
bird 9, *14*, *23*, 34, *50*, 104, *105*, 180, *181*, 197, 208f., *219*, *249*, 268; bird-man *187*; *see also* eagle; vulture
Bīr-kōṭ-ghwaṇḍai (-ghuṇḍai) *141*, *158*, 159, *236*
birth 50, 54, 190, 194, 206–9, 217f., 220f., 224f., 228f., 234, 237–40, 258f., 262, 268f., *275*, 298; birthday 207, 209, 258, 269; birth star 207–10; birth water 190
Bisht, R.S. *113*
bison 11, 54, *131f.*, 180, *181*, 219, 248, 254, *256*, 300
Bīsutūn 42, *129*
bits, *see* horse
bitumen 6, 15
black 14f., 197, 215, 217f., 267, 270, 274, *275*, 297
black-and-red pottery 22, *193*
Black-and-Red Ware (BRW) 169, 172, 295
Black Sea *144*, 145, *146*, *155f.*, 172; *see also* Pontic
Bloch, J. 161
'block' 50, 60, 96
blood 194, 235, 237, 259, 266f., 269f., *275*, 301
Bloomfield, M. 231, 263
BMAC *25*, 54, 148–52, 154, *155f.*, 158, 168, 201, 203, 223, *255f.*, 287, 294, 298; BMAC seal 148, 152, 168, 203, *255f.*, 298; *see also* Bactria; Margiana
boar 9, *107*, 157, 237
boat, *see* ship
Bodh Gaya 244
Bodhi tree *229*
body, part of body, 47, 49f., 56, 78, 104, 110, 191 (dead), 196, 221, 232, 245, *253*, 255, 258
Boğazköy 43
Bolan Pass 15, 149, *164*
Bon 142
bone 9, 15, 17, 29, 110, 157–9, 191, 194, 201, 203
bonfire 206, 221; *see also* fire
book, *see* manuscript
booty 263, 269
Bork, F. *35*
borrowing: of sign forms and their values 58, 289; structural 47; linguistic, *see also* loanword
Bos indicus, *see* zebu (humped domestic) cattle
Bos gaurus, *see* bison
Bos taurus, *see* (non-humped domestic) cattle
boss (knob) of a seal 9, 11, 116; inscribed 91, *92*, 291
Bothmer, D. von, 149
boucranium, *see* bull's head
bound grapheme or morpheme 79
boundary: political 54; sign 69, 290; syntactic 82–4, 90, 96–8, *99*
boustrophedon *66*
bow (and arrow) 80, 109, *112*, *200*, *234*, 237, 239
bow-drill 15
boy 197; *see also* man
Brahma (Brahmā, god) 56, 215, 223f., 226, 233, 241
Brahmagupta 204
Brāhmaṇa texts 169, 175, 188, 197, 207f., 215, 217f., 222, 234, 238, 262, 296; *see also* Middle Vedic
Brahmāṇī 259
Brahma-Purāṇa 259
Brahmasiddhānta 263
Brahmavaivarta-Purāṇa 241, 259
Brāhmī script 6, 18, *37*, 38, 56–8, 104, 117, 172, 196, 287–9
Brahmin (Brahman) class/caste 133, 205, 207, 209, 220, 267, 270
Brāhūī (Brāhōī) 59, 128, *136*, 160, *161*, 162–5, *166*, 171, 174, *175*, 265, 295, 301; *a-* 162; *-ā* 162; *Brāhūī*/*Brāhōī* 162; *kan-* 162; *ki* 162; *ṭik* 265; *χōlum* 165
Braj *135*, *166*
branch 39, 104, 184, *185f.*, 228f., 234, *235f.*, 237, *241*, 244, 246, *250f.*, *253f.*, 259, *260*
Brasseur de Bourbourg, Ch. E. 49
Bray, D. DeS. 160f., 265
Bray, W. 54
bread 33
breakthrough 45, 48f., 101
breast 258
Bṛhaddevatā 181, 195, *275*
Bṛhadīśvara 262
Bṛhaspati 262f.
Bṛhatsaṃhitā, *see* Varāhamihira
brick 5f., 8f., 11, 15, 21f., 24, 201, 216, 298
bride 184, 208f., 240f., 243, 245f., 263, 265–7, 272, 275
bridegroom 208, 241, 243, 245f., 266, 269
brightness 203, 209, 216, 220, 231, 233, 238, 244, 263, 266, 269
Broach (Bharuch) *161*, 163
bronze 9, 14, 24, *35*, 82, 106, *107f.*, 117, 149; brass 270
brow, *see* forehead
Brunton, W. 5, 285
BRW, *see* Black-and-Red Ware
Bubalus arnee, *see* water buffalo (wild)
Bubalus bubalis, *see* water buffalo (domestic)
Buddha, Buddhism 6, *14*, 57f., 107, 109, 133f., 172, 184, *186*, 188, 197, 201, 205, 208, *227*, *229*, 232, 258f., 262; *see also* Lamaism
Budha 208, 262
buffalo, *see* water buffalo
Buffalo demon, *see* Mahiṣa Asura
buff ware 148
builder, building 117, 190
Buitenen, J. A. B. van, 216
bull (ox) 9, 14, *21*, *32*, 33, *37*, 58, *91*, 188, 211, *213*, 214, *219*, 224, 234, *235*, 246f., *248–51*, 254, 256, *269*, 272, 298, 300f.; 'Bull of Heaven' 213, 269, *275*; bull-man *248*, *252*; inscribed bull 110, 292; Śiva's bull 116; *see also* bison; buffalo; cow; 'unicorn'; zebu
bull's head 32, 104, *106*, 188, *277*, 292
bulla of clay with tokens 18, 30, *31*, 287

Bundi 259
'bundle' 109
Bunge, M. 4
bureaucracy, *see* administration
Buren, E. D. Van, 186, 191, 270
burial (grave) 15, 45, 142, *152*, 153, 171f., 244; flexed 148f.; unburied skeletons 24; *see also* cemetery; cremation
Burlingame, E. W. 229
Burmese, Burmic 134, *143*, *166*
Burnes, A. 5, 285
burning 8, 11, 22, 113, *114*, 206, 220f., 224, 231, 299; *see also* cremation
Burrow, T. 142, 148, 165, 168, 175, 182, 223
Burushaski *141*, 142, *166*, 217, 294; *śi* 217, 298
Burzahom *141*, 142, 168, *251*
butter, melted (ghee) 214f., 221
Byblos 128, *147*

cabin *13f.*
cake 109; rice 197; terracotta 221
Calah *190*
Caland, W. 243
Calcutta 262
Caldwell, R. 181
calendar, *see* star calendar; time reckoning
calf 224
calque, *see* translation loan
camel *37*; two-humped 149, 152, 157
Camelus bactrianus, *see* camel
Canaan, Canaanite *37*, 38, 297; language 128; *mlk* 197; Linear alphabet 38
Cāṇḍāla 244
Caṇḍikā 259
Candragupta 115, 208f.
Candra-prabha 209
Caṅkam (Sangam) literature, *see* Tamil
cannibalism 256, 259
Canopus 195, *202*
Cappadocia 83, 149, 293
Cappieri, M. 142
Capra aegagrus, *see* goat (wild)
Capra hircus, *see* goat (domestic)
captive 150, 259
caravan trade 17, 22, 114–15
Carian 126
carnelian 11, 14, 22, 211, 286
carp 184, 189, 191, 263, *264*, 267, 269f., *271*, 272, *275*
carpentry 172
carrying, carrier (bearer, porter) 33, 61, 95, 109f., 117, *183*, 186, *187*, 217; carrying yoke 109f., 191, 226; *see also* yoke-carrier
cart 9, 21, 263, 269f.
cartouche *41*
carving, *see* engraving
Casal, J.-M. 53
cases, *see* declension; nominative, etc.
Caspian Sea *10*, *144*, *146*, 148, *155f.*
caste 110, 116, 133, 170f., 208, 244
casting of copper 9, 107
castration 191, 220, 224
cat 229, 258
catchword 34, 268
category, *see* determinative; type
catfish 263, *264*
cattle 9, 15, 33, 130, 150, 157, 213, 234, 237; domestic humped, *see* zebu; *see also* bull; cow
Caucasian languages 43, 46, 126, *127*, 196, 297
Caucasus 129, *146*, 158, 172
caul, *see* embryonic cover
Cavalli-Sforza, L. L. 46
Caxor *χare* 196
cedar 9, *35*
Cedi *154*, 268
Celtic 168
cemetery *12*, 15, 149, 151, *152*, 244
Cemetery H *8*, *236*; Cemetery H culture *25*, 154, *155*, *236*, 295
Cemetery R37 *8*, *236*
cenotaph 148f.
Central America 39, 49, 57, 126
Central Asia 4, *10*, 15–17, 21–6, 56, 126, 129, 144, *146*, 147–52, *155f.*, 172, 213, 224
Central Dravidian *136*, 165, 170, 174, *175*, 223, 227, 264; *kūli*, *kūḍi* 165; *l* 217; *l-* 223
Central India 61, 110, 134, 137, 140, 161, 165, 198, 221
centralization 24
centre 134, 145, 198, *200*, 222–4, 245
Centum 145, 294
ceramics, *see* pottery
Ce-v-vēl 235
Ce-v-vēḷ 230, 235
Cēy, Cēyōṉ, Ceyyavaṉ, Ceyyōṉ 235, 237
Chadic 128
Chadwick, J. xv, 45, 58, 277
chair 14, *30*; *see also* seat; throne
Chalcolithic 15–17, 19, 54, 153, *155*, 171f., 174, 203
Chalmers, R. 232
Champa tree 228
Champollion, J.-F. 41
change: of language 167; linguistic 46; of script 54
Chanhu(jo)-Daro *7*, *10*, *16*, 24, *25*, 62, 118f., 216, 219, *256*, 300
Channa striatus 263, *264*
charcoal 221
chariot 145, *148*, 149–51, *152*, 158, 216, 226, 295; *see also* vehicle
charm 116, 208, 228, 239; *see also* magic
chastity (conjugal fidelity, marital faithfulness), chaste (faithful) 206, 224, 240, *241*, 243–5, 265, 268, 272; *see also* firm; infidelity
'cheese' 34
Chelyabinsk *152*
Cheremis 145
Cherkaskul' *146*
chert (flint) 8f., 15, 168, *247*
Chettiar, C. 231
Chilas 142, 152
child 9, *132*, 133, 197, 206–10, 217f., 221, 224–6, *228*, 229f., 237, *238*, 239–41, 258f., 262, *275f.*, 297, 299; *see also* embryo; fertility; man (boy); pregnancy; son; young, youth
Childe, V. G. 144
China, Chinese 24, 57, 107, 110, 119, 125, *136*, 137, *139–41*, 142, *143*, 145, 168, 201, 203f., 224, 292–4, 298; language 39, 82, 86, 125: *àn* 39; *b'i̯og* *58*; *k'i̯ŭg* *58*; *săn* *58*; *si* 107; *xiu* 201, 204; script 33, 39, *58*, 287; seals 119, 293
Chitral *253*
chlorite (vessels) 22, *23*, *249*, 286
Cholistan 6, *20*
Chorasmian *129*
Choṭā Nāgpur 161, 163, 174
chronology, *see* dating; time reckoning
Chukchi 224
churning 199
Cilappatikāram 227, 243, 270
circle(s), circular 8, 22, 30, 41, 44, 78, 104, 183, *200*, 206, 214, 216, 218, 227, 265f., 268, 270; of protection 228; worship 256; concentric 22, 110, 204, 211; intersecting 9, 21, 206, 298; (Indus sign) 53, *226–8*, 229f.; semicircle 52, 78, 82, 107, *108*; stone 172; *see also* dot-in-circle; round
circumambulation 226
circumgraph 43, 69
circumpolar star 206, 222, 224, *243*
Ciṟupāṇ. 233
CISI 62, *106*, *108*, *114*, *192f.*
cists, portholed stone, 172
citadel, *see* acropolis
Citra 208
Citrā *202*, 207
city (town, urban) 3–6, *8*, 9, *12*, 14, 17, 24, 26, 34, 43, 45, 49, 54, 61, 103, 110, *113*, 114, *115*, 117, 119, 130, 149, 160, 170, 190, 201, 256, 258f., 270, 285; lower town 6, *12*, 221; *see also* urbanization
Civil, M. 35
civilization, collapse of, 3f., 24f., 49, 55
clan 116, 207
class: (grammatical) 130; (of society) 205, 270
Classical Sanskrit, *see* Sanskrit
classifier, *see* determinative
claw 232, *276*
clay 11, 30, 64, *65*, 69, 107, *113f.*, 221–4; *see also* tag
cleansing, *see* lustration
Cleopatra *41*
climate 9, 285
cloak, *see* dress
cloth 9, 11, *30*, 45, 54, *113f.*, 200, 214, 259
Clothey, F. W. 226
cloud 214, 259
club *91*, *249*
clue, *see* key
'coal' 209
cobra, *see* snake
cock 235
codex, *see* manuscript
cognate 42, 47, 87, 126
coin 5, 55, 117, 184, 288, 293, 296f.
collective concept 82
Collon, D. *132*
colonization, colony (outpost) 11, 14, 17, 22, 38, 148
colour 49, 64, 200f.; of skin 14f., 150, 196f., 235, *251*, *275*; *see also* black, etc.
column *35*, 89, 100f.; 'miniature columns' 148f.
comb *21*, 22, 104
Comb- and Pit-marked Pottery 145
'combinatory method' 47
comet 199, 245
commentary, commentator 243, 259, 269
commodities (goods, merchandise) 13f., 30, 44, 54, 113, *114*, 115; luxury 14, 17, 22, 148, 152
communication 21, 29, 287
comparative linguistics, *see* linguistics
compartments 32
compartmented seals 17, 152, *255*
compass point, *see* direction
complementary distribution 69, 137
completeness of grammar 97; of inscription 80–4, 95, 195, 215, 230; of sentence 96; of sign 78
component (element) 69, 79f., 95, 100
composite sign, *see* ligature
compound (word) xvi, 80, 82, 147, 151, 196f., 230–3, 246, 265, 267, 272, 274, *275–7*
computer (automatic method) xvf, 24, *36*, 60, 62, 64, 88, 90, 97–101, 289, 291
concentric 149, *150*; circles 22, 110, 204, 211
conception 184, 189, 228, 238f., 268; *see also* pregnancy
conch shell 104, 110; *see also* shell
concordance xvi, 62, *63*, 66, 69, 78f., 88, 131, 232, 289, 299
cone, conical 78, 218f.; inscribed 110
conflation of signs 33, 68, 78
conjunction, astral, 203–9, 241, 263, 265
connecting line 33, 69, 79f.
connection, syntactic, 98–101, 194–6
connective (particle) 45
conquest (invasion) 4, 22, 35, 49, 134, 149, 151f., 172, 174, 207,

259, 269; *see also* immigration; subjugation; victory; war
consecration 215f., 218, 224, 246, 262
consistency 35, 38, 60
consonant 35f., 48; alphabet 36, *37*, 38, 56; cluster 56; final 50; initial 194; shared 44, *45*; short and long 175, 298; 'weak' 36, 38
'constant' sign 60, 96
constellation, *see* asterism
constituents of sentence 87–90, *99*
contact 9, 15, 17, 22, 46f., 117, 137, 140, 142, 145, 255
contest (battle, combat, fight) 36, 246, *247–9*, *251–3*, 254, 259, 261, 269f., 272, 300; *see also* war
continuity/discontinuity, biological, cultural, linguistic 21f., 49, 53, 56, 104, 117, 167f., 171f., 174, 288
contract 54, 273
contraction 246, 263
control of trade 114f., 117
conventions in writing 32, 34, 36
co-occurrence (juxtaposition, pairwise occurrence) of signs 94, 97–9, *100f.*, 109, 131, 195f., 226
cook 117
Coomaraswamy, A. K. 229
copper 8f., 13–15, 17, 22, *57*, 106f., 130, *155*, *158*, 174; hoard *108*, 117, 293; tablet *57*, 69, 107, 110, *111f.*, 233, *234*, 237, 239, 274, *276*, 292
Copper Hoards *25*, 54, *55*, 154, *155*, 295
Coptic 35f., 40, 46, 128
cord, *see* rope
Corded Ware *144*
corn, *see* grain
corpus 47, 61–4; *see also CISI*
correspondences: language/culture 137; spoken/written, *see* fit; text/iconography, *see* parallelism; phonemic 46f.
cosmic: forces 247; law and order 14, *106*, 151, 190, 214f., 226 (*see also dharma*); tree 221, 244; *see also* world
cosmogony 268
cosmology 245f.
cotton 9, 15, 54, 170, 241
counting 29f., 44, 169; *see also* number
country (land) 12–15, 33f., *35*, 43, *58*, 117, 121, 130, 133, 170, 245
country fig = udumbara 258
couple 184, 186, *219*, 225, *256*, 263, 265, 267, 269; *see also* pair
courier 117
courtesan 189
courtyard 8, 55, *56*, 194, 258
cover(ing) 197, 274
cow (bovine) *32*, 104, *106*, 109, 188, 196, *219*, 221, 224, 258, 268, *277*; cow shed 238; *see also* bull; cattle
Cowell, E. B. 232
cowherd 221
Cowley, A. E. 44
cowry shell *253*; *see also* shell
crab 59, 232; (Indus sign) *232*, 233, *234f.*, 239f., *276*, 299
crafts 8f., 17, 30, 190, 270
crane 232
creation, creator 49, 51, 56, 85, 189, 197, 206, 224, 228, 238, 268, 301
creeper plant 244, 246
cremation 153, 171f., 194, 244
crescent, *see* moon
Crete 43, 45
crime, criminal 113–15, 234
criticism xvf, 42f., 58–61, 88, 218, 284, 286, 288f.
crocodile, *see* alligator
Crooke, W. 189, 228, 267
cross 30, 78; of St Andrew *55*
cross-checking, *see* testing
cross-cousin marriage 170, *171*
crow *14*, 197, 286
crown 34; *see also* head-dress
cruelty 191, 234
cry(ing) (lamenting) 14, 225, 235, 237, 299
cryptography 48
crystalline rock *113*
cult image, *see* statue(tte)
'cult-object' in front of 'unicorn' *21*, *113*, 131, *132*, 286
cult, orgiastic, 189, 191, 194, 256, 264; *see also* sexuality
culture, archaeological/human, 24, 47, 64, 137
cuneiform script and texts 11–15, 18, 32–5, 41–3, 53, 80, 83, 85, 103, *107*, 113–15, 126, 128, 130, *131f.*, 183, *187*, 190, 205, 213f., 248, *252*, 273, *274*, 287, 293, 302; *see also* Akkadian/Eblaite/Old Persian/Ugaritic cuneiform
Cunningham, A. 6, 58
cupbearer 117, 119
Curinyā 228
curse 14, 224, 268
Curtius Rufus, Q. 149
Cushitic 128
'cutting' 269
customs house 114, *115*
cycle, astronomical or temporal, 49, 203–5, 217, 263; of phrases *90*, 92
cylinder seal *10f.*, 18, 23, 30, 54, *57*, 116, *120*, 131, *132*, *148*, 149, 180, *181*, 183, *184*, *186f.*, 188, *219*, *247–50*, *252–4*, 255, *256*, 260, 287, 297, 300
Cyprinidae 264
Cypriniformes 263
Cyprinus rohita 263, *264*
Cypriot script 42–5, 55, 287
Cypro-Minoan script 43
Cyprus 43, 55

dagger 172; inscribed 117; dagger sheath 14; *see also* knife; sword
Daha *5*, 149f., 294
Daic *143*
Daimabad *10*, *25*, 54f., *55*, 174, 288
dais, *see* throne
Ḍākinī 301
Dakkhini *135*
Dakṣa 238f.
Dākṣāyaṇa 239
Dalbergia sissoo Roxburgh 13f.
Dales, G. F. 24, 104, 218f.
Damb Sadaat *16*, 17, *20*, 52, *269*
Damelī 134
Damerow, P. *36*
dance 9, 14, 194, 221, 259
Daṇḍin 233
Dane, Danish 11
danger(ous) 228, 237, 258, 263, 270
Dardic 134, *135*, 142, 152, *156*, *166*
Darius 4, 13, 41f., 117
dark(-skinned) 14f., 150, 196f., 218, *251*, 259, 274; darkness 215, 217f., 226, 233, 247, 259, 298; *see also* black; night
Dāsa 4, 149–52, 154, *155*, 170, 189, 209, 214, 256, 294
Dashly *16*, *25*, *150*, 151, *213*, *255*, 256, 300
Dasyu 149–51
date palm 15, *23*
dating (chronology, radiocarbon) 3f., 9, 11, 15, *18f.*, 21, 30, 38, 49f., *84*, 85, 107, 133f., 137, 140, 144f., 148, 151, 153, 157f., 169, 171, 204, 234, 243, 263, *274*, 286
dative 34, *94*, 96
daughter 119, 206, 229, 244, 259, 263, 265, 267f., 270; language 46
dawn 203, 206f., 209, 231, 233, 263, 268; *see also* morning; sun (rising)
day, daily 29, 36, 49, 54, 104, 198, 201, 203–5, 207, 209, 215, 221, 228, 233, 239, 241, 245, 247, *251*, 258f., 262–4, 267, 269; *see also* birthday; Vijaya-Daśamī; week
Daybāl 163
dead, death, dying *13*, 15, 54, 188, 190f., 194, 197, 201, 205, 217f., 220f., *228*, 235, *241*, 244f., 247f., *251*, 254, *257*, 259, 264, 269f., *275*, 298; *see also* ancestors
debt 29–31
decapitation (beheading) 191, 199, 220, 235, 239, 260, 270; *see also* head
Deccan, *see* western India (also Central India, South India)
Deccan Chalcolithic *155*, 172, 174; graffiti 54, *55*, 288
decimal system 44, 169
decipherment 3f., 6, 35, 39–51, 58f., 84, 87, 92, 100–3, 106, 121, 125, 133, 174f., 273f., 277f., 285, 287f., 296, 302; acceptance of 3, 41f., 49f., 61, 277; attempts at deciphering the Indus script 57–71, 289; key (clue) to 40, 42, 49, 103, 106f., 110; impossibility of 48; obstacles to 3, 42, 45, 47f., 50, 119, 133, 278, 285; partial 51, 278; routine procedure of 51; types of 47–9; validation of 42f., 45, *46*, 60f., 273; *see also* testing
declension 41f., *44*, 60, 86f., *94*, 95–8, 100, 107, 174; *see also* inflection
De Clercq, L. *132*, *186*, *252*
dedication (votive gift) *35*, 36, 45, *107*, 109f., 116, 119, 228, *248*; votive seal 119; *see also* sacrifice
deer 9, *111*, 157
Deh-bid *105*
deity, *see* god
Delhi *136*, 154
deluge, *see* flood
demon, demoness, demoniac (ghost), 149–51, 191, 194, 199, 201, 208f., 228, 233, 237f., 248, *253*, 254, 258–60, 262, 267f., 270, 272, *276*; *see also* Asura; Mahiṣa Asura
demonstrative *88*
demotic, *see* Egyptian script
deodar 168
Dereivka 157
de Sacy, *see* Silvestre de Sacy
descent, *see* genealogy
desire (lust) 191, 220f., 230f., 238f., 258, *276*, 299; *see also* Kāma; love
destruction 151, 261, 269; *see also* burning
determinative 34–6, 38f., 79f., 109; numerical 51; phonetic 34, 38f., 48, 50f., 196, 234, 240, *276*; semantic 34, 36, 38f., *41*, 42f., 48, 109, 121, 183, 196, 240
Deva 147, 150f.,
Devanāgarī 56
Devapāla 208
Devī, *see* goddess
Devī-Māhātmya 254
devotee, *see* worshipper
Dhammapada Atthakathā 229
dharma 191, 268; *see also* cosmic law and order; law
Dharmapada 133
Dharmasindhu 263, 301
Dhātupāṭha 296
dhiṣṇ(i)ya 207, 216f., 221f., *223*; *see also* fireplace
Dholavira *7*, *10*, 110, *113*, 285, 292
Dhruva 224, 300; *see also* Pole Star
diacritic 33, 44, 48, 56, 59, 79, 95, 97, 104, 179, 196
diadem 265
diagram (maṇḍala) *56f.*, 198, *200*, *254*, 256, 259, 261, 270, 300
dialect 46, 125, 134, 152, 170
dice 22, 244; inscribed 110
differentiation (divergence) 46f., 68, 78, 98

Digambara 172, 184, 217
Dilmun 11–14, 129f., *219*, 273, *274*, 286, 302; seal *11*, 114, *115*, 130, *183*, *219*, 273, *274*, 286, 302
'dim' 197
diminutive 230, *276*
Diodorus Siculus 41
Dionysus 214
direction: (compass point) 6, 47, 110, 119, 195, 198f., *200*, 201, 205, 245, 263; direction-crow *14*, 286; of writing 32f., 41, 44, 56, 62, 64–7, 88, *109*, 110, *111–12*, 290; reversed 98, *109*, 110, *111–12*, *246*
disaspiration 152, 235
disc(s) *30*, 213
discovery (of the Indus Civilization) 6, 285
disease (illness) 24, 190, 198, 218, 228, 233f., 237f., 261, 263, 299; *see also* health; medicine
distribution, *see* position
divergence, *see* differentiation
'dividing' 196, 297
division of texts (into 'words' and phrases) 60, 68, 82–4, 90–2, 95–9, 290f.; *see also* word divider
divination, diviner (omen) 49, 110, 119, *132*, 190
Dnieper *144*, *146*, 157
doab 26, 140, 154, 168
dockyard 11, *12*
documentation 24, 60, 62, 289f.
dog 9, *50*, 121, 142
Dogri *166*
domestication 15, 157, 189
donkey 157
door 8, *37*, *118*, 183f., 199, 205, 301; doorkeeper 119
dot (spot) 49, *250*, *260*, 261–4, *265f.*, 267–70, *271*, 272, 274, *275*, 301; *see also* 'frame' of four dots; dot-in-a-circle 11, *194*, 211, 215f., 269f., *275*; *see also* circle(s)
doublet (duplicate, multiform) 188, 190, 233, 237f., 244, 259, *271*
doubling, of consonant, 194; *see also* repetition
Draco *202*, *243*
drain(age) 6, 8, *12*, 22; inscribed drainpipe 110
drama 49, 133, *271*
Dravidian (Proto-Dravidian) 46, 59–61, 87, 117, 128, 134, *136*, 137, 140, 142, *156*, 160–3, 165, *166*, 167–70, *171*, 172, 174, *175*, 179, 180–2, 188, 194–7, 201, 206f., 209, 217, 223, 225–31, 233f., 237, 245f., 261, 264, 267f., 270, 272, 274–7, 289, 295f., 298; *ā* 188, *277*; *-ā/-a (±-tu)* 188, 261, *277*; *akal, āl* 246, 300; *āḷ/āṇ* 96, 188, 261, *277*, 297; *āl, āla-maram* 246, *276*, 300; *ampara* 61; *ampu* 61; *ara(cu)* 61; *at(t)i* 60; *-at(tu)* 60, 96; *-ay-/-ey-* 197, 201, 297; *c-* 163, 217; *caṯu/caṟu* *275*; *cūl* 217, 228, *276*, 298; *cūl/culay/cullV* 217, 228, *276*, 298; *eḻu* 195, 223, *275*; *eṇ* 169; *k-* 163, 165, 169; *-k-* 165, 170, 201; *kaṇ : kāṇ* 181, 215, *275*; *ke-, kē-* 237; *kiṭa* 165; *-k(k)u* 96; *koḷ* 232–4, 239, 299; *kōḷ(i)* 233–5, 240, *276*, 299; *kōṭṭam* 170; *-ḷ-* 217; *-ḻ-* 217, 230; *may* 197, *275*, 297; *mēl-akam* 170; *min/vin/miṇ/viṇ* 59, 181–2, 195, *275*, 296f.; *mīn/vīṇ/vīṇṭ-V-kk-* 181–2, 218, 241, *275*, 296; *mīn* 59, 180–2, 188, 194–7, 241, *275*, 296; *mu-* 194, 218, *275*; *mukam* 165; *murV* 227, 299; *muruku* 227–30, *276*, 297; *n-* 223, 246, 299f.; *ñ-* 168, 223, 246, 299f.; *nāl* 246, *276*, 300; *ñāl/nāl/āl* 246, *276*, 300; *ñāṅgal/nāṅgal* 168; *ñiṅg-/niṅg-/ñig-/nig-/ñikk-/nikk-* 223, 299; *nūṯu* 169; *pacu* 196f., *275*, 297; *paḵtu* 169; *paḻam* 168; *paṭu* 170; *peḷḷ-/piḷḷ-* 230, *276*, 299; *poṭṭu* 264, 267, 269, 272, *275*, 301; *poṭu-poṭu* 267, 301; *sukka* 60; *-ṯ-* 201, 298; *uṟu/uṯV* 201, 298; *v-* 163, 201; *v-/m-* 197, 297; *vaṭam* 240f., 245f., *276*, 300; *vaṭam, vaṭi* 241, 245f., *276*, 300; *vay/vey/mey* 197, *275*, 297; *vay-k-/vey-k-* 201, 298; *vē* 231, 299; *veḷ* *220*, *231*, *276*, 299; *vēḷ* 231, *276*, 299; *veḷi* 231, *276*, 299; *viḻal, viḻutu, viḻu* 245; *see also* Central/North/South Dravidian; Tamil
Dravidology 174f.
dream 184
Dresden Codex 49, *50*
dress (cloak, garment, robe) 13, *30*, 109, 116, *132*, 197, 211, *212*, 213, *214*, 215–18, 235, 241, 245, 261f., 298; *see also* cloth; skirt; 'sky garment'; tārpya
drill, drilling 11, 15, 24, 211
drink *132*, 149, 151f., 194, 222, 259
'driving' (chariot) 158
drop 220, 261, 264, 267f., 272, *275*, 301; first 268, 301
Dṛṣadvatī 5, *154*
drum(mer) *188*, *227*
Drupada 243
dryad 258f.; *see also* tree
dual 44; dual deity 209, 298
dualism 247
Dubois, J. A. 56, 233
Ḍumākī 134
dung 221
Dun Huang 142
duplication (of inscription) 62, 64, 107, 109f., *111f.*, 119, *120*; *see also* repetition
Dur Khan 18
Durgā 189, 191, 194, 207, 227f., 230, *253*, 254, 256, 258–64, 267, 269f., *271*, 272, 297, 300f.; *see also* Nine Durgās
dust 206
Dutch 57
dyeing 9

Ea, *see* Enki
eagle *23*, 104, *105*, *249*; *see also* vulture
E-anna 186
ear 104, *106*, 211; ear-ring *227*, 230
Early Dynastic period 14, 18, 22, 32, 34, 53, *57*, 85, *106*, 117, 183, 186, *187*, *219*, *247–9*, *254*, 255; seal *106*, 117, *219*, *247f.*
Early Harappan period/culture(s) 17, 19, *20*, 21f., *53*, 104, *105f.*, 126, 130, 142, 153–5, 157, 160, 165, 167–70, 180, 183f., *192f.*, 206f., 234, *236*, 240, *241*, 248, *251*, 263, 286; graffiti *10*, 52, *53*, 62, 288; seal *10*, 17, 21, 53, 152
Early Mature Harappan phase 19, 22, 24, *236*
Early (Ṛg)vedic 152–4, *156*, 168
Early West Iranian Grey Ware 148, *156*
earth (soil) 59, 189, 195, 268; *see also* ground
east 104, *200*, 203–6, 222, 237, 298
East Iranian 129, 133, 142, 150, 155
East Semitic *127*, 128; *see also* Akkadian
Easter Island 57, 126, 289
eastern India 4, 133, 137, 140, 142, 151, 154f., 165, 169f., 266
Eastern Neolithic 137, *140*, 294
eating 33, 184, 191, 197, 259, 263f., 268, 270; *see also* food
Ebla 214; Eblaite cuneiform 18, 38; Eblaitic 128
Ecbatana *129*
eclipse 49, 199, 203, 208, 233, *276*, 301
ecliptic 181, *202*, 204, 206, *243*, 268
economy, economic 6, 8f., 16f., 148, 297; text 32, 34
edict, royal, *see* inscription monumental
edition of inscriptions/texts 44, 61f., 289f.
Edzard, D. O. 85, 88, 117, 119
Eggeling, J. 217, 245
Egypt(ian) 4, 6, 24, 35f., 43, 45, *84*, 128, 148f., 203, *247*, 287–9, 293; art 35f., 148; demotic script 35, 40, 287; hieratic script 35, 287; hieroglyphic script 18, 35f., *37*, 39–43, 48, 54, 57, *58*, 60f., 64, 79, *84*, 103f., 109, 174, 179, 184, 196, 277, 287, 290, 292; language 35, 40f., 46, 57, *127*, 128, 183; *ʿ* 36; *ḏw* *58*; *ẖ3st* *58*; *mn* 36; *n* 36; *nt* 36; *r* 36; *rʿ* 36; *sb* 183; *sb3* 183; names 121; New Kingdom *147*; seals 119
Eka-parṇā/Eka-pāṭalā 259
Elam *10*, *17*, 30, *35*, 53, *84*, 152, 247, 256, *262*, 286; (Middle, Neo-)Elamite language 41f., *107*, *127*, 128, 130, 161, 293, 295; *sunki, -k, -p, -r, -t* 130; *sunki-me, -me-k, -me-p, -me-r* 130; *see* Linear/Proto-Elamite
Elburz 148
electrum *254*, 260
element, *see* component
elephant (*Elephas maximus*) *11*, *106*, *111*, *114*, 115f., 157, *188*, 191, 232, 235, 246; *see also* ivory
Elfenbein, J. H. 161–3, 165
élite, élite dominance 149, 154, 168, 174
Ellamma 228
emblem 61, 184, 186, 188f., 191, 265, *275*, 297; *see also* attribute; flag; mount
'emblem glyph' 50
embryo, embryonic cover 216–18, 228, 238f., 268, 272, 298
Emeneau, M. B. 161, 163, 165, 175, 182, 244
emerald 196
Emir Ware 17, *192*
emphasis, marking of, 87
'enclosure' ligatures 69, 290
end (final, last): of Indus Civilization 24, 26, 149; of text or word 38, 44, 50, 58, 61, *65*, 66, 69, 82–4, 90–8, 100, *108*, 116–18, *120*, 121, 215, 218, 246; of time-period or event 191, 205, 217, 220f.
enemy 140, 149–50, 154f., 189, 191, 201, 207, 215, 230, 245, 247f., 258f., 269f.
Eneolithic 145
English 33, 87, 91, 97, *98–100*, 134; (Old English) *eoh* 158; *slave* 150; *touring* 299; *wheel* 47
Englund, R. K. 33
engraving (carving) 29, 64, 69, 104, 107, 116, 195
Enki (Ea) 14, 102, 183, 186, *187*, 188f., *190*, 191, 204, *252*, 254, 291, 297
Enlil 121, 204
Enuma Anu [d]Enlil 214
Ephedra 149, 152
epic 49, 51, 58, 133, 180, 182, 206, 222, 224, 268, 272; *see also* Mahābhārata; Rāmāyaṇa
Epic Sanskrit, *see* Sanskrit
epidendron 234
epigraphy 45, 47, 60, 209
epithet, *see* atribute
equator(ial pole) *202*, 204
equinox 110, *202*, 203–6, 221, 241, 256, 262, 268
Equus asinus 157
Equus caballus, *see* horse
Equus hemionus khur 157
Equus hemionus onager 157
Eratosthenes 150
'erect' 223, 299
Eridu 191

erotic(s), *see* sex(ual)
Estonian 145
Ethiopia(n) 14, 128
ethnology 104, 137; *see also* tribe
Etruscan 45–8, 57, 126, 287, 289
etymology 43, 47, 56, 137, 140, 158, 162, 165, 170, 175, 180f., 206f., 217, 220, 223, 231, 233–5, 239, 241, 246, 265, 267, *276*; folk-etymology 56, 244, 296, 300
Euphrates 4, 31, *129*, 130
Eurasiatic forests 161; steppes 129, 143
Europe(an) 53, 116, 134, *144*, 145, 158
Evans, A. 44f.
evening 196, 203, 217, 231; star 262; *see also* sun (setting); twilight
evil (sin) 190, 215, 217f., 228, 245, 267, 298, 301; eye 265
evolution: of culture 24; of Indus script 52–6; of language 29, 287; multilinear 24; of writing 29–39
excarnation 172, 244
excavations 6, 11, 13, 15, 21f., 24, 43f., 54, 62, 148f., 286, 290
exclusiveness, in pronoun *166*, 167, 170
exemplar (model) 240, 243–5, 264, 268, 272
exorcist 190
expiation 217f., 268, 301
eye *37*, 181, *194*, 215f., 218, 234, *235*, 237, 239, 244, 265, 267, 270, 272, *275*, 301; evil 265; eye-seed 270; fish-eye(d) *194*, 215, 270, 302; third eye 215, 265, *269*, 270, *271*, *275*, 301

face 206, 234, *235*, 237, *238f.*, 261, 265, 270, 300; goat-faced, *see* goat; many-faced *250*; *see also* head
faience 3, 9, *103*, 107, *110*, *226*, 228
Failaka *10*, 11–13, *23*, 130, *219*
Fairservis, W. A. 61, 289
faithful, *see* chaste
Faiz Mohammad (Muhammad) *16*, 17, *20*
Faiz Mohammad Ware 17, *20*, *192f.*
falling down 224, 245, 267, 269, *276*, 301
family 17, 45, 50, 162, 207; *see also* language family
fan 269
Fara 32, 34, 204, *248*
farmer 121; *see also* agriculture
Fars *105*, 129
fasting 240f.
fate 14, 197
Fatehgarh *25*, 154, *155*
father 38, 119, 121, 130, 162, 191, 206–9, 234, 237, 239, 262, 267f., 270
fauna, *see* animals
fear(ed) 109, 197; *see also* ferocity
feather 104
Fedorov *146*
feedback effect 51
feline 255; *see also* cat; lion; tiger
female/feminine, *see* woman
female organ 32, 184, 217–21, 224, 238, 259, 264, 301; *see also* womb; yoni
ferocity, fierce (terrifying) 188f., 208, 233, 238 (negated), 258f., 263, 268f.; *see also* fear(ed)
fertility 4, 110, *132*, 184, 188–91, 194, 206, 225f., 228f., *238*, 239, 247, *251*, 255, 258, 261–4, 267–9, 272, *275*, 297; *see also* child; creation; embryo; pregnancy
festival 54f., *56*, 110, 191, 194, 196, 203, 206, 220f., 254, 256, 259f., 263, 267f., *271*
fetter, *see* noose
fever, 234, 237, 239
Ficus bengalensis, *see* banyan
Ficus glomerata, *see* udumbara
Ficus indica, *see* banyan
Ficus infectoria, *see* plakṣa
Ficus religiosa, *see* pipal
fidelity, *see* chastity
field 54, *105*
fig: 'fig deity', 'fig deity' seal 60, 104, *110*, 116, 121, 188, 237, 246, 256, 258f., *260*, 261, 263, 267, 269f., 272, 274, 293, 301; fig leaf 61, *185f.*, 234, 238, 240, *241*, *246*, *250f.*, 258f., *260*, *276*; fig tree 9, *21*, 60, 104, *110*, 121, 184, *185f.*, 228f., 234, *236*, 237, *239*, 240, *241f.*, *244*, 245, 256, 258f., *260*, 263, *276*, 292, 299–301; (Indus sign) *231f.*, *234f.*, 237, 239–41, *243*, *246*, *276*; *see also* banyan; plakṣa, pipal; udumbara
fight, *see* contest
'figure-of-eight' 211, 215
figurine, *see* statue(tte)
fillet 266, 301
Filliozat, J. 205
fin 64, 179f.
final, *see* end
find-places of Indus seals and inscriptions *10*, 61, 64, *115*, 117, *118*
finger 267
Finnic 145
Finnish language 86, 267; *kehrä* 145; *mustalainen* 150; *orja* 150; *sata* 145; *tippa, tippua* 267
Finnish team xvf, 61f., 69, *94*, 284, 289
Finno-Ugric 47, 145; *kešträ/kesträ* 145; *śata* 145
fire, fiery 21, 33, 150, 191, 197, 199, 205–8, 216f., 220f., 224, 226, 228, 231, 234f., 237–9, 247, 263, 268, 298; *see also* Agni; bonfire
fire-altar *12*, 154, 201, 206, 216, 221, *222*, 223f., 268, 298f.
firefly 182
fire-kindler 216, 222
fireplace (hearth) 207, 216–18, 221, *222f.*, 224, 228, *276*, 298f.; *see also* dhiṣṇ(i)ya
firing of pottery 52, *65*, 107, 227
firmness (fixity, steadfastness) 224, 243, 245, 300; *see also* chastity
fish 9, 32, 34, *37*, 54, *55*, 109, 121, 179, *180f.*, 182, *183f.*, *186f.*, 188f., *190*, 191, *192–5*, 196f., *215*, 230, 232, 241, 259, 263, *264*, 266–8, 270, *271*, 272, 274, *275*, 288, 296f., 301; (Indus sign) 59, 64, 69, 81f., 91f., *93f.*, 121, 179f., 183f., *185*, *188*, 190f., *194f.*, 196f., 201, 207, 209, 211, *215*, 218, 226, 230, *231*, 232f., 241, *243*, *260*, 261–4, 267f., 270, 272, 274, *275–7*, 296f., 301; bones 9, 191, 194, 264; broth 189; fish-eye(d) *194*, 215, 270, 302; hook 9, 194; fishing, fisherman 9, *13*, 121, 130, 145, 181, 191, 194, 196, 233, 268, 285, 297; net 9, 194; 'fish-man' *190*; offering 190f., *194*, 259, 263f., 297; fish-pair 184, *186f.*, 188, 190, 195, 264, *271*, *275*, 297; ration 194, *195*, 297; rotting 191, 194; scale 9, 21, 264, 267, 272, *275*; fish-water 194, 297; 'horn-fish' 188f.; *see also* shark
fit between written and spoken language 33–6, 38f., 48, 51, 88f., 96f., 125, 287
flag (banner) 189, 199, *200*, 229, 261; *see also* emblem
flame 239, 301
'flashing' 182, 296
flesh-water 194
flint, *see* chert
flood (deluge) 4, 6, 9, 17, 22, 24, 203; flood myth 188, 190, 297
floor 6, 8, 11, *113*
flour 55, *56*, 267; *see also* powder
flower 109, 209, 234f., 239
flying 104, *105*, 238, 245
folklore, folk religion, folk-art 196, 228f., 232, 246, 272, 287, 299
food 9, 121, 186, 189–91, 194, 200f., 244, 263; *see also* eating
foot 59, 197, 232, 237, *252*, *254*, 260, 270; footprint 57; footstool 186, 188
forehead (mark) *21*, 56, 264, *265f.*, 267f., *269*, 270, *271*, 272, *275*, 300–2
foreign(er) 4, 12, 22, 24, 33, 38, 41, *58*, 62, 131, *132*, 170, 208; language 119
foreman 117
forest (grove, jungle) 9, 17, 82, 110, 145, 208, 229, 237, 243, 259
formative era 24; stage 33
formula (textual) 33, 42f., 45, 47, 89, 106; *see also* mantra
Forschungsprojekt Mohenjo-daro, Aachen 24
Förstemann, E. 49
fort(ress) 148f., *150*, 151f., 170, 256, 258, 261, 294; *see also* acropolis; walls
fowl 9, 14
'frame' of four dots 69, *94*, 290
Franke-Vogt, U. 62
fraud 30
French 15, 46, 88, 149, 168
frequency of occurrence (statistics) 33, 41f., 44–8, 60f., 64, 69, *78*, 79, 83f., 90f., *93*, 94, 97f., 100, 117f., 131, 194, 209, 226f., 232, 278, 289; interval statistics 60
fricative, fricativization 36, 163, 165, 169f., 295
Friday 259, 262
friend 244
frog 58
fruit 109, 168, 184, 194, 221, 234, 239, 258
fuchsite 11, 286
fuel 9, 200f., 239, 285
fumigation, *see* smoke
Funambulus pennanti 103
function 64, 89, 97, 106, 110, 291
Fürer-Haimendorf, C. von, 171
furnace 8, 11, 217

Gad(a)bā *136*, *139*, *166*, 175, 182
Gadd, C. J. 66, *132*, 170, 211, 213
Gaja-Lakṣmī 116
galbanum 170
Gama, Vasco da, 134
game(-piece) 9, 22, 194, 220
Gand(h)āra *5*, 13, 133, 209
Gandhara Grave culture *26*, 151f., *156*, 294; *see also* Ghalegay IV–V
Gāndhārī 133, *154*
Gandharva 206f., 216, 222, 229
Gaṇeśa 230
Ganges (Gaṅgā) *25*, 54, 133, 140, *141*, 152, *153–6*, 168f., 181, 206, 224, 268, 294
Gangetic Copper Hoards *25*, 54, *55*, 154, *155*, 174
Ganweriwala Ther 6, *7*, *16*
garden(er) 194, 258
Garga-trirātra 216
garland 235, 260
garment, *see* dress
gate *8*, 22, 110, *113*, 114, *115*, 259
gaur, *see* bison
Gautama-Dharmasūtra 248
Gautamī 243
gavial, *see* alligator
Gawar-bati 134, *166*
gazelle 9, 157
Gebel el-ʿAraq 36, *247*
Gedrōsia 162
Gelb, I. J. 117
gem 196, 201, 209, 214
gender 44, 96, 162, 225
genealogy (descent) 42f., 50, 54, 119, 208
genetics 46
genitive (possessive) 34, 42, 51, *88*, *94*, 95–7, 117, 121, 130, 169, 188, 218, 227, 261, *277*

geography, *see* location
Geoksyur *16*, 17
geometric motif or shape 9, 15, 17, 24, 55, 62, 78, 110, *200*, 201
German 24, 87
Germanic 145
gerund 152, 168
GGS 207–9, 221, 243, 245f., 259
Ghaggar 7, 9, 21
Ghalegay (Ghaligai) *141*, 142, 152f., *156*, *158*, 159, 168, *236*, 294
gharial, *see* alligator
ghee, *see* butter
Ghirshman, R. 148
Gidwani, P. J. 209
gift 248; *see also* dedication; giving; sacrifice
Gilund *26*
Gimbutas, M. *144*
'giving' 32f., 109, 208–10, 216, 229, 238, 258; *see also* gift
glass *228*
'glittering' 181f., 195f., 296
Globular Amphora *144*
gloss 45
glyph (Maya) *49f.*, 51; full figure 50
glyptics, *see* iconography
gnomon 206
goat 9, 15, 161, 191, *219*, 234, *235*, 237, *238*, 239, *251*, 259, 261, 300; domestic 157, 189; wild 157, 189, 237, 261; *see also* markhor
'goat-fish' 188
Gobhila, *see* GGS
'goblet' 25
god (deity) 3f., 14, 24, *32*, 34, *35*, 36, 41, 43, 45, 48–51, 54, 56, *91*, 97, 107, 109, *110*, *111f.*, 116f., 119–21, 128, 130, *132*, 145, 147, 149–51, 171f., 180, 183f., *185–8*, 189–91, 194–8, *199f.*, 201, 205–18, 220–2, 224f., *226*, 227–34, *235*, 237, *238f.*, *241*, 244, 247f., *249–52*, 256, *257*, *258f.*, *260*, 261f., 264f., 267–9, 274, *275–7*, 297, 299–301; dual and triadic god 209, 298; *see also* Deva
Godar-i Shah *16*, *25*, 148
goddess 4, *32*, 48, 59, 102, *107*, 116, 119, *120*, *132*, 183, 189, 191, 194, 206f., 210, 215, 218, 220f., 224, 227, *228*, 229f., 235, 238, 240f., *248*, *253–5*, 256, 258–61, *262*, 263–5, 267–70, *271*, 272, 297, 299–302
'going' 33
gold(en) 9, 14, 45, *106*, 148–50, 190f., 196, 213, *214*, 221, 233, 235, 245, 247, *255*, 263, 266, 268, 301
Gomal *7*, *16*, 21
Gōṇḍī *136*, *166*, *175*, 182, 209, 264; *verce* 230; *viyā sukum* 207; *warcē* 230
Gonur *16*, *25*, 149
goods, *see* commodities
goose 181, 296
Gordon, D. H. 155
Gorgan, *see* Gurgan
Gorresio, G. 189, 263, 265
Gothic *aihwa-* 158
graffito *10*, 12, 22, 52–5, 57, 64, 78, 107, 179, 288; *see also* potter's marks
Gragg, G. *127*
grain (corn) 6, 8, 15, 22, 30, 59, 165, 248, *249*
grammar, grammatical morpheme or feature 31, 33f., 38, 42, 46–8, 51, 60, 82, 85–101, 125f.; context-free/formal/notional 97–101; intermediate *100*
granary 6, *8*, 11, 15, 17, 113f., 117, 285
grapheme (distinct sign) 33, 62, 68–79, 84f., 98, 290; bound/free 79; *see also* fit; number of graphemes
'grasping', *see* seizer
grave, *see* burial
great (in royal titles and theophoric names) 117, 119, 121, 130
Great Bear, *see* Ursa Major
Greater Indus Valley 15–26, 234, 256, 293
Greek: alphabet 18, 35f., *37*, 38, 40f., 58, 126, 287, 290; people, culture and language 4f, 13, 40–5, *46*, 47, 87, 117, 144f., 149f., 162, 172, 208, 214, 270, 285, 301; *álpha* 38; *anõwes* *46*; *árktos* 222; *Bēl astrokhitōn* *214*; *doero (doũlos)* 150; *eikṓn* 32; *e-ruthrós* 235; *éstō* 43; *Gedrōsia* 162; *ikhthús* 191; *Indiē*, *Indós* 4; *kúklos* 47; *leipō:élipon* 87; *Mákai* 13; *ōkús* 158; *parádeigma* 89; *pōlō* 44; *qʷetrõwes* *46*; *suntássein* 89; *triõwee*, *triõwes* *46*; *trípōs*, *trípode* *46*; *see also* Indo-Greeks
Green, M. W. 33
Greenberg, J. H. 87
green(ness) 196f., 216, 228, 265, *275*, 297
grey ware 148, 155, *156*, *192f.*; *see also* PGW
Gṛhyāsaṁgraha 267
Gṛhyasūtra 207–9, 243, 245, 265f.
grid (tabulation) 44, *45*, 48, 64, 87f., *89*, 90, 97, 100f.
Grotefend, G. F. 41f.
ground (soil) 34, 110; *see also* earth
ground-plan, *see* layout
grove, *see* forest
Groves, C. P. 157
guardian, *see* protector
Guatemala 49
Gudea 14, 18, 213
guess 3f., 43, 61, 100f., 106, 274, 302
Guha 228, 238
Guhyaka 216
guilloche *23*
Gujarat 8f., 11f., 22, *25*, 26, *57*, *113*, *136*, 140, *161*, 163, 165, 170, 172, 174, 191, 209, 287, 297
Gujarati 134, *135*, *166*, 170, 174; *paṭṭan* 170; *-vāḍ(ā)* < Old G. *vāṭa*, *-vāṭi* 170
Gulf *5*, 11–14, *17*, 22, 53f., 114, *115*, 126, *127*, 129f., 285f., 293; seals *10*, 11, 114, *115*, 130f., 133, *219*, 286
Gullick, C. B. 191
Gumla *7*, *10*, *16*, *20*, 53, *251*
Gungunum *274*
Gupta dynasty 116, 198
Gupte, B. A. 265
Gurgān (Gorgān) *10*, *25*, 148, 152, *155f.*, 158
Gurgan Buff Ware 148, *156*
Gurgan Grey Ware 148, 152, *155f.*
Gurjara 163, 165
Gurung 142, *166*
Guti *127*, 128
guttural 145
Gypsy 150

hair 59, *132*, 209, *253*, 255, 260f., 300; 'double-bun' hairstyle 24, *253f.*, 255, 260, 300; matted hair 243f., 300; parting of 265; with six locks *247f.*, *252*, 254; hair-whorls *213*, 214; *see also* plait
Hakra 6, *7*, 21
Hāla's Sattasaī 174
Halaf period 18
'half', 'halving' 196f, 205, 263, *275*
Halim, M. A. 53
Hallur *173*, 174
'Hamitic' 128
Hammurapi 9; dynasty 18
Han dynasty 119
hand 14, *37*, 69, 109, 186, *187*, 211, 240, *241*, 246, 248, *249*, *253*, 255, 261; raised 109, *110*, 256, *260*; *see also* arm
'hanging' 244f., *276*, 300
Hansman, J. 170
hapax legomenon (unique occurrence) 47, 69, 183
Harappa 5f., *7*, *8*, 9, *10*, 11, *16*, *20*, 24, *25*, 54, 62, 64, *65f.*, *82*, *91f.*, 107, *109f.*, 117, 142, 149, 157, 179, *180*, 190f., *193f.*, *195*, *226–9*, *231f.*, *236*, *239*, *244*, *246*, 259, 264, 269, 285, 293; excavations 3, 6, 24, 54, 149, 286, 290
Harappan culture, *see* Early/Mature/Late Harappan; Indus Civilization
hare *111*
Hari-Ṇegameṣin 238
Hariparigom *141*
Hariścandra 208, 237
Harivaṁśa 189, 209
Harris, Z. *98f.*; 'Harris' approach 98f.
Hart, G. L. 196, 265
Hartland, E. S. 228
Hartner, W. 269
harvest(ing) 9, 15
Haryana 6, *136*
Hasanlu 152
Hassuna 30
Hassuna-Samarra period 18
Hastings, W. 5
hatching 33, 234
Hathial 168
Ḫatti(c) 43, 126, *127*
Hattusha *147*
Hausa 87
havirdhāna *223*
head 33, *37*, 50f., *103*, 104, *106f.*, *183*, 189, 194, 196, 199, 205, 211, 213, *219*, 226, 237, *238f.*, 240, *241*, 247f., *249*, *251*, *252f.*, 254f., 258, *260*, 268f., *277*, 299, 301; *see also* decapitation; face; hair
head-dress (crown) 121, *132*, 184, *185–8*, 211, 229, *253f*, 255, 258, 261; *see also* hair
head word 88, 97, 126, 130, 169
health 43; *see also* disease; medicine
hearing 244
hearth, *see* fireplace
heaven, *see* sky
Hebrew 87, 128; *ḥawwā* 102; *ḥrṣ* 56; *ṣēlaʿ* 102
Heesterman, J. C. 216
heliacal rise/observation 203f., 206, 263
Hellenistic period/tradition 18, 201, 262
Helmand *16*, *25*, *129*
helmet *254*, 255, 260
Hemacandra 244
Hemādri 241
Hemphill, B. E. 167
Herakles 270
Heras, H. *57*, 59f., 277, 289
hermitage 224, 243
hero 14, 119, 121, 150, 209, 216, 230, 234, 237, 246, *247f.*, *252*, 254, 259f., 270; *see also* warrior
Herodotus 117, 126
HGS 221, 237, 243, 245
hide (of animal) *213*
Hiebert, F. 148
Hierapolis 191
hieratic, *see* Egyptian script
hieroglyph 35
'hieroglyphic alphabet' 36, *37*
hieroglyphic script, *see* Egyptian; Hittite; Maya; Minoan
high priest 106, *107*, 121, 258, 261, 293
highland 14f., 162, *164*, 165, 170
Himachal Pradesh *136*, 168
Himalaya 9, 259
Himalayan languages 142
Hincks, E. 42
Hindi 56, 134, *135*, 137; *bahut bahut* 82; *cānd(a)nī* 265; *saur, saurī* 263; *ṭipkā* 267
Hindu, Hinduism 21, 56, 150, 183f., 188–91, 194, 196–201, 206–10, 218, 220f., 224, 226, 230, 234, 237f., *241*, *253*, 260–2, 264, *265*, 272, 285

Hindu Kush 4, 134, 142f., *146*, 168
Hinduš (satrapy) 4, *5*, 285
history, historical (textual) information 3–6, 36, 42f., 45, 47, 54, 58, 117, 125, 134, 137, 273, 277f., 285, 294, 296; *see also* literature; monumental inscriptions
Hittite: bilingual seal 43; civilization/empire 42, *147*; cuneiform texts 43, 126, 145, 158; hieroglyphic script 18, 42f., 57, *58*, 59, 83, 126, 287, 289; language 43, 58, 126, *127*, 145, 293; *e-es-tu* 43; *harnas* *58*; *-mi* 43; *na* *58*; *-ti* 43
hoard, *see* copper/Copper Hoard
hoe(ing) *105*
holes 211, *214*, 228, 261
Holi 206, 221, 299
holiness, *see* saintliness
Homer 222
homonym 33
homophone, homophony 33, 39, 51, 79, 102f., 121, 175, 179f., 188, 195–7, 217, 220, 223, 231, 234, 241, 245f., 264, 267, 287, 296; *see also* pun
honorific plural 230
hoof(ed leg) 157, *186*, *248*, *250*, 258
hook 9, 15, *37*, 194, 211
horizon 203–6, *275*
horizontal 32f., 104, 180, *181*, 301
horn *21*, 32, 104, *106*, 110, *111f.*, 116f., 121, *132*, 159, 183f., *185f.*, *188*, 211, *213*, 229, *234f.*, 239, *244*, 247f., *250–4*, 258, 261, 265, 269, 299; 'horn-fish' 188f.
horoscope 208, 298
horse 44, 59, 61, *106*, 126, 145, *148*, 149–52, 155, 157, *158*, 159, 171f., 174, 224, 256, 269f., 295; horse sacrifice 158, 184, 219, 235, 256, 264, 269f., 300
'hot' 231
house (abode, housing) 6, 8, 13, 15, 17, *23*, 30, *32*, *37*, 43, 55, 117, *118*, *120*, 130, 142 (underground), 168, 172, 190, 197, 220f., *228*, 239, 243, 245, 256, 258f., 267; lunar house 201, 204
Houston, S. D. 49
Hrozný, B. 43, 58f., 277, 289
Hsiung-nu (Hun) 293
HŚS 216
human being, *see* anthropomorphic; man; statuette
human sacrifice 256, 258–62, 269, 297, 300f.,
humped cattle, *see* zebu
Hun (Hsiung-nu) 293
Hungarian 145
hunter, hunting 9, 15, 234f., 239, 260, 268
hunter-gatherers 11, 137, 145
Hunter G. R. 62, 66, 131
Hunza 142
Hurrian 126, *127*, 130, 145, 148, 174, 293
husband 97, 162, 184, 188f., 191, 206, 220f., 224, 235, 238, 240, *241*, 243, 261–5, 267f., 270, 272, 301; *see also* bridegroom
Hut Grave culture 145, *155*
Hyksos 36
hypocorism 210
hypothesis 3, 47, 60
Hystaspes 42

Ibbi-Sin 130
Ibnišarrum *252*
Ibrāhīm(ī) 162
icon(icity), iconic meaning, *see* picture
iconography xvi, 3f., 9, 11, 17, 21, 24, 41, 49, 53f., 60, 62, 64, 78, 104, 107, *109–12*, 113, 115f., 119, *120*, 121, 130f., *132*, 148, 179f., *181*, *183–8*, 197f., 201, 220, 233f., 238, *246*, 247, 256, 260–2, 269, 272, 292f.; parallelism between text and iconography 49, *91*, *109*, 110, *111f.*, 115f., 121, 233
idea 32, 41
ideogram, ideography 32, 34, 36, 38f., 41–4, *46*, 49f., 59, 80, 103, 174, 216, 234
identification of language 4, 15, 40, 44, 86, 125, 130f.
idol, *see* statue
Ikhthus 191
Iliad 222
illiteracy 54
illness, *see* disease
Illustrated London News 6
imbricate *23*
immigration into South Asia 24, 26, 58; *see also* conquest; migration; transhumance
immortality 199
impersonator 237
imports 36
impotency 189
impression: of packing materials 11, *113*; of a seal 6, *11*, 61, 64, *65f.*, *83*, 107, *108*, *113f.*, 115f., *131f.*, *148*, 149, *181*, *183f.*, *186f.*, 215, *219*, *228*, *231f.*, *247–50*, *252–4*, *256*, 273, *274*, 293; *see also* sealing; stamp
Inanna *32*, 119, 183, 191, *248*, 255, 262, 300
incest 206, 234, 263, 267f., 270, 301
incision, incised 29f., 52, *53*, 55, 64, *65*, 107, 110, 226, *246*, 287
inclusiveness, in pronoun *166*, 167, 170
index 62, 79
India 62; classical India 60, 104, *106*, 107, 109f., 114–19 (seals), 131, 180, 292f.; India's name 4; *see also* eastern/North/South/western India; South Asia
Indian fig, *see* banyan
individual, *see* man; woman
Indo-Aryan 60, 104, 133f., *135*, 137, 140, 142f., 147, 149–59, 163, 165, *166*, 169–71, 195f., 217, 225, 241, 261, 266f., 270, 293–6; *ṭVp* 267, 301; *see also* Neo-Indo-Aryan; Prakrit; Proto-Indo-Aryan; Sanskrit
Indo-European 4f., 43, 46f., 58f., 86f., 126, 133, 137, 142, *144*, 145, 155, 157f., *166*, 167, 180, 217, 222f., 233, 235, 294f.; (H_1)*ék̑wos* 158; (H_1)*ōk̑ús* 158; k^w*ek*^{w}*los* 47; *l* *155*; *ster-* 262
Indo-Greeks 5, 285, 288
'Indo-Hittite' hypothesis 58f., 289
Indo-Iranian: borderlands 12, *16*, 17, *25*, 126, 286; languages, *see* Aryan
Indology 285
'Indo-Mediterranean' 59
'Indo-Mexican' hypothesis 289
Indonesian 57, 82, 289
Indo-Scythian 133
'Indo-Sumerian' hypothesis 58, 286, 289
Indra 147, 149, 151, 207f., 215f., 222, 235, 237, 258, 270, 294
Indrajit 259
Indus Civilization 3f., 6–9, 21f., 24, 159f., 240, 284f.; *see also* Mature Harappan; discovery 6, 285; end 24f., 149; extent and sites 5f., *7*, 125f., 285
Indus river 4f., *7*, 9, *16*, *25*, *141*, *153f.*, 168, 285
Indus script 3, 18, 48f., *84*, 104, 117, 125, 131, *132*, 174f., 248, 288; attempts at decipherment 57–71, 289; diachronic change 54, 288; evolution 52–6; first known sample *6*, 58; origin 22, 53f., 288; *see also* types of texts
Indus Valley 3f., *7*, *16*, 17, 19, *20*, 21–2, 25, 103, 128, 133, 137, 174, 209, 240, 247f., 259, 285, 293
infidelity 241, 243; *see also* chastity
infix(ation) 96, 151
'infix' sign 50
inflection 36, *44f.*, 83, 87, 89, 92, 94–8, 174, 291; of nouns, *see* declension
inheritance 47
inhumation 153, 172
initiation, initiated 207f., 210, 237
inlay *21*, *113*, 211, *213*, *218*, 269
innovation, linguistic, 46, 163
inscription, *see* text
institution 32, 107, 119
Inšušinak *35*
intaglio 64
intensification 82, 195, *275*
interchangeability of allographs 69
'intercultural style' 22, *23*, *249*, 286
interdependence, *see* parallelism
interior of sign 33, 50, 69, 79, 232, 234, 239, 261, 267, 270, *276*; *see also* middle
Intermediate Mature Harappan phase 19, 22, 24
interpreter 131, *132*, 133, 293
interrelationship between signs 44f., 48, 51, 79, 89, 97–102
interrogative *88*
intersecting circles, *see* circle
'intervening space' 231, *276*, 299
intervocalic position 165, 170
intoxicant (alcohol) 191, 194, 259
invasion, *see* conquest
inventory (recording, registering) 33, 44, 54, 107, 115; *see also* archives
invincibility 258f., 263, 268
invisibility 245, *276*
Inzak 130
Irākavaiyaṅkār, Mu. 230
Iran 11, 12f., 30, 52, *84*, 104, *105–7*, 126, 129f., 144, 148, 171, 294; eastern *10*, 13, 151, 170, *192*; northern 15, 17, 25, 148, 162, 172; southeastern 161, 163, 247, *250*; southwestern 22, 128f., 161, 186, *187*; western 152
Iranian: peoples and languages 126, 128, *129*, 133f., 142f., 145, 147f., 152, *154*, *156*, 161, *166*, 172, 180, 203, 262, 293–5; plateau 4, 14–17, 21–3, 25, 126, 128f., 143, 147, 155, 157, 256; seal *187*
Iraq 30, *84*, *113*
Irish (Old) *ech* 158
iron, Iron Age 145, 152, 232; in South Asia 19, 55, 153, 169, 171f.
irrigation 9, 15, 17, 24, 30, 148, 172
Iruḷa 137, *138*
Irwin, J. 220
Ishkashmi 129, *166*
Ishtar 183, 191, 230, *254*, 255, 262, 270, 300
Isimu (Usimu) 34, *187*
Isin II 18
Isin and Larsa dynasties 9, 14, 18
Islam(ic) (Muslim) 13, 134, 163, 165, 228, 265
IsMEO 24
isogloss xvi, 152, 167
isolation: of dialect 134, 160; of language 48, 126, 128, 137, 142, *166*; of position in text 44, 67, 118
isolating (analytic) language 86, 98
Israel 30
Italian language 45f., 168
Italic language(s) and alphabets 45–7
iteration *100f.*
ithyphallic 149, *219*, 224, 238, *257*; *see also* phallus
ivory 11, 14, 22, 110, 213, *247*; stick 81, 292
Ixtlilxochitl 54

jackal 196, 297
Jacobsen, T. 190

Jaḍgālī, *see* Jaṭṭ
Jaggayyapeṭa *106*
jaguar 51
Jahangir 267
Jaina, Jainism 109, 133f., 170–2, 184, 197, 201, 217, *238*
Jalilpur *7*, *10*, *16*, *20*, 52, 157
Jamison, S. 199
Jansen, M. 22, 24
Japanese 46, 48, 87
jar, *see* pot
Jartika 163
Jarmo 29
Jarrige, J.-F. 15, 149, *192*
Jātaka *14*, 189, 194, 196, 232, 258f., 286
Jaṭilā 239, 243f., 300
Jaṭṭ, Jaṭṭa, Jāṭ, Jaṭkī, Jaḍgālī 162f., 266
Jaya-Durgā 259, 261, 301
Jayākhya-Saṁhitā 210
JB 5, 181, 206, 217, 226, 268
Jehol 293
Jemdet Nasr 32; period and pottery 18, 32, 130, 191, 213, *247*, 293
Jettmar, K. 151
JGS 196, *200*, 201, 207, 209, 221, 243
Jhukar *7*, *10*, *25*; culture *25*, 149, 154, *155*, 168, 174, 216, 295; seal 168, 174
Jīmūtavāhana 258
Johnson, S. 5
joint, syntactic, *see* connection
Jones, W. 5
Jorwe *25*; Jorwe Ware and culture *25*, 174, 296
Joshi, J. P. 62
Jotimuttu, P. 231
JŚS 207
JUB 217, 222, 233, 263
Judeirjo-daro 6, *7*
judge 117
jujube 15
Jumna, *see* Yamunā
'jump(ing)' 261, 268
juncture, syntactic, *see* boundary
jungle, *see* forest
Jupiter *200*, 201, 209, 262f.
juxtaposition, *see* co-occurrence of signs
Jyeṣṭha, Jyeṣṭhā *202*, 241
Jyotiṣaratnamālā 263

Kacchi *166*
Kachi plain 15–17, 19, 24, 26, 140, *192*, 287
'Kafir' 134
Kalāšā 134, *166*
Kalat 15, *16*, 17, *161*, 162f., *164*, 165
Kalhaṇa 189
Kālī 262, 300f.; Kālī-nautch 259; Bhadrakālī 259; Mahākālī *255*
Kalibangan *7*, *10*, *16*, *20*, 21, 24, 62, 64, *65*, 115, *120*, 179, *193*, 221, *222*, 223f., *253f.*, 255, 258, 260, 299–301
Kālidāsa (1) *106*, 174, 224, 243f., 261; (2) 263
Kallur 174
Kalpasūtra 238
Kāma 189, 191, 220f., 230f., 239; *see also* desire; love
Kāma-vēḷ 230
Kanara 267; *see also* South Kanara
Kanauri 142, *166*
Kandahar *16*, 149
Kane, P. V. 208
Kangle, R. P. 115
Kaṅkālī Ṭīlā 238
Kannaḍa 134, *136*, *166*, *175*, 182, 195f.; *l-* 223; *ole* 217
Kaṇṇapuram 220
Kansu *141*
Kanta-Purāṇam 230
Kanta-vēḷ 230
KapS 206
Karachi 171, 191, *212*, *218*, 297
Karakorum 142
Karatepe 43
Karen(ic) *143*, *166*
Karlgren, B. 110
Karmāna *5*, 13
Karmania 13
Karnataka 11, 134, *136*, 165, 172, 174, 226, 228, 260
Kārttikeya 206, 224f., 298; *see also* Skanda
Kartvelian 46, *127*
Kashmir 134, *136*, *141*, 142, 168, 248, *251*, 258, 267
Kashmiri 134, *135*, 142, *166*
Kashmir Neolithic, *see* Northern Neolithic
Kassite 18, 126, *127*, 128, *147*; *Šu-ri-ya-áš* 128
Kaštiliaš 126
Kathāsaritsāgara 209, 246, 258f.
KāṭhGS 208, 265
Katī 134, *135*, *166*
Kātyāyana-Śulbasūtra 206
Kaumārī 259
Kauśikasūtra 233, 239, 266
Kauśikī *154*
Kauṭilya 114f.
kāvaṭi 110, 292
Kaye, G. R. 200, *202*
Kazakhstan 145, *146*, 151
KB 205f.
Kechi Beg *16*, 17, 20
Keith, A. B. 269
Kelley, D. H. 51
Kenoyer, J. M. 24, 104
Kerala *136*, 172, *173*, 226
Kerman 17, *23*, *25*, 26, 152, *250*
Ketu 199, *200*, 201, 300
key (clue) to decipherment/meaning 40, 42, 49, 103, 106f., 110
keying 88f.
Khafajeh *23*, 183, 186, 191, 247, *249*, 300
Kharoṣṭhī 6, 38, 56, 117
Khasi 137, *139*, *166*
Khila 238
Khmer *139*
Khotan *129*, 142
Khotanese (Saka) *129*; *daha* 150
Khowār 134, *135*, 142, *166*
khur 157
Kikkuli 145, 158
Kili Ghul Muhammad 15, *16*, 17, *20*, 52
killer, killing 206, 229f., 234, 247, 254, 259–63, 267f., 270, 272, 299
kiln 11, *12*, 24, 217
kindling (stick) 239, 263
kindness (benevolence) 234, 258
king, kingship (royalty) 3, 13f., *35*, 41–3, 48, 50, 54, 58f., 61, 97, 104, *106–8*, 110, 116f., 119, 121, 129f., *132*, 133, 145, 148–52, 154, 158f., 184, 189, 190f., 196f., 208f., 213–18, 224, 226, *227*, 230, 237, 240, 243, 245f., 248, *252*, *254*, 255f., 258–60, 262f., 267f., 270, *274*, *276*, 292, 298f., 301
Kinnara 299
Kinnier Wilson, J. V. 58, 194
kinship 45, 47, 170, *171*, 296
Kiririsha *107*
Kish 9, *10*, *23*, 131, *132*
kitchen 216
knee 211
kneeling *109*, 121, *132*, 226, 229, 256, *260*, 261
knife 15, *57*, 266; stone knife 142, *247*
knob of a seal, *see* boss
Knorozov, Yu. V. 49f., 60, *96*, 277
Knossos 43, 45
knot 113; 'Brahma's knot', 'endless knot' 56, *57*, *111*, 288
knowledge, knowing 190
known/unknown 48
Knudtzon, J. A. 43
Kober, A. *44f.*, 48, 87, 97
Koḍagu *136*, 165, *166*, *175*, 182; *ole* 217
Kohistani dialects *135*
koine 133
Koivulehto, J. 145
Kōlāmi̇œ *136*, *166*, 174, *175*
Koldihwa 140
Koṇḍa *136*, *175*, 182; *solu* 217
Koṇḍa Dora 209
Kopet Dagh 148
Koraga 165, 209
Korava 265
Korean 46
Koskenniemi, K. 62, 97, 232
Koskenniemi, S. 62, 97
Kōta *136*, *166*, *175*, 182
Kot Diji *7*, *10*, *16*, 17, *20*, 21f., 52, 183, *251*, 286; Kot Dijian Ware and culture 19, *20*, 21–2, 52, 142, 168, 183, 206, *251*; Late Kot Dijian *7*, 53, 168
Koṭṭavī 256, 261
KP 191, 260f., 263, 270
Kramer, S. N. 14, 189
Kṛṣṇa 196f., 221, 269, *275*
Kṛttikāḥ *202*, 204–6, 224f., 238; = Pleiades, q.v.
KS 5, 188, 201, 205f., 215, 221, 234, 239, 241, 262, 269
kṣatriya 205, 270
Kṣemendra 189
KŚS 109, 269
KU 244
Kuban 172
Kui *136*, *166*, *175*, 182; *vēgam boḍuri* 207
Kulli *7*, *16*, *20*; Kulli Ware *21*, *25*, 53, 269, 286
Kumaon 199, 221
Kumaoni (Kumauni) *166*
Kumāra 225, 227f., 230, 234f., 237f.
Kumara-vēḷ 230
Kumārī 227
Kunjalal Bhishagratna 238
Kuntī 216
Kuṟavar *56*
Kurdish *129*
'Kurgan culture' 144, 294
Kürin (Lezgi) *γed* 196
Kuriñcippāṭṭu 230
Kurku *139*, *166*
Kurukh (Orāōn) 110, *136*, *161*, 163, 165, *166*, 174, *175*, 182, 267, 292, 295, 301; *bēlas* 230; *kurχ* 163, 165; *χall* 165
Kuṣāṇa 129, 133, 254
Kutch 157, *161*
Kutik-Inšušinak 35
Kutlug-Tepe *150*
Kuwi (Kūvī) *136*, 174, *175*, 182; *hollu*, *holu* 217

Labeo rohita 263, *264*
lac 244
Ladakh *253*
Ladakhi *166*
ladder 104
ladle 104, 221; inscribed 110
Lagash *10*, 14, *147*
Lahnda *135*, 162f., *166*
Lahore 5
Lakṣmaṇa (1) 259; (2) 270
Lakṣmī 116, 259
Lal, B. B. 104
Lalitavistara 205
Lamaism 188, 220, *227*, 256, *257*, 262, 269, *276*, 299
Lamberg-Karlovsky, C. C. 148
'lame' 197
lament(ing), *see* cry(ing)
land, *see* country
Landa, D. de *49*, 50
language(s) 29, 32f., 47, 64, 134, 137, 195, 273, 277; adstratum *155f*, 167; agglutinative 86, 126, 130; analytic (isolating) 86, 98; daughter 46; evolution of 29, 287; exchange of 142; extinct 137, 142; family 42–8, 125f., 128, 133f., 137, *166*; fit between written and spoken 33–6, 38f., 48, 51, 88f., 96f., 125, 287; foreign 119; fusional 86f.; Harappan 3f., 6, 15, 54, 86–101, 103, 119, 121, 125, 130f., 134, 140, 142, 155, 159, 161, 167, 169, 171, 174f., 179, 207, 225, 274, 293, 295; identification of

4, 15, 40, 44, 86, 125, 130f.; inflecting 86f., 130; linguistic innovation 46, 163; isolated 48, 126, 128, 137, 142, *166*; link 133f.; matched with archaeology xvi, 134, 137; matched with script 48, 51; *see also* fit; natural 97–9, 125f., 293; Near Eastern 4, 126, *127*, 128–33, 293; of prestige 133; protolanguage 46f.; relict 137, *138*; South Asian xvi, 4, 133–42, *166*, 293–5; spoken (speech) 29, 33–6, 38f., 88f., 96, 99, 125; *see also* fit; substratum 128, 140, 142, 167–9, 295; superstratum *143*, 167; synthetic 98; universals 87, *88*, 291; unknown/vanished 44–8, 126; *see also* Anatolia(n); linguistics; unit, linguistic; and names of individual languages and language families
Laṅkā 259
lapidary, *see* stone
lapis lazuli 15, 17, 22, 211, *213*
Lapp 145
Larsa 130, *147*, *247*; *see also* Isin-Larsa
laryngeal 38
Las Bela *161*, 172
last, *see* end
Late Harappan period/cultures 19, 22, 24, *25*, 26, *55*, *113*, 126, 149, 153f., 158, 167–9, 216, 234, *236*, 286f., 295; seals or graffiti *10*, 54, *55*, 62, 288
Late Kot Dijian *7*, 53, *236*
Late Ṛvedic 152f., *156*
Late Vedic 153, *156*, 168, 198, *200*, 201, 208, 217, 222
Late West Iranian Buff Ware 148, *156*
Latin: alphabet 45, 58; authors 149f.; language 31, 44–7, 87, 168; *decemviri* 293; *duumviri* 293; *equus* 158; *estō* 43; ligare 33; *-ō* 87; *quattuorviri* 293; *quindecimviri* 293; *rebus* 33; *septem triones* 224; *septemviri* 293; *servus, -um, -o* 44; *triumviri* 293
law 14, 24, 54, 190f., 208f., 215, 243, 267, 270; *see also* dharma; judge
layout: of city 6, *8*, *12*, 21, 149, 285; of fort 149, *150*; of palace *254*, 256
leaf 21, 61, 216, 220f., 229, 234f., 238f., 244, 258, 268; *see also* fig leaf
learning, learned 33, 38, 121
leather 34
Lebanon 128
Leemans, W. F. 170
'left-hand' cult 264
leg 33, *91*, 234, 247f., *249f.*, 258; legged pots *46*
legend 163, 165
Leibnitz, G. W. von 40
Lemnos 126
length (shortness): of vowel 181; of word or text 3, 41f., 45, 48, 60, 64, 68, 83, 85, 87–90, 92, 96, 103f., 106f., 109f.; *see also* text(s), long(est)
Lepcha 134, *166*
Leslie, J. 264
letter (postal) 43, 106; (character) 98
Lewan-dheri *10*, *20*, *192f.*, *251*, 300
Lewis, J. 285
lexical text 31–4, 39, 42, 48, 128, 130, 182, 203, 214, 218, 243, 302
lexicon (vocabulary) 46–8, 134, 160, 162f., 165, 196, 217, 230f., 273
Lezgi (Kürin) *γed* 196, 297
libation 221, 268
liberties 59
life 102, 245, 247, 259
lifetime 50
ligature 33, 43, 56, 61, 69, 79–81, *81*, 84f., 90, 95, 97, 104, 110, 116, 196f., 231, *232*, 233, *234f.*, 239f., 274, *276*, 290; 'double' 80f.
light 104, 206, 216, 226, 247
Lilyan *17*
Limet, H. 121
liminality 237
limitation, *see* obstacles to decipherment
line 30, 32f., 41, 44, 64, *65*, *66*, 67, 69, 79, 82–4, 110, *111f.*, 113, 116–18, 121, 196, 301; curved 32, 78; *see also* row; text (second line)
Linear A 18, 43, *84*
Linear B 18, 43, *44–6*, 48, 55, 58f., 79, 83, 87, 92, 97, 100f., 117, 234, 274, 287, 291
Linear Elamite *17*, 18, *35*, 38, 53, 128, 287
liṅga 189, *218*, 219, *220*, 221–4, 245, 298; *see also* phallus
'liṅga stand' (pedestal) *218*, 220f.
linguistics, linguistic analysis 47, 60, 64, 79, 287f., 294; areal linguistics/relationship xvi, 140, 142, 162f., *166*, 167, 169, 295; comparative (historical) linguistics 4, 42f., 46–8, 125, 134, 137, 174f., 288; typological linguistics, *see* types/typology
linkage, syntactic, *see* connection
link language 133f.
lion(ess) 36, *107*, 213, 246, *247–9*, *252–5*, 256, *262*, 269f., 300
literature, literary text 5, 34, 133f., 142, 171, 174, 196, 225, 230, 235, 239f., 244, 246, 258, 296, 299; *see also* history
Lithuanian: *ašva* 158; *ešva* 158
Livonian 145
load 61
loanword 45, 47, 59f., 137, 145, 162f., 165, 167–71, 180, 182, 196, 223, 268, 270, 294, 296
location, geographic, 137, 142, 144, 153, 169, 201, *202*, 208, 293; *see also* position
locative 51
Loebanr *10*, *141*, 142
logogram, logography 34f., 38f., 42–4, 51, 59, 85, 214
logo-syllabic (morphemic) writing 18, 31–6, 38f., 48f., 60, *84*, 85, 96f., 101f., 125, 174f., 179, 277
Lolo 57, 289
looking, *see* 'seeing'
loop 179, *185*, *244*, 296
Loralai 15, *16*
lord (master) 34, *35*, 80, 91, 97, 117, 119, 151, 210
loss, *see* omission
Lothal 6, *7*, 8, *10*, 11, *12*, *25*, 62, 113, *114*, 183, 221, *232*, 286, 293, 299
lotus 200, 268
love, lover 183, 189, 191, 194, 206, 221, 225, 230f., 239, 262f., 265, *276*, 301; *see also* desire; Kāma
Löwenstern, I. 42
LŚS *5*, 206, 244
Lullubi *127*, 128
Lurewala Ther 6, *7*
lust, *see* desire
lustration (purification) 119, 190, 217, 256, 263
Lustrous Red Ware *25*
Luvian 42, 126, *127*
Lycian 126
Lydian 126

Macchendra, Macchinda 189
Macdonell, A. A. 181
macehead 117, *158*
McIntosh, J. R. 172
Mackay, E. J. H. 5, 9, 117, 184, 211, 214, 216, 219f.
Maclean, C. D. 265
madder 9
Madhyadeśa 153, 168
Madhya Pradesh *136*, 137, 163
Madra *154*, 209
Madrid Codex 49, *50*
Madurai 270
Magadha 133, *154*, 155, 209
Māgadhī 133f., 151, 154, *155*, 169f.
Magahi *135*, *166*
Magan (Makan, Makkan) 12–14, 130, 286
magic (witchcraft) 116, 151, 190, 199, 209, 228, 233, 269
Mahābalipuram, *see* Māmallapuram
Mahābhārata 133, 151, *153*, 181, 188–90, 199, 201, 209f., 214, 216, 220, 224, 227, 237f., 240f., 243f., 258, 263, 268f., 298
Mahadevan, I. 60–2, 64, 66, 277, 289
Mahākālī *255*; *see also* Kālī
Mahānirvāṇa-Tantra 264
Mahapatra, P. K. 258
Maharashtra *25*, 26, *55*, 133, *136*, 170, 172, *173*, 174, 221
Mahārāṣṭrī 133, 172, 174
Mahāvastu 205
Mahāvīra Jina 133, 184, 238
mahāvrata 256, 264, 300
Maheswar *153*, 296
Mahinda 133
Mahiṣa Asura (Buffalo demon) 189, 220, *253*, 254, 260f., 270, 272, 300; *see also* Asura; demon; water buffalo
Maier, J. 14, 189
Maitr(āyaṇ)ī Upaniṣad 201, 233, 244f.
Maiyā 134, *166*
Majumdar, N. G. 15
Maka *5*, 13
Mákai 13
Makan, Makkan, *see* Magan
Makran *10*, 11–13, 17, 22, 162f.
malaria 24
Malayālam 134, *136*, *166*, *175*, 182, 191, 217; *ñāli* 246; *poṭṭan* 264, 301; *viṣu* 205
Maldives 57, 289
Mallory, J. P. 144
Malto *136*, *161*, 163, 165, *166*, 174, *175*, 182; *bindke* *182*, 296
Malwa 172, 174, 240; Malwa Ware and culture *26*, *55*, 296
Malwi *135*, *166*
Māmallapuram (Mahābalipuram) 197, *253*
mammal 34
man (male, masculine, boy, person) 9, 14f., 17, 21, 24, 34, 44, 50, 78, 96, 119, 130, 150, 183, 188–91, 194, 209, 219, 221f., 224–6, *227*, 228–30, 234, *235*, 237–9, *247–50*, *252–4*, 255, 258, 261, 264–6, 268, 270, 272, *276f.*, 299; 'man' (Indus sign) 69, 79, 81, *93f.*, 95f., 121, 188, *215*, 231, *260*, 261, *277*, 297; 'man' ligature 80, *81f.*, 104, *109*, *120*, 290; first man 190
Māna 195
Mānava-Śulbasūtra 205
Manchu 47
Manchuria 293
Maṇḍa *136*, *175*, 182; *huli* 217
maṇḍala, *see* diagram
Mandhal 238
Maṅgala-dāsu 209
manger 11
mango 184, 194
mangrove 14
Maṇimēkalai 171
Manipur(i) 134, *166*
Mannewār 221
mantra 58, 109, 200f., 206, 210, 216f., 233, 237, 239f., 243, 245f., 268, 270
Manu 180, 182, 188, 190, 203, 208, 217, 248
manuscript 40f., 45, 47, 49, *50*, 54, 57, 133, 142
map 5f.
Marathi 134, *135*, *166*, 170, 174; *baṭa* 300
Margiana *25*, 26, 148–52, *155f.*; *see*

also BMAC
Marglin, F. A. 184
Margos 150
margosa 220
Marguš *5*
Maria Gondi 209
Māriyammaṉ 221
mark 222f.; visual, 29, *37*, 269; *see also* mason's mark; potter's mark; sign
Mārkaṇḍeya-Purāṇa 254
markedness 95–7
markhor (wild goat) *111f.*, *186*, 189, 234, 237, *254*, *260*, 261, 301
marriage 170, *171*, 184, 189, 196, 200, 205, 208 (mixed), 220, 230f., 240f., 243–6, 263–7, 270, 272, *275*, 299–301; badge 266; marital faithfulness, *see* chastity; sacred 256
Mars 197, *200*, 201, 209, 233, 237, 261, 301
marshes 17
Marshall, J. 6, 9, 59, 66, 161, 211, 218f.
mask 194, *271*, 234, *235*, 237, 299
mason's mark *57*
mass-production 8f., 21, 24, 26, 107, 116, 119
master, *see* lord
mat(ting) *23*, 113
Mātali 216
material(s): control material 60, 100; of manufacture 64, 69, 107, 116; of study 3, 40, 47, 61f., 277f.; of writing 54, 288
mathematics 24
Mathurā 133, *153*, *238*
Matsya *154*, 268
Matsya-Purāṇa 237, 245, 259, 265
Matsyendra(nātha) 189, 297
Matsyodara 189
Maturaikkāñci 207
Mature Harappan period/culture 6–9, 19, 21–4, 53f., 130, 148f., 153, 155, 157, 159, 168f., 174, 181, *183*, *192f.*, 206f., 209, 221, *222*, 234, *236*, *241*
Maurya period 19, 114f., 168, 172, 209
Maya 39, 49–51, 59f., 89, 277f., 288; 'alphabet' *49*, 50; languages 49–51, 89, 277; *balam* 51; *kan*/*kān* 51; *kutz* 50; *tzul* 50
Mazák, V. 157
Māzandarān 148
Meadow, R. 157
meaning 4, 33, 38, 47, 49–51, 79, 87, 95, 97, 100–4, 106, 110, 174, 196, 215, 217, 230, 232, 234, 241, 245, 273f., *275–7*; extended 32–4, 36, 121; intended 103, 121, 230f., 233, *275–7*, 278; primary 32–4, 49, *58*, 180; *see also* polysemy
measures, *see* weights and measures
meat 194
medallion 43, *229*, *266*
Median 128, *129*, *156*
medicine (Āyurveda, medical) 24, 225, 237, 239, 244; *see also* disease; health
meditation 200
Mediterranean 128, 256
Megalithic culture *156*, 171f., *173*, 174, 296; graffiti 55, 288
Megasthenes 270
Meghanāda 259
Mehi *10*, *16*, *21*, *25*, *193*
Mehrgarh *10*, 15, *16*, 17, 19, *20*, 24, *25*, 52, 149, 157, *183*, *192*, 269, 286, 301
Meluḫḫa 12–15, 131, *132*, 133, 170, 248, 286, 293, 295
memorandum 34
memorial, *see* token
memory 29, 32
Ménant, J. 43
menstruation 267, *275*
merchandise, *see* commodities
merchant *14*, 54, 56, 115, 117, 119, 129–31, 133, 270, 273
Mercury 196f., *200*, 201, 208f., 262, *275* (rising)
merger, *see* conflation
Meriggi, P. 43, 59
Meru 245
Mer 148
Mesoamerica 24, 289
Mesolithic 137, 287, 294
Mesopotamia, *passim*
messenger 119
metal, metallurgy, 8f., 15, 17, 64, 82, 148, 172, 174, 200f., 209, 214
metathesis 46, 170
meteor 199, 245
method(ology) 3, 6, 40–51, 58, 61, 97–102, 134, 137, 174f., 277f., 291
metronym 206
Mexico 289
Meyer, J. J. 228
MGS 209f., 265
Michelia champaka 228
microlithic sites *138*
middle: of sign 196, 204f., 234, *235*, 264; of text or word 42, 45, 84, 94–7; *see also* interior
Middle Babylonian 18, 126
Middle Elamite, *see* Elamite
Middle Indo-Aryan, *see* Pali; Prakrit
Middle Iranian *129*
Middle Persian 41, *129*
Middle Vedic 153f., *156*, 168f.
midnight 259
migration 17, 46, 149, 163, *164*, 295; *see also* conquest; immigration; mobility; transhumance
milk 109, 194, 199, 221, 258
miller 80, 117
millstone 221
Mīna 189
Minagara 170
Mīnākṣī 270, 302
minister *106*, 115, 244, 258
Minnagara 170
Minoan: civilization 43, 45; hieroglyphic script 18, 43, 57, 234; language, names 43f., 117; seals 43
Mir Ahmad 162
mirror 148f., *266*
mirror image 64, 81
Mitanni 126, *127*, 128, 145, *147*, 148f., 151f., *156*, 158, 174, 294f.
Miθra 151
Mitra 147, 151, 214f., 268
Mitra, S. C. 259
Mitramiśra 270, 301
Mizar 241, *243*
mlēccha 170, 296
Mnaseas 191
mobility 17, 152; *see also* migration
model, *see* exemplar; statuette
Modern Indo-Aryan, *see* Neo-Indo-Aryan
Modern Iranian *129*
Modern Persian, *see* Persian
modification of signs 33
modifier (grammatical) 88, 97, 169
Moen-jo-daro *13*
Moghul Ghundai *16*, 172
Moguls (Mughals) 9, *57*
Mohāna 13
Mohenjo-daro *7*, *8*, 9, *10*, 11f., *14*, *16*, 22, *25*, 26, *55*, 62, *65f.*, *83*, *92*, *103*, 106, 107, *108f.*, 110, *111f.*, 117, *118*, 131, *132*, 157, *180f.*, 184, *185f.*, *188*, 205, *212f.*, *215*, 216, *218f.*, *226f.*, 228, *231*, 233, *234f.*, *243*, *247*, *250*, *252*, 256, 258, *260*, 286, 290, 297–9; excavations 6, 15, 22, *23*, 24, 286, 290: DK-B 62; DK-G *108*; DK-I 62; HR 117; HR-A *118*; HR-B *108*; name *13*
mole 264f.
Moloch 197
Mon *139*, *166*
Monday 265
Mongolia(n) 46f., 126, 142, 161
Mongoloid race 142, 294
mongoose 230
monkey *37*
Mon-Khmer *139*
monosyllable 39, 48
month 49, 54, 196, 203–5, 207, 228, 241; *see also* moon
moon (crescent, lunar) 29, 58, 104, 191, 199, *200*, 201, 203–9, *213*, 215f., 222, 237, 241, 243, 247f., 262f., *265*, 267, 269, *270*; ascending and descending node 199; full moon 203, 205, 233, 241, 263, 265; new moon 204f., 241
Moor, E. *265*
Mordvin 145
Morgenstierne, G. 161
morning 203, 217, 231, 268, 297; *see also* dawn; sunrise
morning star 197, 207, 231, 262f., 268
morpheme, morphology 34, 38, 46f., 82, 85f., 89, 96–8, *99*, 102, 126, 162f., 175, 287; bound/free morpheme 79; *see also* fit
morphemic writing, *see* logo-syllabic writing
mortar and pestle 80
mosaic *187*, *213*, 256
mother 50, 162, 189, 208, 228, 237, 239, 243, 258f., 261, 268, *275*, 301
motif, *see* iconography; painted motif
mould, moulded tablet 3, *14*, 107, *109*, *180*, 184, *186*, *215*, *219*, 220, *226f.*, *229*, *239*, *244*, *252*, 254, 259, 261, 274
mound, *see* ruin mound
mount (draught-animal, vehicle) 188f., 191, 197, 226f., 237–9, 248, *253*, 254f., *257*, *271*, 274, *275*
mountain 4, 33, *58*, 82, 104, 109f., 208, 235, 245, 292
mouth 36, *37*, 165, 168, 205
Mṛgaśīrṣa 194, *202*, 218
Mṛtyu 218; Mṛtyu Dhūmaketu 201
MS 188, 197, 201, 206, 215f., 221, 235, 239, 241, 262
Mughal, M. R. 21
Mughals (Moguls) 9, *57*
Muggur Pir 191, 297
Mūjavat 109
Mūla *202*, 208f.
Mūla-mitra 208
MUL.APIN 205
Mūlasthāna 240
Mūl-candu 209
Multan 5, *16*, 240
multiform, *see* doublet
mummy 45
Munda, Mundari 137, *139*, 140, *166*
Mundigak *10*, *16*, 17, *20*, 21–2, *25*, 52, *236*, 286
Munjani, Munji 129, *166*
Münter, F. 41f.
Murg(h)ab river *16*, *25*, 148, 150
murrel 263
Murukaṉ, Muruku 109f., 191, 225–7, 229–31, 235, 237, *276*, 299; *see also* Skanda; Subrahmaṇya
Muruka-vēḷ 230, *276*
Musa Sohag 228
music, musician 117
Muslim, *see* Islam(ic)
'must' 231
Mycenaean 117; *doero* 150
myth(ology) 4, 33, 102, 110, 150, 183, 188–90, 194f., 199, 205–7, 209, 220–2, 224–6, 234, 237, 240f., 243f., 254, 256, 258, 262f., 265, 267f., *275*, 291, 297, 301

Nabû 214
Nad-i Ali 16
Naga *166*
Nagada II 288
Nagir 142

Nagpur 238
Nahāli (Nihāli) 137, *138f.*, *166*
Naigameṣa, Naigameṣin, Naigameya *238*, 239, 300
Naikī *136*, *175*
nakedness, *see* nudity
Nakht *105*
nakṣatra, *see* asterism; star calendar
Nal *10*, *16*, *20*, *25*, *105*, *193*; Nal Ware 17, *20*, *105*, *193*
Namazga V period 22, 152
Namazga VI period 148
Namazga Tepe *16*, 17, *25*, 148, 152
name (onomastics) 3f., 11, 14, 33, 38, 40–3, 45, 50, 59–61, 80, 91, 97, 106, *107*, 110, 115–17, 119, *120*, 121, 128–31, 133, 140, 145, 149, 151, 158, 180, 183, 198, 204, 206–10, 222, 225–31, 233–5, 237–9, 243f., 256, 259, 261f., 268, 273, *274–6*, 293, 295, 298; ethnic 150, *154*, 161–3, 165, 170; pet 210; secret 207f.; theophoric 121, 209; *see also* place; star; Sumerian
Nandin 116
Nåhaiθya 147
Napoleon 40
Naqsh-i Rustam *129*
Nārada 237
Narâm-Sîn 14, 132, *252*
Nārāyaṇa 196, 208
Narbada (Narmada) *25*, *153*, *161*, 163, 165, 172
Naṟṟiṇai 195, 207, 232
Narunde *262*
nasal(ization) 151, 223, 246, 267
Nāsatya 147
Nath, Bhola 157
nationalism 58
nature, naturalistic 47, 103, 208, 220, 247
Nauclea cadamba 235
Nausharo *7*, *10*, 15, *16*, 17, 19, *20f.*, 22, 24, *25*, 26, 54, 149, 157, 234, *236*, 269, 286, 301
Nava-Durgā, *see* Nine Durgās
nava-graha, *see* planet
navarātri 256, 259f., 263, 267, *271*
Navdatoli *25*, *55*
NBPW, *see* Northern Black Polished Ware
neck 266; necklace 15, 116, 266
nectar 199f.
Needham, J. 202
Nejameṣa, Nejameya 238
Nemeṣa *238*
Neminātha-Carita 238
Neo-Assyrian period 18
Neo-Elamite, *see* Elamite
Neo-Babylonian: language 41f.; period 18; texts 213f.
Neo-Indo-Aryan 134, *135*, 267
Neo-Iranian 129
Neolithic 8, 15, 19, 29, 52, 137, *140f.*, 142, 160, 165, 168, 172, 174, 203, 255, 294
Neo-Sumerian 18, 119, 188
Nepal 134, *136*, 142, *161*, 163, 194, *228*, 297
Nepali *135*, *166*; *dasaĩ* 194
nephrite 142
net 9, 194
new year 204–6, 241, 243, 263f., 268–70, *275*
Newari 134, *166*
Nicobar Islands 137, *139*
Nicobarese 137, *139*, *166*
Niebuhr, C. 41
Nigeria 128
night 197, 203, 205, 207, 214f., 217f., 231, 245, 247f., *251*, 259, 265, 268; midnight 259
Nihāli, *see* Nahāli
Nikumbha, Nikumbhilā 259
Nilagiri 137, 197, 209
Nile 4, 38, 203
Nindowari *7*, *10*, *16*, *20*, 53, *103*
Nine Durgās 194; nine gems 196; nine planets, *see* planet; nine years 267
Ninḫursag 14, 189
Ninni 191
Nintu 189
Nippur *10*, *23*, 107, 219, *248*
Niṣāda 181
Nissen, H. J. 33
Niśumbha 259
node, ascending and descending, 199
nomad(ism) 6, 26, 126, 130, 137, 151f., 157, 160–2, *164*, 165, 167, 172, 203, 293
nominative 42, *94*, 96
non-Aryan 133f., 137–42, 150f., *154*, 159, 207f., 223, 233, 241, 266, 294
non-Harappan 255
Nonnos 214
non-Vedic 189, 208
noose (fetter, snare) 217f., 237, 241, 245, 298f.; *see also* rope
normalizing 66, 110
north, northern 109, *200*, 203–6, 216, 221f., *223*, 241, 245f., 265, *276*, 300
North Dravidian 110, *136*, *161*, 163, 165, 169, 174, *175*, 207, 230, 267, 295; *b-* 163, 207; *-ē-* 207; *k-* 163; *-k-* 163; *l* 217; *l-* 223; *χ-* 163, 165, 295
northeast *200*, 263, 301
Northeast Caucasian *127*
Northern Black Polished Ware *153*
Northern (Kashmir) Neolithic *141*, 142, 168, *251*, 294
North India(n) 4, 58, 109, 117, 133f., 137, 152, *153*, 170f., 174, 194, 196, 198f., 225, 264–6
northwest *200*
Northwest Caucasian *127*
Northwest Frontier Province *251*
northwest of the Indian subcontinent 4, 13, 133f., 143, 151–4, 157, 170f., 174, 201, 203, 207
Northwest Semetic 128
nose 208; nose-ring 227
Nostratic 46f., 288
nostril 221
noun, nominal *44*, 51, 86f., *88*, 95–8, 130, 174, 181; *see also* declension
Nṛsiṁha Bhaṭṭa 270
Nubia 14
nudity (nakedness) 9, *184*, 186, 189f., 219, *247*, *252*, 254, 259, 261, 267
Nuhato *10*
number 44, 88, 107, 110, 180, 191, 194, *195*, 196, 293, 296f.; (grammatical) 86f., *94*, 95; of alternatives/possibilities 48, 61, 98, *99*; of signs/graphemes 33–9, 41–4, 48, 50, 52, 55, 60, 68, *78*, 79, *84*, 85, 110, 291; of words 47
numeral 30–3, 43f., *46*, 49, 52, 69, 81f., 87, *88*, 100, *101*, 104, 107, *108*, *120*, 126, 142, 163, 169, 191, 194, *195*, 196, 246, 267, 277, 290, 292, 297; 'eight' 169, 198f., *200*; octonary system 169, 296; 'five' 49, 199, 221; 'four' 51, 59, 107, *109*, 110, 119, 190f., *194*, 245, *246*, 269, *276*, 292, 300; fourth day 267; *see also* 'frame' of four dots; 'hundred' 145, 150, 169; 'hundred and eight' 259; 'hundred thousand' 240; 'one' *46*, 49, 80, 96, 107, 211, 216, 237, 261, 267; 'seven' 88, 194, *195*, 201, 209, 216, 221, *222f.*, 224, 228, 241, *243*, 246, 261f., 270, *275*, 277, 297; 'six' 194, 206, 216, 221f., 226, 237, 239, 241, 243, *247f.*, *252*, 254, 258, 261, *275*, 277; 'sixth' 258; 'sixteen' 237; 'ten' 52, 82, 107, 169, 205; 'thirty' 203f., 216; 'thirty-six' 204; 'thousand' 215f., 237, 259; 'three' 104, 107, 109, *110*, *150*, 191, 194, 209, 215–18, *219*, 228, 234, *235f.*, 240, *241*, 267, 270, *275f.*, 277, 298f.; 'twelve' 201, 203f., 259; 'twenty' 49; 'twenty-four' 203f.; 'twenty-six' 203; 'twenty-seven' 201, 203f., 207, 222; 'twenty-eight' 201, 203f.; 'twenty-nine' 203f.; 'two' 44, *46*, 66, 96, 104, 107, *109*, 191, 196, 207, 209, 211, 215f., 221, 230, *231*, *247*, *253*, 255, 299; *see also* couple; pair
numerical: classifier 51; tablet 30, *31*
nun 262
Nuristan(i) 134, *135*, 143, 152, *156*, 165, *166*, 294
nurse, nursing 206, 224, 261, 268, *275*
nymph 195, 268

oath 145, 147, 151, 190
obelisk 41
object (thing) 8f., 29, 32f., 51, 69, 102–4, 216; inscribed (*see also* text) 64, 69, 82f., 89, 106–21, 227, 273, 292; (grammatical) 87, *88*, 89, 98
oblique case 60, *94*, 96
obstacles to decipherment (difficulties) 3, 42, 45, 47f., 50, 119, 133, 278, 285
obverse of seal/tablet *11*, *32*, *36*, 83, 91, *92*, *108–12*, *113*, *226f.*, 233, *234*, *246*, *255*
ocean, *see* sea
occupation (profession) 8, 45, 117, 119
occurrence, *see* co-occurrence; frequency of occurrence; position (distribution)
Ochre Coloured Pottery (OCP) 153f., *155*, 295
Odyssey 222
offering, *see* sacrifice
office, official 115–17, 119f., 162, 180, 293; *see also* administration
O'Flaherty, W. D. 224, 264
oil 9, 30; oil lamp 216
Okhos 150
Old Akkadian, *see* Akkadian
Old Assyrian 115
Old Babylonian period 18, 119, *132*, 170, *181*, 204; seal 119
Old Indo-Aryan, *see* Sanskrit
Old Iranian *129*, 262, 295
Old Ossetic *129*
Old Persian cuneiform script and inscriptions 41f., 83, 129, 149; language 4, *5*, 41f., *129*, 133, 143, *156*: *Anāhitā* 262; *Bābiruš* *5*, 14; *Bāxtriš* *5*; *Daha* *5*, 149f.; *dahyu* 150; *dipi* 56; *Gandāra* *5*, 13; *Hinduš* 4, *5*; *Karmana* 13; *Maka* *5*, 13; *Marguš* *5*; *yakā-* 13
Old Slavonic: *bogŭ* 147
Old Tamil, *see* Tamil
Oman *10*, 12f., 17, 22, 130, 286
omen 201, 259, 265, 292
omission (absence, loss) 34, 36, 38, 42f., 51, *80*, 83, 85, 88–91, 95–7, 119, 121, 174, 220, 234, *235*, 246, 265, 296; *see also* zero variant
onager 157
onomastics, *see* name
onomatopoeia 47, 168, 267
Ophiocephalus striatus 263, *264*
Oppenheim, A. L. 213f.
opposition, astronomical, 203, 206, 263
optional(ity) 36, 80, 88, 95–7, *99*, 126
oracle bones 201
oral tradition 33, 49, 54
Oraon, *see* Kurukh
order 12, 14, 103, 201; of sides 82f.; of signs 33f., 55, 64, 69, 78f., 84, 95, *132*; *see also* cosmic order; word order
Ordos 203, 298
organization, social, 22, 24f.
orientation of planetary icons 201; of signs 32f., 64, 104; of streets and buildings 6, 205f., 298

Orissa *136*, 137, 151, 163, 184, 220
Oriya 134, *135*, *166*; *sindūra-ṭapā* 267, 301; *ṭip-ṭip* 267; *ṭopā*, *ṭopī* 267
Ormuri *129*, *166*
ornament 9, 15, 209, 213–15, 220, 266
Oscan 46f.,
Ossetic 129
ossuary 172
osteology, *see* bone
Ostyak 145
Oṭṭakkuttār 270
otter 196, 297
outpost, *see* colony
oven, *see* fireplace
overanalysis of signs 61, 80, 290
overlap 64, *65*, 137
overseer 80, 215, 275
Ovis aries, *see* sheep (domestic)
Ovis orientalis, *see* sheep (wild), urial
owner, ownership 4, 17, 29, 52, 54, 61, 69, 78, 91f., 97, 106f., 115–17, 119, *132*, 209f., 227; *see also* property
ox, *see* bull
Oxus 148, 150

pacification, *see* propitiation
pack animals 114
package, packing materials (bale of goods) 11, 13, 30, *113*, 114f., 227
Paddhati 199
Padma-Purāṇa 241, 259, 269f.
Pahari *135*, *166*
Pahlava 133
Pahlavi (Pehlevi) 41, *129*; *anāhīd* 262
Painted Grey Ware (PGW) 152, *153*, 155, *156*, 169, 295
painting, painted motif 9, 15, 17, *21*, 22, 29, 52, *53*, 54, 104, *105f.*, *158*, 159, *180*, 181, *183*, 184, 190, *192f.*, 206, 234, *236*, 240, *241*, 246, 248, *251*; script 107
pair 230, *251*; of anklets 227; of bangles *228*; of eyes 215; of ear-rings *227*; of fishes 184, *186f.*, 188, 190, 195, 264, *271*, *275*, 297; *see also* couple
Pakistan 4, 6, 11, 62, 129, 133f., *136*, 294
palace 14, 41, 43, 130, 148, *255*, 256, 258
Palaeolithic 29, 203, 287
Palaic 126, *127*
palette 36
Pāli 133f., 168, 170; *Bāveru 14*; *kakkaṭa* 232; *milakkha* 170; *pākāra 229; r* 14; *sugahaṇam* 232; *vaṭa-rukkha* 241, 300
Pallava 197, *253*
Pallavaram *173*
palm tree 15, *23*, *249*; palm leaf 54, 69
palm squirrel, *see* squirrel
Pamir 129, 168
Pañcāla *154*, 172
Pañcatantra 181, 232
Pandaiē 270
Pāṇḍava *156*, 199, 216, 243
Pāṇḍya 184, 270
Paṇi 149–51
Pāṇini 133, 168, 204, 208, 266
Panjab(i), *see* Punjab(i)
papyrus 35
paradigm(atic alternation) *44*, 79, *80*, 81f., 88–92, *93f.*, 95, *96*, 97–8, *99f.*
paradise myth 102
Paṟaiya 220
'parallel' 230
parallelism (interdependence) between text and iconography 49, *91*, *109*, 110, *111f.*, 115f., 121, 233
Parāśara-Smṛti 267
parasol *106*
Paraśu-Rāma 172
Paripāṭal 181, 230
Parjī *136*, *166*, 174, *175*, 182; *colngel* 217; *kel* 217; *piṛca* 230, 299; *ṛ* 230
park 248
Parnoi 150
Parpola, A. 4, 62, 171, 219, 232, 235
Parpola, P. 97
parrot 230
Parsee 41
parsing *100*
pars pro toto 32
part of speech 100
Parthia *5*
Parthian *129*, 133, 162
participle 96
particle, connective 45
Pārvatī 220, 226, 238, 259, 265
Pashai (Pašaī) 134, *135*, *166*
Pashto *129*, 133, 162, *166*; *cāṣai* 145
passport 115
paste (pigment) 211, *212f.*, 216, 220f., 229, 264, 267
'path' 230, 245
Pathan 129, 162
Patiṟṟuppattu 244
Patna *153*, *161*, 163
Paṭṭiṉappālai 230, 233
PB 5, 206, 208, 224
pea 9
peace 39, 270
peacock 9, 14, 22, 226, 238, *271*
'pedestal' in Indus signs 79; *see also* 'liṅga stand'
'peg' *37*
Pehlevi, *see* Pahlavi
pendant *253*, 258
Pēngo *136*, *175*, 182; *boṭu mīn* 264; *hol* 217
perforation 31
Periplous 170
Persepolis 41f., *129*
Persian: cuneiform, *see* Old Persian; (Achaemenid) empire 4, *5*, 13, 38, 41f., 128f., 133, *156*, 285; Gulf, *see* Gulf; (modern) language 41f., *129*, *166*: *lālā* 265; *see also* Iranian; Old Persian
Perso-Arabic 134, 163
Peru 24
Perumpāṇ. 207, 232, 270
Peruntokai 230
petroglyphs 142, 152, 294
Pfeiffer, M. 165
PGS 221, 237, 243
PGW, *see* Painted Grey Ware
Phalgunī(ḥ) *202*, 205, 208
Phalūṛa 134
phallus, phallic 69, 189f., 218, *219*, 220–4, 239, 298; *see also* ithyphallic; liṅga
pharyngeal 36
philology 47, 134, 137, 143
Phoenician 106; alphabet and texts *37*, 38, 292; language 43, 128
phoneme, phonology 33, 35, 38, 45–7, 56, *84*, 89, 97f., *99*, 101, 162f., 168f., 171, 175, 196, 217, 287; phonemic writing 38f., *84*; *see also* fit
phonetic indicator, *see* determinative
phonetic sign, *see* phonogram
phonetic value of a sign 41–5, 48–51, *58*, 78f., 102–4, 133, 179, 231, 240, 272, 274, *275–7*
phonetization 33f., 38, 102
phonogram, phonography 32–6, 38, 41, 44, 59, 103, 174, 272, 274
photography xvi, xviiif, 24, 61f., 290
phrase 87–92, 95, 126, 287
phylum, linguistic, 46
physical anthropology 142, 167, 294f.
pictogram, pictography *30*, 32–9, 49, 54f., *58*, 69, 102–4, 216, 267f., 272, 274, 277, 292
picture, pictorial meaning (icon, iconic, iconicity) 29, 32, 44, 47, 49, 51, *58*, 60f., 64, 78, 100, 102–4, 121, 174f., 179, 180, 188, 194, 196, 230f., 239, 246, 261–4, 267, 270, 272, 274, *275–7*, 278, 291f., 296, 299
pig 9
pigment, *see* paste
pilgrim(age) 107, 225, 244, 300
pillar (post) 6, 220f., 223f., 245, 299; *see also* sacrificial stake
pin 116, 148
pincers (tongs) 232
pine 9, 168
Piṅkala-Nikaṇṭu 194, 217
pipal (aśvattha, *Ficus religiosa*) 22, 61, 234, 238f., 244, 258f., 263, 292; *see also* fig tree
Pipru 150f.
Pirak *10*, *16*, 19, *25*, 140, 152, 155, *156*, 157–9, 295
Pisces *202*, 204
Pit Grave culture *144*, 145, 157f., 294
pit house 142
place, place-name 13f., 34, 36, 45, 50, 107, 115, 117f., 128, 149, *153f.*, 170, 293, 296
plait 149 (motif in seals), 261 (hair)
plakṣa = wavy-leaf fig 244, 258
planet(s) 49, 183, 196–8, *199*, 201, 204, 207–9, 211, 214, 231, 233f., 237, 261, *262*, 263, 274, *275–7*, 297–9, 301; eight planets 199; five planets 199; nine planets (*nava-graha*) 196, 198, *199f.*, 201, 237
planning 24
plant 9, 17, 32, 34, 49, 78, 137, 149, *251*, 285
plantain 184, 194
planting 258
plaque *248*, 255; inscribed 110
plate 233, 268
platform 6, 8, *12*, 22, 221, *222*
Pleiades 194, *202*, 204–6, 224–6, 239, 241, 243, 261, 263, 268–70, 272, *275*, 277; = Kṛttikāḥ, q.v.
plough 9, 168
plural 42, 82, 86f., *94*, 95, 230
point, *see* dot; of compass, *see* direction
Polaris *243*
pole *202*, 206, *243*
Pole Star 224, *243*, 245f., 299f.; *see also* Dhruva; Polaris; Thuban
police(man) 117, *120*
pollution 190
Poltavka 152
polyandry 243
polyphony 33, 48, 58f.
polysemy 33, 42, 48, 58f., 85, 87, 102
pompom *251*
Pomponius Mela 150
Pontic-Caspian steppes *144*, 145, *146*, 152, *155f.*, 157f., 172
pool 189, 191, 232, 267
Pope, M. 40, 277
Popol Vuh 49, 51
population 6, 17, 21, 167–9, 295
Porada, E. 183
porter, *see* carrier
Portuguese 46, 134; *albero de laiz* 241; *marraxo* 188
position and distribution of sign(s)/word(s), etc. 40–5, 48f., 60, 62, *63*, 64, 68f., 78f., 82, 84, 88–101, 104, 116–18, 121, 125, 195, 209, 291; *see also* co-occurrence of signs; location, geographic; word order
'positional schematism' 51, 89
possession 97
possessive case, *see* genitive
post, *see* pillar; sacrifical stake
posthole 172, 221
postfix 45, 50
Post-Harappan period/cultures 19, *25*, 26, 157–9, 286f.; seals/graffiti *10*, 152
postposition *88*, 98
post-Proto-Elamite 248
Post-Urban phase 22

post-Vedic 237, 239
pot, pottery, potsherd (jar, vessel) 3, 5, 8f., 12, 15, 17, 21–2, 24, 26, 30, 33, 36, *46*, 52, 54f., 61, 64, *65*, 82, 95, 104, *105*, 107, *109f.*, 113, 130, *132*, 142, 149, 168, 174, 179, *180*, 181, *183*, 186, 190f., *192–4*, 195, 206, 234, *236*, 240, *241*, *277*, 286, 292, 297, 300; (Indus sign) *see* sacrificial vessel; bichrome 17; black-and-red 22, *193*; body of the pot 107; firing of pottery 52, *65*, 107, 227; 'goblet' 25; grey ware 148, 155, *156*, *192f.*; handled *46*; handmade 15, 17; with inscriptions 3, 22, 64, *65*, 82, 95, 107, 179, 292; *see also* potter's marks; legged *46*; plain 15, 22, 24, 52; polychrome 17, *192f.*, 216; rim 107; pot with seal stamp 107, 113, 215, 248, *250*, *275*; storage jar 17, 22, 107; *see also* names of specific ceramics; graffiti; painted motif; potter's mark; sacrificial pot; water-pot
potency, *see* virility
potter's mark 17f., 29, 52f., *53*, 54, 57, 62, 69, 107, 179, 183, 233, 287f.; *see also* graffito
potter's wheel 15, 168
Potwar 142
powder *56*, 259, 265–7, 270, 272; *see also* flour
power 224, 270
Prabhās(a) Pāṭan *7*, *10*, *25*, 258
Pradyumna 189, 297
Prajāpati 197, 206, 221, 234, 238, 262f., 267f., 270, 301
Prakrit (Middle Indo-Aryan) 133, 143, 151, 154f., 170, 241, 267; *ayya* 172; *dipi* 56; *magara, mayara* 188; *miṇa* 182; *nemeso* 238; *-sa* 117; *sukka* 60; *ṭippī* 267; **vaṭṭa* 300
Prakritization 169
Praśna-Upaniṣad 208
Prasun 134, *135*, *166*
Prater, S. H. 103
pravargya 221
prayer 256, *276*
Pre-Aryan 145
pre-Aryan 207–9
precession of the equinoxes 204, *243*
predicative 121
prefix 45, 48, 50, 84, 96, 151
pregnancy, pregnant 206, 217, 224, *228*, 229, 238f., 259, 262, 267f., 272, *276*, 301; *see also* conception
pre-Harappan culture *10*, 21
Pre-Indo-European 145
premodification 97, 125f.
preposition 48, *88*, 106, 130; 'to' 48, 106, 130
preservation 62, 78f., 110, *111f.*
pre-Vedic Indian elements in the Veda xvi, 4, 184, 234, 264
priest 61, 106, *107*, 110, 116f., 119, 121, *132*, 171, 175, 180, 188, *190*, 191, 201, 209, 211, 216, 222, *223*, 258f., 261f., 268, 270, *277*
priestess 219, *256*, 258, 261, 300
'priest-king' statue 211, *212*, 214–18, 266, 298, 301
prince 13, *106*, 241, 258f.
princess 240f., 270
Prinsep, J. 5f.
procession 110
profession, *see* occupation
prohibitions 208–10, 267
pronoun, personal 43, *166*, 167, 170; first person sing. 43, *107*, 117, 119; first person pl. *166*, 167, 170; second person sing. and pl. 43, 119, 121, *252*; third person sing. 119
pronunciation 34, 40, 42, 102f.
proof, *see* validation
property 17, 29, 97, 115, 121; *see also* owner
prophecy 241
propitiation (appeasement, pacification) 198, 224, 233, 237f., 258, 263
Proskouriakoff, T. 50
Prosopis spicigera 239
protection, protector (guardian, tutelary) 6, 112f., 116, 199, 207–9, 214, 222, 228, 237–9, 245, 256, 258f., 262f., 265, 270, 301
Proto-Aryan 144f., *155*, 157f., 294; *aśva-* 157f.
Proto-Dardic 152, *156*
Proto-Dravidian, *see* Dravidian
Proto-Elamite 128, 130; art and civilization 17, 21–2, 53, *106*, 152, 186, *187*, 247f., *249–51*, 286; influence on Indus Civilization 53, *91*; script and tablets *17*, 18, 30, *31*, 35, *36*, 53, 57, *84*, 128, 130, 287–9; seal *106*, *187*, *249f.*, 287; *see also* Elam(ite); Linear Elamite
'Proto-Euphratic' 128
Proto-Finno-Permic 145
Proto-Finno-Ugric, *see* Finno-Ugric
Proto-Indo-Aryan 126, *127*, 147–9, 152, *156*
Proto-Indo-European, *see* Indo-European
Proto-Iranian 148f., *156*
protolanguage 46f.
Protoliterate period *187*
Proto-Māgadhī, *see* Māgadhī
Proto-Nuristani, *see* Nuristani
Proto-Ṛgvedic 152, *156*
Proto-Samoyedic, *see* Samoyedic
Proto-Sauma Aryan, *see* Sauma Aryan
Proto-Scythian, *see* Scythian
Proto-Semitic *127*, 130; *see also* Semitic
'Proto-Śiva' (seal) 116, 121, 183f., *188*, 191, 194, 211, 248, 261, 293, 297, 300
Proto-South Dravidian, *see* South Dravidian
Proto-Uralic, *see* Uralic
Proto-Volga-Finnic 145
Proto-Yajurvedic 154, *155*, 169
Ptolemy *41*, 149, 170
publication, *see* edition
'public space' 61, 231, 299
pugilist 255
Pulayan 265
pun 33, 103, 175, 183, 194–6, 199, 244, 262; *see also* homophony
punch-marks on coins 55, 288, 296
Punic 45
punishing 190, 215, 234, 263, 267f., 301
Punjab 3, 5, 9, *26*, *136*, 152, *154–6*, 162, 168, 172, *236*, 266
Punjabi (Panjabi) 134, *135*, *166*; *chattrā* 266; *ṭikā* 266
Puṟam 171, 197, 233f., 241, 270
Purāṇa text 240, 243, 245f., 262
Puri 220
purification, *see* lustration
Puṣya *202*, 204, 208f.
Puṣya-gupta 209
Puṣya-yaśas 208
Puzur-Inšušinak *35*
puzzle, crossword, 273f., 302
Pylos *46*
Pyrgi 45

Qala'at al-Bahrain *115*
Qatar 130
quality of a seal 24, 54, 116, 119, 121, 195, 293; of a 'liṅga stand' 218
quantity 30, 60f., 191, 194, 196
quarter: of space, *see* direction; of year 110, 203
quatrefoil 211, *213*, 269
queen 50, 59, *106*, *132*, 184, 189, 191, 219, *227*, 256, 258f., 264, 301
Quetta *7*, 15, *16*, 24, *25*, 149, 213
Quetta Valley 52, *193*, *269*, 301
Quetta Ware 17
quiver 239
quotative 168

Rabinal Achi 49
race 142, 160
Rādhā-Kṛṣṇa 209
radiocarbon, *see* dating
Rahman Dheri *10*, *16*, *20*, 21–2, 52f., 104, *106*, 192f., *236*, *251*, 286
Rāhu 199, *200*, 201, 208, 233, 299
Rāhūgaṇa 208
Rāhula 208
raiding, *see* robbing
Raigarh 163
railing 109, *229*, *238*, 259, 299
rain, rainy season 9, *106*, 110, 201, 203, 205, 214, 217, 254
Rājasthān *25*, *136*, *161*, 165, 174, *193*
Rajasthani *135*
Rājataraṅgiṇī, *see* Kalhaṇa
Rājmahāl Hills *161*, 163
Rajput 259, 263
Rakhigarhi 6, *7*, *10*, *20*
ram 9, 235, 237f., *239*, 266, 285
Rāma 205, 244, 259
Rāma-Kṛṣṇa 209
Rāmāyaṇa *153*, 189, 205, 244, 259, 263, 265f.,
ramparts, *see* walls
Ramses III 148
Ranchi *161*, 163
Rangpur *7*, *10*, *25*, 288
Rann of Kutch 157
Rao, S. R. 221
Ra's al-Hadd *10*, 286
Ra's al-Junayz *10*, 12, 22, 286
Ras Shamra *107*, 128
Rask, R. 42
Rāṣṭrakūṭa *57*
Rati 221
rational marker 225
rattle 9
Rau, W. 149
Rauhiṇa, Rauhiṇāyana 208
Rāvaṇa 259
Ravi 5, *7*, 8, *16*, *25*, *153f.*
Rawlinson, H. C. 42
ray 206, 215, 237, 239, 245, 247, 268
razor 269
reading 62; aid 34; 79; mistaken 47, 56, 61f.
rebellion 14
rebirth (renewal, resurrection, revival) 191, 194, 206, 217f., 221, 228, 241
rebus 33, 38f., 60, 88, 102f., 121, 174f., 179, 183f., 231, 274, *277*, 299
reconstruction xvi, 4, 42, 46f., 49, 51, 59, 61, 96, *111f.*, *118*, 125, 134, 137, 158, 167, 174f., 180f., 230, 277
recording, *see* archives; inventory
rectangle, rectangular *200*; copper tablet 110, *111f.*; seal 17, 113
red 9, 11, 14, 191, 206, 211, *212f.*, 216, *218*, 221, 230, 235, 237, 239, 241, 244f., 262–70, 272, *275*, 299; *see also* vermilion
redundancy 79f., 97, 99
reduplication 195
reed 11, 14, 33, 35, 113
referent of the sign *84*
refutation 94
registering, *see* archives; inventory
regularity, *see* system(atic)
relationship, genetic: of languages 42–8, 87, 89, 126, 133f., 167, 288; distant 46f., 128, 161, 288; of scripts and marking systems 53, 56, 58, 104; *see also* interrelationship
relative clause *88*
relief, inscriptions in, 64, 107
religion 47, 51, 148f., 203f., 287; Harappan xvi, 3, 6, 8, 62, 107, 109f., 116, 183–91, 194–8, 211, 213, 215f., 218–21, 256, 274, 277; Indian xvi, 104, 107, 109f.,

171, 181, 183f., 188–91, 194–8, *199f.*, 201, 205–10, 214–25, 256, 272, 274, *275f.*, 277, 299; Near Eastern 104, 183, 186–91, 197, 211, 213f., *219*, 235, 274, 277; pre-Vedic xvi, 4, 184, 234, 264; *see also* e.g. god; goddess; demon; myth; priest(ess); ritual; sacrifice; Veda; worship; Zarathustra
renewal, *see* rebirth
Renfrew, C. 167
repetition 30, 40, *41*, 47, 49, 52f., 64, 69, 81f., 90f., *92*, 96, 107, *109*, 110, *114*, 117, 119, *120*, 125, 131, 195f., 215, 218, *275*, 290, 297; *see also* duplicate; iteration
'responsibility' 32, 61
resurrection, *see* rebirth
retroflex 140, 163, 165, *166*, 167f.
'returning' 33
Revatī *202*, 204
reverence 256, 258; *see also* worship
reverse of seals/tablets/tags 9, *11*, *32*, *36*, 81, 83, 91, *92*, 107, *108–12*, *113*, 116, *131*, *180*, *226f.*, 233, *234*, *246*, *255*, *276*; reversed order/direction 64, 67, 98f., *109*, 110, *111f.*, 205; sequences 66; signs 64; smoothed reverse 115
'revision' of history 58f.
revival, *see* rebirth
Ṛgveda, *see* ṚS
Ṛgvidhāna 238
rhinoceros 9, *11*, *111*, 131, 157, *186*, *188*, 191
rhotacism 223
rhyme 33
'rib' 102, 291
rice 9, *56*, 140, 152, 172, 194, 197, 200, 229, 259, 267
rider, riding 149, 172, 293; *see also* mount
righteousness *106*, 190, 215
ring 9, 213, 227, *276*, 299; ear-ring *227*, *276*, 299; nose-ring 227; *sse also* anklet; bangle
'rising' 223, 299
ritual 6, 45, 50f., 54, 115, 148f., 151, 154, 172, 204f., 214–22, *223*, 224, 256
river (stream) 4–6, *7*, 8f., *12*, *16*, 21, 24, *25*, 34, 121, 150, 168, 181, 183, *184*, 186, *187*, 188f, 204, 206, 208f., 224, 248, *249*, *252*, 254, 268, 285, 296
road 115, 230
robber, robbery 24, 234, 237, 239, 256, *276*, 299
robe, *see* dress
Roberts, T.J. 103, 157
Rodiya 137, *138*
Rohiṇī, *rohiṇī 202*, 204, 206f., 243f., 262–5, 267–70, 272, *275*, 301; = Aldebaran, q.v.
Rohita, *rohita* 189, 237, 263, *264*, 265, 267f., 272, *275*, 301
Rohri hills 9
Roh(i)tās *161*, 163
Rojdi *7*, *10*, *57*
Romance languages 46
Romanian 46
Rome, Romans 22, 172, 224, 293; *see also* Latin
roof 6, 39, 197, *220*, 274, *275*, 297
room 6, 8, 15, 21, *108*, *113*, *115*, 117, *118*, 149, *183*, 221, *254*, 258
root 39, 241; aerial 221, 234, 239, *241f.*, 243–6, 300; lexical 34, 36, 38, 60, 85, 87, 96, 174f., 181, 195–7, 215, 233, 298
rope (cord, thread) 11, 31, 113, *114*, 116, 186, *187*, 206, 237, 241, 245f., 266, *276*, 300; *see also* noose
Rose, H.A. 266
Rosetta Stone 40f., 45f.
rosette *23*, 183, 213, *214*, *249*, *251*, 301
route of transport/migration *16*, 17, 21f., 30, *141*, 144, 148
routine, *see* formula
row 8, 30, 32f., 44, 64, 89, 100, 198, 216, 221, *222*, 226, *227*, 243, 261; *see also* line
ṚS 3–5, 133, 140, 143, 147, 149–53, *154*, 156, 158, 165, 167–9, 181, 190, 195, 199, 201, 203, 205f., 208, 214f., 217, 222f., 228, 234f., 238–40, 244–6, 262f., 268, 294, 300; *see also* Early (Ṛg)vedic
Rudhira, *rudhira* 235, 237
Rudra 4, 109, 189, 199, 206, 210, 224–8, 234f., 237–9, 261, 268f., *276*, 299, 301; *see also* Śiva; Skanda
Rudra-datta 210
ruins, ruin mound 3–6, *13*
rule-forming 83, 98, *100*
Russian language 87
Russian (Soviet) scholars xv, 60, *96*, 144f., 148, 151, 277, 289
Rutul *χœdei* 196

ŚĀ 208
Śabara 151, *154*
sacrifice (offering) 61, 107, 115, *132*, 188, 190f., 194, 197, 200f., 207, 210, 214–22, *223*, 224, 226, 228f., 231, 235, 237, 239f., 246, *252*, 254, 258–64, 268–70, 272, *276*, 292, 297, 299–301; 'sacrificial inscription' 60, 107, *109f.*; sacrificial stake *21*, 220f., 224, 245, 298; sacrificial vessel 107, *109f.*, 190f., *194*, 195, *226*, 259–61, 274, *277*, 292; *see also* dedication; horse sacrifice; human sacrifice; ritual; votive
sacrificer(s) 216–18, 221f.; 231; first 190, 222
saffron 264
sage (seer) 195, 216, 222, 237, 241, 243–5, 268, *275*; *see also* Seven Sages
Sahni, D. R. 6
saint, saintliness 216, 228
St Andrew's cross *55*
Saka (Śaka) *5*, 129, 133, 145, 149, 172; *see also* Khotanese; Tumshuq
Śakti(sm), Śākta Tantrism 189, 256, 300
salination of fields 24
Sālivāhana 61
salutation 256
salvation 270
Samara 145
Śambara 140, 151, 189, 294
śamī 239, 263
Samoyedic 47
Samsu-iluna 9
Saṁvara 151, 294
Sanchi (Sāñcī) *153*, *186*
Sangam (Caṅkam) literature, *see* Tamil
Śaṅkara 243
Sanskrit (Old Indo-Aryan: Vedic q.v.; Epic 133, *156*, 169; Classical 133, 168, 223) 4f., 42f., 58, 82, 91, 104, 133f., 142, 168–70, 174, 196–8, 201, 205, 207–9, 217, 222f., 233, 239, 245, 261–4, 266f; *abhrayantī* 205; *adhṛṣya* 258f.; *ádhyakṣa* 215; *aghāḥ* 205; *aghora* 238; *agni* 199, 206, 215, 217, 221; *agnīdh*, *āgnīdhra*, *āgnīdhrīya* 216, *223*; *aiṁ* 270; *aja* 189; *aja ekapād* 237; *ajānana* 239; *ākāśa-gaṅgā* 181; *akṣa* 158; *akṣamālā* 244; *akṣaya-vaṭa* 244; *ambara* 262; *ambhasāṁ pati* 188; *aṅgāra(ka)* 209; *aṅgāra-prabha* 209; *aṅgāra-setu* 209; *apabharaṇīḥ* *202*, 216–18; *apabhraṁśa* 134; *apāṁ pati* 188; *aparājitā (pur, diś)* 256, 263; *apsaras* 268; *apūpa* 109; *arjunīḥ* 208; *arkabimbam arundhata* 244; *arma(ka)* 5, 285; *aru* 244; *aruṇa* 235, 245; *arundhatī* 241, 243f.; *arundhatī-vaṭa* 244; *aruṣa* 235; *ārya* 172; *aṣāḍha* 208; *aṣāḍhā* 269; *aṣāḍhāḥ 202*, 207; *āṣāḍhi* 208; *āśāpūrṇā* 259; *astu* 43; *āśu* 158; *asura* 149–52, 154; *āsura* 199; *aśva* 158; *aśvamedha*, *see* horse sacrifice; *aśvattha 202*, 239, 244, 258f.; *aśvatthā* 259; *aśvattha-parṇa* 238; *aśvayuj(au)* *202*; *aśvin* 147; *aśvinī 202*, 204; *avabhṛtha* 217f.; *āvīrotsava* 206; *babhluśa* 235; *babhru* 235; *bāhu*, *bāhū 202*; *baka* 232; *bāla-pitṛ* 239; *bali* 109, 239; *bāṇa 200*; *bekurā*, *bekuri* 206, 268, 298; *bhaga* 217, 301; *bhākuri* 206; *bhāṁ hi nakṣatrāṇi kurvanti* 206; *bhar-* 61; *bharaṇī(ḥ) 202*, 216–18; *bhekuri* 206; *bhūta* 259; *bhūtamātā* 258; *bhūtapriyā* 258; *bilva 220*, 299; *bindu* 264, 267, 301; *bodhi-nyagrodha* 240; *bṛhaspati* 201, 262f.; *budha* 208, 262; *caitya* 109, 259; *cakraḥ 47*, *158*; *cakra-vartin* 106; *calākṣibhrū* 239; *caṇḍa* 233; *candra* 58, 208f., 265, 267; *candra-bindu* 267; *candra-gupta* 208f.; *candramā nakṣatre vasati* 207; *candra-prabha* 209; *caṣa* 189; *cattra*, *cāttra* 145; *caturaśra* *200*; *cedi 154*, 268; *citrā 202*, 207; *cullī* 217; *cullī-pāṣāṇa* 217; *ḍākinī* 301; *dasa* 150, 294; *dāsa* 4, 149–52, 154, *155*, 170, 189, 209, 214, 256, 294; *dāśa 151*; *dasyu* 149–51; *deva* 147, 150f.; *dhaniṣṭhā 202*, 205; *dhanus 200*; *dharma* 191, 268; *dharma-cakra* 106; *dhiṣṇ(i)ya* 207, 216f., 221f., *223*; *dhruva* 224, 243, 300; *dhruvaṁ sadaḥ 246*; *dhūma-ketu* 201; *dhvaja 200*; *dine dine* 82; *dīrghacaturaśra* *200*; *divicarā grahāḥ* 201, 233; *-dra* 235; *dramila*, *draviḍa* 170; *drapsa* 268, 272; *dṛṣac-cullī* 217; *dṛṣad* 217; *dṛṣadvatī* 5, *154*; *durādharṣa* 259; *durga*, *durgā* 256, 258, 261; *durga-taraṇī* 263; *eka* 232; *ekaparṇā* 259; *ekapaṭālā* 259; *gaṅgā 26*, 54, 133, 140, *141*, 152, *153–6*; *garbha* 228, 239, 268; *garbhagṛha* 228; *godhūma* 165; *grabh-* 233, 239; *grah-* 233, 269; *graha* 199, 201, 232f., 237–9, *276*, 299; *grāha* 188, 191; *gṛbhīta* 239; *gṛhīta* 237; *guha*, *guhā* 228; *guhya* 207f.; *hara* 234, *276*; *hastin* 191; *hiraṇya* 266; *hiraṇya-garbha* 268; *hotrā*, *hotrāḥ* 222; *hrīṁ* 270; *īṣā* 158; *jaṭā* 243, 300; *jaṭila* 243f., 300; *jaṭilā* 239, 243f., 300; *jaya-durgā* 259, 261, 301; *jayantī* 269; *jhaṣa* 188–90; *jyeṣṭha* 241; *jyeṣṭhā 202*, 241, 263; *jyotiṣām agryā* 263; *-k-* 207; *kacchapa* 197; *kāma* 230f., 239; *kamaṭha* 197; *karkaṭa* 232; *kārttika* 204; *kārttikeya* 206, 224f.; *karttṛ* 145; *ketavaḥ*, *ketu* 199, *200*, 245, 300; *khaḍga* 191; *khála* 165, 168; *khara 223*; *kharoṣṭha* 56; *kinnara* 299; *koṭṭa* 170, 256; *koṭṭavī* 256, 261; *kṛt-kṛṇátti* 145, 269; *kṛttikāḥ 202*, 204–6, 224f., 269; *kṣurā*, *kṣura-dhārā* 269; *kumāra* 225, 228, 230, 235, 237; *kumāra-pitṛ-meṣa* 239; *kumāra-saṁbhava* 224; *kumārī* 227; *kuṅkuma* 264; *kūrma* 188, 197; *l-* 168, 299; *lalāma* 269; *lalāṭa* 266; *lalāṭikā*, *lālāṭikā* 266; *lāṅgala* 168; *lipi* 56; *lohita* 269; *magadha* 133, *154*, 155; *maghāḥ* *202*, 205; *mahāvrata* 205; *mahiṣa*, *mahiṣī* 219; *makara* 188f., 297; *makara-dhvaja* 189; **makaraśa* 188; *maṇḍūka* 58; *maṅgala* 209; *maṅgalaka* 184; *mahāvrata* 256, 300; *mahiṣa* 191;

mahiṣāsura 254 etc.; *mahiṣāsura-mardinī* 254; *mātaraḥ* 259, 301; *matsya* 59, *154*, 188–91, 263; *matsya-dvādaśī-vrata* 190; *matsya-nyāya* 270; *matsya-sūpa* 189; *matsya-yuga* 184; *matsya-yūṣa* 189; *matsyo mahādyutiḥ* 195; *māyā* 151, 190, 199; *meghayantī* 205; *meṣānana* 238; *methī* 224; *mīna* 59, 180, 182, 189, 268, 272, 296; *mīnākāra* 270; *mīnākṣī* 270; *mīna-mithuna* 184; *miñj-* 182, 296; *mithuna* 184, 263; *mitra* 147, 151; *mleccha* 170, 296; *mṛgaśiras*, *mṛgaśīrṣa* 194, *202*, 218, *275*; *mṛtyu* 201, 218; *múkha* 165, 168; *mūla* *202*, 208f.; *munayaḥ*, *muni* 245; *mūṭa* 109; *nāga* 194; *nagara* 170; *naigameṣa*, *naigameya* *238*; *nākra* 188, 297; *nakṣatra* 201, etc.; *nara* 191; *nāsatya* 147; *nava-graha* 198, etc.; *nava-maṇi* 196; *nava-rātri* 256, etc.; *nejameṣa*, *nejameya* 238; *netra-bīja* 270; *nihitāsa uccā* 245; *nikumbha*, *nikumbhilā* 259; *niśumbha* 259; *nyagrodha* 240, 244–6, 258f.; *nyañco nyagrodhā rohanti* 246; *nyāya* 243; *oṁ* 270; *palli* 170; *pañcagavya* 221; *pañcakoṇa* *200*; *paṅgu* 197; *paṇi* 149–51; *pāpman* 218; *pāṣāṇa* 217; *paśu* 196; *paṭa* 54; *pāṭa(ka)*, *pāṭi* 170; *pāṭhīna* 264; *pati-vratā* 240, 264; *paṭṭa* 54; *paṭṭana* 170; *phála* 168; *phalgunī(ḥ)* *202*, 205, 208; *pippala* 258; *pipru* 150f.; *plakṣa* 244; *pṛ- (piparti, pṛṇāti)* 150; *prākāra* 229; *prākṛta-bhāṣā* 133; *puṁsavana* 221; *puṇḍra* *154*, 169; *pur* 256, 294; *pūrṇa-kumbha* 184; *puruṣa* 268; *pūrva*, *pūrve* *202*, 204; *puṣya* *202*, 204, 208f.; *puṣya-gupta* 209; *-r-* 207; *rabh-* 233; *rahasya* 207; *rāhu* 109, *200*, 201, 208, 233, 299; *rāja-rāja* 82; *rājasūya* 215; *rajju* 300; *rāktī-patī* [*sic* for *rātri-pati*] 265; *raṇa-tilaka* 270; *raṅgavalli* 288; *rāśi* 201; *raśmi* 237, 245; *ratha* 185; *raudrī* 269; *rauhiṇa* 244; *revatī* *202*, 204; *ṛkṣāḥ* 222; *rohin*, *rohiṇa* 244; *rohiṇī* *202*, 204, 206f., 243f., 262–5, 267–70, 272, *275*, 301; *rohiṇī-candra-śayana-vrata* 265; *rohit* 206; *rohita* 189, 237, 263, *264*, 265, 267f., 270, 272, *275*; *rohita-matsya* 191; *ṛṣi*, *ṛṣayaḥ* 222, 245; *ṛta* 151; *rud-* 225, 235, 237; *ruddhā* 243; *rudh-* 243f.; *rudhira* 235, 237; *rudra* 235 and *passim*; *ruh-* 244, 246; *sa-* 151; *śabara* 151, *154*; *sahamānā* 269; *śakaṭa* 263, 269f.; *śakaṭacakrākṣa* 270; *śakula*, *śāla* 184, 189, 194, 263, *264*, 272, 301; *śalya* 61; *sam-* 151; *śambara* 140, 151, 294; *śamī* 239, 263; *sam-rāj* 151; *saṁskṛta-bhāṣā* 133; *saṁvara* 151, 294; *saṁvaraṇa* 151; *śanaiścara* 197; *śani* 197, 201; *śānti* 198; *sapta hotrāḥ* 222; **sapta-liṅga* 222; *sapta ṛṣayaḥ* 222; *śarabha* 189, 261; *śarabha-dhvaja* 261, 301; *śāradā* 256; *śāradī pur* 256; *sarasvatī* 5, 9, *154*; *śārdūla* 191; *śarva* 147; *ṣaṣṭhī* 229, 258, 301; *sata* 61; *śata* 145; *śatarudriya* 299; *saubhāgya* 264; *sautrāmaṇī* 218; *savitṛ* 263; *sāvitrī* 203, 240f., 263; *sāvitrī-vrata* 240; *śayana* 265; *śiṁśumāra* 189, 297; *sindhu* 4, *154*; *sindūra-dāna* 265f; *śiśumāra* 188, 297; *śiva* 234; *skambha* 220f.; *skand-*, *caskanda* 268; *skanda* 230, 261, etc.; *skanda-graha* 237, 300; *soma* 149, 151f., 205, 207f.; *śravaṇa* *202*, 208; *śraviṣṭhāḥ* *202*, 205; *śrīṁ* 270; *śrī-vṛkṣa* 259; *śṛṅga* 188; *stambha* 220; *su-grahaṇa* 232; *śukra* 60, 201; *su-palāśa* 244; *su-parṇa-kṛta-lakṣaṇa* 244; *surā* 259; *śūrpa* *200*; *sūrya* 128, 208, 215, 221; *suvastu* *154*; *sva-*, *svāmin* 97; *svar* 215; *svarbhānu* 199, 301; *-sya* 117; *śyāma* 197; *śyāmāṅga* 197; *tāmra* 235; *tapas* 224; *tārā* 209, 233, 262f., 301; *tārāgaṇapati* 265; *tārayati* 262; *tārpya* 215–18, 298; *ṭikā*, *ṭīkā* 264, 266; *tila* 264; *tilaka* 264–7, 270, *275*; *timi* 188; *timi-dhvaja* 189; *timiṅgila* 188; *trikoṇa* *200*; *tripura*, *tripurā* 150, 238, 256; *triśūla* 270; *tṛp-* 215; *tveṣá-ratha* 158; *-tvī* 152; *ugra-tārā* 263; *ulūkhala* 175; *urukara* 175; *uttara*, *uttare* *202*, 204; *uttara-madra* *154*; *vāc* 206, 268; *vah-* 158; *vahana* 61; *vana-durgā* 259, 301; *vandanīyā* 259; *varcin* 151; *varṇabījakoṣa* 289; *varṣayantī* 205; *varuṇa* 147, 151, 245; *varuṇa-sava* 215; *vas-* 207; *vasāti* 154; *vaśīkaraṇa* 302; *vaṭa* 240f., 245, 258, 300; *vaṭa-druma* 241; *vaṭa-mātaraḥ* 259; *vāta-rajju* 245; *vāta-raśana* 245; *vāta-raśmi* 245; *vaṭa-sāvitrī-vrata* 241; *vaṭa-vṛkṣa* *239*, 241; *vaṭa-yakṣiṇī* 259; *vedikā* *229*; *vekurā*, *vekuri* 206; *veṇu-yaṣṭi* 109; *vijaya-daśamī* 194, 256; *vilohita* 235; *virāṭ*, *virāṭa* 268; *viśākha* 237f.; *viśākhe* *202*, 205; *viṣuvat* 205, 298; *vīvadha* 109; *vṛ-* 151; *vrata* 240f., 265; *vrātya* 256, 300; *vrātya-stoma* 256, 300; *vrīhi* 140; *vṛkṣa-śāyikā* 103; *vṛkṣikā* 258; *vṛta* 241, 300; *vṛtta* *200*, 241, 300; *vyāghra* 191; *yādasāṁ pati* 188; *yakṣa*, *yakṣī*, *yakṣiṇī* 194, 229, 259, 301; *yamunā* *26*, 130, *154*; *yoginī* 301; *yoni* 217–21, 224, 259, 301; *yuga* 201; *yūpa* 221, *223*

Santali 137, *166*

Śāradā 256

Sarai Khola *7*, *10*, *20*, 52f., *141*, 142, 168

Sarasvatī 5, 9, *154*, 181, 206f., *271*

Šargališarri *252*

Sargon 14, 18, 248, 254

Sarianidi, V. I. 148f.

Sarikoli 129, *166*

Sarmatian 129, 294

Sarre cylinder *252*

Šarva 147

Sassanid 41f.

Ṣaṣṭhī 229, 258, 301

Sātavāhana 61

Satəm 145, 158, 294

Saturday 259

Saturn 197, *199f.*, 201, 237, 274, *275*, 297

Satyavat *241*, 245

Saudi Arabia 30, 130

Sauma Aryan 149, 151f., *156*; *see also* Soma

Saumāyana 208

Śaurasenī 133

Saurashtra 11, 170, 258

Saurāyaṇi 208

Saurva 147

sautrāmaṇī 218

Sauvīra *154*, 209

Sāvatthī 229

Savitṛ 263, 265

Sāvitrī 203, 210, 240, *241*, 244, 263–5, 300

Sāvitrī-vrata 240f., 300

Sāyaṇa 233

Sayce, A. H. 42f.

ŚB 109, 150, 154, 170, 175, 190, 205–8, 215–18, 222, 224–6, 228, 234f., 237f., 241, 245f., 268–70

ṢB 207

sceptre 80, 270

Schlegel, A. W. 189

Schmidt, M. 43

school (scribal) 32, 117

Schrapel, D. 289

science, scientific research 3, 54, 285

Scorpio *202*

scorpion *23*, *249*

scribe 31–4, 36, 38, 42, 54, 117, 119, *187*, *252*

script(s) 18; matched with language 48, 51; *see also* fit; unknown 44, 47f.; *see also* scripts mentioned under alphabetic, cuneiform and hieroglyphic scripts; Aegean; Aramaic; Chinese; Cypriot; Cypro-Minoan; Indus; Linear A/B; Linear Elamite; Proto-Elamite; Sumerian archaic

Scythian 145, *156*, 172, 294

Scytho-Sarmatian *129*

sea (ocean) 9, 11–14, 22, 38, 53, 129–31, 133f., 170, 172, 188–91, 199, 222, *275*, 296

sea-wood 14

seal(s) 30–2, 88, 91f., 97, 113–21, 292; Akkadian xvi, 85, 117, 119, 131, *132*, *187*, 188, *252*, *254*, 255; from Altin Tepe *10*, 22, 286; BMAC 148, 152, 168, 203, *255f.*, 298; carelessly/carefully carved 69, 116, 121; Chinese 119, 293; compartmented 17, 152, *255*; copper 17; Dilmun 130, *183*, *219*, 273, *274*, 286, 302; Early Dynastic *106*, 117, *219*, *247f.*; Early Harappan *10*, 17, 21, 53, 152; edge 183; Egyptian 119; find places *10*, 61, 64, *115*, 117, *118*; foreign in Indus Valley 62; forged seal stamp 115; with geometrical motifs 17, 24, 62; golden *255*; Gulf *10*, 11, 114, *115*, 130f., 133, *219*, 286; Harappan 3f., *6*, 9, *10*, 21f., 54, 58, 62, *65f.*, *82*, 88, 91, *92*, 107, *108*, 113–21, *180f.*, 184, *185*, *188*, 194, *195*, 215, 224, 226, *228*, *231f.*, 234, *243*, 246, *250*, *252–4*, *256*, *260*, 261, 292f.; from the Near East 9, *10*, 11, *113*, 125, 130, *131f.*, 133, *181*, *186*, *219*, 273, 286, 293, 297; Hittite bilingual 43; hollow 116, 293; (classical) Indian 115–17, 119, 293; inscription 54, 59, 85, 116–21, *252*, *254*, 256, 260f., 263, 270, 293; Iranian *187*; Jhukar 168, 174; large *108*, 116f., 121, *195*; Late Harappan *10*, 54, *55*; manufacture 116, 292; mass-produced 116; Mesopotamian xvi, 11, 113–17, 119, 121, 194, 287, 292f.; Minoan 43; official 116, 119, *120*; Old Babylonian 119; Ordos 203, 298; Post-Harappan (Pirak, Swat) *10*, 152; presentation 119; prismatic *10*; Proto-Elamite *106*, *187*, *249f.*, 287; quality of 24, 54, 116, 119, 121, 195, 293; rectangular 17, 113; round *10*, 11, 17, 130f., *132*, *183*, *187*, *219*; square 9, *10*, 22, 54, *113*, *120*, *131f.*, *254*, 255, 288; stamp(ing of a) 18, 30, 64, *113*, 114f. (forged), 227, 273; as status symbol 116; Sumerian 36, *57*, *219*, 287; Syrian-style *184*; as talisman 116, 293; types 9, *10*, 11, 113, 292f.; Ur III 117, 119; use of 91, 107, *113–15*, 116–21, 292f.; votive 119; worn on person 116; *see also* cylinder; 'fig deity'; impression of; 'Proto-Śiva'; pot with seal stamp; size

sealing 30, 107, 292f.; *see also* impression; stamp(ing of a) seal

season 17, 162, *164*, 165, 203–7, 254

seat(ed) 17, 36, 50, *132*, 183, *185*, 203, 211, 247f., *249*, *252*; *see*

also chair; throne
secrecy, secret 189f., 215, 228, 256; name 207f.
sectarian mark 56, 264, 269, 301
security 113, *114*
seed, *see* semen
'seeing' (looking) 181, 190, 215, 220, 243–5, 270
seer, *see* sage
segmentation of texts, *see* division
Sehwan 11
Seistan (Sistan) *10*, 17, 21–2, *25*, 26, 52, 128, 148, 152, *155f.*, 161f., *192*
seizer, seizing, seizure (grasping) 131, 190, 201, 232–4, 237, 239f., 244, 269, 276f., 299
semantic indicator, *see* determinative
semantic(s), *see* meaning
semen (seed) 189, 195, 206f., 220f., 224, 268, 272
semicircle 52, 78, 82, 107, *108*
Semitic: (West Semitic) alphabet 18, 36, *37*, 38, 56, *84*, 174, 287; languages 31, 34–6, 42, 86, *127*, 128, 130f., 293; *'āleph* 38; *'b* 38; *mw* 36; *see also* East/South/(North)west Semitic
'semi-variable' sign 60, 96
semivowel 38
Sennacherib 191
sentence 87–9, 98, *99f.*, 287
separation 206, 241, 260
sequence: cultural 15–25; of signs 29, *35*, 53, 59, 64, 66, 69, *93*, 98f., 131, *132*, 194–6, 222f., *226f.*, 230, 232, *275–7*, 293
serpentine, *see* steatite
servant, servile 119, 121, 186, 188, 190, 215, *252*, 254, 261, 270, 277
Sesamum indicum 9, 169, 296; sesamum seed 264
settlement, *see* site(s)
Seven Mothers 228, 261, 301
Seven Sages 190, 195, 206, 222, 224, 241, 243–5, 261, 268, *275*, 297f.
Sewell, R. B. S. 157
sewing 214, 216
sexuality 189, 218–21, 223f., 230f., 239, 256, 262, 270
sexual intercourse 184, 206f., *219*, 220f., 224, 226, 238f., *256f.*, 264, 267f., 270, 298
ŚGS 238, 243
shadow 206
Shahdad *17*, *23*, *25*, 152
Shahr-i Sokhta *10*, *16*, *17*, 22, *23*, *25*, 52, 128, 148, *192*, 269, 286, 301
Shah, S. G. M. 62
Shang dynasty 107, 201
Shankara Bhat, D. N. 165
shape (form) 11, 17, 30, 38, 42, 44, 50, 54, 56, 64, 69, 78f., 103, 107, *111f.*, *113*, 191, *194*, 196f., 216f., 219, 224, 237, 239, 246, 255, 258f., 261, 263, 266f., 269f., 272, 278, 292; abstract 32, 35, 38, 50, 103, 278; linear 53, 55f., 69; round 104, 198, 266, 290
shark 188f.
Sharma, A. K. 157
sheep 9, 15, *30*, *32*, 119, 259; domestic 157; ewe *30*; urial (wild) ram 9, 157, 285
shell 9, 15, 49, 104, 110, 117, 197, 209, *213*, *253*; conch 104, 110; cowry *253*
shell-cutter 117
sheora tree 259
Sheorajpur 54, *55*, 288
shepherd 119
Shina (Ṣiṇā) 134, *135*, 142, *166*
'shining' 59f., 181f., 195f., 220, 235, *275*
ship (boat) 8, 11f., *13–14*, 21f., 36, 172, 188, 190f., *215*, 218, 248, *275*, 292
shoot (of tree) 221, 244
shorthand 34
Shortug(h)ai *7*, *10*, *16*, 22, *25*, 148
shoulder pole, *see* carrying-yoke
shrine, *see* temple
Shughni *129*, *166*
Shulman, D. D. 270
Sialk 17, 172
Siberia 47, 126, 142, 145, 161, 224, 293
sibilant 151
Sibri *10*, 24, *25*, 149, 157
sickle 15
side 237; of inscribed object *65*, 82f., 107, 110, *215*, 218, *219*; uninscribed 62; *see also* obverse; reverse
sign(s) (of a script); abstract 32, 35, 38, 50, 278; angular 32, 53, 69, 104, 290; boundaries 69, 290; composition of Maya 50; conflation of 33, 68, 78; 'constant' 60, 96; cramped 64, *65*; definition of 98; distinct, *see* grapheme; elimination of rare 33; identical *35*, 42, 98f.; nearly identical 44; intermediate forms 69; modification 33; new 79; non-terminal 100; order of 33f., 55, 64, 69, 78f., 84, 95, *132*; orientation of 32f., 64; overanalysis of 61, 80, 290; painted 107; 'semi-variable' 60, 96; 'simple' 79, 81, 90, 97, 195f.; simplification of forms 38, 69, 103f., 196, 278; single *55*, 80, *82*, 83–5, *91*, 95, 97, 107, 110, *111f.*, *120*, 183, *227*, *276*; syllabic 34f., 43, 48, 50, 58, 85, 96; 'variable' 60, 96; variant, *see* allograph; *see also* co-occurrence of; frequency of occurrence of; interior of; interrelationships between; ligature; logogram; meaning; number of; phonetic interrelationships between; phonetic value of; phonogram; pictogram; position and distribution of; sequence; shape
sign list 31, 33, 42, 62, *70–8*, 79, 287, 289f.
Sikkim 134, *136*, 142
silt 24
Silurus pelorius 264
Silva Figueroa, Don Garcia 41
silver 14, *107*, 148, 191
Silvestre de Sacy, A. I. 40–2
Šimbišhuk *35*
similarity 32f., 44, 47, 53, 55f., *58*, 59, 61, 69, 78–81, 87, 97–9, *100–1*, 102–4, 196
simile 209
simplification: of sign forms 38, 69, 103f., 196, 278; of the writing system 35f., 38
sin, *see* evil
Ṣiṇā, *see* Shina
Sinai 36, *37*, 38
Sind(h) 4, 6, 9, 11, 14–17, 21, *25*, 26, 134, *136*, 149, 152, *155f.*, *161*, 162f., *164*, 165, 170, 174, 209, *236*, 248, *251*
Sindhi language and people *13*, 134, *135*, 162f., *166*, 170, 209, 289; (related to the Indus script) 298; *ḇerī 13*; *candu* 209; *dāsu* 209; *ḏūndī 13*; *Moen-jo-ḍaro 13*; *Mohan-jo-daro*, *Mohen-jo-daro 13*; *tharo 13*; *ṭipo* 267
Sindhu 4, *154*, 285
singular 42, 86f., *94*, 95
Sinhalese 134, *135*, *166*, 181f.; *mōrā*, *muvarā* 188
Sinitic *143*
Sino-Tibetan 134, 142, *143*, *166*, 294
Sintashta 151, *152*
Siraiki 162f.; *brāhō* 162
Sirius 203
sissoo tree 13f.
sister 162, 259 (elder)
Sītā 205
sites (settlements): Early Harappan 17, *20*, 21; Mature Harappan and late Kot Dijian 5f., *7*, 285; Megalithic of South India *173*; Mitanni *147*; Late and Post-Harappan *25*; NBPW *153*; Northern Neolithic *141*; Painted Grey Ware *153*; Proto-Elamite and Elamite *17*; Timber Grave and Andronovo *146*; and traffic routes in Indo-Iranian borderlands *16*; Yang Shao Neolithic of China *141*; *see also* find places of Indus seals and inscriptions
Śiva 4, 116, 189, 198, *199*, 206, 218, *220*, 221f., 224, 226, 233f., 238f., 264f., 268, 300f.; *see also* Rudra; Skanda
Śiva-Purāṇa 224, 239
size 6, 8, 21f., 30, 32f., 64, 107, *108*, 110, *111*, *113*, 116f., 216, 243, 293; *see also* seals, large
Skanda 109, 189, 206, 224–30, 234f., 237–9, 258f., 261, 268, *271*, 299f.; *see also* Kārttikeya; Murukaṉ; Rudra; Śiva; Subrahmaṇya
Skanda-graha 237, 300
Skandāpasmāra 238
Skanda-Purāṇa 189, 237, 240f., 244, 259, 263
skeletons 142; unburied 24
skin 109, 217, 226, 247; colour 14f., 150, 196f., 235, *251*, *275*; *see also* hide
skirt *253*, *260*, 261
skull 194
sky (heaven) 51, 79, 181, 183f., 196, 201, 203–7, 213–16, 218, 221f., 231, 233, *244*, 245, 247, 258, 262f., 265, 268f., 272, *275*, 296; *see also* An
'sky garment' 214, 218, 298
slab, inscribed, 110
Slav 150
slave 33, 117, 121, 150, 208
Slavic 145
sling 9
slot (sentence position) 89–94
smell 194, 244
smith 8, 117, 232
Smith, G. 43
Smith, S. 66
smoke (fumigation) 199, 201, 221, 237, 239
snake (cobra) 9, *23*, *37*, 51, 59, 109, 184, *186*, 194, 199, 208, 217, *226*, 233, 248, *249*, *252*
snakehead fish 263, *264*
snare, *see* noose
social: class 205, 270; structure 17, 22, 24, 30, 61, 116, 133, 148, 170, *171*, 207–9, 285
soda 11
Sogdian *129*
soil, *see* ground; earth
solstice 110, 203, 205, 298
Soma 149, 151f., 205, 207f., 216, 221f., *223*, 240, 262f., 268, 294, 301; *see also* moon; Sauma
Somali(a) 128
Son *161*, 163
son *35*, 43, 48, 61, 119, 121, 130, 162, 184, 188f., 191, 206, 208f., 221, 224, 228–30, 234, 237–9, *252*, 258f., 262, 268; *see also* child
son-in-law 119
song (singing) 54, 221
Sora *139*, 151, *166*
sorceress, sorcery 5, 208
Sothi *20*; Sothi Ware and culture *20*, 21, 154
sound 32f., 41, 46, 102f.
sources, primary, 61f.
south 195, *200*, 203–5, 221
South Asia(n) 126, 143f.; history and culture 285 (*see also* history); languages xvi, 4, 133–42, *166*, 293–5
South Canara, *see* South Kanara
South Caucasian *127*
South-Central Dravidian *136*, 174, *175*

South Dravidian *136*, *155*, 169, 174f., 217, 227, 234f., 264, 296; θ- 217; *el(ḷu)* 169; *kōḷ* 235, 299; *kōḷi* 234, 237, 239f., *276*, 299; *ñāl* 246; *paḷḷi* 170; *uṭay* 97
southeast *200*
Southeast Asia 57, 137
Southern Neolithic 172, 174, 296
South India 11, 55, *56f.*, 59, 109, 117, 134, 137, 161, 168–72, *173*, 174, 191, 197f., *199f.*, 208f., 217, 220f., 225f., 243, *253*, 258, 260, 262, 264, 266f., 269f., 288, 296
South Kanara (Canara) 165, 209; *see also* Kanara
South Semitic *127*, 128
southwest *200*
Soviet, *see* Russian
space 65, 69; enclosed 231, 299; intervening 231, *276*, 299; public 61, 231, 299; saving of 54, 104, 179
spacing 64f., 69
Spanish 41, 46, 49f., 59
'sparkling' 181f., 195f.
spear(head) 24, 117, 238, *252f.*, 254f., 260, 270; (Indus sign) 53f., 61
speech, *see* language, spoken
spelling 13, 33–5, 50, 69, 79, 81, 95f., 107
spindle 145
spirant(ization), *see* fricative
spirit, *see* god/demon
spot, *see* dot
'spreading' 246, 300
spring (vernal) 9, 110, 204–6, 221, 226, 241, 256, 262, 268, *275*, 298
spy 115, 214f.
square 22, 50, 78, *111*, 149, 151, 198, *200*; bevelled *23*; seal 9, *10*, 22, 54, *113*, *120*, *131f.*, *254*, 255, 288
squirrel *103*, 229f., *276*, 291, 299
Śrautasūtra 215
Śravaṇa-datta 208
Śrāvastī 153
Srednij Stog 157
Śrī 259
Sri Lanka 133, *136*, 137, 170, 172, 221, 259
Srubnaya, *see* Timber Grave culture
Stacul, G. 168
stag 206
stairs 8, 104, *115*
stamp(ing of a) seal 18, 30, 64, *113*, 114f., 227, 273; *see also* impression; sealing; pot with seal stamp
'standing' 33, *186*, 203, *219*, 220, 223, *238*, 248, *249*, 258, *260*
standardization 8, 21f., 24, 29, 54, 78
star (astral) xvi, 34, 59f., *111*, 181f., *183–5*, *187*, 188, 194–8, 201, *202*, 203–11, *213*, 214–18, 220, 222–4, 226, 230–3, 237, 241, *243f.*, 245f., *249*, 261–5, 268–70, 272, 274, *275–7*, 296f., 301; culmination 203; rising 263, 301; (nakṣatra) calendar 194, 201, *202*, 203–7, 217, 224f., 233f., 243, 263, 270, 298; 'Starclad God' 214; name 207–10; *see also* asterism; morning star
state level 6, 22, 24, 116
statistics, *see* frequency of occurrence
status 36, 69, 116, 119, 162, 211; seal as status symbol 116
statue(tte; cult image; figurine; idol; model): animal 9, 17, 21; bull 9, 15 (zebu), 110, 292 (inscribed), *213*, 298 (with trefoils), *21*, *269*, 272, 301 (with a forehead mark); fish 190f., *194*; horse 149 (with a rider), 158; palm squirrel *103*; urial ram 9, 285; water buffalo 9; anthropomorphic 9, 15, 17, 149, 298; female 9, 21, 191, 241, 254, 259, *262*; male 21, 24, 116, 191, 198, *199*, 214f., 219, 221, 234, 237f., 241, 254, 268; *see also* 'priest-king' statue
steadfastness, *see* firmness
steatite (and serpentine) 9, 107, 149, *212f.*, 255; vessels 22, *23*, 148, 183, *213*, 247, *249*, 286
Stein, M. A. 160, 189
stele of clay 221–4
stem (of word) 34, 96
steppe 129f., 143, *144*, 145, *146*, 151f., *155f.*, 157f., 172, 294
steps 104, 221
stereotype, *see* formula
Steward, J. H. 24
stick 80, 109; inscribed 110, 292
stimulus diffusion 53f.
stomach, *see* belly
stone 8f., 11, 14f., 17, *23*, 34, 49, 110, *113*, 196, 201, 218, 220f., 228; axe 15, 137, *140*, 174; bull 213; circle 172; knife 142; pierced 228, 299; three stones 216f., *276*, 298; vessel, *see* steatite vessel
stone-cutter 117, 119
stoneware bangle *227*, 274, *276*
storage jar 17, 22, 107
Strabo 5, 150
stratigraphy 24, 107
stream, *see* river
street 6, 8, *12*, 21, 24, 117, 194, 221
string, syntactic, 89, 97–100, 209
stroke(s) 36, 44, 49, 52, 59, 69, 78, 81f., 107, 228, 246, 291; double 43, 230, *231*; long 82, 230, *231*; single 41f., 44, 48, 261, 267
'strong' (in title) 91, 119
structure of language, *see* grammar
study tools 61–4
stupa 6, *8*, *106*, 107, 117, *186*, *229*, *238*, *266*
style 87, 104, *247–9*, 255
stylus 32
Subandhu 262
subject, grammatical, 34, 87
subjugation 270, 302
Subrahmaṇya 225f.; *see also* Murukaṉ; Skanda
Subrahmanyam, P. S. 165
subscript 33
substitution 89
śūdra 270
Śūdraka 234
suffix 34, *41*, 43, 45, 48, 60, 95f., 116f., 121, 130, 225, 261, *277*; derivational 60, 96f.
suicide 244, 246
Šu-ilušu 131, *132*
Śukranīti 194
sum, *see* total
Šumaṣṭī 134
Sumer(ian) *10*, 14, 21, 54, *57*, *84*, 129, 184, 211, *213*, *247*, *254*, *275*, 288, 291, 293, 302; archaic script and texts 13, 18, *30*, 31, *32*, 33–6, 38, 43, 48, 56, *58*, 59, 64, *84*, 85, 88, 96, 102–4, 174, 183f., 189, 194, *195*, 196, 223, 262, 287, 290, 296; language 31, 35, 48, 58, 82, 88, 96, 102, 119, 121, 125, *127*, 128, 130f., 133, 189f., 204, 289, 293: *ab* *32*; *abgal (apkallu)* 190, 297; *-ak* 130; *alim* 34; *an* *32*, 183f.; *an.ma* 214; *apsû* 188, 190; *ba* 33; *dar* 14; *dé* 34; *dingir* 34, 121, 183f.; *du* 33; *dumu* 130; *e* 130; *e-gal* 130; *en* 34; ^{d}*en-ki(- ke*$_{4}$*)* 34; *see* Enki; *ga'ar* 34; *ga-ar*$_{3}$ 34; *gal* 130; *gemé* 33, 121; *gi* 33; *gin* 33; *gù* 34; *gub* 33; ^{na4}*gug* 14; *ig* 35; *ilu/ili* 169; *ir*$_{11}$ 121; *(*^{d}*)isimud(-ra)* 34; *1 ḫa kešda (du)* 191; *ḫaia* 14; *ki* 34; *kur* 14, 33, *58*, 82; *kur-gi*$_{6}$ 14; *-lá* 121; *lú* 121, 130; *lu-gal* 130; *ma* 34; *mar-tu* 130; *me* 14; *men* 34; *mêsu* 13f.; *mul* 183, 216; *mul.guškin* 213; ^{mul}*mul* 205; *(mu-un-na-)dé(-e)* 34; *ŋá* 34; *ŋen* 34; *ninsun* 130; *nin-ti* 102; ^{d}*nu-dím-mud* 189; *purādu* 190; *ti* 102; *túm* 33; *ú* 34; *udu* 32; *uga* 34; *ur* 121; *uru* 34; *ušū* 14; names 119, 121, 293; seal 36, *57*, *219*, *287*; *see also* Mesopotamia; Near East; Neo-Sumerian period
summer 17, 162, *164*, 165, 203–5, 247, 298
sun (solar) 36, 104, *106*, 128, 198f., *200*, 201, 203–6, 208f., *213*, 215—18, 221, 228, 233, 235, 237, 239, 241, 243–5, *251*, 263, 265, 268, *275*, 301; rising sun, sunrise 104, 196f., 203, 205f., 209, 217f., 221, 226, 233, 235, 237, 241, 245, 248, 263, 268, 272; *see also* dawn; morning; setting sun, sunset 165, 196f., 203f., 209, 217, 235, 237, 248; *see also* evening; twilight
sunspot 301
Śūrpāraka 172
survival of Harappan traditions *55*, 56, *57*, 58, 60f., 104, 118, 288
Sūrya 128, 208, 215, 221
Sūryā 205
Sūrya-datta 208
Sūrya-Siddhānta 216
Susa, Susiana *5*, *9*, *10*, 11, 17, *23*, 30, *31*, *35*, *105*, *107*, 128, 130, 186, *187*, *247*, 248, *249f.*, *262*, 287
Šu-Sin 130
Suśruta-Saṁhitā 103, 237–9
Sus scrofa, *see* boar
Sutkagen-Dor *7*, 11, *16*
Sutlej *7*, *25*, 142, *153f.*
Šu-Turul 106
Suvastu *154*; *see also* Swat
svarabhakti 169
Svar 215
Svarbhānu 199, 301
SVB 208
Śvetāmbara 134, 217, 238
swastika 24, 62, 119, 226, *227*
Swat (Suvastu) *25*, 140, *141*, 142, 152f., *154*, *156*, *158*, 159, 168f., 189, *236*, 294f.
'swift' 158
swimming 181, *187*, *275*, 296
sword 154, *155*, 174, 266, 270; *see also* dagger, knife
syllabogram 34f., 43, 48, 50, 58, 85, 96
syllable 33, 48, 50, 82, *84*, 85, 169, 174, 244, 270, 298; closed 35, 43, 48; monosyllabic 39, 48; open 35, 43f., *45*, 48; *see also* alphabet, syllabic; writing, syllabic
symbol 29, 61, 198, *200*, 201, 245, 247, 272, 274, *275*, 288, 302; *see also* emblem
symmetry 64, 67, 247
synonym 61, 79, 100, 196, 231, 233, 241, 244
syntagm(atic) 89, *98*, 99–101
syntax 33, 46, 51, 82–4, 88f., 97–101, 125, 162, 168, 194–6
Syria 30, 36–8, 40, 42, 48, *84*, *107*, 121, 126, 128, 130, 145, *147*, 149, 151f., *156*, 183, *184*, 191, 214, 261; Syrian-style seal *184*
Syriac 128
Syro-Arabian pastoral technocomplex *127*, 130
system(atic) (regularity) 46–8, 102, 196, 274

TĀ 244f.
Tabasaran *χæž* 196
table 33, 39, 59, 191
tablets, inscribed 9, 17, 30f., *32*, 33, *36*, 42, *46*, 48, 62, 83, 107, *108–12*, *120*, 191, 287, 292, 297; 'miniature' 54, 64, 81, 107, *108*, 190f., *194*, *226*, *246*; numerical 30, *31*; *see also* copper; moulded

tabulation, *see* grid
Tadzhikistan 168

tags, clay, 11, 31f., *108*, *113f.*, 115f.
Tai, *see* Thai
tail 110, *111f.*, 196, 199, 234
Taip-depe *16*, *25*, 149
Tajik *129*, *166*
Takht-i Jamshīd 41
Takht-i Sulaimān *129*
talisman (seal as) 116
Tamil (inc. Old Tamil) 59–61, 86, 91, 109, 134, *136*, *166*, 170–2, 174, *175*, 182, 184, 196, 198, 207, 209, 217, 221, 225, 227–35, 237, 243, 245, 258, 261, 269f., *275*–7, 296f., 299, 301; *ā-* 196; *akam* 170; *āḷ / āṉ* 188, 261, *277*; *āl, āla-maram* 246, 276; *-aṉ* 225; *aṉil* 229f.; *aṇiṟ piḷḷai* 229; *aṅ-kayaṟ-kaṇ-ṇ-ammaiyār* 270; *arici* 140; *aṟu-mīṉ* 194, 225f., *275*; *ātaṉ* 61; *-attu* 60; *cakaṭam* 265; *carppa-k-kāvaṭi* 226; *ce-m-mīṉ* 244; *ceṅ-kaya-ṉeṭuṅ-kaṇ* 270; *ce-v-vēl* 235; *ce-v-vēḷ* 230, 235; *cēy* 237; *cēyōṉ* 237; *ceyyavaṉ* 237; *ceyyōṉ* 235, 237; *cilampu* 227; *ciṉa-miku* 231; *cūl* 217; *cūl kāppu* 228, 276; *cūḷai, cuḷḷai* 217; *cuṟā mīṉ* 188; *eḷu-mīṉ* 195, *275*; *iṉai* 184; *iṉai-kayal* 184; *kaḷam* 165; *kāma-vēḷ* 230; *kampam* 220f.; *kaṇ* 270; *kaṇ-kāṇi* 215, *275*; *kanta-p-piḷḷai* 230; *kanta-vēḷ* 230; *kāppu* 228; *kaṟpu* 241; *kaṭā* 235; *kātalaṉ* 225; *kaṭampu* 235; *kāvaṭi* 109f.; *kayal* 184, 270; *kiḷi* 230; *kīri* 230; *koḷ* 232–4, 239; *kōḷ* 233f., 239f., *276f.*; *kōlam* *56*, *57*, 288; *kōḷi* 234, 237, 239f., *276*, 299; *kōṉ-mīṉ* 233, *277*; *kōṭṭu mīṉ* 189; *kūlam* 165; *kumara-vēḷ* 230; *kuṟavar* 110; *kuṭa* 165; *kuṭakku* 165; *macca-k-kāvaṭi* 191; *mai* 197; *mai-m-mīṉ* 197, *275*; *māl* 196; *marakata-mēṉiyaṉ* 196; *miṉ, miṉṉu, miṉuṅku* 182; *mīṉ* 181f., 230f.; *mīṉ ēṟu* 188; *mīṉ-kāvaṭi* 191; *miṉṉi miṉuṅku, miṉu-miṉukkam* 195, *275*; *mīṉ-ūrti* 188f.; *mu-k-kūṭṭu* 217; *mu-m-mīṉ* 194, 218, *275*; *muruka-k-kaṭavuḷ* 230; *murukaṉ* 225f.; *muruka-vēḷ* 230, *276*; *muruku* 225, 227, 230, *276*; *muruku-p-piḷḷai* 230, *276*; *muṭavaṉ* 197; *nāḷ* 233; *nāl-vāy* 246; *nāṉ-mīṉ* 233; *nāṉūl* 246; *paca* 196; *pacal* 197; *paccai, paccai-veyil* 196, *275*; *pacu* 196; *pacumai* 196; *pacu-v-ā-mīṉ* 196; *paiyaṉ* 197; *pala pala* 82; *pāmpu* 233; *piḷḷai* 229f., *276*; *piḷḷaiyār* 230; *poṭṭu* 264–6; *poṭṭu-k-kārai* 264, 301; *puṉar* 184; *puṉar-mīṉ* 184; *tāli, tāli-p-poṭṭu* 266; *tamiḻ* 170; *tamiḻakam* 170; *tiṟam* 241; *-tt-āṉ* 96; *ulai* 217; *uruḷ, uruḷi* 270; *uṭai, uṭaiyavaṉ* 97; *vaikal mīṉ* 207, 298; *vaikuṟu mīṉ* 207, 268, 298; *vāṉ* 231; *vāṉ-mīṉ* 231; *vaṭam* 241; *vaṭa-maram* 241, 246; *vaṭa-mīṉ* 241, 243–6, *276*; *veḷ* 220, 231; *vēḷ* 230f., *276*, 299; *vēḷ-āḷaṉ* 231; *veḷi* 231; *veḷḷi* 220, 231, 241, *276*; *veḷḷil* 220; *veḷḷi-mīṉ* 231; *vēlu-p-piḷḷai* 230; *vēḷvi-y-āḷaṉ* 231; *veṉ-mīṉ* 231, *276*; *veṭi, viṭi* 231; *viḻu-mīṉ* 245; *viṉ* 231, 296; *viṉ-mīṉ* 231, 296; *viṭi-mīṉ* 231; *viṭi-veḷḷi* 231; *yāmai* 197
Tamil-Brāhmī 172, 196, 288
Tamil Nadu *136*, 137, 170–2, *173*, 196, *220*, 226, 228
Tammuz 235
Tantra, Tantric 189, *255*, 256, 263f., 300; 'code' 58, 289
Tantrākhyāyika 237
Tārā 209, 262f., 301
Tārā-candu 209
tārpya garment 215–18, 298
Tarut 12f., *23*
tattoo 265
Taurus *202*, 213, 269, 272, *275*, 301
taxes 6, 13, 26, 115
Taxila *57*, *153*, 259
Tazmin 142
TB 5, 204f., 217, 237, 263, 268
Tchoga-Zanbil *107*
teacher 201, 207–9, 262
technology 24
Te(d)jend river *25*, 150
Tell Abada 29
Tell Asmar *10*, *11*, *187*
Tell as-Sulema *10*, 11, 180, *181*
Tell el-Amarna 43, *147*
Tello 9, *10*, *23*, 131, 213
Tell Uhaimir 9
Telugu 134, *136*, *166*, 174, *175*, 182, 195, 231, 235, 266; *boṭṭu* 265; *l-* 223; *-ti* 60
temple (shrine) 13f., *23*, 29f., *32*, 45, 54, 64, *107*, 109, 117, *118*, 119, *150*, 186, 189, 191, 197f., *199*, 214, *220*, 225f., 228, 240, *248*, 256, 259, *262*, 299
Tepe Gawra *10*, *214*
Tepe Hissar *17*, *25*, *148*, 152, 158
Tepe Yahya *10*, *17*, 22, *23*, *36*, 183, 247f., *250*, 286
terracotta 3, 9, 12, 17, 107, 110, *215*, 218, 221, 234, *235*, 237, *244*, 269; triangular 'cakes' 21
testicle 221
testing (control, cross-checking) 3f., 41f., 47, 49, 59–61, 100, 107, 133, 196, 230f., 233, 246, 261, 274, *277*, 278
tethering, *see* tying
text (inscription): complete 80–4, 95, 195, 215, 230; long(est) 3, 45, *83*, *90*, 92, 96, 103f., 107, 109f.; *see also* length; monumental 5, 13, 38, 41–3, 49f., 56, 69, 110, *113*, 129, 134, 143, 292; parallelism between text and iconography 49, *91*, *109*, 110, *111f.*, 115f., 121, 233; second line 66, *111f.*, 116, 118, 121; single-sign texts *55*, 80, *82*, 83–5, *91*, 95, 97, 107, 110, *111f.*, *120*, 183, 227, *276*; types of texts/objects 3, 9, *10*, 11, 30, 47, 54, 61, 64, 69, 88f., 106–21, 292; *see also* Asoka; bilingual; cuneiform; division; epigraphy; formula; history (textual sources); length; Sassanid; seal; trilingual
textiles 9, 11, 115
Thai (Tai) *143*
thang-ka *257*
Thanjavur 200, 262
Thapar, B. K. 221
Tharu *228*
thatch(ing) 197
Thebes *105*
theology 24
theophoric name 121, 209
Theravāda 134
Thieme, P. 147
thill 158
thirst *252*, *254*
thread, *see* rope
threshing floor 165, 168, 224
throne 14, 109, 184, *186–8*, *226*, *238*, *250*, *260*, 261, *262*
Thuban *202*, *243*, *276*
thumb 266
thunderbolt 237
Thurston, E. 265
Tibet(an) 87, 134, 142, *166*, 299; *see also* Lamaism
Tibetic 142, *143*
Tibeto-Burman 126, 134, 142, *143*
tiger 9, *82*, *112*, 115, *186*, 188, 191, 226, *227*, 246, *247*, 248, *253f.*, 255, 258
Tigris 4, 31
Tikkanen, B. *166*, 167
tilaka 264f., 270, *275*; *see also* forehead mark
timber, *see* wood
Timber Grave culture 145, *146*, *156*, 294
time-reckoning 29, 45, 49, 54, 104, 110, 201–7, 298; *see also* dating; star calendar
tin 9, 14, 149
Tipura, *see* Tripurī
Tirāhī 134, *166*
Tirumurukāṟṟuppaṭai 230
title 4, 41f., 45, 50, 59–61, 80, 91, 97, 107, *108*, 116f., 119–21, 133, 180, 190, 209, 219, *275*, *277*
Tiṭṭaguḍi *199*, *220*
TL xvi, 196, 230f.
Tocharian 145; *yakwe* 157
Toda *136*, *116*, *175*, 182, 197, 209; *Kwïṭnaṣpïḷy* 209
Togau 15, *16*, 17, *20*
Togolok *16*, *25*, 148f., 152
Toilet objects 148
tokens for accounting 18, 29–32, *30–1*, 33, 38, 287
token (memorial) of offerings 107, 191
tomb *105*, 228
Tongan 87
tongs (pincers) 232
tool 11, 104, *105*, 106, 117, 137, *140*, 172, 174; for study 61–4
'tooth' *37*, 233
torch 33
tortoise 191; *see also* turtle
Tōrwālī 134, *166*
total(ity) (sum) *32*, *36*, 44, 64, 79, 88, 137
totem(ic) 116, 258
town, *see* city
toy 9
trade 9, 11–14, 17, 21f., 26, 30, 38, 53f., 62, 113–15, 117, 129–31, 133f., *141*, 142, 149, 169f., 172, 203, 273; *see also* routes; transport
traffic, *see* transport
traffic sign 39
transaction 30, *32*
Transcaucasia 158
transcription 33
transhumance 17, 162, *164*, 165; *see also* migration
Transitional Harappan phase 19, 21–2, 53, *236*, 269
translation 3, 31, 41, 46, 60, 102, 223, 273; loan 233, 245; *see also* bilingual
transliteration *36*, *41*, *46*
transport (traffic) 8f., *16*, 21f., 31, 113–15, 168; *see also* routes; trade
Trasadasyu 151
Trautmann, T. 170
Travancore 265
treaty 145, 147, 151
tree 9, 13–15, *21*, 34, 39, 82, *103*, *109f.*, 121, 168, 170, *186*, 194, 208f., *219*, 220f., 228, *229*, 230, 234, *235f.*, 237f., *239*, 240, *241f.*, *244*, 245f., *248f.*, *252f.*, 256, 258f., *260*, 261, 264, *276*, 292, 297, 299–301; wishing-tree 258; *see also* dryad; fig tree
tree diagram *98f.*, 134, *175*
'trefoil' 211, *212f.*, 214–17, *218*, *220*, 269, 298
Tregamī 134
triangle *21*, 30, 53, *200*, 216f., 228, 269
tribe, tribal people 11, *13*, 116, 137, 150f., *154*, 155, 160–3, *164*, 165, 191, 208, 258, 266, 297
trident 270
trilingual 41f.
Tripurā 256, 261
Tripuri *26*, *153*, *166*
Triśalā 184
Triticum sativum, *see* wheat
Trophis aspera 259
trough 114, *186*
trumpet 148
Tryambakahoma 109

Tryambakayajvan 264
TS 5, 188, 201, 215f., 226, 234f., 239, 262f., 269
Tsien, T-h. 107
Tuareg 128
Tucci, G. 189
Tuesday 259
Tu(i)š(e)ratta 158
Tulissos 45
Tulu (Tuḷu) *136*, 165, *166*, 174, *175*, 182, 195, 234f.; *nēla* 246
Tumshuq (Saka) *129*
Tungusic 46f.
Tureng Tepe *26*, 148
Turkestan 133, 145
turkey *50*
Turkic 46f., 126, 224, 293
Turkish 86
Turkmenistan *10*, 17, 25
turmeric 259
turquoise 15, *253*
turtle 197, 274, *275*, 297; *see also* tortoise
tusk 235
tutelary, *see* protection
twilight 262; *see also* evening; sunset
twin 268
'twinkling' 181f., 195f.
twisting, *see* bending
tying (binding, fixing, tethering) *21*, 31, 33, 79, 113, 186, *187*, 221, 224, 241, 245, 259, 266, *276*
types/typology: of decipherment 47–9, 288; of languages, typological features 4, 60, 86–8, 96, 125f., 130, 142, 169, 291; of seals 9, *10*, 11, 113, 292f.; of texts/objects 3, 11, 30, 47, 54, 61, 64, 69, 89, 106–21, 292; of writing 4, 38f., 48, 68, 83, *84*, 85, 287, 290f.
Tyre (Tyrus) *147*, 197, 214

U-shape 78; U-shaped Indus sign 107, *109–11*, 190f., *194*
'Ubaid period and pottery 18, 30, 130
udumbara = country fig 258
Ugarit(ic) 38, 43, 45, 48, *107*, *147*; cuneiform alphabet 18, 38, 48, 106, *107*, 288; language 128
Ugra-Tārā 263
Ujjain *153*, *161*, 163
Ukin-Ulmash *252*
Ukraine 157
Umā 238
Umbrian 46f.
Umma *10*, *113*
UMS 243
unction 215f., 218
ungulates 157
'unicorn' 9, 11, *21*, 22, 58, *111*, *113*, 115f., 131, *132*, 159, 180, *181*, *248*, 286
uniformity 6, 21f., 25, 125, 286
unit, linguistic 38, 83, 89, 96, 102; of analysis 82f., 98
United Arab Emirates 130
universals of language 87, *88*, 291
universe 245; *see also* cosmic order; world
Untash-Napirisha *107*
untouchable 220
uprooting 220, 224
Ur *10*, 11, 14, *23*, 32, 116, 130, *131*, *147*, 180, *181*, *183*, *187*, *213*, *219*, *254*, 260; Ur I period 18; Ur III period 14, 18, 107, 117, 119, 121, 130f., 204, 213; seal 117, 119
Uralic 46f., 145, 161, 288, 294f.
Urals 145, *146*, 151, *152*
Urartian 126, *127*, 293
urbanization, urban culture 4, 15, 21f., 24, 49, 203, 286, 298; *see also* city
Urdu 134, 162f.
urine 21
Ursa Major 190, 195, *202*, 206, 222–4, 241, *243*, 245, 261, 268, *275*, 299
Ursa Minor *243*
Uruk *23*, *30*, *32*, *195*, 186, 194, *195*, 211, *213*; Uruk period 18, *214*; Uruk III–IV period 13, 18, 30–4, 128, *195*
* Urvaśī 195, 268
Uśanas Kāvya 262
Uṣas 206, 263
Usimu (Isimu) 34, *187*
ušū wood 14
Uttar Pradesh *136*, 172, *238*
utterance 82, 98

Vāc 206, 268
VādhS 189, 235
Vaigai (Vaiyai) *173*, 181
Vaikhānasa Āgama 261
VaikhGS 198, 208
Vaiṣṇava 210; *see also* Viṣṇu
vaiśya 205, 270
Vaiyai (Vaigai) *173*, 181
validation of decipherment 42f., 45, *46*, 60f., 273; *see also* testing
Vāmana-Paddhati 270, 301
Vāmana-Purāṇa 270
Vaṁśa-Brāhmaṇa 208
Vana-Durgā (Bana-Durgā) 259, 301
Vandanīyā 259
Varāhamihira 194, 199
Varāha-Purāṇa 190
Varanasi 194, *271*
Varcin 151
variable 48f., 64, 79
'variable' sign 60, 96
variant, graphic, *see* allograph
Varuṇa 147, 151, 188–91, 195, 214–18, 221, 224, 237, 244–6, 248, 258, 268, *275*, 294, 298
Vasiṣṭha 195, 206, 224, 241, 243f., 268
Vāsiṣṭha-Dharmaśāstra 267
Vasiṣṭha-Saṁhitā 216
Vasu 268
Vaṭa-Sāvitrī(-vrata) *241*
Vaṭa-yakṣiṇi 259
Vats, M. S. 6, 114, 269
Veda, *passim*; Vedic language, *see* Sanskrit; *see also* AS, etc.; Brāhmaṇa texts; Early/Late/Middle/pre-/post-Vedic
Vedda 137, *138*
Veenhof, K. R. 114f.
vehicle 158, 295; *see also* chariot; mount
Vēḷ 230f.
velar 163, 165, 170
Venetic 46
Ventris, M. 44f., *46*, 48, 58, 87, 97
Venus 49, 183, *200*, 201, 209, 220, 231, *262*, 265, *276*, 301
Veps 145
verb 33f., 51, 87, *88*, 89, 96, 150, 174, 181, 215, 227, 231–5, 239
vermilion 189, 206, 266; box 266f., 272
vertical 32f., 67, 78, 104, 179, 180, *181*, 230, *231*, 246, 290
vessel, *see* pot
Vetāla-Pañcaviṁśatikā 244
Vibhīṣaṇa 259
victim 21, 184, 191, 194, 220f., 224, 237, 239, 259–62, 264, 269f., 272, 301
victory 207, 227, *249*, *253*, 254, 258–61, *262*, 263, 269f., 272; *see also* Vijaya-Daśamī
Vidarbha *154*, 172, *173*
Vīdevdāt 145
Vidiśā 134
Vidyādhara 258
Vietnamese 86f.
vigil(ance) 215, 301
Vijaya-Daśamī 194, 256, 263f., 269, 301
Vijayanagar 228
village 5, 14, 17, 26, 49, 54, 61, 103, 117, 131, 149, 170, 172, 220, 259, 293
Vinča 53, 288
vine 246
violence 270
virgin 227, 301
virility (potency) 188, 191, 238, 261
Virolleaud, Ch. 106
Viśākha 237f.
visibility 203f., 206
Viṣṇu 190, 196, 199, 210, 233, 237, 264; Vaiṣṇava 210
Viṣṇudharmottara-Purāṇa 189, 198f.
Viṣṇu-Purāṇa 245, 262
vocabulary, *see* lexicon
Vodva stupa *238*
Vogul 145
Volga *144*, 145, *146*, 152
Volgaic 145
votive gift, *see* dedication; sacrifice
Votyak 145
vow (vrata) 224, 229, 241, 265
vowel 36, 42–5, *45*, 50, 56, 175, 267; intrusive 169; long and short 38, 175, 181, 298; pure 45; 'synharmony' 50
vrata, *see* vow
vrātya rituals 256, 300
vrātya-stoma 256, 300
VS(M) 184, 188, 206, 216, 234f., 237, 264, 269
vulture *186*, 197; *see also* eagle
vulva, *see* female organ

Waddell, L. A. 58
Wadi Asimah 22, 286
Waigali 134, *135*, *166*
Wakhi *129*, 133, 142, *166*; *dāi*, *δayək* 150
Walker, B. 208
wall(s) (ramparts) 6, *8*, *12*, 21f., 55, *105*, *115*, 130, 148f., *150*, 216, 229, 256
Wanzke, H. 201, 205
war, warrior (army, militarism) 9, 14, 24, 50, 61, 80, *120*, 148–52, 154f., 171, 174, 188, 216, 226f., 237, *253*, 255, 259–61, 263, 270, 272, 286, 301; of stars 262; war-god(dess) 24, 109, 183, 197, 206f., 224f., 227, 230f., 234f., 237–9, *253f.*, 255, 258–61, *262*, 263, 268–70, *271*, 272, *275f.*; *see also* contest; conquest; hero
warehouse 11, *12*, 113, *114*, 115
washing, washerman 117, 200, 217
water (aquatic) 6, 8f., 14, 21f., 32, 36, *37*, 110, 116, *132*, 181, *183*, 184, 186, *187*, 188–91, 194f., 204, 214f., 217f., 221, 241, 247f., *249*, *251f.*, 262, 267f., 270, 274; birth water 190; fish-water 194; flesh-water 194; water-basin 11, *12*; water-god 14, 32, *183f.*, *186f.*, 188–91, 215, 217f., 248, *252*, 254, *275*; *see also* Enki; Varuṇa; water nymph 195, 268; water-pot 184, 190, *252*, 254, 259; water table 15
water buffalo 9, *111*, 115, 158, 183f., *185f.*, *188*, 189, 191, 197, 211, 219f., 248, *250–3*, 254, 256, *257*, 259–61, 263, 269f., 272, 300; domestic 157; wild 157, 260
wavy-leaf fig 244, 258
Wayman, A. 206
wealth 9, 30, 116, 237, 270
weapon 9, 14, 24, *37*, 104, 109, 117, 148, 150, 171f., 174, 230f., 234f., 237, 259; inscribed 106, *107f.*, 117, 292
Weber, A. 263, 268
week(day) 198, 201, 209, 262
weights and measures, weighing 8, 22, 43, 107, 113f., *115*, 169, 295
well 6, 8, 22, 114, *115*
Welsh 87
west, western(er) 130, 165, *200*, 203, 206, 222, 259
West Bengal *136*, 163
western India (Deccan) 129, 133, 172, 174, 198
West Iranian 129
West Semitic: alphabet, *see* Semitic alphabet; languages 36, 48, *127*, 128, 130, 133; *bʿl*, *bʿlt*

48; *bn* 48; *ḫrṣn 107*; *khnm 107*; *l* 48, 106; *mlk* 48; *rb 107*
wheat 8f., 15, 165, 295
wheel 104, *106*, *148*, 151, 157f., 270, 292, 295; (Indus sign) 104, *108*, 110, *113*, 116f.; potter's 15, 168; spoked 148, 151
Wheeler, R. E. M. 149
whistle 9
white 11, 104, 150, 216, 220, 231, 241, 265, 270, *276*, 299
whorl 149
widow 184, 220, 241, 267
wife 43, 119, *132*, 162, 205f., 217, 221, 224, 237, *241*, 243f., 258, 261–5, 268, 272, *275*
Winckler, H. 43
wind 245
window 8
wine, *see* intoxicant
wing *255*
winking of eyes 215
Winn, Sh. M. M. 53
winter 17, 162, *164*, 165, 203–5, 247
Winternitz, M. 238
wisdom, wise 151, 190, 215, 262
wish(ing) 231, 259; tree 258
witchcraft, *see* magic
witness 30, 113
wolf 149
woman (female, feminine) 21, 32, 34, 39, *41* 44, 50, 59, 119, *132*, 133, 184, 194, 208f., 219f., 226, *228*, 229, *238*, 239, 241, 243, *253*, 256, *257*, 258f., 261f., 264f., *266*, 267f., 270, 272; married 264, 267, 272; *see also* bride; statue(tte); virgin; wife
womb 190, 208, 217f., 220f., 228, 238f., 267f., 272, 301; *see also* female organ; yoni
wood (timber) 9, 11, 13f., 34, *35*, 39, 69, *113*, 168, 170, 201, 220f., 239
wood-apple 220, 239
wool *30*
word 32–4, 38, 41, 44–8, 50, 59f., 83, *84*, 85, 91, 95–8, *100*, 106, 131, 137, 230, 268, 287; likely 48, 121; *see also* length of
word divider 41, 43f., 48, 59, 82f., 85, 290f.
word order 86–9, 96, 126, 130, 142, 162, 169
word sign, *see* logogram
workshop 6, 8, 11, 15, 17, 22
world 14, 215, 224, 226, 233, 270; *see also* cosmic order; universe
worship(per) 3, 107, *109f.*, 116, 121, 188, 191, 194, 197f., *199f.*, 201, 215, 218f., *220*, 222, 224, *226*, *228f.*, 231, 237, *238*, 241, 248, *254*, 256, 258f., 261, 263, 265, 268, 270, 298f.; *see also* sacrifice
Woṭapurī 134
wrestling-ground 233
Wright, G. R. H. 191
writing 24, 39, 49, 53, 55, 190, 206, 287; cursive 35; fit between written and spoken language 33–6, 38f., 48, 51, 88f., 96f., 125, 287; forerunner/prehistory of 52, 287; history of 4, 18, 29–39, 59, 273; material 54; syllabic 18, 35, 38f., 41f., 48, 50, *84*, 85, 96, 102; type of 4, 38f., 48, 68, 83, *84*, 85, 287, 290f.; use of 54; *see also* alphabetic/logo-syllabic/phonemic/syllabic writing; script(s)

Xerxes 42
X-raying 30

Yahya, *see* Tepe Yahya
Yājñavalkya-Smṛti 200
Yajurveda 154, *155*, 165, 169, 201, 208; White 269f.
Yakṣa, Yakṣī, Yakṣiṇī 194, 229, 301
Yama 188, 190, 197, 205, 217f., 220, 241, 244f., 248, 256, *257*
Yamna culture, *see* Pit Grave culture
Yamunā (Jumna) *26*, 130, *154*, 268
Yang Shao *140f.*, 142, 294
Yasin 142
Yašt 148, 151, 214
Yaz (Depe) *156*
Yazgulami *129*
year(ly) 33, 54, 104, 110, 201, 203–5, 207, 217, 220, 240f., 260, 263, 268; *see also* new year
'yellow' 196, 208, 237, 265, 270
Yellow River 142
Yidgha *129*, *166*
Yi-jing 107
yoga, 'yogic' posture 184, *185f.*, *188*, 189, *226*, 248, *250*
Yoginī 301
'yoke carrier' *183*; (Indus sign) 61, 69, *94*, 95f., 109, *110*, *183*, 292; *see also* carrying (yoke)
yoni 217–21, 224; *see also* female organ; womb
young, youth 197, 225, 227, 230, 234f., 237f., 243, 258f., 262, *276*, 299; *see also* child
Young, T. 40, 277
Young, T. C. 148
Yudhiṣṭhira 243
yūpa 222, *223*
yurt 172

Zagros 15, 128
Zarathustra, Zoroastrianism 41, 129, 143, 147–9, 151f., *156*, 214, 262, 294
zebu (humped cattle) 15, 17, *21*, *23*, *92*, *108*, *111*, 115–17, 157, *213*, 247, *249*, *251*, 293
Zend, *see* Avestan language
zenith 203
zero 49
zero variant 90, *94*, 95–7, 121, 150f., 174
Zhang Zhung 142
Zhob 15, *16*
Zide, A. R, K. 60
Ziusudra 190
zodiac 201
Zoroaster, *see* Zarathustra
Zvelebil, K. V. xvi, 60, 96, 161, 169, 188, 231, 235
Zyrian 145